The AMERICAN PANORAMA

Michael H. Collins

The
AMERICAN PANORAMA

A Comprehensive Guide to the Culture of the United States

Outskirts Press, Inc.
Denver, Colorado

To those who have taught me and those whom I have taught

Make no little plans. They have no magic to stir men's blood.
Daniel Burnham, the planner of Chicago

Also written by Michael Collins
St. George and the Dragons: The Making of English Identity

The American Panorama
A Comprehensive Guide to the Culture of the United States
All Rights Reserved.
Copyright © 2012 Michael H. Collins
v6.0

Cover Photo © 2012 JupiterImages Corporation. All rights reserved - used with permission.

Outskirts Press, Inc.
http://www.outskirtspress.com

PB ISBN: 978-1-4327-4533-2
HB ISBN: 978-1-4327-4045-0

Library of Congress Control Number: 2010921974

Outskirts Press and the "OP" logo are trademarks belonging to Outskirts Press, Inc.

PRINTED IN THE UNITED STATES OF AMERICA

CONTENTS

The frontier of hope that we all innately pursue will never close.
Alan Greenspan

I had always hoped that this land might become a safe and agreeable asylum to the virtuous and persecuted part of mankind, to whatever nation they might belong.
George Washington, letter to Francis Van der Kamp, May 28, 1788

Governments are instituted among men, deriving their just powers from the consent of the governed.
Declaration of Independence, July 4, 1776

The leading object of government is, to elevate the condition of men—to lift artificial weights from all shoulders—to clear the paths of laudable pursuit for all—to afford all, an unfettered start, and a fair chance, in the race of life.
Abraham Lincoln, Message to Congress, July 4, 1861

The Constitution: a charter to assure the rule of law and the rights of man.
Barack Obama

The American dream, to me, means having the opportunity to achieve . . . because I don't think you should be guaranteed anything other than opportunity.
Lenny Wilkens
Knowledge will forever govern ignorance. And people who mean to be their own governors must arm themselves with the power knowledge gives.
James Madison, letter to W. T. Barry, August 4, 1822

Foreword

*T*he American Panorama is a book which accurately depicts the United States of America and its people through well crafted historical, documented data. This skillfully crafted biography of America contains significant history and science in an informative package that is not just entertaining but challenges your mind and imagination.

Michael Collins has created word images so vivid it is almost like living in the action. The depth of the research is astonishing! There is more to be learned about the American culture here than in any other source I've found. The topics are broad, but woven together brilliantly keeping me continuously engaged.

The American Panorama is a delight to read. One can only hope that from a writer of this talent there will be many more books to come.

Jim R. Graham, CEO,
jimrgraham.com

Acknowledgements

A number of people have helped me with the preparation of *The American Panorama*. My deep and lasting gratitude is especially due to two old friends: Dan Brown, Professor Emeritus, Educational Studies, University of British Columbia, who read the whole text in draft and greatly assisted me to improve it from the point of view of the reader; and Don Ringe, Chair of Linguistics, University of Pennsylvania, who also spent more hours than I could either claim or deserve in reading and commenting on parts of this lengthy text. By both of their efforts the quality of the book has been immeasurably enhanced. Dr. Roger Highfield, formerly Senior Tutor in Modern History and now Fellow Emeritus of Merton College, Oxford, read an earlier draft of the whole book and gave me valuable advice about how to take it forward. My special thanks are also due to Jim Graham, CEO of jimrgraham.com, for providing the Foreword. Professor Jack Ruebensaal, Vice Chairperson, Behavioral & Social Sciences, West Los Angeles College, read and commented on an earlier draft of Chapter 1. The Reverend Dr. Carolyn Stapleton, Associate Pastor of the Chinese United Methodist Church, New York City, read through the chapter on religion as it then stood and made helpful comments. My understanding of the political influence of the Religious Right has also been greatly enhanced by Stephen Bates' *God's Own Country: Religion and Politics in the USA*, Hodder, 2007. Professor Wang Keping, Distinguished Returned Overseas Scholar of the China Academy of Social Sciences, was always ready to give advice and support and particularly emphasized the importance of Locke's *Second Treatise of Civil Government* on the Founders' political thought. Professor David Boozen, Director of the Hartford Institute for Religion Study, enlightened me on the question of how the US came to be home to so many denominations. Instructional materials expert and literary agent, Suzanne H. Robare, gave me much needed encouragement at an earlier stage of writing to persevere with this mammoth undertaking. Duncan J. D. Smith, author of the *Only In* guides, gave me an invaluable introduction to the complexities of author contracts. Jonathan Camilleri, Dr. Henry Davis, the Reverend Dr. Nicholas Henderson, Tim Jackson, Dr. David Jago, Matthew Jay, Professor Jerome Mandel, James Piercy and Mark Stafinski made numerous useful suggestions and provided friendly support. The gestation of the book was like adding a new and demanding member to my circle of family and friends. To the forbearance of all of them I owe more than I can say.

Several authors and organizations have given me permission to make use of copyright material. Among these I am especially grateful to The Pew Research Center for the People & the Press, a project of the Pew Research Center, for permission to make use of the summaries of the findings of the following surveys: January 5, 2006, *Strong Public Support for Right to Die*; March 30, 2006, *America's Immigration Quandary*; August 3, 2006, *Pragmatic Americans Liberal and Conservative on Social Issues*; April 23, 2007, *Little Boost for Gun Control or Agreement on Causes*; and May 22, 2007, *Muslim Americans: Middle Class and Mostly Mainstream*. I am also grateful to Professor Abraham Davidson for permission to make use of his authoritative article on American art, which appears on Encarta. In addition, Professor Larry Sabato, Director of the Center for Politics at the University of Virginia, gave me permission to make use of his chapter on PACs and Parties taken from the website of the Hoover Institution, material which originally appeared in *Money, Elections, and Democracy*. It was at the prompting of Professor Hu Zi Xin (Peter Hu) of Beijing International Studies University that I attempted a section on American philosophy and gave weight to the thought of Jonathan Edwards. Professor David Boersma helped me locate Edwards within American philosophy and allowed me to make extensive use of his Internet Encyclopedia of Philosophy article "American Philosophy" (full article: http://www.iep.utm.edu/, August 9, 2009.) Cornelius Grove & Willa Hallowell, 1998, GROVEWELL LLC, and Grovewell.com have allowed me to make copious use of their article on diversity in the workplace. Similarly, Elizabeth Warren, Leo Gottlieb Professor of Law, Harvard Law School, allowed me to make use of material from her book *The Two-Income Trap*. Professor James B. Twitchell, University of Florida, and Steve Orlando, Director for Print Media, University of Florida News Bureau, gave me permission to reproduce Professor Twitchell's interview about advertising dated April 1, 1996. Polly Skinner, Head of School, Villa Academy, Seattle, made available for my use the material on the Resilient Child that appeared in *Pollysletter*, February, 2009; *The American Magazine* gave permission for me to make use of "The Luxury City vs. the Middle Class" by Joel Kotkin, *American online magazine*, May 13, 2009; and Vijay Joshi, Fellow of St John's College, Oxford, allowed me to quote from his article on the "credit crunch" which appeared in *Postmaster and the Merton Record*, Michaelmas 2008. The RAND Corporation of Santa Monica, California, permitted me to make use of John Despres' article on American Interests with China. My old friend, Richard Mullen, editor of the *Contemporary Review*, has allowed me to re-use my own article on the American character, which appeared in February, 2004.

The index was prepared by Ann Yager and the proofreader was Carolyn Gray.

Every effort has been made to trace copyright holders and to obtain their permission for the use of copyright material. The publisher apologizes for any errors or omissions in the above list and would be grateful if notified of any corrections that should be incorporated in future reprints or editions of this book.

To all those mentioned my gratitude is due, but for what appears within these pages, including, regrettably, errors of commission and omission, I alone am responsible.

Preface

The founding of the United States is the most important political event in modern history. America marks something new in the Western experience: a political entity entirely removed from the dynastic struggles of the European powers. The framers of the US Constitution, which has been adopted as a model around the world, were one of the most brilliant galaxies of political talent in Western history. How well will their modern successors safeguard their heritage? Millions have been attracted to study in the US and millions more to immigrate. But is America now over-extending itself, and beginning to decline like previous empires?

Despite shifts in the balance of world economic power, recent predictions of American decline are somewhat exaggerated. The US, despite current and coming challenges, is and will remain for the foreseeable future the world's leading economic, military, political and cultural power. America has a unique ability to innovate, integrate and renew – to generate solutions to problems, to produce what people want and enjoy, and hire any passing talent to do it. Even though it has lost the capacity to determine the direction of the global economy, the US still leads the world in many critical services and goods sectors. This has made, and will sustain the US as the world's economic superpower, although it will no longer dominate the global economy, orchestrate geopolitics, or overwhelm other cultures unrivaled or unchallenged. In all likelihood, the self-correcting mechanisms in its political and economic systems will enable the US to recover from its current setbacks. Yet it faces unprecedented challenges to its creativity and flexibility, and world economic power will have to be shared with the BRIC countries – Brazil, Russia, India and China – and the financial power centres of the Middle East.

The past two generations, conveniently dated to the reform of the immigration laws in 1965, but by no means solely because of changing patterns of immigration, have seen unique challenges to the traditional model of American culture. So far these have led to tensions and traumas, but not to a transformation. Americans remain tenaciously conservative despite economic and social upheavals. The values of Protestant Christianity have been decisive in the success of the American experiment. This is not to say that the settlers marched into the wilderness towards the frontier waving their Bibles in one hand and copies of the Constitution in the other. The record is far too flawed and ambiguous for that, as Americans are the first to admit. But religion in its American forms was and remains a potent factor in American society and politics, far more than in many other countries. How successfully will America resolve its cultural debates as its population becomes increasingly multicultural and white Protestants become the minority?

Americans, more than any other people, are distinctly suspicious of government and adhere to a complex system of legal and cultural checks and balances to avert the abuse of power. But has the Executive become too strong, or is it not strong enough? What is its role as the forces of globalization reshape Americans' lives and cast doubt on their dreams? Americans also tolerate far wider disparities in wealth than other developed countries, even when they could narrow them. Yet the federal government plays a much greater part in the economy and society than is often realized.

Americans have traditionally veered between two opposed conceptions of the United States' place in the world, from an isolationism that avoids "foreign entanglements" to the fervent promotion of democracy abroad, even by military means. In today's world, America is dominant but cannot dominate. By 2020 China will be the world's largest economy and seven of the ten biggest economies will lie in Asia. The book, however, does not include detailed treatment of the "war on terror," the conflicts in Iraq and Afghanistan, or the instability in the Middle East and elsewhere.

These issues inform and unify the book. Yet it is not a history, nor is it an exercise in boosterism or futurology, but assumes the more modest role as a guide to American culture which readers may refer to in order to engage in debate and draw their own conclusions. Although the author's viewpoint and opinions will be evident, the book attempts to give a balanced picture of the American panorama, making clear what America's heritage is and what its current internal and external debates are about, and referring to further sources of information and analysis for the reader who wishes to study topics further. Many will disagree with the author's selections, omissions and emphases, and specialists will deplore the frequent simplifications and generalizations. Even so, the book contains within one cover a breadth of treatment that will, the author makes bold to believe, rarely be found elsewhere.

The American Panorama will be useful to Americans who have no or limited access to university libraries and academic databases. The book can also be used in the classroom or as a study aid, especially in American Studies, social studies and language arts. Instructors may like to use the appended Questions or Reflection and Discussion for pre-reading reflection and post-reading discussion.

The book also introduces the fundamental concepts of American democracy and the rights and responsibilities of citizenship. It includes material that will be useful for those studying for the new Naturalization (Citizenship) Test. The book does NOT contain US citizenship application instructions or any application forms.

The book will also be of interest to travelers and people who have contact with the US for business or other purposes.

The American Panorama grew out of Culture and Communication classes conducted for junior English language majors at Beijing International Studies University (formerly Beijing Second Foreign Language Institute) in 2003-5 and American Culture classes for seniors there in 2007. The juniors were using the famous textbook Current Issues, Enduring Questions by Barnet and Bedau. Excellent though that book is for stimulating debate on a range of current social, cultural, and political issues, it is not designed for students who come to it with English as a foreign language and with limited exposure to American culture. Such students find many of the assumptions, much of the context, and some of the debates unfamiliar and even inaccessible. The course was offered on the assumption that the instructor would provide supplementary background materials, both factual and analytical, to help the students engage profitably with the texts. As Daniel T. Willingham argues in *Why Don't Students Like School?* students cannot apply generic critical thinking skills to new material unless they first understand that material. And they cannot understand it without the requisite background knowledge. These materials, greatly extended in range and depth, form the basis of the book.

Books like this inevitably date when they turn from principles and summaries to specific details. For that reason, readers who wish to go further into the aspects of America here described are urged to pursue the sources of information listed and to prospect others for themselves. In particular, the statistics presented are offered to stimulate reflection and research and not as headlines for debating complex problems. Reference to, quotations from or summaries of other publications do not necessarily imply that the views expressed in them are the views of this author. Nor can the author accept any responsibility for use made of websites referred to in the book. References to ˜President Bush˜ mean President George W. Bush, except where President George H. W. Bush is specified. Statistics have sometimes been rounded.

CHAPTER 1

THE AMERICAN PANORAMA: THE REGIONS, THE CITIES, AND THE ENVIRONMENT

The frontier of hope that we all innately pursue will never close. Alan Greenspan

Describing the landscape of the United States is like calling home and describing a new girlfriend or boyfriend. Words alone cannot convey the impact of this tremendous country on the traveler and on those who live there. Six factors – size, isolation, topography, climate, resources and patterns of settlement – characterize the material context within which America's uniquely dynamic history and culture have formed the power and personality of the world's greatest nation. America's enormous size and its geographical isolation, the extremes of its climate and the variety of its regions, the richness of its natural resources, and the dispersal of its rural population across vast stretches of the interior, together with the concentration of its urban population in five great areas along the periphery, constitute one sweeping vision—the American panorama. Today that panorama is set in two new contexts: globalization, and communications by air and over the airwaves, which reduce the impact of distance and isolation, and the relative importance of natural resources and topography. The accompanying shift from manufacturing to services is reflected in changing relations between capital and labor, altered patterns of settlements and cities, adaptations in lifestyles, and keenly contested, finely balanced political struggles, not least about protection of the environment. And *place*, that is, where Americans cluster within their panorama and where their culture is set, is still a critical factor to the nation's economic success and Americans' personal fulfillment.

More than half a century ago, Octavio Paz Lozano, the Mexican writer and Nobel Prizewinner, wrote that while all of the New World represented a rejuvenating historical force, the razor's edge of Anglo-Saxon utopianism was honed in North America's unique geography: "pure space, open to human action," which freed men from fighting "against history"—against the class divisions, feudal hierarchies and encrusted traditions that stifled Europe. They instead concentrated their struggle "against nature," formidable though ultimately pliable. Peoples and machines turned forests into farms, deserts into gardens, making the world young again. Native societies that stood in their way were cast out of history, rendered into the "evil that is outside, part of the natural world," like rivers, mountains and other obstacles that must be "domesticated or destroyed." Since "the American reality is the reinvention of itself," Paz continued, then "whatever is found in any way irreducible or unassimilable is not American."

LANDSCAPE

America on the globe

Set between the North Atlantic Ocean to the east and the North Pacific to the west, Canada to the north and Mexico to the south, the mainland United States (US) comprises 48 states, plus the District of Columbia, located on the landmass of North America. The 48 states are often referred to as the "contiguous" or "coterminous" or simply the "lower" states. They stretch over 2,000 miles* (3,200 km) from latitude 50°N to 25°S and extend between longitude 67°W and 127°W. The other two states are Alaska and Hawaii. Alaska is in the North Pacific to the west of Canada, between the 60th and 70th parallels. Hawaii lies at 160°W, 2,000 miles from North America on almost the same latitude as Hong Kong. Alaska is the largest state, with an area of 591,004 square miles (1,530,699 sq km), somewhat smaller than Iran. Rhode Island, on the east coast, is the smallest state, with an area of 1,545 square miles (4,002 sq km). There are 17 other dependencies, mostly islands in the Pacific, which are controlled by the US but do not form part of it. All told, the 50 states form an area of 3.8 million square miles (9.8 million sq km), making the US the third largest country in the world after Russia and Canada. Stretching 2,800 miles (4,500 km) from the Atlantic coast to the Pacific, the US spans four time zones: Eastern, Central, Mountain and Pacific. They are respectively 4, 5, 6, and 7 hours "behind" Universal Time, Coordinated (UTC), which is sometimes referred to as Greenwich Mean Time.

*Distance in the US is measured in miles, feet and inches, and temperature in Fahrenheit, although metric measures are increasingly used in international trade.

The American panorama

The traveler arriving in the US is soon confronted with its enormous landscapes and skylines. Even non-stop, a car trip from coast to coast typically takes at least five days. Nor is it unusual for the gap between the warmest and coldest *high* temperatures on a given day to span 70 degrees Fahrenheit (about 40 degrees Celsius). The physical features of America range from rain forest to waterless desert to bald mountain peaks. Mt McKinley in Alaska, the highest point in the US, stands at 20,320 ft (6,198 m), while Death Valley in California, the lowest point, is actually 282 ft (86 m) below sea level.

The eastern coastal area of the country consists of gently rolling lowlands known as the *coastal plains*. These, which stretch from Maine in the extreme northeast to Texas in the far south, are flat and often swampy. Nowhere in Florida, for example, is more than 350 ft (120 m) above sea level. The soil of the coastal plain is generally very poor, except in the southern part, where it extends many miles inland. Here can be found the Cotton Belt of the Old South and the citrus country of central Florida. The western edge of the coastal plain is marked by a chain of low, almost unbroken mountains, the Appalachians, which stretches southwest from Maine to Alabama in the Deep South. The Appalachians contain huge quantities of easily mined coal and iron, which helps to explain the concentration of heavy industry in the lower region of the Great Lakes, which straddle the Canadian border.

The heart of the US consists of a vast plain known as the *Prairies*, which stretch from central Canada to Mexico and from the Appalachians westwards to the Cordillera. Broken only by the Superior Upland and Black Hills in the north and the Ozark Plateau in the south, the Prairies have been compared to an enormous saucer, since they rise to higher land on all sides. The Prairies are divided into two parts, both of which have rich soil: the wetter, eastern portion is called the *Central Plains*, and the western portion is known as the *Great Plains*.

To the west of the Great Plains rise the Cordillera, which occupies as much as one-third of the US. This is a region of tremendous variety containing several subdivisions. On its eastern border, the Rockies, a high discontinuous chain, rise sharply from the Great Plains. These rugged mountains contain many important minerals such as lead, uranium and gold. The western edge of the Cordillera is marked by a coastal chain of high mountains, among which are broad, fertile valleys. The most important ranges in the western Cordillera are the Sierra Nevada and the Cascades. Between these is a large plateau, with steep cliffs and canyons, basins and isolated smaller ranges. There is no Pacific coastal plain.

Across this enormous area flow some of the world's longest rivers, mostly in the eastern part of the country. The longest is the Missouri (2,540 miles, 3,942km), a tributary of the Mississippi (2,320 miles, 3,760km), which enters the Gulf of Mexico near New Orleans. The Mississippi-Missouri-Red Rock river system is the third longest in the world. Two other tributaries of the Mississippi, the Ohio and the Tennessee, are 981 miles (1,578 km) and 652 miles (1,049 km) long. In the west, the Rio Grande forms part of the US-Mexico border, and flows for almost 2,000 miles (3016 km). The biggest rivers reaching the Pacific are the Colorado 1, 441 miles, (2,320 km), sometimes known as the Red River and is the site of the Hoover Dam, which flows through the Grand Canyon; the Columbia (1,391 miles, 2,240 km) whose heavy flow and 14 dams make it the largest source of hydroelectric power in North America; and the San Joaquin-Sacramento (770 miles, 1,239 km), whose fan-like delta is among the most fertile land in the nation.

Climate

Almost every type of climate can be found in the US, ranging from arctic in Alaska to subtropical in Florida. In fact, despite the latitude, the climate is continental rather than temperate, as the tremendous size of the North American landmass heightens the variations in temperature and precipitation, especially in the Great Plains. Temperatures in South Dakota have reached a maximum of 49°C and a minimum of -60°C.

Most of the country has a humid continental climate with hot summers and cold winters. The lack of natural barriers either to the north or to the south allows cold, dry air to flow southward from Canada and warm, humid air to flow north from Mexico, giving rise to extreme weather of every possible type in the Great Plains and Midwest. Summers are hot and very humid in this region, and rainfall decreases to the west as a result of the rain shadow created by the West Pacific range and the Sierra Nevada. The southwest portion of the Great Plains is the hottest and most arid region, with precipitation, mostly in the form of showers, averaging less than 10 inches (250 mm) a year.

The Pacific coast is almost rainless in the summer, although there is often fog. In the winter there is frequent drizzle, but the climate remains generally warm and dry, especially in California. The eastern part of the country is moderately rainy, with the precipitation fairly well distributed throughout the year. Summers tend to be extremely humid, especially along the coasts of Texas and Florida.

Natural resources

The US possesses vast natural resources. Coal is the most abundant fossil fuel, with production second only to China. The US has the world's largest recoverable coal reserves, sufficient to last for 225 years at present rates of consumption. The three largest coal-producing states are Wyoming, West Virginia and Texas. About half of the nation's electric power comes from coal-fired stations, while natural gas supplies 20%. The main gas fields are found together with the main oil fields in Texas, Louisiana and Alaska. Although the world's third-largest producer of oil, the US is also the world's largest consumer and produces only 40% of its needs. Energy security has become a political issue, as exploration and exploitation of oil and gas reserves are weighed alongside environmental concerns. As of 2008 proven US petroleum reserves had a life of just eight years. The emergency supply in the Strategic Petroleum Reserve was enough as of 2009 for 33 days at current rates of consumption. According to the U.S. Energy Information Administration, the US will require 9% more energy in 2030 than in 2007, about 70% of which will have to be met from oil and gas. Nuclear power, using uranium mined in New Mexico and Wyoming, produces 20% of the nation's energy output. In addition, the US possesses major mineral resources, principally iron ore, and also copper, gold, zinc, magnesium, lead and silver. The US also possesses the world's largest reserves of wood, salt and phosphate rock (used for fertilizers). The most important mineral-producing areas are Texas and California. Mining and quarrying, however, account for only 1% of Gross National Product (GNP).

FACTFILE 1 GEOGRAPHY OF AMERICA

Location:	North America, bordering both the North Atlantic Ocean and the North Pacific Ocean, between Canada and Mexico
Geographic coordinates:	38 00 N, 97 00 W
Map references:	North America
Area:	*total:* 9,826,630 sq km *land:* 9,161,923 sq km *water:* 664,707 sq km *note:* includes only the 50 states and District of Columbia
Area - comparative:	about half the size of Russia; about three-tenths the size of Africa; about half the size of South America (or slightly larger than Brazil); slightly larger than China; more than twice the size of the European Union
Land boundaries:	*total:* 12,034 km *border countries:* Canada 8,893 km (including 2,477 km with Alaska), Mexico 3,141 km *note:* US Naval Base at Guantanamo Bay, Cuba is leased by the US and is part of Cuba; the base boundary is 28 km
Coastline:	19,924 km

Maritime claims:	*territorial sea:* 12 nm *contiguous zone:* 24 nm *exclusive economic zone:* 200 nm *continental shelf:* not specified
Climate:	mostly temperate, but tropical in Hawaii and Florida, arctic in Alaska, semiarid in the great plains west of the Mississippi River, and arid in the Great Basin of the southwest; low winter temperatures in the northwest are ameliorated occasionally in January and February by warm chinook winds from the eastern slopes of the Rocky Mountains
Terrain:	vast central plain, mountains in west, hills and low mountains in east; rugged mountains and broad river valleys in Alaska; rugged, volcanic topography in Hawaii
Elevation extremes:	*lowest point:* Death Valley -86 m *highest point:* Mount McKinley 6,198 m
Natural resources:	coal, copper, lead, molybdenum, phosphates, uranium, bauxite, gold, iron, mercury, nickel, potash, silver, tungsten, zinc, petroleum, natural gas, timber *note:* the US has the world's largest coal reserves with 491 billion short tons accounting for 27% of the world's total
Land use:	*arable land:* 18.01% *permanent crops:* 0.21% *other:* 81.78% (2005)
Irrigated land:	223,850 sq km (2003)
Total renewable water resources:	3,069 cu km (1985)
Freshwater withdrawal (domestic/industrial/agricultural):	*total:* 477 cu km/yr (13%/46%/41% *per capita:* 1,600 cu m/yr (2000)
Natural hazards:	tsunamis; volcanoes; earthquake activity around Pacific Basin; hurricanes along the Atlantic and Gulf of Mexico coasts; tornadoes in the midwest and southeast; mud slides in California; forest fires in the west; flooding; permafrost in northern Alaska, a major impediment to development
Environment - current issues:	air pollution resulting in acid rain in both the US and Canada; the US is the largest single emitter of carbon dioxide from the burning of fossil fuels; water pollution from runoff of pesticides and fertilizers; limited natural fresh water resources in much of the western part of the country require careful management; desertification

Environment - international agreements:	*party to:* Air Pollution, Air Pollution-Nitrogen Oxides, Antarctic-Environmental Protocol, Antarctic-Marine Living Resources, Antarctic Seals, Antarctic Treaty, Climate Change, Desertification, Endangered Species, Environmental Modification, Marine Dumping, Marine Life Conservation, Ozone Layer Protection, Ship Pollution, Tropical Timber 83, Tropical Timber 94, Wetlands, Whaling *signed, but not ratified:* Air Pollution-Persistent Organic Pollutants, Air Pollution-Volatile Organic Compounds, Biodiversity, Climate Change-Kyoto Protocol, Hazardous Wastes
Geography - note:	world's third-largest country by size (after Russia and Canada) and by population (after China and India); Mt. McKinley is highest point in North America and Death Valley the lowest point on the continent

REGIONS

The US owes much of its character and wealth to its good fortune in possessing such a large and varied landmass for its people to inhabit, cultivate and exploit. The country is marked by strong regional characteristics. Indeed, one way in which Americans come to terms with the vast size and variety of their country is to think of themselves as having regional identities indicated by certain traits, such as New England self-reliance, Southern hospitality, Midwestern wholesomeness or Western mellowness.

FACTFILE 2 AMERICA'S REGIONS

- **New England**, made up of Maine, New Hampshire, Vermont, Massachusetts, Connecticut, and Rhode Island
- **The Middle Atlantic**, comprising New York, New Jersey, Pennsylvania, Delaware and Maryland
- **The South**, which runs from Virginia south to Florida and west as far as central Texas. This region also includes West Virginia, Kentucky, Tennessee, North Carolina, South Carolina, Georgia, Alabama, Mississippi, Arkansas, Louisiana, and parts of Missouri and Oklahoma
- **The Midwest**, a broad collection of states sweeping westward from Ohio to Nebraska and including Michigan, Indiana, Wisconsin, Illinois, Minnesota, Iowa, parts of Missouri, North Dakota, South Dakota, Kansas and eastern Colorado
- **The Southwest**, made up of western Texas, portions of Oklahoma, New Mexico, Arizona, Nevada and the southern interior part of California
- **The West**, comprising Colorado, Wyoming, Montana, Utah, California, Nevada, Idaho, Oregon, Washington, Alaska and Hawaii

In fact, the US is not officially divided into regions; and the lists of which states fall into which region are flexible according to one's viewpoint. These groupings are offered simply as a way to begin the otherwise daunting task of getting acquainted with the US.

New England

Traditionally it has been believed that the region was named *New England* by Capt. John Smith because it looked like the coast of England. Some scholars, however, believe that it was Prince Charles, afterward Charles I, who marked the name on Smith's map of the country. Topographically New England is partly separated from the rest of the nation by the Appalachian Mts. to the west. From the Green Mts., the White Mts., and the Berkshire Hills the land slopes gradually toward the Atlantic Ocean. Many short, swift rivers furnish water power; the Connecticut is the region's longest. The six states of New England form the most compact and accessible region in the US. While one state, Rhode Island, can soon be crossed, the others could all fit comfortably inside Oklahoma. America's smallest region, New England has not been blessed with large expanses of rich farmland or a mild climate. Yet it played a dominant role in American development. From the 17th century until well into the 19th, New England was the country's economic and cultural center. The earliest European settlers of New England were English Protestants of firm and settled doctrine, many of whom came in search of religious liberty. They gave the region its distinctive political institution - the town meeting (an outgrowth of meetings held by church elders) in which citizens gathered to discuss issues of the day. Only men of property could vote. Nonetheless, town meetings afforded New Englanders an unusually high level of participation in government. Such meetings still function in many New England communities, in Minnesota and Michigan, and occasionally in the Western states. They have been revived in recent Presidential election campaigns.

Because of the generally poor soil, New Englanders found it difficult to farm the land in large lots, as was common in the South, and agriculture was never a major part of the region's economy. By 1750, many settlers had turned to other pursuits. Excellent harbors and nearby shallow banks teeming with fish made New England a fishing and commercial center, and shipbuilding was important until the end of the era of wooden ships in the mid-1800s. During the colonial period, the region carried on a more extensive foreign commerce than the other colonies and was therefore more affected by the British Navigation Acts, which regulated trade between the Mother Country and the colonies. These were a key issue in relations with Britain, and New England was the focus of the events leading up to the American Revolution, such as the opening engagements at Lexington and Concord in 1775. The return of peace necessitated a reorganization of commerce, with the result that connections were made with the American Northwest and China. The War of 1812 with Britain, however, had an adverse effect on the region's trade, so much so that New England threatened secession from the US. After the war, the growth of manufacturing (especially of cotton textiles) was rapid, and the region became highly industrialized. Such agriculture as there was dwindled with the growth of the West. A large proportion of the immigrants to the Old Northwest Territory came from New England.

New Englanders gained a reputation for hard work, shrewdness, thrift, and ingenuity, characteristics associated with small towns. This ethic of self-reliance and robust individualism is what the poet Emily Dickinson referred to when she wrote, "I think New Englandy." These traits proved invaluable as the Industrial Revolution reached America in the first half of the 19th century. In Massachusetts, Connecticut, and Rhode Island, new factories sprang up to manufacture such goods as clothing, rifles, and clocks. Most of the capital for these businesses came from Boston, which at that time was the financial heart of the nation. New England prosperity supported a vibrant cultural life. Indeed the creation of a distinctive American literature in the first half of the

19th century has been called "the flowering of New England." Prior to the Civil War (1861-65) the region also began to furnish many social and humanitarian leaders and movements. Education is another of the region's greatest legacies. Its cluster of top-ranking universities and colleges - Harvard, Yale, Brown, Dartmouth, Wellesley, Smith, Mt. Holyoke, Williams, Amherst, Wesleyan and others - is unequalled by any other region. As some of the original New England settlers migrated westward, immigrants from Canada, Ireland, Italy, and eastern Europe moved into the region. But despite a changing population, much of the original spirit of New England still remains. It can be seen in the simple, woodframe houses and white church steeples that are features of many small towns, and in the traditional lighthouses that dot the Atlantic coast.

Since World War II, and increasingly in recent years, the character of New England industry has changed. Most traditional manufacturing has relocated to other American states, or to foreign countries such as China, where the products can be made more cheaply. In more than a few factory towns, skilled workers have been left without jobs, and this has fuelled demands for restrictions on imports of foreign goods such as steel, textiles and shoes. Some new employment, however, has been generated by the microelectronics and computer industries, and by tourism, which, long a source of income for the region, remains important throughout the year. There is also stone quarrying, dairying, and potato farming. Boston remains the chief urban center of New England; a number of companies, however, have relocated to many of the smaller cities and suburbs. New England's identities today are many, from the artistic and culturally rejuvenated city of Providence to the booming biotech world of Boston; from the serenity of the Cape Cod National Seashore and the jagged rocky coast of Maine to the skyscraping granite peaks of New Hampshire's White Mountains. And although this region was the heartland of the original English American colonies, New England's heritage today is also Irish and Italian, Vietnamese and Cambodian, Haitian and Portuguese.

The Middle Atlantic

The U.S. Information Agency (USIA) online publication *Portrait of the USA* describes the Middle Atlantic and the South like this: "The Middle Atlantic region was settled by a wider range of people than New England. Dutch immigrants moved into the lower Hudson River Valley in what is now New York State. Swedes went to Delaware. English Catholics founded Maryland, and an English Protestant sect, the Friends (Quakers), settled Pennsylvania. In time, all these settlements became part of the Thirteen Colonies, but the region continued to be a magnet for people of diverse nationalities. Early settlers were mostly farmers and traders, and the region served as a bridge between North and South. Philadelphia, in Pennsylvania, midway between the northern and southern colonies, was home to the Continental Congress, the convention of delegates from the original colonies that organized the American Revolution. The same city was the birthplace of the Declaration of Independence in 1776 and the US Constitution in 1787.

"If New England provided the brains and dollars for 19th-century American expansion, the Middle Atlantic states provided the industrial muscle. The region's largest states, New York and Pennsylvania, became centers of heavy industry (iron, glass, and steel). As heavy industry spread throughout the region, rivers such as the Hudson and Delaware were transformed into vital shipping lanes. Cities on waterways - New York on the Hudson, Philadelphia on the Delaware, Baltimore on Chesapeake Bay - grew dramatically. New York is still the nation's largest city, its financial hub, and its cultural center. Like New England, the Middle Atlantic region has seen much of its heavy industry relocate elsewhere. The city of Buffalo, New York state, for instance, has lost over half its population since 1950. Other industries, such as drug manufacturing and communications, and, in New Jersey, casinos, have taken up the slack. But the declining older industrial base of the region still makes up much of what is called 'the rustbelt'.

The South

"The South is perhaps the most distinctive and colorful American region. The Civil War devastated the South socially and economically. Nevertheless, it retained its unmistakable identity. Like New England, the South was first settled by English Protestants. But whereas New Englanders tended to stress their differences from the old country, Southerners tended to emulate the English. Even so, Southerners were prominent among the leaders of the American Revolution, and four of America's first five presidents were Virginians. After 1800, however, the interests of the manufacturing North and the agrarian South began to diverge.

"Especially in coastal areas, southern settlers grew wealthy by raising and selling cotton and tobacco. The most economical way to raise these crops was on large farms, called *plantations*, which required the work of many laborers. To supply this need, plantation owners relied on slaves brought from Africa, and slavery spread throughout the South (see Chapter 2). Slavery was the most contentious issue dividing North and South. To northerners it was immoral; to southerners it was integral to their way of life. In 1860, 11 southern states left the Union intending to form a separate nation, the Confederate States of America. This rupture led to the Civil War which ended in the Confederacy's defeat and the abolition of slavery. The scars left by the war took decades to heal, and the abolition of slavery failed to provide African Americans with political or economic equality, as Southern towns and cities legalized and refined the practice of racial segregation.

"It took a long, concerted effort by African Americans and their supporters to end segregation. In the meantime, however, the South could point with pride to a 20th-century regional outpouring of literature by, among others, William Faulkner, Thomas Wolfe, Robert Penn Warren, Katherine Anne Porter, Tennessee Williams, Eudora Welty, and Flannery O'Connor. As southerners, black and white, shook off the effects of slavery and racial division, a new regional pride expressed itself under the banner of 'the New South' characterized by such events as the annual Spoleto Music Festival in Charleston, South Carolina, and the 1996 summer Olympic Games in Atlanta, Georgia. Today the South has evolved into a manufacturing region, and high-rise buildings crowd the skylines of such cities as Atlanta and Little Rock, Arkansas. Owing to its mild weather, the South has become a mecca for retirees from other US regions and Canada."

FACTFILE 3 THE SOUTH

Sources of Southern distinctiveness

- Climate and temperament
- Evangelical religion
- Isolation – geographical and social
- Historically a rural economy
- The legacy of slavery, the Civil War, Reconstruction, segregation and pockets of continued poverty

Characteristics of Southern identity

- Self-identification as a Southerner
- An affection for the South
- Similarity to other Southerners
- Dislike of Northerners and "The North"
- A sense of grievance against the North
- A taste for things "Southern" (e.g., food)

The Midwest

The term "Midwest" means different things to different people. For some it includes the "Old Northwest" from Ohio westwards to Iowa and Minnesota. For others it also includes the Dakotas, Nebraska, and Kansas; and for some of those people it does not extend as far east as Ohio. No one seems to include the southern plains (Oklahoma and Texas) in the Midwest, probably because they are so different politically and culturally. Most of the Midwest is prairie. The Mississippi River has acted as a regional lifeline, moving settlers to new homes and foodstuffs to market. The river inspired two classic books, *Life on the Mississippi* and *The Adventures of Huckleberry Finn*, both written by a native Missourian, Samuel Clemens, who took the pseudonym Mark Twain, this being a call by Mississippi river-pilots signifying that there was two fathoms' depth of water, and so the river was safe to navigate.

Portrait of the USA has this to say about the Midwest: "The Midwest is a cultural crossroads. Starting in the early 1800s, easterners moved there in search of better farmland, and soon Europeans bypassed the East Coast to migrate directly to the interior: Germans to eastern Missouri, Swedes and Norwegians to Wisconsin and Minnesota. The region's fertile soil made it possible for farmers to produce abundant harvests of cereal crops such as wheat, oats, and corn. The region was soon known as the nation's "breadbasket." Midwesterners are praised as being open, friendly, and straightforward. They tend to be cautious in politics, but their caution is sometimes peppered with protest. The Midwest gave birth to one of America's two major political parties, the Republican Party, which was formed in the 1850s to oppose the spread of slavery into new states. At the turn of the century, the region also spawned the Progressive Movement, which largely consisted of farmers and merchants intent on making government less corrupt and more responsive to the will of the people. Perhaps because of their geographic location, many midwesterners have been strong adherents of isolationism, the belief that Americans should not concern themselves with foreign wars and problems. "

Lincoln, Grant, Truman and Obama are among Presidents from the Midwest, as was President Eisenhower (1952-60). Also from the region was the notorious Senator Joseph McCarthy, who represented Wisconsin from 1946 to 1957. He was noted for claiming that there were large numbers of Communists and Soviet spies and sympathizers inside the federal government and elsewhere. Ultimately, McCarthy's methods, and his inability to substantiate his claims led him to be discredited and in effect censured by the Senate. Today the term *McCarthyism* is used to describe demagogic, reckless, and unsubstantiated accusations, as well as public attacks on the character or patriotism of political opponents. The character of Senator John Iselin in the 1959 novel *The Manchurian Candidate* by Richard Condon (filmed 1962) was closely modeled on McCarthy.

The region's hub is Chicago, Illinois, the nation's third largest city. This major Great Lakes port is a connecting point for rail lines and air traffic to far-flung parts of the nation and the world. At its heart stands Willis Tower, at 1353 ft (447m), one of the world's tallest buildings. Post-industrial Chicago emphasizes aesthetic improvements, and encouragement of neighborhood redevelopment (i.e., gentrification). These strategies aim to make Chicago more attractive to talented knowledge workers.

The Southwest

"The Southwest differs from the adjoining Midwest in weather (drier), population (less dense), and ethnicity (strong Spanish-American and Native-American minorities). Outside the cities, the region is a land of open spaces, mostly desert. The magnificent Grand Canyon is located in this region, as is Monument Valley, the starkly beautiful backdrop for many western films. Monument Valley is within the Navajo Reservation, home of the most populous American Indian tribe. To the south and east lie dozens of other Indian reservations, including those of the Hopi, Zuni, and Apache tribes.

"Large parts of the Southwest once belonged to Mexico. The US obtained this land following the Mexican-American War of 1846-48. Its Mexican heritage continues to exert a strong influence on the region, which is a convenient place for immigrants (legal or illegal) from farther south to settle. The region's population is growing rapidly, with Arizona in particular rivaling the southern states as a destination for retired Americans in search of a warm climate.

"Population growth in the hot, arid Southwest has depended on two human artifacts: the dam and the air conditioner. Dams on the Colorado and other rivers, and aqueducts such as those of the Central Arizona Project have brought water to once-small towns such as Las Vegas, Nevada; Phoenix, Arizona; and Albuquerque, New Mexico, allowing them to become metropolises. Las Vegas is renowned as one of the world's centers for gambling, while Santa Fe, New Mexico, is famous as a center for the arts, especially painting, sculpture, and opera. Another system of dams and irrigation projects supplies water to the Central Valley of California, which is noted for producing large harvests of fruits and vegetables" (USIA, *op. cit.*).

The West

"Americans have long regarded the West as the last frontier. Yet California has a history of European settlement older than that of most Midwestern states. Spanish priests founded missions along the California coast a few years before the outbreak of the American Revolution. In the 19th century, California and Oregon entered the Union ahead of many states to the east.

"The West is a region of scenic beauty on a grand scale. All of its 11 states are partly mountainous, and the ranges are the sources of startling contrasts. To the west of the peaks, winds from the Pacific Ocean carry enough moisture to keep the land well-watered. To the east, however, the land is very dry. Parts of western Washington State, for example, receive 20 times the amount of rain that falls on the eastern side of the state's Cascade Range" (*op. cit.*).

The western economy is varied. California, for example, is both an agricultural and a high-technology manufacturing state. In much of the West the population is sparse, and the federal government owns and manages millions of hectares of undeveloped land. Aside from grazing, lumbering, and mining, Americans use these areas for recreational and commercial activities, such as fishing, boating, camping and hiking. In recent years some local residents who earn their livelihoods on federal land have come into conflict with the land's managers, who are required to keep land use within environmentally acceptable limits.

"Alaska, the northernmost state in the Union, is a vast land of few, but hardy, people and great stretches of wilderness, protected in national parks and wildlife refuges. Hawaii is the only state in the union in which Asian Americans outnumber residents of European stock. Beginning in the 1980s large numbers of Asians have also settled in California, mainly around Los Angeles. In 1869 the western territory of Wyoming became the first place that allowed women to vote and to hold elected office.

"Western cities are known for their tolerance. Perhaps because so many westerners have moved there from other regions to make a new start, interpersonal relations are as a rule marked by a live-and-let-live attitude. After the Civil War a large number of black Americans moved west in search of equal opportunities, and many of them gained some fame and fortune as cowboys, miners, and prairie settlers. Los Angeles - and Southern California as a whole - bears the stamp of its large Mexican-American population. Now the second largest city in the nation, Los Angeles is best known as the home of the Hollywood film industry. Fuelled by the growth of Los Angeles and the "Silicon Valley" area near San José, California has become the most populous of all the states."

Regional variety

How much sense does it make to talk about American 'regions' when practically all Americans can watch the same television shows and go to the same fast-food restaurants for dinner? One way to answer the question is by giving examples of lingering regional differences in food, speech, attitudes and outlook. Consider the food Americans eat. Most of it is standard everywhere. A person can buy packages of frozen peas bearing the same label in Idaho, Missouri, and Virginia. Cereals, candy bars, and many other items also come in identical packages from Alaska to Florida. Generally, the quality of fresh fruits and vegetables does not vary much from one state to the next. On the other hand, it would be unusual to be served hush puppies (a kind of fried dough) or grits (boiled and ground corn prepared in a variety of ways) in Massachusetts or Illinois, but normal in Georgia. Other regions also have favorites that are hard to find elsewhere. Moreover, while American English is generally standard, American *speech* often differs according to the part of the country. Southerners tend to speak slowly, in what is referred to as a "Southern drawl," Midwesterners use "flat" a's (as in "bad" or "cat"), while the New York City patois features a number of Yiddish words such as "schlep," "nosh" and "nebbish" contributed by the city's large Jewish population. Regional differences make themselves felt in less tangible ways, too, such as in attitudes and outlooks. An example is the attention paid to foreign events in newspapers. In the East, where people look out across the Atlantic Ocean, papers tend to show greater concern with what is happening in Europe, the Middle East, Africa, and western Asia. On the West Coast, by contrast, news editors give more attention to events in East Asia and Australia" (*op. cit.*).

CITIES AND METRO AREAS

Four-in-five Americans live in cities. According to the U.S. Census Bureau, there are 251 cities of over 100,000 population and 27 with over 500,000. Most of the urban centers lie along the Atlantic and Pacific coasts, the Gulf of Mexico and the Great Lakes. The most densely populated area is the relatively small Northeast, where nearly a quarter of America's people live. Overall, cities expanded rapidly during the 1990s, growing nearly twice as fast as in the 1980s. Western and southern cities grew the fastest, especially in Texas and Arizona, while urban industrial centers in the Midwest and Northeast declined in population. New York remains the country's largest city, with a population of 8.4 million in 2008. Census figures show that all of the metropolitan areas with populations of at least 5 million have experienced growth since 2000, ranging from 29% for Dallas to 5% for Philadelphia. New York has gained 355,000 residents, more than the total number of people who live in St. Louis, and is growing faster than any other city, followed by Phoenix and Houston. The total population within metropolitan areas increased by 14%, while the non-metropolitan population grew by 10%. Many of the older cities are losing population from their core areas while the suburbs around them are still growing. But even taking into account total metro area, the newer sunbelt cities are growing at a faster rate than older, industrial ones. The fastest growing cities are in Texas, North Carolina, Arizona and California. For example, Phoenix passed Philadelphia, which lost about 70,000 residents during the 2000s, to become the fifth biggest American city. The top 10 cities of a hundred years ago would have included places like Baltimore (now at 631,366, the 19th largest), Boston (590,763, 22nd), Cleveland (444,313, 40th) and St. Louis (347,181, 52nd). During the 2000s, however, 80,000 people left Detroit, while Cleveland (- 6.9 percent), Pittsburgh (-6.5 percent) and Buffalo (-5.7 percent) also continued to experience big losses. New Orleans lost more than half its residents owing to Hurricane Katrina in 2005, but since then, it has been one of the country's fastest growing cities from a post-storm population of 223,000. Its population grew 8.2% in the 12 months that ended July 1, 2008, gaining 23,740 people to reach 311,853, according to the Census Bureau. That still leaves the population well below its pre-storm level of 484,674, however.

FACTFILE 4 TOP 10 CITIES IN THE U.S. BY POPULATION AND SIZE RANK

Rank	Core city	State	Population	Metro area rank	Metro area population	Region
1	**New York City**	New York	8,250,567	1	18,818,536	Northeast
2	**Los Angeles**	California	3,849,378	2	12,950,129	West
3	**Chicago**	Illinois	2,833,321	3	9,505,748	Midwest
4	**Houston**	Texas	2,169,248	6	5,539,949	South
5	**Phoenix**	Arizona	1,512,986	13	4,039,182	West
6	**Philadelphia**	Pennsylvania	1,448,394	5	5,826,742	Northeast
7	**San Antonio**	Texas	1,296,682	29	1,942,217	South
8	**San Diego**	California	1,256,951	17	2,941,454	West
9	**Dallas**	Texas	1,232,940	4	6,003,967	South
10	**San Jose**	California	929,936	30	1,787,123	West

FACTFILE 5 TOP TEN US CITIES BY PERCENT POPULATION CHANGE, 1990–2000

Rank	Place name	Population		Change, 1990 to 2000	
		April 1, 2000	*April 1, 1990*	*Number*	*Percent*
1.	Augusta-Richmond County, Ga.	199,775	44,639	155,136	347.5
2.	Gilbert, Ariz.	109,697	29,188	80,509	275.8
3.	Vancouver, Wash.	143,560	46,380	97,180	209.5
4.	Henderson, Nev.	175,381	64,942	110,439	170.1
5.	North Las Vegas, Nev.	115,488	47,707	67,781	142.1
6.	Athens-Clark County, Ga.	101,489	45,734	55,755	121.9
7.	Peoria, Ariz.	108,364	50,618	57,746	114.1
8.	Pembroke Pines, Fla.	137,427	65,452	71,975	110.0
9.	Chandler, Ariz.	176,581	90,533	86,048	95.0
10.	Las Vegas, Nev.	478,434	258,295	220,139	85.2

Migration and segregation

In the 1990s, 100 million Americans resettled across a county border. As they have moved over the past three decades, Americans have clustered in communities with similar ways of life, beliefs and politics. They have sought out or gravitated toward those who share their lifeworlds, made up of fundamental factors such as race, class, gender, and age, but also, now more than ever, personal tastes, styles, opinions and values. The population is segregating itself into endless variations of political and lifestyle enclave. In particular, creatives, people who think for a living, such as managers, artists, writers, engineers, and teachers, have moved to high-tech cities: Atlanta, Phoenix, San Francisco, Denver, Portland, Austin, Dallas, Raleigh-Durham, Washington, Seattle, Minneapolis, and Boise. City life is essential for economies of ideas to flourish. They provide a social network for problem solving, discovery, and innovation. In response, corporations have begun moving where pools of talent are deepening. The cities that have grown the fastest and become the richest are the ones where people with college degrees have congregated. Migration patterns have thus created segregation by income. It is noticeable that few cities have both a large creative class and a sizeable working class.

To a large degree, this clustering is a defensive reaction to a society, a country, and a world that seem largely beyond an individual's control or understanding. For generations, people used local networks of affiliation, their trust in a national government, and long-established religious denominations to make sense of the world. But for many people those old institutions no longer provide a safe harbor, and the general anxiety the country feels is building.

But homogeneous suburbs lend themselves to isolation and groupthink. The consequences are balkanized communities whose inhabitants find other Americans to be culturally incomprehensible; a growing intolerance for political differences that has made national consensus difficult if not impossible; and politics so polarized that Congress is gridlocked and elections are no longer just contests over policies, but bitter choices between ways of life. Statistics show that in the 1976 presidential election only 20% of Americans lived in counties that voted for one candidate or the other by more than a 20% margin. By 2004, 48% of America's counties recorded over 20% margins for one of the candidates. Consequently, political leaders are more and more reflecting the segregation of American communities which themselves are becoming more isolated and self-absorbed.

Rather than becoming more tolerant, Americans who have severed traditional community, faith, and family ties have forged new affiliations based on lifestyle preferences. Politically, the nation is divided between Democrat urban areas and rural Republican ones. Hence there is growing difficulty for bipartisan compromise in a country where politicians win office by satisfying their most radical constituents. Mixed company moderates; like-minded company polarizes, enforces conformity and tends to grow more extreme in the majority view.

Big-city revival

Despite the decline of America's larger old cities, some are on the upswing after a wave of reformist mayors who held office in the 1990s. Even before the economic boom of that decade, innovations in school, welfare, and crime policy had begun to revive the fortunes of Cleveland, Milwaukee, Indianapolis, Denver, Philadelphia, and Pittsburgh, "the renaissance city." But most older cities will need several more successful administrations for the revival to be sustained, and must transform their dysfunctional political cultures. Unlike the crusading mayors of the Progressive era, none of the recent reformers were part of a broad social movement to institutionalize reform.

The prosperity of the 1990s was different from earlier expansions. The 1960s boom had been accompanied by riots, rapidly rising crime rates, and social breakdown. In the 1980s, many major cities, including Detroit and Baltimore, never caught the economic wave, while those that did suffered from increasing crime and welfare dependency. Inequality still reigns in the industrial city. Nightmare landscapes of poverty with their zones of devastation are a feature of all former industrial cities in the US. Yet the bulk of the population does not live with hunger and economic insecurity as in the Depression of the 1930s. In the 1990s, in fact, urban home ownership reached historic highs, and poverty dropped sharply to its lowest rate for 20 years. The trend was particularly pronounced in New York, where the greatest gains occurred in poor outer-borough neighborhoods. Even so, American cities continue to face serious problems, due to inadequate tax bases, years of neglect, and weak government regulation and oversight. The quality of drinking water, for example, is deteriorating in major cities such as Washington, D.C., where the levels of lead have been found to be too high.

The 2000 Census in fact suggests that cities all across America have been "returning to the future" as incubators of new businesses and catalysts of upward mobility for immigrants. Fuelled by immigration, New York, Los Angeles, and Miami have reached record population levels. Some degree of prosperity has returned not only to these and other fast-growing cities like Denver, Charlotte, and Columbus, but also to so-called "dinosaurs" like Chicago, Boston, and Kansas City, all once written off as dying. Eight of the ten largest cities grew in the 1990s, and even those that continued to shrink, such as Detroit, Philadelphia, and Cleveland, did so at much slower rates or in some cases nearly stopped shrinking. It would be a mistake, however, to assume that the big cities can ever again achieve the dominant position they once held. America continues to become more suburban, as city populations continue to decline. For every three households that return to the city, five depart for the suburbs. Growth is fastest in overwhelmingly white suburbia, but minorities have joined the move out of the cities as well. As recently as the early 1990s, rising crime, welfare dependency, and unemployment rates, as well as riots in Los Angeles and New York, led many to assume that central cities were dying if not already dead. What happened to turn things around? One of the causes was the surging economy. Another was immigration. But both of those elements were present in the 1980s and failed to spur an urban revival.

Three broad social changes in the 1990s made an enormous difference to American cities. First, the storm created by the rise of black political power in the 1960s had largely passed. Day-to-day racial tensions eased, and African American leaders were incorporated into the political classes of all the major cities. Race remains a major factor in local politics, but after three decades of black mayors, whites are far less fearful of blacks in power, while blacks have, for the most part, come to recognize that black mayors are fully capable of failing their own core constituency.

Secondly, the decline of manufacturing began to offer opportunities in many cities. The reduction of manufacturing production in the past half-century occurred almost entirely within city boundaries, while non-urban manufacturing held steady. The first phase of the high-tech revolution occurred largely in suburbia, but the second phase, involving designing software content, has found milieus of innovation in the creative quarters of older cities. Deindustrialization, a disaster for some cities, has been an opportunity for others to upgrade their quality of life by turning manufacturing lofts into living spaces and once-polluted waterways into recreation areas. Old manufacturing districts, like Soho in New York and Lodo in Denver, are now fashionable places to live. In San Francisco, loft spaces are popular office locations for internet site and software producers. In Chicago, warehouse spaces now house nightclubs and restaurants. The mix of industrial heritage, high tech, and exotic consumption is a characteristic of the modern American urban experience. College graduates have flocked back to the centers of cities, which have become the place to meet other young, single twenty-somethings. Refurbished lofts and a newly developed nightlife like that of Baltimore's harbor neighborhood, Fell's Point, attract young professionals, while empty-nesters are drawn to the city's museums, restaurants, and theatres. Many of those who work in Fell's Point are part of the software and graphics industry. Even famously conservative Cincinnati, a city torn apart by riots, is home to a thriving software sector.

Thirdly, retailers have discovered the untapped buying power of the underserved inner-city market. Thus cities have benefited from the saturation of suburban markets. But although the new elite co-exists in the old industrial spaces alongside a spatially concentrated underclass, social groups are sharply segregated, and urban elites often cordon off the underprivileged from the revived zones of consumption, sometimes creating the gated neighborhoods common to many underdeveloped countries.

City policies that made a difference

But these changes would not have brought about the resurgence of big cities without a concurrent reconceptualisation of urban issues. In Washington, D.C., mayor Marion Barry captured the essence of many 1980s mayoralties when he insisted that he should not be held accountable for the mayhem in his city. He blamed the federal government for not giving the District enough money. Over the course of the 1990s, in fact the federal government's involvement in cities declined, while the cities, newly skeptical of Washington, revived. If Barry depicted himself as a cork on the ocean, the reform mayors of the 1990s, beginning with Milwaukee's John Norquist, assumed responsibility for the condition of their cities. Denver mayor Wellington Webb encapsulated their approach when he described mayors as CEOs, fully accountable for the performance of city government.

All the new mayors recognized that city centers would continue to lose population and jobs to their suburbs unless steps were taken to bring taxes under control and improve the quality of life. This conclusion led to a new concern with the details of daily existence. Mayor Richard Michael Daley of Chicago planted trees throughout the city, even on the roof of City Hall, and has recently leased parts of the city's infrastructure. Cleveland's mayor Mike White effaced graffiti and filled in potholes. John Norquist encouraged excellence in the architectural design for new projects in Milwaukee, arguing that the strength of cities was their public spaces. Cities offer pleasures of public life unavailable in suburbs, he noted, where "life is filtered through a two screen experience - the TV and the windshield."

Less dramatic, but almost as significant, has been the new attention paid to neighborhood vitality. Mayors now recognize that retail is crucial to a neighborhood's revival. Boston has built 12 new supermarkets. "Commerce isn't the last step in a community's comeback; more often, it has to be the first," Mayor Merino explains. "A supermarket is the focal point of a community; you need it to get the foot traffic." Mayor Graham Richard of Fort Wayne, Indiana (pop. 206,000) and Supervisor Mary Ellen Heyman of Irondequoit, New York (pop. 52,000) have announced ambitious and expensive plans to modernize their cities' infrastructure.

But the greatest achievement of the 1990s was bringing crime under control. New York, under its famous mayor, Rudy Giuliani, led the way with the "broken windows" policing strategy. Broken-windows policing takes seriously small crimes, such as public drinking and urination, that can make a neighborhood seem threatening to residents and inviting to would-be felons. In the most famous example of the broken-windows approach, the New York City Transit Police began arresting turnstile jumpers in the early 1990s and found that one in seven was wanted on outstanding felony warrants.

The quality of life in cities has also been improved by the conversion of unused facilities into public recreational spaces. Disused industrial land, derelict warehouses and even decommissioned military sites are being converted into play areas and parks. In California, Los Angeles has introduced Fitness Zones into its parks, with free cardio and strength-training machines, while Irvine's former military airport has been transformed into Great Park, America's largest landscaped municipal green space in over a century, one and a half times the size of Central Park in New York. It contains a sports area with football fields, a wooded canyon and a botanical garden. Meanwhile in New York, the High Line, the derelict elevated freight railroad around west Manhattan, has been turned into a scenic urban walkway.

City renewal - Detroit

Detroit, the strategically- sited Great Lakes city where Henry Ford and others began manufacturing cars, is the home of the US auto industry. But it has become an icon of the failed American city, arguably a test case for the future of the cities of industrial America; and its future direction may as likely be downhill as up. Detroit's population has declined from 1.8 million in 1950 to just over 900,000 in 2008 (over 80% of whom are African American), the first US city of over 1 million to fall below that size. The nation's fourth-largest city in the 1930s, it now ranks eleventh. The city is as small as it was in the 1920s, before the auto industry boom that made it an industrial powerhouse. The automakers have laid off over 100,000 workers. GM, for example, at one time employed 460,000, but now employs 60,000 and is expected to lay off one-third of those. White flight to the suburbs, triggered by the 1967 race riots, and facilitated by the freeway system, has eroded the city's tax base. Detroit's poverty rate, 28.5%, is the nation's highest, as is its unemployment rate (among major metropolitan areas) at 22%. Its functional illiteracy rate is 47%, and its foreclosure rate on homes whose owners cannot pay their mortgages is among the highest in the nation. Detroit has numerous neighborhoods suffering from urban decay. In 2009 there were 80,000 abandoned buildings. Approximately one-third of the city lies empty or unused, an area about the size of San Francisco.

Detroit has been near collapse for years. The government at times has barely functioned. City Hall has long been racked by corruption and cronyism, and in 2008 former mayor Kwame Kilpatrick was jailed. In the early '90s, murder and arson soared. The city did not even plow residential streets after snowstorms. Detroit's downtown was so vacant that it was proposed that the empty skyscrapers be turned into a necropolis, a monument to urban failure. When the city cut back on power for lighting to save money, people joked that the last one to leave should turn off the lights. For decades, city leaders and local business executives have been predicting an imminent revival of their desolate downtown. For all their cheerleading, though, nothing much has changed. One of the biggest obstacles to revival is the city's reputation as a civic failure. Even the Renaissance Center, an enormous office and hotel complex with seven soaring glass towers built 30 years ago on the city's riverfront, did not spark the turnaround that its name promised. Yet like Philadelphia, the city caught something of the 1990s rising tide and there are pockets where revival is starting to happen.

Thus far, the city has had some success, most notably the addition of the Compuware World Headquarters, GM's OnStar (car security) headquarters, and the offices of GM-owned EDS at the Renaissance Center; the PricewaterhouseCoopers Plaza offices adjacent to Ford Field; and the 2006 completion of Ernst & Young's offices at One Kennedy Square. In 2007, Quicken Loans announced its development agreement with the city to move its world headquarters, and 4,000 employees, to Detroit, a move considered highly important by city planners to reestablish the historic downtown. GM have also have moved their headquarters there. The Westin Book Cadillac Hotel has undergone a $200 million renovation, creating 455 rooms and 67 condominiums, including the first in the city to sell for more than $1 million. Three new casinos, the MGM Grand Hotel and Casino, MotorCity Casino and Greektown Casino have been built and are contributing valuable tax revenues. They have created thousands of jobs, and brought luxury hotel rooms to a city which had hardly any. The Russell Industrial Center, a former auto-body manufacturing plant converted into more than 1 million sq ft (93,000 sq m) of studio space, is one example of how new uses are being found for Detroit's vacant structures. The developers have leased large parcels at bargain-basement prices, and a small-business community has flourished. The city's baseball team, the Tigers, and football team, the Lions, have returned to new downtown stadiums. Luxury highrises at Riverfront Towers and New Center are drawing upwardly mobile professionals downtown. In April 2008, the city announced a $300-million stimulus plan to create jobs, demolish blighted properties and revitalize neighborhoods, financed by city bonds and paid for by earmarking about 15% of the wagering (gambling) tax. A neighborhood already revitalized is the Lafayette Park residential district laid out by Mies van der Rohe in the 1950s and '60s.

Detroit's waterfront meanwhile shows a variety of architectural styles. The postmodern neo-gothic spires of the Comerica Tower at Detroit Center (1993) were designed to blend with the city's Art Deco skyscrapers. The first phase of the Detroit International Riverfront includes a partially completed three and one-half mile riverfront promenade with a combination of parks, residential buildings, and commercial areas accessing Belle Isle (the largest island park in a US city). Modernization of the city's streetlights has boosted the number of working lights from 60 percent to 95 percent. Famed as Motown, a center for jazz, rock and techno, Detroit has a thriving entertainment scene, including the nation's largest theatre district outside New York. In 2007, downtown Detroit was named among the best big city neighborhoods in which to retire by *CNN Money Magazine*.

But the city's projected budget deficit recently spurred ratings agencies to downgrade its municipal bonds to junk status. Moreover, experts like Kevin Boyle, a Detroit native and professor of history at Ohio State University, deny that a revitalized downtown will lead to a revitalized city. Despite the new investments downtown, there are not enough new jobs in neighborhoods, and many problems still remain in public services. Detroit in the opinion of some still has not decided whether city government exists to provide jobs for organized interests or services to citizens. The auto industry is slumping and severely affected by the financial crisis. Even so, there is hope of new growth from fuel-efficient cars and company restructuring. But the city has a long way to go. It will need to become smaller, greener and denser, and will need better times throughout the state of Michigan before it can be called vibrant. At present, many streets are largely deserted after dark and new developments are surrounded by empty buildings.

The city of the future

Unlike most urban cultures, that of the US has been dominated not by the dictates of princes or priests, but by the efforts of ambitious entrepreneurs and immigrants. American cities have been driven by a protean, ever-shifting commercial and middle-class culture, willing to break the bonds of tradition. As the sociologist E. Digby Baltzell (1915-1996) noted, the population in New York and other American cities has been heterogeneous from top to bottom. Social mobility, Baltzell said, constituted the fundamental reality of American urbanism. In this country, cities emerged as the principal North American bastion for those who sought to improve their lives. The newcomers were joined by others from rural America, including, by the early 20th century, many African Americans.

The American city is made up of distinct zones: the downtown; the lower middle-class suburbs; the middle class inner-ring suburbs, once inhabited by the elite; the immigrant enclaves typified by strip malls; the postwar suburbs with more green spaces; and the new exurbs with 3,200 square-foot middle-class homes for the nouveaux riche. Such cities often were not pleasant or culturally edifying. Indeed, the modern American city has become synonymous with cookie cutter, strip mall consumerism and flash-bang glitter, but it became increasingly difficult there to restrict a person into tight caste boundaries.

New York and other top cities, including Chicago, Los Angeles, San Francisco and Boston, have been suffering the largest net outflow of residents to the suburbs of virtually all places in the country, although migration has slowed with the recession. Despite the many improvements over the past decade in New York, over 8% more residents, 150,000 in all, left in 2006 than in 1993. New York now has the smallest share of middle-income families in the nation, according to a 2008 Brookings Institution study. Since the 1990s virtually all the gains made in the New York economy have accrued to the highest income earners. Much the same pattern can be seen in Chicago, which is widely touted as America's "model city," Chicago has lost its largely white middle class 40 percent faster than elsewhere and remains America's most segregated big city. Its black population remains among the poorest, and most isolated, of any ethnic population in America. Meanwhile, like other American cities, Chicago now has a growing surplus of luxury condos.

Urban dwellers face multiple problems: high taxes and regulation, poor schools, a lack of middle class jobs, and crime. Urban residents generally pay higher taxes, and more for utilities, insurance, trash collection, and sewer services than those living elsewhere. Manhattan is by far the most expensive urban area in the US, with an average cost of living more than twice as high as the national average. San Francisco, another city that has seen large-scale middle-class flight, ranks second. The Washington, D.C. area, Los Angeles, and Boston also suffer extremely high living costs. These costs are most onerous on the middle class, particularly as their children age and as families expand. For instance, since most middle-class families in big cities need to have two working parents just to get by, child care becomes a necessity for those without grandparents or other relatives to look after young children. In places like Chicago, Washington, Boston, San Francisco, New York, or Los Angeles these costs typically run from $13,000 to $25,000 per child annually. Later, because of the poor schools, many of these families must then contemplate paying considerable sums to send their children to private schools, particularly after the elementary level. This can add from a few thousand dollars to $30,000 a year to their annual costs. Hence the rapidly declining numbers of students in most urban school districts, including those of Chicago, Seattle, Portland, Washington, and San Francisco, cities which have been hailed as urban renewal success stories. Since 2002, for example, Chicago's school system has declined by 41,000 students. America's core cities have among the lowest percentage of children under 17 in the nation. The cities are losing their historic role as incubators of upward mobility. In the New York's Bronx, the city's most heavily Latino county, roughly one in three households lives in poverty, the highest rate for any urban county in the nation.

Three constructs offer competing visions of the city of the future: the Luxury City, the Creative Age City, and the Traditional City. According to Joel Kotkin, "Most urban areas have focused on creating what New York Mayor Michael Bloomberg famously dubbed the 'luxury city.' To pay for often high public employee costs, the luxury city can only survive off the taxes and spending of the wealthy, and because other groups—empty nesters, singles and students—demand relatively little in the way of basic services like schools and public health facilities…. A key group coveted by cities are the legions of baby boomer 'empty nesters', who are expected to rediscover the allure of a fast-paced youthful lifestyle" (*ibid.*). They are supposedly interested in indulging the sophistication of city dwelling. "Despite an enormous amount of publicity about empty nesters moving back to the city, however, surveys conducted by the housing industry find that most aging boomers—upwards of 70 percent—are aging in place, mostly in the suburbs. The numbers moving back into the urban core remain negligible….In Manhattan, where the rich [of New York] are concentrated, the disparities between the classes have been rising steadily. In 1980 it ranked 17th among the nation's counties for social inequality; today it ranks first, with the top fifth of wage earners earning 52 times that of the lowest fifth…."

The University of Chicago's Terry Nichols Clark says cultural activities are crucial to urban economic vitality and cities should focus less on being vehicles for class mobility. Workers in the elite sectors of the postindustrial city make "quality of life" demands, emphasizing aesthetic concerns, and in their consumption practices can experience their own urban location as if tourists. Cities are thus what he calls "entertainment machines" for the privileged. Therefore cities should adopt smart growth strategies to attract educated, mobile knowledge workers engaged in finance, IT and media production: "what matters is the continuing influence which the city as a socially structured space exerts in the conduct of human life." Even Pullman's railroad car factory in Chicago is being rehabilitated as a potential tourist destination. For these elite residents, the lures are not economic opportunity, but rather consumption opportunities in the fashionable restaurants, bars, shops, and boutiques abundant in restructured urban neighborhoods. In this formulation, cities become the domicile primarily of the young, the rich (and their servants), and those members of the underclass who have nowhere else to go. What emerges, in the end, Kotkin observes, is a city largely without children, particularly of school-age, and with a diminishing middle class.

City planners and urban developers who are proponents of the Creative Age City favor the unattached: the so-called "yuspies," young urban single professionals. But surveys of this group—the other large age cohort in the population aside from seniors—show that most prefer a single-family home and, like their parents, seem most likely to head to the suburbs. Scholars such as Richard Florida argue that in the "creative age," places of residence should be leased like cars. In his mind, single-family homes, the ideal of homeownership, should be replaced by a new kind of housing that embraces higher forms of density without long-term commitment by residents to a particular residence or location. This model of urbanism is characterized by a European-style pattern of elite urbanism in the core, with a growing concentration of low-wage workers in the least favored parts of the urban periphery. Another example quoted is the San Francisco-Oakland-San Jose triangle, the premier zone of advanced technological enterprise in the country. Seattle, Portland, and Austin, Texas have seen thriving youth cultures match the growth of their technology sectors in a convergence of bohemian and bourgeois cultures.

Those who wish to revive the traditional city focus on middle-class neighborhoods and the institutions that create a sense of community which satisfies needs for belonging, esteem and intellectual and aesthetic satisfaction. Environmental psychology, specifically a sense of place, is a critical factor in housing choice. Oakland, across the bay from San Francisco, continues to be dogged by Gertrude Stein's famous proclamation that "there is no there there." The sustainable city of the future, according to revival thinkers, will depend on commitment and long-term residents. It will feature moderate density housing and shopping streets, good schools, green spaces and a safe environment. The revival of some neighborhoods in Chicago, New York and San Francisco, the south and west of St Louis, and the San Fernando Valley neighborhoods of Los Angeles, suggests that cities can still nurture a middle class. Falling urban rents and residential housing prices may make urban living affordable and desirable enough for middle class younger people, including families, earning $50-$60K a year for them to eschew the move to the suburbs.

To be successful in the longer term, however, the cities depend on developing an economic base for the people who might settle there. Many traditional industries such as heavy manufacturing and warehousing, and the middle management jobs that go with them, are disappearing. But a new urban economy may arise, built around people working in small firms, or independently in growing fields such as information, education, healthcare, and culture, or as specialists in a wide array of business services. In San Francisco, for example, by 2006 there were an estimated 70,000 home-based businesses and a thriving culture of self-employed "Bedouins" working in post-industrial professions. Similarly, the close-in communities of the San Fernando Valley are home to large contingents of entertainment industry workers, many of them self-employed. Workers in media, graphic arts, and other specialized services have also been among the few groups of middle and upper-middle income earners to see rapid growth in New York's outer boroughs. Advocates for urban revival believe that these post–industrial age artisans, along with more traditional members of the middle class such as civil servants, teachers, nurses, and other service workers, could provide the critical mass of committed residents needed to make urban neighborhoods work.

Public health

Americans' urban lifestyle is based on the car, where cheap 700-calorie cheeseburgers can be only a 10-minute drive away. But junk food and lack of exercise is literally killing thousands. According to the Centers for Disease Control Behavioral Risk Factor Surveillance System, obesity is associated with 112,000 deaths each year, and contributes to an increased risk of contracting chronic illnesses, including heart disease, diabetes, and some cancers. Urban sprawl is also commonly cited as a contributory factor in public health risks. Carol Coletta, president of CEOs for Cities, points out that the economically bifurcated population, lack of transit options, unwalkable neighborhoods, and favored Southern cuisine are a deadly formula.

Experts talk of "reshaping the environment" to foster increased physical activity, while cities are experimenting with new approaches to promote public health. Many cities are aware of public health challenges such as obesity and inactivity and are working to improve access to amenities like parks, while also mounting advertising campaigns on the dangers of leading a sedentary life. Consultants and grassroots organizations have lobbied officials in Memphis, Tennessee, to dedicate more funding to outdoor recreation and parks. According to the consultants, the city provides 16.1 acres of parkland per 1,000 residents whereas Austin, Texas, for example, offers 35.4.

Focusing on such public amenities as parks is just one strategy of an urban planning movement that emphasizes the built environment as the answer to obesity and inactivity. Dr. Thomas Glass, an associate professor of epidemiology at the Johns Hopkins Bloomberg School of Public Health, says that further studies of cities' physical characteristics, like neighborhood walkability and street connectivity, will improve understanding of how the sedentary lifestyle wins out over the active one. Glass says "suburban sprawl is a major player. There are very different scales of urban density and finding the best ones could be a prescription for reducing inactivity." He points out too that rates of obesity and inactivity vary according to the availability of healthy food and perceptions of neighborhood safety. Meanwhile a study published in 2006 in the *American Journal of Preventive Medicine* identified 10 components of an "activity-friendly" community, including access to exercise facilities, transportation environment, aesthetics and land-use economics.

Gated communities

A growing reaction to city problems is gated communities. In the transition from agrarian to industrial and then post-industrial society, land went from being a necessity for livelihood to a refuge from a stressful world, at least for those who could afford it. The rural retreat became a refuge for the wealthy, while a house in the suburbs became the paradise for the middle class. Now, what Evan McKenzie has called "Privatopia" has arisen. Privatopia consists of common interest developments. In Privatopia, house owners must paint their house a certain color, keep cars parked off the street, and avoid such practices as using clotheslines, as stipulated in the covenants, convents and restrictions (CCRs) in the house deed of ownership. The CCRs help maintain the value of the property and exclude "outsiders." According to the Community Associations Institute, by 2006 there were 286,000 such communities housing 57 million people, or about 19% of the population. These self-segregated owners, protected behind their guarded security gates, have exchanged the self-reliance of Jefferson, Locke and the frontier for collective economic power and class cohesiveness. Yet the ideals of unfettered individual ownership and the freedom of the frontier life are still powerful symbols although increasingly less in touch with reality. The frontier is long gone, neighbors are here to stay, no paradise is undiscovered and all predictions of future trends indicate a larger population and an increase in competing and potentially conflicting property demands.

Place names

In America, the sense of place is arguably more important than the sense of history. A sense of place is represented by place names. Many US place names are derived from Native American words: Chicago means *place of the onion*; Natchez is named for a tribe; Seattle is named for a chief, for just a few examples. Many towns are named for Presidents, especially Lincoln, Jackson and Jefferson. Others are named for famous Americans, such as Houston, Texas, named for Sam Houston, and Cody, Wyoming named for Buffalo Bill. A few towns are named for companies, such as Hershey, Pennsylvania. Many other places are named for places in Britain or other countries from which settlers originally came. British names, like Boston and Cambridge, are especially common in New England. Other British names are New York and Birmingham. Names from other countries include Athens, Moscow, Naples, New Holland, New Orleans, Paris and Vienna. A large number of place names in the South-West are of Spanish origin. These include San Francisco, San Diego, Las Vegas and Los Angeles. Some names, such as Anaheim, now famous for Disneyland, combine words from different languages, the Spanish name Ana with the German heim (home). A few towns, such as Brick Church, High Bridge and House, are named for buildings. Atlanta, Georgia, is named for a railroad. Americans enjoy creating unusual or humorous names like Bitter End, Tennessee, Hot Coffee, Mississippi, Monkey's Eyebrow, Kentucky and Tombstone, Arizona. This type of name is particularly common in the South and South-West.

THE ENVIRONMENT

The Conservation and Environmental Movements

Because the resources of the West seemed limitless, Americans developed wasteful attitudes and practices. The great herds of buffalo (American bison) were slaughtered until only remnants remained, and many other species were driven to the brink of extinction. Rivers were dammed and natural communities disrupted. Forests were destroyed by excessive logging, and landscapes scarred by careless mining. A counterweight to the abuse of natural resources took form in the American conservation movement, which owes much of its success to Americans' reluctance to see frontier conditions disappear entirely from the landscape. Conservationists led by John Muir were instrumental in establishing the first National Park, Yellowstone, in 1872, and helped stem the tide of extinctions. Caring about wild animals has since become a common middle-class attitude and reports that a species is endangered may inspire campaigns to save them. Some people have stickers on the rear bumper of their cars "Warning – I brake for animals." Many people feed wild birds in the winter; the National Wildlife Federation (NWF) among its many activities helps people create their own backyard habitat. In rural areas, people tend to be unsentimental about animals, however: bears and wolves can kill livestock. Road signs like "DEER CROSSING" are for the driver's protection, not the animal's.

National Parks

The mission of the National Parks includes the preservation of natural and historic places and the promotion of outdoor recreation. Roughly 60% of the park areas have been set aside as symbols and evidence of American history and prehistory. The National Park System comprises some 388 areas, encompassing approximately 83.6 million acres in nearly every state and US possession. The Parks are as diverse and far-flung as Hawaii Volcanoes National Park and the Statue of Liberty National Monument and attract over 250 million visitors each year. Aside from Yellowstone, other famous Parks include Yosemite, Grand Canyon, Great Smoky Mountain and Rocky Mountain. The largest Park is Wrangell-St. Elias National Park and Preserve, Alaska. At 13,200,000 acres it forms 16.3 percent of the entire system. As many as five National Parks were created by President Theodore Roosevelt. Public opinion surveys have consistently rated the National Park Service among the most popular federal agencies.

The modern environmental movement

The roots of environmentalism lie far back in the 19th century, beginning with *Man and Nature* (1864), in which George Perkins Marsh called attention to the human impact on the land, influencing John Muir, founder of the national parks system. Other leading figures in what was then called the *conservation movement* were Henry David Thoreau and President Theodore Roosevelt.

The modern environmental movement began in 1962 with the publication of *Silent Spring* by Rachel Carson. The book alerted the public to the dangers of pesticides, particularly to humans. Summarizing her main argument, she said, "The 'control of nature' is a phrase conceived in arrogance, born of the Neanderthal age of biology and philosophy, when it was supposed that nature exists for the convenience of man." Since the 1960's, the Environmental Movement has evolved into what one author has called "a fierce green fire," a campaign that has affected American politics, education, economics, law and culture. Robert Nisbet, social analyst, wrote in 1982 that it was entirely possible that when the history of the 20th century was finally written, the single most important social movement of the period would be judged to be environmentalism.

In 1964 the Wilderness Act was passed, establishing a process for permanently protecting some lands from development. The following year the Sierra Club, a leading grassroots organization, brought suit to protect New York State's Storm King Mountain from a power project. The case established a precedent, allowing protest groups to go to court even when they themselves had no economic interest in a case. In June, 1966, the Sierra Club published full-page newspaper ads in the *New York Times* and *Washington Post* against building a dam that would flood the Grand Canyon. This action boosted the Club's prestige and membership and helped in the fight to save the Canyon. The ad in question said simply: "This time it's the Grand Canyon they want to flood. *The Grand Canyon.*" In 1968 the Grand Canyon dam plan was killed. Attention shifted to the potentially devastating effects of oil spills on wildlife when in 1969 the Santa Barbara oil spill from offshore wells fouled beaches in Southern California and aroused public anger. That same year the National Environmental Policy Act was passed and the Environmental Protection Agency created. In this, the first major US environmental legislation, Congress declared: "it is the continuing policy of the Federal Government… to create and maintain conditions under which man and nature can exist in productive harmony, and fulfill the social, economic, and other requirements of present and future generations of Americans." A stronger Clean Air Act was passed in the next year.

Environmentalists celebrated April 22 as Earth Day for the first time in 1972 and in that same year, DDT, one of the chief chemical pollutants Rachel Carson had campaigned against, was banned in the US and the Water Pollution Control Act was passed. Then, in 1973, one of the pillars of environmental legislation, the Endangered Species Act, was made law. Later, in 1977, the Supreme Court upheld the Act and stopped construction of the Tellico Dam to protect from extinction the snail darter, a small fish that lives in the Little Tennessee River below the dam site.

The notorious Love Canal scandal of 1978 alerted the country to the long-term, hidden dangers of pollution of soil and groundwater, in this case by wastes from a chemical plant. Shortly after, on March 28, 1979, the Three Mile Island nuclear power plant almost had a meltdown, severely damaging the reputation of the nuclear power industry, although after intensive study no evidence of the alleged increase of thyroid cancer arising from the incident was found. In 1996 a US district court rejected such claims and was upheld by the US Third Court of Appeals.

Attention turned to Alaska in 1980, when Congress passed the Alaska National Interest Lands Conservation Act, designating over100 million acres of parks, wildlife refuges, and wilderness areas. At the end of that decade, the ecosystem of the coast of Alaska was seriously damaged by oil spilled from a sinking supertanker, the Exxon Valdez in March, 1989.

Activists increasingly scored nationwide publicity for the environmental cause. In 1997 a 23-year-old woman named Julia Butterfly Hill climbed into a 55-meter (180 foot) tall California Coast Redwood tree. Her aim was to prevent the destruction of the tree and of the forest where it had lived for a millennium. She came down two years later after concluding a deal with Pacific Lumber/Maxxam Corporation to save the tree and a three-acre buffer zone around it.

Progress in protection

The US has made significant progress in the conservation of natural resources. In the name of protecting nature - a goal Americans embrace wholeheartedly - over the last two decades Congress has passed more than 300 major environmental laws and regulations. In addition, thousands more laws have been enacted at the state and local levels, and more are being added every year. For example, about a third of the millions of tons of garbage generated in the US annually is recycled or otherwise repurposed.

The Environmental Protection Agency reported in 2006 that the environment has substantially improved. Emissions of the six principal air pollutants have decreased by 53%. Carbon monoxide emissions have dropped from 197 million tons per year to 89 million; nitrogen oxides from 27 million tons to 19 million, and sulfur dioxide from 31 million to 15 million. Particulates are down 80%, and lead emissions have declined by more than 98%.

When it comes to visible environmental improvements, America is also making substantial progress:
- The number of days the city of Los Angeles exceeded the one-hour ozone standard has declined from just under 200 a year in the late 1970s to 27 in 2004. The one-hour standard is to be replaced by an 8-hour standard. These standards set the times for which ozone in the atmosphere must be below a set limit and the number of days per year when the standard is not met.
- The Pacific Research Institute's Index of Leading Environmental Indicators shows that US forests expanded by 9.5 million acres between 1990 and 2000.

- While wetlands were declining at the rate of 500,000 acres a year at midcentury, they have shown a net gain of about 26,000 acres per year in the past five years, according to the Institute. Also according to the Institute, bald eagles, down to fewer than 500 nesting pairs in 1965, are now estimated to number more than 7,500 nesting pairs.

The Environmental Protection Agency is continually devising and refining the indicators by which the state of the environment can be measured.

Americans are increasingly concerned about the state of the environment. Polls show that 63 percent would roll back tax cuts to finance environmental protection and that 95 percent want environmental education in public schools. Despite decreased air pollution, America has much to do in energy conservation and combating global warming. The Obama administration has granted California permission to issue tough greenhouse gas emissions standards while at the same time combining those standards with a new national Corporate Automotive Fuel Economy (CAFE) standard. The result will be a unified national fuel standard of 42 miles per gallon for passenger cars by 2016. The Recovery Act included more than $60 billion in clean energy investments: $11 billion for a better electricity grid, and other sums for 40 million smart meters, low-income home weatherization projects, state and local renewable energy and energy efficiency efforts, green job training programs, competitive grants to develop the next generation of batteries, and funds to green federal buildings.

Environmental measures taken or proposed by the Obama administration by May, 2009:
- increasing fuel economy standards for Model Year 2011 for cars and trucks;
- tougher efficiency standards for common household appliances, like dishwashers and refrigerators;
- measures to develop the renewable energy projects on the waters of the Outer Continental Shelf that produce electricity from wind, wave, and ocean currents;
- legislation to advance energy and climate security to promote economic recovery efforts, accelerate job creation, and drive clean energy manufacturing by developing an American clean energy industry; energy research and development to transition to a clean energy economy;
- investments in clean energy sources that will curb dependence on fossil fuels and make America energy independent;
- promote the next generation of cars and trucks and the fuels they run on;
- enhance US energy supplies through responsible development of domestic renewable energy, fossil fuels, advanced biofuels and nuclear energy;
- promoting investments that reduce energy bills in the transportation, electricity, industrial, building and agricultural sectors;
- stemming carbon pollution through a market-based cap.

Environmental controversy
The early successes of the environmental movement won broad public support, but the statements of some of its leading figures have begun to stir controversy, and something of a backlash has set in. People are now beginning to ask exactly what the scientific evidence is for supposed threats to the environment, since much of the evidence, especially about the long-term effects of human activity, is contradictory and incomplete. Critics claim that environmentalists have gone way beyond

the original aims of counteracting the obvious dangers of uncontrolled human activity and have become a countercultural movement. As such, environmentalism seems to a growing number of Americans to be mounting an attack on private property, capitalism, free enterprise, technology, western culture and even the human species itself. Radical environmental authors have indeed made numerous statements clearly stating that their ideal is a socialist, redistributionist society which they see as nature's proper steward and society's only hope. Respected environmental scholar William Ophuls has declared that "the golden age of individualism, liberty, and democracy is all but over and thus the need for a world government with enough coercive power over fractious nation states to achieve what reasonable people would regard as the planetary common interest has become overwhelming." Another of these authors states: "The only really good technology is no technology at all. Technology is taxation without representation levied by an elitist species upon the rest of the natural world." Beginning early in the 20th century as an effort by a few far-seeing individuals to bring about the prudent use of natural resources in the interest of prolonging economic growth as far as possible, the environmentalist cause has today become the most significant social movement in America. The objective of radical environmentalists is little less than the transformation of government, economy, and society in the interest of what its proponents see as the liberation of nature from human exploitation.

Most Americans, however, although they are concerned about the environment, do not take the radical position, not least because of the widespread concern about the effect on jobs. Today's environmentalists largely fight the same battles they took on at the first Earth Day gathering more than three decades ago. The issues still revolve around cleaner air, cleaner water, cleaner energy and an awareness of how such phenomena as global warming and climate change are tied to the quality of life. There is continuing debate between environmentalists and free-market conservatives over the effects of the modern environmental movement. Conservatives are likely to point out the past successes of the movement, the establishment of governmental bodies to enforce environmental policies, and the increasing efficiencies of technology, and to conclude that the environmentalists should claim victory and move on. Progressive environmentalists are more likely to look to the challenges that still lie ahead. Issues like environmental racism, "smart growth," alternative fuels, greenhouse gases, ozone depletion, deforestation and species extinction are but some of the environmental concerns of the 21st Century.

CHAPTER 2

THE PEOPLES OF AMERICA

I had always hoped that this land might become a safe and agreeable asylum to the virtuous and persecuted part of mankind, to whatever nation they might belong.
George Washington, letter to Francis Van der Kamp, May 28, 1788

E pluribus Unum (Out of Many, One), which appears on the seals of the US and generally on its notes and coins, originally referred to the union of the Thirteen Colonies in one United States. The motto has since come to refer to the unity among the peoples of many heritages and identities who make up America. (The official motto of the nation is *In God We Trust*, which was put on the dollar bill towards the end of the Civil War). The story of the peoples of America is one of the comings of many immigrants and their conformity to American values, and at the same time of continuing discrimination and inequality, and of conflict between some Americans and some newcomers, between groups of newcomers, and with particular protracted tragedy, between African Americans and white Americans. Finally, a new chapter is opening: the prospective doubling of the population between 1965 and 2050; the aging of the white population; and the aggregation of the non-white minorities into a new majority. Even now, perhaps the most significant demographic fact about America is the rise in its population to over 300 million and the prospect of the population growing by 100 million more by mid-century. Immigration policy has been magnificently successful insofar as increasing the population has been the long-term aim. As a result of continuing high rates of immigration and rates of fertility at replacement levels, America is the most populous developed country, accounting for 5% of the world population and one-quarter of the developed world. This fact, together with America's vast natural resources and its deep and expanding reserves of intangible human capital, make it likely, beyond some unforeseen catastrophe, that the US will always have a firm foundation for the future, despite capitalism's recurrent crises, and however much other countries may develop.

America now faces the question of how large its population should be in the future. The answer will have serious economic, political, social and environmental implications for America and the rest of the world. Some of America's leading policymakers believe that an expanding population with increased immigration is good for America, ensuring its prosperity, power and harmonious relations with other nations, with few if any adverse effects. Future immigration policies, however, will have a major effect on the composition of America's population, since the dominant factor in America's demographic growth is immigration, not natural increase. Immigrants not only add their own numbers to the population, but also contribute a disproportionate number of births, whose effects are compounded over time. Since 1776, migrants and their descendants have accounted for at least 60% of America's population growth.

Immigration also has a significant effect on the country's age structure. Notably, immigration slows the aging of the population. As time goes on, however, the immigrants themselves age and eventually retire, so that by itself immigration does not reduce the age of the population. Immigration is also altering America's ethnic composition and culture, which is becoming less European and more Latin American, Asian and African. By mid-century, one out five Americans is expected to be an immigrant – a higher proportion than ever before - with Hispanics accounting for 30% of the nation's population. With current demographic trends likely to continue for some time, immigration can be expected to continue to play a major role in the future size, age-structure and ethnic composition of America, although these trends are not inevitable, since they may be affected by behavioral changes and unanticipated events impacting fertility and mortality as well as changes in America's immigration practices and policies.

High-level committees have advised that, in the long run, the further growth of the nation's population would bring no significant benefits. In particular, they have recognized that America cannot grow indefinitely and have recommended that the country welcome and plan for a gradual stabilization of its population. This would contribute significantly to America's ability to solve its domestic problems as well as many of those affecting other countries, especially energy and resource consumption, climate change and environmental sustainability. In fact, without US efforts to stabilize its population and thereby mitigate further damage to the environment, other nations might be reluctant to stabilize their own populations and work toward sustainable development and ecological policies. Given the current economic and political climate, however, it seems doubtful that Congress will be able to address immigration reform any time soon.

FACTFILE 6 KEY POPULATION STATISTICS

Population: 307,212,123
Age structure: 0-14 years: 20.2% (male 31,639,127/female 30,305,704)
                15-64 years: 67% (male 102,665,043/female 103,129,321)
                65 years and over: 12.8% (male 16,901,232/female 22,571,696)
Population growth rate: 0.975%
Biggest state: California 36,756,666
Smallest state: Wyoming 532,668
Net migration rate: 4.31 migrant(s)/1,000 population
Net migration numbers: 1.3 million

The changing population
The population of the US increased almost 60% from 194 million in 1965 to 307 million in 2009. Immigrants and their descendants account for almost half of the growth. The population has been continuously evolving throughout its history. New immigrants have flocked to America from scores of countries all over the world. Pioneers have made their passage across the Atlantic and Pacific Oceans, and into the interior, to every part of the US. Subsequently their families and descendants have followed in their footsteps to new homes and new occupations, and a new identity as US

citizens. And invariably as one generation gives way to another, the population is affected. Since 1965 both the number of immigrants and the immigrant share of the population have increased each decade. According to the Census Bureau's 2007 American Community Survey, there were 38.1 million foreign born people in the US, which represents 12.6% of the population, double the percentage in 1970, although below the record level of 15% in 1900. A report from the Census in 2008, however, projected that by 2042 non-Hispanic Whites will no longer make up the majority of the population. The Hispanic and Asian populations are projected to double by 2050 and African Americans to increase by 25%.

The "baby boomer" generation, born just after World War II, dominated American society for much of the second half of the 20th century. Now, thanks to longer life expectancy and their own dynamism, seniors are assuming an important role in the US as the new century begins. The role of baby boomers is being enhanced by the "baby bust" of the 1970s, when fertility among women in the US dropped sharply, reaching a record low average of 1.7 births per family by 1976, well below the rate needed to replace the population. That the rate of population growth now hovers around the replacement rate (that needed to keep the size of the population constant) is increasingly a consequence of immigration. As everywhere in industrialized societies, couples are marrying later (if they marry at all), waiting longer to have babies, and then having fewer of them. Many women experience childlessness or late parenthood as liberating: it allows them to spend more of their lives exploring careers, traveling and learning. America's baby boomers established this pattern of reproduction. Now immigrants and their descendants account for almost half of the growth in the population. In the mid-1970s, when the women's liberation movement was at its peak, the number of childless women in their 20s doubled; in the next decade, births tripled for women between the ages of 30 and 35. Most of these older mothers worked and had fewer babies, often only one.

NATIVE AMERICANS

The original American immigrants, who arrived more than 20,000 years ago, were hunters and gatherers whose families followed animal herds from Asia across a land bridge where the Bering Strait is today. Although their languages, clothes and customs differed, most tribes prior to contact with Europeans used similar weaponry. The most common weapons were the bow and arrow, the war club, and the spear, whose quality, material, and design varied widely. The Great Plains tribes had turned to hunting the bison thousands of years before they first encountered the Europeans. The acquisition of the horse and horsemanship from the Spanish in the 17th century greatly altered Native American culture, changing the way in which bison were hunted and making them a central feature of Plains Native American life.

"Native Americans" or "Indians"?
About 1.5 million Native Americans are believed to have been living in the now continental US when Columbus landed in San Salvador in the Bahamas in 1492. Mistaking the place for the Indies, Columbus called the Native Americans "Indians." (Another translation of *Indian* is "in Dios" or "People of God.")

Despite Columbus's mistake, the name *Indian* or *American Indian* remained in use for centuries to denote the people who first came to the Americas. The problem with this traditional term is that the peoples of India are also known as *Indians*. The term *Red Man* was common among the early settlers of New England because the northeastern tribes colored their bodies with red pigments, but during the western expansion this term became a pejorative and insulting epithet, with the corruption *redskin* becoming its most virulent form.

Anthropologists introduced the term *Native American* in the US as a more accurate description of the indigenous people of the Americas, as distinct from the people of India. (The equivalent term in Alaska is Alaska Native.) Now that *Native American* has become widely accepted, some people believe that *Indians* is outdated or offensive. People from India (and their descendants) who are citizens of the US are known as *Indian Americans*.

The term *Native American*, however, has been criticized. Some American Indians have doubts about it because it was introduced by the government without the consent of American Indians. Furthermore, some American Indians argue, the term serves to ease the conscience of "white America" over past injustices done to American Indians, by effectively eliminating "Indians" from the present. Still others (both Indians and non-Indians) argue that *Native American* is problematic because "native of" literally means "born in," so that any person born in the Americas could be considered "native." Very often, however, the compound "Native American" is capitalized in order to differentiate this intended meaning from others. A 1996 survey revealed that more American Indians still preferred *American Indian* to *Native American*. Nonetheless, most American Indians are comfortable with *Indian, American Indian*, and *Native American*, and the terms are now used interchangeably. The continued usage of the traditional term is reflected in the name chosen for the National Museum of the American Indian, which opened in 2004 in Washington, D.C. Recently, the U.S. Census introduced the "Asian Indian" category to sample the Indian American population more accurately.

Interaction with Europeans

During the centuries after Columbus, people from several European countries arrived to explore America and set up trading posts and colonies. At first the Native Americans were positive about the newcomers, welcoming their metal cooking pots, cloth and guns. The native peoples engaged in trade with the explorers and settlers, exchanging food, crafts, and furs for trinkets, blankets, iron and steel implements, horses, firearms, and alcoholic beverages. The Native Americans taught Europeans how to cultivate crops that are now staples throughout the world, such as corn, tomatoes, potatoes and tobacco. Canoes, snowshoes and moccasins are among the Native Americans' many inventions.

But Native Americans soon began to suffer greatly from the influx of Europeans. The transfer of land from Native American to European and later American hands was accomplished mostly through unequal treaties, wars, trickery and coercion. Some tribes fought to prevent giving up land they had traditionally used. They were accustomed to moving from one area to another as they pleased and sharing the land with other tribes that were friendly. They had no concept of exclusive ownership of land. But despite resistance by chiefs like Tecumseh (1768-1813), Sitting Bull (1831?-1890), and Geronimo (1829-1909), the Native Americans were constantly pushed back as the newcomers moved west. Tecumseh was a chief of the Shawnee people who tried to unite them in resistance to the settlers. Their resistance collapsed when his brother, Tenskwatawa, was defeated at the Battle of Tippecanoe in 1813. (The American general at that battle, William Henry Harrison, was elected President in 1840, having campaigned on the slogan "Tippecanoe and Tyler too.") Sitting Bull (1831?–1890) was a leader of one of the Sioux peoples who, together with Crazy Horse (1849-1877), defeated General George A. Custer at the Battle of the Little Big Horn, North Dakota in 1876. The next year Crazy Horse was captured, imprisoned, and killed when trying to escape. Later, Sitting Bull was killed by US troops and Native American police sent to arrest him because he persuaded his people to keep to the Ghost Dance religion. This religion was started in Nevada in 1870 and featured a dance that lasted five days. It was supposed to help the Native Americans regain their lands. Followers wore special shirts which they believed would stop bullets. The Indian wars came to an end when US soldiers killed 200 Native Americans at the Battle of Wounded Knee, South Dakota, December 29, 1890.

During the 19th century, the Native Americans were not respected as a people but regarded as a problem. To solve the "Indian problem," the government forced the tribes to live on plots of land called "reservations." In many cases this land was of poor quality. Thus the Native Americans came to depend on government assistance. Where the land proved fertile, however, or where gold was discovered, the government broke its promises that the Native Americans could live there for ever, and moved them on. In the tragic case of the Trail of Tears (1838-9), 4,000 Native Americans died when 17,000 Cherokees and others were moved during a cold winter from their lands in Georgia to Oklahoma. The Indian Citizenship Act of 1924 made Native Americans citizens of the US. The goal of the Act was to assimilate them into the mainstream culture and to eliminate the reservations. This policy continued into the 1970s.

The way American artists have chosen to depict Native Americans has varied over the centuries. When America was first being colonized, there was great curiosity about Native American cultures among Europeans. The artist John White faithfully depicted the people native to the southeastern states in watercolors and engravings. Later, Theodore de Bry used White's original watercolors to make a book of engravings entitled *A briefe and true report of the new found land of Virginia*. In his book, de Bry often altered the poses and features of White's figures to make them appear more European, probably in order to market his book to a European audience. Much later, during the reconstruction of the Capitol building in the early 19th century, the US government commissioned a series of four relief panels to crown the doorway of the Rotunda. The reliefs represent the mythology of European--Native American relations that had developed by then. The four panels depict: *The Preservation of Captain Smith by Pocahontas* (1825) by Antonio Capellano, *The Landing of the Pilgrims* (1825), *The Conflict of Daniel Boone and the Indians* (1826-27) by Enrico Causici, and *William Penn's Treaty with the Indians* (1827) by Nicholas Gevelot. The reliefs present idealized versions of the Europeans and the Native Americans, in which the Europeans appear refined and gentle, and the natives appear ferocious and savage. While many 19th-century images of Native Americans conveyed negative messages, there were artists, such as Charles Bird King, who sought to express a more positive image of the Native Americans as noble savages.

Whites have explained their treatment of Native Americans in different ways. When Native Americans fought and killed white people, the whites said this proved that Native Americans were wild and had to be controlled. It was also believed, under the influence of John Locke's teaching, that the Native Americans were wasting the land by not developing it. Whites were thus economically as well as morally superior. There was also an ideology of expansion called *manifest destiny*. Popularized by John L. O'Sullivan, editor of the *United States Magazine and Democratic Review,* who first used the phrase in 1845, manifest destiny meant the God-given right of the US to own and occupy all the land of America as far as the Pacific Ocean. This idea was used to justify taking Oregon from the Native Americans and Texas and California from Mexico, which led to the Mexican War of 1846-48. Americans generally thought it would be better for the Native Americans to learn to live with white people and adopt Christianity. Many Native American children were taken away from their tribe and sent to schools where they were not allowed to speak their native language. Among these was the athlete, Jim Thorpe (1888-1953), regarded by some as the 20th century's finest. He was the first to win the Olympic decathlon and pentathlon (in 1912). He later played professional baseball (1917-19) and professional football (1917-29).

The territorial wars, along with Old World diseases to which the Native Americans had no immunity, and the effects of alcohol, sent their population plummeting to a low of 350,000 in 1920. Some tribes disappeared altogether. Nonetheless, Native Americans have proved to be resilient, retaining their own languages, customs and traditions and in some cases their own form of government. When the Europeans arrived, there were some 300 Native American languages. Today there are around 250, many spoken by only a few older people. Some languages, like Cherokee, are widely spoken among Native Americans. Most Native Americans speak English, some as their first language, others as their second. Countless US place-names derive from Native American words, including the states of Idaho, Massachusetts, Michigan, Mississippi, Missouri and Ohio. The words *teepee* (a kind of tent) and *wampum* (a string or belt made of beads which was so valuable the word came to mean *money*) have entered the English language. Wampum originated among the Iroquois, who lived around the Great Lakes, and served a dual function: the knots and beaded designs mnemonically chronicled tribal stories and legends, and also served as a medium of exchange and a unit of measure.

Native Americans today

Today Native Americans number about two million (0.8% of the total US population). Most of them still live on reservations, and poverty and joblessness are endemic among them. According to U.S. Census Bureau estimates, in 2003 a little over one-third of the 2,786,652 Native Americans live in three states: California 413,382, Arizona 294,137, and Oklahoma 279,559. As of 2000, the largest tribes were Navajo, Cherokee, Choctaw, Sioux, Chippewa, Apache, Lumbee, Blackfeet, Iroquois, and Pueblo. In 2000, eight out of ten Americans with Native American ancestry were of mixed blood. It is estimated that by 2100 that figure will rise to nine out of ten. In addition, there are a number of tribes that are recognized by individual states, but not by the federal government. Federal recognition confers some benefits, including the right to label arts and crafts as Native American and permission to apply for grants that are specifically reserved for Native Americans. The rights and benefits associated with state recognition vary from state to state.

Intermarriage among Native American tribes has made it difficult to determine which tribe an individual belongs to. Occasionally, bands or entire tribes split or merged in response to the pressures of climate, disease and warfare. A number of tribes used to adopt captives from other tribes, or Europeans, to replace members who had been captured or killed in battle. White traders, runaway slaves and Native American-owned slaves were also adopted. In later years, such mixing proved an obstacle to qualifying for recognition and assistance from the federal government or for tribal money and services. To receive such support, Native Americans must belong to and be certified by a recognized tribal entity. Some tribes have begun requiring DNA testing. To obtain a federal scholarship requires both enrollment in a federally recognized tribe and a Certificate of Degree of Indian Blood Card showing at least one-quarter Native American descent.

Recently there has been a fashion among white ethnic groups and some African Americans to claim descent from an "American Indian princess," "king" or "brave," often a Cherokee. Descent from Pocahontas is frequently claimed. The term "princess," however, is a misnomer derived from the application of European concepts to Native Americans. The desire to establish Native American ancestry may be based on a wish for prestige, association with distinct folkways, or envy of recent immigrants with cultures distinct from the mainstream. The use of Native American themed team names in US professional sports is widespread and often controversial, with examples such as Chief Wahoo of the Cleveland Indians, and the Washington Redskins.

Tribal governments (563) have the right to self-government, tribal sovereignty (including control of natural resources such as coal and uranium) and self-determination. They form their own administration, enforce laws (both civil and criminal), raise taxes, establish membership, license and regulate activities, administer zoning, and exclude persons from tribal territories. Limitations on tribal self-government include the same limitations applicable to states: for example, neither tribes nor states have the power to make war, engage in foreign relations, or coin money. Native American community governments administer services like firefighting, natural resource management, and law enforcement. Most have court systems to adjudicate matters related to local ordinances, and most also look to various forms of moral and social authority vested in traditional affiliations within the community. There are 20 community colleges on the reservations serving some 4,500 students, and D-Q university at Davis, California.

Numerous problems that afflict Native Americans arise from their unhappy history of interaction with Europeans: military defeat, cultural pressure, confinement on reservations, forced assimilation, the outlawing of native languages, loss of lands, and slavery. Native Americans suffer disproportionately from poverty and from modern health problems including alcoholism, heart disease, diabetes, mental illness and New World Syndrome (a set of non-communicable diseases caused by eating junk food). Many are addicted to gambling. Gambling has become a leading industry on the reservations. Casinos operated by some Native American governments are, however, creating revenues that communities are using to help build diversified economies and lift their people from poverty. But casinos are a source of conflict. Most tribes, especially the smaller ones, feel that casinos and their proceeds will destroy their culture, and they refuse to participate. To address the housing needs of Native Americans, Congress passed the *Native American Housing and Self Determination Act* (NAHASDA) in 1996, which provides block grants to tribes for housing programs.

Occasionally disputes between federal law enforcement officials, the US military and Native Americans have erupted into violence. One of the more notorious incidents took place at Wounded Knee, South Dakota on February 27, 1973. The town itself was under the control of members of the American Indian Movement, which was protesting a variety of issues. Two members of AIM were killed and one U.S. Marshal was paralyzed as a result of gunshot wounds.

Native American Culture

Religion

Many Native Americans would describe their religious practices as a form of spirituality rather than religion, although in practice the terms may sometimes be used interchangeably. The most widespread religion among Native Americans is known as the Native American Church. This is a syncretistic church incorporating elements of native spiritual practice from a number of different tribes as well as symbolic elements from Christianity. Its main rite is the peyote ceremony. In the Southwest, especially New Mexico, a syncretism between the Catholicism brought by Spanish missionaries and the native religion is common; the religious drums, chants, and dances of the Pueblo People are regularly part of mass at Santa Fe's Saint Francis Cathedral. Native American-Catholic syncretism is also found elsewhere in the US, for example, at the National Kateri Tekakwitha Shrine in Fonda, New York and the National Shrine of the North American Martyrs in Auriesville, New York. Native Americans are the only ethnic group in the US who require a federal permit to practice a part of their religion. The eagle feather law stipulates that only individuals of certifiable Native American ancestry enrolled in a feather law stipulates that only individuals of certifiable Native American ancestry enrolled in a federally recognized tribe may obtain eagle feathers for religious or spiritual use.

Music and art

Native American music usually consists of one line, although more than one is not unknown. The music often includes drumming and the playing of rattles or other percussion instruments. There is little other instrumentation aside from flutes and whistles made of wood, cane, or bone. These are usually played by individuals, but in former times were played by large ensembles.

Native American popular music performers have included Rita Coolidge, Wayne Newton, Gene Clark, and Tori Amos. John Trudell has used music to comment on Native American life, and others, such as R. Carlos Nakai, integrate traditional with modern sounds in instrumental recordings. A variety of small and medium-sized recording companies offer an abundance of recent music by Native American performers young and old, ranging from pow-wow drum music to hard-driving rock-and-roll and rap.

Most indigenous communities maintain traditional songs and ceremonies, some of which are shared and practiced exclusively within the community. The pow-wow is the most widespread type of Native American public musical performance. At pow-wows, members of drum groups sit in a circle around a large drum. They play in unison while singing in a native language and performers in colorful regalia dance clockwise around them. Pow-wow songs include honor songs, intertribal songs, crow-hops, sneak-up songs, grass-dances, two-steps, welcome songs, going-home songs, and war songs. The annual Gathering of Nations in Albuquerque, New Mexico is the most famous pow-wow.

Native American art includes pottery, paintings, jewelry, weavings, sculptures, basketry, and carvings and is recognized as significant in world art. Ancient Native American art often exhibited a sophisticated and well-developed style. In modern times, some artists have falsely claimed to have native parentage. The integrity of certain Native American artworks is now protected by a law that prohibits the representation of art as Native American when it is not the product of an enrolled Native American artist.

IMMIGRATION

Immigration and diversity are leading themes in the American story. The US has welcomed more immigrants than any other country - more than 50 million in all - and still admits as many as a million people a year. Almost every person in the US is descended from someone who arrived from another country. Americans are proud to descend from ancestors who came as immigrants with very little and made a better life for themselves. Life was tough for the first arrivals. Often weak and ill after the voyage, they typically had to live one family to a room in tenement blocks, and work in factories where the work was hard, dirty and dangerous, wages were low and conditions atrocious by modern standards.

European immigration: the Golden Door

Give me your tired, your poor, Your huddled masses yearning to breathe free, The wretched refuse of your teeming shore Send these, the homeless, tempest-tossed to me:I lift my lamp beside the golden door.

Emma Lazarus, 1883, inscribed on a bronze plaque at the base of the Statue of Liberty, 1903

HISTORICAL TRENDS IN AMERICAN IMMIGRATION LEVELS

Period	Annual average
1607-1775	3,500
1776-1819	6,500
1820-1879	162,000
1880-1924	584,000
1925-1965	178,000

The English were the dominant ethnic group among the early settlers, and English became the prevalent American language. The English came in four waves: the Puritans from East Anglia to Massachusetts in the 1630s; the Cavaliers and indentured servants from the south of England to Virginia in the mid-17th century; the Quakers from the north Midlands to the Delaware valley in the second half of the 17th century and the first decades of the 18th; and the borderers from the England-Scotland border and from Ulster to the Appalachians in the 18th century. In 1780 three out of every four of the 2.5 million citizens of the US were of English or Irish descent.

But people from other European countries, including Spain, Portugal, France, Holland, Germany and Sweden, were not long in following. Indeed so many German-speakers arrived that in 1795 Congress debated translating federal laws into German. But the belief that German nearly became the official language of the US is a myth. Even in Pennsylvania the number of German-speakers never exceeded one-third.

In the 1820s, immigration averaged no more than 15,000 a year. But by 1832, it had reached 71,000. (In considering immigration, it is essential to keep in mind the difference between the *numbers* of immigrants and the *rate* of immigration i.e., the numbers per 1,000 of the existing population.) The first great wave of immigrants arrived between 1840 and 1860 and the population rose from 17 million to 31 million. In this period, poor harvests, famine, rising populations and political unrest were affecting the whole of Europe. In the peak years 1847-1854, immigration reached an annual average of 334,000, 45% from Ireland, 32% from the German states. In one year alone, 1847, as many as 118,120 people arrived from Ireland as a result of the potato famine. Today there are about 39 million Americans of Irish descent. The failure of the German Confederation's revolution of 1848-49 led many of its people to emigrate at that time.

The yearly volume of immigration fluctuated considerably before 1914. The main reason was changes in economic and political conditions in the US. Periods of lower immigration corresponded with US economic depressions or times of widespread opposition to immigrants. In particular, immigration declined during the period of nativist opposition to immigrants in the 1850s, the major depressions of the 1870s and 1890s, and the Great Depression of the 1930s.

After the peak around 1850, immigration fluctuated through 1930. The average yearly volume was 434,000. In this period, the peak of immigration was reached between 1900 and 1914. At that time an average of almost 900,000 immigrants arrived each year. Immigration fell to low levels between 1931 and 1946, though by the 1970s the volume had again reached that experienced between 1847 and 1930. The rise in volume continued through the 1980s and 1990s, and during the 1990s, the average annual volume surpassed the previous peak experienced between 1900 and 1914, though the rate per one thousand American residents remained well below that experienced before 1915.

Until the 1850s, immigration was unrestricted and largely unopposed. But the mid-century immigrations brought more unskilled workers and also changed the religious balance by bringing more Catholics to the great cities and to the farmlands of the Midwest. Conflicts took place between the newcomers and the "natives" with riots in New York and Philadelphia. From this period arose the traditional suspicion of immigrants among some Americans, who stereotyped the newcomers as dirty, lazy, ignorant and immoral. From this period also dates the association of the Irish and Catholics with the Democratic Party. During the Civil War (1861-65), the US government helped fill its roster of troops by encouraging immigration from Europe, especially from the German states. By 1865, about one in five Union soldiers was a wartime immigrant. Today, 22% of Americans are of German ancestry. Many immigrants also came from Italy, Scandinavia and eastern Europe.

The late 19th century saw several enormous waves of immigration from continental Europe, Russia and the British Isles, doubling or tripling the size of many major cities within a matter of years. During this period, in some regions of the country more than 50% of the residents were foreign born. Between 1865 and 1890, 10 million immigrants arrived, mostly from Germany, Ireland and Scandinavia. Between 1890 and 1914, more than 15 million immigrants, mostly from southern and eastern Europe, arrived. The newcomers not only faced economic hardship. They faced racism and resentment. Unscientific theories such as eugenics were peddled in an attempt to prove the racial superiority of the settlers from northern Europe.

Sources of immigration

Before 1881, the vast majority of immigrants, almost 86%, arrived from northwest Europe, principally Great Britain, Ireland, Germany, and Scandinavia. The years between 1881 and 1893 saw a change in the principal sources of immigrants. The numbers of immigrants from central, eastern, and southern Europe began to increase rapidly. Between 1894 and 1914, immigrants from these regions accounted for 69% of the total. With the onset of World War I in 1914, the sources of immigration again changed. From 1915 to the present day, a major source of immigrants has been the Western Hemisphere, accounting for 46% of the total. In the period between 1915 and 1960, virtually all of the remaining immigrants came from Europe, though no one part of Europe was dominant. Beginning in the 1960s, immigration from Europe fell off substantially and was replaced by a much larger percentage of immigrants from Asia. Currently most immigrants come from the Americas or Asia.

Reasons for immigration

Economic historians generally believe no single factor led to immigration. They have identified five different causes: the difference in real wages between the source country and the US; the rate of population growth in that country during the previous 20 or 30 years; the degree of industrialization and urbanization in the home country (displacing people from the land); the volume of previous immigrants from that country or region; and economic and political conditions in the US. To this list can be added the movement from sail to steam, and the presence or absence of immigration restrictions. After the Civil War, by substantially reducing the length of the trip and increasing comfort and safety, the steamship encouraged immigration. This was partly because, with shorter voyages, temporary immigration became more likely. Individuals came to the US planning to work for a time before returning home. All in all, the period from 1865 through 1914, when immigration was not restricted and steamships were dominant, saw an average yearly immigrant volume of almost 529,000. In contrast, average yearly immigration between 1820 and 1860 by sailing ship was only 123,000, and even between 1847 and 1860 was only 266,000.

Reasons for changes in the source countries

Each source country went through stages where immigration increased, reached a peak, and then declined. Immigration from any particular country initially increased as a consequence of rapid population growth and industrialization, and the existence of a large gap in real wages between that country and the US. After a number of years, the volume of immigrants increased further, since potential immigrants now had friends or relatives who could smooth their transition to living and working in America. Immigration remained high until slower population growth, and industrialization in Europe caused immigration to decline. Partly due to the previous immigration, real wages rose at home and became closer to American rates. These effects were first seen in northwest Europe, and in the late 19th century in central, eastern and southern Europe. A similar pattern is unfolding today in the rest of the Americas and in Asia.

Ellis Island and Angel Island

Most immigrants arrived at New York, Philadelphia, Boston, New Orleans, or Baltimore. Over time, New York became the main port of arrival. Until 1855, when New York established Castle Garden at the tip of Manhattan as its landing depot, there were no immigration facilities. During the late 19th century, so many people were entering the country that the government opened a port of entry on Ellis Island in New York harbor. Between 1892, when it opened, and 1954, when it closed, Ellis Island was the entry port for 12 million people. The Statue of Liberty on nearby Liberty Island was the first landmark these people saw of their homeland-to-be. During the peak "Ellis Island" period, 1902-1914, 12.4 million immigrants entered the country. For immigrants in the West, the government established Angel Island Immigration Station in San Francisco Bay in 1905, which processed one million Asian immigrants between 1910 and 1940.

Limits on Newcomers

The Constitution laid down that there could be no limits on immigration until 1808. While immigration was reaching its peak between 1880 and 1920 many native-born Americans began to worry that the country was admitting too many immigrants, and sought to restrict immigration. Some Americans feared that their culture was being threatened by immigrants from central, eastern and southern Europe or that they would lose their jobs to newcomers willing to accept lower wages. In 1907, Congress set up the Immigration Commission, chaired by Senator William Dillingham, to investigate the matter. This body issued a report, now viewed as flawed, concluding that immigrants from the newer European source countries did not assimilate easily and, in general, blaming them for various economic ills. The Immigration Act of 1917, passed over President Wilson's veto, required immigrants to pass a literacy test, and banned immigrants from Asia altogether. Even so, after World War I the volume of immigration resumed its pre-war levels. Restrictionists then turned to setting stricter limits to the number of arrivals.

US immigration policy was fundamentally changed by the Quota Act of 1921, which limited the number of immigrants from Europe to about 350,000 per year. National quotas for immigrants from each country were established in direct proportion to the presence of immigrants from that country in 1910. In addition, the Act assigned Asian countries quotas near zero. Three years later, in 1924, the National Origins Act instituted a requirement that visas be obtained from an American consulate abroad before immigrating, reduced the total European quota to about 165,000, and determined the quotas in proportion to the presence of immigrants from each country in 1890. Because relatively few individuals had immigrated from southern, central, and eastern Europe before 1890, the effect of this law was a drastic reduction in the numbers of immigrants from these countries. Yet total immigration remained fairly high until the Great Depression because neither the 1921 nor the 1924 law restricted immigration from the Western Hemisphere i.e., west of the 0° median of longitude, which passes through Greenwich, near London, England. As a result, immigration patterns over the next 40 years reflected the existing immigrant population.

A new immigration system

The immigration system was radically reformed by the Immigration and Nationality Act of 1965, the last major change in US immigration policy. Under this Act, the US began to grant immigrant visas ("green cards") in order of application, and national quotas were replaced with hemispheric ones. Preference was given to relatives of US citizens and of permanent resident aliens, and to immigrants with job skills that were in short supply in the US. Preference was also given to professionals, scientists, and artists. The law originally set a quota of 170,000 for total immigration from Eastern Hemisphere countries; and no more than 20,000 were allowed to immigrate from any one country. It is important to note that immediate relatives of US citizens and amnestied illegal immigrants, such as spouses, parents, and minor children, were exempt from the quotas. As a result, family preferences have led to a marked increase in the volume of immigration. The law was designed to treat all countries equally. Thus the virtual prohibition on immigration from Asia disappeared and Asia has become a more important source of immigrants. Moreover, for the first time, the law limited the number of immigrants from Western Hemisphere countries, with the original overall quota set at 120,000.

The total number of legal immigrants since 1965 has always been larger than the combined quotas. The US has at various times also admitted large numbers of refugees from Vietnam, Cuba, and other countries. Additionally, many individuals enter the US on student visas, enroll in colleges and universities, and eventually find companies to sponsor them for a work visa. The government caps employment-based permanent visas for foreign workers and their families at 140,000 per year. In 1978 Congress replaced hemispheric quotas with a worldwide ceiling. No country can receive more than 7% (approximately 25,600) of the total number of annual worldwide visas.

The most important modifications to the 1965 law were made in 1986 with the Immigration Reform and Control Act (IRCA), when penalties were introduced for employers who hire illegal immigrants. But IRCA gave temporary resident status, that would eventually permit them to stay in the country permanently, to many individuals who had lived illegally in the US since before 1982. The latter provision led to very high volumes of legal immigration being recorded in 1989, 1990, and 1991. In 1990, nearly 900,000 people took advantage of this law to obtain legal status. Some three million people (75% of them Mexicans) have become legalized under IRCA.

Current trends in immigration

The US continues to accept more immigrants than any other country. The current wave of immigrants is the only one so far that has not been followed by a period of low immigration. According to the Census Bureau, legal immigration jumped fourfold from 2.5 million admissions between 1951 and 1960 to 9,095,417 between 1991 and 2000. By the early 1990s more than 1 million new legal immigrants were arriving every year. The nation absorbed 11-14 million legal and illegal immigrants in that decade, more than in any other. The U.S. Commission on Immigration Reform (the Jordan Commission) recommended the abolition of the extended family categories, currently capped at 480,000, in order to curb the number of legal and illegal immigrants and to clear the backlogs of qualified immigrants awaiting visas. Another, smaller wave of immigration took place in the 2000s. The largest group of immigrants since 1990 have come from Mexico.

In 2007, 38.1 million foreign-born people were living in the US. Of these, 42.9% entered before 1990, as many as 29.4% between 1990 and 1999, and 27.7% in 2000 or later. Of the total, 30.8% were Mexican-born, the largest group by far. Among the remaining countries of origin of the foreign-born population, the Philippines accounted for 4.5%, followed by India and China (excluding Hong Kong and Taiwan) with 3.9% and 3.6%, respectively. These four countries — together with El Salvador (2.9%), Vietnam (2.9%), Korea (2.7%), Cuba (2.6%), Canada (2.2%), and the Dominican Republic (2.0%) — made up 58.1% of all foreign born people living in the US.

Recent immigrants

In 2006, one million foreign nationals obtained lawful permanent resident (LPR) status, according to the Department of Homeland Security's Yearbook of Immigration Statistics 2007. The total represents a 25.1% increase from 2000 (840,000). Of the new LPRs, 47% were an immediate relative of a US citizen, 18.5% came through a family-sponsored preference, and 15.4% through an employment-based preference. Another 12.9% adjusted from a refugee or asylee status, and 4.0% were diversity-lottery winners. Mexico accounted for 14.1% of new legal immigrants. The top five countries of birth — Mexico, China (7.3%), the Philippines (6.9%), India (6.2%), and Colombia (3.2%) — accounted for 37.7% of such immigrants. Persons born in the next five countries — Haiti (2.9%), Cuba (2.8%), Vietnam (2.7%), the Dominican Republic (2.7%), and Korea (2.1%) — made up another 13.2% of all LPRs, so that the top 10 countries of birth made up more than half of the total.

Mexican immigrants

Immigrants from Mexico amounted to 11.7 million in 2007. They were overwhelmingly concentrated in the West and Southwest, including California (37.7%), Texas (20.6%), Arizona (5.5%), and Florida (2.7%). The foreign born from Mexico accounted for over half of the immigrant population in New Mexico (73.5%), Arizona (65.6%), Texas (63.1%), Idaho (58.8%), and Colorado (50.2%). According to Mexico's National Survey of Occupations and Employment (ENOE), the emigration rate from Mexico appears to have slowed recently from 11.1 migrants per 1,000 Mexican residents in spring 2006 to 7.5 in spring 2007 and 4.7 in spring 2008. (This survey does not include entire families).

Children with immigrant parents

The increase in the number of children of immigrants has halved since 2000 but is still significant. In 2007, there were about 16 million children aged 17 or younger who had at least one immigrant parent. They accounted for 22.9% of the 69.9 million children aged 17 or younger in the US. Between 1990 and 2000, the number of such children with immigrant parents grew 59.7% from 8.2 million to 13.1 million. Between 2000 and 2007, the number of such children grew a further 22.3% to 16 million.

The number of first generation i.e., foreign-born immigrant children, is meanwhile declining. While between 1990 and 2000 the number grew 42.8% from 1.9 million to 2.7 million, the number declined 8.4% between 2000 and 2007 to 2.5 million. On the other hand, the number of second generation immigrant children i.e., those born in the US to at least one foreign-born parent, has grown steadily since 1990. Between 1990 and 2000, the number grew 64.8% from 6.3 million to 10.4 million, and between 2000 and 2007 the number grew another 30.2% to 13.5 million. Thus, while the percentage of children with immigrant parents is growing, so is the percentage of second generation children. In 1990, children with immigrant parents were 13.4% of all children, but they were 19.1% in 2000 and 22.9% in 2007. Meanwhile the share of second-generation children among all children with immigrant parents grew steadily from 77.0% in 1990 to 79.5% in 2000 and to 84.6% in 2007.

Immigrant destinations

In 2007, the five states with the most foreign-born residents were California (10 million), New York (4.2 million), Texas (3.8 million), Florida (3.4 million), and Illinois (1.7 million). Between 2000 and 2007, the five states with the largest growth in the foreign-born population were California (1.1 million), Texas (929,000), Florida (770,000), New York (337,000), and Arizona (335,000). When classified by the share of foreign born in the total population, the top five states in 2007 were California (27.4%), New York (21.8%), New Jersey (19.9%), Nevada (19.4%), and Florida (18.9%). The share of immigrants in the six major receiving states is declining, however, owing to a rapid dispersal of immigrants to states which have not received significant numbers of new immigrants for over a century. The 22 "new growth" states form a broad band across the middle of the country in the Southeast, Midwest, and Rocky Mountain regions, with the highest levels of growth occurring in North Carolina, Georgia, Nevada, and Arkansas. During the 1990s the immigrant population more than doubled in 19 states. (This was because jobs and higher wages were available, not because welfare benefits were higher). Between 2000 and 2007, the five states with the largest percentage growth in the foreign-born population were South Carolina (63.8%), Arkansas (60.7%), Nevada (57.2%), Tennessee (56.9%), and Alabama (56.4%).

Integration issues previously confined to only a handful of states - issues such as access to language classes, health care, welfare benefits, and jobs - are now central concerns for most states. This is because the newest immigrants are arriving in regions that historically have attracted relatively few immigrants. While most taxes paid by immigrants go to the federal government, most of the services they use are paid for by state and local governments, thus raising the issue of financial equity. Additionally, immigrants settling in states with relatively weak social safety nets may not fare as well as those in more generous states in times of decline in the economy. One in four low-wage workers is foreign born.

Illegal Immigrants

The figures for illegal (undocumented) immigrants are subject to a significant margin of error because data is either incomplete or not collected at all. The US Bureau of Citizenship and Immigration Services (formerly the Immigration and Naturalization Service) estimates that some 11-12 million people are living in the US illegally. Similarly the Pew Hispanic Center estimates there were 11.9 million unauthorized immigrants in March 2008. (Other estimates are considerably higher.)

The share of the foreign-born population who are illegal immigrants (also called "illegal aliens" or "illegals") has risen steadily. Illegal immigrants made up 21% of the foreign born in 1980, 25% in 2000, and 28% in 2005. Reversing a long-term trend, however, the flow of unauthorized immigrants (500,000 per year) grew more slowly between 2005 and 2008 than it did between 2000 and 2004 when the flow grew by about 800,000 per year, exceeding that of legal permanent residents. Illegal immigrants either cross the border illegally or overstay their visa (40%). About 44% of the nation's unauthorized immigrants have arrived since 2000.

Uniquely for a First World country, the US has a land border with a Third World country, Mexico. The border stretches two thousand miles. Mexico is the primary source of illegal immigrants, the vast majority of whom (80%) are from Mexico itself and other Latin American countries. The majority of undocumented Mexican workers are men, but the number of women is growing. Over 1,600 Mexican immigrants died trying to reach the US in the period 1998-2004. About 12% of illegal immigrants are from Asia, and the remaining 8% are from Europe, Canada, Africa, and other countries. More than half of the Mexicans in the US in 2000 were illegal aliens. The temptation for Mexicans to cross the border legally or illegally is unsurprising, since the average Mexican earns a twelfth of an American's wages and is much better off in the US despite higher prices.

Another factor in illegal immigration is that a Supreme Court interpretation of the Fourteenth Amendment grants automatic citizenship to virtually everyone born on American soil, including the children of illegal aliens. Hence immigration authorities are highly unlikely to try to deport an illegal alien whose child is an American citizen. Thus, through "birthright citizenship," illegal aliens with an "anchor baby" are relatively sure of permanent residence, if not legal status. According to Census data, an estimated one-tenth, or 380,000, of US births in 2002 were to illegal aliens.

Economic effects of immigration

Most economists and economic historians believe the effects of immigration have been in many ways beneficial, and much less harmful than commonly supposed. The US has benefited through attracting immigrants who have inventive and scientific skills and providing an environment for them to flourish. Immigrants also expand the size of markets for various goods, which may lead to a decrease in the price of those goods. Moreover, most immigrants are between the ages of 15 and 35, so the expenses of their basic schooling have already been paid. At times when most immigrants get a job, the average standard of living rises. Although immigrants may place a strain on government services, they also pay taxes. Even illegal immigrants directly pay sales taxes on goods and indirectly pay property taxes through rent. The large-scale immigration from Europe contributed to the rapid westward expansion of the US during most of the 19th century. This in turn increased the amounts of land and natural resources available to the US, which almost certainly kept immigration from lowering wage rates. The large inflow apparently led to little change in the wages of unskilled workers, because employers adopted new methods of production that used a greater number of them. Skilled artisans who had previously done many of the jobs that now required less skill, however, lost jobs. For recent times, most studies have found that immigration has had little effect on the level of wages. Although immigration has been a factor in the fall in the wages of high school dropouts since the mid-'70s, a bigger factor has been their lack of computer skills.

Labor Market Discrimination

In the labor market, immigrants may be discriminated against in wages and jobs. Yet immigrants have generally been paid the same wage for a given job as a native worker. If immigrants have received lower wages than native workers, the differences have reflected the lower skills of the immigrants. In fact, historically, the skill levels of immigrants were similar to those of the native labor force, so that wages did not differ much between the two groups. During more recent years, however, the immigrant stream has been less skilled than the native labor force, leading to lower wages for immigrants. A second form of discrimination immigrants may face is in the jobs they are able to obtain. This type of discrimination may have occurred against Catholics during the 1840s and 1850s and against the immigrants from central, southern, and eastern Europe after 1890. For example, in 1910, immigrants accounted for over half of the workers in mining, apparel-making, steel manufacturing, meat packing, baking, and tailoring. Yet the open nature of the US schooling system and economy was such that job discrimination usually did not affect the fortunes of the immigrants' children or did so only to a small extent.

Job mobility and wealth

Job mobility for some immigrants has been quite high. Those arriving between 1840 and 1850 from Britain and Germany generally improved their job status over time. Over 75% of those who were low-skilled according to the Passenger Lists, on which ships had to keep details of immigrants, had moved up into a higher-skilled job by 1860, while fewer than 25% of those reporting a high-skilled job had moved down into a lower-skilled job. For immigrants from Ireland, however, the experience was quite different. The percentage moving up was only 40% and the percentage moving down was over 50%. It is not clear if the Irish did worse because they had less education and fewer skills or whether the differences were due to discrimination. As to wealth, all immigrant groups in this period accumulated greater wealth the longer they were in the US, although they did less well than natives. The job mobility of immigrants since the Civil War is not clear. Most researchers have thought that immigrants, even from northwest Europe, who arrived before 1915 had a difficult time. For the period after World War II, the degree of success experienced by immigrants remains an area of controversy.

Public attitudes to immigration

Americans are increasingly concerned about immigration, according to a survey released on March 30, 2006 by the Pew Research Center for the People & the Press, a project of the Pew Research

Center, used by permission. A growing number believe that immigrants are a burden to the country, taking jobs and housing and creating strains on the health care system. Many people also worry about the cultural impact of the increasing numbers of newcomers. Yet the public remains largely divided in its views of the overall effect of immigration. Roughly as many believe that newcomers to the US strengthen American society as say they threaten traditional American values. Reflecting this ambivalence, the public is split over many of the policy proposals aimed at dealing with unauthorized migrants. Overall, 53% say that people who are in the US illegally should be required to go home, while 40% say they should be granted some kind of legal status that allows them to stay. But nearly half of those who believe illegal immigrants should be required to leave nonetheless say that some could stay under a temporary work program. Overall, the public divides about evenly among three main approaches for dealing with people who are in the country illegally: 32% think it should be possible for them to stay permanently; 32% believe some should be allowed to stay under a temporary worker program, under the condition that they leave eventually; and 27% think that all illegal immigrants should be required to go home.

There is also a division of opinion over how to stem the flow of illegal immigrants across the Mexican border. When asked to choose among three options, roughly half of Americans (49%) say increasing the penalties for employers who hire illegal immigrants would be most effective in reducing illegal cross-border immigration, while a third prefer boosting the number of border patrol agents. Just 9% of the public says the construction of more fences along the Mexican border would be most effective. In general, however, the issue of immigration is not a pressing problem for most Americans. Just 4% volunteer it as the most important problem facing the country, far fewer than the number mentioning the war in Iraq, dissatisfaction with the government, terrorism, and several other issues. Nor does immigration loom particularly large as a local community issue. Immigration emerges as a dominant local concern only in Phoenix, Arizona, near a major entry point for illegal immigrants, where 55% say it is a very big problem. In other metropolitan areas, traffic congestion rates as a bigger problem than immigration.

Ambivalent attitudes to immigrants

The Pew survey found ambivalent attitudes toward immigration on a number of points, especially in areas where immigrants are most numerous. First, attitudes toward both Latin American and Asian immigrants are more positive now than in the 1990s, even as concern over the problems associated with immigration has increased. Both groups are overwhelmingly seen as very hard working and having strong family values. Impressions of Latin American immigrants in particular have grown much more positive, with 80% describing them as very hard working compared with 63% nearly a decade ago. And while there is concern about the impact of immigration on the availability of jobs, nearly two-thirds (65%) say that immigrants coming to the country mostly take jobs that Americans do not want, rather than take jobs away from Americans. Yet at the same time, a sizable minority (16%) says they or a family member have lost a job to an immigrant worker. And the perception of being passed over – more common among those with less education and lower incomes – is strongly associated with negative views of immigrants and high levels of support for tough measures to deal with illegal aliens. Moreover, native-born Americans who live in areas with the highest concentration of immigrants hold more positive opinions of them: experience of immigrants results in a better impression of them. Many more of those in areas with relatively low concentrations of foreign-born people see immigrants as a burden to the nation and as a threat to

American customs. People living in areas with few immigrants have a considerably more negative opinion of Hispanics and a slightly more negative view of Asians. As many as 49% nationwide say they often come in contact with people who speak little or no English, up from 28% in 1997. This experience is very common in Las Vegas and Phoenix: 68% of Las Vegas residents and 66% of Phoenix residents say they often encounter people who speak little or no English. Most Americans who come in contact with people with little English say it does not bother them (61%), compared with 38% who say that it does.

Opinions on policy options

The public's divisions over illegal immigration mirror their views of legal immigration; 40% say the current level of legal immigration should be decreased, but almost the same number (37%) believe it should be kept at its present level, while 17% would prefer to see it increased. The immigration of skilled workers has been advocated as a way to sustain critical sectors of the economy and reduce income concentration by narrowing the wage gap between skilled and unskilled workers. But it is illegal immigration, far more than legal immigration, that stirs public anxiety. Six in ten say illegal immigration represents a bigger problem than legal immigration. Just 4% say that legal immigration is a bigger problem, though nearly a quarter (22%) says both forms of immigration are equally problematic.

Besides economic concerns, many express worries that illegal immigrants contribute to crime and increase the danger of terrorism. Yet fewer see tougher border controls, rather than sanctions on employers, as the most effective way to reduce illegal immigration along the Mexican border. Even those who are most worried about the threat of terrorism associated with illegal immigration favor employer fines over border fences and more agents. In line with these attitudes, two-thirds of the public favors the creation of a new government database for all of those eligible to work – citizens and legal immigrants alike – and a requirement that employers check this database before hiring new workers. Even more Americans support a form of national identification card – either a Social Security card or a new form of driver's license – that job applicants would be required to show before obtaining a job.

Like policymakers, the public is conflicted about how to treat immigrants who are in the US illegally. Beyond questions of their legal status, Americans express very different opinions about providing government services for such people and their children. By a wide margin (67%-29%), Americans believe that illegal immigrants should be ineligible for social services provided by state and local governments. Yet by about the same margin (71%-26%), most feel that the children of illegal immigrants should be permitted to attend public schools. Almost all Americans take a dim view of the actions of successive governments on immigration reform. Compelling state and local governments to help enforce the border, which is currently a federal responsibility, has been a flash point in recent years, with state and local governments refusing to help enforce the nation's borders for reasons ranging from the costs to cities declaring themselves sanctuaries for immigrants who are in the country illegally.

Immigration reform

Each new group of immigrants has faced prejudice from those who have already arrived. While they are proud of their own immigrant ancestors, many Americans want to keep other people out. The reason often given is that immigrants are a threat to jobs, but a stronger motive is the fear that immigrants who are not white and from northern Europe may change mainstream American culture in ways Americans do not want, particularly by speaking languages other than English and practicing religions other than Christianity. There is no doubt that there is a large proportion of immigrants in the population and that, unless more restrictions are imposed, their numbers will continue to grow. It is generally accepted that previous groups of immigrants have integrated into American society, and that the current groups are integrating also. But some analysts argue that there is a mismatch between the nation's liberal, if highly-regulated, immigration policies and the relatively little the US does to help immigrants integrate (Fix, Zimmermann, and Passel, 2001). Yet the successful integration of immigrants and their children will be a crucial factor in the country's future. An integration agenda would include promoting the social and economic mobility of immigrants and their families, particularly refugees and people who speak little English, the treatment of legal immigrants with citizen children, and how to deal with the undocumented. Other issues are the categories of people who should be eligible for sponsored immigration, and how an integration agenda should be equitably funded at each level of government.

In 2005 through 2007 no fewer than four immigration reform bills were introduced in the Senate and another in the House. All of them failed. The Secure Borders, Economic Opportunity and Immigration Reform bill of 2007 (S.1348), known as the Comprehensive Immigration Reform bill, built on three previous bills: the Secure America and Orderly Immigration Act (S.1033), proposed by Senators Ted Kennedy and John McCain; the Comprehensive Enforcement and Immigration Reform Act of 2005 (S. 1438), proposed by Senators John Cornyn and Jon Kyl; and the Comprehensive Immigration Reform Act of 2006 (S. 2611), sponsored by Senator Arlen Specter, which was passed in the Senate in May 2006 but never passed in the House. The new bill was crafted by the sponsors of the previous bills plus others, collectively known as "the Gang of 12."

The Secure Borders Bill would have provided legal status and a responsible path to citizenship for currently undocumented immigrants. The Bill was portrayed as a compromise between an amnesty and increased border enforcement. It included funding for 300 miles (480 km) of vehicle barriers, 105 camera and radar towers, and 20,000 more border patrol agents, while changing visa criteria to favor high skill workers. The Bill met heated criticism from both sides of the immigration debate and eventually failed. At the same time, the Security Through Regularized Immigration and a Vibrant Economy Act of 2007 was being considered in the House but also failed.

An amended version of the Secure Borders Bill was introduced at the urging of President Bush as bill S.1639. This too was lost. The amended bill would have created a new class of visa, the "Z visa," that would be given to everyone who was living in the US without a valid visa on January 1, 2008; this visa would have given its holder the legal right to remain in the US for the rest of their life, and access to a Social Security number. After eight years, the holder of a "Z" visa would be eligible for a US Permanent Resident Card (a "green card") if they wanted; they would first have to pay a $2000 fine and back taxes for some of the period in which they had worked. Under the current rules, five years after that the immigrant could begin the process of becoming a citizen.

Bill S.1639 would have required an undocumented immigrant to be in their home country when they applied for a green card. The Bill would also have closed most family reunification categories. Only the spouse and children of a new citizen would be made eligible for green cards. The Bill would also have eliminated employer-sponsored visas and replaced them with a points-based "merit" system similar to that in other developed countries. Points would be awarded by the US Citizenship and Immigration Services for education, job skills, family connections and English proficiency. Additional points would be awarded if a job offer were available. The labor certification process, by which the employer had to state that no suitable American could be found for the job, would also have been eliminated. Several family-based immigration categories would have been folded into the points system. Another new category of visa, the "Y," would have been created to allow guest workers into the country for two years, after which they would have to return home. The original Bill set the number of guest workers at 400,000 a year, but amendments reduced the number of entrants to 200,000 and limited the life of the program to five years.

The Bill would have strengthened enforcement of the US - Mexico border, including increasing the number of border patrol agents to 20,000 and adding another 370 miles (600 km) of fencing, among other measures. The Bill would also have created a new program, the Employment Eligibility Verification System, a central database to hold information on the immigrant status of all workers living in the US. Eventually all employers, whatever the size of the company, would have been required to submit such information and keep the system updated. No further part of the Bill would have taken effect until these measures had been implemented.

The Secure Borders Bill also contained the Development, Relief and Education for Alien Minors Act (the DREAM Act), a Bill that has been introduced unsuccessfully several times in the House and Senate to provide a path to citizenship for undocumented immigrant minors who either go to college or serve in the military, and that would also restore the states' right to determine eligibility for in-state tuition.

Conservatives rejected providing a path to citizenship for undocumented immigrants, on the ground that it would reward them for breaking US immigration laws. Liberals criticized the points system as unfair to less qualified workers, and the limits on family reunification visas as unfair to extended families. Labor unions, human rights, and some Hispanic organizations attacked the guest worker program, claiming it would create an underclass of workers with no benefits. It was also alleged that because guest workers would be required to return home for a year before renewing their visa, they would instead overstay their visa, becoming undocumented immigrants. High-tech industry criticized the points-based green card system because it would have eliminated priority visa-processing for highly skilled workers. Many immigration practitioners, while supporting aspects of the proposal, criticized the Bill as unworkable and called for it to be fundamentally revised. The Obama administration has expressed itself in favor of comprehensive immigration reform.

AFRICAN AMERICANS (see also Chapters 9 and 10)

One group of immigrants came unwillingly, as slaves from Africa. Half a million were shipped between 1619 and 1808, when the importation of slaves into the US became illegal. Slave-owning continued, however, particularly in the South, where crops like cotton required large numbers of laborers to work the fields. Laws were passed to prevent intermarriage with whites (miscegenation), which were only struck down by the Supreme Court in 1867. On January 1, 1863, midway through the Civil War between the free states of the North and the slave states of the South, President Lincoln's Emancipation Proclamation, which abolished slavery in the 11 states that had left the Union, came into force. Slavery was abolished throughout the US with the passage of the Thirteenth Amendment to the Constitution in 1865.

Terminology

The preferred terms for referring to Black or African Americans changed several times during the 20th century, from *colored* to *Negro* to *Black* and then to *Afro-American* and *African American*. The direction of change was to put more emphasis on heritage rather than color. In the 1960s and 1970s, *Afro-American* was prominent along with related terms such as *Afro-American Studies* (1970), *Afro* hair styles (1968), *Afro-beat* music (1974) and *Afro-rock* (1977). The term *African American* was widely adopted after a speech by the Reverend Jesse Jackson in 1988.

During colonial and early national times, black slaves and freemen alike were often referred to as *Africans*, even if their families had lived in America for several generations. That this practice was common among blacks as well as whites is shown by the number of churches and institutions with names such as the African Methodist Episcopal church and the Free African Society founded during this period. This usage fell out of favor in the 19th century, however, and it was not until the Black Power movement of the late 1960s and early 1970s that black Americans' African heritage was again reflected in popular speech. *Afro-American*, which quickly became popular for a while alongside *black*, expressed a growing, sometimes defiant pride in black American culture and its African origins.

But in the following decades *Afro-American* lost some of its popularity, especially in referring to people, and has to a large extent been replaced by *African American*, in line with the standard form of ethnic American names such as *Asian American*, and *Italian American*. Like *Native American*, it is most appropriately used by outsiders in public discourse, as in articles, broadcasts, and speeches, where it communicates respect by emphasizing ethnicity over race. But there is little sign that *African American* will replace *black* in the way that term earlier replaced *Negro*. Indeed, recent surveys among black Americans, while confirming widespread acceptance of *African American*, indicate a strong continued preference for *black*. One reason for this is that there has been increasing immigration from Africa, and the term *African American* cannot distinguish between recent immigrants and people descended from slaves, whose roots in the US go back centuries. Hence, in areas with large African immigrant populations, a shift back toward *black American* has become increasingly common among the non-immigrant black population.

Demographics

The African American population count has been controversial for decades. The NAACP (National Association for the Advancement of Colored People) has claimed that the black population has been under-counted intentionally to minimize its political significance. The only self-reported ancestral groups larger than African Americans are Irish and German Americans. (It has been suggested that, due to the fact that many African Americans trace their ancestry to colonial American origins, some simply self-report as "American.")

THE AFRICAN AMERICAN POPULATION OVER TIME

Year	Number	% of total population	Slaves	% in slavery
1790	757,208	19.3% (highest)	697,681	92%
1800	1,002,037	18.9%	893,602	89%
1810	1,377,808	19.0%	1,191,362	86%
1820	1,771,656	18.4%	1,538,022	87%
1830	2,328,642	18.1%	2,009,043	86%
1840	2,873,648	16.8%	2,487,355	87%
1850	3,638,808	15.7%	3,204,287	88%
1860	4,441,830	14.1%	3,953,731	89%
1870	4,880,009	12.7%	-	-
1880	6,580,793	13.1%	-	-
1890	7,488,788	11.9%	-	-
1900	8,833,994	11.6%	-	-
1910	9,827,763	10.7%	-	-
1920	10.5 million	9.9%	-	-
1930	11.9 million	9.7% (lowest)	-	-
1940	12.9 million	9.8%	-	-
1950	15.0 million	10.0%	-	-
1960	18.9 million	10.5%	-	-
1970	22.6 million	11.1%	-	-
1980	26.5 million	11.7%	-	-
1990	30.0 million	12.1%	-	-
2000	36.6 million	12.3%	-	-

The percentage of blacks in the total population has varied considerably over the centuries. In 1790, when the first US Census was taken, Africans (including slaves and free people) numbered about 760,000—19.3%. By 1860, at the start of the Civil War, the African American population had increased to 4.4 million, but the percentage had dropped to 14%. The vast majority of blacks were slaves, with only 488,000 counted as "freemen." By 1900, although the black population had doubled and reached 8.8 million, the percentage was 11.6%. By 1990, the African American population had reached about 30 million and represented 12% of the total, roughly the same proportion as in 1900. Currently, according to 2005 Census figures, some 39.9 million African Americans live in the US, comprising 13.8% of the total population.

The distribution of the black population has also changed dramatically. In 1910, about 90% of African Americans lived in the South, but large numbers began migrating north in hopes of finding better jobs, voting, enjoying greater equality, obtaining education for their children and escaping violence. The Great Migration, as it was called, spanned the 1890s to the 1970s. This was the greatest internal population shift in US history. Starting about 1910, over five million African Americans moved from the South to northern cities, the West and Midwest. In the 1920s, the concentration of blacks in New York led to the cultural movement known as the Harlem Renaissance, whose influence reached nationwide. The South Side of Chicago, a destination for many on the trains from Mississippi and Louisiana, became the black capital of America, generating flourishing businesses, music and arts. After World War II a new generation of powerful African American political leaders and organizations came to the fore. Membership in the NAACP rapidly increased as it mounted an anti-lynching campaign in reaction to ongoing southern white violence against blacks.

The trend reversed in the 1970s and 1980s, with more blacks moving south to the Sun Belt than leaving it. The 2000 Census reported that 54.8% of African Americans lived in the South, 17.6% in the Northeast and 18.7% in the Midwest, while only 8.9% lived in the western states. The West does have a sizeable black population in certain areas, however. California, the nation's most populous state, has the fifth largest African American population, only behind New York, Texas, Georgia, and Florida.

The majority of African Americans, almost 58%, nowadays live in metropolitan areas (Census 2000). New York City has the largest black urban population, with over 2 million black residents, 28%. Chicago has the second largest black population, with almost 1.6 million African Americans, about 18%. Of the 253 cities with a population over 100,000, Detroit, Michigan, was the "blackest," with an 82% African American population. Other large cities with African American majorities include New Orleans, Louisiana (67%), Baltimore, Maryland (64%), Atlanta, Georgia (61%), Memphis, Tennessee (61%), and Washington, D.C. (60%). Queens County, New York is the only county with a population of 65,000 or more where African Americans have a higher median household income than European Americans.

African Americans are mostly Christians and a small minority Muslims. The majority of Christians are affiliated with the historically black churches of Protestant type. The US Census does not collect data on religious affiliation, but other sources give an indication. According to The Pew Forum on Religion and Public Life (U.S. Religious Landscape Survey), the historical black churches are 92% black, the Jehovah's Witnesses (22% black) and other denominations are typically 11% black.

The African American population is 40.7 million, 13.5% of the total US population. There are 36.6 million non-Hispanic Blacks (12.15% of the population); and 677,290 Black Hispanics (0.23%).

Most African Americans are the descendants of slaves. Blacks whose ancestors immigrated from the Caribbean, or who themselves immigrated, are also generally considered African Americans, as they mostly share common roots in West or Central Africa, the Middle Passage and slavery. Others sometimes referred to as African Americans, and who are so called by the US government, include relatively recent black immigrants from Africa, South America and elsewhere who self-identify as being of African descent.

ORIGINS AND PERCENTAGES OF AFRICAN AMERICANS IMPORTED INTO BRITISH NORTH AMERICA AND LOUISIANA (1700-1820)

Region/modern country	Percentage
West Central Africa, Congo, Angola	26.1%
Bight of Biafra (S.E. Nigeria, Cameroon, Gabon)	24.4%
Sierra Leone (Guinea-Bissau, Guinea, Sierra Leone, Liberia and Côte d'Ivoire)	15.8%
Senegal, Gambia, Niger	14.5%
Gold Coast (Ghana)	13.1%
Bight of Benin (Togo, Benin, S.W. Nigeria)	4.3%
Mozambique, Madagascar, Tanzania	1.8%

Slavery

Slaves were either sold as prisoners of war by African states or kidnapped by Europeans or Americans. British colonists made use of slaves as labor on their American plantations. The slave population was made up of various African ethnic groups. Over time, tribal differences disappeared and the slaves created a new history and culture out of their common pasts and present.

The first slaves were brought to Jamestown, Virginia, by English settlers in 1619 as indentured servants and were released after a number of years. Gradually, however, blacks in America were relegated to slavery as they were in the Caribbean, since freed servants became competitors with the colonists, and were in any case expensive to replace. In 1641 Massachusetts was the first colony to legalize slavery. Soon, other colonies followed suit. Non-Christian imported servants were made slaves for life, and slavery became a heritable status, by which the children of slaves were slaves themselves.

In the Revolutionary period, the Second Continental Congress (1775-1781) considered freeing the slaves in order to disrupt British commerce. But the Congress removed language from the Declaration of Independence that included the promotion of slavery amongst the alleged offenses of King George III. The Declaration, that would later become a manifesto for human rights and personal freedom, was largely written by Thomas Jefferson, who himself owned over 200 slaves. (The extent to which Jefferson agonized over slavery has been much debated; he probably fathered a son by a slave, Sally Hemings.) Other Southern statesmen were also major slaveholders. Several people pointed out the hypocrisy of slaveholders demanding freedom for themselves, and a number of free blacks, most notably Prince Hall, submitted petitions for the end of slavery. But these were largely ignored. This, however, did not deter some 5,000 blacks, both free and slave, from enlisting in the Continental Army. But when George Washington took command in 1775 he barred any further recruitment of blacks. At the end of the Revolutionary War, the Americans demanded that the British hand over their slaves.

The Constitutional Convention of 1787, in drafting the Constitution, in effect provided for the continuation of slavery through the "fugitive slave" clause (which did not include the word "slave" but referred to persons who owed "labor or service") and the "three-fifths compromise" clause which counted a black as 3/5 when reckoning the population. This clause simply referred to "other persons" in contrast to "free persons." In addition, the rights of free blacks were restricted in many places. Most were denied the right to vote and were excluded from public schools. Some blacks sought to fight these restrictions in court. In 1790, Elizabeth Freeman and Quock Walker used language from the new Massachusetts constitution of 1780, that declared all men were born free and equal, to sue successfully for freedom. In 1787 Congress passed the Northwest Ordinance, which barred slavery from the Northwest Territory (north and west of the Ohio river and east of the Mississippi.) Congress also restricted the slave trade. In 1790, a law prohibited US citizens from engaging in the slave trade to foreign ports, and in 1794 it became illegal to manufacture, equip, or otherwise assist any vessels destined for the slave trade. The Atlantic slave trade was abolished with effect from January 1, 1808. But even though Congress passed a law in 1820 making participation in the slave trade an act of piracy and punishable by death, the law was not strongly enforced and the slave trade continued in the South, especially in Texas, Florida and South Carolina.

In the Northern states, widespread anti-slavery sentiment developed from around 1750. Emancipation acts were passed in all the Northern states between 1780 and 1804. The acts mostly provided for gradual emancipation and a special status for freedmen. Pennsylvania was the first state to abolish slavery, passing an act in 1780 for the gradual abolition of slavery. New Jersey and Rhode Island followed in 1787, and Massachusetts (1788), Connecticut (1788) and New York (1799) did so soon after. By 1806, only South Carolina had not forbidden the importation of slaves. In 1790, there were more than 59,000 free blacks in the US. By 1810, the number had risen to 186,446. Most of them were in the North, but some Southern slaveholders also freed their slaves, sometimes by manumission or in wills to be accomplished after the slaveholder's death. In the Upper South, the percentage of free blacks rose from about 1% before the Revolution to more than 10% by 1810. Quakers and Moravians were particularly active in trying to persuade slaveholders to free slave families. In Virginia the number of free blacks increased from 10,000 in 1790 to nearly 30,000 in 1810, but 95% of blacks were still enslaved. In Delaware, three-quarters of all blacks were free by 1810. By 1860 just over 91% of Delaware's blacks were free, and 49.1% of those in Maryland.

As the US grew, slavery became more entrenched in the Southern states, while the Northern states began to abolish it. A number of events combined to polarize the issue. The invention of the cotton gin in 1793 allowed the cultivation of short staple cotton, which could be grown in inland areas. This triggered a huge demand for imported slave labor to develop new cotton plantations. In only 20 years the number of slaves increased by 70%. They were overwhelmingly concentrated in the Deep South (South Carolina, Mississippi, Florida, Alabama, Georgia, Louisiana, and Texas.)

Although the Atlantic slave trade was abolished in 1808, this apparent victory for African Americans actually increased the demand for slaves. Changes in farming in the Upper South (North Carolina, Tennessee, Virginia, Kentucky, and West Virginia) from tobacco to mixed farming meanwhile decreased demand for labor there, and slaves were sold to traders who sold them on in the Deep South. In addition, the Fugitive Slave Act of 1793 allowed any black person to be claimed as a runaway unless a white person testified on their behalf. A number of free blacks, especially indentured children, were kidnapped and sold into slavery with little or no hope of rescue. By 1819 there were exactly 11 free and 11 slave states, which increased sectionalism. Fears of an imbalance in Congress between slave and free states led to the 1820 Missouri Compromise that required states to be admitted to the Union in pairs, one slave and one free.

The number of free blacks grew during this time as well. By 1830 there were 319,000, of whom 150,000 lived in the Northern states. While the majority of free blacks lived in poverty, some were able to establish successful businesses that catered to the black community. Racial discrimination, however, often meant that blacks were not welcome or would be mistreated in white businesses and other white establishments. To counter this, blacks developed their own communities with black-owned businesses. Black doctors, lawyers and businessmen formed a black middle class.

African Americans founded community organizations to help poor blacks and maintain their fight against slavery. Schools were established for black children, who were often barred from public schools. Starting in the early 1790s with such churches as the African Methodist Episcopal Church and the African Methodist Episcopal Zion Church, black churches grew to be the focal point of black communities. They were an expression both of community and of a unique African American spirituality, and were also a reaction to European American discrimination. At first, black preachers formed separate congregations within existing denominations, but because of discrimination at the higher levels of the church hierarchies, some black preachers founded separate black denominations. Free blacks established black churches in the South before 1800. After the Second Great Awakening (1790-1840s), many blacks joined the Baptist Church, which allowed for their participation, including as elders and preachers. (See also Chapter 8.)

The legal status of slaves was brought to an issue by Dred Scott (1799 – 1858), a slave who sued unsuccessfully for his freedom in the infamous *Dred Scott v. Sandford* case of 1857. His case was based on the fact that although he and his wife Harriet were slaves, they had lived in states and territories where slavery was illegal, including Illinois and Minnesota (which was then part of the Wisconsin Territory). But Congress had not asserted whether slaves were free once they set foot on Northern soil. The Supreme Court ruled seven to two against Scott, finding that neither he, nor any person of African ancestry, could claim citizenship in the US, and that therefore Scott could not bring suit in federal court. Moreover, said the Court, Scott's temporary residence outside Missouri did not effect his emancipation under the Missouri Compromise, since that would deprive Scott's owner of his property. The ruling arguably violated the Compromise because, based on the court's logic, a slave owner could purchase slaves in a slave state and then, as Scott's owner had done, bring his slaves to a state where slavery was illegal without losing the right to own the slaves. The Court also ruled that since Scott was an object of private property, he was subject to the Fifth Amendment which prohibits taking property from its owner "without due process." The result of the case upset the Northern Republicans and further worsened relations between North and South. Scott was ultimately manumitted.

African Americans in the Civil War (1861-65)
During the Civil War, African Americans in the Union Army, both free and runaway slaves, comprised 163 units, a total of 186,097 men (7,122 officers, 178,975 enlisted men) and many others served in the Union navy. On the Confederate side, blacks, both free and slave, were used for labor, but the issue of whether to arm them, and on what terms, became a major source of debate in the South.

Most Union leaders, including Lincoln, hesitated to raise black regiments because of concerns about the reaction of the border states (of which one, Maryland, surrounded Washington D.C.), and the response of white soldiers and officers, as well as doubts about the effectiveness of a colored fighting force. Official enrollment began only after the Emancipation Proclamation was issued in September 1862, although state and local militias had already started enrollment.

African American soldiers came to comprise 10% of the Union army, but their death rate was over 20%. Of the total of slightly over two million troops in the US Volunteers, over 316,000 were killed, 15.2%. Of the 67,000 Regular Army (white) troops, 8.6%, or not quite 6,000, died. Of the approximately 180,000 US Colored Troops, however, over 36,000, or 20.5%, were killed, although blacks were not enrolled until some eighteen months after fighting began (Aptheker, "Negro Casualties in the Civil War," *The Journal of Negro History*).

African American soldiers proved they could fight well, indeed heroically, at such engagements as Island Mound, Missouri; Port Hudson, Louisiana; Fort Wagner; Fort Pillow, Tennessee; and Chaffin's Farm, Virginia (*Official Record of the War of the Rebellion*, Ser. I, Vol. XXVI Pt. 1, p. 45). But although black soldiers proved themselves, discrimination in pay and duties was widespread until, on June 15, 1864, Congress enacted equal pay for black soldiers. Besides lower pay, colored units were often disproportionately assigned laborer work (McPherson, *The Negro's Civil War*).

Like the army, the Union navy at first had mixed feelings about the use of blacks until the constant stream of escaped slaves seeking refuge aboard Union ships induced the navy to employ them. In time, almost 16% of sailors were African Americans performing a wide range of duties. In contrast to the Army, though, the Navy from the outset not only paid equal wages to black and white sailors, but paid much better. Rations and medical care were also better than the Army. Becoming a commissioned officer, however, was still impossible for black sailors. Only the rank of petty officer was open to them and, in practice, only to free blacks.

In the Confederacy, nearly 40% of the population were unfree. Civilian work thus fell mainly to the blacks, since many white men were serving in the army. Hence several states impressed slaves and conscripted free blacks to military labor. Slave labor was used in a wide variety of support roles, from construction and mining to teamsters and medical orderlies and nurses. The idea of using slaves as soldiers was debated from the onset of the war, but blacks were only recruited from March 1865. Even so, some 3,000 African Americans took part in "Stonewall" Jackson's occupation of Frederick, Maryland in September 1862, and several African Americans are known to have participated on the Southern side in the Battle of Gettysburg, July 1863. Meanwhile there were some state militias made up of free blacks. The 1st Louisiana Native Guard was the first of any North American unit to have African American officers but was not allowed to fight. When African Americans were allowed to enlist, slaves were offered emancipation if their masters consented. To offer unconditional emancipation, Southern legislators argued, would contradict the reason for fighting the war. Very few blacks were enlisted before the war ended in April 1865.

In the Confederate Navy, it was possible for free blacks to enlist; slaves could serve with their master's consent. No draft of seamen to a newly commissioned vessel could number more than 5% blacks, however. Though precise figures are lacking, a fair number of blacks served as coal heavers, officers' stewards, or sometimes as highly skilled tidewater pilots. Although runaway slaves captured in Union uniform were legally liable to be put to death, it seems that they were returned to their owners. Freemen were confined and put to hard labor.

The Emancipation Proclamation

In 1863, the Emancipation Proclamation freed the slaves in the Southern states (the Confederacy). The 13th Amendment to the Constitution, ratified in 1865, outlawed slavery in every state. The 14th amendment granted full US citizenship to African Americans in 1868. The 15th amendment, ratified in 1870, extended the right to vote to black males.

In the Reconstruction period (1865-1877) which followed the Union victory, some progress was made, with the help of Union troops, toward equal rights for blacks. Southern black men began to vote and were elected to Congress and to local offices such as sheriff. Coalitions of white and black Republicans passed bills to establish the first open public school systems in most states of the South, although sufficient funding was hard to find. Blacks meanwhile continued to establish their own churches, towns and businesses. Tens of thousands, for example, migrated to Mississippi for the chance to clear and own their own land, as 90% of the bottomlands were undeveloped. By the end of the century, two-thirds of the farmers who owned land in the Mississippi Delta bottomlands were black. Tens of thousands of black Northerners also migrated to the South, building schools, printing newspapers, and opening businesses. Many went as teachers sponsored by a dozen or so benevolent societies. Others went to organize relief for refugees. Still others went as missionaries. Finally, thousands of blacks who had gone to the South as soldiers remained to settle. The South became a black frontier.

Yet these years saw increasing intimidation of African Americans and whites sympathetic to their cause. After the disputed state elections of 1872 in Louisiana, for instance, the Colfax and Coushatta massacres took place in 1873 and 1874. (Historians have called numerous such events "massacres" because of the disproportionate number of blacks killed as opposed to whites. The mob violence at Colfax resulted in 40 to 50 blacks killed and three whites. A state historical marker erected in 1950 noted that 150 blacks died and three whites.) According to newspaper records kept at the Tuskegee Institute, about 5,000 men, women, and children were murdered outright, or tortured to death in documented lynchings. Many more are believed to have suffered in undocumented incidents. It is reported that fewer than 50 whites were ever indicted for such crimes, and only four sentenced. (For the story of the lynchings, see Philip Dray, *At the Hands of Persons Unknown: The Lynching of Black America*. For the systematic oppression and terror inflicted, see Leon F. Litwack, *Trouble in Mind: Black Southerners in the Age of Jim Crow*.)

The federal government withdrew its troops from the South in 1877 as part of a compromise deal over the disputed Presidential election of 1876 which allowed Rutherford Hayes to take office. White Democratic Southerners acted quickly to reverse the groundbreaking advances of Reconstruction. Exploiting racial fear and attacking the corruption (real or perceived) of Reconstruction Republican governments, they took over state governments in the South in the 1870s and dominated them for nearly 100 years, chiefly as a result of disenfranchisement of most blacks through statutes and constitutions. To reduce black voting and regain control of state legislatures, Democrats used a combination of violence, fraud, and intimidation from the election of 1868 onward. These techniques were prevalent among paramilitary groups made up of Confederate veterans, such as the White League (1874) and Red Shirts (1875) in Louisiana, Mississippi, and Florida prior to the 1876 elections. In South Carolina an estimated 150 blacks were killed in the weeks before the election. While not as widely known as the Ku Klux Klan (KKK), the paramilitary organizations were more effective than the Klan in challenging Republican governments, suppressing the black vote and achieving political goals. Unlike the Klan, paramilitary members operated openly, and often solicited newspaper coverage.

In contrast, the Ku Klux Klan, a secret vigilante group sworn to perpetuate white supremacy, was formed in 1865 and quickly became powerful across the South. The Klan tried to keep blacks from voting and from participating in the new governments. It carried out lynchings and intimidation, burned houses and churches, and made other attacks against the persons and property of blacks and their white allies. In 1870 Congress passed The Force Act imposing fines and damages for conspiracy to deprive blacks of the suffrage, and banning the use of terror, force or bribery to prevent someone from voting because of his race. It empowered the President to employ the armed forces to suppress organizations which deprived people of rights guaranteed by the 14th Amendment. For such organizations to appear in arms was made rebellion against the US. The President could even suspend habeas corpus in that area. As paramilitary violence against African Americans intensified, however, many blacks like Benjamin "Pap" Singleton began speaking of separating from the South. This idea culminated in the 1879-1880 movement of the Exodusters, who migrated to Kansas (Lemann, *Redemption: The Last Battle of the Civil War.*)

White Democrats then passed laws to make it more difficult for blacks to register to vote. Blacks lost not only the right to vote but also the right to serve on juries, run for local office or keep and bear arms. Many poor whites were also disenfranchised by these laws. Additionally, new laws were passed to reintroduce social barriers in order to segregate society along racial lines (Jim Crow laws). These limited black access to transportation, schools, restaurants and other public facilities. When the Democrats took control of Tennessee in 1888, they ended the most competitive politics in the South. Voting by blacks in rural areas and small towns dropped sharply, as did voting by poor whites. From 1890 to 1908, 10 of the 11 Southern states adopted new constitutions or amendments that effectively disenfranchised most blacks and many poor whites. Using a combination of poll taxes, residency requirements and literacy tests, states dramatically decreased black voter registration and turnout, in some cases to zero. Grandfather clauses were used in many states temporarily to exempt illiterate white voters from literacy tests. As the Democratic Party assumed control, the party positioned itself as a private club and instituted white primaries, closing blacks out of the contests. By 1910 one-party white rule was firmly established across the South. By that year, only 0.5% of eligible black men in Louisiana were registered to vote. As a result, the Southern Democrat bloc in Congress was greatly out of proportion to the population they represented. In this period, the Democrats in the House of Representatives managed to nullify investigations into contested elections by the House Elections Committee, and after the *Dantzler v. Lever* contest in South Carolina in 1904, the House advised complainants to take their cases to the courts.

Although African Americans quickly started litigation, early court decisions at state and federal level went against them. In *Plessy v. Ferguson* (1896), the Supreme Court ruled that "separate but equal" facilities were constitutional. In *Williams v. Mississippi* (1898) the Supreme Court upheld state laws that required applicants for voter registration to pass a literacy test and pay poll taxes. This encouraged other Southern states to adopt similar measures over the next few years. Booker T. Washington of the Tuskegee Institute secretly worked with Northern supporters to raise funds and provide representation for blacks in further cases, such as *Giles v. Harris* (1903) and *Giles v. Teasley* (1904), but again the Supreme Court upheld the states.

White supremacists defended the political subordination of African Americans by claiming that when blacks had taken part in government, they had proved to be incompetent. This view was promoted in school textbooks and in such movies as *The Birth of a Nation* in 1915. For decades after the abolition of slavery, most Southern blacks continued to struggle in grinding poverty as agricultural, domestic and menial laborers, and many became sharecroppers, their economic status little changed by emancipation. Moreover, even where segregation was not enforced legally, it created a segregated culture which persisted through the 1960s. Indeed, in 1913, President Woodrow Wilson, a Southern Democrat, introduced segregation into federal offices, over much protest.

The Civil Rights Movement

In response to the failure of Reconstruction, and the discrimination and oppression African Americans suffered in the generations after the Civil War, in 1905, W. E. B. DuBois and 28 other prominent African American men met at Niagara Falls, Ontario, Canada. There they produced a manifesto calling for full civil liberties for African Americans and an end to racial discrimination. The organization they established came to be called the Niagara Movement. Later, concerned European Americans joined and the NAACP was formed a year later. The NAACP mounted legal challenges to segregation and lobbied legislatures on behalf of black Americans. During this period, blacks continued to create independent community and institutional lives for themselves by establishing schools, churches, social welfare institutions, banks, newspapers and small businesses.

After World War II, in 1946, President Truman desegregated the military, and African Americans increasingly challenged all segregation, as they believed they had earned the right to complete equality by their military service in the two world wars. In World War II, for example, famous segregated units, such as the Tuskegee Airmen and the U.S. 761st Tank Battalion proved their value in combat.

The Civil Rights movement began in response to incidents such as the attack on veteran Isaac Woodard while he was in army uniform. As the Movement gained momentum it used the federal courts to challenge Jim Crow laws, while the white-dominated governments of many of the Southern states countered with alternative forms of restriction. In 1955 Rosa Parks' act of civil disobedience, when she refused to give up her seat on a bus to a white man, sparked a number of demonstrations and a series of legislative and court decisions that undermined the Jim Crow laws. The Montgomery Bus Boycott led by the Reverend Dr. Martin Luther King, Jr., which followed Rosa Parks' action, was not, however, the first of its kind. Numerous boycotts and demonstrations against segregation had occurred throughout the 1930s and 1940s. These early demonstrations achieved limited results but did help promote black political consciousness.

Groups such as the Southern Christian Leadership Conference (SCLC) organized voter registration campaigns, boycotts and other nonviolent action, including pickets, sit-ins and marches, in support of equal access and voting rights. Southern segregationists fought back to block reform. Some used violence, bombings and intimidation. Law enforcement responded to protesters with violence and mass arrests which shocked people across the nation and aroused sympathy for the protesters. State legislators, school board members and other public officials mounted campaigns of obstruction and outright defiance to integration including denying state funding to integrated schools and funding privately run "segregation academies" for white students.

In this era, the Supreme Court began to overturn Jim Crow laws on constitutional grounds through rulings in a number of cases. The Court in *Irene Morgan v. Virginia* (1946) ruled that segregation in interstate transportation was unconstitutional, under the commerce clause of the Constitution. In

1954 the NAACP Legal Defense Committee, through its lawyer, Thurgood Marshall, brought the landmark case *Brown v. Board of Education of Topeka, 347 U.S. 48,3* before the Supreme Court. In its decision, the Court found unanimously that legally mandated public school segregation was unconstitutional since separate facilities were inherently unequal. The decision did not end school segregation based on residence, which still continues today, and school boards continue to grapple with issues of equality. But *Brown* had far-reaching effects in other areas, since it effectively overturned *Plessy v. Ferguson*. In 1971 the Supreme Court, in *Swann v. Charlotte-Mecklenburg Board of Education*, upheld the busing of students to achieve integration.

As well as the Jim Crow laws, businesses, unions and political parties enforced their own forms of segregation, barring blacks from working at certain trades, buying homes in certain neighborhoods, and shopping or working in certain stores. The Supreme Court outlawed some forms of private discrimination in *Shelley v. Kraemer* 334 US 1 (1948), in which it held that "restrictive covenants" that barred the sale of homes to blacks or Jews or Asians were unconstitutional, on the ground that they represented state-sponsored discrimination, since they were only effective if the courts enforced them. The Supreme Court was unwilling, however, to outlaw other forms of private discrimination. It reasoned that private parties did not violate the Equal Protection clause of the 14th Amendment when they discriminated, because they were not the "state actors" covered by that clause. The Court had held in the *Civil Rights Cases* 109 US 3 (1883) that the 14th Amendment did not give the federal government the power to outlaw private discrimination.

The climax of the Civil Rights Movement was the March on Washington for Jobs and Freedom in 1963. This attracted over 250,000 marchers to the grounds of the Lincoln Memorial and the National Mall in Washington, D.C. There speakers demanded equal opportunity in employment, equal access to education and public accommodations, and an end to Southern racial violence and police brutality. It was at this event, on the steps of the Lincoln Memorial, that Martin Luther King delivered his historic "I Have a Dream" speech. The March and the conditions which brought it into being are credited with putting pressure on Presidents John F. Kennedy and Lyndon B. Johnson that culminated in the passage of the Civil Rights Act of 1964.

On January 8, 1964, President Johnson, in his first State of the Union address, asked Congress to "let this session of Congress be known as the session which did more for civil rights than the last hundred sessions combined." Through building a coalition of Northern Democrats and Republicans, Johnson was able to win a majority in Congress for legislation on discrimination and on July 2 he signed the Civil Rights Act. This outlawed discrimination in employment, labor unions and public accommodations (privately owned restaurants, hotels, and stores) and in private schools. By 1965, however, although efforts to achieve effective voting rights had been under way for some time, they had met with only modest success and in some areas had proved almost entirely ineffectual. The murder of three voting rights activists in Mississippi the previous year, along with numerous other acts of racial violence, attracted national attention. The escalating injustices of the "Mississippi Blood Summer," as it had come to be known, and the brutality of the murders, sparked outrage. Finally, the unprovoked attack on March 7, 1965 by Alabama state troopers on peaceful marchers crossing the Edmund Pettus Bridge in Selma, on their way to the state capitol in Montgomery, persuaded the President and Congress to override Southern legislators' resistance and enact the Voting Rights Act of 1965. This ended legally sanctioned state barriers to voting for all federal, state and local elections. It also provided for Federal oversight and monitoring of counties with historically low voter turnout.

Meanwhile, a group of militant black leaders like Eldridge Cleaver of the Black Panther Party and Malcolm X of the Nation of Islam arose. They called on blacks to use violence if necessary to obtain their rights, asserting that non-violent protest was ineffective. From the mid-1960s to the mid-1970s, the Black Power movement urged African Americans to look to Africa for inspiration, and emphasized black solidarity rather than integration. These movements represented only a minority, however. Malcolm X left the Nation of Islam and was assassinated in 1965, while by the 1980s Cleaver had become a conservative Republican. The effect of black casualties in the Vietnam War on the development of subsequent African American leadership remains a matter of controversy.

Politically and economically, blacks have made substantial strides in the post-civil rights era, although the NAACP is still protesting and litigating against discrimination by individual companies, and by industries such as advertizing which historically have not recruited blacks. Civil rights leader Jesse Jackson, who ran for the Democratic Party's presidential nomination in 1984 and 1988, brought unprecedented support and leverage to blacks in politics. In 1989, Virginia elected Douglas Wilder, the first African American governor in US history. In 1992 Carol Moseley-Braun of Illinois became the first black woman elected to the Senate. In 2008 black Senator Barack Obama, whose father was Kenyan, was elected President.

The 42 African American members of Congress (all in the House) form the Congressional Black Caucus, which serves as a political bloc for issues relating to African Americans. The appointment of blacks to high federal offices—including Attorney General Eric H. Holder, Jr., General Colin Powell, Chairman of the U.S. Armed Forces Joint Chiefs of Staff, 1989-1993 and U.S. Secretary of State, 2001- 2005; Condoleezza Rice, Assistant to the President for National Security Affairs, 2001-2004 and Secretary of State 2005-2009; Ron Brown, U.S. Secretary of Commerce, 1993-1996; and Supreme Court justices Thurgood Marshall and Clarence Thomas—also demonstrates the increasing visibility of blacks.

Although blacks make up 13% of the population, they currently comprise only 0.25% of America's economic elite. According to the *Forbes 400* list of the richest people, Oprah Winfrey was the richest African American of the 20th century and was the world's only black billionaire in 2004, 2005, and 2006. She has been the only black on the list nearly every year since 1995. BET founder Bob Johnson briefly joined her from 2001-2003 before his ex-wife acquired part of his fortune, but although he returned in 2006, he did not make it in 2007.

According to the NAACP's *Year One: Toward Safe Communities, Good Schools and A Fair Chance for All Americans, 2009:* "Black unemployment is perennially twice that of white Americans. Several studies found that a majority of employers preferred to hire a white criminal than a black man without a criminal record. African American children disproportionately attend segregated, poor quality schools. Mass incarceration is harming far too many people of color when drug treatment and other approaches would have better outcomes. The health disparities in our communities are well known."

Cultural influence of African Americans

The most influential ethnic vernacular tradition in America is the African American. One of the most pervasive African American cultural influences is to be found in mainstream popular music. Hip-hop, R&B, funk, rock and roll, soul, blues, and other contemporary American musical forms originated in black communities and evolved from other black forms of music, including blues, ragtime, jazz, and gospel music. African American-derived musical forms have also influenced and been incorporated into virtually every other popular musical genre in the world, including country and techno (see Chapter 10).

African Americans have also had an important role in American dance. Bill T. Jones, a prominent modern choreographer and dancer, has included historical African American themes in his work, particularly in the piece "Last Supper at Uncle Tom's Cabin/The Promised Land." Likewise, Alvin Ailey's artistic work, including "Revelations" based on his experience of growing up as an African American in the South during the 1930s, has had a significant influence on modern dance. Another form of dance, Stepping, is an African American tradition.

African American is also a major genre in American literature. Many African American authors have written novels, poems, and essays influenced by their experiences as African Americans. Famous examples include Langston Hughes, James Baldwin, Richard Wright, Zora Neale Hurston, Ralph Ellison, Nobel Prize winner Toni Morrison, and Maya Angelou.

By around 1890, the world of art and culture had accepted black entertainers, musicians, and literary figures. But black athletes found themselves barred from competing alongside whites. Until after World War II, white opposition to African American boxers, baseball players, track athletes, and basketball players kept them segregated and limited in what they could do. But their prowess and abilities in all-African American teams and sporting events could not be denied. Changing social attitudes and leadership by pioneers such as Jackie Robinson, who entered formerly all-white professional baseball in 1947, aided in lowering the barriers. African American participation in all the major sports began to increase rapidly in the 1950s and 1960s.

African American inventors have created many widely used devices. By 1913 over 1,000 inventions had been patented by black Americans. Among the most notable industrial inventors were Jan Matzeliger, who developed the first machine to mass-produce shoes. In transportation, Elijah McCoy invented automatic lubrication devices for steam engines. Later, Granville Woods registered 35 patents to improve electric railways, including the first system to allow moving trains to communicate. Other African American inventors include Lewis Howard Latimer, who created an inexpensive cotton-thread filament, which made long-burning electric light bulbs practicable; and Garrett A. Morgan, who developed the first automatic traffic signal and the gas mask. In agriculture, Norbert Rillieux invented the technique for converting sugar cane juice into white sugar crystals, while George Washington Carver created 300 products from peanuts, 118 products from sweet potatoes, and 75 from pecans. George Crum invented the potato chip in 1853. More recent inventors include Frederick McKinley Jones, who invented the movable refrigeration unit for food transport in trucks and trains. Jones also patented the air conditioner. Lloyd Quarterman worked with six other black scientists on the creation of the atomic bomb (the Manhattan Project). Quarterman also helped develop the first nuclear reactor, which was used in the atomically powered submarine *Nautilus*. Meanwhile Dr. Mark Dean holds three of the original nine patents on the computer on which all PCs are based. More recent inventors include Otis Boykin, who invented several novel methods for manufacturing electrical components used in guided missile systems and computers. Colonel Frederick Gregory was not only the first black astronaut pilot but redesigned the cockpits for the space shuttles. Gregory was on the team that pioneered the microwave instrumentation landing system as well. African Americans have also made notable contributions to medicine. Dr Daniel Hale Williams, for example, performed the first successful open heart surgery, and Dr. Charles R. Drew pioneered the use of blood banks.

Jewish Americans

Sephardic Jews, most of whom came from Spain or Portugal to escape persecution, lived in North America long before the Revolution. At least five of Columbus's crew were *conversos* (Spanish or Portuguese who were outwardly Christian but secretly Jewish.) Some scholars speculate that Columbus may have been a converso himself. In 1520, Bernando Lopez de Mendizabel, a converso, became the Spanish governor of the New Mexico territory but was discovered changing his linen and bathing just before the Jewish Sabbath. As a result, he was dismissed and imprisoned. In the 1660s some 23 Jewish refugees fled from the Portuguese colony of Brazil to the then Dutch colony of New Amsterdam (now New York) and joined the two Jews already there. More arrived, mostly from Holland. In 1655, they petitioned for the right to "stand guard" with the other citizens on the wall built against potential attacks on what is now Wall Street. They also petitioned for a cemetery and in 1656 were granted a tiny plot on today's Chatham Square in Chinatown. This is the oldest known Jewish cemetery in the US and continued in use until 1831. In 1664 the British acquired New Amsterdam, which they renamed New York, and encouraged traders and adventurers, Jews and Christians alike, to set up trading posts in the remote areas of New England.

Other Jewish communities were established around this time in Newport (which has the oldest surviving synagogue), Philadelphia, Baltimore, Savannah and Charleston, South Carolina, which was the largest settlement of Jews until 1830. In 1733, the colony of Georgia was founded by James Oglethorpe, who welcomed new immigrants, including Jewish colonists from England. Georgia sought to establish wine-making as a major industry and one of the first Jewish colonists was Abraham de Lyon, an experienced vintner. The colony was plagued with malaria; fortunately, another Jewish immigrant was Samuel Nunez Ribiero, a doctor with experience in treating the dread disease with success.

In 1773, Francis Salvador from England settled in South Carolina. A representative in the first Provincial Congress of the state, he took up arms for the Revolutionary cause. With a force of five hundred men, Salvador led several attacks against loyalists and their Indian allies. During one such attack he was badly wounded and later killed, unaware that the Declaration of Independence, which he had passionately urged, had been adopted.

A Polish Jew, Haym Salomon, arrived in New York in 1772. During the Revolutionary War, Salomon ensured that the young United States remained solvent and could pay its troops and borrow on its international credit. After the war, Salomon gave away much of his wealth to the poor of Philadelphia, among them a future President, James Madison. Other Jewish fighters for the Revolution were Benjamin Sheftall and his son from England who helped supply the Continental Army. Following the War of 1812, Gershom Seixas, the first American-born rabbi, was elected by the New York state legislature as a member of the first Board of Regents of the University of the State of New York.

At the beginning of the 19th century there were only about 6,000 Jews in the US. Many would-be immigrants stayed away for fear of discrimination, until in the 1820s the Ashkenazi German Jews began to arrive. They lived as merchants or shop owners, and were either Reform Jews, who had ceased to observe the ordinances on diet, purity and dress, and some of the ceremonies of traditional Judaism, or secular Jews who had left Judaism altogether. By 1850 there were about 17,000 Jews in America. After the famines of the 1840s, the failure of the 1848 uprisings throughout Europe, and increased persecution in the Russian empire (particularly in Poland, Lithuania, Belarus, Ukraine and Moldova), the next generation saw a flood of Ashkenazi Jewish immigrants. By 1880 the Jewish population was about 270,000. Between 1880 and 1924, two million Jews immigrated to the US. Most Jewish immigrants went to the New York area, which in the 1880s had a Jewish population of 180,000. This soon grew to 1.8 million. The Jewish area of New York was the Lower East Side of Manhattan. Successful Jews quickly moved to the Upper East Side. They included Marcus Goldman, founder of Goldman, Sachs & Co., the bank; Bloomingdale, founder of the department store, Bloomingdales; Henry, Emanuel and Mayer Lehman, founders of Lehman Brothers; and Joseph Seligman, who started out as a peddler and became one of the most important bankers in America.

At the turn of the 20th century, American Jewry was joined by Jews from Eastern Europe. Between 1881 and 1914, some 50,000 Jews left Eastern Europe every year, most of whom went to America, although their rabbis preached against doing so, fearing that in America the Jews would lose their heritage and identity. The vast majority of these Jews were poor and arrived in New York with little or nothing. On the Lower East Side of Manhattan at the beginning of the 1900s, 6,000 tenements housed as many as 64,000 families. Many of the new arrivals found jobs in the garment industry working in the sweatshops. It was miserable work for minimal wages, 15 -18 hours a day, often under appalling conditions, particularly bad ventilation, which promoted tuberculosis, and dreadful sanitation. (Many other immigrants suffered similarly.) The Jews assimilated quickly. Desperate for a wage, they ceased to observe the Sabbath, since Saturday was a workday. Those who tried to keep the Sabbath by not going to work were immediately fired. Given the terrible conditions and the strong sense of justice that has always been a part of Jewish culture, it is no wonder that Jews played a key role in creating labor unions and fighting for workers' rights and against child labor. One of the leaders was Chaim Nachman Bialik (1873-1934) who is considered the poet laureate of modern Hebrew and one of the leading Jewish intellectuals of his age. Meanwhile a number of important rabbis arrived and began to lay the foundations for what would later become the thriving Orthodox Jewish community.

While the German Jews for the most part rapidly succeeded in America, life was much harder for the Eastern European Jews. The German Jews felt that these poor, Yiddish-speaking, religious Jews gave all Jews a bad name and worked to get them to acculturate as quickly as possible. Their underlying fear was anti-Semitism. This fear was well-founded, because despite the religious tolerance of America, anti-Semitism was active. Jews were isolated and excluded. In 1894, Henry Adams (a descendant of John Quincy Adams) organized the Immigration Restriction League to limit the admission to America of "unhealthy elements," Jews being first among them. But in 1906, President Theodore Roosevelt appointed Oscar Straus as the Secretary of Commerce and Labor, the first Jew to serve in the US cabinet. His responsibilities included immigration.

There were some 200 synagogues in America by 1880. Almost all the early ones were Reform. Temple Emanuel on the Upper East Side of Manhattan, built by the German Jews, was the largest Reform synagogue in the world. Indeed, the focus of the Reform Movement shifted from Germany to America. Reform Jews no longer consider themselves a nation, but a religious community, and expect neither a return to Palestine, nor the revival of a sacrificial worship led by descendants of Aaron, nor the restoration of any of the Biblical laws concerning the Jewish state. Thus American Reform Jews did not support the Zionist Movement or the foundation of the State of Israel at first. Reform Jews are tolerant. There is no religious action a Reform rabbi could take for which he or she would be expelled from the Central Conference of American Rabbis, the official body of Reform rabbis. More traditional Jews who believed that the Reform had gone too far, but who did not want to return to the traditional Orthodox form of Judaism, founded the purely-American Conservative Movement in 1886. The Conservative Movement upholds the Torah (the first five books of the Bible) as the revealed Word of God, but says that the interpretation need not uphold the exact tradition as passed down from Moses but can adapt to modern conditions, in principle as well as practice. Thus the behavior of Conservative Jews is virtually indistinguishable from Reform Jews.

The American Jewish community has had a profound influence, playing vital roles in commerce, law, education, politics, philanthropy, the fine arts, music and theater. Jews were active in the Civil Rights movement from the 1920s and took part in the March on Washington. There are African American Jews. Sammy Davis, Jr. (1925-1990) was one. But the alliance between Jewish and African American political organizations is in decline. Jews have never voted less than around 70% Democratic. In 2008 they voted 78% for President Obama. Of the 13 Jews in the Senate, 10 are Democrats; two (Joe Lieberman and Bernie Sanders) are independents, although both caucus with the Democrats. Senator Lieberman has played a distinguished part in public life and ran as Democratic Vice-Presidential candidate in 2004, the first Jew to run for national office on the ticket of a major party. Of the 32 Jews elected to the House in 2008, only one (Eric Cantor) is a Republican. The Democrats include Jared Polis, 33, the openly gay multimillionaire internet entrepreneur. Two states have two Jewish Senators: Wisconsin (Herb Kohl and Russ Feingold) and California (Dianne Feinstein and Barbara Boxer). All are high-profile legislators. Increasing prosperity has meant suburbanization and, some believe, increasing secularization. So successful have Jews in America been that their struggle for inclusion has become a fight against assimilation. Mass culture, as in the case of Woody Allen, has appropriated some of the defining traits of Jewish humor.

Zionism is a minority but influential opinion among American Jews. The immediate recognition of Israel by the American government in 1948 was an indication of both the American policy of exporting capitalism and democracy, and of the influence of political Zionism. Since then the vast majority of American Jews have become supporters of the State of Israel, although the wars between Israel and its neighbors have given rise to heart-searching among some Jews.

The US Jewish population today is nearly six million. Jews mostly live in major metropolitan areas like New York, and also in South Florida, Philadelphia, California, New England, Ohio, and Illinois. The rate of increase of their population has slowed due a 50% rate of intermarriage with non-Jews.

Hispanic and Latino Americans

Hispanics and Latinos are Americans with origins in the Hispanic countries of Latin America or in Spain (except for the state of New York, where only people of Latin American origin are included in the figures.) The term *Hispanic* does not include Brazilian Americans or Portuguese Americans. Hispanics and Latinos are the largest ethnic minority in the US, 15.1% of the population or 45.4 million people in 2007, and the second largest ethnic group after non–Hispanic White Americans. (African Americans are the largest racial minority.) Hispanic or Latino identity is self-reported, as in the Census. Owing to the popular use of "Latino" in the Western states, the government has adopted the term as an alternative to "Hispanic."

Since 1565, when Augustine in what is now Florida was founded by the Spanish, there has been an unbroken history of settlement by Hispanic or Latino people in America. Augustine was the first European settlement in the continental US. Hispanics are thus the oldest among European

American ethnic groups. The Spanish also established a Jesuit mission at Chesapeake Bay in 1570. Hispanics have lived continuously in the Southwest since near the end of the 16th century, with settlements in New Mexico that began in 1598 and were transferred to the area of El Paso, Texas in 1680. Spanish settlement of New Mexico resumed in 1692, and new settlements were established in the 18th century. These included San Antonio, Texas (1716), San Diego (1769), Tucson, Arizona (1775), San Francisco (1776) and Los Angeles (1781).

As of 2007, according to figures released by the U.S. Census Bureau, Hispanics accounted for 47.5% of the foreign-born population, whereas in 1950 fewer than four million US residents were from Spanish-speaking countries. Hispanic migration to the US due to rural unemployment and overall lack of jobs is estimated to have doubled between 1990 and 2000, especially since the North American Free Trade Agreement (NAFTA) came into force in 1994. Many Hispanics come to the US to work on farms and in the garment, electronic and apparel industries. The growth rate of the Hispanic population from 2000 to 2007 was 28.7%, about four times the rate of growth of the nation's total population (7.2%). Half the Hispanic population (49%, 21.5 million) live in California or Texas. Several other states have large Hispanic populations, including New York, Illinois and Florida. New Mexico has the highest proportion of Hispanics (44.7%), followed by California and Texas, with 35.9% and 35.6%, respectively. Places like East Los Angeles, Laredo, Texas, and Brownsville, Texas, are almost entirely Latino, 97%, 94% and 91% respectively. While two-thirds of the Hispanic population are of Mexican origin, the majority of them in the Southeast, who are concentrated in Florida, are of Cuban origin. The Hispanic population in the Northeast, concentrated in New York and New Jersey, is composed mostly of Puerto Ricans. In northern New Mexico and southern Colorado live peoples who trace their ancestry to Spanish settlers of the late 16th through the 17th century. Many of these settlers intermarried with local Amerindians, creating a mestizo population. Likewise, southern Louisiana is home to communities of people of Canary Islands descent, known as *Isleños*. Immigration has been so massive that some people refer to California as "Mexifornia." A major question is whether the majority of Hispanics will assimilate by learning English as other immigrants have done, or whether they will form an almost separate region within the US, resulting in a "Balkanization" of America.

Estimates put the high school graduation rate for the majority population at around 80%. The figure for Hispanics is highest among Cuban Americans (68.7%) and lowest among Mexican Americans (48.7%). On the same basis, it has been calculated that the rate for Puerto Ricans is 63.2%, that of Central and South Americans 60.4%, and that of Dominican Americans 51.7%. According to the 2000 census, Cuban Americans and Central and South Americans had the highest college graduation rates, with 19.4% of Cuban Americans and 16% of Central and South Americans 25 years and older possessing a 4-year college degree. On the other hand, only 6.2% of Mexican Americans, 9.9% of Puerto Ricans and 10.9% of Dominican Americans did so. This compares with 43.3% for Asian Americans and 26.1% for white Americans. The figure for blacks is 14.4%. As for graduate degrees, Cuban Americans have the highest attainment among Hispanic or Latino groups, with 6.7%. The Central and South American rate is 4.2%. Both are lower than those of Asian Americans (15.6%) and white Americans (8.7%). Black Americans (4.1%) have a lower percentage than most Hispanic or Latino groups.

The income of the average Hispanic American is lower than the national average of $36,764. In 2002, the average individual income among Hispanic and Latino Americans was highest for Cuban Americans ($38,733) and lowest for Dominican Americans ($28,467) and Mexican

Americans ($27,877). For Puerto Ricans it was $33,927 and for Central and South Americans $30,444. Among Hispanics, Cuban Americans (28.5%) had the highest percentage in professional–managerial occupations, compared with the national average of 36.2%. The percentage for Puerto Ricans was 20.7, Central and South Americans 16.8, and Mexican Americans 13.2. According to the American Community Survey (ACS), the poverty rate among Hispanic groups is highest among Dominican Americans (28.1%), Honduran Americans and Puerto Ricans (23.7% both), and Mexican Americans (23.6%). Poverty is lowest among South Americans, such as Colombian Americans (10.6%) and Peruvian Americans (13.6%), and relatively low poverty rates are found among Salvadoran Americans (15.0%) and Cuban Americans (15.2%). In comparison, the average poverty rates for non-Hispanic White Americans (8.8%) and Asian Americans (7.1%) were lower than those for any Hispanic group. African Americans (21.3%) have a higher poverty rate than most Hispanic or Latino groups.

The achievements of Hispanics and Latinos have been notable in every area of American life. The positions held by Hispanic Americans in government are various. The federal cabinet under President Obama includes Ken Salazar, Secretary of the Interior, and Hilda Solis, Secretary of Labor. Hispanic governors include Bill Richardson of New Mexico, former Secretary of Energy and Ambassador to the United Nations. There are currently 23 Hispanic Congresspeople. In 2009 Sonia Sotomayor was appointed to the Supreme Court. Cuban immigrant Roberto Goizueta rose to become head of The Coca-Cola Company.

Hispanics and Latinos have excelled in all fields of culture too. In science, Luis Walter Alvarez, the physicist, won the Nobel Prize, and his son Walter Alvarez, the geologist, was the first to propose that the dinosaurs were made extinct as a result of an asteroid collision. Ellen Ochoa was a pioneer of spacecraft technology and an astronaut. Several other Latinos have made a name for themselves in aerospace: France A. Cordóva, former NASA chief scientist; and Franklin Chang-Diaz, who holds the record for the most flights into space, and is the leading researcher on the plasma engine for rockets. Notable among Hispanic authors are Sandra Cisneros (*The House on Mango Street* and *Woman Hollering Creek and Other Stories*) and Oscar Hijuelos (The *Mambo Kings Play Songs of Love*). Many Hispanic musicians, such as Jennifer Lopez and Joan Baez, have achieved international fame. Hispanics have also contributed prominent actors and others in the television and film industries. Oscar de la Renta is among Hispanics prominent in fashion. In sports, such as baseball, boxing, football, soccer, tennis and golf (Lee Travino) many Hispanic Americans have excelled.

With 40% of Hispanic and Latino Americans being immigrants, and with many of the rest the children or grandchildren of immigrants, at least 2/3 of the community is bilingual. While 90% speak English, 80% speak Spanish, the oldest European language in the US. The leading Spanish–language media are the Univision and Telemundo TV networks, the ConSentido TV, radio and newspaper network of north Texas, the newspapers *La Opinión* of Los Angeles, *El Nuevo Herald* and *Diario Las Americas* of Miami and Hispanic Business (English language) and *Vida Latina* magazine of the Southern states. In addition there are thousands of smaller outlets. Latino Public Broadcasting funds programs of educational and cultural significance for Hispanic Americans. The National Hispanic Media Coalition (NHMC) has advocated for more Latinos to be included in television, radio, and film and to be hired by the media, and has signed diversity agreements with the TV networks.

The political outlooks of Hispanics and Latinos differ according to where they live and their place in the social structure. Cuban Americans and Colombian Americans tend to hold conservative views and support the Republicans, while Mexican Americans, Puerto Ricans, and Dominican Americans tend to favor liberal views and support the Democrats. Because the latter groups are far more numerous, however – Mexican Americans alone are 64% of Hispanics and Latinos – Democratic support is far stronger. In the 2008 Presidential election, 67% of Hispanics and Latinos voted for Obama (compared with 72% for Clinton in 1996). Political organizations concerned with Hispanic and Latino issues are the League of United Latin American Citizens (LULAC), the United Farm Workers, the Cuban American National Foundation and the National Institute for Latino Policy. The economy, employment and immigration are their prime concerns; views on illegal immigration are mixed. Analysts believe, however, that Republican opposition to immigration reform, particularly that offering a pathway to citizenship for illegal immigrants, has damaged their support among Latinos in the swing states of Florida, Nevada and New Mexico.

Hatred of Hispanics and crimes against them (hispanophobia) have always existed, based on ethnicity, race, culture, their Catholic religion, and their use of Spanish. In 2006, *Time* reported that the number of hate groups in the US had increased by 33% since 2000, primarily due to anti-illegal immigrant and anti-Mexican sentiment. According to the FBI, anti–Latino hate crimes have increased by 35% since 2003. In California, the state with the largest Latino population, the number of hate crimes against Latinos has almost doubled. Unlike the Chinese, however, Latinos have never been subjected to legal exclusion.

Asian Americans

Asian Americans are Americans of Asian ancestry. They include Chinese Americans, Filipino Americans, Indian Americans, Vietnamese Americans, Korean Americans, Japanese Americans and others, such as Asians from Pakistan, Sri Lanka and Thailand. In the Census, people who originate from the Far East, Southeast Asia and the Indian subcontinent are classified as of Asian race. But although demographic statistics describe Asian Americans as a single group, there are significant differences among the Asian ethnicities. Because they total less than 5% of the population, however, their diversity is often disregarded. As Asian American author Stewart Ikeda has noted: "The definition of 'Asian American' also frequently depends on who's asking, who's defining, in what context, and why...." Asian Americans now comprise the second largest minority in the US, and the Asian American Movement has asked the government to legitimize "Asian American" as a category alongside other minorities such as African American, Hispanic/Latino American and Native American. Classification is important, among other things, for eligibility for equal opportunity programs.

First generation Asian immigrants, however, still generally identify themselves with their country of origin rather than as Asian Americans, which is an issue of controversy because it is said to perpetuate ancient ethnic divisions in the American context and prevent the creation of an American cultural solidarity for later generations of Asians. The barriers within the Asian community may be strengthened by linguistic differences until the Asians become primarily an English-speaking community. Meanwhile Asian Americans are one of the fastest-growing ethnic groups and are among the most successful of all immigrants, despite the fact that most of them have arrived recently. Asians have higher incomes than many other ethnic groups, and large numbers of their children study at the best universities as undergraduate and graduate students.

The development of some degree of Asian American consciousness is resulting from the shared experiences of Far Eastern Asian Americans as the excluded "yellow people." The Chinese Exclusion Act of 1882, the Watsonville Riot of 1929, the Japanese American Internment Act of 1942, the Vincent Chin incident of 1982 (for which his killers received only a $3,700 fine and served no jail time), the LA Riots of 1992 (when stores owned by Koreans and other Asians were targeted), as well as the Virginia Tech Massacre and the 2009 Binghamton shootings all generate memories and stories of conflict that Asian Americans of various ethnic origins share in their continuing struggle for equality.

In the 19th century, driven by poverty to seek work in America, immigrants from China, Korea and Japan started arriving in Hawaii to labor on the sugar plantations. Later, Filipinos joined them. Many immigrants from China and Japan arrived on the mainland in the mid-19th century looking for work. Although the numbers of Asian immigrants were relatively small, they were concentrated in California, and increased immigration caused a fear among some Americans of what was known as the "yellow peril." In response the federal government passed the Chinese Exclusion Act (1882) and the Asian Exclusion Act (1924) which sharply restricted Asian immigration.

Asian America has been transformed by legislation such as the McCarran-Walter Act of 1952 and the Immigration and Nationality Act of 1965. The former repealed the restriction of citizenship to "free white persons" of the Naturalization Act of 1790 (already abolished for African Americans), but it retained the quota system that effectively banned nearly all immigration from Asia. For example, the annual quota of Chinese was only 50. The Immigration and Nationality Act (INA) enabled significant immigration from every nation in Asia, which has led to dramatic and ongoing changes in the Asian American population and perceptions of who is an Asian American. The preference given to relatives of existing immigrants, initially designed to reduce the number of Asian immigrants, eventually acted to increase their numbers. The INA replaced the immigration rules of the Chinese Exclusion Act of 1882 and its successors such as the 1924 Immigration Act, which effectively excluded Asians. The Luce-Celler Act of 1946 helped immigrants from India and the Philippines. Immigration of Asian Americans was also affected by US involvement in wars from the 1940s to the 1970s. The end of the Korean and Vietnam wars brought a new wave of Asian American immigration, as people from Korea, Vietnam, Laos and Cambodia arrived. Some of the new immigrants were war brides who had married American servicemen and who were soon joined by their families. Others, like the Southeast Asians, were either highly skilled and educated, or refugees.

The 2006 American Community Survey recorded 14.6 million people who identified themselves as having either full or partial Asian heritage, 4.9% of the population. The largest Asian subgroups were Chinese (3.6 million), Filipinos (2.9 million), Asian Indians (2.7 million), Vietnamese (1.6 million), Koreans (1.5 million), and Japanese (1.2 million). Other Asian groups are Cambodians/Khmers (206,000), Pakistanis (204,000), Laotians (198,000), Hmong (186,000), and Thais (150,000). Currently, Indians, Chinese, and Filipinos are the largest Asian groups immigrating to the US.

Half of all Asian Americans (5.4 million) live in Hawaii or on the West Coast, mostly in California (4.2 million). Most Asian Americans live in urban areas, nearly three-quarters of them in metropolises with a population greater than 2.5 million. Asian Americans are concentrated in the largest cities, with 40% living in the Los Angeles, San Francisco, New York and Chicago areas. Census data shows that Asian American populations are also developing in major metropolises away from the West Coast, with visible communities in areas such as Baltimore-Washington and Greater Houston, to name the largest examples. In regions with large numbers of Asian

Americans, suburban communities have developed that are heavily or predominantly Asian. The schools in these areas may offer languages such as Mandarin as a second language. Since the 1970s, Little Manilas, Koreatowns and Little Saigons have appeared in several cities in addition to Chinatowns. Large Japantowns once existed up and down the West Coast because of extensive Japanese immigration. The ones that remain are vestiges of once vibrant pre-World War II communities whose members, like other Americans, have moved out into the suburbs and larger communities. Japanese Americans are underrepresented in several of the largest areas, including Chicago, Boston and Dallas-Fort Worth, although sizable concentrations, double their national percentage, can be found in some urban neighborhoods, such as Albany Park in Chicago and Olney in Philadelphia. Other Asian populations are found in suburbs such as Naperville and Evanston near Chicago; Millbourne, King of Prussia, and Cherry Hill near Philadelphia; Lowell and Lexington near Boston and in Las Vegas. This pattern reflects their later arrival and response to changing economic conditions in some cities.

Asian Americans are the best educated of all of America's ethnic groups. According to the Census Bureau, they graduate from high school at the same rate as other Americans, while 48% attain at least a bachelor's degree as compared with the national average of 27%, and 29% for non-Hispanic Whites. Indian Americans have some of the highest education rates, with nearly 68% having attained at least a bachelor's degree. Asians are the most numerous group who obtain graduate degrees.

As for earnings, Asian American households, at $57,518, have the highest median income of any group, $57.518 (Current Population Survey Annual Social and Economic Supplement 2005). But poverty among Asians, at 9.8%, was higher in 2004 than the 8.2% rate for non-Hispanic whites, and poverty was much higher for some southeast Asian ethnic groups. Much of the poverty is concentrated in ethnic enclaves such as Chinatowns. Census figures also show that a white male with a college diploma earns in excess of $66,000 a year, far more than similarly educated Asian men, who earn more than $52,000 a year.

Impact of Asian Americans

Politics

Gary Locke, a Chinese American, has become Commerce Secretary, after serving as governor of Washington state. In 2009, Steven Chu, another Chinese American, became the Secretary of Energy. The Veteran Affairs Secretary is Eric Shinseki, a Japanese American. Chinese American Elaine Chao was Secretary of Labor 2001-2009. Japanese American Norman Mineta was Secretary of Transportation 2001-2006. Former Congressman Bobby Jindal, an Indian American, is governor of Louisiana. George Ryoichi Ariyoshi of Hawaii was the first Asian American to be elected a governor. The Congressional delegation of Hawaii has been filled by Asian Americans for most of its history. Senator Daniel Inouye, Hawaii's first representative after it became a state and currently the third most senior member of the Senate, was recently named to be chair of the Senate Appropriations Committee beginning in 2009. In 1976, the Japanese American academic S. I. Hayakawa was elected to the Senate from California. In 2000 Japanese American Mike Honda was elected to the House from that state. Robert C. Scott, the congressman from Virginia's 3rd District, has Filipino ancestry. In 2008, Anh "Joseph" Cao became the first Vietnamese American congressman after being elected for Louisiana.

Business

Asian Americans have made major contributions to business. Their widespread success in that field has brought them influence. They are heavily involved in the high-tech industries of Silicon Valley, Silicon Forest (Portland, Oregon), the Research Triangle (North Carolina), the Washington metropolitan area, and Texas. In 1951 An Wang founded Wang Laboratories, an innovative designer and manufacturer of computers and related systems. Amar Bose founded the Bose Corporation, the audio products company in 1964. Jen-Hsun Huang co-founded the NVIDIA corporation, the graphics processing and chipset company, in 1993. Yahoo! was co-founded in 1994 by Jerry Yang, who later became the CEO. Steve Chen and Jawed Karim were the co-creators of YouTube in 2005. Asian Americans are well represented in the professions such as medicine and law, and have started ventures in many other fields. But it was not always so. When Asian Americans were largely excluded from labor markets in the 19th century, they started their own businesses such as convenience and grocery stores, restaurants and laundries.

Many Asian Americans have penetrated the fashion world. Vera Wang, whose famous collections include wedding gowns for the stars, has been a leading fashion designer for years and retails a broad range of luxury fashion products. Anna Sui's clothing, fragrance, cosmetic, and accessories retail in her stores and independent boutiques in over 50 countries. Filipina Monique Lhullier's sophisticated dresses have paraded on the Hollywood red carpet, and Vietnamese American Chloe Dao is a winner of Project Runway, the reality-TV fashion design-based series. Other designers include Phillip Lim, Derek Lam (the 2005 Council of Fashion Designers of America (CFDA) Emerging Talent Award winner) and Korean American Doo-Ri Chung, the 2006 winner of the Award. Andrea Jung serves as Chairman and CEO of Avon Products.

The arts and literature

The distinguished architect I. M. Pei is one of the most famous Asian Americans. He has designed buildings around the world. In the US he designed the National Center for Atmospheric Research in Boulder, Colorado (1961-67), the East Wing of the National Gallery in Washington (1968-78), the John F. Kennedy Library in Boston (1979), and the Morton H. Meyerson Symphony Center in Dallas (1989). Among his many awards and distinctions, in 1983 Pei was chosen the Laureate of the Pritzker Architecture Prize. He used the award to establish a scholarship fund for Chinese students to study architecture in the US (with the strict proviso that they return to China to practice their profession). Meanwhile Maya Lin designed the Museum of Chinese in America (1980) near New York City's Chinatown, the Vietnam Veterans Memorial (1982), which, although a controversial design, has become one of America's best loved buildings, and the Civil Rights Memorial at Montgomery, Alabama (1989). (Lin believes that if the competition for the war memorial had not been "blind" she would not have won it.) In 1994, she was the subject of the Academy Award-winning documentary *Maya Lin: A Strong Clear Vision*. Minoru Yamasaki designed the World Trade Center and fellow Japanese American, Gyo Obata, the National Air and Space Museum in Washington. In literature, Asian American writers have received numerous awards. Jim Lee is considered to be one of the most popular comic book artists and is one of the founders of Image Comics. Adrian Tomine is well known for his comic book series *Optic Nerve*. His cartoons are also featured in *The New Yorker* and *Esquire*.

Theater, film and music

C. Y. Lee's novel *Flower Drum Song* (1957) was the basis of a musical by Rodgers and Hammerstein, but would not be produced with an all-Asian cast until a Broadway revival in 2002. Major films have been based on Asian American novels such as Jhumpa Lahiri's *The Namesake* (2007) and Amy Tan's *The Joy Luck Club*. In 1988, David Henry Hwang's Broadway hit *M. Butterfly* won a Tony Award for Best Play among other awards. Renowned singer and actress Lea Salonga is active on Broadway.

A series of critically acclaimed films including *Brokeback Mountain, Eat Drink Man Woman, Sense and Sensibility, Crouching Tiger, Hidden Dragon* and *Lust, Caution* have brought Ang Lee world renown. Fellow director Justin Lin drew attention to the experiences of Asian Americans through his movie *Better Luck Tomorrow*, a drama/dark comedy focusing on the travails of a group of Asian Americans living in Southern California who are academically successful but socially discontented, and as a result engage in wantonly violent, criminal behavior. The film has an almost exclusively Asian American cast. Lin is also responsible for blockbusters such as *The Fast and the Furious: Tokyo Drift* and its prequel *Fast & Furious*. John Woo is famous for directing such films as *Mission: Impossible 2, Windtalkers,* and *Paycheck*. The Indian American director M. Night Shyamalan has directed a number of movies, including *Signs, The Village, Unbreakable,* and the Academy award-nominated *The Sixth Sense*. Another well-known Indian American director, Mira Nair, has made acclaimed movies like *Salaam Bombay, Monsoon Wedding* and *The Namesake*.

Thai Americans Chang and Eng Bunker (the original Siamese twins) became famous entertainers in the 19th century. Few Asian Americans so far have obtained acting roles in theater, cinema and television, however, and many of those have been narrow, stereotyped characters. In 1965, a group of actors formed East West Players (EWP) in Los Angeles, to provide Asian American actors greater opportunity to perform in leading roles. Several other Asian American theater companies have been formed in other cities.

The Academy Award for Best Supporting Actor was won by Cambodian American Haing Ngor in 1985 for *The Killing Fields*. The career of Lucy Liu the television and film actress took off when she played one of the lead roles in the *Charlie's Angels* movie series (1976-81). Cambodian American Francois Chau has become a well known TV actor in shows such as ABC's *Lost,* and in video games. Margaret Cho won the American Comedy Award for Best Female Comedian in 1994. Wah Chang was the designer for many of the props for the *Star Trek* series as well as for *The Time Machine*, which received an Academy Award for special effects. Film and TV actor John Cho starred in *American Beauty,* the *American Pie* films and as helmsman Hikaru Sulu in *Star Trek* (2009). Up-and-coming actors include Ethan Le Phong, *Naked Boys Singing* (2007). Yo-Yo Ma, world renowned cellist, includes in his discography new recordings of world music, as in *The Silk Road Project*. The composer Bright Chang has received extensive recognition for his work, including being invited to be composer-in-residence at the New York City Ballet. The three Filipino Tenors have made a hit with their mixed-genre repertoire.

Science and technology

In physics, several Nobel Prize winners have been Asian American: Tsun-Dao Lee and Chen Ning Yan (1957); Samuel Chao Chung Ting (1976) for discovery of the subatomic particle; Indian-born Subrahmanyan Chandrasekhar (1983, shared) for his work on the structure and evolution of stars; Steven Chu (1997, shared); Daniel Tsui (1998, shared); and Yoichiro Nambu (2008). In 2008, biochemist Roger Tsien won the Nobel Prize in Chemistry. Har Gobind Khorana shared the 1968 Nobel Prize in Physiology or Medicine for his work in genetics and protein synthesis. Dr. David D. Ho is a leading HIV vaccine researcher. In 1984 he first reported the "healthy carrier state" of HIV infection. Chien-Shiung Wu was well known to scientists as the "First Lady of Physics" or "the Chinese Marie Curie" for her work in radioactivity. In addition, Tsie Hsue-shen co-founded the Jet Propulsion Laboratory in the 1940s.

Health and Medicine

Encouraged by the government, Asian immigrant physicians and dentists, especially from the Philippines and India, are becoming visible, especially in primary care and rural medicine, where they are in demand. Traditional Asian concepts and practices in health and medicine are also attracting greater acceptance and practice by American doctors. India's Ayuveda and traditional Chinese medicine (TCM) and acupuncture are alternative therapy systems that have been studied and adopted. Since the 1970s some studies have shown the efficacy of acupuncture, especially for the treatment of chronic pain. Acupuncture is now covered by many health insurance plans. Meditation and mindfulness practices are taught in mainstream medical schools and hospitals. Increasingly they are seen as part of a holistic approach to health. Ayurvedic herbalism and massage, together with meditation and yoga, have been widely adopted by health spas. These practices are also part of the spiritual practice of the many Americans who are not affiliated with a mainline religious group.

Sport

Since the 1940s, Asian Americans have been making an impact on Olympic sports. The women's gymnastics team which won the gold medal at the Games in 1996 included Amy Chow, who also won an individual silver medal on the uneven bars. At the 2004 Games, gymnast Mohini Bhardwai won a team silver medal, while Hapa Bryan Clay who won the decathlon silver, was the sport's world champion in 2005 and went on to win the decathlon gold in 2008. Wataru Msaka broke the NBA color barrier when he played for the New York Nicks in the 1947–48 season. Michael Chang, the youngest ever winner of a Grand Slam men's tennis tournament, the French Open in 1989, aged 17 years and 3 months, was a top-ranked tennis player for most of his career. Since Tiffany Chin won the women's figure skating championship in 1985, Asian Americans have been prominent in that sport. Kristi Yamaguchi won three national championships, two world titles, and the 1992 Olympic gold medal in figure skating, while Michelle Kwan has won nine national championships and five world titles, as well as two Olympic medals (silver in 1998, bronze in 2002). In football, Asian Americans' contributions are also gaining notice through players like Dat Nguyen (Vietnamese American) and Hines Ward (Korean American). Tiger Woods is ranked as the most successful golfer of all time. In skateboard, Eric Koston (Thai American) is one of the top street skateboarders and placed first in the 2003 X-games street competition.

Popular music

There is an extensive roll-call of Asian Americans in popular music: Amerie, Ne-Yo and Cassie, the R&B singers; Utada Hikaru, who has become world-famous, with two songs in the Kingdom Hearts video games, as has Lea Salonga, who has performed for three US presidents. Vanessa Hudgens and Nicole Scherzinger are also well-known recording artists. Joey Santiago is the lead guitarist for the *Pixies,* while James Iha is best-known as guitarist with *The Smashing Pumpkins.* Tony Kanal, also a songwriter and record producer, is the bassist for the popular rock band *No Doubt*. Mike Shinoda and Korean American Joseph Hahn are members of the rap rock band *Linkin Park*. Kenny Choi is the lead singer and guitarist of the indie rock band *Daphne Loves Derby*, as well as having solo projects. In hip-hop, Apl.de.ap is a member of *The Black Eyed Peas*. A colorful video by rapper Jin spiraled him to fame in 2003. Leehom Wang played in Ang Lee's *Lust, Caution*. In the heavy metal genre, female singer-songwriter Aja Kim of *Z-Band* achieved notoriety as lead vocalist in the role of Bruce "Lee" Chickinson for the tribute band, *The Iron Maidens,* and has since built an illustrious solo career.

Television

The first Asian Americans to become really well-known on television were George Takei and Pat Morita. They sprang to fame through supporting roles in *Star Trek* and *Happy Days*, two of the best known series of the 1960s and 1970s. The stand-up comedian and actress Margaret Cho had a leading role in her own TV comedy series *All American Girl* in the 1990s, reputedly the first Asian American themed sitcom. Her character was a Korean American (as Cho is), who struggled with her family and cultural issues in San Francisco. Despite being a breakthrough in prime-time television, the show was cancelled in two seasons due to low ratings. Lucy Liu had a big part in the *Ally McBeal* TV show from 1998 to 2002 before going on to lead roles in feature films. Daniel Dae Kim and Sendhil Ramamurthy have achieved some recognition as sex symbols from their respective roles on *Lost* and *Heroes*; B. D. Wong currently stars in *Law & Order: Special Victims Unit* after being featured in the critically acclaimed series *Oz*. Benda Song is a Thai-Hmong American actress known to younger audiences for starring in several Disney Channel productions including *The Suite Life Of Zack and Cody*, *Wendy Wu: Homecoming Warrior 1* and 2, *Stuck in the Suburbs* and most recently *The Suite Life on Deck*. Leyna Nguyen, a news anchor, is also heavily portrayed in news anchor roles in major television shows and movies. Some examples include *Boston Legal*, *Without a Trace*, *Las Vegas*, *Two and a Half Men* and *Austin Powers in Goldmember*. Tila Tequila is the star of the MTV show *A Shot at Love with Tila Tequila*. Kal Penn is one of the lead actors in the medical drama *House*. Recently the hit TV series *Survivor* created teams along racial lines during *Survivor: Cook Islands*. People of East and South East Asian ancestry composed the Asian tribe. Asian American Yul Kwon won the season.

Journalism

As early as 1971, CBS national correspondent Connie Chung became one of the first Asian American national correspondents for a major TV news network. Later she co-anchored the *CBS Evening News* from 1993 to 1995. Ken Kashiwahara began reporting nationally for ABC in 1974. Ann Curry joined NBC News as a reporter in 1990, later becoming prominently associated with *The Today Show* in 1997. Carol Lin is perhaps best known for being the first to break the news of 9/11 on CNN. Dr. Sanjay Gupta, the Indian American neurosurgeon, is CNN's chief health correspondent. Lisa Ling, a former co-host on *The View*, now provides special reports for CNN and *The Oprah Winfrey Show*, as well as hosting National Geographic Channel's *Explorer*. Fareed Zakaria, a naturalized Indian-born immigrant, is a prominent journalist and author specializing in international affairs. He is the editor of *Newsweek International*, and the host of the Fareed Zakaria GPS foreign affairs program on CNN. Recently, Juju Chang, Julie Chen, James Hatori, Veronica De La Cruz, Betty Nguyen, and John Yang have become familiar faces on television news.

Aside from the quality of their contributions in these many fields, it is difficult to draw conclusions about the social mobility of Asian Americans from these individual examples, except for noting that they have helped to increase the visibility of their minority and serve as role models. After all, many of these successful individuals are from professional, sometimes wealthy backgrounds in their country of origin or within the US.

Religious Trends

While Buddhism and Hinduism, and the practice of yoga, meditation, Ayurveda and vegetarianism have entered American culture, Christianity has been adopted by more East Asians. Most Filipinos and many South Koreans are already Christian when they immigrate. Beats on the West Coast were among those attracted to Buddhism in the 1950s. American Buddhist groups established then and in the 1970s have built temples, ordained numerous American Buddhist monks, and taught generations of new practitioners. Buddhist concepts and practices such as mindfulness have penetrated mainstream culture. While much West Coast practice was first influenced by Japanese Zen Buddhism, more recent generations throughout the country have been influenced also by Vietnamese and Tibetan monks.

Stereotyping

Most non-Asian Americans do not differentiate between Asian Americans and Chinese Americans. A 2002 survey indicated that 24% of the respondents disapproved of intermarriage with an Asian American; 23% would be uncomfortable supporting an Asian American presidential candidate, compared to 15% for an African American, 14% for a woman and 11% for a Jew; 17% would be upset if a substantial number of Asian Americans moved into their neighborhood; 68% had a somewhat negative or very negative attitude toward Chinese Americans in general. The study did find several positive perceptions of Chinese Americans: strong family values (91%); honesty as business people (77%); and high value on education (67%). Most of the people who responded negatively to Asian Americans lived in the South and parts of the Midwest. There is a widespread perception that Asian Americans are not "American" but are instead "perpetual foreigners." Asian Americans often report being asked the question, "Where are you really from?" by other Americans, regardless of how long they or their ancestors have lived in the US.

Asian Americans are sometimes seen as an élite characterized by high intelligence and education, success and wealth. Some people refer to them as a *model minority*. They assign them this status because of certain well-regarded characteristics typical of Asian American culture: a high work ethic, respect for elders, a high degree of professional and academic success, and a high valuation of family, education and religion. Statistics such as high household incomes and low incarceration rates, low rates of many diseases and higher than average life expectancy are also regarded as positive aspects. But it can also be considered a narrow and one-dimensional portrayal, which neglects other qualities such as vocal leadership, risk taking, the ability to learn from mistakes, and the desire for creative expression. Furthermore, Asian Americans who do not fit into the model minority mold can face challenges when people's expectations do not match reality. Traits omitted from the model minority stereotype such as risk taking, confidence, and empowerment can be seen as character flaws for Asian Americans despite those very same traits being positive for the majority. For this reason, some believe Asian Americans encounter a "bamboo ceiling."

Asians often achieve higher test scores and grades compared to other Americans. But stereotyping Asian American children as over-achievers can be emotionally damaging if schools or peers expect them all to perform higher than average. Studies have shown that Asian Americans suffer from higher rates of stress, depression, mental illnesses, and suicide attempts in comparison to other races. Recently, the discriminatory effects of being perceived as a minority have led some Asian Americans to assert a diasporic, transnational identity, not based solely on Asian cultural traditions, or acculturation to America, or even biculturalism.

Political attitudes

Asian Americans hold diverse political views, which tend to vary more by ethnicity than any other factor. The Democrats tend to be supported by Chinese Americans, Indian Americans, Cambodian Americans, and Hmong Americans. Pakistani Americans and Filipino Americans have traditionally voted Republican but now tend to vote for the Democrats. Vietnamese Americans tend to vote overwhelmingly Republican owing to the Republican Party's strong anti-communist stance and the arrival of Vietnamese immigrants during the Reagan administration, although newer immigrants and younger Vietnamese Americans tend to vote Democrat. Japanese Americans and Korean Americans are nearly evenly split between the two parties with Japanese Americans leaning slightly Democrat and Korean Americans leaning slightly Republican. Younger Asian Americans of all ethnicities tend to vote for the Democratic Party.

The political views of Asian Americans have slowly changed over the last generation. On first arriving in the US, Asian immigrants tend to retain inherited attitudes toward the parties based on perceptions of how favorable that party has been to their ethnic group. In the 1992 presidential election, Republican George H. W. Bush received 55% of the Asian American vote compared to 31% for Democrat Bill Clinton. The Asian American vote has slowly shifted since then with Democrats John Kerry winning 56% of the Asian American vote in the 2004 Presidential election and Barack Obama 62% in 2008. The shift may be attributable to demographic changes. In the early 1990s the vast majority of Asian Americans were anti-communist refugees, such as Vietnamese Americans, Chinese Americans, and conservative Filipino Americans. Since then, more liberal groups such as well-educated Chinese and Indian immigrants and a large proportion of younger Asian Americans, many of whom have completed college degrees in the best universities, have greatly changed the political landscape. There is evidence, for example, that Filipino Americans are becoming more liberal, partly due to the group's increasingly younger average age. Asian Americans as a whole now tend to vote for the Democrats, but this trend has been fairly recent.

Individual Asian American groups

Chinese

Trading ships brought the Chinese to California as early as the 16th century. The fledgling US joined the China trade with the voyage of the *Empress of China* in 1784, and as trade between the two countries expanded, Chinese immigrants trickled into the US. By 1851, 25,000 Chinese had left their homes for California, the land of *gum saan*, or "gold mountain." Between 1871 and 1880, 123,201 Chinese are recorded as arriving, and 61,711 arrived between 1881 and 1890. Most of these immigrants were part of a larger exodus of people who left Guangdong Province in search of better economic opportunities and political freedom.

Some of the first Chinese gold prospectors to arrive in California staked claims along the American River north of Sacramento. At first, when surface gold was plentiful, the Chinese were well tolerated and well received. As gold became harder to find and competition increased, however, animosity to the Chinese and other foreigners mounted. They were often forced to work older claims or to assist other miners. Legislation also created obstacles for Chinese immigrants. Federal law reserved the right of naturalization for white immigrants, making it impossible for Chinese immigrants to own land or file mining claims. At the same time, California passed a law taxing only Chinese miners. Thus the Chinese were effectively excluded from the mines.

Despite the hostile reception that many Chinese immigrants received from Americans, they established thriving communities in urban centers throughout the country, the largest and most notable being San Francisco's Chinatown. The restaurants and theaters, and the novelty of Chinatown, eventually attracted tourism that boosted the city's economy. Aside from the interest in Chinatown, however, anti-Chinese sentiment overshadowed the contributions of Chinese immigrants. Public opinion was so hostile that few were willing to recognize the successes of Chinese businessmen, the contributions of laborers in fishing and agriculture, or the development of a silk industry in California.

Perhaps the most famous contribution of Chinese immigrants was the construction of the first transcontinental railroad in the 1860s. Chinese immigrants comprised 90% of the 10,000 laborers who laid tracks eastward from Sacramento across the Sierra Nevada and Rocky Mountains to connect with the crews laying tracks across the Great Plains at Promontory, Utah on May 10, 1869. The Chinese laborers were assigned the most menial and dangerous jobs, which paid less, although railroad officials appreciated their reliability and cleanliness and railroad entrepreneurs even began a campaign to recruit workers in China.

At the heart of the Chinese community in San Francisco was an organization called the *Six Companies*. Also known as the *Chinese Consolidated Benevolent Association*, the Six Companies provided a variety of services, organizing a private patrol force for Chinatown, assisting with translations, securing necessary permits, organizing a Chinese Boy Scout Troop, and establishing health and hygiene programs. The Six Companies also represented the entire Chinese community throughout the US, dealing with local and national governments on issues such as immigration and persecution.

Although most Chinese immigrants came to the US of their own free will, the belief that there was a slave trade took hold even in the US government, and the Senate discussed a bill "To Prohibit Contracts for Servile Labor" in July 1870. The Committee of the Chinese Merchants of San Francisco responded to assertions that there was a "coolie" slave trade with the assurance that "the Chinese in this country are not slaves or serfs of any description but are working for themselves."

Anti-Chinese sentiment in California grew so quickly that it began appearing in poltical campaigns as early as 1852. By the 1867 race for governor, the "Chinese Question" had become such a heated issue that the Union Party's candidate, George Gorham, was the only one opposed to the anti-Chinese movement, and in consequence lost many votes and impaired his future political prospects. Two years later, anti-Chinese sentiment only increased when the completion of the transcontinental railroad released 9,000 Chinese laborers. American workers, like the miners before them, resented the Chinese immigrants for the competition they presented at a time of recession. The Supreme Order of Caucasians, founded in 1876 to expel the Chinese from California, attracted 5,000 members. Tensions came to a head on July 23, 1877, when a labor rally held in a sand lot in San Francisco to support railroad strikers in the eastern US turned to violence (the Sand Lot Riots). A group of young vagrants, aged 15 to 20, attacked a Chinese man near the rally, igniting three days of riots. As a result, a Committee of Public Safety was established which worked to quash anti-Chinese riots. These were blamed on the demagoguery of Dennis Kearney and his Workingman's Party. Kearney was an Irish immigrant who considered the Chinese to be pawns in the hands of capitalists bent on destroying the workers' unions. Supported by governor Bigler, he championed the expulsion of the Chinese, rallying workers under the banner "The Chinese Must Go." The prevalence of hate crimes against the Chinese, and the passage of discriminatory legislation, led the Six Companies to defend the Chinese community through the courts. Carroll Cook, counsel for them in San Francisco, was involved in a number of cases involving the treatment of Chinese residents in California, Texas, and the Arizona Territory in the early 1900s.

Much of the anti-Chinese agitation of the 19th century took the form of opposition to immigration. The US government adopted its first official stance on the issue in 1868 when, pressured by railroad companies wanting cheap labor, it negotiated a policy of open immigration with China in the Burlingame Treaty. After the Sand Lot Riots, however, calls for Chinese exclusion increased and in 1879 Congress passed a bill abrogating the section of the Burlingame Treaty that permitted unrestricted Chinese immigration. President Hayes vetoed the bill but had the treaty renegotiated to the same effect. In 1882, with President Chester Arthur in office, Congress finally passed the Chinese Exclusion Act, prohibiting the immigration of Chinese laborers and miners for ten years and excluding them from citizenship. The Chinese Exclusion Act was the first significant restriction on immigration in US history. The effect was to deny entry to upwards of 30% of would-be immigrants. The Act was renewed in 1892 for 10 years by the Geary Act and again in 1902 without limit. It stayed in effect until repealed in 1943, when resident Chinese were permitted to be naturalized and become citizens. The California law that Chinese Americans were not able to marry whites was not repealed until 1948. (In 1907, Japanese immigration had been substantially reduced through a Gentlemen's Agreement between Japan and the US.) It is noteworthy that the Chinese Exclusion Act also prohibited the immigration of "convicts, lunatics, idiots" and those individuals who might need to be supported by government assistance. The latter provision was used to some extent during periods of high unemployment, though immigration fell anyway because of the lack of jobs. The Act was strongly supported by the Knights of Labor, a labor union, which argued that Chinese workers were being used to keep wages low and conditions poor. Among labor and leftist organizations, the Industrial Workers of the World were the sole exception in opposing the Act, which they did from their inception in 1905. The fact that immigration of other races was permitted at this time suggests that the Act was motivated by racism.

Debate over the Exclusion Act did not end with its passage in 1882. The following years saw the right of the US to exclude Chinese immigrants challenged in the courts. In 1889, however, the Supreme Court upheld the Act in *Chae Chan Ping v. The United States* on the ground that Congress's right to restrict immigration was a fundamental aspect of national sovereignty. In 1888, Congress also passed the Scott Act prohibiting the return of Chinese laborers who had temporarily left the US. Even Chinese fishermen who had ventured out of coastal waters were expelled.

A convention which met in San Francisco in 1901 to discuss the re-enactment of the Chinese Exclusion Act addressed the President and Congress in a pamphlet *For the re-enactment of the Chinese Exclusion Law*. After providing a brief history of Chinese exclusion legislation, the pamphlet argued in favor of re-enactment, reiterating the dangers of a supposed Chinese slave trade and of labor competition. The racism pervading the pamphlet was the keynote for early 20th-century immigration policy, which sought to exclude not only the Chinese, but the Japanese, Koreans, and Indians as well. A few voices were raised against exclusion. The 1902 pamphlet *Truth versus Fiction: Justice versus Prejudice* opposed re-enactment of the Chinese Exclusion Law. Yet the law was not only re-enacted, but was strengthened in 1924, when all Chinese immigration was effectively stopped, forcing the Chinese American population to live separate, self-sufficient lives excluded from society and prevented from assimilating. The immigrants were mostly, but not all, unaccompanied men, and after the Scott Act had little chance of reuniting with their wives or marrying in the US. Thus the Chinese community did not grow. The attorney for the Chinese Chamber of Commerce, Oliver Stidger, discussed the injustices of the 1924 Act in *Immigration Law in Highlights on Exclusion and Expulsion*. Large-scale Chinese immigration did not begin again until after the 1965 Immigration Act.

Filipinos

The earliest Filipino community in the US consisted of sailors from Mexico who settled in Louisiana from the 1830s. Filipinos became increasingly numerous in the US after having become colonial subjects in 1898 following the Spanish-American War. Aside from California and Hawaii, Filipinos spread to other parts of the US in search of jobs. Seasonal farm workers found their way to Arizona, Utah, Colorado, Montana, and North Dakota. Some Filipinos reached as far as New York. In summer, thousands of Filipinos journeyed to Alaska to work in the fishing and fish canning industries. In Chicago the earliest Filipino community consisted of *pensionados*, scholars sent by the Philippines colonial government to study in the US from 1903. While many completed their studies and went back to the Philippines, there were others who remained, finding employment in the post office and the Pullman Company. Many intermarried with Americans and people from other ethnic groups.

Because they blamed Filipinos for taking their jobs, Caucasian Americans precipitated racial violence against them. The first race riot occurred in Exeter, California, on the night of October 24, 1929 after the Americans were displaced by Filipinos harvesting Kadota figs and Emperor grapes. A mob of 300 men stormed a Filipino camp, stoned and clubbed about 50 Filipinos, and burned the barn. About 200 Filipinos were driven out of the district. The most explosive riots occurred in January 1930 in Watsonville near Monterey, where Filipinos had been constantly harassed. After a Filipino club leased a dance hall in Palm Beach, about 200 Americans, angered by the thought of Filipinos dancing with white women, hunted Filipinos on the streets, and on the following day, the dance hall was raided. Two days later, Filipinos were beaten and one was killed by a mob of 500 Americans, who also destroyed the Filipino quarters. On January 28, a Filipino clubhouse in Stockton was dynamited. In August, a bundle of dynamite was thrown into the camp of 100 sleeping Filipinos near Reedley in protest over the presence of 500 Filipinos in the region who had taken over the jobs of the Americans. The Filipinos were blamed for the decline in the wages of fig, lettuce, and asparagus harvesters. For several years, groups in California lobbied to bar Filipinos from the US. In 1935, Congress passed the Filipino Repatriation Act, offering free passages home, but most of the Filipinos preferred to remain. In 1940, after only 2,190 Filipinos had returned home, the Act was declared unconstitutional.

Indians

In 1990, there were slightly fewer South Asians in the US than Japanese Americans. But by 2000,

Indian Americans had nearly doubled in population to become the third largest group of Asian Americans, forming 16.4% of the Asian American population. The US is host to the second largest Indian diaspora on the planet, 1.2 million.

Indians are among the largest ethnic groups immigrating to the US. They have come in several waves since they first arrived as indentured servants brought by the East India Company in the 1600s and others came as maritime workers around 1800. The first wave, mostly Sikh farmers and laborers from the Punjab, started arriving at Angel Island via Hong Kong in the years before World War I. They found employment on farms and in lumber mills in California, Oregon and Washington. In 1917 the Immigration Act (the Barred Zone Act) barred Asians, including Indians, from immigrating to the US, and in 1923 the Supreme Court decided that no person of Indian origin could become a citizen. In 1943 Republican Clara Booth Luce and Democrat Emanuel Celler, supported by prominent Americans including Pearl Buck and Albert Einstein, introduced a bill to open immigration and naturalization to Indians. President Franklin Roosevelt also endorsed the bill, calling for an end to the "statutory discrimination against the Indians." The Luce-Celler Act became law in 1946 and a second wave of immigration, mostly students and professionals, followed in the 1950s. The elimination of quotas in 1965 drew successively larger waves of immigrants in the late 1970s and early 1980s. With the technology boom of the 1990s, a large influx of Indians arrived between 1995 and 2000. Between 1990 and 2000, the Indian population in the US grew 130% — many times the national average. According to the American Community Survey of the Census Bureau, the Asian Indian population grew from almost 1,679,000 in 2000 to 2,570,000 in 2007: a growth rate of 53%, the highest for any Asian American community, and among the fastest among ethnic groups.

A number of Indian Americans came to the US via Indian communities in other countries such as Fiji, the nations of East Africa, the UK, the West Indies, South Africa, Canada, Guyana, Mauritius and nations of Southeast Asia such as Malaysia and Singapore. A large group of Indian Americans are presently second or third generation. Recently, however, there has been a drop in the immigration of Indians from India to the US. This is generally attributed to the improving economy of India. In contrast with East Asian Americans, who tend to be concentrated near the Pacific coast, Indian Americans are more evenly distributed throughout the US. The states with the largest Indian American populations are California, New York, New Jersey, Texas and Illinois. There are also large Indian American populations in Pennsylvania, Florida, Michigan, Maryland, Virginia, Georgia, and Ohio.

Education and employment

Indians have the highest educational qualifications of all ethnic groups. According to the 2000 Census, almost 67% have a bachelor's or higher degree (compared to 28% nationally and 44% for all Asian American groups). Almost 40% of Indians have a master's, doctorate or other professional degree, five times the national average, according to The Indian American Centre for Political Awareness. Even so, a quarter of Indian immigrants are *limited English proficient*, speaking Hindi at home.

High levels of education have enabled Indian Americans to become a productive segment of the American population, with 57.7% of them employed in managerial and professional specialties. According to the American Association of Physicians of Indian Origin, there are also close to 35,000 Indian American doctors. In 2002, there were over 223,000 Asian Indian-owned firms, employing more than 610,000 workers, and generating more than $88 billion in revenue. Indian Americans own 50% of all economy lodges and 35% of all hotels, which have a combined market value of almost $40 billion, according to *Little India* magazine. A University of California, Berkeley, study, the *Silicon India Leadership Survey*, reported that one-third of the engineers in Silicon Valley are of Indian descent, while 7% of the hi-tech firms are led by Indian CEOs. According to the 2000 Census, Indian American men had the highest year-round, full-time median earnings ($51,094), while Indian American women had a medium income of $35,173.

Culture

There are a number of signs of the growing Indian presence in American culture. Indian American cuisine has become popular, with Indian restaurants available nationwide. There are also many Indian markets and convenience stores. Several cable and satellite providers offer Indian content and whole channels for subscription. Hindi radio stations are available in New York, New Jersey, Connecticut, Chicago and Texas. Many metropolitan areas with high Indian American populations now have movie theatres which specialize in Bollywood movies, sometimes with English subtitles. Although the Indian American media are mostly in Indian languages, there is some English content and films such as *The Sixth Sense* have become hits.

Religions

The first center of an Indian religion in the US was a Sikh temple in Stockton, California opened in 1912. Today there are thousands of Hindu, Sikh and Jain temples as well as Indian churches in all 50 states. As of 2000, the American Hindu population was around a million, the majority of them Indian Americans. There is growing interest in Hindu philosophy and spirituality. More than 18 million Americans are now practicing some form of Yoga. A number of Indians worship in mainstream churches. A large percentage of American Muslims are of Indian origin. They generally congregate with other American Muslims, including those from Pakistan. There is also a large Parsi (Zoroastrian) community. Indian Jews are perhaps the smallest organized religious group among Indian Americans, consisting of approximately 350 members headquartered in New York. (See also Chapter 8.)

Assimilation

The term "Indian American" is an umbrella label covering a variety of views, values, lifestyles and appearances. Although Indian Americans retain a strong ethnic identity, they assimilate into American culture while at the same time keeping the culture of their ancestors. They may assimilate more easily than many other immigrant groups because English is widely spoken in India among the professional classes, they have more educational credentials, and they come from a democratic society. Additionally, Indian culture lays great stress on achievement.

Discrimination

Discrimination is not widespread but is not unknown. Studies have correlated racial discrimination against Indian Americans in the workplace with Indophobia due to the rise in outsourcing. Indian Americans are sometimes blamed for US companies offshoring white collar jobs labor to India. Numerous cases of religious stereotyping of American Hindus (mainly of Indian origin) have also been documented. Muslims among Indian Americans face the same religious prejudices as Muslims in general. Since 9/11, there have been scattered incidents of Indian Americans becoming mistaken targets for hate crimes; a Sikh was murdered at a Phoenix gas station by a white supremacist. In Massachusetts, a pizza deliverer was mugged and beaten for "being Muslim" though the victim pleaded with the assailants that he was in fact Hindu. On August 11, 2006, Senator George Allen singled out in a crowd a political staffer of his opponent, an American-born man of Indian ancestry, by calling him *macaca* and saying "welcome to America." A video of the insult was uploaded to YouTube, and the resulting backlash is believed to have been a factor that led to Allen losing his re-election bid. On April 5, 2006, the Hindu Mandir (temple) of Minnesota was vandalized.

Politics

Only one Indian American has so far been elected to Congress. This was Dalip Singh Saund, who was elected to the House of Representatives from California. He was re-elected to a 2nd and 3rd term, winning over 60% of the votes. In 2007, Republican Congressman Bobby Jindal became the first governor of Indian descent when he was elected governor of Louisiana. Several groups, such as the India PAC (Political Action Committee), have tried to create a unified or dominant voice for the Indian American community in political affairs. There are also industry-wide Indian American groupings including the Asian American Hotel Owners Association and the Association of American Physicians of Indian Origin. Despite being highly religious and having the highest average household income among all ancestry groups, two traits that usually favor conservatism, Indian Americans tend to be more liberal and vote overwhelmingly for the Democrats. Yet Indian American voters have shown support for both the Democratic and Republican parties and have had political candidates of both parties.

Japanese

Before World War II, Japanese immigrants had founded vibrant communities, mostly on the West Coast. During the war, the US declared Japanese Americans a risk to national security and in 1942 interned them. This was a result of war hysteria, racial discrimination, and economic competition. Between 112,000 to 120,000 Japanese and Japanese Americans were relocated from the West Coast to War Relocation Centers in remote parts of the interior. Sixty-two percent of those forced to relocate were US citizens. Starting in 1990, the government paid some reparations to the surviving internees in recognition of the harm internment had caused them and their families. Despite the internment, many Japanese American men served in World War II in the American forces. The 442nd Regimental Combat Team/100th Infantry Battalion, composed of Japanese Americans, is indeed the most highly decorated unit in US military history. They fought valiantly in the European theater even while many of their families remained in detention camps. The 100th was one of the first units to liberate the Nazi concentration camp at Dachau.

Today, given relatively low rates of birth and immigration, Japanese Americans are only the sixth-largest Asian American group, although they have a high profile. There were nearly 600,000 of them in 1970. Then they were the largest of Asian American sub-groups, but the greatest period of immigration was past. In 2000, there were between 800,000 and 1.2 million Japanese Americans (depending on whether multi-ethnics are included). Japanese Americans have the highest rates of native-birth, citizenship, and assimilation into American values and customs. The contrasts between Japanese Americans and South Asian Americans demonstrate the dramatic changes in immigration since the reforms of the mid-20th century.

The legacy of immigration

The steady stream of people coming to the US has had a profound effect on the American character. It takes courage and flexibility to leave one's homeland and come to a new country. The American people have been noted for their willingness to take risks and try new ventures, as well as for their independence and optimism. If Americans whose families have been in the US longer tend to take their material comfort and political freedoms for granted, immigrants are on hand to remind them how important those are. The presence of immigrants with their different values, traditions and languages is beginning to create a more pluralistic, multicultural society where diversity is seen as a source of enrichment and strength. At the same time, second- and third-generation Americans are beginning to change their lifestyles so that they become more like the mainstream.

Immigrants enrich American communities by bringing aspects of their native cultures with them. Some Americans now celebrate both Christmas and Kwanzaa, a festival drawn from African rituals. Hispanic Americans celebrate their traditions with street fairs and other festivities on Cinco de Mayo (May 5). Ethnic restaurants and neighborhoods abound in many US cities. President John F. Kennedy, himself the grandson of Irish immigrants, summed up this blend of the old and the new when he called the US "a society of immigrants, each of whom had begun life anew, on an equal footing." "This is the secret of America," he exclaimed, "a nation of people with the fresh memory of old traditions who dare to explore new frontiers. …" (USIA, *Portrait of the USA*)

In the past, American society was described as a "melting pot", an image that suggested that newcomers should discard their old customs and adopt New World ways i.e., be melded together into a new American identity. Typically, for example, the children of immigrants learned English but not their parents' first language. Recently, however, Americans have placed greater value on diversity, ethnic groups have renewed and celebrated their heritage, and the children of immigrants often grow up bilingual. Thus, American society nowadays is increasingly being described as a "salad bowl."

The end of white America?

The election of Barack Obama exhibits the gradual erosion of "whiteness" as the test of what it means to be genuinely American. As pointed out by Hua Hsu of Harvard in the *Atlantic* ("The End of White America? State of the Union", Jan/Feb 2009), *the* demographically and culturally predictable end of white America poses a number of questions: what will happen when white people actually become a minority? what will the new mainstream look like and how will white Americans fit into it? what will it mean to be white when whiteness is no longer the norm? and will a post-white America be less racially divided or more? What ideas or values might the new mainstream rally to? Will anyone mourn the end of white America? Will anyone try to preserve it?

Whether conceived as the dawning of a post-racial age or just the end of white America, the US is approaching a demographic tipping point. According to an August 2008 report by the U.S. Census Bureau, four groups currently categorized as racial minorities - blacks and Hispanics, East Asians and South Asians - will account for a majority of the population by the year 2042. Among Americans under the age of 18, the shift is projected to take place in 2023, which means that every child born in the US from 2005 on will belong to the first post-white generation.

Meanwhile, steadily rising rates of interracial marriage point toward what Michael Lind has described as the "beiging" of America. Possibly "beige Americans" will self-identify as "white" in sufficient numbers to delay the tipping point, but even if they do, the odds are that the label "white" will be adopted out of convenience and even indifference, rather than aspiration or necessity. For an earlier generation of minorities and immigrants, whether Italians or Poles or Hungarians, to be recognized as a "white American" was to enter the mainstream of American life. Today, whiteness is no longer a precondition for entry into the highest levels of public office: a half-Kenyan, half-Kansan politician can self-identify as black and be elected President. Instead of assimilation toward a common center, the culture is being remade in the image of white America's multiethnic, multicolored heirs.

In 1998, President Clinton, in a now-famous address to students at Portland State University, remarked:

> Today, largely because of immigration, there is no majority race in Hawaii or Houston or New York City. Within five years, there will be no majority race in our largest state, California. In a little more than 50 years, there will be no majority race in the United States. No other nation in history has gone through demographic change of this magnitude in so short a time .... [These immigrants] are energizing our culture and broadening our vision of the world. They are renewing our most basic values and reminding us all of what it truly means to be American.

The new cultural mainstream prizes diversity above all else. Their ultimate goal is to transcend race, rather than subvert white culture or assimilate to it; they appropriate elements of the culture they seek to join. The American panorama now hosts a culture of collisions where newly confident minorities assert their arrival and provoke various responses from the whites. For example, hip-hop mogul Sean Combs, one of the most famous African Americans, gives opulent "white parties" (attendees are required to wear white) and is hailed as a modern-day Gatsby. Successful network television shows like *Lost*, *Heroes*, and *Grey's Anatomy* feature widely diverse casts, and an entire genre of half-hour comedy, from *The Colbert Report* to *The Office*, seems dedicated to having fun with the persona of the clueless white male. The youth market is following the same pattern. Pop culture today has become ethnically ambiguous, rallying around an ethic of multicultural inclusion that seems to value every identity except whiteness. The multicultural, multiplatform Cheetah Girls, teenyboppers who do not conform to the white, middle-class mould, have sold over two million copies of several albums and have starred in their third movie. Dora the Explorer, the precocious bilingual 7-year-old Latina adventurer, is arguably the most successful animated character on children's television today.

Meanwhile whites, especially the working class, are fearful and resentful. Some white people feel they are under siege and losing control. Since the future will apparently belong to people who can successfully navigate a post-racial, multicultural landscape, many white Americans are eager to divest themselves of their whiteness entirely. In 1994, young graffiti artist and activist William Upski Wimsatt published *Bomb the Suburbs*. This argued that "wiggers" (a pejorative term coined in the early 1990s to describe white kids who steep themselves in black culture) can go a long way toward repairing the sickness of race in America because wiggers are immersed in two cultures.

In an attempt to come to terms with whiteness in its past and present forms, academics like Matthew Frye Jacobson, David Roediger and Noel Ignatiev have created a discipline known as *whiteness studies*, They pose such questions as why in America a white woman can have black children but a black woman cannot have white children. In the early 1990s, Ignatiev, author of

How the Irish Became White, set out to "abolish" the idea of the white race by starting the New Abolitionist Movement and founding a journal titled *Race Traitor*, claiming there is nothing positive about white identity.

For some white students, their acceptance of new ideals of diversity has provoked a racial identity crisis which causes them to see themselves as culturally disadvantaged, marginalized without a culture because they are white. This is more important to them than the material advantages that come with being born white. The contrary response is to flee *into* whiteness, as depicted in books like *A Privileged Life: Celebrating WASP Style* by Susanna Salk, or to live in self-contained communities pursuing the authenticity of an imagined past. The white cultural identity crisis has even been the butt of humor, as in reality TV's *The (White) Rapper Show*, and the Smirnoff music video "Tea Partay," an ironic lampooning of WASP culture.

Lower middle class whites have responded by asserting a folksy authenticity that rejects the global, the urban, and what is seen as effete in favor of nostalgia for "the way things used to be." This is reflected in the rise of country music (the highest-selling artist of the '90s was Garth Brooks) of stock car auto racing (NASCAR), the blue collar comedy of Larry the Cable Guy and Jeff Foxworthy, the white rapping of Kid Rock, and the Christian dispensationalism of the *Left Behind* novels. The result is a self-conscious solidarity and feeling of minority empowerment. NASCAR has emerged as professional sports' fastest-growing institution, with ratings second only to the NFL's.

To give voice to their cultural, social and economic grievances, white solidarity has adopted its own identity politics, modeled on civil rights activism, with its own folk heroes, conspiracy theories and lists of injustices. The targets and scapegoats vary from multiculturalism and affirmative action to a loss of moral values, from immigration to an economy that no longer seems to guarantee the American worker a fair chance. The political programs of white solidarity and its representatives range in ideology from Jim Webb to Ron Paul to Mike Huckabee to Sarah Palin. But the core grievance, in each case, is cultural and socioeconomic issues: the sense that the system that used to guarantee the white working class some stability has gone out of balance. The result is a racial pride that dares not speak its name, and that defines itself through cultural cues instead—a suspicion of intellectual elites and city dwellers, a preference for folksiness and plainness of speech (whether real or feigned), and the association of a working-class white minority with "the real America." (In the Scots-Irish belt that runs from Arkansas up through West Virginia, the most common ethnic label offered to census takers is "American.")

The vision of the aggrieved white man lost in a world that no longer values him was given its most vivid expression in the 1993 film *Falling Down*. Michael Douglas plays Bill Foster, a downsized defense worker with a buzz cut and a pocket protector who rampages through a Los Angeles overrun by greedy Korean shop-owners and Hispanic gangsters, railing against the eclipse of the America he used to know. (The film came out just eight years before California became the nation's first majority-minority state i.e., where the non-white minorities together form the majority.) *Falling Down* ends with a soulful police officer apprehending Foster on the Santa Monica Pier, at which point the middle-class vigilante asks, almost innocently: "I'm the bad guy?"

The fact that whites will soon no longer be a majority, however, does not mean that some other race, or combination of races, is set to dominate America. The vision of the racial hierarchy being inverted, shown by John Travolta in *White Man's Burden* (1995) does not reflect reality. There will be dislocations and resentments along the way, but the demographic shifts of the next 40 years are likely to reduce the power of racial hierarchies over everyone's lives, producing a culture that is more likely than any before to treat its inhabitants as individuals, rather than members of a caste or identity group. At the moment, this can be called *the triumph of multiculturalism*, or *post-racialism*. But just as *whiteness* has no inherent meaning—it is a vessel filled with the hopes and anxieties of white people—these terms may prove equally empty in the long run. Does being post-racial mean being past race completely, or merely that race is no longer essential to how Americans identify themselves?

Dalton Conley, the New York University sociologist, presents a much more nuanced picture of the changing ethnic and racial landscape than any film, which is, after all, entertainment. He has written of the effect of social networking media like Facebook and MySpace which are creating what he calls a "network nation," made up of "crosscutting social groups" and new, flexible identities that only vaguely overlap with racial identities. What Conley describes is not merely the displacement of whiteness from America's cultural center; but a social structure that treats race as just one of a seemingly infinite number of possible self-identifications. Perhaps this is where the future of identity after whiteness lies.

Now a black president governs a country whose social networks increasingly cut across every conceivable line of identification, color is arguably becoming less important. Yet while Americans aspire to be post-racial, culture lags behind social reality, and they still live within the structures of privilege, injustice, and racial categorization inherited from an older order. Americans may talk about defining themselves by lifestyle rather than skin color, but their lifestyle choices are still racially coded. They know, more or less, that race is a fiction that often does more harm than good, and yet it is something they cling to as a social and legal fact, a vague sense of belonging and place they make solid through culture and speech, although this is already an outdated way of looking at things. Will the end of white America be the end of anything? Or is it a bridge which some Americans are already crossing? Or will the problem of the 21st century be, as W. E. B. DuBois famously predicted of the 20th, the problem of the color line?

DEMOGRAPHY

During the 20th century, the US population more than tripled. This phenomenon is in sharp contrast to other industrialized countries, such Japan, Korea and the countries of the European Union. Because of immigration, the US, at just under one percent per year, has almost the highest rate of population growth. Growth is fastest among the minorities, who were 102.5 million in 2006. The immigration rate for 2006 is estimated at 3.05 per thousand. The population's distribution by major race and ethnicity in 2006 was: White alone 74% (including 8% White Hispanic and Latinos); Hispanics or Latinos of any race 14.8%; black or African American 13.4%; Asian alone 4.4%. Four-fifths of the population live in suburbs and cities, compared with one-half worldwide. The US has 8 of the 60 "global cities" (cities important to the world economy) and three alpha global cities: New York (population 8.2 million), Los Angeles (3.8 million) and Chicago (2.8 million). The US has 51 metropolitan areas with a population of over one million people each. In 2007, people under 20 years of age made up over a quarter of the population (27.6%), and people age 65 and over made up one-eighth (12.6%). (As it happens, this is the same as the percentage of immigrants in the population.) The national median age was 36.7 years.

Birth, infant mortality and death rates

In 2006, births and fertility rates increased for most states, age groups, and racial and ethnic groups. A total of 4.2 million births were registered, 3 percent more than in 2005, and the largest number of births in more than four decades. Of those, 2.3 million (54.15%) were to non-Hispanic (NH) whites, 617,000 (14.47%) to NH Blacks, 47,000 (1.11%) to American Indians, 239,000 (5.62%) to Asians and 1 million (24.36%) to Hispanics. The crude birth rate per thousand was 14.2: 11.6 for NH whites; 16.5 for NH blacks; 14.8 for American Indians; 16.5 for Asians; and 23.4 for Hispanics. The general fertility rate per thousand was 68.5 and stood at 2.1 per woman, which is about the replacement rate. The average family size was 2.6. Birth rates are increasing most for teenagers and for women aged 20–24 and 40–44 years. Teenage childbearing increased in 2006, interrupting a 14-year decline. The age of the woman at first giving birth was down to 25.0 years. All measures of unmarried childbearing reached record levels. Women were less likely to receive timely prenatal care. The cesarean delivery rate climbed to 31.1%, another all-time high.

The infant mortality rate in 2006 was 6.7 per 1,000 (28,000 deaths), no improvement since 2000, ranking the US 29th among nations including Cuba. In 2005, African American infants suffered a death rate of 13.63 per 1,000 births, by far the highest international average, higher than Russia's 11.5. US infant mortality rates stagnated for the first time in five decades despite significant advances in medical technology. A major factor was the increase in the number of very preterm births. Yet those who need perinatal care the most are likely least able to afford it, according to analysts. Several countries in Scandinavia (Sweden, Norway, Finland) and East Asia (Japan, Hong Kong, Singapore) have an infant mortality rate below 3.5, almost half the US rate.

The death rate in 2005 was 825.9 per 100,000. Life expectancy was 77.8 years, 30th in the world, behind Japan, Canada, Italy, Spain, the UK and Germany. The leading causes of death were heart disease, cancer and stroke. Half of all deaths among Americans younger than 65 are caused by preventable or treatable conditions such as stroke, diabetes, high blood pressure, colon cancer, appendicitis and the flu. These account for nearly 70% of the difference in death rates between blacks and whites.

Shifting demographic patterns

In 2006, the population exceeded 300 million, the third largest in the world behind China and India. It had taken just 39 years to increase 50% from 200 million. Based on Census calculations, one person is added every 11 seconds.

Meanwhile, as immigration of Hispanics and Asians has increased, total population growth is only just about keeping pace with the rate needed to maintain it, largely due to declining fertility rates among non-Hispanic blacks and non-Hispanic whites. As a result, the non-Hispanic white share of the population has fallen since 1970, and the non-Hispanic black share has increased only slightly. Changes in racial and ethnic self-identification have also contributed to the increase in measured racial and ethnic diversity. These changes are most important for the Native American population, which has increased more in recent years than can be accounted for by deaths, births, immigration and improvements in Census coverage. The rise in the numbers of this group suggests that Native Americans are more likely to identify themselves as such in the Census than they were in the past.

While some believe that the population explosion is helping the US remain one of the most prosperous countries in the world, the growth of the population is arousing concerns about the environment and resource consumption, urban sprawl and habitat degradation, congestion and pollution, the increase in greenhouse gas emissions and the loss of agricultural land. Since 1970, more than 30 million immigrants and their descendents have been added to local labor pools and their communities. The influx has dramatically reshaped the social and ecological landscape up and down America's coasts, and has spilled over into the hinterlands, carving out new economic and cultural channels. Millions of new immigrants now pulse through the arteries of most cities from New York City to Dodge City, and an increasing number of non-urban regions, from North Carolina fishing villages to northern Arkansas mountain hamlets. Thus the immigration debate has taken a new turn, toward the issue of population stability. Some are confident that the US can absorb the growing population, reasoning that if the population grows in thriving existing communities, restoring the historic density of older communities, the nation can easily sustain the growth and create a more efficient economy without sacrificing the environment. Others claim that urban sprawl, and its accompanying traffic, has become the predominant form of land use, turning the US into a suburban nation. Broadly speaking, because the population has grown so fast, the time available to expand and update the nation's infrastructure has been shortened from a lifetime to a generation.

Regional differences in the population

National changes in the composition of the population mask differences across and within regions. The population is concentrated in the West (23.9%) and the South (21.7%). The geographical distribution of racial and ethnic groups is also important because it influences the potential for social and economic interaction between them. Most of the nation's minority populations are concentrated along the periphery of the continental US, where the 10 largest states are, and in Hawaii. The West has the highest concentration of minorities, followed by the South, the Northeast, and the Midwest. Non-Hispanic blacks are most likely to live in the South, while Asians, Hispanics and Native Americans are most likely to live in the West.

In several states - California, Connecticut, Illinois, Massachusetts, New Jersey, New York, Pennsylvania and Rhode Island - the share of population growth attributable to immigration is more than 100% because the native-born population decreased at the same time that the immigrant stock was rising. Eight other states have had population increases of more than half a million since 1970. They are Colorado, Georgia, Maryland, Michigan, North Carolina, Pennsylvania, Virginia and Washington.

City centers and suburbs

Minorities have tended to be less mobile than whites, settling in places where they had friends and family who provided support, but now they, too, are more likely to choose where they live based on economic factors such as the availability of jobs and the lower cost of housing. Wherever there is economic growth, the minority population is growing as well. A study by the Brookings Institution in 2006, reported by CityMayors.com, indicated that minority groups are settling much more outside of large metropolitan areas than they used to. The Hispanic population, and some Asians and African Americans, who until recently were clustered in big cities like Los Angeles, Miami, Chicago or New York, are starting to spread out to other parts of the country into a lot of suburban and exurban counties that used to be all-white. The Los Angeles and New York metropolitan areas contained 23% of the nation's Hispanic population in 2004, down from

30% in 1990. Many of the available jobs require people with low skills in construction or retail. These jobs are being created by middle class people who moved first. Thus Hispanics especially are moving to cities like Las Vegas, Nevada, Phoenix, Arizona, and Orlando, Florida. A strong multi-minority presence characterizes 18 large "melting pot" metro areas, and 27 large metro areas now have "majority minority" child populations. Meanwhile, interior California areas such as Riverside and Stockton gained significant numbers of Hispanics and Asians. By contrast, the Midwest and mountain states are still predominantly white and they are aging as people leave to seek opportunities elsewhere. More than for minority groups, white population growth has dispersed towards smaller-sized areas.

As for African Americans, they too are looking for greater economic opportunity. Their grandparents and great-grandparents left rural areas in Mississippi, Alabama and Georgia for jobs in New York and Chicago, but they have been returning to the South since the 1990s. Fully 56% of the nation's blacks now live in the South and around 70% of the growth in the black population is taking place there. The prime destination is Atlanta, Georgia, a city with a large black middle class. Hispanics, Asians, and blacks, however, remain more likely to reside in large metropolitan areas than the population as a whole.

Living arrangements

Currently 50.5% of Americans are married, 30% are single and have never married, 2.2% are separated, 10.5% are divorced, and 6.4% are widowed, according to *America's Families and Living Arrangements*, Census Bureau, 2008. The median age for men at first marriage was 27.4 years, for women 25.6. The percentage of adults ages 45 to 49 who were married varied by race and ethnicity. For example, among women, 79% of Asians, 69% of white non-Hispanics, 62% of Hispanics and 43% of blacks were married. There were 6.8 million opposite-sex couples living together. The US had an estimated 5.5 million "stay-at-home" parents: 5.3 million mothers and 140,000 fathers. The percentage of children living with two parents varied by race and origin. Eighty-five percent of Asian children lived with two parents, as did 78% of white non-Hispanic children, 70% of Hispanic children but only 38% of black children. Despite 12% of the population being mostly non-white immigrants, only about 2% of white men and women marry spouses of another race.

Economic and social factors

Many demographic characteristics affect economic and social status and play a role in explaining differentials in well-being among US citizens. For instance, immigration has lowered the relative socioeconomic status of the US Hispanic population as a whole, since Hispanic immigrants tend to have lower levels of education and income.

Age distribution and household structure are other influential characteristics. There are significant differences in the age distribution of US racial and ethnic populations. On average, the non-Hispanic white population is considerably older than the population as a whole. Only 24% of the non-Hispanic white population is below the age of 18, compared with about 30% of non-Hispanic blacks and Asians and about 35% of Native Americans.

A factor associated with poverty is English ability. The number of people who spoke English less than very well doubled between 1980 and 2000 to 21.3 million.

FACTFILE 7 LANGUAGE SPOKEN AT HOME AND ENGLISH-SPEAKING ABILITY, 1980-2000

	1980	%	1990	%	2000	%	Change
All speakers, age 5+	210,247,455	100.0	230,445,777	100.0	262,375,152	100.0	+24.8%
English only	187,187,415	89.0	198,600,798	86.2	215,423,557	82.1	+15.1%
Other language	23,060,040	11.0	31,844,979	13.8	46,951,595	17.9	+103.6%
Speaks English "very well"	12,879,004	6.1	17,862,477	7.8	25,631,188	9.8	+99.0%
Speaks English less than "very well"	10,181,036	4.8	13,982,502	6.1	21,320,407	8.1	+109.4%
Spanish	11,116,194	5.3	17,339,172	7.5	28,101,052	10.7	+152.8%

Muslim Americans

The first ever nationwide random sample survey of Muslim Americans found them to be largely assimilated, happy with their lives, and moderate with respect to many of the issues that have divided Muslims and Westerners around the world. The study, *Muslim Americans: Middle Class and Mostly Mainstream*, The Pew Research Center for the People & the Press, a project of the Pew Research Center, May 22, 2007, found that Muslim Americans were a highly diverse population largely composed of immigrants. Two-thirds (65%) of adult Muslims were foreign born. A relatively large proportion of Muslim immigrants were from Arab countries, but many came from Pakistan and other South Asian countries. Among native-born Muslims, roughly half were African American (20%), many of whom were converts to Islam. The Pew Center estimated the total Muslim population at 2.35 million.

The survey showed that although many Muslims were relative newcomers, they were highly assimilated into American society and decidedly American in their outlook, values and attitudes, although 47% thought of themselves as Muslim first rather than American first. On balance, they believed that Muslims coming to the US should try to adopt American customs, rather than remaining distinct from the larger society. The study found that Muslim Americans had a generally positive view of American society. Most said their communities were excellent or good places to live, and better for women than Muslim countries. Fully 71% agreed that most people who wanted to get ahead in the US could make it if they were willing to work hard. (Their income and education levels generally mirrored those of the rest of the population.) By nearly two-to-one (63%-32%) Muslim Americans did not see a conflict between being a devout Muslim and living in a modern society.

Muslim Americans reject Islamic extremism by larger margins than do Muslim minorities in

Western European countries. There is, however, some acceptance of Islamic extremism among American Muslims: fewer native-born African American Muslims than others completely condemn al Qaeda. In addition, younger Muslims in the US are much more likely than older Muslim Americans to say that suicide bombing in the defense of Islam can at least sometimes be justified. Nonetheless, absolute levels of support for Islamic extremism among Muslim Americans are quite low, especially when compared with Muslims around the world.

A majority of Muslim Americans (53%) say it has become more difficult to be a Muslim in the US since 9/11. Most also believe that the government singles out Muslims for increased surveillance and monitoring. Relatively few Muslim Americans believe the US-led war on terror is a sincere effort to reduce terrorism, and 40% doubt that Muslims were responsible for the 9/11 attacks. In 2006 Keith Ellison became the first Muslim elected to the federal government, as the representative of Minnesota's 5th congressional district.

The future of the American population

Government figures released in August 2008 reveal that the white population will no longer be a majority by 2042. The main reason is that the percentage of Hispanics in the population will double from 15% to 30% as a result of immigration from throughout Latin America, and their high birthrate. Meanwhile the Asian share of the population will more than double, from 4% to 9%, while the black share will increase slightly to 15%. The total population will increase from 305 million to 439 million by 2050, a rise of over 40%. The social, economic, political and cultural consequences are hard to predict. For example, although the US has been able to assimilate large numbers of immigrants in the past, it is by no means certain that larger numbers of non-whites will mean greater equality. Meanwhile, pressures will likely grow for more restrictions on immigration.

The report *100 Million More* from the Center for Immigration Studies projects that current levels of immigration will add 105 million to the US population by 2060, while having little effect on the rise in the median age of the population. According to the report, each year about 1.6 million legal and illegal immigrants settle in the country and 350,000 people leave, resulting in a net immigration of 1.25 million. If immigration continues at current levels, the nation's population will increase 167 million (56%) to 468 million in 2060. Future immigrants and their descendants will account for 105 million (63%) of the increase. Two-thirds of the increase will come from legal immigration.

American English

There are about twice as many speakers of American English as of the other varieties of English, and about four times as many as speakers of British English. The reason is partly the current position of the US in world affairs, and also the influence of advertising, the media, popular culture (especially films and music) and tourism.

The most distinctive feature of American English is accent, although there are also many differences in vocabulary and idiom between American and other Englishes. American English is based on the dialects of the settlers who arrived from Britain in the 17th century. Soon, American English began to develop separately from British English as the settlers needed words for everyday things such as the food, plants and animals in America that were not found in Britain. Many such words were taken from the languages of the Native Americans. The languages of the early Dutch and French settlers also contributed, as did those of the large numbers of immigrants who arrived in the 19th and 20th centuries. American inventions such as electric lighting, the telephone and the typewriter also added large numbers of words. In the 1980s the political correctness movement introduced a number of expressions to replace those with negative connotations, for example, *Native American* for *Indian*, *visually impaired* for *blind*, *hearing impaired* for *deaf*, and *differently abled* for *disabled*.

Spelling, grammar and pronunciation

American spelling differs slightly from British in several ways. Americans use –*er* instead of –*re* in words like *center*, –*or* instead of –*our* in words like *color* and *flavor*, *-x* for –*ct* in connection, –*l* for –*ll* in *traveler*, *-ize* for –*ise*, as in *summarize*, and *-ed* instead of –*t* in past tenses such as *dreamed* and *learned*. Also –*cks* becomes –*x* as in *Sox*, the name of former President Clinton's cat. American spelling is generally more concise than British. *Programme*, for example, becomes *program*. But this is not always the case, as in *fulfill*, where the Americans retain the final –*ll*. Many of the American variants were introduced by Noah Webster in *The Elementary Spelling Book* as part of a plan to create a distinct form of American English on rational principles. These spellings were also contained in *A Compendious Dictionary of the English Language* (1806), the origin of *Merriam-Webster's Dictionary*. There are also a few differences in grammar. Americans retain *gotten* (received) the old form of the past participle of *got*. They also make more use of *the* with everyday places, for example, "She's in the hospital." The subjunctive, which has virtually disappeared from British English, is quite common in America, for example, "The teacher insisted they *remain* behind after class."

Many American and British idioms are not in common use on the other side of the Atlantic. Polite British forms such as *I'm afraid that…* and *Would you mind if…* sound unnaturally formal to Americans. Several features of pronunciation also make American English distinctive. Among the most prominent is the pronounced (rhotive) *r* in the middle of words like *card* and at the end of words like *dinner*. A *t* pronounced a *d* in words like *letter* is also noticeable. The vowel /ae/ is used in words like *path, cot* and *caught*, which are each pronounced differently in British English. *Tune* is pronounced /tu:n/ not /tju:n/. Vowel lengths can be different too. *Missile* is pronounced like *missal* with no final vowel. Stress patterns can also be different, with more multi-syllable words having the stress on the first syllable.

Accent and dialect

Although America is a large and varied country, Americans rarely have difficulty understanding each other. The standard form of English, known as General American English (GAE), which is particularly common in the Midwest, is spoken in many places elsewhere and is spread throughout the country by television and to a lesser degree by radio. Accents, that is, pronunciation and intonation, vary to some extent according to region, and may also be affected by social class, age and level of education, and by whether the speaker has moved from his or her home area.

There are some differences in vocabulary, grammar and accent in local dialects. The main dialect groups are the Northern, the Coastal Southern, the Midland (from which GAE is derived) and the Western. The main differences between them are in accent, but some words are restricted to particular dialects because what they refer to is not found elsewhere, for example, *hominy*, partly crushed corn that is eaten for breakfast in the Southern states. Northern dialects spread west from New York and Boston, while Midland dialects developed after settlers moved west from

Philadelphia. There are increasing differences between Western dialects because southwestern dialects have been influenced by Mexican Spanish. The Southern dialects are the most distinctive. They contain old words no longer used elsewhere such as *kinfolk* (relatives). Southern dialects have been influenced by French, Spanish and Native American languages. In the distinctive Southern accent called the drawl, a final *r is* often omitted and diphthongs are replaced by simple vowels. Southern speakers may use *y'all* as a plural form of *you*. As well as dialects, there are several specific varieties of English spoken in America such as Black English, Jewish English, Cajun English and Hispanic English.

Accent in America tells the listener little about a speaker's regional origin or social class, except in a few cases such the New York accent, the New England accent, the Boston accent spoken by old, rich families from New England, and the Southern drawl. In cities, people scarcely notice accent, but in small towns and country areas, listeners may be much more sensitive. Many Southerners feel embarrassed about their accent and try to modify it, especially if they are professionals (although former President Carter's accent is still recognizably Southern).

Black English

The speech of black and white Americans has always been different, although since black slaves were mostly taken to the South and most African Americans still live there, Black English and Southern dialects have much in common. Recently, Black English has begun to lose its inferior status and is now considered a dialect called *Black American English* (BAE), *Black English Vernacular* (BEV) or *African-American Vernacular English* (AAVE). The study of Black English has been called *ebonics*. Not all African Americans speak BEV, and some only do so when speaking to other African Americans. There are variations within BEV, which is sometimes the same as a regional dialect of American English.

Black English developed from the pidgin which the slaves, who came from different parts of Africa and spoke different languages, used to communicate with each other. The pidgin first developed into a creole, a language developed from a European and an African language. Later, Black English developed further after contact with other American English dialects. Black English remained distinct, however, because African Americans continued to live very separate lives from other Americans.

There are many differences between BEV and General American English in vocabulary, grammar and pronunciation. Black English contains many words from West Africa, such as *yam* for *sweet potato* and *tote* for *carry*. BEV also has its own slang, where *bad*, for instance, can be used to mean *good*. Some of these expressions have entered American English slang. The verb *to be* is often omitted, as are inflected forms for plurals and possessives. The *l* is likewise left out of words like *help* and *self*. Consonant groups may be reduced. Hence desk is pronounced /des/ and test as /tes/. Final and middle "r" is not pronounced. Words like *this* and *that* are pronounced /dis/ and /daet/. In two-syllable words, the first usually has heavy stress. Black English has much in common with the speech of white Americans from the South.

Black English has some special cultural features such as the dozens (verbal insults about an opponent's mother); rapping (the language of songs and seduction); shucking and jiving (deceiving white people); and sounding (having verbal contests). These traditions were brought from Africa. Some BEV rhetoric is influenced by the Bible.

Since the civil rights movement of the 1960s, the use of Black English in schools has been much debated. Some assert that the use of BEV is a sign of ignorance and should be discouraged in the interests of student development; others argue that students are more likely to learn if they can use a language they know well.

Language policy

The growth of the Spanish-speaking Hispanic population has prompted fears that widespread use of Spanish, especially in the southwestern states, will divide the country, whose many immigrant groups were previously united by English. Some English speakers point to Canada, where the existence of two languages (English and French) has been accompanied by a secessionist movement. The US has been called the "cemetery of foreign languages," referring to the hostility American schools and other institutions have demonstrated toward the retention by immigrants of their native languages. The English Only Movement, comprising two main groups, English First and US English, is campaigning for an English Language Amendment to the Constitution to make English the official language of the US. Supporters say that money spent on providing services in Spanish would be better spent teaching the immigrants English. Others believe an official language is unnecessary. They point out that the children of immigrants, and their children, will learn English as a matter of course, and that studies show that bilingual youngsters tend to do better on almost all cognitive tests and that most of them become fluent in English by age 17. In any case, they add, a common language does not always lead to social harmony. Recognition of English as the official language, opponents argue, would stigmatize speakers of other languages and make it difficult for them to live their daily lives. An English Language Amendment was introduced in Congress in 1981 but a vote has never been taken on it. Meanwhile 26 states have passed English Only laws.

SOCIAL CLASS

Many Americans say with pride that there are no class differences in the US, but this is not the case. Class differences, mainly based on money, do exist, but social mobility can sometimes take place with hard work and good luck. The American dream is based on the belief, not always justified, that if people work hard enough, they can reach any goal they desire. The goal, however, is not to reach the upper classes. Most Americans like to think they are middle class. A middle class lifestyle is seen as the reward of hard work. People who improve their social position are proud of being self-made; people who come from rich families are thought to have an unfair advantage. Another reason for the illusion that almost everyone is middle class is Americans' high degree of social conformity.

It can be difficult to know what class an American belongs to. A person's accent does not usually indicate class, only the part of the country they come from. Even people with a lot of money send their children to public schools, and people who do blue-collar jobs encourage their children to get a good education and enter the professions.

Over the last 30 years, differences between the classes have widened and social mobility has become harder. Mobility is easiest for whites of Northern European origin. These people are called *WASPS*, White Anglo-Saxon Protestants. People of other ethnic origins, particularly African Americans and Hispanics, still face discrimination, and are treated worse and given fewer opportunities than others.

A few Americans belong to a more restricted class system. These people live mostly in the large cities of the East Coast and have "old money" which they inherited. Many are proud of having ancestors who came over on the *Mayflower*. Those who live in Boston are called *Boston Brahmins*. Traditionally living in the best area, Beacon Hill, they are even today among the social and cultural elite. Their social circle is thought to be so restricted that the saying goes *Cabots speak only to Lodges and Lodges speak only to God*. Such people support the *Social Register,* a list of important people in certain cities, and the Daughters of the American Revolution or (in Texas) Daughters of the Alamo. Their children go to expensive secondary schools called *prep schools* and to *Ivy League* universities such as Harvard and Yale. When their daughters are old enough to take part in adult social events they may become debutantes and have coming-out parties. Perhaps class and cultural warfare never reach a boiling point because America's multiple tribes are only dimly aware of one another's existence. There is no one single elite in America.

SENIORS

An aging population

A central demographic fact about America in the 21st century is the aging of the population. According to *The Changing Demographic Profile of the United States,* a report by the Congressional Research Service, June 7, 2006, persons 65 or older numbered 37 million, 12.6% of the population. The number of older Americans has increased by 3.7 million or 12.0% since 1990, compared to an increase of 13.3% for the under-65 population. Today, the 30% of Americans over 50 make up the fastest-growing segment of society. The increase in the number of seniors has been more marked for women. In 2000, there were 20.6 million older women and 14.4 million older men, a ratio of 143:100. The female to male sex ratio increases with age, ranging from 117:100 for the 65-69 age group to a high of 245:100 for persons 85 and over. Looking back over the 20th century, it is noticeable that since 1900, the percentage of Americans aged 65 or older has more than tripled (4.1% in 1900 to 12.4% in 2000), and the number has increased twelvefold (from 3.1 million to 35.0 million). The older population itself is getting older too. In 2000, the 65-74 age group (18.4 million) was eight times larger than in 1900, but the 75-84 group (12.4 million) was 16 times larger and the 85+ group (4.2 million) was 34 times larger. The age group 85 and older is now the fastest-growing segment of the population. There were also 50,000 persons aged 100 or more in 2000, a 35% increase from the 1990 figure of 37,000.

As the US grows more diverse, so does the senior population. In 2003, older Americans were 83% non-Hispanic White, 8% Black, 6% Hispanic and 3% Asian. By 2030, an estimated 72% of older Americans will be non-Hispanic White, 11% Hispanic, 10% Black and 5% Asian.

The older population is growing more in some regions than in others, and is concentrated in metropolitan areas. Three out of four older people lived in metropolitan areas in 2000. Florida (17.6%), Pennsylvania (15.6%) and West Virginia (15.3%) are the "oldest" states, with the highest percentages of people aged 65 and older. Between 1990 and 2000, the largest proportionate increases in the older population were mainly in the Mountain States and in the South Atlantic states.

The face of aging in the US is changing dramatically and rapidly, according to a Census Bureau report, *65+ in the United States: 2005*, commissioned by the National Institute on Aging (NIA). Today's older Americans are very different from their predecessors, living longer, less often living in poverty and having lower rates of disability. The baby boomers, the first of whom celebrated their 60th birthdays in 2006, promise to redefine further what it means to grow older in America.

Life expectancy has increased significantly also. A child born in 2000 could expect to live 76.9 years, about 29 years longer than a child born in 1900, while in 2000, persons reaching age 65 had an average life expectancy of an additional 17.9 years (19.2 years for females and 16.3 years for males). Much of this increase occurred because of reduced death rates for children and young adults. The past two decades, however, have also seen reduced death rates for the population aged 65-84, especially for men. Death rates fell by 19% for men aged 65-74 and by 16% for men aged 75-84. Life expectancy at age 65 increased by only 2.4 years between 1900 and 1960, but has increased by 3.7 years since. The US is, however, relatively young compared with other developed countries. Despite its aging, it has a lower proportion of adults aged 65 and older than most countries in Western Europe.

Changes in the American family have significant implications for future aging. Divorce, for example, is on the rise, and some researchers suggest that fewer children and more stepchildren may reduce the family support available in the future for people at older ages. In 1960, only 1.6% of older men and 1.5% of women aged 65 and older were divorced. But by 2003, 7% of older men and 8.6% of older women were divorced and had not remarried. The trend may be continuing. In 2003, among people in their early 60s, 12.2% of men and 15.9% of women were divorced. Three-quarters of the 10.5 million older Americans living alone in 2003 were women. The proportion varies greatly by age, with 29.6% aged 65 to 74, 47.6% aged 75 to 84, and 57% aged 85 and older living alone. In 2000, 4.5% of people aged 75 to 84 and 18.2% of those 85 or older lived in nursing homes. About three in four older nursing home residents are women.

The increased aging of America was mainly the result of the reproductive outburst (the "baby boom") that took place between 1946 and 1964. Through those years, US births ballooned to an average rate of 3.7 children per family. The number of Americans aged 45-64, the "baby boomers" who will reach 65 over the next two decades, increased by 34% from 1990 to 2000. The first baby boomers will turn 65 in 2011, and people aged 65 and over are projected to represent 20% of the population in 2030. Already in 2000, over 2 million persons celebrated their 65th birthday. In the same year, about 1.8 million persons 65 or older died, resulting in an annual net increase of approximately 238,000 in that age group.

But it is not just in sheer numbers that older Americans increasingly overshadow the young, as Theodore Roszak comments in *The Birth of an Old Generation*. Their share of the national wealth vastly exceeds that of their children and grandchildren. The quarter of the US population over 50 years old at the turn of the 21st century has an annual personal income approaching a trillion dollars. These older Americans control fully half of the country's disposable income, 75% of its financial assets (worth more than $8 trillion) and 80% of its savings and loan accounts.

With a long life expectancy ahead of it, the boomer generation will get richer as it gets older. Boomers will inherit some $10.7 trillion from their parents. The Social Security Administration estimates that, thanks to personal savings, Medicare, home ownership and tax breaks, Americans over 65 years of age now have the largest amount of discretionary income in the nation, more than twice as much as those between 25 and 34. There are already 50 million postmenopausal women. People aged 65 or older are less likely to be in the workforce today than in decades past, but many continue to work. Participation rates for men fell from 46% in 1950 to 19% in 2003. Rates for women did not change. As employed men and women grow older, their likelihood of working part-time increases. In 2003, about half of employed men aged 70 and over and almost two-thirds of employed women aged 70 and over worked part-time. Older adults are far less likely to live in poverty today than in decades past, although poverty rates vary by group. Between 1959 and 2003, the proportion of people aged 65 and over who lived below the poverty line decreased from 35% to 10%, partly due to Social Security. In 2003, older women were more likely than older men to be living in poverty (13% compared with 7%). Older non-Hispanic whites (8%) were less likely than older Blacks (24%) and older Hispanics (20%) to be living in poverty.

The rates of disability and functional limitation among the older population have declined substantially over the past two decades. The proportion with a disability fell from 26.2% in 1982 to 19.7% in 1999. But 14 million seniors report some level of disability, mostly linked to heart disease or arthritis. Death rates for heart disease are declining. However, data comparing people aged 65 to 74 in 1988-94 and 1999-2000 show a startling rise in the percentage of people considered obese. In men, the proportion grew from about 24% to 33% and in women from about 27% to 39%. Although about 80% of seniors have at least one chronic health condition, seniors are increasingly active and independent and, being better educated, take more care of their health and make more use of healthcare services.

A demographic change this dramatic cannot help but be linked to larger political changes in the future. As US society's financial and political center of gravity shifts steadily toward older people, the values that take hold among older Americans become ever more consequential. Seniors are not only the primary property-owners. They are also the country's most conscientious voters. People aged 65 and older consistently vote in higher proportions than other age groups. According to the Census, in the 2006 federal elections, 81.9% of people aged 65-74 reported having voted, the highest participation of any age group.

Studies of voting behavior show that senior voters have no predictable political orientation on anything, except obvious threats to entitlements. As conservative as they may be on many issues, elders are the anchor of the welfare state, and that anchor is getting heavier with each passing year. This inexorable trend accounts for the urgency of the campaigns to reform or privatize entitlement programs such as Medicare and Social Security. For example, the Paul Tsongas Project, a branch of the fiscally conservative Concord Coalition, has been holding public forums on "generational responsibility" and announcing in its literature that "before the baby boom becomes the senior boom, our political leaders have a window of opportunity" to reform entitlements policy. Experts calculate that if Americans were to do nothing to restructure Social Security between now and 2032, the system would be unable to pay 25% of what it owes. Meanwhile, the Social Security Administration has made clear that a series of modest, gradual adjustments in funding and coverage - none of which require privatization - will keep the program solvent for the next century.

Besides, focusing on finance should not distract attention from the fact that the cartoon stereotype of the older American as a little old lady in tennis shoes is far from accurate. America's seniors are expanding the economy's volunteer sector, returning to school in growing numbers, becoming ever more politically engaged, and demonstrating a keen interest in keeping up with modernity by becoming computer literate. The next older generation in the US will be the best educated, most widely traveled and most professionally trained generation the country has ever produced. Judging by their performance as young people in the 1960's, commentators such as

Theodore Roszak believe that the coming senior generation will also be the most politically astute and most culturally creative. They have in their younger days already rallied to many causes: civil rights, nuclear disarmament, sexual freedom, consumer advocacy, environmental issues and women's, gay and ethnic liberation. Not since the days of such independent political figures as Robert LaFollette and President Theodore Roosevelt in the early decades of the 20th century has any generation confronted the power structure by raising such challenging questions about the ethical use of wealth and power.

End of Life Issues

The Right to Die

More Americans are discussing and planning their end-of-life treatment in the event of a terminal illness or incapacitating medical condition, according to the survey *Strong Public Support for Right to Die*, January 5, 2006, The Pew Research Center for the People & the Press, a project of the Pew Research Center. An overwhelming majority support laws that give patients the right to decide whether they want to be kept alive through medical treatment. Public attitudes on these and many other end-of-life issues are unchanged from 1990, despite advances in lifesaving technology, the aging of the population, and the controversy associated with the Terri Schiavo case, where a woman in a persistent vegetative state (coma) was kept alive against the wishes of her husband despite showing no signs of recovery for years. Most Americans believe it should be up to individuals, not the government or medical professionals, to determine their end-of-life decisions.

Public awareness of living wills, already widespread in 1990, is now virtually universal, and the number of people saying they have a living will has more than doubled from just 12% in 1990 to 29%. People are also much more willing to discuss sensitive end-of-life issues with their loved ones than they were a generation ago. Of those who are married, 69% say they have had a conversation with their husband or wife about their spouse's wishes for end-of-life medical care; only 51% reported doing so in 1990. Among those with living parents, 57% say they have spoken with their mother and 48% with their father about the parent's requests for end-of-life treatment. There is strong sentiment (74%) in favor of letting close family members decide whether to continue medical treatment for a terminally ill loved one who is unable to communicate their own wishes, little changed from 1990 (71%).

But Americans are deeply divided over legalizing physician-assisted suicide: 46% approve of laws permitting doctors to help patients to end their lives, while about as many are opposed (45%). On this issue, Americans are divided along religious and political lines. By two-to-one (61%-30%) white evangelical Protestants oppose physician-assisted suicide laws; by nearly identical margins, white mainline Protestants and seculars approve of such laws. Catholics, on balance, oppose such laws (by 50%-40%). Small majorities of Democrats (52%) and independents (52%) approve of allowing physician-assisted suicide. Most Republicans oppose these laws (by 55%-34%), and conservative Republicans oppose them by a margin of two-to-one (62%-29%).

Though most Americans say it is sometimes morally acceptable for people with dire medical conditions to take their own lives, acceptance of this practice is highly dependent on circumstances. Six-in-ten feel that people have a moral right to end their lives if they suffer from great pain and have no chance for improvement. A majority also believes it is at least sometimes justifiable for a person to kill their spouse "mercy killing," again in extreme circumstances.

People's views of end-of-life policies and practices do not perfectly mirror their own treatment preferences. There has in fact been an increase in the percentage who say they would want everything possible done to save their lives in many situations. Opponents of abortion and of the death penalty are more likely than those who accept these practices to favor doing everything possible to save a life, as well as to oppose physician-assisted suicide. The number of people who think there are times when medical treatment should be ended has changed little since 1990, though the percentage believing that all possible efforts should be made has grown modestly during the period. Only among African Americans does a majority (51%) think doctors and nurses should always do everything possible to save a patient.

Views on Aging

The Pew survey also found that a plurality of Americans view the prospect of having more free time as what they look forward to most about getting old, while health concerns are seen as the biggest negative. Among the positives, about a third (35%) say that not having to work or having more free time is what they look forward to most, while 19% mention being able to spend time with their children, grandchildren and other family. Smaller percentages say having good health and being active (10%), travel (4%), and being able to experience changes in the world (2%) are what they most look forward to about old age. The public expresses a broader array of worries about getting old. Health concerns including worries about cancer and other diseases, mental health, and insurance worries are mentioned most frequently (39%). Roughly one-in-five (19%) worry most about not having enough money in old age and 8% voice concern about losing their ability to care for themselves and being a burden on others. These worries have changed only modestly over the past 15 years. Nearly a third of those aged 65 and older (31%) say "nothing" when asked what worries them most about getting old. Only about one in ten or fewer in other age categories express no worries about getting old. Health concerns are mentioned most frequently by people ages 50-64. Compared with other age groups, those ages 18-29 express a relatively high level of concern over dying. One in ten of those under 30 say that their biggest worry about getting old is dying; far fewer people in older age categories, especially those ages 65 and older (2%) express that concern.

Roughly four in ten Americans (43%) say they would like to live to be 100 years old, while 47% say they would not like to live to be that old. These findings have not changed much since 1990, when 39% said they would like to live to be 100. There has, however, been an increase since 1990 in the percentages of African Americans, young people and women who say they would like to live to 100. Nearly two-thirds of blacks (65%) say they would like to live to see the century mark, up from 53% in 1990. That compares with just 39% of whites who want to live to 100. Half of those under age 30 (55%) say they would like to live to be 100, up from 44% in 1990. By comparison, just 36% of those aged 50 or older want to live that long. More women also express a desire to live to 100 than did so 15 years ago (39% v. 31%); still, more men than women continue to say they want to live to 100. In addition, people who register the highest levels of personal happiness are more likely than those who are less happy with their lives to want to live to 100 (51% v. 40%).

CHAPTER 3

GOVERNMENT

Governments are instituted among men, deriving their just powers from the consent of the governed.
Declaration of Independence, July 4, 1776

The leading object of government is, to elevate the condition of men—to lift artificial weights from all shoulders—to clear the paths of laudable pursuit for all—to afford all, an unfettered start, and a fair chance, in the race of life.
Abraham Lincoln, Message to Congress, July 4, 1861

The Constitution: a charter to assure the rule of law and the rights of man.
Barack Obama

FACTFILE 8 THE AMERICAN STATES

50 states and 1 district*; Alabama, Alaska, Arizona, Arkansas, California, Colorado, Connecticut, Delaware, District of Columbia*, Florida, Georgia, Hawaii, Idaho, Illinois, Indiana, Iowa, Kansas, Kentucky, Louisiana, Maine, Maryland, Massachusetts, Michigan, Minnesota, Mississippi, Missouri, Montana, Nebraska, Nevada, New Hampshire, New Jersey, New Mexico, New York, North Carolina, North Dakota, Ohio, Oklahoma, Oregon, Pennsylvania, Rhode Island, South Carolina, South Dakota, Tennessee, Texas, Utah, Vermont, Virginia, Washington, West Virginia, Wisconsin, Wyoming.

Dependent areas
American Samoa, Baker Island, Guam, Howland Island, Jarvis Island, Johnston Atoll, Kingman Reef, Midway Islands, Navassa Island, Northern Mariana Islands, Palmyra Atoll, Puerto Rico, Virgin Islands, Wake Island

Note: from July 18, 1947 until October 1, 1994, the US administered the Trust Territory of the Pacific Islands, but then entered into a new relationship with all four political units: the Northern Mariana Islands is a commonwealth in political union with the US (effective November 3, 1986); Palau concluded a Compact of Free Association with the US (effective October 1, 1994); the Federated

States of Micronesia signed a Compact of Free Association with the US (effective November 3, 1986); the Republic of the Marshall Islands signed a Compact of Free Association with the US (effective October 21, 1986). In the US, "State" can mean any State of the United States, the District of Columbia, Puerto Rico, the Virgin Islands, Guam, American Samoa, the Commonwealth of the Northern Mariana Islands, or the Trust Territory of the Pacific Islands.

Type of Government

"A Government of the People, by the People, and for the People...."
Abraham Lincoln, Gettysburg Address, 1865

The USA is a federal republic with a strong democratic tradition. Its Constitution, adopted September 17, 1787, became effective March 4, 1789. Voting is by universal suffrage from 18 years of age. The national government is the Federal Government, which has three co-equal branches, the executive, the legislative and the judicial. These branches are designed to cooperate in a system of mutual checks and balances. The separation of powers between the branches, the checks and balances between them, and the federal system of government were designed to prevent autocracy and maintain the freedom of the people. Hence analysis of the American political process should take into account the balance of powers between the branches of government and not focus on the Presidency alone

The influence of the French thinker, Montesquieu, on the Constitution is still a matter of debate among political scientists. Donald Lutz has found that Montesquieu was the most frequently quoted authority on government and politics in pre-revolutionary America. Montesquieu himself, however, advocated the English model, in which the laws were made by the Parliament, upheld by the King and interpreted by the judiciary. The framers of the American Constitution sought to uphold "the freedom of English laws," which they accused the British King George III of violating. The republican form of government they adopted was intended to preserve these freedoms, not to replace them with something entirely different. Democracy was only one element in politics. The framers viewed political parties with distrust; and the mass media did not exist.

Role of government

Americans consider that the government should have only certain limited roles, responsibilities and powers. These are principally to provide security for liberty and property, and to ensure that the government retains the consent of the people. This attitude to government is conditioned by the circumstances of the American Revolution against what the colonists saw as British tyranny, and is summed up by the famous slogan "No taxation without representation." The government is expected to defend the citizens from violence and fraud, and to maximize their freedom to use, develop and sell without hindrance the property they own or produce. The task of government thus is only to ensure that basic rights and services are accessible to all Americans. Beyond that, Americans have the faith—the democratic-republican faith—that all individuals are capable of self-government. Exactly what should be included in "basic" rights and services has been lively debated from the beginning and forms much of the substance of political discourse today on such issues as gun control, abortion and the college education of undocumented immigrants.

Political philosophy

Origins

The intellectual environment of the American Revolutionaries was a compound of classical models, Common Law legal tradition, Enlightenment ideology, covenant theology, and a strong tradition of British intellectual and political dissent that had its roots in the Commonwealth period of the 17th century (1649-1660). The latter tradition was especially important and acted as the principle by which other received ideas were interpreted. This is not to say that these ideas *caused* the American Revolution, but that they helped to make it possible for the colonists to think in revolutionary, republican terms and to explain and defend their actions on that basis. The most important contribution of Common Law to American political thought is probably the doctrine of precedent.

The most important shaper of the American Revolutionary viewpoint was *Cato's Letters,* a series of newspaper articles in England written by John Trenchard and his young disciple Thomas Gordon in the early 1720s. These were eagerly received and widely read in the American colonies. *Cato* transmuted the abstract and often guarded statements of philosophers like John Locke (1632-1704) into a hard-hitting and radical political creed. Not only did men (women were ignored) have natural rights to life, liberty and property, which governments must not invade, but *Cato* declared that government – power – was ever the great enemy of liberty, and stood ready to aggress against it. Hence, power must be limited as far as possible and men must watch it continually with the utmost vigilance, in case it break its bounds and destroy the rights of the individual.

Limited government and property rights

It was the English philosopher, John Locke, himself strongly influenced by the Puritan covenant tradition, who most profoundly affected the principles upon which the government of the US was founded. He actually wrote the Carolina Constitution in 1669; the colony was divided into North and South in 1712. Indeed, his legacy of thoughts on human understanding, religion, economics, and politics still influence the structure, operation, and environment of US public administration. He is most noted for his concept of *separation of powers* and for his ideas about *property as the basis for prosperity*. More than any other teaching, Locke's understanding of property links him to the founding of America and dictates his insistence on the limited role and powers of government. Locke's writings on property make him unique, separating him from peers such as Machiavelli and Hobbes, who believed in absolute monarchy, and from the ancient religious and philosophic traditions of political virtue and the good society. Locke was the philosophical founder of modern liberal democracy, whom Jefferson famously paraphrases at the start of the Declaration of Independence, changing Locke's "life, liberty, and property" to "life, liberty, and the pursuit of happiness."

Locke's ideas on government were most extensively expressed in his *Second Treatise of Civil Government* (1689). There he was above all concerned with private property and its protection. Early capitalist economics was at the heart of what Locke saw as the basis for politics, although his concept of liberty extended to liberty of the person and even included the liberty of an adult to use his reason independently:

> "*Political power*, then, I take to be a *right* of making laws…for the regulating and preserving of property, and in employing the force of the community in the execution of such laws, and in the defence of the commonwealth from foreign injury; and all this only for the public good." *Second Treatise*, Chapter 1.

In the years before the Revolution, as Candy Brown has shown, property law in the thirteen colonies was strongly influenced by Blackstone's *Commentaries on the Laws of England* (1765-69), which drew upon Montesquieu and Locke. Robert A. McGuire has also confirmed in *To Form a More Perfect Union* (2003) that the personal economic interests of the Founders, and those of their constituents, played a determinative role in the development and ratification of the Constitution.

Freedom and equality

In accordance with Locke, the Founders believed in two overriding political values: freedom and equality. "To understand political power right," said Locke in Chapter 2 of the *Second Treatise*,"... we must consider what state all men are naturally in, and that is, *a state of perfect freedom* to order their actions, and dispose of their possessions and persons, as they think fit, within the bounds of the law of nature, without asking leave, or depending on the will of any other man. A *state* also of *equality*, wherein all the power and jurisdiction is reciprocal, no one having more than another; there being nothing more evident, than that creatures of the same species and rank, promiscuously born to all the same advantages of nature, and the use of the same faculties, should also be equal one amongst another without subordination or subjection...."

Yet Locke went on to argue that liberty was not the same as license, and that a person had no right to kill either himself or anyone else except in some "nobler cause" greater than mere self-preservation (for example, doing "justice on an offender.") Reason, the law of nature, made it evident that "all being equal and independent, no one should harm another in life, liberty, health, or possessions." Locke then proceeded to expound the social contract theory of government, which asserts that political society is based on an agreement to give up the absolute individual freedom of the state of nature in exchange for the mutual advantages of political association. It was this theory which the American colonists used to reject the rule of the British monarchy and found the American republic. Since British rule gave the colonists no means of appeal to an independent authority when Britain passed laws affecting them which they considered damaging to their interests, the American political class claimed that they were no longer in the same civil society as the British, and that the British had reduced them to the state of nature.

Locke's social contract theory seemed to the leaders of the American Revolution to fit their political, economic and social situation like a glove. The concept of the *state of nature* which he took as his starting point seemed to mirror the position of the settlers in the American wilderness. Meanwhile, British attempts to raise taxation by in effect changing the charters of the colonies, which were more like the articles of incorporation of a company than the constitutions of states, could be understood as breaches of contract which justified the Americans in declaring their independence. Even at the time, there was substantial inequality in wealth and power in America. Except for a broader ownership of land than in most of Europe, the findings of American scholars do not sustain the traditional portrait of substantial equality.

American society after the Native American period was always characterized by sizable differences in wealth and power. During more than 150 years before the American Revolution, an economic and political elite held sway in just about all the colonies. Bureaucratic capital accumulated as offices in government became a main avenue for the acquisition of land. Prodigious land grants were assigned by high officeholders to themselves or to family, friends, and business associates. Almost invariably, large-scale merchants, landowners and slaveholders, and occasionally professionals, occupied the top rungs of colonial society. Wealth and power were further consolidated during the Revolution and the drafting of the Constitution (1775-1783 and 1787-1788).

Separation of powers

Since, in Locke's view, political society provided only some relatively limited, although important, advantages, its authority over citizens should be limited too. The chief advantage of civil society was the existence of an impartial judge, to whom even the government was subject, to redress wrongs and arbitrate conflicts, especially when the case arose from an action of the government. Based on this philosophy is the separation of the judiciary from the executive, a principle summed up in the famous saying of John Adams that the United States is "a government of laws and not of men."

The Declaration of Independence in 1776 echoed Locke's very words when it declared: "We hold these truths to be self-evident, that all men are created equal, that they are endowed by their Creator with certain unalienable rights...." Accordingly the framers designed a constitution that would prevent on the one hand dictatorship and on the other popular rule. In modern times the American view of government was summed up by President Gerald R. Ford who said, "When you have a government that is big enough to give you all you want, you have a government that can take away everything you've got." (This is actually a paraphrase of paragraph 17 of chapter 3 of Locke's *Second Treatise*.) But although the Constitution is heavily indebted to Locke's *Second Treatise*, the framers did not use it as a textbook. Rather, Locke's teachings were so well known and so suitable to the purpose that they formed part of the framers' mental furniture when they were debating and drafting the Constitution.

CITIZENSHIP TEST FACT BOX THE THIRTEEN COLONIES

Massachusetts, New Hampshire, Connecticut, Rhode Island, New York, New Jersey, Pennsylvania, Maryland, Delaware, Virginia, North Carolina, South Carolina, and Georgia.

Virginia
Founded: 1607 by John Smith and others at Jamestown
Named for: England's "Virgin Queen," Elizabeth I
Major Cities: Jamestown, Williamsburg, Richmond
Products: Tobacco, wheat, corn (grown on plantations)
Became a State: June 25, 1788

New York
Founded: 1626 by Peter Minuit and others on Manhattan Island
Named for: Duke of York 1664; originally named New Amsterdam
Major Cities: New York City, Albany
Products: Ships, iron, cattle, grain, rice, indigo, wheat
Became a State: July 26, 1788

Massachusetts
Founded: 1630 by John Winthrop and others at Massachusetts Bay
Named for: the Massachusetts tribe (word means "large hill")

Major Cities: Boston, Quincy, Plymouth, Salem, Lexington, Concord
Products: Fish, corn, livestock, lumber, ships
Became a State: February 6, 1788

Maryland

Founded: 1633 by Lord Baltimore and others at Baltimore
Named for: Queen Henrietta Maria of England
Major Cities: Baltimore, Annapolis
Products: Ships, iron, corn, wheat, rice, indigo
Became a State: April 28, 1788

Connecticut

Founded: 1636 by Thomas Hooker and others at Hartford
Named for: from an Algonquin word, quinnehtukqut, "beside the long tidal river"
Major Cities: Hartford, New Haven
Products: Wheat, corn, fish
Became a State: February 6, 1788

Rhode Island

Founded: 1636 by Roger Williams and others at Providence
Named for: Dutch for "red island"
Major City: Providence
Products: Livestock, dairy, fish, lumber
Became a State: May 29, 1790

Delaware

Founded: 1638 by Peter Minuit and others
Named for: the Delaware tribe and an early governor of colonial Virginia, Lord De La Warr
Major City: Wilmington
Products: Fish, lumber
Became a State: December 7, 1787

New Hampshire

Founded: 1638 by John Wheelwright and others
Named for: County of Hampshire, England
Major City: Concord
Products: Potatoes, fishing, textiles, ships
Became a State: June 21, 1788

North Carolina

Founded: 1653 by Virginia colonists
Named for: from *Carolus,* the Latin word for "Charles," Charles I of England
Major City: Raleigh
Products: Indigo, rice, tobacco
Became a State: November 21, 1789

South Carolina

Founded: 1663 by English colonists
Named for: from *Carolus,* the Latin word for "Charles," Charles I of England
Products: Plantation agriculture (indigo, rice, tobacco, cotton, cattle)
Major City: Charleston
Became a State: May 23, 1788

New Jersey

Founded: 1664 by English colonists
Named for: Isle of Jersey near England
Major Cities: Trenton, Princeton
Products: Manufacturing (ironworking, lumbering)
Became a State: December 18, 1787

Pennsylvania

Founded: 1682 by William Penn and others at Philadelphia
Named for: William Penn and *sylvania,* Latin for forest
Major Cities: Philadelphia, Lancaster, York
Products: Wheat, corn, cattle, dairy, textiles, papermaking, ships
Became a State: December 12, 1787

Georgia

Founded: 1732 by James Oglethorpe and others
Named for: King George II of England
Major City: Savannah
Products: Indigo, rice, sugar
Became a State: January 2, 1788

It is hoped that material included in the Citizenship Fact Box will be of particular interest to candidates for naturalization. Inclusion does not, however, necessarily imply that that the material will be tested on the Naturalization Test.

A Christian republic?

The political philosophy of rights expressed by the Constitution, being a product of Western culture, is ultimately grounded in Christianity and also owes much to the Jewish ethical ideas expressed in the Old Testament. The core idea of the American Revolution finds its most powerful expression in one of Christianity's central teachings, the Golden Rule: Do unto others as you would have them do unto you. Unlike the Ten Commandments or various other moral codes, the Golden Rule does not list a series of prohibited acts. Instead, it provides a way to think about how to behave toward one's fellow men and women. The Golden Rule is also implicitly egalitarian: If all are obliged to treat others as they themselves wish to be treated, they must regard others as basically like themselves and equally deserving of fair dealing. All politics thus proceeds from the assumption of the dignity of all persons; within this social framework there is no greater transgression than abusing one's power over someone else. Abuse of power is based on the assumption that social and political relations are no more than a zero-sum game wherein one person's gain comes at another's loss.

The Golden Rule proposes that, to the contrary, by identifying themselves with one another, citizens arrive at moral virtue and mutual betterment. Society becomes, as recent writer Tod Lindberg puts it, "a community of goodwill," in which a citizen's every act is constrained only by the limits of the imagination. American democracy thus rests on a principle of equality-in-freedom and a belief in individual rights that is consistent with the political philosophy of Jesus. And because it assumes that the political imagination is unlimited, the Constitution makes unique universal claims, which some have interpreted as a claim to hegemony.

But this is not to say that the framers of the Constitution were founding a Christian state. To the contrary, the Constitution, following John Locke, permits a unique degree of toleration of religious and nonreligious belief, and the state itself is secular. As David Holmes has shown (*The Faiths of the Founding Fathers*, 2006), some of the Founders, like Martha Washington, Samuel Adams, John Jay, Patrick Henry, and Thomas Jefferson's daughters, held orthodox Christian views. But many of the most influential figures, including Benjamin Franklin, George Washington, John and Abigail Adams, Thomas Jefferson, James and Dolly Madison, and James Monroe, were believers of a different stripe. Mostly they admired the ethics of Jesus, and believed that religion could play a beneficial role in society. Thomas Jefferson actually published a book *The Life and Morals of Jesus of Nazareth*. But the Founders tended to deny the divinity of Christ, were at least skeptical about organized religion, and a few seem to have been agnostic about the very existence of God. Although the Founders generally professed religious belief, Holmes shows that it was a faith quite unlike the Christianity of today's Protestant evangelicals. Indeed the Constitution makes no reference to God or Christ. In 1797, John Adams, the second President, signed a treaty that stated: "As the Government of the United States of America, is not, in any sense, founded on the Christian religion...." Alexander Hamilton, the leading theorist among the framers, who explained and defended the Constitution in great detail in *The Federalist Papers*, was once asked why. His reply was simple: "We forgot."

Democracy

Today we see the framers as founding the world's longest-lasting democracy; and we need to understand what democracy actually is. Democracy is not a synonym for unlimited freedom, maximum personal choice, or total individual independence. Democracy is a system invented so that Americans could govern themselves without outside authority — king or the will of God — to preserve order. It is a political culture which allows Americans to live together despite their differences. Democracy is designed to reconcile those differences not eliminate them. It is a system to find among all Americans' discordant personal interests areas of common cause, common agreement and common good.

Yet America between 1776 and 1787 was in chaos. The Founders had created a country with maximum freedom and minimum government. This experiment in liberty nearly fell apart as everyone pursued their own interests and nobody had the means to resolve conflicts. That was why the framers wrote a constitution that created ways to force people to debate and confront their differences, that pushed opinion toward the middle, that slowed action until the people found consensus, that encouraged compromise (Eric Lane and Michael Oreskes, *The Genius of America*, 2007).

The Constitution of the US is the central instrument of American government and the supreme law of the land. For over 200 years, it has guided the evolution of governmental institutions and provided the basis for political stability, individual freedom, economic growth and social progress. The American Constitution, prepared by the Federal Constitutional Convention at Philadelphia in 1787, is the world's oldest written constitution in force, and one that has served as the model for a number of others around the world. The Constitution owes its staying power to its simplicity and flexibility. Originally designed to provide a framework for governing four million people in 13 very different colonies along the Atlantic coast, its basic provisions were so soundly conceived that, with only 27 amendments, it now serves the needs of more than 300 million people in 50 even more diverse states that stretch from the Atlantic to the Pacific.

The authors of the Constitution are known as the *Framers*. The most famous are George Washington, Thomas Jefferson, Benjamin Franklin, Alexander Hamilton, John Adams and James Madison. The thinking of the framers is exposed in great detail in the *Federalist Papers* (1788-89), mostly written by Alexander Hamilton with some contributions from Madison and from John Jay.

Federalism

The primary aim of the Constitution was to create a strong elected central government, with broad powers to regulate relations between the states, sole responsibility in such areas as foreign affairs and defense, and directly responsive to the will of the people. At the same time, the Constitution was intended to limit the powers of government in order to preserve the rights of the people which the American colonists said their former British rulers had infringed. Following Locke, the framers of the Constitution argued that the government of George III, who did not allow the Americans representation in the British Parliament yet still imposed taxation, was a usurpation of natural rights. The primary inspiration of the Constitution was Locke's argument that although political society was necessary for human nature to be fulfilled, forming such a society had to be by consent. British rule was claimed, however unrealistically, to be an absolute rule that had reduced the colonists to the status of slaves, and taxation without representation was literally a declaration of war. This argument was taken from the very words of Locke. Thus the concept of self-government did not originate with the Americans. But the degree to which the Constitution committed the US to rule by the people was unique, even revolutionary, in comparison with other governments around the world.

Federalism and diversity

Centralization proved difficult for many Americans to accept. The interests of the large and small states, and those of the slaveholding and "free" states, differed. America had been settled in large part by Europeans who had left their homelands to escape religious or political oppression, as well as the rigid economic patterns of the Old World, which fixed individuals in a particular station in life regardless of their skill or energy. Personal freedom was highly prized by these settlers and they were wary of any power - especially that of government - which might curtail individual liberties.

Special interest groups

The great diversity of the new nation was a formidable obstacle to unity. The people who were empowered by the Constitution to elect and control their central government were of widely differing origins, beliefs and interests. Most had come from England, but Sweden, Norway, France, Holland, Prussia, Poland and many other countries also sent immigrants to the New World. Their religious beliefs were varied and in most cases strongly held. There were Anglicans, Baptists, Roman Catholics, Calvinists, Huguenots, Lutherans, Quakers, Jews, agnostics and atheists. Economically and socially, the Americans ranged from the landed aristocracy to slaves from Africa and indentured servants working off debts. But the backbone of the country was the middle class - farmers, tradesmen, mechanics, sailors, shipwrights, weavers, carpenters and a host of others. Americans then, as now, had widely differing opinions on virtually all issues, up to and including the wisdom of breaking free of the British Crown. In the past two centuries, the diversity of the American people has increased. Throughout the 19th century and on into the 21st, an endless stream of immigrants have contributed their skills and their cultural heritages to the growing nation.

The wealth of the new nation as it developed generated its own kind of diversity. Special regional and commercial interest groups sprang up. East Coast shipowners advocated free trade. Midwest manufacturers argued for import duties to protect their positions in the growing US market. Farmers wanted low freight rates and high commodity prices; millers and bakers sought low grain prices; railroad operators wanted the highest freight rates they could get. New York bankers, southern cotton growers, Texas cattle ranchers and Oregon lumbermen all had different views on the economy and the government's role in regulating it. It was the continuing job of the Constitution and the government it had created to draw all these disparate interests together, to create a common ground and, at the same time, to protect the fundamental rights of all the people.

Cooperation between governments

Under the Constitution, the federal government stands at the peak of a pyramid above state and local jurisdictions. In the US system, each level of government has a large degree of autonomy with certain powers reserved particularly to itself. Disputes between different jurisdictions are resolved by the courts. There are questions involving the national interest, however, which require the cooperation of all levels of government simultaneously, and the Constitution makes provision for this as well. American public schools, for example, are administered by local jurisdictions, but adhere to statewide standards. But since literacy and educational attainment are matters of vital national interest, the federal government also aids the schools and enforces uniform standards designed to equalize educational opportunity. In other areas, such as housing, health, and welfare, there is a similar partnership between the various levels of government.

The Constitution as supreme law

The US Constitution calls itself the "supreme law of the land." This clause is taken to mean that when state constitutions or laws passed by state legislatures or the national Congress are found to conflict with the federal Constitution, they have no force. Thus the Constitution fulfills the idea of John Locke, *Second Treatise*, Chapter 4, paragraph 22:

> "*freedom of men under government* is, to have a standing rule to live by, common to every one of that society, and made by the legislative power erected in it; a liberty to follow my own will in all things, where the rule prescribes not; and not to be subject to the inconstant, uncertain, unknown, arbitrary will of another man...";

and the Constitution supplies an "*established*, settled, known law, received and allowed by common consent to be the standard of right and wrong, and the common measure to decide all controversies between them." (II:9:129) It was because George III, in the opinion of the colonists, had departed from the settled law by forcing new legislation upon them that they considered themselves justified in leaving his jurisdiction and replacing his rule with a new government of their own.

The power of public officials is limited. Their public actions must conform to the Constitution and to the laws made in accord with it. Elected officials must stand for re-election at periodic intervals, when their records are subject to intense public scrutiny. Appointed officials serve at the pleasure of the person or authority who appointed them, and may be removed when their performance is unsatisfactory. The exception to this practice is the lifetime appointment by the President of justices of the Supreme Court and other federal judges, so that they may be free of political obligations or influence. Most commonly, the American people express their will through the ballot box. The Constitution, however, does make provision for the removal of a public official from office, in cases of extreme misconduct or malfeasance, by the process of impeachment.

Final authority under the Constitution is vested in the American people, who can change the fundamental law, if they wish, by amending the Constitution or - in theory, at least - drafting a new one. The people do not exercise their authority directly, however. They delegate the day-to-day business of government to public officials, both elected and appointed.

Impeachment

Impeachment is a charge of misconduct ("high crimes and misdemeanors") brought against a government official by a legislative body. The process called "impeachment" was drawn from English medieval law. The House of Representatives must bring charges of misconduct by voting a bill of impeachment. The accused official is then tried in the Senate, with the Chief Justice of the Supreme Court presiding at the trial.

Impeachment is considered a drastic measure, one that has been used only on rare occasions. The House of Representatives has voted articles of impeachment just 17 times. Thirteen of the 18 persons who have been impeached were federal judges, as were all eight individuals convicted and removed from office by the Senate. Critics argue that this shows impeachment to be an ineffective threat, and states such as California have passed laws to provide alternative means to discipline judges who show themselves to be incompetent, unreasonable or corrupt.

In 1974, as a result of the Watergate affair, President Richard Nixon resigned from office after the Judiciary Committee of the House recommended impeachment, but before the full House of Representatives could vote on a bill of impeachment. In 1998 President Bill Clinton was impeached by the House of Representatives and tried by the Senate with the Chief Justice presiding. The vote on the first charge, abuse of power, was 55-45 and on the second, obstruction of justice, 50-50. A vote of at least 67 would have been necessary for conviction. State officials are similarly subject to impeachment by the legislatures of their respective states. In 1988, for example, the Arizona state legislature impeached its governor and removed him from office. An office-holder convicted after impeachment can be disqualified from public office by the Senate.

The Principles of Government

Although the Constitution has changed in many respects since it was first adopted, its basic principles remain the same now as in 1789:

1. The three main branches of government are separate and distinct from one another. The powers given to each are delicately balanced by the powers of the other two. Each branch serves as a check on the potential excesses of the others. (The balance of powers as embodied in the Constitution departs from the theory of John Locke, who considered the

legislative to be the supreme power (II: 10: 132, 134). Yet Locke did say (135) that there should be limits on what the legislature could do:

"the (legislative) power ...hath no other end but preservation, and therefore can never have a right to destroy, enslave or designedly to impoverish the subjects."

2. The Constitution, together with laws passed according to its provisions, and treaties entered into by the President and approved by the Senate, stands above all other laws, executive acts and regulations.

3. All persons are equal before the law and are equally entitled to its protection. All states are equal, and none can receive special treatment from the federal government. Within the limits of the Constitution, each state must recognize and respect the laws of the others. State governments, like the federal government, must be democratic in form, with final authority resting with the people.

Equal protection of the laws is one of the cornerstones of American democracy and prosperity. Legal equality, together with safeguards for the rights of minorities, helps to secure political consent to majority rule which in turn ensures the political stability of the country. Political stability has since the 19th century encouraged foreign investment in the US. This played a major role in building the transcontinental railroad network and today helps finance the IT revolution. Equal protection also means the uniform, comprehensive enforcement of laws and regulations, and the almost total absence of corruption, which is not only fair to all parties but further encourages inward investment. The stability and integrity of the US as guaranteed through its Constitution are the foundations of its economic prosperity.

4. The people have the right to change their form of national government by legal means defined in the Constitution itself.

Amendment of the Constitution

The Constitution purposely makes the process of amending it difficult. The Congress, by a two-thirds vote in each House, may initiate an amendment. Alternatively, the legislatures of two-thirds of the states may ask Congress to call a national convention to discuss and draft amendments. In either case, amendments must have the approval of three-fourths of the states before they enter into force.

Aside from the direct process of changing the Constitution itself, the effect of its provisions may be changed by judicial interpretation. This also embraces the power of the Supreme Court to explain the meaning of various sections of the Constitution as they apply to changing legal, political, economic and social conditions. Over the years, a series of Court decisions, on issues ranging from governmental regulation of radio and television to the rights of the accused in criminal cases, has had the effect of altering the thrust of constitutional law, with no substantive change in the Constitution itself.

The Bill of Rights

The Constitution has been amended 27 times since 1789. The most sweeping changes were made within two years of its adoption. In that period, the first 10 amendments, known collectively as the Bill of Rights, were added. This was largely the handiwork of James Madison, who, in turn, echoed Virginia's 1776 Declaration of Rights. These were rights that many had wanted to include in the original draft of the Constitution but had left out in order to persuade all the states to ratify it. They were approved as a block by the Congress in September 1789. At first, these 10 amendments were applicable to American citizens only as citizens of the entire US and not as Virginians or as New Yorkers, where state laws could take precedence according to "states' rights", as acknowledged in the 10th and last of the original amendments. It was not until 1868 that the 14th Amendment forbade the states to make laws counter to the original Bill. The intent was to prevent states (in practice, the Confederate states of the South) passing laws discriminating against black Americans, but for another century, until the Civil Rights Act, some found ways of doing so.

Much of the initial resistance to the Constitution came not from those opposed to strengthening the federal union, but from statesmen who felt that the rights of individuals must be specifically spelled out. By the time the First Congress convened, sentiment for adoption of such amendments was nearly unanimous, and the Congress lost little time in drafting them. These amendments remain intact today, although some have been more successful than others. The First Amendment, guaranteeing freedom of speech and religion, is seen as an essential principle of American life. The fourth, which allows the compulsory purchase of property by the government under "eminent domain", subject to compensation at fair market value, has stood unchallenged, although it has given rise to a number of court cases. This Amendment is an example of where the Constitution has had to be interpreted according to the needs of an infinitely more complex society than when it was enacted, but without the need for further amendment. The 18th Amendment, passed in 1919, making it illegal to make or buy alcoholic drinks, had to be repealed by the 21st Amendment in 1933 after a crime wave in bootleg alcohol made it unworkable. Some Amendments reflect changes in American society. The Constitution was written by white men, mainly to protect their rights. Following the Civil War, the 13th Amendment (1865) and the 15th (1870) gave the same rights to people of all races, although for nearly a century afterwards, some of the Southern states passed laws about voting and segregation in education, transportation, public dining and restrooms to make these amendments ineffective. In 1920 the 19th Amendment gave women the right to vote.

The Bill of Rights (the first ten Amendments to the Constitution)

The first guarantees freedom of worship, speech and the press, the right of peaceful assembly, and the right to petition the government to correct wrongs. The second guarantees the right of citizens to bear arms. The third provides that troops may not be quartered in private homes without the owner's consent. The fourth guards against unreasonable searches, arrests and seizures of property.

The next four amendments deal with the system of justice:

The fifth forbids trial for a major crime except after indictment by a grand jury. It prohibits repeated trials for the same offence; forbids punishment without due process of law and provides that an accused person may not be compelled to testify against himself.

The sixth guarantees a speedy public trial for criminal offences. It requires trial by an unbiased jury and guarantees the right to legal counsel for the accused, and provides that witnesses shall be compelled to attend the trial and testify in the presence of the accused.

The seventh assures trial by jury in civil cases involving anything valued at more than 20 US dollars.

The eighth forbids excessive bail or fines, and cruel or unusual punishment.

The last two of the 10 amendments contain very broad statements of constitutional authority.

The ninth declares that the listing of individual rights is not meant to be comprehensive; that the people have other rights not specifically mentioned in the Constitution.

The tenth provides that powers not delegated by the Constitution to the federal government nor prohibited by it to the states are reserved to the states or the people.

Once again the concept of law embodied in the Constitution can be traced to John Locke, who says (II:6:57) "law, in its true notion, is not so much the limitation as the *direction of a free and intelligent agent* to his proper interest....*the end of law* is not to abolish or restrain, but *to preserve and enlarge freedom.*"

Amendments to the Constitution subsequent to the Bill of Rights cover a wide range of subjects. One of the most far reaching is the 14th, ratified in 1868, by which a clear and simple definition of citizenship was established and a broadened guarantee of equal treatment under the law was confirmed. By other amendments, the judicial power of the national government was limited; the method of electing the President was changed; slavery was forbidden; the right to vote was protected against denial because of race, color, sex or previous condition of servitude; the congressional power to levy taxes was extended to incomes; and the election of US senators by popular vote was instituted.

The most recent amendments include the 22nd, limiting the President to two terms in office; the 23rd, granting citizens of the District of Columbia the right to vote; the 24th giving citizens the right to vote regardless of failure to pay a poll tax; the 25th, providing for filling the office of Vice-President when it becomes vacant in midterm; and the 26th, lowering the voting age to 18.

It is significant that a majority of the 27 amendments stem from continued efforts to expand individual civil or political liberties, while only a few are concerned with amplifying the basic governmental structure drafted in Philadelphia in 1787.

Protection for Individual Liberties

Freedom of the individual is one of the basic values of Americans. They sometimes call the US "the land of the free", a phrase taken from the national anthem. Freedom is generally seen by Americans as civil rights, the right to do certain things, or the right to be treated in a certain way, and the right not to be interfered with by the government. The rights Americans cherish most - freedom of speech, freedom of religion, freedom of the press, freedom of assembly, equality before the law, and the right to a jury trial - are taken from the Constitution and the Bill of Rights. Freedom is also the right to indulge in a broad range of behaviors, even unconventional or challenging behaviors, without restriction. Even when Americans disapprove of a behavior, they will often say "it's a free country" to acknowledge the person's right to do it. This is especially true of the freedoms of worship, speech and the press, which are protected by the First Amendment. There is no censorship in the US. The courts will not, for example, practice *prior restraint* and forbid a newspaper to print something (except to protect national security), though they may penalize the newspaper afterwards, especially in a case of libel. It is because the freedom to publish opinions is guaranteed under the First Amendment that the courts do not order newspapers to withdraw or apologize for items that may have given offence, a policy that people in other countries sometimes find hard to understand or accept. Freedom of speech also covers certain actions considered symbolic, although they may be highly offensive to some, such as burning the American flag during anti-war protests. These have been upheld as constitutional, and therefore permissible, by the Supreme Court. Thus there is a lively tradition of protest in the US, and both individuals and organizations are vigilant to protect and promote freedom. In modern times, freedom of information has become important. Under the Freedom of Information Act (FOIA), citizens have a right to see information about them that is held on a computer and the right to correct it if it is wrong. Journalists often request information under FOIA in their investigations. Freedom of information rights have been abridged in certain narrow circumstances under the USA Patriot Act (as amended) and the Foreign Intelligence Surveillance Act, in order to combat terrorism.

The only Amendment to give rise to serious controversy today is the Second, the right to bear arms. When it was enacted, the Revolutionary War had just concluded and the infant US did not wish (and could not afford) to maintain a standing army in time of peace. Originally, the right for citizen militias to bear arms was meant to discourage a standing federal or state army and all the mischief that an armed state might cause. The British solution to a similar problem in 1689 had been to require Parliament to re-authorize the army every year. The American solution was typically more radical: to dispense with a standing army altogether and rely on a citizen militia in each state. The Second Amendment was passed to put these militias on a legal basis. Changes to the gun laws are vehemently opposed by many as an infringement of freedom. But a significant number of Americans wish to restrict the right of citizens to own guns, or even abolish it, and the ownership of guns has been regulated by federal law and the law of some states. Federal gun laws are enacted under Article 1, section 8, of the Constitution, which authorizes Congress to regulate the militias. Under the Second Amendment, the states have the right to impose such controls as registration and licensing of guns, but they cannot outlaw the private ownership of guns altogether without a constitutional Amendment, because that would limit the states' ability to raise a militia. It is that right that the Supreme Court has consistently held is protected under the Second Amendment. In 2007 the Supreme Court said in *District of Columbia v. Heller*, 07-290, that an individual's right to bear arms was protected under the Second Amendment, ruling that Americans have an individual right to possess firearms "for traditionally lawful purposes, such as self-defense within the home." The court made it clear, however, that, like other rights, the right to bear arms is not unlimited, leaving open the prospect of reasonable governmental regulation.

The Fourteenth Amendment also gives rise to debate, if not to controversy. An issue has arisen whether the Fourteenth Amendment "incorporates" the protections of the Bill of Rights and makes them enforceable against the states. This is one of the most important and longest-lasting debates over the interpretation of the Constitution. The Supreme Court's first interpretation of the scope of the Fourteenth Amendment, adopted in 1868, was rendered in The Slaughterhouse Cases of 1873, deciding against incorporation. Beginning in the early 20th century the Court began to incorporate some of the specific provisions of the Bill of Rights while rejecting the incorporation of others. The Court's test for choosing which was which changed over time. The "modern view", as reflected in cases such as *Duncan v Louisiana* (1968) is that provisions of the Bill of Rights "fundamental to the American scheme of justice" (such as the right to trial by jury in a serious criminal case) were made applicable to the states by the Due Process Clause of the Fourteenth Amendment whereas other provisions (such as the right to a jury trial in a civil case involving more than $20) were not made applicable.

Several positions are taken in the debate. Some argue that the Fourteenth Amendment (either through its Privileges and Immunities clause or the Due Process clause) made the specific provisions of the Bill of Rights enforceable against the states and no more. A second view, the No Incorporation theory, is that the Bill of Rights is irrelevant and that violations of the Due Process Clause of the Amendment are to be determined by natural law tests such as "Does the state's action shock the conscience?" or "Is the state's action inconsistent with the concept of ordered liberty?" Thirdly, the Selective Incorporation Theory, utilized in *Duncan v. Louisiana*, holds that the Amendment incorporates certain fundamental provisions, but not other non-fundamental provisions. Other views hold that, in addition to incorporating some or all of the provisions of the Bill of Rights, the Fourteenth Amendment also prohibits certain other fundamental rights from being abridged by the states.

A related issue is that of the evidence relevant to determining whether a right is fundamental to the American scheme of justice. This might be that history shows that the right has always been respected, or that the right has been respected in recent times; or whether or not the vast majority of states have respected the right. Other tests might be what the framers and ratifiers of the Bill of Rights thought about the right in question, or whether a fair system of justice can be imagined without that right.

Economic, Social and Cultural Rights

The American idea of freedom less often refers to economic, social and cultural (ESC) rights. Indeed, the US has officially told the United Nations that ESC rights are an "aspiration", a "goal", and do not actually exist. The Constitution, therefore, is essentially about what governments can and cannot do.

Constitutional rights and law enforcement

Social critics, libertarians, political dissidents and others, from widely different points of view, have used America's First Amendment right to free speech to protest a number of government actions, mostly arising from the wars on drugs and terrorism. These complaints mainly concern surveillance, searches and seizures, demands for ID and the enforcement of tax law. James Bovard's 1994 book, *Lost Rights,* documents (along with a number of provocative exaggerations) what he claims are widespread violations of the 4th, 5th, and 14th Amendments by government.

Fourth Amendment

The right of the people to be secure in their persons, houses, papers, and effects, against unreasonable searches and seizures, shall not be violated, and no Warrants shall issue, but upon probable cause, supported by Oath or affirmation, and particularly describing the place to be searched, and the persons or things to be seized.

Fifth Amendment

No person shall be held to answer for a capital, or otherwise infamous crime, unless on a presentment or indictment of a Grand Jury, except in cases arising in the land or naval forces, or in the Militia, when in actual service in time of War or public danger; nor shall any person be subject for the same offence to be twice put in jeopardy of life or limb; nor shall be compelled in any criminal case to be a witness against himself, nor be deprived of life, liberty, or property, without due process of law; nor shall private property be taken for public use without just compensation.

Fourteenth Amendment (Section 1)

Section 1. All persons born or naturalized in the United States, and subject to the jurisdiction thereof, are citizens of the United States and of the State wherein they reside. No State shall make or enforce any law which shall abridge the privileges or immunities of citizens of the United States; nor shall any State deprive any person of life, liberty, or property, without due process of law; nor deny to any person within its jurisdiction the equal protection of the laws.

Yet the current trend is for the government to seek greater power in these areas, not less. The George W. Bush Administration, for example, asked Congress to make significant changes to the *Foreign Intelligence Surveillance Act 1978* that would allow warrantless tapping of calls and communications between Americans and their friends and relatives overseas. Meanwhile the extent of warrantless wiretapping inside the US is unknown. The Senate Judiciary Committee has asked the Department of Justice for the figures nine times, but without obtaining them. According to Bovard, the number of federally authorized wiretaps has almost quadrupled since 1980.

Moreover since 1985 federal, state and local governments have seized the property of over 200,000 Americans under asset forfeiture laws. Mostly these seizures have been carried out by the Drug Enforcement Agency, the Bureau of Alcohol, Tobacco and Firearms, and the FBI. In a great many cases seizures have been carried out on the strength of no more evidence than unsubstantiated assertions from anonymous informants. Currently, according to Kopel and Blackman in *No More Wacos*, US and some state laws say that whenever a police officer is permitted, with or without judicial approval, to investigate a potential crime, the officer may seize and keep as much property associated with the alleged criminal as the police officer considers appropriate. This is even if the owner is not convicted of a crime or even charged with one. In *United States v. Sandini* (1987) a federal court held: "The innocence of the owner is irrelevant. It is enough that the property was involved in a violation to which forfeiture attaches."

In response to the erosion of public confidence in drug law enforcement through such seizures, governments have tightened the management of narcotics programs through better-focused outcome measures. In Texas, for example, outcome measures for these programs have been more clearly linked to disrupting the illegal distribution of drugs, and no longer simply focus on the number of arrests or seizures. The new outcome measures include: the number of drug-trafficking organizations dismantled; the percentage of arrests of members of such organizations; and the percentage of arrests of end users (hoping that these reduce).

Critics of the *USA Patriot Act* say the law has made it too easy for law enforcement to spy on people. They contend that, by easing restrictions on the use of surveillance tools once reserved for foreign intelligence investigations, the law cuts too deeply into personal liberties and privacy rights. The Justice Department dismisses these objections, saying there have been no reported abuses of the Act and no substantiated claims that civil rights have been violated. But civil liberties groups say that because the Act mandates secrecy about many of its uses, Americans may never know whether their privacy has been violated by law enforcement investigators relying on the Act's powers.

National Security Letters (NSLs), for example, are a type of subpoena under Section 505 of the *Patriot Act* that can be used by the FBI in intelligence investigations without judicial approval. They allow FBI agents to seize financial records, communications information and other personal documents, by drafting a letter stating that the information being sought is relevant to a national security investigation. The government has used this authority to obtain records from an internet service provider. In April 2004, the American Civil Liberties Union sued on behalf of the service provider, arguing that the seizure violated the First and Fourth Amendments. A federal judge in New York upheld the challenge. The judge found that the way the Letters were executed was coercive;

and recipients were not allowed to challenge the orders. According to *Wired* magazine, the FBI issued 47,000 NSLs in 2005 to such companies as phone carriers AT&T, Verizon and MCI.

Information Sharing

Sections 203(b) and 203(d) of the *Patriot Act* are at the heart of the effort to break down the "wall" that used to separate criminal and intelligence investigations. The government says that existing procedures made investigators afraid of sharing information between the intelligence and criminal sides of the probe. Supporters of the *Patriot Act* say the information sharing provisions have greatly enhanced information sharing within the FBI, and with the intelligence community at large. The Justice Department has frequently blamed the wall for the failure to find and detain September 11 hijackers Nawaf al-Hazmi and Khalid al-Midhar prior to the attacks. CIA agents had information that both men were in the US and were suspected terrorists, but the FBI says it did not receive that information until August 2001. US officials also blame the wall for the failure to fully investigate Zacarias Moussaoui, who has since pleaded guilty in connection with the plot. In contrast, civil libertarians say the failure to share information was largely a result of incompetence and misunderstanding of the law. They say investigators were always allowed to share grand jury information. They warn that the scope of the *Patriot Act* language is far too broad and encourages unlimited sharing of information, regardless of the need. Critics believe that investigators should have to explain why information is being shared, and that only information related to terrorism or espionage should be released. They warn that unrestricted sharing could lead to the development of massive databases about innocent citizens.

Roving Wiretaps

The Justice Department has long complained about restrictions that required separate court authorizations for each device used by the target of an investigation, whether a computer terminal, a cell phone or a Blackberry. The information sharing provisions of the *Patriot Act* specifically allow "roving wiretaps" against suspected spies and terrorists. The government says it has long had this type of flexibility in criminal cases, and that such authority is needed in dealing with technologically sophisticated terrorists. Surveillance experts point out, however, that criminal wiretaps must ascertain whether the person under investigation is going to be using the device before the tap takes place. Civil liberties groups say the language of the *Patriot Act* could lead to privacy violations of anyone who comes into casual contact with the suspect. They want Congress to require investigators to specify just which device is going to be tapped, or that the suspect be clearly identified, in order to protect the innocent from unwarranted snooping.

Access to Records

Probably the most hotly debated provision of the *Patriot Act,* Section 215, has come to be known as the "libraries provision", even though it never mentions libraries or bookstores. Civil liberties groups attack the breadth of this section - which allows investigators to obtain "any tangible thing (including books, records, papers, documents and other items)", as long as the records are sought "in connection with" a terror investigation. Library groups believe the law could be used to demand the reading records of patrons. But the government points out that the First Amendment activities of Americans are specifically protected by the law. The Justice Department has released previously classified statistics to show the law has never been used against libraries or bookstores. But the Act's critics argue that there is no protection against future abuse.

Civil liberties groups have proposed numerous amendments: special protections for libraries and bookstores; a requirement that investigators explain the reason the records are sought; and an end to the "gag rule" that prohibits people who receive a 215 order from talking about it with anyone. The Justice Department has agreed that recipients can consult with an attorney and is open to an amendment that specifies this right. But the government says the controversy over this provision is an overreaction, and that this section merely expands longstanding access to certain business records.

Foreign Intelligence Wiretaps and Searches

Criminal investigators have a high bar to reach when asking for permission to wiretap or search a suspect's home. The bar is lower in counterterror or counterintelligence probes, where investigators must only prove the suspect is an "agent of a foreign power." Previously, investigators had to show that the "primary purpose" of the order was to investigate the gathering of foreign intelligence. The *Patriot Act* lowered that requirement to a "significant purpose." The government said this change takes away another brick in the "wall" separating criminal and intelligence probes.

Critics also say the *Patriot Act* creates a new risk in Section 218: that investigators will too easily use spying and terrorism as an excuse for launching wiretaps and searches. They point to the fact that the number of intelligence wiretaps now exceeds the number of criminal taps. Since these probes are conducted in secret, with little oversight, abuses could be difficult to uncover. Civil liberties groups say one antidote would be to require that the Justice Department release more information about foreign intelligence investigations.

"Sneak & Peek" Warrants

This section allows for "delayed notice" of search warrants, which means the FBI can search a home or business without immediately notifying the target of the investigation. The Justice Department says this provision has already allowed investigators to search the houses of drug dealers and other criminals without providing notice that might have jeopardized an investigation. Investigators still have to explain why they want to delay notice, and must eventually tell the target about the search.

Critics say that investigators already had the power to conduct secret searches in counterterror and counterespionage probes. The *Patriot Act*, they say, authorized the use of this technique for any crime, no matter how minor. They say that "sneak and peek" searches should be narrowly limited to cases in which an investigation could be jeopardized by immediate notice.

Material Support

The antiterrorism law passed in 1996 in the aftermath of the Oklahoma City bombing outlawed providing "material support" to foreign terrorist organizations, and expanded the definition of support to include "personnel" and "training." Section 805 of the *Patriot Act* extended that ban to "expert advice or assistance." The Justice Department has said this expansion is critical to cutting off the networks of support that make terrorism possible. But many legal scholars, and some judges, contend the provision is vague. They say it will lead to guilt by association and might criminalize unwitting contact with a terrorist group. Opponents also argue that it stifles free speech, by raising fears that any charitable contribution could somehow be linked to a terrorist group by the Justice Department, and then construed as "material support." Courts have differed on the constitutionality of these efforts to cut off the "lifeblood" of terrorism. Some have ruled they are unconstitutionally vague. Others have upheld these laws.

Internal Revenue Service seizures

Since 1980, Bovard notes, the number of levies and IRS seizures of bank accounts and pay checks has increased fourfold, reaching 3,253,000 in 1992. The Government Accountability Office (GAO) estimated in 1990 that the IRS imposes over 50,000 incorrect or unjustified levies on citizens and businesses per year. The IRS also imposes almost one and a half million liens each year, an increase of over 200% since 1980. The IRS's director of taxpayer services, Robert LeBaube, spoke out in 1989: "Since 1976 there have been 138 public laws modifying the Internal Revenue Code. Since the Tax Reform Act of 1986 there have been 13 public laws changing the code, and in 1988 alone there were seven public laws affecting the code." As Bovard notes but does not explain: "Tax law is simply the latest creative interpretation by government officials of the mire of tax legislation Congress has enacted. IRS officials can take five, seven, or more years to write the regulations to implement a new tax law. Yet Congress routinely changes the law before new regulations are promulgated. Almost all tax law is provisional, either waiting to be revised according to the last tax bill passed, or already proposed for change in the next tax bill. Corporate tax exemptions are a major part of the tax code and have been alleged as the reason that the IRS is so vigorous in pursuit of individual taxpayers." Congress passed a Taxpayer Bill of Rights in 1998, which shifted the burden of proof from the taxpayer to the IRS in certain limited situations. The IRS retains the legal authority to enforce liens and seize assets without obtaining judgment in court.

According to the ACLU, "There has never been a more urgent need to preserve fundamental privacy protections and our system of checks and balances than the need we face today, as illegal government spying, provisions of the Patriot Act and government-sponsored torture programs - for example, by the CIA at Guantanamo Bay, the prison on the US sovereign base on Cuba where terrorist suspects are held - transcend the bounds of law and our most treasured values in the name of national security. For Americans, the debate over government use of powers to combat terrorism and crime was summed up by constitutional law professor Jonathan Turley in a January 2003 interview with the *Los Angeles Times*: "Since 9/11, the Constitution has gone from an objective to be satisfied to an obstacle to national defense....As these changes mount, at what point do we become something other than a free and democratic nation?"

The US combats terrorism through: The US Antiterrorism and Effective Death Penalty Act of 1996; Executive Order 13224, signed by President George W. Bush Sept. 23, 2001; 2001 Uniting and Strengthening America by Providing Appropriate Tools for Intercepting and Obstructing Terrorism Act (USA PATRIOT Act)(amended March 2006); Homeland Security Act of 2002; Support Anti-Terrorism by Fostering Effective Technologies Act (SAFETY Act) of 2002; Border Protection, Anti-terrorism, and Illegal Immigration Control Act of 2005; REAL ID Act of 2005; and the Military Commissions Act of 2006.

Constitutional Rights and the Patriot Act: Summary of the Debate

Information Sharing

Sec. 203(b) and (d): Allows information from criminal probes to be shared with intelligence agencies and other parts of the government.

Pro: Supporters say the provisions have greatly enhanced information sharing within the FBI, and with the intelligence community at large. *Con:* Critics warn that unrestricted sharing could lead to the development of massive databases about citizens who are not the targets of criminal investigations.

Roving Wiretaps

Sec. 206: Allows one wiretap authorization to cover multiple devices, eliminating the need for separate court authorizations for a suspect's cell phone, PC and Blackberry, for example.

Pro: The government says roving wiretaps are needed to deal with technologically sophisticated terrorists. *Con:* Critics say the language of the Act could lead to privacy violations of anyone who comes into casual contact with a suspect.

Access to Records

Sec. 215: Allows easier access to business records in foreign intelligence investigations.

Pro: The provision allows investigators to obtain books, records, papers, documents and other items sought "in connection with" a terror investigation. *Con:* Critics attack the breadth of the provision, saying the law could be used to demand the reading records of library or bookstore patrons.

Foreign Intelligence Wiretaps and Searches

Sec. 218: Lowers the bar for launching foreign intelligence wiretaps and searches.

Pro: Allows investigators to get a foreign intelligence wiretap or search order, even if they end up bringing criminal charges instead. *Con:* Because foreign intelligence probes are conducted in secret, with little oversight, critics say abuses could be difficult to uncover.

"Sneak & Peek" Warrants

Sec. 213: Allows "sneak and peek" search warrants, which let authorities search a home or business without immediately notifying the target of a probe. Does not expire.

Pro: Supporters say this provision has already allowed investigators to search the houses of drug dealers and other criminals without providing notice that might have jeopardized an investigation. *Con:* Critics say the provision allows the use of "sneak and peek" warrants for even minor crimes, not just terror and espionage cases.

Material Support

Sec. 805: Expands the existing ban on giving "material support" to terrorists to include "expert advice or assistance." **Does not expire.**

Pro: Supporters say it helps cut off the support networks that make terrorism possible. *Con:* Critics say the provision could lead to guilt by association.

Note that these provisions, and the *Patriot Act* itself, mostly have expiry dates and are thus subject to periodic review and amendment. The real issue is political. Even libertarian legislators fear being labeled "soft on terror."

Slavery

The very existence of slavery seems to contradict the assertion in the Declaration of Independence that all men are created equal. Even at that time, however, slavery was considered as a natural, if regrettable, condition, according to a tradition of political philosophy that went back to Aristotle. John Locke summed up contemporary opinion:

"Slaves, who, being captives taken in a just war, are by the right of nature subjected to the absolute dominion and arbitrary power of their masters. These men, as I say, having forfeited their

lives, and with it their liberties, and lost their estates; and being in the *state of slavery*, not capable of any property, cannot in that state be considered as any part of *civil society*; the chief end whereof is the preservation of property." (II: 7: 85) Locke defined *property* as "life, liberty and estate."

The principle of property extended to the ownership of human beings. Colonial American society welcomed the use of slaves. The profits of the slave trade itself, the returns from a growing tobacco output, and the general usefulness of slave labor sufficed as a justification, and the philosophy of individualism facilitated its adoption. To Locke, individualism was founded in man's domain over his own labor resources even to the point of selling them unconditionally. The right to own labor carried no social or moral obligation other than the imperative to buy cheap and sell dear. Enslaving others was thus regarded as another expression of an individual's unceasing drive to accumulate property. And because this drive was alleged to belong to the inborn nature of man, Locke's "state of nature", its every expression in social relations seemed only "natural".

Slavery was the circle the Founders could not square. The wealth of many of them depended on it—without slaves, Southern land was valueless. Many of the Founders, however, had a bad conscience about it. True, they generally believed blacks to be an inferior race, genetically low in intelligence. When, to refute Thomas Jefferson's assertions of black inferiority, an ex-slave and self-taught mathematician sent him a complex almanac of his own devising, Jefferson concluded that the man must have had help. Even so, with unflinching logic, Jefferson insisted that, as far as rights were concerned, all men were created equal. "Whatever be their degree of talent it is no measure of their rights," he wrote. "Because Sir Isaac Newton was superior to others in understanding, he was not therefore lord of the person or property of others."

Slavery did not just contravene America's fundamental principle of liberty but subverted it. As Jefferson said, "Can the liberties of a nation be thought secure when we have removed their only firm basis, a conviction in the minds of the people that these liberties are of the gift of God?" The slave owner inflicts "on his fellow men a bondage one hour of which is fraught with more misery than ages of that which he rose up to oppose." Indeed Jefferson tried (and failed) to make it legal for Virginians to free their slaves. In 1778, he did persuade the state legislature to ban further importation of slaves. He believed that the institution could be limited and then gradually eradicated, after which the slaves would be expatriated—largely because their owners would have much to fear from their resentment.

As a member of Congress under the Articles of Confederation, Jefferson strove to ban slavery in any new states carved out of the western territory won from Britain in the Revolution, but a sick delegate did not show up to cast the winning vote. Four decades later, Congress did exactly the opposite and passed the 1820 Missouri Compromise, permitting slavery in Missouri and in any new states formed in the southern part of the Louisiana Territory, of which, as President, Jefferson had arranged the purchase. He was aghast, viewing it as "the knell of the Union." He correctly predicted that the antagonism between the slavery and antislavery factions would spark a nationwide conflagration. Though he held fast to his original solution, he no longer thought it would come to pass.

The Constitution and political stability

The genius of the Constitution in organizing the federal government is often credited by Americans with keeping the US stable and united over the course of two centuries even in moments of war or national crisis. Yet this belief overlooks the Civil War (1861-65) which, up to that time, was the most deadly war that had ever been fought. There may be other explanations for the stability and unity of the US – its geographical and strategic position, its abundance of natural resources, the availability of cheap land for immigrants, its general economic prosperity (with the exception of the Great Depression), the role of religion, the American Dream held by successive waves of immigrants, and the relative smallness and homogeneity of the ruling class. All these and other factors may better explain why change in America has been evolutionary, indeed, conservative.

THE EXECUTIVE BRANCH

- *Chief of State/Head of Government*: The President is both the chief of state and head of government. The President takes office on January 20 in every fourth odd year, as does the Vice- President.
- *Cabinet*: Members of the Cabinet are appointed by the President subject to the approval of the Senate.
- *Seat of Government*: Washington, D.C. (the District of Columbia), a federal enclave located between the states of Maryland and Virginia on the eastern seaboard. The White House, both the residence and office of the President (the Oval Office), is located there.
- *Elections*: The President and Vice-President stand for election on the same "ticket" i.e., they represent the same political party, although they are not allowed to come from the same state. Candidates are chosen by political parties several months before the election, which is held every four years (in years divisible evenly by four) on the first Tuesday after the first Monday in November.

The Presidency

"The chief magistrate derives all his authority from the people...."
Abraham Lincoln, First Inaugural Address, 1861

- *Qualifications*: Native-born American citizen, at least 35 years old, and at least 14 years a resident of the US. In fact the first 10 Presidents were not born in the US. They were eligible because they were citizens before the Constitution was ratified. The first American-born President was Martin van Buren, elected 1836. Americans like to think that, like Abraham Lincoln, anyone can rise "from log cabin to White House." In fact, unlike van Buren, few Presidents have come from poor backgrounds.
- *Chief Duty*: To protect the Constitution and enforce the laws made by Congress.
- *Term of Office*: A four-year term, limited to two terms by the 22nd Amendment (1951). The presidential term begins with the Inauguration on January 20. The ceremony is traditionally held on the steps of the US Capitol, where Congress meets. The President publicly takes an oath of office, administered by the Chief Justice of the Supreme Court. The words are prescribed in Article II of the Constitution: "I do solemnly swear (or affirm) that I will faithfully execute the office of President of the United States, and will, to the best of my ability, preserve, protect, and defend the Constitution of the United States." Then, after the band plays *Hail to the Chief!*, which is only played in greeting the President, there follows an inaugural address in which the new President outlines the policies and plans of the Administration.
- *Salary*: $400,000 per year plus $50,000 expenses allowance. By comparison with many senior

positions, the Presidential salary is relatively modest. The President and First Family are housed, transported and fed on state occasions at public expense, but they must pay for their own food for private consumption, a rule that President Reagan apparently found out about only when the first bill arrived.

Presidential powers

The office of President of the US is the most powerful in the world and the President is an icon of America. The President, the Constitution says, must "take care that the laws be faithfully executed." To carry out this responsibility, the President presides over the executive branch of the federal government. This is a vast organization numbering about 4 million people, including 1 million active-duty military personnel. In addition, the President has important legislative and judicial powers.

Executive Powers

The President has broad powers to manage national affairs and the workings of the federal government. The President can issue "executive orders", which have the force of law on federal agencies but do not require congressional approval. As commander-in-chief of the armed forces, the President may also call into federal service the state units of the National Guard. In times of war or national emergency, the Congress may grant the President even broader powers to manage the national economy and protect the security of the US.

The President nominates, subject to Senate confirmation, the heads of all executive departments and agencies, together with hundreds of other high-ranking federal officials. The Senate has on occasion rejected Presidential nominees. The large majority of federal workers, however, are selected through the Civil Service system, in which appointment and promotion are based on ability and experience.

Legislative Powers

Despite the provision that "all legislative powers" shall be vested in the Congress, the Constitution does permit the President to recommend legislation. This is done in the annual State of the Union address and other special messages. In practice, the President, as the chief formulator of public policy, has a major legislative role. Much of the legislation dealt with by Congress is drafted at the initiative of the executive branch. The President can also veto any bill passed by Congress and, unless two-thirds of the members of each House vote to override the veto, the bill does not become law. Presidents do veto bills from time to time, especially if they are passed by Congressional majorities of the other party. Presidents also occasionally threaten to veto bills and then withdraw the threat if two-thirds majorities appear to favor the legislation. A bill that has been vetoed may be reintroduced in the next session of Congress. In addition, the President, as leader of a political party and principal executive officer of the government, is in a position to influence public opinion and thereby to affect the course of legislation in Congress. To improve their working relationships with Congress, Presidents in recent years have set up a Congressional Liaison Office in the White House. Presidential aides keep abreast of all important legislative activities and try to persuade senators and representatives of both parties to support Administration policies. A President must sign or veto a bill in its entirety; line item vetoes are illegal (see *Signing Statements*).

Judicial Powers

Among the President's judicial powers is that of appointing important public officials. Presidential nomination of federal judges, including members of the Supreme Court, is subject to confirmation by the Senate. During recent elections, the possibility that a candidate would appoint Supreme Court judges who might overturn the right to abortion has been an issue and it will likely be again in future elections. Another significant power of the President is that of granting a full or conditional pardon to, or commuting the sentence of, anyone convicted of breaking a federal law - except in a case of impeachment - and to shorten prison terms and reduce fines. Presidential pardons are most often granted as the President leaves office.

Powers in Foreign Affairs

The President is the federal official primarily responsible for the relations of the US with foreign countries. The President appoints ambassadors, ministers, and consuls - subject to confirmation by the Senate - and receives foreign ambassadors and other public officials. With the Secretary of State, the President manages all official contacts with foreign governments. On occasion, the President may personally participate in summit conferences where heads of state or government meet for direct consultation. Thus, President Woodrow Wilson headed the American delegation to the Paris conference at the end of World War I; President Franklin D. Roosevelt met with Allied leaders during World War II; and every President since then has sat down with world leaders to discuss economic and political issues and to reach bilateral and multilateral agreements.

Through the Department of State, the President is responsible for the protection of Americans abroad and of foreign nationals in the US. It is the President who decides whether to recognize new nations and new governments, and who negotiates treaties with other nations, which become binding on the US when approved by two-thirds of the Senate. The President may also negotiate "executive agreements" with foreign powers that are not subject to Senate confirmation. Also the President can instruct the Justice Department to alter tariffs and quotas on imports and can thus have a major impact on international trade.

Military Powers

The President, as commander-in-chief, has supreme command and direction of the armed forces, but the right to declare war and to raise and regulate the forces remains with Congress. Congress must also approve any deployment of troops lasting more than 60 days

The Pardon Power

The power to pardon for federal crimes is granted to the President by the Constitution. The pardon power was controversial from the outset; many remembered royal abuses of the pardon power in Europe, and warned that the same would happen in the new republic. On his final day in office, however, George Washington pardoned the leaders of the Whiskey Rebellion. Many pardons since have been controversial; critics argue that pardons have been used more often for the sake of political expediency than to correct judicial error. Perhaps the most famous recent pardon was that granted by President Gerald Ford to former President Richard Nixon on September 8, 1974, for official misconduct which gave rise to the Watergate scandal. At the time, as probably now, a majority disapproved of the pardon. Other controversial uses of the pardon power include Andrew Johnson's sweeping pardons of thousands of former Confederate officials and military personnel after the Civil War, and Jimmy Carter's grant of amnesty to Vietnam-era draft evaders. While some see a legitimate use for the power to pardon in some cases, there are those who see it as being susceptible to abuse if applied inconsistently, selectively, arbitrarily, or without strict, publicly accessible guidelines.

Limits on presidential power

Because of the vast array of presidential roles and responsibilities, coupled with the conspicuous presence of the President on the national and international scene, political analysts have tended to place great emphasis on the President's powers. Some have even spoken of the "the imperial presidency."

In the first place, however, the President is limited by the Constitution. Then in practice a new President inherits a bureaucracy that can be difficult to manage and slow to change direction. The President's power to appoint officials extends only to some 3,000 people out of a civilian government workforce of about 3 million. New Presidents are immediately confronted with a backlog of decisions from the outgoing Administration. They inherit a budget formulated and enacted long before they came to office, as well as major spending programs (such as veterans' benefits, Social Security payments, and Medicare health insurance for the elderly), which are mandated by law. In foreign affairs, Presidents must conform to treaties and informal agreements negotiated by their predecessors.

Gradually also, as time goes by, Congress may become less cooperative and the media more critical. The President is forced to build at least temporary alliances among diverse, often antagonistic interests — economic, geographic, ethnic, and ideological. Compromises with Congress must often be struck if legislation is to be adopted.

Despite these constraints, every President achieves at least some legislative goals and prevents by veto the enactment of other laws. The President's authority in the conduct of war and peace, including the negotiation of treaties, is substantial. Moreover, the President has a unique opportunity to articulate ideas and advocate policies, especially through prime time television and weekly radio addresses. President Theodore Roosevelt called this aspect of the presidency "the bully pulpit", for when a President raises an issue, it inevitably becomes subject to public debate. A President's power and influence have their limits, but they are also greater than those of any other American.

Signing statements

A signing statement is a written pronouncement by the President upon the signing of a bill into law. Signing statements may be constitutional - asserting that the law is constitutionally defective, and directing executive agencies to apply the law according to the president's interpretation of the Constitution; political - defining vague terms in the law for the guidance of executive agencies; or rhetorical - using the signing of the bill to mobilize political constituencies. The first president to issue a signing statement was James Monroe. Until the 1980s signing statements were generally rhetorical and went mostly unannounced. Until Ronald Reagan became President, only 75 statements had been issued. President Reagan issued 250 signing statements, 86 of which (34%) contained objections to one or more of the statutory provisions signed into law. President George H. W. Bush issued 228, 107 of which (47%) raised objections. President Clinton issued 381 statements, only 70 of which (18%) raised constitutional or legal objections. President George W. Bush issued far fewer signing statements (161) than his immediate predecessors, but around 80% of them contained some type of challenge or objection. Hence his practice became controversial, as it was claimed by some members of Congress, by the American Bar Association and others that it was contrary to the rule of law and the separation of powers.

Nothing in the Constitution, law or legal principle explicitly permits or prohibits statements. The President is empowered (Article 1, Section 7, the Presentment Clause) to veto a law in its entirety, or to sign it, while Article 2, Section 3, requires that the Executive "take care that the laws be faithfully executed." Although signing statements do not appear to have legal force in themselves, in practice, they may give notice of the way in which the Executive intends to implement a law, which may make signing statements more significant than the text of the law itself.

The Supreme Court has not directly addressed the issue. *Chevron U.S.A., Inc. v. Natural Resources Defense Council, Inc., 467 U.S. 837 (1984)*, established that the courts should defer to executive agencies' interpretations of a law "if Congress has not directly spoken to the precise question at issue" and if the interpretation is reasonable. This appears to give the President wide authority in practice, because he directs the executive agencies. But another case, *Clinton v. City of New York (1998)* decided that a signing statement could not be used to nullify part or all of a law

In support of signing statements, it has been argued that if the President may decline to enforce a law when it unconstitutionally encroaches on his powers, then he may also announce this to Congress and the public. To the contrary, it is objected that signing statements are a tool to increase the power of the Executive improperly.

President Bush's use of signing statements was controversial, both because of the number of objections he made, and because he seemed to use them to nullify legal restrictions on his actions. They appeared to make the President the interpreter of a law's intent, instead of Congress, and the arbiter of constitutionality, instead of the courts. To the contrary it was argued that the President did have the right to judge of the constitutionality of a law in order to fulfill his sworn duty to uphold the Constitution. A second line of argument in favor of signing statements is the unitary executive theory, according to which it would be unconstitutional to require an executive agency to apply all or part of a law contrary to the President's wishes, because the executive agencies are simply the practical way in which the President performs his constitutional function and have no separate constitutional existence. More specifically, supporters of signing statements assert that any law hindering the President in his capacity as Commander-in-Chief is automatically unconstitutional. The issue shows that the relationship between the Executive and Legislative branches is dynamic and the separation of powers not clear cut. Signing statements are likely to be less of an issue when the President and Congress are of the same party. So far, both parties have allowed the democratic process to take its course rather than apply to the Supreme Court for a ruling. The Congress did not take up a bill to give it the power to enforce its own interpretation of legislation.

The personal Presidency

James M. Burns, noted presidential scholar, has categorized presidents in three ways according to how each enacts policy: *Madisonian*: The President is mainly an administrator and relies on Congress to lead in setting policy; *Hamiltonian*: He or she should be above partisanship and rely on the Constitution and public opinion for support. The President should lead in all areas and ignore Congress if necessary; *Jeffersonian*: The President should lead through his or her party, like a Prime Minister in a parliamentary system. The party, influenced and led by the President, sets policy, and the President assists the party with getting their platform enacted. Arthur Schlesinger theorized his own model of the modern presidency. Concerned about too much power centering on the President, Schlesinger coined the term *The Imperial Presidency* in his book of that name.

The Constitution says nothing about the personal presidency; it defines the office. The President has two types of power: the formal or "delegated" powers laid down by the Constitution; and inherent powers that flow from the former. For instance, as Commander-in-Chief the President can make war, while the Congress can declare war. (Actually the US has not declared war since World War II. War Resolutions have been passed after the war began.) On paper the Congress appears much more powerful than the presidency, having 17 delegated powers; the framers intended that the Congress should be more powerful, although it would take longer to reach decisions. As well, the Congress thinks nationally but often acts locally because local interests have to be satisfied in order for national legislation to pass. The Constitution balances efficiency against limited power because Americans originally, as mostly now, preferred inefficient government to a powerful one.

There had been no Executive under the Articles of Confederation, which preceded the Constitution from 1775 to 1789, because the Founders feared creating a monarchy. The President has to lead a people who dislike being led. Thus the President has to know what the people want before *they* know what they want. What the people generally want is leadership, guidance and reassurance. The President, says Arthur Sanders, must provide a vision and an agenda (*Making Sense of Politics*). In this situation, the presidency has to make up for the deficiencies of the Constitution. Theodore Roosevelt said that unless the Constitution said he could not do something, then he could, and it was a short step to saying that if he could do something, then he should. Some Presidents act as leaders, others as managers. Coolidge was a managerial President. When asked what was his greatest achievement as President, he said that he had left the office as he found it. Leaders are creative, risk-takers, entrepreneurs, change-makers. A presidency may work through "transformational leadership", in which the President and colleagues learn collectively. This was very much the case with the Kennedy Administration. Kennedy had left Harvard with a "C" but he knew his weaknesses and assembled around him a gallery of top talents. Nixon by contrast thought he could do it all and was surprised when he became unpopular. Franklin Roosevelt (FDR) ran a personal presidency and under him the role of the office expanded so much that it was necessary to create the Executive Office of the President, housed in the now famous Executive Office Building. To be a successful President today, the holder of the office must excel in several ways. He or she must be a good communicator, as Ronald Reagan and Bill Clinton were. This includes looking good and projecting a good image, in a word, *charismatic*. It also includes having a mastery of the media. FDR pioneered the weekly radio "fireside chats" that all his successors have also used. The ugly Abraham Lincoln would have failed on TV. Presidents also have to persuade Congress, since they cannot command, and to do that they have to keep their hand on the pulse of public opinion. They must also be decisive but willing to admit their mistakes. Americans, as the fall of Nixon showed, are intolerant of attempts to hide wrongdoing.

The office of President has evolved considerably since 1789 as various Presidents have confronted issues that were not envisaged by the Founders or referred to in the Constitution. Indeed, the personalities of Presidents have greatly affected their performance and have played a significant role in their success or failure. In his book *Presidential Character*, James David Barber classifies presidents from Taft to Bush according to a matrix of four factors: Active or Passive in personality; Positive or Negative about being President. The best combination according to him is Active/Positive, as in the case of FDR; the worst is Active/Negative, as in the case of Nixon, who was paranoid about people trying to undermine him. Woodrow Wilson and Lyndon Johnson also fell into that category. The thesis of Barber's book is that events define or identify the character of a President because the office is inescapably personal.

Electing the President

Only a person who is over 35 and was born in the US can run for President. For that reason, well-qualified candidates like Henry Kissinger and Arnold Schwarzenegger, Governor of California, have been ineligible. Until Senator Barack Obama, a black man (although not a descendant of slaves), was elected in 2008, only white men had become President. Previously Geraldine Ferraro had run for Vice-President on Walter Mondale's Democratic ticket in 1984 but was defeated by George H.W. Bush, who was running on Ronald Reagan's (re-election) Republican ticket. John F. Kennedy in 1960 was the first Roman Catholic President. Before that, it had been widely feared that a Catholic would put loyalty to the Pope, the head of the Catholic church, before his duty as President. Joe Biden is the first Catholic Vice-President. Since President Eisenhower (1952-1960), candidates have been well-known political figures such as governors of states or members of Congress. Eisenhower was drafted (selected) for the Republican Party's nomination because of his national popularity as leader of the US and Allied forces in Europe in World War II. The campaign song devised for him like an advertising jingle might sound childishly simple today: "I like Ike. You like Ike. Everybody likes Ike." This slogan was effective because Americans believe that a President should not only be a good leader but a sincere and honest person. Similarly, because he was so successful at giving the impression that he was a "good guy", President Clinton was widely popular despite his personal conduct. His reply to a woman's appeal for help during an election meeting, "I feel your pain" has become one of the classic sayings of American politics. By contrast, President Nixon, who contributed so much to US-China relations, for example, had problems at home with the public perception that he was dishonest, even before the Watergate scandal of 1974.

But amidst almost universal admiration for American democracy, the question remains whether the American system even these days is more of an oligarchy. What effective role does democracy play in the selection and election of leaders and legislators? How far are elections actually controlled by a small class of rich people, with the campaigning merely an entertainment for the masses? If so, how open is the oligarchy to newcomers to join? How are leaders who are born to parents who are not members of the oligarchy co-opted to it? President Eisenhower's family were poor; President Nixon's father was for a time a bus conductor; President Clinton's parents, though middle class, were not rich. Similarly President Obama's middle class family was not rich by American standards; and he is black. A link between them was that they all studied and practiced law. The Constitution, unlike in a Parliamentary system where Parliament can generally amend the constitution by legislation, is a system of principles and precedents that need to be continually reapplied to changing circumstances. Thus the link between law and politics in America is stronger than elsewhere and the practice of law is a highway to political leadership. But many other factors such as personality, wealth, party organization, trade unions, the media, background and chance are involved. But the significant proportion of well-educated lawyers among America's political leadership is striking.

The primary campaign

Presidents are elected in every fourth even year and candidates begin seeking their parties' nominations at least two years ahead. Early in election year, the parties choose their nominee through a series of primary elections (primaries) or caucuses. The timing, manner and method of these elections is not laid down by the Constitution but is left to the states. This is because the framers of the Constitution could not agree on how the states should elect to the newly-created federal government. Originally House Representatives were elected by property-owners i.e., white men. The Senate was appointed by the states until the 17th Amendment (1913).

The primaries elect delegates pledged to vote for a particular candidate at the party convention (selection conference) that summer. At caucuses, members gather and hear speeches and engage in discussion before voting for a candidate. The numbers at each local caucus can be quite small and the atmosphere relatively informal. The majority of candidates today are selected in primaries. To vote in a primary or caucus, a person must be a member of that party, although some states allow registered Independents to vote in primaries. In a Modified Open primary, voters registered to a party may only select candidates of that party, but Independents may choose candidates from either party. Party memberships are fluid and voters sometimes switch; it has even been known for voters to take part in one party's primary but vote for the other party's candidate come the election. A good start to the primaries is considered vital if a candidate is to become a party's presidential nominee, although George W Bush bucked this trend in 2000.

Since 1952 the first primary election has traditionally been in New Hampshire, which has a state law that it always be first, but in recent polls, Iowa, a Mid-Western farm state, has voted first (January 3 in 2008). This is the first real test of opinion and receives a great deal of publicity from the media. As a result a number of other states have brought their primaries forward. In particular around 20 mostly Southern states have decided to hold their primaries on the same day on what has become known as "Super Tuesday." Originally this was on March 8, 1988, but it is now usually held on the second Tuesday of March, although it was held on March 5 in 2008.

Primaries and caucuses began to be more important in 1972, when the Democratic Party mandated that henceforth its delegates be selected in caucuses or open primaries. They did so to take power away from the state chairs, mayors and political bosses who had supported President Johnson and the Vietnam War. Until then, big states like Ohio had waited until June, but some Democratic primaries have now been brought forward to February 5. Indeed, in 2008 some states, notably Michigan and Florida, broke the rules about the dates of their primaries and the parties threatened to bar all or some of their delegates from the convention. The argument of the big states was that they were more representative because they had more cities and larger and more diverse populations. In rebuttal, the small states pointed to the fact that their voters follow the campaign closely and ask the candidates smart, tough questions. In 2008 there were 14 primaries on February 5 (and seven caucuses). Many believe that holding so many primaries early does not give time to weed out those candidates who look good early but fade under pressure (Edmund Muskie 1972, Gary Hart 1984). There is little prospect for change because the in-fighting which would be entailed in negotiating it would be too great for the politicians to stomach.

Caucuses

The word "caucus" comes from the Native People of America and means "to gather together and make a great noise". A caucus is a series of party meetings at every level of party organization within a state: wards, precincts, districts and counties. At each level, party members vote for delegates who will take their opinions on the choice of presidential candidate forward to the next level. Ultimately the state conventions choose the delegates to the national convention. Caucus meetings tend to be dominated by party activists who are sufficiently committed to the party's cause to take part in each stage. Supporters of the caucus system believe that it leads to the best candidate being selected. However, meetings are closed (i.e., not opened up to anyone other than a party member) and historically they were linked to a small group of men in Congress and in state legislatures who selected party candidates for national and state office including presidential candidates. This system of electing a presidential nominee is becoming less and less popular as it puts a great deal of power in the hands of local party bosses, and the fear is that the beliefs of the people themselves at local level are not necessarily listened to. As a result of this apparent lack of democracy, fewer and fewer states are using this type of selection. In 1980, 25% of the delegates to the national conventions (coming from 18 states) were voted for in this way. The figure has continued to shrink. In 2008 the Democrats held caucuses in only 15 states plus some dependencies and Democrats Abroad, electing 15% of the delegates. The Democratic convention also included a number of *superdelegates*, party leaders and officials. Their votes proved decisive between Senator Obama and Senator Hillary Clinton.The Republicans held 17 caucuses and a few conventions, electing 18% of the delegates.

Primaries

This system allows a broader range of voters to express their views on who should represent the party at the next election. Consequently, primaries, in contrast to caucuses, tend to reduce the effect of party activists in selecting candidates for national office, and activists in primary states are often more involved in choosing candidates for local office. In some primaries, people do not even have to be party members to vote, although the Democratic Party rules state that voters must have publicly identified themselves with the party. There are a number of different types of primary.

Closed primaries offer a greater degree of participation than caucuses in that voting is not confined to party members. Those voters who have declared an affiliation to a party are allowed to participate in that party's primary. This declaration can literally be made as the voter enters the polling office with a statement that s/he voted for the party at the last election and wishes to vote in this primary.

Open primaries allow even greater participation. The voters of a state, regardless of their party affiliation, can participate in either party's primary but not both. The advantage of this system is that it allows the most popular candidate to be put forward, one who will have appeal across party lines. But the highly democratic nature of this system is open to abuse, as in the past there have been cases where supporters of one party have voted at the other party's primary, though not at their own, and have voted for the worst candidate. Yet 29 states use this system.

Blanket primaries offer the widest possible participation. Voters are allowed to vote in both primary elections of the parties i.e., at both the Republican and Democrat primaries.

States vary in the way they allocate primary delegates to the presidential candidates. Some primaries use the "winner-take-all" system (WTA) whereby the candidate who wins the most votes statewide at a primary gets all of the delegates. The alternative system is the proportional representation primary (PR) which allocates delegates in proportion to the number of votes they received. The Democrats have used PR since 1969 in an effort to increase the voice of minority groups and to broaden the appeal of candidates. However in recent years the party has used WTA in larger primaries, and some of the larger states favor such a system as they feel that WTA increases their power over the nomination. The Republicans in California have a unique and complex way of allocating the delegates, in order to ensure a balanced representation for the various parts of that large and widely divergent state.

Some primaries are called *advisory primaries*, as the elected delegates to the national convention do not have to follow the views of the voters and are free to follow their own preference for presidential candidate. However, the voters have expressed their advice - hence the title - on the ballot paper. Other primaries are called *mandatory primaries* or *binding primaries,* as the views of the voters with regard to the presidential candidate are binding and the delegates at the national convention cast their votes accordingly. However, this was successfully challenged in 1981 when the Supreme Court declared in *Democratic Party v La Follette* that a state could not force a delegate to a national convention to support the winner of his/her state's presidential primary. Nowadays the conventions are largely symbolic and serve as the media launch of each campaign.

The primaries timetable is negotiated between states, as primaries are valuable publicity opportunities for small states. Candidates fight hard in the early primaries to get voter recognition and build a momentum, a bandwagon effect, that makes them seem unbeatable and makes their opponents and their supporters, especially their financial backers, give up. As the races take place, it becomes clear which candidate is the strongest. The platform of policies that candidates will advocate in their campaigns is decided at the conventions.

Since 1976 there has been a strong trend to move the primaries to the early part of the year ("front-loading") and the trend shows no signs of abating. Yet almost everyone including academics, newspaper editorialists and most candidates is opposed to it. The general argument against front-loading claims that the real losers under the new calendar are not the candidates but the electorate. Front-loading reduces the time between nomination events and increases the number of multi-event days. As major states move their primaries to early February to maximize their influence, the voters are subjected to a barrage of 30-second TV and radio advertising spots and fleeting glimpses on the news of the candidates' motorcades as they race to the nearest airport in what are known as "tarmac campaigns." (*Tarmac* refers to the airport runways.) This type of campaign is arguably ill equipped to inform voters about what the candidates stand for. Voters receive their information from the media advertisements and have little time to process the news about one event before the next occurs. Many candidates will be eliminated from the field before voters have time to learn about them.

The absence of substantive information about the candidates has two potential consequences. The first is that voters may be unable to express their interests through their vote, instead casting ballots on the basis of non-political considerations, such as the candidate's appearance or what the voter thought of the candidate's advertising. This prospect is far from the democratic ideal. The second consequence of a campaign that fails to inform the primary electorate is that disparities in voter knowledge across candidates may be exacerbated. A non-informative campaign probably did not hurt well-known candidates like Rudy Giuliani or Hillary Clinton in 2008 because voters would already have learned a lot about him or her. But such a campaign also makes it impossible for lesser-known candidates to spread their messages, leaving them at a distinct disadvantage. Voters are likely to cast their ballots for the candidate with whom they are familiar, regardless of whether that candidate's policy proposals best match their political predispositions. Such a shortened, crowded primary schedule gives a huge advantage to those who can raise the most money, have high name recognition or are the preferred choice of party insiders. Should candidates for the most powerful office on Earth be chosen in a few chaotic weeks, critics ask?

Scholars commonly speak of the "nomination campaign", and they often treat it as one national campaign. But in truth the primary calendar is composed of a series of separate, though not completely independent, campaigns. Indeed, the Republican primary in California is more like 53 separate District campaigns because of the way the party's delegates are chosen. Yet the implication of front-loading is that primary races may effectively be over before mid-March, suggesting that nominees now are chosen on the basis of non-political factors. In the 2008 Democratic primary season, however, the contest between Senator Obama and Senator Clinton went on until mid-June. Those who object to front-loading assume that in the traditional primary season, where the primaries were more drawn-out, the candidates would head to Ohio, for example, introduce themselves to the voters there, and Ohioans would be just as informed about them at the time they voted as New Hampshire voters at the time they voted weeks earlier. The evidence, though, does not support the belief that voters were better informed in former times than they are today.

Front-loading may not have reduced the amount of time candidates have to campaign (and the amount of time voters have to process the messages they receive). A detailed study by Travis N. Ridout of the University of Wisconsin of four elections between 1976 and 2000 concludes that the alleged negative effects of front-loading are not borne out by analysis of the available data.

Third parties

Although candidates are usually nominated by the Democrats or Republicans, there are a few "third parties" such as the Green Party, the Libertarian Party and the Communist Party. Their candidates only attract about 2% of the vote, if that. It is also possible to run as an individual with an *ad hoc* campaign team as Lyndon H. LaRouche and Harold Stassen did in the past. In 2000 Ralph Nader, the consumer rights champion, did so, as did Pat Buchanan, TV journalist, author and former speechwriter for President Nixon, who ran on an anti-immigration platform. Such candidates can either organize petitions in each state to get their names put on the ballot, or run write-in campaigns, asking voters to write their names on the ballot paper. Write-in votes are sometimes used to register a protest by writing ridiculous names on the ballot paper. Third party candidates have been unsuccessful in modern times for three main reasons: they lack resources, the other parties steal their issues, and voters think they cannot win and a vote for a third party is wasted. Even so Ross Perot polled around 20% in 1992 when Americans were frustrated with the gridlock in Washington politics. Currently another factor working against third party candidates is what political scientist John Kenneth White calls the "values divide". This, even more than economics ("pocketbook issues") is polarizing voters into two camps.

The Presidential campaign

Presidential candidates spend hundreds of millions of dollars on campaigning, mostly on TV, newspaper and poster advertising. It is estimated that the two parties together spent $1 billion on the 2008 election. In recent elections, the candidate with the biggest campaign "war chest" (funds) was the winner. The money is raised by the parties at fundraising events, through appeals and increasingly by candidates themselves over the internet. Even billionaire Independent, Ross Perot, was not successful, nor did wealthy Steve Forbes, proprietor of *Forbes* magazine, win the Republican nomination in 2000, and nor did multi-millionaire Mitt Romney win the Republican nomination in 2008. There is also Federal funding available in equal amounts for both parties, but if a party receives Federal funding it cannot accept money from other sources. In practice, the parties raise so much money themselves that they can forgo Federal funding and thus evade the effective cap on spending that a Federally-funded election would impose.

Party loyalties, party organization, personality and tradition are key factors in elections as well as money. Candidates criss-cross the country holding rallies, making speeches and meeting voters ("pressing the flesh.") Even so, there have been complaints that election campaigns are just a circus lacking any real interaction between candidates and voters. This is a particular grievance of many smaller states (the "fly over" states). But the Electoral College system puts a premium on the 16 larger "must win" states such as California, New York, Texas and Florida. In some New England states the old tradition of town meetings has been revived for candidates to get into closer contact with voters. A popular candidate may make speeches in favor of candidates from the same party seeking lower offices so that they can benefit from the *coattail effect*. In the last few weeks of the campaign, staff, who are often volunteers, man banks of phones, and actually go to voters' homes to ask them to vote. These Get Out the Vote drives have become extremely sophisticated. The parties do market research and target voters with the demographic characteristics which seem most favorable to them. They do this because Americans are only interested in one or two issues at any one time, and because modern computer databases make profiling and targeting possible. Also, the parties need to tailor their messages because at least one-third of the voters are not registered with either party but are Independents. Karl Rove, the campaign strategist for President Bush, is acknowledged as the pioneer of this technique. According to pollster John Zogby, the characteristic which best predicts voting behavior is whether or not the voter goes to church.

American Presidential elections are the longest in the world. Effectively they start the day after the previous election and hence last four years. They are dominated by media coverage, primarily television, and by the results of polls, principally those of the Roper, Harris and Gallup organizations. The intensive use of TV and other media for advertising makes American elections enormously expensive, and fund raising is perhaps even more important for the candidates than the campaigning itself, since the candidate with more money, and hence more advertising, tends to win. Does this mean that American Presidential elections are bought, and hence rigged by special interests? Many Americans suspect so. Fortunately the competitive nature of the political system, freedom of information, and freedom of media comment counterbalance the effects of advertising to some extent, but many Americans are worried about the health of their electoral system, and question whether it discourages good candidates from running. In any case, since the President cannot guarantee that Congress will pass any particular piece of legislation, money tends to buy access and the opportunity to influence rather than directly affect the process of government. Another effect of the predominance of television is that the voters' choices are made much more on the perceived personalities of the candidates and their positions on particular issues, not only economic management such as taxes but also on cultural "hot button" issues such as gun control, abortion and immigration. Thus personal and single-issue factors overshadow the party policy platforms voted on at the nominating conventions, although it is those that the party's representatives will pursue in Congress. Because the voters' personal preferences are diverse and changeable, the role of television has been to make election campaigns more volatile and the statements of the candidates more bland, as they seek not to offend Independents while reassuring their base. It is Independents, typically aged 18 – 26 and socially more liberal, who decide elections. A third major effect of television campaigning has been to make candidates the mouthpieces of their handlers – speech writers, media consultants, psephologists, consultants - rather than independently-operating public servants. Even the televised "debates" (three presidential and one vice-presidential) are scripted and rehearsed; the questions, format and studio presentation are negotiated between the candidates' teams and the television station in advance. The debates have little influence. They tend to confirm what the viewers already think rather than change their minds.

The election takes place on the Tuesday following the first Monday in November. This date was fixed around 1800 when most people lived in the country and there was little work to do on the farms in November and the weather was good enough to travel to a town or city to vote. Even today, because many Americans are disinclined to vote, the weather can have an impact on turnout. The Democrats tend to benefit from good weather and higher turnout, the Republicans from the reverse.

After the election the President-elect goes to Washington to take the oath of office and give the Inaugural Address setting out the key themes for his or her administration. Then follows a parade along Pennsylvania Avenue, the road that connects the White House and the Capitol and passes the FBI, Federal Trade Commission, Commerce Department and the Treasury. In the evening the Inaugural Ball takes place at the White House. Some weeks before the Inauguration, if the President-elect is new to office, transition teams are appointed by the President-elect and the outgoing President to ensure an orderly handover of power. Between the election and Inauguration an outgoing President has little power and is called a *lame duck*.

Voting

Under the Voting Rights Act (1965), all Americans over the age of 18 who have been resident in the US for one year have the right to vote without the need for property qualifications or to pass a literacy test. Previously some Southern states such as Mississippi had imposed a poll tax as a qualification, while Alabama had imposed a literacy test on blacks which had unreasonable questions. Even so only about half of Americans vote in Presidential elections, even fewer in other elections.

A few weeks before the poll, voters receive a card telling the address of the polling station where they should go to vote, usually a school or church hall. Voting is voluntary. People who will be away on election day or who are ill may use an absentee ballot and post it to officials. Polling stations are open from early morning until night. Voters first have to sign their name in a book that lists all the voters in that precinct (small local area). Voters usually vote in a voting booth that has three sides with a curtain that closes the entrance. In the booth are lists of candidates for each office. Voters pull down a metal lever beside the name of the person they want to vote for. The levers operate mechanical counters that record the number of votes for each candidate. It is possible to vote for all the candidates from one party, and this is called *voting a straight ticket*, But many voters choose candidates from both parties, for example, one for national and one for local office, and vote a *split ticket*.

Sometimes there are complaints that there are not enough staff on duty at the polling stations and voters have to wait in line for hours to cast their vote. In Florida and elsewhere too there have also been complaints about inefficient voting machines. It took weeks and numerous court hearings to determine the result in Florida in 2000 and hence confirm the outcome of the national election. Generally, however, the voting goes smoothly and complaints are few. One reason is that in such big electorates, the numbers are so large that even small percentage differences in popularity between candidates yield clear cut results with numerical majorities too large to be affected by problems at individual polling stations. The Help America Vote Act 2002 provided funds for states to buy or lease new voting machines. These are optical scan or direct recording electronic technology (touch screen), replacing the gear-and-lever and *Votomatic* punch card machines which have been used since around 1960. Better communication with voters, especially posters and signage, have been introduced through the *Design for Democracy* project. Optically read paper ballots have also been introduced in about one-third of voting districts. Voters can mark their ballots at home and drop them off at designated points. Since 2000 all voting in Oregon has been conducted by mail.

Journalists and pollsters are allowed to ask people how they voted and these exit polls help predict election results. However, the results of exit polls may not be announced until polling stations have closed everywhere in case they influence the results. In the past, Western states such as California complained that news of results in Eastern states hours earlier had discouraged Western voters from going to the polls.

The percentage of people voting has been declining since the 1960s and is a matter of concern, but no effective remedy has yet been found. One of the reasons is that people have to re-register to vote when they move to another state, which happens quite often in America's mobile society. A solution that has been effective in some areas is voter registration drives, where supporters of one of the parties or of a candidate call people and offer to help them register. In some places voter registration forms are available in locations such as fast food restaurants. In general, though, Americans tend to believe that voting is only one means of exerting political influence. Besides there is currently a climate of disillusion, even cynicism, about the political process. The turnout of 56.8% in 2008 was the highest since 1968.

The Electoral College

The President and Vice-President are actually chosen by the Electoral College, a method peculiar to the American system created by the 12th Amendment to the Constitution in 1804 after the House of Representatives had had to act to resolve a tie between Thomas Jefferson and Aaron Burr in 1800. The Electoral College at present comprises 538 representatives who are elected from each state and the District of Columbia. The electors in each state are equal in number to the number of senators and representatives that state has in Congress. Thus, although the people vote for the candidates by name, they are actually voting for representatives in the Electoral College. The Electoral College never meets as a body. Instead, the electors in each state gather in their state capital on the first Monday after the second Wednesday in December and cast their votes for the candidate with the largest number of popular votes in their state. (In theory, they could vote for someone else, but this has never happened. In practice, each party has a slate of electors who, if their party's candidate is elected, cast their state's votes for him/her.) Maine and Nebraska award two electoral votes to the statewide winner and one electoral vote to the winner of each Congressional district. Neither state had split electoral votes between candidates as a result of this system in modern elections until 2008, when Barack Obama received one electoral vote by winning Nebraska's 2nd congressional district. The Secretary of State transmits the results to Washington, where they are formally recorded in a ceremony in the Senate presided over by the Vice-President. In theory, the legislature of each state determines who the electors should be. This might have been put into practice by the Florida legislature in 2000 when the state Republican leadership made it clear that if the disputed procedures for recounting the votes in some counties resulted in a statewide majority for the Democratic candidate, Al Gore, the legislature, where they had a majority, would nevertheless elect Republican electors to the Electoral College and thus determine the outcome of the Presidential election. In the event, the Republican candidate, George W. Bush, was declared the winner of the popular vote by 537 votes (a tiny margin in American elections) and a potential constitutional crisis was thereby avoided.

To be successful, a candidate for the presidency must receive 270 electoral votes. The Constitution stipulates that if no candidate has a majority, the decision shall be made by the House of Representatives, with all members from a state voting as a unit. In this event, each state and the District of Columbia would be allotted one vote only. Thus the large states would lose their numerical advantage. The procedure has only been used once, in 1824, when although Andrew Jackson had the most votes, but not a majority, in the Electoral College, the House of Representatives elected John Quincy Adams. In the 2000 election, because of the dispute over the result in Florida, there was speculation that it might have to be "thrown to the House."

From time to time, a President elected in the Electoral College has won only a minority of the popular vote: John Quincy Adams 1824, Abraham Lincoln 1860, Rutherford B. Hayes 1876, Benjamin Harrison 1888, Woodrow Wilson 1912, Harry S. Truman 1948, George W. Bush 2000. In the 2000 election, the Democrat candidate, Al Gore, won the national popular vote by a margin of half a million. But the Republican, George W. Bush, won more Electors through the 25 Electors of the state of Florida, where the result was contested for weeks of court hearings, owing to confusion over which ballot papers should be counted as valid.

The electoral college system makes the large states such as California, Texas and New York very important while allowing reasonable representation to the small states, thus ensuring national unity. Abolishing the Electoral College and determining the Presidential election according to the popular vote in each state, or nationally, has been suggested but rejected, since it would give the Republican Party an advantage. Supporters of the Democratic Party point out that, since every state has two Senators, the 7% of the population that live in the 17 least populous states has effective control of 34 Senate seats, and also have numerically disproportionate influence in the Electoral College, even though the US has not been a predominantly rural country for over a century. California, the biggest state, with a population of 36 million, commands 55 electoral votes. The 12 inland states of the Great Plains and the West have 23 million people but 59 electoral votes. But the opposition of the small states to reform of this part of the Constitution, and their power to block it, since three-quarters of the states must approve a constitutional amendment, means that it is not a serious issue. The small states fear that they would lose influence if the election were decided purely by a mass national vote where they would be in the minority. As it is, the system makes both parties pay attention to the rural Mid-Western and Southern states, particularly the Democrats, who draw most of their support from the cities. Almost always, though, the Electoral College is a formality.

The Vice-President

The Constitution provides for the election of a Vice-President, who succeeds to the presidency in case of the death, resignation, or incapacitation of the President (25th Amendment, 1967). A Vice-President who serves as Acting President for more than two years can only be elected once (22nd Amendment, 1951). The Constitution does not delegate any specific executive powers to the Vice-President, who takes the oath of office immediately after the President at the Inauguration Day ceremony and serves concurrently with the President. In addition to holding the right of succession, the Vice-President is the Presiding Officer of the Senate, where the Vice-President has no vote, except in the case of a tie. When the Vice-President is absent, the Senate elects a President pro tempore. Since World War II, Vice-Presidents have become working figures. They have received assignments to deal with such problems as race relations, the space program, and unemployment. The Vice-President is also a member of the National Security Council. Richard Nixon was the first Vice-President to travel abroad extensively on diplomatic missions. Vice-Presidents have also become partisan defenders of their Presidents' policies. Vice-President Al Gore perhaps worked more closely with his President, Bill Clinton, than any previous Vice-President and played a prominent role diplomatically (especially with Russia) and in reform of the bureaucracy.

The President is empowered to name a Vice-President, with congressional approval, when the second office is vacated. This procedure was used for the first time in 1973, when Representative Gerald R. Ford was named by President Nixon upon the resignation of Spiro T. Agnew. Subsequently, when President Nixon resigned in 1974, Ford became President and Nelson T. Rockefeller, former Governor of New York State, Vice-President, without either of them having been elected to their office by the people.

The Constitution gives Congress the power to establish the order of succession after the Vice-President. At present, should both the President and Vice-President vacate their offices, the Speaker of the House of Representatives would assume the Presidency. Next comes the President pro tempore of the Senate, and then cabinet officers in order of the date of creation of their office.

The Executive Departments

Although the Constitution gives no specific powers to federal officials, day-to-day administration and enforcement of federal laws is in the hands of the various executive departments created by Congress. In addition to the Departments, there are a number of staff organizations grouped into the Executive Office of the President.

The Cabinet

The Constitution makes no provision for a presidential cabinet, which nowadays consists of the 15 heads of the federal Departments. The Constitution simply provides that the President may ask opinions, in writing, from the principal officer in each of the executive departments on any subject in their area of responsibility, but the President is not bound to accept this advice. Similarly, there are no specific constitutional qualifications for service in the cabinet. The cabinet developed outside the Constitution as a matter of practical necessity. Cabinets are what any particular President makes them. Cabinet members are, however, responsible for directing the activities of the government in specific areas and meet regularly with the President. Each Department has thousands of employees, with offices throughout the country as well as in Washington. The Departments are divided into divisions, bureaus, offices, and services.

The President also asks advice from the National Security Council and the Council of Economic Advisers, which consists of three advisers appointed by the President and a staff of economists, mostly academics on secondment from their universities.

Unlike in a Parliamentary system, members of the Cabinet are not members of Congress, in order to safeguard the separation of powers between the executive and legislative branches of government. While this ensures the President a wide choice of officials, it does not ensure that the Congress is free of the effects of Presidential political patronage. Indeed such patronage in the form of financial and other help for local projects supported by members of Congress is often negotiated in order to pass legislation desired by the President.

Most of the people working in departments and agencies are career officials. A number of top appointments, however, are made under the "spoils system", by which an incoming Administration gives certain jobs to party supporters. This can mean a high turnover of top officials, but sometimes a President will make a "holdover" appointment i.e., reappoint a trusted, experienced official from a previous Administration. A long-serving holdover was Alan Greenspan, who was Chairman of the Federal Reserve from 1987- 2006. Heads of departments are called *Secretaries*. The head of the State Department is called the Secretary of State. Well-known Secretaries of State have include Henry Kissinger and Madeleine Albright.

The Independent Agencies
The Executive Departments are the major operating units of the federal government, but many other agencies have important responsibilities for keeping the government and the economy working smoothly. These are often called independent agencies, since they are not part of the Executive Departments.

The nature and purpose of these agencies vary widely. Some are regulatory groups with powers to supervise certain sectors of the economy. Others provide special services either to the government or to the people. In most cases, the agencies have been created by Congress to deal with matters that have become too complex for the scope of ordinary legislation. In 1970, for example, Congress established the Environmental Protection Agency to coordinate governmental action to protect the environment.

THE LEGISLATIVE BRANCH

The legislative branch is known as the *Congress*. The Congress is bicameral i.e., of two chambers. Both meet in the Capitol Building at the opposite end of Pennsylvania Avenue from the White House. In contrast to the British Parliament, where the government and opposition face each other on opposite sides, the members sit in party blocs around a semicircle. The upper chamber is the Senate. It has 100 seats, one-third of which are renewed every two even years. Two members are elected from each state by popular vote (17th Amendment, 1913). Since each state has two Senators, and the inland states have a much lower population than the seaboard ones, they are disproportionately represented. The 12 inland states have 24 Senators for a population of only 23 million out of a total US population of over 300 million. A Senator must have been a US citizen for at least nine years. Senators serve six-year terms to guarantee their independence from short-term political pressures. The lower House is the House of Representatives. It has 435 seats. Members are directly elected by popular vote to serve two-year terms. The number of members per state depends on the population. The population of the average Congressional district is 646,952. It is theoretically possible for the House to be composed entirely of legislative novices. In practice, however, most members are reelected several times, and the House, like the Senate, can always count on a core group of experienced legislators. Critics assert that the system makes it too difficult to remove incumbents.

Regular elections and equal districts are considered key principles. When Locke discussed meetings of the legislature in Chapter 13 of his *Second Treatise,* he did not prescribe the workings of the legislature but described what he considered to be best practice, and discussed the advantages and disadvantages of having either regular elections or of calling the legislature when the public good required it. He was just as concerned about a legislature that was too active as about a President who neglected to summon it when necessary. He was clear, however, on two points. First, the legislature was independent of the executive and retained an independent right to meet and act; and second that the people retained ultimate authority. "...the legislative being only a fiduciary power to act for certain ends, there remains still in the people a supreme power to remove or alter the legislative...." (II:13:149)

Functions and powers

The chief function of Congress is the making of laws. The Congress has proved to be exceedingly active, with broad powers and authority in all matters of national concern. While the balance of power vis-à-vis the executive branch has waxed and waned at different periods, the Congress has never been a rubber stamp for presidential decisions. To balance power between the large and small states, the Constitution's framers agreed that states would be represented equally in the Senate and in proportion to their populations in the House. Members of Congress are expected to act in the interests of their state rather than their party, and their constituents, well informed about the voting record and legislative activity of their members of Congress, will call them to account otherwise. Critics point out, however, that voters may tend to forget the voting record of Senators because of the six-year Senate term. Members of Congress also help individual constituents in their dealings with government agencies, which they do through staffers called "constituent aides".

Members of Congress

The Constitution requires that US Senators be at least 30 years of age, have been citizens of the US for at least nine years, and be residents of the states from which they are elected. Members of the House of Representatives (Congressmen or Congresswomen) must be at least 25, citizens for seven years, and residents of the states from which they are elected. Regardless of its population, every state is constitutionally guaranteed at least one member of the House. At present, six states - Alaska, Montana, North Dakota, South Dakota, Vermont, and Wyoming - have only one representative. On the other hand, six states have more than 20 representatives - California alone has 52. Large states are divided into Districts, each of which has one Representative. Apportionment is revised every 10 years in line with the Census.

Powers of the House and Senate

Each House of Congress has the power to introduce legislation on any subject except raising revenue, which must originate in the House of Representatives. Voting "appropriations" (funding of government programs and the salaries of government officials) is one of the most important powers of the House. In 1994 and again in 1995 the Republican majority in the House shut down all or part of the government for several weeks at the end of the year as part of a struggle with Democratic President Bill Clinton over the budget. Because the large states have more Representatives, they may appear to have more influence over the public purse than the small states. The Senate, however, was created to protect the rights of individual states and safeguard minority opinion in a system of government designed to give greater power to the national government.

In practice, each House can vote against legislation passed by the other House. The Senate may disapprove any House bill or add amendments that change its nature. In that event, a conference committee made up of members from both Houses must work out a compromise before the bill becomes law.

The Senate also has certain powers especially reserved to that body, including the authority to confirm presidential appointments of ambassadors, judges and other high officials, hold impeachment trials, and ratify treaties by a two-thirds vote. The Senate has rejected approximately twenty percent of those nominated to the Supreme Court. Of the thousands of treaties submitted, the Senate has turned down fewer than two dozen, but it routinely influences treaty negotiations with threats of modification through the addition of various amendments, reservations, or understandings. The reason for the two-thirds vote is to prevent groups of states combining for commercial or economic gain.

In the case of impeachment of federal officials, the House of Representatives has the sole right to bring charges of misconduct that can lead to an impeachment trial. The Senate has the sole power to try impeachment cases and to find officials guilty or not guilty. A finding of guilt results in the removal of the official from public office. Impeachment has resulted in only eight guilty findings, all of federal district judges.

The 10th Amendment sets definite limits on congressional authority. Powers not delegated to the federal government are reserved to the states or to the people. In addition, the Constitution specifically forbids certain acts by Congress.

Congress may not:
- Suspend the writ of habeas corpus — a requirement that those accused of crimes be brought before a judge or court before being imprisoned. (This does not apply to foreign nationals sususpected of terrorism.)
- Pass laws that condemn persons for crimes or unlawful acts without a trial.
- Pass any law that retroactively makes a specific act a crime.
- Levy direct taxes on citizens, except on the basis of a census already taken.
- Tax exports from any one state.
- Give specially favorable treatment in commerce or taxation to the seaports of any state or to the vessels using them.
- Authorize any titles of nobility.

Officers of the Congress
At the beginning of each new Congress, members of the political parties select floor leaders and other officials to manage the flow of proposed legislation. These officials, along with the Speaker of the House and President pro tempore of the Senate and committee chairpersons, exercise strong influence over the making of laws. The Speaker of the House is responsible for maintaining order, naming members to committees and referring bills to committees. The Speaker and President pro tempore are always members of the majority party. It has often happened that the majority party in one or both Houses is different from that of the President and Vice-President. In that case, there are often protracted negotiations, and sometimes outright deadlock, between the two branches of government. This happened a lot during the Presidency of Bill Clinton. When important votes are likely to be close the Vice-President presides in the Senate, ready to give a casting vote.

The legislative process

Lawmaking is initiated by the introduction of a proposal in either House in one of two main forms: the bill or the joint resolution. These may be introduced by the President, or by members of Congress, perhaps after lobbying by a special interest group. The framers intentionally made the legislative process long and complicated so that only those proposals that commanded wide support became law.

Bills

A bill is the form used for most legislation. A bill must be introduced by a member of the House concerned called a *sponsor*. The more sponsors a bill has, and the more important and influential they are, the greater chance a bill has of passing. A bill is commonly known by the names of its sponsors. An identical bill may be started in both Houses. In that case, the name of its Senate sponsor comes first. The title of a bill originating in the House of Representatives is followed by the letters "H.R.", and a number that it retains throughout all its parliamentary stages. The titles of bills originating in the Senate are followed by "S" and a number. Bills are presented to the President for action when approved in identical form by both the House of Representatives and the Senate.

Joint Resolutions

Joint resolutions may originate either in the House or the Senate. There is little practical difference between a bill and a joint resolution. Both are subject to the same procedure, although joint resolutions require a two-thirds majority in both the House and the Senate. On approval, a Joint Resolution is sent directly to the Administrator of General Services for submission to the individual states for ratification. It becomes law when three-quarters of the states have ratified it, and does not need the President's signature. A joint resolution originating in the House of Representatives is designated "H. J. Res." followed by its individual number. One originating in the Senate is designated "S. J. Res."

"Sense of" resolutions

One or both Houses of Congress may formally express opinions about subjects of current national interest through freestanding simple or concurrent resolutions (known as "sense of the House", "sense of the Senate", or "sense of the Congress" resolutions) or by floor or committee amendment to a bill. "Sense of" resolutions and amendments are mostly focused on foreign policy matters. Although "sense of" proposals have no force in law, foreign governments pay close attention to them as evidence of shifts in US foreign policy priorities. "Sense of" Resolutions passed by one House are known as H. Res. or S. Res. Those passed by both are known as "H. Con. Res." or "S. Con. Res.", depending where the Resolution originated.

Committees

One of the chief characteristics of the Congress is the dominant role committees have come to play in its proceedings, although the Constitution does not provide for them. At present the Senate has 17 standing (or permanent) committees, the House of Representatives 19. There are four joint standing committees and many sub-committees. Each committee specializes in specific areas of legislation. Almost every bill introduced in either House is referred to a committee for study and recommendation. The committee may approve, revise, kill, or ignore any measure referred to it. Without first winning committee approval, it is nearly impossible for a bill to reach the House or Senate floor. The majority party in each House controls the committee process. Committee chairpersons are selected by a caucus of party members or specially designated groups of members. The minority party is proportionally represented on the committees according to its strength in each House.

Bills are introduced by a variety of methods. Some are drawn up by standing committees; some by special committees created to deal with specific legislative issues; and some may be suggested by the President or other executive officers. Citizens and organizations outside the Congress may suggest legislation to members, and individual members themselves may initiate bills. After introduction, bills are sent to designated committees that, in most cases, schedule a series of public hearings to permit presentation of views by persons who support or oppose the legislation. The hearings, which can last several weeks or months, open the legislative process to public participation. Transcripts are usually published. Another virtue of the committee system is that it permits members of Congress and their staffs to amass a considerable degree of expertise in various legislative fields.

When a committee has acted favorably on a bill, the proposed legislation is sent to the floor for open debate. In the Senate, the rules permit virtually unlimited debate. In the House, because of the large number of members, the Rules Committee usually sets limits. When debate is ended, members vote either to approve the bill, defeat it, table it — which means setting it aside and is tantamount to defeat — or return it to committee. It is quite common for bills to die in committee. Voting on bills may be by a voice vote, when each member says "aye" or "no", or by a recorded vote when an electronic system records how each member votes. The voting records of members of Congress are vital pieces of information for the political process.

A bill passed by one House is sent to the other for action. If the bill is amended by the second House, a conference committee composed of members of both Houses attempts to reconcile the differences; and if they do, the legislation must be voted on again by both Houses. At every stage, lobbyists try to have the bill changed to favor their interest, and the bill may be extensively discussed in the media with consequent effects on public opinion. Sponsors may either accept some changes to make a bill more acceptable or may offer to support other members' bills in return for support. The Houses sometimes become deadlocked over a bill, which may be delayed for many months or die altogether, in which case it may be reintroduced later.

Once passed by both Houses, the bill is sent to the President, for constitutionally the President must act on a bill for it to become law. The President has the option of signing the bill - by which it becomes law - or vetoing it and sending it back to Congress. A bill vetoed by the President must be re-approved by a two-thirds vote of both Houses to become law.

The President may also simply refuse to sign a bill. In that case, the bill becomes law without signature 10 days afterwards (not counting Sundays). The single exception to this rule is when Congress adjourns after sending a bill to the President and before the 10-day period has expired; the President's refusal to take any action then negates the bill — a process known as the "pocket veto." When this has occurred in recent years, the impasse has been resolved by negotiation. A President typically vetoes several bills each term. George W. Bush, however, vetoed no bills until well into his second term. Historically, Congress has overridden fewer than ten percent of all presidential vetoes. A law may be amended or repealed by the same process as it became law.

Congressional investigations

Investigation has proved to be one of the most effective techniques that Congress has to influence the executive branch. Congressional oversight prevents waste and fraud; protects civil liberties and individual rights; ensures executive compliance with the law; gathers information for making laws and educating the public; tests the effectiveness of laws already passed; evaluates the qualifications and performance of members and officials of the other branches; inquires into issues of public concern and, on rare occasions, lays the groundwork for impeachment. Congressional oversight applies to cabinet departments, executive agencies, regulatory commissions, and the presidency. This power is usually delegated to committees or agencies such as the Congressional Budget Office, the Government Accountability Office, and the Office of Technology Assessment.

Frequently, committees call on outside experts to assist in conducting investigative hearings and to make detailed studies of issues. Most committee hearings are open to the public and are widely reported in the mass media. Congressional investigations thus represent one important tool available to lawmakers to inform the citizenry and arouse public interest in national issues.

The oversight power of Congress has helped to force officials out of office, change policies, and provide new statutory controls over the executive. The Senate Foreign Relations Committee's televised hearings in the late 1960s helped to mobilize opposition to the Vietnam War. Congress's 1973 Watergate investigation exposed White House officials who illegally used their positions for political advantage, and the House Judiciary Committee's impeachment proceedings against President Nixon the following year ended his presidency. In 1987, oversight efforts disclosed statutory violations in the executive branch's secret arms sales to Iran and the diversion of arms profits to anti-government forces in Nicaragua, known as the "Contras". Congressional findings resulted in legislation to prevent similar occurrences. More recent hearings have investigated campaign finance in the 1990s, and the energy industry in the early 21st century.

Legislative behavior

In contrast to parliamentary systems, the selection and behavior of US legislators has little to do with central party discipline. Each of the two major American political parties is a coalition of local and state organizations that join together as a national party during the presidential elections. Thus the members of Congress owe their positions to their local or state electorate, not to the national party leadership nor to their congressional colleagues. As a result, the legislative behavior of representatives and senators tends to be individualistic and idiosyncratic, reflecting the great variety of electorates represented and the freedom that comes from having built a loyal personal constituency. In recent years, especially among the Republicans, there has been more Congressional caucus discipline. Even so, the legislative process often involves personal negotiations between executive branch officials and even the President and individual lawmakers. Conversely, lawmakers may try to trade their cooperation for deals that favor their constituency, a process disparagingly known as "pork barrel" politics. Senator Joe Lieberman (Independent Democrat) has claimed that the public sees the Congress as the puppet of special interests. He has said polls showed that 72 percent of Americans believe that the federal government wastes "a great deal". Federal spending will continue to be a key issue in public debate, with Democrats contending that the government does not do enough to level the playing field for those who are dislocated by economic disruption, and Republicans complaining that the Congress is too ready to vote for spending without ensuring that the government has the means to pay for it.

Congress being a collegial and not a hierarchical body, power does not flow from the top down, as in a corporation, but in practically every direction. There is only minimal centralized authority, since the power to punish or reward is slight. An increasingly important reward is the participation of a popular President in raising funds for the reelection campaign of a favored lawmaker. Congressional policies are made by shifting coalitions that may vary from issue to issue. Sometimes, where there are conflicting pressures - from the White House and from important economic or ethnic groups - legislators will use the rules of procedure to delay a decision so as to avoid alienating an influential sector. A matter may be postponed on the grounds that the relevant committee held insufficient public hearings. Or Congress may direct an agency to prepare a detailed report before an issue is considered. Or a measure may be put aside ("tabled") by either House, thus effectively defeating it without rendering a judgment on its substance.

There are informal or unwritten norms of behavior that often determine the assignments and influence of a particular member. "Insiders", representatives and senators who concentrate on their legislative duties, may be more powerful within the halls of Congress than "outsiders", who gain recognition by speaking out on national issues. Members are expected to show courtesy toward their colleagues and to avoid personal attacks, no matter how unpalatable their opponents' policies may be. Members are also expected to specialize in a few policy areas rather than claim expertise in the whole range of legislative concerns. Those who conform to these informal rules are more likely to be appointed to committees that affect the interests of a significant portion of their constituents.

Filibuster

A filibuster, or "talking out a bill," is an attempt to extend debate indefinitely in order to delay the progress of, or completely prevent a vote on a proposal. Sometimes a filibuster is threatened precisely in order to provoke a motion to close a debate. The filibuster is permitted only in the Senate. The filibuster was used in the House until 1842 when rules restricting debate were adopted.

The term first came into use in the Senate, where the rules permit a Senator, or a series of Senators, to speak for as long as they wish and on any topic they choose. The word "filibuster" was first used in 1851. It was derived from the Spanish *filibustero* meaning "pirate" or "freebooter". This had in turn evolved from the French word *flibustier*, which itself evolved from the Dutch *vrijbuiter* (freebooter). The term was applied at the time to American adventurers, mostly from Southern states, who sought to overthrow the governments of Central American states, and was transferred to the users of the filibuster in the Senate, as the tactic was seen as pirating or hijacking debate.

While in a filibuster the Senator talking must remain in the same spot and is only allowed to filibuster twice in a legislative day. A legislative day lasts until the debate is adjourned, which can take several calendar days. Budget bills are governed under special rules called "reconciliation" which do not allow filibusters. Usually proposals for constitutional amendments are not filibustered either. This is because a two-thirds majority is needed to pass such a proposal, which is more than the three-fifths majority needed to invoke cloture (closure).

The filibuster remained a solely theoretical option until 1841, when the Democratic minority tried to block a bank bill favored by the Whig majority by using this political tactic. In 1917 a rule allowing for the cloture of debate and ending a filibuster was adopted by the Democratic Senate at the urging of President Woodrow Wilson. After a series of filibusters led by Southern Democrats in the 1960s over civil rights legislation, the Democratic-controlled Senate in 1975 revised its cloture rule so that three-fifths of the Senators sworn (usually 60 senators) could limit debate. Despite this rule, the filibuster or the threat of one remains an important tactic that allows a minority to affect legislation. It is most effective when a number of Senators are undecided. In current practice, Senate Rule 22 permits filibusters in which actual continuous floor speeches are not required, although the Senate Majority Leader may require an actual traditional filibuster if he or she so chooses. The threat of a filibuster can therefore be as powerful as an actual filibuster. Currently, Senators need only indicate that they are filibustering, thereby preventing the Senate from moving to other business until the motion is withdrawn or enough votes are gathered for cloture. Most attempts at stalling legislation are usually just for show and last a relatively short period of time.

Strom Thurmond of South Carolina set a record in 1957 by filibustering the Civil Rights Act of 1957 for 24 hours and 18 minutes, although the bill ultimately passed. A notorious filibuster of the 1960s took place when southern Democratic Senators attempted to block the passage of the Civil Rights Act 1964 by filibustering for 75 hours. The filibuster has tremendously increased in frequency of use since the 1960s. In the 2007-08 Congress there were a record number of 112 filibuster cloture votes.

A filibuster can be defeated by the majority party if they leave the debated issue on the agenda indefinitely, without adding anything else. Strom Thurmond's attempt to filibuster the Civil Rights Act was defeated when Senate Majority Leader Mike Mansfield refused to refer any further business to the Senate, which in effect required the filibuster to be kept up indefinitely. Instead, the opponents were all given a chance to speak and the matter eventually was forced to a vote.

The Budget

The annual US budget is of the order of $2 trillion. Framing it is a joint exercise between the Executive and Legislative branches and may lead to conflict between them, an example of what is called "gridlock in Washington." The President proposes a budget, prepared by the Office of Management and Budget (OMB) in the White House, and submits it to the Congress. A budget may seek to redeem promises made in the President's election campaign. It will certainly address current needs and probably long term issues as well. The Congress have their own priorities. These have to be reconciled between the two Houses and between the Congress and the President.

The President's Budget Request

The federal budget is produced according to procedures laid out in the Congressional Budget Act of 1974. The Budget Act requires that Congress each year develop a "budget resolution" setting limits on total spending and tax cuts. The limits apply both to legislation developed by congressional committees and to any amendments from the floor.

On or before the first Monday in February, the President submits to Congress a detailed budget request for the coming federal fiscal year, which begins on October 1. The tight timetable puts pressure on the transition team of an incoming Administration to work closely with the staff of the outgoing Administration. The budget request plays three important roles. First, it tells Congress what the President believes federal fiscal policy should be towards spending, tax and the deficit (or surplus). Second, the budget request lays out the President's priorities for federal spending on such programs as defense, agriculture, education and health. The President's budget recommends funding levels for individual programs or small groups of programs called "budget accounts." The budget usually also outlines fiscal policy and priorities for the next five years. Thirdly the

President's budget tells Congress what spending and tax policy changes the President recommends. The President does not need to propose legislation to change those parts of the budget that are governed by permanent law if he feels none is necessary. Nearly all of the federal tax code is set in permanent law and will not expire. Similarly, more than one-half of federal spending, including the three largest entitlement programs, Medicare, Medicaid, and Social Security, is also permanently enacted. Interest paid on the national debt is also paid automatically. (There is, however, a separate "debt ceiling" which limits how much the Treasury can borrow. The debt ceiling is periodically raised through separate legislation.)

The type of spending the President has to ask to be renewed each year is funding for "discretionary" or "appropriated" programs which fall under the jurisdiction of the House and Senate Appropriations Committees. Almost all defense spending is discretionary, as are the budgets for K-12 education, health research, and housing, to name just a few examples. Altogether, discretionary programs make up about one-third of all federal spending.

The President's budget can also include changes to "mandatory" or " entitlement" programs and certain other programs such as food stamps, federal civilian and military retirement benefits, veterans' disability benefits, and unemployment insurance that are not controlled by annual appropriations. For example, when President Bush proposed adding a prescription drug benefit to Medicare, he had to show a corresponding increase in Medicare costs in his budget. Any proposal by the President to increase or decrease taxes should be reflected in a change in the projected amount of federal revenue.

The Congressional Budget Resolution

After receiving the President's budget request, Congress generally holds hearings to question Administration officials about their requests and then the House and Senate Budget Committees each develop a budget resolution. These go to the House and Senate floors, where they can be amended by majority vote. The two resolutions then go to a House-Senate conference to resolve any differences, and a conference report is passed by both Houses. In this context, the term "reconciliation" does not have its ordinary meaning of two parties working out their differences (for example, the House and Senate are often described as going to conference to "reconcile" competing versions of a bill.) Rather, it refers to the process by which congressional committees adjust or "reconcile" existing tax or entitlement law with the new tax or mandatory spending targets called for in the budget resolution.

The resulting budget resolution is a "concurrent" congressional resolution, not an ordinary bill, and therefore does not go to the President for signature or veto. It also requires only a majority vote to pass, and is one of the few pieces of legislation that cannot be filibustered in the Senate. The budget resolution is supposed to be passed by April 15, but it often takes longer. Occasionally, Congress does not pass a budget resolution. If that happens, the previous year's resolution, which is a multi-year plan, stays in effect.

Unlike the President's budget, which is very detailed, the congressional budget resolution is a simple document. It consists of a set of figures stating how much Congress is projected to spend in each of 19 broad spending categories, known as budget "functions", and how much total revenue the government will collect, for at least each of the next five or more years. The spending totals in the budget resolution are stated in two different ways: the total amount of "budget authority" that is to be provided, and the estimated level of expenditures, or "outlays." Budget authority is how much money Congress allows a federal agency to commit to spend; outlays are how much money actually flows out of the federal treasury in a given year. Budget authority and outlays thus serve different purposes. Budget authority represents a limit on how much funding Congress will provide, and is generally what Congress focuses on in making most budgetary decisions. Outlays, because they represent actual cash flow, help determine the size of the overall deficit or surplus.

The budget resolution is accompanied by a report that includes a table called the "302(a) allocation." This table attributes the total spending by budget function to each congressional committee. The two Appropriations Committees receive a single 302(a) allocation for all their programs. They then decide on their own how to divide up this funding among their 12 subcommittees, into what are known as 302(b) sub-allocations. The various committees with jurisdiction over mandatory programs each get an allocation that represents a total dollar ceiling for all of the legislation they produce that year.

The spending totals in the budget resolution do not apply to the "authorizing" legislation produced by most congressional committees. Authorizing legislation typically either changes the rules for a federal program or provides a limit on how much money can be appropriated for it. Unless it involves changes to an entitlement program, authorizing legislation does not have a budgetary impact since none of the money can be spent until the annual appropriations bill sets the dollar level for that funding for the year, which is frequently less than the authorized limit. Often the report accompanying the budget resolution describes the assumptions behind it, including how much it envisions certain programs being cut or increased. These assumptions generally serve only as guidance to the other committees and are not binding on them. Sometimes, though, the budget resolution includes devices intended to ensure that particular programs receive a certain amount of funding. For example, the budget resolution could create a "reserve fund" that could be used only for a specific purpose. The budget resolution may also amend the congressional budget process.

The cost of appropriations bills and amendments must not exceed the allocations and sub-allocations given to the Appropriations Committees and sub-committees for the coming fiscal year. Tax or entitlement bills or amendments must not exceed the budget resolution's spending limit for the relevant committee, or the revenue floor, both in the first year and over the total period covered by the budget resolution. The cost of a tax or entitlement bill is determined or "scored" by the Budget Committees, nearly always by relying on the nonpartisan Congressional Budget Office, which measures it against a budgetary "baseline" that projects entitlement spending or tax receipts under current law. Budget estimators thus have considerable power.

Violations of the budget resolution by the House can in theory be prevented by a single member raising a "point of order" on the floor to block such legislation. For a generation, however, the leadership have been able to nullify this procedure by having the Rules Committee, which they appoint, put a resolution to waive it by majority vote. Instead, the Rules Committee have generally allowed the consideration of only a few "substitute" amendments. These are alternative budgets, typically developed by the minority party, or caucuses within the House that have a particular interest in budget policy. In the Senate, however, any legislation that exceeds a committee's spending allocation, or cuts taxes below the level allowed in the budget resolution, is vulnerable to a budget point of order on the floor that requires 60 votes to waive. A separate rule of the House and Senate prohibits legislation other than Appropriations Acts from providing or rescinding discretionary appropriations. On occasion this rule has been ignored and other legislation (including reconciliation bills) has included items of discretionary appropriations.

THE "PAY-AS-YOU-GO" OR "PAYGO" RULE

Independent of the Congressional Budget Act, the House and Senate each have a rule requiring that all entitlement increases and tax cuts be fully offset. For example, a bill that increased Medicare spending would have to be paid for by cutting somewhere else in Medicare or another entitlement program, by raising revenues, or by a combination of the two. The rule does not apply to discretionary spending, which is limited by the allocations set in the annual budget resolution.

If legislation providing for new tax cuts or entitlement increases is not paid for, the "PAYGO" rule gives any Senator the power to raise a point of order against the bill, which can only be waived by the vote of 60 Senators. In the House, any Member can raise a point of order, and there is no opportunity to vote to waive the PAYGO requirement — the bill is automatically defeated, unless the leadership-appointed Rules Committee has decided in advance to waive PAYGO as part of the broader measure (referred to as a rule) setting the terms of debate on the bill as a whole and the House has agreed to that rule.

PAYGO is an additional requirement, separate and apart from the terms of the budget resolution. A bill that cuts taxes or increases entitlement spending without an offset would violate the PAYGO rule even if the budget resolution had assumed the enactment of tax cuts or entitlement increases and allocated the necessary amounts to the relevant committees. (The PAYGO rule does not directly apply to the budget resolution itself or amendments to it, however.)

In order to satisfy the House and Senate PAYGO rules, a bill must be paid for over the first six years (including the current year), and over the first 11 years (including the current year). The Senate PAYGO rule does not consider the impact of a bill on Social Security and other "off-budget" items, whereas the House PAYGO rule applies to the "unified budget," which includes Social Security. On its face, PAYGO looks like a strong barrier to increasing the deficit, but in the end even PAYGO can be overruled by a majority in the House, and in any case does not apply to mandatory programs.

Congressional Record

Daily events in Congress, including votes and verbatim reports of all speeches, are printed in the *Congressional Record*. Members can add comments and even newspaper articles in the "Extension of Remarks" section.

Political parties

The word *party* can be used in three senses. 1. The party that voters say they support. 2. Parties as political organizations. 3. Parties in government. The two main parties, Democrats and Republicans, are essential to the American political process in all three senses. The framers of the Constitution generally regarded parties as undesirable or even dangerous. Nonetheless, the document they wrote unintentionally provided powerful incentives for like-minded politicians to form permanent coalitions in government and the electorate. Parties were originally formed in Congress as members attempted to build alliances to take control of the machinery of government. Attempts to build majorities within Congress quickly translated into attempts to elect majorities to it.

The Democratic Party originated in 1792 and draws much of its support from trade and labor unions, minorities and the poor. Its support is nowadays strongest in the rustbelt states of the North-East, parts of the South and in the West. It pursues more liberal policies such as government spending on welfare and is thus a party of the Left. The animal symbols for the parties were created by the German American, Thomas Nast (1840-1902). The Democrats' party color is blue and their symbol is a donkey, standing for hard work. Democratic Presidents in the 20th century included Woodrow Wilson, Franklin D. Roosevelt, Harry Truman, John F. Kennedy, Lyndon Johnson and Bill Clinton.

The Republican Party (sometimes called the GOP or "Grand Old Party"), was founded in 1854 by people who wanted to free the slaves (Abolitionists). Nowadays it draws its support from the middle class, the rich and business generally and espouses more conservative policies such as more spending on the armed forces and fewer restrictions on business and trade. It is thus a party of the Right. The Republicans' party color is red and their symbol an elephant, representing strength. Republican support is drawn mostly from the smaller states, especially in the Mid-West, and parts of the South. Some white southerners who might otherwise vote Republican vote for conservative Democrat candidates because it was a Republican President, Abraham Lincoln, who fought the Civil War against the South. These Democrats are sometimes called "Dixiecrats" i.e., Democrats from south of the Mason-Dixon line which marks the boundary between Pennsylvania and Maryland i.e., the free and slave-owning states. In the 20th century, Republican Presidents included Theodore Roosevelt, Dwight Eisenhower, Richard Nixon and Ronald Reagan.

Until recently, when a number of factors including "culture wars" have pushed the parties into taking more overtly ideological positions, both parties have been moderate and non-ideological with little difference between them; and Americans still express a strong preference for politicians who will act in the national, rather than partisan, interest and cooperate with the other party in a bipartisan manner to conduct the business of government.

The advantages of parties in America

Political parties are less important in the US than in some countries because they are less involved in the business of government, owing to the separation of powers. Unlike in Parliamentary systems, the head of the ruling political party is not the head of the Administration of the country. An American party leader, called the National Chairman, is an official appointed by the party's candidate for President to head the party's National Committee, which is responsible for organizing the Presidential nominating convention, raising campaign funds and helping candidates with advertising and organization. The parties encompass more general concerns and push the system toward consensus, although the benefits they provide often go unappreciated by the voters. Indeed, the parties perform essential electoral functions.

Many voters use the reactions of political parties to events as a quick and easy way to interpret and respond to issues they may little comprehend, because identification with a party is at the core of most Americans' view of the world. These voters accept and adopt the parties' values and their views of responsible citizenship. This is especially true of the least informed and least interested. These values include involvement and participation; work for the "public good" in the "national interest" (as conceived in partisan terms, naturally); and patriotism and respect for American society's fundamental institutions and processes. The parties use key words like "choice" and "pro-life" to summarize their attitudes to issues. These words are called "dog whistles." Even better educated and more involved voters find party identification helpful. No one has the time to study every issue carefully or to become fully knowledgeable about every candidate seeking public office. The result of party activity may be increased participation in elections.

The effect of the party cue is exceptionally helpful to elected leaders. They can count on disproportionate support among their partisans in times of difficulty or trouble. Because there are only two major parties, citizens who are interested in politics or public policy are mostly attracted to one or the other, creating natural majorities or near majorities for party officeholders to command. The party creates a community of interest that bonds disparate groups together over time. This eliminates the necessity of creating a coalition anew for every campaign or every issue. The consequence is more effective government that is broadly accepted as legitimate.

In addition, parties act as mechanisms for organizing and containing political change, and are thus a potent force for stability. They represent continuity throughout changing issues and personalities. Because of their unyielding, pragmatic desire to win elections and not just contest them, the parties not only act to promote competition but also to moderate public opinion. The party controls its own extreme elements by pulling them toward an ideological center in order to attract a majority of votes on election day.

The parties indeed play a vital role in maintaining political cohesion and national unity. The fragmented system of government designed by the Founders, that divides and subdivides power, makes it possible to preserve individual liberty but difficult to coordinate and produce timely action. Parties help compensate for this drawback by linking all the institutions and centers of power to one another. Although rivalry between the executive and legislative branches of American government is inevitable, the partisan affiliations of the leaders of each branch constitute a common basis for cooperation, as any President and fellow party members in Congress frequently demonstrate. Similarly, the federalist division of national, state, and local governments, while always an invitation to conflict, is made more workable and easily coordinated by the party relationships that exist among officeholders at all levels. The party's linkage function does not end there. The party connection is one means to ensure or increase accountability in election campaigns and in government. Candidates on the campaign trail and elected party leaders in office are required from time to time to account for their performance at party-sponsored forums and in party nominating primaries and conventions.

"In America the same political labels - Democratic and Republican - cover virtually all public officeholders, and therefore most voters are everywhere mobilized in the name of these two parties," says Nelson W. Polsby in *New Federalist Papers: Essays in Defense of the Constitution*. "Yet Democrats and Republicans are not everywhere the same. Variations - sometimes subtle, sometimes blatant - in the 50 political cultures of the states yield considerable differences overall in what it means to be, or to vote, Democratic or Republican. These differences suggest that one may be justified in referring to the American two-party system as masking something more like a hundred-party system."

Why did America end up with two, and only two, major political parties? Most officials in America are elected from single-member districts and win office by beating their opponents in a system for determining winners called "first-past-the-post": the one who gets the most votes wins, and there is no proportional accounting. This encourages the creation of a duopoly: one party in power, the other out. If those who are "out" band together, they have a better chance of beating those who are "in". Occasionally third parties do arise and receive some share of the votes, for a while at least. The most successful third party candidate was former President Theodore Roosevelt in the 1912 election. The former Republican's Progressive Party a.k.a. the "Bull Moose Party" actually bested the losing *major* party candidate, taking six states and eighty-eight electoral votes, while sitting President William Howard Taft (Republican) took only two states and eight electoral votes, and Democrat Woodrow Wilson took the White House. In recent years H. Ross Perot's Reform Party had some success in the presidential elections of 1992 (taking 19% of the vote but no electoral votes) and 1996. Jesse Ventura became the first Reform Party candidate to win statewide office when he was elected governor of Minnesota in 1998. Third parties have a hard time surviving, though, because one or both of the major parties often adopt their most popular issues, and thus their voters.

To some extent, party support reflects class, working class Americans tending to support the Democratic Party, the middle class and the rich the Republicans. But because some issues cut across class lines, people do not always vote as their class would suggest. For this reason, Karl Rove, George W. Bush's election strategist, arranged for propositions on "wedge issues" such as abortion and gay marriage to appear on the ballot papers in certain states. A third factor is voter perceptions of the candidates. Polls repeatedly showed in the 2008 Presidential campaign that Barack Obama lacked support among the white, male working class.

Although the coalitions, characteristics, and the strength of parties have changed over the years, they have become vital to the proper functioning of the American system of government. Parties recruit and train leaders, organize the activities of government, and facilitate the collective action necessary for government to translate voter preferences into public policy. They also help combine varying interests and groups into coalitions and help channel and constrain political conflict. Finally, they help politicians of all stripes communicate more effectively with voters.

In the House of Representatives' contests, parties are limited to direct gifts of $5,000 per candidate per election (with the primary and general election counted separately). But in House races these party contributions are being multiplied since the national party committee, the state party committee, and the national party's congressional campaign committee are usually each eligible to give the $5,000 maximum. Thus, as much as $30,000 ($5,000 × 2 elections [primary and general] × 3 separate party committees) can be directly contributed to every party nominee for the House. In Senate elections, the national party committee and the senatorial campaign committee may give a combined maximum of $17,500 to each candidate; another $10,000 can be added from the state party committee for a total of $27,500 in direct gifts.

The law allows the parties to coordinate their spending on general election campaign expenditures (for television advertising, polling, etc.) with the candidates' own fundraising and spending. This can significantly augment the funding available for some candidates' campaigns. The coordinated expenditure limits are high. For House candidates the national and state parties may each spend $10,000 plus an inflation adjustment. Senate candidates are the beneficiaries of even higher limits on coordinated expenditures. The national and state parties can each spend $20,000 (plus inflation), or two cents per voter, whichever is greater. Importantly, the national party committee is permitted to act as the state party committee's spending agent; that is, with the state party's agreement, the national committee can assume the state party's permitted portion of the coordinated expenditures. This privilege centralizes power in the national committees and unburdens weaker state party committees that otherwise might not be able to contribute the maximum. The GOP also sends additional aid through cut-rate services for media, polling, and consultants. The Republicans have usually outraised the Democrats by enormous margins in all recent election cycles, never by less than 2 to 1 and usually by a considerably higher ratio. The Republicans have been able to give nearly the legal maximum gift (both in direct contributions and in coordinated expenditures) to every reasonably competitive Senate and House candidate; frequently the money is given "up front," immediately after a primary when a nominee's war chest is depleted and the need is greatest.

The increased money and services from both Democratic and Republican organizations may be drawing candidates much closer to their parties since the parties are contributing in tangible ways to their nominees' election. Whether or not any gratitude or obligation to the party is created in this fashion, such services as training schools, party issue papers, and institutional advertising put officeholders through a "homogenizing" process that may predispose them more favorably to the "party line" in government. Party leaders and political observers differ about whether such a development is really taking place, but all are agreed on one point: the parties remain less influential than they would be otherwise because alternative sources of funding are available to candidates. And the most available "alternative source" for incumbents is PACs.

Parties as organizations are doing well both on the national level (helped by special interest money) and on the state and local levels (with Republican clubs, for example, gaining a foothold in the once solidly Democratic south). As for parties in government, however, the evidence is mixed. Party influence and discipline are not particularly strong in executive branch bureaucracies, and parties are generally absent from the judicial branch. Partisanship in American legislatures, however, is getting stronger. Although in recent years political scientists have complained about the weak and ineffectual state of the American political parties, and their narrow activist base, contemporary political debates and election results have convincingly demonstrated that, for better or worse, political parties are a vital part of American politics today.

Positions within the parties

While prominent Democrats run the wide gamut from the near democratic-socialist left (Barbara Lee, Dennis Kucinich and the Congressional Progressive Caucus) and traditional liberals (Hillary Clinton, Nancy Pelosi) to the center-right (Joe Lieberman, the Congressional Blue Dog Coalition and the New Democrat Network) to the GOP-style conservative right (Ralph Hall and Gene Taylor), most fall somewhere into the pragmatic Democratic Leadership Council's "centrist" moderate-to-liberal style (Evan Bayh). Barack Obama was the most liberal-voting Senator.

Leading Republicans fall into several different ideological factions: traditional conservatives (former President George W. Bush and the Club for Growth), the Religious Right (Trent Lott, the National Federation of Republican Assemblies and the Christian Coalition), the old Nixon/Rockefeller "centrist" or "moderate" wing (Colin Powell, George Pataki, the Republican Main Street Partnership, the Republican Leadership Council and the Republican Mainstream Committee), and libertarians (Ron Paul and the Republican Liberty Caucus).

Trends in political attitudes

Over the last 30 years, the American electorate has been relatively stable in its policy and ideological preferences, while the political parties have become more extreme. At least in terms of what Americans call themselves, however, the nation became gradually a little more conservative. At the same time, the majority of Americans do not identify themselves simply as "liberal" or "conservative." Americans have been remarkably consistent with respect to opinions on abortion, national health insurance, the powers of the federal government, and social safety net issues.

Those who, like E. J. Dionne of Georgetown University, foresaw a progressive future in the US were encouraged when the Republicans lost control of both Houses of Congress in the 2006 mid-term elections. American liberals and the left then seemed to have their greatest political opening since the 1960s and their greatest opportunity to alter the philosophical direction of the public debate since the 1930s. Under the Administration of George W. Bush, the advance of Republican conservatism was broken by three failures: the continuing failure to pacify Iraq after the initial victory, the highly-criticized failure to repair the damage caused to New Orleans by Hurricane Katrina, and the failure to persuade many outside the Republican base to accept a brand of moral conservatism ill-suited to a moderate country. Bush's Iraq policy was further discredited in the eyes of many Americans by the revelation that prisoners had been tortured.

The conservative triumphalism of recent years was itself never justified. Even in 2004, as President in a time of war, George W. Bush won less than 51 percent of the popular vote. Moreover even before support for Bush's Iraq policies collapsed or Hurricane Katrina made landfall, three other controversies weakened the foundations of his presidency and of the conservative cause. First, Bush's decision to push for the partial privatization of Social Security was a choice rooted in ideology that called forth a vigorous defense of social insurance. The more Bush discussed the idea, the less the public liked it. Bush was proposing to weaken guaranteed pensions at a moment when many Americans were experiencing new levels of economic insecurity described by the Yale University political scientist Jacob S. Hacker in *The Great Risk Shift* (2006). Hacker notes that more and more financial risk has been thrown onto individual Americans as collective safety nets, particularly those provided by private employers for pensions and health care, have been shredded.

Second, the decision of the President and a Republican Congress to use federal power to overrule a state-court decision allowing the death of Terri Schiavo, who was deemed brain-dead, was far more damaging than it seemed at the time. Even social moderates and conservatives were uneasy with heavy-handed federal intervention in a matter that seemed more properly handled within families and by state governments. Even opponents of physician-assisted suicide did not view the case as clear-cut. They sensed that the moralistic language used by conservative politicians was inspired not by deep conviction but by the frantic pursuit of a key constituency's votes.

Last was the controversy over leaking the name of Valerie Plame, the CIA operative married to former Ambassador Joseph Wilson. The case came to symbolize the Administration's approach to its critics on Iraq. At the very moment when doubts about the war were building, here was an incident that seemed to embody all that was wrong with the Administration's approach to selling a war that, initially at least, a majority of Americans did not consider either wise or necessary.

All of this happened before Katrina, an Administration failure that carried so many messages: lack of respect for the fundamental functions of government and incompetence at executing its most basic tasks; seeming indifference to the plight of the poor and to the situation of African Americans; rampant cronyism. The source of Bush's political success after 9/11 had been his claim that he could protect Americans. As Dionne puts it: "Leadership, strength, and security were his calling cards. They were lost in the Gulf's surging waters." At the time of writing, however, anger with the Obama Administration over its failure to reduce unemployment, foreclosures and bankruptcies whilst at the same time bailing out the banks made it likely that the Republicans would recapture the House and possibly the Senate in the 2010 midterm elections.

Towards the end of Bush's presidency, conservative policies lost a great deal of credibility when it became apparent that his ideologically-based failure to regulate financial institutions sufficiently had in large part led to the worldwide financial crisis and a severe recession in the US. Moreover, the economic policies of Bush and his aides were not peculiar to his Administration and so the whole Republican party was blamed for the mess. Finally, the Republican party's attempt to inject overt racism into the 2008 presidential campaign (against Senator McCain's better instincts), and the fact that most large cities voted for Obama (even in the south) whereas most rural areas voted for McCain (except in New England), has made the Republicans look more and more like the party of poor rural white reaction against any kind of cosmopolitanism, expertise, and progress.

The end of the Bush era, and, by extension, the conservative era, points to both the opportunities and the challenges for American liberalism and the left. Paul Starr has noted in an essay in *The American Prospect* that "the exhaustion of conservatism is not tantamount to a liberal revival." The challenge is "whether liberals can make their case not just for specific policies and candidates but for an alternative public philosophy." To do so, they must first rediscover the power of their own ideas and their own tradition. At the same time, liberals will be required to deal with a set of conflicts and contradictions not unlike the ones that have derailed conservatism. Although the most ardent battles between multiculturalism and universalism are found in the academy, they have a bearing on practical politics. Liberals will inevitably face a tension between the imperative to stand up for the rights of minority groups, including Muslims, and the liberal commitment to root the rights of all in a set of universal values and principles. Liberalism's commitment to economic justice and greater equality demands the recognition of common ground that transcends any particular identity. Some have argued that progressives need to stand for more than diversity and rights and that both would be better defended within a common-good framework. Yet the discrediting of government in the Bush years has undermined Americans' sense of collective capacity. Also globalization as it is currently organized has undermined the capacity of national governments to regulate and redistribute in the common interest and this has diminished the bargaining power of the least privileged in the wealthy nations. A revival of liberalism depends upon a coherent approach to globalization. It should promote the creation of democratic social market economies that marry competitiveness to social justice. This is more difficult to do in globalized markets.

On foreign policy it is easy enough to reject Bush's unilateralism, his squandering of the post-9/11 opportunity, his failure to understand what the invasion of Iraq entailed and required, and his expansive view of executive power. Far more difficult will be settling arguments between advocates of democracy promotion and opponents of imperialism; between realists who have learned the need for prudence from the Iraq adventure, and idealists who insist (as in Darfur) that there is still a role for American power to promote moral ends, and to avert moral catastrophe. Although, in principle, the model of international cooperation pioneered by Franklin Roosevelt and Harry Truman may be reparable, it would be foolish to assume that such an approach to foreign policy can be easily recreated in a world very different from the one they confronted.

The growing gap between the parties

The gap between the parties in ideology and policies is growing, and so is the gap between the parties and the voters. According to political scientists, the main reason is the demise of the New Deal coalition, which united socially conservative southern whites in the Democratic party and northern liberals. Over the first half of the century, Republicans had no significant presence in the old Confederacy, and southern politicians gained national strength by joining in coalition with northern liberals. For this reason, the race issue was kept off the agenda for several decades until it burst on the national scene with the Civil Rights movement in the early 1960s. Only then did differences on race come into a sharp focus within the Democratic party. In addition to the white southerners and northern liberals, the New Deal coalition included Midwestern anti-Communists, ethnic Catholics, and radical social democrats located in the plains states and in the urban northeast. The coalition united many diverse factions, but despite this it persisted into the 1990s. Conversely, since the Civil Rights Act of 1964, the Republican party has begun to draw much more support from southern conservatives, who felt betrayed by the Democrats, and the party's policies have become more conservative as a result. Hence representation has become more polarized regionally, the party caucuses in Congresses much more cohesive, and partisan differences sharper.

Alienation of voters

The prevailing wisdom is that parties are in some trouble among the electorate, as evidenced by the rise in split ticket voting and the gradual decline in the number of voters who identify themselves as "strong partisans." The demise of the New Deal coalition, the rise of the Republican party in the South, the declining fidelity to party labels, the rising partisanship among political elites in Congress, all point to a growing gap between the interests of political elites and the preferences of average Americans. Analysts say that over the last 30 years the Democratic Party has lost touch with its grassroots blue-collar supporters. Mostly among conservative Republican supporters, the Tea Party movement (motto:"Don't Tread on Me") arose in 2009 through a series of locally and nationally-coordinated protests to campaign mainly against both the Republican and Democrat recovery legislation and the Obama plans to refinance mortgages and widen access to healthcare. Tea Party candidates, some of them supported by 2008 Vice-Presidential candidate, Sarah Palin, had a number of surprise victories in Republican primaries ahead of the 2010 mid-term elections. The name *Tea Party* refers to the protest against British commerce regulations which took place in Boston in 1775. Tea Party activists have sent teabags to Congresspeople whose votes they disapprove. A Coffee Party has been formed as an alternative.

Fundamental demographic shifts are creating greater divides between the urban areas which tend to support the Democrats, and the suburban and rural areas which tend to support the Republicans. Districts are becoming more homogeneous and there is no longer a middle. The result is polarization, alienation of voters and voter frustration with partisanship in Congress. The growing gap between the two main parties and the voters is not being filled by third parties because the electoral system is profoundly hostile to third parties. The growing gap between elites and the electorate is being filled with cynicism, mistrust, and frustration that America's leaders do not care about voters' problems. At the same time, it is difficult for the parties to adopt policies with broader appeal because they are dominated by activists who are mainly responsible for raising the necessary funds, and select the candidates based on their personal opinions as much as political skill or experience. The activists are even willing to sacrifice votes for the sake of ideological purity. As Bill Bishop points out in *The Big Sort*, like-minded groups tend to become more extreme. Part of the answer may lie with the union, corporate and interest group backers who control the flow of funds to the parties.

Political Action Committees (PACs)

FACTFILE 8A MAIN TYPES OF ADVOCACY GROUPS

Political Action Committee (PAC) – A political committee that raises and spends limited "hard" money contributions for the express purpose of electing or defeating candidates. Organizations that raise soft money for issue advocacy may also set up a PAC. Most PACs represent business, such as the Microsoft PAC; labor, such as the Teamsters PAC; or ideological interests, such as the EMILY's List PAC or the National Rifle Association PAC. An organization's PAC will collect money from the group's employees or members and make contributions in the name of the PAC to candidates and political parties. A PAC can give $5,000 to a candidate per election (primary, general or special) and up to $15,000 annually to a national political party. PACs may receive up to $5,000 each from individuals, other PACs and party committees per year. A PAC must register with the Federal Election Commission.

501(c) Groups – Nonprofit, tax-exempt groups organized under section 501(c) of the Internal Revenue Code that can engage in varying amounts of political activity, depending on the type of group. For example, 501(c)(3) groups operate for religious, charitable, scientific or educational purposes. These groups are not supposed to engage in any political activities, though some voter registration activities are permitted. 501(c)(4) groups are commonly called "social welfare" organizations that may engage in political activities, as long as these do not become their primary purpose. Similar restrictions apply to Section 501(c)(5) labor and agricultural groups, and to Section 501(c)(6) business leagues, chambers of commerce, real estate boards and boards of trade.

527 Group – A tax-exempt group organized under section 527 of the Internal Revenue Code to raise money for political activities including voter mobilization efforts, issue advocacy and the like. Many 527s run by special interest groups raise unlimited "soft money", which they use for voter mobilization and certain types of issue advocacy, but not for efforts that expressly advocate the election or defeat of a federal candidate or amount to electioneering communications. Currently, the FEC only requires a 527 group to file regular disclosure reports if it is a political party or PAC that engages in either activities expressly advocating the election or defeat of a federal candidate, or in electioneering communications. Otherwise, it must file either with the government of the state in which it is located or the Internal Revenue Service.

Non-Federal Group – A group set up to raise unlimited contributions called "soft money", which it spends on voter mobilization efforts and so-called issue ads that often criticize or tout a candidate's record just before an election in an effort to influence the outcome.

The largest and arguably the most successful PAC is Emily's List, which is devoted to electing pro-choice women and claims to have helped elect 69 Representatives, 13 Senators and 8 Governors (2007). Emily's List is associated with the American Federation of State, County and Municipal Employees and the American Federation of Teachers.

Relationship with the parties

The Political Action Committees (PACs) have received more publicity of recent years, but the parties, which present an important check to abuse of power by PACs, are holding their own in the struggle for political supremacy, despite the fact that the party system in the US has declined and deteriorated in major ways in the last several decades. Prematurely counted out by many political observers, the parties have surprised many critics by regenerating themselves at the national level through the use of direct mail and other tools of the new campaign technology. The Republican Party has led the way, spurred by the hope of breaking out of its minority status, and the Democrats have lately followed, prompted by the need to catch up with the GOP. Despite the press's focus on political action committees, the parties are about as healthy as the PACs.

PACs and parties both raise money from the same limited pool of political givers, large and small. They both try to elect candidates, but in doing so they adopt very different perspectives. Most PACs act on the basis of relatively narrow or even single-interest viewpoints, while the parties operate from a broad-based, overarching vantage point. And they both vie for the attention, affection, and loyalty of candidates and officeholders. Republican and Democratic leaders alike may understand the competing nature of PACs and parties, but they also realize that, under the current system of campaign finance, PAC money gives congressional contenders an often crucial competitive edge.

Thus although there is evidence of considerable competition between PACs and parties, the two have learned to coexist, despite their natural tensions. PACs need the information about candidates, intelligence about congressional contests, and access to political leaders that parties can provide. The parties seek PAC money for their candidates and their own organizations, which of late have modernized and expanded at a rate that matches the growth of PACs. Fortunately for both parties, the independent, non-connected ideological PACs have fallen on hard financial times, and many are mere shadows of their former selves. The parties have easily withstood the assaults of the anti-party PACs, and the latter's heyday may well be over.

Most PACs are indifferent to parties. This does not mean they have no effects on party organization and development, but, according to political scientists, there is little evidence for the widespread claim that PACs have contributed greatly to the long-term decline of the American party system. Rather, PACs may be one more sign of the atomizing forces that have made the parties less appealing to Americans. Nonetheless, PACs provide an alternative source of funding and support services for a candidate, weakening his or her ties with the party and lessening his fear of severe electoral consequences if he is disloyal to his party. But at the same time the competition from PACs is one of many factors stimulating a dramatic surge in party organization, technology, programs, and fund-raising that has drawn candidates much closer to the national parties. Parties can now do - or refuse to do - much more to elect their nominees than in the past.

Finally, since candidates want campaign cash and PACs have it, the two negotiate with the political parties' help. A multicandidate PAC is permitted to give $15,000 each year to all national party political committees combined, and although few contribute that large an amount, about a third of all multicandidate PACs have donated some amount to the parties in recent years.

Most PACs secure some of their information about candidates and elections at regular party briefings and through party newsletters, but PACs are naturally somewhat wary of the slant they receive at briefings. As PACs have become more sophisticated, they have begun to demand more precise and accurate information from the parties, and both parties are attempting to provide it. The Republican National Committee (RNC) and associated committees have established numerous programs and channels of communication with the PACs. For example, any PAC contributing $5,000 or more to the RNC each year gains a PAC 40 membership, entitling it to meet with Republican congressional leaders for off-the-record breakfasts once a month at the Capitol Hill Club in Washington.

Also, briefings for the PACs are provided by both the congressional and senatorial committees on a quarterly basis in Washington and in major cities around the country. And the GOP usually pays attention to the needs of its candidates, particularly unknown challengers. When a challenger comes to Washington, the appropriate Republican committee will help to set up appointments with PAC managers in the capital and to design a PAC solicitation program tailor-made to the candidate's strengths.

The Democrats have also recently devoted greater efforts to securing corporate and trade PAC money. Democrats have followed the Republican lead in using exclusive clubs and offering special access to attract the PACs. For instance, the Democratic National Committee (DNC) has a Business Council which PACs can join with a $15,000 annual contribution, and a $2,500-per-year PAC Council, which is the rough equivalent of the Republican National Committee's PAC 40 Club. Like its GOP counterpart, the PAC Council gathers together legislators and PAC officials for monthly breakfasts. Reflecting labor's prominent role in the Democratic Party, there is a separate DNC Labor Council whose price is $15,000 a year for a PAC and $50,000 for a labor union proper. Democratic Party services to PACs and party candidates have improved, too. The party committees have expanded the size of their PAC liaison staffs, conduct regular briefing sessions for PACs, and distribute informational newsletters about key races.

Special interest groups

A special interest group is an organization composed of people who share common goals and actively seek to influence government policy. Special interest groups often arise from social movements such as the environmental movement or the women's movement. They express the rights of association, petition and freedom of speech guaranteed by the First Amendment and embodied in American culture. Among the best-known of the countless special interest groups are the AARP, the AFL-CIO (representing unions), the American Civil Liberties Union, the Environmental Defense Fund, the National Education Association, and the National Rifle Association.

Poll data show that about 70% of Americans belong to at least one group or association, a significant minority of which are special interest groups. Groups spring up because they can influence government at many points in the political structure, from neighborhoods to the halls of Congress, and because they offer members material, social and purposive incentives. Groups offer companionship, a sense of belonging and the pleasure of associating with like-minded others, what political scientists call "solidarity incentives." Groups can also give people a feeling that their voice is being heard and they are making a difference on specific issues that are of concern to them. In addition, groups may offer material benefits such as discounts, insurance and subsidized travel. By material incentives, especially low annual dues, the AARP has become the largest interest group in the US.

Special interest groups, operating out of offices on or near Capitol Hill, mostly lobby government on economic issues affecting business or agriculture, employers or unions, or professions. These issues may be of little interest to the general public and hence receive little attention, but, according to the Cato Institute, lobbyists' continual successful efforts to gain tax breaks, tariffs, subsidies and exemptions for those they represent cost nearly $100 million per year. Some interest groups, especially those listed in "Power 25", *Fortune* magazine's annual list of the most effective interest groups, are truly powerful. Representing three million member companies, the US Chamber of Commerce, for example, can bring constituent influence to bear on every member of Congress to award government contracts. Similarly the agricultural lobby, whose members are widely spread across congressional districts, have obtained massive subsidies and credits for farmers in recent years.

A third category of lobbying organizations is public interest groups. Although in a population of over 300 million, there are many publics and no one public policy is likely to benefit everybody, a number of groups have been formed "in the public interest." The most effective and probably best known of these are the more than 60 organized under the leadership of consumer activist Ralph Nader. Then there are regional groupings of public interest law firms such as the Mountain States Legal Defense Foundation. Other public interest groups include the League of Women Voters, the Consumer Federation of America and the American Civil Liberties Union.

Fourthly, there are a number of single-issue groups which represent people who care passionately about particular issues, such as abortion, guns, or Israel. These groups have the advantage of highly-motivated members and clear-cut goals. One of them, the National Rifle Association (NRA) is among the most powerful single issue groups in the US. A fifth category includes groups that represent Americans with particular characteristics like age or ethnicity, such as the AARP and the NAACP.

Successful special interest groups gain their reputation through four main factors: size, leadership, financial resources and cohesiveness. For example the AARP has 35 million members and a budget of $770 million, and claims to represent all older Americans, some 20% of the population. Strong leaders with effective strategies are also a factor. Such a leader is John Sweeney, who since his election as President of the AFL-CIO in 1995 has made it a renewed force in American politics. Cohesive organizations are those, like the US Chamber of Commerce, which excel at motivating their members to campaign, communicate with their representatives, and contribute extra money when asked.

Interest groups use an array of techniques to influence government. They frequently campaign to influence the climate of opinion and rally public sentiment (or at least generate an appearance of public support) through advertising, mass mailings, TV publicity and websites. Sometimes they commission polls and publicize the results. At other times they may publicize corporate research that is in the public interest. This technique is commonly used by oil companies who wish to make themselves appear more environmentally friendly. Some campaigns target the constituents of particular lawmakers, asking them to write, telephone or email their lawmakers or the President, and often providing them with postcards and form letters. These "shotgun" campaigns need to generate very large numbers of responses because legislators are well aware of such techniques (and indeed may have used them themselves). Grassroots activity which has been generated artificially has been labeled *astroturf lobbying*. A more effective variant may be the "rifle" approach or "Utah plant manager theory", where the interest group persuades an influential constituent such as a plant manager to approach a lawmaker, because an approach from such a person will carry more weight. (It may also be cheaper.) Such indirect techniques may appear to represent a spontaneous expression of public opinion and can thus have a greater effect than direct approaches from lobbyists. Marches, rallies and demonstrations may occasionally be used. It is doubtful, however, how much direct effect these forms of protest have beyond publicity, and even that may be a two-edged sword, since the public tend to react adversely to scenes of violence.

Interest groups also lobby directly by testifying before Congressional committees and regulatory agencies such as the Federal Trade Commission, providing information to legislators, rating and publicizing legislators' voting records, endorsing and helping political campaigns and building coalitions with like-minded groups. The core role of a lobbyist, though, is to obtain access to officials and build relationships with them that enable an interest group to express its views, in return for giving useful information and assistance with crafting legislation and regulations. Helping at elections is a third method of direct campaigning. The AFL-CIO devotes $30 million in each two-year electoral cycle to supporting Democratic candidates and also mobilizes large corps of precinct workers and volunteers who can significantly increase the turnout for a Democratic candidate. Business organizations make similar, though less sustained and targeted, efforts on behalf of Republican candidates. While few groups can win the full endorsement of their claims from the President and Congress, many are able to block or weaken proposals they see as prejudicial to their interests.

Criticisms of PACs

Lobbying arguably makes the legislative process work better, but often results in legislation that represents pragmatic compromises rather than principled policy. On the other hand most Americans would say that this process ensures a healthy pluralist democracy and prevents any interest from becoming too powerful, although there would be some disagreement over particular cases such as the so-called "military-industrial complex" (a phrase coined by President Eisenhower, a Republican). There are also concerns that lobbyists as a profession may become too powerful. In response, Congress enacted in 1995 that any organization spending $20,000 or more to influence legislation, or any individual who is paid more than $5,000 annually for lobbying and spends at least 20% of his or her time doing so must register. Almost all gifts and expenses-paid trips were also banned, curtailing the socializing ("schmoozing") that had given rise to scandals. Grassroots lobbyists and tax-exempt organizations such as religious groups do not have to register. There are also rules that limit former government employees or congresspersons from lobbying immediately after their retirement. Even so, some people believe that interest groups (or businesses) that hire former government employees gain an improper influence on government.

From a different point of view it has been objected that poor Americans, particularly single parents, disabled people and the young, those who cannot speak English, and non-citizens (who cannot vote) do not benefit from lobbying. They cannot afford the time or the money to join special interest groups, and may not have the knowledge or time to find out what group might represent them. Thus lobbying is of benefit only to the better off and to union members. Studies have shown that the poor largely depend on indirect representation by public officials, welfare workers, religious organizations, public interest groups and some liberal general interest groups.

The relationships between political action committees and political parties are at once symbiotic and parasitic. Both parties work hard to cultivate PACs and secure their money, and most PACs energetically endeavor to be bipartisan (at least to incumbents of both parties). At the same time, PACs and parties are rivals for the attentions of candidates, the favors of officeholders, and the devotions of voters. More important, the success of narrow-based PACs necessarily comes partly at the expense of broad-based parties. As parties decline, PACs gain, and in some ways PACS have hastened party decline.

PACS provide avenues for participation and political liberty but have questionable effects on competition, accountability, governmental legitimacy, and effectiveness. Parties allow for the expression of more broad-based interests, provide channels for representation and accountability, legitimacy and effectiveness. Given the symbiotic relationship of parties and PACs, both have a valuable role in the campaign finance system, but some argue that democratic values could be better served by increasing the significance of the parties and diminishing that of PACs.

Although a good number of PACs of all political persuasions existed before the 1970s, it was during this decade—the decade of campaign reform following the Watergate scandal—that the modern PAC era began. The rapid rise of PACs has inevitably proven controversial, yet many of the charges made against political action committees are exaggerated and dubious.

It is said that PACs are dangerously novel and have flooded the political system with money, mainly from business. Although the widespread use of the PAC structure is new, the fact remains that special interest money of all types has always found its way into politics and that before the 1970s, it did so in less traceable and far more disturbing and unsavory ways. In absolute terms PACs contribute a massive sum to candidates, but it is not clear that there is proportionately more interest group money in the system than before. The proportion of House and Senate campaign funds provided by PACs has certainly increased since the early 1970s, but individuals, most of whom are unaffiliated with PACs, together with the political parties, still supply about three-fifths of all the money spent by or on behalf of House candidates and three-quarters of the campaign expenditures for Senate contenders. So although the importance of PAC spending has grown, PACs clearly remain secondary as a source of election funding and therefore pose no overwhelming threat to the system's legitimacy.

Apart from the argument over the relative weight of PAC funds, critics claim that political action committees are making it more expensive to run for office. Money provided to one side funds the purchase of campaign tools, which the other side must then match in order to stay competitive. In the aggregate, American campaign expenditures seem huge. Yet they are far less than the annual advertising budgets of many individual commercial enterprises. These days it is expensive to communicate, whether the message is political or commercial. Television time, polling costs, consultants' fees, direct mail investment, and other standard campaign expenditures have been soaring in price, over and above inflation. PACs have been fuelling the use of new campaign techniques, but a reasonable case can be made that such expenses are necessary and that more, and better, communication is required between candidates and an electorate that often appears woefully uninformed about politics. PACs therefore may be making a positive contribution by providing the means to increase the flow of information during elections and thus enhancing political liberty.

PACs are also charged with reducing competition, and, except for the ideological ones, PACs do display a clear, overwhelming preference for incumbents. But the same bias is apparent in contributions from individuals. On the other hand, the best challengers are usually generously funded by PACs. PACs limit the number of strong challengers by giving so much early money to incumbents, money that helps to deter potential opponents from declaring their candidacies. But the money that PACs channel to competitive challengers late in the election season may then increase the turnover of officeholders on election day. PAC money also normally invigorates competitiveness in open seat congressional races—races without an incumbent candidate.

The fourth major criticism of PACs concerns their influence on legislative behavior—or "vote buying." There is the potential for influence under certain circumstances, but the magnitude of the problem is hard to judge. Furthermore, PACs are influential in the same cases where traditional lobbies—many of whom have allied with PACs—also succeed.

One last line of attack on PACs is more justified. Many PACs are inadequately accountable to donors or voters—a condition most apparent in many of the ideological non-connected PACs, which lack a parent body and whose freestyle organization makes them accountable to no one and responsive mainly to their own whims. In any democracy, and particularly in one as pluralistic as the US, however, it is essential that groups be relatively unrestricted in advocating their interests and positions. Not only is unrestricted political activity by interest groups a natural feature of American society, but it provides a safety valve for the competitive pressures that build on all fronts in a capitalistic democracy. It also provides a means to keep representatives responsive to legitimate needs.

Campaign finance reform

One of the most talked-about political issues is campaign finance reform. This is particularly designed to curb the activities of PACs. There is intense debate over whether PACs have a legitimate and important role in the political process. Some say that the huge sums contributed to parties is a form of corruption, rather than free speech, and contributes to the contemporary cynicism and mistrust expressed by American voters. Critics say PACs are essentially computer-driven mail-order operations that have no membership and are accountable to nobody. Yet their defenders assert that PACs are what James Madison called *factions*. Through the flourishing of competing interest groups or factions, said Madison in his *Federalist Paper No. 10*, liberty would be preserved. Special interest money has always found its way into the political arena. The growth of PACs is its current manifestation and makes special interest money more visible than it was before reporting requirements were instituted by legislation in the 1970s.

Considerable attention was given to campaign finance reform by the Republican primary campaign of Senator John McCain in 2000. Subsequently, reform was partly achieved by the McCain-Feingold Act of 2002. The main thrust of reform has been to make soft money illegal from November, 2002 and to limit how much PACs and individuals may contribute to political parties. Others have suggested that contributions to political parties be made tax-deductible. Critics respond that this in effect makes political participation universal and compulsory.

FACTLILE 9 THE MCCAIN-FEINGOLD ACT

A Ban on Soft Money. The Act prohibits all soft i.e., unregulated, money contributions to the national political parties from corporations, labor unions, and individuals. State parties that are permitted under state law to accept these unregulated contributions would be prohibited from spending them on activities relating to federal elections, including advertising that supports or opposes a federal candidate. In addition, federal candidates would be prohibited from raising soft money.

Limits on Hard Money. The Act also doubles the amount of hard i.e. regulated money individuals may contribute to state parties for use in federal elections, from $5,000 to $10,000. It increases the amount of hard money an individual may contribute in aggregate to all federal candidates, parties, and PACs in a single year from $25,000 to $30,000.

Restrictions on Issue Ads run by Corporations and Unions.

These ads skirt federal election law by avoiding the use of direct requests to vote for or against a particular candidate. Labor unions and for-profit corporations are prohibited from spending funds on election communications such as radio or TV ads that refer to a clearly identified candidate or candidates and appear within 30 days of a primary or 60 days of a general election. This definition does not include any printed communication, direct mail, voter guides, or the Internet. Non-profits may run ads but only using individual contributions and they must disclose the source.

This provision gives the public crucial information about the election activities of independent groups and prevents corporate and union money from being spent to influence elections.

Foreign Money. Foreign nationals are entirely prohibited from making any contributions in a federal, state or local election.

It is also now illegal to raise election funds on federal property, including the White House and the US Congress.

In *Citizens United v. Federal Election Commission 2010,* however, the US Supreme Court ruled that the McCain-Feingold Act was in violation of corporations' and unions' First Amendment rights. Under the ruling, corporations and unions are no longer barred from promoting the election of one candidate over another candidate.

Until national TV is provided free for national candidates and local TV for local candidates, as in some other countries, there will likely be arguments over campaign finance. Even free airtime is problematic, since it would have to be paid for by taxpayers, although there is already a box on federal income forms which taxpayers can check to have $3 of their taxes allocated to funds for better voting facilities.

Public perceptions of politics

American politics is highly transparent. The two-party system is generally effective, the media are active, and the law requires a great deal of disclosure of information about elected officials' activities in office, especially about how and why decisions were reached. This makes it difficult for politicians to get away with corruption and impropriety, at least for long. Political misbehavior (shenanigans) is more likely where one of the parties has an unchallenged majority for a long time and falls under the control of a party machine. This happened in New York in the 19th century, and the building that housed the Democratic headquarters, Tammany Hall, gave its name to that type of politics. The Republicans had their share of scandal in the Watergate affair in the 1970s, when it was alleged that President Nixon authorized members of the White House staff to commit a burglary. Americans expect high standards of their elected officials and are shocked when they behave badly. A number of Congress people failed to win re-election in 2006 because of alleged corruption.

Americans have little interest in politics and little trust in politicians. Voters, unlike theorists, respond less to ideas than to performance, less to grand promises than to results. They look to political parties and movements, as the Republican pollster David Winston likes to say, less as repositories of ideology than as tools to solve problems. Many people do not like either of the two main parties, and the number of people voting at elections is in long-term decline; only about half of those who could vote for the President actually do so. There is also the problem of *fall-off* i.e., people will vote for the most important positions like state governor but not for city judge. Party loyalties are fluid because people become suspicious of the party in power and like to have a turnover of officeholders in the hope of keeping them honest. Some people favor term limits for members of Congress, as there are for Presidents; others say this would mean the loss of competent, experienced legislators. Americans like to choose candidates because of their character more than their policies. One reason is that the legislative system is so complex and involves so many compromises to get legislation passed that it is not always practicable for the parties to guarantee that certain legislation will be passed if they are elected. Thus in election campaigns, politicians try to avoid seeming overly partisan, and instead talk about their beliefs and values, such as religion and the family, rather than issues and programs. For example, although an increasing number of Americans do not regularly attend worship, it is very rare to find a politician who does not profess to believe in God. This is partly because the American identity is still basically a Christian one, and partly because belief in God suggests morality and honesty. Candidates use soundbites, short, memorable phrases, which they hope will be repeated often and lodge in voters' minds, to encapsulate what they stand for. For instance, in 2000, Senator John McCain used the slogan "Real reform from a real reformer." Even so, some issues, such as abortion and gun control, do come to the fore in elections, and an otherwise bland contest can be become acrimonious and hard-fought.

Americans tend only to see the problems in their political system, rather than its strengths, and try not to get involved, which makes the problems worse. Although they may threaten to write their member of Congress, many do not know who that is or where to find out. To some extent, though, this is being counteracted by the internet, and politics on the internet is having an increasing effect.

The health of American democracy

In *Habits of the Heart*, Robert Bellah and co-authors identify six American visions of the public good, which they see as three contrasting pairs: the Establishment versus populism; neocapitalism versus welfare liberalism; and the administered society versus economic democracy. These illustrate the American inability to reconcile liberal economic philosophy derived from the utilitarian individualism of Hobbes with the expressive individualism of Whitman and Emerson. Yet the contrasting visions have much in common. From the late 19th century until the Depression both the Establishment and populists recognized there was and needed to be a moral component in American public life. Both neocapitalism (personified by Ronald Reagan and George Bush) and welfare liberalism (exemplified by FDR) seek to equip the citizens and the country to be competitive, the former by unraveling the safety net, the latter by strengthening it, according to their optimism or pessimism about the market. The administered society is a continuation of the Progressive ideal of scientific "mastery" which represents economic democracy. The question is whether this should be run by a partnership of elites who work to adjust and balance political, economic and social interests, or whether decision-making should somehow be spread out to include the people at least nominally. But ultimately both sides endorse a similar kind of governance by expert, without moral content. Thus, in the view of some critics, government by a managerial elite, the kind of "democratic despotism" which de Tocqueville saw as a potential of individualistic American mores has arrived.

Voter participation is generally considered a good thing and those who vote are regarded as model citizens. Voting is believed to be a symptom of civic health and virtue. Yet the incentives to cast a ballot are few, and America has been described by Michael McHugh in *The Second Gilded Age* as "a deeply flawed democracy, heavily manipulated by mass advertising and organized money, that could best be described as 'oligarchic pluralism'." Voting costs time and opportunity, yet no election of any importance will turn on a single vote. Presidential elections never turn on a single ballot. Even the controversial vote in Florida in the Presidential election in 2000 was decided by 537 votes. Indeed one reason why the inefficiency of some voting machines had not become an issue before was that American elections are decided by significant margins, thousands, even tens of thousands of votes, so that the results from a few machines or even a few districts will not be material. Yet 100 million people may turn out to vote and wait in line for hours to do so. There is, however, a minority opinion, advocated by economists such as Bryan Caplan, that increasing voter participation is a bad thing. He advances his views in *The Myth of the Rational Voter: Why Democracies Choose Bad Policies* (2008). The argument of his book, perhaps surprisingly, is not that most voters are ignorant about political issues but that they are wrong about the issues, and that their mistaken ideas lead to policies that leave society as a whole worse off. Caplan thinks that voter ignorance, manipulative politicians and lobbying by special interests are endemic to democracy. They are what you would expect to find in a system designed to serve the wishes of the people. Unusually for an American, Caplan argues that the best cure for the ills of democracy is not more democracy but less.

Think tanks

Think tanks, or policy institutes, play an important part in policy debate as they seek to shape the preferences and choices of Presidents, legislators and administrators. As a source of new and independent ideas, think tanks are seen to be different from interest groups and lobbyists, although the difference is not always clear cut. They can play a decisive role because of weaker party discipline, decentralized government, and the periodic turnover in the senior civil service as Administrations of the two parties take office. Moreover think tanks may feel freer to propose and debate controversial ideas than people within government. Having many opportunities and few constraints, the think tanks can become involved at many points in the political process. There are some 1,500 of them, ranging from tiny bodies with one or two staff and budgets of $100,000 - $200,000 to the RAND Corporation (founded 1946) with a budget of $100 million. They vary widely in mission, ideological orientation, areas of specialization, leadership and research output. Although the majority of think tanks are small and have modest resources, they benefit from the array of access points provided by the fragmented political system.

Originally meetings between defense scientists and military planners in a secure environment, until around 1970, there were only a few dozen think tanks, mostly offering non-partisan policy and military advice to the government, and generally with large staffs and research budgets. After 1970, a plethora of organizations sprang up to populate the political landscape, as many smaller think tanks were formed to express various ideological views. Nowadays virtually every interest or issue has a think tank, creating a crowded, competitive market. Some think tanks, such as the Heritage Foundation, are clearly aligned with conservative causes. Others, especially those focused on social and environmental reforms, such as the Tellus Institute, are viewed as clearly liberal. Still others, such as the Cato Institute, promote libertarian social and economic reforms. Globalization has led to increased connectedness between people, issues and ideas and collaboration between think tanks across continents. For instance, the Brookings Institution (founded 1916) collaborates with the Ministry of Foreign Affairs of Qatar for an initiative on West-Islam relations.

Most think tanks are private organizations and sometimes take the form of institutes or corporations. They generally receive funding from private donors. Other sources of income include consulting and commissioned research. Think tanks are tax-exempt and usually nonprofit. To maintain their tax-exempt status, they must refrain from open partisanship. The increased polarization of politics, however, is making it harder for think tanks to remain nonpartisan, and the number of centrist think tanks is diminishing. Consequently some think tanks have become more cautious about what they will publish. Policy makers, however, are increasingly turning to think tanks for research and analysis, on security and defense particularly. Think tanks in this area include the Center for Naval Warfare Studies at the Naval War College, the Center for Technology and National Security Policy at the National Defense University, the Institute for Homeland Security Studies, the Institute for National Strategic Studies, and the Strategic Studies Institute at the U. S. Army War College. The federal government also funds some or all of the work of around 30 nonprofit Federally Funded Research and Development Centers (FFRDCs) to meet specific long-term technical needs that cannot be met by any other single organization. FFRDCs typically assist government agencies with scientific research and analysis, systems development, and systems acquisition, through bringing together the expertise and approach of government, industry, and academia. The FFRDCs include the Aerospace Corporation, the Institute for Defense Analysis and the MIT Lincoln Laboratory. A special type of think tank are the 1,000 or so Federal Advisory Committees or Commissions which advise the President or executive agencies on specific issues, but have come under some degree of oversight and are required to make formal records available to the public.

Think tanks lobby all levels and branches of government, testify before Congressional committees and fill acres of column inches with proposals, op eds (opinion editorials) and even full-length books, some of which are blueprints for an Administration and become best sellers. Among the many ways think tanks seek to influence the political system, contact with Presidential campaign and transition teams is important. The media watchgroup Fairness and Accuracy in Reporting (FAIR) has identified the top 25 think tanks by media citations, which it classifies by ideology as 37% conservative, 47% centrist, and 16% progressive. The most-cited think tank was the Brookings Institution, followed by the Council on Foreign Relations, the American Enterprise Intitute, the Heritage Foundation, and the Center for Strategic and International Studies. The Center for Economic and Policy Research estimates that it is the most cost-effective of the think tanks, measured by the citations per $10,000 budgeted. Media coverage, however, although a commonly-used metric, does not prove that a think tank is effective, only that its input is being talked about. Access does not equate to influence either. The fact that a think tank may gain face time with decision makers, airtime on television and radio and widespread exposure in the press only shows that their issue is being considered, not that the think tank has actually achieved anything. Indeed, given the multitude of organizations involved in politics, it is impossible generally to attribute a policy or a law to anyone in particular.

Lacking long run support from government or universities, think tanks tend to pursue aims and do research that are most likely to attract funding, and this tends to limit depth of analysis and innovation and the ability to attract and retain the best scholars. With the increase in the number of think tanks has come greater competition for funding, a tighter focus on dissemination, as think tanks seek to demonstrate that they make a difference, and a louder clamor for attention from policymakers and the media. Real-time media are also a mixed blessing for think tanks. The emergence of a 24/7 media, and the immediacy of the internet, place more demands on think tanks to demonstrate their influence on policy by increasing their output. This may lead to loss of control over the way they use their staff and where they direct their research, and diminish the quality of dialogue on certain issues by shifting the focus of debate onto the provocative and sensational. Op-eds, brief reports and sound bites may replace in-depth analysis. Undeniably, though, the internet provides a larger audience and connects them with other policy elites and the public. Making think tanks more visible may also help engage an apathetic electorate on issues of national and international importance.

Think tanks have attracted a degree of controversy. Supporters like the National Institute for Research Advancement, itself a think tank, hail them as "one of the main policy actors in democratic societies ... assuring a pluralistic, open and accountable process of policy analysis, research, decision-making and evaluation" (NIRA's *World Directory of Think Tanks*: Introduction, 2002). Critics, however, have suggested that, because most think tanks are privately funded, their results are to some extent biased. In fact, think tanks have something of an image problem. It is easy to assert that they will be inclined to disseminate only research results which ensure the continued flow of funds from private donors. Indeed it could be claimed that think tanks are little more than propaganda tools for promoting the ideological arguments or commercial interests of whatever group established them. For example, The Advancement of Sound Science Coalition was formed in the mid 1990s to dispute research that had found a link between second-hand smoke and cancer. Meanwhile the Discovery Institute has generated a great deal of controversy by injecting the concept of intelligent design into public debate.

Online politics

Talk radio, internet bulletin boards and blogs have become an important part of political communication, not only at grassroots level but between candidates and voters. About 60 million people take part. Both parties now raise large sums through the internet. Websites and online discussions fuel and shape populist protest on left and right, against the Iraq war, for example, or against the "good ol' boys" in Washington. When a bi-partisan bill on illegal immigration was published online, the fierce negative reaction led to its rejection. Even long-serving legislators like Joe Biden (Democrat) and John McCain (Republican) in 2008 had to ride these groundswells of popular protest as if they themselves were insurgents, pointing out at the same time that the other party's nominee was in fact a Washington insider.

THE JUDICIAL BRANCH

The US legal system is based on English Common, or judge-made, law. In addition, the balance of powers created by the Constitution calls for judicial review of legislative acts. Indeed the very fact of having a Constitution requires a judicial authority to interpret it.

The Federal Court System

The judiciary consists of a system of courts spread throughout the country, headed by the Supreme Court of the US. The first Congress divided the nation into districts and created federal courts for each one. The present structure comprises the Supreme Court, 13 courts of appeal, 94 district courts, and three courts of special jurisdiction, the US Tax Court, the US Court of Federal Claims and the Court of International Trade. There is also the Foreign Intelligence Surveillance Court, which supervises government electronic surveillance and the physical search of persons engaged in espionage or international terrorism against the US on behalf of a foreign power. Congress today retains the power to create and abolish federal courts, as well as to determine the number of judges in the federal judiciary system. It cannot, however, abolish the Supreme Court.

Federal jurisdiction

The judicial power encompasses cases arising under the Constitution, an act of Congress, or a treaty of the US; cases affecting ambassadors, ministers, and consuls of foreign countries in the US; controversies to which the US government is a party; controversies between states (or their citizens) and foreign nations (or their citizens or subjects); and bankruptcy cases. Included are cases in which a state government is a plaintiff and a citizen of another state the defendant, but not vice versa. The Supreme Court has original jurisdiction in only two kinds of cases: those involving foreign dignitaries and those in which a state is a party. All other cases reach the Court on appeal from lower courts.

Powers

The power of the federal courts extends both to civil actions for damages and other redress, and to criminal cases arising under federal law. Ordinarily, federal courts do not hear cases arising under the laws of individual states. However, some cases over which federal courts have jurisdiction may also be heard and decided by state courts.

Independence

The Constitution safeguards judicial independence by providing that federal judges shall hold office "during good behavior". In practice, this means until they die, retire, or resign, although a judge who commits an offence while in office may be impeached. US judges are appointed by the President and confirmed by the Senate. Congress also determines the pay scale of judges.

The Supreme Court

The Supreme Court is the highest court of the US, and the only one specifically created by the Constitution. A decision of the Supreme Court cannot be appealed to any other court. Congress has the power to fix the number of judges sitting on the Court and, within limits, decide what kind of cases it may hear, but it cannot change the powers given to the Supreme Court by the Constitution itself. The Constitution is silent on the qualifications for judges. There is no requirement that judges be lawyers, although, in fact, all federal judges and Supreme Court justices have been members of the bar. The Supreme Court consists of the Chief Justice of the US and eight associate justices. The Chief Justice is the executive officer of the Court but, in deciding cases, has only one vote, as do the associate justices.

Of the several thousand cases filed annually, the Court usually hears only about 150. Most of the cases involve important principles of interpretation of the law or of the intent of Congress in passing a piece of legislation. A ruling by the Supreme Court sets a precedent which is binding on lower courts in similar cases. A significant amount of the work of the Supreme Court consists of *constitutionality* cases, determining whether legislation or executive acts conform to the Constitution. The task is particularly important because in some instances the Constitution is vague or ambiguous and in many cases is silent. This power of judicial review is not specifically provided for by the Constitution. Rather, it is doctrine inferred by the Court from its reading of the Constitution, and forcefully stated in the landmark *Marbury v. Madison* case of 1803. In that case, the Court held that "a legislative act contrary to the Constitution is not law," and further observed that "it is emphatically the province and duty of the judicial department to say what the law is." The doctrine has also been extended to cover the activities of state and local governments.

Decisions of the Court need not be unanimous; a simple majority prevails, provided that at least six justices — the legal quorum — participate in the decision. In split decisions, the Court usually issues a majority and a minority (or dissenting) opinion, both of which may form the basis for future decisions by the Court. Often justices will write separate concurring opinions when they agree with a decision, but for reasons other than those cited by the majority.

There are three main schools of thought about how the Constitution should be interpreted. Some believe it is best to follow exactly what the Constitution says (*strict constructionists*). Others such as Justice Antonin Scalia think it is necessary to consider what was in the minds of the people who wrote it (the *Framers*), as evidenced by such classic texts as *The Federalist Papers,* in which Alexander Hamilton (assisted a little by John Jay and James Madison) wrote commentaries on all the articles of the Constitution. This theory is called *originalism.* Today, the Second Amendment, which gives the people the right to bear arms, is in controversy between the two schools of constitutional thought. Some, like the National Rifle Association, say that laws limiting this right are unconstitutional; others say that the Second Amendment was passed so that Americans could defend themselves against a possible attack by the British, and since this is unimaginable today, limiting the right to bear arms would not go against the intentions of the Framers. Modernist theories such as the doctrine of the Living Constitution hold that justices should adapt interpretations to changing circumstances. In some decisions, the Supreme Court draws on pre-Revolutionary precedents and on the English common law tradition.

Another factor is the claim by the Religious Right that the nation was founded on religious principles and that the Court should give these priority in its secular judgments. From this standpoint "the judiciary are regarded as dangerously out of control and in need of being reined in if they exercise any independence of view." (Bates. *God's Own Country: Religion and Politics in the USA,* Hodder, 2008, p. 97).

The idea of a separate supreme court which could rule on the constitutionality of laws was foreshadowed by John Locke when he said (II:11:137) "Absolute arbitrary power, or government without *settled standing laws*, can neither of them consist with the ends of society and government…." According to Locke, the most important reason for controlling the legislature was to preserve property: "The *supreme power* cannot take any part of his *property* from any man without his own consent" (II:11:137).

The growing activism of the Supreme Court (called "judicial activism" by those who disapprove) and fear of its increase has become a matter of political debate and an aspect of the "culture wars" that currently divide America. On the whole, though, the Court's decisions in such landmark cases as *Brown v. Board of Education* (which helped end the segregation of schools), *Roe v. Wade* (which legalized abortion) and *Miranda v. Arizona* (which made police formally warn suspects of their rights to remain silent and to see a lawyer) have won general acceptance, although abortion rights are still limited in a number of states.

Courts of Appeals and District Courts

The second highest level of the federal judiciary is made up of the courts of appeal. Congress has established 12 regional circuit courts of appeal and the US Court of Appeals for the Federal Circuit. The number of judges sitting on each of these courts varies considerably (from 6 to 28), but most circuits have between 10 and 15 judges.

The courts of appeal review decisions of the district courts (trial courts with federal jurisdiction) within their areas. They are also empowered to review orders of the independent regulatory agencies in cases where the internal review mechanisms of the agencies have been exhausted and there still exists substantial disagreement over points of law. In addition, the Court of Appeals for the Federal Circuit has nationwide jurisdiction to hear appeals in specialized cases, such as those involving patent laws and cases decided by the courts of special jurisdiction.

Below the courts of appeal are the district courts. The 50 states and US territories are divided into 94 districts so that litigants may have a trial within easy reach. Each district court has at least two judges, many have several, and the most populous districts have more than two dozen. Where there are many judges, they do not all sit in the same court. Depending on caseload, a judge from one district may temporarily sit in another district. Congress fixes the boundaries of the districts according to population, size, and volume of work. Some of the smaller states constitute a district by themselves, while the larger states, such as New York, California, and Texas, have four districts each. Except in the District of Columbia, judges must be residents of the district in which they permanently serve. District courts hold their sessions at periodic intervals in different cities of the district.

Most cases heard by these courts involve federal offences such as theft of federal property, violations of pure-food, banking, and counterfeiting laws and misuse of the mails. These are the only federal courts where grand juries indict those accused of crimes, and juries decide the cases.

Each judicial district also includes a US bankruptcy court, because Congress has determined that bankruptcy matters should be addressed in federal courts rather than state courts. Through the bankruptcy process, individuals or businesses that can no longer pay their creditors may either seek a court-supervised liquidation of their assets, or they may reorganize their financial affairs and work out a plan to pay off their debts.

Special courts

In addition to the courts of general jurisdiction, there are three federal courts for special purposes. These are known as "legislative" courts because they were created by congressional action. Judges in these courts, like their peers in other federal courts, are appointed for life terms by the President, with Senate approval. The Court of International Trade addresses cases involving international trade and customs issues. The US Court of Federal Claims has jurisdiction over most claims for money damages against the US, disputes over federal contracts, unlawful "takings" of private property by the federal government, and a variety of other claims against the US. The Foreign Intelligence Surveillance Act Court hears applications by federal police agencies, primarily the FBI, for warrants to wiretap suspected foreign intelligence agents inside the US.

The International Court of Justice

The US accepts the jurisdiction of the International Court of Justice with certain reservations, but does not accept the International Criminal Court.

State courts

There are also state, county and city courts. Most states have trial courts which have a general jurisdiction and are known as *courts of common pleas*. Above them are appeals courts, sometimes called *district courts*. Finally there is usually a supreme court. Many states have family courts to hear divorce cases, and small claims courts to hear civil claims for small sums. Each state has its own criminal code, but some crimes are federal offenses. Crimes may come under federal jurisdiction if the crime took place in more than one state. Most of these courts have only one judge, who may be elected rather than appointed.

Court procedure

The judge manages the trial and the parties are represented by lawyers called *attorneys-at-law*. In a criminal trial, the parties are called the *prosecution* and the *defense*. A prosecution is led by an Assistant District Attorney, or in federal cases by a federal attorney. In each county, the people elect a District Attorney (DA), who hires other attorneys. It is because the DA is elected that cases are often referred to as "The People against..." and when the prosecution finish presenting their case, the attorney says "The People rest (their case)." The defendant is represented by a defense attorney, or if too poor to afford one, by a public defender. In a civil case over a small amount, people go to a court of common pleas or small claims court and represent themselves.

When the judge enters to begin the trial, the bailiff calls "All rise!" and everyone stands. The attorneys then make opening statements setting out their case. The judge is addressed as "Your Honor." Testimony is given by witnesses who may be cross-examined by the attorney for the other side. Sometimes expert witnesses will be called. The court bailiff calls the witnesses when they are needed and the court reporter keeps a record of proceedings. As each witness takes the (witness) stand, the bailiff swears them in. Witnesses swear to tell "the truth, the whole truth and nothing but the truth." Those who do not believe in God may make an affirmation, which is equally binding. Lying on oath is a serious offense called *perjury*, which can result in a jail sentence. Attorneys must not *lead* the witness by suggesting the answer they want to hear, and they must not keep repeating the question. An attorney who thinks another is breaking the rules shouts "Objection!" or "Move to strike!" i.e., request that the words be deleted from the record. Almost all cases in America are heard in open court i.e., the court is open to the media and the public. There is a TV channel called *Court TV* which shows only court cases.

At the end of a case, the jury deliberate. If there is a lot of media attention to the case, the judge may sequester the jury i.e., order them to a hotel where they will not be allowed to meet anyone else or receive the media and thus will not be influenced by outside opinions. They are looked after by bailiffs. In a criminal trial, the jury decide the verdict, "Guilty" or "Not Guilty." A defendant is innocent until proved guilty. This bedrock principle of American justice is very important to Americans. In a civil trial the jury will decide for the plaintiff (complainant) or the defendant and may assess the amount of damages.

The virtue of the jury system is that the jury has a direct and emotional engagement with the individual case, and the judgments of jurors are unclouded by the professional bias, ways of thinking or even cynicism of justice system professionals. The jurors are the exclusive judges of fact, while the judge is the judge of the applicable law. This division of responsibility is designed to maintain the supremacy of concrete facts and particulars and to ensure that the courts remain aware that every case is ultimately unique.

Problems with the legal system

African Americans in particular tend to think that the criminal justice system is biased against them. In trials where defendants have been remanded in custody (kept in prison) before the hearing, they often have to wear a prison uniform, which may subconsciously bias the jury against them. African Americans also complain that they are too often denied bail, or that the bail conditions are too onerous (expensive and unduly restrictive). Poor people generally may not be well served by public defenders, who may be inexperienced, incompetent or insufficiently motivated by the low fees to investigate and pursue the defendant's case. In contrast, white people are believed to be able to avoid conviction if they are rich enough to hire a smart lawyer. Also the jury may not be sufficiently representative of the local population; and defendants whose first language is not English may have particular difficulties.

Americans, despite their dislike of lawyers, are a litigious people, and many civil suits that are brought are unnecessary, even frivolous, wasting resources and delaying genuine cases. This is especially serious in cases against doctors, which add greatly to the costs of medical malpractice insurance and hence of medical care, especially in gynecology and obstetrics, sometimes pricing poorer people, particularly African Americans, out of the market altogether. Civil lawyers are generally expensive, which in practice denies poorer litigants their constitutional right to equal protection of the laws. Some lawyers will work for a contingency fee, earning a proportion of the damages if they win and nothing if they lose. A few lawyers known as *ambulance chasers* encourage people hurt in road accidents to sue because they hope to earn a large contingency fee as their share of a payout from the defendant's insurance company. Insurance companies often settle out of court to save the expense of an action. But contingency fees tend to increase the number of cases which have little merit. Ironically, it is partly because of the "equal protection" clause of the Constitution that it has not proved possible to devise a deterrent to trivial lawsuits that would be constitutional.

STATE, CITY AND LOCAL GOVERNMENTS

The federal entity created by the Constitution is the dominant feature of the American governmental system. But the system itself is in reality a mosaic, composed of thousands of smaller units. There are 50 state governments plus the government of the District of Columbia, and further down the scale are still smaller units that govern counties, cities, towns, and villages. "Local government" means any county, city, village, town, district, or other political subdivision of any state, and includes any rural community or unincorporated town or village.

This multiplicity of governmental units is the outcome of how the US evolved. The federal system was actually the last step. The governments of the separate colonies (later states) and, prior to those, the governments of counties and smaller units all preceded the Constitution. And as the new nation pushed westward, each frontier outpost created its own government to manage its affairs.

Today, Americans have come to rely on their state, city and local governments to perform a large number of tasks and provide a variety of services. Hence the bewildering array of jurisdictions.

State governments

In general, matters that lie entirely within state borders are the exclusive concern of state governments. These include internal communications; regulations relating to property, industry, business, and public utilities; the state criminal code; and working conditions within the state. Within this context, the federal government requires that state governments be democratic in form and that they adopt no laws that contradict or violate the federal Constitution or the laws and treaties of the US. States set the local income tax and sales tax, decide the ages at which people can buy alcohol, drive and get married, and determine the school curriculum.

There are, of course, many areas of overlap between state and federal jurisdictions. Particularly in recent years, the federal government has assumed ever broadening responsibility in such matters as health, education, welfare, transportation, and housing and urban development. But where the federal government exercises such responsibility in the states, programs are usually adopted on the basis of cooperation between the two levels of government, rather than as an imposition from above. In fact, under the George W. Bush Administration, cost-sharing with the states became a priority of federal policy.

Like the national government, state governments have three branches: executive, legislative, and judicial; these are roughly equivalent in function and scope to their national counterparts. The chief executive of a state is the governor, elected by popular vote, typically for a four-year term (although in a few states the term is two years). The governor has a deputy known as the lieutenant governor. Except for Nebraska, which has a single legislative body, all states have a bicameral legislature, with the upper house usually called the Senate and the lower house the House of Representatives, the House of Delegates, or the General Assembly. In most states, senators serve four-year terms, and members of the lower house serve two-year terms. Laws are made in basically the same way as in Congress. In some states, for example, California, it is common for a few laws to be made directly through a vote of the people, called an *initiative*. A group may write a law and circulate a petition to win support. If the petition attracts enough signatures, the law is put on the next ballot. These votes usually take place at the same time as state elections. Another way laws are made is by referendum on a statement of principle. If a majority vote in favor, legislation will likely be made.

The constitutions of the various states differ in some details but generally follow a pattern similar to that of the federal Constitution, including a statement of the rights of the people and a plan for organizing the government. On such matters as the operation of businesses, banks, public utilities, and charitable institutions, state constitutions are often more detailed and explicit than the federal one. Each state constitution, however, provides that the final authority belongs to the people, and sets certain standards and principles as the foundation of government.

City governments

About 80 percent of Americans now live in towns, large cities, or suburbs of cities. This makes city governments critically important in the pattern of American government. To a greater extent than on the federal or state level, the city directly serves the needs of the people, providing everything from police and fire protection to sanitary codes, health regulations, education, public transportation, and housing. Local laws called *ordinances* may be made by a council or occasionally by voters in a town meeting.

City governments are chartered by states, and the charters detail the objectives and powers of the municipal government. But in many respects the cities function independently of the states. For most big cities, however, cooperation with both state and federal organizations is essential.

Types of city governments vary widely across the nation. But almost all have some kind of central council, elected by the voters, and an executive officer, assisted by various department heads, to manage the city's affairs. There are three general types of city government: the mayor-council, the commission, and the city manager. These are the pure forms; many cities have developed a combination of two or three of them.

Mayor-Council. This is the oldest form of city government in the US. Its structure is similar to that of the state and national governments, with an elected mayor as chief of the executive branch while an elected council representing the various neighborhoods forms the legislative branch. The mayor appoints heads of city departments and other officials, sometimes with the approval of the council. He or she has the power of veto over ordinances - the laws of the city - and is frequently responsible for preparing the city's budget. The council passes city ordinances, sets the tax rate on property, and apportions money among the various city departments.

The Commission. This combines both the legislative and executive functions in one group of officials, usually three or more in number, elected city-wide. Each commissioner supervises the work of one or more city departments. One is named chairperson of the body and is often called the *mayor,* although his or her power is equivalent to that of the other commissioners.

The City Manager. The appointment of highly trained and experienced professional city managers is a response to the increasing complexity of urban problems, which require management expertise not often possessed by elected public officials.

With a city manager, a small, elected council makes the city ordinances and sets policy, but hires a manager to carry out its decisions. The manager draws up the city budget and supervises most of the departments. Usually there is no set term: the manager serves as long as the council is satisfied with his or her work.

The business of running America's major cities is enormously complex. In terms of population alone, New York City is larger than 41 of the 50 states. It is often said that, next to the presidency, the most difficult executive position in the country is that of Mayor of New York. Yet no Mayor has become President since Coolidge (1923-27). In 2008, former Mayor Rudi Giuliani ran unsuccessfully for the Republican nomination as presidential candidate.

County governments

The county is a subdivision of the state, usually, but not always, containing two or more townships and several villages. New York City is so large that it is divided into five separate boroughs, each a county in its own right: the Bronx, Manhattan, Brooklyn, Queens, and Staten Island. On the other hand, Arlington County, Virginia, just across the Potomac River from Washington, D.C., is both an urbanized and suburban area, governed by a unitary county administration.

In most US counties, one town or city is designated as the county seat, where the government offices are located and where the board of commissioners or supervisors meets. In small counties, boards are elected by the county as a whole; in the larger ones, supervisors represent separate districts or townships. The board levies taxes; borrows and appropriates money; fixes the salaries of county employees; supervises elections; builds and maintains highways and bridges; and administers national, state, and county welfare programs. Counties also have a local police called *sheriff's deputies* who work for the sheriff's department; crimes are prosecuted in the county court by the district attorney. Rural counties may provide schools. Often urban counties cooperate with nearby city governments to provide services.

Town and village governments

Thousands of municipal jurisdictions are too small to qualify as city governments. These are chartered as towns and villages and deal with such strictly local needs as paving and lighting the streets; ensuring a water supply; providing police and fire protection; establishing local health regulations; arranging for garbage, sewage, and other waste disposal; collecting local taxes to support governmental operations; and, in cooperation with the state and county, directly administering the local school system.

The government is usually entrusted to an elected board or council, which may be known by a variety of names: town or village council, board of selectmen, board of supervisors, board of commissioners. The board may have a chairperson or president who functions as chief executive officer, or there may be an elected mayor. Governmental employees may include a clerk, treasurer, police and fire officers, and health and welfare officers. There may be a separate elected school board.

One unique aspect of local government, found mostly in New England, is the "town meeting." Once a year, sometimes more often if needed, the registered voters of the town meet in open session to elect officers, debate local issues, and pass laws for operating the government. As a body, they decide on road construction and repair, construction of public buildings and facilities, tax rates, and the town budget. The town meeting, which has existed for more than two centuries, is often cited as the purest form of direct democracy, in which the governmental power is not delegated, but is exercised directly and regularly by all the people. It has on occasion been revived by presidential candidates, although some object that the meetings are not really town meetings.

Other local governments

The federal, state, and local governments covered here by no means include the whole spectrum of American governmental units. The US Bureau of the Census has in fact identified no fewer than 84,955 local governmental units, including counties, municipalities, townships, school districts, and special districts.

CITIZENSHIP FACT BOX THE FLAG OF THE UNITED STATES

The American flag consists of thirteen equal horizontal stripes of seven red (top and bottom) alternating with six white. In the upper corner near the staff ("the hoist side") there is a rectangle (or "canton") bearing 50 small, white, five-pointed stars arranged in nine offset horizontal rows of six stars (top and bottom) alternating with rows of five stars. The 50 stars represent the 50 states, the 13 stripes represent the 13 original colonies. The 49th and 50th stars were added in 1959 and 1960 respectively, after Alaska and Hawaii were admitted to the Union. White signifies purity and innocence; red, hardiness and valor; and blue, vigilance, perseverance and justice. Because of its stars, stripes, and colors, the American flag is frequently called the *Star-Spangled Banner*, the *Stars and Stripes*, or the *Red, White, and Blue*. Another name is "Old Glory." The design and colors have been the basis for a number of other flags, including those of Chile, Liberia, Malaysia, and Puerto Rico.

Most Americans are very particular about showing proper respect for the flag, and Congress has established a uniform code for displaying it. On certain holidays, the flag is displayed on or near the main administration buildings of all public institutions. It is also displayed in or near every polling place on election days and in or near every schoolhouse during school days. In most of the states there are laws which prohibit the use of the US flag for advertising purposes, although since 9/11 practice has been somewhat relaxed.

CITIZENSHIP FACT BOX THE NATIONAL ANTHEM

The national anthem of the United States of America is "The Star-Spangled Banner", three verses dedicated to the national flag. Usually only the first verse is sung. Written by Francis Scott Key in 1814, as he watched British ships unsuccessfully attempt to take Fort McHenry, Maryland, in the war of 1812, it was officially made the anthem by Congress in 1931. The melody to which Key's words are sung, one of the world's great tunes, originated in Britain.

Oh, say, can you see by the dawn's early light What so proudly we hailed at the twilight's last gleaming? Whose broad stripes and bright stars, through the perilous fight O'er the ramparts we watched were so gallantly streaming? And the rockets' red glare, the bombs bursting in air; Gave proof through the night that our flag was still there. Oh, say, does that star-spangled banner yet wave O'er the land of the free and the home of the brave?

CHAPTER 4

CAPITAL AND LABOR:
THE ECONOMIC SYSTEM AND SOCIAL SECURITY

The American dream, to me, means having the opportunity to achieve . . . because I don't think you should be guaranteed anything other than opportunity.
Lenny Wilkens

A CAPITALIST ECONOMY

In the same year as the US declared its independence, 1776, Scottish economist Adam Smith published *The Wealth of Nations,* which has since become known as "the Bible of capitalism." Smith argued that the apparently selfish activity of individuals to make themselves rich was actually beneficial, since it led to increased production and sharpened competition. As a result, goods circulated more widely and at lower prices, jobs were created and wealth was spread. An "invisible hand" guided individuals to enrich and improve all of society. Smith identified six key success factors for the modern economy: capital accumulation, free trade, limited government, the rule of law (especially the protection of property rights), individual initiative, and competition. Most Americans believe that the rise of their nation as a great economic power could not have occurred under any other than the capitalist system, which is also known as *free enterprise* after a corollary to Smith's thinking: that government should interfere in commerce as little as possible. Americans believe they have surpassed other peoples because their self-discipline and self-sacrifice are greater, and because they obey the dictates of their peers rather than their own egos. Americans think that if other nations wish to attain power and prosperity they should do as they do.

Even so, capitalism creates winners and losers, and there is persistent widespread criticism of the justice, from an egalitarian point of view, of how unfettered competition distributes its rewards. The market and the state have tended to act as coadjutors in a duopoly, to the exclusion of civil society, regulating a consumerist and hedonistic pattern of economic activity, rather than one directed towards improved wealth creation and social development which promotes solidarity in relations between citizens. The American economy, for some people, is perennially pervaded by anxiety about the future, in which fear of losing one's job includes not only the financial consequences but also loss of social status and self-esteem. Competition involves "the uprooting of many previously stable sources of identity and security" (Alan Greenspan, *The Age of Turbulence*, p.18). Naomi, a character in *Portnoy's Complaint* by Philip Roth protests: "American society...not only sanctions gross and unfair relations among men, but it encourages them....Rivalry, competition, envy, jealousy, all that is malignant in human character is nourished by the system. Possessions, money, property – on such corrupt standards as these do you people measure happiness and success. Meanwhile... great segments of your population are deprived of the minimal prerequisites for a decent life.... Because your system is basically exploitive (sic), inherently debasing and unjust....There can never be anything resembling genuine equality in such an environment" (p.261).

In every economic system, entrepreneurs and managers bring together natural resources, labor, and technology to produce and distribute goods and services. But the way these different elements are organized and used also reflects a nation's political ideals and culture. Capitalism is characterized by certain key elements which are conditioned by further elements. The key elements are: (1) private ownership of the means of production; (2) a social class structure of private owners and free wage-earners organized to favor the growth of profits for private owners; and (3) the production of commodities for sale. The conditioning elements are: (a) division of labor; (b) a dependable supply of labor; (c) enough productivity to encourage sustained investment; (d) commercial market organization, including banks, which matches the productivity of the community; (e) a political process whereby economic power can be translated into government policy; (f) a legal system that protects private property; and (g) toleration of new ways of making money.

The US is a capitalist economy, in which a small group of people who control large amounts of money make the most important economic decisions. Marx contrasted capitalist economies to "socialist" ones, which vest more power in the political system. He said little about the American economy, and did not distinguish the important contributions of free, semi-free and unfree labor in American economic development. Although governments in the US have intervened to limit concentrations of wealth and address many of the social problems associated with unchecked private commercial interests, the American economy is predominantly capitalist and becoming more so. In the globalized economy, with billions of transactions involving new forms of credit being made simultaneously, capital flows are too many, too fast and too complex for governments to regulate with much effect. Thus free markets, property rights, and the rule of law, together with its unique culture, education and geography, are what determine America's economic progress. It remains to be seen what effect, if any, new forms of financial regulation proposed after the 2007 financial crisis have on American business behavior and economic development.

The American economy became predominantly capitalist only around 1900. The previous economic history of America falls into three periods. The first, from 1600 to 1790, was a period of subsistence agriculture and handicraft production, with some semi-capitalist production of tobacco. The workers in the most commercialized sectors were mostly slaves and indentured servants. Subsequently, 1790-1865, several industries, including agriculture, became organized on capitalist lines. Classes of free and unfree workers grew rapidly. In the third period, 1865-1920, economic development grew extremely fast as industry and agriculture became almost entirely capitalized. The state of relations between capital and labor at any time in America is the product of the dynamic interplay between enterprises, the workforce, the financial system and the government.

In normal times, the banking system, operating through the bond, stock and commodity markets, is a uniquely effective way of sharing financial risk, and hence of raising capital and fueling economic growth. Unlike many countries, the American financial markets are also the main source of pensions, since retirement accounts are heavily dependent on the performance of the markets and there are relatively few state pensions, funded by the taxpayer. Yet, according to the Dahlem Report, the reason that economists failed to warn sufficiently of the sub-prime crisis and subsequent recession was that they did not give enough weight to the role of the banks in the economy. The sub-prime crisis has made bank chartering (licensing) and regulation a key issue and President Obama has submitted proposals to Congress for a radical overhaul of the bank regulatory system.

The American economy, however, is geared to consumption, not saving. Consequently, Americans save less than their counterparts in other developed countries. Indeed, the rates of capital taxation discourage them from doing so. Lack of savings is one reason the 2008 recession has been so severe. In the last few years, more Americans have declared bankruptcy than have graduated from college.

The cultural factors affecting the economy, such as laws and institutions, traditions and conventions, values and attitudes, although observable, are by their nature hard to measure. The transparency and freedom of information is crucial and is assisted by advanced trading software and the internet. Unfortunately, as the sub-prime crisis has shown, the quality of financial information, such as the asset pricing of newly-created derivatives like collateralized mortgages, is not always good enough, even for experts to understand and assess. Another key cultural factor is optimism. Americans have always believed they live in a land of opportunity, where anybody who has a good idea, determination, and a willingness to work hard can start a business and prosper. This belief in entrepreneurship and willingness to take risks sustains the small businesses that employ half the workforce.

But the unique and arguably most important American contribution to business organization is the corporation. No institution has been more significant in the growth of America as an economic superpower. It has overcome distance and time to create a national market and an international presence. The unique feature of a corporation is that, although an abstraction, it can act in many respects like a person. But because ownership of shares in a corporation is dispersed among many people, ownership and control of a public corporation are separate and this has given rise to controversy over the role and remuneration of the CEO. Even more significant are the tendency of successful corporations to become monopolies, and the role of government, through laws and regulators, in counteracting this by maximizing the access of new players to the market.

The success of the corporation has also given employers greater power over workers. Unions' attempts to counterbalance this power by organizing for collective bargaining over pay and working conditions have had at best mixed success. This is the result of many factors: the large number of scattered small businesses; resistance by employers; large pools of unskilled workers; labor mobility; globalization; past links between union leaders and organized crime; and court decisions that unions cannot enforce agency shops and that employers can fire workers for going on strike. Unions have been relatively successful in the automobile, aerospace, docks, trucking and utilities industries and in the public sector. But US labor standards remain below international norms, and despite trumpeted levels of productivity, a relatively large number of Americans remain in low-paying jobs living paycheck-to-paycheck. There are indeed those like Robert Reich who claim that the process of upward social mobility has broken down. Even so, there is growing evidence of diversity and gender equality in employment and of more equality between dual-earner couples in the home. Indeed, women take more degrees at all levels than men. America's changing workforce is today beginning to adopt new versions of the American Dream of success, fame and wealth alongside the traditional one based on thrift and hard work. For some this means a philosophy of "get rich quick." For others it means sustainable, greener consumption and a new balance between life and work.

THE FINANCIAL SYSTEM

Banks and banking

There are nearly 8,000 different commercial banks in the US. This is because banks may either be chartered nationally or by individual states. Some banks form holding companies, which own banks with the same name in different states. American banks are almost all banks of deposit and credit. Banking is dominated by large money center banks such as Citigroup, which raise money by dealing in the international money markets and lending it to businesses and other banks.

Until the Financial Services Modernization Act of 1999, the Gramm-Leach-Bliley Act, the law limited the ability of different parts of the finance industry to enter one another's markets and freely invest in each other's businesses. Now commercial banks, brokerage firms, hedge funds, institutional investors, pension funds and insurance companies can offer one-stop shops which provide a whole range of financial services. (A hedge fund is allowed to use aggressive strategies unavailable to other mutual funds and is exempt from many of the rules and regulations governing them. Hedge funds are restricted by law to no more than 100 investors per fund, and as a result most hedge funds set extremely high minimum investment amounts, ranging anywhere from $250,000 to over $1 million.)

Whether or not the liberalization of financial services contributed to the sub-prime crisis is a matter of dispute. Another focus of debate is how far the internet enables currency speculators to evade regulatory controls and destabilize the financial system. In any case, since the 1990s, the foreign currency reserves in private hands have outstripped those held by central banks. Hence the central banks are limited in what they can do to stabilize exchange rates. At the same time, their power to set interest rates is being limited through the financial services giants acting in concert. Moreover, the oligopoly (semi-monopoly) power of these companies may be seen as a potential threat to local banks. Meanwhile some Wall Street giants have obtained "national bank" status in several countries. Citigroup, for instance, is now Argentina's second largest bank.

Smaller players in the markets are credit unions. These are independent, not-for-profit, cooperative financial institutions. They are owned and controlled by their members, and operated for the purpose of promoting thrift, providing credit at reasonable rates, and offering other financial services to members. Credit unions are typically smaller than banks; for example, the average US credit union had $93 million in assets, while the average bank had $1.53 billion, as of 2007. Many credit unions exist to further community development. They can be chartered by either the federal government or by a state and are tax-exempt. All federal credit unions and 95% of state-chartered credit unions have "share insurance" (deposit insurance) of at least $250,000 per member through the National Credit Union Share Insurance Fund (NCUSIF). The insurance is backed by the full faith and credit of the US government and is administered by the National Credit Union Administration. Credit unions typically have higher equity capital ratios than banks. As of 2005, credit unions had 86 million members, 43% of the economically active population. As of April 2008, the world's largest credit union was the Navy Federal Credit Union, serving U.S. Department of Defense employees, contractors, and the families of servicepeople, with over $35 billion in assets and over 3 million members.

Individuals hold their bank accounts in commercial banks, which must have a charter (license to operate) from the US or a state government. Each state decides whether to allow customers to do branch banking i.e., do business at any branch of a bank, not just the one where they have an account. People also keep money in savings and loans associations. The most common accounts are checking and savings accounts. US banks issue checkbooks and offer card services. Many banks offer free banking, but some make customers pay a charge for a checking account. This may be a few dollars a month or a few cents per check. Customers get a monthly statement, and the bank cancels and returns any checks they have written. To deposit a check in their bank account, the person to whom it is made out must endorse it by signing his or her name on the back. To get cash for the check, it is necessary to go to the bank that issued it. Banks are open during most of the day, and when they are closed, many transactions can be done through an Automated Teller Machine (ATM). Credit cards are widely used and debit cards are becoming popular, but checks are used to pay for many goods, although personal checks are often not accepted from out-of-state customers.

Americans, as is often observed, save too little. The national saving rate was only 5.7% of GDP in April, 2009. Historically, the American saving rate has been one of the lowest among developed countries, perhaps because the US has one of the world's highest effective tax rates on capital. Fortunately, the capital markets in America deploy savings very efficiently and waste little, so that the capital stock of the US has produced the highest rate of productivity growth among the G7 nations (Greenspan, op. cit., p. 369).

The US dollar is made up of 100 cents. The Department of the Treasury prints bills in denominations of $1, $2, $5, $10, $20, $50 and $100. US dollars are all the same size (8 x 6 inches, 6.5 x 15.5 cms). All bills are green and for this reason are sometimes called greenbacks. On the front, each has the picture of a famous American. The dollar bill, for instance, shows George Washington. Dollars are sometimes informally known as bucks because the early settlers traded in buckskins and prices would sometimes be given as a number of buckskins. The $ refers to the dollar, as in $500, not the bill itself. The coins that make up the dollar are the 1-cent piece (1¢, the penny), the nickel (5¢), the dime (10¢) and the quarter (25¢). Since 2005, there have been $1 coins as well as notes. There are also half-dollars and silver dollars but these are rarely seen, as is the $2 bill.

The Federal Reserve

The US central bank (founded 1913 and dating in its modern form from 1935) is the U.S. Federal Reserve Bank, often called the Fed. In addition, there are 12 regional reserves, which lend to and regulate the commercial banks in their region. The system is governed by seven people appointed by the President. From 1987-2006 the Chairman of the Federal Reserve System was Alan Greenspan. It is now Ben Bernanke. The Chairman serves for four years and may be reappointed an indefinite number of times. The Chairman can do little alone but needs the support of the other governors. While the governors are all appointed by the President, they serve for 14 years, longer than any appointees except justices of the Supreme Court. Congress made the terms of governors long in order to shield them from political pressures. The Fed maintains its independence by funding itself with interest income from the Treasury securities and other assets it holds.

All national banks must belong to the reserve system, and state banks, savings and loan associations, and credit unions may join with the Fed's approval. The Fed regulates private banking institutions, works to contain risk to the financial system in financial markets, and provides certain financial services to the US government, the public, and financial institutions. The Fed is in charge of the electronic payment systems that transfer more than $4 trillion a day in money and securities among banks all over the country and much of the rest of the world. The Fed tells commercial banks how much money they must keep in reserve and decides what rate of interest to charge when lending them money, the "discount rate." The Fed influences interest rates by announcing the funds rate the Fed is seeking and through having its traders in New York buy and sell Treasury securities on the open market. When they buy, they put billions of dollars into the system, and interest rates fall. When they sell, the opposite happens. Decisions on interest rates are made by an expanded Board known as the Federal Open Market Committee (FOMC), which consists of the Chairman and the six other board members plus the Presidents of the 12 regional Federal Reserve Banks, only five of whom can vote at any one time. Decisions are by majority. By tradition the Chairman of the Fed is elected annually to the Chair of the FOMC; by statute the Chairman only controls the agenda for the Board of Governors. All other Board matters are decided by majority. Board and FOMC meetings are held in secret but the FOMC announces moves on rates right afterwards; minutes are published after five years.

The statutory mission of the Fed is to put in place the monetary conditions needed for maximum sustainable long-term growth and employment. This means that the Fed has to work to keep prices stable beyond the current electoral cycle. There is thus sometimes tension between the economic management of the country, led by the Fed, and the priorities of politicians, who decide public spending.

The Fed is constantly in touch with banks and businesspeople and has the most up to date information on the performance of the economy. The quarterly meetings of the Fed are closely watched since its decisions on money supply and lending rates (Fed fund rates) have a crucial impact on the economy, and its statements are an indicator of the economy's performance and prospects, which can affect rates and markets around the world. The Fed does not issue money. Dollar bills and coins are issued by the Department of the Treasury.

Even during a credit crisis, the Fed cannot instruct banks to make loans to businesses. That would be an abuse of government power. What it can do is put heavy pressure on the banks to maintain the liquidity of the financial system. The Fed these days does not try to correct stock market bubbles, for three reasons. No one can know with certainty whether stocks are over- or under-priced. Market sentiment does not take notice of warnings alone and the Fed has only limited room to manoeuver when changing rates because it would otherwise damage the economy. And if the Fed made a misjudgment it would lose credibility.

When banks start lending again as the economy pulls out of recession, the Fed will act to reduce the deficit, which has been enlarged by the stimulus package. To do so, it will need to be able to offer banks something else to hold in place of cash, and thus reduce the money supply. The solution the Fed is proposing is to allow it to create additional kinds of liabilities on its balance sheet. If Congress grants it the power to accept not just interest-free but interest-paying reserve deposits (which it has) and the power to issue and sell its own interest-bearing bonds (which it may), then the Fed will be able to take money back out of the system.

The Repo market

The repurchase agreement ("repo") market is one of the largest and most active sectors in the US money market. Repos are widely used for investing surplus funds short term, or for borrowing short term against collateral. Dealers in securities use repos to manage their liquidity, finance their inventories, and speculate in various ways. The Fed uses repos to manage the aggregate reserves of the banking system. The repo market plays a crucial role in allowing financial companies to secure short-term funding. At its peak, the repo market was worth $5 trillion and provided up to a third of the total funding for some banks, including Bear Stearns and Lehman Brothers.

The repo market is one in which two participants agree that one will sell securities, most often Treasury securities, to another and make a commitment to repurchase the securities on a future specified date, or on call, at a specified price. In effect, it is a way of borrowing or lending stock for cash, with the stock serving as collateral. There are three types of repo maturities: overnight, maturing the next day; term, with a specified end date; and open repo with no end date. Although repos are typically short-term, it is not unusual to see repos with a maturity as long as two years. Under a repo agreement, the borrower pays a fixed rate of interest, the repo rate. The interest is represented by the difference between the forward price (future) and the spot price (present). The overnight repo rate normally runs slightly below the Fed funds rate for two reasons. First a repo transaction is a secured loan, whereas the sale of Fed funds is an unsecured loan. Second, many who can invest in repos cannot sell Fed funds. Even though the return is modest, overnight lending in the repo market offers several advantages to investors. By rolling overnight repos, they can keep surplus funds invested without losing liquidity or incurring risk of the price falling. They also incur very little credit risk because the collateral is always high-grade paper.

The credit risk of a repo is subject to many factors, including the term of the repo, the liquidity of the security, and the strength of the counterparties. If the seller fails to repurchase the security at the maturity date, the buyer may sell it in order to recover the cash lent. The security, however, may have lost value since the transaction. To mitigate the credit risk, sellers often have to provide a margin of 2% to 5% on the collateral, and if the price of the security falls, make a margin payment. During the 2008 crisis, lenders would not buy mortgage-based securities because of the high risk. Hence the repo market shrank. Existing transactions failed because the risky securities lost value and yielded lenders no profit. Lenders therefore bought government bonds instead. The Federal Reserve has since recommended a clearing house to backstop repo transactions and the NYSE has announced a clearing house for certain repos. The banks would not be able to provide a complete clearing house even in normal times because of the huge sums involved.

The Stock Markets

Raising capital

The lifeblood of capitalism, capital itself, is provided through the stock and other capital markets. Brought first to Wall Street, New York City, in 1792, the institution has flourished in the US. Today the New York Stock Exchange (NYSE) is the world's largest and the nation's financial hub. The Council of Economic Advisers has calculated that in September, 2005, the market value of publicly traded US corporations was $15 trillion, although since the sub-prime crisis, values have gone down by around 40%. While small entrepreneurs usually borrow the money they need from friends, relatives, or banks, larger businesses are more likely to acquire cash through a stock exchange (although they can also raise short-term capital - usually to finance inventories - by getting loans from banks or other lenders). Funds are raised on the stock exchange for buildings, machinery, vehicles and other assets; to finance research and development; and to support a host of other essential activities. There are several different types of stock – bonds, preferred stock and common stock.

Bonds

A bond is a written promise to pay back a specific amount of money at a certain date or dates in the future. Meanwhile, bondholders receive interest payments at fixed rates on specified dates. Holders can sell bonds to someone else before they are due. Corporations benefit from issuing bonds because the interest rates they must pay investors are generally lower than the rates for most other types of borrowing and because interest paid on bonds is a tax-deductible business expense. Corporations must make interest payments, however, even when they are not showing profits. If investors doubt a company's ability to meet its interest obligations, they will either refuse to buy its bonds or will demand a higher rate of interest to compensate them for the increased risk. For this reason, smaller corporations can seldom raise much capital by issuing bonds. Moreover, events have shown that it is not always possible for banks to estimate risks correctly. Although the stock market gets much more publicity, the bond market is much bigger. At the end of 2006, according to the Securities Industry and Financial Markets Association, the bond market was worth $27.4 trillion and the stock market $21.6 trillion.

Preferred Stock

A company may choose to issue new "preferred" stock to raise capital. Buyers of these shares have special status in the event the company encounters financial trouble. If profits are limited, preferred-stock owners will be paid their dividends after bondholders receive their guaranteed interest payments but before any common stock dividends are paid.

Common Stock

If a company is in good financial health, it can raise capital by issuing common stock. Typically, investment banks help companies issue stock, agreeing to buy any new shares issued at a set price if the public refuses to buy the stock at a certain minimum price. (An investment bank is an individual or institution which acts as an underwriter or agent for corporations and municipalities issuing securities. Most also maintain broker/dealer operations, maintain markets for previously issued securities, and offer advisory services to investors. Investment banks also have a large role in facilitating mergers and acquisitions, private equity placements and corporate restructuring. Unlike traditional banks, investment banks do not accept deposits from and provide loans to individuals. Although common shareholders have the exclusive right to elect a corporation's board of directors, they rank behind holders of bonds and preferred stock when it comes to sharing profits. Investors are attracted to stocks in two ways. Some companies pay large dividends, offering investors a steady income. But others pay small or no dividends, hoping instead to attract shareholders by improving corporate profitability, and hence the value of the shares themselves. In general, the value of shares increases as investors come to expect corporate earnings to rise. Companies whose stock prices rise substantially often "split" the shares, paying each holder, for example, one additional share for each share held. This does not raise any capital for the corporation, but it makes it easier for stockholders to sell shares on the open market.

Investors

Most capital investment comes from such major institutions as pension funds, insurance companies, banks, foundations, and colleges and universities. Increasingly also, it comes from individuals. Since, in general, prices for shares of stock in the US are relatively low, even Americans of modest means buy and sell shares in hopes of making profits in the form of periodic dividends. They also hope that the price of the stock will go up over time, so that in selling their shares they will make an additional profit. (There is no guarantee, of course, that the business behind the stock will perform well. If it does not, dividends may be low or non-existent, and the stock's price may go down.) More than 40% of US families owned some stock in the mid-1990s, although these were mostly investments made for pensions. The average holding is worth about $25,000, not a great deal in American terms. Very few investors would be willing to buy shares, however, unless they knew they could sell them later. The stock market and other capital markets allow investors to buy and sell stocks continuously. Hence, except for weekends and holidays, the stock exchanges are very busy every day.

Market signals

The markets play several other roles in the American economy as well. When stocks or other financial assets rise in value, investors become wealthier and often they spend some of this additional wealth, bolstering sales and promoting economic growth. Moreover, because investors buy and sell shares daily, stock prices provide instant feedback to corporate executives about how investors judge their performance. Stock values also reflect investor reactions to government policy. If the government adopts policies that investors believe will hurt the economy and company profits, the market declines; if investors believe the policies will help the economy, the market rises. Critics have sometimes suggested that American investors focus too much on short-term profits; often, these analysts say, companies or policymakers are discouraged from taking steps that will prove beneficial in the long run because they may require short-term adjustments that will depress stock prices. Because the market reflects the sum of decisions by millions of investors, however, there is no good way to test this theory.

The importance of trust

Americans pride themselves on the efficiency of their capital markets, which enable vast numbers of sellers and buyers to engage in millions of transactions each day. The markets owe their success in part to computers, but they also depend on cultural factors and perhaps above all trust - the trust of one broker for another, and the trust of both in the good faith of the customers they represent to deliver securities after a sale or to pay for purchases. Occasionally, this trust is abused. But during the last half century, the federal government has played an increasingly important role in ensuring honest and equitable dealing to maintain the reputation all types of America's public companies. As a result, markets have thrived as continuing sources of investment funds that keep the economy growing and as devices for letting many Americans share in the nation's wealth. How far this trust has been damaged by the financial crisis of 2008, and how it will be repaired have yet to be seen.

Market information

To work effectively, markets require the free flow of information. Without it, investors cannot keep abreast of developments or gauge the true value of stocks. Numerous sources of information enable investors to follow the fortunes of the market daily, hourly, or even minute-by-minute. Companies are required by law to issue quarterly earnings reports, more elaborate annual reports, and proxy statements to tell stockholders how they are doing. In addition, investors can surf websites and read the market pages of daily newspapers to find out the price at which particular stocks were traded during the previous trading session. They can review a variety of indexes that measure the overall pace of market activity. The most notable of these are the Dow Jones Industrial Average (DJIA, the Dow), which tracks 30 prominent stocks, and the S&P (Standard & Poors) 500, which tracks 500 leading stocks. Investors also can turn to magazines and newsletters devoted to analyzing particular stocks and markets. Certain cable television programs provide a constant flow of news about movements in stock prices. And now, investors can use the internet to get up-to-the-minute information about individual stocks and even to arrange stock transactions.

The Stock Exchanges

There are thousands of stocks, but shares of the largest, best-known, and most actively traded corporations generally are listed on the New York Stock Exchange (NYSE). In 2008 there were about 8,500 stocks listed on the NYSE, trading at an average price around $26 per share. The exchange has 1,366 members, or "seats," which are bought by brokerage houses at hefty prices and are used for buying and selling stocks for the public. Information travels electronically between brokerage offices and the exchange, which requires 200 miles (320 km) of fiber-optic cable and 8,000 phone connections to handle quotes and orders. The smaller American Stock Exchange, which lists numerous energy-related stocks, operates in much the same way and is located in the same Wall Street area. Other large US cities including Boston, Chicago, Cincinnati, Kansas City, Los Angeles and Philadelphia, host smaller, regional stock exchanges.

NASDAQ

The largest number of stocks and bonds is traded on the National Association of Securities Dealers Automated Quotation system, or Nasdaq. This so-called over-the-counter exchange, which handles trading in about 3,600 stocks, is not located in any one place; rather, it is an electronic communications network of stock and bond dealers. The National Association of Securities Dealers, which oversees the market, has the power to expel companies or dealers that it determines are dishonest or insolvent. Because many of the stocks traded in this market are from smaller and less stable companies, the Nasdaq is considered a riskier market than either of the major stock exchanges, but it offers many opportunities for investors. Today NASDAQ trades in the shares of many leading companies in the retail, communications, media, financial services and biotechnology sectors.

A Nation of Investors

An unprecedented boom in the stock market, combined with the ease of investing in stocks, led to a sharp increase in public participation in securities markets during the 1990s. The annual trading volume on the NYSE, or "Big Board," soared from 11,400 million shares in 1980 to 169,000 million shares in 1998. Between 1989 and 1995, the portion of all US households owning stocks, directly or through intermediaries like pension funds, rose from 31% to 41% and in 2001 slightly over 52% of US households owned stock. Stock prices peaked in the spring of 2000. After that investors suffered three straight losing years on Wall Street, something that last happened at the end of the Great Depression in the 1930s. From 2003, however, the market was in an uptrend until 2008, when a correction brought values off 30-40%. Price to earnings (P/E) ratios - meaning the number of years it takes for a company's shares to recoup their purchase price - now stand around 20. The average P/E ratio from 1900 to 2005 was 14 (or 16, depending on whether the geometric mean or the arithmetic mean is used to average.) Although stock ownership is at a record level, most people still participate indirectly through their 401(k) retirement accounts or other mutual funds. The percentage of families holding stock directly is 21.3 while 52.2% of all families hold retirement accounts.

Mutual funds

Public participation in the market has been greatly facilitated by mutual funds, which collect money from individuals and invest it on their behalf in varied portfolios of stocks. Mutual funds enable small investors, who may not feel qualified or have the time to choose among thousands of individual stocks, to have their money invested by professionals. And because mutual funds hold diversified groups of stocks, they shelter investors somewhat from the sharp swings that can occur in the value of individual shares. On the other hand, investing in mutual funds is generally less profitable than investing directly in stocks. There are dozens of kinds of mutual funds, each designed to meet the needs and preferences of different kinds of investors. Some funds seek to realize current income, while others aim for long-term capital appreciation. Some invest conservatively, while others are more aggressive in accepting risk in hopes of realizing greater gains. Some deal only with stocks of specific industries or stocks of foreign companies, and others pursue varying market strategies. Overall, the number of funds jumped from 524 in 1980 to 8,015 by 2007.

Attracted by healthy returns and the wide array of choices, Americans invested substantial sums in mutual funds during the 1980s and 1990s. In 2009, they held $5 trillion in mutual funds, and the portion of US households holding mutual fund shares had increased from 6% in 1979 to 45% in 2008, despite the worst bear market in decades. (A bear market is a prolonged period in which investment prices fall, accompanied by widespread pessimism.) Mass participation in the stock markets has arguably made markets more susceptible to investor sentiment i.e., investors' opinions of whether stocks, sectors, industries or the market as a whole are likely to go up or down. Energy stocks, for example, are particularly liable to be affected by sentiment. This has increased volatility in the markets and made stock market regulation a political issue.

How stock prices are determined

Stock prices are set by a combination of factors that no analyst can consistently understand or predict. In general, economists say, they reflect the long-term earnings potential of companies. Investors are attracted to the stocks of companies they expect will earn substantial profits in the future, and because many people wish to buy these stocks, their prices tend to rise. On the other hand, investors are reluctant to purchase the stocks of companies that face bleak earnings prospects, and because fewer people wish to buy and more wish to sell these stocks, prices fall.

When deciding whether to purchase or sell stocks, investors consider the general business climate and outlook, the financial condition and prospects of the individual companies they are considering, and whether stock prices relative to earnings already are above or below traditional norms. Investors may also consider patterns in the previous price of the stock. Interest rate trends also influence stock prices significantly. Rising interest rates tend to depress stock prices, partly because they can foreshadow a general slowdown in economic activity and corporate profits, and partly because they lure investors out of the stock market and into new issues of interest-bearing investments. Falling rates, conversely, often lead to higher stock prices, both because they suggest easier borrowing and faster growth, and because they make new interest-paying investments less attractive.

A number of other factors complicate matters, however. For one thing, investors generally buy stocks according to their expectations about the unpredictable future, not according to current earnings. Expectations can be influenced by a variety of factors, many of them not necessarily rational or justified. As a result, the short-term connection between prices and earnings can be tenuous.

Momentum can also distort stock prices. Rising prices typically woo more buyers into the market, and the increased demand, in turn, drives prices higher still. Speculators often add to this upward pressure by purchasing shares in the expectation they will be able to sell them later to other buyers at even higher prices. Analysts describe a prolonged period in which investment prices rise faster than their historical average as a bull market. When speculative fever can no longer be sustained, prices start to fall. If enough investors become worried about falling prices, they may rush to sell their shares, adding to downward momentum and creating a bear market.

There are two main theories of stock prices. The classical theory states that the stock price is a rational reflection of the value of the company because the market enables all the relevant information to be reflected in the price. The alternative theory, the "random walk" theory denies that there can ever be perfect information and hence stock prices are to some extent irrational. It is certainly observable that when the stock price of some companies in a sector rises, the price of other stocks in that sector also tend to rise, not necessarily because of their performance, but rather because their prices look cheap relative to their competitors and offer greater potential profits to investors.

Market Strategies

During most of the 20th century, investors could earn more by investing in stocks than in other types of financial investments, provided they were willing to hold the stocks for the long term. In the short term, stock prices can be quite volatile, and impatient investors who sell during periods of market decline can easily suffer losses. In 1998, an expert noted that US stocks had lost value in 20 of the previous 72 years. Investors who held their stock 20 years or more never lost money (although inflation reduced the real value of their returns.) According to the federal government's Government Accountability Office, even in the worst 20-year period since 1926, stock prices increased 3%. In the best two decades, they rose 17%. By contrast, the returns on 20-year bonds, a common investment alternative to stocks, ranged between 1% and 10%. Economists conclude from analyses like these that small investors fare best if they can put their money into a diversified portfolio of stocks and hold them for the long term. But some investors are willing to take higher risks in hopes of realizing bigger gains in the short term, and have devised a number of strategies for doing this.

How stocks are traded

Transactions can be simple and swift, but buyers and sellers can also put conditions on their trades. Increasingly, also, stock trades are placed using the internet or software without telephoning a broker. Suppose a schoolteacher in California wants to take an ocean cruise. To finance the trip, she decides to sell 100 shares of stock she owns. So she calls her brokers and directs them to sell the shares at the best price they can get, with a specified minimum. At the same time, an engineer in Florida decides to use some of his savings to buy 100 shares in the same company, so he calls his broker and places a "buy" order for 100 shares. Both brokers wire their orders to the NYSE, where their representatives negotiate the transaction. All this can occur in less than a minute. In the end, the schoolteacher gets her cash and the engineer gets his stock, and both pay their brokers a commission. The transaction, like all others handled on the exchange, is carried out in public, and the results are sent electronically to every brokerage office in the nation.

Stock exchange specialists called "market makers" play a crucial role in the process, helping to keep an orderly market by deftly matching buy and sell orders. They make their not inconsiderable profits by taking a percentage of the difference between the buying and selling price of a stock. If necessary, market makers buy or sell stock themselves when there is a shortage of buyers or sellers.

Computers have allowed trading to take place round the clock in real time in the world's linked markets, although individual investors usually have to wait until the market opens to place trades. More than this, computers have enabled trading to take place in complex products such as derivatives that spread financial risks across financial products, geography and time. The NYSE now trades some two billion shares a day as millions of trades worldwide seek to buy undervalued assets and sell those that appear overpriced. The process continually improves the efficiency of directing scarce savings to their most productive investment, thereby raising productivity and standards of living. The distinctions between investment banks, hedge funds and private equity funds are gradually becoming blurred. (A private equity fund invests in private equity, often in attempts to gain control over companies in order to restructure them.) More radically, the distinction between what constitutes finance and commerce will largely disappear (Greenspan, *op. cit.*, p. 489.)

Buying on Margin

Americans buy many things on credit, and stocks are no exception. Investors who qualify can buy "on margin," making a stock purchase by paying 50% down and getting a loan from their brokers for the remainder. Buying stock on margin is an example of "leveraged trading." If the price of stock rises, the investors can sell the stock, repay their brokers the borrowed amount plus interest and commissions, and still make a profit greater than they might have made through a straight purchase, or at any rate more quickly. If the price goes down, however, brokers issue "margin calls," forcing the investors to pay additional money into their accounts so that their loans still equal no more than half of the value of the stock. If an owner cannot produce the cash, the broker can sell the stock - at the investor's loss - to cover the debt. The Federal Reserve sets the minimum margin requirements investors must put down when they buy stock. If the Fed wishes to stimulate the market, it can set low margins; if it sees a need to curb speculation, it sets high margins. For much of the time during the last decades of the 20th century, it left the margin rate at 50%. (Margin calls are not legally required and the broker can sell an investor's stocks without notice to cover deficits in the investor's trading account, but in the interests of good customer relations, margin calls have become customary.)

Selling Short

One particular group of speculators is known as "short sellers." They expect the price of a stock to fall, so they sell shares borrowed from their broker, hoping to profit by replacing the stocks later with shares purchased on the open market at a lower price. While this approach offers an opportunity for gains in a bear market, it is one of the riskiest ways to trade stocks. If a short seller guesses wrong, the price of stock he or she has sold short may rise sharply, hitting the investor with large losses. Experts now think that short selling was not as great a factor in the 2008 financial crisis as was believed at the time.

Options

Another form of leveraged trading for a relatively small outlay of cash is to buy "call" options to purchase a particular stock later at close to its current price. If the market price rises, the trader can exercise the option, making a big profit by then selling the shares at the higher market price. Alternatively, the trader can sell the option itself, which will have risen in value as the price of the underlying stock has gone up. Investors can also buy an option to sell stock, called a "put" option. This works in the opposite way, committing the trader to sell a particular stock later at close to its current price. Much like short selling, put options enable traders to profit from a declining market. But investors also can lose a lot of money if stock prices do not move as they hope.

Commodities and other Futures

Commodity "futures" are contracts to buy or sell certain goods at set prices at a predetermined time in the future. Futures traditionally have been linked to commodities such as wheat, livestock, copper and gold, but in recent years growing numbers of futures have been tied to foreign currencies or other financial assets. Commodities are traded on about a dozen commodity exchanges in the US, the most prominent of which are the Chicago Board of Trade, the Chicago Mercantile Exchange, and several exchanges in New York City. Chicago is the historic center of America's agriculture-based industries.

Commodities traders fall into two broad categories: hedgers and speculators. Hedgers are business firms, farmers, or individuals who enter into commodity contracts to gain assured access to a commodity, or the ability to sell it, at a guaranteed price. They use futures to protect themselves against unanticipated fluctuations in the commodity's price. Thousands of individuals, willing to absorb that risk, trade in commodity futures as *speculators*. They are lured to commodity trading by the prospect of making huge profits on small margins. Futures contracts, like many stocks, are traded on margin, typically as low as 10 to 20 percent.

Speculating in commodity futures is not for people who are averse to risk. Unforeseen forces like weather can affect supply and demand, and send commodity prices up or down very rapidly, creating great profits or losses. While professional traders who are well versed in the futures market are most likely to gain in futures trading, it is estimated that as many as 90% of small futures traders lose money in this volatile market.

Commodity futures are a form of "derivative," complex instruments for financial speculation derived from underlying assets. Derivatives proliferated in the 1990s to cover a wide range of assets, including mortgages and interest rates. This growing trade caught the attention of regulators and members of Congress after some banks, securities firms, and wealthy individuals suffered big losses through financially distressed, highly leveraged funds that bought derivatives, and in some cases avoided regulatory scrutiny by registering outside the US.

Hedge funds

As the name implies, hedge funds often seek to offset potential losses in the principal markets in which they invest by hedging their investments. They do so by using a variety of methods, notably short selling. Hedge funds are permitted by regulators to undertake a wider range of investment and trading than other investment funds. This provides them with an exemption in many jurisdictions from regulations governing short selling, derivative contracts, leverage, fee structures and the liquidity of interests in the funds. Each fund has its own strategy which determines the type of investments it makes, the methods of investment it undertakes and the leverage levels it assumes. Hedge funds invest in a broad range of investments including shares, debt and commodities. The net asset value of a hedge fund can run into billions of dollars, and this will usually be multiplied by leverage. Hedge funds dominate certain specialty markets such as trading within derivatives with high-yield ratings and distressed debt, for example, bonds from bankrupt companies. Hedge funds are typically open only to a limited range of professional or wealthy investors. The remuneration of investment managers is partly determined by performance. The term "hedge fund" has also come to be applied to many funds that do not actually hedge their investments, and in particular to funds using short selling and other "hedging" methods to increase rather than reduce risk, with the expectation of increasing return.

Private equity funds

Private equity funds are typically limited partnerships with a fixed term of 10 years (often with annual extensions). At inception, institutional investors make an unfunded commitment to the partnership, which is then drawn on over the term of the fund for making investments in various equity (and to a lesser extent debt) securities. A private equity fund is raised and managed by investment professionals. Typically, a firm will manage a number of different private equity funds and will attempt to raise a new fund every 3 to 5 years as the previous fund is fully invested.

The Regulators

The Securities and Exchange Commission (SEC), created in 1934, is the principal regulator of securities markets. The SEC has five commissioners, who are appointed by the President. No more than three can be members of the same political party. The five-year term of one of the commissioners expires each year. The Securities Act 1933, the Securities Exchange Act 1934 and the Sarbanes-Oxley Act 2002 gave the federal government a preeminent role in protecting small investors in stocks and bonds from fraud and making it easier for them to understand companies' financial reports.

Companies that plan to raise money by selling their own securities are required to file reports about their operations with the SEC, so that investors have access to all material information. The SEC determines whether these disclosures are full and fair so that investors can make well-informed and realistic evaluations. The SEC also oversees trading and administers rules designed to prevent price manipulation. Brokers and dealers in the over-the-counter market and the stock exchanges must register with the SEC. The agency also seeks to prevent insiders from trading in stock based on information that has not yet become public. The SEC requires companies to tell the public when their own officers buy or sell shares of their stock, since these people presumably possess intimate information about their companies, and their trades may indicate to other investors their degree of confidence in their companies' future (although they may be buying or selling for other reasons).

Companies must also make public what percentage of their stock is held by institutions such as pension funds, as their decisions to buy or sell can greatly affect the price of the stock. The SEC has powers to prevent or punish fraud in the sale of securities and is authorized to regulate stock exchanges. The Commodity Futures Trading Commission oversees the futures markets.

Stock market crashes

Black Monday, October 19, 1987 saw the largest one-day fall in the history of the New York Stock Exchange. The value of stocks fell 22.6%, overshooting the collapse of October 28, 1929 (12.8%), which prompted the Wall Street crash and the beginning of the Great Depression. Since then financial power has become concentrated in the hands of institutional investors operating solely in the financial markets who have the power to bankrupt industrial companies and small investors.

After Black Monday, the federal government introduced a number of safeguards. Automated trading by computer program has to be suspended whenever the Dow Jones Industrial Average rises or falls 2% in a single day from a certain average recent close. There is also a "circuit-breaker" mechanism to halt all trading temporarily any time the DJIA drops 1,050 points.

Those reforms may have helped restore confidence, but a strong performance by the economy may be even more important. In addition, the Federal Reserve said it would ease credit to ensure that investors could meet their margin calls and continue operating. Partly as a result, the crash of 1987 was quickly erased as the market surged to new highs. In the early 1990s, the Dow topped 3,000, and in 1999 it topped the 11,000 mark. What is more, the volume of trading has risen enormously. While trading 5 million shares was considered a hectic day on the NYSE in the 1960s, more than a billion shares were exchanged on some days in 1997 and 1998, and such days are now routine.

Much of the increased activity was generated by day traders who would typically buy and sell the same stock several times in one day, hoping to make quick profits on short-term swings. These traders were among the growing legions of persons using the internet to do their trading. In early 1999, 13% of all stock trades by individuals and 25% of individual transactions in securities of all kinds were occurring over the internet. With greater trading volumes has come greater volatility, and the circuit-breaker mechanism has been triggered several times. The crash which took place on October 27, 1997 was far more devastating and destructive than previous financial meltdowns, especially in Asia. The stock market and currency markets collapsed at the same time. On that occasion the decline amounted to about 7% of the overall value of stocks, and a similar crash occurred in September, 1998. Arguably it was because of the strong economy that investors stayed in the market, which quickly rebounded.

In the crisis of 2008, the Dow fell around 40% over the year, the circuit breakers proving even less effective than they had in 1997. This triggered fresh concern over whether failure of regulation was responsible for the crash, as individuals were indicted for corruption, manipulation and insider trading. In some cases this was alleged to have gone on for many years and to have led to the collapse of banks and other financial services companies.

FACTFILE 10 THE US ECONOMY

The US has the largest and most technologically powerful economy in the world, with a per capita GDP of $48,000. In this market-oriented economy, private individuals and business firms make most of the decisions, and the federal and state governments buy needed goods and services predominantly in the private marketplace. US business firms enjoy greater flexibility than their counterparts in Western Europe and Japan in decisions to expand capital plant, lay off surplus workers, and develop new products. At the same time, they face higher barriers to enter their rivals' home markets than foreign firms do entering US markets. US firms are at or near the forefront in technological advances, especially in computers and in medical, aerospace, and military equipment; their advantage has narrowed since the end of World War II. The onrush of technology largely explains the gradual development of a "two-tier labor market" in which those at the bottom lack the education and the professional/technical skills of those at the top and, more and more, fail to get comparable pay raises, health insurance coverage, and other benefits. Since 1975, practically all the gains in household income have gone to the top 20% of households. The war in March-April 2003 between a US-led coalition and Iraq, and the subsequent occupation of Iraq, required major shifts in national resources to the military. Hurricane Katrina caused extensive damage in the Gulf Coast region in August 2005, but had small impact on GDP growth for the year. Soaring oil prices between 2005 and the first half of 2008 threatened inflation and unemployment, as higher gasoline prices ate into consumers' budgets. Imported oil accounts for about two-thirds of US consumption. Long-term problems include inadequate investment in economic infrastructure, the rapidly rising medical and pension costs of an aging population, sizable trade and budget deficits, and stagnation of family income in the lower economic groups. The merchandise trade deficit reached a record $847 billion in 2007, but declined to $810 billion in 2008, as a depreciating exchange rate for the dollar against most major currencies discouraged US imports and made US exports more competitive abroad. The global economic downturn, the sub-prime mortgage crisis, investment bank failures, falling home prices, and tight credit pushed the US into a recession by mid-2008. To help stabilize financial markets, Congress established a $700 billion Troubled Asset Relief Program (TARP) in October 2008. The government used some of these funds to purchase equity in US banks and other industrial corporations. In January 2009 the US Congress passed and President Barack Obama signed a bill providing an additional $787 billion fiscal stimulus - two-thirds on additional spending and one-third on tax cuts - to create jobs and to help the economy recover.

Gross domestic product

The gross domestic product (GDP) measures the total output of goods and services of a country in a given year. In the US, GDP has been growing steadily, rising from more than $3.4 trillion in 1983 to $14.29 trillion (2008 est.). According to the World Bank, gross national income (GNI) per head had reached $46,040 by 2007. The US economy accounts for 20% of world GDP. But while these figures help measure the economy's health, they do not gauge every aspect of national well-being. GDP shows the market value of the goods and services an economy produces, but it does not weigh a nation's quality of life. And some important variables - personal happiness and security, for instance, or a clean environment and good health - are entirely beyond its scope.

Basic elements of the US economy

Natural resources

The biggest factor in American pre-capitalist economic development was the conquest of the land. During the 17th and 18th centuries, land was the principal means of production and politics was largely about the distribution of land. Wealth and income were concentrated in extreme fashion both before and after the Revolutionary War, although the European immigrants who were not semi-slaves in the form of indentured servants stood a better chance of becoming landowners than if they had remained in Europe. Few outside a tiny circle of insiders received free land, however. Fully half the adult white males owned no land in the decades around the Civil War (1850-1870), although the proportion grew thereafter. By the end of the 19th century, land had been superseded by manufacturing, railroads and finance as the principal means of production. The distribution of wealth and income in the US was less concentrated than in Europe because of easier access to land, but this ended around 1900. Thereafter, concentration of wealth in the US exceeded or matched that of industrial capitalist countries elsewhere.

The US is enormously rich in mineral resources and fertile farm soil, and is blessed for the most part with a tolerable climate. It also has extensive waterways: coastlines on both the Atlantic and Pacific Oceans, and on the Gulf of Mexico; rivers flowing from far within the continent; and the Great Lakes — five large, inland lakes along the border with Canada — which provide access for shipping. These waterways have helped shape the country's economic growth and helped bind America's individual states together into a single economic unit. Americans have traditionally regarded natural resources, especially energy, as inexhaustible, inexpensive and benign. Now fluctuations in the oil price, energy insecurity and environmental concerns are posing tough challenges as energy independence and environmental protection claim competing priorities.

The labor force

In addition, the number of available workers and, more importantly, their productivity help determine the health of an economy. Throughout its history, the US has experienced steady growth in the labor force, and that in turn has helped fuel almost constant economic expansion. Until shortly after World War I, most workers were immigrants from Europe, their immediate descendants, or African Americans whose ancestors were brought to America as slaves. In the 20th century, large numbers of Hispanics and Asians also immigrated to the US.

The quality of available labor - how hard people are willing to work - and how skilled they are (specialization of labor) - is at least as important to a country's economic success as the number of workers. In the early days of the US, frontier life required hard work, and what is known as the *Protestant work ethic* reinforced that trait. A strong emphasis on education, including technical and vocational training, has also contributed to America's economic success, as does a willingness to experiment and to change. The quality of the labor force continues to be an important economic issue. Today, Americans consider "human resources" a key to success in numerous modern, high-technology industries. As a result, government leaders and business officials increasingly stress the importance of education and training to develop workers with the kind of nimble minds and adaptable skills needed in new industries such as computers and telecommunications.

Labor mobility has likewise been important to the capacity of the American economy to adapt to changing conditions. When immigrants flooded labor markets on the East Coast, many workers moved inland, often to farmland waiting to be tilled. Similarly, economic opportunities in northern industrial cities attracted black Americans from southern farms in the first half of the 20th century. More recently, there has been a shift of population from the North and East to the Sunbelt of the South and West in response to economic opportunities. "Today Americans change employers on a truly stupendous scale," observes Alan Greenspan. "Out of nearly 150 million people employed in the workforce, 1 million leave their jobs each week. Some 600,000 quit voluntarily, while roughly 400,000 get laid off, often when their companies are acquired or downsized. At the same time, a million workers are hired or return from layoffs each week as new industries expand and new companies come on stream" *op. cit.,* pp. 169-70.

Technology and innovation

Modern large-scale corporations are on a scale far greater than that envisaged by Adam Smith. Harvard professor Joseph Schumpeter (1883-1950) in *Theory of Economic Development* (1911) was the first to explain how modern capitalism works. He identified the roles of technological and organizational innovation in driving and shaping the growth of capitalist economies. Schumpeter characterized the dynamism, turbulence, and intrinsic uncertainty of the capitalist economy as *creative destruction*. "A market economy will incessantly revitalize itself from within by scrapping old and failing businesses and then reallocating resources to newer, more productive ones" (*ibid,* p. 48).

Schumpeter stressed the key role of the entrepreneur. The entrepreneur is the one who first sees the economic viability of a new product or technique of production, overcomes obstacles, gains entry into the market, and eventually succeeds or fails. Each success means profit for the entrepreneur and his or her investors, and also adds to the economy. A successful innovation, in Schumpeter's view, confers at least a temporary monopoly. Without the lure of monopoly profits, there would be no incentive for anyone to bear the risks of entrepreneurship. The monopoly profits achieved by a successful entrepreneurial firm attract imitators and competitors, many of whom are financed by fresh credit. This activity eventually erodes the profits of the innovation; and then the time is ripe for another. In the course of this competition, which cannot possibly run smoothly, many businesses, individuals, and institutions, themselves founded on earlier successful innovations, will be undermined and swept away. Schumpeter summarizes his analysis in a characteristically strong statement: "Without innovations, no entrepreneurs; without entrepreneurial achievement, no capitalist returns and no capitalist propulsion. The atmosphere of industrial revolutions - of 'progress' - is the only one in which capitalism can survive." Schumpeter believed that large firms were both the source and the result of successful innovation. Reviewers of Schumpeter's theory have found much evidence that having to compete with best practice is an important spur both to innovation and to other aspects of industrial performance, although some speculate that there is an optimal intensity of competition.

Yet as Alan Greenspan observes, "It's no surprise that demands for protection against the forces of market competition are on the rise – as well as nostalgia for a slower and simpler time. America's material standard of living continues to improve, yet the dynamism of that same economy puts hundreds of thousands of people per week involuntarily out of work. Nothing is more stressful for people than the perennial gale of creative destruction" *op. cit.,* p.181.

Business management and organization

Americans have always believed they live in a land of opportunity, where anybody who has a good idea, determination, and a willingness to work hard can start a business and prosper. This belief in entrepreneurship has taken many forms, from the self-employed individual to the global conglomerate. The 20th century saw an enormous leap in the scale and complexity of economic activity. In many industries, small enterprises had trouble raising sufficient funds and operating on a scale large enough to produce most efficiently all of the goods demanded by an increasingly sophisticated and affluent population. In this environment, the modern corporation, often employing hundreds or even thousands of workers, assumed increased importance. Today, the American economy boasts a wide array of enterprises, ranging from one-person sole proprietorships i.e., one-person companies, to some of the world's largest corporations. There are 15-20 million non-farm, sole proprietorships, about 1.75 million partnerships, and 5 million corporations in the US.

Corporations

Although there are many small and medium-sized companies, most large businesses are organized as corporations. A corporation is a specific legal form of business organization, chartered by one of the states and treated under the law like a person. Corporations may own property, sue or be sued in court, and make contracts. Because a corporation has legal standing itself, its owners are partially sheltered from responsibility for its actions. Owners of a corporation also have limited financial liability; they are not responsible for corporate debts, for instance. Because corporate stock is transferable, a corporation is not damaged by the death or disinterest of a particular owner. The owner can sell his or her shares at any time, or leave them to heirs.

The modern business corporation was created in America, first in order to extend local markets, then to create a national one. The corporation was crucial to the development of American industry and to the creation of capitalism itself. No institution has been more significant in the growth of America as an economic superpower than the business corporation. Hence the corporation is one of the most significant features of American culture. In colonial America, the business corporation was almost unknown. Adam Smith barely discussed it and only 30 such firms were formed before 1789, almost all of which failed. But foreign countries undergoing their own industrial revolutions needed American cotton, meat, wool, grain, lumber and coal, and the turnpikes, steamboats, railroads and canals to transport these raw materials to market. Foreigners therefore bought shares in American corporations to raise and deploy the requisite large amounts of capital and to sustain the business over unprecedented timescales. At first, corporations were hampered by lack of legal status. They were not real persons and could not enter into federal legal procedures and sue or be sued (*Bank of the United States v. Devaux*, 1809). But in 1844 the law caught up with practice and the Court reversed itself.

As distinct legal entities, corporations must pay taxes. The *Devaux* case effectively denied corporations tax-exempt status. The dividends they pay to shareholders, unlike interest on bonds, are not tax-deductible business expenses. And when a corporation distributes these dividends, the stockholders are taxed on the dividends. (Since the corporation already has paid taxes on its earnings, critics say that taxing dividends amounts to double taxation of corporate profits.) Many large corporations have a great number of owners, or shareholders. A major company may be owned by a million or more people, many of whom hold fewer than 100 shares of stock each. This widespread ownership has given many Americans a direct stake in some of the nation's biggest companies.

But widely dispersed ownership also implies a separation of ownership and control. Because shareholders generally cannot know and manage the full details of a corporation's business, they elect a board of directors to make broad corporate policy. Because institutions typically hold the majority of the stock, they control board elections, although control has been passing to CEOs. Typically, even members of a corporation's board of directors and managers own less than 5% of the common stock, though some may own far more than that. Individuals, banks, or retirement funds often own blocks of stock, but these holdings generally account for only a small fraction of the total. Some directors are nominated by the company to give prestige to the board, others to provide certain skills or to represent lending institutions. It is not unusual for one person to serve on several different corporate boards at the same time. Usually, only a minority of board members are operating officers of the corporation.

Corporate boards place day-to-day management decisions in the hands of a chief executive officer (CEO), who may also be a board's chair or president. The CEO supervises other executives, including a number of vice presidents who oversee various corporate functions and the chief financial officer, the chief operating officer, and the chief information officer (CIO). The CIO came onto the corporate scene as high technology became a crucial part of US business affairs in the late 1990s. As long as a CEO has the confidence of the board of directors, he or she generally is permitted a great deal of freedom in running a corporation. But sometimes, individual and institutional stockholders, acting in concert and backing dissident candidates for the board, can exert enough power to force a change in management.

Generally, only a few people attend annual shareholder meetings. Most shareholders vote on the election of directors and important policy proposals by "proxy," that is, by mailing in election forms. In recent years, however, some annual meetings have seen more shareholders - perhaps several hundred - in attendance. The US Securities and Exchange Commission (SEC) requires corporations to give groups who are challenging management mailing lists of stockholders so they can present their views.

There are several reasons why corporations play a major role in the American economy. Large companies can supply goods and services to a greater number of people, and they frequently operate more efficiently than small ones. In addition, they often can sell their products at lower prices because of the large volume and small costs per unit sold. Corporations have an advantage in the marketplace because many consumers are attracted to well-known brand names, which they believe guarantee a certain level of quality. Large businesses tend to have more financial resources than small firms to conduct research and develop new products. And they generally offer more varied job opportunities and greater job stability, higher wages, and better health and retirement benefits.

Nevertheless, Americans have viewed large companies with some ambivalence, recognizing their important contribution to economic well-being but worrying that they could become so powerful as to stifle new enterprises and deprive consumers of choice. What is more, large corporations at times have shown themselves to be inflexible in adapting to changing economic conditions. US auto-makers, for example, have been slow to recognize the demand for reliable, safe, comfortable, fuel efficient and greener vehicles. As a result, they have lost a sizable share of the domestic market to foreign manufacturers, mostly from Japan.

Natural and human resources must be organized and directed as efficiently as possible to maximize productivity and exploit innovation. In the American economy, managers perform this function, responding to signals from markets. The traditional managerial structure in America is based on *The Principles of Scientific Management* published by Frederick Winslow Taylor in 1911. Taylorism is characterized by its top-down chain of command: authority flows from the chief executive in the boardroom, who makes sure that the entire business runs smoothly and efficiently, through various lower levels of management responsible for coordinating different parts of the enterprise, down to the supervisor on the shop floor. Numerous tasks are divided among different divisions and workers.

Many enterprises continue to operate with this traditional structure, but others have taken changing views on management. Facing heightened global competition, American businesses are seeking more flexible organizational structures, especially in high-technology industries that employ skilled workers and must develop, modify, and even customize products rapidly. Excessive hierarchy and division of labor are increasingly thought to inhibit creativity. As a result, many companies have flattened their managerial structures, reduced the number of managers, and delegated more authority to interdisciplinary teams of workers.

Before managers or teams of workers can produce anything, they must be organized into business ventures. In the US, the corporation has proved to be an effective device for accumulating the funds needed to launch a new business or to expand an existing one. The corporation is a voluntary association of owners, known as stockholders, who form a business enterprise governed by a complex set of rules and customs. Corporations must have sufficient capital to acquire the resources they need. They raise the necessary finance largely by selling stock (ownership shares in their assets) or bonds (long-term loans of money) to insurance companies, banks, pension funds, individuals, and other investors. Some institutions, especially banks, also lend money directly to corporations and other business enterprises.

If any single person invented the modern corporation, that was Alfred P. Sloan, President, later Chairman, of General Motors (GM). Sloan turned the corporation into a bureaucracy, governed by data derived from rigorous accounting and statistical tools, and focused on relentless marketing. Yet the business Sloan created went on for decades to produce shoddy products, foolish responses to criticism, and failed attempts at reorganization. GM also became risk-averse, opening the door to faster, freer, and more aggressive competitors, and losing market share to them. Although, unlike Ford, Sloan was a leader in using consumer surveys and dealer reports to find out what kind of cars people wanted to buy, GM became too big and their product development process so complicated that they were hard-pressed to change their product line quickly if consumer preferences shifted because of some external event like an energy crisis or if a competitor like Honda adopted a different approach to car sales.

Sloan was the first celebrity CEO. He made GM into an icon of productivity, market dominance, and stable profits. Sloan fought during the New Deal and into the 1940s to keep GM free from government regulation and to persuade Americans that a relatively unfettered private sector, led by profit-minded corporate managers, was the key to prosperity. He convinced Americans, in particular through his biography, *My Years at General Motors* (1923-56), that the rationally managed business corporation was the beating heart of America's political, cultural, and economic life, and that people like him were indispensable to the nation's security and prosperity. He built GM out of a morass of merged companies into a giant corporation that dominated the market through financial muscle, international distribution systems, and economies of scale. Sloan was not, however, obsessed with the share price, as critics say too many of today's CEOs are. Yet Sloan cared little about the common good. He (and Ford) refused to concede labor rights until forced to do so by Congress. Sloan also spent little on the safety or fuel efficiency of his vehicles. Biographer David Farber says Sloan's story helps to explain both the strengths of the American corporate-based economy and the weaknesses of its corporate-influenced polity.

CEOs are the heroes and villains of popular culture, featured in news and lifestyle magazines. Books by CEOs are regularly bestsellers. Under Sloan, GM became a major presence. Among today's CEOs, one much resembling Sloan was the retired CEO of IBM, Louis Gerstner. First, and most importantly, Gerstner used a results-oriented strategy to reverse IBM's decline, not unlike what Sloan achieved with GM in the early 1920s. Second, Gerstner championed the idea that America's public schools could only be saved if they modeled themselves after business corporations, listened to customers, decentralized decision-making, measured performance, and achieved continuous improvement. Sloan made a similar case regarding university education. He gave tens of millions of dollars to the Massachusetts Institute of Technology (MIT) to fund a now world-famous graduate program in management that would directly prepare technically sophisticated people for corporate leadership. MIT honored their benefactor in 1964 by naming the program the Alfred P. Sloan School of Management.

Small Business

Many people outside the US are surprised to learn that, even today, the US economy is by no means dominated by giant corporations. Fully 99% of all independent US enterprises employ fewer than 500 people. These small enterprises account for 52% of all US workers, according to the US Small Business Administration (SBA). Some 19.6 million Americans work for companies employing fewer than 20 workers, 18.4 million work for firms employing between 20 and 99 workers, and 14.6 million work for firms with 100 to 499 workers. By contrast, 47.7 million Americans work for firms with 500 or more employees.

Small businesses help keep the economy dynamic. They generate more than half of nonfarm private gross domestic product. They produce many new jobs. They also provide an entry point into the economy for new groups. Women, for instance, participate heavily in small businesses. The number of female-owned businesses climbed by 89%, to an estimated 8.1 million, between 1987 and 1997, and women-owned sole proprietorships reached 35% of all such ventures by the year 2000. Small firms also tend to hire a greater number of older workers and people who prefer to work part-time. The average small employer has one location and 10 employees, compared with 62 locations and 3,313 employees for the average large business.

A particular strength of small businesses is their ability to respond quickly to changing economic conditions. They often know their customers personally and are especially suited to meet local needs. They may also benefit from outsourcing by big corporations. Small businesses - computer-related ventures in California's "Silicon Valley" and other high-tech enclaves, for instance - are a source of technical innovation. Many computer-industry innovators began as "tinkerers," working on hand-assembled machines in their garages, and quickly grew into large, powerful corporations. Small companies that rapidly became major players in the national and international economies include the computer software company Microsoft; the package delivery service Federal Express; sports clothing manufacturer Nike; the computer networking firm America

OnLine, and ice cream maker Ben & Jerry's.

Of course, many small businesses fail. The market for a product or service may decline or be taken over by a competitor. The small business owner may lack the necessary knowledge and skills, particularly in business planning. Or the business may be unable to raise enough capital or credit. In some industries, for example, the auto industry, the small businesses may be dependent on the fortunes of the large corporations they supply. But in the US, a business failure does not carry the social stigma it does in some countries. Often, failure is seen as a valuable learning experience for the entrepreneur, who may succeed on a later try. As the Depression-era song put it: "Pick yourself up, dust yourself off and start right over again!" Failures demonstrate how market forces work to foster greater efficiency, economists say.

The high regard that people hold for small business translates into considerable lobbying clout for small firms in the Congress and state legislatures. Small companies have won exemptions from many federal regulations, such as health and safety rules. Congress also created the Small Business Administration (SBA) in 1953 to provide professional expertise and financial assistance to persons wishing to run small businesses. Thirty-five percent of federal dollars awarded for contracts is set aside for small businesses. In a typical year, the SBA guarantees $10 billion in loans to small businesses, usually for working capital or the purchase of buildings, machinery, and equipment. SBA-backed small business investment companies invest another $2 billion as venture capital. The SBA runs aggressive programs to identify markets and joint-venture opportunities for small businesses that have export potential, especially for African, Asian, and Hispanic American businesses.

The Sole Proprietor

Most businesses are sole proprietorships, that is, they are owned and operated by a single person. In a sole proprietorship, the owner is entirely responsible for the business's success or failure. He or she collects any profits, but if the venture loses money and the business cannot cover the loss, the owner is responsible for paying the bills even if doing so depletes his or her personal assets. Sole proprietorships have certain advantages over other forms of business organization. They suit the temperament of people who like to exercise initiative and be their own boss. They are flexible, since owners can make decisions quickly without having to consult others. By law, individual proprietors pay fewer taxes than corporations. And customers often are attracted to sole proprietorships, believing that an individual who is accountable will do a good job. This form of business organization has some disadvantages, however. A sole proprietorship legally ends when an owner dies or becomes incapacitated, although someone may inherit the assets and continue to operate the business. Also, since sole proprietorships generally are dependent on the amount of money their owners can save or borrow, they usually lack the resources to develop into large-scale enterprises.

The Business Partnership

One way to start or expand a venture is to create a partnership with two or more co-owners. Partnerships enable entrepreneurs to pool their talents; one partner may be qualified in production, while another may excel at marketing. Partnerships are exempt from most reporting requirements the government imposes on corporations, and they are taxed favorably compared with corporations. Partners pay taxes on their personal share of earnings, but their businesses are not taxed. States regulate the rights and duties of partnerships. Co-owners generally sign legal agreements specifying each partner's duties. Partnership agreements also may provide for "silent partners," who invest money in a business but do not take part in its management. A major disadvantage of partnerships is that each member is liable for all of a partnership's debts, and the action of any partner legally binds all the others. If one partner squanders money from the business, for instance, the others must share in paying the debt. Another major disadvantage can arise if partners have serious and constant disagreements.

Franchising and Chain Stores

Successful small businesses sometimes grow through a practice known as *franchising*. In a typical franchising arrangement, a successful company authorizes an individual or small group of entrepreneurs to use its name and products in exchange for a percentage of the sales revenue. The founding company lends its marketing expertise and reputation, while the entrepreneur who is granted the franchise manages individual outlets and assumes most of the financial liabilities and risks associated with the expansion. While it is somewhat more expensive to get into the franchise business than to start an enterprise from scratch, franchises are less costly to operate and less likely to fail. That is partly because franchises can take advantage of economies of scale in advertising, distribution, and worker training.

Franchising is so complex and far-flung that no one has a truly accurate idea of its scope. The SBA estimates the US had about 535,000 franchised establishments in 1992. These included including auto dealers, gasoline stations, restaurants, real estate firms, hotels and motels, and dry cleaning stores. That was about 35% more than in 1970. Sales increases by retail franchises between 1975 and 1990 far outpaced those of non-franchise retail outlets, and franchise companies accounted for about 50% of US retail sales.

Franchising probably slowed down in the 1990s, as the strong economy created many other businesses. Some franchisors also sought to consolidate, buying out other units of the same business and building their own networks. Company-owned chains of stores such as Sears Roebuck & Co. also provided stiff competition. By purchasing in large quantities, selling in high volumes, and stressing self-service, these chains often can charge lower prices than small-owner operations. Chain supermarkets like Safeway, for example, which offer lower prices to attract customers, have driven out many independent small grocers. Nonetheless, many franchise establishments do survive. Some individual proprietors have joined forces with others to form chains of their own or cooperatives. Often, these chains serve specialized, or niche, markets.

Monopolies, Mergers, and Restructuring

In the late 19th century, many Americans feared that corporations could raise vast amounts of capital to absorb smaller ones or could combine and collude with other firms to inhibit competition. In either case, critics said, business monopolies would force consumers to pay high prices and deprive them of choice. Such concerns gave rise to two major laws aimed at taking apart or preventing monopolies: the Sherman Antitrust Act of 1890 and the Clayton Antitrust Act of 1914. Government continued to use these laws to limit monopolies throughout the 20th century. In 1984, government "trustbusters" broke a near monopoly of telephone service by American Telephone and Telegraph. In the late 1990s, the Justice Department sought to reduce dominance of the burgeoning computer software market by Microsoft Corporation, which in just a few years had grown into a major corporation with assets of over $22 billion.

In general, government antitrust officials see a threat of monopoly power when a company gains control of 30% of the market for a commodity or service. But that is just a rule of thumb. A lot depends on the size of other competitors in the market. A company can be judged to lack monopolistic power even if it controls more than 30% of its market provided other companies have comparable market shares.

While antitrust laws may have increased competition, they have not kept US companies from getting bigger. Seven corporate giants had assets of more than $300 billion each in 1999, dwarfing the largest corporations of earlier periods, although values fell in the 2008 crisis. Some critics have voiced concern about the growing control of basic industries by a few large firms, asserting that industries such as automobile manufacture and steel production have become oligopolies dominated by a few major corporations. Others note, however, that many of these large corporations cannot exercise undue power despite their size because they face formidable global competition. If consumers are unhappy with domestic auto-makers, for instance, they can buy cars from foreign companies. In addition, consumers or manufacturers sometimes can thwart would-be monopolies by switching to substitute products. For example, aluminum, glass, plastics, or concrete can all substitute for steel. But because auto-makers Chrysler and GM were so important to the economy, it was judged politically necessary for the government to bail them out in 2009.

Attitudes among business leaders concerning corporate size have varied. In the late 1960s and early 1970s, many ambitious companies sought to diversify by acquiring unrelated businesses, at least partly because strict federal antitrust enforcement tended to block mergers within the same field. As business leaders saw it, conglomerates - a type of business organization usually consisting of a holding company and a group of subsidiary firms engaged in dissimilar activities - are inherently more stable. If demand for one product slackens, the theory goes, another line of business can provide balance. But this advantage sometimes is offset by the difficulty of managing diverse activities rather than specializing in the production of narrowly defined product lines. Many business leaders who engineered the mergers of the 1960s and 1970s found themselves overextended or unable to manage all of their newly acquired subsidiaries. In many cases, they divested the weaker acquisitions.

Mergers

The 1980s and 1990s brought waves of both friendly mergers and "hostile" takeovers in some industries, as corporations tried to position themselves to meet changing economic conditions. Mergers were prevalent, for example, in the oil, retail, and railroad industries, all of which were undergoing substantial change. Many airlines sought to combine after deregulation unleashed competition beginning in 1978. Deregulation and technological change helped spur a series of mergers in the telecommunications industry as well. Several companies that provide local telephone service sought to merge after the government moved to require more competition in their markets.

Also in the late 1990s, Travelers Group merged with Citicorp, forming the world's largest financial services company, while Ford Motor Company bought the car business of Sweden's AB Volvo. Following a wave of Japanese takeovers of US companies in the 1980s, German firms took the spotlight in the 1990s, as Chrysler Corporation merged into Germany's Daimler-Benz AG, and Deutsche Bank AG took over Bankers Trust. Marking one of business history's deepest ironies, Exxon Corporation and Mobil Corporation merged, restoring more than half of the former industry-dominating Standard Oil Company empire, which had been broken up by the Justice Department in 1911. The Federal Trade Commission did, however, require Exxon and Mobil to sell or sever supply contracts with 2,143 gas stations in the Northeast and mid-Atlantic states, California, and Texas, and to divest a large California refinery, oil terminals, a pipeline, and other assets. That represented one of the largest divestitures ever mandated by antitrust agencies.

Instead of merging, some firms have tried to bolster their business clout through joint ventures with competitors. Because these arrangements eliminate competition in the product areas in which companies agree to cooperate, they can pose the same threat to market disciplines that monopolies do. But federal antitrust agencies have given their blessings to some joint ventures they believe will yield benefits.

Many American companies also have joined in cooperative research and development activities. Traditionally, companies have conducted cooperative research mainly through trade organizations, and only then to meet environmental and health regulations. But as American companies observed foreign manufacturers cooperating in product development and manufacturing, they concluded that they could not afford the time and money to do all the research themselves. Some major research consortiums include Semiconductor Research Corporation and Software Productivity Consortium.

A spectacular example of cooperation among fierce competitors occurred in 1991 when IBM, which was the world's largest computer company, agreed to work with Apple Computer, the pioneer of personal computers, to create a new computer software operating system that could be used by a variety of computers. A similar proposed software operating system arrangement between IBM and Microsoft had fallen apart in the mid-1980s, and Microsoft then moved ahead with its own market-dominating Windows system. By 1999, IBM had also agreed to develop new computer technologies jointly with Dell Computer, a strong new entry into that market.

Just as the merger wave of the 1960s and 1970s led to a series of corporate reorganizations and divestitures, the next round of mergers also was accompanied by corporate efforts to restructure their operations. Indeed, heightened global competition led American companies to launch major efforts to become leaner and more efficient. Many companies dropped product lines they deemed unpromising, spun off subsidiaries or other units, and consolidated or closed numerous factories, warehouses, and retail outlets. In the midst of this downsizing wave, many companies - including such giants as Boeing, AT&T, and General Motors - released numerous managers and lower-level employees.

The role of the market

The American free enterprise system emphasizes private ownership. Private businesses produce most goods and services, and almost two-thirds of the nation's total economic output goes to individuals for personal use (the remaining one-third is bought by government and business). The consumer role is so great, in fact, that the nation is sometimes said to have a "consumer economy."

The emphasis on private ownership arises, in part, from American beliefs about personal freedom. From the time the nation was created, Americans have feared excessive government power, and have sought to limit government authority over individuals, including its role in the economic realm. In addition, Americans generally believe that an economy characterized by private ownership is likely to operate more efficiently than one with substantial government ownership. When economic forces are unfettered, Americans believe, supply and demand determine the prices of goods and services. Prices, in turn, tell businesses what to produce; if people want more of a particular good than the economy is producing, the price of the good rises. That catches the attention of new or other companies that, sensing an opportunity to earn profits, start producing more of that good. On the other hand, if people want less of the good, prices fall and less competitive producers either go out of business or start producing different goods. Such is the "market economy." The dynamism and flexibility of markets are pointed to by Americans as evidence of the superiority of market economies over planned ones. Competitive markets, however, are seen by some Americans as open to "manipulation by advertisers and marketers who trivialize life by promoting superficial and ephemeral values" (*ibid.*, p. 141).

The role of government

There are limits to the scope of free enterprise, however. Americans have always believed that some services are better performed by public rather than private enterprise. For instance, in the US, government is primarily responsible for the administration of justice, education (90% of all schools are public, although there are many private schools, universities and training centers), the road system, social services, environmental protection, statistical reporting, and national defense. In addition, government often is asked to intervene in the economy to correct situations in which the price system does not work, as in the sub-prime crisis. It regulates "natural monopolies," electricity companies, for example, and it uses antitrust laws to control or break up other business combinations that have become so powerful that they can defy the market. Government also addresses issues beyond the reach of market forces. It provides welfare and unemployment benefits to people who cannot support themselves, either because they encounter problems in their personal lives or lose their jobs as a result of economic upheaval; it pays much of the cost of medical care for the aged and those who live in poverty; it regulates private industry to limit air and water pollution; it provides low-cost loans to people who suffer losses as a result of natural disasters; and it has played the leading role in the exploration of space, which is too expensive for any private enterprise to undertake. US government spending accounts for about 20% of GDP.

Moreover, despite their advocacy of market principles, Americans have at times looked to government to provide tax breaks and subsidies for businesses. In particular, they have used government to nurture new industries, and to protect American companies and farms from domestic and overseas competition. Americans have also demanded government action to safeguard consumers and workers. Entrepreneurs have on occasion taken advantage of lack of government oversight to enrich themselves by forming monopolies and eliminating competition, setting high prices for products and selling shoddy goods. In hiring workers, they have followed unfair and discriminatory practices, especially against black Americans, and imposed poor wages and unhealthy and sometimes dangerous working conditions.

In response to these evils, Congress has enacted laws to break up or regulate monopolies, require accurate labeling of food and drugs, and ensure the inspection of meat. In addition there are laws to regulate the sale of stock, set wages and hours in various industries, and put stricter controls on the manufacture and sale of food, drugs, and cosmetics. New federal agencies, such as the Environmental Protection Agency, have come into being to ensure that businesses do not pollute air, soil or water and that they leave an ample supply of green space for people to enjoy. After the Enron scandal of 2002, the Public Company Accounting Reform and Investor Protection Act of 2002, known as the Sarbanes-Oxley Act, commonly called *SOX* or *Sarbox*, was passed to ensure more accurate reporting in company accounts. Under Sarbox, CEOs have to sign forms to say, under penalty of perjury, that the accounts are accurate, there is nothing "off the books" (unreported transactions), there is no offshore bank account (which would be illegal), and that if they are shown to be wrong they can go to jail. Corporations have to pay for external audits to check that their claims are correct. The US takes white collar crime very seriously to protect the capitalist system, and in several highly-publicized cases, top executives have been sent to jail for fraud and insider trading. (*Insider trading* is the trading of a corporation's stock or other securities e.g., bonds or stock options by officers, key employees, directors, or holders of more than 10% of the firm's shares, based on material non-public information obtained during the performance of the insider's duties at the corporation, or that is dishonestly obtained.) All insider trades, which may be perfectly legal if they do not use non-public information, must be reported to the US Securities and Exchange Commission (SEC).

The sum total of these laws and regulations has changed American capitalism, in the words of one writer, from a "freely running horse to one that is bridled and saddled." There is scarcely anything a person can buy in the US today that is not affected by government regulation of some kind. Because of complaints about the costs that regulation imposes on business, however, the style of regulation has begun to change of late. Nowadays it is more likely to require standards to be met than detailed rules to be followed. There is also a school of thought that believes that the Administration may lighten the burden of Sarbox on business in return for improvements to worker representation and collective bargaining laws that are more favorable to workers.

The role of individuals

Individuals can help guide the economy not only through the choices they make as consumers but through the votes they cast for officials who shape economic policy. In recent years, consumers have voiced concerns about product safety, environmental threats posed by certain industrial practices, and potential health risks citizens may face; government has responded by creating agencies to protect consumer interests and promote the general public welfare.

Changes in the economy

The pragmatism and flexibility of Americans has resulted in an unusually dynamic economy, which has changed dramatically since World War II. The population and the labor force have shifted away from farms to cities, from fields to factories, and, above all, to service industries. This once agrarian country is far more urban - and suburban - today than it was 100, or even 50, years ago.

In some industries, mass production has given way to more specialized production that emphasizes product diversity and customization. Large corporations have merged, split up, and reorganized in numerous ways. New industries and companies that did not exist at the midpoint of the 20th century now play a major role in the nation's economic life. In today's economy, the providers of personal and public services far outnumber producers of agricultural and manufactured goods. As the economy has grown more complex, statistics also reveal a sharp long-term trend over the last century away from self-employment toward working for others. But employers are becoming less paternalistic, and employees are expected to be more self-reliant. And increasingly, government and business leaders emphasize the importance of developing a highly skilled and flexible work force in order to ensure the country's future economic success.

The American economy today is characterized by five factors – flexibility, openness, self-correction, fast change and resilience. Perhaps the greatest of these is resilience. In the last generation the economy has survived a number of crises: the largest one-day crash in the history of the stock market in 1987, the real estate boom and bust of the 1980s, the savings and loan crisis, the Asian currency crisis, the 1990 recession, the dot.com crash, 9/11 and the sub-prime crisis. Meanwhile the 1990s saw the longest strongest boom in history. After growing 1.4% per year since the mid-1970s, productivity – the output of goods and services per hour worked – accelerated to 2.5% a year from 1995 to 2000, and then jumped to 3.1% a year from 2000 to 2005. This acceleration in productivity growth, partly attributed to the spread and more efficient use of information technology, has sometimes been labeled the "new economy." Deregulated financial markets, far more flexible labor markets and major advances in IT have enhanced the economy's ability to absorb disruptions and recover, says Alan Greenspan, ibid., pp. 8-10, although he has conceded in Congressional testimony that he was "partially wrong" about the ability of banks to regulate themselves.

Even so, Americans are increasingly worried about international competition, especially from India and China, whose low wages are enabling them to capture American markets, and whose competition for energy is believed by many Americans to be responsible for the rising costs of energy and commodities. Meanwhile American firms are being taken over by foreign companies, and American banks are having to seek new capital from Asia and the Persian Gulf, while the infrastructure of many countries is making America's look poor and out of date. In 2000 US exchanges accounted for about half the value of global stock markets; at the beginning of 2008 they accounted for just 33%. Altogether these signs of the diffusion of economic power indicate that the US has lost its capacity to determine the direction of the global economy. In foreign affairs too, the US no longer has the ability to use economic power as a tool of statecraft when foreign governments own hundreds of billions of dollars of US debt. Yet globalization need not be a zero-sum game; and the US still leads the world in agricultural exports, high tech, biotech, entertainment, marketing, higher education, branded goods and, despite the credit crisis which started in 2007, finance. Manufacturing exports are principally computers and electrical machinery, vehicles, chemical products, food and live animals, military equipment and aircraft.

SECTORS OF THE ECONOMY

Agriculture

Agriculture is a major part of the American success story and an enduring influence on American culture. Food is abundant, affordable and safe, while the individualism and egalitarianism of farmers is admired and emulated by the rest of society. Farming in America has attained a richness and variety unmatched in most other parts of the world, owing to the quality of the land and the ready supplies of water from precipitation, rivers and underground basins. Large stretches of level or gently rolling land, especially in the Midwest, provide ideal conditions for large-scale agriculture. Even in the drier areas of the West (apart from a relatively small area in the South West), there is sufficient water for irrigation.

Because in most parts of the US, land was abundant but labor scarce, agriculture came to be based on a multitude of family farms. The tendency was reinforced by government policy such as the Homestead Act of 1862 which offered, for modest payment, farms of up to 160 acres (65 hectares) to any family that would settle west of the Mississippi. Moreover, these farms tended to be scattered and isolated, enhancing the farmer's individualism and self-reliance. Shortage of labor and the good prices available for produce spurred the invention and adoption of new technology. By the time of the Civil War (1861-65) this had revolutionized every step of growing arable crops and made farming highly productive, so much so that the period 1870-1900 saw oversupply and falling prices.

Today fewer than 2% of Americans work on the land. In the 1950s and again in the 1980s many farmers got into debt and sold up and left the land for the cities. Nowadays 36% of farmland is owned by corporations. Farming is no longer a family business but big business - "agribusiness" - which employs over 22 million people, more than any other sector of the economy. Only four companies control 84% of American cereal production. Likewise four companies control 81% of the US beef market. Joel Dyer writes in *Harvest of Rage*, "Only five to eight multinational companies have, for all intents and purposes, been the sole purchasers and transporters not only of the American grain supply but that of the entire world." Many groups concerned to secure the future of family farmers are calling for a moratorium on mergers and acquisitions in agribusiness, transportation, food processing, manufacturing and retail companies. The average size of a modern farm is 470 acres (190 hectares) compared with 174 acres (70 hectares) in 1940. Even so, there are still many small farms, 85% of which are owned by individuals or families. In 2007 net total farm income was more than $66 billion, but despite this, many farmers have large debts.

US farming is carried out in four main areas. In the Corn Belt of the Midwest, corn (maize) and soybeans are grown. The US grows 36% of the world's corn and 47% of its soybeans. Wheat farming is mainly practiced in the Wheat Belt of the Great Plains. Most livestock farming is done around the Great Lakes in the Dairy Belt, or further south in states like Texas where cattle are bred for beef on ranches. The Cotton Belt is found in the South. In addition, citrus fruits such as oranges are grown in Florida, Southern California and Hawaii, and tobacco is grown in the south-east.

Ethanol

A large and rapid expansion in ethanol production is underway in the US for use in hybrid cars in response both to market conditions and government incentives. A rapid rise in oil prices over the past several years has combined with the Energy Policy Act of 2005 and federal and state biofuel programs to provide impetus for this expansion. The strong global demand for crude oil results from world economic growth, including rapid manufacturing gains in China and India. Although discovery of new oil reserves, new technologies for finding and extracting oil, and continued expansion and improvement in renewable energy are likely to offset increases in part, oil prices are expected to remain high by historical standards. Further contributing to the interest in ethanol, the Energy Policy Act mandated that renewable fuel use in gasoline and biodiesel reach 7.5 billion gallons by 2012, with gains in later years in line with growth in the volume of gasoline sold. Additionally, the legislation did not provide liability protection for MTBE, an additive in gasoline blending that has been found to contaminate drinking water. This has led to sharp reductions in the use of MBTE and a switch to ethanol as a fuel additive. Federal tax laws also provide incentives for biofuels. Under current law, tax credits are available to blenders equal to 51 cents for each gallon of ethanol blended with gasoline. Additionally, an import tariff of 54 cents per gallon is assessed on most imported ethanol. In combination, these factors have made ethanol more economical to produce.

The expansion of ethanol production affects every aspect of the field crops sector, particularly corn, soybeans and cotton, as more acreage is devoted to corn (the primary feedstock for ethanol) and less to the other crops. In 2006, ethanol represented about 3.5% of motor vehicle gasoline by volume. About 14% of corn use went to ethanol production in the 2005/06 crop year and the proportion is expected to rise to at least 30%. Many aspects of the livestock sector are also being affected by ethanol production because the price of feed is going up. Ethanol production totaled almost 5 billion gallons in 2006, about 1 billion gallons more than in 2005. While this was a significant increase, expansion in the industry is continuing, with production expected to exceed 10 billion gallons by 2009 and 12 billion by 2015, according to the U.S. Department of Agriculture (USDA). Still, even by 2017, ethanol production by volume will represent less than 8% of annual gasoline use. Changes in US agriculture will continue for many years as interest grows in renewable sources of energy. In the medium term, the corn market is likely to become more volatile in response to changing patterns of production, and more vulnerable to weather and pests because demand for ethanol is much less elastic than demand for feedstock and exports, but the market is expected to regain equilibrium in the long term. Farm income is expected to grow as the expansion in ethanol creates more demand for corn. As incomes rise, however, government support payments, which currently represent 8% of farm incomes, will fall, and the agriculture sector will have to rely on the market for more of its income. Prices will also rise for red meat, poultry and eggs and for farmland itself.

Alan Greenspan warns, however, that corn ethanol, though valuable, can play only a limited role in America's energy security because of its limited ability to replace gasoline. "One bushel of corn yields only 7.2 gallons of ethanol, which means that all 11 billion bushels of corn that the US produced in 2006 would have yielded only 5.2 million barrels of ethanol a day, the energy equivalent of 3.9 million barrels a day of gasoline, or only a third of US highway use, and less than a fifth of the 21 million barrels a day Americans consumed in 2006" op. cit., p. 461. There are also already claims that selling corn for ethanol production is pushing up the price of corn sold for export and hence the price of food in foreign countries such as Mexico.

Government encouragement to agriculture
Beginning with the creation of the USDA in 1862, the federal government took a direct role in agricultural affairs, including teaching farmers how to make their land more productive. After a period of prosperity in the early 20th century, however, farm prices declined in the 1920s. The Great Depression of the 1930s drove prices still lower, and by 1932 farm prices had dropped, on average, to less than one-third of their 1920 levels. Farmers went bankrupt by the tens of thousands. Many present-day farm policies have their roots in the desperate decade of the 1930s and the rescue effort contained in the New Deal.

Today a maze of legislation embodies US farm policies. On the theory that overproduction is a chief cause of low farm prices, in some circumstances the government pays farmers to plant fewer crops. Deficiency payments reimburse farmers for the difference between the target price set by Congress for a given crop and the actual price paid when the crop is sold. In 1996, however, partly in response to pressure from the WTO, the Freedom to Farm Act was passed which will phase out these payments and leave farmers free to grow what they want in response to demand. In the Western states a federal system of dams and irrigation canals delivers water to farmers at subsidized prices. There is growing concern, however, about the long-term future of water supplies.

The Farm Service Agency (FSA) of the USDA, working through the Commodity Credit Corporation

(CCC) also administers commodity marketing loan programs for wheat, rice, corn, grain sorghum, barley, oats, upland cotton, oilseeds, peanuts, mohair, wool, honey, small chickpeas, lentils, and dry peas. These programs allow producers to receive a loan from the government at a low rate of interest by pledging production as collateral. After harvest, a farmer may obtain a loan for all or part of the new commodity production.

Price supports and deficiency payments apply only to such basic commodities as grains, dairy products, and cotton; many other crops are not federally subsidized. Moreover, farm subsidy programs have been criticized on the grounds that they benefit large farms most and accelerate the trend toward larger and fewer farms. In one recent year, for example, farms with more than $250,000 in sales - only 5% of the total number of farms - received 24% of government farm payments.

American agriculture has been a notable success. American consumers pay less for their food than those in many other industrial countries, and one-third of the cropland in the US produces crops destined for export. In 1995 agricultural exports exceeded imports by nearly two to one. But agricultural success has had its price. Conservationists assert that American farmers have damaged the environment by excessive use of artificial fertilizers and chemicals to kill weeds and pests. Toxic farm chemicals have at times found their way into the nation's water, food, and air, although government officials at the state and federal levels are vigilant in their efforts to protect these resources. By promoting cheap grain production for animal feed, current government policy gives an advantage to livestock farmers at the expense of diversified family farmers who raise their own grain, maintain crop rotations and recycle animal waste as crop nutrients. Employing such innovative (though controversial) techniques as gene-splicing, scientists at research centers across the US hope to develop genetically-modified (GM) crops that grow rapidly and resist pests without the use of toxic chemicals. Agricultural colleges attached to universities have extension officers who act as a link between researchers and farmers.

Family farms

The self-sufficient, independent family farm which Jefferson had envisaged as the basis of American society had been overtaken by the early 19th century by large farms owned by speculators and corporations; the majority of industrial workers and the slaves owned no land. US farm policy today, reinforced by America's agricultural trade agenda, is designed to favor agribusiness groups geared to export production, through subsidies (which many people in other countries consider to be unfair), low commodity prices, and (so some allege) by dumping food on the markets of other countries. Agribusiness corporations, joined by most commodity organizations, wield influence in Washington to ensure that the nation's farm programs, trade agreements, and anti-trust laws guarantee an abundance of cheap commodities for food processors.

This approach has severely impacted small, mostly family, farmers. Farm gate prices paid to farmers for their crops have declined. Since the 1985 Farm Bill, US agricultural prices have been artificially depressed in the interest of exporters, thus forcing many farmers to accept far less than their costs of production in revenue. This trend was reinforced in both the 1996 and 2002 farm bills. In the September 2003 report *Re-thinking US Agricultural Policy: Changing Course to Secure Farmer Livelihoods Worldwide*, Darryl Ray of the University of Tennessee Agricultural Policy Analysis Center wrote: "Despite large increases in taxpayer-provided farm payments, net farm income declined 16.5% between 1996 and 2001." Farmers receive, on average, nine cents of every food dollar. While some farmers do receive a share of government farm payments, these subsidies, they say, do not adequately compensate for losses incurred from low prices. Meanwhile in addition to receiving less income, farmers are paying higher costs for inputs such as fuel, equipment and supplies. At the same time they are receiving inadequate healthcare and insurance. As a result, an increasing number of US farm families are working multiple off-farm jobs just to make ends meet, creating an unsustainable situation for small farms and local farm communities. More than 72,000 family farms disappeared in the US between 1992 and 1999. Legislative pressure is mounting to change eligibility for USDA programs, especially credit and financing programs, to better meet the needs of small, especially minority, farmers.

Farm workers, the majority foreign born and from Mexico, are among the poorest laborers in the US. Giant corporate purchasers award contracts to the lowest bidders, and growers compete by paying farm workers poverty wages and (as documented in the September 2003 issue of *National Geographic*) practicing a modern form of slavery. Most farm workers earn well below the poverty threshold. African American farmers have been hardest hit by the decline in family farms and have lost their land at more than twice the rate of white farmers, according to a 1990 report of the House Committee on Government Operations. Moreover, when they have needed and requested assistance from the USDA, they have been systematically discriminated against, as findings in a recent class action lawsuit indicate. Women farm workers face particular discrimination in getting semi-skilled and skilled farm jobs. Men account for 80% of farm workers and the few women farm workers are concentrated in the packing houses and processing plants rather than in the fields. Pay inequality between women and men continues and women often need to work longer hours in order to earn the same income as men. Ninety-nine percent of all farm workers do not have social security or disability insurance and 95% do not have health insurance for non-work related injuries or illness. Migratory and seasonal work separates families, a burden further intensified by declining benefits. Rural unemployment and poverty continues to rise along with the rates of violence and suicide. In the Midwest, suicide is the fifth largest cause of death among farmers.

To address the problems of family farms, the National Family Farm Coalition seeks to force multinational grain traders and processors to pay farmers at least the cost of production for their crops. Attempts to reform current policy and promote the viability of small, family farms may, however, be threatened with the increasing limits trade agreements place on domestic policy options.

Meanwhile, from other quarters there is a growing movement to cut back the government's role in agriculture and to reduce the subsidies paid to farmers. Important economic interests defend current farm policy, however, and proposals for change have stirred vigorous debate in Congress. Farmers are represented by the American Farm Bureau Federation and county farm bureaus. The Federation seeks to protect farmers' interests and influence government policy and also carries out agricultural research.

Fishing

The US fishing industry is very large, especially for sea fish, with $3.9 billion worth of fish landed in US waters in 2005. The federal government supports the industry through the Fish and Wildlife Service, but states are responsible for the fishing industry off their own shores. More than 60 types of fish are reared at national fish hatcheries, so that each year there are about 200 million new fish available. Beset by overfishing and falling catches, and battered by imports from Asia, Europe, and

Latin America, however, the old way of American fishing no longer seems sustainable and major reform of fisheries management has been urged by the independent Pew Oceans Commission.

Industry

Most industry was originally in the Northeast, but California and Texas soon became major manufacturing centers too. The products of American industry include chemicals, industrial machinery, food processing and electronic goods. Mining for a variety of metals, including iron and gold, continues to be important. The US also produces very large quantities of oil, natural gas and coal (see Chapter 1). Since World War II there has been a huge growth in service industries, such as finance and insurance, and these now employ 75% of the workforce. Some areas which were formerly centers of heavy industry, such as Chicago and Detroit, are experiencing high unemployment.

Mass production

American industrial growth has been powered by three factors: the ready supply of workers through immigration; the desire of Americans to succeed and enjoy a higher standard of living; and the entrepreneurial spirit. The particular contribution of America to industrial capitalism was the system of mass production in factories using precision engineering to transform manufacturing into the assembly of interchangeable parts. This, in turn, allowed the final product to be made in stages, with each worker specializing in a discrete task. In addition, the construction of railroads, beginning in the 1830s, and accelerated after 1862, linked far-flung sections of the country into the world's first transcontinental market. Railroad construction also generated a demand for coal, iron, and steel. By 1890 the output of America's factories exceeded the output of its farms, and by 1913 more than one-third of the world's industrial production came from the US.

In the same year, automaker Henry Ford introduced the moving assembly line, by which conveyor belts brought the parts to the workers. This innovation made possible large savings in labor costs and inspired managers to seek even greater economies of process and scale. Lower costs made possible both higher wages for workers and lower prices for consumers. Mass production of consumer goods such as cars, refrigerators, and kitchen stoves helped to revolutionize the American way of life.

The moving assembly line, however, has been criticized for its effect on workers' conditions and health. Moreover, factory managers have found that bored, depressed workers tend to do inferior work. The assembly line has therefore been modified in many US factories, where "quality circles" assemble, for example, an entire car from start to finish, with workers sometimes performing several different tasks. Recently, many repetitive tasks have been taken over by robots and computers. Workers nowadays do more to supervise the production line and carry out quality inspection. These changes have made jobs more interesting but have reduced the number of jobs available.

In recent years, there have been big job losses in manufacturing, particularly in the eastern and northern industrial belts. The reason is generally not any failure in quality or productivity, but competition from foreign imports, which are cheap because they are made in countries such as China whose currency is kept low against the dollar. The US authorities have allowed the value of the dollar to fall, and some see this an opportunity to recapture lost markets, but many economists believe that, in the long term, manufacturing will be forced to undergo even greater changes than it has already. Meanwhile a degree of protectionism has been advocated to help the industries adjust. But some commentators feel that protection will simply prolong the pain and might even provoke a trade war in which countries block imports of each other's goods, and thereby reduce world economic growth.

By the end of World War II, the US had the greatest productive capacity of any country, and the words "Made in the U.S.A." were a seal of high quality. But the 20th century saw the rise and decline of several industries in the US. The auto industry, long the mainstay of the American economy, has struggled to meet the challenge of foreign competition. The garment industry has also declined in the face of competition from countries where labor is cheaper. But other manufacturing industries have appeared and flourished, including airplanes and cellular telephones, microchips and space satellites, microwave ovens, high-speed computers and nanotechnology (used in semiconductors, medicine, and materials manufacturing).

As high-tech industries have grown and older industries have declined, however, the proportion of American workers employed in manufacturing has dropped. The sector has been hit hard by the trade liberalization brought about by NAFTA and the WTO. Since 1990, the value of US land trade with Canada and Mexico has grown at an average annual rate of 8% per year, compared with about 6% for all US trade. Since the NAFTA agreement was signed in 1993, the US trade deficit with Mexico and Canada has been rising. Robert Scott of the Economic Policy Institute (EPI) calculates that the trade deficit has "caused the displacement of production that supported 879,280 US jobs" i.e., the production, and hence these jobs, has moved to Canada and Mexico. Scott then notes that "most of those lost jobs were high-wage positions in manufacturing industries."

Moreover, technological advances in communications and transportation, and liberalized trade and investment rules, open the door for corporations to move production to countries where wages for low-skilled workers are lower. The manufacturing sectors that have been hardest hit are generally those that have employed a higher percentage of low-skilled labor. While there have been labor abuses in the US, low-skilled manufacturing jobs have often provided disadvantaged persons and families with a first step in moving out of poverty. Even so, the experience of the migrant and immigrant Latino workforce in the US highlights the need for better enforcement of basic labor rights for both legal and illegal migrant and immigrant workers.

Service industries now dominate the economy, leading some observers to call America a "postindustrial" society. Selling a service rather than making a product, these industries include entertainment and recreation, hotels and restaurants, communications and education, office administration, and banking and finance. Most new jobs are in services and the EPI reports that wages in the industries in which jobs are being created are, on average, 21% lower than wages in those industries in which jobs are disappearing. In addition, expanding industries are less likely to provide workers with health insurance than industries that are cutting jobs.

The Knowledge Economy

In the new economy, sometimes referred to as the "knowledge economy," a great deal of activity involves intellectual property, especially information technology, software and communications, which, together with pharmaceuticals, accounted for 20% of GDP in 2003. The economy is no longer solely dependent on the fixed assets of the industrial revolution like energy and physical labor, but rather on intangible assets like knowledge and creativity. In this economy, a product such as a software program is produced and replicated many times rather than created afresh each time. Little or no labor or raw materials are needed to produce new products based on the original.

The US economy has multiplied sevenfold since World War II with little more material input. Almost all the real value added reflects the embodiment of ideas.

Even in industries where one product is manufactured for each sale, the overall transaction cost has been significantly reduced due to the enhanced flow of information, which enables companies to react quickly to changing market needs. Inventories have shrunk due to enhanced supply chain management resulting from information sharing among suppliers and producers. New players gain market dominance by taking advantage of lower transaction cost channels such as the internet.

In 1975, Gordon Moore, a founder of Intel, calculated that computing power would double every two years (Moore's Law), Greenspan, *op. cit.*, p. 474n. With enhanced information flows, the economy is developing the following characteristics:

1. Markets which were once regional or national are becoming global. This is increasing the number of potential suppliers, customers and competitors.

2. Lower transaction costs are encouraging people to make more transactions. For example, $10-$20 fees for trading stocks on the internet have opened the doors to a fully fledged day trading industry not possible previously due to the lack of real-time information and high transaction costs.

3. Lower transaction costs are enabling companies to offset the cost of higher labor and raw materials, thereby enhancing productivity.

These developments have been brilliantly illustrated in Thomas L. Friedman's prize-winning book *The World is Flat*. But critics point out that, while global supply chains are making the world flat, the world is being tilted towards the Far East.

The industrial economy, though still large and growing, is becoming a smaller portion of US GDP, much as the agricultural economy did in the 19th and 20th centuries. Even so, both sectors produce more agricultural products than they did in earlier centuries due to more capital investment and the application of scientific knowledge to agricultural production.

Manufacturing is changing radically, however, in response to international competition and changing market opportunities. From the 1940s to the 1970s, industries were dominated by oligopolies, two, three or four companies which benefited from large economies of scale. This benefited consumers, who could buy acceptable products at acceptable prices. Workers also were content, as the company could afford regular raises and improvements to benefits. Oligopoly produced only average returns for investors, however, and lacked the incentive to innovate. After the Vietnam War, container ships, computers and satellites, all developed for the military, created global supply chains. These enabled smaller, nimbler companies to break into markets with new products at lower prices, which forced the market leaders to respond. This more dynamic, competitive market, that Robert Reich has called *super capitalism,* has created greater choice for consumers and investors but greater inequality and instability for workers.

Globalization

The presence of American business in overseas markets has drawn a mixed response in the rest of the world. People in some countries resent what they see as the Americanization of their cultures, sometimes called "Coca-colonization," while others accuse American firms of pressuring foreign governments to serve US political and economic interests rather than local interests. On the other hand, many foreigners welcome American products and investment as a means of raising their own standards of living. Some Americans are also concerned that by investing abroad, American business is nurturing future competitors. The ratification of NAFTA, however, and the continuing negotiations to form a Free Trade Area of the Americas have confirmed the continuing American commitment to free trade.

The effects of globalization on American workers have been fiercely debated. Economists such as W. J. Wilson claim that globalization allows cheap imports from China to reduce US light manufacturing jobs and opportunities for less skilled workers, while new immigrants and outsourcing fill service jobs. As a result, poverty is increasing among the most vulnerable groups, particularly young unskilled workers, the urban poor, and single mothers. But, in the 1990s, unemployment fell to lows not seen since the boom of the 1960s (under 4%). Meanwhile urban poverty in high poverty urban areas (over 40%) fell by one-third, according to Paul A. Jargowsky in *Stunning Progress, Hidden Problems*. Poverty fell fastest among African Americans and Hispanics with the sharpest decline since the 1960s, driven by a sharp fall in unemployment (see Council of Economic Advisers Report 2000, particularly chapter 5). The recession which started in 2008 was not due to globalization.

Globalization has made expansions last longer, as imports and immigrants dampen inflation. Wages increase more slowly, but more jobs are created. There is, however, debate about the quality of those jobs, and the effect on higher-paid workers. The lower cost of imports meanwhile leaves people more to spend on goods such as clothing, microwaves and DVD players, and households spend their savings on services. The 1993-99 expansion was the longest peacetime boom the US economy has ever experienced. Normally, labor shortages and higher prices force the Federal Reserve to raise interest rates to prevent inflation, but globalization filled shortages of labor with immigrants and shortages of goods with cheap imports. US companies that invested in China and Mexico, such as Wal-Mart and McDonalds, earned large profits.

The economy today

The US entered the 21st century with an economy that was bigger, and by many measures more successful, than ever. It had surmounted challenges ranging from a 40-year Cold War with the Soviet Union to extended bouts of sharp inflation, high unemployment, and enormous government budget deficits in the second half of the previous century. The nation finally enjoyed a period of economic calm in the 1990s: prices were stable, unemployment dropped to its lowest level in almost 30 years, the government posted a budget surplus, and the stock market experienced an unprecedented boom. In 1998, America's gross domestic product exceeded $8.5 trillion. Though the US held less than 5% of the world's population, it accounted for more than 25% of the world's economic output. Japan, the world's second largest economy, produced about half as much.

As in earlier periods, however, the US had been undergoing profound economic change. A wave of technological innovations in computing, telecommunications, and the biological sciences were profoundly affecting how Americans work and play. At the same time, the collapse of communism in the Soviet Union and Eastern Europe, the growing economic strength of the European Union, the emergence of powerful economies in Asia, expanding economic opportunities in Latin America and Africa, and the increased global integration of business and finance posed new opportunities and risks. All of these changes were leading Americans to re-examine everything from how they organize their workplaces to the role of government. Perhaps as a result, many workers, while content with their current status, looked to the future with uncertainty.

Global competition was a critical issue for Americans as the 21st century began. In the 1990s, 2.7 billion people from China, India and the former Soviet bloc joined the global economy and 1.5 billion were added to the global workforce. China, in particular, presented a number of challenges, because it was developing universities and research parks at dizzying rates and on an enormous scale; making remarkable achievements in mathematics; and producing more engineers at a faster pace than the US. Assuming stable politics and sound policies for Brazil, Russia, India and China (the BRIC economies), experts predict that by 2040, China will become the world's largest economy; India will boast the third largest economy and the largest population; and the BRIC economies will be larger than the combined G6 economies of the US, Japan, the UK, Germany and France.

America also faced a number of other continuing long-term challenges. Although many Americans had achieved economic security and some had accumulated great wealth, significant numbers continued to live in poverty. Disparities in wealth, while not as great as in some countries, were larger than in many. Substantial numbers of Americans lacked health insurance. The aging of the large baby-boom generation threatened to strain the nation's pension and health-care systems. Environmental quality also remained a major concern.

Global economic integration has brought some dislocation along with many advantages. In particular, traditional manufacturing industries, especially steel, automobiles, textiles and chemicals, have suffered setbacks, and the nation has developed a large and seemingly irreversible trade deficit. The liberalization of trade and investment contained in NAFTA has given employers the credible threat of relocating plants and jobs to other countries, thus weakening labor's bargaining position. AFL-CIO analysts project that 3.4 million white-collar jobs and $136 billion in wages will move overseas by 2015. Trade liberalization has reduced not only the number of jobs, but also real wages. Robert Scott of EPI has calculated that wages in the growing service sector are only 81% of those in manufacturing. Thus more people are working for less. Also the influx of displaced manufacturing workers into other sectors depresses wages in the expanding sectors as more workers compete for jobs.

According to research by the AFL-CIO, the majority of the new jobs being created are non-union, whereas many jobs lost to globalization were union jobs. The loss of union jobs lowers average wages. Union workers earn 27% more than non-union workers, according to the Department of Labor's Bureau of Labor Statistics. Union women earn 33% more than non-union women. African American union members earn 35% more than their non-union counterparts, Latino workers 51% more, Asian workers 11% more. Labor representatives assert that the US does not currently have industrial policies which support the creation of good jobs.

Labor critics also blame the Jobs for Americans Act 2005 for some unemployment. That Act encourages corporations to build business overseas. The intention was to create a virtuous circle in which large overseas profits are repatriated to create American jobs, and generate tax revenues. There is no tax on profits or capital appreciation until the funds are repatriated and the tax rate on repatriated profits is only 5%, instead of the usual 30%, leading skeptics to assert that corporations have no incentive to create jobs in the US after establishing functioning divisions overseas, but will instead use the extra profits to support their share price through stock buybacks, dividends, and further expansion overseas. Supporters point out that the Act needs time to have its intended effect.

The loss of thousands of good-paying jobs in the manufacturing sector has had an impact not only on individual workers but also on local communities. Research is just beginning on the impact of trade liberalization on communities. Rural areas like North Carolina have been the hardest hit. A study by Professor Leslie Hossfeld from the University of North Carolina at Pembroke on the impact of globalization on textile manufacturing on Robeson County, a small rural county, has revealed the "multiplier effect" that job dislocation can have on a community.

The implementation of the WTO and NAFTA meant displacement for thousands of North Carolina rural workers, with a loss of 100,000 jobs between 1994 and 2000. Between 1997 and 2000, Robeson County lost 41% of its manufacturing and saw significant increases in unemployment and bankruptcies, and substantial reductions in household income and business taxes. Individuals, families and the entire community were all been affected by the loss of jobs and also by the loss of an entire way of life. The effect was not confined to the individual worker or plant: workers' salaries flow back into the community when they buy goods and services. Similarly, a manufacturing plant uses utilities and services from the community, and generates considerable property tax for the county. When these salaries and taxes are lost, the "multiplier effect"' is tremendous. In 1993, manufacturing accounted for 31% of all jobs in the county. Ten years later, it accounted for only 18%. Robeson County lost approximately 8,708 manufacturing jobs. The loss of these jobs resulted in an estimated total reduction in regional employment of 18,345 jobs (full- and part-time) over ten years. This included hospital and eating and drinking establishment jobs, as well as many others in the county. Moreover by 2004 regional governments were collecting $39 million less per year in indirect business taxes. In 1993-2004, Robeson County lost a cumulative total of $4,784,293,080 in payroll, income, and business taxes.

When considering this research, however, it is important, as Hossfeld points out, to keep in mind that it is restricted to one county, and that the impacts reported are estimates of what *would have occurred* in the region over the study period *if* the manufacturing decline *had been* the *only* change to occur in the regional economy. Even so, both national statistics and the North Carolina case study indicate the difficulty workers may have in adjusting to the changing economy. New jobs being created generally offer lower wages and fewer benefits (such as health insurance) and may be temporary.

Intangible wealth

The US currently has more machinery, tools and natural resources than any other nation and is the world's most productive economy. The reason, according to some remarkable research by the World Bank ("Where is the Wealth of Nations?: Measuring Capital for the 21st Century"), is that the average American has access to over $418,000 in intangible wealth. The World Bank defines *natural capital* as the sum of nonrenewable resources (including oil, natural gas, coal and mineral resources), cropland, pasture land, forested areas and protected areas. In addition there is produced, or built, capital: the sum of machinery, equipment, and structures (including infrastructure) and urban land. But once the value of all these is added up, the economists found that the vast majority of the world's wealth was still unaccounted for.

This is because of "intangible" factors such as the trust among people in a society, an efficient judicial system, clear property rights, and effective government. This *intangible capital* also boosts the productivity of labor and results in higher total wealth. In fact, the World Bank finds, "Human capital and the value of institutions constitute the largest share of wealth in virtually all countries." Even taking into account all of the world's natural resources and produced capital, 80% of the wealth of rich countries and 60% of the wealth of poor countries is of this intangible type. The World Bank concluded: "Rich countries are largely rich because of the skills of their populations and the quality of the institutions supporting economic activity."

What the World Bank economists did was to quantify the intangible value of education and social institutions. According to their analyses, the rule of law explains 57% of countries' intangible capital. Education accounts for 36%. The rule-of-law index was devised using several hundred individual variables measuring perceptions of governance, drawn from 25 separate data sources constructed by 18 different organizations. The latter include civil society groups, political and business risk-rating agencies (such as the Economist Intelligence Unit) and indices produced by think tanks (such as the International Budget, Open Budget Index). On the rule-of-law index the US scores 91.8. The natural wealth in rich countries like the US is a tiny proportion of their overall wealth—typically 1% to 3%—yet they derive more value from what they have. Cropland, pastures and forests are more valuable in rich countries because they can be combined with other capital like machinery and strong property rights to produce more value. Machinery, buildings, roads and so forth account for 17% of the rich countries' total wealth. Overall, the average per capita wealth in the US totals $513,000, made up of natural capital ($15,000 per person), produced capital ($80,000) and intangible capital ($418,000). The annual purchasing power parity GDP per capita of the US is $43,800.

It is because of the enormous potential for future growth and jobs that can be leveraged through America's intangible wealth that newer manufacturing industries, and the service industries, have a different outlook from their traditional counterparts. A company like Google, for instance, seeks to attract and train the best talent from overseas as well as within the US, and argues that it benefits America in so doing. About half of Google's web traffic comes from outside the US, and this is true of other successful American global companies. In 2008, American inventors were awarded 92,000 US patents, twice the combined total given to South Korean and Japanese inventors. Asia's two giants, China and India, still lag far behind in this respect.

Stabilizing the economy

Ideas about the best tools for stabilizing the economy changed substantially between the 1960s and the 1990s. In the 1960s, governments had great faith in fiscal policy – manipulation of government revenues to influence the economy. Since spending and taxes are controlled by the President and the Congress, these elected officials played a leading role in directing the economy. A period of high inflation, high unemployment, and huge government deficits, however, weakened confidence in fiscal policy as a tool for regulating the pace of economic activity. Instead, monetary policy - controlling the nation's money supply through such devices as interest rates - assumed growing prominence. Monetary policy is directed by the Federal Reserve Board, which has considerable independence from the President and the Congress.

The budget deficit, current account and the national debt

The US budget deficit, current account deficit and the national debt have attracted much comment domestically and internationally. Much of this is partisan advocacy for spending programs or tax cuts. More objective surveys are published regularly by the Congressional Budget Office (CBO) and the Government Accountability Office (GAO), which make both short- and long-term projections of current trends and the likely effects of proposed policies. By law the CBO must base its estimates on assumptions that are endorsed by both parties, in particular the Joint Committee on Taxation (JCT). Analyses are also published by the Bureau of Economic Analysis.

The CBO estimated that the budget deficit for the 2009-10 budget year would range from $1.67 trillion to $1.85 trillion, between 11.9% and 13.1% of GDP, compared with $459 billion in 2008. Both parties promised to eliminate the deficit by 2012, although they had greatly divergent views on how to achieve the goal. The Republicans insisted on extension of the 2001 and 2003 tax cuts when they expired at the end of 2010, while the Democrats demanded more spending on social programs and cuts to military spending. A two-year extension was agreed.

Economists say the best way to measure the deficit is in relation to the size of the economy. In normal times, the rising ratio of household and business debt to income, or nonfinancial debt (bank debt) to GDP is not a concern so long as there continues to be an ever-increasing division of labor and specialization of tasks, and rising productivity, because these create assets which also rise as a percentage of national income.

The current account deficit for 2008 was $706.1 billion, a drop of 2.8% from a 2007 deficit of $726.6 billion, which was caused by depressed imports of oil and other goods. 2008 marked the second straight year the current account deficit had fallen after five straight increases which drove it to record highs. The current account is closely monitored by economists because it reflects the amount of borrowing from foreigners the US needs to do to finance its total trade deficit. The trade deficit climbed from zero in 1991 to 6.5% of GDP in 2006. While it is true that there must come a time when foreign investors do not wish to acquire any more US assets and the dollar will have to decline, as it has actually already done, such a decline is unlikely to be dramatic. In theory, foreign investors could suddenly switch out of US assets, but in practice this is unlikely because ongoing developments in the world economy now enable far greater deficits to occur without incident. Moreover, the lack of profitable, safe investments in many developing countries make it likely that funds will continue to flow into the US. The use by foreign countries of the dollar as their foremost reserve currency is a third factor enabling the US to finance its imports, which stood at 18% of GDP in 2006. (In 2008, imports as a percentage of GDP fell by a startling 36.5%.) China and Japan, for example, have bought hundreds of billions worth of dollars. The main reasons for the growth in the current account deficit are globalization and accelerating productivity growth. With globalization, foreign investors are more willing to invest abroad. At the same time, they have been finding that relatively more and higher risk-adjusted rates of return are available in the US. Thus foreign holdings in the US totaled $2.5 trillion at the end of 2005. Meanwhile the rate of return on the over $2 trillion worth of US investments abroad was 11% in 2005, comfortably enough to service the US debt to foreigners. Analysts disagree about how serious the problem of the deficits will be in the long term. Meanwhile the dire predictions made in the media have not come to pass and at time of writing the deficit looked to be correcting itself, Greenspan *op. cit.*, pp. 348-62.

The National Debt

- The total national debt as of June 2009 was $11.3 trillion, which is equal to 82.5% of GDP. This amounts to $36,989 per person (GAO).
- The national debt can be divided into $6.4 trillion of publicly held debt (domestic and foreign), and $4.5 trillion of debt held by government accounts (trust funds), the largest of which is Social Security.
- Because trust fund debt is a matter of internal governmental bookkeeping, economists focus

on the publicly held debt. It is this number that reflects the impact of federal borrowing on the economy and the budget.

Publicly Held Debt
- The publicly held debt is currently $4.790 trillion, a historic high in nominal terms i.e., not allowing for inflation over past years.
- A more important measure of the debt is its size in relation to the nation's economy, generally stated in terms of GDP. Currently, the publicly held debt equals nearly 38.9% of GDP. Its post-World War II high was 109% of GDP in 1946. Its post-WWII low was reached in 1974 at 24% of GDP.
- According to the January 2006 CBO baseline, the level of publicly held debt will expand from $4.790 trillion to $6.092 trillion in 2011. According to the GAO long-term budget outlook, publicly held debt will be 72.5% of GDP by 2020.

Foreign Holdings of Debt
- The amount of the debt held by foreigners is at a historic high. As of July 2006, foreign investors held $2.066 trillion of Treasury Securities, $1.312 trillion of which was held by official institutions.
- Foreign investors hold roughly 43.13% of the publicly held debt.
- Foreign holdings of Treasury securities have increased by $1.049 trillion since 2000.

Interest on the Publicly Held Debt:
- Every borrowed dollar carries an interest cost. The most direct impact of public debt on the federal budget is therefore the amount of money that has to be spent each year to finance past borrowing.
- Net interest on the publicly held debt in fiscal year 2006 amounted to $218 billion, 8.2% of the federal budget.
- Spending on interest on the debt in fiscal year 2006 ($218 billion) was equal to 23.5% of all personal income tax revenue and more than the entire federal share of the Medicaid program ($190 billion).
- During the 1980s and 1990s, before the 1998-2001 surpluses, interest regularly consumed 13% or more of the annual federal budget, reaching a high point of 15.4% in 1996.
- For fiscal year 2006, interest on the publicly held debt equaled 1.8% of GDP. Its recent high point was 3.3% of GDP in 1991.
- Under GAO's long-term budget scenario, net interest costs will reach 3.3% of GDP by 2020.

Trust Fund Debt:
- While trust fund debt does not have the same economic and budgetary effects as publicly held debt, it is nevertheless a relevant, if incomplete, indicator of future burdens such as Social Security, Medicare and federal government pension payments.
- As explained by the GAO: "Because debt held by the trust funds is neither equal to future benefit payments, nor a measure of the commitments of the current system, it cannot be seen as a measure of this future burden. Nevertheless, it provides an important signal of the existence of this burden.

- As a technical matter, trust fund balances are credited with interest. But trust fund interest is simply a credit of IOUs (a promise to pay) to the respective trust fund. It does not involve an outlay of federal dollars and thus has no economic or budgetary effect.
- According to the April 2006 Monthly Treasury Statement, the five largest trust funds were:
  1. Social Security's Federal Old Age and Survivors Insurance, $1.715 trillion
  2. Civil Service Retirement, $658 billion
  3. Medicare's Federal Hospital Insurance, $295 billion
  4. Social Security's Federal Disability Insurance, $198 billion
  5. Unemployment, $49 billion

The figures above do not include private debt. The total of public and private debt together may be 350% of GDP, some analysts believe.

Regulation and Control

Free enterprise and regulation

America points to its open, competitive markets as a model for other nations. But a complex web of government regulations shapes many aspects of American business. In recent years, regulations have grown tighter in some areas and been relaxed in others. Indeed, one enduring theme of recent American economic history has been a continuous debate about when, and how extensively, government should intervene in business affairs.

Government regulation of private industry can be divided into two categories: economic regulation and social regulation. *Economic regulation* seeks primarily to control prices. Designed in theory to protect consumers and certain companies (usually small businesses) from more powerful companies, it is often justified on the grounds that fully competitive market conditions do not exist and therefore do not provide such protections. *Social regulation* promotes objectives that are not economic, such as safer workplaces or a cleaner environment. The government controls smokestack emissions from factories, for instance, and provides tax breaks to companies which offer their employees health and retirement benefits that meet certain standards.

Economic regulation

By the early 1990s, Congress had created more than 100 federal regulatory agencies in fields ranging from trade to communications, nuclear energy to product safety, and from medicines to employment opportunity. Among them are the Federal Aviation Administration, which was established in 1966 and enforces safety rules governing airlines, and the National Highway Traffic Safety Administration (NHSTA), which was created in 1971 and oversees automobile and driver safety. Both are part of the federal Department of Transportation.

Many regulatory agencies are structured so as to be insulated from the President and, in theory, from political pressures. They are run by independent boards whose members are appointed by the President and must be confirmed by the Senate. By law, these boards must include commissioners from both political parties who serve for fixed terms, usually of five to seven years. Congress appropriates funds to the agencies and oversees their operations. In some ways, regulatory agencies work like courts. They hold hearings that resemble court trials, and their rulings are subject to review by federal courts.

Despite the official independence of regulatory agencies, members of Congress often seek to influence commissioners on behalf of their constituents. Some critics charge that businesses at times have gained undue influence over the agencies that regulate them. Agency officials often acquire intimate knowledge of the businesses they regulate, and many are offered high-paying jobs in those industries once their tenure as regulators ends. Companies have their own complaints, however. Among other things, some corporate critics complain that government regulations dealing with business often become obsolete as soon as they are written because business conditions change so rapidly.

Control of monopolies

Monopolies were among the first business entities the US government and courts attempted to regulate in the public interest. Consolidation of smaller companies into larger ones enabled some very large corporations to escape market discipline by "fixing" prices or undercutting competitors. Reformers argued that these practices ultimately saddled consumers with higher prices, restricted choice and limited the access of new companies to the market. In 1997, a federal court concluded that even though retailing is generally unconcentrated, certain retailers such as office supply "superstores" compete in distinct economic markets, and in those markets, merger of two substantial firms would be anti-competitive. The case involved a well-known home office supply company, Staples, and a well-known building supply company, Home Depot. The planned merger was dropped.

Corporate arrangements that appear to pose antitrust threats in one era may appear less threatening in another, however. Concerns about the enormous power of the Standard Oil monopoly in the early 1900s, for instance, led to the breakup of Rockefeller's petroleum empire into numerous companies, including the companies that became Exxon and Mobil. But in the late 1990s, when Exxon and Mobil announced that they planned to merge, there was hardly a whimper of public concern, although the government required some concessions before approving the combination. Gas prices were low, and other, powerful oil companies seemed strong enough to ensure competition.

The Federal Trade Commission (FTC) enforces federal antitrust and consumer protection laws by investigating complaints against individual companies initiated by consumers, businesses, congressional inquiries, or reports in the media. The Commission seeks to ensure that the nation's markets function competitively by eliminating unfair or deceptive practices.

Deregulation

Since the mid-'70s, regulation has been eased in a number of cases where it shielded companies from market pressures and hence acted to the disadvantage of consumers, thus inhibiting growth. The most important cases were transportation, airlines, telephone companies, utilities and banking.

Airlines

Deregulation created enormous upheaval in affected industries such as airlines. After controls were lifted, airline companies scrambled to find their way in a new, far less certain environment. New competitors emerged, often employing lower-wage non-union pilots and other workers and offering cheap, "no-frills" services. Large companies, which had grown accustomed to government-set fares that guaranteed they could cover all their costs, found themselves hard-pressed to meet the competition. Some - including Pan American World Airways, which to many Americans was synonymous with the era of passenger airline travel, and Eastern Airlines, which carried more passengers per year than any other American airline - failed. United Airlines, the nation's largest single airline, also ran into trouble and was rescued when its own workers agreed to buy it. United announced in 2010 that it would merge with Continental Airlines.

Customers were affected too. Many found the emergence of new companies and new service options bewildering. Changes in fares also were confusing, and not to the liking of some customers. With deregulation, small competitors realized they could win business by concentrating on the more lucrative high-volume markets, where rates were artificially high. As established airlines cut fares to meet this challenge, they often decided to cut back or even drop service to smaller, less-profitable markets. Some of this service later was restored when new "commuter" airlines, often divisions of larger carriers, sprang up. Nevertheless, analysts generally agree that air fares are lower than they would have been had regulation continued.

Telephones

Until the 1980s, the term "telephone company" was synonymous with American Telephone & Telegraph (AT&T). Its regional subsidiaries, known as "Baby Bells," were regulated monopolies, holding exclusive rights to operate in specific areas. The Federal Communications Commission regulated rates on long-distance calls between states, while state regulators had to approve rates for local and in-state long-distance calls.

Government regulation was justified on the theory that telephone companies, like electric utilities, were natural monopolies. Competition, which was assumed to require stringing multiple wires across the countryside, was seen as wasteful and inefficient. That thinking changed beginning around the 1970s, as sweeping technological developments promised rapid advances in telecommunications. Independent companies asserted that they could compete with AT&T. But they said the telephone monopoly effectively shut them out by refusing to allow them to interconnect with the massive AT&T network.

Telecommunications deregulation came in two stages. In 1984, a court effectively ended AT&T's telephone monopoly, forcing the giant to spin off its regional subsidiaries. AT&T continued to hold a substantial share of the long-distance telephone business, but vigorous competitors such as MCI Communications and Sprint Communications won some of it, showing that competition could bring lower prices and improved service.

A decade later, pressure grew to break up the Baby Bells' monopoly over local telephone service. New technologies - including cable television, cellular (or wireless) service, and the internet - offered alternatives to the local telephone companies. But economists said the enormous power of the regional monopolies inhibited the development of these alternatives. In particular, competitors would have no chance of surviving unless they could connect, at least temporarily, to the established companies' networks, something the Baby Bells resisted in numerous ways.

In 1996, Congress responded by passing the Telecommunications Act, which opened the local telephone business both to long-distance telephone companies including AT&T, and also cable television and other start-up companies. The regional monopolies had to allow new competitors to link with their networks. To encourage the regional firms to welcome competition, the law allowed them to enter the long-distance business once new competition was established in their domains.

At the end of the 1990s, there were some positive signs. Numerous smaller companies had begun offering local telephone service, especially in urban areas where they could reach large numbers of customers at low cost. The number of cellular telephone subscribers soared. Countless internet service providers sprang up to link households to the internet. But there were also developments that

Congress had not anticipated or intended. A great number of telephone companies merged, and the Baby Bells mounted numerous barriers to thwart competition. The regional firms, accordingly, were slow to expand into long-distance service. Meanwhile, for some consumers - especially residential telephone users and people in rural areas whose service previously had been subsidized by business and urban customers - deregulation was bringing higher, not lower, prices.

Banking

Banks are a special case when it comes to regulation. On the one hand, they are private businesses. But they also play a central role in the economy and therefore affect the well-being of everybody, not just their own customers. One of the most important bank regulations is the requirement to have deposit insurance, which is designed to protect bank deposits in times of economic difficulty and hence prevent runs on banks, as happened during the Great Depression. Nowadays, if a bank appears to be in trouble, the government's bank insurance agency, the Federal Deposit Insurance Corporation, pays off the depositors, using funds collected in the form of premiums from the banks themselves. If necessary, the government will also use general tax revenues to protect depositors from losses. To protect the government from undue financial risk, regulators supervise banks and order corrective action if the banks are found to be taking undue risks. The government has a continuing responsibility to supervise failing institutions and prevent them from engaging in unnecessarily risky behavior that could damage the entire economy. In addition to direct supervision, regulators increasingly require banks to raise a substantial amount of their own capital. Besides giving banks funds that can be used to absorb losses, capital requirements encourage bank owners to operate responsibly, since they will lose these funds in the event their banks fail. Regulators also require banks to disclose their financial status; banks are likely to behave more responsibly if their activities and conditions are publicly known.

Faced with threats to the profitability of banks from financial services companies, in late 1999, Congress enacted the Financial Services Modernization Act. The new law allowed banks, securities, and insurance firms to form financial conglomerates that could market a range of financial products including mutual funds, stocks and bonds, insurance, and automobile loans. The regulatory system failed in the sub-prime crisis, however, partly because the risks the banks were taking were poorly understood.

In 2010 Congress passed the Wall Street Reform and Consumer Protection Act. The stated aim of the legislation is: "To promote the financial stability of the United States by improving accountability and transparency in the financial system, to end 'too big to fail', to protect the American taxpayer by ending bailouts, to protect consumers from abusive financial services practices, and for other purposes." The Act changes the existing regulatory structure by creating new agencies, such as the Financial Stability Oversight Council, the Office of Financial Research, and the Bureau of Consumer Financial Protection, while merging and removing others. The Act streamlines the regulatory process, increases oversight of institutions regarded as a risk to the financial system and promotes transparency. and corporate governance, and eliminates the loopholes in regulation that led to the recession. All of the new agencies, and some existing ones which are not currently required to do so, are also compelled to report to Congress on an annual (or biannual) basis.

In addition, the Act provides for an advance warning system on the stability of the economy, creates rules on executive compensation and corporate governance, and eliminates the loopholes in regulation that led to the recession. All of the new agencies, and some existing ones not currently required to do so, are also compelled to report to Congress on an annual (or biannual) basis.

Savings and Loans

After World War II, the government had been eager to foster home ownership through the building of new suburbs. To do so, it helped create a new banking sector - the "savings and loan" (S&L) industry - to concentrate on making long-term home loans, mortgages secured on deposits. The mortgages typically earned 6% interest, while only 3% was paid on deposits. Thus S&Ls were assured of good profits while interest rates remained stable. By 1987 there were 3,600 S&Ls with $1.5 trillion in assets.

Savings and loans faced one major problem, however: mortgages typically ran for 30 years and carried fixed interest rates. When short-term interest rates rose above the rate on long-term mortgages, savings and loans lost money, because they were unable to afford to increase their interest rates to depositors enough to prevent them withdrawing their savings to invest elsewhere. Meanwhile the S&L was unable to write enough new mortgage business to cover the cost of its higher rates for depositors. To protect savings and loan associations and banks, regulators decided to de-control interest rates on deposits.

But by the 1980s, many depositors had started seeking higher returns by putting their savings into new forms of investment such as money market funds and other non-bank assets. This put savings and loans in a dire financial squeeze, unable to attract enough new deposits to cover their large portfolios of long-term loans. By 1989 most S&Ls were technically insolvent.

Responding to their problems, in 1980 Congress allowed S&Ls to engage in consumer, business, and commercial real estate lending, so that the profits would help balance out the losses on the mortgage portfolios. S&Ls expanded into highly risky speculative real estate ventures which in many cases proved unprofitable. Many S&Ls ran up huge losses, and the problem was made worse when some S&L executives committed fraud. The government was slow to detect the unfolding crisis because budgetary stringency and political pressures combined to shrink regulators' staffs.

The S&L crisis in a few years mushroomed into the biggest financial scandal in American history. By the end of the 1980s, not only had large numbers of S&Ls tumbled into insolvency. The Federal Savings and Loan Insurance Corporation, which insured depositors' money, itself became insolvent. In 1989, Congress and the President agreed on a taxpayer-financed bailout measure known as the Financial Institutions Reform, Recovery, and Enforcement Act (FIRREA). This Act provided $50 billion to close failed S&Ls, totally changed the regulatory apparatus for savings institutions, and imposed new constraints on portfolios. A new government agency called the Resolution Trust Corporation (RTC) was set up to liquidate insolvent institutions. In March 1990, another $78 billion was pumped into the RTC. But estimates of the total cost of the S&L cleanup continued to mount until they topped $200 billion, and by 1995 the RTC had liquidated 744 S&Ls, more than a quarter of the industry. But through selling off the S&Ls' assets in $1 billion blocks, the cost to the taxpayer, although huge, was limited to $87 billion.

After energy commodities trading was exempted from federal regulation, the Enron scandal occurred in 2002. The Sarbanes-Oxley Act of 2002 made a number of reforms in an attempt to prevent and detect fraud. For example, it gave CEOs discretion to choose which recognized accounting system to use in presenting their company's accounts, Generally Accepted Accounting Principles (GAAP), or Financial Accounting Standards Board (FASB). In addition the chairmen of company audit committees have now to be professionally qualified. Section 404 of the Act has become controversial, however, because it requires certain accounting best practices to be enforced by companies' auditors, who are overseen by a new agency, the Public Company Accounting Oversight Board (PCAOB). Yet it is rare for auditors or regulators to detect fraud. Almost always, illegal dealings are reported by whistleblowers within the company. Sarb-Ox also encourages "independent"' directors who, critics point out, generally lack enough experience in the business they are overseeing to detect fraud. They may also represent potential investors seeking to take over the company. Thus critics of Sarb-Ox claim the Act damages the competitive flexibility of American companies, imposes costs which do not pay for themselves by detecting fraud, and tends to undermine CEOs by encouraging dissident voices on boards Thus, in practice, it is claimed, board meetings become limited to the bare legal requirements and meaningful discussions take place elsewhere between the CEO and "friendly" directors, with the loss of the useful exchange of ideas which are one of the most valuable parts of board meetings.

The sub-prime crisis

In 2007-08, a somewhat similar financial crisis to S&L hit the American economy and stock markets, when a number of financial institutions which had made mortgage loans on insufficient security (sub-prime loans) lost $500 billion as interest rates and unemployment went up and many homeowners were unable to meet their mortgage payments. The loans had often been made on inflated valuations that created false collateral. As a result, several banks which had bought the mortgages to earn interest from them failed, the stock markets lost confidence and share values crashed. This provoked a raft of emergency responses by the Federal Reserve and the Congress to ensure that banks could borrow what they needed, and to give limited help to homeowners unable to pay their mortgages. A key issue in deciding what measures to take to stabilize the financial system was how to share the cost among the banks, the borrowers, the taxpayers, and the overseas bondholders such as the governments who had bought bank debt and faced the writedown or wipeout of their investments.

The most serious losses were those incurred by Fannie Mae (the Federal National Mortgage Association, founded 1938) and Freddie Mac (the Federal Home Loans Mortgage Corporation, founded 1970), government-sponsored enterprises (GSEs) which held 50% of the mortgages in the US to a value of $5 trillion and had lost about $12 billion. Fannie and Freddie do not themselves sell mortgages. They buy them and sell shares in themselves backed by the payments due on the mortgages. Fannie buys bank mortgages and Freddie was set up to do the same for S&Ls, at their request. Some legislators and officials were reluctant to give government help to these enterprises, pointing to the danger to which government financial safety nets give rise: "moral hazard." This arises when people take actions they would not so readily consider if they were not insured against the adverse consequences of their behavior. In September 2008, however, the danger to the entire financial system if the government did not fully guarantee Freddie and Fannie, as the banks were demanding, was considered so great that the government took over 80% of these corporations' liabilities under a procedure known as "government conservatorship" run by the Federal Housing Finance Agency. Fannie and Freddie had to issue convertible stock certificates called "warrants," which took priority for payment over the existing shares. Additionally the government stood ready to inject $200bn into Fannie and Freddie. In this way, they were stabilized, the financial system safeguarded, the stock markets reassured, and foreign bondholders, including 66 governments, protected.

By controlling Freddie and Fannie, the government gained the power to lower mortgage rates and thus help homeowners. Conservatorship, however, did not directly help the people who were struggling to pay their mortgages and had fallen into debt because they were behind with their payments. The shareholders meanwhile suffered, at least in the short term, as their shares lost around 85% of their value and traded at $1 per share. The conservatorship, however, is not permanent. A future administration can allow Fannie and Freddie to return to normal operations. In that case the shareholders could eventually get back the money they lost.

The attitude of regulators to sub-prime lending before the crisis was as much governed by political considerations as by economic ones. Alan Greenspan explains it thus: "I was aware that the loosening of mortgage credit terms for sub-prime borrowers increased financial risk, and that subsidized home ownership initiatives distort market outcomes. But I believed then, as now, that the benefits of broadened home ownership are worth the risk. Protection of property rights, vital to a market economy, requires a critical mass of owners to sustain political support" *op. cit.* , p. 233. Greenspan sums up his view of what regulation causes least interference with the market in three rules of thumb: "1. Regulation approved in a crisis must subsequently be fine-tuned....2. Sometimes several regulators are better than one....3. Regulations outlive their usefulness and should be reviewed periodically...." *ibid.*, pp. 374-75. Meanwhile the alternative to government regulation is *counterparty surveillance,* by which banks, other financial institutions and high-income investors require collateral, for example, to be set against loans.

Social regulation

Labor standards

Copious regulations have been enacted to protect workers and consumers. It is against the law for employers to discriminate in hiring on the basis of age, sex, race, or religious belief. Child labor generally is prohibited. Independent labor unions are guaranteed the right to organize, bargain, and strike, although in practice the usefulness of the right to strike is limited because employers can legally dismiss workers who go on strike. The government issues and enforces workplace safety and health codes through the Occupational Safety and Health Administration to protect workers from hazards they may encounter in their jobs.

Consumer protection

Nearly every product sold in the US is affected by some kind of government regulation: food manufacturers must say exactly what is in a can or box or jar; to protect the public's health and safety, no drug can be sold until it has been thoroughly tested and licensed by the US Food and Drug Administration; automobiles must be built according to safety standards and must meet pollution standards; prices for goods must be clearly marked; and advertisers are not allowed to mislead consumers.

Protecting the environment

The regulation of practices that affect the environment has been a relatively recent development in the US, but is a good example of government intervention in the economy for a social purpose. Beginning in the 1960s, Americans became increasingly concerned about the environmental impact of industrial growth. Engine exhaust from growing numbers of automobiles, for instance, was blamed for smog and other forms of air pollution in larger cities. With market forces unable to address such problems, many environmentalists suggested that the government had a moral obligation to protect the earth's fragile ecosystems, even if doing so meant that some economic growth be sacrificed. A slew of laws was enacted to control pollution, including the 1963 Clean Air Act, the 1972 Clean Water Act, and the 1974 Safe Drinking Water Act (see Chapter 1).

Environmentalists achieved a major goal in December 1970 with the establishment of the US Environmental Protection Agency (EPA), which brought together in a single agency many federal programs charged with protecting the environment. The EPA sets and enforces tolerable limits of air and water pollution, and establishes timetables to bring polluters into line with standards. Since most of the requirements are of recent origin, industries are often given several years to conform. The EPA also has the authority to coordinate and support the research and anti-pollution efforts of state and local governments, private and public groups, and educational institutions.

Data collected since the Agency began its work show significant improvements in environmental quality. There has been a nationwide decline in virtually all air pollutants, for example. Many Americans, however, believe that still greater efforts to combat air pollution are needed. Congress passed important amendments to the Clean Air Act, which were signed into law by President George H. W. Bush. Among other things, the legislation incorporated an innovative market-based system (emissions trading) designed to secure a substantial reduction in sulfur dioxide emissions, which produce what is known as "acid rain." This type of pollution is believed to cause serious damage to forests and lakes, particularly in the eastern part of the US.

The future of regulation

The government has tried to use price mechanisms to achieve regulatory goals, hoping this would be less disruptive to market forces. It has developed a system of air-pollution credits, for example, which allows companies to sell the credits among themselves. Companies able to meet pollution requirements least expensively can sell credits to other companies. By this means, it is hoped, pollution-control goals can be achieved in the most efficient and least costly way.

Social regulation was relaxed somewhat during the presidency of Ronald Reagan in the 1980s. Still, many Americans continued to voice concerns about specific events or trends, prompting the government to issue new regulations in some areas, particularly environmental protection. Some citizens, in fact, have turned to the courts when they feel their elected officials are not addressing certain issues quickly or strongly enough. For instance, in the 1990s, individuals, and eventually government itself, sued tobacco companies over the health risks of cigarette smoking. A large financial settlement provided states with long-term payments to cover the costs of treating smoking-related illnesses.

The market during most of the last hundred years has remained sufficiently open and competitive to generate capital formation, rising real wages, and an increasing supply of goods and services, in spite of rising taxes, increased government spending, and a widening circle of government rules and regulations. Yet reluctance to regulate financial institutions, and to make the bonuses paid to their managers conditional on the longer term consequences of their performance, have been blamed by many for the sub-prime crisis and the growth of inequality and resentment. Moreover, as Robert Reich, former Labor Secretary and now a professor at the University of California at Berkeley points out in *Super Capitalism*, globalization is creating wider inequalities for which an updated model of the market is required.

The 2008 financial crisis

The financial crisis which broke in September 2008 has led many to question the free market economic model in its American form and to claim that the US will lose its status as the superpower of the global financial system. After all, the American government felt obliged in effect to nationalize the country's two largest mortgage lenders and then its biggest insurance company, to spend billions on facilities to help near-bankrupt banks and $700 million on the Troubled Assets Relief Program (TARP), although the net cost of the latter has been estimated to be $60-$100 million. In addition The American Recovery and Reinvestment Act of 2009 distributed $787 billion in tax benefits, contracts, grants and loans, and entitlements in roughly equal thirds. It seemed that the belief in the self-regulating nature of the market, "market fundamentalism," had turned out to be false. In economic management, the pendulum seems likely to swing back toward more regulation.

The symbiotic relationship between America and China is critical to the future of the world economy and hence to US recovery from the financial crisis, according to leading expert, Niall Ferguson of Harvard. Taken as a single economy, the relationship between China and America, which he calls "Chimerica", accounts for around 13% of the world's land surface, a quarter of its population, about a third of its gross domestic product, and somewhere over half of the global economic growth of recent years. Chinese savings have helped Americans to borrow cheaply and buy cheaply, mainly because China kept its currency cheap relative to the dollar and has bought vast reserves of dollar-denominated securities, especially U.S. Treasuries and bonds issued by Fannie Mae and Freddie Mac. Chinese holdings were worth $682 billion in 2009. Meanwhile, other Asian economies have joined China in adopting currency pegs (fixing the value of their currency to another currency such as the dollar, or to a basket of currencies), and accumulating international reserves, thereby financing Western current account deficits. Middle Eastern and other energy exporters have also found themselves running surpluses and recycling petrodollars (profits from oil denominated in dollars) to the Anglosphere (English-speaking countries) and its satellites.

But the wave of defaults in the US sub-prime mortgage market revealed how unstable Chimerica was. In essence, the rest of the world's savings had helped inflate a real estate bubble in the US. As is usual in asset bubbles, easy money was accompanied by lax lending standards and outright fraud. Euphoria eventually gave way to distress and then to panic. What made the property crash so dangerous was that an inverted pyramid of financial assets had been erected upon the flimsy base of American mortgages. Banks had bundled the sound and unsound loans together and resold them to investors around the world as "Collateralized Debt Obligations" and similar instruments. Meanwhile the ratings agencies had pronounced the top tier of these instruments to be AAA-rated. After the crash, the banks were left with liabilities worth many times their assets. According to the Bank of England, total losses could eventually amount to as much as $2.8 trillion.

The failure among financial firms has had three results. First, the share prices of the weaker banks have crashed, particularly those of the investment banks, which do not have reserves of savers' federally insured deposits. As the underlying equity supporting the shares declined in value, the degree of leverage (the ratio between what the firms own and what they owe) rose, and the firms became short of funds (illiquid). Without new capital, the firms soon became unable to pay their debts and became insolvent. Second, the banking crisis has triggered a further crisis in the market for derivatives. Credit default swaps (CDS), a form of derivative used to insure against a borrower's failure to repay a loan, were supposed to act as a safeguard for bondholders. But it is unclear how the derivatives market can cope with defaults on this scale when the notional total amount of CDS is $58 trillion. But thirdly and most importantly, the efforts of banks to stabilize their balance sheets by reducing credit has driven the US economy into a recession, the most severe economic downturn since the early 1930s. The Federal Reserve has cut its effective federal-funds rate to very close to zero. The Federal deficit has already exploded, with an increase in public debt in 2008 alone of around $1.5 trillion. But neither monetarist nor Keynesian measures have been unable to avert a major recession.

Many observers failed to foresee the damage the bubble in the housing market would cause when it burst. (The likes of Robert Shiller of Yale and Nouriel Roubini of New York University are now famous for their prescience.) Indeed, some argue that a free market anti-regulation bias among economists blinded many of them to the danger and made them deny that it would happen. Over the past generation, economists have believed that economic cycles are driven by players in the "real" economy, the producers and consumers of goods and services. Many economists used mathematical models that failed to account for the critical roles that banks and other financial institutions play in the economy. These computerized mathematical models also omitted hard-to-measure factors like psychology and people's expectations about the future. The models assumed that markets and economies are inherently stable, and disregarded differences in the way various economic players make decisions, revise their forecasting methods and are influenced by social factors. Standard analysis also failed, in part, because of the widespread use of new financial products that were poorly understood. Economists badly underestimated the risks of new types of derivatives built upon pools of mortgages, and credit default swaps, which played a key role in the collapse of America's largest insurer, AIG, and one of the largest banks, Lehman Bros. Economists did not firmly grasp the workings of the increasingly interconnected global financial system.

But it was the financial institutions that fomented the crisis, by creating risky products, encouraging excessive borrowing among consumers, and engaging in high-risk behavior themselves, like amassing huge positions in mortgage-backed securities Yet it was obvious that home prices could not continue indefinitely rising faster than household incomes. There was an assumption, however, that all concerned - bankers, lenders, borrowers and consumers - behaved rationally at all times, as if they were economists making the most financially favorable choices. In fact borrowers acted irrationally, taking out mortgages they could not afford, and lenders did so by investing in securities backed by those risky mortgages. Even though some individuals do act rationally, economists were wrong to assume that large groups of people will react to given conditions as an individual would, because they often do not.

Instead, economists assumed that creating a wider variety of new financial products would allow market participants to make ever more refined investments, so that the markets would better reflect the combined wisdom of all the players and greater degrees of leverage could be safely accepted. But because there was not enough historical data to put into the models used to price the new derivatives, risk and return assessments turned out to be wrong. When certain price and risk models came into widespread use, they led many players to make the same assumptions. The market thus lost the benefit of having many participants, since there was no longer a variety of views offsetting one another. The problem was exacerbated by the "control illusion," an unjustified confidence based on the model's apparent mathematical precision.

Much of the financial crisis can also be blamed on an overreliance on ratings agencies, which gave complex securities a seal of approval, using models which grossly underestimated the risks. The false confidence created by asset-pricing models led banks and hedge funds to use excessive leverage, borrowing money to make bigger investments, and laying the groundwork for larger losses when they went wrong. At the time, few people knew that major financial institutions had become so heavily leveraged in assets based on real estate.

Crises in the financial markets have shown that participants can rely too heavily on the belief that they can quickly unload securities that decline in price. The stock market crash of 1987 began with a small drop in prices which triggered an avalanche of sell orders in computerized trading programs, causing a further price decline that triggered more automatic sales. Then in 1998 came the collapse of the Long-Term Capital Management (LTCM) hedge fund. It had built up a huge position in government bonds from the US and other countries, but was forced into a wave of selling after a Russian government bond default deflated bond prices, because a default in one kind of bond causes reassessment of all the risks.

Oxford economist Vijay Joshi advocates five measures of tougher bank regulation "to prevent even bigger financial crises in the future: There is a crying need to remove the dearth of information in the financial sector about how risks are valued, packaged, managed and distributed....; compensation systems in financial institutions must be changed....Investment managers could be required to invest a significant part of their pay in the assets they manage, with the stipulation that their holdings in the funds would be retained for several years (even if they quit their jobs). Thirdly, the rating agencies must be made genuinely independent....the practice of their being paid by issuers of the bonds has to be ended. Fourthly, financial institutions must be compelled to be adequately cushioned against capital losses and liquidity risk....Lastly, financial regulation has to be internationally coordinated" *Postmaster and the Merton Record*, Michaelmas, 2008, pp.48-50.

To some extent also, the sub-prime crisis was the result of the efforts of successive Administrations since 1997 to expand home ownership. In response to political pressure, the banks and GSEs took steps to make homeownership more affordable for lower-income Americans and those with a poor credit history. In 2001/2002, President Bush created "America's Home Ownership Challenge," in which he challenged the private lending sector as well as Fannie Mae and Freddie Mac to make more than 5.5 million new minority and low income mortgage loans. To meet his challenge to the private lending industry, 24 of the largest banking and lending companies pledged to make 1.1 trillion dollars in low income and minority loans (see http://mitchell-langbert. blogspot.com/2008/09/clintons-and-democrats-responsibility.html). Under President Bush, US homeownership in the second quarter of 2004 reached an all-time high of 69.2%, single-family housing affordability was at its highest level in 30 years, and minority homeownership set a new record-high of 51%.

Speaking of its response to the recession, the Obama Administration has stated that the Recovery Act of 2009 "is an unprecedented effort to jumpstart our economy, create or save millions of jobs, and put a down payment on addressing long-neglected challenges so our country can thrive in the 21st century. The Act is an extraordinary response to a crisis unlike any since the Great Depression, and includes measures to modernize our nation's infrastructure, enhance energy independence, expand educational opportunities, preserve and improve affordable health care, provide tax relief, and protect those in greatest need."

THE WORKFORCE

Labor unions

Around 1800, industrial innovation began to reduce the skills required by craft workers such as shoemakers, carpenters, leather workers, and printers, and enable employers to replace them with unskilled workers at lower rates of pay. In response, workers began to organize themselves into trade unions to protect their interests. Union members would agree on the wages they thought were fair, pledge to stop working for employers who paid less, and pressure employers to hire union members only. Originally each trade union represented a particular trade or craft or a group of related trades. A well-known example is the Union of Needletrades, Industrial and Textile Employees. Later on trade unions began to unite to form labor unions to increase their bargaining power. The first labor union was the IWW (Industrial Workers of the World) formed in Chicago in 1905, which united miners and textile workers. Employers resisted union activity in the courts, alleging that concerted activity by workers was an illegal conspiracy against their employer and the community. But by the 1850s peaceful union activity had become widely accepted. Unions extended their efforts beyond wages to campaign for a 10-hour workday and against child labor. Several state legislatures responded favorably.

Struggles and successes

During the great surge of industrial growth between 1865 and 1900, the workforce expanded enormously, especially in heavy industry. But the workers suffered in times of economic depression. Strikes, sometimes accompanied by violence, as in Chicago in 1905, became commonplace and legislatures in many states passed new conspiracy laws aimed at suppressing labor. American capitalists used more violence in the class struggle than their opposite numbers in any other country. In straight contests of strength with both organized and unorganized workers, the capitalists usually triumphed.

In response, workers formed organizations with national scope. The American Federation of Labor (AFL) was founded in 1886 by Samuel Gompers. Comprising craft unions and their members, the AFL had grown to 1.75 million members by 1904, making it the nation's dominant labor organization. Gompers sought to give workers a greater share in the wealth they helped produce. A radical alternative was offered by the IWW, a trade union of 43 organizations. The IWW demanded the overthrow of capitalism through strikes, boycotts, and sabotage. It opposed US participation in World War I. After reaching a peak of 100,000 members in 1912, however, the IWW had almost disappeared by 1925, because of federal imprisonment of its leaders for organizing violent strikes, and a national sentiment against radicalism during and after World War I.

In the early 1900s, an alliance was formed between the AFL and representatives of the American Progressive Movement. Together they campaigned for state and federal laws to aid labor. Their efforts resulted in the passage of state laws prohibiting child labor, limiting the number of hours women could work, and establishing workers' compensation programs for people who were injured on the job. At the federal level, Congress passed laws to protect children, railroad workers, and seamen, and established the Department of Labor. During World War I, labor unions made great strides, and by January 1919, the AFL had more than 3 million members. Violence continued to mark labor protests, as in the Carnegie steelworks strike in Pennsylvania in 1922.

The Depression

During the Progressive Era, Americans had tended to sympathize with labor, but after the Russian Revolution of 1917 they became hostile to it. Once again, the courts restricted union activity. But during the Great Depression, as part of his "New Deal," President Franklin Roosevelt vowed to help "the forgotten man," the farmer who had lost his land or the worker who had lost her job. By the Wagner Act of 1935, Congress guaranteed workers the right to join unions and bargain collectively, and established the National Labor Relations Board to settle disputes between unions and employers. As a result, many new unions were formed.

Not long after, tensions within the AFL between skilled craftspersons and industrial workers led to the founding of a new labor organization, the Congress of Industrial Organizations (CIO). The new organization grew rapidly; by the late 1930s it had more members than the AFL.

The unions today

After World War II a wave of strikes for higher wages swept the nation. Employers charged that unions had too much power, and Congress agreed. It passed the Taft-Hartley Act in 1947 outlawing the "closed shop" agreement (by which employers were required to hire only union members), restricted the right to strike, and permitted states to enact "right-to-work" laws, which ban agreements requiring workers to join a union after being hired. The Act also empowered the President to impose an 80-day "cooling off" period in a strike deemed to create a national emergency.

In response, in 1955 the AFL and CIO merged to form a new organization, the AFL-CIO, whose 75 members represent the majority of labor organizations today. The largest of these are the American Federation of State, County and Municipal Employees, the United Food and Commercial Workers' International Union, and the International Brotherhood of Teamsters (the largest US trade union). The National Education Association (NEA), with 2.3 million members, remains independent, however. The Teamsters was formed in 1903 to represent truck drivers but now covers many occupations including chauffeurs, warehousemen and helpers.

The government, through the Department of Labor, supports the right of workers to belong to unions, and upholds the laws regulating workers' pay and conditions. But when air traffic controllers started an illegal strike in 1981, President Reagan had most of them dismissed. Meanwhile corruption has continued to taint the reputation of labor unions. In the 1960s, two presidents of the Teamsters, Jimmy Hoffa and Dave Beck, were sent to prison, and in 1997, the election for president was found to have involved illegal campaign money. Hoffa (1913-?1975) was investigated by Robert Kennedy for alleged ties to the Mafia and was jailed from 1967-71.

In recent decades there has been a decrease in the percentage of workers who join a union. Among the reasons are the decline of heavy industries, which were union strongholds, and the steady replacement of "blue collar" (manual) workers by automation. Even so, organized labor remains a strong force in the US economy and politics, and working conditions have steadily improved. A Teamsters strike in 1997 against UPS (United Parcel Service) involving 185,000 workers won a pay increase and more jobs. UPS is notorious in labor history for the practice of Taylorism, invented at the turn of the 20th century, which prescribes in minute detail how workers shall perform each task. Even today, UPS truck shelves are designed so that drivers cannot deliver a package unless their GPS (Global Positioning System) shows that they are at the correct address. UPS say that this prevents wrong deliveries and thefts by workers, some of whom are immigrants with low levels of education. Some workers, however, feel that the systems of work at UPS are overly restrictive and demeaning. More recently, union campaigns for better conditions at WalMart have received wide publicity and achieved some success.

According to the US Department of Labor's Bureau of Labor Statistics, in 2008, union members accounted for 12.4% of employed wage and salary workers. The number of workers belonging to a union was 16.1 million. By contrast, in 1983, the first year for which comparable data are available, the union membership rate was 20.1%, and there were 17.7 million union workers. In 2008, government workers (36.8%) were nearly five times more likely to belong to a union than were private sector employees (7.6%). Workers in education, training, and library occupations had the highest unionization rate at 38.7%, followed by protective service occupations at 35.4%. Within the public sector, local government workers had the highest union membership rate, 42.2%. This group includes many workers in several heavily unionized occupations, such as teachers, police officers, and fire fighters. Private sector industries with high unionization rates include transportation and utilities (22.2%), telecommunications (19.3%), and construction (15.6%). In 2008, unionization rates were low in financial activities (1.8%), professional and business services (2.1%), sales and related occupations (3.3%) and farming, fishing, and forestry occupations (4.3%). Black workers were more likely to be union members than were white, Asian, or Hispanic workers. Among states, New York had the highest union membership rate (24.9%) and North Carolina the lowest (3.5%). Behind some of these statistics, say union leaders, the real story is the millions of workers who are denied the right to choose a union because of employer intimidation. Another reason for the decline in union membership is that the struggles over fair pay, shorter hours and decent conditions have mostly been won. The emphasis is now on pay raises, job protection (especially in industries affected by globalization), equal rights and political influence, mainly through the Democratic Party and PACs.

Labor standards

An independent perspective on how the US as a whole measures up to international labor standards comes from Human Rights Watch (HRW): "Researching workers' exercise of [these] rights in different industries, occupations, and regions, Human Rights Watch found that freedom of association is a right under severe, often buckling pressure when workers in the United States try to exercise it." Private employers are the main culprits when it comes to denial of freedom of association to organize and bargain collectively. These employers can and do use a variety legal means to deter workers' exercise of their rights. Some employers drag out legal proceedings for years, fearing little more than an order to post a notice in the workplace promising not to repeat unlawful conduct or to grant back pay to a worker fired for organizing. Many employees have come to view such remedies as a routine cost of doing business.

While US workers, unlike employees in many other countries, may not suffer from direct government repression, "workers' freedom of association is under sustained attack in the US, and the government is often failing its responsibility under international human rights standards to deter such attacks and protect workers' rights," the HRW report says. "Some provisions of US law openly conflict with international norms and create formidable legal obstacles to the exercise of freedom of association. Millions of workers, including agricultural and domestic service workers, are expressly barred from the law's protection of the right to organize. US legal doctrine allowing employers to permanently replace workers who exercise the right to strike effectively nullifies the right. Mutual support among workers and unions recognized in most of the world as legitimate expressions of solidarity is harshly proscribed under US law as illegal secondary boycotting. Labor laws have failed to keep pace with changes in the economy and new forms of employment relationships, creating millions of part-time, temporary, subcontracted, and otherwise 'atypical' or 'contingent' workers whose exercise of the right to freedom of association is frustrated by the law's inadequacy."

The National Labor Relations Act (NLRA) defends the rights of workers to form, join, or assist in organizing a union at their place of employment, to engage in activities that seek to modify wages or working conditions, or to refuse to do any or all of these things. It prohibits employers from unduly interfering in organizing activity, such as threatening to fire or actually firing employees because they are engaged in organizing, and it also protects employees against union pressure on and retaliations against workers who do not participate in or who criticize union activities. But, the HRW report states, the reality of NLRA enforcement falls far short of its goals. "Many workers who try to form and join trade unions to bargain with their employers are spied on, harassed, pressured, threatened, suspended, fired, deported, or otherwise victimized in reprisal for their exercise of the right to freedom of association.... International human rights law makes governments responsible for protecting vulnerable persons and groups from patterns of abuse by private actors. In the US, labor law enforcement efforts often fail to deter unlawful conduct." In 2009, the Employee Free Choice Act was introduced into Congress to remedy these deficiencies.

The changing workforce

In the past 50 years, the size of the US labor force has more than doubled, from 62.2 million in 1950 to 145.9 million in 2007. Over the next 50 years, however, the labor force growth rate is projected to slow to near zero from its peak of 2.6% per year in the 1970s. One reason for this is that while women's share of the labor force has increased dramatically, from 30% in 1950 to 47% in 2000, their share is projected to remain at around 48%. Without a major increase in productivity, therefore, says the Government Accountability Office, low labor force growth will lead to slower growth in the economy and slower growth of federal revenues.

Labor force participation rates are high at around 66% but at least 5% of full time workers moonlight i.e., work at a second job. Although sex discrimination is illegal, women still hold most of the lower-paid secretarial and nursing jobs, and higher-paid jobs are predominantly held by men. Women also complain of having to work a "second shift," cooking and cleaning in the evenings and looking after children, although men say they are in principle willing to share in the housework. Jobs are mainly found by word-of-mouth or through advertisements in newspapers or on the internet. The work week is 40 hours and the 30 minutes spent eating lunch is usually not paid. Factory workers are usually paid by the hour for a 45-hour week, and earn higher rates for night and weekend work; office workers are paid bi-weekly or monthly and often work longer than the scheduled hours. There is a federal minimum wage, currently $7.25 per hour. Depending on the employer, a number of non-pay benefits add to the value of the pay package. The chief of these is a healthcare plan. There are also pensions. Two-thirds of all retirement funds are held in defined contribution plans controlled by workers themselves, such as IRAs (Individual Retirement Accounts) and 401(k)s. A 401(k) plan is a retirement savings plan that is funded by employee contributions and often by matching contributions from the employer. The major attraction of these plans is that the contributions are taken from pre-tax salary, and the funds grow tax-free until withdrawn. Also, the plans are (to some extent) self-directed, and they are portable when an employee changes jobs. Pensions in the US are not always portable but the US claims to be the leading country for pensions portability, a highly important benefit for workers who need to change jobs. The other one-third of pension plans is controlled by employers, unions, or state/local governments. The federal government has created an insurance system for businesses offering private pensions, funded by premiums collected from these employers. Americans typically get two weeks' vacation which increases with length of service. Even with the 10 statutory holidays during the year such as Thanksgiving, this allowance is far less than for workers in Europe. Workers in low-paid jobs may get no vacation at all. Strict laws govern hours, breaks and safety.

Working life is generally between the ages of 18 and 65. Work is seen as part of personal identity, and people of working age who cannot find work often see themselves as without value. Unemployment is typically 6% although much higher for blacks (8.5%). An average spell of unemployment is 15 weeks. Under liberal US labor laws, hiring and firing is easy, so companies can quickly adjust to downturns in the market by laying off workers and downsizing their operations. In theory, this should mean that downtowns are shorter, but only if capital and credit remain available.

While technological changes can create demand for higher-skilled workers, these changes, depending on the industry, can also decrease employer demand for such workers. The growth of the knowledge-based economy, and innovations in management systems, such as the adoption of high-performance practices that emphasize problem solving and teamwork, have also contributed to the need for increased skill levels in many industries. Trade liberalization is also a factor. Liberalization generates winners and losers. The clear winners in the current trade model are people with capital to invest, entrepreneurial ability, education and marketable skills. Conversely, those who are left out of the current model are people in poverty, who often lack basic education, unskilled workers and indigenous people. All of these changes have the potential to increase the wage gap between high- and low-skill workers, with significant implications for society.

Job stability has certainly significantly decreased for blue-collar workers owing to changes in technology and globalization. Offshore sourcing of jobs (the practice of moving business processes or services to another country, especially overseas, to reduce costs) has increased and is likely to continue, since failure to do so may leave companies at a competitive disadvantage. Rapid advances in technology, increased trade, lower transportation costs, and communications innovations have greatly facilitated offshoring, especially in the services sector. Given the high level of education and worker skill development in some countries, the jobs moving offshore are no longer low-wage, low-skilled jobs, but instead are those that attract high-skilled workers. In addition, the high cost of health care in the US and the fact that it is often a factor in employer costs have contributed to employers' decisions to move certain functions overseas.

Foreign competition and offshoring have also led to some redistribution of population. The town of Buffalo, New York State, on the Canadian border, has lost half its population in the last 20 years owing to a loss of manufacturing jobs, while Southern cities like Atlanta, Georgia (which hosted the 1996 Olympic Games) are booming high-tech and service centers. A similar pattern is found throughout the rustbelt states of New England and the Great Lakes, although some jobs have returned, for example, in specialist steel-making. Self-employment and part-time work have increased somewhat.

Low pay

The US still leads the world in productivity and (apart from a few countries with small populations) real income per person, but the American way of organizing work and rewarding workers no longer guarantees hardworking citizens a piece of the American dream. Child poverty rates, homelessness, the urban underclass, and the gap between high-paid and low-paid workers continue to increase. Low-paid US workers have worse standards of living than comparable workers in Europe or Japan. While the US market does better than most other countries in job creation, much of that growth is in low-wage service industries. Many women may have been pushed into those poor-paying jobs by their husbands' falling incomes. The US workforce is very mobile and relatively unregulated compared to that in other advanced countries, moving into and out of employment much more rapidly. This facilitates new employment, but it increases turnover, reduces on-the-job training and minimizes job security and worker representation. In terms of purchasing power, US production of goods and services per capita generates the world's highest living standard. But Americans work longer hours and take shorter vacations. Hence US productivity per hour is generally similar to that of most other advanced countries. Notably, American low-wage workers do much worse compared to the US average than do low-wage European workers in relation to the average in their countries. Low-paid Americans have lower real earnings than workers in all advanced countries for which there are comparable data. This may be a trade-off for creating more jobs. But other advanced economies may have useful solutions to offer in their different ways of determining wages, training workers and creating new kinds of representation and social safety nets.

Women in the Workforce

The proportion of women and men in the wage and salaried workforce is now nearly equal (51% men and 49% women), and men have become far more accepting of women's participation over the past 25 years. Two in five men, however, still think women's place is in the home. Over the past generation, women have achieved increasingly higher educational levels and steadily moved into managerial and professional occupations, so that today women employees are significantly better educated and significantly more likely to hold managerial and professional positions than men. Women's annual earnings, however, are still significantly less than men's ($36,716 versus $52,908), around 80% in 2007. Possible reasons for this persistent gender difference in earnings include women's greater likelihood of working part time and in administrative positions. In addition, employees, whether men or women, who have greater responsibility for care of their children report lower earnings. In dual-earner couples, there is a significant third job that has to be done at home—family work, for which women are still much more likely to assume primary responsibility than men.

Dual-Earner Couples

The proportion of married employees who live in dual-earner couples has increased substantially over the last generation, from 66% in 1977 to 78 % in 2002. And together, these couples are working longer hours. Combined work hours for dual-earner couples with children have risen 10 hours a week, from 81 hours in 1977 to 91. Clearly, today's working couples have less time for their lives off the job. Given this, it comes as a surprise that the combined time that spouses with children spend caring for and doing things with their children on workdays has actually increased from 5.2 hours in 1977 to 6.2 hours today.

According to *Times Are Changing: Gender and Generation at Work and at Home*, from the Families and Work Institute, for the first time, young women (66%) and men (67%) aged under 29 "the Millennials" do not differ in their desire for jobs with more responsibility, whether or not they have children. This was not the case as recently as 2002. As for labor force participation, more men, particularly young men, are not in the labor force. Either men are pursuing postsecondary education, or they are retiring earlier. In 1975, 47% of mothers with children under 18 participated in the labor force. By 2007, the proportion had risen to 71%. One reason is that the average age of women bearing children is higher. Another reason may be that many employed women with children have already completed their education. Women's level of education has in any case increased relative to men's. As for earnings, in 1979, the average full time employed woman earned 62% of male earnings. In the early 1990s, the wage gap narrowed and by 2007, the average full-time employed woman earned 80% of what men earned on a weekly basis and 82% of the hourly pay of men. Meanwhile, attitudes to women's and men's work and family roles have changed. Attitudes to employed women and mothering have shifted as well. Men's roles and behaviors at home are changing too. The percentage of employees who agree that it is better if the man earns the money and the woman takes care of the home and children has dropped from 64% in 1977 to 41% in 2008. For the first time, in 2008 men's and women's views about appropriate work and family roles converged. Employees were also more likely than in 1977 to agree that employed women can be good mothers. Nowadays, employed fathers spend significantly more time per workday with their children under 13 than they did three decades ago, while the amount of time employed mothers spend with their children has not changed significantly. The amount of time fathers spend has increased from two hours to three hours. At the same time, the amount of time mothers spend has remained constant at an average of 3.8 hours. Thus, mothers still spend significantly more time per workday, on average, caring for their children than fathers, but fathers are catching up. Today's Millennial fathers in particular spend an average of 4.3 hours per workday with their children, significantly more than their age counterparts in 1977, who spent an average of 2.4 hours per workday with their children. Mothers under 29 spend an average of 5 hours, up from 4.5 hours in 1977.

Men are also taking more overall responsibility for the care of their children, according to themselves and their wives/partners. Men who say their wives or partners take the most responsibility for childcare are no longer the majority (48% in 2008 compared with 58% in 1992). The nearly half of employed men (49%) who now say they take most or an equal share of childcare responsibilities is up from 41% in 1992. Importantly, employed women agree that their husbands or partners are taking more responsibility for childcare. The percentage of women reporting that they take most responsibility for child care has dropped (from 73% in 1992 to 67% in 2008). Alternatively, the percentage of those who say their spouse takes or shares the responsibility increased significantly from 21% to 31%.

Men are taking more responsibility for other family work as well. The percentage of men who report they do most or an equal share of cooking has increased substantially since 1992, from 34% to 56%, while the percentage of women who say they do most of the cooking has dropped from 75% to 70%, and the percentage of women who say their husbands do most or an equal share of cooking increased from 15% to 25%. Although women agree that their husbands are more involved in cooking, there is still a notable difference between the 70% of women who say they do most of the cooking and the 56% of men who say they take at least an equal share. It may be that some men have different perceptions about what is involved in food preparation than their wives do, and may not be including certain aspects of the meal preparation process, such as meal planning and shopping for ingredients. The gender that has traditionally been assumed to have primary responsibility for particular aspects of family work tends to see itself as doing more in those areas. Whatever the actual degree of responsibility men are assuming, it has clearly become more socially acceptable for men to be and to say they are involved in child care, cooking and cleaning over the past three decades than it was in the past.

Changing gender roles appear to have increased the level of work-life conflict experienced by men. (Work/life conflict occurs when employees (and employers) find their roles within the workplace and outside it are overwhelming them, or interfering with one another.) Men's reported level of work-life conflict has risen significantly over the past three decades, while the level of conflict reported by women has not changed significantly. In 1977, the proportions of men and women reporting some or a lot of work-life conflict were similar. Men's work-life conflict, however, has increased from 34% to 45%, while women's work-life conflict has increased less dramatically from 34% to 39%. The majority of fathers in dual-earner couples (59%) report experiencing some or a lot of such conflict, up from 35% in 1977.

There is no question that the American workforce has changed. Women, and particularly mothers of children under 18, have reached a critical mass in the workplace. Women are also earning the majority of bachelor and advanced degrees. In light of these changes, it is not surprising that young women today are equal with young men in their desire to move to jobs with more responsibility. Young mothers no longer necessarily feel pressured to reduce their career aspirations. Meanwhile, attitudes about working mothers are more favorable today than ever before. In addition, husbands are more likely to be involved in family work, providing much needed support for working mothers, although both are likely to have less time for themselves.

Diversity

"Diversity" is a word used in many US companies. "Human diversity" is widely discussed in publications for American businesspeople, who address the advantages of "workplace diversity" at conferences. Diversity has come to refer to efforts by US business leaders to hire, promote, and retain people of every conceivable type. The objective of these efforts is to move sharply away from the employment pattern that dominated American business for decades: virtually every white collar (professional and managerial) job was held by a native-born white male; many blue collar (manual labor) jobs were, too. Workers who were not native-born or not white males were often relegated to the most menial, lowest paid types of work (if they held jobs at all).

This situation created a conflict of values for many Americans. They felt deep respect for the principles expressed in the Declaration of Independence: "We hold these truths to be self-evident, that all men are created equal, that they are endowed by their Creator with certain unalienable Rights, that among these are Life, Liberty, and the pursuit of Happiness." It was very difficult to reconcile that ethical statement with a reality in which all the interesting, influential, well-paying jobs were held by native-born white males. The social and political history of the US from World War II to the present is marked by the efforts of citizens and government leaders to bring about fairer, more inclusive human resource practices. From the late 1960s through the 1980s, "Affirmative Action" (AA) was heard and discussed as often as diversity is today. Affirmative Action refers to a collection of laws and court decisions that compelled employers to hire and promote other people in addition to native-born white males. Women and blacks benefited most.

Unlike Affirmative Action, diversity has nothing to do with legislation or the judicial process.

Diversity is a social movement organized and promoted by businesspeople themselves, including many white males. Their message to everyone else in US business is that diversity in the workplace is good for business, and the US should quickly move beyond the minimal requirements of Affirmative Action to include people of every variety (in terms of national origin, ethnicity, gender, age, physical ability, and so forth) throughout all levels and functions of our companies. "Good for business" means that profits will increase. The business case for diversity is grounded in the following arguments:

1. Those available to work include more and more people who are not native-born white males; white males are becoming relatively scarce and employers must hire other types of people. Many of the most highly educated, well trained potential employees are not native-born white males. Highly competent people may be few, but they come in every conceivable type and variety.

2. The US is a nation of high immigration, so purchasers of goods and services come from myriad backgrounds. In order to know how to produce, market, and sell things that diverse consumers will want to buy, a firm needs employees who are similar to those consumers. With globalization, the argument is easily extended to consumers in other nations: To know how to attract purchasers abroad, a firm needs employees at all levels and in all functions who are similar to the people to whom the firm is marketing.

3. Research shows that when decision-makers have similar backgrounds, their decisions are less creative because they all view the world from similar perspectives. In a rapidly shifting business environment, a diverse mix of perspectives yields superior decisions.

These arguments may be realistic, persuasive, and supported by research. But force of reasoning is not the sole explanation for why diversity is succeeding in US business. Although the proponents of diversity avoid overt ethical appeals ("diversity is the right thing to do"), the fact is that core American values strongly support the objectives of the diversity movement:

- **Egalitarianism:** People should compete on a "level playing field" to get ahead; equal opportunity and fairness should prevail in the workplace as in all other places.
- **Achievement:** People should get ahead in life on the basis of their own accomplishments, not on the basis of their ascribed traits (such as being a native-born white male).
- **Individualism:** People should be self-sufficient and self-expressive; businesses should give each employee an opportunity to use his or her best individual talents productively.

Diversity is gaining broader acceptance among Americans because it converts deep American values into action. This value-base helps to explain, too, why many proponents of diversity are earnest and full of zeal. They believe that they are doing the right thing, that they are promoting superior principles. Not surprisingly, their efforts to extend the benefits of these values to all people is beginning to spill across the borders of the US and into other nations.

Attempts to export diversity raise an intriguing ethical question. By taking diversity abroad, its advocates are transferring a Made-in-the-USA set of values and behaviors into regions of the world where egalitarianism, achievement, and individualism are not core values, and may even contradict them. In some long-established cultures, hierarchical relationships are seen as more useful than egalitarian ones, ascription is thought a better way to sort people out than achievement, and collectivism is embraced while individualism is viewed as selfish.

There is genuine irony here. American diversity advocates often talk about how important it is to "respect the values of others." But in trying to export American-style diversity, they seem to be making an exception to that rule. They seem to be advocating that people who value human diversity differently from Americans should have their values changed to become like American values.

CREDIT. Cornelius Grove & Willa Hallowell, 1998, GROVEWELL LLC, and Grovewell.com.

The role of technology in employees' lives

Nearly two-thirds of wage and salaried workers use computers for their jobs daily. A majority also use computers for personal reasons at least several times a week. More than one-third of employees sometimes use a computer at home for job-related work, and nearly one-fifth use a computer at home to read and send job-related email. Among employees who use cell phones, beepers, pagers or email for personal reasons, more than half (55%) feel these new ways of communicating help them in managing their work, personal, and family lives. Interestingly, employees who experience the most spillover from their jobs into their home lives rely most heavily on technology to stay in touch with families and friends.

Work-Life supports on the job

Work-life supports on the job, both specific benefit entitlements and less formal policies and practices, have increased somewhat, according to the *National Study of the Changing Workforce* (2002). One work-life program that has increased significantly is elder care resource and referral services. In 1992, only 11% of employees had access to this benefit, compared with nearly a quarter (24%) in 2002. And more and more employees are needing elder care services as the population ages: 35% of workers, men and women alike, say they have provided care for a relative or in-law 65 or older in the past year. Despite somewhat increased work-life supports, however, employees with families report significantly higher levels of interference between their jobs and their family lives than employees 25 years ago (45% versus 34% report this "some" or "a lot.") Men with families report higher levels of interference between their jobs and their family lives than women in the same situation. The National Study finds that when supportive work-life policies and practices, such as flexible work arrangements like starting and finishing early, are available, employees exhibit more positive work attitudes, such as job satisfaction and commitment to the employer, as well as more positive life outcomes, such as less interference between job and family life, less negative spillover from job to home, greater life satisfaction and better mental health.

Labor shortages and the aging workforce

The aging workforce creates a challenge for employers seeking to retain good people, and an opportunity for workers who may want to earn extra in retirement. The US workforce grew at a rate of 30% in the 1970s, and at 12% in the 1990s through the present. But growth is expected to slow to about 3% and to level off by 2010. About 76 million baby boomers, born between 1946 and 1964, are set to retire in large numbers by 2010. Boomers make up about one-third of the US workforce, and there are not enough younger workers to replace them. By 2010, the number of workers aged 35 to 44 - or those typically moving into upper management - will decline by 19%; the number of workers aged 45 to 54 will increase 21%; and the number of workers aged 55 to 64 will increase 52%. This poses a threat to future growth and productivity.

Labor shortages in key industries will force a radical rethinking of recruitment, retention, flexible work schedules and retirement. Retaining mature workers will both meet employers' needs and provide cost savings at a time when global competition will be fiercer than ever. Industries now suffering from a skills shortage include energy, health care and nuclear engineering; and technical and scientific fields generally.

Many boomers say they plan to balance work and leisure in retirement. The AARP (formerly known as the American Association of Retired Persons) and others report that 79% of baby boomers say that for financial and personal reasons they do not plan to stop working at age 65. Many baby boomers have not saved enough to retire completely and will continue to work to meet basic expenses. But others say they plan to continue working, though shorter hours, because they want to continue to be engaged in their fields. Today's staged life plan where education, work and leisure succeed each other is becoming obsolete and being replaced by cyclical careers in which education, work and leisure exist in different proportions throughout life. Boomers want to work on their own terms when and how they wish.

Some companies have set up a Casual Worker Program that allows them to hire or reemploy workers who would receive limited benefits and no pension. Others invite grandparents to work in the company child-care center. Many companies seek to develop ways for older workers to pass their knowledge and skills on to younger workers, and some make a concerted effort to integrate the two groups. Some financial-services companies have discovered that prospective clients often feel more comfortable discussing money with an older representative, since mature workers are viewed as reliable, compassionate and honest. These companies therefore make an effort to retain and hire those with extensive experience. Changes to laws governing tax, pensions and age discrimination, however, will be needed to make such developments widespread, say experts.

The federal government in the labor market

Global interdependence, technological change, and the knowledge-based economy have all helped change the relationship between workers and employers. Because workers are less likely to spend a major portion of their careers with a single employer, they are more likely to seek training that is marketable to a variety of employers instead of training that is employer-specific. For this reason, though, employers may not invest in worker training if the training will make the employees more attractive to other companies. Furthermore, because global interdependence has increased pressure on companies to streamline operations, employers are more willing to lay off workers and move operations to lower-cost locations domestically and internationally. These changes have implications for both the types of skills that workers need and the incentives for individual workers to acquire them or employers to provide training. Indeed, globalization, according to Gabor Steingart, author of *The War for Wealth,* means that workers in future will need higher levels of education. Also, governments will need to re-think the way that markets work in a globalized world, in order to protect the one-third of the workforce who are blue collar and need time to adjust to changing demands for their skills. Much of the debate about how to respond to the massive changes taking place in the economy affecting millions of workers is about how to share between workers and taxpayers, industry and investors the costs of the adaptations that are widely agreed to be needed. But paid those costs must be. For as Bernard Anderson, a former assistant Secretary of Labor in the Clinton administration has put it: "The fundamental process of upward mobility has broken Down," *Newsweek,* September 8, 2008, p.27. There is a higher risk to American society not seen since the Depression that disenchantment with the American Dream will cause an economically disenfranchised class to dissolve into disaffection. The debate on the economy in the 2008 election between Obama (pessimist) and McCain (optimist) was about the degree of that risk and how to address it.

As the US labor force changes, the role of the federal government in the labor market is also likely to change. Currently, the federal government plays an important role in promoting the labor force through a variety of means, including workforce development programs, unemployment insurance, skills development, education, pensions, health care and immigration policies. In 2003, the federal government spent over $148 billion on employment and training programs, education grants, loans, tax credits, and income support programs such as unemployment insurance and assistance to low-income families. At the same time, however, because of the financial crisis, the federal government faces large and growing structural deficits that might constrain government spending on these programs in the future. Given that the US population is aging, the proportion of the federal budget dedicated to mandatory programs such as Medicare and Social Security is likely to grow, and the amount available for discretionary programs such as employment and training assistance is likely to decrease without increases in taxes. According to the Government Accountability Office, from 1964 to 2004, discretionary federal spending decreased from 67% of the federal budget to 39%, while mandatory spending more than doubled. Lower economic growth resulting from low labor force growth, unless accompanied with a significant jump in productivity, will only accentuate the overall pressure on the federal budget. Meanwhile immigration reform is a bitterly contentious issue and its impact remains to be seen.

Working for oneself versus someone else

Approximately one in five employed people in the US work for themselves rather than someone else. Of these, 30% are considered to be small business owners because they employ others for pay, and the remaining 70% are considered self-employed independents because they do not. Owners are much better educated and earn considerably more than wage and salaried employees or the self-employed. Those who work for themselves, however, are significantly less likely to have family or personal health insurance. Small business owners work the longest hours, with 38% working more than 50 hours a week, while self-employed independents have the shortest workweeks, with 38% working fewer than 35 hours a week. Both owners and the self-employed are more likely to say that their jobs require creativity, allow them to develop their skills and abilities, and give them freedom to decide what to do on their jobs. This is partly in response to changes in the corporation. In the new, "re-enchanted" workplace, the employee is required to work harder than before in exchange for the promise, not of an additional material reward, but of an additional emotional one. Today's employee, subject to the new demands of work, is supposed to behave like an entrepreneur without the prospect of an entrepreneur's reward.

A new American dream

Americans are increasingly coming to believe that the "more is better" version of the American dream leaves in its wake less contentment and less free time, disconnection from nature and community, and an environment straining to supply the natural resources and absorb the waste generated by an expanding collection of stuff. A few startling facts offer some perspective:

- America consumes over 40% of the world's gasoline and more paper, steel, aluminum, energy, water, and meat per capita than any other society on the planet.

- The average American produces twice as much garbage as the average European.
- Recent scientific estimates indicate that at least four additional planets would be needed if each of the planet's 6 billion inhabitants consumed at the level of the average American.

Americans' hectic work-and-spend way of life takes its toll on their financial well-being, psychological health, and personal happiness. The commercial culture leads many to accumulate debt and live beyond their means. In the last few years, more Americans have declared bankruptcy than have graduated from college. The average employed American now works more than 47 hours a week in the struggle to keep up with mounting bills. Millions of Americans report feeling exhausted, pressured, and hungry for more balanced lives.

Whose Dream is it anyway?

The "more is better" approach to life widens the growing gap between the "haves" and "have-nots." Globally, the 20% of the world's people in the highest-income countries account for 86% of the total private consumption expenditures, the poorest 20% a minuscule 1.3%. Conspicuous consumption is especially damaging to low-income families in a culture that measures self-worth in material terms.

A new consumer movement is working to create a new American Dream by changing the way Americans consume in order to improve their quality of life, create a greater feeling of purpose, provide more free time to spend with family and friends, protect the environment and promote social justice. They are reconnecting to the land, and to their communities. They are also putting pressure on businesses, institutions and governments to provide products that make sense for the planet while still making a reasonable profit. These critics accept that many services and products do improve people's lives while providing quality jobs. Furthermore, millions of people even in the US live on the edge of poverty and must consume more to become healthy and materially secure. The point the new consumer movement is making is that everyone needs to shift their consumption choices toward environmentally friendly goods and resist excessive consumerism.

To make the new Dream a reality, says this movement, businesses must play a role, by reinventing products that are durable, produced for reuse, and fashioned from recycled materials. Labor must press for living-wage jobs making products designed not to hurt workers or the planet. Governments must create tax incentives and public policies that help individuals and communities feel safer while encouraging responsible consumption. There should also be private and public incentives that encourage flexible work arrangements and options for reducing stress in the workplace. Meanwhile American socio-economic institutions from education to social security in retirement are likely to change in unimagined ways as the economic landscape is reshaped by global forces and new technology.

GOVERNMENT SERVICES, SOCIAL SECURITY AND WELFARE

Direct Services

Each level of government provides many direct services. The federal government, for example, is responsible for national defense, backs research that often leads to the development of new products, conducts space exploration, and runs numerous programs designed to help workers develop workplace skills and find jobs. State governments, meanwhile, are responsible for the construction and maintenance of most highways. State, county, and city governments play the leading role in financing and operating public schools. Local governments are primarily responsible for police and fire protection. Total federal, state, and local spending accounted for around 20% of gross domestic product in 2004.

Direct Assistance

The federal government also provides many kinds of help to businesses and individuals. It offers low-interest loans and technical assistance to small businesses, and loans to help students to attend college. Government-sponsored enterprises buy home mortgages from lenders and turn them into securities that can be bought and sold by investors, thereby encouraging home lending. Government also actively promotes exports and seeks to prevent foreign countries from maintaining trade barriers that restrict imports. About one-quarter of the federal budget goes on social security, housing and welfare. These services are organized in a sometimes un-coordinated way by the Department of Health and Human Services through the Social Security Administration, the Department of Housing and Urban Development, the Veterans Administration, the Department of Agriculture and other bodies. Programs are implemented at state and local level, usually by several separate bodies, sometimes by umbrella agencies for social security and related services.

Most social services spending benefits higher- and middle-income people: welfare accounts for only a quarter of it. Social Security, which is financed by a tax on employers and employees, provides the largest portion of Americans' retirement income. The Medicare program pays for many of the medical costs of the elderly. The Medicaid program finances medical care for low-income families. In many states, the government maintains institutions for the mentally ill or people with severe disabilities, retirement homes, and maternity and child health services. The government also gives tax breaks and subsidies for education and home loans.

US Social spending

Mandatory spending at $1.412 trillion in Financial Year 2006, was over half of the federal budget. The largest mandatory spending programs were Social Security and Medicare:

- Social Security - $544 billion
- Medicare - $325 billion
- Medicaid - $186 billion
- All other mandatory programs - $357 billion. These programs include Food Stamps ($32 billion), Unemployment Compensation, Child Nutrition, Child Tax Credits, Supplemental Security for the blind and disabled, Student Loans, and Retirement / Disability programs for Civil Servants, the Coast Guard and the Military.
- Social security accounts for 20% of federal spending.
- Welfare accounts for 6% of the federal budget.
- 70% of healthcare and social security spending (including pensions, unemployment pay and housing) is borne by the federal government. The remaining 30% is borne by companies and by individuals through insurance.

Tax credits

The federal Earned Income Tax Credit (EITC) is one of the largest anti-poverty measures and enjoys broad bipartisan support. The EITC is a refundable tax credit that reduces or eliminates the taxes such as payroll taxes paid by low-income working people. It thus frequently operates as a wage subsidy. Enacted in 1975, the EITC has been expanded with each major tax bill. For tax year 2006, for a family with two dependent children, the credit was equal to 40% of the first $11,340 earned, leveled out at a maximum credit of $4,536. It began to phase out when earnings increased beyond $14,810, and reached zero when earnings passed $36,348. In addition, 20 states have their own EITC on state taxes, which work in the same way. Almost 21 million American families received more than $36 billion in refunds through the EITC in 2004. EITC has had a significant impact on the nation's lowest-paid working people, lifting an estimated 5 million families above the federal poverty line, although income measures such as the poverty rate generally do not take EITC into account.

Welfare

History

Americans have always prided themselves on their strong sense of individualism and self-reliance. Arriving immigrants depended mainly on predecessors from their homeland to help them start a new life, not on the government. In the late 19th and early 20th centuries, several European nations instituted public welfare programs. But such a movement was slow to take hold in the US because the rapid pace of industrialization and the ready availability of farmland seemed to confirm the belief that anyone who was willing to work could find a job. Indeed, many believed that those who could not take care of themselves were to blame for their own misfortunes.

During the 19th century, local and state governments as well as charities established institutions such as poorhouses and orphanages for destitute individuals and families. Conditions in these institutions were often deliberately made harsh so that only the truly desperate would apply. Local governments (usually counties) also provided relief in the form of food, fuel, and sometimes cash to poor residents. Those capable of it were required to work for the town or county, often at hard labor such as chopping wood and maintaining roads. But most people on general relief were poor dependent persons not capable of working: widows, children, the elderly, and the disabled. Local officials decided who went to the poorhouse or orphanage and who would receive relief at home. Cash relief to the poor depended on local property taxes, which were limited in scale. Also, not only did a general prejudice exist against the poor who were on relief, but local officials commonly discriminated against individuals applying for aid because of their race, nationality, or religion. Single mothers often found themselves in an impossible situation. If they applied for relief, they were frequently branded as morally unfit by the community. If they worked, they were criticized for neglecting their children.

After a conference held by President Theodore Roosevelt in 1909, mother's pensions were introduced for some single parents. These pensions mainly benefited families headed by white widows, since they excluded large numbers of divorced, deserted, and minority mothers and their children. Otherwise, few private and government retirement pensions existed in the US before the Great Depression. The prevailing view was that individuals should save for their old age or be supported by their children. About 30 states provided some welfare aid to poor elderly persons without any source of income. Local officials generally decided who deserved old-age assistance in their community.

During the Great Depression which followed the stock market crash of 1929, when 40% of the population were living in relative or absolute poverty, state and local governments and private charities were overwhelmed by needy families seeking food, clothing, and shelter. The effect of the Depression on poor children was particularly severe. Grace Abbott, head of the federal Children's Bureau, reported that in the spring of 1933, 20% of the nation's schoolchildren showed evidence of poor nutrition, housing, and medical care. School budgets were cut, and in some cases schools were shut down for lack of money to pay teachers. An estimated 200,000 boys left home to wander the streets and beg because of the poverty of their families. Most elderly Americans did not have personal savings or retirement pensions to support them in normal times, let alone during a national economic crisis. Those few who had been able to set aside money for retirement often found their savings and investments wiped out by the financial crash. Even skilled workers, business owners, successful farmers, and professionals of all kinds found themselves in severe economic difficulty as one out of four in the labor force lost their jobs. Desperate times convinced the majority of the American people that individuals could not always provide adequately for themselves in work or old age, and that some form of greater security should be provided by society. Millions of the unemployed, made jobless and desperate by the failure of banks and businesses, demanded that the federal government take action.

New Deal social security

President Franklin D. Roosevelt (1932-45) initially focused on creating jobs for the millions of unemployed workers. Federal money flowed to the states to pay for public works projects which employed the jobless. But he also backed the idea of federal aid for poor children and other dependent persons. By the Social Security Act of 1935, a national welfare system was established for the first time in American history and remained a federal government responsibility for 60 years. The Act set up a federal retirement program for persons over 65, which was financed by a payroll tax paid jointly by employers and their workers. The Act also provided for employer-paid unemployment insurance. These two measures, it was believed, would provide the economic security most people needed during both good and bad times.

Federal Welfare

Under the Social Security Act, the federal government guaranteed one-third of the total amount spent by states for assistance to needy and dependent children under age 16 (but not their mothers). Additional federal welfare aid was provided to destitute old people, the needy blind, and crippled children. Although federal welfare was financed partly by federal tax money, the states could still set their own eligibility requirements and benefit levels. This part of the Act was introduced by the Southern states so that they could control the coverage made available to their African American populations.

At the time, it was believed that the need for federal welfare for dependent children and poor old people would gradually decline as employment improved and those over 65 began to collect Social Security pensions. But many Americans, such as farm laborers and domestic servants, were never included in the pensions program. Also, increasing divorce and father desertion rates have dramatically multiplied the number of poor single mothers with dependent children.

When the federal Aid to Families with Dependent Children (AFDC) program began in 1936, it provided cash aid to about 500,000 children and parents, and by 1969 the number had grown to nearly 7 million. Over the years, Congress added new entitlements. President Lyndon B. Johnson's *War on Poverty* program provided major non-cash benefits to AFDC recipients as well as to other needy persons. In 1964, Congress approved a food stamp program for all low-income households. Food stamps under the Supplemental Nutrition Assistance Program (SNAP) are Department of Agriculture certificates that people can use to purchase food in approved shops at about one-third normal price. Food stamps are now available only for three months unless the recipients are working.

Additionally, New Deal legislation allowed for General Assistance (GA), sometimes called General Relief for childless able-bodied adults living in poverty. Today this benefit is paid only by New Jersey and Utah. Elsewhere, applicants have to show that they cannot qualify for other programs before they can get GA, which usually covers food stamps, school meals and help with housing rental.

During World War II, the Roosevelt Administration passed the Servicemen's Readjustment Act of 1944, known informally as the "GI Bill of Rights." It provided college or vocational education for returning veterans as well as up to one year of unemployment compensation for jobseekers. It also provided low interest, zero down-payment loans for returning veterans to buy homes and start businesses. Although the GI Bill applied equally to African American veterans, the refusal of suburban homeowners to sell to them prevented many from moving out of inner city apartments and into the suburbs. The GI Bill has attracted universal praise as one of the most significant pieces of social legislation of the 20th century because of its effects on both the national economy and its beneficiaries. The benefits offered by the Bill forestalled a widely feared depression, expanded the home-owning middle class, and forever changed the nature of American higher education by greatly increasing college enrolments. Notably, a far greater percentage of Vietnam veterans (72%) took up education benefits than World War II veterans (51%) or Korean Conflict veterans (43%) under similar legislation. Because of the military draft (conscription) between 1940 and 1973, it is calculated that, when dependants are taken into account, as much as one-third of the population benefited from veterans benefits. The Veterans Readjustment Benefits Act of 1966 extended veterans benefits to those who had served in peacetime as well as war, and subsequent Acts raised benefit levels. Contrary to the stereotype of the Vietnam veteran, most who served in Vietnam used their benefits to build productive and successful lives afterwards.

In the 1960s, President Johnson (1963-68) established assistance programs as part of the *Great Society* program. This was developed in response to perceived need, the Civil Rights movement, and a feeling among some Americans that the US should be able to care for more of its citizens. The programs provided major non-cash benefits to AFDC recipients as well as to other needy persons. In 1965, Congress created Medicaid, a federal and state funded healthcare system for the destitute elderly, disabled persons, and AFDC families. Johnson also introduced programs such as *Head Start* which aimed to reduce unemployment and poverty through education, job training and regional development assistance. In 1974, during the presidency of Richard Nixon (1968-73), Congress established the Supplemental Security Income (SSI) program to provide aid to the needy elderly, blind, and disabled. This program made up the last major component of the federal welfare system.

To qualify for most of these benefits, American workers pay Social Security taxes on their earnings. Future benefits are based on these contributions. During the 1970s and 1980s, however, some people began to regard non-contributory benefits as a right and the number of claimants grew. Despite the efforts of President Reagan (1981-89) to restrict the growth of welfare spending, it continued to increase. President George H. W. Bush (1989-93) tried to rein in welfare but was eventually forced to raise taxes to meet the increased demand. The Clinton Administration (1993-2001) tried to introduce universal healthcare in 1993 but could not persuade Congress, mainly because private healthcare providers argued that the proposed system would be too costly. Instead, President Clinton was faced with renewed demands for cuts in welfare by the Republican majority. By 1994, more of the nation's needy families, elderly, and disabled received federal welfare than ever before. AFDC alone was supporting more than 14 million children and their parents.

The majority of Americans live comfortable lives on the salaries they earn. They generally own their own homes and cars, spend some time each year on vacation, and can pay - at least in part - for a college education for their children. Most Americans set aside money in savings accounts to help pay for major expenses. Most also buy insurance, especially life and medical insurance, frequently together with contributions from the companies for which they work. Many companies in addition have retirement plans by which they and their employees put aside money for retirement pensions. When added to Social Security payments, pensions enable many retired Americans to live comfortably. On the other hand, for older Americans who require long-term care outside of a hospital, a nursing home can be very expensive. Some people invest in the stock market. For other Americans, however, the social safety net is essential. Yet the US is witnessing continuing deterioration in basic human services especially among those in poverty.

Housing

The availability of affordable housing is at an all-time low and the government has been cutting back on its housing voucher programs. The number of homeless families, especially women-headed families, is increasing. Cities such as Boston, Cleveland, Detroit, New York and Philadelphia have become home to an increasing concentration of poor households, disproportionately composed of racial and ethnic minorities and mostly located in the city centers. There is a patchwork of federal, state and local programs devoted to addressing the quality of housing and the quality of life in urban areas.

Community Development Block Grant (CDBG) Program

Under the National Affordable Housing Act 1974, Congress extended public housing, which is built at federal expense and made available to persons with low incomes. The Community Development Block Grant (CDBG) program, authorized by the Act, provides annual federal grants to entitled cities, urban counties and states to develop viable urban communities by providing decent housing and a suitable living environment, and by expanding economic opportunities, principally for low- and moderate-income persons. The grants pay for a wide range of community development activities directed toward revitalizing neighborhoods, economic development, and providing improved community facilities and services.

The annual appropriation (budget) for CDBG is split between states and local jurisdictions called "entitlement communities." Entitlement communities are central cities of Metropolitan Statistical Areas (MSAs); other metropolitan cities with populations of at least 50,000; and qualified urban counties with populations of at least 200,000 (excluding the population of entitled cities). States distribute funds to localities which do not qualify as entitlement communities. The Department of Housing and Urban Development (HUD) determines the amount of each grant by a formula which uses several objective measures of community needs, including the extent of poverty, population, housing overcrowding, age of housing, and population growth lag in relationship to other metropolitan areas.

States and entitlement communities must submit to HUD a comprehensive plan, which must identify its housing and community development goals for HOME Investment Partnerships, Housing Opportunities for Persons with AIDS (HOPWA), and Emergency Shelter Grants (ESG). The plan must also state how the jurisdiction will attempt to further fair housing through affirmative action i.e., give preference to minorities, especially blacks and Hispanics. The plan must provide citizens, particularly residents of predominantly low- and moderate-income neighborhoods, slum or blighted areas, and areas in which CDBG funds are to be used, with reasonable access to meetings at which the plan is discussed. The plan must also give citizens an opportunity to review proposed activities and program performance. In addition the plan must provide for timely written answers to written complaints and grievances; and identify how the needs of non-English speaking residents will be met in the case of public hearings where a significant number of such people can be reasonably expected to participate.

Eligible activities for CDBG funds include, but are not limited to: acquisition of real property; relocation and demolition; rehabilitation of residential and non-residential structures; construction of public facilities such as water and sewerage, streets, and neighborhood centers; and assistance to profit-motivated businesses to carry out economic development and job creation/retention. Noticeably CDBG funds are not available for construction of new housing by local governments, which is funded separately.

Financial help for tenants

The Housing Choice Voucher Program under the U.S. Housing Act, the Wagner-Steagall Act of 1937 as amended by the Quality Housing and Work Responsibility (QHWRA) Act of 1998, is the largest housing subsidy program, with more than 1.5 million households participating. Agencies have annual contracts with HUD to operate it. The vouchers can be used to assist residents that must be relocated from public housing because of demolition, and are also used to support welfare recipients who are working toward economic self-sufficiency. Unfortunately, tight rental markets, low fair market rental levels and landlords who are choosing to opt out of the program are reducing the supply of available housing for program participants.

Public housing

The public housing program in the US was first authorized by the U.S. Housing Act of 1937, which was the first major federal program providing low-rent housing to low-income households. Although housing problems had been acknowledged for decades, not until the Great Depression in the 1930s did the federal government become involved with housing on a large scale. The housing initiatives enacted during this period had several goals, including improving housing, creating employment, stimulating the economy, and removing slums.

Today, HUD administers federal aid to local Public Housing Agencies (PHAs) to provide decent shelter for low-income residents at rents they can afford. Local PHAs own and operate low-income public housing developments. HUD furnishes technical and professional assistance in planning, developing and managing these developments. Estimates from 1998 show that the average household monthly rent for public housing residents was $193 and the total number of households being assisted by the public housing program 1,170,444.

Public Housing is a valuable source of accommodation for the most vulnerable elderly and disabled. Elderly and disabled households without children account for 43% of all public housing households. Most households who live in public housing stay there less than 10 years, and 40% remain 3 years or less. Those who stay longer often have no other recourse. Minority populations are overrepresented in public housing. Racial and ethnic minorities in public housing are, for the most part, composed of native-born households.

Case study - Pittsburgh

Research conducted in Pittsburgh has revealed that public housing residents can be classified in six distinct resident segments, each with its own needs, desires and behaviors. Probably these segments are representative of those found in most public housing systems around the US:

1. *Established core.* This group consists primarily of elderly retired residents who are relatively settled in public housing. They do not have strong ties to their communities, have little interest in taking leadership or management roles, and do not wish to move to other housing options. Their needs for transportation, healthcare, etc., are similar to those of other older Americans;

2. *Service seekers.* This group is demographically similar to the previous segment, but its members have greater need of services, chose their current housing because of the services offered, would move to another location if they could obtain better services, and are more likely to consider themselves handicapped. They usually need the same services as the previous group, plus more intensive levels of other human services such as housekeeping assistance.

3. *Community anchors.* These residents are the backbone of most public housing communities. They have strong ties to their communities, often take leadership roles in community organizations, and have little desire to move elsewhere. This group is interested in resident management and other ways of taking an active role in building communities.

4. *Employed movers.* Relatively well educated and well motivated, most of the members of this group are employed and aspire to live outside public or assisted housing. They remain in public housing for three main reasons: they are afraid of losing their jobs and leaving their families homeless; they use community services such as childcare or transportation that enable them to work but may not be available outside their community; and they often have a support system within that community. Their primary need is for enabling services that will allow them to continue working.

5. *Community-involved job seekers.* These are young heads of households, often with larger than average families. Well educated, they are actively looking for work. Though they aspire to live outside public or assisted housing, they take an active leadership role in the communities to which they belong. They are in favor of resident or private management of public housing communities. Their needs focus firstly on their children (daycare and after-school programs) and secondly on job-related training, but they are also interested in services such as help with substance abuse and family counseling.

6. *Emerging core.* These residents are demographically similar to the previous group, except that they tend to have had less education. Few are actively looking for employment, but almost all aspire to leave assisted housing. They have few connections in their communities, seldom take leadership roles, and have little interest in resident management. This group has higher than average needs for child-related services and for more critical human services such as substance abuse counseling.

The public housing systems of most major US cities do not provide a sufficiently safe, quality environment at a reasonable cost to taxpayers. Yet in cities like Charleston, Richmond, and Omaha, public housing does provide an attractive quality of life at sustainable cost. In Charleston public housing the crime rate is actually lower than in the city of Charleston itself. Elsewhere, however, runaway costs plague the system because it is not well-managed, according to research from McKinseys. The current policy of cutting budgets and giving states or cities discretion in how they spend them has not brought about improvements.

The Pittsburgh research provides some revealing insights into the potential for improvement in management practices. The Housing Authority of the City of Pittsburgh (HACP) currently spends $36.2 million per year, $22.4 million of it coming from HUD, and the remaining $13.8 million from rents. HACP owns 9,400 housing units with some 17,200 residents. Roughly 60% of this housing was built before 1960. Communities range in size from 31 to 1,749 units. HACP administers an additional 3,300 rental assistance units, whose residents obtain rent aid through federal vouchers and certificates. These apartments are privately owned and managed. There are currently about 2,500 applicants on the housing waiting list.

At the beginning of 1995, Pittsburgh's public housing system was rated by HUD as one of the poorest performing authorities in terms of physical condition, efficiency, and cost. With strong leadership from Mayor Tom Murphy and HACP executive director, Stanley Lowe, an aggressive turnaround plan, and significant involvement from resident leaders, HACP is now positioned to capture significant performance improvements both in achieving a higher quality of life and by reducing total costs. Specifically, more timely rent collection and reduced vacancies are expected to boost revenues by some $2.2 million, while streamlining preventive maintenance and improving productivity will save $5 million; increasing security will cost an additional $1.2 million. All told, costs should fall by around 30%. At the same time, however, the quality of life will improve significantly: crime should drop by 45%, social violations like leaving trash in the hall should have almost disappeared, and it will take only hours, not days, to get a light replaced or a toilet fixed. At the same time resident leaders are beginning to focus on self-determination and self-governance in communities. Reaching these new levels of performance does not require superhuman efforts. The best practices from the cutting-edge cities would be familiar to any high-performing business leader: simplifying procedures, setting incentives, and listening to customers (residents).

In addition, as the management approaches of individual housing authorities change, and public and private sector leaders take the lead in establishing close working partnerships with residents to begin transforming local housing systems, the role of HUD also needs to evolve. In the past, HUD has allocated money and enforced procedures, but experts recommend that it should also promote effectiveness, efficiency, and the satisfaction of residents' needs. In the coming years, the money HUD gives to local housing systems will shrink. Instead of simply allocating a smaller pool of dollars based on the number of units in a public housing system, as now, HUD could make these grants contingent on satisfactory performance against meaningful measures like reductions in the incidence of violent crime, cuts in the turnaround time for emergency repairs, or the ability of maintenance services to "fix it right first time," say consultants. The 3,300 housing authorities could be segmented into a manageable number of peer groups with similar profiles and problems to enable a more relevant and frequent exchange of ideas, information, and experience. Moreover, if best practice were applied across the whole system, HUD would save a minimum of $400 million per year of its current $2.7 billion subsidy for public housing.

The Debate over Welfare

"Welfare" is an ambiguous term, used in three main senses:

- Welfare commonly refers to "well-being." In welfare economics, welfare is understood in terms of "utility." People's well-being or interests consist of the things they choose to have.
- Welfare also refers to the range of services which are provided to protect people in a number of conditions, including childhood, sickness, and old age. The idea of the "welfare state" is an example.
- In the US, welfare refers specifically to financial assistance to poor people (e.g., Temporary Aid to Needy Families). This usage is not generally reflected elsewhere.

Welfare is often associated with needs, but it goes beyond what people need. To achieve well being, people must have choices, and the scope to choose personal goals and ambitions.

Arguments for welfare

The basic arguments for collective provision are:

- *humanitarian*. Concerns about poverty and need have been central to many developments in welfare.
- *religious*. Several of the world's major religions make charity a religious duty. Beyond charity, Catholicism recognizes a duty of social solidarity (or mutual social responsibility); Judaism, Islam and Lutheran Christianity require collective responsibility for one's community.
- *mutual self-interest*. Many welfare systems have developed, not from state activity, but from a combination of mutualist activities, gradually reinforced by government.
- *democratic*. Social protection has developed in tandem with democratic rights.
- *practical*. Welfare provision has economic and social benefits. Countries with more extensive systems of social protection tend to be richer and have less poverty. (The main difficulty in evaluating this is knowing which comes first, wealth or welfare.)

There is scarcely a government in the world that does not recognize the force of these arguments and make some form of collective social provision. The real disputes are not about whether welfare should exist, but about how much provision there should be, and how it should be made.

Arguments against welfare

Conservative economists like Alan Greenspan point out that "The propensity of Congress to create benefits for constituents without specifying the means by which they are to be funded has led to deficit spending in every fiscal year since 1970, with the exception of the surpluses of 1998 to 2001 generated by the stock-market boom," *op. cit.*, p. 481. This is not strictly an argument against welfare but a warning about how welfare spending affects the public finances in practice.

The main objections to the provision of welfare come from the radical right. They are against welfare in principle, on the basis that it violates people's freedom. On this view, redistribution is theft and taxation forced labor. These arguments rest on some questionable assumptions:

- *People have absolute rights to use property as they wish*. People are interdependent, and the production of property depends on social arrangements. Rights to property are conventional; liability to taxation is part of the conventions.
- *People do not consent to welfare provision; redistributive arrangements are based in*

compulsion. This is not necessarily true.

- *The rights of the individual are paramount.* Property rights are certainly important, but few people would argue that property rights are more important than every other moral value. If one person owns all the food in a region while everybody else is starving, the others have a moral claim on it.

The radical right also claim that the welfare state has undesirable effects in practice. *Economically*, it can be argued that development is more important for welfare than social provision. Some have argued that property rights and a market economy are essential for growth and so for the protection of the poor. The other main argument is that the welfare state undermines economic performance. This position is not supported by the evidence. In *social* terms, the welfare state is accused of fostering dependency and trapping people in poverty. Evidence on the dynamics of poverty, however, shows that poverty and dependency are not always long-term, but may affect people at different stages in the life cycle. The population of welfare claimants is constantly changing. Where poor people are separated and excluded from the rest of society by the receipt of welfare, this is mainly the product of the kinds of restricted welfare the radical right has been arguing for. In the US there may sometimes be an undisclosed racial motive for engineering this separation, which may be said to re-introduce segregation by the back door.

Who is welfare for? *Residual welfare*
Welfare is often seen as being for the poor. This has been the dominant model in English-speaking countries. The English Poor Law (1598-1948) was widely exported. The English system has been taken as the model of a residual system of welfare, in which welfare is a safety net, confined to those who are unable to manage otherwise.

Solidarity
Welfare in much of Europe is based on the principle of solidarity, or mutual responsibility. People in society are part of solidaristic social networks. The responsibilities which people have to each other depend on their relationships. Many of the rights which people have are particular, rather than general. They depend on a person's circumstances, work record or family relationships, not on general rights protected by the state. Those who are not part of such networks are said to be "excluded."

Institutional welfare
An institutional system is one in which need is accepted as a normal part of social life. Welfare is provided for the population as a whole, in the same way as public services like roads or schools might be. In an institutional system, welfare is not just for the poor: it is for everyone.

Industrial achievement/performance
Welfare has often been seen as a "handmaiden" to the economy. It helps employers, by preparing and servicing the capacity of the workforce, and it acts as an economic regulator, stimulating demand when production is low.

Universality and selectivity
Universal benefits and services are benefits available to everyone as a right, or at least to whole

categories of people like old people or children. Selective benefits and services are reserved for people in need. Institutional and residual welfare are principles; universality and selectivity are methods.

Universal services can reach everyone on the same terms. This is the argument for public services, like roads and sewers. It was extended in the 1940s to education and health services. The main objection to universal services is their cost. Selectivity is often presented as being more efficient: less money is spent to better effect. There are problems with selective services, however: because recipients have to be identified, the services can be administratively complex and expensive to run, and there are often boundary problems caused by trying to include some people while excluding others. Selective services also sometimes fail to reach people in need.

Certain aspects of the American welfare system came under criticism in the 1980s and 1990s, and the system itself became an issue in national elections. Many middle-class Americans resent the use of their tax dollars to support those whom they regard (rightly or wrongly) as unwilling to work. Some critics argue that dependency on welfare tends to become a permanent condition, as one generation follows another into the system. Some people believe the system encourages young women to have children out of wedlock, because welfare payments increase with each child born. Other experts maintain that unless the root causes of poverty - lack of education and opportunity - are addressed, the welfare system is all that stands between the poor and utter destitution. Both taxpayers and welfare clients complain that the system is too complex, incomplete, inefficient, costly and open to abuse. The charge that social programs tend to trap the poor in dependency and deny them the power to control their lives has led to the redesign of certain federal programs. For example, the government has been allowing tenants of public housing projects to buy the buildings and take over their management.

Welfare policy

The US welfare regime is sometimes described as "liberal," since the values it represents are individualism, laissez-faire and residualism (welfare is the last resort), and the system takes a punitive view of poverty. Welfare reform has introduced "workfare," excluded many long-term benefit claimants, and has been based on negative assumptions about the "underclass." While there are advocates for increasing welfare, the general view is restrictive, as summed up by President Reagan: "Government exists to protect us from each other. Where government has gone beyond its limits is in deciding to protect us from ourselves." This sidesteps the question of the role of government in natural disaster, catastrophic sickness and economic depressions, and in fact the federal and state governments do help individuals in these circumstances, though not as much as in other developed countries. The US does not, however, have a unified welfare system. Federalism has meant that many important functions are performed by the states, including public assistance, social care and various health schemes. (Minnesota and Hawaii have state-funded health systems.) By comparison with other developed countries, central government has a limited role in social welfare provision. In practice, the US is pluralistic, rather than liberal. There are also significant departures from the residual model e.g., state schooling, social insurance, and the Veterans' Administration, which provides health care for nearly 40 million people. In addition to federal and state activity, there are extensive private, mutualist and corporate welfare providers. The resulting systems are complex and expensive. With the turbulent labor market of a globalized world, many are beginning to say that the whole system is out of date.

Welfare reform

Unlike many countries, the US has not had significant restructuring imposed on its economy through conditions attached to loans, a process which often results in the privatization of public social services or a decrease in their scope. The US has opened few services, and no social services, through commitments made in trade negotiations. Yet in the US the cost of social protection, social security and other welfare provisions is increasingly shifting from the public sector to the household. Whereas other countries have involuntarily reduced the scope of publicly provided services, the US has willingly done so.

After the Great Depression, especially in the 1960s and 1970s, the national welfare system expanded both in coverage and federal regulation. The total cost of all federal assistance programs - including Social Security, Medicare, Medicaid, and various welfare programs - accounts for nearly one-half of all money spent by the federal government. That is a doubling of the percentage that obtained in the 1960s.

From its inception, the system drew critics. Some complained that the system did not do enough to get people to work. Others simply believed the federal government should not administer a welfare system. As the system grew, so did criticism of it, especially in the 1980s and 1990s. In 1992, candidate Bill Clinton, a Democrat, ran for President promising to "end welfare as we know it." In 1996, a Republican Congress passed and President Clinton signed a reform law that returned most control of welfare to the states, thus ending 61 years of federal responsibility.

Aid to Families with Dependent Children (AFDC) drew the greatest criticism of the four major federal welfare programs. By 1994, AFDC was supporting 15% of all US children. In most cases, these children lived at home and were cared for by a single parent, usually the mother, who did not work. This situation provoked complaints that welfare let able-bodied adults avoid work and become dependent on government handouts. Criticism was further fueled by cases of children who grew up in families where no one ever had a paying job and who themselves became dependent on welfare as adults. Moreover, the program generated a vast bureaucracy, overlapping services, and endless regulations. All this placed an increasing burden on the nation's taxpayers (although AFDC made up less than 1% of the federal budget).

Some of those criticizing AFDC were recipients themselves, 70% of whom collected a welfare check for less than two years. For many of these people, going on welfare was a humiliating experience of struggling through a maze of bureaucratic rules in order to feed, clothe, and house themselves and their children. Others, however, saw welfare more positively. Although the program was not perfect, AFDC provided a relatively inexpensive safety net, which prevented people from falling into extreme poverty. Many of the people helped by welfare only needed it for a limited time. Those who needed it longer were usually those with few skills or with learning disorders or other disabilities.

Temporary Assistance for Needy Families (TANF)

ADFC was replaced in 1996 by Temporary Assistance for Needy Families (TANF). The new law was funded by federal block grants and state money. States are given wide discretion in determining eligibility and the conditions under which families may receive public aid. But Congress tied a number of strict work requirements to the federal block grants:

- Adults receiving family cash-aid benefits must go to work within two years. States may exempt a parent with a child under one for no more than 12 months.

- States had to have 25% of their welfare caseloads at work in 1997 and 50% of their caseloads at work by 2002. States who failed to meet these requirements would lose 5% of their federal block grants.
- Each adult is limited to no more than five years of cash assistance during his or her lifetime. But states may exempt up to 20% of their caseloads from this limit.

Stiff new federal standards were mandated in 2007 for moving poor people from welfare to work. States now have to enroll at least 50% of poor parents in work-preparation programs or face hefty penalties in lost federal grants. The regulations strictly define what types of activities qualify as work preparation. In addition, the new rules extend federal oversight to separate state-funded TANF programs.

The states are responding in various different ways according to their politics, wealth, the cost of living and inflation. States are also constrained by pressures to balance their budgets and by federal "matching funding" policies which provide federal funds equal to those that are provided locally and are consequently less helpful to the poorer states.

Wisconsin Works

Moving hundreds of thousands of people from welfare to work requires sufficient suitable jobs to be open. When jobs are not available, local and state governments may have to create community-service jobs like cleaning public parks. Many welfare recipients are poorly educated, have few job skills, and lack the experience and discipline of going to work on a schedule. Thus they may need extra help and training in getting and holding on to a job. Moreover, going to work costs money. Child care has to paid for, clothing purchased, and transportation arranged.

Of all the states, Wisconsin is probably the most advanced in moving welfare recipients to work. Before Congress acted in 1996, the state had already begun major welfare reforms on its own. Wisconsin's Republican governor, Tommy Thompson, together with Democrats in the state legislature, vowed to abolish welfare by 1999.

Wisconsin's welfare reform effort, *Wisconsin Works*, has the nation's strictest work requirements for adults receiving public aid. By the end of 1997, all adult welfare recipients had to be involved in some work-related activity. Even so-called "unemployables," like the mentally ill and drug addicts, had to report to therapy or rehabilitation sessions to try to make themselves job-ready. Only mothers with newborns under three months old were temporarily exempted from going to work. New welfare applicants had first to look for a job before collecting any cash aid. As a result of these requirements, Wisconsin succeeded in cutting 60% of its welfare caseload by the end of 1997.

The success so far of *Wisconsin Works* relies not only on requiring welfare recipients to go to work, but also on providing them with support as they make the transition from dependency to independence. Wisconsin pays for both child care and medical services for all low-income working families. The state also provides job training, helps pay the wages of certain workers in "trial jobs," and places those who cannot get hired into community-service work.

Because of the cost of the support services, moving people from welfare to work in Wisconsin is expensive. The state's welfare budget is currently running 40% higher than it did under the old AFDC program despite the steep drop in the welfare caseload. Typically, a mother with two children who now works at a minimum wage job and also receives food stamps, child care, health insurance, and tax credits from the government earns the equivalent of about $16,500.

Under AFDC she would have earned $9,500. The US poverty level income for a family of three is $17,170 (2007).

Like Wisconsin, the other states are creating their own pathways to try to get more people off welfare and into jobs. Some, like Connecticut, allow a person to keep receiving a welfare check while also collecting a paycheck until the work income rises above the national poverty level. Other states impose severe penalties for not working. For example, Mississippi is experimenting with cutting off all cash and food stamp benefits to families who do not comply with work requirements.

Prior to 1996, the federal welfare program did not require states to help people find jobs and move off welfare. To give states time to craft their welfare-to-work programs, the federal government offered caseload reduction credits each year that welfare rolls were lower than 1995 levels. For example, if rolls were half of the 1995 level, the required work participation rate was reduced by half. Because welfare rolls shrank dramatically during the boom of the late 1990s, the original 50% required work-participation rate was reduced to 25% or lower in every state. From 2007 the base year for calculating caseload reduction credits was shifted to 2005, giving states little to no credits; welfare rolls have fallen very little since then. The objective of federal policy is to make states carry more of the burden of welfare as well as to make state programs more efficient. Whether states will opt to raise welfare spending and possibly taxes, or whether they will choose to deny welfare to more claimants remains to be seen. Although 80% of people who leave welfare do so on finding work, the American system gives no help to the long-term unemployed unless they are entitled to welfare. Already some single mothers who have refused workfare to stay at home with their children have lost their benefits and been forced to seek refuge in homeless shelters.

Privatization of welfare

The rising burden of taxes to pay for expanded government services, as well as the general American distaste for "big government" and increasingly powerful public employee unions, led many policymakers in the 1970s, 1980s, and 1990s to question whether government is the most efficient provider of needed services. A new word, "privatization," was coined and quickly gained acceptance to describe the practice of turning certain government functions over to the private sector. The 1996 welfare law, the Personal Responsibility and Work Opportunity Reconciliation Act of 1996, opened the door to the privatization of welfare by permitting states to contract out the operation of some or all of their welfare programs. Previously, the law required the public administration of welfare programs, and specifically that public employees determine eligibility for public benefits. Trade rules prevent governments from replacing for profit businesses and rehiring workers once the work has been contracted out. According to unions, the privatization of welfare has reduced the number of jobs held by women and has added to gender inequality.

Through various incentive programs, and cutbacks in federal and state funding for human services, governments have been promoting privatization since the early 1980s. To date, however, only Wisconsin, Florida and Texas have privatized welfare because the food stamp and Medicaid programs still require public administration, but this could very well change. At least 40 states already offshored the administration of electronic benefit cards for food stamps. Privatization has occurred primarily at the municipal and regional levels. Major cities such as New York, Los Angeles, Philadelphia, Dallas, and Phoenix have began to employ private companies or nonprofit organizations to perform a wide variety of activities previously performed by the municipalities themselves, ranging from streetlight repair to solid-waste disposal and from data processing to management of prisons. Some federal agencies, meanwhile, are operating more like private enterprises.

Privatization of public services remains controversial. While advocates insist that it reduces costs and increases productivity, others argue the opposite, noting that private contractors need to make a profit and asserting that they are not necessarily more productive. Public sector unions, not surprisingly since the jobs of their members are at stake, adamantly oppose most privatization proposals. They contend that private contractors in some cases have submitted very low bids in order to win contracts, but later have raised prices substantially. Advocates counter that privatization can be effective if it introduces competition. Sometimes even the threat of privatization may encourage local government workers to become more efficient. These claims, however, are disputed by the recipients of the services, several government-sponsored studies of specific programs, and studies by research institutes and unions. These sources point out that private companies do not have the same relationship to their clients as government has to its citizens. Therefore corporations are not inherently obligated to ensure equitable access to basic services for all citizens. The rationale of a private company is to ensure profit. Thus cost-cutting measures such as tightening eligibility standards are common. Moreover in a privatized system, services are rationed by price. In healthcare, for example, services vary from expensive high-tech facilities to underfunded walk-in neighborhood clinics. Quality standards also tend to vary across companies because there are few universally agreed norms and regulations. With weaker regulation, quality of service is at risk. Clients have fewer options for holding corporate service providers accountable and must generally resort to litigation to do so. In contrast, citizens generally have recourse to both legal and political support.

From welfare to work

When the Clinton Administration overhauled welfare in 1996, it provided a state-run system financed by federal grants. Lifetime welfare assistance was limited to five years, required most able-bodied adults to work after two years on welfare, eliminated welfare benefits for legal immigrants who had not become US citizens, and limited food stamps to a period of three months unless the recipients were working.

The reform marked a turning point in national welfare policy. The new policy aimed to encourage personal responsibility by promoting work, reducing non-marital births, and strengthening and supporting marriage. No longer could able-bodied adults remain on welfare year after year without working. Individuals were given strong financial incentives to leave welfare for work; families were given essential support for child care and health care to facilitate the transition to work; states were given equally strong incentives to help parents prepare for and find jobs by making funding for welfare dependent on meeting federal program standards. State and local governments were given more control over welfare than ever before.

Although many Republicans favored Clinton's reforms, critics in Clinton's own party saw two obstacles preventing welfare recipients from going to work. First, many on welfare could not find jobs because they lacked skills or work experience. Second, those who could find work usually ended up in jobs that did not pay enough to support a family. To overcome the latter problem, Clinton persuaded Congress to enlarge the earned income tax credit. This allows low-wage earners who support a family to receive each year a tax refund from the Internal Revenue Service.

The result of the Clinton reform of welfare has been a historic decline in the welfare rolls, substantial increases in employment for low-income mothers, unprecedented increases in earnings by low-income females heading families, and a sustained decline in child poverty, particularly among African American children. In addition, for the first time in several generations, the percentage of children born outside wedlock has leveled off and has remained nearly flat since 2002.

The Bush reforms

In 2007, further welfare reform by the Bush Administration gave even greater incentives for welfare recipients to work. Although nearly three million families had left welfare, most of them for work, there were still over two million remaining on the rolls. The Bush plan committed $22 billion per year to cash welfare, work preparation, and childcare through TANF and Childcare and Development block grants.

Strengthening families was the second major element of the plan. The existing level of spending on childcare was continued, the commitment to providing health insurance to the children of low-income working families was maintained, and the child support enforcement program strengthened so that more payments by fathers were given directly to mothers. In addition, the Earned Income Tax Credit continued to provide income supplements of up to $4,000 per year to single mothers leaving welfare for work.

National policy also continues to promote healthy marriages, supported by research that shows that children reared in intact families are more likely to complete high school and less likely to be poor, to commit crimes, or to have mental health problems than are children reared in single-parent families. For this reason, the plan committed up to $300 million per year for states, often working together with private and faith-based organizations, to design and implement programs that reduced non-marital births and increased the percentage of children in married-couple families. Moreover, nutrition benefits for legal immigrants were restored. Legal immigrants are now allowed to receive food stamps after five years. Federal policy strives to find a balance between the needs of poor immigrants and the obligation to ensure that welfare policy neither attracts noncitizens to the US to take advantage of welfare programs nor induces welfare dependency among immigrants who receive welfare.

The federal government's primary role in welfare nowadays is to set broad goals for social programs, help fund them, evaluate their efficiency and effectiveness, and provide assistance to states trying to implement programs that have a proven track record. This arrangement of federal and state roles is sometimes called *picket fence federalism*: the verticals represent the federal government and the horizontals represent the states and localities. Specifically, the Bush reform included legislation that expanded the authority of cabinet-level agencies to grant waivers to states for the purpose of improving coordination between cash, housing, nutrition, and workforce programs.

Contrary to the stereotype of uncaring governments, Administrations of both parties have not abandoned low-income Americans to their own struggle. But instead, based on optimism about the effectiveness of the traditional values of independence and self-reliance, and faith in the ability of the economy to generate new jobs, successive Presidents have said that there is no acceptable level of despair and hopelessness in America. Time will tell whether welfare reform can deliver on its upbeat promises in bad times as well as good.

Social Security and Medicare

Social security comprises three main programs: The Old Age, Survivors, Disability and Health

Insurance program, known as OASDHI or R(Retirement)SDI; Medicare; and Unemployment Compensation. By dollars paid, the US Social Security program is the largest government program in the world and the single greatest expenditure in the federal budget, of which social security takes up 20.9% and Medicare/Medicaid 20.4%, compared to 20.1% for military expenditure. Social security amounts to 7% of GDP. To finance the system, employees, employers and the self-employed must contribute 6.2% of the first $106,800 of earnings for pensions plus 1.45% for Medicare. For the entire history of Social Security, benefits have been paid almost entirely out of revenue from these payroll taxes. For this reason Social Security is referred to as a *pay-as-you-go* system.

The amount of monthly benefit depends on the worker's earnings record and the age at which the retiree chooses to begin receiving benefits. Reduced pensions can start at age 62, full pensions at between 65 and 67, depending on year of birth. A worker who delays taking retirement benefits until past normal retirement age earns delayed retirement credits that increase the benefit until they reach age 70. In 2009, nearly 51 million Americans received $650 billion in Social Security benefits. Social Security constitutes more than half of the incomes of almost two-thirds of retired Americans and is estimated to keep 40% of elderly Americans out of poverty. For one in six, it is their only income. The average monthly pension for a retired worker was $1158.10 in May 2009.

Almost all workers are covered by Unemployment Compensation, which is run separately by each state under the supervision of the Department of Labor and financed by a modest payroll tax on employers which varies by state and the size of the firm's payroll. The size of the payments and the number of weeks they are made vary widely from state to state. Benefits generally amount to one-third of earnings up to a maximum and are payable for between 26 and 39 weeks. Many Americans arrange to supplement social security through insurance, investments and savings. Other sources of social security include federal and state supplemental payments for the blind, disabled and elderly poor, and benefits paid by employers and unions.

Social Security taxes are paid into the Social Security Trust Fund maintained by the U.S. Treasury. Current expenses are paid from current Social Security tax revenues. When revenues exceed expenditures, as they have in most years, the excess is invested in special non-marketable U.S. government bonds. Thus the Trust Fund indirectly finances the federal government's general purpose spending. The economic significance of the Fund is a subject of considerable dispute because its assets are special Treasury bonds i.e., the monies in the Fund have been loaned back to the federal government to pay for other expenses. Hence the Fund is regarded by some as simply an accounting device that consists of nothing but IOUs. Others, however, argue that the Fund has legal significance because the Treasury securities it holds are backed by the "full faith and credit" of the U.S. government, which has an obligation to repay its debt. Yet although the Treasury guarantees the interest and principal payments it makes to the Fund, the benefit payments have no guarantee at all.

Pensions have become a public issue because Americans are living longer, there is a lower ratio of paying workers to retirees, and the population of elderly Americans is expected to increase dramatically. In 1935, when Social Security began, the average American man lived to be 65. Today life expectancy is about 75 for men and 80 for women. Consequently retirees rely on pension income longer. Men who retired from 1950-55 could expect to live on their pensions for 11.5 years. By 1995-2000 the figure had increased 50% to 18.1 years. Moreover, the birth rate is expected to continue low compared to the baby-boom period. The Social Security Administration (SSA) projects, however, that the demographic balance will stabilize and the cash flow deficit will level off as a share of GDP. The SSA makes three predictions - optimistic, midline, and pessimistic - to project the future solvency of Social Security, but the actuarial calculations that underlie them are necessarily inexact, since they extend 75 years into the future. Demographers indeed disagree about life expectancy. Some argue it will improve more than projected, which would make the shortfall worse, but others think the past gains in life expectancy cannot be repeated, and add that the adverse effect on the system's finances may be partly offset if health improvements induce people to stay in the workforce longer. Meanwhile, some economists believe future productivity growth will be higher than current projections, in which case the shortfall would be smaller than currently projected.

There has been concern for some time that the Social Security Fund may not have enough money to fulfill its obligations even though the Social Security system is currently generating surplus tax revenues. During 2008, for example, an estimated 162 million people paid into the program and 51 million received benefits, roughly 3.2 workers per beneficiary. This compared with 6.1 workers per retiree in 1960 and is projected to decline to 2.1 by 2040. Around 2018, however (estimates vary), payroll tax revenue is projected to be insufficient to cover Social Security benefits. The sub-prime crisis has accelerated the transition from surplus to deficit, because as unemployment rises, payroll tax revenues fall. The estimated annual shortfall averages 1.9% of the payroll tax base or 0.7% of GDP. The value of unfunded Social Security obligations as of January 1, 2009 was approximately $5.3 trillion. This was the amount that would have to be set aside so that the principal and interest would cover the shortfall. Hence the system will at some point begin to withdraw money against the Treasury Notes in the Fund. Under the intermediate assumptions of the Social Security Board of Trustees, the Trust funds i.e., their claim on general revenues that have been built up during the years of surplus, are estimated to run out in 2040, at which point 74% of benefits would be payable with incoming receipts. Without changes to the law, Social Security would have no legal authority to draw other government funds to cover the shortfall and payments would decline without a large tax increase. At the same time, between around 2018 and 2040, redemption of the trust fund balance to pay retirees will draw $3.7trillion in government funds from sources other than payroll taxes, a challenge for the government overall, not just Social Security.

Reform is a political hot potato because it raises the specters of hikes in taxes, or cuts in benefits or other programs, or all of them. The government might also be forced to sell assets and increase borrowing. Social Security is known as the "Third rail of American politics" because touching it means political death. The GAO, the OMB and the Treasury have warned that debt levels will increase dramatically relative to historical levels if entitlement programs are not reformed. The severity of the measures necessary to address the challenge increases the longer changes are delayed. A long-term solution is still being debated, and changes are unlikely during the recession. Moreover, should the recession be succeeded by a bout of inflation, the picture will change again. President Bush called for a transition to a combination of a government-funded program and personal accounts ("individual accounts" or "private accounts") through partial privatization of the system. Under that plan, workers would have been allowed to invest part of their social security contributions in approved schemes of their choice. Supporters contended that the choices opened up through such a substitution would be welcomed and well used. To the contrary, those who defend Social Security's guaranteed minimum retirement income express the fear that too many households might fall victim to bad luck or bad management of their resources and end their lives in poverty. President Obama strongly opposes privatization or raising the retirement age, but supports raising the cap on the payroll tax.

Private pension plans

American Express established the first private pension plan - an employer-run retirement program - in 1875. General Motors implemented the first modern plan in the 1940s. Today there are two types of private pension plan in America: defined benefit pension plans and defined contribution plans. In a *defined contribution plan*, the employee or employer (sometimes both) make contributions to a retirement account that grows with each contribution. Employee contributions are exempt from income tax. The cost of these plans is easily calculated and the benefit risk (how much the pension will cost) is borne by the employee. Defined contribution plans such as a 401(k) are now the most common, in part due to the fact that workers can take a 401(k) plan with them when they change jobs. A *defined benefit plan* uses a formula to determine an employee's benefit, usually based on a combination of earnings, age at retirement, and length of service. The risk is borne by the corporation and the employee has the security of knowing what the benefit will be. Through the 1980s, this was the most common retirement plan. Only defined-benefit plans are eligible for federal Pension Benefit Guaranty Corporation (PBGC) insurance.

Business failures, however, meant that firms did not always pay the pensions to which their workers had contributed. When Studebaker, the car maker, went out of business in 1963, only one-third of the 10,500 workers received full benefits; almost half received 15% and almost one-third received nothing. The outcry from workers and their unions led Senator Jacob Javits (New York) to introduce a pension reform bill in 1967, and eventually, in 1974, Congress passed the Employee Retirement Income Security Act (ERISA), which created the PBGC under the Department of Labor as guarantor. The law also required that pension plan assets cover liabilities. Since ERISA began, more than 160,000 companies have ceased honoring their pensions. In recent years the biggest defaulters have been steel companies and airlines. The PBGC is funded by insurance premiums from those employers who offer insured pension plans. In return, PBGC will pay monthly retirement benefits, up to a maximum adjusted annually by law, should the employer default on the pension plan. Workers who retire at age 65 can currently receive up to $4,500 per month. Those who retire before age 65 have their maximum benefit reduced, while those who retire after age 65 see it increased. Some 44 million American employees (current and future retirees) are covered by the PBGC, whose assets are currently pegged at about $35 billion, $23 billion short of what they themselves say they will need over the coming few years. Current pension plan underfunding increases the likelihood that more pension plans will fail and taxpayers will eventually be called upon to provide a bailout as in the Savings and Loans crisis. In 2004, Congress actually reduced the premiums corporations are required to pay to PBGC by $80 billion over two years and also provided $1.6 billion in relief to the airline and steel industries, on the calculation that this would be less costly than letting the companies fail and making PBGC meet their pension obligations. According to *Investors Business Daily,* the PBGC for years undercharged on its premiums, so companies never had to pay for full cover for the risks to taxpayers. Currently, no taxpayer money is used to fund PBGC. Congress, however, faces the task of determining how to close the PBGC shortfall, which everyone agrees exists. Ultimately, Congress may decide to raise the retirement age.

Medical care

America offers some of the world's best medical care in private, religious and university hospitals, clinics and surgeries, which are well-equipped and well-run, but standards in the public sector can be lower because of underfunding. Although the US spends 15.2% of GDP on healthcare (2008), more than any other OECD country, in 2000, the last time they published rankings, the World Health Organization rated the US 37th out of 191 countries. The WHO found that while the top 10% of Americans were the healthiest people in the world, people on middling incomes received only an average service, and the bottom 5-10% had poor services.

In the last 30 years, the cost of medical care in the US has skyrocketed. Health expenditures rose from $204 per person in 1965 to $7,439 in 2007. Prices for medical services, materials, technologies and drugs are three times as much as in Canada. General Motors spends more on healthcare than it does on steel. One reason for rising health costs is that physicians are among the highest-paid professionals in the US. As justification for their high incomes, they cite the long and expensive preparation they must undergo. Most potential doctors attend four years of college, which can cost $25,000 a year, before going on to four expensive years of medical school, costing up to $50,000 a year. By the time they have a medical degree, many young doctors are deeply in debt and still face three to five years of residency in a hospital, where the hours are long and the pay relatively low. Setting up a medical practice can be costly too. Furthermore, the fragmented American system of healthcare is costly to run.

Moreover, the new machines and technologies for diagnosing and treating illness are expensive, and the technicians who operate them must be well-trained and paid accordingly. In addition, physicians, hospitals and drug companies must buy expensive malpractice or product liability insurance to protect themselves against lawsuits from patients who believe they have received inadequate care. The rates charged for this insurance have risen sharply since the 1970s. Doctors who deliver babies can have to pay premiums of over $100,000 a year. Proposals to reform medical liability have been put before Congress but were not made part of healthcare reform.

The Patient Protection and Affordable Care Act of 2010 will extend coverage to an estimated 32 million uninsured people by 2019, although some 23 million will still be uninsured. Experts predict that a third of those will be illegal immigrants, while the remainder are likely to be those eligible for Medicaid – the government-run healthcare program for the poor – who do not take advantage of the scheme, and those on extremely low incomes, who may be exempt from having to purchase insurance.

Paying medical bills

The US has evolved a very complicated mixed system of private and public responsibility for health care, which is neither uniform nor universal. Access to adequate care depends heavily on income, gender, location and ethnic background. White males on good salaries and some of the poor and elderly are fairly well covered, but people under 65 on average incomes, females, people living in inner cities or in rural locations, and ethnic minorities may find it difficult to get satisfactory healthcare. Unsurprisingly, there is some hostility towards doctors and drug companies. The vast majority of Americans pay some portion of their medical bills through insurance obtained at work. Employers' health insurance covers 120 million people. Some insurance is provided by unions. In addition the government as employer provides coverage to 39.2 million federal, state and local government employees, including the military. About five out of six American workers, along with their families, are covered by group health insurance plans, paid for either jointly by the employer and employee or by the employee alone. Under the most common type of plan, the employee pays a monthly premium or fee. In return, the insurance company pays a percentage of the employee's medical costs above a small amount known as a deductible. Insurance plans vary considerably. Some include coverage for dental work and others for mental health counseling and therapy; others do not. Some people take out several policies to cover themselves adequately. Even so, Americans usually have to pay something towards the cost of their healthcare. The reason for this unusual system is that during the Second World War, wage and price controls were placed on American employers, and in order to compete for employees, they offered health benefits, which in those days were cheap. Thus Americans have become accustomed to getting their health insurance through their employers.

Although most Americans have some form of private health insurance, some people cannot afford it. An estimated 46 million were without insurance before reforms in 2010. Moreover, health care costs have continued to rise, despite the growth of Health Maintenance Organizations (HMOs). An HMO is staffed by a group of physicians who provide all of a person's medical care for a set fee paid in advance. HMOs emphasize preventive care because the HMO must pay the bill when a person needs services that it cannot provide, such as specialized treatment, surgery, or hospitalization. HMOs have grown in popularity and are widely viewed as a means of holding down medical costs. Some Americans, however, are wary of HMOs because they limit the patient's freedom to choose his or her doctor. This has become more common in recent years as HMOs have split into two categories: some that provide insurance, and some that provide care which the insurers buy.

Meanwhile, American physicians have helped slow the increase in costs by reassessing the need for hospitalization. Many surgical procedures that once involved staying in a hospital, for example, are now performed on an "out-patient" basis (the patient comes to the hospital for part of the day and returns home at night). The percentage of hospital surgeries performed on out-patients increased from 16% in 1980 to 60% in 2003. Even when a hospital stay is prescribed, it is typically shorter than in the past.

Medicare

Medical coverage for nearly 45 million Americans is provided through two social programs established in 1965. *Medicare* is the federal health insurance program for all people age 65 and older regardless of their income or medical history. The program was expanded in 1972 to include people under age 65 with permanent disabilities. Most people age 65 and older are entitled to Medicare Part A if they or their spouse are eligible for Social Security payments and have made payroll tax contributions for 10 or more years. People under age 65 who receive Social Security Disability Insurance (SSDI) generally become eligible for Medicare after a two-year waiting period, while those with End Stage Renal Disease and Lou Gehrig's disease become eligible for Medicare when they begin receiving SSDI payments. Medicare plays a vital role in ensuring the health of beneficiaries by covering many important health care services, including prescription drug benefit. There are gaps in coverage, however, notably dental, vision, and long-term care. Medicare benefits were expected to total $374 billion in 2006, accounting for 14% of the federal budget.

Medicare covers a diverse population: 36% have three or more chronic conditions, 29% have a cognitive or mental impairment, 17% are African American or Hispanic, and 12% are age 85 and older. Many people on Medicare have modest incomes and resources: 47% have incomes below 200% of poverty ($20,420 for a single person and $27,380 for a couple in 2007). Fifteen percent - nearly 7 million in 2006 - are under age 65 and permanently disabled.

Medicare is organized into four parts. **Part A** pays for inpatient hospital, skilled nursing, home health, and hospice care. Accounting for 41% of benefit spending in 2006, Part A is funded mainly by a dedicated tax of 2.9% of earnings paid by employers and workers (1.45% each). **Part B** pays for physician, outpatient, and home health visits and preventive services. Part B is funded by taxpayers through general revenues and beneficiary premiums, accounting for 35% of benefit spending in 2006. Medicare beneficiaries pay a monthly Part B premium of about $100. Starting in 2007, those with annual income over $80,000 ($160,000 per couple) pay a higher, income-related monthly Part B premium. **Part C** comprises the Medicare Advantage program, through which beneficiaries can enroll in a private managed care plan, such as an HMO, PPO (Preferred Provider Organization), or private fee-for-service (PFFS) plan. These plans offer combined coverage of Part A, Part B, and in most cases, Part D (prescription drug) benefits. Part C accounted for 14% of benefit spending in 2006. **Part D** is the outpatient prescription drug benefit, delivered through private plans that contract with Medicare. The benefit includes additional assistance with plan premiums and cost-sharing amounts for low-income beneficiaries. Part D, which is funded by general revenues, beneficiary premiums, and state payments, accounted for 8% of benefit spending in 2006. Enrollees in Medicare drug plans pay a monthly premium that averaged $25 across plans in 2006. Enrolment is voluntary but almost all seniors do enroll.

Medicare has relatively high cost-sharing requirements, covering less than half (45%) of beneficiaries' total costs. Medicare premiums and cost-sharing requirements are indexed to rise annually; the monthly Part B premium nearly doubled between 2000 and 2006. In 2006, the Parts A, B, and D (standard) deductibles were $952, $124, and $250, respectively. Unlike most employer-sponsored plans, Medicare has no cap on out-of-pocket spending. A significant share of beneficiary out-of-pocket spending in 2002 was for long-term care (36%) and prescription drugs (22%). Even with the drug benefit, beneficiaries are likely to face significant out-of-pocket costs in the future to meet their long-term care needs.

Private plans are playing a larger role in Medicare through a revitalization of the Medicare managed care program, Medicare Advantage, as well as through the Part D drug benefit. Medicare HMOs have been an option since the 1970s, although the majority of beneficiaries have remained in the traditional fee-for-service program. The Medicare Modernization Act of 2003 (MMA) included several provisions to encourage private plan participation and beneficiary enrollment. By 2006, virtually all beneficiaries had a choice of one or more Medicare Advantage plans, with enrollment now at 16% of the total Medicare population. Medicare pays HMOs and other plans to provide all Medicare-covered benefits. The average Medicare payment to Medicare Advantage plans for Part A and B services is 111% of the cost of similar benefits in the fee-for-service program. Beneficiaries can obtain the Medicare drug benefit through private stand-alone prescription drug plans (PDPs) and Medicare Advantage prescription drug plans (MA-PDs). Medicare pays plans to provide the standard drug benefit, or one that is actuarially equivalent. As of June 2006, 22.5 million beneficiaries were enrolled in Medicare Part D plans, including 16.5 million in PDPs and another 6 million in MA-PDs.

In addition to Medicare, most beneficiaries have some form of supplemental coverage. Employers are a key source, assisting about 11 million retirees who are on Medicare. Retiree health benefits are on the decline, however. Only 33% of large firms offered them in 2005, down from 66% in 1988. An additional 2.6 million Medicare beneficiaries are active workers (or spouses) for whom employer plans are the primary source of coverage.

More than 7 million low-income beneficiaries are dually eligible for Medicare and Medicaid. Most qualify for full Medicaid benefits, including long-term care and dental, and get help with Medicare's premiums and cost-sharing requirements. Some do not qualify for full Medicaid benefits, but get help with Medicare premiums and some cost-sharing requirements under the tax-free Medicare Savings Programs, administered under Medicaid. Many beneficiaries purchase private supplemental policies, known as Medigap (nearly 9 million in 2002). Another 3 million beneficiaries receive supplemental assistance through the Veterans Administration or some other government program.

With the aging of the population, net federal spending on Medicare is estimated by the CBO to grow from $331 billion in 2006 to $524 billion in 2011. Annual growth in Medicare spending is influenced by factors that affect health spending generally, including increasing takeup of services and higher prices. Although Medicare spending increases each year, the average per capita spending growth rate between 1970 and 2004 was lower for Medicare (8.9%) than for private health insurance (9.9%) for common benefits (excluding prescription drugs). Looking to the future, Medicare faces many challenges, but none greater than financing care for an aging population with a declining ratio of workers to beneficiaries. Medicare spending as a share of GDP is expected to increase from 2.7% in 2005 to 4.7% in 2020. The Part A Trust Fund reserves are projected to be exhausted in 2018. In addition to these fiscal challenges, others include: setting fair payments for providers and plans; improving care for those with multiple chronic conditions; providing adequate financial protections for those with low incomes; and ensuring health security for an aging US population.

From 2010, seniors who fall in the coverage gap known as the *doughnut hole* will start getting some help. Seniors fall into the doughnut hole once they exceed the $2,830 coverage limit. Then they have to pay $3,610 out of pocket for drugs before prescription coverage picks up again at $6,440. In 2010, seniors who fell into the hole received a $250 rebate. In 2011, they will receive a 50 percent discount on brand-name drugs. Also, seniors will receive a 7 percent discount on generic drugs, which will increase 7 percent every year thereafter. In 2020, the doughnut hole will close, meaning seniors will have no gap in coverage. Starting in 2011, the reforms also give all seniors free annual wellness exams and preventive tests, like screenings for high blood pressure and certain cancers.

Yet some seniors who make $85,000 or more a year and already pay more in premiums for doctor's visits and prescription drug coverage will see those premiums go even higher depending on which plan they choose. The 11 million seniors who buy Medicare Advantage plans could pay more as well because the reforms will cut the subsidies to private insurers who offer those plans. The insurance industry says premiums will rise but have not said by how much.

Medicaid

Medicaid funds medical care for the poor aged under 65 with dependent children. The requirements for receiving Medicaid and the scope of care available vary widely from state to state. Medicaid is the nation's largest social welfare program, and covered 51 million people in 2004. The program is funded by federal, state and county governments.

State Medicaid programs are generally required to cover:
- inpatient and outpatient hospital services

- physician, midwife, and certified nurse practitioner services
- laboratory and x-ray services
- nursing home and home health care for individuals age 21+
- early and periodic screening, diagnosis, and treatment (EPSDT) for children under age 21
- family planning services and supplies
- rural health clinic/federally qualified health center services

States can also receive federal matching funds for many "optional" services, including prescription drugs, prosthetic devices, hearing aids, and dental care. Until recently, states were required to offer the same Medicaid benefits to all their enrollees statewide. The Deficit Reduction Act 2005 (DRA), however, gave states authority to provide more limited benefits for some groups and to offer different benefit packages to different enrollees. The DRA also expanded states' discretion to use premiums and cost-sharing in Medicaid. In 2005, Medicaid spending was $305.3 billion, of which acute care services comprised over half (60%) and long-term care services made up 34%, while premiums met about 3% of costs.

Medicaid is a key source of coverage for poor and near-poor Americans, most of whom are in working families. Medicaid complements the Medicare program for low-income people who cannot afford Medicare premiums and cost-sharing, and covers critical benefits that Medicare does not cover, such as long-term care. Such "dual eligibles" account for 40% of Medicaid spending. The federal government also matches the supplemental payments that states make to hospitals that serve a disproportionate share of indigent patients. Medicaid accounts for nearly half of national long-term care spending and finances care for 60% of nursing home residents. Many people with the greatest health and long-term care needs depend on Medicaid for their coverage and care. Though they make up a relatively small share of the Medicaid population, spending is sharply skewed toward these enrollees. The 4% of enrollees with costs exceeding $25,000 account for half of all Medicaid expenditure

More than one in four children in the US relies on Medicaid. Together, Medicaid and the smaller State Children's Health Insurance Program (SCHIP) have greatly reduced the uninsured rate among children. The share of low-income children without coverage fell by more than one-third between 1997 and 2005, from 23% to 14%. In recent years, while employer-based insurance steadily eroded, increases in children's enrollment in Medicaid and SCHIP offset the losses of private coverage among low-income children, and the number and rate of uninsured children actually fell. In contrast, among adults, whose eligibility for Medicaid is much more restricted, uninsurance rose. As declines in employer-based coverage continue, Medicaid and SCHIP play an increasingly important role in stemming the ongoing growth in the number of Americans who lack health insurance.

As declines in job-based health insurance continue and the uninsured count rises, initiatives to expand coverage of the uninsured are taking shape in a growing number of states and at the federal level. Though the approaches vary in many respects, most build on Medicaid coverage and financing. At the same time, as the baby-boomers gray and financing long-term care becomes a more pressing issue, the dominant role of Medicaid in this realm is likely to receive more attention. President Obama hoped that Congress would agree on a plan by end 2009.

Under the Medicaid Act 2003, from mid-2004 seniors became eligible for a drug discount card that saves them between 10-25% on their regular drug costs. Low-income seniors receive up to $600 a year to help them with their drug costs in addition to the card. The Act also introduced Association Health Plans to make it easier for small employers to collaborate to offer their employees better health coverage options. The federal government works with states to form state-sponsored purchasing pools, to help ensure that employers have access to a broad range of affordable coverage options. Federal funding to states for Medicaid for families in transition from welfare to work helps to ensure that families do not lose their health coverage when they start jobs.

The Patient Protection and Affordable Care Act has expanded Medicaid to include people on incomes up to 133 percent of the federal poverty level. The Act requires states to expand Medicaid to include childless adults starting in 2014. The federal government will pay 100 percent of the costs of covering newly eligible individuals through 2016. Illegal immigrants were not made eligible for Medicaid.

The uninsured

One of the most troubling health care problems facing the US has been providing care for those who cannot afford health insurance and who are not eligible for either Medicaid or Medicare. Federal funds cover only 40% of total US healthcare spending. It has been estimated that 46 million Americans are without health insurance at least part of the year. Contrary to popular belief, the great majority of people without health insurance are actually members of working families, lower middle class families who do not happen to work for an employer who offers health benefits. Others may be unemployed or live just above the poverty line. The official 2007 poverty threshold for a family of four was $21,027. Poor Americans can go to public hospitals, where they will get treatment in an emergency, but they often fail to obtain routine care that might prevent illness. In recent years, a high point of bipartisan health reform was the 1997 creation of the State Children's Health Insurance Program (SCHIP). While early implementation of SCHIP was slow, it has now grown to reach, over the course of a year, 5.8 million children who would otherwise be uninsured and is widely regarded as a success.

Features of the Obama healthcare reform include: a requirement that all residents purchase health insurance, with premium subsidies for people of modest means; an insurance exchange through which uninsured adults can purchase affordable coverage (eligible adults would select from federally approved private health plans offering about three different standardized benefit packages); the expansion of Medicaid for adults in the 33 states with an eligibility cutoff of 100% of the federal poverty level and, through SCHIP, for children in families with incomes below 250% of the federal poverty level.

Charity and philanthropy (see also Chapter 11)

Organized philanthropy by institutions and individuals for amazingly diverse objectives, social, cultural, and sometimes political in nature, is a notable American phenomenon. For over two centuries, institutional charity has shaped American society in surprising and largely salutary ways. The names of Carnegie, Mellon, Getty and Gates have become world famous. Philanthropic activity in America often has its roots in the desire to promote social ideals or conceptions of truth. The main areas of charitable activity are animals, arts, culture and humanities, education, the environment, health, human services, public benefit and religion.

Protestant missionaries were pioneers of philanthropy before1861 and did much to influence American sensitivity to social issues. Benjamin Franklin recorded in his *Autobiography* the project of the evangelist Whitefield in 1739 to build an orphanage in Georgia. As giving and caring developed from charity into organized philanthropy, it came to have its own legal design and relation to the tax system. The American Indians were included, under the influence of Christianity. Religious philanthropists emphasized salvation, self-control, and social transformation. In the period 1861-1930, blacks benefited from philanthropists' efforts to improve education in the South. The 20th century saw the rise of the foundation, and the work of such figures as Mrs Russell Sage. The Depression and World War II gave a great impetus to philanthropy. American philanthropists, both secular and religious, have since taken the world for their scene of action and have focused on curing evils at their source by "scientific giving." Domestically, philanthropists became involved with the civil rights movement and the politics of racial justice. It has become clear, however, that government action is needed as well as private philanthropy to make a real difference to America's social problems.

When the economy was based on manufacturing, unions undertook the role of seeing that the wealth of the nation was spread equitably. In the years ahead, Americans may have to look to organized grandparent power as the only force strong and compassionate enough to shoulder the task. The Gray Panthers, an intergenerational advocacy and educational organization working for social and economic justice, is such a body. It addresses issues like national health care, jobs, social security, housing, sustainable environment, education and peace. "The old," its founder Maggie Kuhn observed, "having the benefit of life experience, the time to get things done, and the least to lose by sticking their necks out, were in a perfect position to serve as advocates for the larger public good."

Foundations are uniquely positioned to serve as architects of social change because they have the flexibility, creativity and innovation to find effective solutions to complex issues. Public policy work by foundations can create common ground by opening up new lines of communication among diverse groups of citizens and others, and can counteract the efforts of lobbyists paid by special interest groups such as large corporations.

Foundations are also free to take a significant part in the public policy process through activities such as nonpartisan analysis; self-defense lobbying (where they are directly affected by legislation or proposed legislation); technical assistance (when, for example, they are asked for specialist advice by legislators); and discussions of broad social and economic problems. Moreover, they may, subject to certain rules, make grants to public charities that lobby. In particular, private foundations may fund generalized public education messages that discuss, and take clear positions on, broad public policy issues, provided that the communications do not refer to specific legislative proposals or call on the public to undertake lobbying. The major exception is that foundations are not allowed to undertake paid mass media advertisements on "highly publicized" legislation within two weeks of a legislative vote.

Public charities, community foundations and private foundations all benefit from generous tax rules on lobbying, which is an important part of the American political process and protected by the First Amendment. Lobbying is a communication with a legislator, legislative staff, or other government official that refers to, and takes a position on, specific legislation or a specific legislative proposal. Lobbying does not include communications with executive branch officials, who focus on administrative (as distinct from legislative) actions.

Nonprofits are on a par with the world's leading companies, generating substantial revenue and competing for attention. They are increasingly taking a professional approach to managing their brands and ensuring they clearly communicate everything they stand for. The largest nonprofit sector is international needs, but consumers consider that the least familiar and least relevant. The health, education and youth sectors are the most familiar and most relevant to consumers. Although they are less familiar and have less revenue, environmental and animal-related nonprofits are growing the fastest. Domestic social needs is the most valuable sector in revenue terms. Needy Americans can turn to a broad spectrum of private charities and voluntary organizations. According to a 2001 survey by the Independent Sector (IS), 89% of Americans donate to charity, giving an average $1,620 annually. IS also reports that 44% of Americans over age 18 (83.9 million people) do volunteer work, the equivalent of a workforce of 9 million people.

Despite the funding raised and volunteers engaged by nonprofits, critics like Steven Goldberg argue that philanthropy is of little benefit for millions of American families because there is not a direct connection between funding and results. The nonprofit capital market haphazardly distributes more than $300 billion of charitable donations among more than two million nonprofits that compete for funding, with almost no consideration given to which organizations can make the best use of the money. As a result, fragmented funding fails to marshal vital growth capital that strong nonprofits need to achieve meaningful reductions in poverty, illiteracy, violence, and hopelessness.

TOP 10 AMERICAN CHARITIES BY ANNUAL REVENUE IN '000S OF DOLLARS

1. YMCA of the USA, $6,393.6
2. The Salvation Army, $4,702.9
3. United Way of America, $4,516.9
4. American Red Cross, $3,146.2
5. Goodwill Industries International, $2,534.8
6. Catholic Charities USA, $2,361.1
7. Habitat for Humanity International, $1,768.0
8. American Cancer Society, $1,359
9. The Arc of the United States, $1,223.6
10. Boys & Girls Clubs of America, $1,168.3

CHAPTER 5

STUDY, SCIENCE, SPACE AND MEDICINE

Knowledge will forever govern ignorance. And people who mean to be their own governors must arm themselves with the power knowledge gives.
James Madison, letter to W. T. Barry, August 4, 1822

Education in America is provided through a unique combination of local, state, federal and private funding. American education has had enormous success in providing, for the vast majority of students up to high school graduation, a broad and rounded education which fits them both for the labor market and for their role as citizens. American schooling has enabled successive generations of students, particularly immigrants, to acculturate to their society, while studying progressively more advanced curricula. Private universities and colleges play a major part in higher education. American college education, at its best, is world class and acts as a magnet for the best researchers, teachers and students on the planet. Higher education is mainly responsible for the groundbreaking advances in science, space research and medicine that have kept the US at the top of the economic, academic and military league.

Yet a rising chorus of criticism voices widespread concerns about the standards of those who persist with their education and the dropout rates of those who do not. Leading educationists have documented their alarm that the US is losing its competitive position in science, technology, engineering and mathematics. There are two reasons for this: not enough students are choosing those majors and, because of financial barriers, not enough qualified young people are able to go to college at all. As a result of rising costs and falling student aid, American education is losing its power as a motor of social mobility and becoming by default a means of reinforcing inequality. Thus for many from the racial and ethic minorities, the American Dream is an ever-receding frontier. This, says the College Board, is a threat to the long-term health of American democracy. (In his early months in office, President Obama secured from Congress more funds for community colleges.) Even for a significant proportion of those who can afford a four-year college education, tuition and housing costs impose levels of debt that are harder to pay off than in previous generations. Funding, curriculum and control are all at issue as Americans seek to realize their core values of equality and freedom in the education system. None are more keenly aware than Americans that equitable, efficient and effective education is the foundation for full participation in a vibrant democracy and for the fecundity of innovation on which the nation's material prosperity depends.

The educational system

The US does not have a national school system and, with the exception of the military academies and staff colleges, the federal government does not run schools. Education has long been the primary responsibility of state and local governments. Until 1965, the federal role in education was very limited. Although the Founders believed that education was necessary to create an enlightened public, they did not envision a federal role in education. The Constitution does not even mention the words "education" or "school." By default, the responsibility fell to the states under the Tenth Amendment. Even today, Washington meets less than one-tenth of the costs of public education, but its importance in shaping education policy has grown steadily over the past 40 years. In 1867, the federal government began to collect statistics and report to the public about "the condition and progress" of education, but Washington did not get directly involved in changing the way schools work until 1917, when Congress passed a law to encourage vocational education. The federal government's role in education was greatly extended by the Servicemen's Readjustment Act 1944, the "G. I. Bill of Rights." The Act provided returning World War II veterans with federal aid of various kinds, especially education, to help them readjust to civilian life. The Act subsidized tuition, subsistence, books and materials and provided counseling for veterans to attend school, college or on-the-job training. Other initiatives followed, notably the National Defense Education Act in 1958, which supported the teaching of science, mathematics and engineering in response to the Soviet launch of the earth satellite *Sputnik*. But the biggest change in the federal role was the passage of the Elementary and Secondary Education Act (ESEA) in 1965, as part of President Johnson's *Great Society* program. That Act provided federal aid to education, targeted especially at districts with large numbers of poor children. After the passage of ESEA, many more federal education programs were enacted. In 1980, in the closing days of the Carter administration, the U.S. Department of Education was created. The Department provides guidance and funding for federal educational programs, in which both public and private schools take part. And most recently, with the passage of the Bush Administration's *No Child Left Behind* (NCLB) legislation, the federal government has assumed a significant role in determining what children are taught.

Even so, the curriculum, standards for graduation, and the training and certification of teachers are controlled by state boards of education. Local governments appoint, or supervise elections for, school boards, which determine how the local schools are run. School boards may be at the state, county, city or township level. They are made up of people who live in the area, including parents of pupils. School boards hire the *superintendent,* who is in charge of all the schools in a school district, the principals and the teachers. School boards also allocate the education budgets for their district. Because most of their funding comes from local property taxes, schools differ widely in the resources they have available per student, and class sizes vary considerably. The federal government supplies around 8.5% of the public school system funds; of the remainder, 48.7% comes from state governments and 42.8% from local governments, although the proportions vary considerably. The largest public school system is in New York City, where more than one million students are taught in 1,200 separate schools. Local decision-making and funding, and its dependence on the local property market, make the American public school system almost unique in the world. At the primary and secondary levels, most school districts have a Parent-Teacher Association (PTA), which gives all parents a chance to have a say in decisions about how the school is run. Parents regularly visit schools to meet the teachers and discuss their children's progress. Many also volunteer to teach children a skill, take them on trips or help in the library.

Preschool

Just 22 percent of 4-year-olds are enrolled in preschool/nursery school/kindergarten and 3 percent of 3-year-olds. The quality of the programs varies. Preschool may be advocated as a measure of justice or as an investment in society's future. According to the College Board, many studies demonstrate that low-income children with access to high-quality preschool programs have better life outcomes. They are more ready for school when they enter. They are more successful in school. They are more likely to persist to a diploma and subsequently lead fulfilling lives, and are less likely to be unemployed, on public assistance or in the correctional system. Programs like *Head Start* increase the school readiness of young children in low-income families. Funded through the Department of Health and Social Services and administered locally, *Head Start* provides comprehensive education, health, nutrition, and parent involvement services to 900,000 low-income children and their families. Other similar programs are run by the states. In large cities, some preschools cater for the children of the wealthy.

Elementary and secondary schools

All states require young people to attend school. Although some children attend pre-school or day care from an early age, formal education is usually considered to begin at the age of five. The age limit for compulsory education is generally 16, but sometimes 18. In some cases, pupils may be promoted beyond the next regular grade, and some states allow students to leave school between the ages of 14 and 17 with parental permission. Thus, almost all children in America receive at least 11 years of education, regardless of sex, race, language or citizenship. Almost 90 percent of American children below college level attend public elementary and secondary schools. These schools do not charge tuition. Traditionally, elementary school encompasses pre-schooling for three- to five-year-olds at kindergarten and goes through to the eighth grade at age 14. In some places, however, elementary school ends after the sixth grade, and students then attend middle school, or junior high school, from grades seven through nine. Similarly, secondary school, or high school, traditionally comprises grades nine through twelve, but in some places begins at the tenth grade. Together the primary and secondary grades are called *K-12*.

Elementary school students attend from 8.30am to 3.30pm daily Monday through Friday, September through some point in June, having a much longer summer break than students in many other countries. Most of the day is spent with their class and their class teacher. A few times each week they will do physical education, library studies, music or art with another teacher. Elementary school teachers are trained as generalists with emphases on child cognition and psychology and the principles of curriculum development and instruction, earning either a bachelor's or master's degree in Early Childhood and Elementary Education. During each of the morning and afternoon sessions there is a 15-minute recess when, weather permitting, the students can go outside to the playground and play games using the equipment provided. At midday the students eat lunch, either one packed by their parents, or a hot one bought from the school and subsidized for low-income families; the rest of the lunch period is free for play.

The syllabus usually comprises mathematics, language arts (including reading, grammar, writing, and literature), science, social studies (including history, geography, citizenship and economics), physical education, and computing. It is considered vital to expose students to as many different subjects as possible so as to reveal their abilities and help them develop their potential. Since around 1980 the amount of homework assigned has steadily risen, particularly in affluent school districts. It begins in the 1st grade and by the 5th grade, students have 1-2 hours' homework a night, at least Monday through Thursday. Homework increases in middle school and high school, so that many high school students have almost no free time. Many parents now believe that the pendulum has swung too far in this direction, and want homework scaled back. Arrangements for control of the curriculum vary widely. Typically, the curriculum within public elementary education is determined by the school district. The school district selects curriculum guides and textbooks that are reflective of a state's learning standards and benchmarks for a given grade level. *Learning standards* are the goals by which states and school districts must meet adequate yearly progress (AYP) as mandated by the *No Child Left Behind Act*. Teachers receive a textbook to give to the students for each subject and brief overviews of what they are expected to teach.

Discipline is mild and students are not expected to be silent in class. Teachers are called by their title and surname e.g., Ms Johnson. Students do not wear a formal uniform at most public schools, although many schools have dress codes, specifying what is considered appropriate attire. Punishments such as staying behind or being sent to the principal's office for a reprimand are only given if the student is out of control or risks hurting others. Corporal punishment is still permitted in 23 states, however, mostly in the South and West. Because of levels of violence, it has been found necessary for many elementary schools and nearly all high schools to have a police officer, euphemistically titled a "resource officer", on site to screen students for firearms and help avoid disruptions.

Junior high school

Junior high school, or middle school, is any school between elementary school and senior high school. It usually includes seventh and eighth grade, and sometimes fifth, sixth or ninth grade. In some locations, junior high school includes ninth grade only, allowing students to adjust to a high school environment. Students in junior high take lessons from different teachers for different subjects. They follow broadly the same curriculum as high school students but one which is less advanced and usually offers fewer electives.

High school

The rise of the high school at the beginning of the 20th century was unique to the US. High schools are open to all and provide a diploma after study of broad-based curricula tailored to the needs of the economy. Students are required to take a range of science subjects, usually for at least two years, but may choose, for example, physics, chemistry or biology. Mathematics (usually two years minimum) normally includes algebra I, geometry, algebra II, and/or precalculus or trigonometry. Social Science (usually three years minimum) includes history, government or economics. English (usually four years minimum) and physical education (at least one year) are also required. Many states require students to take a health course covering anatomy, nutrition, first aid, sexuality and birth control. Parents are divided over whether schools should provide sex education. Drug education programs are also usually part of health courses. A foreign language and art education are mandatory in some schools. High schools may also teach computer programming alongside academic subjects.

In addition, there are also quite a number of electives, optional subjects which students may take, drop or never take at all. Popular electives include visual arts, performing arts, driver's education, cooking, technology "shop" (use of tools, carpentry, and repair of machinery), publishing (e.g., the school yearbook), French and sports. Some parents and educators believe there may be a connection between the growth of electives and disappointing average scores on standardized tests of mathematics, reading, and science. In addition to their schoolwork, students in junior high and high school are expected to develop more independence and show more responsibility. High school grades have special names. Ninth graders are called *freshmen*, tenth graders *sophomores*, eleventh graders *juniors* and twelfth graders *seniors*. Many schools offer summer courses for students to catch up on work they have missed or courses they could not fit in during term time.

Children are continually assessed by their teachers, and report cards are issued to parents at varying intervals. Generally the scores for individual assignments and tests are recorded for each student in a grade book, along with the maximum number of points for each assignment. At any time, the total number of points for a student when divided by the total number of possible points produces a percent grade which can be translated into a letter grade. Letter grades are often used on report cards, and the current grade may be available at other times, particularly when an electronic grade book connected to an online service is used. Although grading scales differ from school to school, grading is usually based on a scale of 0-100. In some jurisdictions, Texas or Virginia, for example, the "D" grade (or that below 70) is considered a failing grade. In other jurisdictions, such as Hawaii, a "D" grade is considered passing in certain classes and failing in others. Usually, starting in ninth grade, grades become part of a student's official transcript (official list of all subjects studied and grades received). Future employers or colleges may want to see steady improvement in grades and a good attendance record. When they graduate, high school students receive a diploma.

SAT and ACT

High school students, usually in 11th grade, may take one or more standardized tests, depending on their postsecondary education preferences and their local graduation requirements. The SAT and ACT (American College Test) are the most common. In theory, these tests evaluate the students' overall level of knowledge and learning aptitude. Student may take either or both. Most higher education schools also require two or three SAT Subject Tests, short exams that focus strictly on a particular subject. SAT or ACT are not required to graduate high school.

Advanced courses

In states with well-developed community college systems, gifted high school students may get permission to attend community college courses full time. The units earned can often be transferred to a university, facilitating early graduation. Early college entrance programs permit students to enroll as freshmen at a younger-than-traditional age. In the 11th or 12th grade, many high schools provide Advanced Placement (AP) or International Baccalaureate (IB) courses. These are special forms of honors classes where the curriculum is more challenging and lessons more aggressively paced than standard courses. Most post-secondary institutions take AP and IB exam results into consideration in admissions. Because AP and IB courses are intended to be the equivalent of the first year of college courses, institutions may grant unit credit, which enables students to graduate early. Other institutions use the examinations for placement only: students are exempted from introductory course work but may not receive any other credit. Institutions vary in the selection of examinations they accept and the scores they require to grant admission or credit. The lack of AP, IB, and other advanced courses in inner-city high schools is often seen as a major cause of the greatly differing levels of postsecondary education these graduates go on to receive, compared with both public and private schools in wealthier neighborhoods.

Extracurricular activities

A major characteristic of American high schools, and one almost unique to the US, is the high priority given to sports, clubs and activities by the community, the parents, the schools and the students themselves. Student participation in sports programs, drill teams, bands, and spirit groups can take up many hours in practice and performance. Sports programs, especially football and basketball, are very important, and can be a major source of funds for school districts. State high school championship tournaments attract high levels of public interest. School stadiums and gymnasiums are often filled to capacity; schools may sell "spirit" shirts to wear to games. Most states have organizations which develop rules for competitions. High school athletic competitions often also generate intense interest. Inner city schools are heavily scouted by college and even professional coaches offering scholarships and contracts, with national attention given to which colleges outstanding high school athletes choose to attend.

In addition to sports, numerous non-athletic extracurricular activities are available in high schools, both public and private. These typically involve working on the school newspaper or joining a club such as chess, computing, acting or cooking. In addition, there are music groups, marching bands, student government, science fairs, debate teams, and clubs focused on academic areas such as Spanish or community service such as Kiwanis Key Clubs. A teacher will spend time with each group but older students are expected to run their own activities. High school students often travel further to school than before and spend longer in school when they get there. They may be bussed, especially when bussing is practiced to maintain a racial balance. At age 16 many students learn to drive and get a license. Some then drive to school in their own car or borrow one from their parents.

The school year is marked by social activities, starting with homecoming in the autumn, the day when former students revisit the school. The day is celebrated with a big football game and a dance in the evening. Other dances are held throughout the year. The most important of these is the Prom, which is usually limited to juniors and seniors. Students take great care to find the right clothes. Younger students are delighted to be invited as guests of older ones. The graduation of students (and the commencement of their adult life) is marked by the *commencement* ceremony with speeches, including one from a student representative, chosen from among the best achievers, called the *valedictorian*.

Educational understretch

American children have one of the shortest school years anywhere, 180 days compared with an average of 195 for OECD countries and more than 200 for East Asian countries. German children spend 20 more days in school than American ones, and South Koreans over a month more. Over 12 years, a 15-day deficit means American children lose 180 days of school, equivalent to an entire year. American children also have one of the shortest school days, six-and-a-half hours, adding up to 32 hours a week. By contrast, the school week is 37 hours in Luxembourg, 44 in

Belgium, 53 in Denmark and 60 in Sweden. On top of that, many American children do only about an hour's-worth of homework a day, far less than the Japanese and Chinese.

Americans also close their schools for three months in the summer. The long summer vacation acts like a mental eraser, with the average child reportedly forgetting about a month's-worth of instruction in many subjects and almost three times that in mathematics. American academics have even invented a term for this phenomenon: "summer learning loss". This understretch is exacerbating social inequalities. Poorer children frequently have no one to look after them in the long hours between the end of the school day and the end of the average working day. They are also particularly prone to learning loss, falling behind by an average of over two months in their reading. Understretch is also leaving American children ill-equipped to compete. They usually perform relatively poorly in international educational tests, compared with students in Asian countries that spend less on education but work their children harder. California's state universities have to send over a third of their entering class to take remedial courses in English and math. There is evidence that America's poor educational performance is weakening its economy. A recent report from McKinsey even argues that the lagging performance of the country's school pupils, particularly its poor and minority children, has wreaked more devastation on the economy than the 2008 recession.

President Obama has urged school administrators to "rethink the school day," arguing that "we can no longer afford an academic calendar designed for when America was a nation of farmers who needed their children at home plowing the land at the end of each day." About 1,000 of the country's 90,000 schools are experimenting with lengthening the school day. In particular, charter schools in the KIPP (Knowledge is Power) Program start at 7.30am and end at 5pm, hold classes on some Saturdays and teach for a couple of weeks in the summer. All in all, KIPP students get about 60% more class time than their peers and routinely score better in tests.

Still, American schoolchildren are unlikely to end up working as hard as children elsewhere anytime soon. The federal government has only limited influence over the school system, and powerful interest groups, notably the teachers' unions, and also the summer-camp industry, have a vested interest in the status quo. Reformers are also up against the powerful cultural forces of sentimentality and complacency. Parents have protested against attempts to extend the school year into July or August, or to increase the amount of homework. They still find it hard to believe that Chinese students will take their children's jobs. But brain work is going the way of manual work, to whoever will provide the best value for money.

Private schools

Most of the six million students (11% of the total) who do not attend public elementary and secondary schools attend private schools (sometimes called *prep schools*), for which their families pay tuition. The 33,000 private schools make up 25% of US schools. According to the Census Bureau, only 20% of children of families who earn $100,000 a year or more attend private school. Private schools may be religious, for-profit independent or non-profit. Four out of five private schools are run by religious groups, the largest of which is the Catholics (42.5% of the students). In these schools religious instruction is part of the curriculum, which also includes the traditional academic courses. (Religious instruction is not permitted in public schools.) Students in many private and most parochial (religious) schools wear a uniform. Private schools may cater for gifted students, students who need the nurturing, supportive environment of a smaller school, or those with learning disabilities or other special needs. Some private schools cater to college-bound students seeking a competitive edge in admissions. The National Assessment of Educational Progress periodic tests of children aged 4, 8 and 12, run by the National Center for Educational Statistics, consistently show private school students achieve well above average. Most private schools also take sports very seriously. Unlike public schools, private schools have no legal obligation to accept any interested student, and admission to some is highly selective. Private schools also have the ability to exclude persistently unruly students, an option not always legally available to public schools. Private schools offer the advantages of smaller classes, typically under 20 students in an elementary classroom, 16 in high school, allowing more individual attention. The more competitive schools offer expert college placement services. Tuition in a religious school ranges from nominal amounts to $13,000 per year. Catholic schools charge between $1,200 and $2,700. Fees are often subsidized by endowments and donations which may cover half the costs. Elite schools may charge much more. The right of parents to buy a different education for their children is rarely questioned. In fact, private schools have a good public image.

Student development

Through elementary and high school, there is great stress on the development of the full potential of each student, personally and socially as well as academically, in order to fit the students for their roles in society and equip them to be independent and self-directing adults. Public elementary school teachers typically instruct between twenty and thirty students of diverse learning needs. A classroom will include both children with special needs as specified in the Individuals with Disabilities Act (IDEA), and those who are cognitively, athletically or artistically gifted. Children with health impairments or emotional disturbance may be taught in special classes by specially trained teachers. School districts must meet with the parents of a child with special needs to develop an individual education program that determines the best placement for the child, which must be in the least restrictive environment.

Americans are very concerned when there is evidence that developmental objectives have not been met, for they see life as a race or a competition, sometimes to an extreme degree, and believe that no child should be left behind lacking the means to take part. Parents often put pressure on their children to do well, especially when the children get older and start taking exams. Parental attitudes to competition vary somewhat between regions and classes. The most competitive are middle class parents in the cosmopolitan areas, while working class and lower middle class parents are more focused on getting by and less optimistic about their children's life chances, often with good reason (see *Outliers*, Malcolm Gladwell, Little, Brown, 2008). In rural parts of the South and West, even well-off people often do not particularly want to "get ahead" but are more interested in keeping what they already have. Midwesterners (roughly, west of Pennsylvania, north of the Ohio River, and as far west as the edges of the Great Plains) fall somewhere in between: interested in progress but not so likely to see life as a cutthroat, winner-take-all competition. Yet children from some families have little help and encouragement from their parents. Children whose parents' first language is not English have special difficulties.

Magnet schools

Admission to public schools is usually based on residence. To compensate for differences in school quality, and to overcome racial segregation, school systems serving all or parts of large cities often have *magnet schools,* or magnet programs within schools, for all grades. These enroll an additional limited number of non-resident students by lottery, with equal numbers of males and females chosen. Some, but not all, magnet schools cater to gifted students or to students with special interests, such as the sciences or performing arts. Admission to some of these schools is highly competitive. Although they may mean more traveling for the students, and separation from siblings, magnet schools are popular and increasing in number.

Home schooling

There is a small but growing number of parents (1.7%) who educate their children themselves, sometimes for religious or moral reasons, or because they prefer non-standard education. There were 1.5 million home schooled children in 2007, up 74% from 1999. This was 2.9% of all children. Home schoolers may wish to add religious instruction to the curriculum, and may be unable to afford a church-run private school, or the only available school may teach views contrary to theirs. Others feel that they can more effectively tailor a curriculum to an individual child's academic strengths and weaknesses, especially for those with special needs or disabilities. Still others feel that the negative social pressures of schools (such as bullying, drugs, crime, and sex) are detrimental to a child's proper development. Parents often form groups to help each other. Opponents fear home schooling may be of poor academic quality, may inculcate religious or social extremism, and hinder children's socialization. Over half the states monitor or measure the academic progress of home schooled students, and all but ten require parents to notify them that they are home schooling.

Religion in schools

Religious and moral education - whether teachers should be allowed to say prayers in class, and whether there should be sex education lessons, for example - are the greatest areas of conflict in public education. Religious observances have been so contentious that disputes have ended up in the courts, which have usually said that students should not be forced to do something that is against their beliefs.

Presidential Guidelines set out what is, and is not, acceptable, according to the rulings of the Supreme Court. The Guidelines continue to reflect two basic and equally important obligations imposed on public schools by the First Amendment. First, schools may not forbid students acting on their own from expressing their personal religious views or beliefs solely because they are of a religious nature. Schools may not discriminate against private religious expression by students, but must instead give students the same right to engage in religious activity and discussion as they have to engage in other comparable activity. Generally, this means that students may pray in a non-disruptive manner during the school day when they are not engaged in school activities or instruction, subject to the same rules of order that apply to other student speech. The right of religious expression in school does not include the right to have a "captive audience" listen, or to compel other students to participate. (There have been cases of alleged bullying arising from pressure to do so.) School officials should not permit student religious speech to turn into religious harassment aimed at a student or a small group of students. Students do not have the right to make repeated invitations to other students to participate in religious activity in the face of a request to stop. At the same time, public schools may not endorse religious activity or doctrine, nor may they coerce participation in religious activity. Among other things, school administrators and teachers may not organize or encourage prayer in the classroom. Teachers, coaches and other school officials who act as advisors to student groups must remain mindful that they cannot engage in or lead the religious activities of students (*Religious Expression in Public Schools*, U.S. Department of Education, 1998).

Catholics and religious schools

By the time of the Civil War, over one million Irish Catholics had come to the US. In a majority Protestant country, they and Catholics of other backgrounds were subjected to prejudice. Although Catholics were never denied access to public schools, beginning in the 19th century they built institutions of their own, which met accepted standards while observing the tenets of Catholic belief and morality. The Catholic Church, however, does not require its members to go to church-run institutions. Many Catholic students attend public schools and secular colleges. But Catholic schools still educate many Catholic young people, as well as a growing number of non-Catholics, whose parents are attracted by the discipline and the quality of instruction. The Catholic schools of Chicago form the largest private school system in the US.

Catholics have long recognized that the separation of church and state protects them, like members of other religions, in the exercise of their faith. But as the costs of maintaining a separate educational system mounted, Catholics began to question one application of that principle. Catholic parents reasoned that the taxes they paid supported public schools, and that they saved the government money by sending their children to private schools, for which they paid tuition. They sought a way in which they might obtain public funds to defray their educational expenses. Parents who sent their children to other private schools, not necessarily religious ones, joined in this effort. The legislatures of many states were sympathetic, but the Supreme Court ruled that most attempts to aid religious schools were unconstitutional. Too much "entanglement" between state and church, the Court held, violated the First Amendment's ban on establishing religion. Attempts to alter the separation of church and state by amending the Constitution have not been successful.

Concerns about standards

The educational system is the pad from which the US has launched most of its greatest successes. But a 2008 College Board report on the future of American education, *Coming to Our Senses: Education and the American Future*, has produced startling statistics. The US now ranks 21st out of 27 advanced economies in high school completion rates, a stunning drop after leading the world throughout the 20th century. The rate at which students drop out between grades 9 and 10 has tripled and high school graduation rates have fallen from about 77 percent in 1971-72 to 67 percent today. In some high schools, mostly in low-income urban and rural areas, fewer than 60 percent of freshmen earn a diploma within four years. The question thus arises whether many American school students are missing out on a basic human right to have the opportunity to be the best that they can be, as a liberal would worry, or whether, as a conservative would say, the job of the public school system is only to turn out so many students with varying degrees of competence according to the needs of the economy.

As in many countries, there is considerable debate in America about the perceived decline in the intellectual acumen of students, the alleged spread of laziness among them, and the effects of cell phone and iPod use and of excess TV exposure. Television is accused of reducing children's ability to concentrate (their "attention span") and taking up time that they should be spending on their homework. American children watch an average of 25 hours TV a week - too much say critics. There are also those who say that today's young people are overprotected and spend insufficient time outdoors. Moreover they fail to get enough exercise and lack basic knowledge and skills, being unable, for example, to identify basic plants or handle tools. Teachers cite increasing evidence of teenagers' decreasing ability to tackle even the most basic intellectual tasks, from understanding simple history to working through moderately complex ideas, to being able to define basic concepts or to express themselves adequately in written English. College administrators and business executives complain that some high school graduates need remedial courses in the three R's: reading, writing, and arithmetic (reading, 'riting and 'rithmetic). In particular, they say, many high school graduates lack proficiency in math, the one skill above all required to achieve a skilled job. The 2001 American Management Association Survey on Workplace Testing found that 34.1% of applicants tested by respondent firms lacked the basic skills necessary to perform the jobs they sought in 2000. Various reasons have been suggested, including insufficient math qualifications of high school math teachers, and the fact that math graduates have a choice of many jobs that pay better than school teaching (Lou Gerstner, former chairman of IBM, *Christian Science Monitor*, December 13, 2004). Public education is believed by many to be churning out ignorant teenagers who are becoming ignorant adults. Society, it is claimed, will shortly pay a high price for educational failure. Among the chief scapegoats cited for the supposed failings of American youth is the extensive growth of mandatory testing. (In fact test scores correlate strongly with parental income.) Teachers have been criticized for giving students easier material to work with so that all of them can get a diploma, a phenomenon known as "dumbing down" the curriculum. Another factor that has been identified is the crime and violence in inner city schools, where children sometimes take weapons to school. Meanwhile school boards have been criticized for paying teachers too little, with the result that good ones tend to leave the field of education. No single cause has been identified for what ails American secondary education.

Those who are skeptical about educational decline assert that youth are no dumber than they have ever been, and that some of the perceived problems reflect the generation gap. They point out that SAT scores have risen consistently over the past decades, despite the fact that the pool of students taking the test has increased from an academic elite to a much more representative sample of the population. Optimists also point to impressive teen and youth movements and achievements, such as developments in internet software and new forms of entrepreneurship, alongside the achievements of designers, writers, artists, poets, chefs, and so on in their early to mid-20s. The nation's top universities are also still managing to turn out young minds of astonishing ability and acumen. Many affluent parents, and many more who are not, now put their children into private schools, or move into well-funded school districts. They give their children no TV or video games, and minimal junk food. Of course, this in no way guarantees a smart, "attuned" child, but compared to the odds of success in some school districts, it certainly seems to help.

About 99 percent of American adults reported in the 1980 Census that they could read and write. But statistics from the U.S. Education Department show that some 32 million adults cannot read a newspaper or the instructions on a bottle of pills. About 20% of adults, some 40 million, have very limited skills in reading and writing and 4% are actually illiterate. Ultimately, the quality of American universities depends on the quality of the elementary and secondary education American students receive (unless universities are going to maintain overall standards by recruiting well qualified international students).

Goals 2000

In 1989 President George H.W. Bush and the governors of all 50 states gave the movement to improve the outcomes of American education a new impetus when they set six goals to be achieved by the year 2000:

- That all children will start school ready to learn.
- That 90 percent of all high school students will graduate.
- That all students will achieve competence in core subjects at certain key points in their progress.
- That American students will be first in the world in math and science achievement.
- That every American adult will be literate and have the skills to function as a citizen and a worker.
- That all schools will be free of drugs and violence and offer a disciplined environment that is conducive to learning.

In 1994 Congress passed the Educate America Act, establishing a five-year program, *Goals 2000*, by which the states received federal grants to help them reach the goals. Such programs iron out the inequalities in funding that are a significant factor in student under-achievement, especially in the inner cites. By 1996, some progress had been made in the number of students completing high school, scores on national math and science tests, and the number of four-year-olds attending school preparation programs. Meanwhile, there was an effort to establish national standards in math, science, English, and history. Even so, much remains to be done, especially in ethnic minority education. For example, in 2008, the graduation rate from high schools was 67%, below that of most developed countries. A number of organizations have taken on the voluntary challenge of creating educational standards or guidelines in a whole range of subjects that can be used throughout the nation.

Raising standards in public schools

The quality of US schools is judged in part according to the results of benchmark tests administered to students. In the US, testing companies make assumptions about what students at different grade levels will learn, in part by examining textbooks that are widely used across the nation. Thanks to these tests and the similarity of textbooks, there is already something akin to a national curriculum in science, mathematics, reading and history. Some children will do poorly on tests simply because the curriculum in their classroom, school, or even state did not include the material that was tested. Test results send a signal to educators about what is usually taught, as well as what was taught poorly and therefore not learned. Some experts believe that the process should be reversed and the tests based on the curriculum actually taught.

Testing

Perhaps surprisingly, most states and districts have no sequential curriculum. The curriculum amounts to the textbooks each school uses. Because of its immense size, the New York City public school system is nationally influential in determining standards and materials such as textbooks. Some educators such as E. D. Hirsch Jr. in *The Knowledge Deficit* (Houghton Mifflin, 2007) are beginning to advocate a national curriculum. Students in the 800 schools which use the Core Knowledge curriculum he developed for preschoolers through 8th grade achieve at very high levels, while getting a full education in history, literature, and the arts. In addition, some educators advocate national standards and national tests, with states and local districts responsible for acting on the information about student achievement gathered by the federal government in return for the federal funding they receive.

In international assessments of math and science, despite some improvement in the last few years, the performance of US students compared with students in other advanced countries is still disappointing. There are two major tests, the Trends in International Mathematics and Science Study (TIMSS) and the Program for International Student Assessment (PISA). In 2003, on the math portion of the TIMSS, US eighth-grade students ranked 16th among 46 nations (having scored above average in fourth grade). In 2007, according to the National Center for Education Statistics (NCES), part of the U.S. Department of Education, in math, US 4th graders achieved 11th place and 8th graders 9th place, scoring 529 and 508 respectively, against a scale average of 500. Hong Kong SAR 4th graders came first with 607 and Chinese Taipei 8th graders with 598. (Mainland China does not take part in TIMSS. Nor does India.) In science, US 4th graders achieved 8th place and 8th graders 11th place, scoring 539 and 520. Singapore came first in both grades with 587 and 567. Massachusetts 4th graders scored roughly as well as those in high-performing Taiwan and Japan. An OECD report in 2005 ranked the US tied in first place with Switzerland for annual spending per public school student, spending more than $11,000. How realistic it is to draw conclusions from comparisons with countries with much smaller populations, however, is a matter of debate.

On PISA, in 2003 American students' scores in science and math literacy were below the average for the 30 nations of the Organization for Economic Cooperation and Development (OECD.) The American Institutes for Research examined the scores of the 12 nations, including the US, that participated in TIMSS and PISA in 2003 and found that American students consistently ranked eighth or ninth of the 12. Only mathematics and science have been consistently tested, because other subjects are culture-bound. The NCES reported that the PISA results for 2006 also showed that the average combined science literacy scale score for US students was lower than the OECD average, coming in 17th out of 29. In math, US students came 24th. According to the UN Human Development Program, the US spends 5.7% of its GDP on education, around 15th among developed countries. There is controversy about what these figures mean, and what should be done about under-achieving students. It is undeniable, however, that students who under-achieve are likely to remain in lesser-skilled jobs at a time when demand for those jobs is declining. As a result, the country loses productivity and competitiveness, and income disparities are wider than they might be.

To establish whether school standards have declined, there have been consistent measures of academic performance for national samples of students since the 1970s, when a federal testing program, the National Assessment of Educational Progress (NAEP) was created. When the test was first administered in 1971, the average reading proficiency score for nine-year-old children was 208, for thirteen-year-olds 255, and for seventeen-year-olds 285. The results of the most recent test (2008) revealed that the average reading score for nine-year-old children was 220, for thirteen-year-olds 260, and for seventeen-year-olds 287. These scores indicate that, despite a few minor shifts, reading achievement has either stayed slightly better or about flat over the past 37 years. Math scores show similar results. The SAT, previously known as the Scholastic Assessment Test and before that as the Scholastic Aptitude Test, is another measure that has been used since the 1940s, but it tests only students applying for college. Median SAT scores peaked in 1964, then declined steadily until 1980. Median math scores rebounded almost to their earlier levels in the late 1980s, but median verbal scores hovered in the 420s (the mean score earlier was 500). The College Board re-centered the scores in 1994, so that median verbal SATs once again were about 500. Test scores do not tell the whole story, however. American students, at least those in the top classes and schools, study far more demanding programs in mathematics and science than were offered half a century ago. On the other hand, students today are likelier to know less about history and literature than their counterparts of earlier generations.

No Child Left Behind (NCLB)

To improve student achievement, the *No Child Left Behind* Act (NCLB) was passed in 2001. NCLB increases accountability for results, and focuses attention on the lowest-performing students. It requires all states to test all students in every public school that receives federal funding (as nearly all of them do) from grades three through eight in reading and math, to ensure that they are achieving the minimum level of education required by that state. Since 2007, schools have also tested science. The schools must break down these scores into subgroups by race, ethnicity, disability, low-income status and English language proficiency. All schools are to make what the law calls "adequate yearly progress" (AYP) for every one of these subgroups. All students must be 100 percent proficient by 2014. If *any* of the subgroups fails to make AYP in reading or math, then a school faces sanctions that grow more onerous every year. In the second year, for example, the school must offer all of its students the chance to go to another school (even though the failure may involve only one subgroup, for example, students with disabilities). In the third year, the school must offer extra tutoring to the students who need it (this rule has created a bonanza for private tutoring companies). In the following years, if the school continues to fail to meet AYP targets, it may be restructured or its staff removed, the school turned into a charter school, handed over to the state or private managers, or closed.

Under NCLB, America's elementary and middle school students have made some improvements in reading and math. According to the National Assessment of Educational Progress (NAEP) long-term trend report published in 2009, students at ages 9 and 13 did significantly better on 2008 tests than their counterparts of the early 1970s. Black, white and Hispanic 9-year-olds all posted higher scores than in previous years. Unfortunately, the scores of 17-year-olds have stayed flat. Improved performance of younger students, and particularly minorities, can be traced to the standards-based reforms embodied in NCLB and the state efforts that predated it. Moreover although minority students still trail their white counterparts, black and Hispanic students of all age groups have made greater gains in math than white students since 1973. But despite these welcome gains in shrinking the achievement gaps between white and minority students, the gaps did not change significantly from 2004 to 2008. It seems, however, that the NCLB's emphasis on reading and math has helped students to do well in other subjects such as science and history. Even so, although NCLB tests reveal the results of teaching, they do little to help students overcome academic weaknesses, since in most states the results are not known until six months later. Hence many school districts have implemented MAP (Measures of Academic Progress) tests, state-wide computerized assessments that measure each student's progress over time. This test allows elementary school teachers to have ongoing access to data that identifies the strengths and weaknesses of individual students so that they can remediate where necessary.

State officials are unhappy that, through mandatory testing, control over their schools is shifting to Washington. Teachers complain that the unrelenting focus on reading and mathematics has narrowed the curriculum to the detriment of subjects like history, literature, geography, and the arts, none of which counts toward NCLB goals. Also, the law does nothing for top students and may even divert attention away from them. More importantly, the goal of 100 percent proficiency by the year 2014 is impossible to meet, unless "proficiency" is diluted to mean only basic literacy (after all, no school system has ever achieved 100 percent proficiency). As the date grows closer, more and more schools are likely to be labeled as "failing", even if the overwhelming majority of their students are performing well. At some point, according to Professor Diane Ravitch of New York University, Congress will have to revise the law to recognize this reality.

Meanwhile studies have shown that fewer than 5% of students from failing public schools are switching to other schools. This is because some urban districts do not have enough empty seats in good schools for all the eligible students, or the districts are not providing good information about choices. In cases where top-rated schools have failed to meet AYP for a single group, the other students have seen no reason to transfer.

Vouchers

To provide more places, some have advocated voucher programs using public money to send students to private schools. These proposals have been blocked by provisions in many state constitutions that prohibit public money from going to religious schools. Opponents of vouchers are quick to sue and have been generally successful in the courts. In Milwaukee and Cleveland, the two cities where programs have survived legal challenges, children are able to use vouchers to attend nonpublic schools of their choice, including religious schools. In the Cleveland case, the U.S. Supreme Court majority said the parents had a sufficient range of choice among secular and religious schools that Ohio's voucher plan did not violate the First Amendment prohibition against the establishment of religion. These programs are often oversubscribed. The educational research literature, however, abounds with heated debates about whether vouchers actually improve achievement. The evidence narrowly favors vouchers. But because of the constitutional constraints, the limited supply of religious and private schools, limited public funds, and the modest gains registered, vouchers do not seem to be a practical cure for the system as a whole.

Charter schools

Another suggested solution for the problem of failing schools is charter schools. These are elementary or secondary schools that are within public school systems but enjoy more autonomy. Charter schools operate under 3-5 year contracts by which they accept accountability to deliver improved student outcomes in return for being freed from some of the rules, regulations, labor agreements and statutes that apply to other public schools. Some charter schools are run by non-profit groups, and include ones set up by teachers, parents, universities, government entities, and even teaching unions. About 10% are run by for-profit corporations. Charter schools are not allowed to charge tuition and have no religious affiliations. When space is limited, admission is frequently by lottery. Charters are mostly new schools in urban areas. They tend to be small (250 students) and somewhat more racially diverse than regular district schools. They enroll a high proportion of low-income and at risk students. Charters can be laboratories of school reform, demonstrating what can be done by changes in curriculum, governance or teaching methods. Some charter schools specialize in a certain field e.g., arts or mathematics. Others attempt to provide a better general education than other local public schools. Charter schools are mainly funded by transferring funding for each pupil from the school district where the student lives. Federal legislation also authorizes monies for charter schools. Additionally, charter schools may receive funding from private donors or foundations. There are 4,000 charters, with 1.2 million students, in 41 states and the District of Columbia. But 26 states have capped the number of charters and nine had no charters in 2009, when more federal funding was made available.

Charter schools' performance and funding are controversial. There are some excellent charters, but 11% have had to be closed, mostly for academic, financial or managerial reasons. Studies on whether charter schools outperform regular public schools are inconclusive, although the data suggests that, at least after a few years, charters on average outperform traditional public schools. In 2004, the National Bureau of Economic Research found that charters increase competition, thus improving the quality of traditional public schools, even though the students leaving district schools for the charters tended to have above average test scores. But some say that charter schools perform only the same as traditional public schools or worse.

Funding equity between charter schools and traditional public schools is a matter of continuing debate. A study from the Thomas B. Fordham Institute claims that charter schools receive about 22 percent less on average in per-pupil public funding, or $1,800, than the district schools that surround them. The study asserts that the funding gap is wider in most of the 27 urban school districts studied, where it amounts to $2,200 per student, and that in cities like San Diego and Atlanta, charters receive 40% less than traditional public schools. The report suggests that the main reason for the funding gap is charter schools' lack of access to start-up and capital funding and district program funds. Although charter schools may receive less public funding than traditional public schools, a portion of charter schools' operating costs can come from donations and foundations such as the Gates Foundation, the Walton Family Foundation and the Broad Foundation. In the case of D.C. charter schools, private funding has been found to account for $780 per pupil and, combined with a higher level of public funding, results in considerably higher funding for charters than comparable public schools. Some educators claim that for-profit charters divert into profits part of the funding that in a traditional public school would be spent entirely on education. Studies have shown many instances of charter schools cutting programs or refusing to educate students with special needs. Polls, however, show that charters are popular with the public. Former President Bill Clinton saw charter schools, with their emphasis on autonomy and accountability, as a workable political compromise and an alternative to vouchers. Others, such as former President Bush, saw charter schools as a way to improve schools without antagonizing the teachers' unions.

Meanwhile, regular public schools have shown little interest in replicating any of the successful models that have been piloted in charter schools. For example, most people admire the KIPP schools of New York, where there is a longer school year, special emphasis on enrichment, and much encouragement of pupils to persevere in problem solving, especially in math (Gladwell, *op. cit.*, pp. 250-252, 260-269). Yet few public schools are adopting the KIPP model (only 82 in 19 states and the District of Columbia). Similarly, the Achievement First schools in Connecticut have been extraordinarily successful, but few public schools emulate them. Opponents say they siphon off public funds (unless privately funded), compete destructively with the regular schools and may divide the system on racial lines, reintroducing segregation. Indeed, Dennis Parker, Director of the ACLU's Racial Justice Program, says the US is already "a nation where schools are becoming increasingly segregated by race and ethnicity." Even so, almost all studies have shown that charters produce better outcomes for students, and President Obama has made it a condition for receiving Recovery Act funding that states work towards removing the caps on the number of charter schools.

American Recovery and Reinvestment Act (ARRA) 2009

In April 2009, $44 billion was authorized for education reform under the Recovery Act, with strong emphasis on accountability and transparency. States will collect, publish, analyze and act on basic information regarding the quality of classroom teachers, annual student improvements, college readiness, the effectiveness of state standards and assessments, progress on creating charter schools, and interventions in turning around underperforming schools.

Specifically, the Recovery Act requires states to show:

- Improvements in teacher effectiveness and commitments that all schools have highly qualified teachers;
- More rigorous assessments that will improve both teaching and learning;
- Better student achievement in low-performing schools, with intensive support and effective interventions where necessary;
- That they can gather information to improve student learning, teacher performance, and college- and career-readiness.
- Note: KIPP schools will receive more funding.

Reasons for under-achievement

Why a country as rich as the US still struggles with student achievement has been explained in numerous ways. Some observers blame the bureaucracy and the power of teachers' unions. Yet other nations with much higher achievement also have bureaucracy and strong teachers' unions. Some say the problem is a lack of choice and competition. Others argue that students today are distracted by television, the internet, video games and cell phones and are unwilling to spend the time required for serious reading and concentrating on lessons. Yet others argue that the teaching profession has suffered because of the removal of gender barriers in the marketplace, with talented women entering more remunerative jobs when, in the past, they would have become teachers. Another school of thought contends that the schools suffer from a general dumbing-down of the culture; for example, popular movies, once based on the classics, are now likely to feature gratuitous sex and violence. Still others theorize that Americans today care only about degrees and credentials, not about the intrinsic value of a good education. Some say that parents are not as involved with their children's education as they once were. Others add that discipline problems cut into teachers' ability to teach and often make the job impossible, since students know that the punishment for misbehavior will be minor. These arguments all have some truth, but there is an even more important factor, according to Professor Ravitch. The US has raised its sights. For many years the US thrived because of the intellectual success of the top one-third of every graduating class. Now, the country wants to educate *all* children and leave none behind. This is an ambitious goal to which Americans' sense of democracy and belief in fairness impels them. But it will not be easy to achieve. It remains an uncomfortable fact that poverty is a key factor: there are too many poor students because there are too many poor parents. The Forum for Education Accountability has argued that the law's emphasis needs to shift from applying sanctions for failing to raise test scores to holding states and localities accountable for making systemic improvements in teacher training, curriculum development and resources.

Improving results

The objectives of school reformers are generally to increase the rigor of high school programs; to improve students' course selection and financial planning for college; to raise graduation requirements; to narrow the "achievement gap"; and to align course content with the skills required to succeed in higher education and work. According to the College Board report *Coming to our Senses* (2008). curriculum rigor is the best predictor of college success, but no ethnic group attends high schools where such a curriculum is universally available. Just 9% of all college-ready graduates are African American or Hispanic. Too many teachers are inadequately qualified, especially in middle school. While all the best educational systems in the world draw their teachers from the top third of university graduates, American teachers do not meet that standard. President Obama plans to offer scholarships to attract potential science and math teachers to high-needs schools. Moreover, poor pay and conditions lead to teacher attrition rates as high as 60% in five years. Many advocate more and better counseling to raise student and family awareness, expectations and aspirations for college, especially to overcome the skepticism among African Americans, low-income and first-generation families that financial aid will be available. Financial barriers alone prevent nearly one-half of all college-qualified low- and moderate-income high school graduates from enrolling in a four-year program of college study. Annually, more than 405,000 students successfully completing a college-prep curriculum and prepared to enter a four-year college will not do so (4.4 million a decade), and 170,000 will attend neither a two- nor four- year college at all (about 1.7 million a decade). Need-based grant assistance has not kept pace with need. Resources for counseling are limited in many low-income urban and rural areas. Counselors in private schools spend half their time on college counseling, but public school counselors devote just a quarter. Partnerships with universities have been found helpful in encouraging minority recruitment.

In addition to the challenge to be excellent, American schools have been facing novel problems. The difference in quality between inner city and suburban schools is a big issue. Parents who have money are likely to spend it not by sending their children to private schools but by moving to a suburb where the public schools are good. Schools also have to cope with an influx of immigrant children, many of whom speak little or no English, and respond to demands that the curriculum reflect the various cultures of all children. Some 9.7 million children aged 5 to 17 primarily speak a language other than English at home. Of those, about 1.3 million do not speak English well or at all. There is also argument in states like California, for instance, where the first language of many children is not English, over what language should be used in class. Some, mostly Hispanic, groups believe that children have a right to an education in their own language; others say that people who come to the US have a responsibility to learn English and cannot expect special treatment; or that teaching subject classes in English, perhaps with additional English as a Second Language (ESL) classes as well, is actually a more efficient way for children to learn. Schools also have to make sure that students develop basic skills for the job market, and to consider the needs of non-traditional students such as teenage mothers.

Schools are addressing these problems in diverse ways. They are hiring or training large numbers of teachers of English as a second language and, in some communities, setting up bilingual schools. They are also opening up the traditional European-centered curriculum to embrace material from

African, Asian, and other cultures. Schools are also teaching thinking skills to the nearly 40 percent of American students who do not go on to postsecondary education. In the words of a report by the Commission on Achieving Necessary Skills: "A well-developed mind, a continued willingness to learn and the ability to put knowledge to work are the new keys to the future of our young people, the success of our business, and the economic well-being of the nation."

Urban schools, however, are continuing to deteriorate both in academic achievement and in the educational environment. Local and federal governments are turning to voucher programs for private schools which primarily assist the middle class and tend to decrease the educational budget available to the public system. Some municipalities are hiring private companies to run their school systems, but there is scant evidence that the quality of education is thereby improved. The high school completion rate for African Americans aged 18 to 24 has remained relatively flat over the past two decades at about 76 percent. Hispanics still have the lowest rate among all racial/ethnic groups, despite improving their rate of high school completion from 59 percent to 68 percent. Asian Americans have the highest rate of high school completion at 91 percent (National Center for Education Statistics).

Postsecondary education

The US leads the world in the proportion of its young people who receive some form of higher education. About 45% of Americans have some postsecondary or further education, and over 20% graduate from a college or university. In 2008, 68.6 percent of 2008 high school graduates were enrolled in colleges or universities. More than 60 percent of Americans now work in jobs that involve the handling of information, and a high school diploma is seldom adequate for such work. About four in five new jobs will soon require a two-year degree or vocational training and certificates, according to the Bureau of Labor Statistics (BLS). Other careers do not strictly require a college degree, but having one often can improve a person's chances of getting a job and can increase the salary he or she is paid. According to the BLS, in 2004, 27.7% of the workforce had a college degree or more. This share is predicted to rise by just one percentage point by 2014. Yet America's future, not just in competition in the global economy but in individual personal achievements, and in universal participation in a vibrant, democratic society, is dependent on more Americans going to college and completing college, says the College Board.

One of the strengths of the American system of higher education is its great variety. From small colleges with only a few hundred students to large state-supported universities with tens of thousands, and from two-year community colleges with vocational programs to privately funded research universities, American higher education meets a wide variety of needs. For students, the right choice has much to do with possible career paths, financial constraints, and geography. During 2006-07, over 4,000 validly accredited institutions offered degrees at associate level or above. These included 2,450 4-year colleges and universities, and 1,732 2-year community colleges. The US has the second largest number of higher education institutions in the world after China, an average of more than 100 per state. The US also has the highest number of higher education students in the world, a figure of 14.4 million, or roughly 4.75% of the population. Strong research and funding have gained American colleges and universities worldwide prestige. According to the Shanghai Jiao Tong University's Academic Ranking of World Universities, 35 of the highest-ranked 45 institutions, as measured by awards and research output, are in the US.

US HIGHER EDUCATION STATISTICS 2006-07

	Number	Enrollment
Public 4-year institutions	629	6,837,605
Private 4-year institutions	1,845	4,161,815
Public 2-year institutions	1,070	6,184,229
Private 2-year institutions	596	303,826
Total	4,140	17,487,475
Undergraduate		14,473,884
Graduate		2,097,511
Professional		329,076

	Number		Number
Degrees awarded:			
Associate	696,660	Doctorate	52,631
Bachelor's	1,439,264	Professional	87,289
Master's	574,618		
Enrollment highlights:			
Women	57.4%	Minority	30.9%
Full-time	61.7%	Foreign	3.3%

Degree attainment	Percent
attended college no degree	19.5
associate's degree	9.5
bachelor's degree	17.1
graduate or professional degree	9.9

Colleges

In American parlance, a college is a two-year or four-year institution of higher learning that offers courses in related subjects. Americans often use the word "college" as shorthand for either a college or a university. They talk about "going to college" rather than "going to university" because the former sounds more democratic. Institutions that offer four-year courses and call themselves colleges are universities in the international sense of the term. A similar source of confusion is the American use of "school" to include higher education, whilst in the UK and the Commonwealth, "school" refers only to primary and secondary education. Like high school, the four undergraduate grades are commonly called *freshman, sophomore, junior,* and *senior* years (alternately called first year, second year, etc.).

Four-year colleges offer mostly undergraduate programs and bachelor's degrees in arts or science (B.A. or B.S.). A liberal arts college offers courses in literature, languages, history, philosophy, and the sciences, while a business college offers courses in accounting, investment and marketing. Many colleges are independent and award their own bachelor's degrees. Colleges and community colleges can also be components of universities. Liberal arts colleges emphasize taught courses with a high degree of interaction between students and teachers, although research is also undertaken. They aim to develop the person as much as the mind. Proponents believe that the purpose of a liberal arts education is to develop the personal and intellectual capacities of an individual by expanding his or her capacity to think clearly and critically, to judge wisely, to act humanely, responsibly and collaboratively, and to communicate effectively. Liberal arts colleges are known for being residential communities of learning and living, and for having smaller enrollment, class size, and teacher-student ratios than universities. Most are private although there are public ones. Some offer experimental curricula.

Community colleges offer specialized vocational and technical training. Typical courses include IT, electronics, auto repair and nursing. Community colleges are primarily two-year public institutions, which offer associate's degrees or vocational certificate programs. States usually require community colleges to accept all local residents who seek admission. Community colleges have seen a dramatic increase in enrolment for their two-year vocational courses from 2.1 million in 1961 to 6.5 million in 2004. Numbers surged during the economic crisis of 2008, though at different rates between states. Almost a third of postsecondary students are 30 or older. Many community colleges have relationships with four-year state universities and colleges, and even private universities, which enable students to transfer relatively smoothly to complete a four-year degree after completing a two-year program at the community college. In most states, community colleges are operated either by a division of the state university or by local special districts subject to guidance from a state agency. In junior colleges, students can generally complete their first two years of college courses for an associate degree in arts or science (A.A. or A.S.) at low cost and remain close to home. Adults may also attend universities run for their employees by such companies as General Motors and McDonalds. Some of the McDonalds courses are accredited for credit toward 2- or 4-year degree programs at a college or university.

Universities

Each state maintains its own public university system, which is always non-profit. Some states operate large networks of colleges and universities. The State University of New York (SUNY) and California State University are the largest. SUNY has more than 60 campuses. Some cities also have their own public universities. Most areas also have private institutions which may be for-profit or non-profit. Unlike many other nations, there are no public universities at the national level in the US apart from the military academies. Universities are research-oriented institutions which provide both undergraduate and graduate education. For historical reasons, some universities—such as Boston College, Dartmouth College, and the College of William & Mary—have retained the term "college," while some institutions granting few graduate degrees, such as Wesleyan University, use the term "university."

A large university typically comprises several colleges, graduate programs in various fields, one or more professional schools (for example, a school of law, medicine, journalism or dentistry) and one or more research facilities. A common practice is to refer to different units within universities as *colleges* or *schools* (what are referred to in other countries as *faculties*. Some units may be divided into *departments,* such as an anthropology department within a college of liberal arts and sciences within a larger university. Typically, thus, a university is composed of an academically-diverse set of units called schools or colleges, whereas a college—whether a stand-alone institution of higher learning or a constituent of a university— focuses on one academic sector chosen by that institution, and the college is composed of departments within that sector. Neighboring universities organize themselves into *conferences* and undertake certain activities such as sports together.

Admissions criteria for college or university include the rigor of high school courses taken and grades earned, the student's grade point average (GPA), class ranking, and standardized test scores (such as SAT or ACT, the American College Test). International students may also need to take the IELTS (International English Language Testing System) or TOEFL (Test of English as a Foreign Language). Each institution decides on the minimum score it will accept. While test scores and GPAs are never the only factor taken into account, they are very important; each college usually has a rough threshold below which admission is unlikely. Most colleges also consider more subjective factors such as a commitment to extracurricular activities, a personal essay, and an interview. Students apply directly to colleges during their last year at high school. Each college or university has its own application form and most include an essay question. Applicants also have to submit a transcript and letters of reference. Three-quarters of students study at public universities; and 92 of the largest universities are public.

There is no limit to the number of colleges or universities to which a student may apply, though a separate application must be submitted for each. With a few exceptions, most undergraduate colleges and universities maintain the policy that students are to be admitted to (or rejected from) the entire college, not to a particular department or major. Some students, rather than being rejected, are "wait-listed" for a particular college and may be admitted if another student who was admitted decides not to attend. A group of 346 colleges allows students to apply using the same Common Application form, sending a copy to each college of their choice.

The most common college course consists of four years of study leading to a Bachelor of Arts (B.A.), a Bachelor of Science (B.S.), or sometimes another bachelor's degree such as Bachelor of Fine Arts (B.F.A.), Bachelor of Social Work (B.S.W.), Bachelor of Engineering (B.Eng.) or Bachelor of Philosophy (B.Phil.). Five-Year Professional Architecture programs offer the Bachelor of Architecture Degree (B.Arch.).

The US academic year is usually divided into two semesters of about 15 weeks or four quarters typically of 10 weeks each. Students take courses in a variety of subjects because the aim of the curriculum is to produce well-rounded people with good critical skills. At the end of their sophomore (second) year, students choose a major and sometimes a minor which they study for the next two years. Students also take electives and study a total of four or five courses each semester. Courses consist mainly of lectures but may include seminars or lab sessions. It has been estimated that American colleges and universities offer more than 1,000 majors.

Most teachers at American universities have a doctorate and are addressed as *professor.* Most are tenured and employed full-time by their institutions. While not as diverse as the student population, some 13 percent of college and university faculty are members of minority groups. As well, colleges and universities have a low student/faculty ratio of 15 students for every two instructors. Graduate students working towards a higher degree may teach undergraduate courses at larger universities. These grad students are called *teaching assistants* (TAs). TAs receive a small stipend and do not have to pay tuition. Class sizes can be large, with introductory classes having hundreds of students.

Private universities

The major private schools occupy all but three or four of the top 25 slots in most rankings of American universities. Thus, the private research university appears to be held in especially high regard in the US and around the world. About 25 percent of colleges and universities are privately operated by religious groups, although most of these are open to students of all faiths. Many private institutions have no religious ties. Whether public or private, colleges depend on three sources of income: student tuition, endowments (gifts made by benefactors), and government funding. Most universities, public and private, have endowments. The largest endowment is Harvard's $29 billion.

There is, however, no clear difference between the quality of teaching, faculty, scholarship and research, and hence the quality of education, at private and public universities. The public universities of California and Virginia, for example, are generally rated on a par with the *Ivy League*, an association of eight prestigious private schools with a very high academic reputation in the northeast: Brown, Columbia, Cornell, Dartmouth, Harvard, Pennsylvania, Princeton and Yale. Certain public engineering and medical schools currently also place among the elite. (The name *Ivy League* comes from the ivy that grows on the old buildings of the colleges.)

What makes private universities different from public ones is their financial flexibility, international presence and small size. Private universities draw their resources from alumni, philanthropic foundations, and scientific and other professional organizations, all of which support the universities by funding programs, scholarships, buildings, and professorships. These sources of funding enable private universities to move in bold new directions, creating specialized centers of study and distinctive programs. Notable is New York University's other anchor campus in Abu Dhabi., which NYU's president, John Sexton, predicts will become one of the world's "idea capitals." For students, this flexibility often translates into the opportunity to stay in fields where they might otherwise find little encouragement. Their financial independence generally allows private universities to open international portals for research, service, and teaching more easily. Moreover the smaller scale of private campuses makes possible the easy interaction of scholars across disciplines. In a world where the most important discoveries are being made through collaboration across boundaries, the capacity of the private university to foster and intensify collaborations both within its confines and to the far reaches of the globe may be the private university's greatest attraction.

Today, the distinction between public and private remains ambiguous as "flagship" state universities raise billions of dollars toward the establishment of private endowments. The University of Virginia now receives only 8 percent of its funding from the Commonwealth (state) of Virginia, down from nearly 30 percent a quarter-century ago. At the University of Wisconsin, in a state with a long progressive tradition, only about 19 percent of revenue comes from public funds, down from around 30 percent a decade ago. Meanwhile at the University of Michigan, after a $4 billion capital campaign, there is periodic talk of "going private" (becoming a private university), which, supporters say, would allow it to raise the discounted tuition rate for Michigan residents and thereby compensate for the loss of public funds.

Many Americans would also recognize the top colleges to include the so-called *Little Ivies*, a handful of liberal arts colleges known for their high-quality instruction and academic rigor. *Little Ivies* is a colloquialism referring to a group of old, small, exclusive, liberal arts colleges and universities in New England founded between 1793 and 1855. They include Amherst College, Wesleyan University and Williams College (the *Little Three*) and Bates College, Bowdoin College,

Colby College, Connecticut College, Hamilton College, Haverford College, Middlebury College, Swarthmore College, Trinity College and Tufts University. Hillary Clinton of Wellesley is probably the most famous alumna.

Women's and minority colleges

The majority of both liberal arts colleges and public universities are coeducational. There are 63 women-only colleges. Their distinguished alumnas include: government officials Hillary Clinton, Nancy Pelosi, Madeleine Albright, Jeane Kirkpatrick and Geraldine Ferraro; scientists Rachel Carson and Margaret Mead; journalist Barbara Walters; authors and poets Margaret Atwood, Elizabeth Bishop, Pearl Buck, Emily Dickinson, Helen Keller, Flannery O'Connor and Sylvia Plath; and actresses Katharine Hepburn and Meryl Streep. There are five men's colleges. There are also 104 historically black colleges and universities (HBCUs), some private, some public. Today their student bodies are around 75% black. HBCUs educate one-quarter of black college students, about 575,000, and take a disproportionate number of low-income students, but they produce an outsized number of future black graduate students and leaders. That group is largely female. Women on average are 61% of the students, and HBCUs award twice as many degrees to women as to men. Just 29% of HBCU males complete a bachelor's degree within six years, according to Associated Press.

Rankings and accreditation

A student who has graduated from a highly regarded college may have a distinct advantage as he or she seeks employment. Many political leaders come from the Ivy League. Thus, competition to get into the more renowned schools can be intense. Larger universities put more emphasis on research and hiring distinguished faculty. Smaller ones put more emphasis on teaching and give more attention to individual students. Aside from the top schools, academic reputations vary widely among the middle-tier and even among academic departments within each of these schools. Some schools include honors or other rigorous programs that challenge academically exceptional students.

Rankings publications include *Top American Research Universities* from The Center for Measuring University Performance, University of Florida and *Academic Ranking of World Universities* by Shanghai Jiao Tong University. Rankings are also produced by magazines such as *U.S. News and World Report, Washington Monthly* and *Times Higher Educational Supplement,* which publishes *THE- QS World University Rankings*; and test preparation services such as *The Princeton Review.* These rankings are based on factors like brand recognition, selectivity in admissions, generosity of alumni donors, and volume of faculty research. Only a small percentage of students who apply to these schools gain admission. Rankings have attracted some criticism, and most experts feel they are only one of many factors a student should consider when seeking admission. American universities have developed independent accreditation organizations to vouch for the quality of the degrees they offer. The accreditation agencies rate universities and colleges on criteria such as the quality of their libraries, the publishing records of their faculty, and the degrees which their faculty hold.

Military academies

Prospective students applying to attend one of the five military academies require, with limited exceptions, nomination by a member of Congress. Like acceptance to a top university, competition for these limited nominations is intense and must be supported by superior scholastic achievement and evidence of leadership potential.

Graduate study

At the graduate level, colleges and universities offer both research and professional degrees. Entrance into graduate programs usually depends upon a student's undergraduate academic performance (sometimes just three years of study) or professional experience, and his or her score on a standardized entrance exam like the Graduate Record Examination (GRE), the Medical College Admission Test (MCAT), or the Law School Admissions Test (LSAT). Professional degrees such as law, medicine, pharmacy and dentistry do not require a specific undergraduate major, though medicine, pharmacy, and dentistry have set prerequisite courses that must be taken before enrollment. Many graduate and law schools do not require experience after earning a bachelor's degree to enter their programs, but business school candidates are sometimes required to gain a few years of professional work experience before applying. Students whose native language is not English, or who have not been educated in a country or region where English is a native language, may be required to present the results of an English proficiency test, such as IELTS or TOEFL. Graduate applicants who seek a teaching assistantship may also be required to take the Test of Spoken English (TSE) as evidence of their ability in English.

Of all university students, 8.9 percent receive postgraduate degrees. Graduate study leads to a more advanced degree such as a master's, which could be a Master of Arts (MA), Master of Science (MS), Master of Business Administration (MBA), Master of Public Administration (MPA) or other less common master's degrees such as Master of Education (MEd), and Master of Fine Arts (MFA). After additional years of study and sometimes in conjunction with the completion of a master's degree, students may earn a Doctor of Philosophy (Ph.D.) or other doctoral degree, such as Doctor of Arts, Doctor of Education, Doctor of Theology, Doctor of Medicine, Doctor of Pharmacy, Doctor of Physical Therapy, Doctor of Veterinary Medicine or Doctor of Jurisprudence. Some programs, such as medicine, have formal apprenticeship procedures post-graduation which must be completed after graduation and before one is considered to be fully trained. Other professional programs like law and business have no formal apprenticeship requirements after graduation, although law school graduates must usually take the state bar exam to practice.

International students

America has a reputation as a world leader in higher education and attracts a large segment of the international student population to benefit from its excellence in science, empirical studies and in creative thinking. US postsecondary education has long been recognized as a model of quality, diversity, and opportunity. International students help create this experience. Over 600,000 undergraduate and graduate students from all over the world come to the US each year, although institutions in their own countries offer excellent programs developed and adapted to their needs. International students are engaged in undergraduate, research, professional, English language and summer programs. The vast majority of these students return home as fluent English speakers. English proficiency is a tremendous asset and indeed, in some cases, a necessary skill. Social activities, like experiencing cuisine, music, movies and other customs together with American and other international students, offer additional enrichments and a better understanding of each other's cultures. The learning, the language, and the intercultural environment can make the US study experience a uniquely rich one. With such a solid and broad background, the foreign student who has completed studies in the US is better prepared for successfully working in many locations around the world.

The US remains the premier destination for international students. US colleges and universities have raised their profile overseas and are devoting more resources and improving infrastructures to support international students on their campuses. America's universities not only accept and welcome international students warmly, but also transform those students' lives. The number of non-U.S. students enrolled in higher education institutions during the 2007-2008 academic year jumped 7 percent to a record 623,805, according to the annual *Open Doors* survey from the Institute of International Education (IIE). First-time enrolments increased 10 percent in 2007-2008, following a similar 10 percent rise the previous year. The field growing the fastest in popularity is intensive English language (up 30 percent from the previous year). The State Department supports English language programs, like the English Access Microscholarship Program for underserved high school students in more than 60 countries, to prepare future generations of international students to pursue educational opportunities in the US. The program provides scholarships for after-school classes and intensive summer learning activities to disadvantaged youth in predominantly Muslim communities around the world. About 44,000 students have participated to date.

MOST POPULAR FIELDS OF STUDY FOR INTERNATIONAL STUDENTS

	Percentage of total
Business and management	20
Engineering	17
Physical and life sciences	9
Social sciences	9
Mathematics and computer sciences	8
Fine and applied arts	6
Health professions	5
Intensive English language	5
Education	3
Humanities	3
Agriculture	2

The University of Southern California in Los Angeles has the highest international student enrolment, with New York University second. Other leading recruiters are: Columbia University in New York; the University of Illinois at Urbana-Champaign; Purdue University in West Lafayette, Indiana; the University of Michigan in Ann Arbor; the University of California, Los Angeles; the University of Texas at Austin; Harvard in Cambridge, Massachusetts; Boston University; and the University of Pennsylvania in Philadelphia.

The leading country of origin for international students is India (94,563 in 2007-08), an increase of 13 percent over 2006-2007. China ranks second with 81,127 students (an even larger increase - 20 percent), and South Korea is third with 69,124 (up 11 percent). Other countries sending sharply higher numbers of students to study include Saudi Arabia (ranking nine, with 9,873 students, up 25 percent after a 129 percent increase), Nepal (11th with 8,936 students, up 9.3 percent) and Vietnam (13th with 8,769 students, up 45 percent after a 31 percent increase). The IIE report also found that the number of US students studying abroad continues to grow, by 8 percent in the 2006-2007 academic year to a total of 241,791, and up close to 150 percent over the past decade.

Classroom culture

First impressions of academic life in the US may be confusing for non-Americans. International students often comment that American students are competitive but do not seem to study very hard, and that beyond the informality of the classroom, the professors are very demanding. Some of these apparent contradictions can be explained by the values that underpin them. Creativity, tolerance, and flexibility are, in general, valued above tradition and respect for authority. Teaching styles and classroom attitudes vary widely and are influenced by many different factors.

Professors and Instructors

Professors are the core of the teaching staff at most institutions. Professors generally teach lecture courses, seminars, and courses for graduate students and upper-class undergraduates. Informal attire and the omission of titles in interpersonal communication are common in American university teaching; but beneath this largely informal surface lie a wide variety of individual expectations and preferences concerning student behavior.

A professor's informal style of dress or speech must not be taken to mean that he or she has a relaxed attitude toward assignments, class attendance, or the quality of students' work. Students may dress casually, eat and drink in class, address their instructors by their first names, and possibly even get comfortable enough to put their feet on the chair in front of them. Though informality may be misinterpreted as a sign of disrespect, this is not what Americans are trying to communicate by being informal. Rather it is a feeling of comfort and a sign of democratic values.

American teachers treat education as a process of inquiry. They expect students to think critically and creatively and ask questions. They place rather little value on skills that some other cultures emphasize, such as memorizing and summarizing. In an American classroom, instructors often seek to affirm the knowledge that students bring to the classroom and encourage them to develop from that level. In classroom discussions, students' own knowledge and experience are often the focus. The instructor acts as a facilitator who helps students discover knowledge, rather than an authority who solely possesses a body of knowledge which must be transmitted to the passive students.

That is the ideal picture. But the 2007 *Your First College Year* survey, conducted by the Higher Education Research Institute, found that only 29 percent of students reported studying more than 10 hours per week. Seventy-nine percent of them "frequently" or "occasionally" turned in material that did not "reflect their best work," 70 percent skipped class, 62 percent "came late," and 44 percent fell asleep. Their engagement with instructors outside of class was similarly tenuous. On the 2008 National Survey of Student Engagement, 38 percent of first-year students "never" discussed ideas from readings or classes, and 39 percent did so only "sometimes."

Teacher's role

It is in order for the teacher to say, "I don't know." (No one knows everything.) The teacher attempts to challenge the students intellectually. They, in turn, are expected to respond. The teacher may conduct class any way he or she chooses and may sit on desks or chairs, or walk around the room. Students are expected to participate in class discussion; the teacher may pair students in class or ask several students to work as a group for an activity. Students are also expected to attend class in person, on time and regularly.

Student's role

Class participation is important. Silence may be misconstrued as lack of interest. Students are usually free to ask questions of the teacher at any time during the class. In turn, they are expected to give their personal opinion when asked and during discussions. Students may express an opinion that is opposed to the teacher's provided there is a rational explanation for the alternative viewpoint. They are commonly involved in study groups outside of class. Students may dress extremely casually.

Students who miss class are expected to contact the professor by email or telephone and explain. Also they should ask the professor or a reliable classmate if there are any assignments due for the next class period and hand in that assignment when they return to class. In addition they should get any notes they missed from the lecture or class discussion. If there was a major assignment due the day they were absent, they are supposed, if at all possible, to pass it in that day, possibly by emailing it to the professor or having someone take it to the professor's office. Students should never miss class days when there is an exam except in case of emergency or illness, and if they do they should contact the professor immediately and arrange a time to make up the exam.

Problems and preparation

If students do not understand material in a class, they are expected initially to make sure they have made an honest attempt to understand the material themselves. Many colleges offer tutoring or help services. After that, students may stop by the professor's office, preferably during office hours, to ask for help. The professors assume that students will have read all assigned materials before coming to any class so as to be able to discuss the material. Similarly all assigned homework should have been done by the deadline. In some cases the teacher will collect homework on certain days. In any case, students may receive no credit for an assignment if they turn it in late.

Teacher's Responsibility

Professors give students a syllabus on the first day or week of class with a schedule of readings and material to be covered, due dates for assignments, a breakdown of how the grade will be determined, contact information including email address, office number, and office hours, required materials for the course, including textbooks and other materials, and an attendance policy.

Office Hours

A professor is required to hold office hours weekly, usually about 3-4 per week. These will be listed on the syllabus. During these hours, the professor will be available to help with course material or to discuss concerns students may have about the course.

Assignments

Most courses require at least two hours of work outside the classroom for every hour spent in class. The ability to use computers is essential. Most professors do not accept handwritten papers (except exams). Computers are usually available for students in the library or computer lab. When a professor gives a major assignment for the course, he or she will give it in writing. The written description will state what the objectives and rationale are for the assignment and in particular state what the expected outcomes are and how the assignment will be graded. When the professor gives back the assignment, which is usually within one or two weeks, he or she gives a grade and a justification for the grade stating the criteria used and an evaluation of how well the work fulfilled the requirements.

Grades

International students sometimes find that their US classmates are preoccupied with grades, which are given at the end of each course. This can be explained partly by the spirit of individual competition that is fostered by American society. It is also a practical matter, as grades are an important factor in gaining admission to graduate school or getting a job after graduation. The basis for grading in each course will be determined by the professor. The weight given to exams, papers, class participation, and other factors will be clearly specified at the beginning of the course. The highest grade is A; the lowest is F, which means the student will not get credit for taking the course. To check a student's overall progress, the university calculates a grade point average or GPA. An A scores 4 points, B 3, C2, D 1 and F 0. Students with high GPAs may be awarded Latin honors, that is, have one of three Latin phrases written on their diploma. The phrases are *cum laude* (with praise), *magna cum laude* (with great praise) *and summa cum laude* (with highest praise). Students with low GPAs can be dismissed.

Quizzes and Examinations

US colleges and universities test students, particularly undergraduates, frequently. Quizzes, short tests on assigned material, are used most frequently in language and mathematics courses. "Pop quizzes" are unannounced tests that are given by the professor to see if students are keeping up with their reading assignments or to verify that students understand the material being presented in the course. Examinations may call for specific, short replies or for longer responses in the form of essays. Multiple-choice tests are common. Often examinations are a combination of both forms. They cover a broad range of material and demand a particular type of study.

Homework

International students are sometimes dismayed by the amount of reading assigned for their courses, especially if English is not their native language. It is important, therefore, to be clear about the role of the reading assignments in a course. In some courses, the reading is central; students must read the texts closely and know the material for exams. In other courses, readings may be supplementary or optional.

In writing, students are be expected to know when and how to "paraphrase" or summarize another writer's ideas in one's own words. It may be tempting to use a source word for word, but because this practice can lead to a charge of plagiarism, it is essential for students to acquire the skill of paraphrasing and to understand clearly the definition of plagiarism.

Plagiarism

Plagiarism is one of the most difficult changes for students new to American culture to adjust to. But in American universities, plagiarism is a serious offence. The penalty can be a failing grade or expulsion from the class or the university. Plagiarism is the use of another's words or ideas without acknowledgment of their source. Therefore, it is important to be able to give the proper credit to the other authors. Although in some cultures the incorporation of the words of revered scholars is an important part of the style of academic writing, it is not acceptable in the US; indeed, it is considered a serious and severe offense. *Borrowed words and ideas must always be clearly documented. Any source must be cited.* There are two basic guidelines:

If copying exactly what appears in another source, put double quotation marks around it and cite the source. If borrowing specific ideas, arguments, data, or other information from another source, cite the source even if the material is put into one's own words. Professors will give guidance on how to avoid plagiarism.

FACTFILE 11 STUDYING IN THE US

Studying in the United States
U.S. Network for Education Information on international exchanges and study in the U.S.
- http://usinfo.org/enus/education/edu_studyteach.html

Undergraduate Study, Graduate and Professional Study and Research, Short-Term Study, English Language Programs, Distance Education and Accreditation
U.S. Department of State, Bureau of Educational and Cultural Affairs
- http://www.educationusa.state.gov/

Exchanges
- http://exchanges.state.gov/student.html

Exchange Visitor (J) Visas
U.S. Department of State, Bureau of Consular Affairs
- http://exchanges.state.gov/education/advise/

Technical and Vocational Studies
U.S. Information Agency (Sept 1993)
- http://usinfo.org/facts/edu1/techvoca.htm

FACTFILE 12 LINKS FOR PROSPECTIVE GRADUATE STUDENTS

America's Best Graduate Schools
U.S. News and World Report
- http://www.usnews.com/usnews/edu/beyond/bchome.htm

College Board OnLine
The Board's online ExPAN College Information Search can be searched to identify degree-granting institutions by specific criteria (e.g., location, majors offered, enrollment).
- http://www.collegeboard.org

Educational Testing Service
Internet users can register online for the various pre-admission tests such as the SAT, TOEFL, GMAT and Law School Admission Test.
- http://www.ets.org/

Financial Aid Information Page
Under the heading, International Students, information is provided on sources of financial assistance for foreign students who wish to study in the U.S.

- http://finaid.org

Higher Education: College Entrance
YAHOO's list of sites opens with a broad range of resources useful to prospective university students

- http://www.bestschoolsusa.com/press/yahoo!highereducation.html

IELTS
Internet users can register online for IELTS.

- http://www.ielts.org/usa/

Institute of International Education
Study abroad portal and many other resources

- http://www.iie.org/

International Admissions to U.S. Colleges

- http://www.america.gov/st/peopleplace-english/2008/April/20080530124432xjsnomm is0.9839899.html

National Center for Educational Statistics College Navigator

- http://nces.ed.gov/collegenavigator/

The cost of college

Except for the five Service academies and a handful of institutions whose role is to provide tuition-free education, all universities charge tuition, although scholarships (both merit-based and need-based) are widely available. Annual undergraduate tuition varies widely from state to state, and many additional fees apply. Because each state supports its university system through state taxes, most public universities charge much higher rates for out-of-state students, comparable to private school prices, although students can generally get state residency after their first year. The average surcharge for full-time out-of-state students at public four-year institutions is $10,867 (College Board). Generally, private universities charge much higher tuition than their public counterparts, which can rely on state funds, although prices vary widely depending upon the type of school and program. Tuition is not the only cost of college. Living expenses (room and board, books and supplies, travel, clothing, entertainment and telephone) and additional fees such as activities fees and health insurance must also be met. College costs are rising at the same time that state appropriations for student aid are shrinking. This has led to debate over funding at both the state and local levels. Between 1982 and 2007, college tuition and fees rose three times as fast as median family income in constant dollars.

The College Board estimates that in 2008-09 the average annual cost of community college was $2,402, compared to $6,585 in tuition and fees for in-state students at four-year schools, and $25,143 for private four-year schools, before factoring in financial aid. About 56 percent of full-time students at four-year colleges attended institutions that charged less than $9,000 per year; while 38 percent attended institutions that charged tuition and fees between $3,000 and $6,000. While private four-year institutions have a much wider range of tuition and fee charges, only about 9 percent of all students attend colleges with tuition and fees totaling $33,000 or higher per year. Annual graduate tuition can vary from $15,000 to as high as $40,000. Two-thirds of students rely on student loans and scholarships from their university, the federal government, or a private lender; some also do work-study, and work part-time job at the college. In 2008-09, estimated aid in the form of grants and tax benefits averaged about $2,300 per student at public two-year colleges, about $3,700 at public four-year colleges, and about $10,200 per student at private four-year colleges.

Financial barriers to college access are significant, however, and growing higher. In 2002, a federal advisory committee issued a report entitled *Empty Promises: The Myth of College Access in America* which estimated, according to author Donald E. Heller, a leading authority on the economics of higher education, that "more than 400,000 students nationally from families with incomes below $50,000" met the standards for college admission "and yet were unable to enroll in a four-year college because of financial barriers. More than 160,000 of these students did not attend any college because of these barriers, not even a two-year institution." Two years later, Heller pointed out that "the college-going rates of the highest-socioeconomic-status students with the lowest achievement levels is the same level as the poorest students with the highest achievement levels."

College funding is complex and confusing, and the College Board recommends that obtaining it be made simpler. Half of student loan funding is managed by the Department of Education directly, through the Federal Direct Student Loan Program (FDSLP) which charges 6.8% interest. The other half is managed by commercial entities such as banks, credit unions, and financial services firms such as Sallie Mae, under the Federal Family Education Loan Program (FFELP). Some schools accept only FFELP loans; others accept only FDSLP. Still others accept both, and a few schools will not accept either, in which case students must seek out private alternatives. President Obama wishes to shift all loans to the federal program and use the savings to make the Pell need-based grants to families earning less than $30,000 an entitlement. Meanwhile he has eased the eligibility criteria and increased the amount of the Grant. According to the National Endowment for Financial Education, student loan balances in 2006 were on average $14,379; revolving debt, including credit cards $5,781; and total installment debt, including student and personal loans $17,208.

Issues in higher education

Curriculums and degree choice

Most Americans agree that a good education gives people the best chance of getting a good job and improving their social position. More people are completing college. Both high schools and colleges and universities, however, are sometimes criticized for discarding required courses and offering too many electives. In the mid-1980s the Association of American Colleges issued a report that called for teaching a body of common knowledge to all college students. A similar report, *Involvement in Learning*, issued by the National Institute of Education, concluded that the college curriculum had become "excessively...work-related." The report also warned that college education may no longer be developing in students "the shared values and knowledge" that traditionally bind Americans together. These reports coincided with a trend away from the liberal arts. Instead, students were choosing major fields designed to prepare them for specific jobs. Public opinion meanwhile was stirred by a bestselling book *The Closing of the American Mind* by Allan Bloom (Simon & Schuster, 1987) which severely criticized universities for their failure to teach students to think and students' lack of coherent moral and philosophical ideas.

From 1991 through 2006, between 63 and 66 percent of bachelor's degrees were awarded in seven fields: business; social sciences and history; education; health professions; psychology; visual and performing arts; and engineering. In 2005–06, some 318,000 degrees were awarded in business, 161,000 in social sciences and history, 107,000 in health professions, and between 81,600 and 92,000 degrees in each of the other four fields. Overall, 320,000 more bachelor's degrees were awarded that year than in 1995–96 (a 28 percent increase). The pattern of bachelor's degrees by field of study has shifted noticeably in recent years. Significant declines are taking place in engineering and mathematics. Engineering, engineering technologies and mathematics degrees have declined about 20 percent since 1990. Enrollments in computer science dropped 40 percent between 2001 and 2006. There is concern that China and India graduate five times as many engineers as the US. That, together with their low-cost labor could, say some economists, seriously affect the US trade deficit.

In response, there are proposals to reverse the cuts in higher education spending made by state legislatures and for incentives for more American students to study math and engineering. Since 2003 the number of bachelor's degrees in engineering has hovered around 76,000 per year and master's degrees around 38,000, according to *Engineering & Technology Degrees, 2007*, a report from the Engineering Workforce Commission (EWC). Increased risk for job loss in IT due to offshoring, and more employers moving toward "on-demand" employment are believed to be major factors making engineering a less attractive career. Fragmented career patterns leave STEM (science, technology, engineering and mathematics) professionals especially vulnerable, since keeping up with the pace of technology is critical to their employability. Meanwhile, although efforts have been made to encourage women and underrepresented minorities (collectively, the *majority*) to enter STEM fields, it is clear that more effort is needed. At the same time, many STEM workers, particularly older ones, report unemployment and underemployment. It is widely accepted that the STEM workforce has a disproportionate impact on America's ability to compete in a global economy. The report *Policy and the STEM Workforce System*, Commission on Professionals in Science and Technology (CPST), 2007 on the state of the nation's STEM workforce and the policy implications, calls on policymakers to develop a healthy STEM workforce system and for degree production, employment levels and salaries to rise. One bright spot is the fact that the number of engineering doctorates rose again in 2007, increasing 6.1% to a record 8,612 from 8,116 the previous year. This follows an 11.5% increase in 2006 and an 11.9% increase in 2005.

The trends in degree choice among American students raise questions that apply to the educational philosophy of all industrialized countries. In an age of technological breakthroughs and highly specialized disciplines, is there still a need for the generalist with a broad background and well-developed abilities to reason and communicate? And if the answer to that question is yes, should society take steps to encourage its colleges and universities to produce more generalists? At the same time, should the education of graduates in the numeracy-based disciplines include a grounding in the humanities? Like their counterparts in other countries, American educators continue to debate these questions.

Women and minorities

The percentage of women in American colleges has grown steadily. Indeed, in 2006, 44 percent of young women aged 18 – 24 were enrolled in college compared with 36 percent of young men. More women than men earn associate, bachelor's, and master's degrees, and the number of women receiving all types of degrees has increased at a faster rate than for men. Between 1989-90 and 1999-2000 the number of bachelor's degrees awarded to men increased by 8 percent, while those awarded to women rose by 26 percent. According to NCES, in 2003 women received 54 percent of all degrees awarded, compared to 24 percent in 1950. Is the gender balance now about right, or are too few men completing degrees?

With the end of racial segregation in the 1950s and 1960s, African Americans also entered college in record numbers. Total minority enrollment at the nation's colleges and universities rose by 50 percent from 3.4 million students to 5 million between 1995 and 2005; and students of color made up 29 percent of the nearly 17.5 million students. White enrollment increased from 9.9 million to 10.7 million, a gain of 8 percent. The percentage of African Americans who go on to college, however, is still lower than the general population, although enrollment among African Americans rose by 46 percent between 1995 and 2005 to nearly 2 million. Meanwhile the increase in Hispanic enrollment led all racial/ethnic groups, up by 66 percent to more than 1.7 million students in that period. Asian American enrollment increased by 57 percent to more than 1 million. In 2006, 61 percent of Asian Americans aged 18 to 24 were enrolled in college compared with 44 percent of whites, 32 percent of African Americans, and 25 percent of Hispanics and American Indians respectively.

More minority students than ever are earning degrees. The number earning bachelor's degrees grew 65 percent to 355,000 over the period 1995-2005. Hispanics nearly doubled their total to more than 105,000. African Americans more than doubled the number of master's degrees earned from nearly 25,000 in 1995 to nearly 53,000 in 2005. During the same period, the number of doctoral degrees earned by African Americans increased 84 percent from nearly 1,600 to nearly 2,900. Hispanics also made dramatic gains in doctoral degrees earned, from 950 in 1995 to more than 1,700 in 2005, an increase of 83 percent. But the number of Asian American men receiving doctorates dropped by 10 percent, while the number of Asian American women receiving them increased by 74 percent (The *Minorities in Higher Education 2008. Twenty-third Status Report*, American Council on Education (ACE)).

In recent years, however, concern has grown that access to postsecondary educational opportunity has become more elusive for a growing number of students and, to an even greater degree, for those historically underrepresented in the college population. Just 26 percent of African Americans, 18 percent of Latino and Hispanic Americans, and 24 percent of Native Americans and Pacific Islanders have at least an associate degree. Although enrolment by minorities is increasing, persistence rates remain in the 50th percentile. Just 36 percent of first-time, full-time undergraduates at four-year colleges, who enroll intending to earn a bachelor's degree, attain their goal within four years, according to a June 2008 report from NCES. Only 58 percent achieve it within six years. Most estimates indicate that even among students who enroll in postsecondary education planning to transfer to a four-year institution, only about 25 percent do so. The Lumina Foundation for Education reports that only about a third of community college students who "attempted the highest level of developmental math, English or reading actually completed that course within a three-year period." Among the likely reasons are motivation, the costs and being offered a job meanwhile. The US ranks 11th in the world for college completion rates for workers between the ages of 25-34, down from an all-time high of second in the world – a phenomenon described by Fareed Zakaria as "the rise of the rest." For the first time the US faces the prospect that the educational level of one generation of Americans will not exceed or even equal the level of its parents.

According to expert bodies like the American Council on Education and the College Board, educational progress, while significant, is not keeping pace with changing demographic realities. Despite significant gains in college enrollment rates for young people from all races, progress is uneven and gaps have widened. According to the College Board report *Coming to Our Senses* (2008), the US needs to pay much greater attention to the educational success of low-income and underrepresented minority students. The US is entering a period of dramatic demographic change where any increase in college-bound students will be coming from groups that are traditionally underprepared for and underrepresented in colleges and universities. Demographers project that the number of high school graduates will grow by 17 percent between 2000 and 2020 and that all of that growth will represent students of color. The number of white graduates is expected to decline by about 10 percent, while the number of African American and Native American students will grow by 3 percent and 7 percent indicate, respectively. The number of Asian American high school graduates will increase slightly, while the number of Hispanic graduates will grow by 54 percent. Erasing disparities in educational attainment will be vital to the future success of America and its peoples, says the College Board.

Yet, the College Board points out, seven severe, chronic and interrelated obstacles stand between where the US P-16 educational system (prekindergarten through college) stands today and where the US needs to be tomorrow:

- many poor and minority children arriving at kindergarten educationally well behind their peers;
- high attrition rates at crucial stages of the educational pipeline;
- shortcomings in K-12 student preparation and college readiness and lack of alignment between high school and college;
- disparities in the quality of K-12 teaching;
- significant challenges on… college campuses, including complex admissions and financial aid processes, affordability challenges and disappointing completion rates; outdated college credit and transfer practices that inhibit student mobility;
- and inadequate investment in adult education. State higher education budgets face severe shortfalls through 2013.

The College Board came up with a 10-part action agenda or recommendations:

1. Provide a program of voluntary preschool education, universally available to children from low-income families.
2. Improve middle-school and high school college counseling.
3. Implement the best research-based dropout prevention programs.
4. Align the K-12 education systems with international standards and college admissions expectations.
5. Improve teacher quality and focus on recruitment and retention.
6. Clarify and simplify the admissions process.
7. Provide more need-based grant aid while simplifying and making financial aid processes more transparent.
8. Keep college affordable.
9. Dramatically increase college completion rates.
10. Provide postsecondary opportunities as an essential element of adult education programs.

The College Board report set a goal for the US to reclaim its world leadership ranking in postsecondary education with 55 percent of young Americans completing their schooling with a community college degree or higher by 2025. Meanwhile, financial aid administered by the states is being allocated more and more on the basis of "merit" rather than need—meaning that scholarships are going increasingly to high-achieving students from high-income families, leaving deserving students from low-income families without the means to pay for college; "merit" is the ubiquitous slogan but disparity of opportunity is often the reality

Illegal immigrants

Whether or not the children of illegal immigrants should be entitled to postsecondary public education is hotly debated. In 1982, the U.S. Supreme Court ruled that undocumented immigrant children are entitled to free public education K-12. The College Board estimates that 5-10 percent of the 65,000 illegal immigrants who graduate from high school each year actually go to college. Many illegal immigrants cannot register for college, however, because they do not have a social security number. The Supreme Court has not said whether illegal immigrants are entitled to postsecondary education, and federal legislation is still pending on major proposals. Under the DREAM Act (see Chapter 2), illegal immigrants who entered the US at age 15 or under and who have lived in the US for five years could apply to the Department of Homeland Security for conditional legal status after graduating from high school. This would make them eligible for in-state college tuition rates and some forms of federal financial aid. Then, if they attended college or did military service for at least two years, they would qualify for permanent legal residence and ultimately citizenship.

States such as California, Illinois, Kansas, Nebraska, New Mexico, New York, Texas, Utah and Washington already allow illegal aliens in-state tuition rates. New Jersey is reviewing whether to offer in-state tuition, while California is considering whether to let immigrants compete for financial aid. But Georgia, Oklahoma, Colorado and Arizona generally prohibit illegal immigrants from paying in-state tuition, and South Carolina bars illegal immigrants from public colleges altogether, while Alabama bars them from two-year colleges. Opponents of the DREAM Act say it would in effect reward illegal behaviour and attract more illegal immigrants, whom the border authorities would find hard to keep out, and who if they entered the country would overburden local housing and services. The College Board says that about 360,000 illegal immigrants who have a high school diploma could qualify for tuition aid, and another 715,000 between the ages of 5 and 17 would also benefit if tuition aid motivated them to finish high school and pursue a college degree. Education of these students would eventually benefit the nation. There is an unresolved debate over the effect of tuition aid on college finances. Some say that aid would increase college revenues through attracting students who would not otherwise attend, while others say that aid would lead to an influx of poor students replacing some who would have paid full tuition.

Distance education

Distance education is defined as a formal education process in which the students and instructor are not in the same place. Thus, instruction may or may not take place in real time, may involve communication through the use of video, audio, or computer technologies, or by correspondence (including written correspondence and the use of technology such as CD-ROM). According to NCES, in the 2006- 07 academic year, 66 percent of degree-granting postsecondary institutions offered college-level distance education courses. The overall percentage includes 97 percent of public 2-year institutions, 18 percent of private for-profit 2-year institutions, 89 percent of public 4-year institutions, 53 percent of private not-for-profit institutions, and 70 percent of private for-profit 4-year institutions. There was an estimated total of 12.2 million enrolments. Of these, 77 percent were reported in online courses, 12 percent were reported in hybrid/blended online/onground courses, and 10 percent were reported in other types of distance education courses. There were 11,200 programs designed to be completed totally through distance education; 66 percent of these programs were reported as degree programs and the remaining 34 percent were reported as certificate programs.

Online education

Online education is a legitimate extension of the role of established universities and colleges. There are also purely online institutions, particularly in the vocational field. The University of Phoenix is the largest American private university with campuses in 40 states and in the District of Columbia. It has nearly 350,000 students worldwide, and offers over 100 degree programs at all levels, with a mixture of online (75 percent) and onground courses aimed at working adults. Students spend 20-24 hours per course with an instructor compared with 40 hours at a traditional university. Tuition averages $12,000 per year. Not all websites offering online degrees, however, are legitimate. They may claim to be accredited by bodies that are not legally authorized to grant accreditation. Applicants in any doubt should check with the U.S. Department of Education's Office of Postsecondary Education or an accrediting body recognized by them before paying any money for an online course. A list of U S universities is held at the University of Texas at Austin website http://www.utexas.edu/world/univ/alpha/. Information may also be obtained at http://www.onlinedegreereviews.org/college/.

FACTFILE 13 EDUCATIONAL ATTAINMENT

Population 25 years and over	182,211,639	100.0
Less than 9th grade	13,755,477	7.5
9th to 12th grade, no diploma	21,960,148	12.1
High school graduate (includes equivalency)	52,168,981	28.6
Some college, no degree	38,351,595	21.0
Associate degree	11,512,833	6.3
Bachelor's degree	28,317,792	15.5
Graduate or professional degree	16,144,813	8.9

SCIENCE

The US came into being during the Age of Enlightenment (circa 1680 to 1800), a period in which writers and thinkers rejected what they saw as the superstitions of the past. Instead, they emphasized the powers of reason and unbiased inquiry, especially inquiry into the workings of the natural world. Enlightenment philosophers envisioned a "republic of science," where ideas would be exchanged freely and useful knowledge would improve the lot of all citizens. From its emergence as an independent nation, the US has encouraged science and invention by promoting a free flow of ideas, by encouraging the growth of "useful knowledge," and by welcoming talented people from all over the world. In the 19th century, Alexander Graham Bell, who arrived from Scotland by way of Canada in 1872, developed and patented the telephone. Charles P. Steinmetz, who came from Germany in 1889, developed new alternating-current electrical systems at the General Electric Company. More recently, the German theoretical physicist, Albert Einstein, arrived in 1933; Enrico Fermi came from Italy in 1938 and produced the world's first self-sustaining nuclear chain reaction; and Vladimir K. Zworykin left Russia for the US in 1919 and later invented the television camera. Scientists and inventors continue to be drawn to the US by state-of-the-art research facilities and considerable material as well as intellectual rewards.

The Constitution itself reflects the desire to encourage scientific creativity. It gives Congress the power "to promote the progress of science and useful arts, by securing for limited times to authors and inventors the exclusive right to their respective writings and discoveries." This clause has formed the basis for the US patent and copyright systems, which ensure that inventions and other creative works cannot be copied or used without the inventor receiving some kind of compensation.

Two of America's Founders were scientists of some repute. Benjamin Franklin conducted a series of experiments that deepened human understanding of electricity. Among other things, he proved what had been suspected but never before shown: that lightning is a form of electricity. Franklin also invented such conveniences as bifocal eyeglasses and a stove that bears his name. Thomas Jefferson was a student of agriculture who introduced various types of rice, olive trees, and grasses into the New World.

Applied science

The US has long excelled in using theory to solve problems: applied science. The great American inventors include Robert Fulton (the steamboat); Samuel F.B. Morse (the telegraph); Eli Whitney (the cotton gin); Cyrus McCormick (the reaper); and Thomas Alva Edison, the most fertile of them all, with more than a thousand inventions patented in his name. Edison was not always the first to devise a scientific application, but he was frequently the one to make an idea commercially viable. Perhaps his most significant invention was the development of electrical generating systems. Between the 1890s and the 1920s his inventions had introduced electric lighting into millions of businesses and homes. Another landmark application of scientific ideas to practical uses was made by the brothers Wilbur and Orville Wright. Combining scientific knowledge and mechanical skills, the Wright brothers built and flew several gliders. Then, on December 17, 1903, they successfully flew the first heavier-than-air, mechanically propelled airplane.

The transistor, an American invention of 1947 that was barely noticed at the time, has ushered in a new age of information sharing. The transistor employs sophisticated principles of theoretical physics to replace bulky vacuum tubes. This, together with a device invented in 1958-59, the integrated circuit or chip, has made it possible to package enormous amounts of electronic circuitry in tiny containers. As a result, book-sized computers of today can outperform room-sized computers of the 1960s, and there has been a revolution in the way people live, in how they work, study, conduct business, and engage in research. Subsequently, satellites, the microprocessor, and the joining of laser and fiber-optic technologies set the stage for the arrival of the internet. Jack Kilby, co-inventor of the chip, went on to invent the electronic calculator in 1967. Robert Noyce, the other co-inventor, went on to found Intel, the company responsible for the invention of the microprocessor.

Pure science

In the second half of the 20th century, American scientists became known for more than their practical inventions and applications. Suddenly, they were being recognized for their contributions to "pure" science, the formulation of concepts and theories. The changing pattern can be seen in the Nobel Laureates in physics and chemistry. During the first half-century of Nobel Prizes, from 1901 to 1950, American winners were in a distinct minority. Since 1950, Americans have won approximately half of the Nobel Prizes awarded in the sciences.

Nuclear energy

One of the most spectacular, and controversial, accomplishments of US technology has been the harnessing of nuclear energy. The concepts that led to the splitting of the atom were developed by the scientists of many countries, but the conversion of these ideas into the reality of nuclear fission was the achievement of US scientists in the early 1940s. After German physicists split a uranium nucleus in 1938, Albert Einstein, Enrico Fermi, and Leo Szilard concluded that a nuclear chain reaction was feasible. In a letter to President Roosevelt, Einstein advised that this breakthrough would permit the construction of "extremely powerful bombs." His letter inspired the Manhattan Project, led by Robert Oppenheimer, the US effort to be the first to build an atomic bomb. The project bore fruit when the first such bomb was exploded in New Mexico on July 16, 1945. The development of the bomb and its use against Japan in August, 1945 initiated the Atomic Age, a time of anxiety over weapons of mass destruction that has lasted through the Cold War and down to the anti-proliferation efforts of today. But the Atomic Age has also been characterized by peaceful uses of atomic energy, as in nuclear power and nuclear medicine.

The first US commercial nuclear power plant started operation in Illinois in 1956. At the time, the future for nuclear energy in the US looked bright. But opponents criticized the safety of power plants and questioned whether safe disposal of nuclear waste could be assured. An accident at Three Mile Island in Pennsylvania in 1979 turned many Americans against nuclear power. The cost of building a nuclear power plant escalated, and other, more economical sources of power began to look more appealing. During the 1970s and 1980s, plans for several nuclear plants were cancelled, and the future of nuclear power remained uncertain. The Energy Policy Act 2005 changed US energy policy by providing tax incentives and loan guarantees for energy production of various types. Nuclear energy provides almost 20 percent of US electricity and is its leading source of emission-free electricity. The US has 104 reactors (35 boiling water, 69 pressurized water), five built since 1990, operated by 32 companies in 31 states. In six states – Vermont, South Carolina, New Jersey, Connecticut, Illinois, New Hampshire – nuclear made up the largest percentage of electricity generated in 2007 (Nuclear Energy Institute). In 2007-09, companies announced plans to submit applications to the U.S. Nuclear Regulatory Commission for 26 new units. Support for nuclear energy has risen to its highest level for a generation. A survey conducted for the Nuclear Energy Institute in 2009 found that 70 percent of Americans favor nuclear energy and express a willingness to have a new reactor built at the nearest existing nuclear plant. Specifically, 62 percent agree that the US should definitely build more plants in the future. However, 26 percent of respondents voiced opposition; 12 percent were strongly opposed.

Solar power

Meanwhile, American scientists have been experimenting with other renewable sources of energy, including solar power. Although solar power generation is still not economical in much of the US, two recent developments might make it more affordable. In the early 1990s, photovoltaic solar cells that generate energy from the rays of the sun became a commercial proposition. By 1996 another innovation had come off the assembly line: solar shingles that can be nailed directly onto the roof. The shingles are made from stainless steel sheeting, coated with nine layers of silicon, a semiconducting film and protective plastic. Roofers install the shingles just as they do normal ones, but they must drill a hole in the roof for electrical leads from each shingle. On average, one-third of a home's roof covered with solar shingles should provide enough power to meet all electrical needs when the sun is shining. Shingles may be economical in some parts of the US. Another solar power invention that came to fruition in 1996 is the Solar Two power plant that began operation in the Mojave Desert in California, generating enough electricity for 10,000 homes. On a 38-hectare site, nearly 2,000 huge mirrors point toward a 90-meter "power tower" that heats molten salt which flows to a steam generator that turns a turbine. The molten salt stores heat energy more effectively than water, and proponents of Solar Two believe this innovation can make large, commercial plants economically feasible in areas with plenty of sun and high energy costs.

The Department of Defense is playing a leading role in the development of renewable energy. Itself accounting for 1.5% of US energy consumption, the Department plans to use the uniquely wide scope of its mandate to develop products and technologies that will enable the US military to draw 25% of its energy from renewable sources by 2025, and to develop machines and methods to help Main Street America reach similar targets. The biggest solar power array in the US is at Nellis Air Force Base, Las Vegas, Nevada.

The 2009 budget presented by President Obama gave increased funds to US science: $2.7 billion (a 35% increase) to the Environmental Protection Agency, which also got $7 billion in the 2009 stimulus package; the National Science Foundation received an 8.5 percent increase to its budget, combined with $3 billion from the stimulus package; NASA received $700 million from the budget and an extra billion dollars in stimulus cash; the Department of Energy gained $39 billion from the stimulus package and $2.4 billion from the budget. The Advanced Research Projects Agency – Energy, created by President Bush in 2008, got $400 million to begin operations (*Wired Science*).

Particle physics

America led the world in physics in the 20th century. The *Tevatron* particle collider at Fermilab, Chicago, was the world's fastest, enabling physicists to probe into the very earliest moments of the universe and discover what the universe is fundamentally made up of and how it works. In 2008, a much faster machine, the *Large Hadron Collider* at Geneva, Switzerland demonstrated that Europe had at least temporarily overtaken the US in this vital field. The US contributed 5% of the $8 billion cost of the *LHC*, which was shared by a number of countries. America had looked to maintain its lead through the *Superconducting Collider*, authorized by President Reagan, as an all-American venture which would have been bigger than the LHC, but funding was withdrawn by Congress in 1993 because of budget overruns. Some scientists feel that the loss of the project has discouraged American students from majoring in physics and that, since the *LHC* is in Europe, fewer students and scientists may come to the US to study and conduct research. This loss of human capital might in time weaken America's competitive position.

SPACE

Exploration

Running almost in tandem with the Atomic Age has been the Space Age. American Robert H. Goddard was one of the first scientists to experiment with rocket propulsion systems. In his small laboratory in Worcester, Massachusetts, Goddard worked with liquid oxygen and gasoline to propel rockets into the atmosphere. In 1926 he successfully fired the world's first liquid-fuel rocket, which reached a height of 12.5m. Over the next 10 years, Goddard's rockets achieved modest altitudes of nearly two kilometers, and interest in rocketry increased in the US, Great Britain, Germany, and the Soviet Union. Expendable rockets provided the means for launching artificial satellites, as well as manned spacecraft. In 1957 the Soviet Union launched the first satellite, *Sputnik I*, and the US followed with *Explorer I* in 1958. The first manned space flights were made in the spring of 1961, first by Soviet cosmonaut Yuri Gagarin and then by American astronaut Alan B. Shepard, Jr.

NASA

The National Aeronautics and Space Administration (NASA) was created on October 1, 1958 in response to pressures of national defense. After World War II, the US and the Soviet Union were engaged in the Cold War, a broad contest over the ideologies and allegiances of the nonaligned nations. During this period, space exploration emerged as a major area of contest and became known as the "space race."

Earlier, President Dwight D. Eisenhower had approved a plan to orbit a scientific satellite as part of the International Geophysical Year (IGY), 1957-58. The Soviet Union quickly followed suit, announcing plans to orbit its own satellite. A full-scale crisis resulted on October 4, 1957 when the Soviets launched *Sputnik 1*, the world's first artificial satellite. This had a dramatic effect on American public opinion, creating an illusion of a technological gap between the US and the Soviets and providing the impetus for greatly increased spending on aerospace.

Shortly afterwards, the US launched its own first Earth satellite from Cape Canaveral, Florida, on January 31, 1958, when *Explorer 1* began the exploration of the Earth's own space environment, leading to the discovery of the radiation belts named after James van Allen and the magnetosphere, the magnetic bubble around the planet that protects it from the direct effects of solar wind.

NASA began to conduct space missions within months of its creation, and during its first twenty years NASA conducted several major programs:

- *Human space flight*: The *Mercury* program (flights of a single astronaut during 1961-1963) to ascertain if a human could survive in space; *Project Gemini* (flights during 1965-1966) with two astronauts to practice space operations, especially the rendezvous and docking of spacecraft and human activity outside the spacecraft; and *Project Apollo* (flights during 1968-1972) to explore the Moon.
- Robotic missions to the Moon (*Ranger*, *Surveyor* and *Lunar Orbiter*), Venus (*Pioneer Venus*), Mars (*Mariner 4*, *Viking 1* and 2), and the outer planets (*Pioneer 10* and *11*, *Voyager 1* and 2).
- Aeronautics research to enhance air transport safety, reliability, efficiency, and speed (X-15 hypersonic flight, avionics and electronics studies, propulsion technologies, and aerodynamics investigations).

- Remote-sensing Earth satellites for information gathering (Landsat satellites for monitoring the environment).
- Communications satellites (*Echo 1*, *TIROS* and *Telstar*) and weather monitoring.
- An orbital workshop for astronauts, *Skylab*.
- A reusable spacecraft for traveling to and from Earth orbit, the Space Shuttle, *Columbia*.

Early Spaceflights: Mercury and Gemini

NASA's first high-profile program involving human spaceflight was *Project Mercury*, an effort to learn whether humans could survive the rigors of spaceflight. On May 5, 1961, Alan B. Shepard, Jr. became the first American to fly into space, when he rode his *Mercury* capsule on a 15-minute suborbital mission. In the following year, on February 20, 1962, John H. Glenn, Jr. became the first US astronaut to orbit the Earth. With six flights, *Project Mercury* achieved its goal of putting piloted spacecraft into Earth orbit and, essential for the later Moon mission, retrieving the astronauts safely. (Rocket designs at this time were also meant to double as Intercontinental Ballistic Missiles (ICBMs)).

Project Gemini extended NASA's human spaceflight program to spacecraft built for two astronauts. *Gemini's* 10 flights also provided NASA scientists and engineers with more data on weightlessness, perfected re-entry and splashdown procedures, and demonstrated rendezvous and docking in space. One of the highlights of the program occurred during *Gemini 4*, on June 3, 1965, when Edward H. White, Jr., became the first US astronaut to conduct a spacewalk.

Going to the Moon - Project Apollo

The greatest achievement of NASA during its early years was *Project Apollo*. The program became a priority when, on May 25, 1961, President John F. Kennedy announced: "I believe that this nation should commit itself to achieving the goal, before this decade is out, of landing a man on the Moon and returning him safely to the Earth." A direct response to Soviet successes in space, *Apollo* was a "giant step" that would convince the world and reassure the American public that the US had scientific and technological superiority over its Cold War adversary and could do what nobody else could do, recognizing that the most important and most convincing force in international politics is the perception of superiority.

Project Apollo took 11 years in all and cost $25.4 billion ($150 billion in current terms), which the world's largest economy paid for with relative ease. Only the building of the Panama Canal rivaled it as the largest non-military technological endeavor ever undertaken by the US; only the *Manhattan Project* was comparable and that was in wartime. There was tragedy on the way: a fire involving the command module of *Apollo 1* during pre-flight tests on January 27th, 1967 killed astronauts Gus Grissom, Ed White (the first US astronaut to walk in space) and Roger Chaffee. But less than two years later, in October 1968, the *Apollo 7* mission orbited the Earth and tested the redesigned command module. Then on December 24-25, Christmas Eve, *Apollo 8* orbited the Moon and its three astronauts made an emotional live television broadcast of greetings to the Earth. *Apollo 9* carried out further tests and *Apollo 10* went to within 15km of the Moon's surface, sending back William Anders' iconic image, *Earthrise*, the first-ever picture of our "blue marble" the Earth from space.

It was the *Apollo 11* mission that fulfilled Kennedy's vision by successfully landing Neil A.

Armstrong and Edwin E. "Buzz" Aldrin, Jr. on the Moon on July 20, 1969. "That's one small step for [a] man, one giant leap for mankind," said Armstrong as he took the first human step on the Moon after dramatically piloting the lunar module to the surface with less than 30 seconds' worth of fuel remaining. Having taken soil samples and photographs, and done other tasks on the Moon, Armstrong and Aldrin rendezvoused with their colleague Michael Collins in lunar orbit for a safe voyage back to Earth.

Five further successful lunar landing missions followed, each more successful than the previous ones, sending increasingly higher quality television images including that of the Moon buggy racing across the lunar landscape. Even the flight of *Apollo 13* of April, 1970, the aborted mission that gave rise to the famous phrase "Houston, we have a problem," is memorable for the remarkable technical recovery from a desperate situation, when the astronauts and ground crews had to improvise to end the mission safely after an oxygen tank burst midway through the journey to the Moon. Although this mission never landed on the Moon, it reinforced the notion that NASA had a remarkable ability to adapt to the unforeseen technical difficulties inherent in spaceflight. With the Apollo 17 mission of December 1972, NASA completed the *Apollo* program. While the *Apollo* program was wholly motivated by strategic political considerations, the Moon landings also brought important scientific results through observations made on the Moon's surface and by bringing back a total of about 368kg of lunar samples. Scientists began to understand from these the structure and past history of the Moon, which had been almost completely unknown before the *Apollo* program. The findings of the *Apollo* mission also support the belief that in its early history a body the size of Mars collided with the Earth, ejecting enough material to form the Moon. In total, 12 astronauts walked on the Moon during the six Apollo lunar landing missions. The *Apollo* mission flew the American flag and displayed the might of US technology and resources to massive global audiences in what remains, arguably, the greatest technical achievement of mankind. Apollo was the response of a technically fast-developing and confident nation with bewildering reserves of money and talent. It was also symbolic of the American mentality, optimistic, can-do and willing to confront the most awe-inspiring challenges.

Three years later, in 1975, NASA cooperated with the Soviet Union to achieve the first international human spaceflight, the *Apollo-Soyuz Test Project*. This project successfully tested joint rendezvous and docking procedures for spacecraft from the US and the USSR. After being launched separately from their respective countries, the *Apollo* and *Soyuz* crews met in space and conducted various experiments for two days.

The Space Shuttle

After a gap of six years, NASA returned to human spaceflight in 1981, with the advent of the *Space Shuttle*. The *Shuttle's* first mission, STS-1, took off on April 12, demonstrating that it could take off vertically and glide to an unpowered airplane-like landing. On mission 6, during April 4-9, 1983, F. Story Musgrave and Donald H. Peterson conducted the first activity outside the command module, to test new spacesuits and work in the *Shuttle's* cargo bay. Other *Shuttle* experiments have studied how things can be manufactured in space. The *Shuttle* astronauts also launched satellites from the shuttle and even repaired satellites already out in space. Sally K. Ride became the first American woman to fly in space when STS-7 lifted off on June 18, 1983. In the same year Guion Bluford became the first African American astronaut.

Tragedy struck the program on January 28, 1986, when a leak in the joints of one of two solid rocket boosters attached to the *Challenger* orbiter caused the main liquid fuel tank to explode 73 seconds after launch, killing all seven crew members. In honor of those who lost their lives, President Reagan addressed the nation in a speech which has lodged in the memory of many Americans. In a passage addressed to schoolchildren, the President expressed the optimistic faith of Americans when he said: "The future doesn't belong to the fainthearted; it belongs to the brave. The *Challenger* crew was pulling us into the future, and we'll continue to follow them." And then in words that have become famous, he concluded: "The crew of the space shuttle *Challenger* honored us by the manner in which they lived their lives. We will never forget them, nor the last time we saw them, this morning, as they prepared for their journey and waved good-bye and 'slipped the surly bonds of earth' to 'touch the face of God'."

The *Shuttle* program was grounded for over two years, while NASA and its contractors worked to redesign the boosters and implement management reforms to increase safety. On September 29, 1988, the *Shuttle* returned to flight and launched some 70 scientific and engineering missions but ceased to be used to launch satellites. As well as *Challenger*, there were four *Shuttle* orbiters in NASA's fleet: *Atlantis, Discovery, Endeavour* and *Columbia*. Tragedy struck again, however, when on February 1, 2003, the shuttle *Columbia* burned up on reentry to the Earth's atmosphere. Commemorating the dead crew, President Bush expressed the motivation behind the program: "Mankind is led into the darkness beyond our world by the inspiration of discovery and the longing to understand. Our journey into space will go on." Even so, the official report into the disaster in August, 2003, contained severe criticisms of management failures, lack of a safety culture and budget cuts, which it said were the main causes of the disaster. The report suggested, however, that it was in the nation's interest to replace the *Shuttle* as soon as possible as the primary means for transporting humans to and from Earth orbit. *Columbia* will be replaced by a new vehicle, *Orion*, in 2015. The core mission of any future space exploration will be journeying to Mars, this time for extended and perhaps permanent stays. Research into hypersonic space vehicles continues.

Three deep-space probes were launched on the *Space Shuttle*: the *Ulysses* Sun probe, the *Galileo* spacecraft to Jupiter, and the *Magellan* probe to Venus. *Magellan* was the first unmanned interplanetary spacecraft launched by NASA since its successful *Pioneer Orbiter*, also to Venus, in 1978. It was also the first spacecraft to employ aerobraking to lower its orbit and thus save fuel. *Magellan* created the first (and currently the best) near-photographic quality, high resolution mapping of Venus's surface features. *Magellan* finally allowed detailed imaging and analysis of craters, hills, ridges, and other geologic formations that was comparable to the visible-light photographic mapping of other planets. Built largely from spare parts from both the *Voyager* and *Galileo* missions, the *Magellan* spacecraft was 15.4 feet (4.6m) long, topped with a 12ft (3.7m) parabolic antenna. *Magellan* was powered by two solar panels. During the mission they gradually degraded, as expected. Because Venus is shrouded by a dense, opaque atmosphere, conventional optical cameras could not be used to image its surface. Instead, *Magellan's* imaging radar used bursts of microwave energy somewhat like a camera flash to illuminate the planet's surface. On October 11, 1994, *Magellan's* orbit was lowered a final time and radio contact was lost the next day. Within two days, the spacecraft became caught in the atmosphere and plunged to the surface. Although much of *Magellan* was vaporized, some sections are thought to have hit the planet's surface intact. Study of the *Magellan* images is providing evidence to better understand the geology of Venus, and the role of impacts, volcanoes, and tectonism in the formation of the surface.

Skylab

The first US space station was NASA's *Skylab* program, started in 1973. NASA used its huge *Saturn 5* rockets to launch a relatively small orbital workshop. The purpose was to prove that people could live and work in space for an extended period. Compared to the *Apollo* capsule, it was spacious, about the size of a small house. Inside, the astronauts did not have to wear spacesuits all the time as in the previous space capsules. Studies were conducted on how well humans adapted to life in space, and data was collected for earth and solar research. Experiments were also conducted in a field called "microgravity" (very close to no gravity at all) to observe how substances behave. One discovery, made by a solar telescope carried on *Skylab*, revealed that the ebbing and waning of the large dark areas of the Sun's atmosphere, called *coronal holes*, affected climatic change on Earth. There were three human *Skylab* missions, with the crews staying aboard the orbital workshop for 28, 59, and 84 days. The first crew manually fixed a broken meteoroid shield, demonstrating that humans could successfully work in space. The *Skylab* program also served as a successful experiment in long-duration human spaceflight.

The International Space Station

In 1984, Congress authorized NASA to build a major new space station as a base for further exploration of space. By 1993, after two re-designs, the facility became known as *Space Station Alpha*. In that same year, Russia, which had many years of experience in long-duration human spaceflight, joined with the US and 14 other international partners to build a joint facility that became known formally as the *International Space Station* (ISS). The ISS is the largest scientific collaboration in history, so expensive that no one country could create and support it. To prepare for building the ISS, NASA participated in a series of *Shuttle* missions to the Russian space station *Mir*, and seven American astronauts lived aboard *Mir* for extended stays. (*Mir* was safely disposed of at the end of its life in March, 2001, through a controlled de-orbit and re-entry and final splashdown in the Pacific.) In 1998, the first two modules of the ISS were launched and joined together in orbit. Other modules soon followed and the first crew arrived in 2000. The ISS was completed in 2004. ISS projects have explored the influence of gravity on a wide range of natural phenomena including its effect on blood flow. Additionally, attempts have been made to grow protein crystals in space, which has prompted major advances in our understanding of the structures of complex biomolecules. Now the *Shuttle* fleet is retired, the ISS is to be supplied with crew and goods by *Soyuz* and the newly developed unmanned European cargo ship, the *Automated Transfer Vehicle*. The use of the ISS will thus be restricted because of the limited numbers of crew who can be transported. Meanwhile the maintenance costs are as high as the cost of *Apollo* while the further usefulness of the ISS is questioned by scientists.

The Science of Space

In addition to human spaceflight programs, scientific probes have explored the Moon, the planets, and other areas of the solar system. Two similar spacecraft, *Pioneer 10* and *Pioneer 11*, launched on March 2, 1972 and April 5, 1973, respectively, traveled to Jupiter and Saturn to study the composition of interplanetary space. *Voyagers 1* and *2*, launched on September 5, 1977 and August 20, 1977, respectively, conducted a "Grand Tour" of the solar system.

In 1990, the *Hubble Space Telescope (HST)* was launched into orbit around the Earth from the *Space Shuttle*. One of the largest and most versatile telescopes, the *HST* has become a vital research tool. Hubble's *Ultra Deep Field* image, for instance, is the most detailed visible-light image ever made of the universe's most distant objects. The *HST* is a collaboration between NASA and the European Space Agency, and is one of NASA's Great Observatories, along with the *Compton Gamma Ray Observatory*, the *Chandra X-ray Observatory*, and the *Spitzer Space Telescope*. Unfortunately, NASA scientists soon discovered that, in the polishing of the *Hubble's* mirror, the edge had been ground too flat. Even this microscopic error significantly limited the instrument's observing power. During a previously scheduled servicing mission, in December, 1993, a team of astronauts performed a dramatic series of spacewalks to install a corrective optics package and other hardware. The hardware functioned like a contact lens and the elegant solution worked perfectly to restore *Hubble's* capabilities. This greatly improved public confidence in NASA, which had been damaged by the disappearance of the *Mars Observer* spacecraft August 21, 1993, just three days before it was to go into orbit around the red planet. There have been five *Hubble* servicing missions, the last occurring in May 2009.

Hubble has helped to resolve some long-standing problems in astronomy, as well as producing results that have required new theories to explain them. Among the primary mission targets it achieved was to measure more accurately the Hubble constant, the rate at which the universe is expanding. *Hubble* also helped to refine estimates of the age of the universe. Moreover it uncovered evidence that, far from decelerating under the influence of gravity, the expansion of the universe may in fact be accelerating. The high-resolution spectra and images provided by the *Hubble* have established the prevalence of black holes in the nuclei of nearby galaxies, showing that black holes are probably common to the centers of all galaxies. Servicing Mission 1 enabled *Hubble* to take sharper images of Jupiter than any since the passage of *Voyager 2* in 1979. The images were crucial in studying the dynamics of the collision of *Comet Shoemaker-Levy 9* in 1994, a kind of event believed to occur once every few centuries. *Hubble* has also enabled discoveries to be made about planets outside the solar system and gamma-ray bursts. While only a small fraction of astronomical objects are accessible to high-resolution ground-based imaging; *Hubble* can perform high-resolution observations of any part of the night sky, and on objects that are extremely faint. Furthermore, space telescopes can study the heavens across the entire electromagnetic spectrum, most of which is blocked by Earth's atmosphere. Finally, the background sky is darker in space than on the ground, because atmospheric airglow washes out faint, low-contrast astronomical objects.

After *Hubble*, *Mars Global Surveyor* was launched on November 7, 1996, and has been mapping Mars since 1998. Using innovative technologies, the *Mars Pathfinder* spacecraft landed on Mars on July 4, 1997 and explored the surface of the planet with its miniature rover, *Sojourner*. The mission was a scientific and popular success, with the world following along via the internet. Additionally, the *Galaxy Evolution Explorer (Galex)* is an orbiting ultraviolet space telescope that was launched on April 28, 2003. During its mission it is making observations at ultraviolet wavelengths to measure the history of star formation in the universe, even beyond the Milky Way, 80 percent of the way back to the Big Bang (10 billion years ago). Partnering with JPL on the mission are the California Institute of Technology, Orbital Sciences Corporation, University of California, Berkeley, Yonsei University, Seoul, Korea, Johns Hopkins University, Columbia University, and Laboratoire d'Astrophysique de Marseille, France.

Over the years, NASA has continued to look for life beyond our planet. In 1996 a probe from the *Galileo* spacecraft that was examining Jupiter and its moon, Europa, revealed that Europa may contain ice or even liquid water, thought to be a key component in any life-sustaining environment.

NASA also continues to investigate whether any Martian meteorites contain microbiological organisms. In March 2009 a rocket bearing the *Kepler* telescope was launched into solar orbit on a three-year mission to scan 100,000 stars for planets which might sustain life.

The *James Webb Space Telescope (JWST)* is a planned infrared space observatory that will partly replace the aging *Hubble Space Telescope* but will not be sensitive to all of the light wavelengths that *Hubble* can see. The main scientific goal is to observe the most distant objects in the universe, those beyond the reach of either ground based instruments or the *Hubble*. The *JWST* project is a NASA-led international collaboration with contributors in 15 nations, including NASA, the European Space Agency and the Canadian Space Agency. The *JWST* will be launched by a European *Ariane 5* rocket. The proposed *Advanced Technology Large-Aperture Space Telescope (AT-LAST)* would be a true replacement for the *Hubble*, able to observe and photograph in the optical, ultraviolet, and infrared wavelengths, but with substantially better resolution than the *Hubble*.

The *New Horizons* robotic spacecraft mission is currently en route to the dwarf planet Pluto. It is expected to be the first spacecraft to fly by and study Pluto and its moons, Charon, Nix, and Hydra. NASA may also approve flybys of one or more other Kuiper Belt Objects. *New Horizons* was launched on January 19, 2006 directly into an Earth-and-solar-escape trajectory, leaving Earth at the fastest speed to date. It flew by Jupiter on February 28, 2007 and Saturn's orbit on June 8, 2008. It will arrive at Pluto on July 14, 2015 then continue into the Kuiper belt.

The *Messenger* mission meanwhile will orbit Mercury after making three flybys of the planet, using data collected during the flybys as an initial guide to perform a more focused investigation of this mysterious world. *Messenger* will investigate six key scientific questions about Mercury's characteristics and environment with a set of miniaturized instruments. The spacecraft will enter Mercury orbit in March 2011 and carry out measurements for one full Earth year.

Aeronautics research

NASA has continued to conduct many types of cutting-edge aeronautics research on aerodynamics, wind shear, and other important topics using wind tunnels, flight testing, and computer simulations. The *National Aerospace Plane* did advanced hypersonic research in such areas as structures, materials, propulsion, and aerodynamics. NASA has also done significant research on flight maneuverability on high speed aircraft which has had a significant impact on civil aircraft design such as that of the *Boeing 777*.

Applications Satellites

NASA did pioneering work on communications satellites in the 1960s. Communications satellites transmit computer data, telephone calls, and radio and television broadcasts. In the 1970s, NASA's *Landsat* program literally changed the way we look at our planet Earth. *Landsat* data has been used in a variety of practical commercial applications such as crop management and fault line detection, and to track many kinds of weather such as droughts, forest fires, and ice floes. NASA has been involved in a variety of other Earth science projects which have yielded important scientific results in such areas as tropical deforestation, global warming, and climate change. Weather satellites furnish the data necessary to provide early warnings of severe storms. Space technology has generated thousands of products for everyday use - everything from velcro, lightweight materials used in running shoes, to respiratory monitors used in hospitals. At the same time, there is a growing problem of space junk, that is old satellites and discarded hardware still in orbit, that may cause an accident.

Exploration of space has taught us to view the Earth, ourselves, and the universe in a new way. While the tremendous technical and scientific accomplishments of NASA demonstrate vividly that humans can achieve previously inconceivable feats, we also are humbled by the realization that Earth is just a tiny "blue marble" in the cosmos.

The future of US space exploration

Under proposals put to Congress by President Obama in 2010, the Shuttle was to be retired as planned. The four-person Orion Crew Exploration Vehicle was to be reinvented as an on-call rescue vehicle for orbiting space crews. The life of the International Space Station was to be extended by at least five years to 2020. Keeping the orbiting outpost open was to provide a laboratory for preparing for long-duration missions further from home. Mr. Obama has called for NASA to focus on exploring more far-flung destinations, where no one has gone before, rather than return to the Moon. Near-Earth asteroids are one possible destination. Another are the "Lagrange points" — areas of space balanced between the Earth and the moon that could serve as gravitational islands for long-term research and even potential fueling depots. The challenge in the Station's second decade will be getting crews to and from it. After the shuttle, NASA and its international partners will be dependent on the small three-person Russian Soyuz spacecraft. The Obama administration's primary focus is to help start a new industry — corporate spacecraft builders that will sell transportation services instead of vehicles to NASA and its partners. Interplanetary missions and other forms of deep-space exploration would require rockets that could provide a much bigger boost, so the President has proposed to invest $3.1 billion in designing a new heavy-lift launch vehicle by 2015. At the time of writing, Congress was still considering amendments to the President's proposals.

MEDICINE

As in physics and chemistry, Americans have dominated the Nobel Prize for physiology or medicine since World War II. About one in three of the new drugs released worldwide each year are developed in the US. The National Institutes of Health, the focal point for biomedical research, have played a key role in this achievement. Consisting of 27 separate institutes, the NIH has a budget of $30.5 billion. The goal of NIH research is knowledge that helps prevent, detect, diagnose, and treat disease and disability - everything from the rarest genetic disorder to the common cold. At any given time, grants from the NIH support the research of about 325,000 investigators, working in every US state and foreign countries around the world. Among these grantees have been 91 Nobel Laureates. Five Nobel winners have made their prize-winning discoveries in NIH laboratories.

NIH research has helped make possible numerous medical achievements. For example, mortality from heart disease, the number-one killer in the US, dropped 41 percent between 1971 and 1991. The death rate for strokes decreased by 59 percent during the same period. Between 1991 and 1995, the cancer death rate fell by nearly 3 percent, the first sustained decline since national record-keeping began in the 1930s. And today more than 70 percent of children who get cancer are cured.

With the help of the NIH, molecular genetics and genomics research have revolutionized biomedical science. In the 1980s and 1990s, researchers performed the first trial of gene therapy in humans and are now able to locate, identify, and describe the function of many genes in the human genome. Scientists predict that this new knowledge will lead to genetic tests for susceptibility to diseases such as colon, breast and other cancers and to the eventual development of preventive drug treatments for persons in families known to be at risk. Perhaps the most exciting scientific development of recent years is the NIH's human genome project. This has constructed a genetic map of humans by analyzing the chemical composition of each of the 30,000-40,000 human genes. The project is expected to take 15 years to complete, at a cost of at least $3 billion.

Research conducted by universities, hospitals, and corporations also contributes to improvement in diagnosis and treatment of disease. NIH funded the basic research on Acquired Immune Deficiency Syndrome (AIDS), for example, but many of the drugs used to treat the disease have emerged from the laboratories of the American pharmaceutical industry; those drugs are being tested in research centers across the country.

One type of drug that has shown promise in treating the AIDS virus is the protease inhibitor. After several years of laboratory testing, protease inhibitors were first given to patients in the US in 1994. One of the first tests (on a group of 20 volunteers) showed that not only did the drug make the amount of virus in the patients' blood almost disappear, but also that their immune systems rebounded faster than anyone had thought possible.

Doctors have combined protease inhibitors with other drugs in "combination therapy." While the results are encouraging, combination therapy is not a cure, and, so far, it works only in the blood; it does not reach into the other parts of the body – the brain, lymph nodes, spinal fluid, and male testes – where the virus hides. Scientists continue to experiment with combination therapy and other ways to treat AIDS, and are making progress in their search for the ultimate solution - a vaccine. NIH has already developed a vaccine for cervical cancer.

The work of Nobel winner Robert Furchgott helped lead to the development of the anti-impotence drug Viagra.

Preventive medicine

While the American medical community has been making strides in the diagnosis and treatment of disease, the American public also has become more aware of the relationship between disease and personal behavior. Since the U.S. Surgeon-General first warned Americans about the dangers of smoking in 1964, the percentage of Americans who smoke has declined from almost 50 percent to approximately 25 percent. Smoking is no longer permitted in most public buildings or on trains, buses, and airplanes traveling within the US, and most American restaurants are divided into areas where smoking is permitted and those where it is not. Studies have linked a significant drop in the rate of lung cancer to a nationwide decline in cigarette smoking.

The federal government also encourages Americans to exercise regularly and to eat healthy diets, including large quantities of fruits and vegetables. More than 40 percent of Americans today exercise or play a sport as part of their regular routine. The per capita consumption of fruits and vegetables has increased by about 20 percent since 1970.

The future

The complexity of biology remains a daunting challenge. In response, the NIH has set out a plan called the *NIH Roadmap* to revolutionize the aims and methods of biomedical research, and in 2002 President Bush doubled the NIH research budget. Under the theme, *New Pathways to*

Discovery, the *NIH Roadmap* addresses the need to understand complex biological systems: future progress in medicine will require quantitative knowledge about the many interconnected networks of molecules that comprise cells and tissues, along with improved insights into how these networks are regulated and interact with each other. After the successful completion of the Human Genome Project, the next frontier is to understand all of the myriad elements of cells and organs that are encoded by DNA and determine how this enormously complex machinery functions in health and disease.

New Pathways to Discovery sets out to capitalize on the sequencing of the human genome. Among the resources to be produced are libraries of chemical molecules that can provide probes of biological networks, innovative tools for capturing real-time images of molecular and cellular events, improved computational infrastructure for biomedical research and tiny, nanotechnology devices capable of viewing and interacting with basic life processes. A long-term goal is to create materials and devices at the level of molecules and atoms to cure disease or repair damaged tissues, such as bone, muscle, or nerve.

Biological, physical and information sciences have converged at an incredible pace. The era of the single-purpose clinical trial conducted in isolation with no standardization across trials is coming to a close. In the future, research will be largely multidisciplinary. Academic centers, community physicians and patients will work together, sometimes internationally.

CHAPTER **6**

THE MEDIA AND TRANSPORTATION

To the press alone, checkered as it is with abuses, the world is indebted for all the triumphs which have been gained by reason and humanity over error and oppression. James Madison, Report on the Virginia Resolutions, 1798

The media and transportation present two complementary images of America, as successive innovations in both fields make yesterday's miracles seem mundane. The print media, which played such an important role in the American Revolution and during the industrial age, often look outmoded and unresponsive when compared with the instant individualism offered by the internet and cell phone technologies of the information age. But a short-focused contrast on the differences between modes of media communication excludes the real importance of the newspaper-based gathering of news for the internet, the range and vitality of radio, and the attention commanded by the fast-paced entertainment and information presented on television, which has by no means lost the battle to dominate popular culture. While no one has yet found a way for newspapers to make money on their websites, innovative partnerships - for example, between professional journalists and citizen journalists, the TV tube and YouTube, bloggers and printed books - are engaging with editors and audiences. This enables higher volumes of trading in the openness of fact and freedom of opinion which gives American democratic culture its unique and essential vitality. In fact the very success of social networking and technologies which provide instant access to facts are giving rise to information overload. No one wants to find themselves on the wrong side of the digital divide, out of business in the marketplace of ideas and short of advertising dollars. As a result, the American media, amongst a wealth of content, present much that is bland and trivial spiced with sensational exaggeration, at times displaying poor news judgment and leaving Americans dangerously uninformed. The blandness, sameness and mediocrity of much of the media, and the ubiquity of advertising, can be attributed to several things: the lack of a significant left wing party, the natural monopolies or near-monopolies of the media in America's scattered cities, and the ownership of media by large chains dependent on the interests of advertisers and the shifts of stock market sentiment. Meanwhile book reading, although not growing, at least remains steady, aided by e-book readers and print-on-demand. Physical communications, on the other hand, present a quite different picture. America's infrastructure is aging, underfunded and short of capacity and short of intermodal connections, although the vehicles that undertake America's human and freight transportation are becoming greener and more fuel-efficient. Most of the cities and suburbs in which America's increasingly urban population now lives are shapeless sprawls produced by affordable automobiles and cheap gasoline. Freedom of movement by car across America's long distances has been bought at the price of more commuting, congestion and pollution, and of severely crimped public transport that limits some citizens' equal opportunity to participate in American life.

FREEDOM OF THE PRESS

The US has the most highly-developed mass media in the world. Nowhere have more consumers gained more access to a supply of daily changing news and information in a common language than in the US. American media companies have a global reach. Google, News Corporation, Apple, Time Warner and others are at the forefront of the digital revolution that will determine the fate of all 21st century economies.

The average American, according to one study, spends about eight hours a day with the print and electronic media—at home, at work, and traveling by car. This total includes four hours watching television, three hours listening to radio, half an hour listening to recorded music, and another half hour reading the newspaper.

The central role of information in American society harks back to a fundamental belief held by the framers of the Constitution: that a well-informed people is the strongest guardian of its own liberties. The framers embodied that assumption in the First Amendment to the Constitution, which provides in part that "Congress shall make no law...abridging the freedom of speech or of the press." A corollary to this clause is that the press functions as a watchdog over government actions and calls attention to official misdeeds and violations of individual rights.

The First Amendment and the political philosophy behind it have allowed the American media extraordinary freedom in reporting the news and expressing opinions. In the 1970s, American newspapers printed the "Pentagon papers," classified documents related to US involvement in the Vietnam War, and investigative *Washington Post* journalists Woodward and Bernstein uncovered the Watergate scandal. In the 1980s, American reporters uncovered the Iran-Contra scandal, and in the 1990s reported the Monica Lewinsky affair, which led to the impeachment of President Clinton. Press reports of official corruption that in some countries would bring arrests and the shutdown of newspapers are made freely in the US, where the media cannot be shut down, where government itself cannot be libeled, and where public officials must prove that a statement is not only false but was made with actual malice before they can recover damages (*New York Times Co. v. Sullivan*, Supreme Court, 1964). Moreover in 1988 the Supreme Court held that public figures cannot circumvent the First Amendment by attempting to recover damages based on emotional distress suffered from parodies.

The tradition of the American newspaper reporter as portrayed in films and literature is one of toughness, controversy, and conflicts between honest reporting and the desire to sell newspapers. Today the newspaper is more of a business (and less of a labor of love) often owned by a large conglomerate or newspaper chain. Although journalists attempt to be objective, and American newspapers and magazines set store by fact-checking, the latter can come under pressure from advertisers, their major source of revenue, threatening to withdraw advertising if certain statements are published. For example, it is noticeable that financial analysts more often recommend that readers buy shares than sell them. Fortunately the range of print and electronic media, which nowadays include websites, forums, wikis and bloggers, counteracts this tendency to some extent. Journalists who have been found to have falsified stories or quotations have been forced to resign. In some cases, newspaper proprietors, such as Australian-born Rupert Murdoch of News Corp, who is now an American citizen, are major business people in their own right and exert considerable influence. Editors, however, decide day-to-day what to print, while the publisher or owner decides general policy. Publishers usually retain the right to veto editorials and to determine political endorsements for high office.

NEWSPAPERS

There are 1,439 daily newspapers, most of them with a local or regional readership. But hard-copy circulations are in decline and 85% of newspapers no longer win more than 50,000 readers per day, as readers turn to the web. In 1990 the press celebrated its 300th anniversary as an American institution.

America's first continuously published newspaper was the *Boston News-Letter,* launched in 1704, which contained, besides the shipping news, government pronouncements, letters from Europe, and whatever smattering of local news was bland enough to pass the censor. Its most sensational story was that of the death of Blackbeard the Pirate. But Benjamin Franklin's elder brother James's *New-England Courant,* launched in 1721 in Boston, marks the real birth of the American newspaper. It was the first unlicensed paper in the colonies—published without authority. The *Courant* contained mostly political essays, opinion, satire, and some word of goings on. James Franklin was the first newspaperman in the world to report the results of a legislative vote count. Newspapers played a large part in stoking opposition to British rule and maintaining American morale during the Revolutionary War. In his *Apology for Printers* (1731) Ben Franklin, with typical Enlightenment optimism, summed up the contemporary journalist's view of the role of newspapers: "when Men differ in Opinion, both Sides ought equally to have the Advantage of being heard by the Publick; and that when Truth and Error have fair Play, the former is always an overmatch for the latter." Newspapers were also critical to the development of American democracy. Marcus Daniel argues in *Scandal & Civility: Journalism and the Birth of American Democracy* (OUP USA, 2009) that without partisan and even scurrilous printers pushing the limits of a free press in the 1790s, the legitimacy of a loyal opposition never would have been established and the new nation, with its vigorous and democratizing political culture, might never have found its feet.

Newspapers multiplied after independence, and American newspaper history features the great battles between editors and proprietors and their rivals. This led to the developments in practice and organization which enabled newspapers to gather news from great distances and circulate it quickly. Two men stand out in early newspaper history: James Gordon Bennett, Sr. (1795-1872) and his son, James Gordon Bennett, Jr. The senior Bennett, who founded the *New York Herald* in 1835, was the pioneer of the newspaper interview, and created the newspaper as a voice in American politics through his endorsement of candidates. He was the first to interview a President, Martin Van Buren, although he endorsed his rival, William Henry Harrison. Bennett created the role of managing editor to coordinate the many activities of newsgathering and newspaper production. The man he appointed, Frederic Harrison, became known as "the father of American journalism."

In 1841 Horace Greeley founded *The New York Tribune*, which quickly became the nation's most influential newspaper until challenged by Henry Raymond's *New York Times* founded 1851. Two media giants, Joseph Pulitzer with *World* (1887) and William Randolph Hearst with the *Journal* (1895), began building newspaper empires after the Civil War. Fiercely competitive, they resorted to "yellow journalism"— sensational and often inaccurate reporting aimed at attracting more readers. Early in the 20th century, newspaper editors found that the best way to attract readers was to give them all sides of a story, without bias. This standard of objective, balanced reporting, with high emphasis on fact-checking, has become one of American journalism's most important traditions. Another dominant feature of early 20th-century journalism was the creation of chains of newspapers operating under the same ownership, led by a group owned by Hearst. This trend accelerated after World War II, and today about 75 percent of all US daily papers are owned by newspaper chains.

Newspapers rather than radio were the real casualty of television. With the advent of television in the 1940s and 1950s, the new electronic medium made inroads on newspaper circulation. Readers began to overlook the afternoon paper, especially as women started to go out to work, because they could watch the day's news on TV. Even so, most cities and communities still have a daily newspaper, appearing either mornings or evenings. But the number of cities with more than one daily paper has continued its downward trend, from 55 in 1999 to 49 in 2000. The number of Sunday papers by contrast rose from 497 in 1946 to 914 in 2005. The combined figure in 2008 was the highest number of newspapers with the highest total circulation - 147 million - in the world. Each weekday, 120 million Americans read a newspaper and 135 million do so on Sundays. Nonetheless, the largest US newspapers have been losing circulation in recent years. The trend can be attributed to the increasing availability of news from television and the internet. Through these, consumers can follow their own preferences. Newspapers, meanwhile, are produced in a uniform general-interest format according to the editors' judgment of the greatest common interest of the average reader, at a time when there are fewer and fewer average readers. Consumers have gone online primarily to access content that they cannot get from traditional mass media packages. Online news coverage can be more up-to-date and offer multimedia, although consumers find newspapers and magazines more convenient and easier to read. Indeed the average user of the average American newspaper's website visits it only two to six times per month, seeing only two to four story pages per visit, compared with the average newspaper's print edition reader reading at least something on all pages and doing so 17 to 20 times per month (i.e., four to five days per week). Content is no longer "king," readers now live in a digital republic.

Most readers (75%) subscribe to a newspaper, which is delivered to their home, rather than buying single issues of it. This is the cheapest way to obtain a newspaper. Otherwise, newspapers can be bought at supermarkets, stores and, in the larger cities, newsstands. There are also vending machines for newspapers. The average daily newspaper has 50-75 pages, divided into sections - news, business, sport, etc. - with the major stories, plus the beginnings of four or five others, on the front page, and color photographs. The news section comes first and as well as current events includes op-eds (opinion-editorials) and letters to the editor. The sports section comes near the end, along with the features section, which contains comics (the funny pages) and advice columns such as *Dear Abby*. Many columns and articles are syndicated from newswires and other services. There are advertisements throughout the paper. This type of newspaper is called a *broadsheet* because of its size; the other type is *tabloid*, which is more a magazine size and focuses on photo spreads and gossip. These can be bought in supermarkets, although actually many customers just glance at them without buying while they are waiting in line at the checkout. Famous among tabloids is New York's *Daily News* ("New York's Hometown Newspaper") founded 1919, winner of ten Pulitzer Prizes, and known for its colorful, blunt headlines. The thick Sunday papers are an American tradition. These carry fewer news stories but more analysis of recent events, together with features, and specialized sections such as sports, lifestyle, travel, regional and community events, and color comics. Often a Sunday paper will have its own magazine section and plenty of advertising inserts.

Tabloid weeklies exist in both newspaper and magazine form. Their subject matter is more sensational than factual: gossip about television and movie stars, UFOs, astrology and the occult, health miracles and, of course, the latest sighting of Elvis Presley. Their headlines scream in an effort to sell. The *National Enquirer*, *Globe* and *National Star* are the three biggest tabloid weeklies. Two publishing companies control the six largest supermarket tabloid weekly newspapers. At least 50 million Americans read these newspapers regularly, read only those newspapers, and rely on television for all their other information.

The top selling newspaper, *USA TODAY*, is the youngest of the market leaders. It was launched as a national newspaper in 1982, after exhaustive research by the Gannett chain. It relies on bold graphic design, color photos, and brief articles to capture an audience of urban readers interested in news "bites" rather than traditional, longer stories. *USA TODAY* is the only truly national American newspaper. *The New York Times*, *Washington Post* and the *Wall Street Journal*, however, are read all over the country. These newspapers put their local area news in a section separate from the world and national news so that it can be omitted in the national editions. The most widely circulated newspaper in New England is the *Boston Globe*, founded 1872 and now owned by The New York Times Company. Investigations by *Globe* reporters uncovered the child sex abuse scandal in Roman Catholic parishes in Massachusetts in 2001-3. The paper was awarded the Pulitzer Prize. The *Globe* also started Peter Gammons' Notes section on baseball, which is syndicated nationwide.

This is a time of crisis for the daily newspaper industry. The rise of cable and satellite television in the 1970s, topical magazines in the 1980s, and the internet has spectacularly altered how individuals choose which information they consume and how. Thus in the 1990s and 2000s, newspaper circulation declined, generally gently, but steadily, and for some papers precipitously. Circulation peaked in 1984 at 63.3 million and has declined since to 53 million in 2008, mostly due to the effect of TV news on afternoon papers. The morning papers actually increased their circulation from 35.7 million in 1984 to 44.5 million in 2007. Ad revenue, $23 billion in 1984, went to a peak of $49.4 billion in 2005 before declining steeply since. While 54 million daily print readers (about 75 percent of all circulation) subscribed for $11 billion, online ad revenue was only $2 billion. Audience share is in long-term decline. In 1992, 71 percent of survey respondents said they read a paper "regularly," but in 2008 only 34 percent read a newspaper "yesterday," and the decline is particularly large among young people. For example, the British newspaper, *The Guardian*, apparently has eclipsed *The New York Times*, *Washington Post,* and *The Boston Globe* as what most American liberals online read each day. Although the British daily circulates a negligible number of printed copies in America, perhaps as many as half *The Guardian* website's 20 million users are from the US, probably more than the number of *The New York Times* website's readers who are. Meanwhile, data from the firms that track American newspaper websites' traffic

(Nielsen and ComScore) show that the average visitor uses the web daily and will visit not one newspaper website but half a dozen or more on any given day.

Much of what has happened to the news industry has been the result of broader economic, technological, demographic and social changes. Most newspapers now belong to giant, publicly owned corporations far removed from the communities they serve. They face the unrelenting quarterly profit pressures from Wall Street now typical of American capitalism. Media owners are accustomed to profit margins that would be impossible in most traditional industries. For example, the now troubled Tribune Company of Chicago, which owns newspapers all across the country, for example, used to expect a 30 percent margin. At the same time, newspapers are no longer the ubiquitous, pervasive news and advertising medium they once were. They are facing fiercer competition from cell phones and the internet, especially from bloggers. In 1964, 81 percent of American adults were regular newspaper readers; by 2000 that number was 55 percent. Young people were the least likely to read a paper. The ways people obtain and share information are becoming more complex, more varied and more flexible. Newspapers are no longer undisputed authorities. A Pew survey showed that 52 percent of Americans only followed national news when something major happened; 63 percent said the same about international news. Editors were shaken by public opinion polls that showed a sharp decline in the credibility of newspapers.

In addition, newspapers are struggling with the profound disruption brought on both by the internet and the rising costs of newsprint and transportation. Online competitors have threatened to capture much of print newspapers' classified advertising, the source of 20 to 40 percent of all newspaper revenues. In 2009 the New York Sun and the Seattle Post-Intelligencer folded, and the Minneapolis Star-Tribune was in bankruptcy. The Audit Bureau of Circulations reported that the *San Francisco Chronicle* had suffered a 25.8% drop in circulation for the six-month period ending September 2009, to 251,782 subscribers, the largest percentage drop in circulation of any major newspaper. The paper has moved to a business model that focuses more on increased subscription fees and less on advertizing and subscriptions, and claims the new strategy is producing significantly improved financial results. For the first nine months of 2008, the Washington Post newspaper business lost $178 million on $600 million of revenue; the company is bailed out by its educational subsidiary and cable television. Even The New York Times has sold off real estate and taken on new borrowing on distress-financing terms.

The key issue is advertising revenue. Newspapers, print or online, are not worth as much to advertisers (mostly auto dealers, realtors and retailers) now as 20 years ago because online outlets such as Autotrader.com, Craigslist, DoubleClick, eBay, Google, Monster.com and local call spots on digital phones give them more outlets. Thus they can drive down advertising rates. The newspapers then cannot afford to produce enough attractive content, they lose readers, and a downward spiral begins. Publishers are at a disadvantage in promoting the efficacy of their product to advertisers when online metrics provide much greater certainty about who is clicking and buying. Circulation revenues only ever covered printing and distribution; advertising revenues are essential for realizing a profit.

The future of newspapers and news-gathering organizations is not clear. There seem to be several options. *The Detroit Free Press* and *The Detroit News* offer a daily digital version, with home delivery of the paper reduced to Thursday, Friday and Sunday. For other papers, an all-digital model supported by advertising is being mooted. *The New York Times* has already abandoned its online subscription-only *Times Select* and is now seeking online advertising revenue; other papers have followed suit. A third option is a voluntary pay model, a form of shareware like public radio or television. Fourthly, the paywall model relies on subscriptions for online versions, at least partly. How these options play out will depend on various factors, including the rate of adoption of SmartPhones with iPhone-sized screens, the pricing and availability of e-readers such as Kindle, and the price for wireless broadband. The survival of a news industry with a full range of news-gathering, content, analysis and comment is a matter of serious concern. Americans look to the press to keep the government accountable, honest and fair.

Changes in the concept of news and the economics of newspapers hit the *Christian Science Monitor* first, because of its relatively small size and the complex logistics of national distribution. The century-old *Monitor*, highly respected, especially for its foreign affairs coverage, turned itself, from April 2009, into the first newspaper with a national audience to shift from a daily print format to an online publication updated continuously each day, together with a daily email edition and weekly print run. The *Monitor's* mission, stated in its first edition is "journalism that seeks to bless humanity, not injure, and that shines light on the world's challenges in an effort to seek solutions." The *Monitor* has won seven Pulitzer prizes and numerous other awards. But the *Monitor's* print circulation, mainly delivered by mail, has trended downward for nearly 40 years. The *Monitor* believes that focusing resources on the fast-growing web audience for news through an online edition will make the *Monitor* quicker with the news and hence more relevant. The *Monitor* hopes that the people who subscribe to the daily will shift to the weekly and that many more who may not have had time to read the daily will find the weekly appeals to them. Going online should increase revenue and reduce costs, cutting the net operating loss by almost 45%. The *Monitor's* website currently attracts about 1.5 million visitors a month. The newspaper wants to encourage much more two-way conversation between readers and *Monitor* staffers to build a community who share the *Monitor's* values. To do so, the paper will offer a portal where editors will point visitors to other areas on the web that are attempting journalism in the same spirit as the *Monitor*. The weekly will feature an in-depth cover story on a major global issue or trend; brief dispatches from *Monitor* correspondents around the globe; the best photographs of the week; special sections on innovation, the environment, and personal finance; as well as Home Forum essays, and a single religious article, as has been the *Monitor's* practice since 1908. The *Monitor* will continue to operate at its current level of international and domestic coverage, with bureaus throughout the globe, and a strong presence in Washington, distinct competitive advantages at a time when other news organizations are cutting back on staff coverage from outside their circulation regions. So far, however, the *Wall Street Journal* is one of the few newspapers to succeed with a subscription model, presumably because businesses will pay for information on which they can base decisions. *The New York Post* also plans to charge for access from 2010.

New technology is enabling newspapers to enlarge their international audiences. *USA TODAY* is edited and composed in Arlington, Virginia, then transmitted via satellite to 32 printing plants around the country and two printing plants serving Europe and Asia. The *International Herald Tribune*, owned jointly by the *New York Times* and the *Washington Post*, is another global newspaper, printed via satellite in 12 cities around the world, and distributed in 181 countries and 100 airlines. In 1992, the *Chicago Sun-Times* began to offer articles through *America Online*, one of the first companies that connected personal computers with the internet. Now, most American newspapers are available on the internet, and anyone with a personal computer and a link to the internet can scan papers from across the country in his or her own home or office. Many newspapers also host blogs.

American newspapers obtain news, especially foreign news, from staff reporters, foreign correspondents, and a number of outside sources, especially press agencies like AP, UPI and Bloomberg LP, and wire services. Larger newspapers also have their own features writers. Features are usually syndicated, which means that one newspaper in an area can buy the sole right to print them. Associated Press (AP), founded by a syndicate of New York newspapers in 1846 and headquartered in New York, is a non-profit news service with 243 bureaus all over the world, serving thousands of daily newspaper, radio, television and online customers with fast coverage in all media and news in all formats—news, photos, graphics, audio and video. AP is known for its high quality, reliability and objectivity and reports that are accurate, balanced and informed. AP is a cooperative owned by its 1,500 US daily newspaper members, who elect a board of directors. AP also operates a radio network for broadcasters in the US. AP has received 49 Pulitzer Prizes, more than any other news organization in the categories for which it can compete, including 30 photo Pulitzers, again the most of any news organization. On any given day, more than half the world's population sees news from AP.

Another international news source, headquartered in Washington D.C., is UPI (United Press International), which since 1907 has been a leading provider of critical news and analysis to media outlets, businesses, governments and researchers worldwide. UPI is a global operation with offices in Beirut, Hong Kong, London, Santiago, Seoul and Tokyo. UPI licenses content directly to print outlets, online media and institutions of all types. In addition, UPI's distribution partners provide content to thousands of businesses, policy groups and academic institutions. Each day UPI publishes its content directly to a growing audience on UPI.com. This includes the NewsTrack newswire consisting of seven topic-specific channels: Top News, Entertainment, Business, Health, Science, Sports and Quirks in the News. UPI's three premium news channels are Emerging Threats, Energy Resources, and Security Industry. Similar products are offered in Spanish and Arabic. UPI's award-winning photo product, Newspictures, covers each day's most compelling scenes of newsmakers from around the globe and includes an Historical Collection. UPI also offers videos: White House Weekly, Man on the Street Issue of the Day, Special Segments, Seiff on Strategy, and Medill Videos. Over 2.8 million unique visitors visit the website every month.

Additionally, Bloomberg L.P., with 135 offices around the world and 10,000 staff, provides real-time business data and analysis. Founded in 1981 by the now Mayor of New York, Michael Bloomberg, who is no longer the CEO, Bloomberg prides itself on innovation, speed and accuracy. Claiming to be the fastest-growing financial information network in the world providing news to 350 newspapers and magazines, Bloomberg holds about one-third of the market. Other news services companies include Dow Jones Newswires, FactSet Research Systems and smaller companies such as New York Financial Press. British-owned Thomson Reuters plc is also headquartered in New York.

Thousands of weekly newspapers serve communities and neighborhoods. Some are given out free and supported by advertising. These weeklies are quite different from the dailies and serve a different purpose. Both kinds of newspapers are used as sources of information about consumer issues, local events, employment and business opportunities, and about the life and needs of the community in general.

TOP US NEWSPAPERS BY CIRCULATION 2008

	Daily	Sunday
USA TODAY	2,284,219	N/A
The Wall Street Journal	2,069,463	N/A
The New York Times	1,077,256	1,476,400
Los Angeles Times	773,884	1,101,981
The Daily News - New York, NY	703,137	704,157
The New York Post	702,488	401,315
Washington Post	673,180	890,163
Chicago Tribune	541,663	898,703
Houston Chronicle	494,131	632,797
Arizona Republic - Phoenix, AZ	413,332	515,523

The Pulitzer Prizes

The Pulitzer Prizes, awarded annually in April, are regarded as the highest national honor in newspaper journalism, literary achievement and musical composition. First awarded under the will of Joseph Pulitzer in 1917, they have achieved worldwide fame. Pulitzer endowed the prizes to inspire journalists to strive for excellence and thus maintain a free press. In an article in the *North American Review* in May 1904 Pulitzer wrote:

> "Our Republic and its press will rise or fall together. An able, disinterested, public-spirited press, with trained intelligence to know the right and courage to do it, can preserve that public virtue without which popular government is a sham and a mockery. A cynical, mercenary, demagogic press will produce in time a people as base as itself. The power to mould the future of the Republic will be in the hands of the journalists of future generations."

Pulitzer himself was a Hungarian immigrant who arrived practically penniless and followed a distinguished journalistic career. A passionate fighter against crime and corruption, he transformed the daily *St Louis Post-Dispatch* into one of the great independent newspapers of America. He introduced the meaningful headline so that the reader grasped the essence of an article in the first paragraph. His motto, "Accuracy! Accuracy! Accuracy!" was displayed in every one of his newsrooms. He made journalistic history with his crusades for principles and ideas rather than the prejudices of interest groups. He left $2 million to fund a School of Journalism at Columbia University, New York City, and the Pulitzer Prizes. The award in poetry was established in 1922 and that for nonfiction in 1962.

The Pulitzer Prizes are nowadays available in 21 categories. Since the inception of the prizes, the journalism categories have been expanded and repeatedly redefined to keep abreast of the evolution of American journalism. The cartoons prize was created in 1922, the prize for photography in 1942; and in 1968 photography was divided into spot or breaking news, and feature. With the development of computer-altered photos, the board stipulated in 1995 that "no entry whose content is manipulated or altered, apart from standard newspaper cropping and editing, will be deemed acceptable."

The other categories of Pulitzer Prize are: fiction, preferably dealing with American life; history of the United States; biography or autobiography; a volume of original verse; nonfiction that is not eligible for consideration in any other category; and a musical composition that has had its first performance or recording in the US during the year.

A Pulitzer Prize Winner may be an individual, a group of individuals, or a newspaper's staff. Only US citizens are eligible to apply for the Prizes in Letters, Drama and Music (with the exception of the History category in Letters where the book must be a history of the US but the author may be of any nationality). For the Journalism competition, entrants may be of any nationality, but work must have appeared in a US newspaper published at least once a week or on a newspaper's website. Online-only US websites that are published at least weekly, that are primarily dedicated to original news reporting and coverage of ongoing stories, and that adhere to the highest journalistic principles, are eligible, as are US newspaper websites. Prizes are not awarded to printed magazines and broadcast media and their respective websites.

More than 2,400 entries are submitted each year, and only 21 awards are normally made by the 102 distinguished judges, who serve on 20 separate juries and are asked to make three nominations in each of the 21 categories. It is up to the Nominating Juries and The Pulitzer Prize Board to determine what makes a work "distinguished" and eligible for a Prize. Nominations are often hotly debated. In 20 categories the winners receive a $10,000 cash award and a certificate. The winner in the Public Service category of the Journalism competition is awarded a gold medal. The Public Service prize is always awarded to a newspaper, not an individual, although an individual may be named in the citation. Since 1984, Pulitzer winners have received their prizes from the president of Columbia University at a modest luncheon. (The board has declined offers to transform the occasion into a television extravaganza.) For most recipients of the Pulitzer Prizes, the cash award is only incidental to the prestige accruing to them and their works. Numerous competitions bestow far larger cash awards, yet do not rank in public perception with the Pulitzers. The Pulitzer accolade usually translates into commercial gain.

John F. Kennedy, the only US President to be awarded a Pulitzer Prize, was awarded the 1957 Prize in Biography for his book *Profiles in Courage*. Gwendolyn Brooks, awarded the 1950 Pulitzer Prize in Poetry for "Annie Allen," was the first African American to be awarded the Prize. Famous recipients of the Pulitzer Prize also include Margaret Mitchell, Ernest Hemingway, Eudora Welty, Harper Lee, and William Faulkner for Fiction; Robert Frost for Poetry; Roger Ebert for Criticism; and Tennessee Williams, Arthur Miller, Rodgers and Hammerstein, and Stephen Sondheim for Drama.

Criticisms of the American press

Over the last 20 years, a growing chorus of criticism has voiced its concerns about the priorities, standards and sustainability of the American press. Critics allege that the press as a whole has ceased to do its job competently, let alone aspire to the ideals of Pulitzer.

Aggressive, independent journalism is widely believed to strengthen democracy, check the abuse of power, support the weaker members of society, and connect all citizens to one another. Good journalism, it is held, enriches Americans by giving them both useful information for their daily lives and a sense of participation in the wider world. It makes possible the cooperation among citizens critical to a civilized society. But citizens cannot function as a community unless they share a common body of information about their neighbors, their governing bodies, their community, and their environment. That information is the essence of the news. The best journalism probes into it, makes sense of it and makes it accessible to everyone. Good journalism entertains as well as educates. But bad journalism - failing to report important news, or shallow, sensational, inaccurate or unfair reporting - can leave people dangerously uninformed. Yet at a time when nearly half of eligible Americans do not vote, the news media have steadily reduced their coverage of government and elections. Although Americans are more globally connected than ever, most news media have steadily and substantially reduced their coverage of foreign news. This fact was widely discussed after the terrorist attacks of September 2001, when foreign stories suddenly became fashionable again.

Bad journalism can misinform. Many newspapers, for example, routinely overemphasize crime news: "If it bleeds, it leads." Thus, Americans continue to fear that crime is getting worse when it has actually been decreasing for years. Bad journalism can mislead. Glowing, uncritical coverage of new technology companies in the late 1990s encouraged many Americans to sink their savings into speculative stocks and mutual funds that soon crashed, collectively costing them billions of dollars. Much bad journalism is just lazy and superficial. Newspapers fill columns with fluffy trivia and rewrites of press releases, and as entertainment this may be harmless in itself. But bad news judgment is more damaging; and too much news in recent years seems to critics to have been untrustworthy, irresponsible, misleading or incomplete. Too many of those who own and lead the nation's news media have evaded their responsibility to provide a service, critics claim.

Before the crisis of 2008, many in the news business had become convinced that in an era of unparalleled prosperity and security, Americans would rather be entertained than informed. Papers tried to attract readers and advertisers with light features – shopping was a favorite - reducing serious reporting on business, government, the country and the world. Most newspapers shrank their reporting staffs, along with the space they devoted to news. In the eighties, newspapers all over America copied the color and graphics of *USA TODAY* (but rarely if ever gained new readers). The temptation to push serious news aside in favor of glitz and melodrama has too often been irresistible. A national infatuation with celebrities, both encouraged and exploited by news media, has had a profound influence on journalism. It has also tempted many journalists to try to become celebrities themselves. At the same time, there is debate about how much of a person's private life should become public if he or she runs for public office. Politicians from both parties complain that the press is "out to get" them, and some people claim that investigative reporting deters people from seeking public office. To the contrary, veteran blogger Bob Somerby is among those who claim that the relationship between newspapers and those in power is too cozy.

Aside from criticisms of journalists, critics allege that concentration of ownership reduces the quality, diversity and trustworthiness of newspapers, although little data about concentration is in the public domain. Single company ownership of media in a given market is now permitted up to 45% (up from 25% in 1985). In order to ensure the viability of America's newspapers, in 2007 the Federal Communications Commission (FCC) eliminated some media ownership rules which forbade a single company to own both a newspaper and a television or radio station in the same city. The Commission will presume that newspaper-broadcast combinations in the top 20 markets are in the public interest, so long as eight independent voices, including newspapers, remain and the stations are not among the top four in the market. The FCC will also allow newspaper-radio combinations but require no voices test.

Newspapers are being challenged to reinvent themselves in ways that profitably combine their past strengths and high brand recognition with the power of the internet. The alternative, if newspapers are to survive to carry out their vital social and economic roles, seems to be a government-funded news service, possibly supplemented by private capital, and consequently less independent. Pundits predict that as many as half of the existing dailies will disappear, starting with the regionals and smaller papers, and that even some of the best-known titles will not appear in print for more than a decade more.

MAGAZINES

The first American magazines appeared a half-century after the first newspapers and took longer to attain a wide audience. Most magazines contain news, feature articles, reviews, stories and color pictures, which establish their identity. They often have a page of readers' letters commenting on articles in previous issues or asking for advice. American magazines usually carry advertisements, and some publish their articles in widely separated sections within the magazines, with advertisements and parts of other articles appearing between, which can be confusing for readers unfamiliar with this type of layout. In 1893, *Munsey's Magazine,* the first mass-circulation magazine, appeared, and in 1923, Henry Luce launched *Time,* the first weekly news magazine. *Time,* with its distinctive writing style, is now published in four international versions. To appear on the front cover, or to be named *Time* Man or Woman of the Year, is considered a great honor. Other weeklies are the New York-based *Newsweek,* which covers politics, science, society and culture for its three million readers, and the conservative opinion-magazine, The *Weekly Standard.*

Newsweek has decided to reposition itself as a high-end magazine selling in-depth commentary, following *Time* magazine's emergency retrenchment along similar lines. This accelerates a process by which the 76-year-old *Newsweek* will purposely reduce its circulation from 2.7 million to a little more than half of that. (Its circulation was nearly 3.5 million in 1988.) Likewise, *Time's* circulation, which 20 years ago was close to 5 million, is now 3.4 million. Both newsweeklies are seeking to avoid the fate of *U.S. News & World Report,* which, after years of decline, has become bi-weekly with a monthly magazine. It has a particular focus on economic and business news and a more conservative viewpoint. With ever-shorter news cycles, daily newspapers have effectively become newsweekly-style digests themselves and made the traditional newsweeklies out of date. By contrast, though, one weekly news digest, the British-owned *Economist,* is thriving. Its advertising revenues increased in 2008 by 25 percent, according to the Publisher's Information Bureau, while *Newsweek's* and *Time's* dropped 27 percent and 14 percent, respectively.

Famous among magazines which present longer articles is the weekly *New Yorker* (founded 1925) which, as well as news and politics, contains fiction, humor and the world famous cartoons. Writers have included Ogden Nash, Dorothy Parker, S. J. Perelman and James Thurber. The *New Yorker* regularly sponsors readings and author and artist appearances, and even has an annual three-day festival. The monthlies *National Geographic* and *Scientific American* have become famous for in-depth treatment of their specialist subjects. The *National Geographic* is renowned especially for its beautiful photographs and maps as well as its coverage of different countries, peoples and animals. Its nine million readers must join the National Geographic Society to receive the magazine. The Society also publishes books and other magazines and has an associated TV series. *Scientific American* covers discoveries and research in a more technical way than general interest magazines. It too has an associated PBS TV program, *Scientific American Frontiers*. The *Atlantic* magazine is the oldest and leading literary magazine. Among the most popular *general interest* magazines (also called *consumer magazines*) are the weekly *TV Guide* and *People*. Apart from information about times and channels, stars and shows, the *TV Guide* publishes serious articles about television for its 13 million readers. *People* publishes photographs and gossip about the stars and also news articles.

The arrival of television cut into the advertising revenues enjoyed by mass-circulation magazines, and some weekly magazines eventually folded. (Even *Life* magazine, famous for its large photographs, went out of circulation for a few years before being revived.) Publishers responded by trying to appeal more to carefully defined audiences than to the public at large. Magazines on virtually any topic imaginable have appeared, including *AutoWeek, Model Railroading, and Tennis*. Other magazines have targeted segments within their audience for special attention. *TV Guide, Time*, and *Newsweek*, for example, publish regional editions, and there are many regional magazines such as *Alaska* and *New York Magazine*. There are also a large number of specialist magazines catering to industries, trades and professions. Several magazines are attempting to personalize the contents of each issue according to an individual reader's interests.

Women generally buy more magazines than men. There are about two dozen major women's magazines. Upmarket glossy magazines such as *Vogue* (founded 1892) and *Harper's Bazaar* (1867) focus on fashion, beauty and the arts. Magazines aimed at younger women tend to be written in a franker, more chatty style. They contain articles on fashion, makeup, food, dieting and fitness, offer advice on careers and personal problems, and may also include film and book reviews. The monthly *Cosmopolitan* (founded 1972) was the first to write frankly about sex, although many people now find its viewpoint old fashioned. *Cosmopolitan* remains the top-selling US magazine with 1.8 million single-copy sales at newsstands in 2008, according to the Audit Bureau of Circulations. Meanwhile *Good Housekeeping* (founded 1885), also a monthly, covers houses, decoration, fashion and food.

A growing magazine market is targeted at men. Highly-illustrated magazines such as *Esquire* (founded 1933) have gained an international following for their articles on arts, sport, fashion and business, aimed at men aged 20-40, while *Gentlemen's Quarterly* is also famous. Magazines for younger men focus on cars, clothes and music. Teen magazines contain information and advice about clothes, school, friends and entertainment. Aimed mostly at older girls, they are sometimes read by younger teens. Some parents disapprove of these magazines because they contain stories about boys and sex.

Specialization more than quadrupled the number of magazines published in the US from 6,960 in 1970 to 31, 390 in 2001, but, according to the Magazine Publishers of America, the number has since fallen by over a quarter to 22,652 in 2007, when 90 magazines had a circulation of over one million. As many as 289 magazines were launched in 2002 alone, ranging in coverage from sports (*Total Sport, Top Gear* and *Regatta*) to automotive and computers, ethnic interest (*Ebony*, a highly-illustrated magazine aimed at African American women), food, movies and home service. Among the best-known movie magazines are *Empire, Neon,* and *Sight and Sound*. The average household now buys six different magazines in a year, and surveys show that magazines, perhaps surprisingly, still reach a significantly greater proportion of all age groups than television. Restricted circulation magazines aimed at customers can be bought at supermarkets or read on airline flights. Clubs and associations often publish magazines for their members.

TOP US CONSUMER MAGAZINES BY CIRCULATION 2008

1. *AARP The Magazine* 24,444,293
2. *AARP Bulletin* 23,815,128
3. *Reader's Digest* 9,322,833
4. *Better Homes And Gardens* 7,638,912
5. *National Geographic* 5,042,672
6. *Good Housekeeping* 4,632,531
7. *Family Circle* 4,011,530
8. *Woman's Day* 3,930,566
9. *Ladies' Home Journal* 3,911,188
10. *AAA Westways* 3,775,228

The first two are aimed at retired persons.

In 1993, *Time* became the first magazine to offer an on-line edition that subscribers can call up on their computers before it hits the newsstands. In 1996, software magnate Bill Gates started *Slate*, a magazine covering politics and culture that was intended to be available exclusively on-line (*Slate*'s publisher soon decided to add a print version.)

As with newspapers, many Americans buy magazines by subscription, because it is cheaper than buying them singly. Nearly all libraries have a periodicals section offering the newest issues of magazines and access to back issues, often many years' worth in microfilm or bound volumes. These might include *People*, *Money* (about a subject dear to American hearts), news-magazines, journals of opinion like *Harpers*, *National Review* or the *New Republic*, possibly fashion-oriented woman's magazines like *Cosmopolitan* or *Vogue* and family-oriented ones like *Family Circle*, business magazines, and perhaps a few of the specialty magazines, like high-tech *Wired* or *Fast Company*.

Newsletters

Meanwhile, a new hybrid of newspaper and magazine became popular, starting in the 1970s: the newsletter. Printed on inexpensive paper and often as short as four to six pages, the typical newsletter appears weekly or biweekly. Newsletters gather and analyze information on specialized topics. *Southern Political Report*, for example, covers election races in the southern states, while *FTC Watch* covers the actions of the Federal Trade Commission. Newsletters can be the product of small staffs, sometimes only a single reporter who produces the issue by computer. An estimated 300,000 US newsletters are published on the web. The newsletter has been joined by the "'zine," highly personalized magazines of relatively small circulation, sometimes with contents that are meant to shock. *Afraid*, for instance, is a monthly 'zine devoted to horror stories. Fanzines are devoted to singers, groups and sports clubs.

BLOGS

A blog (short for *weblog*) is a website, usually maintained by an individual, with regular descriptions of events, commentary, or other material such as graphics or video. "Blog" can also be used as a verb, meaning to maintain or add content to a blog. The term 'blog' and its cognates were coined at the end of 1997.

Many blogs provide news or commentary on a particular subject. Others serve as online diaries where people keep a running account of their personal lives. Indeed the modern blog evolved from the online diary. A typical blog combines text, images, and links to other blogs, web pages, and other media related to its topic. Entries are commonly displayed in reverse-chronological order. The facility for readers to leave comments and interact with the author and other blog users is an important feature of many blogs.

Dave Winer's *Scripting News* (http://www.scripting.com/) is credited with being one of the oldest and longest running weblogs. But the first proper blog, defined as web based commentary with links to other articles, was started by Dr. Glen Barry in 1993. His *Forest Protection Blog* (originally entitled *Gaia's Forest Conservation Archives*) at http://forests.org/blog/ was also the first political blog, as Dr. Barry campaigned there for forest protection. The blog has been on the web continuously since January 1995, making it the web's first and longest continuously running blog. The work has since evolved into one of the world's largest environmental portals. Other early blogs which are still running include *Open Diary*, launched in October 1998, which innovated the reader comment, where readers could add comments to other writers' blog entries. Brad Fitzpatrick started *LiveJournal* in March 1999 to keep high school friends updated on his activities. The blog is still most popular with people aged 18-24, who enjoy such forums as *Oh No They Didn't* (ONTD) celebrity gossip. *LiveJournal* users each have a webpage of their own, which includes the comments left by other users. In addition, each user has a journal page, which shows all of his or her most recent journal entries, along with links to the comment pages. The most distinctive feature of *LiveJournal* is the "friends list," which gives the site a strong social aspect in addition to the blog services. Each user has a "friends" page, which collects the most recent journal entries of the people on his or her friends list. Who should count as a "friend" has been controversial here and on other social networking sites. In 2005 the operating company was sold and *Live Journal* is currently operated from Russia. *Pitas.com* (http://pitas.com/) was created in July 1999 by Andrew Smales as an easier alternative to maintaining a "news page" on a web site. The site's software saves time on editing and uploading. Smales followed up with *Diaryland* (http://members.diaryland.com/edit/welcome.phtml) in September 1999, offering a personal diary community where users could control who sees the diary and what it looks like. The first major political blog in the US was Bob Somerby's *The Daily Howler*, which was started in 1998, followed by Mickey Kaus's kausfiles, now on *Slate* in 1999.

Blogs have sparked controversies over privacy and personal security, inappropriate use, advertisements (which can be crucial to the blog host's survival), paid services, and the fear that users' posts may be monitored by governments. One consequence of blogging is the possibility of attacks or threats against the blogger, sometimes without apparent reason. Internet trolls who would attack a blogger with threats or insults can be emboldened by anonymity. It is common for blogs to feature advertisements either to benefit the blogger financially or to promote the blogger's favorite causes. The popularity of blogs has also given rise to fake blogs where a company will create a fictional blog as a marketing tool to promote a product.

Types of Blogs

There are many different types of blogs, differing not only in the type of content, but also in the way that content is delivered or written.

Personal Blogs

The personal blog, an ongoing diary or commentary by an individual, is the traditional, most common blog. Few personal blogs are widely read, but some have gained an extensive following. A special type of personal blog is *microblogging*, an extremely detailed blog that seeks to capture a single moment. Sites such as *Twitter* allow bloggers to share thoughts and feelings instantly with friends and family and is much faster than e-mailing or writing. This form of social media is popular with people who are too busy to keep in touch.

Corporate Blogs

A blog can be for business purposes, either used internally to enhance the communication and culture in a corporation, or externally for marketing, branding or public relations.

Question Blogging

Qlogs are devoted to answering questions. Questions can be submitted on a form, or through email or other means such as telephone or VOIP. Qlogs can be used to display shownotes from podcasts. Many question logs use publication tools such as RSS.

By Media Type

A blog comprising videos is called a *vlog*, one comprising links is called a *linklog*, a site containing a portfolio of sketches is called a *sketchblog*, one comprising photos is called a *photoblog*. Blogs with shorter posts and mixed media types are called *tumblelogs*. Blogs written on typewriters and then scanned are called *typecast* or *typecast* blogs. A rare type of blog hosted on the Gopher Protocol is known as a *Phlog*. Most blogs are primarily textual, although some focus on art (*artlog*), photographs (*photoblog*), sketches (*sketchblog*), videos (*vlog*), music (*MP3 blog*), audio (*podcasting*). These form part of a wider network of social media. With the advent of video blogging, the word *blog* has come to mean any type of media where the blogger expresses an opinion or simply talks about something.

By Device

A blog can also be defined by which type of device is used to compose it. A blog written on a mobile phone or PDA can be called a *moblog*.

By Genre

Some blogs focus on a particular subject, such as politics, travel, houses, fashion, projects, education, niches, classical music, quizzing and law (often referred to as a *blawg*) or *dreamlogs*. While not a legitimate type of blog, one used for the sole purpose of spamming is known as a *Splog*.

The community of all blogs is known as the *blogosphere*. Blogs can be interconnected through blogrolls, comments, linkbacks (refbacks, trackbacks or pingbacks) and backlinks. Discussions in the blogosphere have been used by the media as a gauge of public opinion on various issues. A collection of local blogs is sometimes referred to as a *bloghood*. Several blog search engines are used to search blog contents. These include *Bloglines*, *BlogScope*, and *Technorati*. *Technorati*, which is among the most popular blog search engines, provides current information on both popular searches and tags used to categorize blog postings. There are several online communities that connect people to blogs, and bloggers to other bloggers, including *BlogCatalog* and *MyBlogLog*. As of December 2007, blog search engine *Technorati* was tracking more than 112 million blogs. Blogs are given rankings by *Technorati* based on the number of incoming links and by *Alexa Internet* based on the Web hits of *Alexa Toolbar* users. *Technorati* has rated *Boing Boing* (http://boingboing. net/) the most-read group-written blog.

Researchers such as *tailrank.com* have analyzed how blogs become popular. There are essentially two measures of popularity: citations and affiliation (i.e., blogroll). These studies have concluded that, while it takes time for a blog to become popular through blogrolls, links (permalinks) can boost popularity more quickly, and are perhaps a better indication of popularity than blogrolls, since they show that people are actually reading the blog and deem it valuable.

Many bloggers, particularly those in participatory journalism, distance themselves from the mainstream media, while others are members of those media working through a different channel. Some institutions see blogging as a means of getting around the media filter and pushing messages directly to the public. This has led some critics to worry that bloggers respect neither copyright nor the role of the mass media in presenting credible news. Bloggers and other contributors to user-generated content were responsible for *Time* magazine naming their 2006 Person of the Year as "You." Many mainstream journalists, meanwhile, write their own blogs, well over 300, according to *CyberJournalist.net's J-blog* list. Some bloggers have appeared on radio and television: Duncan Black (known widely by his pseudonym, *Atrios*), Glenn Reynolds (*Instapundit* – libertarian Republican), Markos Moulitsas Zúniga (*Daily Kos* – liberal Democrat), Alex Steffen (*Worldchanging*) and Ana Marie Cox (*Wonkette*). In contrast, Hugh Hewitt is a mass-media personality who adds to his reach in "old media" by being an influential blogger. Equally, many established authors, for example, Mitzi Szereto have started using blogs to update fans on their current works and also to expand into new areas of writing. Author Andrew Sullivan's influential *Daily Dish* now appears on *Atlantic Monthly*.

Many bloggers, such as Salam Pax, Ellen Simonetti, Jessica Cutler, and ScrappleFace have published books based on their blogs. Blog-based books have been given the name *blook*. Christian Lander in January 2008 started a blog called *Stuff White People Like* (stuffwhitepeoplelike.com), which pokes fun at the manners and mores of a specific species of young, hip, upwardly mobile whites. Lander's site, which formed the basis for a book of the same name, distills the identity crisis and apologetic attitudes plaguing well-meaning, well-off white kids in a post-white American panorama. Yet many of these books have not sold as well as expected, only Tucker Max reaching the *New York Times Bestseller List*.

Several cases of defamation or liability against bloggers have been brought before the national courts, with mixed results. Internet Service Providers (ISPs), in general, are immune from liability for information that originates with third parties. But in *John Doe v. Patrick Cahill*, the Delaware Supreme Court held that great efforts had to be made to identify anonymous bloggers. Aaron Wall was sued by *Traffic Power* for defamation and publication of trade secrets in 2005. According to *Wired* magazine, *Traffic Power* had been "banned from Google for allegedly rigging search engine results." Wall and other "white hat" search engine optimization consultants had exposed *Traffic Power* in what they claimed was an effort to protect the public. But the case was dismissed.

In general, anonymity has proved ineffective in protecting the blogger. In particular, employees who blog about their employer are liable to be held responsible for blogging that affects the brand recognition of their employer. In fall 2004, flight attendant Ellen Simonetti was fired for what were deemed by her employer, Delta Air Lines, to be inappropriate photographs of herself in uniform on an airplane, and because of comments posted on her blog "Queen of Sky: Diary of a Flight Attendant." She subsequently wrote a book based on her blog. This case highlighted the issue of freedom of expression v. employer rights and responsibilities, and received wide media attention. Simonetti took legal action against the airline for "wrongful termination, defamation of character and lost future wages." The suit was postponed while Delta was in bankruptcy proceedings. Mark Jen was terminated in 2005 as an Assistant Product Manager at Google for discussing corporate secrets on his personal blog, then called *99zeros* and hosted on the Google-owned Blogger service. He blogged about unreleased products and company finances a week before the company's earnings announcement. In another case, Mark Cuban, owner of the Dallas Mavericks, was fined $250,000 by the NBA during the 2006 playoffs for criticizing officials on the court and in his blog. Jessica Cutler, aka "The Washingtonienne," blogged about her sex life while employed as a congressional assistant. After she was fired, she wrote a novel based on her experiences and blog: *The Washingtonienne: A Novel*. Cutler was sued by one of her former lovers in a case that could establish the extent to which bloggers are obligated to protect the privacy of their real life associates.

Blogs have attracted increasing attention for their role in breaking, shaping, and spinning news stories. The Iraq war saw bloggers taking measured and passionate points of view that went beyond the traditional left-right divide. In December 2002, Josh Marshall's *talkingpointsmemo. com* blog and many others called attention to comments made by Senate Majority Leader Tent Lott at a party honoring Senator Strom Thurmond, suggesting that the US would have been better off had Thurmond been elected President in 1948. Lott's critics saw these comments as tacit approval of racial segregation, a policy advocated by Thurmond's campaign. This view was reinforced by documents and recorded interviews dug up by bloggers. Though Lott's comments were made at a public event attended by the media, no major media organizations reported on his controversial comments until after blogs broke the story. Blogging helped to create a political crisis that forced Lott to step down as majority leader. Similarly, blogs were among the driving forces behind the "Rathergate" scandal, when television journalist Dan Rather presented documents on the CBS show *60 Minutes* on September 8, 2004 that conflicted with accepted accounts of President Bush's military service record. Bloggers declared the documents to be forgeries and presented evidence and arguments in support of that view. Subsequently, CBS apologized for what it said were inadequate reporting techniques (see *Little Green Footballs* http://littlegreenfootballs.com/weblog/). Many bloggers view this scandal as the advent of blogs' acceptance by the mass media, both as a news and opinion source and as a means of applying political pressure. Though often seen as partisan gossips, bloggers sometimes lead the way in bringing key information to public light, with mainstream media having to follow their lead. More often, however, news blogs tend to react to material already published by the mainstream media. Meanwhile, an increasing number of experts are blogging. By 2004, the role of blogs became increasingly mainstream, as political consultants, news services, and candidates began using them as tools for outreach and opinion forming. Blogging was established by politicians and political candidates, such as Howard Dean and Wesley Clark, to express opinions on war and other issues, and cemented blogs' role as a news source. Even politicians not actively campaigning began to blog to bond with constituents. In January 2005, *Fortune* magazine listed eight bloggers that business people "could not ignore": Peter Rojas, Xeni Jardin, Ben Trott, Mena Trott, Jonathan Schwartz, Jason Goldman, Robert Scoble, and Jason Calacanis.

POPULAR BLOGS

Rank	Blog	Links*
1	Huffington Post, huffingtonpost.com	24,166
2	TechCrunch, techcrunch.com	23,264
3	Engadge, engadget.com	22,365
4	Gizmodo, gizmodo.com	22,073
5	Boing Boing, boingboing.net	16,974
6	LifeHacker, lifehacker.com	15,446
7	Ars-Technica (CA), arstechnica.com	14,725
8	I Can Has Cheezburger?, icanhascheezburger.com	11,770
9	Mashable! The Social Network Blog, mashable.com	11,739
10	Daily Kos, dailykos.com	10,192
11	ReadWriteWeb, readwriteweb.com	10,175
12	Smashing Magazine, smashingmagazine.com	9,452
13	Official Google Blog, googleblog.blogspot.com	8,867
14	Seth's Blog, sethgodin.typepad.com	8,785
15	Blog Tips To Help You Make Money Blogging, problogger.net	8,566
16	Dosh Dosh, doshdosh.com	8,448
17	Perez Hilton, perezhilton.com	8,440
18	Gawker, gawker.com	7,993
19	PostSecret, postsecret.blogspot.com	7,773
20	TreeHugger, treehugger.com	7,599
21	Copyblogger, copyblogger.com	6,627
22	Valleywag, valleywag.com	6,329
23	Think Progress, thinkprogress.org	6,251
24	Shoemoney, shoemoney.com	6,071
25	The Consumerist, consumerist.com	6,047

* Number of other distinct blogs linked to it in the previous 6 months

BOOKS

More new books are published in America than anywhere else except, sometimes, Britain. The size of the economy, the scope of science, technology and engineering, and the high value that Americans place on freedom of speech and freedom of information all help to explain why. Book publishing is a fast-paced world of thousands of publishing companies employing over 70,000 staff, issuing thousands of new titles annually (172,000 in 2005), keeping 1.5 million titles in print and generating $19 billion annually in sales. Then there are the printing, distribution and bookselling industries that work closely with publishing. Historically the book industry was centered in New York, Boston, Philadelphia and Chicago but, while New York City still headquarters the most companies, the next most important publishing centers are now California, New Jersey and Florida.

Book publishing has been revolutionized by the internet. Nowadays, for example, academics produce electronic journals and distribute academic materials without the need for publishers. The number of published papers doubles about every ten years. Traditional academic publishers, however, provide the key benefit of peer review, the impartial assessment of research by academic colleagues, and this vital role has not yet been taken over by online publishing, even with the advent of social networking and online document sharing.

Writers in a specialized field or with a narrower appeal have found alternatives to the mass market in the form of small presses and self-publishing. Niche publishers sell through all available outlets. Book clubs market almost entirely to retailers. More recently, alternatives to traditional publishing have come to include print on demand and ebook format, such as those available from market leader, *Outskirts Press*. These provide an outlet for authors who believe that mainstream publishing will not meet their needs, or who can make more money from direct sales than they could from bookstore sales because of the high royalties they can get. Such authors include popular speakers who sell books after speeches. Ebooks have been multiplying since 2005. Google, Amazon and Sony have been leaders in working with publishers and libraries to digitize books. Meanwhile several ebook readers have been launched, including Amazon's *Kindle*, the Apple *iPhone*, the *Palm* reader and the *Sony Reader*. Accessible publishing uses the digitization of books to mark them up into XML and sell in multiple formats such as audiobooks, Braille and DAISY, and large print sizes, for those with difficulty reading.

In contrast to commercial publishing, there is nonprofit publishing, by such organizations as university presses or medical charities. A third approach is open access publishing, the online distribution of individual articles and academic journals without charge to readers and libraries. The pioneers of Open Access journals are *BioMed* and the *Public Library of Science* (PloS). There is also open source publishing, where volunteers participate in editing. Well-known examples are the various wiki projects, such as *Wikiprofessional, Wikipedia, Wikiuniversity*, and *Citizendium*.

Many other media engage in publishing. Radio, television, cinemas, VCDs, DVDs, music systems, games, computer hardware and mobile telephony publish to their audiences. The marketing of a major film often includes spin-offs such as a novel, comic version, soundtrack album, game, model, toys and promotional items. For example, Ballantine Del Rey Lucasbooks has the exclusive rights to *Star Wars* in the US. The game industry self-publishes through BL Publishing/Black Library (*Warhammer*) and Wizards of the Coast (*Dragonlance, Forgotten Realms*, etc.). Sales of these multimedia works frequently outperform the average stand-alone published work.

e-books

Digital books are starting to transform reading. A budding niche market in the $25 billion per year publishing industry, they have had a major growth spurt. The Association of American Publishers (AAP), the industry's primary trade group, has tracked digital book sales since 2003, when wholesale revenues amounted to $20 million. By 2007, that number had tripled to $67 million. But in 2008, the figure nearly doubled again to some $113 million with a173 percent jump in sales from January 2008.

There are many reasons for this explosion, including in no small part Google's determination to scan all of human knowledge into its Library Project, which was formatted for mobile devices in February 2009. Another driver is the proliferation of portable gadgets for reading digital books, most notably the Amazon Kindle and Sony Digital Reader. The Plastic Logic reader is expected to be flexible so readers can bend the pages back as they would with a book.

On such devices the reader can annotate the digital book, save the annotations, pull up footnotes instantly, bookmark, excerpt and archive books and even share them by phones such as iPhone. Because digital books are portable, they are more accessible; readers commonly have bound copies at home.

A new method of reading, writing and interacting is promised by *Sophie*, open source software for writing and reading rich media documents in a networked environment developed at the Institute for the Future of the Book. In a Sophie-created "book," the pages are "thick" or full of information sources. These might include video clips, music, narration, or a wide range of textual sources. The tools allow readers to go as far into the potentially unlimited additional material as they want. What distinguishes Sophie as a coherent "book" is that the additional material is not opened through hyperlinks. The reader never leaves the material assembled by the author, and has no need to search the internet for further sources.

Many publishers have embraced the multi-media concept, and are moving into the fully digital era, particularly for non-fiction. Sourcebooks, for example, launched in 1987 as an interactive, multimedia firm devoted to exploring all the possibilities of new media. Now that the social networking world of *Twitter, Facebook*, and *MySpace* define so much of the digisphere, the company has adapted its content. An author can build an online community, cultivated via extensive blogs and postings, before a book is even published. As so often with new technology, though, format wars can hinder its progress. In May 2008, AAP issued a call for industry e-publishing standards in the hopes that hardware and software can be made interoperable.

Meanwhile Amazon has launched the Kindle DX with a larger screen—9.7 inches as opposed to the 6 inches of the early model (the better to see charts and graphs with)—a built-in PDF reader, and the ability to add annotations in addition to notes and highlights. It is also tailored to newspaper and periodical reading. Amazon believes the larger Kindle will encourage people to subscribe to newspapers in digital form. *The New York Times, Boston Globe* and *The Washington Post* offer the DX at a reduced price to readers where home delivery of those newspapers is not available. Case Western and five other universities—Pace, Princeton, Reed, Arizona State, and the University of Virginia—have signed a deal with Amazon under which some students are given large-screen Kindles with textbooks for chemistry and computer science. The schools will then compare the experiences of these students with those using traditional textbooks. Two dozen competitors have already entered the market.

Reading habits

For years, people have been predicting the death of the book. While reading books may be declining, Americans are in fact reading. While one in ten (9%) tell pollsters they typically read no books in an average year, over one-third (37%) of Americans say they read more then ten books. The average number is 7.9 for women, 5 for men. In 2004, a National Endowment for the Arts report titled *Reading at Risk* found only 57 percent of American adults had read a book in 2002, a four percent point drop in a decade. Analysts say the reasons are mainly competition from the internet and other media. Book sales have been flat in recent years and are expected to stay that way indefinitely. One in five Americans (20%) say they have not purchased any books in the past year. Of those who do read, women and older people are most avid, while non-readers tend to be older, less educated, lower income, minorities, from rural areas and less religious. Figures indicate that those with college degrees read the most, and people aged 50 and up read more than those who are younger, who say they have less time. The greatest readers live in the Midwest and the suburbs and are white.

The Bible and religious works were read by two-thirds according to one survey: popular fiction, histories, biographies and mysteries were cited by about half, while one in five read romance novels. Every other genre, including politics, poetry and classical literature were named by fewer than five percent of readers. The largest single genre is mystery, thriller and crime (48% read) followed by history (35%), biographies (31%), religious and spirituality (28%) and literature (27%). Men and women have different tastes in the type of books they read. Women are more likely to read mysteries (57% versus 38%), religious books (32% versus 24%), and romance novels (38% versus 3%). Men, on the other hand, are more likely to read history (44% versus 27%), science fiction (34% versus 18%) and political (22% versus 9%).

The great majority of books (85%) are sold through bookstore chains like Barnes & Noble and Borders, the rest through independent booksellers. In recent years, the chains have developed internet sales in competition with each other and with online retailers such as amazon.com. Recently chains such as Borders have found the market very difficult. They have even experimented with instore digital kiosks so that customers can buy from the store's website and stores have to carry less inventory. The company has reorganised itself around its e-commerce operations and made them key to its short-term and long-term strategies. Books-on-demand, by which customers simply print off a book they are purchasing, has been developed by publishers. The *Espresso* book machine is found in over 20 US locations and more overseas. Meanwhile, even Barnes & Noble, the world's largest retail bookseller, has also seen profits fall.

RADIO

The beginning of commercial radio broadcasts in 1920 brought a new source of information and entertainment directly into American homes. Radio became important to politics in 1924, when the proceedings of the national political party conventions were first broadcast live. In that year, the political parties began paying for radio advertisements. Their competition started the upward spiral in campaign spending that has accelerated in recent years. Perhaps the most famous incident on American radio, however, took place on Halloween, October 30, 1938, when Orson Welles' Mercury Theatre dramatization of H.G. Wells' *War of the Worlds* engendered a mass panic in which millions of Americans believed they were being invaded by Martians. President Franklin Roosevelt understood the usefulness of radio as a medium of communication: His "fireside chats" kept the nation abreast of economic developments during the Depression and of military operations during World War II. American Presidents still give a weekly radio address.

The widespread availability of television after World War II brought predictions of a quick death for radio and caused radio executives to rethink their programming. Radio could hardly compete with television's visual presentation of drama, comedy, and variety acts, and many radio stations switched to a format of recorded music mixed with news and features. Radio in the US is broadcast in two bands, amplitude modulation (AM) and frequency modulation (FM). The FM signal is weak but of a better sound quality, suitable for music or stereo broadcasting. The much more numerous AM stations are more powerful and more suitable for talk. Just as with television, the national broadcast networks have affiliations with local stations around the country, though usually the only national programs are news and some interview shows. Starting in the 1950s, radios became standard accessories in American automobiles. The medium enjoyed a renaissance as American commuters tuned in their car radios on the way to work. In fact despite the importance of TV, the reach of radio is still impressive. Just about every American household has at least one radio, with an average of five per household. ABC and CBS both have radio networks. Clear Channel, the largest commercial radio operator, owns more than 1,200 stations.

The expansion of FM radio led to a split in radio programming in the 1970s and 1980s. FM came to dominate the music side of programming, while AM has shifted mainly to all-news, sport and talk formats. There is a long-term trend towards more talk and less music on radio. Most radio stations have frequent weather and traffic reports, with the largest operating special helicopters for following traffic conditions in major cities.

Barely in existence 25 years ago, talk radio has become big business, airing 24 hours a day. Shows usually feature a host, a celebrity or an expert on some subject, and the opportunity for listeners to call in and ask questions or express opinions on the air. Even interview shows will bring their guests on by telephone. Many talk radio hosts are controversial, even abusive to their listeners. Some talk radio stations are 100% news. The call-in format is now heard on nearly 1,000 stations. Stations give airtime to every hue of political and religious thinking. Elsewhere, outspoken radio "shock jocks" push at the boundaries of taste.

Music radio, either AM or FM, airs in many formats. "Easy listening" stations play soft, undemanding music, often called "elevator music" because similar music is sometimes piped into elevators in large buildings. Many ethnic groups have their own stations. Specialized stations play jazz, country music, classical music or even classic rock and roll. But the most distinctive and most American type of radio station is the "Top-40" pop station. These stations play the most popular pop songs accompanied by commercials and commentary from a rapid-fire professional announcer (a "disk-jockey" or DJ). These stations also have frequent promotions and contests to encourage people to listen.

Satellite radio, a relatively new phenomenon, is provided by Sirius XM Inc., which, with 18.5 million subscribers, is the second largest radio company in the country, with 10 percent of the home and car radio market. The company broadcasts more than 300 channels of programming, including exclusive radio broadcasts from shock-jock Howard Stern, television magnate Oprah Winfrey and home-decorating guru Martha Stewart. Subscribers can access the signals from their homes or cars anywhere in the US. In return for a monthly or annual fee, most satellite music stations have no commercials.

Besides the 10,000 commercial radio stations, the US has more than 1,400 commercial-free public radio stations. Most of these are run by universities, cities and other public institutions for educational purposes and are financed by public funds and listener donations. National Public Radio (NPR) was founded in 1970 and provides news, debate, information and music. NPR serves a growing audience of 21 million Americans each week via more than 730 stations and the internet, and in Europe, Asia, Australia and Africa via NPR Worldwide. Over 2,000 stations broadcast on the internet.

The FCC has auctioned $15 billion of public airwaves abandoned by television broadcasters moving to digital programming, which are ideal for carrying wireless signals. The major US cellular carriers and Google have spent millions of dollars on lobbying to influence the outcome, which could dramatically alter the nation's cellphone industry. Google, the giant internet search company, wants to extend its popular tools, which include email and video, to the rapidly expanding mobile phone market. According to Canalsys, its Android operating system has taken 17% of the market, second only to Nokia with 37%. Currently, the major US wireless carriers, including AT&T and Verizon Wireless, largely decide which websites, music-download services and search engines their customers can access on their cell phones by determining which cell phones will receive their services. AT&T, for example, is the only carrier available to users of Apple's *iPhone*.

TELEVISION

Since World War II, television has become the most popular over-the-air medium, with enormous influence on the nation's politics and way of life. American TV dramas, comedies, soap operas, animations, music videos and films have a global audience and are part of the staple fare of broadcasters worldwide. In a huge country of over 300 million people, television programs are among the few experiences that nearly all Americans can share. Television reflects American culture and it also makes American culture, amid much comment and controversy. Television reflects a great deal about American life and values, but does not tell the whole story. America is a culturally diverse nation, and television often misses the mark.

History

Television was first commercialized in the early 1940s by RCA (through NBC, which it owned) and CBS. Development was initially hampered by lack of a standard for transmission, but in 1941 the National Television System Committee (NTSC) recommended the 525-line broadcast that would provide the basis for TV across the country through the end of the century. At first there were only a few dozen stations, which were concentrated on the East and West coasts. But when the FCC began handing out licenses to communities of all sizes in the early 1950s, an explosion of growth took place. (The FCC grants, for a fee, licenses to the spectrum to broadcasters for commercial use, so long as the broadcasters act in the public interest by providing news programming. Half of all households had TV sets by 1955, though color was a premium feature for many years. Most households could only afford black-and-white models, and few programs were shown in color until the mid-1960s. In 1950 only 9% of American households owned a television set. By 1961 nearly 90 percent of US homes had a television. By 2001, according to the Census Bureau, 98.2 percent of American households owned at least one of the 248 million TVs in the country, for an average of 2.4 per home. American adults watch about 4.6 hours of television per day, or 1,669 hours per year.

Many of the earliest TV programs were modified versions of well-established radio shows. The '50s saw the first flowering of the genres that would distinguish TV from movies and radio: talk shows like *The Jack Paar Show* and sitcoms like *I Love Lucy*. The first television broadcast of a political convention was of the GOP convention in 1940, with an audience of 100,000 viewers.

The 1960 Kennedy-Nixon debates clinched the crucial role of television in modern campaigning. The people who heard the debate on radio thought Nixon won, while the majority who saw it on TV gave the victory to Kennedy. Apparently this was because Nixon, who had sustained a minor injury a fortnight before, looked tired and unattractive compared with his opponent. Virtually every American home – over 100 million in 2001 – has at least one TV set, and 76 percent have two or more; 88% percent receive cable TV, 32% paying for the service.

Stations across the country also produced their own local programs. Usually carried live, they ranged from simple advertisements to game shows, and children's shows that often featured clowns and other offbeat characters. Local shows could often be popular and profitable, but concerns about product promotions on the shows and other issues led them to disappear almost completely by the mid-1970s. Over-the-air stations ceased airing in analog by June 12, 2009.

Channels and networks

There are three basic kinds of television in the US: broadcast, or 'over-the-air', which is freely available to anyone who can receive it; cable; and satellite television. Cable and satellite require a subscription to receive. The three major commercial television networks in the US are NBC and CBS, which both began in the 1920s as radio networks, and ABC, founded in its modern form in 1953. The privately owned networks that offered free programming financed by commercials – NBC (owned by General Electric), ABC and CBS (since 1999 part of Viacom) - controlled 90 percent of the TV market from the 1950s to the 1970s. In the 1980s the rapid spread of pay cable TV transmitted by satellite undermined that privileged position. Among the new cable channels were several that show news 24 hours a day such as Cable News Network (CNN), the creation of Ted Turner, and MTV, which shows popular culture shows aimed at teenagers and young adults. CNN airs both domestic and international streams and was the first major network to air in HD. CNN was also the first to use holograms; on election night, November 5, 2008, correspondent Jessica Yellin was beamed in to the New York City studio from Chicago. In the meantime, a fourth major commercial network, Fox, has come into being and challenged the big three networks; several local TV stations have switched their affiliation from one of the big three to the newcomer. Two more national networks - WB and UPN - have also come along, and the number of cable television channels continues to expand. Each of the four major networks now has around 14% of the audience. The networks have news departments with bureaus and reporters all over the world. They also have sports departments that cover major national sporting events like the Superbowl (football) and the World Series (baseball). NBC, for example, produced 3,600 hours of Olympics coverage over seven networks in 2008 at a cost of over $1 billion. The major product of the networks, however, is entertainment programming.

Broadcast television

The US has a decentralized, market-based television system. Unlike many other countries, the US has no national television stations. Instead, local media markets have their own television stations, which may be affiliated to one of the national networks. Except in very small markets with few stations, affiliation agreements are usually exclusive: If a station is an ABC affiliate, for example, the station would not air programs from CBS, NBC or other networks. To maintain a minimum amount of local programming, federal law restricts the amount of network programming local stations can run. Because of the costs of production, however, many stations produce only local news shows.

They fill the rest of their schedule with syndicated shows, or material produced independently and sold to individual local stations.

Scheduling

Major-network affiliates air very similar schedules. Typically, they begin weekdays with a locally produced early morning news show, followed by a network morning show, such as NBC's *Today* or ABC's *Good Morning America,* which mixes news, weather, interviews and music. The major networks all offer a morning news program. Syndicated programming, especially talk shows, fills the late morning, often followed by local news at noon.

Soap operas, game and contest shows and daily dramatic serials dominate the early afternoon. (Soap operas are so called because they were originally sponsored by soap and household products companies; some were even produced by these companies.) Soap operas are filled with drama: murders, trials, abortions, treachery, mistaken identity, and strange diseases. American soap operas have been running for over six decades, initially on radio and subsequently on television. Primetime soap operas of note have included *Peyton Place, Dallas, Dynasty,* and *Beverly Hills, 90210.* Of the nine current daytime soaps, seven have been on the air for over thirty years: *The Guiding Light, As the World Turns, General Hospital, Days of Our Lives, One Life to Live, All My Children,* and *The Young and the Restless.*

Syndicated talk shows such as *The Oprah Winfrey Show* appear in the late afternoon. Late afternoon television is often given over to certain types of audience participation talk shows. They will usually feature a panel of people with some strange problem that the audience can comment on or ask questions about, like nephews of alcoholic uncles or people born with twelve fingers. Sometimes screaming, shouting, even violence occurs on these programs, which have begun to be shown at all hours.

Local news comes on again in the early evening, followed by the national network's news program at 5:30 or 6:30 p.m. and more news. This may be followed by early evening syndicated game shows like *Wheel of Fortune* or *Jeopardy* for the next hour or ½ hour, called the *prime access slot,* before the networks take over for *prime time,* between 8pm and 11pm, the most-watched three hours of television. Prime time is filled with dramatic and comedy series that feature major actors and receive heavy media coverage. Most of these shows last only one or two 13-week seasons, but some run for many years. Family-oriented comedy programs used to lead in the early part of prime time, although in recent years reality television like *Dancing with the Stars* has largely replaced them. Later in the evening, dramas like *CSI: Crime Scene Investigation* and *Grey's Anatomy* are aired.

At 10 or 11 p.m. another local news program comes on, usually followed by late night talk shows, such as the *Late Show with David Letterman.* For many years, the *Tonight Show* with Johnny Carson had the best following among late night talk shows, and so it set the standard for the genre. Carson would interview celebrities, make humorous comments on current controversies and news stories, and perhaps have a singer or comedian do an act, with frequent commercials. Most present-day programs of this sort follow a similar format. Rather than sign off for the small hours, as was standard practice until the 1980s, TV stations now fill the time with syndicated programming or 30-minute advertisements, known as infomercials.

Primetime comedy has included situation comedies such as *I Love Lucy, M*A*S*H, All in the Family, The Jeffersons, The Cosby Show, Seinfeld, Friends* and *Everybody Loves Raymond,* as well as sketch comedy/variety series such as the early shows of Milton Berle, *The Carol Burnett Show*, *Rowan and Martin's Laugh-In* and the late night *Saturday Night Live*.

Dramatic series have taken many forms over the years. Westerns such as *Gunsmoke* had their greatest popularity in the '50s and '60s. Medical dramas have endured (*Marcus Welby, M.D.*, *St. Elsewhere*, *ER*), as have family dramas (*Eight is Enough*, *The Waltons*, *Little House on the Prairie*) and crime dramas (*Dragnet*, *Hawaii Five-O*, *Hill Street Blues*, *Law & Order* and *CSI: Crime Scene Investigation* - the last two of which have spawned multiple spin-offs). Some series, such as HBO's *The Sopranos*, successfully bend the traditional drama categories.

The early evening newscasters have come to personify American TV news. Successful news magazines have included *60 Minutes*, *20/20*, *Dateline* in primetime and *Meet the Press*, the US's oldest series, having debuted in 1947. *Face the Nation* and *This Week* air on Sunday mornings.

Reality television has long existed in the US, both played for laughs (*Candid Camera*, *Real People*) and as drama (*COPS*, *The Real World*). A new variant - competition series - exploded in popularity in 2000 with the launch of *Survivor*. Then *Big Brother*, *The Amazing Race*, *America's Next Top Model*, and *American Idol* followed.

Daytime has also been home to many popular game shows over the years (particularly during the 1970s). *The Price is Right*, *Family Feud*, *Match Game*, *The Newlywed Game*, *Concentration*, *Wheel of Fortune* and *Jeopardy!* have found their greatest success in the early evening slot before primetime, while game shows actually aired within primetime had great popularity in the 1950s and 1960s (*What's My Line?*, *I've Got a Secret*, *To Tell the Truth*) and again, intermittently, in the 2000s (*Who Wants to Be a Millionaire?*, *The Weakest Link*, *Deal or No Deal*). The only daytime game show remaining on the networks is *The Price Is Right*, which has appeared on CBS since 1972.

The most successful talk show has been NBC's late night (after 11:30 PM Eastern/Pacific) *Tonight Show*, particularly when hosted by Johnny Carson. *Tonight* ushered in a multi-decade period of dominance by one network in American late night programming, and paved the way for many similar combinations of comedy and celebrity interviews, such as those hosted by Merv Griffin and David Letterman. Daytime talk show hits have included *The Oprah Winfrey Show*, *Phil Donahue*, *The Ellen DeGeneres Show*, and *Live with Regis and Kelly*, and run the gamut from serious to lighthearted. A subset of so-called trash TV talk shows such as *The Jerry Springer Show* also veered into titillation and exploitation. Variety shows have gone out of fashion. *The Carol Burnett Show* ceased production in 1978, and is generally regarded as the last successful major network variety show.

Saturday mornings usually feature network programming aimed at children, such as animated cartoons, while Sunday mornings include public affairs programs that help fulfill stations' legal obligations to provide public service programming. Sports and infomercials can be found on weekend afternoons, followed again by the same type of prime-time shows aired during the week.

Mainstream TV is slick, fast moving and awash with advertising. The success of American television has inspired television networks across the world to make shows of similar types or air these shows in their own country. The opposite is also true; a number of popular American programs have been based on shows from other countries, especially the UK and Canada.

Other over-the-air commercial television
Until 1987, all English-language stations not affiliated with the big three networks were independent,

airing only locally produced and syndicated programming. Many independent stations still exist. Syndicated shows, often reruns of old TV series and old movies, take up much of their schedule. In 1986, however, the Fox Broadcasting Company launched a challenge to the big three networks. Thanks largely to the success of shows like *The Simpsons* and *American Idol*, as well as the network's acquisition of rights to show National Football League games, Fox has established itself as a major player in television. However, Fox differs from the three older networks in that it does not air a nightly news program, and its prime-time schedule is only two hours long. In the 1990s, three new networks - The WB, UPN and PAX - joined the scene. The fledging WB and UPN merged into The CW in fall 2006, while News Corp's MyNetworkTV also debuted that fall. PAX, now known as ION Television, has had very low ratings since its launch and is no longer considered a competitor to the larger over-the-air network. The CW broadcasts 15 hours a week in prime time and 10 hours in daytime. MyNetworkTV broadcasts 12 hours a week, Monday through Saturday. UPN broadcasts 10 hours a week Monday through Friday, with an optional weekend rerun block. ION broadcasts 24 hours a day, 7 days a week, making the ION network totally responsible for its affiliates.

Over-the-air television in languages other than English.

Univision, a network of Spanish language stations, is the fifth-largest TV network behind NBC, CBS, ABC and Fox. Its major competition is Telemundo, a sister network of NBC. Univision-owned TeleFutura, aimed at a younger Hispanic audience, and Azteca America, the American version of Mexico's TV Azteca, are two other popular Spanish-language over-the-air networks. In addition, the Miami-based Haitian Television Network offers locally produced Haitian Creole and French language programming in Miami and parts of New Jersey, New York City, and Boston.

Non-commercial television

Public television has a far smaller role in the US than in most other countries, although public television stations exist in most parts of America. There is no state-owned network. Instead, the federal government subsidizes non-commercial television stations through the Corporation for Public Broadcasting which runs PBS, a private non-profit organization founded in 1969. The income received from the government, however, is insufficient to cover expenses, and stations rely on corporate sponsorships and viewer contributions.

American public television stations air programming that commercial stations do not offer, particularly educational, cultural, and public affairs. Most such stations will show children's and educational programs during the day. During prime time, they will show quality documentaries, performing arts, public affairs programs, and a great number of British-made dramatic, mystery, and comedy series.

Most public TV stations are affiliates of the Public Broadcasting Service, sharing programs like *Sesame Street* and *Masterpiece Theatre*. Unlike the commercial networks, PBS does not produce its own programming; instead, individual PBS stations create programming and provide these to other affiliates. New York City's municipally-owned broadcast service, NYCTV, creates original programming that airs in several markets. Few other cities, however, have major municipally-owned stations. Many religious stations exist, funded by viewer contributions.

There are 349 public television stations across the US, each of which is independent and serves its local community. The stations are owned by community organizations, colleges and universities, state authorities and local educational or municipal authorities. PBS supplies much of the programming. In October, 2002, 75.7 million households representing 143.6 million people watched public television, with the average home tuning in for over seven and a half hours during the month. Among the most popular programs is *Sesame Street*, a children's show that teaches beginning reading and mathematics through the use of puppets, cartoons, songs, and comedy skits.

Cable and satellite

Cable television is a rapidly expanding segment of the industry. Until the 1970s, cable television was used only to re-send over-the-air TV to areas that had trouble receiving signals. But in that decade, national networks dedicated exclusively to cable appeared, along with cable TV systems that provided service to major cities. Today, most American households receive cable TV, and cable networks collectively have greater viewership than traditional networks.

Unlike over-the-air networks, most cable networks air the same programming nationwide. Top cable networks include ESPN (sports), MTV (popular culture), CNN (news), Sci Fi (science fiction) and Discovery Channel (documentaries). The cable channels with the greatest impact, however, are parts of Atlanta-based Turner Broadcasting System. Turner's *Cable News Network* (CNN) has the widest news coverage in the nation. Turner's other national stations, *TBS* and *TNT,* show programs from Turner's inventory of thousands of classic American films of the past.

Cable programming is extremely varied. The *Discovery Channel*, for example, shows nature shows and documentaries, while *History Channel* tells about the past. *Arts and Entertainment* (A&E) shows various documentaries, dramas and performing arts programs. The *Disney Channel* has programs geared for children and family audiences. *Nickelodeon* is largely children's programming. *Animal Planet* is 100% animal programs, while *House and Garden* covers home issues. Dozens of other specialized networks, from country music to prayer, exist around the country. In any local area, the local cable company will offer some but rarely all of them.

Cable TV subscribers receive these channels through local cable system operators, who in turn receive them from the networks and transmit them into homes. Usually, local governments award a monopoly to a system operator to provide cable TV service in a given area. By law, cable systems must include local over-the-air stations in their offerings to customers.

Basic cable service includes all the network and public stations (though with much better reception) and many cable-only stations that the local cable company offers for no extra charge. Premium channels, like the movie channels, certain sports channels, and even some foreign language channels, are also available for an extra monthly fee. "Pay-per-view" movies and special sporting events are available for a one-time charge per viewing.

Several cable television channels like Home Box Office (HBO) and Showtime show movies all day long without commercials for a monthly fee in addition to the basic cable TV connection charge. HBO has originated some of the most critically acclaimed programs. Over-the-air television stations also show movies, but these are usually interrupted by commercials and often edited, except on certain public stations. Home video has also changed American film-viewing habits. Within a short time of its theater release, a film will become available on a DVD, which can be played on a DVD player. Video stores either sell or rent the film for a small fee. Public access cable also exists in all communities. Many of these programs are produced by amateurs or local community affairs groups. Ethnic groups often have television programming in various languages for certain hours of the day. These programs are shown on UHF over-the-air stations, some public stations and on some public access cable channels. They are easiest to access through cable. Some cable

TV companies such as Comcast started carrying HDTV in 2003. At least some HD programming is now carried by all major networks, while .ScreenSleuth reports that 53 percent of American households have at least one flat-screen TV.

Satellite TV

Satellite dish TV systems are becoming more common. Direct broadcast satellite (DBS) television services, which became available in the US in the 1990s, offer programming similar to cable TV. Dish Network and News Corporation's DirecTV are the major DBS providers. Satellites were originally launched and used by the television networks as a method of distributing their programs from headquarters to local affiliates. In the 1970s, people in remote locations without access to terrestrial television found they could get free television by installing large satellite dishes and aiming them at the various satellites owned by the networks. This had the additional benefit of providing channels that others could not receive, such as programs without commercials, live feeds not intended for airing, programs from other countries, and eventually cable television programming. To prevent people receiving pay content for free, satellite transmissions are now scrambled. Meanwhile newer transmission technology has enabled satellite dishes to be much smaller, and subscription services have been developed. Houses with satellite dishes can receive hundreds of channels directly from satellites orbiting in outer space, although they may have to pay for a descrambler to receive certain pay stations. As a result, cable television is now often "cable" in name only.

Beginning in the late 1970s, US cable companies have offered services to selected segments of the population. Programs aired by the Silent Network come with sign language and captions for the network's audience of people with hearing problems. In 1988, Christopher Whittle founded Channel One cable network, which provides educational programming - along with commercials - to about 40 percent of American high school students.

Internet TV

The convergence of the computer, TV, and fiber optics has created the possibility of interactive TV, which allows viewers to select specific programs they wish to see from an archive of programs or from a channel directory and watch them at times of their choosing. Internet television (otherwise known as Internet TV, or Online TV), not to be confused with Web television or IPTV, has become very popular and every major network now has a TV presence. The two forms of viewing Internet television are streaming the content directly to a media player or simply downloading the program to the user's computer.

Web TV

Web television (Web TV) is an emerging genre of digital entertainment that is distinct from traditional broadcast television. Delivered originally online via broadband and mobile networks, Web television shows, or Web series, are short-form (2–9 minutes per episode), episodic, and produced in seasons. Major web television networks include The WB.com, Hulu, MySpace, YouTube, Newgrounds, Blip. tv, and Crackle. (MSN TV (formerly WebTV) is the name of both a thin client which uses a television for display (rather than a computer monitor) and the online service that supports it).

African American television and radio

There are some who assert that news media coverage of African American news, concerns or dilemmas is inadequate, and that the news media present distorted images of African Americans. In response, African Americans have founded their own television and radio networks. Black Entertainment Television (BET), founded by Robert L. Johnson, targets young African Americans and urban audiences. Most of the programming consists of rap and R&B music videos and urban-oriented movies and series. Additionally, the channel shows syndicated television series, original programs, and some public affairs programs. On Sunday mornings, BET broadcasts a lineup of network-produced Christian programming. Other, non-affiliated Christian programs are also shown daily during the early morning hours. There is also BET J (BET Jazz), a spin-off cable television channel, created originally to showcase jazz-related programming, especially that of black jazz musicians. While jazz remains the focus, programming has been expanded to include urban programs as well as some R&B, neo soul, and alternative hip hop. Another African American-oriented network, TV One, targets African American adults with a broad range of programming, and competes directly with BET. The network airs original lifestyle and entertainment shows, movies, fashion and music, as well as classic series such as *227, Good Times, Martin, Boston Public* and *It's Showtime at the Apollo*. A black-owned radio network, Radio One, Inc., is of the nation's largest radio broadcasting companies. Other African American networks, the Black Television News Channel founded by former Congressman J. C. Watts, and Better Black Television founded by Percy Miller, are set to launch in 2010.

TV financing

Over-the-air commercial stations and networks generate the vast majority of their revenue from advertisements.. According to a 2001 survey, these stations allocated 16 to 21 minutes per hour to commercials. Most cable networks also generate income from advertisements, although most basic cable networks also receive subscription fees. However, premium cable networks, such as the movie network HBO, do not air commercials. Instead, cable-TV subscribers must pay extra to receive these programs.

Production cycle of shows

Television production companies either commission teleplays to serve as pilots or buy "specs" (proposals for a show with sample scripts). Those which the production company thinks might be commercially viable are then marketed to television networks or television distributors for first-run syndication. (KingWorld distributes Oprah in first-run syndication, for example, because that show is syndicated, not affiliated with a particular network.)

Networks sometimes buy pilots simply to prevent other networks from controlling them, and the purchase of a pilot is no guarantee that a show will win an order for more episodes. Those that do get "picked up" win either a full or partial-season order, and the show goes into production, usually establishing itself with permanent sets, a full crew and production offices. Writers are hired, directors are selected and work begins, usually during the late spring and summer before the fall season-series premieres. (Shows can also be mid-season replacements, meaning they are ordered specifically to fill holes in a network schedule created by the failure and cancellation of shows which premiered in the fall. *Buffy the Vampire Slayer* is an example of a successful mid-season replacement.

The standard broadcast television season is 22 episodes per season; sitcoms may have 24 or more; animated programs may have more (or fewer) episodes; cable networks with original programming seem to have settled on about 10 or 12 episodes per season.

American soap operas air in the afternoon, five days a week, without any significant break in taping and airing schedules throughout the year. This means that these serials air approximately 260 episodes a year, making their casts and crews the busiest in show business. These shows are rarely, if ever, repeated, making it difficult for viewers to "catch up" when they miss a month, or even a week, of programming.

Networks use profits from commercials run during the show to pay the production company, which in turn pays the cast and crew, and keeps a share of the profits for itself. (Networks sometimes act as both production companies and distributors.) As advertising rates are based on the size of the audience, measuring the number of people watching a network is very important. This measurement is known as a show or network's ratings. Sweeps months (November, February, May, and to a lesser extent, July) are important landmarks in the television year. Ratings earned during these periods determine advertising rates until the next sweeps period. Therefore shows often have their most exciting plot developments happen during sweeps.

Shows that are successful with audiences and advertisers receive authorization from the network to continue production; the others are quickly cancelled. Instances of initially low-rated shows surviving cancellation and later becoming highly popular are rare. For the most part, shows that are not immediately even moderately successful will be cancelled by the end of November sweeps.

A revolution in television

In 2002 there was a sharp decline of 20% in revenues for terrestrial TV, which since the 1940s had experienced steady growth. Even cable had failed to achieve any significant share of advertising revenues. But certain trends had been quietly building up to bring about this sudden change. Perhaps the main cause of the current crisis in the TV industry is a change in the model of television demand. Demand for information, services, entertainment and education is disappearing. Some young people are beginning to switch over to the internet, as it is already possible to watch entire programs online. In October 2003, Microsoft announced software to enable cable TV and telephone companies to deliver internet television (IPTV). Meanwhile educated viewers are moving to niche cable channels. Video-on-demand (VOD) and technologies such as TiVo, which enables viewers to skip advertisements, are also cutting into profits. At the same time, the shift from analog to digital broadcasting is at its height. This shift not only involves enormous capital investment in technical refitting, but requires a change in production itself. The poorly produced programs which have brought American TV into some derision accounted until recently for 70-80% of production on both terrestrial and cable TV. But the technical bar has risen with the appearance of new technologies: shooting with high definition cameras requires more careful preparation and better lighting, for example. These challenges will soon be compounded by competition with telephone companies that are ready to begin transmitting cable signal, and with software producers. On the bright side, approximately 50% of US TV programs pay for themselves from international sales alone. The companies that survive the current revolution will have to take their international viewership into account more than they have before, which promises more variety and better quality for domestic viewers.

Current issues in television

Most television networks and local television stations now belong to giant, publicly owned corporations which expect to keep high percentages of their revenue as profit. Protecting such high profits can easily undermine the notion that journalism is a public service. The national television networks have trimmed their reporting staffs and closed foreign reporting bureaus to cut costs. They have tried to attract viewers by diluting their expensive newscasts with lifestyle, celebrity and entertainment features, and by filling their low budget, high profit, prime time "newsmagazines" with sensational sex, crime and court stories. News directors routinely make gory crime stories the first items on the 11 p.m. news. Sensational trivia, such as a celebrity divorce, or a police raid on a massage parlor, all too often displaces serious news. Thus, say critics, television newscasts overemphasize crime.

Local television stations weight their newscasts with dramatic video fragments of relatively minor but sensational fires and auto accidents. Broadcast and cable networks devote news time to pointless chat and debate. Local stations provide little real news, no matter how many hours they devote to "news" programs. Their reporting staffs are dramatically smaller than even the shrunken staffs of newspapers in the same cities. The television stations have attracted viewers - and the advertising that rewards their owners with extraordinary profits - with the melodrama, violence and entertainment of "action news" formulas, the frivolity of "happy talk" among their anchors, and the technological gimmicks of computer graphics and "live" remote broadcasting.

All-news cable television channels, to which the networks have ceded much of the routine coverage of national and foreign news, fill many of their hours as cheaply as possible with repetitive, barebones news summaries and talk shows that present biased opinions and argument as though they were news. The shortfall in real news and serious discussion, claim critics, leaves citizens vulnerable to the negative and misleading political advertising ("attack ads") that fills the airwaves during election campaigns.

A variety of groups mobilized outside government in the 1980s to counter what was perceived as a moral degeneration in the media. These included Dr. James Dobson's Focus on the Family, the Rev. Louis Sheldon's Coalition for Traditional Values, and Pat Robertson's Christian Coalition. In 1985, the Parents Music Resource Center, led by Tipper Gore (wife of then-Senator Al Gore of Tennessee), lobbied in Senate hearings for content labeling of popular music because of concerns about sex and violence. That same year, evangelical Protestant organizations, led by the Rev. Jerry Falwell, founder of the Moral Majority, and the Rev. Donald Wildmon, founder of the National Federation for Decency (since renamed the American Family Association) allied with anti-pornography feminists to pressure 7-11 and other national chains of convenience stores to ban the sale of *Playboy* and *Penthouse* magazines. That effort succeeded, but may have been a pyrrhic victory insofar as it immediately stimulated the market for pornographic videos, introduced into homes by the then-new technology of the VCR.

Many Americans are disturbed by the amount of violence their children see on television. In response to citizens' complaints and pressure from Congress, the four major TV networks - ABC, CBS, NBC, and Fox - agreed in 1993 to inform parents of violent content at the beginning of a program, and cable networks have agreed to give similar warnings. In 1996, the commercial and cable networks went a step further and established a rating system, based on the amount of violence, sexual content, and/or profane language that a program contains. A symbol indicating the show's rating appears on the television screen at the beginning of, and intermittently during, the show.

Such voluntary measures seem preferable to most Americans to government regulation of programming content, which would probably violate the First Amendment. Another possible solution to the problem is technological. Beginning in 1998 new television sets sold in the US have been equipped with a "V-chip," a device that enables parents to block out programs they would rather their children not see.

As with the print media, privacy is another controversial issue. Whilst Americans generally believe that investigative reporting safeguards democracy by exposing scandals and abuses, politicians especially allege that journalists' intrusions into the private lives of people seeking public office will deter capable people from going into politics.

Regulation

Over-the-air television is regulated by the Federal Communications Commission. The FCC awards licenses to local stations, stipulating stations' commitments to educational and public interest programming. The FCC also prohibits the airing of "indecent" material over the air between 6 a.m. and 10 p.m. Although stations can legally air almost anything they want late at night, and cable networks can do so at any time, nudity and profanity are very rare on American television. Producers fear that airing such material will discourage advertisers, and encourage the federal government to strengthen its regulation of TV content. Premium cable networks are exceptions, and often air very racy programming at night. Some networks, such as Playboy TV, are devoted exclusively to "adult" content. Cable television is largely, but not entirely, unregulated. Cable systems must include local over-the-air stations in their offerings and give them low channel numbers. The systems cannot show over-the-air network affiliates from other parts of the country. Regulation is much less than in other countries. The drawback is that it leads to an overabundance of suppliers through competition to produce minimum acceptable quality; the first newscast to release even a partial story wins the traffic.

Government funded external broadcasting

- Voice of America - programs for global audiences in many languages
- Radio Free Europe/Radio Liberty - targets eastern Europe, former Soviet Union and
- the Caucasus in local languages.
- Radio Free Asia - targets North Korea and southeast Asia.
- Al-Hurra - satellite TV for Middle East
- Radio Sawa - Arabic-language radio for Middle East
- Radio Farda - Persian-language radio
- Radio and TV Marti - services for Cuba

Bias in the news media

Most scholars have concluded there is no significant bias in the news media, although outlets often have definite standpoints. On TV, "NewsHour with Jim Lehrer" (PBS) is considered the most centrist, with other networks somewhat to the left and Fox News to the right. *USA TODAY* is regarded as a centrist newspaper, with the *New York Times* and the *LA Times* to the left and the *Wall Street Journal* to the right. A more serious problem may be the uniformity of the media, and their failure to report fully on some news such as the insurgency in Iraq.

Opinion polls

News reporting in all the media bears constant reference to opinion polls, especially on political issues. George Gallup began conducting public opinion polls in 1934, starting with small samples in key districts. He believed that these polls would provide "a swift and efficient method by which legislators, educators, experts, and editors, as well as ordinary citizens throughout the length and breadth of the country, can have a more reliable measure of the pulse of democracy." Today, polling has become highly sophisticated, as questioning has been refined by experience, and analysis has been aided by the introduction of modern technology. In spite of occasional errors, polling is generally considered to be an effective way to keep track of public opinion and has thus become a part of everyday public discourse.

There are numerous polling organizations, which include Gallup, Harris, Polling Report and the Roper Center. In addition, extensive polling is carried out by the print and broadcasting media, especially the *Los Angeles Times*, the *New York Times*, *Newsweek*, *Time*, *USA TODAY*, the *Washington Post*, CNN, ABC, CBS, *Fox News* and NBC.

THE INTERNET

The internet was created by the Department of Defense through the networking of computers at UCLA and the Stanford Research Institute in 1969. In 1980, Bill Gates's deal to put a Microsoft Operating System on IBM's computers paved the way for almost universal computer ownership. Apple launched the first successful "modern" computer interface using graphics to represent files and folders, drop-down menus and, crucially, mouse control in 1984. The worldwide web, rapidly taken up at Stanford, was invented in 1989 by British physicist, Tim Berners-Lee. It made internet communication simple using browsers, pages and links. Search engines were soon developed. Google, originally a research project at Stanford, began in 1996. Although a great advance, Google Search, and other search engines such as *Yahoo!*, still have problems generating relevant answers to questions without including irrelevant results. British physicist, Stephen Wolfram, launched the Wolfram Alpha computational knowledge engine in 2009 which appeared to offer a solution by presenting data, not pages, but it depends on the search engine understanding the question. Google has also announced upgraded searching.

The swiftness of the worldwide web's ascent from obscure experiment to cultural icon has been truly remarkable. In the space of less than a decade, the Web extended into nearly every facet of society, from commerce to education, and is employed in a variety of uses, from scholarly research to casual browsing. By 2008, three in four Americans had internet access. Like other transformational technologies that preceded it, the Web has spawned (and consumed) vast fortunes. The "dot-com bust" (2000-2001) was a sobering indication to organizations of all descriptions that the nature and extent of the Web's impact is still unsettled.

Size and Growth

The size of the Web is hard to estimate, but according to WorldWideWebSize.com, the Indexed Web contains at least 2.97 billion pages (Wednesday, 03 November, 2010). On July 25, 2008, Google software engineers announced that Google Search had discovered one trillion unique URLs. Of these 74% were commercial or other sites operating in the .com generic top-level domain. About one-third of the world's websites are in English and one-half are in America. Some experts say that only a fraction of the Web's information can be considered useful, and conclude that the Web is unimpressive as an information resource, since it hosts too many rumors, distortions and fabrications. But the Web encompasses digital resources of many varieties beyond plain text, often combined and re-combined into rich multi-media information objects. Furthermore, many Web analysts now recognize the distinction between the "surface Web" (accessed by most search engines) and the "deep Web" (inaccessible to search engines which crawl link-to-link), which is believed to be large and growing. About 41% of the surface web is believed to be in the public domain. This implies that the information on the surface Web was roughly equivalent in size to between 14 and 28 million books, possibly as many as twice the number in Harvard University Library. The conclusion, however, that the Web is equivalent to, or perhaps even surpasses, the largest library collections is probably unwarranted. A significant percentage of the surface Web is taken up by "format overhead," for example, HTML or XML tagging. What is probably most remarkable about the size of the Web is how rapidly it rose from relatively insignificant proportions to a scale at least comparable to that of research library collections.

Continuing growth

The extravagant, unrealistic expectations that prevailed in the dot-com sector during the late 1990s have vanished. Yet the role that the internet plays in the lives of millions is stronger than ever. The internet is regarded by increasing percentages of users as valuable, interesting, and important. In 2002, the UCLA Internet Project found that about 71 percent of Americans use the internet. Even though 47 percent of non-users said they were likely to go online in 2003, the flip side of that positive response means that 53 percent of those who do not go online had no plans to do so in the next year. Lack of interest or lack of know-how seem more important barriers than cost, according to the 2010 World Internet Project survey from the Center for the Digital Future at the USC Annenberg School for Communication & Journalism. The survey also found that 78% of Ameicans used the internet with only a slightly higher proportion of men doing so, and 87% bought online. The question is whether the US will become a society in which about three-quarters of its citizens use a powerful interactive communications tool, while one-quarter does not. If so, what will be the price for voluntarily not using the internet?

Closely related to the possible peaking of internet use is the question of how to define the "digital divide." It was once perceived by politicians and policymakers as a social and educational problem, but the issue is no longer as simple as it once seemed. Using the narrowest definition – comparing those with no internet access to those with internet access from one or more locations – the divide has indeed narrowed considerably. Studies show that online use has increased to include nearly three-quarters of Americans; the vast majority of children have access to the internet where they live or at school; and more than half of adults use the internet at work. Although the number of online users has flattened – even if only temporarily – the number of users who access the internet at home continues to increase. By 2002, almost 60 percent of users had access to the internet at home, nearly triple the rate of home use in 1995. The divide today is not only between those who have access and those who do not, but between access by broadband v. access by telephone modem, and between those who fear technology v. those who embrace it. A $4.7bn Broadband Technology Opportunities Program was included in the Recovery Act 2009.

According to MostPopularWebsites.net, the world's five most visited websites are Google, Facebook, YouTube, Yahoo! and Live.com, all of them American. The majority of Web users visit newspaper sites only a few times per month but visit a search engine several times per day.

The internet as a tool for political power

American politicians use the internet as a powerful tool for delivering political messages and attracting campaign contributions. Barack Obama's internet outreach was one of the things that built his massive Presidential nomination "war chest," made up almost entirely of small contributions from voters. Public officials are increasingly linking to their constituencies through their internet pages or email. Moreover, advocacy groups in growing numbers are building civic dialogue and mass expression of opinion through broadcast emailings and opportunities for automated responses. The UCLA Internet Project found that more than one-quarter of email users in 2002 had communicated online with a government official.

The internet and television

In 1998 television viewing by children under the age of 14 in the US dropped for the first time in the 50-year history of television. For the very first time children found something more appealing than television: computers and the Internet. While television has had an unprecedented influence on American culture (witness the debate after the April 1999 Colorado school shootings), television has been primarily about entertainment and leisure. It is now becoming clear that computers and especially the Internet are producing effects comparable to television on work, school and play.

Internet users are frequently switching from television to go online, and this is already affecting the profits of the TV networks. How programming and marketing will adjust has yet to be seen, as has the effect of the experience of online interactivity compared with passive television watching. Americans still watch more TV than online videos, but video-watching is growing exponentially and Americans watch 12 billion online videos per month.

Information reliability and accuracy

Whilst the internet is viewed as a vital source of information by users, troublingly many users do not trust large amounts of the information they find online. While nearly three-quarters of users consider the internet to be a very important or extremely important source of information – a ranking higher than for books, television, radio, newspapers, or magazines – only half of users believe that most or all of the information online is reliable and accurate. Even worse, more than one-third of users say that only about half of the information they find online is reliable and accurate. How this credibility gap is addressed is another issue to watch.

Privacy, credit card security and buying online

Although the twin problems of online privacy and credit card security decline somewhat as internet use increases, they nevertheless remain an important factor in online purchasing and information exchange. In response, some credit card companies have begun to offer zero liability i.e., if a card is used by an unauthorized person to make a transaction, the cardholder will not be liable for the cost. The 2002 UCLA Internet Project produced several revealing findings about buying online and the attitudes of purchasers. While fewer adults bought online in 2002, the number of purchases and the amount they spent had increased over 2001. Nearly two-thirds of internet purchasers in 2002 said that online purchasing had reduced their purchasing in retail stores, even though concerns about using credit cards online remain high, and online purchasers do not generally consider the internet as a source of better prices than traditional stores. More than 70 percent of internet users say their online purchasing will increase.

Indecency and crime

Many complaints about the words and images accessible on the internet have been voiced on grounds of public decency and the protection of children. In 1996, Congress passed a law attempting to keep indecent language or pictures from being transmitted through cyberspace, but the Supreme Court struck it down as unconstitutional. If this problem has a solution, it probably lies either in close parental supervision of children's time on the computer or the development of software filters to bar access to sites not rated safe for children. A number of these are now on the market for about the price of a computer game. In October 2003, Microsoft shut down most of its internet chatrooms because of public concern about child abusers (pedophiles) posing as children or teenagers in order to meet and molest children.

The rise of broadband

Finally, many new issues may arise as internet access switches from telephone modem to faster methods on broadband. Already it has been found that broadband users spend more time online than telephone modem users in all of the most popular internet activities; and more broadband users than telephone modem users consider the internet an important source of information. Yet broadband access is far from universal and President Obama has said that "it is unacceptable that the United States ranks 15th in the world in broadband adoption."

The dramatic growth of the internet shows no sign of abating. There are more than a billion people online worldwide. By 2020, experts say, the internet will have gone beyond personal communications to become a thriving, low-cost network of billions of devices. Mobiles are predicted to play a big part in the net's future. Many more of the 10 billion new micros embedded each year will be on the internet. By 2020, most mobile networks are expected to provide universal one-gigabit-per-second minimum speed.

Key builders of the next generation of internet often agree on the direction technology will change, for example, in the addressing system and search engines, but there is much less agreement about the social and political impact those changes will have. Some have serious reservations about interoperability between systems (different formats working together), privacy, control over the internet architecture, and the emergence of a counter culture of isolated Luddites resorting to violence. Nor is the internet immune to media consolidation. The largest telephone and cable companies which own the infrastructure of the internet have been accused of attempting to control the speed in which users can access various websites. The debate surrounding the independence and public control of the internet is called *net neutrality*. Competing commercial interests, and government regulation, may preclude a universal internet. Thus the digital divide will remain. There could also be dangers in letting machines take over some tasks such as surveillance and security. Opinions are divided about whether English will become the common language of the internet. Experts are also divided over the effect of people's lives becoming increasingly online. A growing number of people are likely to be working within virtual worlds, more productive online than offline, but for most people it will make no difference in productivity; virtual reality will only change what type of work people do and how it is done. Many hope that giving all people access to information and a context to understand it will be an advance in civilization. Use of the internet will continue to grow (though probably through wireless and television devices rather than through computers) until it reaches television-type levels of 98.3% (World Internet Project. *Surveying the Digital Future: A Longitudinal International Study of the Individual and Social Effects of PC/Internet Technology*).

POSTS AND TELECOMMUNICATIONS

The U.S. Postal Service (USPS) is a quasi-independent agency of the federal government. The President nominates nine of the Board of Governors for confirmation by the Senate. The nine then select the U.S. Postmaster General, who serves as the board's tenth member and oversees the day to day activities of the service as Chief Executive Officer. The ten nominate to the remaining seat a Deputy Postmaster General, who acts as Chief Operating Officer.

The mission of USPS is to provide trusted, reliable, affordable universal service. Each day USPS delivers mail to 150 million US addresses and countless more worldwide, helping customers build and maintain relationships, share sensitive information, and exchange goods and services, thereby helping the economy grow. The USPS employs over 635,000 workers, making it the third-largest employer in the US, after the Department of Defense and Wal-Mart, and operates the largest civilian vehicle fleet in the world, with an estimated 260,000 vehicles.

Under the Constitution, Congress has a monopoly over the delivery of mail. Congress has delegated to USPS the power to decide whether others may compete with it, and USPS has made an exception to its monopoly for extremely urgent letters. USPS also has a monopoly of access to mailboxes. To provide a universal postal service covering every state and territory of the US means providing a range of products, access to services and facilities, ensuring delivery frequency, service quality, and security of the mail, and all at affordable and uniform pricing.

Mail is delivered once a day on-site to nearly all private homes and businesses Monday through Saturday except on observed federal holidays. The USPS still distinguishes between city delivery (where carriers generally walk and deliver to mailboxes hung on exterior walls or porches, or to commercial reception areas) and rural delivery (where carriers generally drive). With "curbside delivery," mailboxes are at the ends of driveways, on the nearest convenient road. "Central point delivery" is used in some locations, where several nearby residences share a "cluster" of individual mailboxes in a single housing. Some customers choose to use post office boxes for an additional fee, for privacy or convenience. This provides a locked box at the post office to which mail is addressed and delivered, usually earlier in the day than home delivery. High volume business customers can also arrange for special pickup. Another option is the old-style general delivery, for people who have neither post office boxes nor street addresses. Mail is held at the post office until they present identification and pick it up.

Through competition from email and private operations such as United Parcel Service (UPS) and FedEx, and the economic downturn, USPS has incurred heavy losses and been forced to adjust its business strategy and to modernize its products and services. First Class mail volume has declined 30% since 1998. Lower volume means lower revenues, but many of the costs of providing a universal six-day-a-week service are fixed. These include retiree pensions and health premiums for postal workers. Other costs, such as energy, are rising faster than inflation, while prices for services that generate 90 percent of USPS revenue are capped at the rate of inflation. Meanwhile every year the USPS must accommodate somewhere one million new addresses. USPS is facing a total debt of $10 billion. Moreover experts forecast a steady decline of direct mail volumes in favor of less expensive email advertising. At the same time, an improving economy will not necessarily increase conventional mail volume.

To meet these challenges, USPS went through a transformation while continuing to provide an affordable, universal mail service. This process is typical of what big companies in America do from time to time to refashion themselves to meet changed market conditions. Significant features are good business practice combined with use of the latest technology, good citizenship initiatives, and a smart use of public relations. USPS has increased productivity each year since 2000, through increased automation, better routing, and consolidation of facilities. Over 7,000 routes were eliminated in 2008 alone. First-Class service performance has reached record levels and customer satisfaction is among the highest levels ever achieved.

Through the transformation begun in 2002, aggressively balancing work hours and workload, reducing career positions through attrition, realigning the headquarters and field management structure, and postponing most capital spending, the USPS has reduced or avoided costs by $2.8 billion. More pricing flexibility has been introduced. For example, periodicals mailers can now get discounts if they share some of the work of preparing their publications for mailing. In 2008, USPS offered a 30 percent summer discount on larger volumes of standard mail. USPS is planning three operational initiatives to secure its future: maximizing address quality; automating every possible stage of mail handling through the Intelligent Mail Barcode (IMb); and reducing and outsourcing as many labor-intensive tasks as possible. The first will be achieved by charging extra for undeliverable addresses; and mailers who submit inaccurate mailing lists will not receive discounts on them. USPS is depending on IMb to be the cornerstone of the future efficiencies it plans in order to contain its escalating burden of labor costs. IMb enhances the sorting and tracking of letters and other flat mail items, and the tracking of individual mail pieces. The benefits to mailers include the incorporation of several functions into the IMb that used to require a second or third data set on the address label, including eligibility for automation discounts.

New automated technology brings the processing efficiency of letter mail to flat-size mail, oversized envelopes, magazines and catalogues. By sorting three times faster than the last generation of flat-sorting equipment, costs are controlled and the mail service gives better value. Building on its experience as a leader in innovation, the Postal Service has tested the revolutionary Segway Human Transporter on delivery routes in seven cities across the country, with more tests to follow. (The Segway HT is a battery-powered two-wheel platform which travels on pavements at 5 mph (8 kph) and can carry a load of over 30kg as well as a person.) The CONFIRM service lets customers track their mail as it moves through the system. The information helps businesses plan and manage inventory and other resources better. Click-N-Ship, available at *www.usps.com*, allows customers to print postage and mailing labels from their own home or office computers. The Postal Inspection Service takes a lead role in protecting senior citizens against fraud. At the same time, it is helping to combat identify theft, one of the fastest-growing and most devastating crimes. The Post Office was one of the first government departments to regulate obscene materials on a national basis. When the U.S. Congress passed the Comstock laws of 1873, it became illegal to send through the U.S. mail any material considered obscene, indecent or which promoted abortion issues, contraception, or alcohol consumption.

USPS lost its monopoly on the mailing of packages in the 1970s. Its network of bulk mailing centers was engineered to handle primarily packages and secondarily the less lucrative mail. Then FedEx, and shortly after UPS, came in and took over 90 percent of the business within a few years, because USPS could not react effectively to defend its market share. The corporation's pricing flexibility is limited to negotiated service agreements and high-volume packaging arrangements. Given the regulatory framework, it is likely that USPS will have to keep on raising prices, although this will reduce mail volumes. Hence, annual downsizing could be the norm until an alternative private sector service is allowed by Congress. Federal elected officials seem disinclined to consider privatization.

UPS and FedEx deliver packages which are larger and heavier than those the USPS will accept. A variety of other transportation companies move cargo around the country, but either have a limited range of delivery points, or specialize in items too large to be mailed. Many of the thousands of courier companies focus on same day delivery, for example by bicycle messenger.

Without question, the U.S. Postal Service has made an extraordinary contribution to the economic health and unity of the nation. But tough choices have been required in order to overcome significant challenges to the institution's continued ability to ensure universal mail service at affordable rates. Like some private sector delivery services, the Postal Service is suffering from weak mail volumes and rising labor and infrastructure-related costs. In addition to these pressures, significant debt loads, network inefficiencies and rigid statutes governing the institution's management are preventing the Postal Service from adequately adapting to fundamental market and technology changes. While many of these trends are exacerbated by a weak economy and other factors, the most significant threat is not. To the contrary, it appears that the nation is at the beginning of a long-term decline in First-Class Mail volumes as more and more Americans take greater advantage of cheaper electronic alternatives. In this new environment, unless Postal Service operating expenses can be reduced correspondingly, it is questionable whether affordable universal mail service via a self-financing public institution is sustainable. Rural residents meanwhile fear that relaxation of the universal service obligation would either mean they will have to pay more for mail, or will have to rely on the internet and satellite phones, which in some areas can be unreliable and expensive. In a report to the Postal Regulatory Commission in 2008, USPS said that increased regulatory flexibility was required to ensure affordable universal service in the future. In 2009, the Postmaster General floated the idea of reducing delivery days from 6 to 5, due to declining mail volume and increasing costs.

FACTFILE 14 MODES OF COMMUNICATION

Telephones - main lines in use:	163.2 million (2007)
Telephones - mobile cellular:	255 million (2007)
Telephone system:	*general assessment*: a large, technologically advanced, multipurpose communications system *domestic*: a large system of fiber-optic cable, microwave radio relay, coaxial cable, and domestic satellites carries every form of telephone traffic; a rapidly growing cellular system carries mobile telephone traffic throughout the country *international*: country code - 1; multiple ocean cable systems provide international connectivity; satellite earth stations - 61 Intelsat (45 Atlantic Ocean and 16 Pacific Ocean), 5 Intersputnik (Atlantic Ocean region), and 4 Inmarsat (Pacific and Atlantic Ocean regions) (2000)
Radio broadcast stations:	AM 4,789; FM 8,961; shortwave 19 (2006)
Television broadcast stations:	2,218 (2006)
Internet country code:	.us
Internet hosts:	316 million (2008); note - the US Internet total host count includes the following top level domain host addresses: .us, .com, .edu, .gov, .mil, .net, and .org.
Internet users:	223 million (2008)

Cell phones

The development of the telephone and radio have gone hand-in-hand. Alexander Graham Bell invented the telephone in 1876. The following year, the first private telephone was installed in the home of Charles Williams of Somerville, MA. By the end of 1880, 47,900 telephones were in use in the US. But it was Italian inventor, Guglielmo Marconi, who proved the feasibility of radio communications by sending and receiving the first signal in 1903. From Cape Cod he sent a 54-word greeting from President Theodore Roosevelt across the Atlantic to Britain's King Edward VII. Reginald Fessenden, who had worked for Edison, and in 1900 pioneered AM radio, in 1906 successfully completed an 11-mile wireless telephone call from his laboratory in Brant Rock, MA. It was the Detroit Police Department who started the first one-way radio messaging service in 1921. Again, it was a police cruiser that had the first two-way radio installed, by Motorola in 1941. The first commercial mobile radiotelephone service was introduced in 1946 in St. Louis, but it was not till 1965 that AT&T eliminated push-to-talk operation and offered automatic dialing. Then in 1972, Bell Labs made wider mobile telephone communication possible, enabling experimental cellular systems to be launched in Chicago and the Washington, D.C./Baltimore region in 1977 which were activated in 1983. The first standardized cellular service in the world became available then, and that same year Motorola introduced the first truly "mobile" radiotelephone. Nicknamed the "brick," it had one hour of talk time and eight hours of standby. On October 13, 1983 from a Chrysler convertible in a parking lot at Soldier Field, Chicago, the first international cell phone call was made to Bell's grandson in Germany. Skeptics said the service would never become popular. Units weighed 40 oz (2 1/2 lbs) and cost $4000. Calls cost several dollars per minute. Yet subscribership topped two million in 1986, using 1,000 cell sites across America. Nationwide services began in 1988. Motorola announced the first cell phone with a flip-lid mouthpiece. It sold for $3000. Cellular subscribership surpassed 5 million by 1990 and 10 million by 1992, using 10,000 cell sites across America. That year the now almost universal use of texting began. Bell Atlantic Mobile launched the first commercial CDMA network in 1996. Use of cell phones passed 38 million in 1996, then 50 million in 1997, using 50,000 cell sites. That year the 2G service began. The next year the average consumer was using a phone for over 2 hours per month, and WAP (Wireless Application Protocol) began. At the millennium, wireless subscribership exceeded 100 million and digital wireless users outnumbered analog subscribers. The average wireless consumer was using a phone for 320 minutes per month. There are now 200 million customers and projected to be 500-800 million, using cell phones as a universal tool for entertainment, education, credit card payments, safety and other purposes.

Since 2005, mobile wireless has been the fastest-growing form of high-speed telephony (over 200 kbps). Almost all new high-speed subscriptions are for advanced services, with the number of subscribers with 3G devices almost doubling to 64.2 million. By June 2008, 28.4 percent of subscribers had 3G, equal to the five largest countries in Europe (which have a combined population equal to the US). According to the FCC, the percentage of mobile subscribers who use their cell phones to browse the mobile Web for such services as news, information, sports, news, entertainment, maps and directions, financial account access, financial news, business directories and travel is slightly higher in the US than in Europe. Interestingly, both Hispanics and African Americans use mobile laptops to access the internet at a greater rate than the average internet user (*The Pew Internet & American Life Project*). Currently 62% of Americans have some experience with mobile access to digital data and tools using a handheld wireless device or laptop (*Pew*). There are more than 600 unique wireless handsets/devices for sale. Handsets range from simple, voice-only models like the Jitterbug, to multifunction devices like the Apple iPhone, Smartphones and multimedia devices. Mobile calls are significantly less expensive per minute ($0.05) than in Western Europe ($0.20) and Japan ($0.25). In return, services include camera phones, ringtones, social networks and E-911 calls. Wireless broadband also has economic benefits for productivity and employment. A full 3G mobile broadband coverage will, however, require an increase and upgrading of the towers and access to more spectrums. Although a nationally available service, cell phone networks are still subject to inconsistent state requirements. The FCC began in April 2009 the process of developing a national broadband plan that will seek to ensure that every American has access to broadband capability. In conjunction with the Broadband Technology Opportunities Program established by the Recovery Act, the FCC is working with the National Telecommunications and Information Administration (NTIA).

According to a National Health Interview Survey conducted by the Centers for Disease Control, the number of households opting for cell phones only is greater than those that just have traditional landlines. In 2008, 20% of households had only cells compared to 17% with landlines but no cells. By contrast, in 2003, 3% of households were wireless only, while 43% were landline only. The growth of cell-only households is partly due to the recession. Six in 10 households have both landline and cell phones, while only one in 50 have no phones at all. Some households (15%) have both landlines and cells but take few or no calls on their landlines, often because these are wired into computers. Thus 35% of American households are usually reachable only on cells. About a third of people age

18 to 29 live in households with only cell phones. Wireless use is accelerating and could reach almost one-third of households by 2012. Wireless consumers are paying less today than they did 10 years ago while enjoying almost seven times as many minutes of use per month.

PHYSICAL COMMUNICATIONS AND TRANSPORTATION

The US is the most mobile nation in history. Transportation accounts for 19 percent of spending by the average household in America - as much as for food and health care combined - and is second only to spending on housing. The independence of the US, by uniting the former Thirteen Colonies, created the largest area without internal tariff barriers, or internal market, in the world at that time. The first such area was Great Britain, created by the Union of England and Scotland in 1707. Then in 1753 an internal market was created in Russia. Shortly after the US, Napoleon made an internal market in France. A key factor in the efficient working of internal markets is the unimpeded movement of people and goods, as well as services and capital. Across the American panorama, vast arteries of physical communication enable the unimpeded transportation which is vital to the economy and valuable in binding the nation together as one people.

Businesses and consumers in America's advanced economy depend on the interconnected transportation network to move myriads of goods, from raw materials such as lumber, coal, and petroleum products to manufactures including medical supplies, furniture, household appliances, and computers. More than ever before, Americans take for granted buying imported fresh fruits, vegetables, and flowers at their local supermarkets; receiving next day delivery of goods purchased over the internet; and tracking express packages online to know their whereabouts at any given time. These everyday occurrences result from the availability of a vast transportation network, changes in freight delivery services and freight carrier operations, and improvements in freight logistics, due in part to advancements in information technology and the internet.

In addition to roads, there are 120,000 miles (192,000 km) of major railroads, over 25,000 miles (40,000 km) of commercially navigable waterways, over 5,000 public-use airports and two million miles (3.2 million km) of oil and natural gas pipelines. This vast system also includes over 500 major urban public transit operators and more than 300 ports on the coasts, Great Lakes, and inland waterways. According to *Freight in America* (Bureau of Transportation Statistics, 2006) trucking is the most frequently used mode of freight transportation, hauling an estimated 70 percent of the total value, 60 percent of the weight, and 34 percent of the overall ton-miles, and is increasing its market share. Trucking is followed by rail at 31 percent of ton-miles, pipeline at 16 percent, and water with 11 percent. In general, trucking dominates shipment distances of less than 500 miles (800 km) while rail dominates longer distance shipments. Air freight and express delivery are growing the most rapidly, although air cargo remains a small and specialized part of freighting in terms of tonnage. Intermodal freight, where more than one type of vehicle is used, is increasing, and use of containers for multimodal shipments is rising. Growing demand for more efficient and faster delivery of high value, low weight products is changing the structure of the freight industry, creating new alliances among shippers, carriers, and logistics providers. At the same time, enormous volumes of bulk commodities—whether grains, lumber, ores, coal, or oil—continue to move into, out of, and within the US. One out of every six tons shipped is gravel and crushed stone, 11 percent is electronic, electrical, and office equipment. The top commodity by ton-miles in 2002 was coal, accounting for about 22 percent.

The leading state of origin of traded goods by value is California with 11 percent, followed by Texas with 7 percent; other leading states of origin include Ohio and Illinois. By weight, the leading metropolitan areas of origin are Houston, Chicago and Los Angeles. Smaller sized shipments (less than 500 pounds) account for about 25 percent of the value. Of these, those weighing less than 100 pounds are growing fastest.

Transportation accounts for 10% of GDP and 16% of the labor force. The wide range of transportation services includes for-hire freight carriers, private transportation providers, freight forwarders, logistics providers, and firms that service and maintain vehicles. During the decade to 2002, labor productivity rose 53 percent for rail, 23 percent for trucking, and 143 percent for pipeline.

Roads

There are 3.9 million miles (6.24 million km) of public roads. Between 1970 and 2008, passenger travel increased two-and-one-half times while road capacity only increased five percent. U.S. Department of Transportation (DOT) data show that a minimum $65 billion per year federal investment in highway improvements is necessary simply to maintain the current physical conditions and system performance of the nation's highway and bridge network. Some commentators believe that road use will increase by nearly two-thirds in the next 20 years. The Recovery Act 2009 provided $27 billion for roads and bridges

Interstate highways

The interstate highway system is an interconnected network of controlled-access freeways (highways without intersections) that stretches for more than 46,380 miles (74,600 km) and reaches nearly every major city. On many of these roads, a toll has to be paid, and there are speed limits. In 1941, President Franklin Roosevelt set up a committee to look into the creation of a network of highways as a way to provide jobs for people out of work, and the Federal-Aid Highway Act of 1944 authorized the designation of "Interstate Highways," but not funding for them, because of World War II. It was President Eisenhower who made the interstate highway system a reality. When he crossed the country in a military convoy in 1919, the journey took 62 days because of the poor roads and bridges. Years later, during World War II, he observed the advantages of the German autobahn network. In 1956, after a long, bitter debate between various interests such as rail, truck, tire, oil, and farm groups over who would pay for the new highways and how, he persuaded Congress to authorize a huge program of state aid for highways under a further Federal-Aid Highway Act. Later, the Surface Transportation Assistance Act of 1982 standardized truck size and weight limits across the country for traffic on the Interstate Highways. This made trucking fully transcontinental. In a country with the world's largest auto industry, a national highway system makes sense. The system is aging, however. The most serious problem is structurally deficient bridges.

A standard design

- The system has uniform design standards, including:
- a minimum of two lanes in each direction
- lanes that are 12 ft in width
- a 10-foot paved shoulder on the right
- design speeds of 50–70 mph

Naming the Interstates

The procedure for naming the highways is systematic. Major routes are designated by single- or two-digit numbers. If a route runs north-south, it is given an odd number, and if a route runs east-west, an even number. For north-south routes, numbering conventions begin in the west. Thus I-5 runs north and south along the West Coast, while I-95 runs north and south along the East Coast. For east-west routes, numbers begin in the south. Major routes usually traverse cities and are the shortest and most direct line of travel. Connecting interstate routes that travel around a city carry three-digit numbers.

Interstate highways have contributed to the economic growth and quality of life in America. Indeed, the system has been a major factor in making the US the homogeneous nation it has become. All demographic trends indicate overwhelmingly that people will continue to pursue the American Dream of a house in the suburbs and a high degree of personal mobility. Thus the highway system will continue to be a vital feature of transport.

The National Highway System

The National Highway System (NHS) is the largest highway system in the world. The NHS was mandated by Congress in 1995 to extend the benefits of the interstate highways to areas not served directly. By providing essential linkages to other modes of transportation, the NHS creates a seamless transportation system for the rapid movement of people and products.

The NHS does not replace the interstates but supplements them by adding 2% to the total mileage. The NHS covers 163,000 miles (261,000 km) of roads important to the nation's economy, defense, and mobility which at many points are linked to train and bus stations, ports and airports. The NHS will function as the backbone of the nation's 21st century transportation system. Although containing 4% of the nation's roads, the NHS carries carry 40% of the traffic, 75 percent of heavy truck traffic, and 90 percent of tourist traffic. The NHS links 190 rail/truck terminals for the transfer of containerized cargo to and from markets. About 90 percent of America's population lives within 8 km of an NHS road. Another measure of the significance of the NHS is that counties that contain NHS highways also host 99 percent of all jobs in the nation. A valuable benefit of the NHS is reducing the $40 billion per year cost of congestion.

THE NATIONAL HIGHWAY SYSTEM

- Interstate Highway System 70,000 km, 30% of the NHS
- 21 high priority corridors 7,200 km
- Strategic Highway Corridor Network, or STRAHNET, identified by the Department of Defense in cooperation with DOT. 25,000 km
- Strategic Highway Corridor Network connectors 3,000 km
- Arterial highways 148,000 km connections to major ports, airports, public transportation facilities, and other intermodal facilities

Waterways

Originally, the vast network of rivers and lakes were the main arteries of communication in the eastern part of the country and played a great part in economic development. The Mississippi and its tributaries are easily navigable, and the five Great Lakes, four of which are shared with Canada, are linked to these rivers by a series of canals.

Together with pipelines and railways, America's 25,000 miles (40,000 km) of commercially navigable waterways are still important for the transport of bulk freight. About 29% of the GDP and 13 million jobs rely on international trade, and 95% of overseas trade travels by water for at least part of the journey. The marine transportation system moves more than two billion tons of freight, over 60% of the nation's grain exports, and 95% of soybean exports. Over 99% of US international freight by volume – 1.3 billion tons – moves on federally maintained waterways. The US maintains 321 ports.

Inland and intracoastal waterways directly serve 38 states. The Gulf Coast states, the Midwest and the Ohio Valley especially depend on them. Almost all of the navigable rivers and canals are in the eastern half of the country. The steep grades and variable flows of most of the West Coast rivers make them unsuitable for navigation. Also, most of the large rivers there are dammed to supply water for hydroelectricity and other uses. A shortage of water and the mountainous terrain in the West make canals unfeasible as well.

The U.S. Army Corps of Engineers (USACE) is responsible for most of the commercially important inland waterways together with their 191 commercially active locks and 237 lock chambers. The locks allow barges to "stair-step" their way through the system and reach distant inland ports such as Minneapolis, Chicago, and Pittsburgh. These 12,000 miles (19,000 km) include 11,000 miles (18,000 km) of fuel taxed waterways, where commercial operators pay a fuel tax, which is deposited in the Inland Waterways Trust Fund to pay for half the cost of new construction and major rehabilitation. The Mississippi River System, including the Gulf Intracoastal Waterway (GIWW) connects Gulf Coast ports, such as Mobile, New Orleans, Baton Rouge, Houston, and Corpus Christi, with major inland ports, including Memphis, St. Louis, Chicago, St. Paul, Cincinnati, and Pittsburgh. The Lower Mississippi from Baton Rouge to the Gulf of Mexico allows ocean shipping to connect with barge traffic, thereby making this segment vital to both domestic and foreign trade. In the Pacific Northwest, the Columbia-Snake River System allows navigation 465 miles (750 km) inland to Lewiston, Idaho.

The waterways have the ability to convey large volumes of bulk commodities or primary manufactured products long distances at relatively low cost. Towboats push strings of barges which are lashed together to form a "tow." A tow may consist of four or six barges on smaller waterways up to over 40 barges on the Mississippi below its confluence with the Ohio. A 15-barge tow is common on the larger rivers with locks, such as the Ohio, Upper Mississippi, Illinois and Tennessee. A single 15-barge tow is equivalent to about 225 railroad cars or 870 tractor-trailer trucks. The ability to move more cargo per shipment makes barge transport both fuel efficient and environmentally advantageous. On average, a gallon of fuel allows one ton of cargo to be shipped 59 miles by truck, 202 miles by railway, and 514 miles by barge (95 km, 325 km, and 827 km, respectively). Carbon dioxide emissions from water transportation are significantly less than rail. Inland waterways also help reduce traffic congestion, accidents and noise.

The inland and intracoastal waterway system handles about 17 percent of all intercity freight by volume. Coal is the largest commodity moved by inland waterways. The electricity industry depends on the waterways for over 20 percent of the coal it uses. Petroleum products are the next largest item. Grain and other farm products for export are mostly moved by waterway to ports on the Lower Mississippi or Columbia. In all, 60 percent of farm exports travel by inland waterway. Other major commodities include aggregates, such as stone, sand and gravel used in construction; chemicals, including fertilizers; metal ores, minerals and products, such as steel; and many other manufactured products.

Over 50 percent of the locks operated by the U.S. Army Corps of Engineers (USACE) are over 50 years old and approaching the end of their design lives. They are in need of modernization or major repair. Many locks are simply too small and tows of 12 or more barges have to be split into two sections to pass through, causing long delays. In the 1960s, USACE began to modernize and enlarge the locks on the Ohio. Modernization continues today with over $3.5 billion to be spent over the next decade. Additionally, over 70 million Americans participate in recreational boating, using 16 million boats of all types. Millions of Americans enjoy passenger vessels that provide sightseeing, excursion, dining, gaming, wind jamming, whale watching, and nature cruises.

Trucking

Truckers (truck drivers) have been romanticized as modern-day cowboys and outlaws, using Citizens Band (CB) radio to relay information to each other about police patrols and transportation authorities. In the 1970s, plaid shirts, trucker hats, CB radios, and using CB slang became a fashion. In 1976, "Convoy," a novelty song about a convoy of truck drivers evading speed traps and toll booths across America, was the number one hit on the Billboard chart. The following year, *Smokey and the Bandit* was the second highest grossing film from that year, while *CB Bears*, a Saturday morning cartoon featuring mystery-solving bears who communicate by CB radio, made its debut. Since then cell phones have largely, but not entirely, displaced CB.

The trucking, transportation or logistics industry is the transport and distribution of industrial and commercial goods by commercial motor vehicle. According to size and design these are most commonly semi-truck, box trucks or dump trucks. A heavy truck may weigh as much as 80,000 pounds (36,000 kg), be 60-foot (18 m) long and have 18 wheels. The trucking industry is essential to the American economy, transporting large quantities of raw materials, works in process and finished goods, mostly from manufacturing plants to retail distribution outlets. Retail stores, hospitals, gas stations, garbage disposal, construction sites, banks, and even a clean water supply depend on trucks to distribute vital cargo. Over 80% of communities rely exclusively on trucks to deliver their fuel, clothing, medicine, and other consumer goods. Unless a manufacturing or distribution facility has a direct connection to a railroad, the remainder of the trip must be handled by truck. Railroads are primarily used to haul bulk quantities of cargo over long distances. The spread of cost-saving just-in-time logistics has increased the use of trucks to make more frequent deliveries. The busiest gas stations, for example, require deliveries of fuel several times per day, while grocery stores require deliveries of perishable food every two to three days. Trucks are also vital in construction, as dump trucks and portable concrete mixers are necessary to move large amounts of building materials and waste. By 2006 there were over 26 million trucks on America's roads, hauling over 10 billion tons of freight. Trucking is responsible for around 70% of freight and contributes around 5% to the GDP annually.

Truckers must undertake special education and training, obtain a commercial driver's license, and observe the hours of service laid down by the Federal Motor Carrier Safety Administration, a division of the U.S. Department of Transportation. Truck drivers are limited in the number of daily and weekly hours they may drive, the roads and highways they may drive upon, and in the amount of alcohol they may have in their blood. A driver may not drive more than 11 hours in any 14-hour period, after which he/she must rest for 10 hours. Three hours may be spent in such duties as fueling, filling out paperwork, obtaining vehicle repairs, and conducting mandatory vehicle inspections. The Federal Highway Administration has set a blood alcohol limit that is no higher than half that permissible for other drivers. In some states there are special speed limits for trucks; and trucks may be excluded from the outside (fast) lanes. Interstate trucking is generally limited to the interstates and to state highways on the National Highway Network.

Long-haul drivers often spend weeks away from home, spending their time off and sleeping at truck stops or rest areas. Driving is relatively dangerous work. Truck drivers are five times more likely to die on the job than the average worker, accounting for 12% of all work-related deaths, the highest number of all fatalities. Computers, satellites and the internet have increased productivity, made drivers' jobs easier, and provided more in-cab entertainment on what is often a lonely job. Using a keyboard, a driver can now, for example, input the information from a bill of lading into a simple text-only dot matrix screen which displays an automated system of pre-formatted messages known as *macros*. There are macros for each stage of the delivery, such as "loaded and leaving shipper" and "arrived at final destination." Drivers no longer need to contact their dispatcher by public phone. Better communication means fewer miles traveling with an empty truck and less time waiting between loads. The system also allows the company to track such data as the driver's fuel usage, speed, location, direction and time spent driving. GPS satellite navigation is replacing paper maps. Indeed a UPS truck's rear doors cannot be opened until the vehicle is at the right location. For entertainment, drivers can listen to satellite radio coast-to-coast without the signal being interrupted. Off duty, drivers can watch the wider range of channels available on satellite television. Technology is also changing the relationship between carriers and freight brokers. Traditional freight brokers acted as intermediaries to manage the coordination of freight, helping independent companies and drivers match loads with available trucks. Brokerage over the internet enables shippers to post loads and solicit bids directly from carriers, without the need for human brokers.

The trucking industry is made up of small businesses. Ninety-three per cent of the 500,000-plus interstate carriers operate fewer than 20 trucks. The industry employed 10 million people, including 1.8 million drivers of heavy trucks in 2006. The Motor Carrier Act of 1980 deregulated the industry, dramatically increasing the number of trucking companies. The trucking workforce was drastically de-unionized, resulting in lower average pay for drivers. Many long-haul drivers are nearing retirement and very few new hires are expected in the near future (although this may change in the recession), due to the long working hours, long periods away from home, the dangerous nature of the work, and the relatively low pay compared to other forms of unskilled labor. In 2005 there was an estimated shortage of 20,000 long haul drivers, which is expected to increase to 111,000 by 2014. Meanwhile employee turnover is extremely high. Many more drivers are quitting their jobs than being hired. Moreover, many of the trucks themselves are inefficient and polluting. "The nation's eight million heavy trucks…average less than seven miles to the gallon. By themselves, those heavy trucks consume as much petroleum as all of Germany" (Greenspan, *op. cit.*, p. 460).

International trade

While over 400 seaports, airports, and land border crossings handle international merchandise trade, most of that trade passes through a relatively small number of gateways. In 2003 the nation's top five freight transportation gateways handled more than one-fourth of the total value of the trade, and the top 14 gateways handled more than 50 percent. That year, according to *Connecting Our Nation to Places and Markets Abroad*, Bureau of Transportation Statistics, 2004, the Port of Los Angeles was the leading gateway for international trade by value. John F. Kennedy (JFK) International Airport, New York, ranked second, and the Port of Long Beach third, followed by the land border crossing of Detroit, and the Port of New York and New Jersey. The growth of Los Angeles reflects a major increase in trade with Asia and Pacific Rim countries, especially growth in goods from China. China now ranks as the second largest supplier of merchandise imports by value of shipments. The water transportation system carries more trade, both in tonnage and value, than any other mode: 78 percent of the weight and 41 percent of the value in 2003. Pound for pound, water cargo tends to be lower in value than cargo carried by other modes. Freight moving through land gateways accounts for 22 percent of the weight of US trade, but 28 percent of the value. Air cargo's share of total trade tonnage was less than 1 percent, but that cargo accounted for 26 percent of the value of all US trade.

In 2003 nearly one-third (32 percent) of the value of all US merchandise trade was with the two largest trading partners, Canada and Mexico. Land trade—carried by truck, rail, and pipeline—accounted for 89 percent of this value. Even though there are over 75 land ports along the US-Canadian border and over 25 along the US-Mexican border, the land freight across the borders is heavily concentrated at a few gateways. This concentration affects traffic and congestion at the border as well as the growth of major transportation corridors. In 2003, the top three ports for US-NAFTA land trade by value were Detroit, Michigan; Laredo, Texas; and Port Huron, Michigan. In total, these three ports accounted for over 41 percent of the value.

Most of the main land border ports serve as national and multistate regional trade gateways in addition to serving local markets. The proportions vary quite a bit among gateways. Only about 30 percent of the value of shipments passing through Detroit originates or terminates in Michigan, and, for Laredo, only 25 percent of the value of shipments starts or ends within Texas. In contrast, 91 percent of the freight shipments passing through Otay Mesa, the largest California port on the US-Mexican border, originates or terminates in that state.

In value terms, trucks carried nearly three-quarters (72 percent) of all land trade in 2003. But many border crossings are important rail gateways, facilitating the transport of long-haul freight to and from origins and destinations in several states. Over half of the value of US-NAFTA rail trade passes through just two gateways, Laredo and Port Huron. These two ports, along with Eagle Pass, Texas, have seen large growth in the value of rail cargo in recent years, in part due to rail privatization in Mexico and new North American rail alliances. Rail marketing alliances, such as the NAFTA Railway formed by Kansas City Southern and other rail lines, provide integrated service from the US into Mexico and Canada with a single freight rate. Regarding modal shares, in 2003, trucks moved 37 percent of the tonnage of total land trade imports, rail moved 32 percent, and pipelines accounted for 31 percent. Trucks hauled a much larger percentage of the tonnage of US land imports from Mexico (74 percent) than from Canada (32 percent). The US has the largest network of energy pipelines in the world: oil (stretching 55,000 miles), natural gas (20,000 miles), gasoline (95,000 miles), and those moving many chemicals such as ammonia. Pipelines remain the safest, most efficient and economical way to move these resources.

Over two-thirds (68 percent) of the value of US international merchandise trade is to and from countries other than Canada and Mexico. Maritime trade accounts for about 60 percent of this; air freight accounts for the rest. The Port of Los Angeles' prominence as a gateway by value of goods reflects the specialization among seaports. The Pacific and Atlantic ports are heavily involved in container trade, while the Gulf Coast ports are primarily involved in dry bulk and tanker trade.

Gulf ports such as Houston lead other US ports in tonnage of international cargo shipments— agricultural, petroleum, coal, and other bulk commodities. In general, bulk commodities are lower value per ton, and containerized commodities are higher. In 2003, the top three seaport gateways by weight were Houston, followed by South Louisiana and New York and New Jersey. Maritime cargo exports account for 30 percent and imports 70 percent of trade. Air freight accounted for 26 percent of the total US merchandise trade in 2003. JFK International Airport was the leading airport for international freight by value, handling over one-fifth (21 percent) of imports and exports. Because the types of commodities transported by air e.g., cut flowers, electronics, and clothing are higher in value per ton than those transported by other freight modes, the value of shipments is a much better indicator than weight in revealing the importance of air gateways to the nation's international commerce.

Container ships

Five decades ago, the containership revolution started in America. Today, one container in every nine in global trade is bound for or coming from the US. The year 1956 saw the US pioneer the world's first use of containers for intermodal sea-land movements between Newark, New Jersey, and Houston, Texas, seamlessly moving cargo from sea to land and land to sea in standard metal containers. Containers have greatly changed the movement of US-international freight, port operations, and the distribution of ports' share of ocean-borne trade. They have also impacted rail and trucking operations to and from seaports. With the exception of a few products, such as cars transported in specialized vessels, huge container vessels carry manufactured products of nearly every description. Although the US remained the leading trading nation, accounting for 12 percent of total world merchandise trade in 2005, it has ranked second in container traffic to China since 1998. Container ports are operating at or near capacity, which is causing concern to shippers. Economists estimate that over the next 20 years seaborne commerce will double and inland navigation increase by more than 35%. Today's mega-containerships require deep-draft channels and harbors (45-50 feet) to avoid running aground, but few US ports meet this requirement.

Public transportation

Railroads

By 1869 it was possible to travel and ship goods from the Atlantic to the Pacific by rail, and there is now a railroad network extending over almost the entire country. There are 122,000 miles of major railroads, of which 10,572 miles and 2,825 rail stations are run by transit authorities, mostly urban, but the majority by private railroads and Amtrak. The North American railway landscape has changed significantly in the last few years. A "NAFTA railroad" has emerged with the acquisition of the Illinois Central (IC) by Canadian National (CN) and the subsequent marketing agreement with the Kansas City Southern (KCS). There is now a direct rail link starting in Canada between the US and Mexico. The newly integrated NAFTA rail network promises to be particularly important for trade in agricultural products. Some freight railroads are high-tech structures allowing double-deck trains carrying 250 20-ton containers each to run efficiently cross-country. Many of the other railroads, however, are in bad repair resulting from lack of investment.

The National Railroad Passenger Corporation (Amtrak) is a federal entity organized in 1971 to provide intercity passenger train service. "Amtrak" is a combination of the words "American" and "track." It operates passenger service on 21,000 miles (34,000 km) of track primarily owned by freight railroads and connecting 500 destinations in 46 states. Amtrak serves some states only nominally through stations along borders or away from major population areas, as in Idaho. Several significant Amtrak routes have been eliminated because of lack of funding, leaving gaps in service. There is no service in South Dakota or Wyoming. Alaska is served by Alaska Railroad. In Hawaii there are only a few tourist lines. Some railroads also serve Canada. In fiscal year 2008, Amtrak served 28.7 million passengers, compared with 16 million plus in 1971. According to Amtrak, an average of more than 70,000 passengers per day ride on up to 300 of its trains. In the 2000s, ridership increased continuously, partly because of the upgrading of the network's tracks, trains and stations, which made schedules faster and more reliable. Meanwhile Amtrak's competitors, particularly airlines, were affected by bankruptcies, 9/11, and rising fuel costs. Commuter rail is also making a comeback. There are almost 3,825 route miles of commuter rail service in operation in the US. An additional 134 miles are under construction and 300 miles are in design, with over 2,300 miles in planning and 1,100 additional miles under consideration for commuter rail projects. But despite recent growth, the US has one of the lowest intercity rail usages in the developed world.

Amtrak is no longer required by law, but is encouraged, to operate a national route system. Routes vary widely in frequency of service, from three trips weekly on the *Sunset Limited*, from Los Angeles to New Orleans, to weekday service several times per hour on the Northeast Corridor (NEC) from New York City to Washington, D.C. Many commuter railways offer service during peak times only, and on a round trip basis, running during the morning and evening rush hours. Amtrak also operates a captive bus service, *Thruway Motorcoach*, which provides connections to train routes, especially in California. The most heavily used services are those on the NEC, which include the *Acela Express* and *Northeast Regional*, and in the Chicago metro area. The NEC serves Boston, New York, Philadelphia, Baltimore, Washington, D.C. and many communities between. The 600 mile-long (960 km) electrified line is shared with commuter trains and regional and intercity trains. The NEC services accounted for 10 million of Amtrak's 25.7 million passengers in 2007. Two-thirds of the nation's rail riders live in the New York City metro area. Regional services in California subsidized by the California Department of Transportation are the most popular services outside of the NEC and the only other services boasting over one million passengers per year. The *Pacific Surfliner*, *Capitol Corridor* and *San Joaquins* services accounted for a combined 5 million passengers in 2007. Connections between Amtrak trains and other transportation are available at many stations, especially downtown and a few airports. Amtrak trains have both names and numbers. Train routes are named to reflect the rich and complex history of the routes and the areas they traverse. Each scheduled run of the route is assigned a number. Generally, even numbered routes run northward and eastward, while odd-numbered routes run southward and westward. Some routes, however, such as the *Pacific Surfliner*, use the opposite system. Many major cities in the Midwest, West, and South have two or fewer trains per day.

Although passenger traffic has declined steeply since World War 11, railroads are still important for the carriage of many types of freight. Amtrak Express provides small package and less-than-truckload shipping among more than 100 cities. Amtrak Express also offers station-to-station shipment of human remains to many express cities.

For its entire existence, Amtrak has been subject to political cross-winds and insufficient capital. The formation of Amtrak in 1971 was criticized as a bailout serving corporate rail interests and union railroaders, not the traveling public. In fact, Amtrak only owns track in the Northeast Corridor and has to pay fees to other railroads elsewhere. When other railroads have gone out of business, Amtrak has sometimes had to discontinue services because it has been unable to afford to take over and maintain the track and bridges.

When the federal government began to construct the National Highway System, the railroads found themselves faced with unprecedented competition for passengers and freight with automobiles, buses, trucks, and aircraft, all of which were subsidized by the billions of dollars spent in construction and maintenance of highways, government-owned airports and the air traffic control system. Amtrak has never operated at a profit. Critics assert that Amtrak has proven incapable of operating as a business and that it does not provide valuable transportation services meriting public support. They argue that subsidies should be ended, national rail service terminated, and the Northeast Corridor turned over to private interests. Advocates assert that Amtrak should only be expected to be as self-sufficient as those competing modes of transit. Arguably, no form of passenger transportation in the US is self-sufficient. Highways, airports, and air traffic control are funded through the Highway Trust Fund, Aviation Trust Fund and the General Fund, paid for by user fees, highway fuel and road taxes and general taxation. Former Amtrak President Alex Kummant claimed that Amtrak received $40 in federal funds per passenger, while highways are subsidized at a rate of $500–$700 per automobile. Moreover, Amtrak provides all of its own security, while airport security is a separate federal subsidy, Kummant added. The Rail Safety Improvement Act 2008 appropriated $2.6 billion for year in Amtrak through 2013.

The influence of unions is a strong force against change. Amtrak has 14 separate unions to negotiate with, because of the fragmentation of railroad unions by job. It has 24 separate contracts with those unions. This makes it difficult to make substantial changes, in contrast to a situation where one union negotiates with one employer. In recent times, efforts at reforming passenger rail have addressed labor issues. In 1997 Congress released Amtrak from a prohibition on contracting for labor outside of the corporation (and outside its unions). Since that time, many of Amtrak's employees have been working without a contract.

President Obama has adopted a much more rail-friendly policy. His strategy is a network of new and upgraded 100-mile to 600-mile high-speed rail corridors that will connect underserved cities. The projects will be developed through a partnership between the public sector and private industry, which the Administration hopes will stimulate the economy through the creation of a range of new jobs. The US also faces pressure to decrease its dependence on oil and strive towards a more sustainable eco-friendly future. The U.S. Department of Energy considers Amtrak among the most energy-efficient forms of transportation. Per passenger mile, Amtrak is 18 percent more energy-efficient than commercial airlines and automobiles. Even so, the Administration's investment of $13 billion is only a fraction of that in Europe and Japan, and the maximum railroad speeds of 100 mph (62kph) much lower.

Air transport

Air transport has largely replaced rail for long-distance passenger travel, especially for transcontinental journeys, because it is cheaper. The nation's airlines survived their post-9/11 tailspin but that was not their only problem The US airline industry is apparently sputtering back to life. But the airlines may be in more precarious shape than ever. To reach profitability, the airlines have slashed pay, furloughed workers, cut service, and grounded hundreds of aircraft. Yet every major carrier except Southwest is losing money. Revenues will still need to grow by a hefty 10 percent for the industry just to break even.

September 11 was not a temporary setback. Nearly 600 aircraft – about 15 percent of the US fleet – had to be taken out of service because of decreased demand. The market for air travel is changing in ways few airlines expected. As a percentage of GDP, airline revenue has fallen 20 to 30 percent from levels of the past 25 years. Long security lines and other inconveniences make air travel slower, while videoconferencing and webcasting are becoming viable alternatives for business travelers—the airlines' main source of cash. There are no big, strong airlines, excluding Southwest, which could merge with troubled competitors, even if regulators gave permission. In future, say industry analysts, the big carriers, unable to cut costs further, will focus on more profitable long-distance and international routes. Air travel will probably become more expensive and less convenient, although there will be better benefits such as individual TV sets. More airline mergers, such as that between United and Continental, are likely, according to analysts.

The 30 largest airports in the US handle nearly 70 percent of all commercial aviation traffic. During the past 20 years, these airports have become increasingly congested. In the last twenty-five years, only one major airport has been built: Denver International Airport. From 1995 to 1999, runway capacity increased only three percent while passenger demand increased 16 percent.

Flying has changed the American lifestyle. Cross-country family reunions and international business meetings so commonplace today would have been impossible not long ago. Dining on fresh Alaskan salmon in Topeka, Kansas, receiving overnight deliveries from Europe or Asia, and moving emergency relief supplies from across the country are among the many remarkable innovations made possible by safe, affordable and abundant air service.

According to the Federal Aviation Administration (FAA), the airline fleet included 7,816 aircraft at the end of 2007, comprising 6,808 (3,972 mainline and 2,836 regional) passenger aircraft and 1,008 cargo jets. US airlines posted record passenger and cargo traffic in 2007 with 769.2 million passengers. Traffic growth was particularly strong across the Atlantic and in the Latin American market. The New York metropolitan area appeared in 11 of the 12 most traveled domestic origin-and-destination (O&D) city pairs, led by New York-Chicago, which averaged 4,839 O&D passengers per day, each way. Atlanta ranked number one in annual passengers (42.7 million) and aircraft takeoffs and landings (991,627). Chicago O'Hare ranked second in both categories, with 34.2 million passengers and 926,973 operations. Memphis remained the busiest air cargo facility, enplaning 2.2 million tons of freight and mail, followed by Louisville, Anchorage and Miami. E-ticketing and web check-in are becoming common and at some airports, passengers are already able to check in using bar codes on some hand-held mobile devices. Extended delays account for only one out of 5,000 flights. The FAA forecast in 2008 that US airlines would carry more than one billion passengers on scheduled services in 2016.

Air travelers continue to benefit from the competition unleashed by deregulation in 1978. Since then, in real terms, domestic airfares have fallen 51.9 percent, dropping 2.5 percent per year from 1978 to 2007. This is largely responsible for the long-term growth of air travel. Profit margins for airlines have consistently trailed the average profitability of US corporations and, since 2000, they have been overwhelmingly negative. However, in 2007, through restructuring and aggressive fuel conservation programs, the industry generated an operating margin of 5.3 percent on operating profits of $9.2 billion, despite some record-breaking fuel prices, an antiquated, delay-stricken air traffic control system, and a decline in spending on air travel. For example, despite critical airspace issues in the New York region, passenger airlines filled four out of every five seats. The industry remains highly leveraged, especially after factoring in the airlines' sizable off-balance-sheet debt associated with aircraft operating leases. It will take several years of sizable profits to reduce the industry's debt load to an acceptable level. Notably, of the 10 US passenger airlines rated by Standard & Poor's, only one is considered "investment grade." In the airfreight arena, only two airlines carry investment-grade credit, helping them borrow money at reasonable interest rates. In contrast, 75 of the 76 US airport authorities rated by S&P enjoy investment-grade credit.

In 2007, the National Transportation Safety Board (NTSB) recorded zero fatal airline accidents on US airlines in approximately 11 million departures. According to the National Safety Council, airlines are consistently the safest mode of intercity travel, followed by bus, rail and the automobile.

The airline industry has intensified efforts to increase fuel efficiency. In addition to retiring less fuel-efficient aircraft, airlines have retrofitted aircraft with winglets, employed more efficient operational procedures, and reduced aircraft weight. Consequently, in 2007 they were able to carry 20.4 percent more passenger and cargo traffic while using nearly 3 percent (538 million) fewer gallons of fuel than in 2000. As the industry continues to migrate to quieter and cleaner jets, and as engine and airframe technologies evolve, per-operation noise and air quality impacts will diminish accordingly.

The steep increase in fuel prices in 2008, coupled with a deteriorating US economy, is taking a toll on airlines. National energy policy is crucial. Possibly the recession will result in a permanently much smaller air transport network, hindering economic growth and seriously crimping American mobility, just-in-time movement of goods and the lifestyle to which Americans have become accustomed. Meanwhile airline restructuring will likely continue. Moreover, the air traffic control system is outdated, inefficient and overwhelmed by the volume of flights, including the tremendous growth in business jet traffic. This growth and unnecessarily complex routings lead to increased delays and emissions. An improved system called *NowGen* will help airlines move even more aggressively on maximizing and eliminating unnecessary emissions. NowGen includes improved separation of aircraft, better air/ground communications, improved navigation, and streamlined traffic flows. The industry is seeking to persuade the government to invest in the Next Generation Air Transportation System (*NextGen*), a satellite-based system which will open new airways, improve efficiency and significantly ease flight delays.

FAA statistics reveal that the number of people affected by aircraft noise has diminished by 94 percent since 1975, though passenger boardings have more than tripled. Airlines' practices in fuel handling and de-icing at airports continue to be cited as exemplary around the world. The airlines' advances on aircraft emissions are no less impressive. US airlines (passenger and cargo combined) improved their fuel and greenhouse gas efficiency by 110 percent between 1978 and 2007, resulting in 2.5 billion metric tons of carbon dioxide (CO_2) savings, roughly equivalent to taking 18.7 million cars off the road each of those years. US.airlines emitted 11.2 billion fewer pounds of carbon dioxide in 2007 than in 2000 while carrying more than 20.4 percent more passenger/cargo traffic on nearly 3 percent less fuel. The U.S. Environmental Protection Agency (EPA) states that US commercial aviation contributes just 2 percent of domestic greenhouse gas emissions. The airlines are committed to improving fuel efficiency another 30 percent through 2025 by reinvestment in technology and more fuel efficient operations. That equates to an additional 1.2 billion metric tons of CO_2 saved or another 13 million cars taken off the road each year. The industry is also committed to the development and implementation of commercially viable, environmentally friendly alternative jet fuels. The industry is leveraging 75% of its R&D on environmental improvements for future aircraft generations with an emphasis on CO_2, noise, and alternative fuels.

Mass transit

According to the American Public Transportation Association, approximately 59 percent of riders use transit to get to and from work; 11 percent to and from school; and 9 percent for shopping and dining. Mass transit is most associated with New York City, which, after horsecars and streetcars appeared, also had its first elevated railroad in 1876. This was the nation's first rapid transit running on an exclusive right-of-way between fixed stations. By the late 1890s, mass transit had become indispensable to the life of large American cities. Street transit was meanwhile provided by streetcars, also known as trolleys, inaugurated in Richmond, Virginia. By 1902, 94 percent of street railway mileage was electrically powered. The Boston subway opened in 1897 and in 1904 the now famous New York subway, where electric trains ran at high speed the entire length of Manhattan and into the Bronx. In 1912, San Francisco launched its municipal railway, to be followed by public systems in Seattle and Detroit.

Competition from affordable mass-produced automobiles fueled by cheap gasoline, such as the Model T Ford, spelled the decline of mass transit, and following World War II, ridership quickly collapsed. Not only were cars available and affordable, but so were suburban houses, built so far from central employment areas and scattered so sparsely that mass transit was simply impractical. Moreover, the construction of new roads, including federally-financed expressways, encouraged automobile commuting, whether by driving alone or in a carpool. About a quarter of all transit riders were found in New York, whose island geography made automobile ownership less desirable.

The history of urban transit has been fiercely debated. At one extreme are those who believe that mass transit was victim of a criminal conspiracy of automobile, rubber, and oil producers who hoped to force Americans to depend on their cars. At the other are those who see the decline of transit as the product of market forces, as a free and wealthy people chose the automobile in preference to streetcars and buses. In between, most scholars emphasize the importance of policy choices which encouraged driving and hampered the transit industry's ability to compete. But even within this interpretation, the degree to which these policies were the product of an open and democratic political system or were imposed by a small elite remains the subject of debate.

At the start of the twenty-first century, mass transit remains an industry defined by public ownership, high costs, and low revenues. But few would argue it is unnecessary. Indeed, several trends - increased congestion, concerns about energy shortages, citizen resistance to highway-building, and an aging population - suggest that mass transit will continue as a vital component of metropolitan America.

Buses

As the backbone of the US economy, transportation comprises 11 percent of GDP, approximately $1.1 trillion annually. The US transportation system includes 800 public transit operators in 417 urbanized areas, 300 transit systems serving rural areas, and 4,000 transit agencies that provide mobility to elderly and disabled people. The transit systems operate 154,244 transit vehicles (buses and trains). Transit ridership is at a 40-year high and growing faster than any other mode of transportation. Ridership on the nation's public transportation systems has grown 21 percent over the last five years; 14 million Americans use public transportation every day and 25 million use transit on a regular basis. Transit ridership is expected to increase by 40 percent over the next ten years.

But the nation's public transportation infrastructure is declining due to inadequate funding, according to the American Society of Civil Engineers (ASCE). Aging facilities and fleets, increased demand for services, and record-high numbers of riders have created severe stress on America's transit systems. The nation's buses are aging and need replacement: 22 percent of the nation's bus fleet is over the federal age limit; and an additional 47 percent of buses will become too old to meet these recommendations during the next federal funding program. President Obama has recommended to Congress $1.83 billion in funding for major transit projects that will create jobs and increase transportation options throughout the nation. More than $600 million of those funds are being recommended by the Federal Transit Administration for new projects in areas as diverse as Northern New Jersey; Austin, Texas; and Roaring Fork Valley, CO.

Motorcoaches

In this country dominated by the car, motorcoach travel is surprisingly important. (Although the industry itself refers to *coaches* and *motorcoach companies*, most Americans would call them *buses* and *buslines*). More passengers travel by motorcoach than by any other commercial mode (U.S. Department of Transportation). Twelve percent of carriers provide scheduled service between cities, accounting for 50 percent of motorcoach mileage. Working people use motorcoaches to commute; senior citizens use them to travel to places of cultural and historical significance; airline passengers use them to shuttle to and from airports; ocean-going cruise line passengers use motorcoaches to shuttle to and from ports; students use them for field trips, band trips, and sports outings. One-third of motorcoach mileage is logged on charters, while eight percent of motorcoach miles are logged on tours and sightseeing. The eight most popular cities to visit by motorcoach (unranked) are: Atlantic City, N.J., Chicago, Las Vegas, Los Angeles, Nashville, New York, Orlando, and Washington, D.C. Motorcoaches service 89% (15 million) of rural residents, while air services cover 70% and intercity rail covers only 42%. For 14.4 million rural residents, motorcoaches are the only available mode of intercity commercial transportation. Rural residents depend on motorcoaches for transportation to medical facilities. People stranded after Hurricane Katrina relied on motorcoaches to transport them to safety. Motorcoaches in 2007 provided 9% more passenger trips than airplanes and 20 times more than Amtrak and commuter rail combined. The national network of locations served by motorcoaches includes more than five times the number of airports and intercity rail stations.

The industry consists of 3,400 mostly small businesses operating a fleet of 33,400 coaches, providing scheduled, charter, tour, sightseeing, airport shuttle, commuter, and special operation services, and supporting 800,000 jobs. Only about 50 companies own more than 100 coaches, and these account for 56 percent of passengers. Hundreds of local economies benefit from visitors who travel by motorcoach. Motorcoaches are the safest and most cost effective mode of transportation. The fatality rate is half that of cars and one-third that of airplanes. Motorcoaches before the industry was deregulated generally used to be outmoded, inefficient, dirty and noisy but in 2007, for example, the industry spent $978 million on new vehicles. Motorcoaches are now the greenest mode of transportation. Motorcoach passenger miles per gallon of fuel are more than twice the fuel efficiency of commuter and intercity rail, and more than four times greater than domestic air carriers and transit buses. Motorcoach emission of CO_2 gases are lower than any other mode. Motorcoaches provide seamless, affordable, safe, and green nationwide service which plays a part in binding the nation together.

Greyhound buses

The iconic Greyhound buses are the largest provider of intercity bus transportation, with 10,500 daily departures to serve 1,700 destinations across the country. Greyhound buses are equipped with air conditioning, sometimes Wi-Fi, an on-board restroom, reclining seats with headrests, and tinted windows. Greyhound buses travel around the clock. They carry 25 million passengers a year and operate more than 5.8 billion passenger miles. The company's busiest route is New York to Atlantic City, New Jersey, with well over 2,000 passengers traveling between these locations daily. New York to Washington, D.C. is second with an average of 1,300 passengers on the route each day.

Intercity bus is the safest mode of transportation in the US over cars, trucks, trains, planes and other commercial vehicles, according to the Bureau of Transportation Statistics. The Greyhound fleet consists of more than 1,250 buses, with an average age of 7.2 years. One Greyhound bus takes an average of 34 cars off the road, and achieves 184 passenger miles per gallon of fuel. In many cases, Greyhound passengers report that they travel by bus because it is safe and more economical. Most Greyhound passengers travel to visit family and friends and 21% for business. The average ticket price is $45.

Ferries

The US has 640 ferry terminals, 296 of which are in the scheduled public transportation system, while the rest primarily carry vehicles between two stretches of highway that are unlikely to be used by nonvehicular passengers, or are tourist or attraction ferries. Ferry terminals are classified as either transit (189) or intercity (107). A transit facility is one where the majority of departures are to locations within the same city or metropolitan area. Examples are those ferries that run between San Francisco and Oakland, CA, and those between New York City and points across the Hudson River in New Jersey. An intercity facility is one where the majority of departures are to locations outside of the metropolitan area. Examples are those that operate between Fort Myers and Key West, FL and Long Beach and Catalina Island, CA. The Alaska Marine Highway System ferries operate intercity service within Alaska and to the State of Washington.

The Achilles heel of the ferry services is lack of connectivity with other scheduled public transportation. As many as 59 percent (175 facilities) do not have direct connections. Even in metropolitan areas, only half the ferries connect with other public services. One-third (99) are served by one other mode (most commonly transit bus); 20 are served by two other modes; and there are two facilities - Boston Logan Airport and the Hoboken, NJ Terminal - that are served by three other modes. Of the facilities served by multiple connecting modes, 16 are located in the northeast, where there is generally more public transportation than in most other parts of the country. Ferries are less connected than intercity rail, where 53 percent of stations have links with other modes, but more connected than airports where only 24 percent are served by another mode. More data are needed to determine how serious a problem ferries' lack of connectivity is.

Problems of the infrastructure

A significant portion of America's infrastructure is at an age where years of accumulated wear and tear are a concern. The nation's roads, bridges, levees, schools, water pipes and inland waterways are in such bad shape that it would take $2.2 trillion over five years to put them right. But even that would only raise their grade from a "D" average to a "B," according to the latest *Report Card for America's Infrastructure* released in 2008 by the ASCE. The US has been patching instead of providing regular improvements for aging facilities. Many bridges, sewers and water treatment plants were built during the great suburban expansion of the 1950s, '60s, and '70s. They were not built to last longer than 50 years, and are now approaching the end of their lifespans. The 2003 failure of the Silver Lake Dam in Michigan caused over $100 million in damage. In 2005 the ASCE concluded that 27 per cent of the 600,000 bridges in the US are structurally deficient or functionally obsolete. The report estimated that it would cost $9 billion annually for 20 years to fix the bridges alone. Moreover changes in freight movement require investment for air and marine facilities, land border crossings, and connecting infrastructure linking gateways to commercial and population centers.

According to experts, the most important water resources challenge facing the nation is improving and updating ports and inland waterways to allow greater capacity and efficiency. This is essential to enable the US to remain competitive in the world's marketplace, because global competition affects the cost of goods. Many would add that these improvements should be made without damaging aquatic ecosystems or unnecessarily impinging on water related recreation. Inland waterway transportation offers low-cost bulk transportation that affords low consumer prices, while also reducing road and rail congestion, and reducing emissions. Yet lock delays attributed to waiting in line to use the lock currently run at over 550,000 hours annually, translating into about $385 million in increased transportation costs. Most of the locks on the inland navigation system were built in the 1930s with a design life of 50 years. The deepening of harbors and shipping channels in the Great Lakes is particularly important. In Alaska, where the water transportation system is the equivalent of the road system in the lower 48 states, water transportation improvements for poor, isolated communities are vital to the survival of the communities themselves.

Americans take the infrastructure for granted, which makes it difficult to generate awareness until there is a major event, such as levee failures during Hurricane Katrina in 2005, and the 2007 fatal bridge collapse in Minneapolis. Many roads are funded through a tax on gasoline. Few Americans would support an increase in the gas tax; Americans have become increasingly tax-averse over the past 25 years. Popular limited government ideology explains why Americans continue to build more bridges, roads, and sewers than they can afford to maintain, and why so few American leaders are unwilling to do much about it. It is also politically difficult for many mayors to make a case for more funding for a problem that is not readily apparent. The occasional catastrophic failure is dismissed as a fluke. Roads, sewers, and so forth are owned and maintained by federal, state, or local governments. In 2006, these levels of government spent a total of US $112 billion to build and repair infrastructure, not enough in a nation that leads the world in sprawling, low-density, automobile-oriented development. Under the Recovery Act 2009, $26.6 billion of this funding was available to the states for highway investment.

CARS

Cars and trucks are the most important means of transport for passengers and goods. There are 237.2 million cars in the US, and 765 vehicles per 1,000 population (UN). According to the Department of Transportation, neither higher gas prices, nor pollution, nor traffic congestion can break up Americans' love affair with the car. Indeed, in 2003, for the first time, in the average US household there were more vehicles than people to drive them. There are 107 million US households, each with an average of 1.9 cars, trucks or sport utility vehicles (SUVs) and 1.8 drivers i.e., 204 million vehicles and 191 million drivers. Rising gas prices and national energy security concerns, however, have prompted calls for higher taxes on gasoline, as were imposed in the 1970s by President Carter, to encourage drivers to modify their behavior.

For the last two decades, car ownership has increased while the number of people per household has been declining. More families with two breadwinners are driving separately to work, more teenagers own cars of their own, and more families own recreational or weekend vehicles.

Cars once were sent to the scrap heap with 100,000 or fewer miles on their odometers. Now they are more reliable it is common to drive them for 200,000 miles or more. People are buying 10-year-old cars. Low-cost automobiles are readily available.

Americans love cars so much that in many areas they have replaced downtown apartment buildings with suburban subdivisions and in the process remade their communities. The result is more daily trips to buy groceries or go to the mall. Cars have become a necessity. In fact the average person in the US takes four trips per day, covering 40 miles. Nearly half (45%) are for shopping or running errands. "The average number of miles driven per licensed driver has continued to drift upward: from 10,500 miles in 1980 to 14,800 miles in 2006" (Greenspan, *op. cit.*, p. 462).

While 91% of people who commute use their own cars or trucks, 85% of all leisure trips are taken by car. In fact, only 8% of US households do not have cars. Of all personal vehicles, 57% are cars or station wagons, 21% are vans or sport utility vehicles and 19% are light trucks. Some people buy high-mileage cars for commutes and keep a gas-guzzling SUV for weekends and vacations. Convenience, status, self-expression, personal security and the sheer pleasure of driving America's comfortable, air-conditioned cars on good quality roads are all reasons to explain Americans' continued love of the car. Most Americans like the thought of being able to fill up and take off, without permission, any time they want to. Private transportation means mobility for the common man and woman. Among the many abiding American themes is the lure of the road. Compare Jack Kerouac's *On the Road* and recall Huckleberry Finn and Jim on their raft.

Commuting

For all the concerns about road rage, environmental costs, and up to $78 billion in lost productivity through congestion, it is becoming evident that the American commute - growing ever longer and more extreme according to the Texas Transportation Institute's *2007 Urban Mobility Report* - is a sophisticated personal, even philosophical, journey as well as a testimony to the lengths that Americans will go to chase their dreams. People are willing to make tough commutes in order to enjoy the perceived benefits of suburban living that mean a lot to them.

"It's a thickening jungle out there in sprawl city," according to the report. "The big picture is we see congestion increasing in cities of all sizes," says Tim Lomax, an author of the study. Despite high gas prices, 9 of 10 Americans still drive to work each day, the vast majority of them alone, according to Census figures released in June 2007. What is more, the average commute has lengthened by a minute a year since 2000, now topping out at 38 minutes, according to the report. In 2006, Atlanta alone added 6,684 "extreme commuters" who travel three or more hours daily, pushing up the total to 88,023. Longer commutes have unfortunate effects on society. Robert Putnam, a political scientist at Harvard, has found that every 10 minutes added to a person's commute decreases by 10 percent the time that person dedicates to their family and community.

The long commute mostly stems from a design problem, having less to do with workers' decisions to drive than by unruly and often nonsensical development patterns that undermine communities, some critics say. "Everyone says it's their choice to [commute], but, in a way, there's no choice at all," says Dean Terry, creator of *Subdivided*, a documentary about suburban disconnectedness. "You're going to live in a suburban sprawl pattern no matter what, once you get outside of ... any city from Atlanta to Phoenix."

But many commuters accept sprawl. Drivers are changing habits, choosing flex-time schedules, and encroaching on the early morning trucking hours, affecting everything from their news consumption to their food consumption, with McDonald's promoting 5 a.m. specials. All their coping measures are spreading out the rush hour, says Tim Lomax. Some commuters are switching to carpools, spurred, for example, by the Clean Air Campaign's "Cash-For-Commuters" program that gives as much as $180 to participants who agree to leave their car in the garage. Besides cutting fuel costs by three-quarters, the real benefit is the potential for a nap on the way. States that are unable to pay for megaprojects such as massive lane additions and major new arteries are instead altering drivers' commutes by such means as ramp meters that spread out rush hour by controlling on-ramp flow, and dedicated phone lines that give drivers personalized traffic tips. The authors of the *Mobility Report* say small adjustments like these can yield big dividends for drivers, if only to keep speeds up and overall commuting times steady. The question is when employers are going to put an end to extreme commutes, and support governments in efforts to improve transportation, or decide to re-locate businesses to locations such as business parks outside city centers.

A few Americans dislike cars. They say that the American love affair with the car is a myth and that Americans love their cars like a chain smoker loves tobacco. They point to traffic congestion, road rage, accident fatalities, fuel consumption and pollution, as well as the effects on city design, working and social life and the burden of cars on the household budget. But these critics are in a distinct minority. Growing concern about pollution and energy use, however, is prompting experimentation with fuel-cell vehicles such as the Hypercar.

According to the Department of Labor's Bureau of Labor Statistics, car ownership costs are the second largest household expense in the US. In fact, the average household spends almost as much on their cars as they do on food and health care combined for their entire family.

ANNUAL COSTS OF CAR OWNERSHIP

vehicle purchase costs (do not include finance charges)	$3579
finance charges on vehicle loan(s)	$359
gasoline and motor oil	$1279
car insurance expenses	$819
maintenance and repair expenses	$662
Total	**$6698**

Accidents

As cars became more attainable for most Americans, this newfound freedom and individualization of transit became the norm. Every year, though, there are more than 6 million automobile accidents on US roads. But traffic deaths in 2008 reached a record low, while seat belt use continued to climb. According to the National Highway Traffic Safety Administration (NHTSA) 37,313 people were killed in motor vehicle traffic crashes in 2008, the lowest number since 1961 (36,285). The nation also saw the lowest fatality rate ever recorded: 1.28 fatalities per 100 million vehicle miles traveled, down from 1.36 in 2007. There were 2,491,000 people injured in 2007, about 25% less than in 2000. Notably, however, reductions in fatalities since 1979 have been far greater in Great Britain, Canada and Australia. As measured by the number of traffic deaths per million vehicles, the US has slipped from 1st to13th place in the world. The major causes of accidents are running red lights, speeding and tailgating – all illegal. Drunk driving is also a problem. Nearly 40 percent of all fatal traffic accidents involve drinking, resulting in an annual death toll of 17,000, according to the NHTSA. While most Americans believe you should not drink and drive, they also believe you should not drink at home. But most cannot walk to a bar, because neighborhoods will not accept bars, and because of lack of mass transit, Americans who want to drink have to drive to and from a commercial area. The reason there is less of a road safety culture in the US than in other countries is probably because litigation, laying the blame elsewhere than on the road user, is thought to be the answer to fatalities and injuries, while crashes are considered inevitable.

CHAPTER **7**

THE AMERICAN CHARACTER

It is part of the American character to consider nothing as desperate —to surmount every difficulty by resolution and contrivance.
Thomas Jefferson

Cultural heritage

The American character has some strongly marked traits that people from other countries find very noticeable, sometimes admirable, sometimes puzzling, sometimes bothersome. Knowing something of the American character is therefore important for understanding American culture and interacting with Americans.

Theodore Roosevelt once told a reporter that the grizzly bear should be the symbol of America, not the eagle. He likened America to the grizzly bear because it is solitary. He went on to say: "The world will never love us. They may respect us, they might one day fear us, but they will never love us, for we have too much audacity." It has been said that while most empires turned complacent as they grew successful, America has turned more anxious and industrious. There are many reasons for this, but the American cultural inheritance is crucial.

Americans are the descendants of immigrants, sometimes quite recent. Immigrants are typically people who, for whatever reason, believe that, through effort and endurance, they can win a better life. Life in a new country, especially with a new language, is not easy. Yet immigrants are uprooting their lives, leaving most of their friends and family behind, and going to America. So it is no mystery that Americans have a drive to work hard and succeed. Children learn from their parents, and the parents of Americans were not a random sample of the nations from which they came but a self-selected group who had particular energy and drive.

There has been much comment in recent years that Americans are very independent and not much inclined to pay attention to international opinion. Given their cultural heritage, this is unsurprising. Their ancestors cared little about the opinions of the countries that they left. What would make their descendants think differently?

Alexis de Tocqueville, the French aristocrat who wrote the celebrated and widely quoted study *Democracy in America*, warned about the potentially fatal flaws in the American character: a tendency toward self-indulgence and apathy toward the public good paves the way for the threat of tyranny. Americans often seem content to barter material success for the control over their government which their Constitution is designed to provide and public rhetoric still enjoins. "I confess," says de Tocqueville, "that in America I saw more than America. I sought the image of democracy itself, with its inclinations, its character, its prejudices, and its passions, in order to learn what we have to fear or hope from its progress."

The Frontier Spirit

"Every country in the world loved the folklore of the West—the music, the dress, the excitement, everything that was associated with the opening of a new territory. It took everybody out of their own little world. The cowboy lasted a hundred years, created more songs and prose and poetry than any other folk figure. The closest thing was the Japanese samurai."
John Wayne

The common thread that binds Americans stems from their individualism, self-reliance, independence, courage to take risks and readiness to challenge the impossible. Americans believe that no frontier was or is beyond them. Indeed, no other nation uses the word *frontier* in the special way Americans do. During the 19th century, American settlers relentlessly pushed westward, plowing the plains, killing the Indians, crossing the Rocky Mountains, and exploring the Pacific Ocean. Then they wondered where to go next. The answer: around the world and into outer space.

The philosophy of American expansion has been described by Brian Schofield as a "cocktail of Puritan fervour, geographical predestination and, predominantly, political cynicism." One cannot deny the powerful impact the settlement made on the national consciousness and pride of Americans. Stories and images of the frontier and the settling of the West have shaped American identity and values. Log cabins and wagon trains, cowboys and Indians, Buffalo Bill and General Custer: these and other frontier images pervade American life, from fiction to films to advertising, where they attach themselves to products from pancake syrup to cologne, blue jeans to banks. There is a national preoccupation with this uniquely American image.

Why have these images exerted such a strong appeal to Americans for more than a century? Why do advertisers and politicians alike continue to invoke these images when they want Americans to associate their products and proposals with resourcefulness, courage, and a progressive spirit? How has a single set of icons come to resonate so powerfully among a diverse national population?

To understand the attractiveness and influence of the frontier ideal, it is necessary to consider the stories that were told about it. The two most enduring stories of the frontier were both told in Chicago in 1893, the year of the World's Columbian Exposition, an enormous fair held to mark the four-hundredth anniversary of Columbus' voyage, which created widespread European awareness of the existence of the American continents. One of the stories was Harvard historian Frederick Jackson Turner's remarkably influential lecture and article, "The Significance of the Frontier in American History," which has been called "the single most influential piece of writing in the history of American history." "The existence of an area of free land, its continuous recession, and the advance of American settlement westward explain American development." With these words, Turner laid the foundation for modern historical study of the American West and presented a "frontier thesis" that continues to influence historical thinking even today. Turner claimed that the frontier was the "cradle of American democracy." He recounted the peaceful settlement of an empty continent, a tale of a pioneer experience that shaped American individualism and democracy, a story that placed the Indians at the margins. The frontier was a place of "open road[s] [where] the game [could] be played according to the rules. . .no artificial stifling of equality of opportunity, no closed doors to the able, no stopping the free game before it was played to the end."

Turner's account may have seemed more credible because of the Indians' transitory way of life, and because the settlers developed the land materially. "As much land as a man tills, plants, improves, cultivates, and can use the product of, so much is his property," John Locke had argued (*Second Treatise*, 5:32). Indeed, such development, because it added to the preservation of the cultivator, was God's will. "God gave the world…to the use of the industrious and rational (and *labour* was to be his *title* to it)," Locke concluded (paragraph 34) before actually advising "let him plant in some inland vacant places of America," where it was assumed that the presence of settlers would not do any injury to the Indians but might even benefit them through the production of corn. Indeed, Locke concluded (5:42) "the increase of lands, and the right employing of them, is the great art of government." This attitude had been expressed long before in Thomas More's influential book *Utopia* (1516): "For they count this the most just cause of war, when any people holdeth a piece of ground void and vacant, to no good nor profitable use, keeping other from the use and possession of it, which notwithstanding by the law of nature ought thereof to be nourished and relieved," *Utopia*, Book 2, chapter 4. Three years before Turner's pronouncement of the frontier thesis, the U.S. Census Bureau had declared the disappearance of a contiguous frontier line, when the population of most parts of the Western states had reached at least two people per square mile.

The other story about the frontier was told in William "Buffalo Bill" Cody's flamboyant extravaganza, *The Wild West and Congress of Rough Riders of the World*. Cody's story put Indians, and bloody battles, at center stage, and culminated in the Battle of the Little Bighorn (1876), popularly known as "Custer's Last Stand." The way Cody told the American story placed great emphasis on rugged individualism and on the exercise of *male* strength, what is today called *macho*. This story of national pride is also laced with racism.

Seemingly contradictory stories about peace and war in the West, these are in fact complementary interpretations of America's frontier past, revealing two sides of a complicated national identity: the ways in which Americans think about their history and what they believe it means to be an American. In fact these two stories depended for their influence on a set of images, or cultural icons, that were already widely familiar to 19th-century Americans. Among them were log cabins, wagon trains, frontier farms, and skirmishes between Indians and settlers. Both Turner and Buffalo Bill were geniuses in their use of these symbols and images. They used them to make their stories seem merely everyday experiences on the frontier, even as they paved the way for these images and others to achieve even greater prominence as elements of the American identity. The stories took on a life of their own in the 20th century and were then reshaped by additional voices, those of Indians, Mexicans, African Americans, and others, whose versions revisit the question of what it means to be an American.

Turner's history and Buffalo Bill's performances were interpretations of the West. They insisted that the true meaning of America lay out there toward the setting sun. To them, and the many Americans who even today accept their version of "Western" history, the essence of the frontier experience was the spirit of competition with nature, enemies and one's own weaknesses, desires and disabilities. Under the influence of these stories, Americans have come to believe that the difference in American institutions from those of any other nation is that they have a way of adapting themselves to the growing, changing nation on which they were imposed. In addition, modern American development has shown itself to be not only an advance along a land frontier, but a cycle of returning to primitive conditions in many fields of endeavor along a constantly moving frontier line, then moving in, taking control and making a profit.

Historians no longer see the country so simply, however, and still hotly debate Turner's ideas and approach. Mainstream historians have long since discarded Turner's assumption that the frontier is the key to American history. They point instead to the critical influence of such factors as slavery and the Civil War, immigration, and the development of industrial capitalism. Many critics have sought to replace the idea of a moving frontier with the idea of the West as a distinctive region, much like the American South. But even within "Western" and frontier history, a growing body of historians has contested Turner's approach. Some have long disputed the very idea of a frontier of "free land" because of the presence of the numerous Indian peoples whose subjugation was required by the nation's westward march. John Locke's idea that America was like the primitive "state of nature" (*Second Treatise*, 5:49) is seen as a gross misunderstanding of the Indians' economy and way of life. Moreover, the bulk of the newly acquired lands were not democratically distributed to yeomen pioneers. Thus the American frontier was not such a sharp contrast with European nations' borders with other states. Furthermore, critics point out, far from the frontier promoting a distinctly American democracy, the opposite was the case. Cooperation and communities of various sorts, not isolated individuals, made possible the absorption of the West into the US. Most migrant wagon trains, for example, were composed of extended kinship networks. Moreover, as the 19th century wore on, the role of the federal government and large corporations grew increasingly important. Corporate investors headquartered in New York laid the railroads (19 million miles (30.4 million km) of track by 1871, fueled by federal land grants); government troops defeated Indian nations who refused to get out of the way of "manifest destiny"; and even the cowboys, enshrined in popular mythology as rugged loners, were generally low-level employees of sometimes foreign-owned cattle corporations. Finally, but also significant, revisionist scholars argue that the West has not been the land of freedom and opportunity that both Turner's history and popular mythology would have us believe. For many women, Chinese and other Asians, whose labor was often exploited, Mexicans who found themselves residents of the US, and, of course, Indians, the West was no Promised Land. Commentators also say that the belief that modern Americans are rugged individualists is self-deception.

Even if not historical, the frontier still serves as a powerful myth. In the stories Americans tell each other about their country's past, the West and all the images, virtues, and conflicts associated with it, remain central. Images from these stories—images of movement and settlement, of suffering and eventual triumph—have become paramount symbols of American life. Last stands and log cabins, wagon trains and racial conflicts say as much about America's present conflicts and divisions as about its past. That is why so many Americans, new and old, claim a part of this past. A common stock of stories helps them to explain what it means to be an American. When Americans assume the right to become a part of and retell a common American past, then there seems to be a unity that transcends, but does not erase, their differences.

Effects of the frontier heritage

The frontier days are long past, but the attitude of individualism, the practice of self-reliance, and the ethic of no retreat continue to shape everything from entertainment to foreign policy (consider President Bush's "America will not run.")

1. *Politics.* People on the frontier had to deal with whatever life brought them and make the best of it. They learned to be highly self-reliant. This has led Americans to develop a political culture that facilitates individualism. Americans are suspicious of government because they prefer to solve their own problems. This mentality is shown in criticism of the government's increasing intervention in Americans' personal lives. With its frontier heritage, it is no accident that the West is the area where the vast majority of recent political reforms have originated. These include, at state level, the *initiative*, the right of citizens to initiate a new law into the legislature; the *referendum*, the citizens' right to vote law directly into action instead of passing it through the legislature; and the *recall*, the citizens' right to vote a legislator out of office by way of petition, as when Gray Davis of California was replaced by Arnold Schwarzenegger in 2003; and at federal level *campaign finance reform* embodied in the McCain-Feingold Act sponsored by Senator John McCain of Arizona and Senator Russell Feingold of Wisconsin; and *term limits*. All these reforms were born in the West.

2. *Economics.* The frontier also affected the modern American economy. During settlement, people did not need or want a government to interfere overly with the country's economy. Thus a laissez-faire economic system was established. The economy in America is one of speculation and risk taking, but because America was settled so quickly, speculation was often no great risk at all. Setbacks such as successful Indian resistance to the conquest of their lands were very much the exception, quickly overcome. Even now, Americans will take great risks believing, often with justice, that the odds are in their favor. The late '90s dot.com boom illustrated how Americans will throw their money into whatever new company they think has a chance. While there are many losers, there are enough winners, sometimes big winners, to encourage newcomers. Americans also have a strong technological bias, and are a people of tools and gadgets, so to speak. Americans have been such an inventive country because they have so often needed to devise some way to get around an obstacle or threat found in nature. At the same time, labor has been scarce, as on the frontier, or expensive, as generally today.

3. *Psychology.* Another way, perhaps one of the most important, in which the frontier has profoundly affected modern American life is psychologically. Americans in general enjoy solving problems or puzzles, and will usually at least make an attempt to solve any problems that confront them. This problem-solving trait has its root in the fact that there were innumerable tasks and problems set before the average settler each day: How do I get across this stream? through this forest? build something on this plot? keep the wild animals away? get food to eat? The frontier heritage also reinforced American egalitarianism, the belief that everyone is equal in status. On the frontier there were simply so many types of people that made their living in the same way that a class system was not important.

4. *Violence.* Life on the frontier was harsh, lonely, poverty-stricken, precarious and downright dangerous, plagued with drunkenness, sexual license and violence. Since solving the problems of frontier life was often literally a matter of life or death, and in the period 1865-1890 there was no effective government in the West, each man (and it usually was a man) would have

to settle his own scores, even if it involved killing. And that could be justified by reference to the argument of John Locke (*Second Treatise*, 3:18, 19), that anyone who threatened the self-preservation of anyone else, for example, by robbery, should be deemed to be willing to kill him. In frontier society, everyone would always be armed because they knew what people would do to solve a conflict. The state of war, which Locke had discussed as a theory, could become an actual fact. The right to stand one's ground, however, appeared relatively recently in law. Under English common law, the threatened party had a legal duty to retreat "to the wall" before fighting back. But from the 19th century on, such authorities as Justice Oliver Wendell Holmes rejected this doctrine as unsuited to both the American mind and the age of firearms. Hence, in the face of a deadly threat, Americans now claim the right to stand their ground and fight. They acknowledge no duty to retreat. As the Battle Hymn of the Republic (1861) puts it: "He has sounded forth the trumpet that shall never sound retreat."

Famous gunmen such as Wild Bill Hickok (1837-1876) and Wyatt Earp (1848-1929) and grassroots gunfighters—men who resorted to their guns at a moment's notice—had a tremendous impact on frontier life. Their duels, ambushes, and firefights were more than personal vendettas. They were part of what historian Richard Maxwell Brown calls a "Western Civil War of Incorporation," pitting gunmen—usually Republicans and Unionists, who sided with the expanding banks, railroads, and businesses—against cowboys and independent farmers, who were often Democrats sympathizing with the Confederacy. In such lesser-known battles as the Mussel Slough war (May 11, 1880), resisting farmers, imbued with the ethic of no retreat, fought for their independent lifestyle against the encroaching rail barons. This civil war fed the culture of violence of the West and reinforced the legal doctrine of "no duty to retreat." Thus frontier violence helps to explain why America has become the most violent of all developed nations. Even now, in the capitol building in Madison, Wisconsin, the state where Frederick Jackson Turner was born and spent much of his life, there is a notice requiring legislators to check in their guns before taking their seats. And in 2003, a New Mexico lawyer began court proceedings to carry out DNA tests on the supposed body of Billy the Kid (died 1881?), and his mother, to find out whether stories that the Kid was not really killed by sheriff Pat Garrett were founded on fact. (In 2004 permission was denied and the "mystery" remains).

It has also been argued that the frontier experience made America a more tolerant and inclusive society, gave a higher status to women than in many other countries and stimulated the desire for public education. In the West many different types of people were able to settle without upsetting one another because of the vast empty space to separate them. This is only partly true, however, since farmers, cattlemen and railroads all competed, sometimes violently, for resources. In addition, women gained rights because during the settlement their labor was needed. Thus American women could own land, vote, and perform traditionally men's jobs earlier than elsewhere. Education, too, was crucial in frontier life to develop local human capital. America today is still possessed by a thirst for education, and a college education is virtually mandatory for membership of the middle class.

Though challenged as never before by the values of peace and social activism, the frontier remains a central theme in American thought and character. Not least of the reasons for this is that the idea of the frontier elevated the role of the common folk in American history. For most Americans, regardless of their differences, the efforts of the nation's cultural forebears represent the value of the search for challenges, particularly those posed by the unknown. During the 20th-century, many frontiers, both physical (Antarctica, Mars) and figurative (The Last Frontier, The Great Society), were located and claimed by American culture. The Republican Vice-Presidential candidate in the 2008 election, Sarah Palin, governor of Alaska, was described by *Newsweek* as "a surprise from the last frontier" (*Newsweek*, September 8, 2008, p. 36).

The pioneer then, as now, exemplifies the treasured instinct of "man" (and increasingly of woman as well) to pursue adventure and innovation. These pursuits no longer involve a place, except in regard to space ("the final frontier") but rather the opportunities of technological and commercial enterprise, and the aspirations toward a better society. Velcro, Teflon, and latterly cyberspace, and a myriad other scientific and technological advances, have been promoted as advances on the frontier of invention and innovation. Pioneering has also come to denote the activities of Americans of racial minorities. Hence the frontier remains a powerful myth even today.

AMERICAN VALUES

FACTFILE 15 GENERAL AMERICAN CULTURAL VALUES

1. An individual's most important concern is his/her self-interest, self-expression, self-development, self-gratification, and independence.
2. The privacy of an individual is a basic right. Intrusion into it by others is permitted only by invitation.
3. Because government exists for the benefit of the individual, all forms of authority are slightly suspect.
4. Being accepted by peers is an important factor in the American concept of success.
5. Religion and religious affiliation are important. Most Americans belong to an organized church or religious institution even although they may not be regular attenders.
6. Women and men are equal.
7. All human beings are equal.
8. Progress is good and inevitable. An individual must improve him/herself: institutions must modernize to make themselves more responsive to change.
9. America is the utmost symbol of progress.
10. Time is a commodity to be tallied and managed.
11. Conservation and ecology are practiced virtues as long as they do not affect the individual's self-interest too severely.
12. Singlehood as a chosen way of life is modestly suspect.

Values and relationships

Stereotypes

There are a number of stereotypes about Americans. But even the ones that are true in general may not be true about specific individuals or a large segment of the population. For example, although Americans tend to be louder and more boisterous than people from other cultures (especially at athletic events), many are quiet and polite. Some people may be intolerant and xenophobic, but most will be pleasant and welcoming. American films and television exaggerate in order to generate excitement, and so present a rather distorted picture of what life in the US is really like. Likewise, American tourists are not always on their best behavior when visiting other countries. Asked about his favorite pop culture icons, Presidential candidate Barack Obama chose Spider-Man and Batman because "they have some inner turmoil." Senator John McCain also chose Batman, calling him a quiet hero who pursues justice "against insurmountable odds" (Reuters).

COMMON STEREOTYPES OF AMERICANS

- Boastful and arrogant
- Disrespectful of authority
- Extravagant and wasteful
- Generous
- Ignorant of other countries and cultures
- Informal
- Insensitive
- Loud and obnoxious
- Promiscuous.
- Racist
- Rich
- Rude and immature
- Stingy
- Think they know everything
- Think every country should imitate the US
- Uninformed about politics

PERSONAL CHARACTERISTICS

1. Friendliness

Americans tend to form friendships easily, quickly, and shallowly, and allow their friendships to dissolve with little more effort or time. The early European settlers in America lived on the frontier, often very distant from their nearest neighbors. A tradition of friendliness and openness developed that visitors from abroad noticed even 200 years ago. This is one of the first things that people from other countries recognize in Americans, and it can be misleading, as friendliness can be confused with true friendship. In the US, as anywhere else, true friendships take time to develop. Most Americans actually have many acquaintances but relatively few close friends. In America it is rare for friendships to outlast distance. Once an American becomes your friend, however, the friendship is a strong one.

2. Individualism and self-reliance

Most Americans value independence. They speak a lot about freedom: freedom from control by government, nobility and church, and freedom to do what they want, the way they want. Americans generally believe that the ideal person is an autonomous, self-reliant individual. Most Americans see themselves as separate individuals, not as representatives of a family, community, or other group. Self-made and self-reliant people are often highly respected. Unlike people from many European or Oriental countries, Americans do not expect to rely heavily on their families, friends or teachers. They dislike being dependent on other people, or having others dependent on them. Americans are encouraged at an early age to be independent and to develop their own goals in life. Some people from other countries view this attitude as "selfishness." Others view it as a healthy freedom from the constraints of ties to family, clan, or social class. Because Americans cherish personal independence so much, asking about private matters, like income and age, is regarded inappropriate in most situations. Critic Charles Churchyard, however, finds that the American belief in individual freedom is false. Americans, he says, are far more likely to submit themselves to the influence and controls of groups than most people around the world. This, he says, is especially true in the workplace.

3. Egalitarianism (love of equality)

Americans are taught that "all men (and women) are created equal" and have equal rights. While they obviously violate that ideal in some aspects of life, in others they uphold it by law, especially with regard to women and minority ethnic and cultural groups. The general lack of deference to people in authority is one example of equality. Titles, such as "sir" and "madam" are seldom used in most of America, although they are still customary in the South. Managers, directors, presidents and even university instructors are often addressed by their first or given name. More than 150 years ago, Alexis de Tocqueville saw America's lack of class consciousness as one of its greatest strengths, in contrast to the rigid class structure of Europe. Americans still view themselves as essentially classless.

There is a general lack of class consciousness in America and no serious support for redistributing wealth or imposing income equality. A poll from AARP suggests why. Firstly, the survey found, money plays less of a role in people's happiness than is generally assumed. Only 27 percent consider earning a lot of money to be absolutely necessary for success; 23 percent say it has little or no importance. Most consider non-monetary factors to be more important, including having a good marriage, having a good relationship with one's children, helping those in need, having an interesting job and being well-educated. In the poll, each of these was considered essential for happiness by between 79 percent and 94 percent of respondents.

Key findings:
- People still believe strongly that it is possible to get ahead in America.
- Sixty-nine percent of those polled say they are better off than their parents were at the same age.
- 67 percent think their children will be better off than they are.
- Remarkably, the percentages of blacks and Hispanics agreeing were significantly higher at 80 percent and 81 percent respectively.

4. Conformity

Americans like people to be "regular" and "like folks." They are uncomfortable with difference. This attitude stems in part from the New England Puritans, who laid great stress on social cohesion and saw difference as a threat to their tightly-organized society based on their covenant with God. Similar attitudes can be found in the South, where God- fearing folks are supposed to think, feel, and react in similar ways and follow approved traditional customs. "The struggle to control dangerous others... rather than (as Tocqueville thought) escaping from controls shapes American political thought and culture in every era" (Morone, *Hellfire Nation*, p. 124). These attitudes are both based on the assumption that there are optimum ways to behave which will be best for the individual and hence for society. Those who believe this assume that they know what is best, often claiming in religious contexts scriptural sanction for their views and for their claim to the right to force them on others. In the Midwest, too, conformity is valued. In settler days, where margins of survival were tight, conformity meant material safety. While conflict with the Indians lasted, conveniently dated to 1876, after when the army revenged the defeat of "Custer's last stand" and herded the Indians into reservations, conformity meant safety. In modern times, the mass marketing of big corporations has also fostered conformity: standard consumers buy standard products. Because they are predictable they are commercially less risky. There is a lack of variety in certain product lines outside the big cities. Eccentricity, by contrast, tends to flourish in aristocratic societies, where the aristocrats themselves are contemptuous of the opinions of their social inferiors, some of whom may take license for their own eccentricities from the example of their superiors.

5. Informality

Americans treat each other in very informal ways, for example, even in the presence of great differences in age or social standing. American society tolerates a considerable degree of informality in dress, speech, and methods of communication. From the point of view of some people from other cultures, this kind of behavior shows lack of respect. From the point of view of Americans, it reflects a healthy lack of concern for social ritual.

Americans frequently use first names in addressing one another, even when they first meet. Calling people by their first names often implies friendliness and creates a more relaxed atmosphere. American lifestyle is generally casual. You will see students going to class in shorts and T-shirts. Male instructors seldom wear a tie and some may even wear blue jeans. Female instructors often wear slacks along with comfortable walking shoes. Greetings and farewells are usually short, informal and friendly. Students may greet each other with "hi," "how are you?" and "what's up?" The farewell can be as brief as: "see you," "take it easy," or, "come by some time" (although they generally do not really mean it). Friendships are also casual, as Americans develop and end friendships easily.

Informality is often linked with spontaneity. Americans like to do things off-the-cuff on the spur of the moment more than in some cultures. Partly this stems from their creativity and adaptability. The downside is, as they themselves admit, Americans tend to rush ahead enthusiastically and then have to backtrack to correct mistakes they could have avoided with more foresight and deliberation.

There are situations and environments, however, in which formality is the norm. Some businesses require their employees to wear a uniform or a suit. It would usually be inappropriate to wear a T-shirt and blue jeans to a job interview. Some of the more prestigious restaurants require that male patrons wear a coat (jacket) and tie. Americans tend to dress up for cultural events (the opera, theatre and ballet) and to dress down for athletic events. Formal wear is required at weddings and funerals, or any other event with religious overtones.

6. Directness

Directness is an aspect of American self-confidence. Sometimes it can appear arrogant, and Americans may be direct to a point that would seem offensive in many other countries. In the

US, however, people feel that by asking direct questions and making direct statements, they are demonstrating honesty. Foreigners should not feel offended if an American asks them a direct question; the American is genuinely trying to get to know them. Americans try to work out differences face-to-face and without a mediator. They are encouraged to speak up and give their opinions. Students are often invited to challenge or disagree with certain points in the lecture.

In the business setting, Americans generally get right to the point and argue logically, rather than warming up to a subject with small talk or humor, or approaching their objective by indirect hints. This may appear rude to people from some other cultures where polite, personal conversation comes before a business discussion. It can also hamper Americans in negotiations if the party from another culture feels too pressured or that he or she is being pushed into a corner. Americans act like this out of respect for the other person's time and their own, and to appear honest in their dealings.

7. Time Consciousness

Americans take pride in making the best use of their time. In the business world, "time is money." Americans try hard to do things in a timely fashion. They tend to organize their activities by means of schedules and apologize if they are late. For business meetings or gatherings involving a group of people, a date, or a dinner invitation especially, punctuality is very important. As a result Americans may sometimes seem harried, tense, and impatient, always running from one thing to the next, not able to relax and enjoy themselves. "Sorry. I have to run" is a frequently-heard excuse. Wasting one's own time or others' time is very much discouraged. Foreign observers sometimes see this as being "ruled by the clock." Other times they see it as a helpful way of assuring that things get done. Being on time for class is important. Some instructors give demerits to students who are late to class, and students at most universities have institutional permission to leave the classroom if their instructor is 10 or 15 minutes late.

8. Materialism

Success in American society is often marked by the amount of money or the quantity of material goods a person is able to accumulate. A person is expected to become successful by such means as hard work, intelligence, and persistence. Some foreigners see this as a lack of appreciation for the spiritual or human things in life. Americans see it as a way of assuring a comparatively high standard of living and higher social status, and more social respect.

Related to this is the almost reverent regard accorded to *newness* by Americans. *New and improved* is the ceaseless refrain of advertisers as they hawk their products. Sometimes the product is not new at all in any meaningful sense. *New and improved* is often a spurious commercial catch phrase, used simply to ensure the perpetual consumption of material goods, which is the chief source of economic wealth in the US. *New* also sums up the key American belief that success depends on being creative and innovative, especially in business, and then working hard to promote that innovation.

The obsession with newness is reflected in virtually every aspect of American life, from the most insignificant consumer product to the highest expressions of art, science, and culture. Older people are sometimes regarded as being somehow less deserving of respect and dignity (and therefore of less value to the nation) than younger people. Young people have been elevated by consumerism to a higher status. Partly as a consequence, Americans collectively have a poorly developed sense of the importance of preserving things (historical, social, architectural, natural) in their haste to tear everything down and put up something new in its place. The most direct end result (lamented by only a few) is that aside from a few remnants of the colonial period and the Civil War, there is very little in the way of observable history left in the US to remind Americans of the discovery and development of their country.

9. Competition and Achievement

The foreigner is often impressed at how achievement-oriented Americans are and how hard they both work and play. The American system of free enterprise is based on competition, and Americans are encouraged to be competitive from an early age. Their competitiveness may initially appear overbearing or rude at times, but it is an inherent part of American culture. Americans admire a winner, and a competitive spirit is often the motivating factor to work harder. When an American friend or acquaintance makes a competitive remark, it is not meant as an insult or put down. Friendly competition is normal in American society. Americans often compete with themselves as well as others. They feel good when they "beat their own record" in an athletic event or other type of competition. Americans always seem to be "on the go," because sitting quietly doing nothing seems like a waste of time.

10. Asking Questions

Americans ask a lot of questions and these may seem silly, intrusive, or even stupid to people from other countries. To the American, however, this is part of the process of getting to know you and a mark of sincere interest in the other person and their country. Therefore when interacting with Americans, one should not hesitate to ask a question if one does not understand something.

One delicate matter is that Americans sometimes ask direct questions about money—how much something costs or how much money one earns. At times these questions are even too intrusive for some Americans. The question, however, is usually not meant to offend and a person has every right to say politely and firmly say that they do not wish to discuss such things.

11. Silence

"It is only natural that Americans would invent chewing gum; they aren't alive unless their jaws are moving."
Will Rogers, American humorist

Americans are uncomfortable with long periods of silence. Often when two people are speaking and one becomes silent, the American will bring up the subject of the weather or ask a question rather than allow the silence to continue. Unlike in many countries, especially in Europe and Latin America, one seldom sees Americans silently taking a meal together; they will generally talk right through dinner. Americans are great talkers and debaters. They are passionate about truth, justice, and equal opportunity, and optimistic about the potential of free and open discussion to solve problems.

12. Privacy

For most Americans, the home is a sanctuary, a place of privacy. Americans like their privacy and enjoy spending time alone. Only the closest friends and family members are usually entertained at home. The right to privacy is a major principle in American law and custom. Americans react strongly when strangers or government pry into their private business without cause. In the US the police cannot search an automobile or a home without a search warrant issued by a court of law. To ask the question "What is on your mind?" may be considered by some to be intrusive.

13. Overt Patriotism

One trait of Americans that surprises many people from other countries is their serious overt sense of patriotism, regardless of political views, ethnic background, or age. Although the open expression of patriotism may be unsettling, because in many countries such feelings are considered personal, American patriotic sentiment is a form of celebrating American identity and is not generally directed against non-Americans. The National Anthem ("The Star-Spangled Banner") is played before virtually every sporting event, political rally, and a variety of other public events. Americans also commonly fly the flag, which can be found in classrooms, churches, public halls, and many homes. Indeed, proper respect for the flag has even been a national political issue, something unlikely elsewhere. A large number of cultures coexist in the US. This fact has given American society a high level of tolerance for different cultures and peoples. Americans are usually very friendly to foreigners and are ready to help them.

14. Pride in one's job

Most Americans have very positive work ethics. Hard work is an essential part of the American self-image. No matter what kind of job they do, they cherish the employment opportunity and try hard to be as professional as possible. The pace of career life is often fast and many American people spend a lot of time at work.

15. Optimism: looking to the future and to change

Americans are determined optimists. As Alan Greenspan has remarked, "the frontier of hope that we all innately pursue will never close" op. cit., p.505. They believe that everyone has the potential for a worthwhile future and that that future will be better than the past. Children are often asked what they want to be "when they grow up"; college students are asked what they will do when they graduate; and professors plan what they will do when they retire. Progress is often equated with change, and holding onto traditional ways of doing things seems to imply outdated attitudes. Many Americans have developed what Alvin Toffler has called "throw-away lifestyles," based on the belief that as circumstances change one can and should reinvent oneself. Nevertheless, Americans' unique characteristics and core values are changing remarkably little even in these times of transformation in the economy, society and America's place in the world. In fact, when times are tough, Americans tend to say it is because the country has strayed too far from traditional values, not that it has failed to adopt new ones.

16. Respect for data

Americans have great respect for numerical data. What they can measure, they can more likely believe. The management consultant, W. Edwards Deming had on his desk a sign that read "In God we trust. All others must bring data" (although he did acknowledge the role of unquantifiable factors). To refer to someone as a "quant jock" is not usually an insult. It shows respect for a person with ability in mathematical calculation and analysis. The long list of American Nobel Prizewinners in economics is probably no accident. In fact the science of econometrics, the measurement of small scale highly specific economic movements, was pioneered in America.

17. Attitude to animals

The treatment of animals has become a public issue as part of the environmental and animal rights debates. About 60% of families have a pet. Americans are sometimes considered sentimental about animals and are accused of treating them as well as they treat people, but although Americans love their pets they generally put people's interests before those of animals. At weekends they may visit zoos and aquaria, and amusement parks with animals such as Busch Gardens and Disney's Animal Kingdom. TV programs about animals, ranging from documentaries to cartoons such as *Lassie* and *Tom and Jerry*, are popular. Children get interested in animals from an early age when they are given cuddly toy animals, and picture books about famous characters such as Brer (Brother) Rabbit, the main animal character in the Uncle Remus books by Joel Chandler Harris (1848-1908). Fictional animals have their own typical character: lions are brave, foxes are cunning and cats are proud.

News stories about animals appear regularly in the media. Many newspapers regularly feature photographs of an animal being cared for by an animal charity, in the hope that somebody will adopt it. Americans' fondness for animals has also led to animals' names being used for sports teams such as the Chicago Bears and Philadelphia Eagles.

Cruelty to animals is illegal and anyone found guilty of ill-treating animals may be forbidden to keep one, fined or even jailed. People give generously to animal charities and the money helps set up animal hospitals and rescue centers for injured or abandoned animals. Each spring, charities celebrate a "be kind to animals week." The American Society for the Prevention of Cruelty to Animals runs an animal adoption program in many cities. There has been concern over the way animals are treated in zoos. Most American zoos are fairly modern and many animals live in a large enclosure similar to their natural habitat, rather than in a cage. Many zoos now only keep animals that cannot survive in the wild or which were born in captivity. Some breed animals to put back into the wild, and try to raise public awareness about the need for conservation.

There are several animal rights groups, and some products bear labels saying they have not been tested on animals, but most Americans accept the need for animal research. Some people oppose the use of animals in circuses and other entertainment. Many do not believe that people should wear furs, and in New York and some other cities paint has been thrown at people wearing furs. There have also been campaigns against factory farming as cruel, but most Americans accept it. After Hurricane Katrina, many thousands of animals were abandoned in New Orleans when their owners were not allowed to evacuate them, a policy that has since been changed in response to public protest.

18. Consumerism

Americans are full of restless energy and spiritual striving, sometimes expressed through consumerism, which is not so much about having what they can afford now as it is about getting rich by working hard so that they can have something more luxurious in future. Hence comes the perception that Americans are shallow, greedy, self-absorbed and workaholic, and own far more "stuff" than they really need.

ETHICS

America is an incredibly diverse society but many of its traditional values endure despite the transformation of large areas of American life. Indeed it is scarcely possible to overestimate the effect of the strict morality of the Puritan Founders and their Protestant coreligionists. "Their stress on individual virtue and personal development as a sign of worth, hard work as an indication of merit and material success as the reward for diligence, remains central to many Americans' sense of their country's strengths" (Bates, *op. cit.*, p. 58). Thus even today there is a real connection between the values of hard work, perseverance and obedience to God's will (or at least to ethical principles) and the optimism which is so marked a trait in the American character. Yet there is also a tension in American values between individual initiative and social discipline.

The Josephson Institute of Ethics has set out what it believes to be a consensus on American values that would be accepted by Americans of all political, racial, religious, gender, or socioeconomic sensibilities. These six core values they call *The Six Pillars of Character*. Some 40 states and 500 municipalities, school districts and business groups have joined the President and both Houses of Congress to endorse the Josephson Institute's campaign CHARACTER COUNTS!

Even so, it is important to remember that US society is made up of a diversity of ethnic groups and cultures that have helped shape American values. Some individuals and groups have a set of respected values that are quite different from those of mainstream America.

The Six Pillars of Character

1. Trustworthiness

Americans believe there is no more fundamental ethical value than honesty. They associate honesty with people of honor, and admire and rely on those who are honest. Honesty is a broader concept than many may realize. It involves both communications and conduct. *Honesty in communications* is expressing the truth as best we know it and not conveying it in a way likely to mislead or deceive. It has three dimensions. *Truthfulness* is presenting the facts to the best of our knowledge. *Sincerity* is genuineness, being without trickery or duplicity. It precludes any act that is intended to create beliefs or leave impressions that are untrue or misleading. *Candor* may require forthrightness and frankness, volunteering information that another person needs to know.

Honesty in conduct is playing by the rules, without stealing, cheating, fraud, subterfuge and other trickery. Americans think that cheating on a test or exam, for example, is disgusting and disgraceful, because one not only seeks to deceive but to take advantage of those who are not cheating. It violates both trust and fairness.

Americans believe that honesty includes integrity, that is, always acting in accordance with one's beliefs and not for expediency or for any immoral purpose. A person with integrity acts consistently at work, at home, in public or alone. Because they must know who they are and what they value, the person of integrity takes time for self-reflection, so that events do not determine the course of their moral life. They are trusted because people know who they are: what you see is what you get. People without integrity are called "hypocrites" or "two-faced."

Americans put great store by *reliability* or *promise-keeping*. This means accepting the responsibility of making all reasonable efforts to fulfill commitments. Americans are firm believers in the written word and contractual agreements. A broader aspect of honesty and integrity is *loyalty*. The American ideal is that some relationships, such as husband-wife, employer-employee, citizen-country, create an expectation of allegiance, fidelity and devotion. Loyalty exacts a special responsibility to promote the interests of certain people, organizations or affiliations. Loyalty does not, however, go beyond ethical considerations.

Americans see themselves as people who do not deceive, cheat or steal; are reliable and do what they say they will do; have the courage to do the right thing and maintain a good reputation; and are loyal to family, friends and country. Even on the most cynical estimate, a reputation for honesty is good for business.

2. Respect

In America's increasingly diverse society, the traditional value of *respect* is acquiring even greater importance. Everyone has a right to be treated with dignity and respect, regardless of who they are and what they have done. Respect prohibits violence, humiliation, manipulation and exploitation. It reflects notions such as civility, courtesy, decency, dignity, autonomy, tolerance and acceptance. Intimidation, coercion or violence should only be resorted to, Americans believe, in extraordinary and limited situations: to defend others, teach discipline, maintain order or achieve social justice. Judicial punishment should be used in moderation and only to advance important social goals and purposes. Dignity and autonomy require all individuals, including maturing children, to have a say in the decisions that affect them. Respect also involves tolerance and acceptance, accepting individual differences and beliefs without prejudice and judging others only on their character, abilities and conduct. In American schools, pupils are taught to use good manners, not to use bad language; to be considerate of the feelings of others; and not to threaten, hit or hurt anyone but to deal peacefully with anger, insults and disagreements. Nevertheless, the persistence of violent behavior in schools across the country is a standing contradiction of this professed ideal.

3. Responsibility

To an American, responsibility means being accountable (responding to other people's reasonable expectations), pursuing excellence and exercising self-restraint. Our capacity to reason and our freedom to choose make us morally autonomous and, therefore, answerable for whether we honor or degrade the ethical principles that give life meaning and purpose. An accountable person is not a victim and does not shift blame or claim credit for the work of others. But, to Americans, accountability goes further. They feel they are responsible for the triumph of evil when nothing is done to stop it and they seek to lead by example. This moral theory is enormously powerful in American culture and does much to explain the attitudes and actions of the US.

Americans sometimes give the impression of wanting to be the only ones in charge. This of course is far from being always desirable or justified but, again, the desire can be understood from within their culture. To them, being responsible means being in charge of our choices and, thus, of our lives. What they sometimes forget is that it does not authorize them to be in charge of other people's lives without their consent.

Responsibility also means doing one's best. Americans believe this is a moral obligation, that they should be diligent, reliable, careful, prepared and informed. People should in addition finish what they start, overcoming rather than surrendering to obstacles and avoid excuses for giving up. Indeed, they should seek continuous improvement, always looking for ways to do their work better.

The pursuit of excellence may mask greed or ruthlessness but at its best is an acknowledgement that others should be able to rely upon an American's knowledge, ability or willingness to perform tasks well. Indeed, responsible people exercise self-control, restraining passions and appetites (such as greed, gluttony, lust, hatred and fear) for the sake of longer-term vision and better judgment. They delay gratification if necessary and rarely feel it necessary to win at any cost.

4. Fairness

Fairness is difficult to define and apply and probably more subject to legitimate debate and interpretation than any other ethical value. Most Americans would agree it involves issues of equality, impartiality, proportionality, openness and due process. Most would also agree that it is unfair to handle similar matters inconsistently. Most would agree that it is unfair to impose punishment that is not commensurate with the offense. But, essentially, fairness implies adherence to a balanced standard of justice without relevance to one's own feelings or inclinations, or in the famous saying, "the very definition of a republic is 'an empire of laws, and not of men'" (John Adams, *Thoughts on Government*, January, 1776). *Due process* is a crucial principle of American law and in settling disputes, both to reach the fairest results and to minimize complaints. A fair person scrupulously employs open and impartial processes for gathering and evaluating the information necessary to make decisions. But fair people do not wait for the truth to come to them; they seek out relevant information and conflicting perspectives before making important judgments. Thus in America there are continual enquiries into problems, scandals and disasters, with hearings often held in public. Decisions are supposed to be made without favoritism or prejudice and considerable effort goes into ensuring that they are, although not always with success. America has never overcome the prevalence of institutional racism, for instance, despite some improvements. An individual, company or society is expected to correct mistakes promptly and voluntarily and not to take advantage of the weakness or ignorance of others.

5. Caring

Americans see themselves as a generous people, and indeed it is true that as a nation they give more, and a higher proportion of their GDP, in foreign aid than any other country. Americans see caring as the heart of ethics, since it is scarcely possible to be truly ethical and yet unconcerned with the welfare of others. That is because ethics as Americans understand it is ultimately about good relations with other people. For Americans, sincere caring involves an emotional response to both the pain and pleasure of others. Americans as individuals and corporations give to charitable causes both domestic and international on a big scale. Of course, sometimes these donations are hypocritical and fraudulent, meant to advance personal or corporate interests. In that case, though, most Americans would see them for what they are, investments or tax write-offs.

6. Citizenship

Citizenship includes civic virtues and duties that prescribe how we ought to behave as part of a community. The good citizen knows the laws and obeys them. But for Americans that is not all. A good citizen stays informed on the issues of the day, the better to execute the duties and privileges as a member of a self-governing democratic society. The good citizen volunteers and does more than a "fair" share to make society work, now and for future generations. Such a commitment to the public sphere can have many expressions, such as conserving resources, recycling, using public transportation and cleaning up litter. Good citizens give more than they take.

Americans argue passionately about how to put their ethical principles into practice and what to do about ethical failure by private citizens or public authorities. Americans may take less part in organized religion than they used, but to assume that America has thereby become an amoral culture is wide of the mark. In an age of expressive individualism and rampant consumerism, Americans still hew to the traditional virtues of loyalty, honesty, self-restraint and forgiveness. Even though they reject what they believe are outmoded versions of these virtues, Americans struggle to fashion their own versions of them. Moral freedom means to them that individuals should determine for themselves what it means to lead a good and virtuous life. Americans debate and demand moral standards because they believe that they desperately matter and that they, the Americans, are a special people with a special purpose within the purposes of God.

Yet Americans are often not active citizens. The enormous success of the American economy has created such prosperity for the great majority that they feel totally secure with no need to interest themselves in politics. Although they may take an interest in the personalities of the protagonists, political "shows" are really a form of entertainment. Secondly, there is no ideology in mainstream American politics and the results of elections, owing to the constitutional limitations on government, will be no worse than broadly neutral for most Americans, whoever wins. Thirdly, the pressures of today's work, family and social lives leave little time for the average person to devote to an interest in public affairs. In any case, significant involvement in politics is limited by the expense of campaigning to those who have or can raise millions of dollars. The reason is that the First Amendment is generally taken to mean that just as there can be few limitations on what a person or corporation or union says, so there should be minimal limits on how much they spend to promote their message. After all, it is argued, the message has to go out to over 300 million people of diverse ethnicity and education spread across a continent.

MARRIAGE AND THE FAMILY

The family unit
The American family today is usually taken to mean a mother, father and their children, the *nuclear family,* living in the same house and closely involved in each other's lives. Fifty years ago, the father spent all day at work and made most of the decisions about how the money he earned was spent. The mother stayed at home to manage the house and look after the children. Children were expected to obey their parents. Many modern families live rather differently, and because of this some people think the family is dying and society being weakened. Ironically, though, many people when questioned about their own family report that they are happy in it and with it.

Relationships
Americans often feel closer to their friends than to their family, because family members often live far apart, and people can choose their friends. But family ties are still strong in the South, and reunions may attract 40 or more from all over the country.

In the US, being outgoing and ready to talk to others is considered a positive quality. Americans are quick to get onto first name terms because they are afraid of seeming too formal, and they make friends easily, but the relationship often does not go very deep. Americans in cities do not often invite friends to their homes; they prefer to socialize at a restaurant, ball game or other place of relaxation or entertainment. People distinguish between best friends, close friends and acquaintances. College and professional friendships may last for many years even although the people see each other only occasionally. Some Americans are very open and tell others a great deal about their private lives, but they like to choose whether to share these confidences, so it is generally rude to ask such personal questions as how old a person is or how much money they earn. Company colleagues may spend a lot of time together at formal and informal company gatherings at bars, parties and sports. There can be strong social pressure to be present on these occasions and to take a spouse or partner along.

MARRIAGE

Americans expect to get married. Marriage is associated with stability and happiness. Despite a 48 percent divorce rate, America remains a "marriage-happy" society. In fact, 54 percent of women remarry within five years after a divorce (Centers for Disease Control, 2002).

Young people generally start to have romantic relationships at school or college. The age of puberty is now around 13. The accepted way for couples to get to know each other is dating. If the children are still at home, families generally make rules for what dating activities are acceptable, what time of day dates may take place, and whether the date is to be group or single, according to the age, personality and maturity of the children. It is common for young people to hold hands with their boyfriend or girlfriend and to kiss in public. People who find it difficult to get a boyfriend or girlfriend may use a dating agency or advertise in the personal column of a newspaper.

Love between the couple is believed to be a prerequisite to marriage. The man is usually expected to make the proposal of marriage and acceptance by the woman results in an engagement. Sometimes the decision is a joint one. The engagement is marked by the gift of an engagement ring from the man to the woman (fiancée). The couple then set a date for the wedding and decide who will perform the ceremony, a religious leader or a secular official such as a judge, and where the ceremony will be held. All states require the couple to get a marriage license, some require a blood test, and there is sometimes a prescribed waiting period, which varies from state to state, before they can marry.

Customs and traditions associated with the wedding ceremony that marks the beginning of the marriage vary widely. The couple send out printed invitations and the guests buy a gift, usually something for the home. A dinner is usually celebrated between the immediate families of spouses in the late afternoon the day before the wedding, after the wedding rehearsal. The bridegroom's family traditionally provides for this celebration.

A bachelor party (stag party) is held for the groom and usually sponsored by the Best Man (groom's assistant at the wedding ceremony) shortly before the wedding. Stag parties are meant to celebrate the groom's remaining freedom and can often be quite lively, with lots of alcohol consumed. A Bridal Shower (bachelorette party) for the bride, typically a rather quieter event, is usually sponsored by the Bride's Maid.

The wedding is most often performed as part of a religious ceremony at a church or synagogue with its own specific customs and traditions. On the day of the wedding, the groom does not see the bride until the ceremony. The groom's best male friend (usually an unmarried one,) called the *best man,* stands next to the groom during the wedding. One of his most important duties is to bring the wedding ring. Other friends act as ushers and show guests where to sit. The bride's closest woman friend is called the *maid of honor* (if married, *matron of honor*). Other friends and children act as bridesmaids. Rings are exchanged to mark the permanent commitment of the new spouses to each other.

Many women choose to have a *white wedding,* so called because the bride wears a long, white wedding dress with a veil covering her face. Her wedding clothes traditionally include "something old, something new, something borrowed, something blue" for luck. The bridesmaids wear matching dresses specially made for the occasion and, like the bride, carry bouquets of flowers. The bridegroom, best man and other men may wear a *tuxedo,* a black suit with a satin collar to the jacket and satin seams to the trousers and a white dress shirt. The bride enters accompanied by her father, who will *give her away,* and, to the sound of a wedding march usually played on the organ, moves to the front to stand beside the waiting groom. Some brides today find giving away offensive, particularly as, with increasing divorce, the then father of her family may not be her natural father, but the custom is still generally observed as a symbol of the goodwill of her family towards the marriage. Typically the person performing the ceremony talks about the importance of marriage, and a friend of the couple may read a poem. Then the bride and groom exchange vows, promising to stay together and support each other. The groom places a wedding ring on the third finger of the bride's left hand, and sometimes the bride gives him a ring too. The couple are then declared man and wife. They sign the register, the official record of marriages, and, as they leave, guests may shower them with rice or confetti (small pieces of colored paper in lucky shapes, such as horseshoes and bells).

The happy couple then usually go to a hotel or restaurant or the bride's home for the wedding reception for family and friends to celebrate. The bride's family usually arranges and pays for this celebration, which may be either a formal meal or a party. The couple and their parents then greet the guests, who say "Congratulations!" to the groom and "Felicitations!" to the bride. (The reason for not congratulating the bride is that, traditionally, congratulating was thought to imply that the woman had planned to marry the man for money or some other material benefit.) There are speeches towards the end of the meal by the best man, the bride's father and the bridegroom. The best man is supposed to make a humorous speech about the groom; the bride's father is supposed to praise the bride; and the bridegroom is to supposed to thank everyone, especially the maid or matron of honor and the bridesmaids. (Naturally these speeches vary widely in quality and the guests are sometimes relieved when they are over.) The bride and groom then jointly cut the wedding cake, with the groom placing his hand over the bride's as she holds the knife. (Sometimes two cuts are made in the cake beforehand to make it easier for the couple to take out the first slice.) The cake has several tiers covered with white frosting (icing) with figures of a bride and groom on the top one. Pieces of the cake are put into boxes to give to guests who cannot be present. It has become customary at many wedding receptions to leave a camera on each table for guests to take souvenir snapshots. A honeymoon is taken by the bride and groom immediately after the reception at a secret place where they go off for their first nights together in marriage. Before the couple leave, the bride throws her bouquet into the air; there is a belief that the woman who catches it will soon be married herself. The car the couple leave in has usually been decorated by their friends with the words "JUST MARRIED" and with old tin cans or shoes tied to the back.

Weddings can be very expensive and sometimes the reception and even the ceremony itself are just small family gatherings. The average wedding budget is $20,000, and the average cost of a wedding ring over $1,000. Total spending on honeymoons is $8 billion a year, $3,657 each on average. Traditionally, the father of the bride would pay for everything. Today, the bride and groom themselves pay for the wedding about 30 percent of the time; the bride's parents pay about 17 percent of the time; otherwise the cost is shared between the couple and one or both sets of parents. Over 91 percent of all to-be-weds open a bride's book at a store to register for gifts and say what gifts they would like. Most wedding guests spend between $70 and $100 on a gift. The couple receives gifts from an average of 200 guests, and an average 178 attend a wedding.

Americans used to be, and sometimes still are, more conservative about marriage, religion, sexuality and contraception than people in such areas as Northern Europe, where long-term cohabitation and having children outside of marriage are quite common. Even so, marriage and the family in the US are being affected by the tremendous social and technological changes taking place and are changing in a number of major respects. Age at first marriage continues to rise and is now 26.7 years for men and 25.1 for women; couples are having fewer children and later in life; and society is becoming more accepting of interracial marriage and gay and lesbian couples. Indeed, there is no longer a generally accepted moral code about sex, and no one type of household predominates. Ideas about when sex is appropriate are based on individuals' own standards and are very varied. Sex is not necessarily linked to marriage or a long-term relationship and is now part of most romantic relationships. This is due not only to a change in attitudes but also to the ready availability of contraception for women. The average age of first sexual intercourse is between 16 and 17. Sleeping around, however, that is, having sex with many people, or having sex for money, are generally disapproved of. People now talk about sexual relationships more easily, though many prefer to talk to a doctor or counselor, rather than friends, or write to an agony aunt (advice columnist) in a magazine.

Many couples still get married but many live together without doing so. A few years ago, couples living together usually got married when they wanted to start a family (have children) but this happens less now. Even so, couples expect each other to be loyal and not to have an affair or sleep with (have sex with) anyone else. Couples living together find it difficult to get a joint health insurance policy. Among the findings of a survey by University of Chicago researchers is that the percentage of American households made up of married couples with children dropped from 45 percent in the early 1970s to just 26 percent in 1998. Today, 32 percent of all children in the US are born out of wedlock. People who are in a long-term relationship refer to their *boyfriend* or *girlfriend, significant other, a person who is special and important,* or POSSLQ. The latter is a humorous name that comes from the way the government refers to people living together as "persons of the opposite sex sharing living quarters." An increasing number of organizations are recognizing the new family structures so that, for example, family tickets, which were traditionally for two adults and children, are now sometimes available for one adult and children.

Divorce

Americans believe that the purpose of marriage is to maximize the happiness of each partner and that, if it does not, the partners are free to divorce and seek other soulmates. With greater economic equality between the sexes, it is easier than ever before for women to escape unhappy marriages. According to the National Center for Health Statistics, in 2005 the number of marriages was 2,230,000, the marriage rate was 7.5 per 1,000 total population, and the divorce rate was 3.6 per 1,000 population (48%). Broadly speaking, the marriage rate has declined by about 8% since 1980 and the divorce rate has remained stable. The population of unmarried women aged 15 or over will soon surpass the number of married women. The number of children living with only one parent increased from 9% in 1960 to 30% (29.52%) in 2005. Of those 83% of the children live with the mother.

Greater acceptance of divorce and remarriage (or "serial monogamy", as sociologists term it) is reflected in a steady, high divorce rate and a growing number of stepfamilies and single-parent households. The children of single (or lone) parents may only see the other parent occasionally, or may have two homes and divide their time between them. Children in step-families often have to fit in with siblings from one or both of their parents' previous marriages. They may also have to relate to more than one set of grandparents, a new version of the extended family. Where the latter is the case, the family is called a *blended* family. (The author used to know a family where, as a result of both parents' remarriages, some of the children were not related to each other.) Today, the number of stepfamilies in the US is almost equal to the number of intact families. Families in which some children are adopted, legally made permanently part of another family, or fostered, looked after by another family for a time because their own parents cannot look after them, are not uncommon. Because many mothers now go out to work, either by choice or economic necessity, the parenting role for part of the day is more and more being shared by child minders or the staff of daycare centers or after-school centers. Some politicians, religious leaders and others have criticized working mothers, but most Americans accept that the traditional home can often not be provided and that other forms of family life can be loving, caring, and sufficient for adequate parenting.

One result of people getting married later in life and having fewer children is that the size of the average family is shrinking. But even though families are having fewer children, usually only one or two, America is still a very child-friendly society. Fewer children and longer life spans have also led to what one writer terms "beanpole families." In the past, families were broad, with two or three generations living in the same residence and many children in each nuclear family. Now, couples may have just one or two children, but it is not uncommon for as many as four generations to be alive at one time, though usually not residing together. The positive side of today's reality is more intergenerational contact. The challenge is that baby boomers and the generations that follow will have to deal with issues of elder care in addition to child care.

Homosexual and lesbian relationships, sometimes known as "alternative lifestyles," are now heard of and talked about more frequently. Many gay couples have "come out" and publicly admitted their sexuality and talk freely about their partner. Formerly, many Americans were hostile to homosexuals but gay couples are now generally tolerated, though many people do not approve. Even so, a state governor who left his wife and children for another man was forced to resign by public disapproval; and there are few homosexual characters on TV or in the movies. Civil unions (forms of marriage, but not legally the same) for gay people are recognized in several states. The term *domestic partnership* often connotes a lesser status that may or may not be recognized by local law. Oregon, Washington, California, Maine and Hawaii, however, do recognize committed gay couples as domestic partnerships. However, the terminology is still evolving. These forms of relationship have met fierce resistance in places, and only a few states recognize civil unions. The Defense of Marriage Act was passed in 1996 and signed into law by President Clinton. DOMA, as it has come to be known, officially barred federal benefits to same-sex partners. Under DOMA, states do not have to recognize same-sex relationships authorized by another state. In 32 states, state benefits cannot be paid to same-sex couples.

As society transforms ever more rapidly, ideals, mythologies, even laws cannot keep up, a situation known as "cultural lag." As such, Americans' current idealization of marriage is more a reflection of the past than of the present realities of marital and family life. It is tacitly assumed that the "family" in "family values" is the one of 50 years ago. In many cases, family values are a cultural and political symbol of security in a time of rapid, sometimes threatening change.

CHILD-RAISING

Babies

About 4 million babies are born in the US each year. The infant mortality rate is 7.2 per 1,000 live births, which is very high compared with most developed countries. The rate for whites is 6 per 1,000 but for blacks 14.2. These figures are explained by the fact that good medical care in the US is too expensive for poorer people, who are mostly black, to afford.

Contraception is widely used to help in family planning. Thus childbearing is largely a matter of choice. Only 10% of US babies are unwanted or unplanned. Many couples are now choosing to have children later in life. More than a third of babies are born to mothers over 30. Advances in fertility treatment mean that it is now possible for mothers who are too old to conceive naturally to have a baby. This possibility has raised a number of ethical and practical issues such as whether it is a good thing for a child to be born to an older mother.

During pregnancy, women go to prenatal classes to prepare for the birth. Fathers are also encouraged to attend. American women often have strong feelings about how and where they want to give birth. Most have their babies in a homely hospital birthing center. Women can choose to have the baby delivered by a specialist doctor called an *obstetrician*, or by a midwife. Fathers are often present and help at the birth.

Some women want to experience a natural birth without pain-relieving drugs. Doctors give the mother as much control over the birth as possible but take over when it seems necessary, since there is a high rate of litigation (court cases) over difficult births. This may also explain why one baby in five in the US is born by caesarean section, a surgical operation to remove the baby from the mother.

Babies in America are cause for celebration. Relatives and friends visit the mother and baby in hospital and take cards and gifts. Many American women are sentimental about babies, coo over them (talk lovingly in a soft voice) and want to hold them. After the parents choose the baby's name, they may send out a printed card giving the baby's name, weight and date of birth, or put a notice in the local newspaper. Births are registered at the local courthouse. Later there may be a christening (baptism) service at a local church, though these are less common now than in the past.

POPULAR NAMES

Girl baby names	Boy baby names
Mia	Emerson
Mallory	Austin
Kaylee	Brodin
Olive	Myles
Fiona	Jordan
Gweneth	Spencer
Elena	Ryan
Amber	Henry
Adrienne	Noland
Ellie	John
Renata	Jacob
Alyce	Michael
Brooklynn	Christopher
Bonnie	Carter

Naming customs

Junior, Senior, and Roman numerals

Words placed after a name to distinguish people of different generations who have the same name are not unique to America. In France, for example, the words *père* and *fils* denote father and son, as in the case of the two authors named Alexandre Dumas. Social name suffixes are far more frequently applied to men than to women. *Senior* and *junior* are the most common suffixes. When spelled out in full they are written with the first letter in lower case, and when abbreviated may be written with a capital first letter (Sr.) or in lower case (jr.), with or without an interceding comma. The term *junior* is only correctly used if a child is given exactly the same name as his or her parent. (See, for example, *Emily Post's Etiquette* by Elizabeth L. Post, 1985.) Sons with a different middle name or initial may, however, also be called *Junior*. An example is Ronald P. Reagan, the son of the President, who is still titled *junior* even though his middle name, Prescott, differs from his late father's middle name, which was Wilson. A son may also be nicknamed "Junior" even if he is not titled as such, as "Junior" is a popular family nickname. An instance of this is George W. Bush, who is nicknamed "Junior" by his family. Similarly the singer Hank Williams' son, Randall Hank Williams, is professionally known as Hank Williams, Jr. Randall's son, Shelton Hank Williams, is known professionally as Hank Williams III.

One case of a woman bearing the name suffix *jr.* was that of Eleanor Roosevelt (Anna Eleanor Roosevelt, Jr.), the wife of President Franklin D. Roosevelt. She used the suffix "jr." because she was named after her mother. A woman named after her mother or grandmother could also bear the suffix "II," but again, this is not common. Usually, the namesake is given a different middle name and so would not need a suffix for differentiation. The title "Jr." is sometimes used in legal documents, particularly those pertaining to wills and estates, to distinguish among female family members of the same name. A wife who uses the title *Mrs.* would also use her husband's full name, including the suffix. In less formal situations, the suffix may be omitted. Hence: Mrs. Lon Chaney Jr. on a wedding invitation, but Mrs. L. Chaney or simply Shannon Chaney for a friendly note. Widows are entitled to retain their late husband's full names and suffixes but divorcees may not, even if they retain the surname.

It can easily be imagined what confusion may arise when someone bearing the suffix *sr* dies. Neither tradition nor etiquette provide a certain guide. Do the men retain their titles, or do they all "move up" one? Upon the death of John Smith, Sr., his son, John Smith, Jr. may decide to style himself John Smith Sr. (causing confusion if his widowed mother and his wife both use the formal style Mrs. John Smith, Sr., and necessitating that his son and grandson change their titles as well) or he may remain John Smith, Jr. for the rest of his life. One effect of moving up is that it reduces the extension of Roman numerals over the generations: i.e., a John Smith III, IV, and V. A disadvantage is that it may cause confusion with respect to birth certificates, credit cards, and the like. In practice it is quite uncommon for families to go beyond "III" in naming children, although there are notable exceptions. The legal name of Tom Cruise, for instance, is actually Thomas Cruise Mapother IV, and the oldest sons of U.S. Senator Jay Rockefeller (legal name John Davison Rockefeller IV) have "V" as their suffix. Former boxer George Foreman named his five sons after himself: George Edward Foreman II through VI.

There is a good reason for using numerical suffixes as well as *sr.* and *jr.* For example, a child named Michael James Taylor, after his uncle Michael James Taylor, would properly be considered Michael James Taylor II, as opposed to "Junior." Junior is not used because, in this example, Michael James Taylor is not the child of Michael James Taylor, senior. If Michael James Taylor II were to have a son, he could then be named Michael James Taylor III or Michael James Taylor, Jr., depending upon the family. While it is not *technically* the social norm to use "II" in place of "junior" for children born directly to a same named parent, there is no social rule against the usage of "II" instead of "junior" for a same named child. Often, II is used by families who want to avoid having their children referred to as "junior" as a nickname. Finally, common nicknames for a junior or II include "Chip" (as in "chip off the old block") and "Bud" (predominantly in the South). Likewise, a common nickname for a III is "Trey" which denotes that the nameholder is the third in a line.

Christening

Christening (baptism) is the ceremony by which a person officially becomes a member of the Christian church, usually while still a baby. The clergyperson pours holy water on the child's head from a special bowl called a *font* and gives the child a name. The most popular names are Jacob for a boy and Emily for a girl (Social Security Administration). Promises are made on behalf of the child by three adults, two of whom must be of the same sex as the child. Afterwards a party may be held for family and friends.

Looking after the baby

Most Americans believe that breastfeeding a baby is better than bottle feeding with *formula*, a product made from cow's milk mixed with water. About 55% of babies are breastfed, particularly among better educated and older women; mothers who choose to bottlefeed, or are unable to breastfeed, may be made to feel guilty. There has also been controversy over whether breastfeeding should be allowed in public places such as restaurants, but nowadays the practice is widely accepted.

Fathers are encouraged to help with babycare, as this is thought to help them and the child bond i.e., form a close emotional relationship. In practice women do most of the work, because men cannot usually stay at home long after the baby is born. In the US, workers have no legal right to take time off work, unless they work for an employer who employs more than 50 workers. Leave depends on individual employers, and the concepts of "maternity leave" and "paternity leave" have been slow to catch on, although more employers are granting it. There is some limited financial help for mothers, but no universal state maternity benefits as in other developed countries. Most Americans believe that people who cannot afford to support a baby should not have one. Some women give up their jobs to care for their baby; others return to work and must find a babysitter or daycare center to care for it.

ABORTION (see also Chapter 11)

The US has one of the highest abortion rates in the developed world. Abortion is one of the defining issues in the "culture wars" that have raged in the US since the 1960s. It has provoked passionate, sometimes bitter debate and even the murder of abortion doctors. Abortion has also become a leading political issue, since a President in favor of limiting abortion could nominate justices to the Supreme Court who would vote to do so if a case came before them. In 1973 abortion became legal all over the US through the Supreme Court decision *Roe v Wade*.

Since then there has been much debate between people on the *pro-choice* side, who believe that women have the right to decide what happens to their bodies, and *right-to-life* supporters, who believe that abortion is murder. For pro-choice it is said that if parents have taken all reasonable precautions against having a child, they do not simply by virtue of their biological relationship to the child who comes into existence have a special responsibility for it.

The most common reasons a woman chooses abortion are because she:
- is not ready to become a parent.
- cannot afford a baby.
- does not want to be a single parent.
- does not want anyone to know she has had sex or is pregnant.
- is too young or too immature to have a child.
- has all the children she wants.
- is asked to by her husband, partner, or parent.
- (she or) the fetus has a health problem.
- was a survivor of rape or incest.

Pro-lifers say that abortion, especially late-term, is inhumane and the procedures used are abhorrent. Many pro-lifers are Christians who believe that their religion requires them to uphold the "sanctity of life." Pro-lifers' opinions vary as to precisely when a fetus becomes a human being, but they agree that once the fetus is viable outside the womb, it has an absolute right to life. Most pro-lifers are peaceable citizens, but on a few occasions, pro-life groups have gone so far as to bomb clinics where abortions are performed and kill doctors who perform them. Alongside the moral and religious issues is the question of who should bear the cost of reproductive health education, and the fear by some that if governments begin to pay for such programs, they will subsequently fund further healthcare programs and start to raise extra taxes to pay for them. A government healthcare system that might seem normal and desirable in some countries is seen as undesirable and even a threat to freedom by some Americans.

Induced abortions usually result from unintended pregnancies, which often occur despite the use of contraception. The US rate of unintended pregnancies is higher than the world average, and much higher than that in other industrialized nations. More than 3 million pregnancies per year are unintended, resulting in about 1.3 million abortions. Of the 800,000 and rising teen pregnancies per year, over 80% were unintended in 2001. One-third of teen pregnancies result in abortion. It is estimated that 52% of unintended pregnancies result from couples not using contraception in the month the woman got pregnant, and 43% result from inconsistent or incorrect contraceptive use; only 5% result from contraceptive failure, according to a report from the Guttmacher Institute. Unintended pregnancy is a problem not just for adolescents, unmarried women, or poor women; it is a pervasive public health problem for all women of reproductive age.

After increasing gradually until it peaked at a high of over 1.6 million in 1990, the number of abortions annually performed in the US has dropped back to levels not seen since the late 1970s. In 2005, 1.21 million abortions were performed, down from 1.31 million in 2000. (The Centers for Disease Control point out that these figures are conservative estimates because reporting is voluntary. The Alan Guttmacher Institute, a private organization that contacts abortion providers directly, consistently reports figures that are 12%-20% higher. Both sources, however, report the same downward trend.) For a long time, nearly 90% of abortions have taken place in the first trimester, and in recent years, women having an abortion have been able to do so earlier within the first trimester. Currently, more than six in 10 abortions occur within the first eight weeks of pregnancy, and almost three in 10 take place at six weeks or earlier. Almost all (97%) abortions are performed by curettage (suction).

The Guttmacher Institute has documented a widening reproductive health gap between poor women and higher-income women, however. From the 1980s to the mid-1990s, women of all income groups became more likely to use contraceptives and less likely to experience unintended pregnancies. But since 1994, unplanned pregnancy rates among poor women have increased by 29%, while rates among higher-income women have decreased by 20%. Today, a poor woman is four times as likely to experience an unplanned pregnancy as a higher-income woman. Approximately 55% of women who obtain abortions are white, 35% black and 7% of other races; for 3% of the women, race is unknown. The abortion ratio for black women (503 per 1,000 live births) is 3.0 times the ratio for white women (167 per 1,000 live births), a disparity that has been increasing since 1990. Additionally, the abortion ratio for women of other races (329 per 1,000 live births) was 2.0 times the ratio for white women. The abortion rate for black women (30 per 1,000) was 3.1 times the rate for white women (10 per 1,000), whereas the abortion rate for women of other races (22 per 1,000) was 2.2 times the rate for white women. Notably 78% of women who obtained abortions were known to be unmarried. The abortion ratio for unmarried women was 8.8 times the ratio for married women (570 versus 65 abortions per 1,000 live births). The abortion ratio was highest for women who had three previous live births (285 per 1,000 live births) and lowest for women who had one previous live birth (194 per 1,000). In 2000, 53% of women who obtained an abortion were reported to have obtained one for the first time. Eighteen percent of women were reported to have had two or more previous abortions. The number of women who die in the US as a result of legal abortions is tiny, less than 20, sometimes only a handful a year.

The National Organization for Women (NOW), however, point out that the Hyde Amendment in 1976 and state parental involvement laws have resulted in the deaths of women driven to back alley abortions. The Hyde Amendment cut off funding for abortion to women who cannot afford health care. NOW also points out that 87% of US counties have no abortion provider, and fewer new doctors are being trained to perform abortion procedures.

The US backed away a little from what was once a core principle, the "woman's right to choose," when, on April 18, 2007, the Supreme Court, by a vote of 5–4, upheld the constitutionality of the Partial-Birth Abortion Ban Act of 2003, which banned a form of late-term abortion. There is no exception under this Act for the health of the mother, unless her life is in danger. Many women seeking late-term abortions are those who have had amniocentesis and have discovered genetic abnormalities. The procedure involves partially delivering the fetus, before collapsing or piercing its skull and then removing the fetus entirely. This procedure is called *intact D&E* (dilation and evacuation). After the first trimester, D&E is the most common abortion procedure. The procedure is completed by emptying the uterus using a combination of suction and medical instruments. Inconsistently, it is still permitted to dismember the fetus inside the womb and remove it piece by piece (partial D&E), a method that is more widely used. Arguably, the reasons for this illogical compromise were political, to assuage the demands by pro-lifers, who are more likely to vote Republican, and, some allege, to set a precedent by which abortion can be limited further in the future. In 2000, however, only 2,200 abortions used this method, a figure that has varied very little since 1992. Doctors who perform the banned procedure could now face criminal prosecution, fines and up to two years in prison. Why the Supreme Court accepted the case as a constitutional issue is another interesting point. The reason was that the practice of abortion is deemed to fall within the Court's competence under the Constitution to regulate interstate commerce, since many patients travel to states where the laws on abortion are more liberal than their own; and some abortion centers belong to national or multistate businesses.

Family life

Weekdays generally follow a regular pattern. The parents get up and make sure the children are up and getting ready to go to school. There may be a rush for everyone to use the bathroom, find clean clothes, and eat breakfast and often for the children to catch a bus (sometimes the typical American school bus) to school. Meanwhile the parents have to get ready for work and arrange to do errands such as picking up neighbors' children and giving them a lift to school. The school day usually ends around 3 p.m. and the working day at 5 p.m. or later, so many parents have to make arrangements for younger children to be cared for after school, staying with a neighbor's children or at an after school center. Older children may do activities such as sports or music at school, or go home and do their homework. These children often go home to an empty house, let themselves in and have to fend for themselves. They are called "latchkey kids." Finding good, affordable childcare for children until their parents come home is a problem. Some wealthier parents employ nannies who live in the family home, while others use daycare providers who take care of a group of children. Others send their children to a daycare center or a nursery school. Childcare may take a large proportion of the parents' income.

The closest families eat meals at the same time and spend their free time together. Some families are even child-centered, putting the children's interests first. Some families, however, only see each other for a short time in the evening, and though the children are still considered important, they have to fit in with the lives of their parents. In many families, the children eat when they get home and their parents eat later. In the evenings the children may complete their homework, play or go and see friends. If everyone is staying in, they may spend time in the yard or watch television together. The backyard is the main play area, and during warm weather Americans spend a lot of time there. It may contain sandboxes, slides, swings or climbing frames for the children and, in richer homes, a swimming pool. Americans like to eat outside, often preparing meals on a barbecue. There may also be a patio or a *deck,* a wooden platform attached to the house. The backyard may be decorated with birdfeeders and lamps for use after dark. The front yard contains a lawn, trees, shrubs and bushes. Americans like to keep their front yards tidy and they mow them often. Front yards may be open or fenced. All the children living in an area go freely into each other's backyards.

Once children in America start grade school, parents believe that children's education is the responsibility of teachers. Thus parents play little direct part in educating their school-age children beyond checking that they are doing their homework and encouraging them to get good grades. Many parents make an effort to spend at least an hour of quality time together with their children when they give them their full attention. But the children are encouraged to have their own hobbies and develop their own personalities. At the weekend, families may go together to a sports game, or on trips to parks, museums, wildlife parks or places of entertainment. In school vacations they may visit other family members or go to the beach. Children in poor homes have few of these opportunities and for some it is a treat to visit the local hamburger restaurant.

American families are often criticized for the way they do things separately, and for the freedom that they allow the children, but Americans believe that the purpose of the family is to maximize the happiness of each member, and that it is vital for children to learn to be independent, to make choices and abide by the consequences. This is based on the belief that adults are responsible for their own destiny and that an adult is one who has reached maturity and developed sufficient understanding and discretion to be able to exercise rational free choice. Thus parents are seen as guides and guardians rather than as dominating authorities. Ultimately this view of the relations between parents and children may be traced back to Chapter 6 of John Locke's *Second Treatise.* Locke's describes the parents' role like this:

> "(father's) power reaches no farther than by such a discipline, as he finds most effectual, to give such strength and health to their bodies, such vigour and rectitude to their minds, as may best fit his children to be most useful to themselves and others; and, if it be necessary to his condition, to make them work, when they are able, for their own subsistence. But in this power the *mother* too has her share with the *father.*"

Thus from an early age, children are encouraged to decide what they want to do, eat or wear, and their parents try to respect their wishes. Children owe their parents, in Locke's words (*Second Treatise*: 6:66): "honour, respect, gratitude and assistance... (not) absolute obedience and submission." Moreover the degree of respect and compliance varies as the "care, cost and kindness in his education, has been more or less." Fundamental to the American concept of family relations is the statement by Locke (*Second Treatise*: 6:71) that political and paternal power are distinct. Indeed he points out earlier in the chapter that parents who bring up their children to be independent are thereby creating a society in which the absolute monarchy of the past cannot return.

Unfortunately, lack of parental supervision can mean lack of discipline and in some cases anti-social behavior by children. One of the factors in the Columbine school shooting in 2000, where two psychologically disturbed teenage boys shot many of their classmates and some teachers before shooting themselves, was that they had spent many hours unsupervised in their bedrooms playing violent video games without their parents' knowledge.

In fact, American parents generally encourage their children to be caring and responsible. Over half of American families have pets, and children usually have some responsibility for looking after them. The most popular pets for children include cats, dogs, birds, fish, rabbits, guinea pigs, hamsters and mice. Pure-bred dogs may be taken to shows, but most people are happy with a mutt (a mixed-breed dog). Most pets are treated as members of the family. Pets have their own place to sleep, bowls to eat from, and toys to play with. A few dogs sleep outside in a doghouse, but most, and cats too, are allowed to go where they like inside the house. They may eat special pet food and biscuits, or meat, fish, and milk. There are special salons for pets where their fur is washed and cut. Dogs (and sometimes cats) wear a collar with a small disc attached giving a name and address. Dog owners have to buy a dog license and usually in public places have to keep the dog on a leash. People generally teach their dogs heeling (walking close to their owner) and not to jump up at people. They may also teach tricks like fetching or begging. Some owners take their dogs to obedience school. People are also supposed to clean up if a dog makes a mess in a public place and may be fined if they do not. Looking after pets costs Americans over $20 billion a year. Particularly expensive items are pet motels when the owners go on vacation, medical insurance and, for pets with emotional problems, a pet psychologist. When a pet dies it may be buried in a pet cemetery after a special ceremony.

As well as helping look after pets, children are also expected to do chores like washing dishes and keeping the house (and garden if there is one) clean and tidy. Most children receive regular pocket money or an allowance to spend as they wish. From an early age also children are encouraged to make friends with other children; and they may go through fads or crazes where they want to have the same toys or clothes as their friends. Most parents exercise discipline. This often takes the form of restrictions such as *grounding,* not being allowed to go out with their friends, or loss of privileges such as watching television. Nowadays children are spanked much less than in the past, and indeed are thought to have certain rights such as the right to have their interests taken into consideration, not to be abused, and to have their opinions taken into account.

Most children in America have a happy childhood. Some have lots of toys, games and books, and even their own TV and computer, where they surf the internet, in their bedroom. Young children are given soft, stuffed, cuddly toys, also known as plush animals, such as a teddy bear. In fact the practice of keeping, collecting, naming, and ascribing personalities to these toys is also widespread among American adults of both genders and of all ages. Teddy bears, large and small, are probably the most popular, but in most American homes can be found plush dogs, rabbits, pigs and other stylized cute animals. Antique plush animals are highly sought after, but there is also a collectors market for styles of plush animals that have only recently gone out of production. In shopping malls and theme parks, companies offer "build your own bear" services. The customer (not always a child) can have a bear in a chosen style custom-stuffed and custom-dressed, usually accompanied by a birth certificate. A large market exists for commemorative bears, usually small and floppy, celebrating a state, city, region, special event or sports team, or simply showing a sentimental phrase like "I Love You" or "I'm Sorry". Collectors often insist that the identification tags be left on the ears of these animals to maintain their resale value.

After soft toys, children accumulate building blocks, dolls, balls, toy cars, paints and, in some homes, toy guns. Most children spend part of each day watching television. There are special programs for children during the day and in the early evening. Parents often use the television to keep children amused when they are busy.

Young children go to a local playground where there are swings and slides. Older ones like to play on bikes, skateboards or Rollerblades, or just socialize with their friends. Some congregate in the local shopping mall. Sports are popular, especially basketball. In cities, children play on parking lots or waste ground. Children from middle class homes take part in a lot of organized activities such as sport, music and drama. In many homes the parents put up an organizer in the kitchen to keep track of where their children are and when they need to ferry them by car to and from these activities, public transport generally being non-existent. In the past, children regularly went out alone, but now in cities parents worry about the danger from traffic, or that their children might become involved in drugs or crime, or be the victim of a pedophile. Many families find it hard to strike a balance between encouraging their children to be responsible and independent and trying to protect them.

There are, unfortunately, a significant number of children who do not have a happy family life. Some suffer emotionally because of family problems such as unemployment, debt, drugs and divorce. Some do not receive enough attention and grow up lacking in confidence, or get in trouble with the police. Some beg in the streets. A few suffer physical or mental abuse.

Teens

Teenagers love pop music. They spend money on CDs and DVDs and on going to discos and concerts. Teenagers also become interested in fashion and may have a clothing allowance to buy their own clothes. Girls start using makeup and worrying about their weight and figure. At 13 or 14 some teens get part-time jobs such as delivering newspapers. Later they may work in shops or fast food restaurants. Most want to earn extra money and are encouraged to do so by their parents. By 14 or 15 many teenagers are interested in the opposite sex and may have regular boyfriends or girlfriends. On their 18th birthday, when they become adults, they usually have a party and richer parents may give them money, for example, towards their college expenses. Teenagers often develop tastes and opinions different from their parents and, because they are considered to have the right to have their say, there are often *run-ins* (arguments) in the family. Usually these are minor and blow over but some adolescents become difficult and rebellious.

Fathers

Fathers in America today are expected to take a more active part in child-raising than in the past. Instead of letting their partner pluck a crying or smelly baby from their arms, they are expected to handle things, and maybe ask for advice. American fathers learn by doing, just like anything else. Men are increasingly unafraid to get help if they are uncertain or feel ill prepared to be a father. Programs are available to help fathers learn the basics of caregiving.

Naturally, men and women have different ways of interacting with their children. Men tend to stress physical and high-energy activities; women, the social and emotional. Safely wrestling, bouncing on the bed, and other "guy things" are considered just as important as the "girl things" mothers do with their kids. Children with physically active dads have been shown to be more popular and more successful in their relationships with other children. American men tend to be more emotionally available to their children these days and able to empathize with their children's feelings.

All in all, the modern American dad is more of a partner than a helper, sharing responsibility for the household and childcare in an active fashion, and not just on weekends. Despite the nostalgia of some social critics for the idealized Ozzie-and-Harriet families of the 1950s (so called after a popular soap opera of that time), the traditional father-as-helper model is outdated and inappropriate. Fathers get involved in the day-to-day decisions that affect their children, instead of leaving everything to the mother. Yet they respect the decisions she makes when they are unavailable. Successful parents develop a system to plan parent-child and family activities together. As the children mature, they let them take part in the planning process as well. Taking part in the everyday chores, routines, and activities that make up childhood, fathers get to know their children with the kind of intimacy that they generally did not do in the past. Changes in the law have given fathers more rights to help them balance home and work. They may now be eligible for family leave under the Family and Medical Leave Act.

Nevertheless, it remains a fact that when a marriage ends, fewer than 15 percent of fathers receive shared or joint custody of their children, and many of those who do not get custody end up slowly fading out of their children's lives. Experts agree that it is critical to stay in touch with the children and make the time they spend with them meaningful. The problem is that some divorced dads try to settle old marital disputes by using the children as pawns, when the parents need to cooperate and support each other for the sake of the children.

Supporting the school

American parents often are in touch with their children's schools. Research shows that when parents actively support the schools, children behave better, earn higher grades, score better on tests and graduate at higher rates. Even parents who cannot volunteer in the classroom on a regular basis may use an occasional vacation day to chaperone a field trip or help with a special class project. And if they cannot get to school, they may send in cupcakes or help plan a class party. Most schools have parent-teacher organizations. Parents' employers can be valuable partners for schools too. Some parents get their firms to donate supplies or equipment, for example. Others may print a brochure, give door prizes for a fund-raising event, provide small incentives for kids to read a certain number of books, host a work-site tour for students or supply speakers for career day. Parents vary a good deal in their attitude to supporting the school at home. Conscientious ones read to their children every day, making sure (s)he completes homework, and seeing that (s)he gets enough sleep and has a good breakfast.

Children's activities outside the home

Middle class parents are keen to enroll their child in extracurricular activities to cultivate a child's interest or innate talent. Sometimes this puts excess stress on themselves and the children, not least because the parents have to drive the children to and from the activities. For two- to five-year-olds these may include music class, ballet or gymnastics. When a child begins kindergarten, parents feel pressure from their parenting peers, who are buying soccer shoes and a piano so their child can join a team and begin lessons. For parents in a neighborhood isolated from other families with young children, a class can supply the opportunity for the child to interact with peers and a place for parents to meet other parents. Ambitious parents believe an early start with enrichment activities will foster a lifelong interest in the subject, give the child a competitive edge in high school, or even start the child in a career in sports or music.

Some commentators believe that American children these days are over-scheduled and over-stressed. When family members are all going in so many different directions, homework may be neglected and family meals skipped, and the children become accustomed to grazing from the refrigerator or simply grabbing fast food from the nearest mall. Children may indeed never develop the ability to entertain themselves with a game, hobby or project, and instead become bored and restless. Others, overly stimulated from going from one event to the next, have trouble concentrating or sleeping, and fail to absorb all they are experiencing.

Youth organizations

Young people have a wide choice of clubs to join. Some clubs concentrate on sports, public service or religion, but most offer a wide range of activities. Parents are often keen to support local youth clubs because they believe the clubs will keep their children and teens usefully occupied. But although many children like to go to clubs, teens are less interested in organized activities and prefer to go to a sports center, drive in movie or bar when they feel like it.

High schools have school professional clubs, student organizations associated with various careers. Junior Achievement, for example, helps students learn about careers and business. Students can actually run small businesses through their schools. Other such clubs include Future Teachers of America and Future Business Leaders of America. The US Army, Navy and Air Force all have ROTC (Reserve Officers Training Corps). Members of these groups are given basic military training and are encouraged to seek a career in the armed forces. Many children go to summer camp during school vacation and take part in sports, craft work and social activities. Many higher school students join fraternities or sororities.

Among the best known youth groups in America are the Boy Scouts of America and the Girl Scouts of America. The Scouts are organized by age group: Tiger Cubs aged 6, Cub Scouts 7-10, Boy Scouts 11-18 and Explorers 15-20. The highest rank is Eagle Scout. The Girl Scouts are Daisy Girl Scouts 5 - 6, Brownie Girl Scouts 6 - 8, Junior Girl Scouts 8 -11, Cadette Girl Scouts 11-14 and Senior Girl Scouts 14-17. Together they have about 8 million members. Scouts can join special troops to learn about careers such as medicine and communications.

Many churches have youth groups that meet to discuss religion. There are also religious organizations not linked to a particular church, established so that young Christians can meet and encourage each other and also take along friends and encourage them to become Christians. There are also youth groups linked to the Jewish, Muslim and other faiths. Examples are Youth for Christ, whose first paid-up member was the evangelist Billy Graham, and Young Life, which has groups in schools and organizes camps. Many towns have branches of the YMCA and YWCA (the Young Men's and Young Women's Christian Association). The Campus Crusade for Christ has branches at colleges and universities.

Some American service clubs are involved in community projects. The Kiwanis, for example, run Key Clubs for young people and members to visit old people and help with collections for charities. Members of the Big Brothers or Little Sisters Clubs spend time with a little brother or sister from a disadvantaged family. They become their friend and give advice like a real elder brother or sister. In 1998 there were 500 groups helping 100,000 people. Many young people from disadvantaged homes belong to the Boys and Girls Clubs of America.

Spoiled children

Spoiling children is a hot topic of conversation and in the media. American children appear to be more assertive and hence noisier than those in other cultures, but this is hard to judge and easy to stereotype. To some extent, the relationship between parents and children is a by-product of raising children to be independent. Some American parents equate indulgence, attention, and instant gratification with love. If a child sees a Barbie doll she must have, such parents buy it to stop the child complaining, even though she already has several. When a group of friends or family gather, the child is allowed to take center stage, interrupt and insist everyone focus attention on him or her. When a child cannot delay gratification and, for example, asks for a cookie right before dinner, whining and pleading until it is given, such parents give in. When it is time to put toys away, the child throws a temper tantrum and the parent ends up completing the job. Many parents, however, take their child-raising responsibilities seriously and discipline their children. Whole columns are given over in newspapers and magazines and on websites to counseling such parents on how to handle naughty children and avoid spoiling them. Spanking is probably commoner than the data suggest, because some parents are embarrassed to admit that they do it. The issue is inconclusively debated, since most of the arguments deployed on either side are *ad hominem* or circular. At any rate, punishment is highly culture-bound ("that's how we raise our kids around here.") Broadly speaking, physical chastisement is more common in the South and in religious homes. Only a few parents allow their children to call them by their first names.

The Resilient Child

According to parenting expert, Jan Faull, M.Ed., the resilient child has certain characteristics:

1. *Good problem-solving skills.* From the preschool years on, resilient children display an interest in finding solutions to problems rather than giving up or depending on others to manage situations for them. They are task- and solution-oriented.

2. *An internal locus of control.* Resilient children believe in their own effectiveness. Although external events may have caused their problem, they assume responsibility for a solution. They do not consider themselves victims.

3. *Elicits support from others.* The resilient child has the knack of finding a nurturing person in or outside the family to support him or her through troubled times. It is a combination of independence coupled with an ability to ask for help when needed.

4. *Cultivates an interest or hobby.* When the resilient child faces turmoil, he turns to a hobby or a special interest for solace. It might be cooking, computer games, or a baseball card collection that brings the world back into focus, builds competency, and provides a source of pride to share with others.

5. *Has an optimistic view of life.* Resiliency goes along with a faith that things will work out as well as can be reasonably expected, and negative events can be surmounted, giving meaning to life and a reason for commitment and caring.

6. *Is helpful to others.* By late elementary school the resilient child works to carry out socially desirable tasks to prevent others in the family, neighborhood, or community from experiencing distress or discomfort.

7. *Has effective communication skills.* The resilient child effectively communicates problems and feelings, thus gaining positive attention, backing, and ideas from interested friends, family, and adults.

8. *Uses intellectual gifts effectively*: The resilient child is not necessarily intellectually gifted, but each uses talents optimally, working to reach his potential. If the child is intelligent and good at school, these are positively associated with the ability to overcome great odds.

The extended family

Americans often move from city to city, and it is common for members of the extended family (grandparents, uncles, aunts, cousins) to live far away. Some grandparents see very little of their grandchildren. Families try to stay in touch by emailing, telephoning (and to a lesser extent nowadays writing) by visiting occasionally and sometimes holding big family reunions. Family loyalty is still important and many people feel they have a duty to care for other members of their family when they need it. Even so, it is not part of American culture for old people to live with other members of their family. Most elderly people live in their own home and when they cannot care for themselves move into an old people's home or a nursing home.

Volunteering

Between 2005 and 2007, the nation had an average volunteer rate of 27.2% per year. In 2007, 60.8 million volunteers dedicated 8.1 billion hours of service to community organizations, according to the Corporation for National and Community Service. There were one million more volunteers in 2007 than 2002. More corporations are giving support to volunteering. In a separate poll taken after the 9/11 terrorist attacks, Independent Sector, an organization of charities and foundations, found that 44 percent of Americans (42 percent men, 46 percent women) reported they volunteered, 60 percent of whom said they did so at least monthly. Volunteers serve as tutors and mentors in underperforming local schools, help homeless and other marginalized people by preparing meals at soup kitchens, teach the underprivileged at neighborhood computer labs, and work on neighborhood beautification and other projects. Among college students, a trend is the "alternative spring break" movement, in which university students perform community service projects during their vacation week in March. Thousands of students each year build houses for low-income families, care for HIV/AIDS patients and tutor inner-city children.

Charities (see also Chapter 4)

Charities are independent organizations that help the poor, children, the elderly, the sick, the homeless and animals. A well-known example is the Red Cross, which gives help to people after disasters. Charities are also involved with campaigning on social issues, education, medical research and the environment. Charities rely on money given by the public, and on volunteers for fund-raising and carrying out their activities. Americans are enthusiastic supporters of charities and give $120 billion a year, about $450 per person. Charities are non-profit and people do not have to pay taxes on charitable contributions. Religious organizations receive most money from the public, followed by those concerned with social services, education and health. Well-known charities include the Salvation Army, the United Negro College Fund, and the American Cancer Society. Local charities run shelters for the homeless and soup kitchens where the poor can eat free. The Salvation Army and Goodwill shops sell secondhand clothes. (Goodwill Industries provide training and employment for people with emotional problems or who have committed crimes.) A lot of the work done by charities, such as caring for the poor and education, is done in other countries by the government. Americans have a strong belief that private groups are responsible for charitable work. Many Americans want to be generous and are happy to give money to charity, but they want giving to be a personal choice. In recent years the telethon has proved an effective method of fund-raising. During an evening of popular television programs, television stars ask the public to telephone and pledge money to a charity. The muscular dystrophy telethon is the most famous. Many workers allow money to be deducted from their pay and sent to charity. Some companies hold fund-raising drives in which different parts of the company compete to see which of them pledges the most. The United Way, a national organization that collects money in an annual fund-raising drive to give to small charities, benefits from this. At Thanksgiving, churches and schools arrange collections of food for old people and the poor called *food drives*. At Halloween children may collect money for the UN charity UNICEF. Many Americans leave money to charities in their wills and some people, instead of sending flowers to the funeral, send the money to a charity.

CHAPTER 8

AMERICAN RELIGION

Although he's regularly asked to do so, God does not take sides in American politics.
George J. Mitchell

If any one feature of the US is different from most Western countries, it is the extensive practice, influence and variety of religion, and religion's constitutional position. The US is well known for its many traditional churches and less formal Christian groups, and for the number of non-Christian religions that have been brought to its shores. According to surveys, large majorities, though smaller in recent years, say they believe in God, and Harris Poll reports that 26 percent of Americans go to church every week or more often. Churches are centers for social events and sometimes business activities as well as places of worship. Prayers are often said at football games and some teams kneel together in prayer before a game. American religiosity has also become well known through the rhetoric of former President George W. Bush and the religious motives of some of his policies such as faith-based initiatives. From the Pilgrim settlers onward, the feeling that America has been chosen and set apart by God to be a light shining in darkness and to have a mission to the nations has been part of the national identity, one that many Americans feel it is their duty to declare, discuss and to demonstrate in their own lives and in their country's actions. Sometimes this extends to legislating morality, whether banning alcohol or abortion.

Separation of church and state

Soon after the formation of the US, Americans rejected the institution of established or state religion that had dominated and divided many European countries. The US was the first country to have no official religion. Most of the initial settlements consisted of Christian zealots, some of them refugees of one sort or another, but by 1700 what Stephen Bates (*op. cit.*, p. 57) has called the "repressive theocracies of the like-minded" had had to accommodate settlers who were not of the same religion and even some who had no religious allegiance. A major theme of the history of the Colonial period was disputes over the position of religion in society and the freedom of religious observance. Even among the Puritans, Roger Williams had argued in the mid-17th century that people could only become good Christians by wanting to and that conscience must not be forced. Separation of church and state was laid down by the First Amendment to the Constitution, which provides in part that "Congress shall make no law respecting an establishment of religion, or prohibiting the free exercise thereof...."

This seems straightforward, but in practice it has at times been difficult even for constitutional scholars to draw a distinction between government and religion. Students in public schools, for instance, may not pray publicly as part of the school day, yet the Pledge of Allegiance that is regularly recited contains the phrase "under God" which was introduced at the request of President Eisenhower in 1954. Although the Constitution states that "no religious test shall ever be required as a qualification to any office or public trust under the United States," it has become tradition for Presidents to end their Presidential Oath with "so help me God." The Vice-President, members of the House of Representatives, the Senate, and the Cabinet, and all other civil and military officers and federal employees are required to take an oath ending with "so help me God." Sessions of the Congress begin with a prayer by a clergyperson, and Presidents attend church regularly. Some cities may not display a Christmas crèche on public property unless symbols of other faiths are shown too, but the slogan "In God We Trust" appears on US currency, and money given to religious institutions can be a deduction for income tax purposes. Students who attend church-affiliated colleges may receive federal loans like other students, but their younger siblings may not receive federal monies specifically to attend religious elementary or secondary schools. In 1963, the Supreme Court ruled that it was unconstitutional for public school students to say the Lord's Prayer or read the Bible in class, but some schools, especially in the Deep South, ignore the ruling. As recently as August, 2003, the Chief Justice of the state of Alabama was removed from office for defying a federal court order to move a carving of the Ten Commandments from the rotunda of the Alabama Supreme Court building. (It was suggested, however, that it would have been constitutional to install the carving in his office.) It may never be possible to resolve these apparent inconsistencies. They derive from a tension built into the First Amendment itself, which tells Congress neither to establish nor to interfere with religion. In an ironic aside, political commentator Gore Vidal once remarked "the only national religion that the United States has ever truly had [is] anti-Communism" ("Shredding the Bill of Rights," *Vanity Fair,* November 1998.)

The First Amendment and religion

One of the first permanent settlements in what became the North American Colonies, Massachusetts, was founded by English Puritans, strict Calvinists, who refused to be included in the Church of England (Episcopal Church), which had been established in England by law. In America they grew and prospered. The Puritans considered their success a sign that God was pleased with them, and they assumed that those who disagreed with their beliefs should not be tolerated.

When the colony's leaders exiled one of the members, Roger Williams, for preaching religious toleration, he responded by founding a separate colony, which became the state of Rhode Island, where everyone enjoyed religious freedom. Two other states also originated as havens for people who were being persecuted for their religious beliefs: Maryland was a refuge for Catholics, and Pennsylvania for the Society of Friends (Quakers), a Protestant group whose members espouse plain living, a meditative spirituality, minimal church structures, and pacifism. Although the Church of England became the established church in the colonies after 1700, it never managed to become the church of the establishment. For one thing, most of the colonies had been founded by religious dissenters and lacked laws to enforce attendance at the established church. The Church of England also lacked the support of the aristocracy it enjoyed at home and had few clergy. As the settlers pushed west, they found the teachings of Presbyterianism more useful and its simpler structures easier to staff and maintain.

Even after the adoption of the Constitution in 1787 and the Bill of Rights (which includes the First Amendment) in 1791, Protestantism continued to enjoy a favored status in some states. Massachusetts, for example, did not disestablish its Congregational church until 1833. (As written, the First Amendment applies only to the federal government, not to the states.) The Fourteenth Amendment, ratified in 1868, forbids states to "deprive any person of life, liberty, or property, without due process of law." This clause has been interpreted to mean that the states must protect the rights, including freedom of religion, that are guaranteed by the Bill of Rights. The claim of the Religious Right, however, that the US was founded as a Christian nation is demonstrably unhistorical. In fact, the Baptist forerunners of the Religious Right were wholehearted in supporting the separation of church and state in order to be free to practice their religion.

In the 20th century, the relationship between church and state became involved in a new mode of conflict, that between civic duty and individual conscience. The broad outlines of that conflict took shape in a number of Supreme Court rulings. Perhaps the most noteworthy of these was *West Virginia State Board of Education v. Barnette* (1943). The suit stemmed from the refusal of certain members of the Jehovah's Witnesses to salute the American flag during the school day, as commanded by state law. Because their creed forbade such pledges of loyalty, the Witnesses argued, they were being forced to violate their consciences. Three years earlier, the Supreme Court had upheld a nearly identical law, a decision that had been roundly criticized. In the 1943 case, the Court in effect overruled itself by invoking a different clause in the First Amendment, the one guaranteeing freedom of speech. Saluting the flag was held to be a form of speech, which the state could not force its citizens to perform. The cases taken to the Supreme Court by the Jehovah's Witnesses have helped to widen the definition of civil liberties, especially the application to the individual of the liberties of free speech, free press and freedom of religion.

Since then the Supreme Court has carved out other immunities to laws on behalf of certain religious groups. There remains, however, a distinction between matters of private conscience and actions that adversely affect other people. Thus, members of the Church of Jesus Christ of Latter-day Saints (Mormons) were jailed in the 19th century for practicing polygamy. (Subsequently the Church of Jesus Christ, as it nowadays often calls itself, withdrew its sanction of the practice.) More recently, parents have been convicted of criminal negligence for refusing to obtain medical help for their ailing children who went on to die, even though the parents' religious beliefs dictated that they refuse treatment because faith would provide a cure.

The absence of an established church, and the existence of a fluid social order and a high degree of mobility in the population have given rise to typically American styles of worship and church organization. This demands greater innovation and an emphasis on what might be called *customer service*. Megachurches (churches with around 2000 or more attendees for a typical weekly service) in particular cater to virtually all the needs of their members, from food courts to addiction counselling. Faced with the challenge of marketing faith in a post-industrial society, contemporary American "pastorpreneurs" have turned to sophisticated business models for inspiration and instruction. Because religion is divorced from the state, religious leaders and communities have to fend for themselves, building their own institutions while competing strenuously for adherents with other religious groups. To an extent unknown elsewhere, Americans change their religious allegiances and church memberships easily. These factors, and arguably, low population density across much of the US, have encouraged churches to split over issues of doctrine and practice, and also over the sharing of resources. In the 1990s, a new branch of the Presbyterian church was formed in Washington state by just five ministers. Thus religion in America has to be marketed and spirituality sold. Many American preachers are independent entrepreneurs. It should also be appreciated that religion in the US is a multicultural tale of Native Americans, African Americans, Catholics, Jews and other groups. It is also as much a tale of popular religion as that of the churches and theology of white male middle class eastern Protestants.

Theology: Jonathan Edwards

Space does not permit a survey of American theology. For an overview, readers are referred to *Theology in America: Christian Thought from the Age of the Puritans to the Civil War,* E. Brooks Holifield, Yale University Press, 2005.

Jonathan Edwards (1703-1758), however, is the most important American religious thinker before William James. Edwards was born to a family of prominent Congregationalist ministers in Connecticut and was educated at Yale. He adopted Locke's psychology and epistemology as the basis for an intellectual defense of Calvinism. His philosophy and theology, however, were more influenced by Malebranche (1638-1715) and the Cambridge Platonists.

Anthologies intended for survey courses in high school or college often include a short extract from Edwards' sermon "Sinners in the hands of an angry God" (1741), which has often been taken to be typical of his thought. In fact, mentions of hell are rare in Edwards' writings: he has far more to say about the love of God than about His wrath. More typical is his sermon "On the Excellencies of Christ." Modern scholarship, greatly aided by the publication of more of Edwards' writings by the Jonathan Edwards Center at Yale, sees him as an important and original philosopher and theologian, and not simply a revivalist and hellfire preacher.

A series of sermons that Edwards preached on justification by faith gave rise to a religious revival at Northampton, Massachusetts in 1733. This became so intense in the winter of 1734-35 that it threatened to bring normal life to a stop. Edwards recorded his observations of the process of conversion in minute detail, publishing *A Faithful Narrative of the Surprising Work of God* in 1737. The Northampton revival was followed in 1739–1740 by the *Great Awakening* under Edwards' leadership. The outcries, convulsions and faintings characteristic of those affected by the revival met with criticism from conservative ministers, who maintained that conduct was the sole mark of conversion. In 1741, Edwards published *The Distinguishing Marks of a Work of the Spirit of God,* dealing particularly with the phenomena most criticized. In this pamphlet, he insisted that, although "bodily effects" did usually occur during conversion, they were not distinguishing marks of conversion but incidental to it. In 1742 he wrote a second defense of the revival, *Thoughts on the Revival in New England,* the burden of which was the great moral improvement of the country that had resulted from the revival. In the same pamphlet, he defended an appeal to the emotions, and advocated preaching terror, even to children. A series of sermons preached during 1742 and 1743 and published under the title *Religious Affections* in 1746 were a restatement in more philosophical guise of Edwards' ideas on the subject of conversion.

Eventually Edwards' views on conversion brought him into conflict with his congregation. Edwards believed that only persons who had undergone conversion ought to be admitted to the Lord's Supper, but the congregation disagreed. He accordingly resigned in 1750 and went to be a missionary to the Housatonic Indians of western Massachusetts and defended them against corrupt officials. He remained with the Indians for seven years, writing *Freedom of the Will* (1754), *True Virtue* (c. 1755) and *Original Sin* (1758), all the while struggling with language difficulties, ill health, and inter-tribal Indian wars. His treatise on free will defends predestination on logical and intellectual grounds and is considered by some to be the definitive analysis.

Edwards' complex theology can only be briefly summarized here. A determinist, he believed that salvation was entirely determined by the will of God; otherwise it would depend partly on human choice, and the sovereignty of God would not be absolute and universal. He also argued that for a person to be self-determining meant starting with an act of will to be so and that something had to cause a person to make that act of will. If we deny that an original act of free will is necessary, he argued, then acts of will happen accidentally and hence cannot make a person better or worse. But if it is not we who make our choices, they are not truly ours and we cannot be held responsible for them. That, he pointed out, leads to the conclusion that acting immorally out of habit is excusable, whereas we usually judge that a habitually immoral person is worse than one who only occasionally acts immorally. (Edwards assumed that every action had to have a complete cause.) He was concerned that, if he were wrong, the doctrines of original sin, grace and election, fundamental to Protestantism, would be unsustainable. He also argued that since God's knowledge of the future is comprehensive, no future human action is genuinely contingent. Even so, Edwards claimed that necessity was consistent with moral responsibility, since we are responsible for our actions when we act as we choose, and our actions often spring from our choices. Nor is necessity incompatible with praise and blame. Even though God necessarily acts for the best, His actions are eminently praiseworthy.

Edwards did not rely only on natural causes to explain events but also appealed to divine decrees and typology. Typology is the practice of interpreting things, persons, or events (the "type") as symbols or prefigurations of future realities (the "antitype.") Protestant divines had tended to restrict typology to figures, actions, and objects in the Old Testament, which in their view prefigured Christ as their antitype. Edwards interpreted the New Testament typologically as well, arguing that relevant passages prefigured events in the church's later history. Most radically, Edwards construed nature typologically.

Edwards went on to give a philosophical interpretation of the absolute sovereignty of God. God is the only real cause and the only true substance. "If second causes were real causes they would be sufficient to produce their effects and God's activity would be redundant and it is not," as William Wainright summarizes it in the *Stanford Encyclopedia of Philosophy*. Secondary causes, however, such as applying heat to water to make it boil, are simply the occasions upon which God produces effects, in this case the boiling water, according to His customary manner of acting. Since God is essentially omnipotent, His will is necessarily effective and He does not need the cooperation of other causal powers to produce His effects. And because sovereignty belongs to Him alone He does not share His causal power with others. God's decrees are thus fully sufficient for their effects. God's sovereignty also extends to criteria of identity. In determining every feature of space and time, God has determined how things will be classified i.e., what counts as a species. One implication is that God can so arrange things that Adam and their posterity count as one thing for purposes of punishment and reward. Edwards believed that it is in his work of redemption that God's sovereignty, holiness, and splendor are most fully displayed.

The sovereignty of God was also expressed in beauty and the grace to appreciate it. Only true benevolence was truly beautiful, and only God was truly benevolent. Hence God was the only thing that was truly beautiful and the foundation of all beauty. Natural virtues were either tainted with self-love or failed to extend to being in general. Edwards himself was especially sensitive to the beauties of nature and the harmony of sounds, but he thought that what were primarily beautiful, second only to God himself, were the Gospel and the providential work of God and the saints (the elect) in history. The saints alone could discern true beauty.

The splendor and holiness of God were discerned by the saints, because their hearts had been regenerated by the indwelling of the Holy Spirit and they had become benevolent. Their sense of the beauty of holiness was a new simple idea that could not be produced from any idea they had before and truly represented divine reality. Edwards tended to identify true beauty with the pleasure that holiness evokes in spiritual people. The saints alone can discern the truths of religion that are dependent on the "excellency of divine things." A person must see the beauty of holiness to appreciate the hatefulness of sin, and thus be convinced of the justice of divine punishment and human inability to make restitution. This spiritual sense is objective because benevolence agrees with the nature of things. The reality of the world, for Edwards, was an interconnected system of minds and ideas in which the only true substance and cause was an infinite and omnipotent love. Human benevolence was thus an appropriate response to reality. Since a delight in benevolence is a perception of its spiritual beauty, the spiritual perceptions of the redeemed are true representations of something besides what is in their own minds. Edwards believed reason could prove that God exists, establish many of His attributes, discern our obligations to Him, and mount a probable case for the credibility of scripture. But he also believed that grace was needed to see the clear evidence of the truth of religion. To reason accurately about God a person must have an actual idea of Him, and to have that one must be truly benevolent.

Moreover, for Edwards, since God was the only real cause of phenomena, He was the only real cause of "thoughts" or "perceptions." Since the idea of a body can be reduced to ideas of color and resistance, and these have only mental existence, "the world is...an ideal one" in the philosophical sense. God, however, was not only the first cause, like Aristotle's Unmoved Mover. He was a concrete entity or substance, a necessarily existing intelligent willing agent, only without our imperfections. Created beings are no more than God's "shadows" or "images." As the only true substance and only true cause, God is the "head" of the system of beings, its "chief part," an absolute sovereign whose power and perfection are so great that "all other beings are as nothing and less than nothing compared with him."

Since, for Edwards, true virtue consisted in benevolence to being and "complacence" or delight in moral excellence, and since God was the "chief part" of being and the source of all excellence, true virtue must necessarily be expressed supremely in love of God. God's ultimate concern must therefore be his own glory, and He had created the world for Himself. But since Edwards also believed that the essence of goodness is to communicate good for its own sake, the happiness of humanity is included in God's ultimate aim. Apparently this means that God *had to* create the world, that it had to be *this* world and that this is the best possible world. God is nevertheless free in the sense that He is aware of alternative worlds he might have created, and he is not constrained by any other being.

In 1757 Jonathan Edwards became president of the College of New Jersey (now Princeton University) but died a year later. Throughout his life, Edwards was concerned to demonstrate the reasonableness and veracity of the Christian faith and Reformed theology. In particular his work was an attempt to make plain how God glorifies Himself in the history of the work of redemption. In addition to the central themes of Calvinist theology, Edwards wrote on the relation of personhood to community, the purpose of history, and America's apocalyptic destiny. The followers of Jonathan

Edwards, who were influential in New England, came to be known as the New Light Calvinist ministers. Edwards' descendants included Vice-President Aaron Burr, the writers O. Henry and Robert Lowell and the publisher Frank Nelson Doubleday.

Jonathan Edwards' thought is relevant to a consideration of what religious thought can contribute to an analysis of American culture. Only America and America's church were created by the Enlightenment. It was Edwards who saw the implications. Robert W Jenson argues that, as a student of the ideas of Newton and Locke, Edwards was very much a figure of the Enlightenment; but unlike most other Americans, also a discerning critic of it. Edwards made use of Enlightenment thought without yielding to its mechanistic and individualistic tendencies. Alone among Christian thinkers of the Enlightenment, Edwards conceived an authentically Christian piety and a creative theology not in spite of Newton and Locke but by virtue of them.

Protestants – conservatives, liberals and evangelicals

Americans have been caught up in many waves of religious enthusiasm. One that occurred in the 1730s and 1740s, called the *Great Awakening*, united several of the Protestant denominations, particularly Presbyterians, Congregationalists and Baptists, in an effort to overcome a sense of complacency that had afflicted organized religion. The fervor aroused by revivalist preachers such as Jonathan Edwards, George Whitefield from England, and James Davenport led people to challenge not only their preachers but the political authorities, and sowed the seeds of discontent with British rule, especially over taxation. A second Great Awakening swept through New England in the early 19th century.

Not all of New England's clergy, however, were sympathetic to the call for revival. Some had abandoned the Calvinist idea of predestination, which holds that God has chosen those who will be saved, the "elect," leaving humans no ability to affect their eternal destinies through good works or other means. Some ministers preached that every person had free will and could be saved. Others, influenced by the idea of Progress that had taken hold in the US generally, took even more liberal positions, giving up many traditional Christian beliefs. Just as science had altered our understanding of the natural world, they argued, reason should prompt reassessments of religious doctrine.

Liberal American Protestantism in the 19th century was allied with similar trends in Europe, where scholars were reading and interpreting the Bible in a new way. They questioned the truth of biblical miracles and traditional beliefs about the authorship of biblical books. There was also the challenge of Charles Darwin's theory of evolution to contend with. If human beings were descended from other animals, as most scientists came to believe, then the story of Adam and Eve, the biblical first parents, could not be literally true, and the authority of the Bible would come into question.

What distinguished 19th-century liberal Protestants from their 20th-century counterparts was optimism about the human capacity for improvement. Some of the early ministers believed that the church could accelerate progress by trying to reform society. In the spirit of the gospels, they began to work on behalf of the urban poor. Today's liberal clergy – not just Protestants but Catholics and others, too – may be less convinced that progress is inevitable, but many of them have continued their efforts on behalf of the poor by establishing shelters for homeless people, feeding the hungry, running day-care centers for children, and speaking out on social issues. Many are active in the ecumenical movement, which seeks to increase cooperation and full recognition of each other's ministries among Christian churches.

While liberal Protestants sought a relaxation of doctrine, conservatives believed that departures from the literal truth of the Bible were unjustified. Their branch of Protestantism is often called "evangelical," after their enthusiasm for the gospels of the New Testament, which were known in the original Greek as *evangelion*. Evangelical Protestantism is America's most distinctive religious tradition. The South in particular became a bastion of this "old-time religion," and the conservative Southern Baptist church is still very influential. Evangelical Christians favor an impassioned, participatory approach to religion, and their services are often highly charged, with group singing and dramatic sermons that evoke spirited responses from the congregation. Where Evangelicals differ from other religious conservatives is in their belief that society can be improved by the reform of institutions, and that this should be attempted because it raises the moral standing of the nation and improves the behavior of its citizens. In the 19th century, evangelicals were prominent in campaigns for women's rights, prison reform, the prohibition of alcohol, and the abolition of slavery. Evangelicals in the South, however, defended slavery and opposed women's rights, based on their own biblical "proof texts." Today, Southern evangelicals preach that progress and prosperity depend on individual effort and ability, not social or government action. In what some call the "Great Reversal," the social concern and political activism of the 19th century evangelicals has become an inward-looking conservative movement which defines itself in opposition to the liberal, the urban and the multicultural.

In 1925 the conflict between conservative faith and modern science crystallized in the Scopes trial. John Scopes, a high school biology teacher in Tennessee, was indicted for violating a state law that forbade teaching the theory of evolution in public schools. Scopes was convicted after a sensational trial that featured America's finest criminal lawyer of the time, Clarence Darrow, for the defense and the renowned populist and former presidential candidate, William Jennings Bryan, for the prosecution. Since then the Supreme Court has ruled that laws banning the teaching of evolution violate the First Amendment's prohibition of establishing religion. The state of Louisiana subsequently tried a different approach, banning the teaching of evolution unless the Bible-based doctrine of special creation was taught as an alternative. This, too, the Supreme Court invalidated as an establishment of religion. Despite the Supreme Court's clear rulings, however, issues pitting reason against faith remain alive. Religious conservatives argue that teaching evolution alone elevates human reason above revealed truth and thus is antireligious. And even some thinkers who might otherwise be considered liberals have argued that the media and other American institutions foster a climate that tends to slight, if not ridicule, organized religion. Meanwhile, the trend toward removing religious teaching and practices from public schools has prompted some parents to send their children to religious schools and others to educate their children at home.

Fundamentalists

Part of the Deep South is called the *Bible Belt* because in that region are found many Protestant fundamentalists, who believe that the Bible is the inspired, inerrant Word of God and therefore has to be taken literally. To fundamentalists "all Scripture is totally true and trustworthy" (Southern Baptist Statement of Belief). In particular, fundamentalists believe that the account of creation in Genesis is literally true. Hence, to be a Christian, a person must, according to fundamentalists, subscribe to certain beliefs and doctrines that are claimed to arise directly from the Bible or to be directly derivable from it: the inerrancy of the Scriptures; the virgin birth and deity of Jesus; the doctrine of substitutionary atonement by God's grace and through human faith; the bodily resurrection of Jesus; and the authenticity of Christ's miracles (or, alternatively, his pre-millennial Second Coming). Evangelicals are not necessarily fundamentalists, although they often are, and the two often share a conservative political stance.

Fundamentalism is a religious reaction to social changes which have occurred since around 1870, and in particular to what are seen as the amoral and atheistic implications of the theory of evolution, which strongly suggests that at least the proximate reason for the existence of humankind is blind chance, not the purposeful design of a beneficent Creator. Seen from the fundamentalist viewpoint, the theory of evolution robs human beings of dignity and life of meaning and purpose, turning people into animals or machines, with disastrous consequences for individuals and society. Thus fundamentalism poses in its sharpest form the dilemma at the heart of Western society: how to react to the social and existential implications of a science which, on the one hand, interprets the universe and humanity's place within it with unexampled explanatory power while at the same time seeming to render meaningless the perennial human search for meaning and truth in areas outside the scope of scientific theory, experiment and calculation. It is because the Bible stands as an alternative to science as a source of authority and explanation that fundamentalists will sing such hymns as:

Cling to the Bible, though all else be taken;
Lose not its precepts, so precious and pure;
Souls that are sleeping its tidings awaken;
Life from the dead in its promises sure.

Refrain
Cling to the Bible!
Cling to the Bible!
Cling to the Bible
Our Lamp and our Guide!

Cling to the Bible! This jewel and treasure
Brings life eternal, and saves fallen man;
Surely its value no mortal can measure:
Seek for its blessing, O soul, while you can!

Creationism

Fundamentalists believe that the world was created exactly as Genesis says it was, and generally that it was made in exactly seven days. Creationism, sometimes called "creation science" or "Intelligent Design," is offered as an alternative to evolution and indeed as better science. The theory is presented as science even though the Supreme Court has ruled that creationism is not science, but religion, and therefore it is unconstitutional to teach it in the public schools (*Edwards v. Aguillard*, 1987). The main argument of intelligent design is that life is too complex to have evolved by chance and must therefore be the product of an intelligent creator. A sophisticated multimedia facility, the Creation Museum, has been built to illustrate the theory at a cost of $25 million raised from private donations. Five miles (8 km) from Cincinnati international airport, the museum has been sited within a day's drive of two-thirds of the population of the Lower 48 states.

The key religious issue is that in *Genesis*, God directly implanted a soul into Adam, hence assuring humanity of a special status and of the ability to know God and be with him in heaven after death. For fundamentalists, the theory of evolution makes doubtful the very existence of the human soul, and therefore the truth of religion and even the existence of God. Despite heavy lobbying, however, the creationists have been unable to win equal time with evolution in school curricula.

Even so, the ridicule and rejection which sometimes replace reasoned argument on the subject of fundamentalism have no place in serious social study. Fundamentalism, from a religious, philosophical, political and social point of view is a serious phenomenon. Without at least trying to appreciate it, an understanding of America cannot be complete. A major reason for refusal to engage seriously with fundamentalism is that many of its exponents have sought to forge an alliance between their version of Christianity and right-wing politics, usually those of the Republican Party. The arrogant, self-righteous tone some fundamentalists adopt, characterizing people and countries that do not share their views as godless and effete, arouses antagonism. Additionally, scientists cannot accept creationism as science, let alone as an alternative to the theory of evolution. Hence there is an irreconcilable standoff, and those who might otherwise be sympathetic to fundamentalists' moral principles and vision of society feel that they cannot become fundamentalists with intellectual integrity.

In contrast, fundamentalism plays into the paranoia, fear of otherness and readiness to believe in conspiracy theories that characterize a defensive, declining social group that sees itself as an oppressed minority and insulates itself as much as possible from external influences. Fundamentalists see the pluralism and tolerance of relative values of a secular society as a conspiracy to overthrow the US by stealth. Fundamentalism is a reaction to insecurity, isolation and fear. The shared values and common beliefs based on the Bible offer security and certainty in an increasingly uncertain and apparently hostile outside world. Fundamentalists see changes in social attitudes as an attack on Christianity itself. In reaction to greater toleration of alternative lifestyles, for example, fundamentalists lay heavy emphasis on traditional views of male sexuality, perhaps playing into fears aroused by feminism and greater social tolerance of homosexuality. But they say little about divorce. Homosexuality was chosen as an issue by evangelical campaigners because it was one on which they could unite. They are also highly suspicious of ecumenical relations and generally oppose the ordination of women. Fundamentalists openly express hatred of secular society in general, and liberal individuals in particular, a hatred that extends to other religious conservatives of differing shades of opinion. In recent years, the Southern Baptists, the largest Protestant denomination, separated themselves (and their money) from the rest of the world's Baptists because they deemed them too liberal on social issues (Bates, *op. cit.*, p. 37). Those fundamentalists, such as Rousas John Rushdoony (1916-2001), who are Christian Reconstructionists or Dominionists aim to replace the secular state with one based on religious principles, and US law with Old Testament law. "In a Reconstructionist America there would be no tolerance for other religions, no public education or welfare and public execution by stoning for a range of 'crimes' such as homosexuality and adultery" (Kimberly Blaker, *The Fundamentals of Extremism*, p. 179).

Political influence of fundamentalists

Over the last generation, especially under the presidency of George W. Bush, himself not a fundamentalist but a United Methodist, the apparent influence of fundamentalism has grown: apparent because although fundamentalist preachers, often well-funded by rich businesspeople, have made noisy pitches for their faith in the media, they have been disregarded when their wishes would have cost votes or harmed the economy. For example, officially atheist China was granted most favored nation status, while only $80 million was given by Bush to Christian groups for faith-based social services, although he did ban late-term abortions in 2003. Indeed there are commentators who say that fundamentalism has passed its peak. A new generation of leaders has not arisen to fill the places of Jerry Falwell and Pat Robertson, and younger people generally seem alienated by the bombastic manner, strident tone and intolerant message of the Religious Right. They expect candidates for public office not to offend their moral standards, but they seem disinclined to elect any preacher as President.

Even so, it would be a mistake to dismiss the influence of fundamentalists and evangelicals. In 2008, 34 percent of adults self-identified as evangelical or born again Christians, 45 percent of all Christians; the Religious Right comprises 11 percent of the electorate. They are pervasive in a great swathe of the nation, they mobilize a coalition of religious groups, they affect public opinion through TV and radio broadcasting, and they undertake sophisticated lobbying. They have brought moral issues such as abortion to the forefront of political debate and made cultural issues a litmus test in many political contests. As an indication of how credible some Americans find the claim that the end of the world is imminent, on July 31, 2006, CNN's *Paula Zahn Now* program featured a segment on whether the crisis in the Middle East was actually a prelude to the end of the world. That marked the third time in eight days that CNN had devoted airtime to those claiming that the ongoing Mideast violence signaled the coming of the Apocalypse. Republican candidates have found it wise to court the support of conservative Christians and lace their speeches with the buzzwords of the Religious Right. During the 2004 presidential election, for example, George W. Bush supported the idea of a constitutional amendment to define marriage as between a man and a woman, although after the election he took no further action. An ex-Baptist preacher and former governor of Arkansas, Mike Huckabee, garnered significant support in the 2008 Republican presidential primaries. Fundamentalists serve on the U.S. Commission on International Religious Freedom, a federal agency created by the International Religious Freedom Act of 1988 for the purpose of monitoring the freedom of conscience, thought and religion or belief abroad. Perhaps most of all, the Religious Right has affected how the rest of the world sees the US (Bates, *op. cit.* pp. 266, 348).

Baptists

One in five Americans identify themselves as Baptist. The origins of the Baptist churches are disputed. According to Baptist historian H. Leon McBeth, Baptists as a distinct denomination originated in England. McBeth writes: "Our best historical evidence says that Baptists came into existence in England in the early seventeenth century. They apparently emerged out of the Puritan-Separatist movement in the Church of England" (McBeth, "Baptist Beginnings," Baptist History and Heritage Society. http://www.baptisthistory.org/baptistbeginnings.htm, accessed 12/14/2008). During the final years of the 16th century, radical groups impatient with the church's slow pace of reform had emerged in the Church of England. Many of these broke away and became known as Separatists. Some Baptists, however, claim that their church originated with the 16th century Anabaptists in Germany. Both Roger Williams and his compatriot in working for religious freedom, Dr. John Clarke, are variously credited as founding the earliest Baptist church in America. In 1639, Williams established a Baptist church in Providence, Rhode Island, and Clarke founded one in nearby

Newport. Which of them was first cannot be proved. The restoration of the British monarchy in 1660 led to renewed persecution of dissenting churches, during which time the Baptist preacher, John Bunyan, author of *Pilgrim's Progress*, spent 12 years in prison, and some English Baptists emigrated to America.

The name *Baptist* is derived from a conviction that followers of Jesus Christ are commanded to attest their faith publicly by being immersed in water. Thus, Baptists reject infant baptism. Baptists share orthodox Christian beliefs with most other moderate or conservative Christian denominations but do not have any creeds or confessions of faith which have binding authority. There are, however, six underlying principles which govern Baptist belief.

1. The Bible alone is a sufficient and authoritative guide to faith.
2. Baptism should only be undertaken by believers and be accompanied by a profession of faith. (No one can be saved by baptism alone.)
3. Only convinced Christians should belong to the church.
4. Each member has an equal say in the running of the church and, therefore, the minister does not have any special priestly authority.
5. Each local church is autonomous.
6. Church and state are separate and the state should guarantee freedom of belief.

Beliefs among Baptists regarding the end of the world vary widely. Baptists generally believe in the literal Second Coming of Christ, at which time God will sit in judgment and divide humanity between the saved and the lost, and Christ will sit in judgment of the believers, according to things done while alive, although works alone will not ensure salvation. Most Baptist traditions believe in the "Four Freedoms" articulated by Baptist historian Walter B. Shurden:

- *Soul freedom*: the soul is competent before God, and capable of making decisions in matters of faith without coercion or compulsion by any larger religious or civil body.
- *Church freedom*: the local church should be free from outside interference, whether government or civilian (subject only to the law where it does not interfere with the religious teachings and practices of the church).
- *Bible freedom*: the individual is free to interpret the Bible for himself or herself, using the best tools of scholarship and biblical study available.
- *Religious freedom*: the individual is free to choose whether to practice his or her religion, another religion, or no religion; separation of church and state is often called the "civil corollary" of religious freedom.

Otherwise, there is great variety of belief among Baptists, which is typical of American Protestantism. Most Baptists worship on Sunday, a few on Saturday. Baptist churches are simple in design and rarely use symbols. Many churches contain baptisteries which provide for baptism through full immersion. Bread and grape juice are used to commemorate the Lord's Supper.

A few Baptists refuse to class themselves as Protestants because they believe Baptists have existed separately since the early days of the Church. Thus Baptists were always independent of the Catholic Church. People who take this position also point out that Baptists have no direct connection to any of the Reformers like Luther, Calvin, or Zwingli. Other Baptists accept the *Protestant* label as a demographic concept that describes churches which share similar beliefs about the Bible, salvation and discipleship to those held by the Reformers.

The Baptists claim 36.7 million adherents in over 50 separate groups. In 2005, according to the annual report of the Southern Baptist Convention, there were 370,000 baptisms and that year saw 1,717 new congregations started. The church sends out 5,000 missionaries, and has chaplains serving in Iraq and Afghanistan. The predominantly African American National Baptists have only slightly fewer adherents. Of the Baptist denominations, five – the Southern Baptist Convention, the National Baptist Convention, USA, Inc., the National Baptist Convention of America, Inc., the American Baptist Churches in the USA and the Baptist Bible Fellowship International – include 92 percent of Baptists. Conservatives gained control of the Southern Baptists' national structure in the late 1970s and have kept control ever since. Former President Bill Clinton is a Southern Baptist.

RELIGIONS FROM AMERICA

Two themes unite many of the Christian-based denominations founded in America: restoring what they believe was Christianity in its original form; and preparing their members and the rest of society for the Second Coming of Christ.

The Church of Jesus Christ of Latter-day Saints

The Church of Jesus Christ of Latter-day Saints (the Church of Jesus Christ, LDS Church or Mormons) was founded by Joseph Smith in 1830. Mormons believe their church restores Christianity to the form it had in the time of the Apostles and is the only true church. Mormonism can be described as a typically American form of religion because, among other things, it is optimistic and entrepreneurial, emphasizes personal growth and sees a special place for America in history. Smith was born into a poor family in Vermont in 1805 and received little education, learning only basic math and literacy, but he did spend much time in Bible study. Later the family moved to Palmyra, New York, at a time of religious revival. Unsure which version of Christianity to follow, the teenage Smith found a Biblical text that told him to ask God what to do. According to the Church, he went out into the country and prayed for guidance, and had a vision of God the Father and Jesus Christ. Christ told Joseph that he should not join any existing church, but should be God's agent to restore the true Church. The vision, and its effect on Joseph, are a close parallel with the vision of Paul on the Damascus Road (Acts 9:3). Joseph went home and told his family, who supported him, although the local churches were highly critical. Three years later, Smith was visited by the angel Moroni and told that he should unearth and translate a holy book written on plates of gold, which contained the writings of the prophets of ancient America. Smith wanted to take the plates immediately but was advised by Moroni not to do so. Four years later Smith removed the plates, and spent three months translating the words engraved on them into the *Book of Mormon*. This text, which reads something like the Old Testament, tells the story of an ancient Hebrew patriarch and prophet named Lehi, who, in roughly 600 B.C., was called by God to lead a group of Jews from Jerusalem to the New World. The group established themselves somewhere in North America and, according to this history, at least some Native Americans descended from the immigrants. Eventually, Jesus appeared to these New World Jews and taught the Christian Gospel to them. From this civilization, God continued to call forth prophets, including one named Mormon, the original author of the text. Along with the plates, Smith said he found the Urim and Thummim, a translating contrivance that allowed him to read the engravings on the plates.

Before Joseph could restore the church, it was necessary for him to be authorized by God to do so. In 1829, he was, he said, visited by John the Baptist. The Baptist laid hands on the heads of Smith and his colleague, Oliver Cowdery, and gave them the authority of the Aaronic Priesthood. (Aaron was the first high priest of Israel (Exodus 29)). Soon afterwards, the Apostles James, Peter, and John appeared to Joseph and Oliver and gave them the authority of the Melchizedek Priesthood. (Melchizedek was the priest of the Most High God, who blessed Abram, who became Abraham, the patriarch of Israel (Genesis 14)). With this priestly authority, Smith founded the Church of Jesus Christ of Latter-day Saints in Fayette, New York State on April 6, 1830.

Joseph continued to receive direct guidance from God on how to build the restored church. He translated further scriptures, and wrote down further revelations from God, and these form a major part of the Church's canon of scripture. Smith also founded the missionary program of the Church, built several towns, and was a candidate for President. In 1836 the first Mormon Temple was dedicated at Kirtland, Ohio. During Smith's lifetime the Church grew from six to 26,000 members. What Smith accomplished was a seamless synthesis of the quintessentially American sense of the boundlessness of human potential together with an authoritative revelation of truth. Moreover, in his church, he invented a system that could duplicate for everyone his vision of God. Joseph Smith has been described by Professor Harold Bloom as "an authentic religious genius."

The Church attracted enemies and was persecuted by mainstream Christians. Smith himself was imprisoned more than thirty times for his faith. Although the Church continued to grow, the persecution continued, notably during the Mormon War in Missouri in 1838, which saw the issue of the Extermination Order by the governor. Eventually the Mormons moved to Illinois, where they built a new city, Nauvoo (Hebrew for "beautiful") on the banks of the Mississippi, where they hoped to live and worship in peace. The persecution continued, however, and Latter-day Saint farms were attacked by mobs who burned crops, destroyed homes, and threatened the people. Joseph Smith was arrested and jailed on several occasions (although never found guilty). The Mormons were persecuted for several reasons. Mormons were considered outsiders because they led a completely different sort of life. They did not keep slaves, which was seen as a threat to the surrounding slave-owning culture at a time when the abolition of slavery was a big issue. Moreover their doctrine of plural marriage (polygamy) was seen as a serious attack on Christian social and ethical norms. Meanwhile the rapidly growing and tightly-knit Mormon communities had the potential to exercise considerable political power. On June 27, 1844 a jail in Illinois where Smith and his brother Hyrum were being held on charges of riot and treason was attacked by an armed mob, and both men were shot and killed.

After the murder of Joseph Smith, the Mormons realised they could not stay safely in the heartland of America, and the Church's new leader, Brigham Young, decided that their future lay in the West. He organized a mass emigration like that of the Israelites, who had been forced to leave Egypt in search of the Promised Land. After great hardships, 16,000 Mormon emigrants reached the Great Salt Lake Basin in the Rocky Mountains in 1847. This was 1,000 miles from the nearest significant town in the East, in fact outside the US, and a long way from their persecutors. The area was an inhospitable desert, but the Mormons were inspired by it and named it *Zion*. They gave the local river the name *Jordan*. And they began to build Salt Lake City, with at its heart a Temple, which was dedicated in 1893 and is still the headquarters of the LDS Church. The Mormons saw Salt Lake City as their holy city. Brigham Young called it a "Kingdom of Heaven on Earth." During his lifetime the Mormons founded another 325 towns.

But theirs was a bleak, cold kingdom, and the Mormons had to work hard to make it a liveable place. Their first task was to irrigate the land to make it fit to plough and grow food. The Mormons mapped out a huge area which they called *Deseret* ("honeybee"), and chose the beehive as a symbol of their ideal community, one filled with industry and co-operation. They asked the federal government to make Deseret a new state. The government gave them a much smaller area called *Utah* (after the local Ute tribe of Native Americans), as a territory, not a state. Brigham Young became Governor. In 1857, however, President Buchanan sent troops to Utah to put down what he had been told was a Mormon uprising, but a settlement was negotiated and Mormon growth resumed. The community grew rapidly, not just by having children, but also by the mass immigration of converts from elsewhere in the US and from abroad. By the time of Brigham Young's death in 1877, there were 140,000 Mormons in Utah, and at one stage more than half of them were immigrants from Britain.

Later, legal action was taken to suppress the Mormon custom of plural marriage. In 1879 the Supreme Court stated that "Laws are made for the government of actions, and while they cannot interfere with mere religious belief and opinions, they may with practices." The Edmunds-Tucker Act of 1887 among other things disincorporated the LDS church and sold its assets, required civil marriage licenses, and required voters, jurors, and public officials to deny polygamy. The Mormons resisted and many were jailed, while others, including church leaders, went underground. The Church abandoned plural marriage in 1890. Utah became the 45th state of the Union in 1896. By reviving the Biblical custom of tithing, by which members give a proportion of their income to the Church, the Church doubled its income within a year, and by 1907 was out of debt.

By the late 1920s the LDS Church had become a respected institution in the eyes of most Americans. The Church gained many members on the West Coast and then in the East and Midwest. Some of this growth was due to a reform of the missionary system that provided proper training for missionaries before they set out, and ensured that they had the funds to support them during their service. The second half of the 20th century saw the Church expand massively outside America. In 1950 only 8 percent of church members lived outside the US. By 1990 the figure was 35 percent. Now less than half the membership lives in the US. In 1950 the Church had eight temples, four of them in Utah; by August 2005 it had 122 around the world. Twenty percent of growth is due to children being born into the faith, while 80 percent is due to new converts. In Utah, 70 percent of the population is Mormon.

The teachings of the LDS Church derive from the Church's Standard Works, primarily the *Book of Mormon*, and secondarily the *Bible*, the *Doctrine and Covenants*, and the *Pearl of Great Price* (compiled from the writings of Smith). The Church also regards parts of the *Apocrypha*, the writings of some Protestant Reformers and non-Christian religious leaders, and the non-religious writings of some philosophers to be inspired, though not canonical. Other sources of doctrine are the Endowment ceremony, and the statements of Presidents of the Church ("Prophets") and lesser figures. The Church recognizes a single ultimate spokesperson for God, often called the Prophet. Many Mormon teachings are shared by some mainstream churches: Restorationism (the belief that there was a Great Apostasy at the end of the Apostolic era and that the church is being restored); Millennialism (belief in a thousand year reign of peace on Earth after the Second Coming of Christ); baptism by immersion; and Continuationism (the belief that the gifts of the Holy Spirit, specifically, speaking in tongues, and prophecy, have continued to the present).

The Church of Jesus Christ, however, has many unique teachings. The doctrine of the Atonement, for example, is much wider in its scope than in traditional Christianity. The concept of sin extends beyond moral offences to encompass all the negative aspects of human life, whether proceeding from internal or external causes. Thus Atonement for Mormons covers not only sin, but all pain, suffering, heartache, or hardship. The Mormons believe that Jesus will establish his kingdom on the American continent. They believe too that Joseph Smith was adopted into the Apostolic Succession through his vision of the Apostles. Mormons reject the doctrines of original sin and the Trinity. They believe that the three Persons of the Godhead are separate and distinct beings united in purpose, and that Jesus and the Father have physical "bodies of flesh and bone," while the Holy Spirit does not, though the Holy Spirit has a "spirit body." God the Father is an exalted, perfected man, immortal, all-powerful and all-knowing, and is understood to be the literal father of the spirits of humanity. The heavenly parenthood of humanity is shared by God the Father and a Heavenly Mother. Mormonism includes a distinctive Mormon cosmology, a unique Plan of Salvation that includes three stages of existence and three heavens, and a doctrine of Exaltation, which includes the ability of humans to become gods and goddesses in the afterlife.

Mormons believe that human life has three stages: pre-existence as spirit children born to the Heavenly Parents, which is a time of preparation; then a time of probation on earth, when people learn to choose between good and evil and accept the missions and callings that have been chosen for them; and, after death, eternal life with the Heavenly Father. Life on earth is when Mormons begin to build their eternal families, first as children, and then as parents. Mormons believe that the family is an eternal unit and central to God's plan. On earth, families may be "sealed"—meaning that they are eternally bound as husband–wife, parents–child—and that these bonds will continue after death. Indeed, eternal progression toward Godhood is limited to those who marry for time and eternity (celestial marriage) in a ceremony conducted by a properly ordained member of the LDS priesthood in a Mormon temple. Celestial marriages can be created after death by proxy marriages performed in temples. Mormons trace their family trees to find the names of ancestors who died without learning about the restored Mormon Gospel so that these relatives from past generations can be baptized by proxy in the temple. Once baptized, if the ancestor's spirit has accepted the Gospel, they will be able to be together with the rest of their baptized Mormon family in the celestial kingdom. The Church does have a process for annulment but sees divorce only as a necessary evil. The LDS Church also teaches that its adherents are members of the House of Israel; patriarchal blessings are received by most individuals in their youth. Among other things, this blessing's purpose is to declare to which of the twelve tribes of Israel the individual belongs. The Church teaches that Jesus is the Jehovah of the Old Testament, and the Holy One of Israel. In the 1990s, Jewish groups vocally opposed the LDS practice of baptism for the dead on behalf of Jewish victims of the Holocaust and Jews in general.

LDS Church life revolves around the family. Marriage is believed to be highly important, and there is a higher rate of marriage among Mormons than in the general population. Mormon families also tend to have more children than members of other Christian traditions. The Church regards each person's gender as eternal and teaches that each gender has equal but different roles and duties in the family that are ordained by God. The Church enjoins what it calls *the law of chastity*, a moral code that its members must follow to be in good standing. At its core, the law of chastity prohibits pre-marital sex and adultery, which includes gay and lesbian sex. The law also prohibits other sexual behavior, such as bestiality and masturbation, as well as mental behavior such as lust, sexual fantasy, and viewing of pornography. The emphasis on the law of chastity apparently leads to a lower rate of pre-marital sex among LDS youth than among their peers. Lesbian, gay, transgender and transsexual members of the church are expected to keep the law of chastity. If they do, they can "go forward as do all other members of the church." If they desire to enter into a heterosexual marriage, they should first learn to deal with their homosexual feelings; otherwise, they must remain celibate. Gay or lesbian sex, in any form, whether the participants are married or not, may be grounds for excommunication. The church favors measures that define marriage as the union of a man and a woman and that do not confer legal status on any other sexual relationship.

Most Mormon families spend about three hours with their local community each Sunday. Some of this time is taken up with adult learning or Sunday School, and with various meetings. The heart of the Sunday is the Sacrament Meeting. This lasts 70 minutes, and involves the whole community including children. The service is led by the bishop, and his two counsellors. (The bishop is the lay ecclesiastical leader of the local Church). Communal worship in the LDS Church is rather informal, without ceremonials or priests. It takes place in a simple chapel, which does not have religious statues or pictures. The service is organised and conducted by unpaid lay members of the congregation, as the Church does not have clergy. The service begins with hymns followed by prayers. There are a number of short talks or sermons given by members of the congregation chosen by the bishop. Although they are not ordained to the priesthood, preaching and instruction by women is an integral part of weekly LDS worship. These talks range from quite formal doctrinal lectures, to more informal chats about the application of faith to family life. During the service the members receive a sacramental communion of bread and water, during which they remember the Last Supper, the Atonement of Jesus Christ, and their own baptismal promises to serve the Lord and keep his commandments. The sacrament is distributed by deacons. Mormons always make a point of dressing smartly and respectfully for services. Non-Mormons are welcome to visit Mormon chapels and attend services, but only Mormons in good standing can enter a temple. The privacy of temples, and the fact that church accounts and disciplinary proceedings are not published, have given rise to adverse comment. Church members fast on the first Sunday of each month by going without food and drink for two consecutive meals. They give the amount of money they would have spent for the meals to the Church. Bishops use these fast offerings to provide food, shelter, clothing, and medical care for the needy. The fast is preceded, accompanied, and followed by prayer. Without prayer the fast is considered to have little, if any, spiritual value.

Mormons participate in many religious activities apart from worship services. They are encouraged to pray several times a day, perform good works, and read scripture daily. Mormons are expected to spend a good deal of their time and talents on church activities. They are also expected to donate their time, money (usually 10 percent), and talents to the Church, and those who have participated in the Endowment ceremony take an oath to donate all that they have, if required of them, to the Lord. As well as attending weekly services, members in good standing are assigned to visit the homes of other members monthly. Members are also expected to conduct a Family Home Evening weekly with their family and to engage in family history research. Church members are encouraged to live self-sufficiently and avoid unnecessary debt. Good standing in the Church also requires that members follow the "Word of Wisdom," a health code laid down by Joseph Smith, which the church interprets as enjoining abstinence from alcoholic beverages, tobacco, coffee, black tea, and recreational drugs. Members must also obey the Church's code for modesty and allowable forms of sexuality, and are strongly counseled against elective abortion, except in rare cases. The Church discourages gambling in all forms, including lotteries. Church members who commit what are considered serious violations of the standards of the Church may be subject to disciplinary action, including shunning (disfellowshiping or marking) or even excommunication. In contrast to overt actions which are prohibited, Church members are generally permitted to think or believe freely on any issue. Missionary work is a key aspect of Mormon practice. As of 2008, there were around 52,000 missionaries serving at 348 mission sites throughout most of the world. Mission is performed in pairs. Every young man who is morally, physically and mentally capable of it is expected to participate. Single young women may also serve. Minimum ages for missionaries are 19 for men and 21 for women. Older married couples also act as missionaries. Missionaries refrain from social activities such as parties, dating, and other forms of entertainment. The average length of a mission for a young man is two years, and a young woman 18 months.

Christian Scientists

Christian Science was founded by Mary Baker Eddy (1821-1910), who in 1875 published *Science and Health with Key to the Scriptures,* which she claimed was the final revelation of God to mankind. The word "Key" in the title refers to her being the Woman of Revelation 12; her writings provided the "key" spoken of in Rev 3:7. In 1879, Eddy and some of her students organized the Church of Christ (Scientist) in Boston. In 1881 Eddy opened a college to train healers for a fee. This church too claims to restore the original New Testament Church and in particular the element of healing, which it believes was lost after the early centuries of Christianity. Christian Scientists contend that faith in the omnipotence of God demands demonstration in healing, which attests to the higher mission of the Christ-power to take away the sins of the world.

Christian Scientists are not creationists or biblical literalists, and they have no ordinances like baptism or the Lord's Supper. They regard the Bible as often having symbolic rather than literal meaning, particularly the early parts of the Book of Genesis. Indeed, Eddy's writings contradicted several mainstream Christian doctrines. Christian Science regards God as both Father and Mother i.e., God has both masculine and feminine characteristics. Jesus himself was not Christ or God and did not die; his blood did not avail. Eddy regarded Christ as completely divine, spiritual and not material. Jesus, the son of God, embodied the Christ to such a degree that he, and he alone, bore the title *Christ*, but as a corporeal being he was not the totality of the Christ. Jesus is "the Wayshower," a proof by example of the divine method of healing sin, sickness and death. To Eddy, the Trinity was polytheism. The Trinity in Christian Science is God the Father-Mother, Christ the spiritual idea of sonship, and divine Science or the Holy Comforter. At the core of Christian Science is the teaching that God and his creation are entirely good and spiritual, harmonious and perfect, and that God has made all things in his likeness; all else is illusion or "error." Eddy taught that love, truth and goodness were real, and matter, sin and sickness were illusions. Sickness is the result of fear, ignorance, or sin, and when that is corrected through a true understanding of God's goodness, the sickness will disappear. Christian Scientists consider that suffering can occur only when one believes (consciously or unconsciously) in the supposed reality of a problem; if one changes one's understanding, the belief is revealed as false, and the acknowledgement that the sickness has no power heals it, since God is the only power. Christian Scientists believe that both material science and literalist theology are concerned with the illusory and mortal rather than the spiritually real and immortal. Christian Science periodicals occasionally cite developments in cosmology and physics as indicating how contemporary science is coming to an understanding of the illusory nature of time and materiality. Eddy believed that, from a material perspective, the Theory of Evolution might be regarded as true but that it misleadingly understood man as a mortal rather than a spiritual being. Christian Science might be considered a form of theistic monism, an extreme example of philosophical idealism: there is but one substance, which is God, in whom we are all embraced in love. Immortality is possible, indeed inevitable, since each person is a spiritual idea. As to whether God punishes evil-doers, Christian Science teaches that any thought or action contrary to humankind's God-given goodness results in some kind of suffering, just as the misunderstanding of a mathematical principle results in incorrect answers.

Christian Science is nondenominational, though many believers in it join the Church of Christ (Scientist). Church services consist of Bible readings interspersed with readings from *Science and Health*, given by lay people who are elected Readers for three years. There are separate public testimony meetings, at which anyone can give testimony to the healing power of Christ in his or her life. Some Christian Scientists, after years of experience of healing, train to become Christian Science Practitioners and go into the full time public practice of healing, charging for their services. There is no manipulation, or laying on of hands, in a Christian Science healing treatment; healings are often accomplished without the Practitioner ever having met the patient. Christian Scientists claim no monopoly on the application of God's healing power through prayer, and welcome it wherever it occurs. Mary Baker Eddy favored women's rights, and rejected the corporal punishment of children. She opposed imperialism and economic monopoly. The *Christian Science Monitor*, which she founded, has traditionally been a staunch defender of civil liberties and individual freedom, though it did support Prohibition. The church does not have an official position on abortion or homosexuality, believing that each individual Christian Scientist should seek their own highest sense of right through prayer. Christian Science churches maintain Reading Rooms in most major cities in the world, where Eddy's writings can be read, borrowed or purchased.

According to Christian Science, there are no limits to the medical conditions that can be healed through prayer: true healings are the result of true belief. Christian Scientists prefer not to use doctors, medicine, or immunizations. They use Christian Science Practitioners to help them through the "false reality" of illness. While there is no obligation on Christian Scientists to eschew medical means, they avoid using conventional medicine and Christian Science simultaneously in the belief that they tend to counteract or contradict each other. In some cases, Christian Scientists will be examined by a doctor for informational purposes (although Christian Scientists sometimes object to detailed descriptions of disease, as tending to reinforce the symptoms described in the consciousness of the viewer or listener, with the consequent danger of externalizing these mental images on the body as physical symptoms). Testimonies of healings reported in Christian Science publications claim 50,000 healings in cases where a doctor confirmed the initial condition and the subsequent healing. Claims are always verified by three other parties. It is unclear how Christian Scientists are to decide when they should have surgery instead of Christian Science treatment before a condition e.g., cancer becomes inoperable.

Although Christian Science acknowledges that experience seems to be of a material existence, it holds that this experience is ultimately spiritual and that this is how healing through prayer is possible. Christian Scientists have a particular view of prayer. To them, it is not intercession, asking God to do something, but rather a process of learning more of God's spiritual reality. Healthcare is attempted through "Christian Science treatment," a specific form of prayer intended to spiritualize thought. The world as it appears to the senses is regarded as a distorted version of the world of spiritual ideas: the latter is the only true reality. Prayer can heal the distortion, bringing spiritual reality into focus and resulting in healing. Eddy held that it is not enough to think true thoughts, however: consciousness must be imbued with the love which is God; and furthermore love must be lived as well as felt. Christian Scientists believe that prayer works through love in its Christian sense of unselfish, unlimited and unconditional awareness of the inherent worth of another, and that this is the way Jesus Christ healed. The Christian Science view is that Jesus taught that we should claim good as being present, right here and now, and that this will result in healing. Effectual prayer and moral regeneration go hand-in-hand. Loving, in a Christian Science sense is "seeing," understanding, witnessing to or upholding the spiritual identity of each individual as God's likeness or expression or idea. Spiritual identity consists of the individual's own particular reflection of the qualities, attributes or ideas of their Creator, God, such as love, innocence, and intelligence. These qualities cannot be perceived materially but only through spiritual sense, which Eddy defined as "a conscious, constant capacity to understand God" (*Science & Health* 209:31-32).

Christian Scientists have been controversial from the outset. Mark Twain wrote a satirical attack on Christian Science in 1903 (although he later spoke well of its principle of healing), and Willa Cather published a critical biography of Mary Baker Eddy in 1908 which outraged Christian Scientists. Joseph Pulitzer's "crusade" against her in 1907 resulted in the latter's establishment of the *Christian Science Monitor*. Christian Scientists have also been controversial for their failure to provide conventional healthcare for children. The constitutional protection of religious practice from intrusion by government has been used by Christian Scientists (and other religious groups) to seek exemption from legislative or regulatory requirements regarding child abuse and neglect. There are now statutes in 44 states which contain provisions that a child is not to be deemed abused or neglected merely because he or she is receiving treatment by spiritual means according to the tenets of a recognized religion. Two important sets of interests are in apparent opposition: those of children in the benefits of medical care, and those of parents in making a decision about their children's well-being. Some parents believe the Constitution allows them to choose the method of healing (spiritual or medical) they feel will best benefit their children. This interpretation of the Constitution, however, is in contradiction to court rulings that parents may not martyr their children and that children cannot be denied what is regarded as essential healthcare.

Jehovah's Witnesses

The Jehovah's Witnesses are a Christian-based religious movement which believes that the mainstream churches have deviated from the teachings of the Bible and fallen into apostasy, willful rebellion against God and rejection of his Word ("the Great Apostasy.") The Witnesses belong to a diverse group of sects known as Restorationists or Christian Primitivists, which believe that pristine, or original Christianity is restored in themselves to an important degree. Jehovah's Witnesses strive to reflect Christianity as they believe it was practiced in the first century, the Apostolic Age.

Jehovah's Witnesses believe that the Great Apostasy was prophesied by Jesus and began before the death of the last Apostle. They consider that the falling away was already complete before the Council of Nicaea in 325, which adopted the Nicene Creed enshrining the doctrine of the Trinity as a central tenet. The Witnesses consider the doctrine to be a distortion of Christianity introduced through Greek Platonic and Sophist philosophy. The traditional Christian Churches do not regard the Witnesses as a mainstream Christian denomination because they reject this doctrine.

Jehovah's Witnesses base their beliefs only on the text of the Bible and dismiss what they call "mere human speculations or religious creeds." They believe that the Bible is the Word of God and consider it to be divinely inspired and historically accurate. According to the Witnesses, Jehovah's first creation was Jesus, his only-begotten Son. Jesus was Michael the archangel, who became a man. He was only a perfect man, not God in flesh. Jesus was born again, but did not rise from the dead in his physical body but was raised a spirit. He began his invisible rule over the earth in 1914. Witnesses say the Holy Spirit is God's impersonal active force, not a Person. Like the Adventists, the Witnesses believe that the soul ceases to exist after death and there is no hell of fire where the wicked are punished. Witnesses do not celebrate Christmas or Easter because they believe that these festivals are based on (or heavily contaminated by) pagan customs and religions. They point out that there is no record that Jesus asked his followers to celebrate his birth. The Witnesses do not use the sign of the cross because they say it is a pagan symbol. This church is strongly millennial and believes that humanity is now in the "last days" and that the final battle between good and evil will happen soon.

Jehovah's Witnesses say that Jesus taught in St John's Gospel that his followers should keep separate from the world. Thus they reject many of the values of secular society, which they regard as sinful, and maintain a degree of separation from non-believers. Witnesses strictly abstain from political involvement and military service, which they regard as forms of apostasy. They also say that blood transfusions are a sin. Jehovah's Witnesses believe that God's kingdom is an actual government in heaven. They therefore refuse to vote, salute the flag, sing the "Star Spangled Banner," or celebrate national holidays.

The denomination was founded towards the end of the 19th century, under the leadership of Charles Taze Russell. There are about 1 million active Witnesses. Witnesses claim to be the only channel of God's truth and that (as stated in the Book of Revelation) only 144,000 people will go to heaven. These will be their church members, who must be born again and do good works such as missionary work They will rule with Jesus as kings and priests over an earthly paradise, where the remaining Christians have the hope of living forever, although it is possible to lose one's salvation. Members of the movement are probably best known for their door-to-door evangelical work, offering their magazines *The Watchtower* and *Awake!,* and converting people to their faith. Witnesses have a conservative morality, though alcohol is permitted in moderation. It has been claimed that the Watch Tower Society exercises control over every aspect of the lives of Jehovah's Witnesses and conditions them to think it is wrong for them to question statements by the Society.

Pentecostalism

Pentecostalism began among poor and disadvantaged people in the US at the start of the 20th century. Pentecostalism is a form of Christianity that emphasises the work of the Holy Spirit and the direct experience of the presence of God by the believer. Pentecostalism is not a church in itself, but a movement that includes many different churches. It is also a movement of renewal or revival within other denominations. Pentecostals hold the basic beliefs of Christianity, although Oneness Pentecostals believe that only Jesus Christ is divine, and baptize in His name alone. Pentecostalism is strong in the African American churches and the megachurches (Protestant congregations with a sustained average weekly attendance of 2000 persons or more in their worship services). The largest Pentecostal denomination is the Assemblies of God, which claims 2.8 million adherents, including the 2008 Republican Vice-Presidential candidate, Sarah Palin.

Pentecostals believe that faith must be powerfully experiential, and not something found simply through ritual or thinking. They believe they are driven by the power of God moving within them and seek to recover for themselves the original experience of the disciples following Christ's resurrection. Pentecostals lay great stress on personal redemption – sin repented, lives transformed, prayers answered – as a visible sign of God's personal intervention in human affairs. Believers assert that only faith in Jesus Christ can save a person from eternal damnation.

Pentecostals believe it is essential to be born again to Christ through baptism in the Holy Spirit. This fills the believer with the strength to live a truly Christian life. Baptism in the Holy Spirit is an experience in which the believer gives control of himself or herself to the Holy Spirit and in return receives charismatic gifts i.e., the ability to speak in a language unknown to the speaker, or ecstatic speech in non-existent languages, prophecy, and healing. Human beings must have come to salvation in Christ and been baptized in water before they can receive the baptism of the Spirit. Pentecostals practise adult baptism by immersion; infants in Pentecostal churches are dedicated to God and blessed. God's grace makes Spirit baptism possible but people must seek the experience or it will not happen.

The baptism of the original twelve disciples by the Holy Spirit on the day of Pentecost is the event from which Pentecostalism draws its inspiration. When the Holy Spirit descended, according to the Bible, they were empowered to speak in many languages as evidence that they had been baptized in the Spirit. Pentecostals claim that this was not a one-time event, but something that can and does happen every day. Most Pentecostals believe their movement is returning the faith to a pure and simple form that has much in common with the very earliest stage in the life of the Christian church. A few Pentecostal churches engage in handling poisonous snakes during services (based on Mark 16:17-18 and Luke 10:19), teaching that doing so successfully is a gift of the Spirit. Although this practice has been given sensational publicity in the media, it was always extremely rare, restricted to small groups, and largely disapproved of by the larger Pentecostal denominations. Although they have the same view of the status of the Bible as fundamentalists, Pentecostals are not fundamentalists because they also accept (as fundamentalists do not) the importance of individual experience of God working in a person's life through the Holy Spirit. Most Pentecostals accept all mainstream Christian beliefs, although the beliefs and customs of Pentecostal churches are diverse. Although the movement is a modern one, its roots go back to the 18th century Wesleyan Holiness tradition, the 19th century Holiness movement and the late-Victorian Keswick *Higher Life* movement. The difference between these earlier traditions and the Pentecostal movement was, on the surface, speaking in tongues. The underlying theological conflict was that members of the Holiness tradition believed that the Pentecost story did not need to be interpreted literally in modern times, while the early Pentecostals saw baptism in the Spirit as a re-enactment of the day of Pentecost.

Modern Pentecostalism began on January 1, 1901, when Agnes Ozman, a theological student in Charles Parham's Bethel Bible College at Topeka, Kansas, spoke in tongues (apparently Chinese) and did not speak English again for several days. On January 3, other students also spoke in tongues. The group later moved to Texas and began a spiritual revival in 1905. This was followed in 1906 by what became known as the Azusa Street revival in Los Angeles, led by the African American preacher William Joseph Seymour, a former student of Parham. (Parham was soon disowned because of his racism and suspect personal conduct.) Seymour preached that God would "send a new Pentecost" if people prayed for one, and was rewarded when he and his congregation began speaking in tongues. This event, greatly influenced by apocalyptic thoughts prompted by the San Francisco earthquake, helped start a powerful religious revival. At first Pentecostalism flourished in individual church groups across North America, and it was not until 1914 that the first Pentecostal denomination, the Church of God in Christ, was founded.

Pentecostalism gives emphasis to the interconnection of body, mind and spirit, which it displays in its highly physical worship, and in healing, speaking in tongues, and the acceptance of dreams and visions as valuable tools of spiritual insight. Pentecostal worship is less formal and more emotionally expressive than that of other Christian traditions since it is designed to bring about an experience of God's presence. The worshippers may dance and clap. Personal testimonies may be given. Preaching may rely more on stories and less on textual analysis. The preaching and teaching of the Christian message is performed through religious ways of thinking and talking that are already familiar to local people. The congregation is likely to respond actively to the sermon with applause or shouts of amen and hallelujah. Services can incorporate trances, speaking in tongues and what are claimed to be healings. The result may well be that participants feel the service is actually led by the Spirit. Pentecostalism adapts easily to local traditions and incorporates local music and other cultural elements in worship, enabling people to retain elements of their own spirituality when they move to a Pentecostal church.

What Pentecostalism offers is spiritual certainty. This is attractive when religious beliefs are under attack, because a direct experience of God is unarguable to those who receive it. As a form of worship, Pentecostalism offers a means of spiritual experience to people who prefer to express themselves through spontaneous emotion rather than through a set ritual. Such people are called "oral" people by contrast with "literary" people. Because Pentecostal worship is spontaneous and oral, rather than anchored in a liturgical text, it allows all members of the congregation to play their part without any fear of doing the wrong thing. It enables each worshipper to share his or her particular experience of God and have it valued by the whole community. Pentecostal churches approach the predicaments of the poor very practically and work as "mutual aid communities" providing alternative solutions to poverty and sickness. Pentecostal churches have flat power structures, and allow a great amount of participation by the laity, both in worship and in the organization. This tends to appeal to people who are otherwise largely deprived of power or influence. Pentecostalism's ability to change, and its devolution of power to individual congregations, allows it to adapt to the needs and desires of people more quickly than hierarchical churches.

There are over 20 million Pentecostals in the US. Theirs are the fastest-growing churches in the country with congregations numbering thousands and annual budgets sometimes running into tens of millions of dollars. Pentecostalism is particularly strong among African Americans. Pentecostals generally have a conservative theology, but 79 percent of Pentecostal respondents to a Pew Forum survey in 2006 said religious groups should express their views on current social and political questions. More than half of those surveyed said the government should take special steps to make America a Christian country, compared with only 25 percent of all Christians, and 64 percent said abortion could not be justified in any circumstances. Pentecostals also oppose stem cell research Pentecostal churches, however, are not very influential among the Christian denominations. This may be because many Pentecostal churches have a minority racial profile, and their members are mostly poor and not in positions of secular power. Given the energy and growth of the movement, however, the influence of Pentecostals will likely grow significantly in future (Bates, *op. cit.*, p.147).

Seventh-Day Adventists

The Seventh-day Adventist Church was founded in the 1860s. The reason it is called "Adventist" is that the church is a Millennialist Protestant denomination which is preparing for the Second Coming of Christ. The term "Seventh-day" refers to the Church's observance of the "biblical Sabbath" on Saturday, the seventh day of the week. "Advent" means *coming* and refers to their belief that Jesus Christ will soon return to this earth. Seventh-day Adventists differ in only four areas of belief from the mainstream Christian denominations: the Sabbath day; the doctrine of the heavenly sanctuary; the status of the writings of Ellen G. White; and eschatology (death, the Second Coming and the millennium). Seventh-day Adventists believe in a literal six-day creation. Baptism is by immersion.

Seventh-day Adventism is derived from the teachings of William Miller (1782-1849). He taught that Jesus would return to earth on a specific day in 1844. This would be the Second Coming or "advent" of Jesus. Many of his followers abandoned Miller when Jesus failed to appear as expected (the *Great Disappointment*). Miller was succeeded by Ellen G. White (1827-1915), a visionary and prophet. White taught that Jesus had indeed come again, but not to Earth. Jesus had actually returned to the "most holy place" of the heavenly temple. Jesus, she said, had started to "cleanse" the heavenly temple, and when he had done that, he would come to start cleansing the Earth. White taught that Christ, as the high priest of the new covenant, ministers in the heavenly sanctuary. The heavenly sanctuary has two areas, the holy place and the most holy place. When Christ went from earth to heaven he went into the holy place. Adventists believe that after 2300 years (in 1844), Christ went into the most holy place to cleanse it before his Second Coming on earth, and that while he is doing so, the Holy Spirit is working to cleanse God's people. Christ's ministry in the heavenly sanctuary is as both priest and sacrifice. His work is one of investigative judgment that reveals which of the dead are righteous and should be resurrected at the Second Coming, and which of the living are also worthy of heaven.

Adventists see themselves as the remnant that announces the arrival of the judgment hour, proclaims salvation through Christ, and heralds the approach of his Second Coming, which they believe will happen soon. Christ's return "will be literal, personal, visible, and worldwide." On that day the righteous dead will be resurrected and taken with him to heaven, together with the righteous living. Prophecy is seen as an identifying mark of the remnant church. Adventists believe this gift was manifested in the ministry of Ellen G. White, whom they regard as God's messenger. The essence of her prophecy was that humanity is involved in a battle between Satan and Christ called the *great controversy* and should choose Christ.

Adventists do not believe that people go to heaven or hell when they die but that the dead remain unconscious until the resurrection at the return of Christ in judgement. Thus there is no surviving soul or spirit, even of saints, to invoke or for spiritualist mediums to contact. The Second Coming will be followed by a period of a thousand years (the Millennium) during which the earth will be deserted except for Satan and his helpers, the righteous live with God in heaven, and the "wicked dead" are judged. After the Millennium, Christ with his saints and the Holy City will return to earth, the unrighteous dead will be resurrected and, together with Satan and his helpers, will be destroyed by fire, leaving behind a universe without sin or sinners. The wicked will be annihilated rather than tormented for eternity.

Seventh-day Adventists keep the Sabbath on Saturday—more specifically, from sunset on Friday to sunset on Saturday. The Sabbath is a special day for rest, Bible study, prayer and worship in the home and in the church, and also for learning from nature, because it is God's creation. Families join together on Friday evenings to celebrate the Sabbath. It is also a time to visit the sick and to work for the salvation of souls. No unnecessary work should be performed, and giving time to secular reading or broadcasts is discouraged. Children are expected to attend Sabbath School. The Saturday Sabbath has brought Adventists into conflict with both commercial interests (because they will not work on Saturdays) and other Christians (because they will not treat Sunday as a holy day). Adventists do not say, however, that any truly born again Christian who is currently worshipping on a Sunday has the "mark of the beast" or is under Satan's influence.

Adventists live modest lives, with a strict, to outsiders puritanical, code of ethics. They do not use tobacco, alcohol or recreational drugs, and recommend a vegetarian diet. Meat is permitted, but only following the Biblical commandments on clean and unclean food. Adventists dress modestly, but do not adopt an antique style of clothing, preferring to wear tasteful conservative and sensible styles that are common at any period. Clothes are chosen for their durability. Profuse ornamentation and gaudy display are unacceptable, an attitude to clothing shared by many Americans. Adventists do not wear jewelry, other than a wedding ring.

Adventist doctrine tells them to regard their bodies as temples of the Holy Spirit and that they should therefore attend to their health. Adventists believe that whatever promotes physical health promotes the development of a strong mind and a well-balanced character. They are instructed that it is their religious duty to observe the laws of health, both for their own well-being and happiness and for more efficient service to God and to others. Adventists were responsible for the popularization of breakfast cereal; the Adventist layman, John Harvey Kellogg, invented cornflakes as a replacement for eggs and bacon. The Adventist Church is heavily involved in education and also operates medical facilities. Adventists believe they have a duty to share their beliefs with others, and missionary work is very important. The Church bases its mission of healing of body, mind, and spirit on the fact that Christ ministered to the whole person.

Adventists are cultural conservatives. Educational, news, current affairs and classical music broadcasts are valued, but programs that are neither "wholesome nor uplifting" are avoided. Adventists are advised not to go to the theatre or movies, which, with other entertainments, are seen as partly responsible for the poor moral state of the world. Social dancing is not permitted. Some music is seen to be of great value, while other forms are dangerous. Jazz, rock and similar music, and any lyrics expressing foolish or trivial sentiments are shunned by Adventists. Adventist social events are usually held in family homes, rather than commercial places of entertainment, and are meant to promote happy fellowship and the improvement of the powers of mind and soul. They are also occasions for the making and carrying out of plans for outreach (missionary work). Adventists adopt the highest standards of sexual behavior. Sex outside marriage is forbidden, and parents are expected to chaperone meetings between young people. Young people, for their part, are expected to take responsibility for avoiding sexual encounters. Adultery, homosexual and lesbian practices, sexual abuse within marriage, incest and sexual abuse of children are forbidden. Pornography is to be avoided (Ellen G. White Estate - http://www.whiteestate.org, accessed July 23, 2009). Seventh-day Adventist ministers will not marry church members to non-members. Adultery, sexual perversion and abandonment by a non-believing spouse are valid grounds for divorce, although the Church will first try to mediate and reconcile the couple. If reconciliation is not possible, the couple can divorce and the spouse who remained faithful has the right to remarry. The spouse who broke the marriage vow may not remarry while his or her ex-partner lives. Adventists regard it as a sacred responsibility to be good citizens but, based on their understanding of the 6th Commandment "Thou shalt not kill," will not take a combatant role in warfare.

Megachurches, Nondenominational and Postdenominational churches

For over a century, entrepreneurial preachers have been willing to reinvent their churches in order to appeal to the unchurched. They have used non-sacred architecture, innovative worship, popular music, drama, and diverse programming to meet the needs of people who felt unwelcome in traditional churches. Their churches are places where worshipers can meet people, network, build relationships and grow spiritually. A few of these new churches grew very large and became megachurches.

Like all American institutions, the churches were challenged to adapt their culture and strategy by the tidal wave of immigrants who landed on US shores in the generations spanning 1900. Immigrants flooded into the cities, and by the outbreak of World War I, one in three Americans was an immigrant or the child of an immigrant. In a few cities, the foreign-born outnumbered the native-born two to one. Newcomers displaced older residents in downtown districts, and downtown churches had to choose either to follow their parishioners uptown or to modify their ministry for the newcomers. Many churches chose to adapt, and the "institutional church" movement was born. To meet the needs of their new congregants, the institutional churches built facilities for new kinds of ministry—gymnasiums, swimming pools, medical dispensaries, employment centers, loan offices, libraries, daycare centers, and classrooms——buildings designed for seven-days-a-week service. They taught English, hygiene, home economics, and work skills. They showed movies, held lectures, and sponsored concerts. They held services in several languages. Shaping ministry programs around the needs of their neighbors made some of these churches huge. Russell Conwell's 3,000-member Baptist Temple in Philadelphia built a hospital and a university (Temple University) as well as a large new church. Of the nondenominational evangelical churches (gospel tabernacles), the most famous was Aimee Semple McPherson's 5,300-seat Angelus Temple in Los Angeles, which at its peak attracted more than 10,000 people every Sunday. Other large evangelical churches, including those affiliated with denominations, took the same approach. In Seattle, the 9,000 members of Mark Matthews's First Presbyterian Church helped operate the church's radio station, hospital, and Bible institute. In Chicago, L. K. Williams's 12,000-member Olivet Baptist Church had 30 paid staff and hundreds of volunteers. In 1950, Hollywood Presbyterian was sponsoring over 300 societies, classes, groups, clubs, auxiliaries, fellowship teams, choirs, camps, circles and flocks.

In the 20th century, nondenominational Christianity became a widespread movement which has persisted into the present. The gospel tabernacles led the way and were followed by many other churches. Among the first of these was Calvary Undenominational Church, founded by Martin DeHaan in Grand Rapids, Michigan in the late 1920s. Originally this church was Calvary Reformed Church (Reformed Church in America). The new version drew in more than 2,000 people every Sunday. William McCarrell withdrew his Chicago-area church from the Congregational fold and renamed it Cicero Bible Church. In 1930 he founded an association of similar churches, the Independent Fundamental Churches of America (IFCA). Over time, the IFCA evolved from an association of nondenominational churches into a denomination, IFCA International. On the liberal side, a number of talented pastors founded large nondenominational churches. When John D. Rockefeller built a grand new church, modeled on Chartres Cathedral, in New York City for moderate Baptist, Harry Emerson Fosdick, in 1930, Fosdick insisted the church be nondenominational. For the next 16 years, crowds packed Riverside Church to hear Fosdick preach and to participate in its extensive ministry activities, which combined the best features of both institutional and evangelical churches. In a suburb just outside of Columbus, Ohio, First Congregational had already become the nondenominational First Community when liberal Roy Burkhart took over in 1935. In his 23 years there, Burkhart built a 3,400-member church which placed strong emphasis on lay-led ministry. Although the excitement surrounding Angelus Temple cooled during the 1930s, the new denomination it birthed grew and prospered as the International Church of the Foursquare Gospel. By the mid-1990s, this included 27,000 churches in North America and 25,000 abroad. The institutional church movement, however, was largely over by the '50s, as congregations moved up the socioeconomic ladder and out to the suburbs, and tastes changed.

In more recent years, there has been a major change in the role of American denominations. In a country where church and state were separate, the European state churches and the groups that dissented from them had to find a new reason for existence once they were transplanted to America. Their initial response was to provide services for local churches, chiefly by establishing institutions to train, ordain, and sustain clergy. Through most of the 19th century, denominations were modest organizations. But in the late 19th century, power shifted from the local church toward the denominational headquarters, which expanded by taking control over a larger share of ministry activities. The purpose of the local church became to support the denomination's central program and generate income for it. Headquarters hired efficiency experts to determine which kinds of churches produced the most income and then developed plans to encourage more of that kind of church. Increasingly they evaluated local pastors on their records of producing income. Now power has shifted back to the local churches. Independent churches are flourishing, and churches within denominations are asserting their autonomy as never before. The headquarters are redefining themselves as servants, not masters, slashing central office programs, laying off staff, and beginning to strengthen programs that directly support the local churches.

Many nondenominational churches, such as Willow Creek Community Church in the Chicago suburb of South Barrington, and Saddleback Church, south of Los Angeles, are identical to Baptist churches in doctrine, and many have Baptist roots. Increasing numbers of moderate evangelical Baptist churches are dropping the term "Baptist" from their names, often choosing names like "Community Church" or "<placename> Church." They are doing this because the fundamentalists and Southern Baptists have engaged in aggressive political action and confrontational evangelism, which have given the impression that all Baptists are combative right-wing partisans. Similar changes are happening in other denominations. There is also growing ecumenical awareness and erasing of denominational boundaries between most Protestants, so that denominational identity is no longer regarded as important by many.

Willow Creek Community Church is a nondenominational, evangelical megachurch in the Chicago suburb of South Barrington. Founded in 1975 by Bill Hybels, currently the Senior Pastor, the church has three weekend services, which average nearly 23,000 attendees, making it the fourth-largest church in the US. Willow Creek has been listed as the most influential church in America in the last several years in a national poll of pastors. Willow Creek states that its mission is to "turn irreligious people into fully devoted followers of Jesus Christ." The church bases its belief on the *Bible*, which it asserts is the inspired Word of God, inerrant, infallible, and the final authority on the matters to which it relates. Based on this understanding, the church holds to the doctrines of mainstream Christianity and asserts that the church's role is to glorify God and serve those in need. Like Saddleback, Willow Creek began with a demographic survey and built itself up using services for seekers (enquirers), and like Saddleback's Purpose-Driven Ministries (PDM), Willow Creek has nearly 100 ministries that are designed to serve the needs of a variety of people and age groups. The ministries include prayer requests (which may be sent online), pastoral care, support communities, workshops, and classes.

Nondenominational churches present interesting programs and comfortable surroundings to attract the unchurched. Once drawn in, they are enveloped in a comprehensive network of activities designed to give them a supportive community and deeper instruction in the faith. Willow Creek's state-of-the-art Worship Center (completed in 2004 at an estimated cost of $73 million) seats over 7,200 people, making it the largest theater in the US. It uses high definition LED screens usually seen in sports stadiums. Weekend services are designed to reach the unchurched (Luke 19:10), while midweek classes are an opportunity for people to move forward in their spiritual growth. The church's regional congregations throughout the Chicago area each has its own worship team, student ministry, children's program, and campus pastoral team. The weekly message is videocast from the South Barrington campus. The first thing visitors might notice about the service at Willow Creek is the music, which is lively, contemporary, and professional. The church also uses its downtown presence to develop its ministries for the homeless and prostitutes. Enthusiasts call Willow Creek the trailblazer of a "second Reformation" that will remake Christianity. Critics insist that Willow Creek represents a complete surrender to the secular values of contemporary North America.

Today Americans are leaving the mainline churches in droves, and many are finding spiritual homes in rapidly-growing "new paradigm" churches that often rent space in shopping malls and warehouses because they have no facilities of their own. The Pentecostal-type congregations of American Protestantism's so-called third wave, like Calvary Chapel, Hope Chapel and Vineyard Christian Fellowship, are built on the faith of those whose lives have been radically changed by their church experience. These churches emphasize a common evangelical theology and are abandoning the staid cultural forms of traditional Protestantism (organs, choirs, and vestments) in favor of newer ones that young people find culturally relevant (guitars, small support groups, and beach baptisms). Dress is casual, ministers are often untrained, and lay people lead Bible studies and healing circles. Adherents are encouraged to take an active role in congregational growth. These new rituals fill a real spiritual need. In particular, where traditional Protestantism has emphasized the rational at the expense of the experiential, new paradigm churches fill the void through physical healings and deeply felt personal conversions. Offering a unique blend of contemporary culture and life-transforming spirituality, with little doctrine or hierarchy, these groups appeal primarily to young, middle class families. A growing number of new believers only know this type of church. Since many new paradigm churches have large attendances, they are able to finance the start of others. These churches are continuing to grow and attract more people (often from non-religious backgrounds). Indeed, some observers believe that new paradigm churches may well become the norm of church life in America. But they have resisted incorporation into denominations, and rather are "postdenominational" churches that reflect their baby-boomer leaders' distrust of established institutions.

The promotion of church growth is a major feature of nondenominational Christianity. The church growth movement has become a multi-million dollar operation. Churches in two new denominations that grew out of other evangelical megachurches—the Calvary Chapel Association and the Association of Vineyard Churches—train and ordain pastors. To teach other churches what his church had learned, Bill Hybels and colleagues founded the Willow Creek Association (WCA) in 1991. The WCA offers training and leadership conferences and workshops, books and curricula, video and audio tape series, newsletters, and networking materials for its more than 13,000 member churches from 90 denominations and 45 different countries. The WCA annual Leadership Summit speakers have included President Bill Clinton, Karen Hughes (Special Advisor to President Bush) and Tim Sanders, former Leadership Coach at Yahoo! The 2007 Leadership Summit served 80,000 leaders in over 130 cities. Speakers included Colin Powell, Jimmy Carter and Richard Curtis, founder of *USA TODAY*. Rick Warren's Purpose-Driven Ministries (PDM) at Saddleback megachurch sponsors conferences and workshops and produces teaching materials to help churches learn from Saddleback's successes. A major difference between PDM and WCA is that PDM advocates the use of a formula for church growth designed to replicate the Saddleback experience. The leaders of Willow Creek, on the other hand, insist that churches need to shift their concern from programming and growth to the real needs of those they are called to serve. Willow Creek's ultimate goal is not to grow churches, nor spawn imitators: it is to renew Christianity by encouraging every church to focus on the people among whom they minister.

Campaigning by Protestants

Protestant evangelists preach, often vehemently and passionately, a democratic message of personal salvation and individual responsibility, reinforced with warnings about the imminent end of the world. They address the fears and aspirations of their hearers in the conviction that theirs is the divine revelation. The great majority of these evangelists are religious and political conservatives. Their political message was summed up by Moral Majority leader, Jerry Falwell, as "pro-life, pro-family, pro-morality, pro-America." They believe they are building a nation whose success rests on their own belief and on the outcome of their mission. Neo-conservative (neo-con) religion is a faith-based ideology which unites the traditional evangelical values of individual virtue and self-reliance with a religion-based view of America's role in history. To neo-cons, the world is black and white, policy should be based on moral absolutes, and there is no need for America to consult or compromise. Most of the evangelists evoke the Puritan us-versus-them outlook on morality as being an integral part of American history. Popular morality is frequently cited as the only thing that can protect "us" from "them," whoever "they" may be. Indeed the US should use its superpower military to enforce God's will on the world. The insecurity which motivates supporters arises, argues Stephen Bates (*ibid.*, pp. 111-12) largely from the effects of desegregation on poor whites: the loss of the slim margin of superiority over their African American neighbors, and the need to associate with them and compete on equal terms. Currently, these fears are exacerbated by globalization and the effects of economic insecurity and unemployment.

Conservative Protestants espouse either of two theories about the end of the world, which they believe to be imminent. *Dispensational Premillennialists* believe that the world is getting worse and worse and soon Christ will return to judge it. They take the biblical books of *Revelation* and *Daniel* absolutely literally and have constructed a complex, detailed account of Christ's return. History is divided into seven ages. The final one, lasting seven years, will see the coming of the Anti-Christ, the Beast of Revelation, a world leader who creates a new Roman Empire and facilitates the return of the Jews to the Promised Land, but then persecutes them. This period of hatred, chaos, and warfare, allegedly predicted in Matthew 24, is called the Tribulation. When it ends, Christ and his armies will arrive and defeat the Beast at the Battle of Armageddon in the Middle East. (Two-thirds of evangelicals believe there will be a literal battle of Armageddon.) True believers will be saved from destruction by being carried up to heaven to meet Christ in a movement known as the Rapture. Then Christ will begin his 1,000-year reign. The Beast is variously identified as the UN, the EU, Iran or Islam. This theory seems to explain on divine authority what its believers see as the moral decay and corruption of the modern world, and to identify them as the Elect who are predestined for a future of happiness. This fatalistic theory makes social action irrelevant. The other version of the theory is called *postmillennialism,* an optimistic faith that the Anti-Christ, today identified by some believers as Islam, will be soon defeated as the world progressively improves and a 1,000-year golden age, blessed with the outpouring of the Holy Spirit, begins. The US will lead humanity to the consummation. This theory thus combines social progressivism and a sense of national righteousness (Bates, *ibid.*, pp. 138-41).

Radio and Television

Both Protestant and Catholic preachers have long used the radio as a medium for evangelism and political commentary. Stations include Family Radio's WYFR and the Bible Broadcasting Network (BBN). In recent decades some have taken their ministry to television as "televangelists" (a term sometimes used derisively) to reach larger audiences. The aim of Christian broadcasting is both to convert people to Christianity and to provide teaching and support to believers. Televangelism began as a peculiarly American phenomenon, resulting from the freedom to air religious broadcasts, and access to television networks open to virtually anyone who can afford it, combined with a large Christian population that is able to provide the necessary funding. The increasing globalization of broadcasting has since enabled some American televangelists to reach an even wider audience through international broadcast networks such as Trinity Broadcasting Network and The God Channel. Some televangelists are also regular clergy in their own places of worship (often a megachurch), but the majority of their followers come from their TV and radio audiences. Others do not have a conventional congregation and work solely through television. Televangelists' preaching combines passionate conviction with homey anecdotes, pathos, humor and sentiment, offering what critics call "cheap grace," suggesting that people can earn their salvation by their own efforts and improve their material lot at the same time. Several media evangelists have made large fortunes, which they believe are a reward from God for hard work and virtue. Some televangelists, however, have been convicted of crimes. Jim Bakker, for example, served six years in jail for defrauding his followers of $158 million. Others, like Jimmy Swaggart, have shown themselves more interested in pleasure than religion.

Many media evangelists are Southern Baptists. *Dr. Richard D. Land,* for example, is the president of The Ethics & Religious Liberty Commission (ERLC), the public policy entity of the Southern Baptist Convention, a post he has held since 1988. He is also the host of *For Faith & Family* and *For Faith & Family's Insight,* two nationally syndicated radio programs. He was the primary author of the *Land letter,* an open letter sent to President Bush by leaders of the Religious Right in October 2002 which outlined a "just war" argument in support of the subsequent invasion of Iraq. Land often speaks on news reports and as a guest on radio talk shows about issues ranging from religion to tax cuts. Among Land's many books is *The Divided States of America? What Liberals AND Conservatives are Missing in the God-and-Country Shouting Match,* Thomas Nelson, 2007, which examines the separation of church and state debate. Land also serves as Executive Editor of *FFV,* a national magazine dedicated to addressing issues of traditional religious values, the challenge of Christian ethics, and other cultural trends. Land even appeared in the movie *Article VI* (2008), in which he discusses religion in politics. He is also a member of the U.S. Commission on International Religious Freedom (USCIRF).

Billy Graham, the Southern Baptist evangelist, has been called the "pastor of America." He has preached in person to more people around the world than any other Protestant in history, appearing before live audiences of nearly 215 million people in more than 185 countries and territories. Graham has also reached hundreds of millions more through television, video, film, and webcasts. As of 2008, Graham's lifetime audience, including radio and television, topped 2.2 billion. As of 1993 more than 2.5 million people had stepped forward at his crusades to accept Jesus Christ as their personal Savior. Graham was converted in 1934 and later attended Bob Jones College (now Bob Jones University) before in 1937 transferring to the then Florida Bible Institute, from which he graduated in 1940 with a B.Th. (Bachelor of Theology degree). Graham then attended Wheaton College, Illinois, from 1939 to 1943, graduating with a B.A. in anthropology. It was during his time at Wheaton that he decided to take the Bible as the infallible word of God.

As a young minister, Graham launched a new radio program in 1944 called "Songs in the Night." While this ministry continued for many years, Graham decided to move on in early 1945 and became the first full time evangelist of the new Youth for Christ International. He held a series of revival meetings in Los Angeles in 1949, which is considered the point when he became a national religious figure. Graham's rise was due in part to publicity from William Randolph Hearst. Most observers believe that Hearst appreciated Graham's patriotism and appeals to youth, and thought that Graham would be helpful in promoting Hearst's conservative anti-communist views. Henry Luce put him on the cover of *TIME* magazine in 1954.

Billy Graham began conducting evangelistic crusades in 1947 and continued until recently. He would rent a large venue, arrange a group of up to 5,000 to sing in a choir, preach the gospel and invite people to come forward for Christ. These *inquirers* were then given the chance to speak one-on-one with a counselor who clarified any questions and would pray with each inquirer. The inquirers were often given a copy of the *Gospel of John* or a Bible study booklet. Graham held missions in both London and New York City in 1957 before leading his first crusade, which took place in Australia in 1959.

In 1950 Graham went on to found the Billy Graham Evangelistic Association. BGEA Ministries have included one of the most famous of all evangelistic broadcasts: *Hour of Decision*, broadcast around the world weekly on radio for more than 50 years; mission television specials regularly broadcast in prime time in almost every market in the US and Canada; a newspaper column, *My Answer*, carried by newspapers across the US; *Decision* magazine, the official publication of the BGEA; *Christianity Today*; Passageway.org, the website for a forthcoming children's program; and World Wide Pictures, which has produced and distributed more than 130 productions. Graham has been careful to take reasonable compensation, far below what other television evangelists would later receive. The Modesto (California) "manifesto" produced by him and some colleagues early in his ministry also noted the dangers of sexual immorality, criticism of local churches, and exaggerated publicity.

Billy Graham took a strong public stand against segregation. He refused to speak to segregated audiences, once dramatically tearing down the ropes that organizers had erected, saying "There is no scriptural basis for segregation.... The ground at the foot of the cross is level." Graham paid bail money to secure the release of Martin Luther King from jail. He later invited King to join him in the pulpit at his revival in New York City, when Graham was heard by 2.3 million listeners. During the Cold War, Graham became the first evangelist of note to speak behind the Iron Curtain, addressing large crowds in countries throughout Eastern Europe and in the Soviet Union, and calling for peace. During the apartheid era, Graham refused to visit South Africa until its government allowed his audiences to sit desegregated. His first crusade there was in 1973, during which he openly denounced apartheid. At one revival in Seoul, South Korea, Graham attracted one million people to a single service. He appeared in China in 1988 and North Korea in 1992. In Moscow in 1992, one-quarter of the 155,000 people in the audience came forward. On June 24, 2005, Billy Graham began what he said, because of failing health, would be his last North American crusade, in New York City. But on the weekend of March 11–12, 2006 he held the "Festival of Hope" with his son, Franklin, in New Orleans, which was recovering from Hurricane Katrina.

Although he is a registered member of the Democratic Party, Billy Graham does not openly endorse political candidates; he has given his support to some. He was a friend of Richard Nixon, but has not fully allied himself with the Religious Right. He says that Jesus did not have a political party. He refused to join Jerry Falwell's Moral Majority in 1979, saying: "I'm for morality, but morality goes beyond sex to human freedom and social justice….We have to stand in the middle in order to preach to all people, right and left." He has been an advisor to every President since Truman, with the exception of Kennedy. He helped George W. Bush overcome alcoholism in the mid-1980s. After a special law was passed on his behalf, Graham was allowed to conduct the first religious service on the steps of the Capitol building in 1952.

Graham was outspoken against communism and supported US policy during the Cold War, including the Vietnam War. But when he discussed his relationship with the late North Korean dictator Kim Il-sung in 1999, he took a more sympathetic view of Communism and praised Kim as a "different kind of communist" and "one of the great fighters for freedom in his country against the Japanese." Graham went on to note that although he had never met Kim's son, the current North Korean leader Kim Jong-il, he had exchanged gifts with him.

Billy Graham's career has not been without controversy. In 2002, declassified tapes captured him agreeing with President Nixon in a 1972 conversation that Jews had a "stranglehold" on the American media. These remarks were characterized by Abraham Foxman of the Anti-Defamation League as anti-Semitic. Graham apologized. According to *Newsweek* magazine, "[The] shock of the revelation was magnified because of Graham's longtime support of Israel and his refusal to join in calls for conversion of the Jews." In his essay "Superchrist of a Superstate," Malcolm Boyd expressed dismay at Graham's silence and alleged hypocrisy about the Vietnam War and the Watergate scandal. In 1993, Graham said he thought AIDS was a judgment of God, but after seeing letters criticizing the comment, he retracted it.

Graham has consistently appeared near the top of rankings of most admired persons in the US and the world. He has received numerous honors, including *Greatest Living American*. He has also received both the Congressional Gold Medal and the Presidential Medal of Freedom (from President Reagan), America's highest civilian honors. On May 31, 2007, the $27 million Billy Graham Library was officially dedicated in Charlotte, South Carolina. Graham has also received the Big Brother of the Year Award for his work on behalf of children and been cited by the George Washington Carver Memorial Institute for his contributions to race relations. He has received the Templeton Foundation Prize for Progress in Religion. A movie has been produced to capture the essence of Graham's journey from a young man at the crossroads of faith and doubt to ultimately facing the moment of decision that made one of history's most influential evangelists. *Billy: The Early Years* premiered in theaters officially on October 10, 2008. Graham himself has authored 28 books. The best known of Evangelical preachers, Billy Graham has made revival Evangelicalism the mainstream American faith

A politically more conservative preacher, *Jerry Falwell* (1933-2007), an Evangelical minister and commentator, founded the Southern Baptist Convention megachurch in Lynchburg, Virginia (1956), Liberty (liberal arts) University (1971), and the Moral Majority (1979). He used to broadcast on *The Old Time Gospel Hour*. The Moral Majority became one of the largest political lobby groups for evangelical Christians during the 1980s. It was founded as being pro-family, pro-life, pro-defense and pro-Israel. (Falwell's staunch pro-Israel stand was sometimes referred to as *Christian Zionism*.) He believed in the patriarchal family in which the father is the breadwinner and the mother takes care of the home and raises the children until they are old enough to leave. Falwell condemned homosexuality as forbidden by the Bible. Falwell also advocated a school voucher system which would allow parents to send their children to either public or private schools, and expressed the hope that, as in the early days of the Republic, there would be no public schools but only schools run by the churches. He was critical of sanctions against the apartheid regime of South Africa, fearing that sanctions would result in a Soviet-backed revolution. The Moral Majority is credited with delivering two thirds of the white, evangelical Christian vote to Ronald Reagan during the 1980 presidential election. Falwell sued and was sued in a number of high profile cases. His legacy is also a source of heated controversy. Many of his detractors have accused him of hate speech and identified him as an "agent of intolerance," finding fault with his views on religious discrimination, racial segregation, the Women's Movement and LGBT (lesbian, gay, bisexual and transgendered) people, and his statements blaming gays, feminists, pagans and abortionists for the September 11 attacks.

Another Southern Baptist, prominent religious broadcaster, *Pat Robertson*, was born in Lexington, Virginia, the son of a conservative Democratic US Senator. Ordained in 1961, he holds to a charismatic Pentecostal-type theology uncommon among Southern Baptists. In 1988 he unsuccessfully campaigned to become the Republican Party's presidential nominee. As a result of seeking political office, he no longer serves in an official role in any church. His media outlets, financial resources and forthright views make him a recognized, influential and controversial public voice for conservative Christianity in the US.

Robertson is the founder of numerous organizations and corporations and is probably the most materially successful of all Christian broadcasters. His American Center for Law and Justice (ACLJ) is a public interest law firm that defends Christians whose First Amendment rights have allegedly been violated. The Christian Broadcasting Network (CBN), which he founded in 1960, is seen in 180 countries and broadcast in 71 languages. The channel was acquired by Disney in 2001 and is now run as ABC Family, which airs Robertson's program, *The 700 Club*, twice a day. *The 700 Club*, which airs on channels throughout the US and affiliates worldwide and is "so-called for the 700 viewers he originally asked to pledge $10 each to keep the station going, mimics the news broadcasts of secular national stations, with Robertson and his fellow presenter sitting behind a studio desk and delivering news, lifestyle advice and improving homilies often featuring individuals helped by their faith, as well as asides and commentaries on the day's events from the host himself" (Bates, *ibid.*, p. 253). Formed by Robertson in 1990, International Family Entertainment, a publicly-held company listed on the New York Stock Exchange, produces and distributes family entertainment and information programming worldwide. IFE's principal business is The Family Channel, a satellite-delivered cable-television network with 63 million US subscribers. Robertson is also founder of the Flying Hospital, Operation Blessing International Relief and Development Corporation, and Regent University (1989).

In 1987, having signed up three million volunteers, and having raised millions of dollars for his campaign fund, Robertson entered the race for President. His campaign, against Vice-President George H. W. Bush, was seen as maverick, however. Robertson ran on a very conservative platform including banning pornography, reforming the education system, and eliminating Departments such as the Department of Education and the Department of Energy. He also supported a constitutional amendment requiring a balanced federal budget. Robertson achieved second place in the Iowa caucus, ahead of Bush, but did poorly in the New Hampshire primary, was uncompetitive once the multiple-state primaries began and ended his campaign before the primaries were over. Afterwards, Robertson started the Christian Coalition, a 1.7 million-member Christian Right organization that campaigned mostly for conservative candidates. He left the Coalition in 2001. Robertson's book *The New World Order* (1991) claims there is a worldwide conspiracy of Freemasons and a secret Order of the Illuminati, a group combining Masons and Jewish bankers. In 2009, Robertson said that he was "adamantly opposed" to the division of Jerusalem between Israel and the Palestinians. He also said that Armageddon was not going to be fought at Megiddo but at Jerusalem when the forces of all nations came together to try to take Jerusalem away from the Jews. Robertson added that Jerusalem was a spiritual symbol that must not be given away because Jesus Christ the Messiah would come down to the part of Jerusalem that the Arabs wanted. While usually associated with the political right, Robertson has recently begun endorsing environmental causes, urging people to join the We campaign against global warming.

Robertson is outspoken in both his faith and his politics, and controversies surrounding him have often made headlines. After 9/11 he concurred with Falwell that it was a punishment of America from God for adopting secular values. In 2005, he suggested that the US arrange the assassination of Venezuelan President, Hugo Chavez. He is also well-known for making predictions around New Year which he claims are based on personal revelations from God. These include "a judgment on the world" to fall in 1982, a tsunami for 2006, a terror attack in 2007, worldwide violence and a recession in 2008, and a stock market crash by 2010. In October 2008 Robertson posted a press release speculating that instability in the Middle East would result in nuclear strikes on US coastal cities.

Psychologist *Dr. James Dobson* is among the most prominent of evangelical writers and broadcasters. By contrast with many of his peers, he is not actually an ordained minister of any denomination but was trained as a psychologist and practiced as one for a number of years. He was an Associate Clinical Professor of Pediatrics at the University of Southern California School of Medicine for 14 years and spent 17 years on the staff of the Division of Child Development and Medical Genetics at the Children's Hospital of Los Angeles. He was raised a member of the Church of the Nazarene, the largest denomination to come out of the 19th century Holiness Movement. Now an evangelical conservative author, and founder in 1977 of Focus on the Family (FOTF), which he chaired until 2003, Dr Dobson has also served on government advisory panels and testified at several official hearings.

James Dobson hosts *Focus on the Family*, a daily radio program with an audience of 20 million tuned to 4,000 stations. According to FOTF, the program is broadcast in more than a dozen languages and on over 7,000 stations worldwide, and is heard by more than 220 million people in 164 countries. The TV version is carried by about 60 US television stations daily. Dobson also publishes monthly bulletins called *Focus on the Family*, which are dispensed as inserts in some Sunday church service bulletins. Dobson uses FOTF to promote the 36 books he has authored or co-authored. He is a frequent guest on Fox News Channel. His syndicated monthly columns are published in many newspapers. In 1981 he founded the Family Research Council as a political arm through which "social conservative causes" could achieve greater political influence.

Dr. Dobson takes an unfashionably traditional view of gender roles. He is a passionate advocate of what he calls "traditional marriage." He defends his position by arguing that while women are not inferior to men, because they, like men, are created in God's image, the role of each gender is laid down in the Bible. He recommends that married women with children under the age of 18 focus on mothering, rather than working outside the home. In his 2004 book *Marriage Under Fire: Why We Must Win This Battle*, Dobson claims that traditional marriage "is rapidly dying," with most young people cohabiting or choosing to live alone, and illegitimacy rates rising. He describes marriage as "the bedrock of culture." Criticizing what he calls "the realities of judicial tyranny," Dobson has written that "[t]here is no issue today that is more significant to our culture than the defense of the family. Not even the war on terror eclipses it." Dobson and Focus on the Family support private school vouchers and tax credits for religious schools, believing that parents are ultimately responsible for their children's education. Dobson opposes sex education curricula that are not abstinence-only. He supports student-led prayer in public schools.

Dobson believes that God defines marriage as between one man and one woman only and describes this as the central stabilizing institution of society; any sexual activity outside of such a union, including homosexual practice, cannot be approved by God. In Dobson's view, homosexuality is a choice that is made through influences in a child's environment rather than an inborn trait. He states that homosexual behavior, specifically "unwanted same-sex attraction," has been and can be "overcome" through clinical means. He claims that tolerance and diversity are almost always buzzwords for promoting homosexual behavior. On October 23, 2008, Dobson published a "Letter from 2012 in Obama's America" that claimed an Obama presidency would lead to mandated homosexual teachings. Dobson's Focus on the Family ministry sponsors the monthly conference Love Won Out, where participants hear "powerful stories of ex-gay men and women." Parents, Families and Friends of Lesbians and Gays (P-FLAG) has protested against the conference, questioning both its methodology and success. Dobson opposed a bill expanding the prohibition of sexual discrimination in public accommodation, housing practices, family planning services and 20 other areas. Fears have been expressed that Dobson's ultimate goal is to pressure lawmakers into outlawing homosexuality and that he favors reinstituting Old Testament-style executions for homosexual practice. Dobson has stated that Focus on the Family has no interest in promoting hatred toward homosexuals or anyone else or depriving them of their constitutional rights. Dobson strongly opposes the movement to legitimize same-sex relationships. Although Dr. Dobson is a licensed clinical psychologist, and discusses homosexuality in psychological terms, his views are not supported by the mainstream mental health community.

Dobson first became well-known with the publication of *Dare to Discipline*, which contradicted the liberal philosophy of child-rearing made famous in the 1950s by Dr. Benjamin Spock. Dobson encouraged parents to spank children up to the age of eight when they misbehaved, but warned that "corporal punishment should not be a frequent occurrence" and that "discipline must not be harsh and destructive to the child's spirit." The spanking should, however, cause the child to cry genuinely. He also warned that anyone who has ever abused a child, lost control during a spanking, has a violent temper or enjoys giving corporal punishment should not do so. In *The Strong-Willed Child*, Dobson suggests that if authority is portrayed correctly by parents, the child will understand how to interact with other authority figures. Thus parents must uphold their authority consistently and not submit to defiance by children. Dobson's position is controversial. Although spanking is legal in the US, as long ago as 1985 *The New York Times* stated that "most child-care experts today disapprove of physical punishment."

Dobson's following is believed to exceed even that of Falwell or Robertson at the height of their popularity. Dobson suggested at one time that evangelicals might withhold their support from the Republican Party if it did not more strongly support conservative family issues. He garnered national media attention in the 2008 Presidential election after saying he would not vote for Senator McCain, as a matter of conscience. At first, he endorsed Mike Huckabee. When he later indicated he "might" vote for McCain, Independent candidate Alan Keyes coined the tongue-in-cheek phrase "Dobson's Choice" to highlight the dilemma conservative voters faced in a two-party system while choosing to endorse the lesser of two evils. After McCain selected a pro-life candidate, Sarah Palin, as his running mate, Dobson said that he was more enthusiastic in his support for the Republican ticket. Dobson advocates intelligent design, has spoken at conferences supporting it, and frequently criticizes evolution. In 2007, Dobson was one of 25 evangelicals who called for the ouster of Rev. Richard Cizik from his position at the National Association of Evangelicals because Cizik had urged evangelicals to take global warming seriously.

Focus on the Family had a budget of $138 million for fiscal year 2009 and employs some 1,100 people – a third of them answering callers with problems. The organization offers a complete child-rearing and family problem service, including advising parents on what films to let their children watch. Its magazine *Citizen* takes a strongly conservative line. FOTF sells self-improvement books and videos and even gives guided tours of the headquarters to 250,000 tourists a year. At one time, the headquarters was receiving 10,000 emails, 50,000 telephone calls and 173,000 letters a month and had a mailing list of six million names. Dobson has been called "the nation's most influential evangelical leader."

Many televangelists hold charismatic or Pentecostal viewpoints. Others preach a prosperity gospel that promises material, financial, physical, and spiritual success to believers, usually subject to their offerings to the "work of God." Televangelists address the needs and tastes of average people, and use psychotherapy and the language of popular culture to compete with great success in the spiritual marketplace. The televised church services of Joel Osteen's Lakewood Church in Houston, Texas, and Robert Schuller's Crystal Cathedral in Garden Grove, California, for example, attract large audiences. Televangelism requires substantial amounts of money to produce programs and purchase airtime on cable and satellite networks. Thus products such as books, CDs, DVDs, and trinkets are promoted to viewers. Some televangelists have significant personal wealth and own large properties, luxury cars and private aircraft. This is seen by critics to be contradictory to traditional Christian thinking. Yet these evangelists pastor some the largest churches in the nation, lead vast spiritual networks, write best-selling books and are among the most influential preachers in American Protestantism.

A new breed of Evangelical leaders with new emphases in doctrine and presentation is coming to the fore. *Robert A. Schuller*, son of televangelist Robert H. Schuller, has teamed up with

GodTube.com co-founder Chris Wyatt to create ComStar Media Fund, a limited partnership that acquires media properties that globally distribute family-values programming through television, mobile and internet platforms. Among their first acquisitions is the popular "baby boomer" network AmericanLife TV Network (ALN), which thrives as the only independent network devoted to America's baby boomer generation and their families. It delivers classic TV, lifestyle, original and socially responsible programming that addresses issues important to boomers. Schuller and Wyatt are not creating another religious network but a new channel with family-values programming that speaks to all generations.

Rick Warren, an evangelical minister of the Southern Baptist Convention, has become one of the most influential religious leaders in the US. He is the founder (1980) and senior pastor of Saddleback Church, a megachurch in Lake Forest, California, currently the eighth-largest church in the US, with an average weekly attendance of 20,000. Warren is a bestselling author of many books, including his guide to ministry and evangelism, *The Purpose Driven Church*, which has been used all over the world. He says his organization has trained 400,000 pastors worldwide in how to balance the five "purposes" - worship, fellowship, discipleship, ministry, and evangelism - in their churches. Warren's methods have led the Saddleback Church to grow rapidly, although some say his techniques can be divisive. *Wall Street Journal* writer Suzanne Sataline cited examples of congregations who have split over the growth strategies and congregations that have expelled members who fought changes, although Warren says he opposes efforts to expel church members. He is perhaps best known for his devotional, *The Purpose Driven Life*, which has sold over 30 million copies, making Warren a *New York Times* bestselling author. Due to the success of his book sales, he and his wife have become "reverse tithers," giving away 90% of their income and living off 10%. Warren has been invited to speak at high-level national and international forums.

Warren regards Billy Graham as among his mentors and, like Graham, holds conservative theological views. But at the same time, Warren has strived to change the narrow focus of the evangelical movement from issues such as abortion, same-sex marriage, and stem-cell research to wider concerns such as poverty. He has also called on churches worldwide to focus their efforts more on fighting disease, including the spread of HIV/AIDS, expanding literacy and educational opportunities, and caring for the environment. Regarding same-sex marriage, he once called divorce a greater threat to the American family. The intention of his P E A C E Plan is to involve every Christian and every church in every nation in the task of serving people in the areas of the greatest global needs. P E A C E is an acronym: "Promote reconciliation - Equip servant leaders - Assist the poor - Care for the sick - Educate the next generation." In February 2006, in one of his most criticized moves, he signed a statement backing a major initiative to combat global warming, thus breaking with other high-profile conservative evangelical leaders who had opposed the move. Polls have indicated that most evangelicals are skeptical of global warming theories, especially those related to human culpability.

Warren played a part in the 2008 Presidential election and in the inauguration of the new President. In August 2008, he hosted the Civil Forum on the Presidency, at which the two candidates answered questions on their religious beliefs and moral attitudes. Warren explained that its purpose was to "restore civility in our civil discourse." During the two-hour event, which was broadcast live on national television, each candidate took the stage separately for about an hour to respond to Warren's questions about faith and moral issues including abortion and human rights. Obama later ignited controversy when he asked Warren to give the invocation at the presidential inauguration in

January 2009. The invitation angered pro-choice and LGBT advocates and led to criticism of both Obama and Warren. Obama defended his choice of Warren, saying that although he disagreed with the minister's positions on abortion and same-sex marriage, there should be room for dialogue on such difficult social issues. The Invocation was generally praised for its positive message.

Warren's conservative views have sparked several controversies. In a *Newsweek* article, he denounced the theory of evolution and advocated its fundamentalist alternative, creationism. When asked whether religion was beneficial to society, he answered by making the point that brutal dictators such as Stalin and Pol Pot were atheists. During the Terri Schiavo controversy (about whether the life-support machine of a patient in a coma should be switched off), Warren called her husband Michael Schiavo's decision to remove her feeding tube "an atrocity worthy of Nazism." (An autopsy showed she would never have recovered.) Two weeks before the 2008 election, consistent with the official position of the Southern Baptist Convention, Warren issued a statement to his congregation endorsing Proposition 8, which would amend the California Constitution to make only heterosexual marriage valid or recognized. After the measure passed, Warren's church and others were targeted by protesters. In an interview with Beliefnet later, Warren again provoked controversy by appearing to equate same-sex marriages to marriages of siblings, multiple partners, and adults and minors. He later released a video saying he does not equate gay relationships with incest or pedophilia.

Joel Osteen, bestselling author and senior pastor of Lakewood Church, stands at the intersection of faith, commerce and politics. Since Osteen succeeded his father as senior pastor in 1999, Lakewood's congregation has increased fivefold and now numbers over 43,000 per week, the largest congregation in the US. Lakewood now occupies the 16,000-seat arena previously home to the Houston Rockets. The church's weekly services are broadcast on both religious and secular TV including *ABC Family*, *Fox News Channel*, and *USA Network*. Osteen's ministry reaches over seven million broadcast media viewers weekly in the US and millions more in over 100 nations around the world. In 2007, Lakewood reported spending nearly $30 million every year on its television ministry.

Joel Osteen served for 17 years as producer of his father's televised church services. Osteen's first book, *Your Best Life Now: 7 Steps to Living at Your Full Potential*, was released in October 2004. In it he details how readers should enlarge their vision, develop self-esteem, discover the power of thought, let go of the past, find strength through adversity, give back to others and choose to be happy Osteen was named one of the year's "Ten Most Fascinating People" by ABC News' Barbara Walters in December 2006.

Osteen is nationally known for the public worship event "A Night of Hope," conducted in large stadiums by himself and several other members of the Lakewood team. The event includes music led by the church's music ministry, a testimony by Joel's mother Dodie and a sermon from Osteen. The tour has expanded to include stops in several other countries, including Canada, England, Northern Ireland, Israel and Australia. Osteen released his second book, titled *Become a Better You: 7 Keys to Improving Your Life Every Day* in October 2007, which also topped the New York Times Best Sellers List. That year Osteen was also named "Most Influential Christian in America" 2006 by *The Church Report*.

Osteen teaches personal growth with a Christian slant, focusing on the goodness of God rather than sin. When asked why he does not include many Bible verses in his books, he says he sees himself as more of a life coach, trying to teach Biblical principles in a simple way, emphasizing the power of love and a positive attitude. Osteen has received much criticism from the evangelical community for the lack of Scripture reference in his sermons also, as well as his downplaying of sin, repentance and atonement. Critics claim that he implies that heaven is on earth, and that the believer who is not enjoying the material abundance that he and his wife enjoy is simply not spiritual. He has been accused of preaching a man-centred materialist gospel focused on what God can do for believers, not how they can serve him, a prosperity gospel that encourages an entitlement mentality and a vacuous spirituality, a worldly, self-centred pop psychology without much theology or eschatology (afterlife, judgment or Second Coming). Osteen has also received criticism for his lack of formal theological training. He studied at Oral Roberts University for two years, but did not study theology or religion in college, and has never attended a theological seminary. Nevertheless he remains enormously popular and his ministry continues to grow.

From another perspective, sociologist Robert Bellah and co-authors critique the way the politically neutralizing individualistic "therapeutic mode" has penetrated into religious life. This, they say, has led to the loss of "communities of memory" based on shared values, along with the "second language" of religious and republican virtue, the language of the Bible and the Founders. Where once there was a language of sin and redemption, there is now only the therapeutic language of the self, by which the individual is encouraged to consider himself or herself and his or her happiness as paramount, thus reinforcing the ideology of the free market.

Coming from a very different background, *Brian McLaren*, the founding pastor of the nondenominational Cedar Ridge Community Church in Spencerville, near Baltimore, Maryland, is a prominent, controversial voice in the Emergent Church movement. After teaching English literature and consulting in higher education, he left to found Cedar Ridge in 1986. The church has grown to several hundred people, many of whom were previously unchurched.

The Emerging Church movement rejects what proponents perceive to be the influence of modernism among evangelicals in favor of a postmodern epistemology (theory of knowledge) which guides their faith and praxis (way of doing things). McLaren believes this epistemology enables him to approach faith from what he considers a more Jewish perspective, which allows personal trust in God without objective, propositional truth. A postfoundationalist, he questions not only the evangelical claim to certainty in faith, but also the ability to interpret according to authorial intent. To him, our interpretations reveal less about God or the Bible than they do about ourselves; meaning comes not from the author or the text but the reader. Often McLaren's view of Biblical interpretation seems to call for others to rethink the whole process of interpretation.

McLaren favors what he calls a "generous" approach to biblical interpretation and explanation (hermeneutics). He claims that the hermeneutical method of evangelicals — taking the Bible as an unassailable foundation for knowledge and that it reveals objective truth - leads them to become oppressive and politically conservative. He has been an outspoken advocate on social justice and peace. Often McLaren takes a less traditional approach towards controversial issues such as homosexuality. He encourages humility to enable productive dialog. McLaren also suggests that new Christian converts should remain within their own religion. To help them, he says, he would enter into their world without judgment but with saving love, as his world has been entered by the Lord. Many of McLaren's books, including *A Generous Orthodoxy, More Ready Than You Realize*, and the trilogy *A New Kind of Christian*, deal with Christianity in the context of the cultural shift towards postmodernity.

McLaren is active in networking and mentoring church planters and pastors. He is on the international steering team and board of directors for Emergent Village; a growing, generative friendship among missional (community-focused) Christian leaders, and serves as a board member for Sojourners and Orientación Cristiana. In spite of the intense criticism leveled at him by some evangelical leaders, he remains a popular speaker nationally and internationally on numerous topics including postmodernism, Biblical studies, evangelism, apologetics, leadership, global mission, church growth, church planting, art and music, pastoral survival and burnout, inter-religious dialogue, ecology, and social justice.

Brian McLaren has come under criticism from both within and without the Emerging Church movement. Generally critics claim that McLaren's epistemology provides no basis for doctrine, which is thus abandoned in favor of "generosity" and "conversation." Conservative Emergents like Mark Driscoll, and a number of evangelicals, have protested that McLaren's philosophical position has led him to unorthodox positions. Driscoll has complained about McLaren's "open theism," his downplaying of substitutionary atonement, and his implicit denial of hell. Evangelical D. A. Carson claims that McLaren has largely abandoned the gospel (*Becoming Conversant with the Emerging Church*, (2005), p.186).

Lobbying

American Christians from various traditions are renowned for their use of lobbying. The Institute for Religion and Democracy campaigns against the progressive national leaderships of mainstream churches such as the Episcopalians, Lutherans and United Methodists, in pursuance of a partisan conservative agenda. IRD is incorporated as a tax-exempt charitable organization as many such bodies are. Groups of this sort do not encourage people to leave their churches but to change them from within. Conservative lobbying groups interact frequently, their board members tend to sit on each other's boards, and they are mainly funded by the same small group of wealthy donors.

Tim LaHaye is a founder of the Moral Majority. His wife, Beverly, founded Concerned Women for America. He is author of the *Left Behind* and *Babylon Rising* series of books which apply a literal, premillennialist interpretation of prophecy to current events to show that we are living in the End Time and should prepare for the physical Second Coming of Christ. These books have sold over 70 million copies and have helped change the way that conservative voters evaluate American foreign policy, particularly in the Middle East.

American Episcopal conservatives, meanwhile, through such organizations as the American Anglican Council, have funded dissident movements in the Anglican communion, the second widest-spread of all Christian churches after the Catholics. These activities have been blamed for the 2008 boycott of Anglicanism's worldwide decennial gathering of bishops, the Lambeth Conference in England, by a quarter of the bishops. American conservatives are also known to be playing a part in changes in the Anglican diocese of Central Africa.

The Sojourners community, by contrast, are mostly Democrats. In the tradition of radical evangelicalism, they stress justice, compassion, humility, repentance and reconciliation. They are much more concerned with child poverty and the environment than gay marriage. Sojourners publish a monthly magazine with a mailing list of 250,000 evangelicals committed to social justice.

The International Christian Embassy in Jerusalem (ICEJ) is an influential group of Christian Zionists, who teach that we are living in the End Time and that world events are moving to a final conflict between Christ and Anti-Christ. As a result, Christ will reign on earth for 1,000 years and the biblical land of Israel will be permanently established. The ICEJ and similar groups pressure the US government always to support Israel and be hostile to the Palestinians. Israeli leaders speak at ICEJ events, and also make use of preachers such as Pat Robertson to spread Israeli propaganda in the US. Dan Cohn-Sherbok (cited by Bates, *ibid.*, p. 326) estimates there are 3,250 pro-Israeli evangelical organizations in the US. Organizations such as Christians United for Israel have encouraged the US government to attack Iran.

The Catholics

The first Catholic congregations were made up of Irish and German immigrants, who were later joined by southern and eastern Europeans around the turn of the 20th century. Catholics were for many years a "ghetto" church, concentrated in New York, Boston, Baltimore and Chicago, where churches and neighborhoods provided refuge from an otherwise unfamiliar and often hostile environment. Yet, beginning in the second half of the 19th century, bishops, priests, and nuns built a remarkable array of Catholic institutions – orphanages, schools, universities and hospitals, for example – right across the nation. Catholics voted Democrat but had no effect on national events. It was not until 1928 that a Catholic ran for President. He was Al Smith, governor of New York, who had come up through the notorious Tammany Hall system of influence. He lost to Herbert Hoover, partly because people thought he would take his orders from the Pope. John F. Kennedy, elected in 1960, was the first Catholic President. Kennedy reassured voters that he could not imagine a situation in which his Catholic faith or the teachings of his Church would prevent him from carrying out his responsibilities as President; and, if such a situation ever arose, Kennedy promised, he would resign from office. Senator John Kerry, a Catholic, ran for President in 2004 and also had to disavow claims that he would be influenced by the church. Indeed some US bishops threatened to deny Kerry the Holy Communion because of his support of abortion rights, although most of the laity disagreed. Catholics are no longer solidly Democrat, although they are not reliably Republican either. Many of the theorists and campaigners of the Religious Right, such as Pat Buchanan, are Catholics. Catholic bishops, as well as campaigning against abortion, have also made influential statements on economic justice and nuclear disarmament. The Catholic church recently met severe criticism over its treatment of pedophile priests. Catholics own radio and TV stations, such as EWTN, the Eternal Word Television Network, which expounds conservative Catholic theology.

The Catholic Church in the US is in a state of profound transition. Affiliation and participation have fallen considerably since the Second Vatican Council closed in 1965. Vocations to the priesthood have fallen 90% and there have been massive defections from the priesthood by priests planning to get married. By 2020, if present trends continue (and there is no sign of a dramatic upsurge in vocations), half the parish priests will be over 70. The increasing affluence and integration of Catholics into society has been responsible for part of this change, as entry into the priesthood became only one of many routes to professional status. Also, the average size of the American family (influenced by affluence and the increased availability of contraception) has dropped from seven to four, meaning fewer men were being born. (Only men can be Catholic priests.) The number of priests per Catholic layperson began to decline as early as the 1940s. Hundreds of priests have been dismissed for sexually abusing children. Yet accusations have been brought against fewer than 2% of Catholic clergy since 1965, and the scandal has not seemed to lessen sacramental participation or even financial contributions to the Church. On any given Sunday as many as 40 percent of American Catholics may be attending Mass even though some of them do not attend Mass regularly. Indeed, statistics suggest that the decline in many areas of

Church life is bottoming out.

There are approximately 69 million Catholics in the US in 195 dioceses. The percentage of Catholics in the population has remained fairly steady in the last forty years, hovering around a quarter of the population. The actual number of Catholics may be millions more, due to illegal immigration by Hispanics. Increasingly the Catholic Church in America is bilingual. On the handling of the Hispanic immigrant population rests the future of the Church in the US. The only religious congregations showing signs of life and attracting many vocations are strongly faithful and evangelizing men's congregations like the Franciscan Friars of the Renewal and the Legionaries of Christ. Similarly, among women, congregations that wear full habit and have a strong prayer and community life are drawing many vocations — the Nashville Dominicans and Mother Angelica's Poor Clares being outstanding examples. The traditional Carmels also continue to attract a steady stream of young vocations.

Almost half the Catholic schools open in 1965 have closed; 4.5 million students attended Catholic schools in the mid-1960s, while today there are about half that many. The number of teaching nuns has fallen 94 percent from the close of the Council, while the number of young men studying to become members of the two principal teaching orders, the Jesuits and Christian Brothers, has fallen by 90 percent and 99 percent respectively. The US bishops recognize 224 colleges and universities as Catholic. Two of them, Georgetown and Notre Dame University, are generally included among the top 25 universities in the US, but only some 15 have theology faculties who have as a whole received authority from the local diocesan bishop allowing faculty to teach Catholic theology. Over the last 30 years, however, over a dozen new Catholic colleges have been founded, and at least six new Catholic colleges and universities are under development.

Among other characteristics of the Catholic population, it is notable that Catholic families have about the same number of children as non-Catholics. Catholics tend to have fewer abortions than the rest of the population, but not by a large percentage. Catholics are 30 percent less likely to divorce than the rest of the population, and active Catholics are 50% less likely to divorce than unaffiliated/secular Americans.

Episcopalians

Episcopalians are part of the worldwide Anglican Communion, a family of churches with 77 million members which stems from the Church of England in Britain. These churches are moderately Protestant in doctrine and semi-catholic in church order and ritual. They lay stress on their historic continuity with the faith of the Western church of the early centuries as declared in the three Catholic Creeds and ministered through an unbroken succession of bishops. They develop their teachings through a dynamic interplay between scripture, reason and tradition. Episcopalians have two million adherents in the US. The Episcopal Church of the USA (ECUSA) is socially liberal and has been fiercely criticized inside and outside the US for the consecration in 2005 of an openly gay man, Gene Robinson, as bishop of New Hampshire and in 2010 of Mary Glasspool as an assistant bishop in California (see *A Church at War: Anglicans and Homosexuality*, Stephen Bates, I. B. Taurus, 2004). The 2006 election of Katharine Jefferts Schori to be Presiding Bishop, the first ever female primate of a major Christian denomination, has also been controversial. Although a small denomination which has nothing like the influence of the Church of England, the Episcopalians are a wealthy church and are associated with the establishment. Senator John McCain is an Episcopalian, as is former President George H. W. Bush. In late 2008 it was announced that some conservative Episcopal parishes planned to seek recognition from the rest of the Anglican Communion as a separate province. They founded the Anglican Church in North America in 2009.

African American churches

Across the country, separate denominations and congregations exist which are predominantly composed of African Americans or European Americans. Reconciliation among European Americans, not integration with African Americans, was the aim of the great majority of Northern Christians after the Civil War, since feelings of racial superiority were almost universal. Although there has been integration in the last 50 years, some separate African American churches do exist and some are in fact growing, often under the influence of the Pentecostal movement.

Enslaved Africans were unable to maintain all of their native religious practices, partly because of restrictions, and also because they were often mixed together with people of different tribes. Knowledge of spirit rituals to honor and call up the spirits of ancestors, cast healing spells, protect against harm and divine the future seems, however, to have been widespread and to have continued through Emancipation. Call and response interactions, shouting, and dance also survived and became incorporated into African American Christian worship.

Segregation was a prime reason for the foundation of separate black churches. The first people to found black congregations were free blacks who wanted to practice religion free from white oversight. Before 1800 they had founded churches in both northern and southern cities. Two black churches were born in Philadelphia out of protest against being relegated to a segregated gallery at St. George's Methodist Church. In 1787, preachers Absalom Jones and Richard Allen, and other black members, left and formed the Free African Society, a mutual aid and worship group. At first, services were non-denominational, but over time Jones began to lead Episcopal services. Finally, with most of the members, he created the African Church in the Episcopal tradition. This was accepted as a parish and in 1794 became the African Episcopal Church of St. Thomas. Richard Allen, however, continued in the Methodist tradition and founded the Bethel African Methodist Episcopal Church, also in 1794. This was active in antislavery campaigns, fought racism in the North, and started schools for black children. In 1816, together with other black congregations, Allen organized the African Methodist Episcopal Church (AME), the first fully independent black denomination. He and Jones continued to work closely together.

Another reason that African Americans began to take leadership roles in worship and to found their own churches was the Great Awakening of the late 18th century. In this period, evangelical preachers, particularly Baptists and Methodists, traveled throughout the South preaching directly to slaves, and many converted. Blacks found opportunities for active roles in new congregations, especially in the Baptist Church, where slaves were appointed as leaders and preachers. (They were excluded from such roles in the Episcopal church of the owners.) From Bible readings, slaves found inspiration in stories of deliverance such as the Exodus from Egypt. Slaveholders also often held prayer meetings at their plantations. Petersburg, Virginia had two of the oldest black congregations in the country, both Baptist, one dating from 1774, followed by Gillfield Baptist Church in 1797. Each congregation moved from rural areas into Petersburg and into their own buildings in the early 1800s. By 1777, a black Baptist congregation was organized in Savannah, Georgia by George Liele, a freedman, encouraged by his master, Henry Sharp, a Baptist deacon and Loyalist. After 1782, when Liele left the city with the British, Andrew Bryan led what became known as the First

African Baptist Church. By 1800 the church had 700 members, free blacks and slaves, and by 1830 it had grown to more than 2,400. The black churches provided mutual aid to the free black community and, along with white churches opposed to slavery, provided aid and comfort to slaves who escaped, and helped new arrivals adjust to city life.

Before Emancipation, however, most African Americans worshiped in unorganized ways, or in underground churches and secret religious meetings, known as the "invisible church," where evangelical Christianity became mixed with African beliefs and ritual. The underground churches provided psychological refuge from the white world. The singing of spirituals gave the church members a secret way to communicate and, in some cases, to plan rebellion. Following slave revolts in the early 1800s, including Nat Turner's Rebellion in 1831, however, Virginia and other states passed laws requiring black congregations to meet only in the presence of a white minister. Nevertheless, the black Baptist congregations in the cities grew rapidly and their members numbered several hundred each before the Civil War. While led by free blacks, most of their members were slaves. Although in the early years of the first Great Awakening, Methodist and Baptist preachers argued for manumission and abolition, by the early decades of the 19th century, they had often found ways to support slavery. Where whites supervised worship and prayer, they used Bible stories such as the Curse of Ham (Genesis 9: 20-27) that taught slaves to be loyal and obedient to their masters, and promoted the idea that loyal and hard-working slaves would be rewarded in the afterlife.

After Emancipation, legal and social segregation continued, and this created an environment in which the separate development of white and black churches could take place. African Americans established more of their own separate congregations and church facilities where worship and community life were conducted in distinct ways developed from the traditions of the underground churches and the freely established black churches. In any case, segregation in the South prevented African Americans from worshiping in the same churches as whites, while in the North segregationist attitudes discouraged it. The tradition of African Americans worshiping together continued to develop during the late 19th century and continues to this day despite the decline of segregationist attitudes and the general acceptability of integrated worship. African American churches have long been the centers of communities, taking up social welfare functions, such as providing for the indigent, and going on to establish schools, orphanages and prison ministries. As a result, black churches have fostered strong community organizations and provided spiritual and political leadership, especially during the civil rights movement.

Meanwhile, Northern churches, both black churches such as the AME, and predominantly white denominations, sent missions to the South to minister to newly freed slaves, including the teaching of reading and writing. In the first year after the Civil War, the AME Church gained 50,000 congregants. By the end of Reconstruction in 1877, there were AME congregations from Florida to Texas, totaling more than 250,000 adherents. Similarly, the African Methodist Episcopal Zion church also gained tens of thousands of Southern members. The AME Zion Church, like the AME Church, is an offshoot of the Methodist Episcopal (ME) Church. Black members of the John Street Methodist Church of New York City left to form their own church after several acts of overt discrimination by white members. In 1796 they asked permission of the bishop to meet independently, though still as part of the ME Church and led by white preachers. This group built Zion chapel in 1800. In 1822, members separated further from the ME Church with the ordination, after some debate, of Abraham Thompson, Leven Smith, and James Varick, as their first superintendent (bishop). After the Civil War, the denomination sent missionaries to the South and attracted thousands of new members, who greatly affected the church's future. These two independent black denominations attracted the most new members in the South.

A flourishing independent African American branch of Methodism was founded in 1870, which grew from 40,000 to 67,000 worshipers within three years. This was as a result of a conference of black Southern ministers, all former slaves, in Jackson, Tennessee. A new denomination, the Colored Methodist Episcopal (CME) Church (now the Christian Methodist Episcopal Church), was established with support from white colleagues in the Methodist Episcopal Church, South, At the same time, black Baptist churches, well-established before the Civil War, continued to grow and add new congregations, so rapidly that in 1894 church officials organized a new association, the National Baptist Convention, USA, Inc., which is now the largest black religious organization in the US. First organized in 1880 as the Foreign Mission Baptist Convention in Montgomery, Alabama, its founders, including Elias Camp Morris, stressed the preaching of the gospel as an answer to the shortcomings of a segregated church. In 1895, Morris moved to Atlanta, Georgia, and founded the Convention through a merger of the Foreign Mission Convention, the American National Baptist Convention, and the Baptist National Education Convention. In 1897, Charles Harrison Mason formed the Church of God in Christ (COGIC) after his Baptist church expelled him for promoting the Holiness Movement. In 1906, he attended the Azusa Street Revival in Los Angeles and on his return to Tennessee began teaching the Pentecostal Holiness message. At a conference in Memphis, Tennessee, Mason reorganized COGIC as an episcopal Pentecostal body. His colleagues Charles Price Jones and J. A. Jeter, however, disagreed with Mason's teachings on the Baptism of the Holy Spirit and separated in 1907, renaming their congregations the Church of Christ (Holiness) USA in 1915. The Assemblies of God separated on racial lines in 1914. In recent years, the COGIC and the Assemblies of God have dedicated themselves to reconciling and healing the two organizations, by working together in common ministries. During the formative years, Mason credentialed both whites and African Americans who would subsequently become leaders within other Pentecostal denominations such as the Assemblies of God, the Pentecostal Assemblies of the World, and the United Pentecostal Church International. COGIC believes in divine healing, but does not advocate forgoing conventional medicine. General Mother/Supervisor Lillian Brooks Coffey (1945-1964) was the organizer of the 1st International Women's Convention (1951). The headquarters of COGIC, Mason Temple in Memphis, is the site of Martin Luther King's final sermon, "I've Been to the Mountaintop," delivered the day before he was assassinated. COGIC began in the southern states of Tennessee, Mississippi, and Arkansas. Since then it has experienced phenomenal growth. As African Americans moved north during the Great Migration, members spread the church north and west. It now claims 5.4 million members.

In the years after the Civil War, black churches were the focal points of black communities, and the secession of their members from white churches demonstrated their desire to manage their own affairs independently of white supervision. This resulted in growing tension between black leaders from the North and those in the South who wanted to run their churches and worship in their own way. It also showed how strong the "invisible church" had been. Black preachers provided leadership, encouraged education and economic growth, and were a link between the black and white communities. The black churches ran the first black schools and encouraged community members to fund these schools and other public services. For most black leaders, the churches always were linked to the political goal of advancing the race. Since the male hierarchy denied them opportunities for ordination, middle class women in the black churches asserted themselves in other ways: they organized missionary societies to address social issues. These societies provided job training and reading education, worked for better living conditions, raised money for African missions, wrote religious periodicals, and promoted Victorian ideals of womanhood, respectability, and racial uplift. Black churches held a leadership role in the American Civil Rights Movement. Their history as a centers of strength for the black community made them natural leaders in this moral struggle. Notable minister-activists of the 1950s and 1960s included Rev. Martin Luther King, Jr. and Ralph David Abernathy. The black churches continue to be a source of support for members of the African American community. Compared to other American churches, black churches tend to focus more on social issues such as poverty, gang violence, drug use, prison ministries and racism. Black churches are typically very conservative on sexual issues such as homosexuality. Most surveys indicate that while blacks tend to vote Democrat in elections, black churches are generally more socially conservative than white evangelicals.

An offshoot of the Civil Rights movement was the black liberation theology movement. It is accepted that this movement originated with the full-page "Black Power Statement" placed in *The New York Times* of July 31, 1966 by a group of 51 black pastors calling themselves the National Committee of Negro Churchmen (NCNC). The ad proposed a more aggressive approach to combating racism using the Bible for inspiration. Black liberation theology was first systematized by James Cone and Dwight Hopkins. In 1969 Cone published the work that laid the basis for black liberation theology, *Black Theology and Black Power*. In it, Cone asserted that not only was black power not alien to the Gospel, it was, in fact, the Gospel message for all of 20th century America. In 2008, approximately one-quarter of African American churches followed a liberation theology. The theology was thrust into the national spotlight after a controversy arose over preaching by Rev. Jeremiah Wright, former pastor to then-Senator Barack Obama at Trinity United Church of Christ, Chicago. Wright had built Trinity into a successful megachurch following the theology developed by Cone, who has said that he would "point to [Trinity] first" as an example of a church embodying his message.

In black urban neighborhoods in cities where industry has moved away and public services such as schools, police and fire protection have lost funding, the churches help to improve the physical and social capital and are an important source of social cohesion. For some African Americans the kind of spirituality learned through these churches works as a protective factor against the corrosive forces of poverty and racism. Churches in Harlem have undertaken real estate ventures and renovated burnt-out and abandoned brownstones to create new housing for residents. Churches have also fought for the right to operate their own schools in place of the often inadequate public schools. For some African Americans the kind of spirituality learned through these churches works as a protective factor against the corrosive forces of poverty and racism

The main black denominations are: the African Union First Colored Methodist Protestant Church and Connection; Apostolic Faith Mission; Christian Methodist Episcopal Church; National Baptist Convention of America, Inc.; National Missionary Baptist Convention of America; Pentecostal Assemblies of the World; Progressive National Baptist Convention; Spiritual Israel Church and Its Army; United House of Prayer for All People; and United Holy Church of America, Inc. While some black churches such as African Methodist Episcopal belong to predominantly African American denominations, many are members of predominantly white denominations such as the United Church of Christ (which developed from the Congregational Church of New England).

Other Christian denominations

Other Christian denominations founded in the US include the Children of God, Christian Churches/Churches of Christ, Christadelphians, Christian and Missionary Alliance, Churches of Christ (undenominational), Christian Church (Disciples of Christ - President Lyndon B. Johnson was a member.), Grace International, and the United Church of Christ. Smaller faith groups include the Amish, Hutterites, Mennonites and Shakers. There are also para-church groups that are not churches, such as the Fellowship of Christian Athletes, Promise Keepers, and Bible Study Fellowship.

Church membership

The 2007 edition of *The Yearbook of Canadian and American Churches,* widely considered the nation's oldest and most reliable source of church membership and growth trends, reports a record number of 224 national church bodies. The figures reflect the continued overall vitality of church participation, and account for the religious affiliation of almost 166 million Americans. Only three mainline Protestant churches are among the ten largest churches: the United Methodist Church (ranked 3); the Evangelical Lutheran Church in America (ranked 7); and the Presbyterian Church, USA (ranked 9). All three churches declined in membership since the 2006 *Yearbook* was released. Pentecostal churches have experienced "remarkable" growth, says the editor. For example, the Assemblies of God reported a membership of 50,386 in the 1925 edition of the *Yearbook.* This year, its reported membership is 2,830,861.

1. The Catholic Church, 69,135,254 members, reporting an increase of 1.94 percent.
2. The Southern Baptist Convention, 16,270,315 members, reporting an increase of .02 percent.
3. The United Methodist Church, 8,075,010 members, reporting a decrease of 1.36 percent.
4. The Church of Jesus Christ of Latter-day Saints, 5,690,672 members, reporting an increase of 1.63 percent.
5. The Church of God in Christ, 5,499,875 members, no increase or decrease reported.
6. National Baptist Convention, USA, Inc., 5,000,000 members, no increase or decrease reported.
7. Evangelical Lutheran Church in America, 4,850,776, reporting a decrease of 1.62 percent.
8. National Baptist Convention of America, 3,500,000, no increase or decrease reported.
9. Presbyterian Church (USA), 3,098,842 members, reporting a decrease of 2.84 percent.
10. Assemblies of God, 2,830,861 members, reporting an increase of 1.86 percent.
11. African Methodist Episcopal Church, 2,500,000 members, no increase or decrease reported.
12. National Missionary Baptist Convention of America, 2,500,000 members, no increase or decrease reported.
13. Progressive National Baptist Convention, Inc., 2,500,000 members, no increase or decrease reported.
14. The Lutheran Church – Missouri Synod (LCMS), 2,440,864, reporting a decrease or .93 percent.
15. Episcopal Church, 2,247,819, reporting a decrease of 1.59 percent.
16. Churches of Christ, 1,639,495 members, reporting an increase of 9.30 percent (This increase reports the church's growth since its last reported figures in 1999.)
17. Greek Orthodox Archdiocese of America, 1,500,000 members, no increase or decrease reported.

18. Pentecostal Assemblies of the World, Inc., 1,500,000 members, no increase or decrease reported.
19. The African Methodist Episcopal Zion Church, 1,440,405 members, reporting an increase of .53 percent.
20. American Baptist Churches in the USA, 1,396,700, reporting a decrease of 1.97 percent.
21. United Church of Christ, 1,224,297, reporting a decrease of 3.28 percent.
22. Baptist Bible Fellowship International, 1,200,000, no increase or decrease reported.
23. Christian Churches and Churches of Christ, 1,071,615 members, no increase or decrease reported.
24. The Orthodox Church in America, 1,064,000 members, no increase or decrease reported.
25. Jehovah's Witnesses, 1,046,006 members, reporting an increase of 1.56 percent.

The total members reported in the largest 25 communions is 149,222,807, an overall increase of .82 percent.

There are several reasons why there are so many churches and religions in America. First and most importantly, the US was founded and continues to be a nation of diverse immigrants, and throughout history there has been a strong interrelationship between ethnic and religious identity and community, in part fostered by the separation of church and state (which gave special protections and other benefits to religious organizations) and in part because several of the early groups were dissenters in their country of origin. This fostered a strong culture of religious identification that continues today e.g., Irish and now Latino Catholics; German and Swedish Lutherans. Similarly, racial segregation played a part. Second, the American form of church-state separation fostered and continues to foster religious innovation e.g., Methodists, Pentecostals and most recently megachurches. No church is supported by government and thus none can have a monopoly. Nor does government act as the secular arm of the church. Moreover the distance from Europe meant weaker control by mother churches. Even in the strictly hierarchical Catholic Church, American Catholics may have different views from European Catholics. For example, they accept the separation of church and state. In the same way, until the mid-19th century especially, distance and difficulties in communications allowed local congregations to develop independently. In modern times, easier access to broadcast communications, and the money to fund it, have opened opportunities to religious entrepreneurs. These have notably been grasped by those with a strong belief in the Second Coming and the need to obey the Great Commission to go out and make disciples of all nations. It is possible also that the absence of a strong communist labor movement left a void for "blue collar" workers that was filled by emergent religious awakenings.

Religion in the US today

The key fact about religion in the US today is the shift away from organized observance of Christianity and other religions, although overall the American Religious Identification Survey (ARIS) 1990-2008 time series, conducted by the Graduate Center, City University of New York, shows that changes in religious self-identification in the first decade of the 21st century have been moderate in comparison to the 1990s, which was a period of significant shifts in the religious composition of the US. According to ARIS 2008, the proportion of the American population that can be classified as Christian had declined from 86 percent in 1990 to 76 percent. The people of the US form the most profusely religious nation on earth. Contrary to widespread assertions, the statistics do not reflect a revival of religion, although they do show an increase in non-Christian and non-traditional religions.

Even so, 81 percent of American adults identify themselves with a specific religion, 76.5 percent (159 million) with Christianity. Of these, 52 percent are Protestant and 24.5 percent Catholic. In addition, 1.3 percent of Americans are Jewish and 0.6 percent Muslim (2.35 million); although some claim the figure for Muslims is between 6 and 8 million. The fastest-growing religion (in terms of percentage) is Wicca, a neopagan religion that is sometimes referred to as *white witchcraft*. Numbers of adherents went from 8,000 in 1990 to 134,000 in 2001 and are doubling about every 30 months. As many as 16.1 percent (some 35 million) of Americans do not follow any organized religion (2007). This is an unusually rapid increase, a doubling, from only 8 percent in 1990. There are now more Americans who say they are not affiliated with any organized religion than there are Episcopalians, Methodists, and Lutherans taken together. The polarization of Christianity by evangelicals has, according to studies, contributed to this trend.

A *USA Today*/Gallup Poll in January 2002 showed that almost half of American adults appear to be alienated from organized religion: about 50 percent consider themselves religious (down from 54 percent in December 1999); about 33 percent consider themselves spiritual but not religious (up from 30 percent); and about 10 percent regard themselves as neither spiritual nor religious.

Exact figures are impossible to obtain, however. Religions count their adherents in different ways, refuse to release membership figures, or do not count them at all. The US Census does not collect data on religious affiliations. Of the 258 identified religious bodies in the US, only 149 cooperated in the Religious Congregations and Membership Study (RCMS) survey. Many of the missing bodies are small, independent churches, but 14 say they have memberships of 100,000 or more. One, the Jehovah's Witnesses, has 990,340 members. Also serious, from a statistical standpoint, is the absence of most major African American churches. Combined, they report 18 million members, but some experts call the figure exaggerated.

Meanwhile there are many people who say they believe in God but do not belong to any religion. Thus there can be a big difference between surveys that report what people say about their religion and surveys that report official church membership figures. Also to be taken into account is a significant and growing group of non-religious secular humanists of various shades of opinion. Nevertheless, although the margin of error varies somewhat throughout the survey, ARIS is considered very accurate and the broad trends it reveals are not in dispute. The National Council of Churches of Christ claims to represent 40 million mainstream worshippers. The Religious Right and liberal/progressive Christians are about equal in number, some 10% of the electorate.

Religion among cultural and ethnic groups

Hispanics comprise the largest minority group in the US. Although many assume that they are overwhelmingly Roman Catholic, their religious identification is quite diverse: 57 percent Roman Catholic, 22 percent Protestant, 5 percent other religion; and 12 percent no organized religion. Jews in America consist of about 5.3 million adults: 53 percent followers of Judaism, 26 percent of other religions, and 20 percent of no organized religion. Native Americans consist of 20 percent Baptist, 17 percent Catholic, 17 percent of no organized religion, and 3 percent tribal religion.

Interfaith marriages

The ARIS survey found that 22 percent of couples reported that they identified with *different* faith groups. Defining the term "couple" broadly to include both married and living together partners, some 28 million adults live in a mixed religion household. Percentages range from a high of 42 percent for Episcopalian to a low of 12 percent for Mormons. Adult groups of whom 30 percent live in mixed faith homes include Buddhists, non-denominational Christians and Jehovah's Witnesses. Adult groups of whom fewer than 20 percent live in mixed-faith homes are members of Protestant denominations such as Baptist, Church of Christ, Assemblies of God, and the Church of God.

Political affiliation

Adults identifying with a specific faith group are almost evenly split among Republicans, Democrats and Independents. The Religious Right claim that demographic shifts since 1964 are moving in their favor, because conservatives have been giving birth to more children than liberals. Even if true, this claim disregards the fact that the children may vote differently from their parents, as their parents have switched from Democrat to Republican. Among Americans who do not identify with a religion are 43 percent Independent, 39 percent Democrat, and 17 percent Republican.

Denominational breakdown

Catholics are easily the largest single religious group in the US with over 69 million adherents (2009) in nearly 22,000 congregations. While the largest single Protestant group is the Southern Baptist Convention with 16 million members, the combined Protestant groups report 66 million adherents. Catholics are one of the four largest groups in every state of the Union as well as in the District of Columbia. United Methodists (8 million) are one of the top four groups in 38 states, and Southern Baptists in 28 states and the District of Columbia. The Latter-day Saints (5.6 million) and Evangelical Lutheran Church in America (4.8 million) are both among the top four in 13 states, and Jewish adherents in 10 states and the District of Columbia. Twelve other groups make the top four in anywhere from one to eight states (*Yearbook* and *Religious Congregations and Membership 2000*, Glenmary Research Center).

In addition, Greek Orthodox number 1.5 million, the Orthodox Church 1 million, Seventh Day Adventists 900,000. The data are not standardized, so that comparisons between groups are difficult. The definition of "church member" is determined by the religious body.

Religious congregations and trends

Among the other major trends found in the ARIS study is that many "mainline" religious groups are aging and declining. The Episcopal (2.4 million), Lutheran (8.6 million including Evangelical Lutheran (4.8 million) and Presbyterian (4.7 million all told) churches are diminishing significantly. Conservative Protestant 'evangelical' churches, however, are growing. Many of these churches have small memberships of less than 1 million, however. The fastest-growing religious group in the country with more than 1 million members is the Mormons. Often viewed as "the typical American," United Methodists are the most widespread religious group in the US, represented in 3,003 (96 percent) of the nation's 3,141 counties.

Regional variations in religion

Sectarian allegiances vary greatly in different regions. Rural parts of the South (except Louisiana and the Hispanic community, which both consist mainly of Catholics) have many evangelicals but very few Catholics, while urbanized areas of the north Atlantic and Great Lakes states, as well as many industrial and mining towns, are heavily Catholic, though still quite mixed. Church attendance varies widely by state and region. In a 2006 Gallup survey, the figures ranged from 58% in Alabama, Louisiana and South Carolina to 24% in Vermont and New Hampshire.

Despite recent trends, the South remains a unique region, with religious membership being a key factor. In the South, 86 percent of people say they believe in God, compared with 59 percent in the West. Often, the difference between Southern culture and Southern religion is blurred. But as the South becomes less rural and more urbanized, religion and culture are not as intertwined as they once were. Some believe this trend is responsible for the increased appeal of conservative churches. Because of the growing political importance of the South over the last 20 years, changes in its traditionally strong religious culture are especially significant. In numbers, the South is still dominated by Baptists, followed by United Methodists. Most Southern states are still less than 10 percent Catholic, with most of the Catholics living in metropolitan areas.

The nine major world religions considered in the ARIS study are centered on the coasts, in the West and in major urban areas. Five of the nine major world religions are represented in every Southern state, and all nine groups are represented in Florida and Texas.

The number of people in the study listed as unclaimed by a religion does not necessarily mean people do not go to church or are irreligious. The figures might suggest that the South is not the most "claimed" region in terms of religion, but this is due to lack of participation in the study by African American churches as well as small, independent European American churches in Appalachia and other rural areas.

Recent Protestant Trends

- De-institutionalization of religion at both the congregational and individual level. This includes the rise in nondenominational church names such as *The Whole Life Center* or *Lifeways*.
- A focus away from religion in favor of "spirituality"
- Religion becoming more individual and private, rather than a social institution.
- The increase of megachurches with an emphasis on intense religious experiences such as being "born again"

Conservative trends

- Fundamentalism has moved from the fringe of Southern life to national prominence.
- The Christian Coalition, the Southern Baptist Convention (SBC), and the Believers' Bible Fellowship, among others, represent a "second coming" of fundamentalism.
- Connections to the political right and an alliance with Catholics on issues such as abortion, homosexuality and the ordination of women. The SBC has terminated the Baptist-Catholic Dialogue.

FACTFILE 16 THE CATHOLIC CHURCH

	Numbers before 1965 (the end of the Second Vatican Council)	Numbers in 2006
Secular (parish) priests	58,000	41,000

Ordinations to the priesthood	1,575	454
Catholic population	45.6 million	69 million (2007)
Seminarians	50,000	5,000
Regular clergy i.e., members of religious communities	22,707	14,137
Religious brothers	12,271	5,451
Women religious	179,954	68,634
Catholics attending Mass every Sunday	75%	32% (2004)

Non-Christian religions

Although the number of adults who classify themselves in non-Christian religious groups has increased from about 5.8 million to about 7.7 million, the proportion of non-Christians in the population has increased only by a very small amount from 3.3 percent to about 3.7 percent.

Jews

There were very few Jews in America until the late 19th century. Most of these were from the German states. Many of them belonged to the Reform movement, a liberal branch of Judaism which had made many adjustments to modern life. Anti-Semitism, or anti-Jewish prejudice, was not a big problem before the Civil War. But when Jews began coming to America in great numbers, anti-Semitism appeared. Jews from Russia and Poland, who as Orthodox Jews strictly observed the traditions and dietary laws of Judaism, clustered in city neighborhoods when they first arrived. Usually, Jewish children attended public schools and took religious instruction in special Hebrew schools. The children of Jewish immigrants moved rapidly into the professions and into American universities, where many became intellectual leaders. Many remained religiously observant, while others continued to think of themselves as ethnically Jewish, but adopted a secular, nonreligious outlook. Some Orthodox Jewish males may be recognized by their black hats and long black coats and by their use of the yarmulke (skull cap) when praying. To combat prejudice and discrimination, Jews formed the Anti-Defamation League, which has played a major role in educating Americans about the injustice of prejudice and making them aware of the rights, not only of Jews, but of all minorities. The ARIS study projected there were 5.3 million adults in the Jewish population: 2.6 million were estimated to be adherents of Judaism; 1.08 million were adherents of no religion; and 1.36 million were estimated to be adherents of a religion other than Judaism. The Jewish proportion of the population has significantly declined from over 3 percent in the 1950s, chiefly due to the relatively low birthrate among Jewish Americans and high rates of out-marriage to non-Jews. According to the National Jewish Population Survey 2001, among those who belong to a synagogue, 38 percent are members of Reform synagogues, 33 percent Conservative, 22 percent Orthodox, 2 percent Reconstructionist, and 5 percent other types. Jews in the Northeast and Midwest are generally more observant than those in the South or West. Reflecting a trend also observed among other religious groups, Jews in the Northwest are typically the least observant. In recent years, there has been a noticeable trend of secular American Jews, called *baalei teshuva* ("returners"), returning to a more religious, in most cases, Orthodox, style of observance. It is uncertain how widespread or demographically important this movement is at present.

Muslims

The number of Muslims in the US is uncertain. ARIS 2008 says there are 1.3 million self-identified Muslims but other estimates claim there are several million. The highest estimate that is generally considered credible is 2.35 million (including children). As many as one-third of American Muslims are black converts. Most of these first joined the Nation of Islam, though many later moved into mainstream Sunnism. Research indicates that Muslims in the US are generally more assimilated and prosperous than Muslims in Europe. Surveys also suggest, however, that they are less assimilated than other American subcultural and religious communities (but see Chapter 2).

According to ARIS, the number of self-identified Hindus is 227,000. Most studies have indicated a Buddhist population of between 1 and 4 million. Sikhs total over 650,000, the majority of them living in California.

Atheism

Those with no religious affiliation are the fastest-growing group in America, even including Muslims. The number of non-religious persons has doubled since 1990. Now the Secular Coalition for America, with five million members, is seeking the political influence in Washington that has made Christian conservatives and the Jewish lobby powerful in politics. One non-religious group launched a case in the Supreme Court claiming that federal support for social services by faith-based groups was a violation of the separation of church and state (Edwin S. Gaustad, *Proclaim Liberty Throughout All the Land: History of Church and State in America*, Oxford, 2003). In 2007, reversing the Court of Appeals, the Supreme Court held that taxpayers had no standing to raise the issue. Polls show atheists to be the most distrusted minority among Americans. A Gallup Poll released in 2007 indicated that 53 percent of Americans would refuse to vote for an atheist as President, up from 48 percent in 1987 and 1999.

Tolerance

It used to be said that American religion came in three flavors: Protestant, Catholic, or Jewish in that order. The order reflects the numerical strength of each group. In the 1990 census, Protestants of all denominations numbered 140 million; Catholics, 62 million; and Jews, 5 million. Today the three-faith formula is obsolete. The Islamic faith also has numerous US adherents, many of whom are African American converts. It is estimated that the number of mosques in the US today, about 1,200, has doubled in the last 15 years. Buddhism and Hinduism are growing with the arrival of immigrants from countries where these are the majority religions. In some cases, inner-city Christian churches whose congregations have moved to the suburbs have sold their buildings to Buddhists, who have refitted them to suit their practices.

Because of its tradition of non-interference in religion, the US has also become a haven for many small sects who have immigrated. A well-known example is the Amish, descendants of German immigrants who mostly live in Pennsylvania and neighboring states. For generations they have lived their traditionally simple lives, wearing plain clothes and shunning modern technology. America has also been a fertile ground for new religions. The LDS, Jehovah's Witnesses and Christian Science churches are perhaps the best-known of the faiths that have sprung up on American soil. Religious intolerance is rare although not unknown.

Some small groups are considered to be religious cults because they profess extremist beliefs and tend to glorify a founding figure. As long as cults and their members abide by the law, however, they are generally left alone. The best known cults are the Unification Church (the "Moonies," so called because they were founded by Rev. Sun Myung Moon in 1954) and the Church of Scientology, of which the film star Tom Cruise is a leading member. The most controversial aspect of religion in the US today is probably its role in politics. In recent decades some Americans have come to believe that separation of church and state has been interpreted in ways hostile to religion. Religious conservatives and fundamentalists have joined forces to become a powerful political movement, the Christian Right. Among their goals is to overturn, by law or constitutional amendment, Supreme Court decisions allowing abortion and banning prayer in public schools. Ralph Reed, former executive director of the Christian Coalition, estimates that one-third of delegates to the 1996 Republican Convention were members of this or similar conservative Christian groups, an indication of the increased involvement of religion in politics.

Although some American religious groups openly demonstrate their faith and seek to convert others, for most Americans religion is a personal matter not usually discussed in everyday conversation. The vast majority practice their faith quietly in whatever manner they choose, as members of one of the traditional religious denominations, as participants in nondenominational congregations, or as individuals who join no organized group or who have no religion. However Americans choose to exercise their faith, they remain a spiritual people. Nine out of ten Americans express some religious preference, and approximately 70 percent are members of religious congregations.

CHAPTER 9

THE ARTS AND LITERATURE

The myths underlying our culture and underlying our common sense have not taught us to feel identical with the universe, but only parts of it, only in it, only confronting it— aliens.
Alan Watts

THE ARTS

The position of the fine arts in America has rarely been secure. This is a practical, commercial, some would say philistine nation where the arts have often been seen as wasteful, frivolous, or unmanly. America is relatively young, and it has never had an aristocracy, the elite class that typically commissions the fine arts and dictates taste. The Puritans who arrived in New England in the early 17th century brought with them the Calvinist hostility or indifference to the visual arts. A motivating principle of the 16th-century Protestant Reformation was the correction of what was considered Roman Catholicism's idolatrous use of images—paintings, statues and stained-glass windows—in medieval churches. The Protestant reformers reasserted the Ten Commandments' ban on graven images, objects that seduced the soul away from the immaterial divine. In particular, Protestants forbade the nude, which has been a symbol of Western art, individualism and freedom since the ancient Greeks.

The development of the arts in America has also been marked by a tension between two strong sources of inspiration: European sophistication and domestic originality. Frequently the best American artists have managed to harness both sources. Yet in her autobiography *A Backward Glance* (1933), novelist Edith Wharton claimed that "the really vital change is that, in my youth, the Americans of the original States, who in moments of crisis still shaped the national point of view, were the heirs of an old tradition of European culture which the country has now totally rejected" (*Backward* 1.2.) If, and to what extent, she was right may be an illuminating debate.

American drama, for instance, is no longer an imitation of European models but a diverse, indigenous art form. Indeed theater is blossoming throughout America, although the numbers of theaters and productions in New York have fallen because of rising costs. The movie, though, is America's premier art form (see Chapter 10.) Another product of photography, the color magazine, pioneered in America, introduced an age of news reporting where the image dominates the words. America's unique contribution to the built environment has also been visual: the skyscraper, whose bold, thrusting lines have given the modern city its visual signature—the skyline.

Not long ago many people in the US were apologetic about the fact that the country had produced few painters, singers, dancers, choreographers, conductors, or musicians of international stature. That deficit no longer exists. There is a degree of pride that at least some Americans feel at the great reputations and legacies of artists such as Isaac Stern, Leonard Bernstein, Jackson Pollock, Jessye Norman, Suzanne Farrell and Martha Graham.

American literature has combined many traditions, genres and voices to produce a uniquely American body of world class novels of unrivalled scope and unparalleled impact, if sometimes diffuse in form and undisciplined in fecundity, that have on occasion blurred the boundary between high and low culture. America has also produced some of the world's finest poetry in English in the 20th century. American literature expresses the national second nature: the urge to purify bound up in the simplifying power of "American pastoral", in which Nature, the preserve of the rural, the pre-modern, the authentic, and the masculine, a world of innocence, is defined in contrast with the Unnatural, the Babylon of modernity, urban foppery, effeminacy, and intellectuality. That said, it remains a fact that almost all of America's great contemporary writers were born in the age of Franklin Roosevelt. Meanwhile American philosophy has a strong naturalistic bent, proposing a set of principles, perspectives, and commitments that seek an understanding of phenomena and concepts in terms of how they arose and how they play a part in our engagement with the world. But only a minority of voices, such as C. Wright Mills and Reinhold Niebuhr, have advocated for engaging with the world in order to change it. Similarly, American history writing, while distinguished for its scholarship, has until recently dwelt almost exclusively on what has unified the country and not on what has divided it.

Theater

In September, 1951, *Theatre Arts* magazine (the word *theater* can also be spelled *theatre* in American English) noted that "the American theatre" was, of course, the New York theatre. "It is an unfortunate fact that very little of genuine worth or national interest originates outside Manhattan Island," the article observed.

Even then, however, new plays, notably *Summer* and *Smoke* by Tennessee Williams, were being performed in Dallas, Texas, while Eugene O'Neill had unveiled *Lazarus Laughed* at the Pasadena Playhouse in southern California as far back as 1928. But in effect what existed was Broadway and Off Broadway. Everywhere else - Boston, Cleveland, Denver, Los Angeles, Chicago - was "out of town."

Broadway

Broadway is the name of a street that runs north-south the length of Manhattan in New York through the heart of the city's theater district. The 40 theaters are actually to be found clustered in the side streets between W41st St and W57th St, especially between 44th and 45th Sts, near Times Square. This part of Broadway is known as the *Great White Way* because of the bright lights outside the theaters. The first modern theater was built in 1894 and the subway was actually extended north to help audiences get there. *Broadway* has also come to mean US theater in general. The smaller theaters, where less commercial works are performed, are known as *Off Broadway*; and some shoestring operations housed in the lofts of the SoHo district, are called *Off-Off-Broadway.* (*SoHo* means "south of West Houston Street," which separates SoHo from Greenwich Village.) The classification of theaters is governed by language in Actors' Equity Association contracts, rather than by whether the theater has a Broadway address. There are probably more Off-Off-Broadway shows than Broadway or Off Broadway combined. This is where some really exciting cutting-edge productions happen. Most of these productions run for only a short time, however, many for just a weekend.

In the 1920s, before the rise of the movie industry, Broadway had 80 theaters and was the place for young actors to make their mark, and Broadway is still the most prestigious and lucrative location to develop a theater career. Since the 1970s, however, the high cost of productions – a production can cost $10-$15 million - has forced many theaters to close or become movie theaters, leaving 40 playhouses mounting some two dozen shows a season. Three venues, the Lincoln Center Theater, the Roundabout Theater, and the Manhattan Theatre Club have regular non-commercial subscription seasons. Broadway never developed large permanent corporations like the movie industry, and retained a transient, anarchic mode of organization. Most Broadway shows, however, are commercial productions intended to make a profit for the producers and investors ("backers") and are therefore intended to have open-ended runs, meaning that they may be presented for a varying number of weeks depending on critical response, word of mouth, and the effectiveness of the show's advertising. A bad review by the drama critic of the *New York Times* can close a play. Commercial pressures have meant that most of the longest running plays in recent years have been musicals, revivals or successful plays transferred from the West End of London, England. Although serious American stage plays such as Arthur Miller's *Death of a Salesman, Long Day's Journey into Night* by Eugene O'Neill, and Edward Albee's *Who's Afraid Of Virginia Woolf?* have had long runs, most straight plays nowadays appear Off Broadway. As Arthur Miller himself has lamented: "I'm the end of the line; absurd and appalling as it may seem, serious New York theater has died in my lifetime." Both musicals and stage plays on Broadway often rely on casting well-known performers, especially from movies and television, in leading roles to draw larger audiences or bring in new audience members. There are still, however, performers who are primarily stage actors, spending most of their time on the boards, and appearing in television and in screen roles only secondarily. Famous US actors who have appeared on Broadway include Dustin Hoffman, Robert Redford, Elizabeth Taylor and Lisa Minnelli. On average 25,000 people per night see a Broadway show at a cost of around $65 per seat.

Off Broadway

Off Broadway denotes a widely dispersed group of small theaters away from the principal commercial theater center near Times Square which have 100 to 499 seats. Many of these playhouses are to be found in basements, lofts and converted churches, and they regularly produce plays deemed too risky for commercial production. Many of the plays first presented in these theaters later transfer to traditional Broadway houses, while others remain in their original playhouses for their entire runs, which can be long. Off Broadway theaters are often considered to be among the most exciting theater in New York. Playwrights, such as Edward Albee (1928-), A. R. Gurney Jr (1930-), Lanford Wilson (1937-) and Sam Shepard (1943-) have been presented in New York almost solely in Off Broadway houses, and several, such as Tennessee Williams, announced a preference for Off Broadway after their later plays were not well received uptown. Off Broadway has its own prestigious award, the Obie.

Off-off-Broadway

From 1958, theaters that served as an alternative to Off Broadway and Broadway started springing up across Manhattan and in the boroughs. Deemed the most experimental and least compromising of the three venues, Off- Off-Broadway often has a specific agenda: gay or lesbian, feminist, ethnic theatre, and so on. The spaces are small and mostly found in such unconventional places as church basements, community centers, former storefronts, even garages and warehouses. Off-Off-Broadway theaters are generally defined as theaters that have fewer than 100 seats. Longer-established OOB theaters include Richard Foreman's Ontological Hysteric Theater in the East Village, and the Flea Theater in Tribeca. Some professional theater companies, such as the Two-River Theater Company in Red Bank, New Jersey, consider themselves to be Off-Off-Broadway despite the fact they are not housed within New York.

Many Off-Off-Broadway productions are non-union, others are "Equity showcases," and some are defiantly amateur. Equity maintains very strict rules about working in such productions, including restrictions on price, the length of the run and rehearsal times. Professional actors' participation in showcase productions in fact comprises the bulk of stage work for the majority of New York actors. OOB theaters tend to be formed, sometimes quickly blossom, and just as often disappear in a year or two without a trace. It is estimated that in any one season there are more than sixty such groups in New York. There is currently a movement to rebrand Off-Off-Broadway as "Indie Theatre" (independent theater.) The New York Innovative Theatre Awards (the IT Awards) are given annually to honor artistic excellence in Off-Off-Broadway theater.

By the late 1990's, theater was blossoming all over America. *The Lion King,* a celebrated adaptation of the Walt Disney animated film, had its pre-New York engagement in Minneapolis. The national touring company of the musical *Ragtime,* a colorful evocation of early 20th-century America, was on the road, as was *Chicago.*

In addition to long runs in Broadway theaters, producers often remount their productions with a new cast and crew for the Broadway national tour, which travels to theaters in major cities across the country. The bigger and more successful shows may have several of these touring companies out at a time, some of them "sitting down" in other cities for their own long runs. Smaller cities are eventually serviced by "bus & truck" tours, so-called because the cast generally travels by bus (instead of by air) and the sets and equipment by truck. Tours of this type, which frequently feature a reduced physical production to accommodate smaller venues and tighter schedules, often play "split weeks" (half a week in one town and the second half in another) or "one-nighters," whereas the larger tours will generally play for one or two weeks per city at a minimum.

In the last generation, the theater world's pendulum has swung from Broadway to the regions, with New York theater frequently beholden to the rest of the country for an infusion of activity. These days, although new companies are not springing up all over, the ones that were established between 1950 and 1975 tend to be constructing new homes, and second stages, to expand their activities. Now there are over 200 resident theaters from Hawaii to Maine. Asian American theatre in particular is flourishing.

But because of the need to fill theaters and keep foundations and corporate sponsors happy, a sense of danger, of experimentation, is certainly not in the air. Even so, a young US playwright finds it easier to get a hearing today than ever before. African American women dramatists are especially visible. Playwright David Henry Hwang (1957-), author of such Broadway dramas as

M. Butterfly and *Golden Child,* is the most successful Asian American playwright today. There is room for more black, Asian American and Hispanic theaters to meet the enthusiasm of expanding multicultural audiences.

Tony awards

Tony Awards are given each spring by the American Theater Wing to the best Broadway plays, actors and other professional theater people. The Tonys were named for Antoinette "Tony" Perry (1888-1946), who produced and directed Broadway plays and founded the American Theater Wing in 1941.

DRAMA

The beginnings of American theater were stormy. Performances of plays were opposed by governments and by certain religious groups. Several colonies passed anti-theater laws based on the Puritan belief that the seventh of the Ten Commandments ("Thou shalt not commit adultery") prohibited dancing and stage plays. Bankruptcy was a common hazard for theater managers, and playwrights were constantly subjected to abuse by theater managers, actors, and the public. American drama before 1800 was imitative and immature and the theater was dominated by British plays until around 1910.

The first American play in English was possibly *The Lost Lady* (1641) by Sir William Berkeley, Governor of Virginia. The first play actually printed in America was *Androborus* by Robert Hunter, 1714. Intended for a reading public rather than a viewing audience, it established a tradition of political satire that became common fare in the American drama of the 1700s. In 1767 The American Company staged *The Prince of Parthia,* a tragedy by Thomas Godfrey, in Philadelphia. This is usually considered the first professional production in America of a play written by an American. Satirical plays were written as propaganda during the American Revolution, either attacking British control of the colonies or supporting it. Mercy Otis Warren created several biting satires of the British. The earliest play to treat a native subject was *Ponteach or The Savages of America* by Robert Rogers (1766). In 1787, Royall Tyler wrote *The Contrast,* the finest American play of the 18th century. This five-act comedy of manners satirizes the customs of the upper classes. It compares British and American fashions and values and ultimately sides with what it sees as American candor and patriotism over British duplicity and artificiality.

The most popular form of drama in the 19th century was melodrama. These productions were an emotional form of entertainment with simple plots and a basic stock of characters. The plays were set in mysterious locations, and peopled with stereotypical characters: heartless villains, heroines in distress, and strong heroes who faced almost insurmountable odds in rescuing those heroines. *Gothic melodramas,* which emphasized horror, mystery, and the supernatural, and *tragic melodramas* with unhappy endings appeared regularly in American theaters from the 1790s, in many cases adapted or translated from German, French, and British plays. The first prolific American writer of melodramas was William Dunlap. He adapted Revolutionary War history in *André* (1798), a fictionalized account of the final days of British spy Major John André. In 1803 Dunlap reshaped the play as a musical, *Glory of Columbia.* It was an early example of spectacle dominating dramatic content. Dunlap took spectacle even further in *A Trip to Niagara* (1828).

Replication of local color became the norm in 19th-century American melodrama and encompassed details of scenery, dialects, and gestures representative of specific locations, contemporary slang, and historical incidents.

Although American drama of the 19th century usually followed European models, its subject matter often came from specifically American situations. *Superstition* (1824), a romantic tragedy by James Nelson Barker, for example, was set in the New England of 1675. It discussed conflicts between Native Americans and white settlers, British interference in local affairs, Puritan *xenophobia* (fear and dislike of foreigners), and the idea of witchcraft. This play, in which the hero is tried and executed for witchcraft, was the first of many American plays to explore themes of isolationism, bigotry, and intolerance.

The Native Americans were long ignored in professional drama. It was not until the 1820s that a fashion for so-called Indian plays began which lasted until the 1840s. Before that only one professionally produced play had explored Native American characters and themes. This was Barker's *The Indian Princess* (1808), which told the story of Pocahontas, a Native American who married an English colonist. While the Pocahontas story was popular, the most famous such drama was *Metamora, or The Last of the Wampanoags* (1829) by John Augustus Stone. Metamora was viewed as natural but uncivilized, that is, living in harmony with nature but unfamiliar with what European settlers saw as civilized ways. The sentiments of the play harmonized with white values. It ended with Metamora's inevitable death as the representative of a displaced race that could not co-exist with the white man.

As the US began to expand, opened up by the exploration and settlement of the West, audiences were excited by spectacular romantic plays spiced with danger, known as *Frontier melodrama*. The most famous of these was *Nick of the Woods* (1838) by Louisa Medina, which capitalized on the spectacle, romance, and danger of the frontier—for example, when the title character escapes his pursuers by plunging over a waterfall in a burning canoe. Playwrights repeatedly glorified backwoodsmen and moved toward making Native American characters into villains. One of the most successful frontier melodramas, *Davy Crockett* (1872) by Frank Murdoch, featured the so-called natural gentleman. This character had developed from an earlier view of the Native American but was now white and considered a gentleman, despite his life outside society and his uncouth ways. Another form of melodrama was the *temperance play*, for example, *The Drunkard; or, The Fallen Saved* (1844) by W. H. Smith, which illustrated the evils of alcohol and supported a ban on its sale. Temperance plays were staged frequently from the 1830s until the Civil War. Because the formulas of these plays accommodated moral lessons important to social reformers, temperance plays attracted audiences formerly opposed to the theater. *Melodramatic comedy* appeared frequently in the 1800s, while comedies of manners, so popular in the previous century, became rare. A notable exception and one of the most successful and well-written plays of the 19th century was *Fashion* (1845) by Anna Cora Mowatt, which urged Americans to resist British cultural models.

In the generation before the Civil War, the drama began to take on darker tones. Playwrights explored contemporary social themes, particularly racial tensions and social and economic conflict. Far and away the most successful of these productions were stage adaptations of the novel *Uncle Tom's Cabin* (1852) by Harriet Beecher Stowe. Sentimental versions of the novel filled so many professional stages that this material was performed more often than any other American play of the time. An 1852 adaptation by George Aiken was the most enduring version. Dion Boucicault's

The Octoroon (1859), a stage adaptation of the novel *The Quadroon* (1856) by Mayne Reid, was the most well-crafted melodrama on the subject of slavery and racism in the mid-19th century. It combined local color from Louisiana, ethnic mixes, spectacle in the form of a burning steamboat, and a tragic heroine whose ancestry (a black great-grandparent) prevents her from marrying the man she loves.

By the end of the 19th century, American drama was moving steadily toward realism and naturalism, illuminating the sordid side of ordinary life and creating more believable characters acting in natural settings and speaking natural dialogue. These plays included the hugely popular *Shenandoah* (1888), set in the Civil War, which combined melodramatic tension and comic romance. A master of melodrama in a realistic style was actor and playwright William Gillette. Other realist playwrights included Steele Mackaye and William Dean Howells. While realistic plays assumed that people were in control of their destinies, naturalistic plays were more pessimistic, assuming that people were controlled by their animal instincts and their environment, fate, or chance. The hero struggled to survive against insurmountable odds. Realism reached new levels after 1900 in the work of David Belasco and Clyde Fitch. Belasco's *The Girl of the Golden West* (1905) sentimentally recreated a rural California town of the mid-19th century Gold Rush days, while Fitch's *The City* (1909) explored the evils of shady business deals and drug addiction. Realistic portrayals of sensational subjects also flourished in many plays of this era. For example, *The Easiest Way* (1909), by Eugene Walter, dramatized the situation of a kept woman whose acceptance of financial support from one man leads to her rejection by the man she loves.

The enormous flood of immigration around the turn of the 20th century, and mounting criticism of the appalling working conditions in the factories and the living environments of the cities led dramatists to concentrate on social issues in the years leading up to World War I. An early example was *The Great Divide* (1906) by William Vaughn Moody. The story of a New England woman's move to Arizona, the play contrasted Western, rural sensibilities against Eastern, urban ones. The most prolific of prewar playwrights with a social agenda was Rachel Crothers, who addressed such issues as society's double standard for men and women in *A Man's World* (1909). *The New York Idea* (1906), a social satire by Langdon Mitchell, managed to entertain while commenting meaningfully on divorce. The American family, and its development and disintegration, was a recurring theme of playwrights at this time, and it would dominate much American playwriting for the rest of the 20th century.

Twentieth century Drama

Until 1910 the American stage was dominated by British repertoire. American drama lagged behind other genres because it was entirely controlled by businessmen and played before largely conservative audiences. But by the end of World War I, a better balance of power between the various interests of actors, playwrights, producers and theater owners was brought about, largely by the Actors' Equity strike in 1917, which shut all New York theaters.

The Little Theater Movement

Small but significant developments took place in theater in the second decade of the 20th century. The year 1912 alone saw three new theaters founded: Winthrop Ames' The Little Theatre in New York, Maurice Brown's Little Theatre in Chicago, and Mrs. Lyman Gale's Toy Theatre in Boston. Another theater for serious drama was founded in New York in 1915 by Alice and Irene Lewisohn.

This was The Neighborhood Theatre on Lower East Side, which offered American plays as well as some from Europe, Japan, and India. Its first production was *Jephthah's Daughter*. The following year, The Provincetown Players, which began in the artist-colony at Cape Cod, and was devoted to offering only works by American writers, also opened in New York, at the Playwrights Theatre. Other prominent participants in the Little Theatre Movement were Edna St. Vincent Millay, and couples George "Jig" Cram Cook and Susan Glaspell, John Reed and Louise Bryant, Max Eastman and Ida Rauh. From 1916 to 1922, this group presented 16 plays by Eugene O'Neill, 11 by Glaspell, and a total of 93 works by nearly 50 American writers. *Trifles* (1916) by Susan Glaspell, a subtle study in sexism, was among its first productions. O'Neill was the most experimental of 1920s playwrights and with *The Hairy Ape* (1922).was one of the first to introduce expressionism in America. *The Hairy Ape* depicts a rejected ship laborer who feels he belongs nowhere until he confronts an ape in a zoo. He sets the caged animal free only to be destroyed by it. Eugene O'Neill (1888-1953) was the first important American dramatist. He drew upon classical mythology, the Bible, and the new science of psychology to explore inner life. He wrote frankly about sex and family quarrels, but his preoccupation was with the individual's search for identity. His plays *Beyond the Horizon* (1920), *Anna Christie* (1922), and *Strange Interlude* (1928) won Pulitzer Prizes and were followed by *Mourning Becomes Electra* (1931), a trilogy recounting the far-reaching consequences of adultery, incest, jealousy, and vengeance. In 1936 O'Neill became the first American playwright to win a Nobel Prize in literature.

At this time, a reaction against realism set in and a new movement imported from Germany, Expressionism, became the dominant mode of the drama. Influencing all the art forms, Expressionism emphasized feelings and emotions rather than the objective depiction of reality. The characters and the setting may be realistic but the stage, lighting, costumes, music, and scenery could be highly elaborate or bare. Expressionistic writing has no recognizable plot, conflicts or character developments and is more like a dream, albeit one the audience can follow. The most famous example is *The Adding Machine* (1923) by Elmer Rice, that focuses on the emotional journey of the leading character, Mr. Zero, after he is replaced at his job by an adding machine. Another such play is *Processional* (1925), a depiction of a West Virginia miners' strike by John Howard Lawson. This play made use of collage-like scenic effects and cacophonous musical and sound techniques.

The Washington Square Players meanwhile organized to produce plays of merit which had been turned down by Broadway producers. The Players received critical praise for their professional productions. Authors presented were Europeans Ibsen, Chekov, Shaw, Wilde, and Americans Elmer Rice, John Reed, Alice Gerstenberg, Glaspell, and O'Neill. After a three season run, the company became the Theatre Guild. Outside New York, 1916 saw the opening of The Cleveland Playhouse, the Pasadena Community Playhouse and the Detroit Arts and Crafts Theatre. Soon after, in 1919, the Petit Theatre du Vieux Carre opened in New Orleans.

Realism, both in comedies and tragedies, continued to be a major form of drama, even as experiment in both the content and production of plays became increasingly important. The 1920s were a rich period in American drama, which achieved international recognition through the psychological realism of plays by Eugene O'Neill with their searing investigation of characters' inner lives. As the century advanced, the number of subjects considered suitable for drama broadened to include race, gender, sexuality, and death.

The drama of the 1930s was preoccupied with reaction to the Depression, which inspired a wave of hard-edged plays about the sufferings of the working class. These plays not only tackled the contemporary theme of economic suffering, but also explored the rival political solutions offered by left-wing ideologies and fascism, and the fears of another world war. The most famous is *Waiting for Lefty* (1935) by Clifford Odets, a play about a taxi drivers' strike, which examined the pros and cons of capitalism. Odets also wrote one of the finest expressions of 1930s anxieties, *Awake and Sing!* (1935), in which a Marxist grandfather commits suicide for his family's financial benefit, and his grandson ultimately dedicates himself and the life insurance money to helping his community rather than seeking better opportunities elsewhere. The plays of Lillian Hellman also displayed a social conscience. Hellman's *The Children's Hour* (1934), later filmed, in which a child's vengeful lies cause the downfall of a school and the two women who run it, explored the devastating effects of malicious gossip and the willingness to believe it.

Perhaps the most frequently produced play by an American playwright comes from the late 1930s. *Our Town* by Thornton Wilder (1938), set in fictional Grover's Corners, New Hampshire, was inspired by Wilder's friend Gertrude Stein's novel *The Making of Americans. Our Town* employs a choric narrator called the "Stage Manager" and a minimalist set to underscore the universality of human experience. Through following the daily lives of the Gibbs and Webb families and their neighbors, the play illustrates the importance of the lives of all people, however simple. A master of comedy as well, Wilder wrote *The Matchmaker* (1955) which later became the "book" for the musical *Hello! Dolly*.

African American characters became more visible in plays after World War I. The main character of *In Abraham's Bosom* (1926) by Paul Green (1894-1981), whose father is white and mother black, works to help his black community but is defeated by the racial prejudice of both whites and blacks. Paul Green was the first playwright from the South to gain national and international recognition. In Abraham's Bosom won the 1927 Pulitzer Prize for drama. Green created and promoted a new dramatic form, the symphonic drama, a type of history play, usually set on the very site depicted in the action, and including music, dance, pantomime and poetic dialogue. Following the first of these, *The Lost Colony* (1937), about Sir Walter Raleigh's failed colony on Roanoke Island, he wrote sixteen more. The symphonic drama is one of the two uniquely American dramatic forms, the other being the musical. Green stood almost alone in preaching the equality of the races, and the richness of Southern tradition as a source of great literature. It was Langston Hughes who paved the way for acceptance of drama by African Americans with his successful play *Mulatto* (1935) about the complexity of race relations. Otherwise, however, black playwrights remained on the margins of the theater world until the 1950s.

Theater since 1945

Mainstream postwar theater expressed a wider range of viewpoints, reflecting the increasingly complex makeup of American society. The most powerful plays spoke to social issues like civil rights and, later, AIDS. Tennessee Williams (1911-1983) and Arthur Miller (1915-2005) plumbed profound new levels of psychological realism. Williams dealt, for example, with how people use illusion to cope with loneliness, and with the hitherto taboo subject of sexual frustration. A strikingly original playwright, Williams expressed his Southern heritage in poetic yet sensational plays, which were often about a sensitive woman trapped in a brutish environment. He wrote many plays about social misfits and outsiders. In *A Streetcar Named Desire* (1947), a neurotic, impoverished Southern woman fights to maintain her illusions of gentility when forced to confront the truth about her life by her sister's working-class husband. The play was three times filmed and was also made into an opera. Williams' *Cat on a Hot Tin Roof* (1955), which won the Pulitzer Prize for drama and was filmed, similarly focused on pretense and its destructiveness and destruction in an unhappy family. Arthur Miller combined realistic characters and a social agenda while also writing modern tragedy, most notably in *Death of a Salesman* (1949), a tale of the life and death of an ordinary working man, Willy Loman. Miller's *The Crucible* (1953), a story about the 17th-century Salem witch trials, was a parable of the hunt for Communists in the 1950s led by Senator Joseph McCarthy.

The 1950s also saw a range of contrasting dramatic styles. Realism continued strongly with character studies of society's forgotten people. *Come Back, Little Sheba* (1950) by William Inge, later filmed, told the story of the unfulfilled lives of an alcoholic doctor and his wife. O'Neill's masterpiece *Long Day's Journey Into Night*, a harrowing drama based largely on his own family, appeared posthumously in 1956 and was twice filmed. The play chronicled a day in the life of the Tyrone family, during which family members inexorably confront one another's flaws and failures. Also at the end of the 1950s the semi-absurdist plays of Edward Albee, starting with *Zoo Story* (1959), caught the American imagination with their psychological danger and intelligent dialogue. Albee's *Who's Afraid of Virginia Woolf?* (1962), later filmed, depicted the destructive relationship of a married couple primarily through their verbal abuse. In the late 1950s, African American playwriting received a tremendous boost with the highly acclaimed *A Raisin in the Sun* (1959), later filmed, the story of a black family and how they handle a financial windfall. Written by Lorraine Hansberry, this play was the first Broadway production to be directed by an African American, Lloyd Richards.

American drama grew rapidly in many directions in response to two political movements of the 1960s and 1970s: the civil rights movement and the antiwar protests. New theaters sprang up all over America. Many of these produced experimental drama, and talented new dramatists came to the fore. Experimental theater companies, including the Living Theater and the Open Theater, used group dynamics, placing performers and audience members in the same space. *The Serpent* (1968) by Jean-Claude Van Itallie, which made use of this elimination of physical barriers between actors and audience, recreated Biblical stories through the depiction of modern events like the assassination of John F. Kennedy. Megan Terry's plays, such as *Calm Down Mother* (1965), featured actor transformations, in which one actor plays multiple roles and switches between characters without apparent transition. A number of playwrights challenged contemporary social codes, giving voice to traditionally disenfranchised members of American culture, and many African American dramatic voices of the 1960s had a confrontational edge. In his violent play *Dutchman* (1964), Amiri Baraka portrayed white society's fear and hatred of an educated black protagonist. The autobiographical *Funnyhouse of a Negro* (1962) by Adrienne Kennedy addressed the difficulties of being an American of mixed racial ancestry. Meanwhile Neil Simon emerged as a major comedic playwright in the 1960s with such works as *Barefoot in the Park* (1963) and *The Odd Couple* (1965), both later filmed.

The leading playwrights of the 1970s and 1980s were Sam Shepard and David Mamet. Shepard explored the stresses within family relationships and took a highly critical view of the myths of the American West. Among his hard-edged plays, the most biting were *Buried Child* (1978) and *True West* (1980). Mamet created a darkly comic style that imitated the fragmented speech of the inarticulate and used profanity as nearly every part of speech. Mamet's *American Buffalo* (1975) used a Chicago junk shop as a symbol of American capitalism, and his Pulitzer Prize-winning *Glengarry Glen Ross* (1983), later filmed, depicted the moral decay brought about by the win-at-all-costs ethic of the American salesman.

There have been few postmodernist playwrights in American theater, but there have been some. The minimalist style of postmodern staging and design entered American theater in the 1970s. Postmodern directors sought to uncover multiple layers of meaning in plays. These approaches were used effectively by feminist playwrights such as Maria Irene Fornés and Wendy Wasserstein. In *Fefu and Her Friends* (1977) and *The Conduct of Life* (1985), Fornés employed spatial experiments such as moving the audience from room to room instead of changing stage scenery. Wasserstein explored the complex social issues raised by the women's movement in *Uncommon Women and Others* (1977) and *The Heidi Chronicles* (1988), which won the 1989 Pulitzer Prize for drama.

Contemporary issues preoccupied playwrights in the 1980s. *Night Mother* (1983) by Marsha Norman discussed the question of when suicide might be justifiable. *The Normal Heart* (1985) by Larry Kramer confronted the devastation wrought by the AIDS crisis in New York. In his *M. Butterfly* (1988), later filmed, David Henry Hwang artfully used the famous opera *Madame Butterfly* (1904), by Italian composer Giacomo Puccini, to examine the ways in which Western civilization feminizes Eastern civilization. During this time two new playwrights took audiences into new territory while expressing themselves in language as different as their subject matter. Eric Overmyer harnessed sophisticated language, satire, and vibrant theatricality to dissect a corrupt social and political infrastructure in *On the Verge* (1986) and *In Perpetuity Throughout the Universe* (1988). African American August Wilson used black vernacular English in his narrowly focused domestic dramas, each of which is set in a different decade of the 20th century. Among the best of these are *Fences* (1985), portraying the conflicts between a father and son, and *The Piano Lesson* (1987), which focuses on the dispute between a brother and sister over selling a family heirloom to buy the land that their ancestors worked as slaves. Both plays won the Pulitzer Prize.

Audiences and critics were excited in the 1990s by the return of gripping domestic drama by two famous playwrights: Arthur Miller (*Broken Glass*, 1994) and Edward Albee (*Three Tall Women*, 1994). Both plays were widely acclaimed, with Albee's work capturing the Pulitzer Prize. Younger playwrights continued to challenge audiences, often in small or regional theaters. Mamet's *Oleanna* (1992), later filmed, investigated sexual harassment. Overmyer's *Dark Rapture* (1992) combined crime, greed, and sex in the style of motion-picture thrillers. Wilson's *Two Trains Running* (1990) revisited the black experience in 1960s America, while *Seven Guitars* (1995) did the same for the 1940s, *King Hedley II* (1999) for the 1980s, and *Gem of the Ocean* (2003) for the first decade of the 20th century. Wasserstein's *An American Daughter* (1997) looked at gender politics in Washington, D.C. Meanwhile Stephen Sondheim's musicals became darker, tackling topics such as presidential assassination (*Assassins*, 1990) and out-of-control love and guilt (*Passion*, 1994).

Another important young playwright of this period was Tony Kushner. His *Angels in America*, winner of the 1993 Pulitzer Prize and later filmed, was one of the most successful dramas of the 1990s. The two-part story chronicled the effects of the AIDS epidemic on the lives of eight characters over a six-year period. The two plays, *Millennium Approaches* (1991) and *Perestroika* (1993), each won a Tony Award for best drama.

As the 21st century began, the direction of American drama prompted troubling questions. Economic difficulties at regional and experimental theaters resulted in plays with a single setting and no more than two or three characters, making them less expensive to produce but also less ambitious. The aging of American theater audiences and competition from other forms of entertainment also threatened drama's future. Theaters were rejecting many large-scale plays as too risky and unlikely to cover production expenses. Consequently, crowd-pleasing musicals and revivals dominated Broadway. Almost all nonmusical plays originate in regional theaters. Many playwrights write with film or television adaptation in mind, a tendency encouraged by the fact that motion-picture studios own many theaters and dramatic production companies. Although experimentation and poignant subject matter continue to appear, many playwrights worry that American theater has become too conservative in its mainstream work and too specialized in its alternative productions.

CLASSICAL MUSIC

Until the 20th century, "serious" music in America was shaped by European standards and idioms. A notable exception was the music of composer *Louis Moreau Gottschalk* (1829-1869), son of a British father and a Creole mother. Gottschalk enlivened his music with plantation melodies and Caribbean rhythms that he had heard in his native New Orleans. He was the first American pianist to achieve international recognition, but his early death contributed to his relative obscurity.

A distinctively American classical music came to fruition when such composers as *George Gershwin* (1898-1937) and *Aaron Copland* (1900-1990) incorporated homegrown melodies and rhythms into forms borrowed from Europe. Gershwin's "Rhapsody in Blue" and his opera *Porgy and Bess* were influenced by jazz and African American folk songs. Some of his music is also self-consciously urban. The opening of his *An American in Paris*, for example, mimics taxi horns.

As Harold C. Schonberg writes in *The Lives of the Great Composers*, Copland "helped break the stranglehold of the German domination on American music." He studied in Paris, where he was encouraged to depart from tradition and indulge his interest in jazz. Besides writing symphonies, concertos, and an opera, he composed the scores for several films. He is best known, however, for his ballet scores, which draw on American folk songs. Among them are *Billy the Kid*, *Rodeo*, and *Appalachian Spring*.

Bernstein also wrote a one-act opera, *Trouble in Tahiti*, in 1952, and its sequel, the three-act opera, *A Quiet Place* in 1983. He collaborated with choreographer Jerome Robbins on three major ballets: *Fancy Free* (1944) and *Facsimile* (1946) for the American Ballet Theatre; and *Dybbuk* (1975) for the New York City Ballet. He composed the score for the award-winning movie *On the Waterfront* (1954) and incidental music for two Broadway plays: *Peter Pan* (1950) and *The Lark* (1955). Bernstein contributed substantially to the Broadway musical stage, composing *On The Town* (1944), *Wonderful Town* (1953) and, in collaboration with Richard Wilbur, Lillian Hellman and others, *Candide* (1956). Other versions of *Candide* were written in association with Hugh Wheeler, Stephen Sondheim and others. In 1957 he again collaborated with Jerome Robbins, Stephen Sondheim, and Arthur Laurents, on the landmark musical *West Side Story*, later made into the Academy Award-winning film. In 1976 Bernstein and Alan Jay Lerner wrote *1600 Pennsylvania Avenue*.

In the last decades of the 20th century, there was a trend back toward music that pleases both composer and listener, a development that may be related to the uneasy status of the symphony orchestra in America. Unlike Europe, where it is common for governments to underwrite their orchestras and opera companies, the arts in America get relatively little public support. To survive, symphony orchestras depend largely on philanthropy and paid admissions.

Some orchestra directors have found a way to keep mainstream audiences happy while introducing new music to the public. Rather than segregate the new pieces, these directors program them side-by-side with traditional fare. Meanwhile, opera, old and new, has been flourishing. Because it is so expensive to stage, however, opera depends heavily on the generosity of corporate and private donors.

Classical music is widely appreciated throughout America, with thriving symphony orchestras and opera companies. The repertoire is largely European, however, despite the existence of many fine American composers, like *Philip Glass* (1937-) and *Steve Reich* (1936-), who compose in the traditional European genres. Glass' repertoire spans the genres of opera, orchestra, chamber ensemble, dance, theater, and film and includes collaborations with a variety of distinctive contemporary artists. *Leroy Anderson* (1908 – 1975) was a composer of short, light concert pieces, many of which were introduced by the Boston Pops Orchestra under the direction of Arthur Fiedler. Younger classical composers include Kevin Puts, Steven Weigt, and Trevor Weston. The US has produced a number of world class performers including cellist Yo-Yo Ma, Grammy-winning pianist Emanuel Ax, violinists Isaac Stern (1920-2001) and Itzhak Perlman, singers Maria Callas (1923-1977), Jessye Norman (1945-) and Barbara Bonny (1956-), and conductors Antal Doráti and Leonard Bernstein.

Dance

Closely related to the development of American music in the early 20th century was the emergence of a new and distinctively American art form: modern dance. Among the early innovators was Isadora Duncan (1878-1927), who stressed pure, unstructured movement in lieu of the positions of classical ballet. The main line of development, however, runs from the dance company of Ruth St. Denis (1878-1968) and her husband-partner, Ted Shawn (1891-1972). Her pupil Doris Humphrey (1895-1958) looked outward for inspiration, to society and human conflict. Another pupil of St. Denis, Martha Graham (1893-1991), whose New York-based company became perhaps the best known in modern dance, sought to express an inner passion. Many of Graham's most popular works were produced in collaboration with leading American composers, *Appalachian Spring* with Aaron Copland, for example. Later choreographers searched for new methods of expression. Merce Cunningham (1919-) introduced improvisation and random movement into performances. Alvin Ailey (1931-1989) incorporated African dance elements and black music into his works. Recently such choreographers as Mark Morris (1956-) and Liz Lerman (1947-) have defied the convention that dancers must be thin and young. Their belief, put into action in their hiring practices and performances, is that graceful, exciting movement is not restricted by age or body type.

In the early 20th century, American audiences also were introduced to classical ballet by touring companies of European dancers. The first American ballet troupes were founded in the 1930s, when dancers and choreographers teamed up with visionary lovers of ballet such as Lincoln Kirstein (1907-1996). Kirstein invited Russian choreographer George Balanchine (1904-1983) to the US in 1933, and the two established the School of American Ballet, which became the New York City Ballet in 1948. Ballet manager and publicity agent Richard Pleasant (1909-1961) founded America's second leading ballet organization, American Ballet Theatre, with dancer and patron Lucia Chase (1907-1986) in 1940.

Paradoxically, native-born directors like Pleasant included Russian classics in their repertoires, while Balanchine announced that his new American company was predicated on distinguished music and new works in the classical idiom, not the standard repertory of the past. Since then, the American ballet scene has been a mix of classic revivals and original works, choreographed by such talented former dancers as Jerome Robbins (1918- 1998), Robert Joffrey (1930-1988), Arthur Mitchell (1934-), Eliot Feld (1942-), Suzanne Farrell (1945-) and Mikhail Baryshnikov (1948-).

Opera

One of the most unexpected developments in American culture today is the burgeoning popularity of live opera. Even as symphony attendance declines and movie theater admissions stagnate, opera-going has blossomed. The US has become one of the global leaders in opera, with 125 professional opera companies, 60 percent of them launched since 1970, according to the trade group OPERA America. This is more than Germany and nearly twice as many as Italy. In the most comprehensive recent study, the National Endowment for the Arts found that between 1982 and 2002, total attendance at live opera performances grew 46 percent. Annual admissions are now estimated at 20 million, roughly the same as NFL football games (22 million, including playoffs, in 2006–07). In part, this reflects a perception that seeing opera is cheaper and safer. Consequently, opera travel within America is booming. The Opera Theatre of Saint Louis has drawn attendees from 42 states. The number of American opera productions continues to increase also. As of 2005, OPERA America included companies under its aegis in 44 states. They put on 3,012 performances (up by one-third in just four years) of 420 different productions. Opera companies, moreover, are raising large amounts of money: $387 million in private contributions in 2005 alone. The new opportunities in the US have also made a big difference to singers' careers: the emergence of regional opera in the last 30 years has replaced the necessity for American singers to go to Europe to forge a career.

The new-found popularity of opera has a number of causes. Young people with disposable income may want to try opera for the total aural and visual experience it offers. Modern music videos have helped, too. For many young people, opera is a multimedia art form something like what they know from MTV. Because US companies have to work hard to attract audiences and donors, they put on accessible, if often challenging, productions, and avoid the pretentious and inscrutable. The need to recruit and retain a local audience also means an emphasis on finding the best singers and tailoring the schedule to suit local tastes and interests. Two of America's best opera companies, Santa Fe, founded in 1957, and Glimmerglass, started in 1975, perform during summer festivals in outdoor settings. The regionals can be more flexible than the Metropolitan Opera, New York (the Met) in picking new works and can more easily spot and take advantage of musical trends. Among the operas that have been introduced outside New York are John Adam's *Nixon in China* at the Houston Grand Opera. The acceptance of new works, and of opera generally, may also owe something to the rise of captioning (a typically American technological solution). With the singers' words in supertitles above the stage or on seat titles right in front of the audience (as at Santa Fe and the Met), the experience is more intelligible and comfortable. Many experts would add that the shift toward a local emphasis in American opera reflects the disbanding of the Metropolitan Opera touring company. Moreover singers can easily fly to smaller cities to do single shows. Unlike the touring Met, regional companies typically try to carve out a unique niche for themselves, while recognizing an obligation to make the traditional repertory exciting.

Media coverage, however, still focuses on the Met. With an annual attendance of 800,000, a budget of $200 million, a 125-year history, and an international radio network distributing its Saturday performances, the Met takes up most of the reporting allotted in media arts sections for opera. Yet the Met deserves its reputation, with the world's best singers, a superb orchestra, and lavish spectacle. In 2006, under its new general manager, Peter Gelb, the Met inaugurated high-definition video presentations of several of its operas in movie theaters around the US, Canada, Japan, and Europe. But the Met is unique. Few of today's top singers first made their names on its stage, and the Met's immense size works against both dramatic effect and subtle and refined singing. The Met is designed to hold an audience of nearly 4,000 in a structure with five ascending tiers and broad rows of seats. Into the Met's vast space, singers must project, without amplification, across a stage extending 80 feet back, 103 feet across, and 110 feet up to the rigging. The result is a preference in New York for singers with gargantuan, if sometimes metallic, voices.

Most of the nation's 125 opera companies are small- to medium-size businesses, organized under the tax code as non-profits. In some cases, a strong leader functions both as artistic director and chief administrator. Speight Jenkins, the general director of the Seattle Opera, for example, assumes this dual role. More typical, however, is the setup in Minnesota, where the administrator, Kevin Smith, acts as a buffer between the artistic director, Dale Johnson, and the board. Even if they have excelled in recent years in developing and promoting new singers and repertory, directors are often more occupied with fundraising and marketing than with artistic matters. Tough as it is, the American system is a grassroots system, where companies have to demonstrate their value. Mounting a production is expensive and, even with triple-digit ticket prices, all operas lose money, so the success or failure of each company is tied to its ability to find charismatic and capable leadership and to cultivate local patrons. The rapid growth of the Los Angeles Opera, which was founded only in 1986 but now puts on 10 productions and 75 performances per year with a $54 million budget, is closely connected to the leadership of its general director, the tenor, Placido Domingo, who has attracted contributions from philanthropists. In 2003, Domingo also became general director of the Washington National Opera, a highly regarded company where he does similar work. While the US has more opera companies now than any other nation, total funding remains below that in Germany and other countries. European companies receive massive state subsidies far out of proportion to the occasional NEA, state, and city grants that US groups receive. Government subsidies only come to 5 or 6 percent of the US companies' funding, says OPERA America, but funding from the NEA in particular often influences donors.

Arts funding

In the past 20 years, the arts and culture sector has boomed, especially in new large scale cultural facilities, libraries, museums and concert halls. The number of non-profit performing arts groups, and the revenues from sales and attendance at cultural venues, have risen to all-time highs. Even so, the amount that Americans spend on admission to live, non-profit performing arts is only about half what they spend on flowers, seeds and potted plants. To achieve and sustain such prosperity, artists and arts institutions must rely on a network of allied but independent funding sources which make up the lion's share of contributed income for arts organizations. US arts funding is comprised of public and private entities, tax policies, legislative allocations, donated bequests, restricted endowments, education mandates, and social agendas. The hierarchy of government arts agencies, composed of city, county, state, regional, and federal strata, is a complex scheme, especially compared with nations that have highly centralized, state-directed systems.

In recent years, the main source of federal funding, the National Endowment for the Arts, has been a focus of controversy. In 1989 after acrimonious Congressional debate, the NEA managed to survive, but it was regulated by an obscenity clause. During the 1990s, funding to performers was cut at all levels of government. Prospects for increased federal support for the arts in the 1990s were ruined by four controversies over alleged obscenity: an art photograph by Andres Serrano called *Piss Christ*; an exhibition of the openly gay and sadomasochistic photographs of Robert Mapplethorpe; Madonna's music video for *Like a Prayer*; and British-Nigerian artist Chris Ofili's mixed-media painting *The Holy Virgin Mary*.

The US arts system has no Ministry of Culture. Instead, a variety of public subsidies compose roughly 13% of the nation's total investment in non-profit arts groups. The NEA is the largest single funder of the arts across America, but the majority of direct public funding still flows from a combination of other federal, state, regional and local agencies. Direct public support is not used to impose arts policy. Instead, government decisions on arts funding tend to be driven by experts within a given field or discipline. Candidates for funding are almost always subject to rigorous peer review, which ensures that the award is based on merit, and not on a policy aim or on political favoritism. In any case, direct grants never finance the bulk of artistic activity in the US, which spends less per head on the arts than other comparable countries. Direct grants fill gaps, enhance arts education, spread new creations, and enable preservation. They thus complement, and do not replace, other means of arts funding. Most of the NEA's grants, for example, require the recipient organization to couple the award funds with other, non-federal donations (matching funding). In Fiscal Year 2006, the agency awarded 2,292 grants, ranging from $5,000 to $1.39 million; the most commonly awarded amount was $10,000. The Recovery Act gave the NEA $50 million for job preservation in the arts.

The revenues from individual and corporate donors and from charity foundations make up 43% of total arts funding. This flows more readily because of incentives in the tax system. Together, private and publics account for roughly 56 percent of total funding of US non-profit arts organizations. Non-profit arts groups realize the other 44 percent of their revenue through earned income (ticket sales, subscriptions, etc.) Earned or contributed, both means of income are unpredictable. Consequently, arts directors face a two-sided challenge. On the one hand, they must cope with rising expenditures for artists, artworks, productions, and educational projects. On the other, they must forecast the revenue needed to support their program goals.

PAINTING

The first works of art created in America after the Europeans arrived were probably watercolor drawings made by English artist John White from 1577 to 1590. They show the animals, plants, and Native Americans in and about English settlements in Virginia. Not until the last half of the 17th century did the American colonies produce a sizable body of paintings, all portraits.

The early colonial portraitists, known as *limners* (from the English word *limn*, meaning "to draw") traveled from town to town and were of low status. Some of their portraits were crude, but masterpieces did appear, such as *Mrs. Elizabeth Freake and Baby Mary* (about 1674.) The painting is notable for its sympathetic portrayal of maternal concern. The two chief areas of artistic activity were eastern Massachusetts, where English models that emphasized the outline prevailed, and New York and surrounding regions, where a more realistic, Dutch-influenced tradition that sometimes included landscape with the figure, was practiced. There was also some Native American influence.

As the population increased (by 1720 there were nearly half a million settlers in the colonies) and commerce spread, prosperity and the pursuit of fashion came to cities. In the decades preceding the Revolution, portrait painters such as Robert Feke caught the elegance of wealthy merchants. In Feke's portraits, however, neither the men nor the women show much individuality. The men are richly and tastefully dressed, and the women are young, amply bosomed, and small of waist.

In the years before the Revolution, Boston-born portraitist, John Singleton Copley (1738-1815) focused most on the character of his subjects. While still using something of the outline method of the Massachusetts limners, he made his subjects more three-dimensional. It was from Copley's portraits that the faces of the Boston revolutionary leaders Samuel Adams, Paul Revere, and John Hancock first became well-known. Copley actually valued history painting above portraiture, but as he found no market for such work, because at that time America lacked a significant history, he followed Benjamin West (1738-1820) to England. West spent most of his career in England as official painter to King George III. In England, West's scenes of historic events on American soil, such as *Penn's Treaty with the Indians* (1771-1772), were viewed as part of British history. Today, both the English and the Americans claim West as one of their own.

The subject matter of painting broadened considerably after independence to include history, landscape, still life, and *genre* (everyday scenes of ordinary people), in addition to portraiture. The new nation was in the process of forging an identity, and artists helped by portraying American heroes, depicting important events, and giving visual expression to unfamiliar landscapes. Yet Europeans still provided the models that American painters sought to equal. Charles Willson Peale (1749-1831) was among the most important artists. In his *Exhumation of the Mastodon* (1806), Peale depicted the digging up of two mastodon skeletons on an upstate New York farm. Peale also was a competent portraitist. His brother, James, and son, Raphaelle, became America's first professional still-life painters.

In the early 19th century, landscape emerged as the dominant subject. After independence, George Washington was the most celebrated man in the Western world, and Gilbert Stuart (1755-1828) became his most noted portraitist. Stuart used the contemporary English approach of loosely applying paint in broad strokes, as opposed to the hard linear approach of Copley and other colonial painters. Stuart endowed Washington with a sense of noble imperturbability by glossing over small details of the face, giving his flesh a ruddy glow, and eliminating unattractive features such as the protuberance of the jaw misshapen by false teeth. John Trumbull (1756-1843) created a visual record of the fight for American independence in neoclassical style. His battle scenes, as in *Surrender of General Burgoyne at Saratoga* (1817), are filled with action. The observer perceives the events as set in motion by shared resolve rather than the decision of a single figure.

Americans were aware that their country marked something new in the Western experience, a political entity entirely removed from the dynastic struggles of the European powers. Painters represented this vision of America in different ways. In landscapes they showed nature untouched by human beings, as a kind of Garden of Eden. In *Kindred Spirits* (1849), Asher B. Durand (1796-1886) portrayed painter Thomas Cole and poet William Cullen Bryant, dressed in their Sunday best, on a ledge in a gorge in the Catskill Mountains in New York State as they commune reverently with the grandeur before them. Durand belonged to the Hudson River School, so-called because, from around 1820, its members started out by painting sites along the Hudson River. Thomas Cole (1801-1848), an accomplished landscape painter, settled in Catskill and his fame drew others to the area. The landscapes of the Hudson River School carried religious connotations, a sense that the blessings and goodness of God are discernible through the contemplation of nature's majestic grandeur, in which craggy mountains and lofty trees overwhelm humankind and their concerns. The Hudson River School conceived of the land as wild and intractable, reinforcing America's view of itself as something new. The religious philosophy, Transcendentalism, which saw God as immanent in creation, was spectacularly embodied in such works as Cole's *River in the Catskills* (1843) or his pupil Frederic Church's (1826-1900) *Niagara* (1857). These artists showed America 's mountains and monumental cataracts glowing with the numinous. Another approach to landscape and to seascape avoided the portrayal of dramatic beauty. A group of painters called *luminists*, whose scenes featured large areas of light-filled sky, favored instead a calm and reassuring nature. In paintings by Fitz Hugh Lane (1804-1865), such as *Gloucester Harbor* (1848), everything seems frozen in time. The subdued landscapes of Martin Johnson Heade (1819-1904) made him one of the most important American artists of his generation.

Genre paintings were also plentiful before the Civil War. William Sidney Mount (1807-1868), George Caleb Bingham (1811-1879) and others typically placed figures out-of-doors, energetically engaged in some group activity. Bingham specialized in scenes of frontier life, such as *Fur Traders on the Missouri* (1845). This painting depicts an old trader, his son, and a bear cub tied to their boat, all bathed in a diffuse, poetic light.

Some artists in this period held the belief that history moved in cycles marked by the rise and fall of empires, cycles they hoped would not control America's destiny. Landscape painter Thomas Cole painted a five-canvas series called *The Course of Empire* (1833-36) that deals with this imagined historical process. Washington Allston (179-1843) was also interested in the idea of young and aging civilizations. He labored for years on *Belshazzar's Feast* (1817-1843).

In the decades before the American Civil War, European settlers and their descendants continued to push westward, displacing Native Americans. The West, with its dramatic landscapes and unfamiliar inhabitants, offered artists new subjects. Some painters and sculptors presented Native Americans as dangerous marauders; others, as undeveloped peoples standing in the way of civilization's progress. George Catlin (1796-1872), however, whose mother had been briefly kidnapped by Native Americans when he was a child, lamented the imminent disappearance of native folkways and wished to preserve a record of them through his art. Closely studying the Native Americans of the Great Plains during the eight years he spent among them, he recorded their dances, hunting expeditions, and other activities as a kind of visual anthropologist.

Another artist to take an interest in colorful and unfamiliar aspects of America was the naturalist John James Audubon (1785-1851), who in his drawings of birds combined a sense of design with detailed observation. His four-volume *Birds of America, from Original Drawings*, with 435 plates showing 1,065 figures of birds, was published in England from 1827 to 1838.

The Hudson River painters' directness and simplicity influenced such later artists as Winslow Homer (1836-1910), who depicted rural America - the sea, the mountains, and the people who lived near them. Middle class city life found its painter in Thomas Eakins (1844-1916), an uncompromising realist whose unflinching honesty undercut the genteel preference for the romantic and the sentimental.

After independence, the training of artists became more professional. In 1794 Charles Willson

Peale organized the Columbianum, the first society of American artists, in Philadelphia, which held its first exhibition in 1795. In 1805 Peale became one of the founders of the Pennsylvania Academy of the Fine Arts, the nation's first art school, as well as the repository of its first permanent public collection. In 1817 John Trumbull became the first head of the New York Academy of Arts (later the American Academy of the Fine Arts.) Despite the presence of Peale and Trumbull, however, businessmen rather than artists played the main role in founding and running both institutions.

At first most artists in America lived along the Eastern seaboard, but starting in the 1830s and 1840s some artists from the East pushed westward, a move reflected in paintings of Native Americans by George Catlin and paintings of animals and Native Americans of the Rocky Mountain region by Albert Bierstadt (1830-1902).

After the Civil War (1861-1865) artists no longer considered it sufficient to achieve a likeness; they began to probe into the national or individual psyche. Nature became far grander in the vast earthscapes of Federick E. Church. In Church's paintings the vista is so overwhelming that the viewer feels utterly lost within it. He suggests the beginnings of Earth's formation through awesome geological processes beyond human comprehension. Historians have linked Church's canvases with Manifest Destiny, the belief that it was the inherent right of the US to expand to the Pacific Ocean.

Painters such as Albert Bierstadt helped people living in the Eastern states envision US territory in the West. His painting *Among the Sierra Nevada Mountains, California* (1868) shows a group of deer grazing at the edge of a lake in the foreground, with the peaks beyond so grand that Easterners could not have imagined them.

Another painter to turn the West into a colorful spectacle was Thomas Moran (1837-1926). Although he started out as a member of the Hudson River School, Moran traveled West and produced dozens of watercolors of Yellowstone and the Grand Canyon. Moran and many others chose times of day with dramatic light—sunrises, sunsets, and twilight—as in *Sunset* (1901).

In his *Sundown* (1894), landscape painter George Inness (1825-1894) also departed from the reassuring vision of the Hudson River School. The scene in *Sundown* is not an attractive gorge in the Catskills or a grand mountain vista, but a rundown farm. The mood that prevails is one of stillness, even sadness, a response to the devastation and social disruption brought about by the Civil War. This mood was found in much American painting of the time.

During the last three decades of the 19th century, American portraitists aimed for more than the recording of likenesses. Thomas Eakins (1844-1916) depicted the distinguished surgeon Dr. Samuel David Gross as he directed an operation before onlookers in the surgical amphitheater of Jefferson Medical College in Philadelphia (*The Gross Clinic*, 1875). Gross appears as the great leader of a team of healers. All action occurs around him as he stands at the center, unperturbed. Light appears to flow from his brightly lit, high forehead, expressing the surgeon's wisdom and kindness as well as his scientific knowledge.

A more distinguished portraitist of this era, John Singer Sargent (1856-1925) received many portrait commissions from wealthy patrons, and also portrayed social climbers. His portrait of *Madame Pierre Gautreau* (1884) reveals the vanity and self-indulgence of its subject, who had married a wealthy French businessman and aspired to advance in European society. Her haughty bearing and shockingly low-cut gown made the painting so scandalous that it came to be known simply as *Madame X*. In *Madame Gautreau Drinking a Toast* (1882-1883), also by Sargent, her shoulders are covered by chiffon but her haughty demeanor remains.

A contemporary of Sargent who also worked mainly in Europe, was Mary Cassatt (1844-1926). Cassatt became a close friend of Edgar Degas, and exhibited with the French impressionists, whose style she adopted. She showed figures in a moment of time, apparently caught off-guard, as in *Mrs. Cassatt Reading to Her Grandchildren* (1880).

Of the variety of approaches to portraiture, none in this period was more advanced than that of James Abbott McNeill Whistler (1834-1903). Most of his life was spent in Europe, where he adopted the slogan "art for art's sake." By this he meant that art need have no other purpose than to please through its beauty and need not have an instructive or morally elevating subject matter, as most painters before and during his lifetime believed. Whistler called his paintings by the musical terms *symphony, nocturne, arrangement,* and *composition* because he claimed that "as music is the poetry of sound, so is painting the poetry of sight, and the subject matter has nothing to do with harmony of sound or of color." The primary title of the portrait of his mother is *An Arrangement in Grey and Black No. 1* (1871). It is a nearly *monochromatic* (single-color) composition of rectangles—the baseboard, the curtain, the picture frames, the rug—that is broken by the asymmetrical profile of the woman. Whistler's adherence to basic geometric forms in this painting anticipated the minimalist art of the 1960s. Ironically, the portrait of Whistler's mother, noted by contemporaries for its lack of sentimentality, is regarded today as a glorification of motherhood.

The pre-Civil War American genre painters, such as Bingham, had been more concerned with portraying a way of life than with exploring the inner life of their subjects. But after the war a meditative atmosphere surrounds the disconnected figures in dimly lit, largely empty interiors painted by African American artist Henry Ossawa Tanner (1857-1937), as in *Interior with Woman Spinning*. Tanner, a pupil of Thomas Eakins, also painted religious subjects, such as *Angels Appearing Before the Shepherds* (about 1910).

Winslow Homer is best known for his seascapes, such as *High Cliff, Coast of Maine* (1894), and his scenes of men struggling against the sea, which emphasize its power. But he also worked as a genre painter from the end of the Civil War to 1881. His *Veteran in a New Field* (1866) shows an ex-soldier, now a farmer, harvesting his wheat with a scythe. But unlike the reaper with a scythe who typically signifies death, this farmer brings forth life and renewal. The painting suggests that swords have been beaten into plowshares, a metaphor of peace.

As the frontier began to disappear toward the end of the 19th century, scenes and sagas of the Old West became more popular than ever. But nostalgia had set in. Where Catlin, in paintings of the 1840s and 1850s, had sought to record a way of life, Frederic Remington (1861-1909) revealed a different interest. He ignored the suffering and hardship undergone by settlers and Native Americans. Instead, Remington evoked for people in the Eastern states the sense of a West that never fully existed, a place of never-ceasing romantic excitement.

Childe Hassam (1859-1935) became known as "the American Monet" because his sensitivity to the effects of light was reminiscent of the French Impressionist. Yet his impressionism was really home-grown. He painted primarily American subjects and, unlike European impressionists, stuck to descriptive color, although he borrowed the Impressionist technique of cutting off figures and objects by the edge of the painting, much as a snapshot might. He helped found an impressionist group called The Ten. In *Celia Thaxter in her Garden* (1892), the bright colors, the loose brush strokes used to paint the flowers, and the dappled light display Hassam's impressionist manner. He kept the figures and objects in his paintings fairly intact, in contrast to contemporary Europeans who tended to dissolve objects into patches of color.

Other noted impressionists were William Merritt Chase (1849-1916) and John Twachtman (1853-1902). Chase favored dark tones and a loose, almost slap-dash application of paint. This approach contrasted with the muted palette of whites and grays of Twachtman. In *Fishing Boats at Gloucester* (1901) Twachtman represented the sky, water, boats, and buildings along the harbor of Gloucester, Massachusetts, in silvery-blue and soft pink tones, unlike the bright colors favored by Monet and other Europeans.

Meanwhile a group of artists known as the visionaries was united neither by style nor by subject, but by a general approach, a certain cast of mind. Their images evoked an inner dream world conjured from the imagination. Visionary painter Albert Pinkham Ryder (1847-1917) painted lone boats beneath a strangely luminous sky in which the moon appears to emit an eerie glow, as in *Moonlight* (1887). In 1872 Ralph Albert Blakelock (1847-1919), another visionary painter, began to depict the Native Americans he had seen on the Great Plains as tiny passive figures within a vast mysterious, moon-drenched realm, as in *Moonlight* (1880s or early 1890s).

Controversy soon became a way of life for American artists. In fact, much of American painting and sculpture since 1900 has been an accelerating series of revolts against tradition. Movement has followed movement at an ever-faster pace and with growing profusion, until at the century's end it had become impossible to identify a dominant trend.

The first artistic rebellion of the 20th century saw the emergence of The Eight, a group of eight artists who showed their work together in 1908 in New York City's Macbeth Gallery. The Eight were linked by their rebellion against the subjects considered proper for painting at the time, but their approach to style remained basically impressionist. Five members of The Eight - Robert Henri, William Glackens, George Luks, Everett Shinn, and John Sloan.- were later dubbed "the Ashcan school," a reference to their brand of realism drawn from portrayal of squalid aspects of city life. (Other names for The Eight were Apostles of Ugliness and the Revolutionary Gang.) "To hell with the artistic values," announced Robert Henri (1865-1929), their leader. Soon the ashcan artists gave way to modernists arriving from Europe, the cubists and abstract painters promoted by the photographer Alfred Stieglitz (1864-1946) at his Gallery 291 in New York City.

The Eight featured as their subject matter the life of the people of New York's Lower East Side, which by the first decade of the 20th century was teeming with immigrants from Italy, eastern Europe, and elsewhere. These artists viewed the paintings of Whistler as elitist (appealing only to a select few), the paintings of the visionaries as too private in meaning, the subjects of the impressionists as irrelevant to modern city life, and the late seascapes of Homer as escapist. The Eight's spokesman, Henri, contended that the working classes were the most suitable subjects for art and that the artist was a social force whose "work creates a stir in the world." The Eight captured the grittiness of New York life.

The best-known members of The Eight are Luks, Sloan, Glackens, and Prendergast. Luks (1867-1933) passed himself off as a working class tough, and painted physically active, straining figures in works such as *The Wrestlers* (1905). He worked with dark tones and expressed disdain for all artists of the past except for the 17th-century Dutch artist, Frans Hals, who also depicted the low-life types of his time. Sloan (1871-1951) was adept at showing the seamy side of city life, in the streets, inside tenements, and even on rooftops. His etching *Turning Out the Lights* (1905), which gives the viewer a glimpse of a drab, dimly lit interior, is part of a series titled *New York Life*. Glackens (1870-1938), who used bright colors closer to those of the French Impressionists, preferred scenes of crowds in parks, in theaters, or at beaches, as in *Beach Umbrellas at Blue Point* (1915). Prendergast (1858-1924) used large spots of vivid color to give an abstract tapestry-like effect to his paintings, such as *Summer, New England* (1912). For Glackens and Prendergast, the city was a place of camaraderie and fulfillment, regardless of the economic status of its inhabitants.

Many historians regard the so-called Armory Show of 1913 in New York as the most important art exhibition in the US in the 20th century, and credit it with having helped to bring the modern movement in art to America. The exhibition featured some 1,300 European and American works, beginning in time with a miniature from 1799 by Spanish master Francisco de Goya. The American artists represented included Hassam, Twachtman, Ryder, Luks, Sloan, Glackens, and Prendergast. Some American painters, notably Stuart Davis, converted to modernism as a result of seeing the exhibition.

In the decades following the Armory Show the views of the city put forth by The Eight would appear rosy, and the ability of artists to find beauty in crowded city life disappeared for the most part. Differences between rich and poor became noticed and resented. In addition to addressing economic hardships, artists observed that loneliness existed in crowded cities and that psychological barriers arose between people in close physical proximity.

The revelation of urban loneliness was the special province of Edward Hopper (1882-1967). He studied under Robert Henri and Kenneth Hayes Miller and exhibited in the Armory Show. His etching *East Side Interior* (1922) shows a woman seated at her sewing machine next to a window in a crowded interior. The artist has placed a chair and other objects in the room so that they hem the woman in as she looks dreamily out of the window, hoping (we are led to assume) to escape her unhappy existence. This is not the active, self-sufficient woman in Sloan's *Turning Out the Lights*. Motion pictures attracted Hopper as a subject, not as spectacle so much as a darkened place of escape from the boredom and harsh realities of life. In his *New York Movie* (1939), the audience sits in a darkened, extravagantly decorated auditorium, while in the hall outside a young, harshly lit usherette, her head bowed, laments her state. The loneliness of city life is also evident in Hopper's *From Williamsburg Bridge* (1928). In this painting nothing is alive, and the bridge railing in the foreground blocks our view of the street and the lower stories of the buildings beyond, leaving a picture of vacant upper-story windows.

If Hopper's figures are passive, those in the works of Reginald Marsh (1898-1954) are boisterous, carried along by the crowds of which they are a part. In many cases these crowds lie on Coney Island's beaches or promenade about its amusement parks, stopping to look at freak shows and other displays. Marsh also depicted the urban poor during the Great Depression. His etching *Tenth Avenue at 27th Street* (1931) shows unemployed men loitering about New York's streets with nowhere to go. Two artists who created less obviously dramatic urban scenes are Isabel Bishop (1902-1988), who studied under Marsh and Miller, and Raphael Soyer (1899-1987). They showed the quiet day-to-day struggles of ordinary people, often women, trying to get along in the city. In Bishop's *Waiting* (1938), a haggard woman, her packages beside her and her child asleep on her lap, waits in a station for a train or a bus. In Soyer's *Office Girls* (1936), young working women pass alertly though tensely along a crowded street.

During the period between the two world wars, modernism burst upon the American scene. Painters discarded realism, choosing instead to break up forms or overlay transparent planes in the manner of European cubism, to distort objects in the manner of European expressionism, and even to paint canvases in which nothing was recognizable. The latter choice was in keeping with the work of Europe's early *nonobjective* (completely abstract or non-representational) artists, such as Piet Mondrian from The Netherlands or the Russians, Kasimir Malevich and Wassily Kandinsky.

Arthur Garfield Dove (1880-1946) was one of America's first nonobjective painters. He began in 1910, independently of Kandinsky, and moved back and forth between realism and abstraction. Some of Dove's nonobjective paintings suggest—without actually picturing—landscapes with moons or suns. In the late work *Sun* (1943), he comes closest to representing a recognizable solar disk.

Skyscrapers quickly became symbols of modernism in America. Early modernist artists tilted and merged these tall buildings in their work to suggest urban dynamism and convey something of the dizzying sensation pedestrians experience while walking by a skyscraper. Max Weber (1881-1961) used this device in *Rush Hour, New York* (1915), and John Marin incorporated it in *Lower Manhattan (Composing Derived from Top of Woolworth)* (1922).

Dove, Marin, Weber, and Marsden Hartley (1877-1943), received emotional and, at times, financial support from the photographer Alfred Stieglitz. Hartley's work featured objects that were flattened in the manner of cubism. Stuart Davis (1892-1964) was another modernist who, under the influence of cubism, flattened objects, rearranged their parts, and changed their relative sizes. By the time Davis painted *Abstraction* (1937), most of the objects in his paintings had become unidentifiable.

Emmanuel Radenski (1890-1976), who took the name Man Ray, used ready made objects, rather than painting them, as demonstrated in *Object to be Destroyed* (1923). This work consisted of a metronome with a paper image of an eye attached to the pendulum, which, when swinging, was meant to have a hypnotic effect on the spectator.

Precisionism prevailed during the 1920s and 1930s. Precisionism depicted simplified but recognizable forms reduced to their essential geometry. Many of the subjects of precisionist art had a distinctly American character—factory buildings, Pennsylvania barns, early American churches, and other structures that were plain and sturdy. The turn to American subject matter can be attributed largely to the growing isolation of the US after World War I. Charles Demuth (1883-1935) and Charles Sheeler (1883-1965) are the best-known American precisionist painters. *After All* (1933), Demuth's painting of parts of factory complexes, demonstrates the simplification of forms that the precisionists favored. Demuth most likely took the title of the painting from a stanza in Walt Whitman's *Leaves of Grass* (1855), a volume that marked the beginning of a uniquely American poetry. In some of Sheeler's paintings of rural buildings, he set them back in space, omitted doors and windows, and left the foreground bare, as in *Bucks County Barn* (1923). In a later painting showing New England barns, *Connecticut Barns in Landscape* (1934), the sharply focused, hard-edged barns contrast with the soft, slightly out-of-focus landscape around them.

Stieglitz's wife Georgia O'Keeffe (1887-1986) applied her precisionist vision to the American Southwest. O'Keeffe painted desert stones and flowers, cows' skulls bleached white by the sun, crosses left by Spanish Catholic missionaries in New Mexico in the 1600s and 1700s, and old adobe churches. An example of the latter is *Ranchos Church* (1930).

Despite the arrival of modernism, realism persisted in American art in the 1920s and 1930s, chiefly in the form of regionalism and social realism. Most of the regionalists were white, American-born, of European ancestry, and antiurban in their outlook. They celebrated in their art the culture of small towns and rural life, which they regarded as authentically American. The social realists, on the other hand, consisted mostly of Jewish and black artists and were urban in their orientation.

They saw the US as a place of discrimination and injustice, and of privilege vested in a wealthy upper class. Both groups sought to portray American subjects in a way that could be understood by all, not just an elite few.

Thomas Hart Benton (1889-1975), the leader of the regionalists, painted vast surveys of different industries and histories of particular regions, including those of his native Missouri. He sympathized with the working clsss and small farmer and peopled his almost sculpted canvases with vigorous horseshoe pitchers, country fiddlers, cowboys, star-crossed country lovers, hay mowers, and cotton pickers. For the Missouri state capitol he painted a large mural entitled *A Social History of Missouri* (1935) which caused controversy by depicting slavery. Grant Wood (1891-1942) from Iowa was exceptional among the regionalists in two respects. First, he drew inspiration from Flemish and German paintings of the 14th and 15th centuries, which he had seen in Europe. Like these artists, he painted some areas of his canvases meticulously in minute detail. Secondly, he lampooned some of the country folk he pictured, as in his *American Gothic* (1930).

Ben Shahn (1898-1969), a social realist, painted *The Passion of Sacco and Vanzetti* (1931-1932). In the painting the men controversially executed for murder are shown as Christian martyrs with their final accusers standing next to their coffins like attending saints. African American artist Jacob Lawrence (1917-2000) focused on the history and sufferings of his race. His painting *Tombstones* (1942) is marked by irony. It shows a black family living above a shop for tombstones. William Henry Johnson (1901-1970) dealt with experiences of African Americans, such as *Ferry Boat Trip* (1943-1944).

Several notable American painters had their own distinctive styles. Charles Burchfield (1893-1967) was sensitive to the frightening appearance of old, decaying buildings in backwater towns. In his *Church Bells Ringing, Rainy Winter Night* (1917), he encases human faces within the facades of houses and makes the church steeple suggest a human head. Ivan Le Lorraine Albright (1897-1983) painted old and decrepit people, whose wrinkles, cracked skin, blemishes, and protruding veins he recorded in great detail, as in *The Farmer's Kitchen* (1933-1934).

Because of the divergence between religion and the fine arts, fewer great artists painted overtly religious subjects. William Sallman's *Head of Christ*, a 1940 oil painting inspired by Victorian precedents, showed a long-haired Jesus as the gentle, benevolent Good Shepherd, bathed in light and gazing raptly toward heaven. In *Icons of American Protestantism*, David Morgan notes that *Head of Christ* was reproduced five hundred million times over the next four decades. Many critics, even believers, however, rejected the painting as sentimental kitsch and denounced its portrayal of Christ as effeminate as well as overly Nordic Caucasian. (Sallman was in fact the son of Scandinavian immigrants.)

CONTEMPORARY AFRICAN AMERICAN ARTISTS

Simmie Knox portraitist
Alma Thomas abstract expressionist
Edward Bannister landscapes
Lois Mailou watercolors
Hale Woodruff murals
Charles Alston murals
William H. Johnson modernist

After World War II, New York City became the world's major art center, and American artists no longer saw themselves as following in the shadow of European art. A number of painters who would become noted abstract expressionists had immigrated to the US before the war. They included Arshile Gorky, Mark Rothko, Willem de Kooning, and Hans Hofmann. During the war, Mondrian, Marc Chagall, and other important European artists sought refuge in the US.

In this period, a group of young New York abstract expressionists formed the first American movement to exert major influence on foreign artists. Among the movement's leaders were Jackson Pollock (1912-1956), Willem de Kooning (1904-1997), and Mark Rothko (1903-1970). The abstract expressionists abandoned formal composition and representation of real objects to concentrate on instinctual arrangements of space and color and to demonstrate the effects of the physical action of painting on the canvas. Later 20th-century American art movements, such as pop art and minimal art, also had an international impact. Abstract expressionism was the foremost modernist art form of the 1940s and 1950s, producing daring, adventurous, and forceful art such as Richard Diebenkorn's. Stylistically, abstract expressionists fell into two groups. The first applied paint in rapid gestures, flinging, splattering, or dribbling it, or laying it on in slashing, dramatic brushstrokes. This branch of abstract expressionism is sometimes called *action painting*. Artists in the second group applied paint in broad areas, and their branch is sometimes referred to as *color field* painting. Painters in both groups insisted that their paintings were not merely decorative, but had content and referred to universal concepts, feelings, or ideas.

The best-known action painters are Jackson Pollock, Gorky, Franz Kline, and de Kooning. Pollock developed a method of dripping paint onto canvas in intricate webs from which an image or emotion might—or might not—eventually emerge. His *Cathedral* (1947) suggests vertical extension, as in a cathedral, that defies the pull of gravity. The glowing colors and network of forms in Arshile Gorky's (1895-1948) *Waterfall* (1943) are meant to suggest the landscape near his Connecticut home. This painting is one of a series of waterfalls and landscapes that he painted in the 1940s. Franz Kline's (1910-1962) black-and-white *Meryon* (1960-1961), its black streaks pushing outward at the edges of the canvas, implies an essentially American idea of boundlessness. In de Kooning's (1918-1989) *Marilyn* (1949), the broken forms and lines seem to assert the figure of a woman within a pervasive chaos.

The best-known color field painters are Rothko, Clyfford Still, William Baziotes, Robert Motherwell and Josef Albers. The floating rectangles of color in Mark Rothko's (1903-1970) paintings evoke a sense of calmness and surrender rather than the feeling of ceaseless activity conveyed by the action painters. The flamelike jagged forms in Still's (1904-1980) paintings bring to mind both constructive and destructive processes in nature, such as burning forests that clear the way for new growth. In Baziotes's (1912-1963) paintings, such as *Primeval Landscape* (1953), semitransparent floating shapes resemble primitive, single-celled organisms. Motherwell (1915-1991) created a series of black-and-white paintings titled *Elegies to the Spanish Republic,* in which he placed egg-shaped forms between vertical bars, presumably with the intention of recalling the Spanish Civil War.

A second generation of abstract expressionists, including Grace Hartigan and Joan Mitchell, carried the movement into the 1960s and 1970s. But by the mid-1950s other directions in avant-garde art had emerged, for example in the work of Jasper Johns, Robert Rauschenberg, and Larry Rivers. Johns' (1930-) paintings of common objects—including flags, targets, numbers, and maps—mystified the art world, coming as they did during the heyday of abstract expressionism.

What Johns wished to do was to subvert the meanings of these objects. Is a painting of a flag still a flag? Or when an entire painting is the image of a flag, does the sense of a flag as a symbol of the country then slip away? Does the flag become simply a pattern? Where abstract expressionists had sought to express meaning through abstract form, gesture, and color, Johns aimed to remove the meaning from objects that are laden with connotations. Rauschenberg (1925-2008) retained something of abstract expressionism in the streaks of paint applied to his work *Estate* (1963), but he composed most of the surface of images from photographs and newspapers that he silk-screened onto the canvas. Some of the images he chose for this composition refer to freedom and control: traffic signs, the Statue of Liberty, and the Sistine Chapel during the Second Vatican Council, a period of openness in the Roman Catholic Church. Rivers (1923-2002), too, stands at the edge of abstract expressionism, having retained its splatters of paint while deriving his images from cigar box lids and famous paintings of the past. His gift for facial characterization is evident in *Parts of the Face* (1961).

Representational art portraying recognizable objects continued alongside abstract expressionism, primarily outside New York. On the West Coast, the Bay Area Figurative School emerged in the 1950s and became known for its landscapes and paintings of the human figure. One of its leading members, San Francisco artist Richard Diebenkorn (1922-1993), created softly colored grids whose compositions suggest boulevards or, in *View of Oakland* (1962), the rooftops of a city. Wayne Thiebaud (1920-) painted pastries and other foodstuffs, taking care to emphasize their gooey and shiny qualities.

Andrew Wyeth (1917-2009) painted country scenes, some marked by a sense of disquieting solitude. One of his most poignant works, *Christina's World* (1948), is set in Maine and shows a physically disabled young woman as she struggles to reach a distant house at the top of a hill. Morrs Graves, a follower of Zen, painted birds and other aspects of nature. He regarded his birds, which he often showed as blind, to have moved beyond their physical presence to become symbols of the inner life, as in *Raven in Moonlight* (1943).

Romare Bearden and Betye Saar dealt with their identities as African Americans, but unlike social realist Jacob Lawrence, they did not focus on the sufferings of their race. Bearden (1911-1988) focused on the solidity of the family and the community (*Family*, 1988), and Saar (1926-) on the mystical aspects of her people's collective past (*Black Girl's Window*, 1969). Robert Colescott (1925-) recast the figures in famous paintings of the past with blackface stereotypes of African Americans, thereby satirizing the paintings and pointing to the absence of African Americans in white histories.

The representational art movement that emerged in New York in the 1960s was pop art, which followed Johns and Rauschenberg in its use of images drawn from popular culture. But unlike them, who incorporated mass-produced objects and images in their art, the pop artists re-created commonplace objects and images—soup cans, comic strips and Coca-cola bottles—as works of art in their own right. The pop art movement began in part as a reaction against abstract expressionism, which pop artists believed was too intellectual and divorced from real life. Rather than glorifying the creative process and the artist's personal touch as abstract expressionism had done, pop art embraced mechanical creation and the impersonality and repetitiveness of the mass media. As with post-painterly abstraction, there seemed to be a lack of involvement on the part of the artist, an absence of allusions or possible interpretations. The writer Susan Sontag characterized the avant-garde art of the 1960s and 1970s as "a flight from interpretation."

The leading pop painters include Andy Warhol, Roy Lichtenstein, James Rosenquist and Edward Ruscha. Warhol, who had enjoyed a successful career as a commercial illustrator, showed as single images, or rows of images, objects so frequently seen and so immediately recognizable that people never stopped to examine them closely. These objects included dollar bills, the face of Marilyn Monroe as displayed on billboards or in magazines, and Campbell's soup cans. Warhol's (1928-1987) attitude toward these objects, positive or negative, cannot be discerned. Surfaces were everything, he claimed. Critics found more behind images of an electric chair or a car crash Warhol re-created from news photos. By repeating the static images, reproducing them in altered colors such as silver and black, and displaying them as art, Warhol restored shock value to the images and what they depicted.

Using greatly enlarged frames of comic strips, Lichtenstein (1923-1997) made paintings dealing with dramatic situations, such as war and romantic entanglements. His large, colorful paintings, such as *Whaam!* (1963), purposefully pointed to their distance from reality. If actual fighting constituted the experience in *Whaam!*, and a photograph that captured that experience was a step away from the reality, then a comic strip based on the photograph would be still another step removed. Finally, a painting based on the comic strip would be at the furthest remove from the actual experience of war.

Rosenquist (1933-) began as a billboard painter, and his pop paintings reveal this background with their enormous size and oversized images. Advertising also influenced his art, and his fragmented images in unrelated juxtaposition capture the visual overload of a consumer culture. Jim Dine (1936-), another pop artist, used as his subjects items found in catalogs, such as ties, bathrobes, and heart-shaped objects (*Putney Winter Heart*, 1971-1972).

The conceptual approach to art was widespread in the last decades of the 20th century. In this approach, introduced by Duchamp in the second decade of the century, the concept or novel idea becomes more important than the art object. The conceptual art movement took off in the 1960s, spearheaded in America by artists Sol Lewitt, Joseph Kosuth, and others. Lewitt's (1928-2007) concepts were so straightforward that he could telephone the instructions for others to execute. Among his works are three-dimensional grids of open cubes and geometric drawings based on straight lines. Kosuth (1945-) explored language and meaning, exhibiting, for example, an object (such as a chair), its photograph, and a printed dictionary definition of the object, leaving the observer to ponder the reality of each.

Some conceptual artists worked with industrial materials. Carl Andre (1935-) employed bricks, squares of metal, and other materials that spread over the floor or ground, usually in flat, rectangular patterns as in *144 Magnesium Squares* (1969). Explaining what he had done, Andre wrote that his work "is atheistic because it is without transcendent form, without spiritual or intellectual qualities; materialistic because it is made out of its own materials without pretension to other materials; and communistic because the form is equally accessible to all men." Dan Flavin (1933-1996) used fluorescent light tubes in different colors, displayed vertically or in various configurations, to transform visually the space they illuminated. These works, as a result, extend beyond the physical object into the onlooker's space, as in *Monument for V. Tatlin* (1969), which pays homage in its composition to the Russian constructivist sculptor Vladimir Tatlin. In some of Flavin's works, the lights flash rhythmically on and off. The work of Andre and Flavin also falls into the category of minimal art, sculpture and painting based on geometric modules or other simple units.

Conceptual art even encompassed nature and natural forces, and some artists brought art out of the gallery through what became known as *earthworks* or *earth art*. Earth art was constructed within and in harmony with the landscape and ordinarily lasted only a limited time before natural processes wore it away. One of the best-known earthworks is *Spiral Jetty,* created in Utah in 1970 by Robert Smithson (1938-1973). After having 6,000 tons of earth deposited in the Great Salt Lake, Smithson built upon this layer a graceful, narrow coil out of black rock and salt crystals. This coil or spiral jetty, which extended into the lake, was 4.6 m (15 ft) wide and 457 m (1,500 ft) long. The presence of the jetty altered the viewer's experience of the lake. Although rising water submerged the jetty soon after its completion, photographs and drawings of it remain.

Many of the art movements of the 1970s continued into the latter part of the 20th century. Some artists altered the outdoor environment in ways related to earth art. Others moved their environment-altering art indoors and created room-size artworks. Artists worked in an ever-greater variety of media, including electronic media, especially videos. Some took their art online. A number of artists sought to raise public consciousness by confronting issues such as racism and feminism.

In the late 1970s and the 1980s a number of artists rejected the constraints of conceptual and minimal art, returning instead to image-based painting. Among the first to do so were Susan Rothenberg and Jennifer Bartlett. Rothenberg (1945-) used thick, expressive strokes of paint, usually in a single color, to depict indistinct human and animal forms in a spectral atmosphere, as in *Vertical Spin* (1986-1987). Bartlett (1941-) created multipart compositions that explore the relationship between light and color. The *Study for Swimmers Atlanta* series (1979) comprises 11 colorful paintings on two of Bartlett's favorite themes: water and swimmers.

The human figure took on greater importance in a movement known as neo-expressionism, which gained strength in Europe in the 1970s and had a great impact in America in the 1980s. Among its leaders in the US were Julian Schnabel, David Salle, and Eric Fischl. These artists broke with the cool and impersonal approach of the minimal and conceptual artists. Like Rothenberg, they used energetic brushwork to raise the emotional temperature and expressiveness of their work. Schnabel (1951-) painted on various surfaces, including broken crockery that he attached to his canvases. Salle (1952-) borrowed imagery from past art and from comics and other mass media. Fischl (1948-) painted suburban life with a loose brush in a realist manner, but with a disturbing, often sexual, subtext.

Other artists depicted figures in almost cartoonish ways. Philip Guston (1913-1980), who had gained prominence as an abstract expressionist, began painting human figures and body parts in a deliberately awkward manner. These distorted images were rendered in unpleasant hues of red and pink, as in *Transition* (1975). Keith Haring (1958-1990) in the 1980s worked cartoonlike outlines of human figures into colorful all-over patterns that drew on many sources, including graffiti.

A group of artists known as *photorealists* carried on the cool, detached attitude of post-painterly abstraction and pop art. They created detailed paintings that look like huge photographs. Richard Estes (1932-) depicted cityscapes, often reflected in plate-glass windows or on shiny car fenders. The city scenes Estes chose were not especially picturesque or identifiable as rich or poor; they did not offer an overview of a part of the city. Nor did they have a focus; they appeared as fragments, cropped and shown with full clarity, like an unseasoned photographer in a snapshot, as in *American Express Downtown* (1979). Chuck Close (1940-) concentrated on the human head in enlarged close-up views. To transfer the image, he created a grid on the original photograph, then painted each section of the grid on the canvas. Close's portraits, such as *Lucas II* (1987), also mimic the three-color separation technique or computer techniques of photography. Audrey Flack (1931-), another photorealist, created brightly colored still-lifes by projecting slides onto canvas and then painting the projected images.

Much of the art of the 1990s was issue-oriented and explored gender and identity through the experiences of women, gays, African Americans, and other groups. Among the important feminist artists were photographer Cindy Sherman (1954-), who took on different female roles in her art, and conceptual artists Jenny Holzer and Barbara Kruger, who questioned clichés and advertising images. African American artist Melvin Edwards (1937-) worked on a series of metal sculptures called *Lynch Fragments,* which deal with violence against African Americans. Faith Ringgold (1930-) commented on the plight of African Americans through her story quilts, which narrate tales of fictional characters through painting, stitchery, and handwritten texts.

A few artists of the late 20th century used their own bodies as art. Sherman featured herself in various guises and roles. In the 1990s she began to re-create famous works of art, using herself as the subject. Other artists explored issues through language. Holzer (1950-) used words in various ways, especially statements that appear to express obvious truths with authority. In presenting these truisms, as carved in marble in the 1987 work *Untitled,* she forces the viewer to consider these statements and decide whether he or she agrees or disagrees with them. In an online work entitled *Please Change Beliefs,* Holzer invited people to read a stream of truisms, choose among them, and add their own. Feminist artist Barbara Kruger (1945-) presented words together with mass media images in collages in the format of a magazine layout. The words function as commentary on the cultural underpinnings of the image, as in *Untitled (No),* a 1985 work that shows a child thumbing its nose. Each image in this series of untitled prints illustrates a single word. Many of her images are angry or aggressive.

At the turn of the 21st century, no one or two main trends dominated American Art, which was in a period of pluralism that encompassed a bewildering variety of styles and techniques. In the last decades of the 20th century, art in America embraced new materials, including industrial metals; vinyl, cloth, and other soft materials; fluorescent lights; and even the earth itself. Today artists in America tend not to restrict themselves to schools, styles, or a single medium. A work of art might be a performance on stage or a hand-written manifesto; it might be a massive design cut into a Western desert or a severe arrangement of marble panels inscribed with the names of American soldiers who died in Vietnam. Perhaps the most influential 20th-century American contribution to world art has been a mocking playfulness, a sense that a central purpose of a new work is to join the ongoing debate over the definition of art itself.

Excerpted with the permission of the author, Professor Abraham Davidson, from "American Art," Microsoft® Encarta® Online Encyclopedia 2007 http://encarta.msn.com © 1997-2007 Microsoft Corporation. All Rights Reserved.

SCULPTURE

Sculpture in the round—sculpture meant to be seen from all sides—did not exist in the colonies in the 17th century. Carved gravestones were abundant, however, and their sculpted motifs of skulls or skeletons with scythes were reminders of the inevitability of death. During the 1700s the colonists began creating sculpture apart from gravestones. Among the items that appeared were copper weather vanes, carved wooden figureheads for the fronts of ships, and wooden figures placed outside shop doors to identify the trade found inside. Woodcarvers generally based ship figureheads on mythical figures such as mermaids. The workshop of Simeon Skillin (1716-1778) and his three sons in Boston turned out some of the best of these. Wooden shop figures included cigar store Indians to identify a tobacconist (Native Americans had introduced Europeans to tobacco) and sailors to identify a ships' supplier. Woodcarvers continued to make these figures throughout the 19th century. American sculptors became more ambitious in style and subject matter as they moved beyond the utilitarian pieces of the crafts tradition to what they considered a higher artistic level. In the early 1800s they began to carve large pieces in marble that carried associations with classical culture. The loftiness of the subject matter was of paramount importance. Like other Americans of their time, these sculptors found a fitting model for their own young republic in ancient Greece and Rome, civilizations in which it was believed that all citizens shared equally in the rights conferred by the state.

Professional sculpture made its appearance in America in the 19th century. Horatio Greenhough (1805-52) is regarded as America's first professional sculptor. It was he who carved the enormous seated *George Washington* (1832-1840) for the Capitol in Washington, D.C. (If standing, the figure would be 3.7 m (12 ft) tall.) Washington, who is shown draped in a Roman toga and wearing Roman sandals, has the pose of an ancient Greek statue of the god Zeus. Though greeted with derision for its portrayal of Washington half-naked and as a mythological god, the work was significant in being the first major sculptural commission given to an American. Hiram Powers' (1805-1873) *Greek Slave* (modeled 1841-1843) was the most admired American sculpture produced before the Civil War. The nude manacled woman has the posture of a classical Roman sculpture of Venus and represents virtue or chastity. Nudity was acceptable in art if it represented a higher ideal rather than a specific woman. In this case the figure represented a Greek woman taken captive by the Turks in the Greek War of Independence in the 1820s.

After the Civil War, sculpture was slower to change than painting. The most common subject was the human figure, either an allegorical one or an historical hero or heroine. One of the most skillful sculptors of the period was William Rimmer (1816-1879). No sculptor in his time was better at rendering human and animal anatomy, yet Rimmer gained little popular acceptance because of the disturbing nature of his nude figures. Based on models from classical antiquity, his figures are invariably presented as wounded or dying, as in *Falling Gladiator* (1861).

Edmonia Lewis (1845-1911), daughter of a Chippewa mother and a black father, carved the marble *Hagar* (1875). This biblical figure is dressed in a classical tunic and stands with her hands clasped in gratitude. In the book *Genesis*, Hagar was Abraham's concubine, who, through the wish of Abraham's wife, Sarah, was expelled from his house into the desert. The subject had special meaning for Lewis, who professed that she had "strong sympathy for all women who have struggled and suffered."

The foremost American sculptor after the Civil War was Augustus Saint-Gaudens (1848-1907), who broke from the limitations of neoclassicism. One of his most unusual sculptures is the *Adams Memorial* (1891), a monument for the grave of Marian Hooper Adams, wife of the writer Henry Adams. The heavily draped seated figure on the monument seems emotionless yet at peace. (Adams had taken her own life.) This contemplative sculpture was not based on any European model.

Daniel Chester French (1850-1931), who worked on some commissions with Saint-Gaudens, was responsible for some of America's best-known statues commemorating historic events and personages. These include *The Minute Men* (1875) and *John Harvard* (1884). French is best remembered for his colossal marble statue of a seated *Abraham Lincoln*, authorized by Congress in 1911 for the Lincoln Memorial in Washington, D.C. His earlier sculpture of a standing *Lincoln* (1912) in Lincoln, Nebraska is similar to a statue of Lincoln by Saint-Gaudens (1887) in Chicago's Lincoln Park.

Over and over, Gaston Lachaise (1882-1935) sculpted parts of his wife's body, especially her breasts and buttocks. In some works these looked like huge clods of earth; in other works, like voluptuous pieces of fruit. A complete figure of his wife, *Standing Woman* (1930-1933), improbably combines the gargantuan proportions of a powerful female with a light gracefulness of stance.

Paul Manship (1885-1966), for whom Lachaise worked from 1913 to 1920, drew inspiration from early Greek art but infused his figures with stylized patterns and carefully repeated curves. His bronze statue *Day* (1938), an allegory of time, shows a fleet figure, nearly horizontal in his hurry, carrying a stylized sun. Elie Nadelman's (1882-1946) elegant and witty figures of dancers, men with bowler hats and bow ties, and fashionable bathers distantly suggest early American folk carvings. John Flannagan (1895-1942) carved stone sculptures whose small size and roughness to the touch may not impress at first glance. But these sculptures have a wonderful compactness and sense of coiled tension. His figure of Jonah embedded in the whale suggests a fetus about to spring forth (*Jonah and the Whale* (1937).)

Chaim Gross (1904-1991) emerged as a figural sculptor during the 1930s. For almost 60 years he carved blocky human figures of wood, such as *Judith* (1960). Isamu Noguchi (1904-1988) made smooth abstract sculptures of wood and marble with elegant curves respectful of the material, such as *Grey Sun* (1967). But while these two artists worked, an entirely new concept took over American sculpture: assemblage. Assemblage involved putting together different elements to create sculpture, for example, by soldering metal parts, rather than working directly on the sculptural medium through hacking, carving, or molding.

The metal assemblagists of the 1940s and on included David Smith (1905-1965), Richard Stankiewicz (1923-83) and Alexander Calder (1898-1976). Smith learned his craft by working in automobile factories and on ships with dockworkers. For some pieces he used sharp, angular shards, and for others, gracefully flowing metal strips. In his *Cubi XIX* (1964) and other burnished metal sculptures in the Cubi series, he used simple geometrical shapes, including cubes. Stankiewicz made his sculptures of discarded remnants—pipes, parts of radios, boilers—that he found by rummaging through junkyards, as in *Untitled* (1959). Calder made a serious enterprise of the mobile, a sculpture whose parts are set in motion by air currents, although he was not the first sculptor to make sculptures with moveable parts. Calder's *Horizontal Yellow* (1972) is a standing version of the mobile.

Louise Nevelson (1899-1988) created assemblages of wood, starting in the 1950s. She collected pieces of wood and door handles, architectural decorations, chair legs, and other discarded wooden objects, which she assembled in boxes and then painted in a single color—black, white, or gold. With their careful arrangements of shape and pattern, these works appear related to abstract art. Joseph Cornell (1903-1972) made assemblages of glass boxes in which he placed tattered labels, bits of newspapers, shells, old movie posters, reproductions of European paintings, or other odds and ends that he carefully collected. His ingenious combination of things often alluded to Europe, whose culture he yearned to experience for himself, though he never managed to do so.

What particularly characterized sculpture in the late-20th century was the use of new media in the form of industrial materials by minimal and conceptual artists. Donald Judd (1928-1994), who created elegant and austere metal boxes of polished metal and Plexiglas, was a leader of the minimal movement. Meanwhile earth artists had advanced this notion by incorporating nature into their sculptures. Christo (1935-) altered the landscape and our experience of it, in many cases by wrapping buildings, trees, or other large objects. Christo's art is of short duration but is documented in models, photographs, and drawings. Other Christo projects include *Surrounded Islands* (1980-1983), in which he floated pink polypropylene fabric around 11 islands in Biscayne Bay near Miami, Florida, and *The Umbrellas,* which placed umbrellas along the coasts of California and Japan in 1991.

Some late-century sculptors transformed interior spaces rather than the outdoors. Known as installation artists, they used a variety of materials to create works that the viewer could walk by or through. Judy Chicago (1939-) created one of the earliest installations, *The Dinner Party* (1979). Each of the 39 place settings in the work represented a different woman in history. Installations by Judy Pfaff (1946-) referred to specific urban environments and to the natural world. She installed enormous constructed reliefs of fruits and vegetables along a brick wall in *Supermercado* (1985). She also created imaginative gardens of glass, colored tubing, wire, and other materials in works such as *Moxibustion* (1994). Ann Hamilton (1956-) sought to overwhelm the spectator's senses in her sculptural installations of the 1980s and 1990s, many of which involved sound, smell, or taste.

Nam June Paik (1932-2006) created sculptural installations from multiple television sets. In these works, an array of rapidly changing images flashes across the TV screens, conveying the fleeting nature of information and the quick cut of television pictures and subjects. The sculpture of Bruce Nauman (1941-) incorporated flashing neon lights and videotaped images that assault the onlooker with disturbing and disagreeable words, thoughts, images, and sounds.

Duane Hanson (1926-1996) created extraordinarily lifelike sculptures of working class people that he cast life-size in synthetic resins and painted. Caught in mid-stride and decked out in actual (usually mismatched) clothing, these figures stare vacantly ahead. In an exhibition, viewers find it easy to confuse Hanson's super-realistic figures with other gallery-goers.

It was the then-unknown young Chinese-American, Maya Lin (1959-) who, after winning a "blind" competition, in which the judges did not know the identities of the contestants, sculpted the Vietnam Veterans Memorial (1982, Washington, D.C.). This turned out to be perhaps the best known and most acclaimed American public monument of the late 20th century. It consists of two highly polished black granite walls 150 m (493 ft) in total length on which are inscribed the names of more than 58,000 American men and women killed or missing as a result of the Vietnam War (1959-1975). The monument was created to harmonize with its setting on the National Mall. As earth art transforms the environment, the memorial not only focuses attention upon itself, but also changes one's perception of the Mall. Yet the memorial also demands a close-up view: relatives, friends, and other visitors can see their own faces reflected as they search for names. Lin also designed a Civil Rights Memorial in Montgomery, Alabama, to honor those who died in the struggle for civil rights.

Pop sculptors, meanwhile, typically used hard and unyielding materials, with the notable exception of Claes Oldenburg (1929-). While using mass-produced objects like other pop sculptors, Oldenburg used vinyl and other flexible materials to create his so-called "soft sculptures" such as *Soft Drum Set* (1972). The soft sculptures sag as though they are going to sleep or deflating and dying, thereby evoking the human condition more poignantly than a representational but hard and unyielding figure of a person in a traditional sculpture material. Oldenburg also constructed giant replicas of tools, such as *Trowel I* (1971-1976), and other common objects, including clothespins, a baseball bat, and a lipstick. Placed out of context, on a city sidewalk or college campus, or in a sculpture park, the pieces elicit from the pedestrian a sense of shock and disassociation. George Segal, who is sometimes grouped with the pop artists, made plaster casts of neighbors and friends from New Jersey standing about or engaged in everyday activities. The white figures placed in settings with actual objects seem ghostlike and estranged from their surroundings. In *The Curtain* (1974), for example, a plaster nude woman stands behind a wooden window frame, pulling back a cloth curtain.

AMERICAN MUSEUMS AND ART GALLERIES

See artists mentioned in this chapter at:
Amon Carter Museum, Fort Worth, Texas http://www.cartermuseum.org
Art Institute of Chicago http://www.artic.edu/
Detroit Institute of Arts http://www.dia.org
Exit Art, New York City http://www.exitart.org/site/pub/main/index.html
Harvard University Art Museums http://www.harvard.edu/museums/index.php
Isabella Stewart Gardner Museum, Boston http://www.gardnermuseum.org/
Nebraska State Capitol http://showcase.netins.net/web/creative/lincoln/art/nebraska.htm
Metropolitan Museum of Art http://www.metmuseum.org/
Museum of Modern Art http://moma.org/
Museum of Fine Arts, Boston http://www.mfa.org/
National Gallery of Art, Washington, D.C. http://www.nga.gov/
New York Public Library http://www.nypl.org/digital/
North Carolina Museum of Art, Raleigh http://www.ncartmuseum.org/
Pace Wildenstein Gallery, New York http://www.pacewildenstein.com/
Philadelphia Museum of Art http://www.philamuseum.org/
Phillips Collection, Washington, D.C. http://www.phillipscollection.org/
Reading Public Museum and Art Garden, Pennsylvania http://www.readingpublicmuseum.org/
Seattle Art Museum http://www.seattleartmuseum.org/
Smithsonian American Art Museum http://americanart.si.edu/index3.cfm
Smithsonian Institution, Washington, D.C. http://www.si.edu/
U.S. Capitol Rotunda http://www.aoc.gov/cc/architecture/index.cfm
Virginia Museum of Fine Arts, Richmond http://www.vmfa.state.va.us/
Whitney Museum of American Art http://www.whitney.org/
Worcester Art Museum, Massachusetts http://www.worcesterart.org/

PHOTOGRAPHY

It was only after the turn of the 20th century that photography began to be taken seriously by the gallery and museum world, and even then only in a limited way. Now, however, photographs can sell for six figures and be presented in fine art museums, not industrial expositions.

Even so, the development of photography coincided with the exploration and settlement of the West, and this simultaneous growth resulted in a complex relationship that has shaped the perception of that region's physical and social landscape through the photographs of Carleton E. Watkin, Stephen Shore, Darius Kinsey, Dorothea Lange, Robert Frank, Cindy Sherman, and Richard Prince. In the early 20th century, photographs imitated painting as the way to claim artistic status, modeling Whistler's famous painting of his mother, or recording a New York skyscraper with compositional devices learned from Japanese prints and a dreamy softness that prevented the image from being confused with an "objective" factual record. Yet this was also the age of picture postcards and the Kodak "Brownie" camera, which offered instant informal photography to everyone; in the words of the ad "You Press the Button, We Do the Rest." Through personal sentimental associations, great slices of social history have been preserved, the past as it was rather than as someone dreamed it into being.

For most of the 19th century, it had not been possible to reproduce photographs in magazines or newspapers. If photos were used in books, they had to be glued in by hand, one at a time. But in 1910 the *National Geographic*'s first color photographs (produced by using color screen plates) appeared. A 24-page series on Korea and China, it was the largest collection of color photographs ever published in a single issue of any magazine to that time. Also around that time, Edward Curtis published a 20-volume set of photographs documenting the lives of Native Americans. Most people's idea of what American Indians look like comes from Curtis' photographs. In 1919 the first tabloids, the *New York Daily News* and *Evening Graphics* appeared.

Also in the first decades of the century, photography both documented America's growing industrial might and was put to work as a tool of the modern assembly line. Factory owners looked to the camera of Frank Gilbreth to help them make their workers move even faster. Some accused Gilbreth's time and motion studies of turning skilled workers into robots, but the bosses loved his techniques.

Then came modernism, and photography adopted sharp focus and new notions of subject matter and treatment. Edward Weston's image of a pepper took something that is familiar and common, isolated it to focus attention, and through careful lighting and printing made it look like a monumental sculpture. Modernism used in print ads helped to bring about a revolution in advertising. By the '20s, advertising was not read, it was seen, because increasingly advertisements were organized around photographic images.

In this era, pictures began to be used to create stars like Rudolph Valentino and Babe Ruth. Photography added a new dimension to fame, and created a uniquely modern phenomenon, the media celebrity. Scientists, gangsters, politicians and preachers all could become famous, as long as they looked good in pictures. Valentino's death in 1926 was just a small preview of what would become a celebrity-obsessed century. For the fans, the loss of a hero they had known only in pictures was as real, perhaps more real, than that of a family member.

During the 1930s, wirephotos changed newspapers. These photos were made famous by the Lindbergh Trial and the 1937 Hindenburg disaster. The day the Hindenburg went down, the image eclipsed the words. From then on, it was not really news without a picture. On November 23, 1936, a new magazine appeared on newsstands. Publisher Henry Luce gave Americans something they had never seen before, a glossy, large-format news magazine which used photographs to tell its stories; the photo essay was born with photographer Ansel Adams. Never one to think small, Luce called the magazine quite simply, *LIFE*. Adams said of some of his landscapes: "I have thought about the land…observing its precarious status quo: beautiful yet on the verge of disaster." Earlier that same year Farm Security Administration photographer Roy Stryker documented the Dust Bowl and the Great Depression. In a total collection of 150,000 photographs, he showed that in this vast country there were many lost souls, that not everybody fitted in, and that the American dream is not a one-size-fits-all. In the early 1940s, the photograph had completed its conquest of America. After the success of *LIFE*, the newsstands were overflowing with picture magazines.

Finally came post-modernism, in the guise of Andy Warhol, who used photographs as the basis for paintings. Many photographers were no longer trying to go out and make pictures from nature in the manner of Ansel Adams. Post-modern photographers appropriated images from other sources such as photojournalism or advertising, or staged their own scenes instead of trying to go out on the streets and capturing real life. Photography became a tool, and a modern and useful one. Beauty was one thing, interesting visual images made using photography was another.

In slightly over a century and a half, photography has gone from outsider to insider status, but now the rules of the art game seem to have changed, as mixed media (collage and installation art, with photography, painting, and sculpture joined) and new media (video and computer) disrupt the old-fashioned divisions into painting, sculpture, and prints and drawings.

On January 24, 1955 the Museum of Modern Art in New York presented an exhibition called *The Family of Man*. Organized by photographer Edward Steichen, it was a fusion of carefully selected photographs and captions, all to support the concept that mankind is one. It said the human heart was beautiful and shared by everyone. This optimistic outlook was challenged by dramatic pictures of racism in the South, the murder of Emmett Till that same year, and the Birmingham marches. Gordon Parks profiled Ella Watson to combat racial discrimination. The photographs helped create change as the reputation of the US was damaged.

Photography had played a controversial role in World Wars I and II, when photographs had been censored. For certain subjects, still photography is widely regarded as the most powerful medium, especially for war. When the photographs of the Holocaust appeared there was an irresistible demand for freedom to publish, in the hope that this would prevent future atrocities. Like the holocaust they documented, the photographs marked a turning point in human consciousness. Thus during the Vietnam War, there was no censorship of photography, and photographs of anti-war demonstrations and end-the-war headlines helped hasten the end of the conflict.

Towards the end of the century, the world became concerned with ecological issues, and it began to seem that the preservation of the planet was as important an issue as any. The still images of the landscape taken by Adams seemed prophetic when the first photos of the whole earth were taken by Apollo 8 on December 24, 1968. Now, iconic photographs appear in the newspapers and magazines, and make not only a first impact, but a second and a third, and soon that picture is imbedded in the consciousness of the country.

LITERATURE

The colonial era

The beliefs of the Puritans and Deists of the colonial era have had a lasting effect on American literature and culture.

The Puritans

The colonial era in American literature was dominated by the Puritans, a separatist sect that seceded from the Church of England and followed the Reformation imperative to put the Bible at the center of their faith. Through direct study of the Bible, made possible by Gutenberg's invention of the printing press in the fifteenth century, believers opened a personal dialog with God. This focus on text and close reading helped inspire the American literary tradition. Both poetry and prose, in the form of diaries, were stimulated by the Puritan practice of self-examination known as *introspection*. The Puritan suspicion of ornamentation, symbolized in the sober black dress of the Pilgrims, was reflected in the style of Puritan authors. The Puritans' attitude toward art was conditioned by the principles of frugality and propriety: art had no inherent purpose except as entertainment, a distraction from duty and ethical action.

The Puritan view of history and the duties of authors

Manifest Destiny

The concept of manifest destiny was implied in the famous words of a sermon by John Winthrop (1588-1649), first governor of Massachusetts, known as the *Arbella Covenant* (1630): "We must consider that we shall be as a city upon a hill, the eyes of all people are upon us...."

Typology

The Puritans believed in the typological theory of history, which taught that it moved in repetitive cycles. The Pilgrims' crossing of the Atlantic to found a New Jerusalem typologically participated in Moses' journey out of Egypt leading the Children of Israel. God's intentions could be seen in human action and natural phenomena. Failure to understand His intentions was due to sin. The Puritans considered themselves heirs of a new covenant like the old one between God and Israel. God's wrath and reward were present in natural phenomena like floods, locusts, lightning and bountiful harvests.

Backsliding

Since "saved" believers could fall into temptation and become sinners, despite having visible signs of grace, they were expected to do constant soul-searching and pray continually. Puritan writers thus had three main functions: to reveal the ways of a mysterious God; to make God more relevant to the world; and to glorify God. Puritan writing also reflected the character of the reading public, which was highly literate and well-grounded in religion. Puritan writers were deeply influenced by the Bible, eschewed ornament in style, and wrote with a religious purpose. Sometimes this was to defend God's inscrutable ways to man and explain the existence of evil (theodicy). The common themes of early Puritan writing were both religious and pragmatic.

A number of factors combined to undermine Puritanism. The economic and demographic bases of the colonies underwent significant change and outgrew the Puritan model of social organization. The spread of farms and the growth of fishing on the frontiers of the settlements took more settlers out of the control of the congregations, which were headquartered in the largest settlements. The outlying settlers developed frontier values of individualism, self-reliance and optimism, which contradicted the corporate, pessimistic values of the Puritans. In addition, more settlers who were not Puritans came into the colonies.

Puritan beliefs

The basic Puritan beliefs can be summed up by the well-known mnemonic (memory aid) TULIP.

Total Depravity. Through the Fall of Adam and Eve, Original Sin, everyone is born sinful.

Unconditional Election. God predestines to salvation only the few whom he Chooses (the Elect).

Limited Atonement. Jesus died only for the Elect.

Irresistible Grace. God's grace, which brings the soul to repentance and obedience, and hence salvation, cannot be earned by good works or denied once given.

Perseverance of the saints. Those elected by God have complete power to interpret His will and live accordingly. As grace could not be resisted, anyone apparently doing so was a backslider and criminal and could be punished both by the church and the secular law.

Thus a relatively large class grew up who resented the power and wealth of the Puritan leaders and began to question their beliefs. They pointed out, for example, that a person's natural desire to do good cast doubt on the doctrine of predestination. The growth of rationalism, which taught that God could be known through the use of the mind, led to less reliance on the Bible and on its interpretation by authorized leaders (theocracy). Capable leaders of dissent such as Anne Hutchinson and Roger Williams arose whilst the Puritan leaders lacked flexibility. Massachusetts became a Crown colony with a royal governor in 1691.

Signs of the decay of the Puritan ideal steadily appeared in religion and society. Quakers and Anabaptists entered New England and did not conform to the Puritan church. There were heresies among the Puritans. The new rich broke Puritan dress codes and flaunted their wealth, emphasizing class divisions. Standards of behavior declined, with Sabbath-breaking (not attending church, and working on Sundays), sleeping during sermons, sexual misconduct, drunkenness, and swearing. Business morality also declined, with lying, underpaying laborers, and a rise in lawsuits. The family unit also became weaker. The Puritan dream became fundamentally compromised when, around 1670, the second generation in America discovered that their parents had, in fact, embarked on a fool's errand, the bitterest kind of all; that the dream of a model society to be built in purity by the elect in the New World in order to redress the wrongs of the Old was now a dream that meant nothing more to Europe. The emigrants were on their own, wondering who they were and what they were to do.

The Puritans left a long-lasting legacy, however. From them, Americans absorbed the belief that there must be a moral justification for private, public, and governmental acts and that America was a city upon a hill with a manifest destiny. To some extent also, the quest for freedom - personal, political, economic, and social – derived from the Puritans. The Puritans also brought their work ethic to America. One particular feature of literature descends from the Puritans: elegiac verse and a fascination with death.

Rationalism

The Age of the Puritans was succeeded by the Age of Reason. In this period, writers saw their role as performing a searching inquiry into all aspects of the world around. They took an interest in the classics as well as the Bible. They were also interested in nature and saw God as an "absentee landlord" or "blind watchmaker" who did not intervene in the world. They were interested in science and scientific experiments too. The rationalists' attitude was optimistic and they sometimes undertook experiments in utopian communities in the belief they could prove their theories. Their optimism led them to believe that a person had a duty to succeed. Rationalists undertook constant introspection with an emphasis on individualism in religion and personal interpretation of the Bible. Benjamin Franklin and Thomas Jefferson, the statesmen, and Thomas Paine, the political writer, were typical rationalists.

Rationalist beliefs

- People were naturally good and born without sin. The mind was a blank slate (*tabula rasa*).
- Human beings and society were perfectible.
- Reason was sovereign.
- Everyone should be benevolent and willing to help others.
- Antisocial behavior was the product of outmoded institutions.

The 18th century saw the dawn of liberalism with its emphasis on freedom from restraint. It was the age of revolutions in America and in France (1789), of experimentation in science, laissez-faire economics, awareness of the frontier, and the development of a rational form of religion known as *Deism*. There was marked growth in nationalism and materialism and belief in progress.

Deists held that God was discovered through reason and life was a never-ending quest for knowledge that brings wisdom. In Deist belief, God designed and created the world, and governs it through natural laws that can be discovered through reasoning, observation, and experience. He does not reveal himself through inspired texts or by supernatural means, but through creation itself. Most Deists believe that after God created the universe he "wound it up" and left it to function.

Deist beliefs

- God cannot be found through organized religions, creeds, rituals or sacraments.
- God has not chosen any people (e.g., Jews or Christians) to receive special revelations or gifts.
- Deists deny the Christian doctrine of the Trinity.
- Deists may see Jesus as a philosopher, teacher and healer, but not as the Son of God.
- Deists do not believe in miracles.
- The laws of nature given by the Creator are sufficient to explain the world.
- Morality can be derived from reason without revelation or dogma.
- Deists do not practice intercession but give thanks to God for his works.

Romanticism

America in the 19th century was basically middle class and English, practicing laissez-faire economics, albeit in a modified form because of the need for subsidies for setting up industries, building railroads, and so forth. There was also the economically primitive institution of slavery in the South, justified by the myth of master and slave. William Gilmore Simms justified modern slavery by references to Greek democracy in Pericles' Athens. This was based on a slave proletariat, but he said it provided order, welfare and security for all.

There was a second great confluence of religion with the arts in 19th century America. The Bible, in its poetic King James translation of 1611, had a huge formative influence on the language, imagery, symbolism, and allegory of such major writers as James Fenimore Cooper, Nathaniel Hawthorne, Ralph Waldo Emerson, Emily Dickinson, Walt Whitman, and Herman Melville. The American literary renaissance was produced by the intersection of the nation's residual Calvinism with British Romanticism, which was hostile to organized religion but which had transferred its concept of spirituality to nature.

Key elements of romanticism
- The idea of the frontier with its vast expanse and freedom from limitations
- Optimism, which was greater than in Europe because of the frontier.
- Experimentation in science and institutions
- The mingling of races through large-scale immigration reinforced the idea of progress and introduced new ideas.
- The growth of industrialization polarized North and South into the industrial North and agricultural South.

Romanticism was concerned with the unusual within normal life with the aim of penetrating beneath the surface of experience and deriving large generalizations on the nature of life. Romantic authors sought pure beauty, especially in nature, without any moral associations. They often set their works in far-away, fanciful, sometimes antique locales. Nature was taken to be the source of the primitive i.e., the pure. The Romantics took an interest in history and sometimes created artificial historic environments. In what is called *American Gothic*, authors made use of the odd, the grotesque, and a sense of terror in characterization and style. To an extent the romantics indulged in escapism from American problems. Nature was seen as a refuge, and also as a source of revelation of God to the individual. Thus, Romantic authors appealed to the imagination and invited their readers to suspend disbelief. By contrast with the Rationalists, the Romantics stressed emotion rather than reason, and subjectivity in form and meaning.

Much early American writing is derivative: European forms and styles transferred to new locales. For example, *Wieland* and other novels by *Charles Brockden Brown* (1771-1810) are energetic imitations of the Gothic novels then being written in England. Even the well-wrought tales of *Washington Irving* (1783-1859), notably *Rip Van Winkle* and *The Legend of Sleepy Hollow*, seem comfortably European despite their New World settings.

Featured Authors—James Fenimore Cooper, Edgar Allan Poe, Nathaniel Hawthorne, Herman Melville
The most prolific and popular author of the early 19th century was *James Fenimore Cooper* (1789-1851), social critic and would-be politician. His works include historical novels as well as numerous sea stories. Cooper's historical romances known as the *Leatherstocking Tales* featured frontiersman Natty Bumppo, a true patriot. Among Cooper's most famous works is the novel *The Last of the Mohicans* (several times filmed), which many people consider his masterpiece. Cooper was an imaginative narrator but lacked literary skill and consistency in characterization, his vocabulary was limited (as Edgar Allan Poe implied), and his style awkward and pretentious. In particular, he had the habit of interrupting the action to make Natty Bumppo deliver improbable-sounding "sermonettes." Cooper was influenced by Mary Rowlandson (1637-1711), who, captured by Indians along with her three children and held hostage for 11 weeks, wrote an account of her experiences which influenced writers of captivity narratives. She is notable for her courage and resilience, eye for detail, ear for dialogue, and sense of suspense and of character.

The first American writer to produce boldly new fiction and poetry was *Edgar Allan Poe* (1809-1849). In 1835, Poe began writing short stories - including "The Masque of the Red Death," "The

Pit and the Pendulum," "The Fall of the House of Usher," and "The Murders in the Rue Morgue" - that explore previously hidden levels of psychology and push the boundaries of fiction toward mystery and fantasy.

Meanwhile, in 1837, the young *Nathaniel Hawthorne* (1804-1864) collected some of his stories as *Twice-Told Tales*, a volume rich in symbolism and occult incidents. Hawthorne went on to write full-length "romances", quasi-allegorical novels that explore such themes as guilt, pride, and emotional repression in his native New England. His masterpiece, *The Scarlet Letter*, is the stark drama of a woman cast out of her community for committing adultery.

Hawthorne's fiction had a profound impact on his friend *Herman Melville* (1819-1891), who first made a name for himself by turning material from his seafaring days into exotic novels. Inspired by Hawthorne's example, Melville went on to write novels rich in philosophical speculation. In *Moby-Dick*, an adventurous whaling voyage becomes the vehicle for examining such themes as obsession, the nature of evil, and human struggle against the elements. In another fine work, the novella *Billy Budd*, Melville dramatizes the conflicting claims of duty and compassion on board a ship in time of war. His more profound books sold poorly, and he had been long forgotten by the time of his death. He was rediscovered in the early decades of the 20th century.

Romantic Techniques

- Settings remote in time and space
- Improbable plots
- Unlikely characters
- Authorial subjectivity
- Morality was considered harmful.
- Form arises from content.
- Experimentation in forms, sometimes adopting obsolete structures
- An individualized, subjective form of writing

The 19th century was marked by the influence of the French Revolution and its concepts of liberty, equality and fraternity. In America, a key political movement was Jacksonian democracy, led by Andrew Jackson, which appealed particularly to farmers, artisans and people in the new frontier states. Jackson, a man of humble origins, was the first presidential candidate from the new states. He unsuccessfully ran for the presidency in 1824, when he won the plurality of votes, but lost to John Quincy Adams when the election was decided in the House of Representatives. In 1828, Jackson convincingly defeated Adams, bringing to an end the monopoly of the presidency by the eastern establishment. There was also an intellectual and spiritual revolution with the rise of Unitarianism.

The Flowering of American Literature

The early 19th century saw the introduction of steamboats, spinning mills, Eli Whitney's cotton gin, clipper ships, railroads, and the telegraph. This industrial revolution raised the issue of overworked laborers. Influenced by the French philosopher Charles Fourier, Albert Brisbane published *The Social Destiny of Men* (1840). In it Brisbane wrote: "monotony, uniformity, intellectual inaction, and torpor reign: distrust, isolation, separation, conflict and antagonisms are almost universal. ... Society is spiritually a desert." To counter these phenomena, several Utopian experiments were made, such as Robert Owen's New Harmony in Indiana, George and Sophia Ripley's Brook Farm, Bronson Alcott's Fruitlands, and many Fourierist colonies. Other social and scientific innovations included Amelia Bloomer's bloomers, worn by women in some Fourierist colonies, mesmerism, phrenology, hydropathy, giving up tobacco or alcohol, and the eating of Dr. Graham's bread.

The success of northern industry made slavery appear anomalous and, to the free laborers of the North, slavery became repugnant. Major reform movements to abolish slavery and advance the rights of women took hold, fed by two impulses, the ideas of evolution and the perfection of the social order. During the American Renaissance, when writing came of age aesthetically, new themes, like abolition and the image of the household as a prison, emerge. From the beginning, American women writers were interested in the interactions of race and culture — romance with Native Americans, abolition, and slavery. Different types of women writers emerged: domestic novelists like the evangelical Susan Warner (1819-1885), whose *The Wide, Wide World,* about the claustrophobic world of a little girl, was a bestseller; Mary Virginia Hawes Terhune (Marion Harland) (1830-1922), who published stories, essays, and even her autobiography under pseudonyms; and the until recently unknown escaped slave, Harriet Jacobs (Linda Brent) (1813-1897), the author of *Incidents in the Life of a Slave Girl, Written by Herself.* But soon, women writers became considered popular literature and were ignored.

In the decade 1850-59, amidst enormous economic, social and political changes, American authors published remarkable works in such a short space of time that this feat is unique in the annals of literary production and has been called "the American Renaissance."

Featured Author —Harriet Elizabeth Beecher Stowe

Harriet Elizabeth Beecher Stowe (1811-1896) was a white abolitionist and novelist, whose *Uncle Tom's Cabin* (1852) attacked the cruelty of slavery; it reached millions as a novel and play, and became influential, even in Britain. It made the issue of slavery tangible, energizing abolitionists in the North, though it angered and embittered the South. The impact of the novel is summed up in a commonly quoted statement apocryphally attributed to Abraham Lincoln when he met Stowe in 1862: "So you're the little woman who wrote the book that started this great war!" Her reputation was overwhelmed by the political debates over *Uncle Tom's Cabin,* but its successor *Dred* is a powerful analysis of the possibilities of violence and insurrection.

Transcendentalism

The Transcendentalist era is usually taken to have begun in 1855, when Walt Whitman published his volume of poems, *Leaves of Grass.* Transcendentalism was a freethinking form of spirituality based on philosophy. It was not so much a movement as a wave of sentiment arising from a ferment of ideas. Transcendentalism was not a religion in the accepted sense because it rejected beliefs common in major religions: a personal God, an afterlife, and that this life has consequences in the next. Transcendentalism does not reject an afterlife, but its emphasis is on this life. In literature, Transcendentalism was Romantic and individualistic. The chief Transcendentalists were Ralph Waldo Emerson, Henry David Thoreau and Margaret Fuller.

Core Transcendentalist beliefs

The Transcendentalists, in keeping with the individualistic nature of this philosophy, disagreed readily with each other, but there were four points of general agreement.

1. Intuition, rather than reason or the senses, was the means of conscious union between the

individual psyche (known as *Atman,* a word taken from Sanskrit) with the world psyche, otherwise known as the Oversoul, life-force, prime mover or God (known in Sanskrit as *Brahma.*)

2. The individual was the spiritual center of the universe, the clue to nature, history and, ultimately, the cosmos itself.
3. The structure of the universe literally *corresponded* with the structure of the individual self. All knowledge, therefore, began with self-knowledge.
4. Transcendentalists believed nature was a living mystery full of signs.

Individual virtue and happiness depended upon self-realization. This in turn depended upon the reconciliation of two universal psychological tendencies: the expansive or self-transcending tendency, a desire to know and become one with the world; and the contracting or self-asserting tendency, the desire to withdraw and remain unique and separate.

Correspondence

The concept of correspondences proposes that the external is united with the internal. Physical or material nature is neutral, indifferent or objective; it is neither helpful nor hurtful; it is neither beautiful nor ugly. What makes one give such attributes to nature is the individual's imposition of her or his temperament, mood or psyche. The Transcendentalists believed that knowing oneself and studying nature is the same activity because nature mirrors our psyche.

Transcendentalism was a response to many changes in American life: the rise of science and new technology, the new industrialism, and the expansion of the middle class. Transcendentalists re-examined the relations of humankind to nature and to each other. Transcendentalism was, at its core, a philosophy of complete individualism, aimed at the creation of the new American, the self-reliant person, self-contained and independent.

Transcendentalism is rooted in the American past. To Puritanism it owed its pervasive morality and the doctrine of divine light, and to the Quakers the doctrine of the inner light. But while these concepts assume acts of God, in Transcendentalism, intuition is an act of the individual. The belief that the individual was the true source of moral light is also found in Unitarianism. From Romanticism, Transcendentalism took the concept of nature as a living mystery, and not a clockwork universe as the Deists taught.

Featured Author—Ralph Waldo Emerson

Ralph Waldo Emerson (1803-1882), a former Unitarian minister, and other like-minded intellectuals, founded the Transcendental Club in September 1835. The following year he published a startling nonfiction work called *Nature,* in which he claimed it was possible to dispense with organized religion and reach a lofty spiritual state by studying and responding to the natural world. His Divinity School Address at Harvard in 1838 shocked the establishment, as he proclaimed that while Jesus was a great man, he was not God. Emerson was strongly influenced by the *Bhagavad Gita* and the *Vedas* and by his early reading of the French essayist Montaigne. From those works he took his conversational, subjective style and the loss of belief in a personal God. Emerson associated much with Nathaniel Hawthorne and Henry David Thoreau. The land on which Thoreau built his cabin on Walden Pond belonged to Emerson. Their close relationship fractured after Emerson gave Thoreau the poor advice to publish his first book, *A Week on the Concord and Merrimack Rivers,* which put Thoreau heavily into debt. Emerson's essay on Thoreau is largely credited with the latter's negative reputation during the 19th century. Emerson was noted as being a highly abstract writer with a dense, concentrated style. While his work is credited with the founding of Transcendentalism, he insisted that he wanted no followers, but sought to give man back to himself, as a self-reliant individual. Asked to sum up his work late in life, he said it was his doctrine of the infinitude of the private man that remained central.

Emerson's most gifted fellow-thinker was *Henry David Thoreau* (1817-1862), a resolute nonconformist. Author, naturalist, transcendentalist, tax resister, development critic, and philosopher, Thoreau is regarded as one of the foremost American writers, both for the modern clarity of his prose style and the prescience of his views on nature and politics. He is best known for *Walden*, a reflection upon simple living in natural surroundings, and his essay, *Civil Disobedience*, an argument for individual resistance to civil government in moral opposition to an unjust state. Thoreau's philosophy of nonviolent resistance influenced the political thoughts and actions of such later figures as Leo Tolstoy, Mahatma Gandhi, and Martin Luther King, Jr. His radical writings express a deep-rooted tendency toward individualism in the American character. Some anarchists claim Thoreau as an inspiration. Though *Civil Disobedience* calls for improving rather than abolishing government, the direction of this improvement aims at anarchism: "That government is best which governs not at all; and when men are prepared for it, that will be the kind of government which they will have."

Transcendentalism had a widespread influence on contemporary and later writers including Poe, Hawthorne, Melville, Whitman, Dickinson, and Longfellow. Modernist writers like Frost, Stevens, O'Neill, and Ginsberg also drew on Transcendentalism. This philosophy also influenced the psychologist, William James and his ideas on the subconscious. Two movements, Mind Cure through Positive Thinking (Christian Science), founded by Mary Baker Eddy, and New Thought, founded by Warren F. Evans, also owed something to Transcendentalist influence. Transcendentalism influenced the "beat" generation of the 1950s and the "young radicals" of the '60s and '70s who practiced dissent and anti-materialism, and held anti-war and anti-work ethic sentiments. Traces of Transcendentalism have also been discerned in the Black Power, feminist and sexual liberation movements, not to mention the modern practice of Transcendental Meditation.

Realism 1865-80

Realism was partly a response to a growing audience of readers in the East who wanted to know what kind of people leading what kind of life there were in the other regions of America being surveyed, mapped, settled and linked by railroads after the Civil War. Americans wanted to know what their country looked like, and how the various races which made up their growing population lived and talked. Realism was also a reaction against Transcendentalism.

Through the "local color" movement, as it came to be called, the literary scene in America, so long a small corner in the East, with a patch on the Southern coast, began to take root throughout the nation. Bret Harte and Mark Twain brought in California, Nevada, and Missouri; Edward Eggleston the hills of Indiana; George W. Cable and William Harben the Delta country and North Georgia; Mary Noailles Murfree the mountains of Tennessee; Sarah O. Jewett and Mary E. Wilkins Freeman the back country of New England; Harold Frederick the upstate valleys of New York; E. W. Howe the village life of Kansas; Hamlin Garland the towns and plains of the Dakotas and Wisconsin; Henry Blake Fuller the cement cliffs of Chicago; and Henry Harland the tenements of Manhattan.

The Western regionalists described the unique dress, speech and social ways of the villages and camps of the remote deserts, canyons, mountains and forests where the only woman was the town whore, and the only currency was gold-dust. Writers of the South told of swamps where the cypress grew out of the green-scummed water and the moss grew down into it, and of the cities where the obsessive blood-consciousness of its inhabitants testified to the mingling of the races. Mid-Western authors narrated tales of the plains where a person could be lost in the dust or ruined by a hailstorm, and of cities where fortunes were made or lost in a day's trading on the beef or grain exchanges. According to Warner Berthoff, American local-color realism presents an imaginative sociology that is at once objective and visionary. Paradoxically, the particular local circumstances begin to appear incidental. The same stories are told by authors from all regions.

Realists believed that humans control their destinies, and characters act on their environment rather than simply reacting to it. Character is superior to circumstance. The Realists generally rejected the idea that natural facts symbolized spiritual facts. Their use of symbolism was controlled and limited. They depended more on the use of images. Although their subject matter was everyday experience, this does not make them superficial. They wrote of life in all its tangled density. Their writing makes room for the simultaneous existence of different levels of reality or of many truths, equally "true" from some point of view.

Featured Authors—Henry James, Mark Twain

Henry James (1843-1916) confronted the Old World-New World dilemma by writing directly about it. Although born in New York City, he spent most of his adult years in England. Many of his novels center on Americans who live in or travel to Europe. With its intricate, highly qualified sentences and dissection of emotional nuance, James's fiction can be daunting. Among his more accessible works are the novellas *Daisy Miller*, about an enchanting American girl in Europe, and *The Turn of the Screw*, an enigmatic ghost story.

Now considered a national writer, *Mark Twain* (the pen name of Samuel Clemens (1835-1910)), was the first major American author who came from elsewhere than the East Coast, from the border state of Missouri. His regional masterpieces are the memoir *Life on the Mississippi* and the novel *Adventures of Huckleberry Finn*. Twain's style - influenced by journalism, wedded to the vernacular, direct and unadorned but also highly evocative and irreverently funny - changed the way Americans write. His characters speak like real people and sound distinctively American, using local dialects, newly invented words, and regional accents.

Techniques of Realism

- Settings thoroughly familiar to the writer
- Plots set in daily experience
- Ordinary characters, studied in depth
- Complete objectivity
- Responsible for reporting the world accurately

Naturalism

Naturalism displays the detailed accuracy of Realism and the philosophical depth of Romanticism. But Naturalism differs from Realism in subject matter, characterization, and in its belief that human actions are largely determined by circumstances (materialistic determinism). The subjects are those raw and unpleasant experiences which reduce characters to "degrading" behavior in their struggle to survive. These characters are mostly from the lower middle or the lower classes. They are poor, uneducated, and unsophisticated. The milieu is the commonplace and the unheroic. Life is usually the dull round of daily existence. But the Naturalist discovers qualities in such characters usually associated with the heroic or adventurous, and portrays acts of violence and passion leading to desperate moments and violent death. The suggestion is that life on its lowest levels is not as simple as it seems to be. There is discussion of the fate and hubris that affect a character. Generally the controlling force is society and the surrounding environment.

The motive of Naturalistic writing was to portray the struggle between people and an environment that threatened to overwhelm their fortunes and destroy their personality. Although Naturalistic characters are conditioned, indeed controlled by their environment, heredity, chance, or instinct, they have compensating human qualities which affirm their individuality. Their struggle for life becomes heroic and they maintain human dignity. The Naturalists introduced new topics and helped broaden the scope of American fiction, in particular the exposure of social conditions and social evils such as prostitution and seduction.

Featured Authors —Jack London, Upton Sinclair

America's first professional author, in that he was the first to make a lucrative career solely from writing, *Jack London* (1876 – 1916), author of *The Call of the Wild* and other novels and stories, was born John Griffith Chaney to poor, working class parents in Oakland, California. As young as 12, in 1889, London had to begin working 12 to 18 hours a day at Hickmott's Cannery. To escape this exhausting labor he borrowed money, bought a sloop and became an oyster pirate. After a few months, however, his sloop was damaged beyond repair and he switched to the side of the law and became a member of the California Fish Patrol. In 1893, he took a job as a sailor. Later he had to do a series of grueling jobs in a jute mill and a street-railway power plant. Leaving in despair, he took up the life of a tramp and actually spent 30 days in jail at Buffalo, New York State. After many experiences as a hobo, and as a sailor, he returned to Oakland and attended Oakland High School. Although he started at the University of California, lack of money forced him to leave in 1897 and he never graduated. In July, 1897, London and his brother-in-law sailed to join the Klondike Gold Rush where he would later set his first successful stories. On returning to Oakland in 1898, he began struggling seriously to break into print, a struggle memorably described in his novel, *Martin Eden*. His first published story was the fine and frequently anthologized "To the Man On Trail." Throughout his life, London saw writing as a business and his ticket out of poverty. He started just as new printing technologies enabled lower-cost production of magazines and a boom in commercial magazine fiction aimed at a wide public.

London became politically aware at an early age and a socialist at 20, adopting a political outlook that was to last the rest of his life. He told in his essay, "How I Became a Socialist," how his views formed. Youthful optimism and individualism had faded after his early struggles. He first joined the Socialist Labor Party in April 1896. In 1901, he left and joined the new Socialist Party of America and twice ran unsuccessfully as the Socialist nominee for mayor of Oakland. Later he published collections of essays on socialism, *The War of the Classes* (1905) and *Revolution, and other Essays* (1910). He often closed his letters "Yours for the Revolution." London regarded the International Workers of the World ("the Wobblies") as a welcome addition to the Socialist cause, although unlike them he never recommended sabotage. A socialist viewpoint is evident throughout his writing, most notably in his novel *The Iron Heel*. Jack London was no theorist or intellectual. His socialism came from the heart and his life experience. After he became rich, London felt some ambivalence toward socialism. Although in 1916 he resigned from the Socialist Party, he stated emphatically that he did so "because of its lack of fire and fight, and its loss of emphasis on the class struggle." Mark Twain, however, thought London was a poseur. Although not a successful farmer, London had pioneering views about ecology and sustainable agriculture. Many of Jack London's short stories are notable for their empathetic portrayal of Mexicans (*The Mexican*), Asians (*The Chinago,*) and Hawaiians (*Koolau the Leper*). In his 1904 essay, *The Yellow Peril*, he said: "The Chinese is the perfect type of industry." He also greatly admired much about the Japanese. But, unlike Mark Twain, for example, Jack London did not depart from the conventional views of his time, and shared the common Californian concerns about Asian immigration.

London excelled at the short story of under 7,500 words, where his ready fund of imagery and gift for narrative were disciplined by the form. In contrast, many of his novels, including *The Call of the Wild*, are weakly constructed and resemble sequences of short stories. "To Build a Fire" is the best known of all his stories. It tells of a new arrival to the Klondike who stubbornly ignores warnings about the folly of traveling alone. Other stories from his Klondike period include: "All Gold Canyon," about a battle between a gold prospector and a claim jumper; "The Law of Life," about an aging man abandoned by his tribe and left to die; and "Love of Life," about a desperate trek by a prospector across the Canadian taiga (arboreal forest). "Moon Face" has been compared to Edgar Allan Poe's "The Tell-Tale Heart." "A Piece of Steak" is an evocative tale about a match between an older boxer and a younger one. "The Mexican" combines boxing with a social theme, as a young Mexican endures an unfair fight and ethnic prejudice in order to earn money with which to aid the Mexican revolution.

A lesser-known part of London's output consists of stories that would today be classified as science fiction and are reminiscent of H.G. Wells (also a socialist). "The Unparalleled Invasion" describes germ warfare against China; "Goliah" revolves around an irresistible energy weapon; "The Shadow and the Flash" is a highly original tale about two competitive brothers who take different routes to achieving invisibility; "A Relic of the Pliocene" is a tall tale about the encounter of a modern-day man with a mammoth. "The Red One," a late story from a period when London was intrigued by the theories of Jung, tells of an island tribe held in thrall by an extraterrestrial object. His dystopian novel, *The Iron Heel*, meets the contemporary definition of "soft" science fiction.

Jack London's reputation today rests largely on a small set of novels: *The Call of the Wild*, *White Fang*, *The Sea-Wolf*, *The Iron Heel* and *Martin Eden*. Even *The Call of the Wild*, which editor Franklin Walker calls a "long short story," is picaresque or episodic. *The Call of the Wild* features a St. Bernard/Shepherd mix named Buck, based on a dog London had been lent by his landlords in Dawson, Klondike. London told some critics of this story that, in his belief, man's actions are the main cause of the behavior of their animals. *The Iron Heel* anticipated and influenced George Orwell's *Nineteen Eighty-Four*. Jack London's socialist politics are explicit in the novel's description of the capitalist class forming an organized, totalitarian, violent oligarchy to crush the working-class, and it forewarned in some detail of the totalitarian dictatorships of Europe. Given the book was written in 1908, this prediction was uncanny, as Trotsky noted while commenting on it in the 1930s. *Martin Eden* is a novel about a struggling young writer with some resemblance to Jack London.

Upton Sinclair (1878-1968) was also an avowedly socialist author, regarded by Conan Doyle as the Zola of America. Believing that all art was propaganda, Sinclair wrote a hundred Realistic novels about the working class, focusing on various groups, industries and regions, for example, *King Coal* (1914) about a coal strike in Colorado, and *Oil!* (1927). His muckraking novel of 1906, *The Jungle*, excoriated the working conditions in the Chicago meat-packing industry. The book made the deepest social impact since *Uncle Tom's Cabin*. It won Sinclair fame and fortune, and led to the implementation of the Pure Food and Drug Act in 1906. *Dragon's Teeth*, about the rise of Nazism in Germany, one of an 11-volume series of contemporary historical novels, won the Pulitzer Prize for fiction in 1943.

THE EARLY 20TH CENTURY AND MODERNISM

Characteristics of Modernism

- Stylistic innovations. Disruption of traditional syntax and form
- Writers self-conscious about questions of form and structure
- Obsession with primitive material and attitudes
- International perspective on culture

Modernism is characterized first and foremost by a different attitude on the part of writers. The writer is seen as generally less appreciated but more sensitive, even more heroic, than the average person, because the writer challenges tradition and reinvigorates it, breaking away from patterned responses and predictable forms. Modernism was really a series of movements and contained writers of many contradictory viewpoints. It was both democratic and elitist. Some modernist writers were traditional, others anti-tradition. Modernists might express national or local patriotism or celebrate international culture. There were also differences between puritanical and freer attitudes to sexual and political matters. Despite these differences, Modernists focused on several contemporary themes. Alienation was a preoccupation of the Modernists and led to heightened awareness of the inner life. The Modernists belonged to a "lost generation" (Gertrude Stein), suffered from a "dissociation of sensibility" (T. S. Eliot), and had "a Dream deferred" (Langston Hughes). The Modernists dramatized the plight of women and created a literature of the urban experience, but also continued the pastoral or rural spirit, regionalism and local color. Experimentation in style and form soon joined the new freedom in subject matter. In 1909, Gertrude Stein (1874-1946), by then an expatriate in Paris, published *Three Lives*, an innovative work of fiction influenced by her familiarity with cubism, jazz, and other movements in contemporary art and music.

Modernist themes

- Collectivism versus the authority of the individual
- The impact of the 1918 Bolshevik Revolution in Russia
- The Jazz Age
- The passage of 19th Amendment in 1920 giving women the right to vote
- Prohibition of the production, sale, and consumption of alcoholic beverages, 1920-33
- The stock-market crash of 1929 and the Depression of the 1930s

Featured Authors—Willa Cather, Edith Wharton

Wilella (Willa) Silbert Cather (1873-1947) is among the most eminent American authors. She is known for her depictions of American life in novels such as *O Pioneers!*, *My Antonia*, and *Death Comes for the Archbishop*. Her first novel, *Alexander's Bridge*, was heavily influenced by Henry James. Cather moved to New York in 1906 to join the editorial staff of *McClure's* and became the managing editor in 1908. As a muckraking journalist, she coauthored a powerful and highly critical biography of Mary Baker Eddy, the founder of Christian Science, published in 1909.

Author Sarah Orne Jewett advised Cather to rely less on the influence of James and more on her native Nebraska, and Cather returned to the prairie for inspiration. Her works began to become popular and critical successes. She won the Pulitzer Prize in 1923 for *One of Ours* (1922). Cather was celebrated by critics like H. L. Mencken for writing about ordinary people in plain language. Later critics, however, tended to favor more experimental authors and attacked Cather, a political conservative, for ignoring the actual plight of ordinary people. Recently feminists have been interested in the sexual themes in Cather's work.

In sharp contrast, in her stories and novels, *Edith Wharton* (1862-1937) scrutinized mostly the upper-class, Eastern-seaboard society in which she had grown up, although *Ethan Frome* deals with poor farmers. One of her finest books, *The Age of Innocence* (1920) (later filmed), centers on a man who chooses to marry a conventional, socially acceptable woman rather than a fascinating outsider. The novel won the 1921 Pulitzer Prize, making Wharton the first woman to win the award. At about the same time, *Stephen Crane* (1871-1900), best known for his Civil War novel *The Red Badge of Courage*, depicted the life of New York City prostitutes in *Maggie: A Girl of the Streets*. And in *Sister Carrie*, Theodore Dreiser (1871-1945) portrayed a country girl who moves to Chicago and becomes a kept woman.

The Lost Generation

Some of the finest American writers are those who expressed disillusionment with Western culture after World War I. Notable among them are the "Lost Generation," a term that refers to a group of American literary notables who lived in Paris and other parts of Europe between the end of World War I and the beginning of the Great Depression.

Featured authors—F. Scott Fitzgerald, John Dos Passos, Ernest Hemingway

The stories and novels of *F. Scott Fitzgerald* (1896-1940) capture the restless, pleasure-hungry, defiant mood of the 1920s. Fitzgerald's characteristic theme, expressed poignantly in *The Great Gatsby*, is the tendency of youth's golden dreams to dissolve in failure and disappointment. The story of Jay Gatsby's quest for Daisy Buchanan expresses a 1920's version of the American Dream. Although Fitzgerald was an avid participant in the stereotypical "Roaring Twenties" lifestyle of wild partying and bootleg liquor, he was also an astute critic of his times. Fitzgerald's social criticism focuses on a group of privileged young people between the ages of 20 and 30. In doing so, he portrays a vision of the "youth and mystery that wealth imprisons and preserves." Throughout the novel, the narrator, Nick Carraway, finds himself surrounded by lavish mansions, fancy cars, and endless wealth. The inhuman attitudes bred by this culture of excess is typified by Tom and Daisy Buchanan. Nick explains: "They were careless people, Tom and Daisy—they smashed up things and creatures and then retreated back into their money or their vast carelessness or whatever it was that kept them together, and let other people clean up the mess they had made." Part of the mess left in the Buchanans' wake at the end of the novel includes the literal and figurative death of Jay Gatsby. Certainly, his undeserved murder by George Wilson evokes sympathy, but the true tragedy lies in the destruction of an American idealist. Gatsby is a true American character, according to the author, because of his firm belief in the American Dream of self-made success: he has, after all, not only invented and self-promoted a whole new persona for himself, but has succeeded both financially and socially. Yet when he makes winning Daisy his sole ambition, he sacrificed the quest for self-improvement that had brought him so far. Indeed, Gatsby seems to realize that his pursuit of Daisy is more rewarding than the actual attainment of her. As Fitzgerald wrote in 1924 while working on the novel, "the whole burden of this novel [is] the loss of those illusions that give such color to the world so that you don't care whether things are true or false as long as they partake of the magical glory."

Another of the Lost Generation writers, *John (Roderigo) Dos Passos (1896-1970)* began his literary career with quite different preoccupations from Fitzgerald: those of an anti-war writer. *One Man's Initiation: 1917* was followed by *Three Soldiers*, which brought him considerable recognition. His 1925 novel about life in New York, titled *Manhattan Transfer*, was a commercial success and introduced experimental stream-of-consciousness techniques into Dos Passos' method. A social revolutionary, Dos Passos came to see the US as two nations, one rich and one poor. His major work is the *U.S.A.* trilogy, comprising *The 42nd Parallel* (1930), *Nineteen Nineteen* (1932), and *The Big Money* (1936). Dos Passos used experimental techniques in these novels, incorporating newspaper clippings, autobiography, biography and fictional realism to paint a vast panorama of American culture during the first decades of the 20th century. Though each novel stands on its own, the trilogy is designed to be read as a whole. Dos Passos' political and social reflections in the novel are deeply pessimistic about the political and economic direction of the US. Few of the characters manage to hold onto their ideals through the First World War. Over his long and successful career, Dos Passos wrote forty-two novels, as well as poems, essays, and plays, but the quality of his novels drastically declined following the triumph reached with *USA*. Dos Passos' pioneering works of nonlinear fiction were a major influence.

Ernest Hemingway (1899-1961), also of the Lost Generation. saw violence and death first-hand as an ambulance driver in World War I. The senseless carnage persuaded him that abstract language was mostly empty and misleading. He cut out unnecessary words from his writing, simplified the sentence structure, and concentrated on concrete objects and actions. He adhered to a moral code that emphasized courage under pressure, and his protagonists were strong, silent men who often dealt awkwardly with women. *The Sun Also Rises* and *A Farewell to Arms* are generally considered his best novels. He won the Nobel Prize in Literature in 1954.

The mid-twentieth century

Featured Authors—Dawn Powell, Sinclair Lewis, Thornton Wilder, John Steinbeck, William Faulkner, Saul Bellow, John Cheever, Shirley Jackson, Flannery O'Connor, Louis Auchincloss

Dawn Powell (1896-1965) is remembered for her witty, quirky, often moving fiction which manages to be satirical and sensitive at the same time. Her enormous output included hundreds of short stories, ten plays, a dozen novels, and an extended diary starting in 1931. In 1922, Powell began work on her first novel, *Whither*, which was published in 1925. She wrote *She Walks in Beauty* in 1925, though this novel was not published until 1928. *The Bride's House* appeared in 1929. During this time, she also wrote book reviews for the *New York Evening Post*. In 1930, *Dance Night* was published. She considered it to be her best work. Her 1936 novel *Turn, Magic Wheel*, however, was the first work that both received critical acclaim and reasonably good sales, and marked a turn to social satire in a New York setting. In 1942, Powell published her first commercially successful novel, *A Time to Be Born*, whose central figure, Amanda Keeler Evans, an egotistical hack writer whose work and media presence are bolstered by the assiduous promotion of her husband, the newspaper magnate Julian Evans, is loosely modeled on Clare Boothe Luce, wife of Henry Luce. Another of Powell's acclaimed New York novels is *The Locusts Have No King* (1948), a portrait of the disintegration and eventual rekindling of a love affair against the background of the city and the onset of the Cold War. Two late novels show Powell's interest in the New York art world of the 1950s: *The Wicked Pavilion* (1954), an ensemble portrait of the characters orbiting around the Café Julien, and a vanished or deceased painter named Marius; and *The Golden Spur* (1962), set in a fictionalized Cedar Tavern, in which a young man's effort to discover who his real father was brings him to New York and eventually to involvement with the circle around a charismatic painter named Hugow. Powell's posthumous reputation has recently revived, thanks partly to being championed by Gore Vidal.

Meanwhile social criticism was represented by *Sinclair Lewis* (1885-1951), novelist, short-story writer, and playwright, author of *Babbitt* (1922), *Arrowsmith* (1925) and *Elmer Gantry* (1927). In *Main Street,* Lewis portrays a small town in a novel that was to become a classic. An educated young woman with a taste for "highbrow" drama and a knack for town planning marries a doctor and begins a crusade against the narrow-mindedness of the natives of their Midwestern community, Gopher Prairie. In 1930 Lewis became the first American to be awarded the Nobel Prize in Literature, "for his vigorous and graphic art of description and his ability to create, with wit and humor, new types of characters." His works are known for their insightful and critical views of American society and capitalist values. His style is droll, satirical, yet sympathetic.

Thornton Wilder (1897-1975), spent part of his childhood in China where his father worked as a diplomat. Wilder later studied in Rome before beginning a career as a playwright and novelist. In 1926 his first novel *The Cabala* was published. In 1927, *The Bridge of San Luis Rey* brought him commercial success and his first Pulitzer Prize in 1928. (In 1938 and 1943 he won the Pulitzer Prize for drama for his plays *Our Town* and *The Skin of Our Teeth*.) *The Bridge of San Luis Rey* tells the story of several unrelated people who happen to be on a bridge in Peru when it collapses, killing them. Philosophically, the book explores the problem of evil, or the question of why unfortunate events occur to people who seem "innocent" or "undeserving." In 1998 it was selected by the editorial board of the American Modern Library as one of the 100 best novels of the 20th century. The book was quoted by British Prime Minister Tony Blair during the memorial service for victims of the September 11 attacks in 2001. Since then its popularity has grown enormously. The book is the progenitor of the modern disaster epic in literature and filmmaking, where a single disaster intertwines the victims, whose lives are then explored by means of flashbacks to events before the disaster.

John Steinbeck (1902-1968) was one of the most famous and widely read American writers of the 20th century. Winner of the Nobel Prize in Literature in 1962, he is best known for *Of Mice and Men* (1937) and the Pulitzer-prize winning novel *The Grapes of Wrath* (1940), both of which examine the lives of the working class and migrant workers during the Dust Bowl and subsequent Great Depression. Steinbeck often populated his works with struggling characters, and his stories drew on real historical conditions and events. His body of work reflects a wide range of interests, which included marine biology, jazz, politics, philosophy, history and myth. Seventeen of his works, including *Cannery Row* (1945), *The Pearl* (1947) and *East of Eden* (1955), went on to become Hollywood films. A pedestrian storyteller and prosaic stylist, Steinbeck remains popular because of his down-to-earth portrayals of the rural poor and deep sympathy with those whose misfortunes are the result of vast economic changes they are powerless to resist.

Five years before Hemingway, another American novelist had won the Nobel Prize: *William Faulkner* (1897-1962). Faulkner managed to encompass an enormous range of humanity in Yoknapatawpha, a Mississippi county of his own invention. He recorded his characters' seemingly unedited ramblings in order to represent their inner states, a technique called "stream of consciousness." (In fact, these passages are carefully crafted, and their seeming randomness is an illusion.) He also jumbled time sequences to show how the past, especially the slave-holding era of the South, endures in the present. Among his great works are *The Sound and the Fury, Absalom, Absalom!, Go Down, Moses,* and *The Unvanquished*.

Faulkner was part of a southern literary renaissance that also included such figures as *Truman Capote* (1924-1984). Although Capote wrote short stories and novels, fiction and nonfiction, his masterpiece was *In Cold Blood* (1965), a factual account of a multiple murder and its aftermath, which fused dogged reporting with a novelist's penetrating psychology and crystalline prose. Other practitioners of the "nonfiction novel" have included *Norman Mailer*, who wrote about an antiwar march on the Pentagon in *Armies of the Night*, and *Tom Wolfe* (1931-), who wrote about American astronauts in *The Right Stuff*.

Saul Bellow (1915-2005) was born in Lachine, Quebec, a suburb of Montreal, Canada, and was raised in Chicago. His first novel, *Dangling Man*, was published in 1944, and his second, *The Victim*, in 1947. In 1954 *The Adventures of Augie March* won the National Book Award for fiction. Later books include *Seize The Day* (1956), *Henderson The Rain King* (1959), *Herzog* (1964), *Mosby's Memoirs and Other Stories* (1968), and *Mr. Sammler's Planet* (1970). *Humboldt's Gift* (1975) was awarded the Pulitzer Prize. Bellow won many other prizes. Both *Herzog* and *Mr. Sammler's Planet* were awarded the National Book Award for fiction. In 1965 Bellow was awarded the International Literary Prize for *Herzog*, becoming the first American so honored. In 1968 he received the B'nai B'rith Jewish Heritage Award for excellence in Jewish literature. A playwright as well as a novelist, Saul Bellow was the author of *The Last Analysis* and of three short plays, collectively entitled *Under the Weather*, which were produced on Broadway in 1966. Saul Bellow was awarded the Nobel Prize in Literature in 1976 for "the human understanding and subtle analysis of contemporary culture that are combined in his work." Bellow's first non-fiction work, *To Jerusalem and Back: A Personal Account* was published that same year.

A self-proclaimed historian of society, Bellow's scathing, unrelenting and darkly comic examination of his heroes' struggle for meaning, gave new vigor to the American novel in the second half of the 20th century. Many of his works are set in Chicago, where he spent most of his life, and almost all of them have a Midwestern earthiness and brashness. Bellow depicted more-than-lifesize characters and equally big themes and ideas in clever, flowing prose. Like their creator, his heroes - Augie March, Henderson, Herzog, Humboldt - tended to be dreamers, questers or bookish intellectuals, but they lived in a lovingly depicted world of cranks, con men, fast-talking salesmen and wheeler-dealers. They fought the battle for selfhood and a sense of human grandeur, a higher truth and a moral purpose in the postwar age of expansive, materialist, Chicago-style capitalism. Characters like Albert Corde, the dean in "The Dean's December" were all men trying to come to grips with what Corde called "the big-scale insanities of the 20th century." All his work, long and short, was written in a distinctive style that blended high and low, colloquial and mandarin, wisecrack and aphorism. Bellow stuck to an individualistic path, and steered clear of cliques, fads and schools of writing. He was frequently classed as a Jewish-American writer, but he rejected the label. He spoke his own mind, without regard for political correctness or fashion, and was often involved, at least at a literary distance, in fierce debates with feminists, black writers and postmodernists.

Meanwhile *John Cheever* (1912-1982), short story writer and novelist, was called the "Chekhov of the suburbs." Cheever's main theme was the spiritual and emotional emptiness of life. He especially described the manners and morals of middle class, suburban America, with an ironic humor which softened his basically dark vision.

Shirley Jackson's (1919-1965) self-portrait - morbidly obese, alcoholic, agoraphobic - revealed in a series of her writings is compelling. *Flannery O'Connor* (1925-1964) was a Catholic and thus an outsider in the heavily Protestant South in which she grew up. Her characters are Protestant fundamentalists obsessed with both God and Satan. She is best known for her tragicomic short stories.

The world of *Louis Auchincloss* (1917-) is Upper East Side New York, the society of Wall Street bankers and lawyers, heiresses and women of fashion. Many will want to pass by this successful lawyer's 60 or so books as irrelevant or distasteful, finding excuses convincing to them for avoiding engagement with a social scene with which they themselves might not feel comfortable. Himself a biographer of Edith Wharton, Auchincloss writes penetrating social history which explores what makes a meaningful life among those who have all they could want materially. His novels, such as *The Scarlet Letters* and *East Side Story* unfold sagas which span the generations, treating the themes of family politics, money, sex, ambition and religion, and snobberies great and small, through shrewdly analysed, finely etched portraits laced with nuanced psychological insights and spiced with shafts of humor. His stories pinpoint the interaction between the characters and their society and the results for themselves and their circles. Auchincloss's greatest novel, *The Rector of Justin,* evaluates the career of the founder of a private Episcopalian school through the testimonies of those who knew him. Auchincloss's novels prompt us to ask what America has lost and gained now that the families he depicts, with their traditions of moral earnestness and public service, rooted within the Presbyterian tradition, no longer command the political scene or set the social tone.

The Harlem Renaissance

The *Harlem Renaissance* is the name given to the period from the end of World War I through the middle of the Depression, during which a group of talented African American writers living in the New York neighborhood of Harlem produced a sizable body of literature in the four prominent genres of drama, fiction, poetry and essay. The Harlem Renaissance brought the black experience clearly within general American cultural history. The black migration from South to North changed their image from rural to urban, from peasant to sophisticate. Black intellectual and cultural circles were influenced by thinkers such as Aime Cesaire and Leopold Sedar Senghor, who celebrated blackness, or négritude, and writers Zora Neale Hurston, Langston Hughes, Claude McKay and Richard Wright gained prominence. Harlem became a crossroads where blacks interacted with and expanded their contacts internationally. The Renaissance profited from the spirit of self-determination which was widespread after World War I; the future of the "New Negro" was accepted without question. The Renaissance echoed American progressivism in its faith in democratic reform, in its belief in art and literature as agents of change, and in its almost uncritical belief in itself and its future. The common themes of Renaissance authors were alienation, marginality, the use of folk material, the use of the blues tradition, and the problems of writing for an elite audience. Peasant folk materials and spirituals provided a rich source for racial imagination.

One of the leading thinkers of the Harlem Renaissance was W. E. B. DuBois. He introduced the notion of *twoness*, a divided awareness of one's identity, and in the influential book *The Souls of Black Folks* (1903): "One ever feels his two-ness - an American, a Negro; two souls, two thoughts, two unreconciled stirrings: two warring ideals in one dark body, whose dogged strength alone keeps it from being torn asunder." DuBois was one of the founders of the National Association for the Advancement of Colored People (NAACP).

The Renaissance was more than a literary movement, however. It included racial consciousness, the "back to Africa" movement led by Marcus Garvey, racial integration, the explosion of music particularly jazz, spirituals and blues, painting, dramatic revues, and others.

The relationship between modernism and the Harlem Renaissance is complex. They shared the important motif of alienation. American modernism, however, was inspired by European avant-garde art while the Harlem Renaissance represented the unique and distinct experience of black Americans. Modernism borrowed from the Harlem Renaissance the themes of marginality and the use of folk or so-called "primitive" material. The use of the blues tradition, important for the Renaissance, was not shared by white modernists. They considered it too limiting, a mere complaint about one's repressed and exploited condition. Actually the blues tradition represents images and themes of liberation and revolt.

The Harlem Renaissance was only a limited success. Its leaders entertained naïve assumptions about the importance of culture and the relationship of culture to economic and social realities. The Harlem intellectuals, while proclaiming a new race consciousness, became mimics of whites, wearing the clothes and using the manners of sophisticated whites, earning the epithet "dicty niggers" (*dicty* is short for *dictionary*) from the very people they were supposed to be championing. Moreover the Harlem Renaissance could not overcome the overwhelming white presence in commerce which defined art and culture. What was needed was a rejection of white values. They needed to see whites and themselves objectively, without myth or fantasy, in order that they could be themselves in life and art.

Ironically, the Harlem Renaissance created an ethnic provincialism, strangely separate from the rest of American culture. Blacks, unlike newer arrivals, had no immediate past and foreign culture to celebrate. But the positive implications of American nativity were never fully appreciated by them. Yet the African American's history and culture is American, more completely so than most others in the country. The 1920s, then, seem to have been too early for blacks to have felt the certainty about native culture that would have freed them from crippling self-doubt.

Even so the Harlem Renaissance became a symbol and a point of reference. The name, more than the place, became synonymous with new vitality, black urbanity, and black militancy. The complexity of the urban setting was important for blacks to truly appreciate the variety of black life. It encouraged a new appreciation of folk roots and culture.

The Harlem Renaissance produced such gifted poets as *Langston Hughes* (1902-1967), *Countee Cullen* (1903-1946), and *Claude McKay* (1889-1948). Hughes, who was also a playwright, was one of the first black authors who could support himself by his writings. The novelist *Zora Neale Hurston* (1903-1960) combined a gift for storytelling with the study of anthropology to write vivid stories from the African American oral tradition. Through such books as the novel *Their Eyes Were*

Watching God, about the life and marriages of a light-skinned African American woman, Hurston influenced a later generation of black women novelists.

CHRONOLOGY OF HARLEM RENAISSANCE PUBLICATIONS

Claude McKay, *Spring in New Hampshire*

W. E. B. Du Bois, *Darkwater* **1922** *The Book of American Negro Poetry* edited by James Weldon Johnson

Claude McKay, *Harlem Shadows* **1923** Jean Toomer, *Cane*

Marcus Garvey, *Philosophy and Opinion of Marcus Garvey*, 2 vols. **1924** W. E. B. Du Bois, *The Gift of Black Folk*

Jessie Fauset, *There is Confusion*

Marcus Garvey, *Aims and Objects for a Solution of the Negro Problem Outlined*

Walter White, *The Fire in the Flint* **1925** Countee Cullen, *Color*

Du Bose Heyward, *Porgy*

James Weldon Johnson and J. Rosamond Johnson (eds.), *The Book of American Negro Spirituals*

Alain Locke, *The New Negro*

Sherwood Anderson, *Dark Laughter*

1926 Wallace Thurman, *Fire!!*

Langston Hughes, *The Weary Blues*

Carl Van Vechten, *Nigger Heaven*

Eric Walrond, *Tropic Death*

W. C. Handy, *Blues*: An Anthology

Walter White, *Flight* **1927** Miguel Covarrubias, *Negro Drawings*

Countee Cullen, *Ballad of the Brown Girl*, *Copper Sun*, and *Caroling Dusk*

Arthur Fauset, *For Freedom: A Biographical Story of the American Negro*

Langston Hughes, *Fine Clothes to the Jew*

James Weldon Johnson, *God's Trombones: Seven Negro Sermons*

In Verse and *The Autobiography of an Ex-Colored Man* (reprint of the 1912 edition)

Alain Locke and Montgomery T. Gregory (eds.), *Plays of Negro Life* **1928** Wallace Thurman, *Harlem: A Forum of Negro Life*

W. E. B. Du Bois, *The Dark Princess*

Rudolph Fisher, *The Walls of Jericho*

Nella Larsen, *Quicksand*

Jessie Fauset, *Plum Bun*

Claude McKay, *Home to Harlem* **1929** Countee Cullen, *The Black Christ and Other Poems*

Claude McKay, *Banjo*

Nella Larsen, *Passing*

Wallace Thurman, *The Blacker the Berry*

Walter White, *Rope and Faggot: The Biography of Judge Lynch* **1930** Randolph Edmonds, *Shades and Shadows*

Charles S. Johnson, *The Negro in American Civilization: A Study of Negro Life and Race Relations*

James Weldon Johnson, *Black Manhattan*

Langston Hughes, *Not Without Laughter* **1931** Arna Bontemps, *God Sends Sunday*

Jessie Fauset, *The Chinaberry Tree*
Langston Hughes, *Dear Lovely Death, The Negro Mother, Scottsboro Limited*
Vernon Loggins, *The Negro Author: His Development in America to 1900*
George S. Schuyler, *Black No More*
Jean Toomer, *Essentials* **1932** Sterling Brown, *Southern Road*
Countee Cullen, *One Way to Heaven*
Rudolph Fisher, *The Conjure Man Dies*
Langston Hughes, *The Dream Keeper*
Claude McKay, *Ginger Town*
George S.Schuyler, *Slaves Today;*
Wallace Thurman, *Infants of the Spring* **1933** Jessie Fauset, *Comedy, American Style*
James Weldon Johnson, *Along This* Way
Claude McKay, *Banana Bottom* **1934** Arna Bontemps, *You Can't Pet a Possum*
Randolph Edmonds, *Six Plays for the Negro Theatre*
Langston Hughes, *The Ways of White Folks*
Zora Neale Hurston, *Jonah's Gourd Vine*
James Weldon Johnson, *Negro Americans: What Now?*
George Lee, *Beale Street: Where the Blues Began* **1935** Langston Hughes, *Mulatto*, first full-
    length play by a black writer, opened on Broadway, October 25
1936 Countee Cullen, *The Medea and Other Poems*
Zora Neale Hurston, *Mules and Men*
Willis Richardson and May Sullivan, *Negro History in Thirteen Plays* **1937** Claude McKay, *Long
    Way From Home*
Zora Neale Hurston, *Their Eyes Were Watching God* **1939** Zora Neale Hurston, *Moses: Man of
    the Mountain* **1940** Langston Hughes, *The Big Sea*
Claude McKay, *Harlem: Negro Metropolis*

Late 20th century and Postmodernism

The postwar novel

After World War II, a new receptivity to diverse voices brought black writers into the mainstream of American literature. *James Baldwin* (1924-1987) expressed his disdain for racism and his celebration of sexuality in *Giovanni's Room*. In *Invisible Man, Ralph Ellison* (1914-1994) linked the plight of African Americans, whose race can render them all but invisible to the majority white culture, with the larger theme of the human search for identity in the modern world.

Two contrasting decades followed. Conventionality was the hallmark of the 1950s. That decade, characterized by poet Robert Lowell as ˜the tranquilized Fifties," has been ridiculed as smug, irresponsible, and materialistic. The outstanding literary work was J. D. Salinger's *The Catcher in the Rye* (1951). Other important works were Ralph Ellison's *Invisible Man* (1952), Norman Vincent Peale's *The Power of Positive Thinking* (1952), and Paul Goodman's *Growing Up Absurd* (1959). With Allen Ginsberg reading aloud his poem, *Howl!*, in San Francisco in 1955, this decade also saw the beginning of the Beat generation led by Ginsburg, Jack Kerouac, and Lawrence Ferlinghetti. *Jack Kerouac* (1922-1969) celebrated the Beats' carefree, hedonistic lifestyle in his episodic novel *On the Road*.

A radical agenda was pursued by writers in the 1960s. By then, discussion of previously ˜taboo˜ topics had become the norm. Sexual fantasies, extremes of adventure, and ˜black humor˜ (satire using shock or cruelty) were commonly used as subjects of literary works. For example, in a series of novels beginning with *A Boy's Own Story*, Edmund White (1940-) captured the anguish and comedy of growing up homosexual in America. The journalistic essay became a popular style of writing. The decade was also marked by freedom movements such as Black Power, women's liberation, and gay rights.

The 1970s marked the emergence of the women's movement led by the 1970 publication of *Sexual Politics*. In this work the author Kate Millet attacked male writers for their anti-female attitudes. Others who picked up Millet's theme were Mary McCarthy, Susan Sontag, and Joan Didion.

Featured Authors—Norman Mailer, Gore Vidal, William Kennedy, E. L. Doctorow, John Updike, Cormac McCarthy, Philip Roth, Joan Didion, Don DeLillo, Thomas Pynchon, Joyce Carol Oates, Anne Tyler, Bret Easton Ellis

Innovator of the nonfiction novel, *Norman Mailer* (1923-2007) developed in the 1960s and 1970s a form of journalism that combines actual events, autobiography and political commentary with the richness of the novel. Like Truman Capote's, Mailer's works have aroused controversy both because of their stylish nonconformity and his controversial views on American life. Mailer placed himself at the center of American political and cultural life and reported his observations on the civil rights movement, political assassinations and other upheavals.

During World War II, Mailer was a sergeant in the US army. *The Naked and Dead* (1948), based on his combat experiences in the Philippines, made him world famous. The story depicts a group of American soldiers. Flashbacks that illuminate their past mix with feverish combat scenes. When the book appeared, it was hailed by some as one of the finest American novels of World War II, and criticized by others as obscene and motivated by personal disgust with army life. The *New York Times* said: ˜Mr. Mailer's soldiers are real persons, speaking the vernacular of human bitterness and agony.˜

In the mid-1950s, Mailer started to gain fame as an anti-establishment essayist. In 1949 he had read Marx's *Das Kapital* and later said that it helped him to become a better writer. He did not believe, however, that Communism would solve all problems. Mailer's third novel, *The Deer Park* (1955) was about the corruption of values in Hollywood. In his notorious essay ˜The White Negro: Superficial Reflections on the Hipster˜ reprinted in *Advertisements for Myself* (1959), Mailer examined violence, hysteria, crimes and confusion in American society. In 1961 Mailer published an open letter to Fidel Castro, saying ˜you are giving us hope,˜ which made him hugely unpopular with many Americans in the era of the Cuban missile crisis.

The Presidential Papers (1963) established Mailer as one of the most vigorous essayists in America. In *Cannibals and Christians* (1966) Mailer accused American writers of not being able to produce works that would ˜clarify a nation's vision of itself.˜ The Pulitzer Prize for non-fiction was awarded him for *The Armies of the Night* (1968) in which he studied his own reactions as a barometer of the events themselves.

In the 1970s Mailer became a target of feminist attack when he proposed in *The Prisoner of Sex* (1971) that gender might determine the way a person perceives and orders reality; and he wrote a biography of the life and career of Marilyn Monroe. *The Fight* (1975) was an account of the legendary bout between Muhammad Ali and George Foreman. Later that decade he published a highly successful true life novel, *The Executioner's Song* (1979) based on the life and death of a convicted killer, Gary Gilmore.

In his writings, Mailer often compared the US to the Roman empire, seeing himself perhaps as a Petronius or Apuleius. His ambitious novel, *Ancient Evenings* (1983), was set in ancient Egypt (1290-1100 BC). Mailer had written it for 11 years. It was characterized by Anthony Burgess as ˜one of the great works of contemporary mythopoesis˜ (story-making related to a myth).

Gore Vidal (1925-) is a novelist, essayist, playwright, and political controversialist. In addition to a major sequence of seven novels about American history, Vidal has written satirical novels, dozens of television plays, film scripts, and even three mystery novels under the pseudonym *Edgar Box*. He has also written well over a hundred essays, gathered in several volumes published between 1962 and 2001. This seemingly varied work has a remarkable unity, exhibiting easy familiarity with the worlds of politics and letters, urbane wit, and supreme self-confidence. Vidal is closest in type to Henry James, the upper class sophisticate with European connections, and to Mark Twain, the raw humorist and critic of American empire.

The tight-lipped, minimalist style of his first novel, *Williwaw* (1946) reflects Vidal's reading of Hemingway and Stephen Crane. The book was an extraordinary achievement which put Vidal in the same league as other young postwar novelists like Mailer and Capote. Vidal went on to publish eight novels in succession between 1946 and 1954. These included *The City and the Pillar* and *The Judgment of Paris*, a dryly witty, deeply ironic story set in Europe. *The City and the Pillar* is notable for being among the first explicitly gay novels in American fiction. As a result his next five novels were dismissed by the mainstream press. Among the best of these was *Messiah*, a prophetic novel that makes deft use of the modernist technique of the journal within the memoir.

Writing as Edgar Box, Vidal then published three clever mystery novels, *Death in the Fifth Position*, *Death before Bedtime*, and *Death likes it Hot*. For financial reasons, Vidal next turned to writing dozens of TV scripts including *I Accuse!* and *Suddenly, Last Summer*. The best of these, *Visit to a Small Planet*, a scathing satire, was later successfully staged on Broadway.

Early in the 1960s Vidal moved to Italy, where he has remained. There he worked on *Julian*, the first novel that demonstrates his mature style. In this historical novel, Vidal writes with massive authority about the ancient Roman world, much as he does when he writes about the American past. It is this authority for which he is probably most valued by his readers.

Vidal's satirical novels include *Myra Breckinridge*, *Myron*, *Duluth*, *Live from Golgotha*, and *The Smithsonian Institution*. These add a unique vein of Swiftian humor to American literature. Ferociously bitter and subversive, they are lauded for their progressive themes. But it is his canny exploration of American history, in such novels as *Washington, D.C.*, *1876*, *Lincoln*, and *The Golden Age*, among others, that is seen by critics as his principal achievement. Writing of *Lincoln*, Harold Bloom called Vidal ˜a masterly American historical novelist.˜

In the 1960s, Vidal became a leading writer for the newly established *New York Review of Books*. His sharp and scolding manner, ranging in tone from the highly formal to the sharply colloquial, became a kind of trademark. Vidal's career as an essayist culminated in 1993 when he won the National Book Award for *United States: Essays, 1952-1992*, a volume of over 100 brilliant, shrewd, uncompromising pieces about literature and politics, including such figures as Scott Fitzgerald, Orson Welles, Eleanor Roosevelt, and Tennessee Williams, whom he had actually known. Though cool, elegant, and witty, the essays comment harshly on American politics and foreign policy. Vidal became, in the '60s, a leading spokesman for the New Left, an iconoclast who was willing to write scathing essays about Richard Nixon. In "Pink Triangle and Yellow Star," he drew stunning parallels between the persecution of homosexuals and Jews. In "The Holy Family," he burst the bubble of awe and admiration that had kept the Kennedy family free of criticism for many years. He poked fun at any number of American icons, even Theodore Roosevelt (whom he called ˜an American sissy.˜) Perhaps more importantly, he singled out neglected writers for praise, raising their profile in the world of letters. Among those he helped to reach a wider audience were Italo Calvino and Dawn Powell, both of whom he knew as friends. In public speeches during a failed political career he supported the recognition of China, shrinking the Pentagon's budget, and putting more federal money into education.

In recent years, Vidal has waged a continual war on those who would attempt to diminish freedom. For example, in an essay "Shredding the Bill of Rights," he protests against post 9/11 surveillance by ˜curious officials and pushy police.˜ His ability to say what everyone secretly knows and to make it unsettling without worrying about his reputation has won him many admirers and numerous enemies. Vidal has been likened to Mark Twain in his effect on American literary culture. In his memoir, *Palimpsest*, he has left a remarkably entertaining record of his life and times, which are also the life and times of the nation.

For some 40 years, *William Kennedy* (1928-) has crafted history and memory into a body of literature that is as remarkable for its variety as it is for erecting an Albany of the imagination. "What James Joyce did for Dublin and Saul Bellow did for Chicago, William has done for Albany, New York.... His cycle of Albany novels is one of the great resurrections of place in our literature," asserted James Atlas in *Vogue*. In them, outcasts and machine politicians, lowlifes and swells populate an imagined Albany as real as any city of bricks. Thanks to Kennedy, Albany occupies a privileged place on America's mythic map as a capital of the national memory, and a metropolis of everyday struggles. Kennedy took a course with Saul Bellow, who said of Kennedy's early work, "I was moved by the characters, by their naïve but human frailties." Matthew Parrish, writing in *The Los Angeles Times Book Review*, called Kennedy's nonfiction book, *O Albany!* (1983). "a book distinguished by intellectual depth and a vibrant prose style...with the humor, nobility and pathos." Kennedy's time as a journalist in Albany provided him with an opportunity to internalize the city thoroughly and use it as a fictional landscape. His first novel, *The Ink Truck* (1969), relates the story of a newspaper strike in a vividly evoked but unnamed Albany.

Legs (1975), the first novel of the Albany Cycle, tells the tale of gangster Jack "Legs" Diamond. The *Hudson Review* said of it, "the speakeasies and gangsters and fast talk seem immediate and legendary, with Irish-Catholic Albany as a microcosm of the thirties." *Billy Phelan's Greatest Game* (1978) then introduces the Phelan family, subsequent generations of which appear in five more novels. Billy is a small-time Depression-era gambler and bookie who becomes mixed up in the kidnapping of a politician's son. Billy's father, Francis, a derelict on the run from his own demons and past mistakes, is the principal character of *Ironweed* (1983), a winner of the Pulitzer Prize and National Book Critics Circle Award for fiction. Writing in the *New York Times Book Review*, Robert Towers called *Ironweed* "a kind of fantasia on the strangeness of human destiny, on the mysterious ways in which a life can be transformed and sometimes redeemed...a work of unusual interest, original in its conception....' While the first three novels unfolded in the Depression, the next three explored various periods in the city's history. *Quinn's Book* (1988) is set in the 19th century and follows the picaresque adventures of a Phelan ancestor, Daniel Quinn. *Very Old*

Bones (1992) takes the Cycle forward to the 1950s, and examines the mental breakdown and redemption of Orson Purcell, the bastard son of artist Peter Phelan. *The New York Times* asserted "Few Irish-American writers have produced more haunting portraits of their ancestors or the ghosts that possessed them." *The Flaming Corsage* (1996) portrays the turbulent courtship and marriage of Katrina Taylor and Edward Daugherty during the decades that precede and follow the turn of the 20th century. Distinguished critic Harold Bloom called it "at once prose-poem, historical novel and theatrical melodrama." *Roscoe*, the next installment in the Cycle, came out in January 2002. Kennedy's literary successes have extended to screenplays, plays and children's books. He co-scripted *The Cotton Club* (1986) with Francis Ford Coppola. He also wrote the film version of *Ironweed* (1987) starring Jack Nicholson and Meryl Streep.

E. L. (Edgar Lawrence) Doctorow's (1931-) critically acclaimed and award-winning fiction vividly evokes 19th and 20th century social history, particularly that of New York, from the Civil War to the present. After military service, he took a job as a reader for a motion picture company where he said he had to read so many Westerns that he was inspired to write what became his first novel, *Welcome to Hard Times*. He began the work as a parody, but the piece evolved into a serious contribution to the Western genre. Becoming an editor at the New American Library, a mass market paperback publisher, he worked with such authors as Ian Fleming and Ayn Rand, and then, in 1964 as Editor-in-chief at The Dial Press, publishing work by Norman Mailer and William Kennedy, among others.

Shortly after, Doctorow became a full time writer himself. In 1969 he took up the position of Visiting Writer at the University of California, Irvine, where he completed *The Book of Daniel* (film, 1983), a freely fictionalized version of the trial and execution of Julius and Ethel Rosenberg for passing nuclear secrets to the Soviet Union during the Cold War. The novel deftly evokes the complex anxieties of Cold War America, shuttling back and forth in time from the 1950s, when Paul and Roselle Isaacson (the fictional Rosenbergs) were convicted and electrocuted, to the late 1960s, when their troubled son, Daniel, a graduate student at Columbia, must deal with the consequences of his unusual birthright. Published in 1971 it was widely acclaimed and launched Doctorow into the first rank of American writers. Doctorow's next book, *Ragtime* (1975) is a dazzling reimagining of America at the dawn of the 20th century by means of a plot that, like *City of God*, ingeniously mingles real-life figures—such as Henry Ford, J. P. Morgan, Harry Houdini, and Emma Goldman—with an array of invented characters. Accounted one of the hundred best novels of the 20th century, *Ragtime* was adapted into a successful Broadway musical in 1998. Doctorow's subsequent work includes the award winning novels *World's Fair* (1985), *Billy Bathgate* (1989) and *The March* (2005); two volumes of short fiction, *Lives of the Poets I* (1984) and *Sweetland Stories* (2004); and two volumes of selected essays, *Jack London, Hemingway, and the Constitution* (1993), *City of God* (2001) and *Creationists* (2006). *City of God* opens a vast window on a range of religious, scientific, historic, and aesthetic concerns and centrally the mysteries of God, creation, and human destiny. The book mixes all sorts of literary forms and genres - Homeric verse poems, prayers, and jazz-like improvisations on pop standards - into a stew of biographical sketches mirroring the consciousness of one New York writer at the dawn of the twenty-first century. All orbits around the narrative's central issue, the mystery of the stolen cross. Doctorow is widely acclaimed for the beauty of his prose, his innovative narratives, his feel for atmosphere, and above all for his talent for evoking the past in a way that makes it at once mysterious and familiar, Doctorow has created one of the most substantial bodies of work of any living American writer. He is published in over thirty languages.

John Updike (1932- 2009), novelist, short story writer and poet, was one of the most successful American writers, celebrated for his novels *Rabbit, Run* (1960), *Rabbit Redux* (1971), *Rabbit is Rich* (1981), and *Rabbit at Rest* (1990), which follow the life of Harry "Rabbit" Angstrom, a star athlete, from his youth during the social and sexual upheavals of the 1960s, to later periods and to final decline. Updike's oeuvre was large, including a great deal of literary criticism.

His first novel, *The Poorhouse Fair* (1959), was about the residents of an old people's home. Updike's purpose was to write a novel, as he expressed it, "which would serve, in its breadth, as a base for further novels." *The Centaur* (1963) used a mythological framework to explore the relationship of a schoolmaster father and his son. Most of Updike's fiction is set in New England. The small town of Ipswich, Massachusetts, became the model for Tarbox in his novel *Couples* (1968). This portrait of sexual passion amongst a group of young suburban married couples was criticized as merely an "uptown Peyton Place." *The Coup* (1979) was an exotic first-person narration by the ex-dictator of a fictitious African state. In 2000 appeared Updike's prequel to *Hamlet*, in which the central character is not the moody prince but his mother, Queen Gertrude, together with her husband, and Claudius, her husband's younger brother. *Terrorist*, Updike's 22nd novel, was about an 18-year-old Islamic extremist and his critique of American culture.

The first book about Updike's famous hero, Harry Angstrom, a naturally athletic, sexually magnetic, blue-eyed Swede, was written in the present tense, giving it a cinematic quality. In *Rabbit, Redux* - Redux is Latin for brought back - Harry is middle-aged and finds his life shattered by the infidelity of his wife. In *Rabbit at Rest*, set in the late 1980s, Rabbit's swollen body, his chest pains, and his feeling that there is "nothing under you but black space" parallels the decay of society in AIDS-plagued America. After leaving Rabbit in 1990, Updike published in 2000 a 182-page novella called "Rabbit Remembered" in *Licks of Love*, a collection of short stories. As in all his Rabbit books, "Rabbit Remembered" ends with a single word, in this case "Gladly."

Updike's literary ideals were felicity in style, accuracy in presenting the subject, precision in describing the external and inner world, and humanistic values. As an essayist, Updike was a gentle satirist, poking fun at American life and customs. He observed the ordinary life he saw around him, and frequently asked the reader to recognize and reconsider preconceptions. In 1958 Updike made his debut as a poet with the volume *The Carpentered Hen and Other Tame Creatures*.

Existential questions were at the center of Updike's work from the beginning. In his autobiographical piece, "The Dogwood Tree: A Boyhood," Updike called sex, art, and religion "the three great secret things" in human experience. His religious consciousness has been characterized as "our sense of an unavoidable, unbearable, and unbelievable Sacred Presence." Updike received many awards, among them the National Book Award in Fiction (1964), the American Book Award (1982), and the National Book Critics Circle Award for fiction (1982, 1990.) His novels *Rabbit is Rich* and *Rabbit at Rest* have won Pulitzer Prizes.

Cormac McCarthy (1933-) was born in Rhode Island. Originally named Charles after his father, he was renamed Cormac, "son of Charles." In 1937 the family moved to Knoxville, where his father became chief counsel for the Tennessee Valley Authority until 1967. Lastly, the McCarthys moved to Washington, D.C., where Charles was the principal attorney in a law firm until retirement.

Cormac was raised Roman Catholic. He attended Catholic High School in Knoxville before studying liberal arts at the University of Tennessee in 1951-52. McCarthy joined the U.S. Air Force in 1953 and served four years, two in Alaska, where he hosted a radio show. From 1957-59,

McCarthy returned to the university, where he published two stories, "A Drowning Incident" and "Wake for Susan" in the student literary magazine, *The Phoenix*, calling himself "C. J. McCarthy, Jr." His university creative writing won him the Ingram-Merrill Award in 1959 and 1960.

McCarthy then moved to Chicago, where he worked, apparently as an auto mechanic, while writing his first novel, *The Orchard Keeper*, published 1965 to favorable reviews. Traveling fellowships from the American Academy of Arts and Letters and the Rockefeller Foundation enabled him to tour extensively in Europe for the next three years, visiting Blarney Castle (built by king Cormac McCarthy), England, France, Switzerland, Italy, and Spain. He and his second wife, Anne DeLisle, settled on the island of Ibiza, which was a kind of artist's colony, where he completed *Outer Dark*. In 1967 he returned to America, to Rockford, Tennessee, near Knoxville. *Outer Dark, set in southern Appalachia,* was published in 1968, again to favorable reviews.

A Guggenheim Fellowship for Creative Writing in 1969 enabled him to purchase a barn near Louisville, which he renovated himself, salvaging bricks for the fireplace from the boyhood home of James Agee, which was being levelled. (Agee was the author of *Let Us Now Praise Famous Men*, a classic study of poor cotton farmers in Depression-era Alabama.) McCarthy's *Child of God*, also set in southern Appalachia, was published in 1973. Inspired by actual events in Sevier County, it garnered mixed reviews, some praising it as great, others finding it despicable. From 1974-75, McCarthy worked on the screenplay for a PBS film *The Gardener's Son*, which premiered in January 1977. Set in South Carolina, this too was based on historical events. After separating from Anne DeLisle, McCarthy moved to El Paso, Texas. In 1979, McCarthy published his fourth novel, *Suttree*, his most autobiographical book, which had occupied him on and off for 20 years. It is said by many to be McCarthy's best work to date.

A MacArthur Fellowship enabled McCarthy to live while writing his next novel, *Blood Meridian*, an apocalyptic western heavily based on historical events in Texas and Mexico during the 1840s, telling of a gang of mercenaries paid to clear Indians from the borderlands, which they do by flaying them and selling their scalps for gold. *Blood Meridian* was published in 1985. It received little attention at the time but is now considered a turning point in McCarthy's career. In a 2006 poll of authors and publishers conducted by *The New York Times Magazine* to list the greatest American novels of the previous quarter-century, *Blood Meridian* placed third, behind only Toni Morrison's *Beloved* and Don DeLillo's *Underworld*. *The Atlantic* called the novel "the most beautifully written, unrelievedly ghastly chronicle of violence, carnage, torture, rapine, plunder, murder and every other conceivable variety of barbarism to be found anywhere in our literature." "In the entire range of American literature, only *Moby-Dick* bears comparison to *Blood Meridian*," believes the critic Steven Shaviro. "Both are epic in scope, cosmically resonant, obsessed with open space and with language, exploring vast uncharted distances with a fanatically patient minuteness." In connection with the book's publication, the reclusive McCarthy granted *The New York Times Magazine* one of the few interviews to which he has ever submitted.

All the Pretty Horses, the first volume of *The Border Trilogy*, was published in 1992. It was released as a movie in 2000 under the direction of Billy Bob Thornton. Unlike McCarthy's earlier books, it became a publishing sensation and a *New York Times* bestseller, giving McCarthy the wide readership that had eluded him for many years and winning a National Book Award. Some critics indeed prefer his Western writing, while others feel that he has strayed too far from his roots. McCarthy edited a play he had written in the mid-1970s for publication in 1994. Called *The Stonemason*, the tragedy explores the fortunes of three generations of a black family in Kentucky.

Shortly after, the second volume of *The Border Trilogy*, *The Crossing*, came out. The novel tells of Billy Parham's attempt to return a trapped she-wolf to its home in the northern Mexican mountains and the tragic consequences of his adventure. The third volume of *The Border Trilogy*, *Cities of the Plain* was published in 1998. In it, John Grady Cole, the main character of *All the Pretty Horses*, unites with *The Crossing's* Billy Parham. The novel centers on Cole's doomed relationship with a Mexican prostitute. Not as well-received by critics as the first two books in the trilogy, *Cities of the Plain* is nonetheless notable for its epilogue, which reaches back to *Suttree* in its imagery and simultaneously casts the entire trilogy in a fascinating new light.

McCarthy now lives with his third wife and their child near Santa Fe, New Mexico. *No Country for Old Men*, a thriller set on the US-Mexico border, appeared in 2005 and was filmed in 2007 by Joel and Ethan Coen, winning four Academy Awards. 2006 saw publication of *The Road*, which won a Pulitzer Prize and was chosen by Oprah Winfrey for her book club. A movie of *The Road* was released in 2009. *The Road* describes a journey taken by a father and son across a post-apocalyptic landscape peopled by violent cannibals after some unnamed cataclysm has destroyed most life and "civilization." McCarthy does not believe that the kind of catastrophe he describes will be brought on by a meteor. "We're going to do ourselves in first," he says. "If I wrote about violence in an exaggerated way, it was looking at a future that I imagined would be a lot more violent," McCarthy said recently. "And it is. Can you remember, 20 years ago, having beheadings on TV? I can't." 2006 also saw publication of a second play, *The Sunset Limited*.

McCarthy is not an author's author. He does not read fiction, and has little time for writers other than Melville, Dostoevsky, Joyce and Faulkner. He prefers the company of scientists. Yet he is regarded by many as the greatest American novelist since William Faulkner. McCarthy's books are implacably grim and violent, sometimes wrenchingly elegiac, and centered on the issues of life and death. His main characters are solitary outsiders, criminals or outcasts. McCarthy has been described as "a poet of violence". If there is a dominant, recurring theme in McCarthy's work, it is the unrelenting imminence of violence. "There is no such thing as life without bloodshed," he says. His early novels "trade in necrophilia, perversion and baby murder, and reading them one is struck repeatedly by the way he displays the bloody-minded glee of the horror writer, the gross-out artist," writes the novelist Michael Chabon. McCarthy's books are also stylistically challenging, often plotless, lacking traditional punctuation and arcane in their vocabulary. In this he is seen as the heir to Faulkner and Joyce. Saul Bellow praised his "absolutely overpowering use of language, his life-giving and death-dealing sentences." Hostile critics disdain McCarthy as the biggest phony in American fiction. *The New Yorker* called him "one of the great hams of American prose." One of his most ardent detractors has been Michiko Kakutani, chief book critic of *The New York Times*, who sneers at his "sentimentality, pretension and windy self-importance." Reviewers most often complain of his writing about women. *The Texas Monthly*: "One can't help suspecting that deep down, McCarthy wonders, Henry Higgins fashion, 'Why can't a woman be more like a horse?' On Oprah, the thrice-married writer admitted: "I don't pretend to understand women."

No other writer working today commands critical acclaim and broad popularity to the extent of *Philip Roth* (1933-). Author of 29, his are the most widely awaited novels on both sides of the Atlantic. A second-generation Jewish-American born in Newark, New Jersey, Roth studied with Saul Bellow at the University of Chicago. His first novel, *Goodbye, Columbus* (1959), won him the National Book Award, the first of many literary prizes, but it was not until the raunchy, hilarious *Portnoy's Complaint* in 1969 that he became a bestseller. Always popular, Roth won all four of

America's leading literary prizes, for four different books in five years, in the 1990s. One of the keys to his success is his ability to discuss the weightiest of topics – faith, marriage, family – while at the same time being the sexiest writer in the business. Roth's work is characterized by a feverish interest in sex that occasionally verges on the pornographic. Yet his work also remains a highly serious discussion of man's tenuous place in an increasingly hostile world. The other hallmark of Roth's work is its playfully autobiographical nature, whether about his feelings toward his mother, his two spectacularly failed marriages or his uneasy relationship with fame. To deflect some of this attention, the reclusive author has created the surrogate character Nathan Zuckerman, a randy Jewish-American author who shot to fame with the publication of a scandalous novel. Zuckerman is one of literature's great creations, a wise-cracking, bed-hopping trickster who allows his author to keep one step ahead of his readership. Male sexuality is his great, overriding theme, seeing the world in terms of male sexual opportunity and experience. His fiction is rife with bawdy, explicit descriptions of sex. In 1974 he wrote a novel called *My Life as a Man*. Roth's men are always on the prowl, even if, like Coleman Silk in *The Human Stain* (2000), they need Viagra to put a spring in their step. Roth writes about sex with a candor that has no equal among serious novelists. This has, of course, drawn the outrage of the prudish, and made Roth as big a target for feminists as Norman Mailer. And it is true that his female characters can often appear rather less than human. His response has always been that he simply "writes about the lives of men."

Although he objects to being a called a Jewish writer, Roth's work has constantly addressed what it means to be a Jew in the modern world. The early books were, in many ways, "complaints" against the stultifying effect of Jewish culture and tradition on his burgeoning artistic imagination, and drew a chorus of criticisms from fellow Jews that Roth was self-hating and even anti-semitic. Roth's later work has proven less mutinous toward his heritage, particularly the loving, nuanced portrait of a Jewish community besieged by a pro-Nazi US government in *The Plot Against America* (2004). Roth may look at his native country through the prism of Jewish assimilation, but that does not prevent him from being one of America's most acute observers, particularly in the series of big novels he has written since 1997. *American Pastoral* (1997), which details a father's search for his radical daughter in post-1960s America, is a brilliant dissection of the limits of prosperity and idealism, while *I Married a Communist* (1998) presents a memorable portrait of the McCarthy witch hunts of the 1950s. *The Human Stain* expands Roth's vision of race and assimilation in an unexpected direction by telling the story of a light-skinned African American writer who was able to "pass" as white. Roth also took on Nixon, in *Our Gang* (1971), and tackled baseball, with *The Great American Novel* (1973). With the possible exception of Saul Bellow, no other novelist provides a fuller portrait of what it meant to be an American intellectual in the latter half of the 20th century.

The notoriety that followed the publication of *Portnoy's Complaint* was so intense that Roth felt compelled to create a fictional surrogate to take the heat: Nathan Zuckerman, a Jewish writer who himself became notorious after writing a book called *Carnovsky* (whose plot sounds suspiciously like that of *Portnoy's Complaint*.) Zuckerman, who has so far featured in 10 of Roth's books, can perhaps best be seen as, so to speak, an alter id, a surrogate who allows Roth to write about his own emotional and intellectual life without indulging in pure autobiography. Roth once famously claimed that "making fake biography, false history, concocting a half-imaginary existence out of the actual drama of my life is my life." Roth loves to wrong-foot readers, to pull their legs. In *Operation Shylock* (1993), he describes with a perfectly straight face how he served as an Israeli spy in

Greece, only to conclude the book by telling the reader that "this confession is false"—a claim he then laces with ambiguity by elsewhere suggesting that Mossad made him put it in the book. In *The Counterlife*, both of Roth's main characters die, only to come back to life. His "novelist's autobiography," *The Facts* (1988), concludes with a long rebuttal by Zuckerman, who accuses Roth of being "the least completely rendered of all your protagonists."

Family relations have always stood at the heart of Roth's work. Portnoy describes his overbearing mother, Sophie, as "The Most Unforgettable Character I've Met," and Roth seems to feel the same about his own mother, Bessie, although she is more saint to him than monster. His father, Herman, an insurance salesman, looms equally large in the author's imagination, inspiring *Patrimony* (1991), a deeply moving account of the elder Roth's last days. As Roth ages, so do his protagonists. Death has almost replaced sex as their central concern. Roth has been twice divorced. He separated from his first wife in 1963 and their train-wreck marriage provided material for several novels. In 1990, he married the British actress Claire Bloom, but they divorced five years later. In response, Roth created the spoilt actress Eve Frame in *I Married a Communist*, a social climber who ruins her husband's life by writing a tell-all autobiography.

Joan Didion (1934-) is concerned about the disintegration of American morals, and what she sees as cultural chaos, which she comments on in her essays and explores in her novels, where the overriding theme is individual and social fragmentation. A sense of anxiety or dread permeates much of her work, and her novels have a reputation for being depressing and even morbid. Didion is heavily influenced by Ernest Hemingway, from whom she learned how the structure of sentences affects a piece of writing and developed her spare, elegant prose. Other influences include Henry James, George Eliot and the Brontës. *Slouching Towards Bethlehem* (1968), exploring the cultural values and experiences of American life in the 1960's, was her first work of non-fiction. It was sequeled by *The White Album*, a collection of journalistic essays. *Play It As It Lays*, set in Hollywood, was published in 1970 and *A Book of Common Prayer* in 1977. She also wrote *Democracy* in 1984, which deals with her concern for the loss of society's traditional values. Her 1987 novel, *Miami*, addresses US foreign policy. In 1992, she published *After Henry*, a collection of twelve geographical essays, and in 1996, *The Last Thing He Wanted*, a romantic thriller. Didion then wrote *The Year of Magical Thinking* (National Book Award 2005) which she later dramatized.

Didion is a practitioner of *New Journalism*, which seeks to communicate facts through a subjective viewpoint and the techniques of narrative fiction. This style is also described as *creative nonfiction*, *intimate journalism*, or *literary nonfiction*. Didion includes her personal feelings and memories in a first person narrative, describing the chaotic way individuals perceive the world. The author's voice is critical to a reader forming opinions in response. New Journalism was popularized by Tom Wolfe, author of *The New Journalism* (1974), who said it was possible to write journalism that would read like a novel. Through a combination of much research, a perceptive eye, and the belief that it is the media that tell us how to live, Joan Didion has become an observer of journalists themselves. She believes that the difference between the process of fiction and nonfiction is the element of discovery that takes place during the research in nonfiction.

Don DeLillo (1936-) first became well known when his novel *White Noise* won the National Book Award in 1985. Born to Italian immigrants in the Bronx, New York City, he attended Fordham University. After graduating, DeLillo took a job in advertising and worked for five years as a copywriter at the agency of Ogilvy & Mather on Fifth Avenue. His first novel, *Americana*, was published in 1971, to modest critical praise. Starting in the late 1970s, he spent several years living in Greece, where he wrote *The Names*. His greatest work, the novel *Underworld* (1997) was widely heralded as a masterpiece. Novelist and critic Martin Amis said it marked "the ascension of a great writer." *Underworld* was the runner-up in the *New York Times'* survey of the best work of American fiction in the last 25 years, announced in May 2006. *White Noise* and *Libra* were also recognized by the anonymous jury of contemporary writers. DeLillo's most recent work, *Falling Man*, 2007, concerns a survivor of the 9/11 terror attacks.

DeLillo's work is not easy to characterize as belonging to any school or tendency. He sees the role of the novelist as facilitating social discourse and prefers not to be labeled. Asked if he accepted the critics' label of *postmodernist,* he said, "I don't react. But I'd prefer not to be labeled. I'm a novelist, period. An American novelist." According to DeLillo himself, the main influences on his work are abstract expressionism, foreign films, and jazz. Unlike other Italian American authors such as Mario Puzo or John Fante, few aspects of his fiction reflect Italian culture. Many of his books (notably *White Noise*) satirize academia and explore the postmodern themes of rampant consumerism, novelty intellectualism, underground conspiracies, the disintegration and re-integration of the family, and the promise of rebirth through violence. In several of his novels, DeLillo explores the idea of the increasing visibility and effectiveness of terrorists: *Players, Mao II, Falling Man*. Another constant theme is the role of mass media in removing an event from its context and altering or draining its inherent meaning: the highway shooter in *Underworld*, the televised disasters longed for in *White Noise*, the planes in *Falling Man*, the evolving story of the interviewee in *Valparaiso*. The psychology of crowds and the capitulation of individuals to group identity is another theme DeLillo examines in several of his novels, especially in the prologue to *Underworld, Mao II*, and *Falling Man*. In a 1993 interview with Maria Nadotti, DeLillo explained: "My book (*Mao II*), in a way, is asking who is speaking to these people. Is it the writer who traditionally thought he could influence the imagination of his contemporaries or is it the totalitarian leader, the military man, the terrorist, those who are twisted by power and who seem capable of imposing their vision on the world, reducing the earth to a place of danger and anger."

Critics are divided over the merits of DeLillo's work. Some feel that his novels, so to speak, take the temperature of society without offering an intellectually satisfying diagnosis of its ills. Bruce Bawer famously condemned DeLillo's novels, insisting they were not actually novels at all but "tracts, designed to batter us, again and again, with a single idea: that life in America today is boring, benumbing, dehumanized....It's better, DeLillo seems to say in one novel after another, to be a marauding murderous maniac—and therefore a *human*—than to sit still for America as it is, with its air conditioners, assembly lines, television sets, supermarkets, synthetic fabrics, and credit cards." DeLillo also figured prominently in B. R. Myers' critique of recent American literary fiction, *A Reader's Manifesto*. Melville Houe, 2002. Many younger authors such as Bret Easton Ellis, Jonathan Franzen and David Foster Wallace have cited DeLillo as an influence. Critic Harold Bloom named him as one of the four major American novelists of his time, along with Thomas Pynchon, Philip Roth, and Cormac McCarthy, though he questions the classification of DeLillo as a "postmodern novelist."

In a short summary, it is unusually difficult to provide even rudimentary signposts to the enormous, many-faceted novels of *Thomas Pynchon* (1937-). This writer works in four genres of fiction: black comedy, historical fiction, satire and science fantasy. Based in New York City, Pynchon is noted for his dense and complex works. Both his fiction and non-fiction are eclectic and wide-ranging, encompassing a vast array of subject matter, styles and themes, including history, science and mathematics. After publishing several short stories in the late 1950s and early 1960s, he began composing the novels for which he is best known: *V.* (1963), *The Crying of Lot 49* (1966), *Gravity's Rainbow* (1973) (his most highly regarded work), *Vineland* (1990), *Mason & Dixon* (1997), *Against the Day* (2006) and *Inherent Vice* (2009). The wildly eccentric characters, frenzied action, frequent digressions, and imposing lengths of Pynchon's novels have led critic James Wood to classify Pynchon's work as hysterical realism. Pynchon is also seen as a progenitor of cyberpunk fiction. Pynchon is regularly cited as a contender for the Nobel Prize in Literature.

Pynchon is a descendant of William Pynchon, who emigrated to the Massachusetts Bay Colony with the Winthrop Fleet in 1630. His third and best-known novel *Gravity's Rainbow* (1963), his last published short story "The Secret Integration" (1964), and the Slothrop family histories make use of this family background as source material. Some of the motifs and subject matter he would use throughout his career – oddball names, sophomoric humour, illicit drug use and paranoia – date back to high school. His first published story, "The Small Rain", appeared in the *Cornell Writer* in May 1959, and narrates an actual experience of a friend who had served in the army; subsequently episodes and characters throughout Pynchon's fiction draw freely upon his own experiences in the navy. Pynchon's work as a technical writer at Boeing inspired his depictions of the "Yoyodyne" corporation in *V.* and *The Crying of Lot 49*. Both that and his background in physics provided much raw material for *Gravity's Rainbow*.

More concise and straightforward than his other novels, the nevertheless labyrinthine plot of *The Crying of Lot 49* features an ancient, underground mail service known as "The Tristero" or "Trystero," a parody of a Jacobean revenge drama called *The Courier's Tragedy*, and a corporate conspiracy involving the bones of World War II American GIs being used as charcoal cigarette filters. The novel proposes a series of seemingly incredible interconnections between these events and other similarly bizarre revelations that confront the novel's protagonist, Oedipa Maas. Like *V.*, the novel contains a wealth of references to science and technology and to obscure historical events, and dwells on the detritus of American society and culture. The novel also investigates homosexuality, celibacy, and both medically-sanctioned and illicit psychedelic drug use. *The Crying of Lot 49* also continues to include parodic song lyrics, punning names, and references to aspects of popular culture.

Pynchon's most celebrated novel is his third, *Gravity's Rainbow*, an intricate and allusive fiction that combines and elaborates on many of the themes of his earlier work, including preterition (the act of being disinherited), paranoia, racism, colonialism, conspiracy, synchronicity, and entropy. *Gravity's Rainbow* describes many varieties of sexual fetishism (including sado-masochism, coprophilia and a borderline case of tentacle rape), and features numerous episodes of drug use, most notably marijuana but also cocaine, naturally occurring hallucinogens, and the mushroom *Amanita muscaria*. The novel is mostly set in London and Europe in the final months of World War II and the weeks immediately following VE Day. The novel has spawned a wealth of commentary and critical material, including two reader's guides, online concordances and discussions, and art works, and is regarded as one of the archetypal texts of American literary postmodernism. Encyclopedic in scope and often playfully self-conscious in style, the novel displays impressive erudition in its treatment of an array of material drawn from the fields of psychology, chemistry, mathematics, history, religion, music, literature and film. *Gravity's Rainbow* was a joint winner of the 1974 National Book Award for Fiction, along with Isaac Bashevis Singer's *A Crown of Feathers and Other Stories*.

A major source for the biography of this reclusive writer is the autobiography he included as an introduction to the collection of early short stories published in 1984 under the title *Slow Learner*. "The Secret Integration" (1964), Pynchon's last published short story, is a sensitively-handled coming-of-age tale in which a group of young boys face the consequences of the American policy of racial integration. In October of the same year he published an article entitled "Is It O.K. to Be a Luddite?" in the *New York Times Book Review*. Another article, entitled "Nearer, My Couch, to Thee," was published in June 1993 in the *New York Times Book Review*, as one in a series of articles in which various writers reflected on each of the Seven Deadly Sins. Pynchon's subject was "Sloth."

Pynchon's fourth novel, *Vineland*, was published in 1990, but disappointed a majority of fans and critics. The novel is set in California in the 1980s and 1960s, and describes the relationship between an FBI cointelpro (anti-subversion) agent and a radical woman filmmaker. Its strong socio-political undercurrents detail the constant battle between authoritarianism and communalism, and the tension between resistance and complicity, but with a typically Pynchonian sense of humor.

Pynchon's fifth novel, *Mason & Dixon*, was published in 1997. Researched in great depth, and written on the scale of a saga, it recounts in postmodernist style the lives of the English astronomer, Charles Mason, and his professional partner, the surveyor Jeremiah Dixon, the surveyors of the Mason-Dixon line. *Mason & Dixon* explores the scientific, theological, and socio-cultural foundations of the Age of Reason whilst also depicting the relationships between actual historical figures and fictional characters in intricate detail, and is another archetypal example of the genre of historiographic metafiction. Some, including Harold Bloom, have hailed it as Pynchon's greatest work.

In his book description, Pynchon described the setting of his latest novel, *Against The Day* (2006) as "a time of unrestrained corporate greed, false religiosity, moronic fecklessness, and evil intent in high places." He went on to say, "No reference to the present day is intended or should be inferred." In fact, the action takes place between the 1893 Chicago World's Fair and the time immediately following World War I. Yet presciently, Pynchon's description refers to "a worldwide disaster looming just a few years ahead." Composed mainly of interwoven pastiches of popular fiction genres from the era in which it is set, the novel drew a mixed reaction from critics. Some said it was a summation of Pynchon's personal philosophy, while others thought it a loose baggy monster which had been pieced together from several long-time works-in-progress and offcuts from others of his novels. A further novel, *Inherent Vice*, is forthcoming.

Along with its emphasis on lofty themes such as racism, imperialism and religion, and its use of many elements of traditional high culture and literary form, Pynchon's work also demonstrates a strong affinity with the practitioners and artifacts of low culture, including comic books and cartoons, pulp fiction, popular films, television programs, cookery, urban myths, conspiracy theories, and folk art. This blurring of the conventional boundary between "High" and "low" culture, sometimes interpreted as a "deconstruction," is one of the defining characteristics of postmodernism. In particular, Pynchon has revealed himself in his fiction and non-fiction as an aficionado of popular music, particularly jazz and rock and roll. Song lyrics and mock musical numbers appear in each of his novels.

By the 1980s and '90s, women, no longer restricted to certain subjects, could write from any perspective, even a male one, for example, about violence and boxing, like *Joyce Carol Oates* (1938-). Brought up in rural, working class New York state, Oates has published over fifty novels, as well as many volumes of short stories, poetry and non-fiction. Her novel *them* (1969) won the National Book Award, and *Black Water* (1992), *What I Lived For* (1994), and *Blonde* (2000) were nominated for the Pulitzer Prize. Oates published her first novel, *With Shuddering Fall* (1964), and in 1966 she published "Where Are You Going, Where Have You Been?", a short story dedicated to Bob Dylan. Based on the serial killer Charles Schmid, the story has been frequently anthologized and was adapted into the 1985 film *Smooth Talk*.

Oates is an enormously productive author, managing to publish on average two books a year, mostly novels. Reflecting her preoccupation with working class America, she frequently deals with rural poverty, sexual abuse, class tensions, desire for power, female childhood and adolescence, and occasionally the supernatural. She has written in a variety of genres, eras and landscapes. From her first novel up to *Kindred Passions* in 1987, Oates built up a literary corpus that mixes Gothic horror with social observation. Her works contain the typical elements of this type of tale: unconscious forces, seduction, incest, violence, and rape, sometimes to the point of sensationalism. Her works contain strong feminist overtones, and use of the Gothic device to explore the ambiguities of gender and the sexual bases of fantasy. In 1996, Oates published *We Were the Mulvaneys*, a novel following the disintegration of an American family, which became a bestseller after being selected by Oprah's Book Club in 2001. In the 1990s and early 2000s, Oates wrote mostly mystery novels, under the pen names "Rosamond Smith" and "Lauren Kelly." Among her characters, Oates favors cunning, hardy survivors, both women and men. In her book-length essay *On Boxing* (1987) she wrote: "Boxing is a celebration of the lost religion of masculinity all the more trenchant for its being lost." Violence is a constant in her work, even leading Oates to write an essay in response to the question, "Why Is Your Writing So Violent?" Joyce Carol Oates' best books include *A Garden of Earthly Delights* (1967), *them* (1969), *Wonderland* (1971), *On Boxing* (1987), *Black Water* (1992), *Blonde* (2000), *I'll Take You There* (2002), *The Falls* (2004) and *High Lonesome: New & Selected Stories, 1966-2006* (2006).

The novels of *Anne Tyler* (1941-) of Baltimore, Maryland, where most of her novels are set, have a Southern flavor. Baltimore's Roland Park, one of the places where her characters live, is, as critics have noted, an epitome of "upper-middle-class Waspdom in all its glory." Her novels focus on middle class families, their secrets, ambitions, dreams, and crises. Tyler's keen ear for dialogue and life-like characters have won critical acclaim.

Tyler considers her ninth novel *Dinner at the Homesick Restaurant* her best work. It explores tensions inside a family - the family is for Tyler the basic battlefield — seeing the events from the perspective from each member in turn. The mother, Pearl Cody Tull, is in turn violently abusive, suspicious, or nurturing, and her children all have their own view of her. *The Accidental Tourist* (1985) won the 1986 National Book Critics Circle Award and in 1988 was made into a successful film starring William Hurt and Kathleen Turner. The protagonist is Macon Leary, who writers travel guides for travel-hating businessmen. Macon spends his time in planes, addicted to routine. As in many of Tyler's novels, the characters are hesitant to flee their present lives. In this story, Tyler reassures that whatever happens, life goes on. *The Amateur Marriage* (2003), Tyler's sixteenth novel, shows on the other hand that domestic conflicts have the tendency to continue several generations. Michael Anton and Pauline Barclay marry during the early World War II years. The dissolving of their marriage takes decades.

In 1989, Tyler won the Pulitzer Prize for *Breathing Lessons*, in which she explores the problems of marriage, love and happiness. "She [Tyler] loves love stories, though she often inventories the woe and entropy of lovelessness. She likes a wedding and all the ways weddings can differ, loves to enumerate the idiosyncrasies of children's sensibilities and of house furnishings. Temperate though she is, she celebrates intemperance, zest and an appetite for whatever, just as long as families stay together. She wants her characters plausibly married and caring for each other" (Edward Hoagland in *The New York Times*, September 11, 1988.)

Identity and integrity are the main themes of much of Tyler's work: guilt in an unhappy middle class family is the theme of *Saint Maybe* (1991); *Ladder of the Year* (1996) is a story about a woman who leaves her marriage and family to discover who she is; in *A Patchwork Planet* (1998), Barnaby Gaitlin, a former delinquent, incurable optimist, and divorced wrestles with the mystery of what makes some people more virtuous than others; in *Back When We Were Grownups* (2001), a mother of a large family, Rebecca Davitch, discovers that "she had turned into the wrong person." She does not believe it is too late to make changes and tries to find her true self from her past.

The generation of writers born during or just after World War II has produced several notable authors. *Russell Banks* (1940-) has produced *Continental Drift, Rule of the Bone, Cloudsplitter, The Sweet Hereafter* and *Affliction*. The latter two were made into films in 1997. His works reflect his working class upbringing and show people facing setbacks and tragedies in everyday life, expressing sadness and self-doubt, but also showing resilience and strength in the face of their difficulties. *John Irving* (1942-) has written bestsellers including *The World According to Garp* (1978), *The Cider House Rules* and *A Prayer for Owen Meany*, and many have been made into movies. *Paul Auster* (1947-) is a Brooklyn-based postmodernist author known for works blending absurdism and crime fiction, such as *The New York Trilogy* (1987), *Moon Palace* (1989) and *The Brooklyn Follies* (2005). Influenced by Jacques Lacan's psychoanalysis and transcendentalism, he explores the basis of individual identity and meaning. *Richard Russo's* (1949-) novel *Empire Falls*, (2001, TV 2005) won the Pulitzer Prize. He has written five other novels: *Mohawk, The Risk Pool, Nobody's Fool* (filmed 1994 starring Paul Newman), *Straight Man*, and *Bridge of Sighs*, as well as a short story collection, *The Whore's Child*. Russo writes about the decline of small working class northeastern towns and the loss of pride of their people. *Jane Smiley's* (1949-) best-selling *A Thousand Acres*, based on *King Lear*, received the Pulitzer Prize in 1992 and was adapted into a film of the same name in 1997. Her novella *The Age of Grief* was made into the 2002 film *The Secret Lives of Dentists. Thirteen Ways of Looking at the Novel* (2005), is her non-fiction meditation on the history and the nature of the novel. *David Guterson* (1956-) is best known for the novel *Snow Falling on Cedars*, which won many awards and was adapted for a motion picture starring Ethan Hawke.

Novelist and short story writer *Bret Easton Ellis* (1964-) is one of the so-called literary Brat Pack which also included Tama Janowitz and Jay McInerney. Ellis is a self-proclaimed "moralist" and is known for transgressive satire. Ellis's novels are linked with common, recurring characters. *Less Than Zero,* his first novel (filmed 1987), a tale of disaffected, rich teenagers in Los Angeles, was praised by critics and sold well. He moved to New York City in 1987 for the publication of his second novel, *The Rules of Attraction* (filmed 2002, with extra footage 2004), which follows a group of sexually promiscuous college students. The novel introduced Patrick Bateman, who would become the principal character of his controversial third novel, the graphically violent *American Psycho*. This novel has achieved cult status. Its protagonist, Patrick Bateman, is a crassly materialistic yuppie and a serial killer, Ellis has also written short stories. A collection titled *The Informers* (1994), dealing with wayward Los Angeles characters ranging from rock stars to vampires, appeared between his third and fourth novels.

After years of struggling with it, Ellis released his fourth novel *Glamorama* in 1998. *Glamorama* is set in the world of high fashion, following a male model who becomes entangled in a bizarre terrorist organization comprised entirely of other models. The book plays with themes of media, celebrity, and political violence, and like its predecessor *American Psycho* uses surrealism to convey a sense of postmodern dread. The author's most recent novel, the semi-autobiographical *Lunar Park* (2005) (film expected 2011), uses the form of a celebrity memoir to tell a ghost story about the novelist "Bret Easton Ellis" and his chilling experiences in the apparently-haunted home he shares with his wife and son. In keeping with his usual style, Ellis mixes absurd comedy with a bleak and violent vision. Critical reaction to the novel was mostly positive, with many critics endeared by its tones of wistfulness and sentimentality. *Imperial Bedrooms,* sequel to *Less Than Zero,* was published in 2010. Ellis recently wrote the screenplay for a film titled *The Frog King.* Ellis often uses recurring characters and settings. Camden College, a fictional New England liberal arts college, is frequently mentioned. Ellis's writings are referred to throughout popular culture.

Minority authors

African American women have produced some of the most powerful fiction of recent decades. The recent emergence of fiction by members of other minority groups has also been striking. Appearing on the literary scene in the 1980s and 1990s were the so-called multicultural writers like *Maxine Hong Kingston* (*Woman Warrior*), *James Welch, Bharati Mukherjee* (*The Middleman and Other Short Stories*), and *Sandra Cisneros. Amy Tan* (1952-), of Chinese descent, has described her parents' early struggles in California in *The Joy Luck Club. Oscar Hijuelos* (1951-), a writer with roots in Cuba, won the 1991 Pulitzer Prize for his novel *The Mambo Kings Play Songs of Love. Chang-Rae-Lee* received the Hemingway Foundation/PEN Award for *Native Speaker* (1995). He has since written *A Gesture Life* and *Aloft. Jhumpa Lahiri* won the 2000 Pulitzer Prize for her short story collection *The Interpreter of Maladies.* Her novel *The Namesake* (2007) was the basis of a movie. *Kiran Desai* won the Man Booker Prize (2006) and National Book Critics Circle Award (2006) for her second novel *The Inheritance of Loss. Naomi Hirahara* won a 2007 Edgar Award for her novel *Snakeskin Shamisen.* Japanese American *Adrian Tomine's Shortcomings* explores issues of race and ethnic heritage along with the vicissitudes of being in love.

Featured Authors—Alice Walker, Toni Morrison

Alice Walker, born in 1944 in Eatonton, Georgia, to sharecropper parents, has become one of the best-known and most highly respected writers in the US. Active in the 1960s Civil Rights movement in the South, she used her own and others' experiences as material for her searing examination of politics and black-white relations in her novel *Meridian* (1976).

Beginning with her first novel, *The Third Life of Grange Copeland,* Walker has focused on sexual and racial realities within black communities as well as the unavoidable connections between family and society. For exposing the former, she has been criticized by some African American male critics and theorists; for exploring the latter, she has been awarded numerous prizes while winning the hearts and minds of countless black and white readers. Perhaps her most famous work is *The Color Purple,* brought to the attention of mainstream America through the film adaptation by Steven Spielberg (1985). In that novel of incest, lesbian love, and sibling devotion, Walker also introduces blues music as a unifying thread in the lives of many of the characters.

Toni Morrison (1931-), author of *Beloved* and other works, won the Nobel Prize in Literature in 1993, the first African American and only the second American woman to be so honored. (The first was Pearl S. Buck in 1938.) *Beloved* was written from an impulse to bring the historical experience of black Americans, and the expressive traditions this experience had produced, into the mainstream of American literature, or, rather, to reveal that it had been there all along, and that race, far from being a special or marginal concern, was a central facet of the American story. *Beloved* deals with the primordial situation of American violence, slavery and its aftermath, in compressed, lyrical language that rises at times to archaic, epic strangeness. Morrison's work (like Ralph Ellison's) combines realism with elements of allegory, folk tale, Gothic and romance.

"When slavery has torn apart one's heritage, when the past is more real than the present, when the rage of a dead baby can literally rock a house, then the traditional novel is no longer an adequate instrument. And so Pulitzer Prize-winner *Beloved* is written in bits and images, smashed like a mirror on the floor and left for the reader to put together. In a novel that is hypnotic, beautiful, and elusive, Toni Morrison portrays the lives of Sethe, an escaped slave and mother, and those around her. There is Sixo, who 'stopped speaking English because there was no future in it,' and … Baby Suggs, who makes her living with her heart because slavery 'had busted her legs, back, head, eyes, hands, kidneys, womb and tongue;' and Paul D, a man with a rusted metal box for a heart and a presence that allows women to cry. At the center is Sethe, whose story makes us think and think again about what we mean when we say we love our children or freedom. The stories circle, swim dreamily to the surface, and are suddenly clear and horrifying. Because of the extraordinary, experimental style as well as the intensity of the subject matter, what we learn from them touches at a level deeper than understanding." From a review by Erica Bauermeister: From *500 Great Books by Women*.

Younger American novelists

A. O. Scott of the *New York Times*, writing in the *International Herald Tribune* of May 16, 2006 about a survey to find "the single best work of American fiction published in the last 25 years found it "startling to see … that the baby boom, long ascendant in popular culture and increasingly so in politics and business, has not produced a great novel. The best writers born immediately after the war seem almost programmatically to disdain the grand, synthesizing ambitions of their elders (and also some of their juniors), trafficking in irony, diffidence and the cultivation of small quirks rather than large idiosyncrasies. Only two books whose authors were born just after the war received more than two votes: *Housekeeping* by Marilynne Robinson, and *The Things They Carried* by Tim O'Brien. These are brilliant books, but they are also careful, small and precise. They do not generalize; they document. Ann Beattie, born in 1947, is among the most gifted and prolific fiction writers of her generation. Add Thomas Pynchon and E.L. Doctorow, Anne Tyler and Cynthia Ozick, John Irving and Joan Didion and Russell Banks and Joyce Carol Oates and you will have a literary pantheon born almost to a person during the presidency of Franklin Roosevelt….few of the highly praised, boldly ambitious books by younger writers - by which I mean writers under 50 - were mentioned. One vote each for *The Corrections* (Jonathan Franzen) and *The Amazing Adventures of Kavalier & Clay* (Michael Chabon), none for *Infinite Jest* (David Foster Wallace) or *The Fortress of Solitude* (Jonathan Lethem), a single vote for Richard Powers, none for William T. Vollmann, and so on."

RECENT WINNERS OF THE PULITZER PRIZE IN FICTION

Cormac McCarthy for *The Road* in 2007
Philip Roth for *American Pastoral* in 1998
John Updike for *Rabbit at Rest* in 1991 and *Rabbi is Rich* in 1982
Anne Tyler for *Breathing Lessons* in 1989
Toni Morrison for *Beloved* in 1988
William Kennedy for *Ironweed* in 1984
Alice Walker for *The Color Purple* in 1983
Norman Mailer for *The Executioner's Song* in 1980
John Cheever for *The Stories of John Cheever* in 1979
Saul Bellow for *Humboldt's Gift* in 1976

POETRY

There was little notable poetry in early America. In the Puritan age, Anne Bradstreet (1612-1672), the first woman American poet, began writing with very formal classical structures and themes and then turned to subjects like pregnancy, childbirth, marriage and grandchildren.

Nineteenth century

America's greatest 19th-century poets could hardly have been more different in temperament and style. *Walt Whitman* (1819-1892) was a working man, a traveler, a volunteer nurse during the American Civil War (1861-1865), and a poetic innovator. His great work was *Leaves of Grass*, in which he uses a free-flowing verse and lines of irregular length to depict the all-inclusiveness of American democracy. Taking that motif one step further, the poet equated the vast range of American experience with himself and managed not to sound like a crass egotist. For example, in "Song of Myself," the long, central poem, Whitman writes: "These are really the thoughts of all men in all ages and lands, they are not original with me...." Whitman was also a poet of the body – "the body electric," as he called it. In *Studies in Classic American Literature*, the English novelist D. H. Lawrence wrote that Whitman "was the first to smash the old moral conception that the soul of man is something `superior' and `above' the flesh."

Emily Dickinson (1830-1886), on the other hand, lived the sheltered life of a genteel unmarried woman in the small town of Concord, Massachusetts. Within its formal structure, her poetry is ingenious, witty, exquisitely wrought, and psychologically penetrating. Her work was unconventional for its day, and little of it was published during her lifetime. Many of her poems dwell on death, often with a mischievous twist: "Because I could not stop for Death," one begins, "He kindly stopped for me." The opening of another Dickinson poem toys with her position as a woman in a male-dominated society and an unrecognized poet: "I'm nobody! Who are you? / Are you nobody too?" Julia Ward Howe's (1819-1910) *Passion-Flowers*, about her unhappy marriage, was brought out anonymously, and when her husband found out, he threatened her with divorce.

The works of *Henry Wadsworth Longfellow* (1807-1882) included *Paul Revere's Ride*, *A Psalm of Life*, *The Song of Hiawatha* and *Evangeline*. He also wrote the first American translation of Dante Alighieri's *Divine Comedy* and was one of the five members of the group known as the *Fireside Poets* along with William Cullen Bryant, John Greenleaf Whittier, James Russell Lowell, and Oliver Wendell Holmes, Sr. Longfellow was such an admired figure during his life that his 70th birthday in 1877 took on the air of a national holiday, with parades, speeches, and the reading of his poetry. He had become one of the first American celebrities. His work was immensely popular during his time and is still today, although some modern critics consider him too sentimental. His poetry is based on familiar and easily understood themes with simple, clear, and flowing language. Longfellow's poetry created an audience for poetry in America and contributed to creating American mythology.

Longfellow's contemporary, *John Greenleaf Whittier* (1807-1892) was a Quaker poet and forceful advocate of the abolition of slavery. Highly regarded in his lifetime and for a period thereafter, he is now remembered largely for the patriotic poem *Barbara Frietchie*, as well as for a number of poems turned into hymns, some of which remain exceedingly popular. Although clearly Victorian in style, and capable of being sentimental, his hymns exhibit both imagination and universality that set them beyond the ordinary. Best known is probably *Dear Lord and Father of Mankind* taken from his poem "The Brewing of Soma," but Whittier's Quaker thought is better illustrated by the hymn that begins "O Brother Man, fold to thy heart thy brother."

Twentieth Century

Edwin Arlington Robinson (1869-1936), winner of three Pulitzer Prizes, wrote grim, intelligent poetry of American failures, *Miniver Cheevy* among them. *Edgar Guest* (1881-1959), the Poet Laureate of Michigan, wrote some 20 books of sentimental, optimistic poems that were widely published in magazines and newspapers and were popular during the Depression. (Alfred) *Joyce Kilmer* (1886-1918), author of *Trees and other Poems,* has received renewed attention recently because of environmentalists' interest in his work.

Robert Frost (1874-1953) frequently used themes from rural life in New England, using the setting to examine complex social and philosophical themes. Frost's poetry was highly popular in his lifetime and remains so. Among his best-known shorter poems are "Stopping by Woods on a Snowy Evening," "Mending Wall," "Nothing Gold Can Stay," "Birches," "Acquainted With the Night," "After Apple-Picking," "The Pasture," "Out Out," "Fire and Ice," "The Road Not Taken," and "Directive." Frost won the Pulitzer Prize four times, an achievement unequalled by any other American poet.

Not a poets' poet, *Wallace Stevens* (1879-1955) paid little attention to the literary world and did not receive widespread recognition until the publication of his *Collected Poems* in 1954. Now he is regarded by critics as among the most significant poets of the 20th century. Stevens explored the dualism between concrete reality and the human imagination. His poems focus on the sound of language, on obscure vocabulary, and on imaginative images. For most of his adult life, Stevens pursued two careers, as an insurance executive and a poet.

Encouraged at Harvard by George Santayana, he was influenced by imagism (itself partly derived from classic Chinese poetry.) Stevens published his first collection of verse, *Harmonium* in 1923. Dismissed at the time by most critics, now the collection is regarded as one of the great works of American poetry. *Harmonium* included "The Emperor of the Ice Cream" (one of Stevens' own favorite poems), "Le Monocle de Mon Oncle," "The Man Whose Pharynx Was Bad," and "Thirteen Ways of Looking at a Blackbird." The poems were partly autobiographical, including references to the failure of his marriage. "The Emperor of the Ice Cream," despite its title, is about death seen in a harsh light. *Ideas and Order* (1935), Stevens' next collection, received mixed reviews, with accusations of indifference to the political and social tensions of the day. In fact, he was a socialist during the 1930's, but did not make his views a public issue. *The Man with the Blue Guitar and Other Poems* (1937) affirmed that "Poetry / Exceeding music must take place / Of empty heaven and its hymns."

Among Stevens' acclaimed poems were "Notes toward a Supreme Fiction," "The Auroras of Autumn," "An Ordinary Evening in New Haven," and "The Planet on the Table." From the early 1940s, he turned gradually away from the playful use of language to a more reflective, abstract style. Echoing the ideas of Baudelaire, Stevens argued in "Esthétique du Mal" that beauty is inextricably linked with evil. In 1955 he was awarded both the Pulitzer Prize and the National Book Award.

Much influenced by Gertrude Stein, and also by Ezra Pound, e. e. *cummings* (1894-1962) was a prolific and popular poet, painter, essayist and playwright. He is one of the greatest 20th-century poets. Despite Cummings's affinity for avant-garde styles, much of his work is traditional. Many of his poems are sonnets, with a recognizable structure of 14 lines and an intricate rhyme scheme, though he occasionally made use of the blues form and acrostics. Cummings' poetry deals much with themes of love, sex, nature and death, as well as the relationship of the individual to society. His poems are also often rife with satire. While his poetic forms, and even themes, show a close continuity with the Romantic tradition, his work universally shows a particular idiosyncrasy of syntax. Some of his poetry is free verse (with no concern for rhyme or scansion.) A number of his poems feature exuberant typography, with words, parts of words, or punctuation symbols scattered across the page, often making little sense until read aloud, at which point the meaning and emotion become clear. Famous poems include "a man who had fallen among thieves," "i carry your heart with me," "next to of course god america i," "my sweet old etcetera," and "since feeling is first."

The two leading Lost Generation poets were friends and colleagues: Ezra Pound and T. S. Eliot. *Ezra Pound* (1885-1972) spent much of his adult life in Europe, although he was born in Idaho. His work is complex, sometimes obscure, with multiple references to other art forms and to a vast range of literature, both Western and Eastern. Pound is generally considered the poet most responsible for defining and promoting a modernist aesthetic in poetry. In the early teens of the 20th century, he opened a seminal exchange of work and ideas between British and American writers, and was famous for the generosity with which he advanced the work of such major contemporaries as W. B. Yeats, Robert Frost, William Carlos Williams, Marianne Moore, H. D. (Hilda Doolittle), James Joyce, Ernest Hemingway, and especially T. S. Eliot. His own significant contributions to poetry begin with his promulgation of *Imagism*, a movement in poetry which derived its technique from classical Chinese and Japanese poetry—stressing clarity, precision, and economy of language, and foregoing traditional rhyme and meter in order to, in Pound's words, "compose in the sequence of the musical phrase, not in the sequence of the metronome." For nearly fifty years, his work focused on the encyclopedic epic poem he entitled *The Cantos*.

T. S. Eliot (1888 – 1965) is the most celebrated English-language poet of the 20th century. He wrote spare, cerebral poetry carried by a dense structure of symbols, often with a tone of ironic elegance and psychological nuance. A Harvard-educated philosopher, Eliot was influenced by Irving Babbitt, George Santayana, Henri Bergson, William James and Bertrand Russell. His wide interests included the psychology of consciousness, anthropology, religion, Sanskrit, and Hindu thought.

His early poems were published in *Prufrock and Other Observations* in 1917. Much influenced by the French symbolist, Jules Laforgue, they include "The Love Song of J. Alfred Prufrock," "Portrait of a Lady," "La Figlia Che Piange," "Preludes," and "Rhapsody on a Windy Night." Combining something of Robert Browning's robust monologues with the elegant incantations of symbolist verse, and uniting poetry of alienation with moral earnestness, these poems explore the subtleties of the unconscious with a caustic wit. Their effect was unique and compelling, and their assurance staggered contemporaries. In 1920 he collected a second slim volume of verse, *Poems*, and a volume of criticism, *The Sacred Wood*. Both displayed a winning combination of erudition and jazzy bravura.

The Waste Land (1922), the greatest of his early poems, was an assemblage of dramatic vignettes based on Eliot's London life. The poem's extraordinary intensity stems from a sudden fusing of diverse materials with a jazz-like syncopation into a whole of great skill and daring. It was a deeply unoptimistic, un-Christian and therefore un-American poem. In its desolation at the breakup of the Judeo-Christian past, the poem turns for salvation to the Buddha and his three ethical commandments: Give, Sympathize, Control. But on the way to its ritually religious close "Shantih, shantih, shantih" (accent on the second syllable), it films a succession of loveless, violent or failed sexual unions among the educated ("My nerves are bad tonight") and the uneducated ("He, the young man carbuncular, arrives"), and in the poet's own life ("your heart would have responded / Gaily".) It speaks of an absent God and of a dead father. Readers felt the desperate spiritual quest behind the poem's fragmented, haunting images and were seduced by the unerring musicality of its free-verse lines. Like Pound's, Eliot's poetry could be highly allusive, and some editions of *The Waste Land* come with footnotes supplied by the poet. *Poems 1909-1925* (1925) featured *The Hollow Men,* a sequel to *The Waste Land.*

Meanwhile Eliot became editor of a high-profile literary journal, the *Criterion*, which appeared 1922-39. In this period he joined the Anglican church and in 1927 took British citizenship. The next year he caused a surprise by collecting a group of politically conservative essays under the title of *For Lancelot Andrewes,* prefacing them with a declaration that he considered himself a "classicist in literature, royalist in politics, and anglo-catholic in religion." Eliot's poetry now addressed explicitly religious themes, as in a series of short poems such as "Journey of the Magi" (1927), "A Song for Simeon" (1928), "Animula" (1929), "Marina" (1930), and 'Triumphal March" (1931). Steeped in his contemporary study of Dante and the late Shakespeare, all of them meditate on spiritual growth and anticipate the longer and more celebrated *Ash-Wednesday* (1930). "Journey of the Magi" and "A Song for Simeon" are also exercises in dramatic monologues in the style of Browning, and exchanged the symbolist fluidity of the psychological lyric for a more traditional dramatic form.

Eliot spent much of the last half of his career writing one kind of drama or another, and attempting to reach and bring together a larger and more varied audience. *Sweeney Agonistes* (unfinished) was an experimental and striking jazz play; *The Rock,* a church pageant with accompanying choruses, and *Murder in the Cathedral,* a masterpiece portraying the murder of Thomas à Becket in Canterbury Cathedral in 1170. The opening stanza of *The Rock* contains the oft-quoted lines:

Where is the Life we have lost in living? Where is the wisdom we have lost in knowledge? Where is the knowledge we have lost in information?

In the late 1930s, Eliot attempted to conflate a drama of spiritual crisis with a Noël Coward-inspired contemporary theater of social manners. *The Family Reunion* was based on the plot of Aeschylus's *Eumenides,* redesigned to tell a story of Christian redemption. It was not a success in the theater. A more popular (though less powerful) combination of similar dramatic elements achieved much greater success: *The Cocktail Party*, modernizing Euripides's *Alcestis* with some of the stylishness of Noël Coward, received a warm critical reception and ran respectably on Broadway in 1950. Eliot's last two plays, *The Confidential Clerk* and *The Elder Statesman* were more labored and fared less well. His humorous *Old Possum's Book of Practical Cats* (1939) with its clever meters has been popularized in the musical *Cats*, ironically the work by which he is now generally best known.

The *Four Quartets* (1935-42), a suite of four somber, five-part poems, opens with "Burnt Norton," which considers humanity's enslavement to time. "East Coker," the second piece, is most concerned with the place of man in the natural order and with the idea of renewal. The third poem is "The Dry Salvages" ("salvages" should be pronounced with the emphasis on the penultimate syllable) reverted to Eliot's experience as a boy on the Mississippi and sailing on the Massachusetts coast. Its title refers to a set of dangerously hidden rocks near Cape Ann. The poem considers human history and cycles of rebirth and renewal. "Little Gidding," the last in the cycle, is an extended meditation on the subject of the individual's duties in a world of human suffering. Its centerpiece was a sustained homage to Dante written in a form of terza rima (a three-line stanza using chain rhyme in the pattern a-b-a, b-c-b,) dramatizing Eliot's meeting with a "familiar compound ghost" he associates with Yeats and Swift. The voice of the *Four Quartets* , meditative, grave, sorrowful, but also dry, experienced and harsh, allowed the conversational tone of everyday life to enter into the discussion of the deepest subjects. The heartbreak under the poised irony of Eliot's work was not lost on his audience, who suddenly felt that in understanding Eliot, they understood themselves. Eliot won the Nobel Prize in Literature in 1948.

Eliot's numerous publications included *Dante* (1929), *Selected Essays 1917-1932* (1950), *The Use of Poetry and the Use of Criticism* (1933), *After Strange Gods* (1934), *The Idea of a Christian Society* (1939) and *Notes towards the Definition of Culture* (1948). By 1950, Eliot's reputation as a poet and man of letters gave him an authority comparable to Samuel Johnson or Samuel Taylor Coleridge. But in the decades after his death, Eliot's reputation declined. He was regarded as too academic and too classical. In recent years, however, the strong affinities of Eliot's post-symbolist style with currently more influential poets like Wallace Stevens (Eliot's contemporary at Harvard and a fellow student of Santayana) have been reassessed, as has the tough philosophical skepticism of his prose.

A contemporary of Eliot and Pound (in fact a friend of Pound's) *Dr. William Carlos Williams* (1883–1963), who was sometimes known as "WCW," was a practicing pediatrician (children's physician) whose poetry was closely associated with early modernism and, at first, imagism. Williams' most anthologized poem is "The Red Wheelbarrow," which is considered a model of the Imagist movement's style and principles.

In addition to his medical practice, Williams had a full literary career. His work consists of short stories, poems, plays, novels, critical essays, an autobiography, translations and correspondence. Williams considered himself a socialist and opponent of capitalism, and in 1935 published "The Yachts," a poem which indicts the rich elite as parasites and the masses as striving for revolution. The poem features an image of the ocean in which the "watery bodies" of the poor masses beat at the hulls of the yachts "in agony, in despair," attempting to sink the yachts and end "the horror of the race." Indeed, in the introduction to his 1944 book of poems, *The Wedge*, he writes of socialism as an inevitable future development and as a necessity for true art to develop. In 1949, he published a booklet/poem, *The Pink Church,* that was about the human body but was understood at the time as being pro-communist.

Williams championed a fully American poetry. He protested against the English influence on American poetry, and disliked Ezra Pound's and T. S. Eliot's frequent use of allusions to foreign languages and classical sources. Williams preferred to draw his themes from what he called "the local." In his modernist epic of place, *Paterson* (1946-58), an account of the history, people and essence of Paterson, New Jersey, he examined the role of the poet in American society. Williams tried to invent a fresh American form of poetry whose subject matter was centered on the everyday lives of common people. He abandoned traditional meter in most of his poems and replaced it with his own, largely based on American speech rhythms and jazz.

Williams was especially important as a mentor for younger poets. He had an especially significant influence on many of the American literary movements of the 1950s: poets of the Beat Generation, particularly Allen Ginsberg, the San Francisco Renaissance, the Black Mountain school, and the New York School. In May 1963 he was posthumously awarded the Pulitzer Prize for *Pictures from Brueghel and Other Poems* (1962).

The *Black Mountain School* was a group of influential poets associated with the school of that name in North Carolina, which existed from 1933 to 1956, and the *Black Mountain Review.* The group included Robert Creeley (*Pieces*), Robert Duncan (*Structure of Rime* and *Passages*), Denise Levertov, and Charles Olson (*Maximus*). Their work was called "projective verse," in which poets removed themselves and projected the energy of their work directly to the reader. It owed much to objectivists like William Carlos Williams and modernists like Ezra Pound. Spontaneity and "the act of the poem" took the place of reason and description.

The New York School of poetry began around 1960 in New York City and included poets such as John Ashbery, Barbara Guest, Kenneth Koch, and Frank O'Hara. Heavily influenced by surrealism and modernism, the poetry of the New York School was serious but also ironic, and incorporated an urban sensibility into much of the work. Abstract expressionist art was also a major influence, and the New York School poets had strong artistic and personal relationships with artists such as Jackson Pollock and Willem de Kooning. Both O'Hara and James Schuyler worked at the Museum of Modern Art, and Guest, Ashbery, and Schuyler were critics for *Art News.* O'Hara also took inspiration from artists, entitling two poems "Joseph Cornell" and "On Seeing Larry Rivers." A second generation of New York School poets arose during the 1960s and included Ted Berrigan, Ron Padgett, Anne Waldman, and Joe Brainard. Their scene grew up around downtown New York and was associated with the Poetry Project at St Mark's Church. The New York School continues to influence poets.

The *San Francisco Renaissance* is the name given to the emergence of writers and artists in the Bay Area at the end of World War II. It was not a single movement, but rather a diverse group of many different communities that migrated to San Francisco during the postwar era seeking out the remnants of bohemian culture in America. Although the poets were united in eschewing a poetic mainstream they felt had turned back toward formalism and abandoned the innovations of modernism, they were not united by a single particular aesthetic style and often were at odds with one another both artistically and politically. Many of their poems, however, shared an elegiac quality, responding to both the devastating aftermath of both World Wars as well as the restrictive cultural climate. Their work often expressed a longing for the lost world and an attempt to restore it with visions of nature and distant cultures. Recalling the expressive exuberance and regionalism of Whitman, the poems of the San Francisco Renaissance were frequently confessional and deeply evocative of their Pacific coast and San Francisco surroundings. The poets' influences ranged from European modernism and surrealism to Eastern religions and literature. Some of the major writers involved in the San Francisco Renaissance included Kenneth Rexroth, William Everson, Jack Spicer, Robin Blaser, and Michael McClure. Though more associated with the Black Mountain movement, Robert Duncan introduced many of the central figures of the San Francisco Renaissance to each other.

Rexroth became a reluctant godfather to the *Beat Movement*, which grew out of the San Francisco Renaissance in the 1950s on the West Coast. The poetry and fiction of the Beat Generation involved the rhythm of jazz music, a sense that postwar society was worn out, and an interest in new forms of experience through drugs, alcohol, and Eastern mysticism. Poet *Allen Ginsberg (1926-1997)*, a protegé of William Carlos Williams, set the tone of social protest and visionary ecstasy in "Howl !"(1955), a Whitmanesque work that begins with this powerful line: "I saw the best minds of my generation destroyed by madness." Colleagues included Michael McClure, Gary Snyder, Philip Whalen and Philip Lamantia. Contemporary *Sylvia Plath (1932-65)* poet, novelist and short story writer, advanced the genre of confessional poetry in such collections as *Ariel*.

Modern poets

Modern poets include *John Ashbery (1927-)* and *Charles Wright (1935- .)* Ashbery, a controversial experimental poet, has received the Pulitzer Prize for Poetry, the National Book Critics Circle Award, and the National Book Award for *Mirror* (1975) and *Self Portrait in a Convex Mirror* . Ashbery has published over 20 books of poetry. Much of his poetry is about the play of the mind. Wright has been widely published, winning the National Book Award in 1983 for *Country Music: Selected Early Poems* and the Pulitzer Prize for Poetry in 1997 for *Black Zodiac*. He has received critical acclaim as a "verbal musician," but some readers feel he lacks the vision of some of his predecessors. *Adrienne Rich (1929-)* has been acclaimed as one of the most widely read and influential of contemporary poets. Native American writer *Leslie Marmon Silko (1948-)* uses colloquial language and traditional stories to fashion haunting, lyrical poems such as "In Cold Storm Light." The collections of the much-respected African American poet *D. A .Powell* (1963-) - *Lunch, Tea, Cocktails,* and *Chronic* - deal with contemporary themes like movies, art, contemporary culture, AIDS and the environment.

Listen to poets
The Poetry Archive. Listen and read at the same time (needs realplayer). Includes John Ashbery, T. S. Eliot, Allen Ginsberg.
http://www.poetryarchive.org/poetryarchive/home.do

E. E. Cummings
"Let's From Some Loud Unworld's Most Rightful Wrong" and "That Melancholy"
http://www.ubu.com/sound/cummings.html
T. S. Eliot "La Figlia Che Piange"
http://www.poets.org/viewmedia.php/prmMID/15305

Robert Frost "Stopping By Woods on a Snowy Evening" and "After Apple-Picking" and Ezra Pound
    excerpt from "The Cantos"
http://www.salon.com/audio/2000/10/05/pound/

Penn Sound Daily (modern poets)
http://www.writing.upenn.edu/pennsound/

Wallace Stevens "The Idea of Order at Key West," "The Poem that Took the Place of a Mountain,"
    "Vacancy in the Park" and "To an Old Philosopher in Rome"
http://town.hall.org/radio/HarperAudio/021594_harp_ITH.html

The short story

From Irving and Hawthorne to the present day, the short story has been a favorite American form. One of its 20th-century masters was *John Cheever* (1912-1982), who brought yet another facet of American life into the realm of literature: the affluent suburbs that have grown up around most major cities. Cheever was long associated with *The New Yorker*, a magazine noted for its wit and sophistication. *Jean Stafford* (1915-1979) has become known for her venomous attacks on the women's movement in the 1970s. She is notable for her accounts of the frustrations, anxieties, and bewilderment over finding her own voice. Award-winner *Cynthia Ozick* (1928-) writes about Jewish-American life among a broad range of subjects, with fascinating female characters. *Donald Barthelme's* (1931-1989) surreal postmodernist short stories are often exceptionally compact (a form sometimes called "short-short story," "flash fiction," or "sudden fiction") focusing only on incidents rather than complete narratives. *Edna Annie Proulx* (pronounced /pru:/) (1935-) won the Pulitzer Prize and the National Book Award for her second novel, *The Shipping News* (1993), which was made into a film in 2001. Her short story with a gay theme "Brokeback Mountain" was adapted for an award-winning and commercially successful movie (2005). *Raymond Carver* (1938-1988) is considered to have revitalized the short story in the 1980s. Currently, *Tobias Wolff* is among the leading American short story writers. His characters are mostly misfits, fantasists and liars, driven by anger, humiliation, boredom, or the need to make better sense of their lives by reinventing the details. Wolff's stories are permeated by what he himself describes as a "sourness of foreboding," a view of the world "where wounds did not heal and things did not work out for the best." Perhaps Wolff is at his best when handling the poetics of place – a sunset, a strip mall – which sometimes redeem the banality of his endings. Carver, Wolff and *Richard Ford* (1944-) write in a brand of minimalist style known as "dirty realistm." Award-winners *Ann Beattie* (1947-) and *Mary Hempel* (1951-) are also noted for their minimalist style.

Popular literature

American popular literature is an immense field. Despite TV, Americans are reading more than ever; women more than men. The best-selling fiction genres are mystery, suspense, horror, romance and historical fiction. The sweeping novel following the fortunes of four generations of Americans is particularly liked. In the world of non-fiction, advice and how-to books are extremely popular. These books cover many health issues and at least one diet book is always on the best-seller list. Personal finance and self-development books of all types are popular, as well as inspirational titles.

Books and book clubs

Compared to many other countries, prices for books in the US are very reasonable. Used books are also for sale in special stores, and even by street peddlers. Books on tape cassette are growing in popularity. Most American libraries allow people to borrow books, audio and even video cassettes. Online booksellers such as Amazon.com and Barnes & Noble, which is also a large retail chain, are winning large shares of the book market. Online transmission of books electronically (Books On Demand) is also available.

The practice of reading is encouraged by book clubs, which are popular as they make it convenient to order books. Book clubs advertise special offers such as "Any five books on this page for $1.00." These are legitimate bargains, but substantial postage and handling charges are made and customers must also usually agree to purchase a certain number of books from the club within a year or two. The book club will send a catalog every few weeks with an order form. A customer who does not want the book the club has selected for any particular month must send back a special form and tell the club "no" or else they will send the book and bill for it.

PHILOSOPHY

American philosophy has both reflected and shaped American identity. Well before the founding of the US, explicit positions were taken by Americans on social and political issues such as the relation of individuals to their communities, and the nature of those communities, secular or religious. While the three most famous American philosophers are Charles Peirce, William James, and John Dewey of the late 19th and early 20th centuries, the founding documents of several colonies, such as the Mayflower Compact of 1620, which referred to the "civil Body Politic" that the Puritans had arrived to form at Plymouth, asserted distinct philosophical beliefs. Similarly, the writings of early colonial leaders, such as John Winthrop (1588-1649) declared that "the care of the public must oversway all private respects...for it is a true rule that particular estates cannot subsist in the ruin of the public." Even so, the Maryland Toleration Act (1649) and the writings of Roger Williams (1603-1683) among others stressed religious tolerance over commitment to the religious covenant of a community.

By far the most important American thinker of the first half of the 18th century was *Jonathan Edwards* (1703-1758), who synthesized Calvinist theology and the scientific worldview of modern physics. The last and greatest of the New England Puritan preachers, Edwards is widely considered America's most important Christian philosopher. Edwards drew on Christian Platonism, with its emphasis on the reality of a spiritual world, an empiricist epistemology (knowledge comes from sense data), Locke's account of sensation, and Newtonian physics. His thought much resembles the idealism of the British philosopher Berkeley (1685-1753), who stressed the necessity of mind (or non-material reality) to make sense of human experience, although scholars now think Edwards reached his idealism independently. For Edwards, non-material reality consisted of understanding and will, both of which were basically passive. Material reality was characterized by *resistance*. Objects remained at rest or in motion unless acted upon by some other force, in accordance with Newton's laws of motion. Edwards is perhaps best known for his rejection of free will. As he remarked, "we can do as we please, but we cannot please as we please." Just as there was natural necessity and natural inability, for Edwards there was moral necessity and moral inability. Every act of will was determined. Echoing the views of Calvin, Edwards saw not good works, but the grace of God as the determinant of human destiny. Edwards' theology is outlined in Chapter 8.

Other American thinkers of the late 18th century, however, largely abandoned theology and adopted the concerns and commitments of their Enlightenment contemporaries. Like them, they relied on reason and believed in scientific and social progress and the perfectibility of humans. They were strong advocates of political democracy and laissez-faire economics. Thus, while they attended very little to metaphysics or epistemology, Founders such as Thomas Jefferson (1743-1826), Benjamin Franklin (1706-1790), and James Madison (1751-1836), wrote voluminously on social and political philosophy, focusing on the appropriate form of the State and its relation to individuals. Jefferson, for example, when he drafted the Declaration of Independence, emphasized the natural, inalienable rights of individuals against the tyranny of the State; the function of the State was only to secure the rights of individuals. Meanwhile Federalists such as James Madison highlighted the dangers of factional democracy, advocating for both individual rights and the public good. Though making explicit references to God, these thinkers tended to commit themselves less to Christianity and more to Deism, seeing God as creator of a world governed by natural laws but not directly involved with human life. In particular, while Franklin acknowledged Jesus as the teacher of a system of morality, he did not commit himself to the divinity of Jesus or to any organized church.

Transcendentalism, or American Romanticism, was the first of several major traditions to characterize philosophy in America's first full century as a nation, with Transcendentalism succeeded by Darwinian evolutionary thought and finally by America's most renowned school of thought, Pragmatism. The Transcendentalists stressed the subjective nature of human experience and existence. Writers such as Ralph Waldo Emerson (1803-1882), Henry David Thoreau (1817-1872), and Walt Whitman (1819-1892) argued for the priority of personal emotional, even mystical connections between humans and nature and the world as a whole. Humans, for these thinkers, were agents in the world more than knowers of the world. "Real" knowledge was intuitive and personal; it transcended scientific understanding based on empirical sense experience. Because of this, those things that constrain or restrict free personal thought, such as conventional morality and political institutions, needed to be transcended as well. This outlook was captured in the poetry of Walt Whitman's "Song of Myself" in which he declared, "I celebrate myself....Unscrew the locks from the doors! Unscrew the doors themselves from their jambs! I speak the past-word primeval, I give the sign of democracy...." The sentiment was echoed in the works of Emerson and Thoreau, both of whom argued for the importance of self-reliance, intuition, and a return to nature i.e., an embracing of what is non-civilized and non-industrial. In his 1836 paper, "Nature", Emerson said: "In the woods, we return to reason and faith...I am nothing; I see all; the currents of the Universal Being circulate through me; I am part or parcel of God...In the wilderness I find something more dear and connate than in streets and villages." Emerson's "The Transcendentalist" (1842) stands as a manifesto of this philosophical movement, in which he explicitly identifies Transcendentalism as a form of philosophical Idealism. Here Emerson declared:

"Society is good when it does not violate me, but best when it is likest to solitude. Everything real is self-existent. Everything divine shares the self-existence of Deity...[Kant showed] there was a very important class of ideas or imperative forms, which did not come by way of experience, but through which experience was acquired; that these were intuitions of the mind itself; and he denominated them Transcendental forms."

At the same time, during the 1830s and 1840s, there were other thinkers who stressed greater social and political equality, particularly several important women writers and activists, such as Sarah Grimké (1792-1873) and Elizabeth Cady Stanton (1815-1902). The call for social and political emancipation also came from those demanding the abolition of slavery, notably William Lloyd Garrison (1805-1879) and Frederick Douglass (1817-1895).

The publication of Charles Darwin's evolutionary theory in 1859 had a great impact on subsequent American philosophy. John Fiske (1842-1901) and Chauncey Wright (1830-1875) stressed the need to understand consciousness and morality in terms of their evolutionary development. It was often under the label of "Social Darwinism" that this view had even greater impact and influence, especially through the writings of William Graham Sumner (1840-1910). Sumner likened societies to organisms engaged in a struggle for survival. If groups within a society, and even societies themselves, were, like biological organisms, in constant competition for survival, Sumner argued, then a sign of their fitness was the fact that they did in fact survive. Sumner and others, such as the industrialist Andrew Carnegie (1835-1919), argued that the social implication of the struggle for survival was that free-market capitalism was the natural economic system and the one that would ensure the greatest economic well-being. In his essay, "The Man of Virtue," Sumner remarks that, "Every man and woman in society has one big duty. That is, to take care of his or her own self…Society, therefore, does not need any care or supervision." Carnegie's "The Gospel of Wealth" echoes this view: " [The law of competition] is here, we cannot evade it; no substitutes for it have been found; and while the law may be sometimes hard for the individual, it is best for the race, because it insures the survival of the fittest in every department…the law of competition [is] not only beneficial, but essential to the future progress of the race." The emphasis on competition as the key to evolutionary thought was not shared by everyone, however. One prominent advocate of Darwin, who nevertheless argued that cooperation rather than competition was the message of evolutionary thought, was Lester Ward (1841-1913). Not only are those groups that cooperate and function together as a group more likely to survive than those that do not, he claimed, but human history showed that government was a natural, emergent feature of human societies, rather than a hindrance and impediment to progress.

After Transcendentalism and evolutionary philosophy, the third and by far the most prominent philosophical movement in 19th-century America was Pragmatism, the philosophy given that name by one of its most famous proponents, Charles Sanders Peirce. Pragmatism is seen by most philosophers today as the classic American philosophical tradition. Not easily definable, Peirce's "pragmatic maxim" captures this stance as follows: "Consider what effects, which might conceivably have practical bearings, we conceive the object of our conception to have. Then, our conception of these effects is the whole of our conception of the object." Pragmatists rejected the foundationalist view of knowledge i.e., that there is some sure starting point such as Descartes' "I think, therefore I am." For Pragmatists, all claims to knowledge were fallible and could be revised. No inquiry was disinterested and beliefs were basically tools for us to cope with experience. The Pragmatists were not pure subjectivists, however, and did not advocate abandoning standards or criteria of judgment beyond the individual. Perhaps the most significant aspect of Pragmatism for an understanding of American culture is that it sees beliefs in terms of consequences and is thus oriented toward the future.

Charles Peirce (1839-1914)

The three chief classical pragmatists were Charles Peirce, William James and John Dewey. Peirce not only coined the term "Pragmatism" in the 1870s, but did ground-breaking work in semiotics (the study of signs) as well as in logic, particularly in the logic of relations. A scientist and mathematician also by profession, he wrote a considerable amount on the philosophy of science (for example, on the nature of explanation), value theory, and metaphysics, including seminal work on categories. From his early writings in the 1860s, in which he criticized Cartesian doubt and the foundationalist search for indubitability, to his later works on cognition and what he termed "evolutionary cosmology," Peirce consistently argued against nominalism and in favor of realism, in the sense that our conceptions are of things independent of us. An important feature of Peirce's pragmatism was a vigorous rejection of subjectivism. He insisted that, as inquirers do not exist in isolation, beliefs are not fulfilled in isolation (an assertion commonly known as the *Pragmatic Maxim*.) Rather, it is the development of successful habit that matters, and it is the verdict of the community of inquirers in the long run that matters in the determination of an inquiry. This, however, is not a "social constructivist" view, in which what is real or true is determined by what society decides. Instead, as in good science, there is a community of inquirers who form a system of checks and balances for any belief, but this community operates within a world of objects, qualities, relations, and laws.

In metaphysics, Peirce identified three fundamental categories of being. One category was that of Quality (or Firstness). This is the conception of being independent of anything else, such as a pure tone or color. A second category was that of Brute Fact (or Secondness), that is being relative to or connected with something else, such as a particular instance of a tone or a color. This is what he sometimes called the "demonstrative application" of a sign. Finally, there was Law, or Habit (or Thirdness), or mediation whereby a First and Second are brought into relation. This is the notion of regularity and representation, and as such involves a regulative as well as descriptive aspect. An example is a red light indicating the need to stop or perhaps indicating danger. Law, habit, and regularity are neither reducible to the particular instances that are true of it (that is, Secondness) nor to the pure material quality of what is instantiated in those particulars (that is, Firstness.) For Peirce, these three categories were all real, were all irreducible to the others, and were all involved in any form or act of inquiry.

William James (1842-1910)

William James, known during his lifetime as much for his work in psychology as for his work in philosophy, did much more than Peirce to popularize Pragmatism, both as a philosophical method for resolving disputes and as a theory of meaning and truth. James stressed the practical effects of belief and assertion, claiming that truth was a species of good (what it was ultimately good for us to believe.) Much of James's philosophical work was aimed at dissolving many of the traditional philosophical puzzles by showing that they made no practical difference in our lives, or that they rested on mistaken and fruitless assumptions. Any stance on, say, the existence of God, will matter only if adopting a belief (for or against) will shape our future experience for the better. Since beliefs are instruments for coping with the world, those beliefs that are good for us, those that indeed help us cope, are the ones that are true. Of course, James admitted that the goodness and coping-value of some beliefs might be negligible. He believed that human freedom was compatible with some forms of determinism. He also argued against a dualist view of mind by which mind and body are separate orders of being. In particular, he claimed that a belief in determinism led to a feeling of fatalism and surrendering to the status quo; hence, it was not better for us.

In metaphysics, James is still known for his view of "radical empiricism," in which he argued that relations between objects are as real as the properties of objects. This view, he claimed, consisted in outline of a postulate, a statement of fact, and a generalized conclusion. The *postulate* is that the only things that shall be debatable among philosophers shall be things definable in terms drawn from experience. The *statement of fact* is that the relations between things are just as much matters of direct particular experience as the things themselves or their properties. For example, when we look at a cat and a mouse, not only are those two objects (and their properties, such as their color and shape) immediate aspects of our visual experience, but we also see the cat is larger than the mouse. This experience is just as immediate as seeing that the cat is black and the mouse is gray. *The generalized conclusion* is that the parts of experience hold together by relations that are themselves parts of experience.

Another important metaphysical position held by James was pluralism i.e., that there is no single correct description or account of the world. Not only can there be different *good* accounts, but different *correct* accounts. In holding this view, James rejected the correspondence view of truth (what he called "the copy theory") in which truth was simply a relation between a belief and a state of affairs. Rather, truth involved both a belief and facts about the world, but also other background beliefs and, indeed, future consequences. For James, then, the distinction between a good account and a correct account was not a sharp one. This does not mean that any account was as good as any other. Rather, there could be different accounts that not only made sense of present and past knowledge and experience, but also led to useful future experiences. What will determine the truth of an account will be its consequences e.g., are predictions based on it borne out in experience? does it promote physical and spiritual flourishing? does it survive scrutiny by others? Though James himself also argued against subjectivism and for the importance of "older truths" (i.e., established facts,) his writings led many others (including Peirce) to see his position as much more relativist and nominalist than theirs.

John Dewey (1859-1952)

John Dewey produced a body of work that reached a far greater audience than either Peirce or James. Dewey engaged in academic philosophical writing, publishing many essays and books on metaphysics, epistemology, and value theory. But, unlike his predecessors, he also wrote a vast amount on social and political philosophy, such as *The Public and Its Problems,* and very often engaged in public dialogue. He became nationally known as an education reformer, producing highly influential works including *Democracy and Education*. Within philosophy proper, Dewey is probably best known for his work on inquiry and logic. Stating that all inquiry was conducted by agents, and not merely by passive information processors, he emphasized the experimental and instrumental nature of human conduct. Dewey argued that logic, formal rules of inference and implication, was ultimately a set of generalizations of warranted, or warrantable, conclusions. Logic was a species of inquiry, and the latter was never disinterested or free of valuation. This emphasis on purposeful interaction between agents and environments points to Dewey's well-known criticism of what he termed "the quest for certainty." Too much human activity, especially philosophy, he claimed, had been a search for absolutes, whether in the area of ontology, epistemology, or ethics, whereas the world is filled with contingencies and is in flux. Human inquiry should be a matter of purposeful action in response to, and ultimately in anticipation of, such contingencies and change. Intelligence was experimental and evaluative; we learn by doing, by engagement with the puzzles and problems presented by a changing environment. While there might not be eternal, absolute standards or criteria for, say, moral judgment, it was also the case that there were criteria that transcended subjective preferences, since there were facts about the contingencies and problems we face.

Like James, Dewey saw human inquiry as the entertainment of hypotheses, and intelligence as evaluative. Preferring to call his philosophical approaches "instrumentalist" rather than "pragmatist," Dewey emphasized the contingent, purposive nature of human action. Thus, an agent can only be fully understood as one pole in a person-environment interaction, not merely as a subject bumping into a world of objects. This position greatly influenced his educational theory. Here he strongly advocated formal schooling as a means to enhance the autonomy of persons i.e., the ability of persons to frame purposes, plans and life goals along with the skills and abilities to carry these into effect. An education that was relevant to meaningful experiences was one that recognized and was based on two principles: a principle of continuity (we are temporal agents and today's experiences are part of a continuum with yesterday's and tomorrow's), and a principle of interaction (we are social beings and one's experiences are inherently and inextricably interwoven with the experiences of others.

For Dewey, what was good (or bad) was relative to contexts and goals, but at the same time was a matter of what helped an organism cope with and flourish in the world. Drawing on Darwin, and writing as an early proponent of evolutionary and naturalistic ethics, Dewey believed that growth was the only moral end. Adaptation and adjustment to different and changing environments, including social and moral environments, were the signs of appropriate action. Although Dewey's philosophy does not, strictly speaking, rule out radical or revolutionary action, it tends to draw attention to immediate goals and purposes and neglects the historical dimension of social structures.

Finally, along with arguing for valuation (judgment) at the level of the individual organism or person, Dewey wrote voluminously on valuation at the level of the group or community. Often speaking of democracy as a way of life, he claimed that full self-realization required participation in community. Social arrangements, indeed, were means of "creating" individuals, and were not oppressive or repressive simply by being social. In contradiction to the tendency of much of American thought, Dewey argued that social arrangements, far from being external impositions on our freedom, were both "natural" and conducive to individual freedom. Dewey expanded this claim by distinguishing two types of freedom: freedom of movement and freedom of intelligence. Freedom of movement was what some philosophers referred to by the expression "freedom from." To be free in this sense meant that one was free from external constraints on one's movements. This said Dewey, was certainly an important sense of freedom, but was only a means toward a fuller sort of freedom i.e., freedom of intelligence (or what some philosophers called "freedom to".) Simply having no significant external constraints on one's movements did not lead to or entail self-realization. What one did with that absence of constraint was much more important. For example, children at play, he said, first established rules and limits for the game, in order to make play possible. Thus, games involved rules, which constrained action but at the same time made meaningful action possible. The important point here is that the rules are not only accepted, but most often self-imposed by the children at play. In addition to being natural, freedom of intelligence, which incorporates social controls, is social in its origin. "Liberty," said Dewey, "is that secure release and fulfillment of personal potentialities which take place only in rich and manifold association with others; the power to be an individualized self making a distinctive contribution and enjoying in its own way the fruits of association."

Other Pragmatists

Besides the three leading classical Pragmatists, there were many other important thinkers of this type. George Herbert Mead (1863-1931) was particularly influential during the earlier 20th century, especially through his work on the social development of the self and of language. A generation later, Clarence Irving Lewis (1883-1964) wrote several significant works on what he termed "conceptualistic pragmatism," stressing how pragmatic grounds shape the interpretation of experience. His contemporary, Alain Locke (1885-1954), blending the thought of earlier pragmatists with that of W.E.B. DuBois (1868-1963), produced a large body of work on the social construction of identity (particularly focusing on race) and advocating cultural pluralism within the context of what he called a philosophy of "critical relativism" or "critical pragmatism."

Another important thinker, often labeled as Pragmatist, but noted more for advocating an explicit version of philosophical Idealism, was Josiah Royce (1855-1916). Though there were other American Idealists (e.g., G. H. Howison of the St. Louis Hegelians and Bordon Parker Bowne (1847-1910), known for his view of "personalism"), Royce is recognized as the most influential of them. In epistemology, Royce noted that any analysis of experience showed that the fact and, indeed, very possibility of error led to the postulation of both mind and external reality, since only minds could be in error, and being in error presupposed something about which mind could be mistaken. The recognition of error presupposed a higher level of awareness (what he called "Absolute Pragmatism") since knowing that one was in error about X presupposed that one recognized both X and what was mistaken about one's judgment. Error, then, presupposed some form or level of truth. Error was really having only partial truth. For Royce, this also pointed to the ultimate communal nature of all interpretation, since knowledge (even of one's self) came from signs, which in turn required some kind of comparison and finally of community. Royce extended this view, and displayed definite affinities to Pragmatism, in his analysis of meaning. The meaning of an idea, he claimed, contained both an external and an internal element, much as we say that terms have both a denotation and a connotation. Ideas had external meaning in the sense that they connected to an external world. But they had an internal meaning in the sense that they embodied or expressed purpose.

20th Century

While pragmatism continued to be the dominant movement in American philosophy in the early 20th century, other movements and schools of thought emerged. In the first several decades, there was a revival of common sense realism and naturalism as well as the emergence of Process Philosophy, which was directly influenced by relativity theory. Mid-20th century philosophy was heavily dominated by empiricism and analytic philosophy, with a strong focus on language. Finally, in the last decades there was a rediscovery and revival of pragmatism as well as the emergence of feminist and "minority" issues and concerns, of people and groups who had been marginalized and underrepresented throughout the nation's history. Some movements and schools of thought that had been prominent in Europe, such as existentialism and phenomenology, though having advocates in America, never gained much attention in American philosophy.

One of the earliest movements in 20th century American thought was a rejection of idealism by such thinkers as Royce's own student, George Santayana (1863-1952), who saw philosophy as having unfortunately abandoned, and in the case of idealism contradicted, common sense. If we pushed the concept of knowledge to the point of requiring indubitability, then skepticism would be the result, since nothing would satisfy this requirement. On the other hand, if knowledge was a kind of faith, much as common sense rested on untested assumptions, then we were led to a view of "animal faith," which Santayana endorsed. This return to common sense, or at least to a naturalist, realist stance was echoed by many philosophers of the time. In 1910 an essay entitled, "The Program and First Platform of Six Realists" announced a strong reaction against idealism and what were seen as idealist elements in pragmatism. Among the platform planks of this program were statements that objects existed independently of mind, that ontology was logically independent of epistemology, that epistemology was not logically fundamental (i.e., that things were known directly to us), that the degree of unity, consistency, or connection subsisting among entities was a matter to be empirically ascertained. This realist stance was exemplified by, for example, Ralph Barton Perry's (1876-1957) *General Theory of Value*. A second school of thought early in the century was known as "Process Philosophy." Having notable proponents such as Charles Hartshorne (1897-2000), process philosophy emphasized events or processes as primary. Thus change and becoming were emphasized over permanence and being.

Despite the revival of Realism and Process Philosophy and the still-present influence of Pragmatism, the middle half of the 20th century was dominated by empiricism and analytic philosophy, with a pronounced turn toward linguistic analysis. Beginning with the powerful influence of the Logical Positivists (or Logical Empiricists), academic philosophy turned in a decided way from social and political concerns to conceptual analysis and self-reflection i.e., to the question of just what the proper role of philosophy was. The most influential American philosopher during this period was W.V.O. Quine (1908-2000). Though Quine was critical of many aspects of Logical Positivism, he nevertheless shared the view that the role of philosophy was not to enlighten persons or serve social and political concerns. Saying that philosophers in the professional sense had no particular fitness for inspiration or "helping to get society on an even keel," he argued instead that philosophy's job is to clear away conceptual muddles and mistakes. Seeing philosophy as in large part continuous with science in the sense of trying to understand what there was and how we could then flourish in the world, he claimed that philosophy was on the abstract, theoretical end of scientific pursuits.

Advocating a physicalist ontology i.e., body and mind are two aspects of one reality, Quine was behaviorist about understanding human agency and knowledge. Criticizing the view that there were truths independent of facts about the world, Quine strongly advocated a naturalized epistemology and ethics. Acknowledging an affinity with some aspects of Pragmatism, Quine claimed a holistic approach to knowledge, insisting that no particular experiences occurred in isolation; rather we experienced a "web of belief," with every belief or statement or experience affecting "the field as a whole," and hence "our statements about the external world face the tribunal of sense experience not individually but only as a corporate body." Reminiscent of Dewey, Quine asserted that while there was no distinction between judgments of fact and judgments of value, the sciences, with their system of checks and balances, did provide the best theories and models of what there was. Besides his commitment to materialism, behaviorism, and holism, Quine urged what he called "semantic ascent," that is, that philosophy should proceed by focusing on an analysis of language. By looking at the language we used and by framing philosophical concerns in terms of language, we could avoid fruitless philosophical disputes and faulty ontological commitments.

Within academic philosophy, Quine is perhaps best known for his work in formal, mathematical logic, and with his doctrine of "the indeterminacy of translation." In his highly influential book, *Word and Object*, he introduced the term "gavagai," a term uttered by a native while pointing at something in the immediate environment, something that appears to us as a rabbit. From that utterance, however, we do not know if "gavagai" should be translated into English as "rabbit" or "undetached rabbit parts" or "rabbit time-slice" or something else. The point is that there is no givenness to the situation, no determinateness of translation. Nor is this a simple matter, as this lack of givenness and determinacy holds in all situations. There are other, pragmatic, factors that allow communication and understanding to be possible.

With this formal, often extremely technical, conceptual analysis dominating mid-century American philosophy, a return to social and political concerns did not become mainstream again until the 1970s. Such a return is often credited to the publication of John Rawls' (1921-2002) *A Theory of Justice*. While other philosophers had been writing on these issues, it was Rawls' book that brought these topics back into mainstream consideration among professional philosophers. Rawls argued for political liberalism based on a system of procedural justice. Though his work was widely influential, it was critiqued by philosophers identified as libertarian, such as Robert Nozick (1938-2002), who saw it as too restrictive of individual liberties, as well as by communitarians, such as Alasdair MacIntyre (1929-) who saw it as focusing too much on procedural justice and not enough on what is good for persons, who are also citizens situated in communities. Outside of academic philosophy, these concerns had not been absent, however, but were present in the writings of social and political leaders, and in popular political philosophy, such as the writings of Ayn Rand (1905-1982) and Martin Luther King, Jr.(1929-1968).

As the century ended, there was a renewal of interest in Pragmatism as a philosophical movement, with two important philosophers in particular adopting the label of Pragmatist, Hilary Putnam (1926-) and Richard Rorty (1931-). They brought the writings and stance of classical pragmatists back into the forefront of professional philosophy, often with their critiques of each other's works. This renewal of pragmatism, along with the revival of social and political philosophy, came at the same time as feminist philosophy emerged, though there had been prominent feminist thinkers in American philosophy prior to this time e.g., Grimké, Stanton, Charlotte Perkins Gilman (1860-1935) and even Anne Hutchinson (1591-1643). Outside academic philosophy, the publication, in the 1960s, of Betty Friedan's *The Feminine Mystique*, struck a popular nerve about the marginalization of women. Inside academic philosophy, feminist philosophers such as Adrienne Rich (1929-) and many others, began comprehensive critiques of traditional philosophical concerns and stances. For example, there were critiques of epistemic values such as objectivity (i.e., detached, disembodied inquiry), as well as what were taken to be masculine approaches to ethics and political philosophy, such as procedural over substantive justice or rights-based ethical theories. Insisting that there was no final distinction between public and private, and no value-neutral inquiry, feminists reformulated philosophical issues and concerns and redirected philosophical attention to issues of power and the social dimensions (and construction) of those very issues and concerns. This demand for pluralism in content was expanded to philosophical methods and goals generally, and was expanded to other traditionally marginalized perspectives. By century's end, traditional philosophical work continued in full force, for example, with a strong surge of interest in philosophy of mind and philosophy of science, accompanied by a sharp increase in newly-demanded foci, such as philosophy of race, philosophy of law and philosophy of power.

Unlike European cultures, there was less of an academic class in America until the 20th century, hence less of a sense of professional philosophy. Even then, much of what has been taken as philosophy by most Americans has been distant from what most professional philosophers regarded as philosophy. Few American philosophers have had the impact outside the academic world of John Dewey. Moreover, many thinkers in American intellectual history lie outside what is today considered philosophy. Hence, although Jonathan Edwards is still studied within the discipline, other important American thinkers, such as Reinhold Niebuhr (1892-1971) and C. Wright Mills (1916-1962) are not. Much like other academic disciplines, philosophy in America has become professionalized. Nevertheless, professional philosophers, for example in their analysis of rights and the question of the meaningfulness of animal rights, or in their application of philosophical ethics to health care contexts, have both reflected and shaped the face of American culture.

Source: This section is adapted from the Internet Encyclopedia of Philosophy article "American Philosophy" by David Boersema and appears here by permission of the author. Full article: http://www.iep.utm.edu/, August 9, 2009

Reinhold Niebuhr (1892 -1972)

Reinhold Niebuhr is widely regarded as one of the most significant Christian intellectuals of the 20th century. Over the years, Niebuhr won the admiration of political figures on the left and the right, including the late historian and Kennedy aide, Arthur Schlesinger, Jr., and the late Jean Kirkpatrick, who served as Ronald Reagan's UN ambassador. Reinhold Niebuhr thought of himself as a preacher and social activist, but the influence of his theological thought on social ethics and society made him a significant intellectual figure.

Niebuhr was born in Missouri in 1892, the son of German immigrants. His father became an ordained minister of the German Evangelical Synod (later part of the United Church of Christ.) This denomination gives more importance to inner spirituality and practical results than dogmatic theology. Niebuhr decided to follow his father's profession. As a seminarian, he was much influenced by the Liberal Protestant theology of Adolf von Harnack.

Niebuhr's professional life of ministry began in 1915, when he was appointed minister of Bethel Evangelical Church in Detroit, where he served until 1928. In Detroit, he personally witnessed the lives of American automobile workers. The extended exposure to their drudgery and frustrations made him critical of capitalism. In *Leaves from the Notebook of A Tamed Cynic* (1929), Niebuhr exposed the tragedy of the workers' lives in passionate denunciations of their inhumane treatment in Henry Ford's factory. By then an outspoken advocate of socialist principles in social and economic matters, in 1932 he supported the socialist candidate for President. His advocacy of socialism continued until he came to support the mixed economics of the New Deal policy in the early 1940s.

Niebuhr criticized both the moral idealism of the liberal-leaning churches and their unconditional rejection of violence. He found the so-called "Neo-Orthodox" theological tendencies more useful. This preference is evident in *Moral Man and Immoral Society* (1932), written during the Great Depression. In this book, Reinhold insists on the necessity of politics in the struggle for social justice because of the sinfulness of human nature, that is, the egotism of individuals and groups. He saw the limitations of reason in solving social problems, since reason was always the servant of interest.

Niebuhr's analysis of moral responsibility drew a radical distinction between individual and group morality. He believed that what he called "group egoism" was inescapable. In Niebuhr's view, individuals were morally capable of considering the interests of others and acting prudently when they sensed conflicts of interest between themselves and others. Societies, however, found it virtually impossible to handle rationally the competing interests of subgroups. Societies, he argued, effectively gather up only individuals' selfish impulses, not their capacities for unselfish consideration toward others. Thus social co-operation on a larger scale than the most intimate social group required a measure of coercion. Hence, he suggested a compromise between uncoerced and perfect peace and justice, and a sufficient degree of non-violent coercion. Harmonious social relations, for Niebuhr, depended upon a sense of justice as much as, or even more than, upon the sentiment of benevolence. This sense of justice was a product of the mind and not of the heart. It was the result of reason's insistence upon consistency. In addition, he saw a role for religion in dealing with social problems by reducing the influence of selfishness through contrition and the spirit of love.

Niebuhr's concept of love as the highest form of morality was developed further in *An Interpretation of Christian Ethics,* in which he criticized orthodox Christianity, modern liberal Christianity and some forms of Marxism. Instead of the direct application of the law of love to political and economic reality, he suggested the principle of justice as an approximation of love, since love was the source of the norms of justice, and the ultimate perspective by which their limitations were discovered.

Niebuhr taught applied Christianity (later Ethics and Theology) at Union Theological Seminary in New York from 1928 to 1960, when he retired. His famous "Christian realism" was developed in *The Nature and Destiny of Man* (two volumes, 1941 and 1943.) He did not confine himself to academic circles but sprang into the political and social worlds of New York City as an activist. He founded several journals and organizations. He edited *The Christian Century* (1922-1940), *Radical Religion* (renamed *Christianity and Society*) (1935), *Nation* (1938-1950), *Christianity and Crisis* (1941), and *New Leader* (1954-1970.) He helped to found the Fellowship of Socialist Christians in the early 1930s and the Union for Democratic Action in 1941.

Interest in Niebuhr is reviving in America. Barack Obama, when the Democratic presidential candidate in 2008, told *New York Times* columnist David Brooks that Niebuhr was "one of my favorite philosophers." Meanwhile the Republican candidate Senator John McCain, in his volume *Hard Call,* wondered what the critic of pacifism during World War II would say today about Iraq.

Niebuhr's unrelenting gaze inward at a US he refused to herald as the world's unquestioned savior runs counter to the renewed sense of American exceptionalism that followed the 9/11 attacks. Niebuhr's Christian realism - his recognition of the persistence of sin, self-interest, and self-righteousness in social conflicts - highlights the distinction between the acknowledgment of evil's existence and America's own involvement in that evil. Niebuhr's own grounding of his political beliefs in his Christian faith may serve as another factor in the increased interest in him. While Republicans have long cloaked their programs and policies in the language of faith, Democrats have increasingly turned to a religious vocabulary to cast foreign and domestic issues in moral terms.

In a keynote address to the United Church of Christ, Niebuhr called the challenges of poverty, racism, war, and unemployment "moral problems rooted in societal indifference and individual callousness, in the imperfections of man, the cruelties of man towards man," in other words, the inescapable fact of sin. But his speech also captured Niebuhr's insistence that neither sin's inevitability, nor the idea that worldly justice can only ever approximate divine justice, should give rise to a "Christian pessimism which becomes an irresponsibility."

C. Wright Mills (1916-1962)

According to Todd Gitlin (to whose work this section is much indebted,) C. Wright Mills was "the most inspiring sociologist of the second half of the 20th century." Philosophically trained in the Marxist tradition, Mills was a radical, skeptic and populist who yet produced rigorous sociology with the aim of transforming America. His tracts against the Cold War and US Latin American policy were more widely read than any other radical's.

C. Wright Mills was born in Waco, Texas in 1916. He died in 1962, academically controversial and personally unpopular. Described by his biographer Irving L. Horowitz as an "American Utopian," he was also heir to key American intellectual traditions such as Pragmatism.

Mills was angered by the oppression he saw around him, and committed to social change. He put himself outside the mainstream of American social comment by his support for Fidel Castro and by his critique of what he saw as US imperialism. He was also critical of what passed for contemporary sociology. Mills believed that knowledge, properly used, could bring about change and that if the good society was not yet here, that was primarily the fault of intellectuals. He made a distinctive contribution to American sociological theory, especially in the areas of class, power and social structure.

His major books were driven by large topics, not method or theory. In them, he attempted to link sociology to social criticism, preferring the term "social studies" to "social sciences." In *The Sociological Imagination*, Mills severely criticized the two dominant tendencies of the mainstream sociology of his time, what he saw as the exaggerated claims of Grand Theory on the one hand and the irrelevance of small, empirical studies on the other. He considered theory ineffective against irresponsible power, dismissing it as class-bound ideology. Similarly he disdained small, empirical studies as merely the supervisory tools of corporate and government bureaucracies.

His forceful prose, his instinct for significant controversy, his reputation for intellectual fearlessness and his passion for craftsmanship (one of his favorite words) made him one of the most famous critics of his day. In a style reminiscent of Whitman and Hemingway that has since been ridiculed as "macho" or simply "male," Mills sought to develop an intelligible way of communicating modern social science to non-specialized publics. As early as his freshman year, in a letter to a student newspaper, Mills asked: "Just who are the men with guts? They are the men...who have the imagination and the intelligence to formulate their own codes; the men who have the courage and the stamina to live their own lives in spite of social pressure and isolation"(Letter to *The Battalion*, April 3, 1935, in ms., p. 36.)

Mills' writing was charged with a keen awareness of human energy and disappointment, a passionate feeling for the human adventure and a commitment to human dignity. Mills insisted that a sociologist's proper subject was the intersection of biography and history. In a vigorous, instantly recognizable prose, he hammered home again and again the notion that people lived lives that were not only bounded by social circumstance but deeply shaped by social forces not of their own making, and that this irreducible fact had two consequences: it lent most human life a tragic aspect with a social root, and also created the potential, if only people saw a way forward, of improving life in a big way by concerted action.

Mills searched for and studied potential history-making classes in his books of the late 1940s and 1950s: labor in *The New Men of Power*; the middle classes in *White Collar*; and the chiefs of top institutions in *The Power Elite*. Labor was not up to the challenge of structural reform, white collar employees were confused and backward, and the power elite was irresponsible. His conclusion after a decade of work was that if one were looking for a fusion of reason and power, at least potential power, there was nowhere else to look but to intellectuals. Intellectuals and only intellectuals had a fighting chance to deploy reason. Since they could embody reason in addressing social problems when no one else could do so, it was incumbent upon them to try, in addressing a problem, to have "a view of the strategic points of intervention, of the 'levers' by which the structure may be maintained or changed; and an assessment of those who are in a position to intervene but are not doing so" (*Sociological Imagination*, p. 131.) While Mills did not fully appreciate just how much enthusiasm Americans could bring to acquiring and using consumer goods, he did anticipate one of the striking ideas of perhaps his most formidable antagonist, Daniel Bell, namely, the centrality, in corporate capitalism, of the tension between getting (via the Protestant ethic) and spending (via the hedonistic ethic) (*The Cultural Contradictions of Capitalism*, Basic Books, 1976.)

Mills himself had a high sense of mission, not only his own mission, but that of intellectuals in general and social scientists in particular. He thought the questions for social study ought to come from values, but the answers should not be decided in advance. Mills also thought that good social science became good politics when it moved into the open and generated public discussion. He came to this activist view of intellectual life partly by temperament but also by deduction and by elimination. For if intellectuals were not going to break the intellectual logjam, who would? This was not, for Mills, a merely rhetorical question. It was a question that required an experimental answer, an answer that would unfold in real life through reflection upon experience. As he wrote in *The Marxists*, a political philosophy had to encompass not only an analysis of society and a set of theories of how it works but "an ethic, an articulation of *ideals*" (*The Marxists*, Dell, 1962, p. 12., Mills' italics.) It followed that intellectuals should be explicit about their values and rigorous in considering contrary positions. It also followed that research work should be supplemented by blunt writing that was meant to inform and mobilize what he called, following John Dewey, "publics." Mills as a freelance politician wished to have on his side a reasoning public without letting it exact a suffocating conformity as the price of its support.

To a degree that is now controversial, Mills was not cynical about the importance of reason, seeing Enlightenment at least as a goal that could be approached ever nearer to, if never reached. The "central goal of Western humanism," he wrote, [was] "...the audacious control by reason of man's fate" (*The Causes of World War Three*, Ballantine, 1958, 1960, pp. 185-6.) He thought the problem at mid-century was not that America had too much Enlightenment but too little, and the tragedy was that the universal worship of technical rationality in the form of scientific research, business calculation, and state planning was the perfect disguise for this great default (*Sociological Imagination*, pp. 165-176.) "Our major orientations, liberalism and socialism, have virtually collapsed as adequate explanations of the world and of ourselves," he wrote (*Sociological Imagination*, p. 166.) Like Weber, he thought that the democratic self-governance of rational men and women was damaged by the bureaucratization of the economy and the state. Democratic prospects were also being damaged, Mills believed, because the West was coping poorly with the entry of the developing countries onto the world stage.

Mills felt alarmed about the state of the world because of the sheer destructive power that had been gathered into the hands of the American national security establishment and its Soviet counterpart. It cannot be overemphasized that much of Mills' work on power was a response to the existence of national strategies for nuclear war. Mills made the point in *The Power Elite* and in *The Causes of World War Three* that the major reason America's most powerful should be considered dangerous was that they controlled weapons of mass destruction and were in a position not only to contemplate their use but to launch them. Mills died a mere seven months before the Cuban missile crisis came within a hair's breadth of triggering a nuclear war. The fact that the decision-makers on both sides did not make the wrong decisions does not detract from Mills' judgment in taking seriously this huge fact about America's elite. Who were these men? How did they get to their commanding positions? How there had turned out to be so much at stake in their choices? These important questions were the subject of Mills' analysis in *The Power Elite*. Meanwhile, he thought that Castro's tyranny, and other harsh features of the Cuban revolution, were "part of a phase, and that I and other North Americans should help the Cubans pass *through* it" (*Listen, Yankee*, p. 183, Mills' italics.)

Mills was seen as a father figure by the student movements of the 1960s. More than any other sociologist of the time, he anticipated the ways in which conventional careers and narrow life plans within and alongside the military-industrial complex would fail to satisfy a growing proto-elite of students trained to take their places in an establishment that they would not judge worthy of their moral vision. If he exaggerated the significance, or goodness, of intellectuals as a social force, this was also a by-product of his faith in the powers of reason. For all that his life was cut short, more of Mills' work endures than that of any other critic of his time.

The American attitude to history

Since the late 19th century, when professional history writing in America began, historians have mostly concentrated on the present, mining historical resources for answers to current problems. The first generation after the Civil War focused on the development of national unity, making the writing of history part of the project of national healing. The Progressives of the succeeding generations, starting with Frederick Jackson Turner, added the socio-economic dimension to historical explanation and began to make use of the social sciences. Later writers, notably the reformist socialist, Charles Beard, emphasized conflict and diversity in the people's struggle against the "interests." Postwar historians, at a time of economic boom and Cold War anxieties, returned to the theme of stability. During the 1960s, however, demonstrations against the Vietnam War, and riots in the ghettoes, attracted attention to the sources of disorder and prompted more history writing from the viewpoint of the working class and minorities. Social history and radical interpretations burgeoned. The "culture wars" since the 1980s have provoked a spate of history written from feminist and black viewpoints. Today political history is often written to draw lessons about leadership and democratic participation. A particular theme is how the churches can mobilize politically under a constitution that separates church and state. Once again, however, the nation's collective memory of the Civil War has come to the fore. As David Blight has shown in *Race and Reunion*, in the generations succeeding the Civil War, Americans came to terms with their divisions through selectively remembering the heroics of ordinary soldiers and forgetting ideological divisions. The moral conflicts over slavery and emancipation were written out of the script and the contribution of African Americans to the war disregarded. "In other words," as Richard Carwardine, Rhodes Professor of American History at Oxford, points out, "the healing of white America came about by denying justice to black Americans." Fitzhugh Brundage adds in *The Southern Parts*, "elite white Southerners systematically refined a version of the past that sanctioned their privilege and power." American history writing is thus predominantly functional, and less concerned with the humanistic understanding of unfamiliar and uncongenial viewpoints. Even so, it exhibits the highest standards of scholarship. Indeed no country has devoted more of its resources to the promotion and dissemination of historical research.

Advertising

Advertising attempts to persuade its audience to purchase a good or a service, to build a corporate reputation, solicit a vote or a contribution. Advertising has responded to changing business demands, media technologies, and cultural contexts. In the18th century, many American colonists enjoyed imported British consumer products such as porcelain, furniture, and musical instruments, but also worried about dependence on imported manufactured goods. Advertisements in colonial America were most frequently announcements of goods on hand, but even in this early period, persuasive appeals accompanied dry descriptions. Benjamin Franklin's *Pennsylvania Gazette* reached out to readers with new devices like headlines, illustrations, and advertising placed next to editorial material. Advertisements in the 18th and 19th centuries were not only for consumer goods. They included notices of slave sales or appeals for the capture of escaped slaves. Despite the ongoing "market revolution", early and mid- 19th century advertisements rarely demonstrate striking changes in advertising appeals. Newspapers almost never printed ads wider than a single column and generally eschewed illustrations and even special typefaces. Magazine ad styles were also restrained, with most publications segregating advertisements on the back pages. Equally significant, until late in the nineteenth century, there were few companies mass producing branded consumer products. Patent medicine ads proved the main exception. In an era when conventional medicine seldom provided cures, manufacturers of potions and pills vied for consumer attention with large, often outrageous, promises and colorful, dramatic advertisements. In the 1880s, industries ranging from soap to canned food to cigarettes introduced new production techniques, created standardized products in enormous quantities, and sought to find and persuade buyers. National advertising of branded goods emerged. Large department stores in rapidly-growing cities, such as Wanamaker's in Philadelphia and New York, Macy's in New York, and Marshall Field's in Chicago, also pioneered new advertising styles. For rural markets, the Sears Roebuck and Montgomery Ward mail-order catalogues offered everything from buttons to kits with designs and materials for building homes. By one commonly used measure, total advertising volume in the US grew from about $200 million in 1880 to nearly $3 billion in 1920. Advertising agencies became servants of the new national advertisers, designing copy and artwork and placing advertisements in the places most likely to attract buyer attention. Workers in the developing advertising industry sought legitimacy and public approval, attempting to disassociate themselves from the patent medicine hucksters and other swindlers.

While advertising generated anxieties about its social and ethical implications, it had nevertheless acquired a central place in US popular culture by the 1920s. Consumer spending, fueled in part by increased credit, on automobiles, radios, household appliances, and leisure time activities like spectator sports and movie going gathered pace in this generally prosperous period. The rise of mass circulation magazines, radio broadcasting and to a lesser extent motion pictures provided new media for advertisements. Advertising, as historian Roland Marchand pointed out, sought to adjust Americans to modern life, a life lived in a consumer society.

Since the 1920s, American advertising has grown massively, and current advertising expenditures are eighty times greater. New media, radio, television, and the internet, deliver commercial messages in ways almost unimaginable 80 years ago. Beneath the obvious changes, however, lie continuities. The triad of advertiser, agency, and medium remains the foundation of the business. Advertising people still fight an uphill battle to establish their professional status and win ethical respect. Perhaps the most striking development in advertising styles has been the shift from attempting to market mass-produced items to a general consuming public to ever more subtle efforts to segment and target particular groups for specific products and brands. In the 1960s, what Madison Avenue (the New York center of the advertising business) liked to call a "creative revolution" also represented a revolution in audience segmentation.

Interview with Professor James Twitchell, University of Florida, author of Adcult USA:The Triumph of Advertising in American Culture by Joe Wilhelm, Jr, writer, University of Florida News:

There are few places left where people can escape the onslaught of advertising. A study by the American Association of Advertising Agencies has shown that of the 3,000 advertisements a person consumes in a day, only 80 will be noticed, and only 12 will cause some reaction. "It all begins when people sit down to breakfast in the morning," Twitchell said. "The cereal box sits staring at them from across the table. On the way to school or to work, people may see billboards, park benches, public buses, inner-city basketball backboards, parking meters and taxis covered with advertisements. Once students arrive at school, they may get Chef Boyardee worksheets showing how to use pasta in home economics class. Prego offers the Prego Science Challenge complete with an 'instructional kit' to test the thickness of various spaghetti sauces. Union Carbide donates a video explaining the benefits of chemicals in their lives. Kodak, Coca-Cola and McDonald's sponsor essay contests about why kids should stay in school.

"Advertisements stare at passengers from the walls and float down from the speakers of the elevator as they travel to work. While at work people on the phone are captive audiences as they listen to advertisements when they are put on hold. On the way home, a stop at the gym puts people face to face with a wall of advertising while they use the Stairmaster. On their right a person is wearing a Nike T-shirt with the statement 'Just do it'. On their left is a person listening to music from a bright yellow Sony Walkman cassette player. Next stop is the supermarket and a shopping cart adorned with small billboards. In order to capitalize on indecisive shoppers, the same products aren't placed in alphabetical order and higher priced merchandise is mixed in with the value items. Finally at home they settle back in their easy chairs and try to escape the advertising attack by watching a program on the public broadcasting channel, but those 'underwriting announcements' seem a lot like commercials," Twitchell said. "The birth of the infomercial has produced hour-long commercials that cut down on the leg work and perils of being a door-to-door salesman. Try taking a trip to escape the reach of advertising. *USA Today* supplies airplane passengers with Sky Radio, complete with eight 30- to 60-second commercials per hour. But there is no vacation from advertising. Chairlift towers now serve as billboards at ski resorts. Advertisements are beamed to clouds over San Francisco by laser. Public parks like Yellowstone and Yosemite, as well as private parks like *Disney World* and *Six Flags*, are covered with advertisements." Twitchell attributes this advertising assault to the public's high tolerance for commercialism and its eagerness to be entertained. He calls that culture "Adcult."

According to this University of Florida English professor, the public almost enjoys being courted by commercialism. "We don't mind being advertised to", he says. "In fact, sometimes we seek it out. A generation ago we would have communicated meaning by referring to literature and religion. Now we use ads," Twitchell says. "Where's the beef?", "You deserve a break today," "I love you man," and "Because I'm worth it" are more than just commercial slogans. They are ways we organize and communicate experience".

CHAPTER 10

MOVIES AND MUSIC, SKYLINES AND SCREENS, FOOD AND FUN

Names, genres, and phrases from American sports and entertainment have, like fast food, the internet, and American products, found their way to all parts of the globe. For better or worse, many nations now have two cultures: their indigenous one and another consisting of the sports, movies, television programs, and music whose energy and broad-based appeal are identifiably American. Popular culture in America has often been criticized as being mere pap to lull the masses into satisfaction with their alienated life under capitalism, and it is undeniable that much American popular culture is undemanding. To others, American popular culture is coarse and saturated with sex. Charles Krauthammer says: "There is no comparing the brutality and cynicism of today's pop culture with that of forty years ago: from *High Noon* to *Robocop* is a long descent."

Yet America's sheer wealth and diversity can often obscure her cultural achievements. Even so, critics tend to underestimate the subversive effect of humor and the critical power of American forms of music, particularly jazz, folk, rock and rap. In no area of culture has America contributed more to the world than in music. The book musical is considered by many to be the unique contribution of America to theatre, while many genres of music that were developed in America, such as R&B, jazz, rock and rap, have become staples of popular culture around the globe.

American popular culture is democratic, often highly visual, and the product of many traditions, especially but not exclusively African American and Jewish. In sport particularly, the spectacle can be an integral part of the activity. Notably also, American popular culture is permeated with the images and catchphrases of advertising. Thus, on the one hand, American leisure provides a wealth of entertainment and recreation and vibrant democratic debate. On the other hand, the democratic may become the mediocre and the accessible merely shallow.

The movie, though, is America's premier art form. Hollywood dominates the world film industry, continuing to produce universally popular entertainment and at the same time make movies the filmmakers can be proud of. Fewer films are being made, however. Again, there is much more diversity of people and genres, although some deplore the prevalence of blockbusters where special effects drown out the narrative. Acting, camera work and animation have become more subtle, if screenwriting and production skills have declined. A much higher proportion of profits comes from spinoffs. America's unique contribution to the built environment has also been visual: the skyscraper, whose bold, thrusting lines have made it the symbol of capitalist energy changing the physical and social spaces of everyday life and giving to the modern city its visual signature—the skyline.

American television, although weak in public education programs compared with other countries, produces a wealth of information and entertainment, and world class children's TV. Talk shows, soap operas and game shows are main ingredients of TV, and many shows are syndicated around the world. There are, however, those who say that in the broadcast media, intelligent discussion has been replaced by images and sound bites, and competitions of knowledge and skill by a noisy carnival of mindless greed.

Contrary, however, to the stereotype of a passive population of car-bound couch potatoes plagued by obesity, Americans take part in a wide range of fitness, recreational and competitive sports. American inventiveness has supplied the world with baseball and basketball, and American competitiveness until recently made the US dominant in almost all international sporting competition except soccer for over 100 years. The idioms of baseball have permeated American speech.

MOVIES

If moving pictures were not an American invention, they have nonetheless been the preeminent American contribution to world entertainment, although Bollywood now makes more money and the movie industry has changed more in the last two decades than it had in the previous 80 years. The classic studio system with thousands on the payroll – actors, producers, directors, writers, stuntmen, craftspersons, and technicians – has almost disappeared. Also the number of movies being made has dropped sharply, even as the average budget has soared because Hollywood wants to offer audiences the kind of spectacle they cannot see on television. Single-auditorium movie houses have given way to 14-screen multiplexes. The contract system at studios has been displaced by freelancing, with each movie's creative team assembled from scratch. Even so, six major Hollywood film studios together control 95 percent of the US film business. Some commentators believe that we are in the midst of a transition in which very few films will have the singular cultural importance some films did in the past. Today, a speedier, bittier television-rooted style is becoming the norm. As screenwriting has lost its edge, for instance, screen acting has grown measurably richer. Some say it has never been more subtle. They point to Sean Penn, Johnny Depp and Gwyneth Paltrow and many others.

Most impressively, there is probably more variety in contemporary US filmmaking than at any previous period. There has been a growing presence of women directors and producers in recent years among them Jodie Foster, Barbra Streisand and Randa Haines. African American filmmakers are far more numerous, not to mention more gifted, than ever before. Directors such as Forrest Whittaker have enough credibility these days to be accepted into the mainstream. With the expanding ethnic population, Hollywood is embracing a wide range of gifted performers from abroad as well.

Many Americans, however, complain about the movie industry's tendency to pitch programs toward the lowest common denominator. And yet the common denominator need not be a low one, and the American knack for making entertainment that appeals to virtually all of humanity is no small gift. The new century promises great leaps, although no one really knows where the next wave of hits is coming from.

Several genres have been particularly strong in American filmmaking. The American Dream, for example, is typified by the best loved of all American films, *The Wizard of Oz* (1939), a fantasy story that has become part of American life. Other films with pure fantasy themes that have caught the American public's imagination are *Star Wars* (1977) and *E.T.: The Extra-Terrestrial* (1982). The American West has likewise been a leading subject of Hollywood since motion pictures began. The lone white male hero brandishing his gun led God-fearing people and hardworking, sanitized cowboys to triumph against crooks, speculators and big government. The hero was allowed to show little emotion except righteous anger and chivalry towards women. (The gay love story *Brokeback Mountain* broke new ground in 2008.) Few American films show business in a favorable light. *Citizen Kane* (1941) is the classic about the rise of a powerful American businessman. Films like the comedy *Trading Places* (1983) also show the negative sides of business. Filmmakers have never been kind to politicians either. *The Candidate* (1972) and *All the President's Men* (1976) are representative examples of the political process gone awry. Two highly romantic films that have become part of American culture are *Gone with the Wind* (1939) and *Casablanca* (1942). More modern treatments of romance are found in *Annie Hall* (1977) and *Moonstruck* (1987).

Meanwhile the subject of youth in America has been treated in many different ways. *The Graduate* (1967) made a statement which became world famous about society's values from a young man's perspective, while *American Graffiti* (1973) shows similar youth having a little more fun growing up. The musical *Saturday Night Fever* (1977) covered restless urban youth, while *Dead Poets Society* (1989) is a moving portrayal of a group of boys in a private school and their iconoclastic teacher. Hollywood has produced many fine movies about war. *The Longest Day* and *The Great Escape* (1963) and *Patton* (1970) are set in World War II. *Apocalypse Now* (1979), *Platoon* (1986) and *Hamburger Hill* (1987) are all very different films about the Vietnam War. Crime movies have always fascinated Americans. The heroes of *Bonnie & Clyde* (1967) are depression-era bank robbers. The tough, flinty American hero shines through in *Dirty Harry* (1971). *The Godfather* (1972) stands alone as the great movie about organized crime. Science fiction films have been registering the search for spiritual meaning since the medium began, perhaps most famously in George Lucas' six-film *Star Wars* saga, with its evocative master myth of the "Force." Sports too always been major film subjects. *Rocky* (1976) and *Raging Bull* (1980) examine boxing. *The Hustler* (1961) and its sequel *The Color of Money* (1986) show the often seedy world of professional pool hustling. Films which explore the immigrant experience in America include *The Color Purple* (1985) and *Terms of Endearment* (1983). Walt Disney stands alone as the great producer of children's and family films. Just some of his animated classics are *Bambi* (1942), *Cinderella* (1950), *Fantasia* (1940), *Pinocchio* (1940), and *Snow White and the Seven Dwarfs* (1937).

Among the most popular films of the 2000s were *The Dark Knight* (2009), a Batman film, and two *Lord of the Rings* films: *The Fellowship of the Ring* (2001) and the *Return of the Ring* (2003). A number of innovative films in those years showed that American filmmaking was still healthy and attracting large audiences and DVD sales. A brief revival of the historical epic has also taken place in the new century. Among the more successful of these films were *Alexander*, *Troy*, and *Gladiator* (2000).

The Hollywood blockbuster may be in crisis, but the art of the cinema is as healthy as ever, led by directors rated by critics as world-class. A basic list might include:

- Wes Anderson *Rushmore, The Royal Tenenbaums*
- Joel and Ethan Coen *Intolerable Cruelty, Fargo, No Country for Old Men.*
- Francis Ford Coppola, *The Godfather, The Conversation, The Godfather Part II. Apocalypse Now*

- David Fincher, *Alien 3, Seven, Fight Club, Panic Room*
- Michael Moore, *Fahrenheit 9/11, Sicko, Bowling for Columbine*
- Errol Morris, *The Thin Blue Line, Mr. Death, Holocaust, Fog of War*
- Alexander Payne, *Election, About Schmidt*
- Martin Scorsese, *Gangs of New York, Taxi Driver, Raging Bull*
- Steven Spielberg, *Jaws, Star Wars, The Color Purple, Schindler's List, Raiders of the Lost Ark, Indiana Jones, Close Encounters of the Third Kind, E.T., Jurassic Park*
- Quentin Tarantino, *Kill Bill, Reservoir Dogs, Pulp Fiction*

The American Film Institute lists the Top 10 movies of all time as:
1. *Citizen Kane*
2. *The Godfather*
3. *Casablanca*
4. *Raging Bull*
5. *Singin' in the Rain*
6. *Gone With the Wind*
7. *Lawrence of Arabia*
8. *Schindler's List*
9. *Vertigo*
10. *The Wizard of Oz*

Ratings

Movies are rated according to their suitability (sex and violence content) for certain viewers. A movie rated "G" (for General Audiences) can be seen by anyone. (This is real "family" entertainment.) A "PG" rating means anyone can be admitted, but parental guidance is suggested. "PG-13" means that some of the material may not be suitable for young children. An "R" rating means some nudity or suggested sex; children under 17 can see the movie only if accompanied by an adult. An "NC-17" rating means that no one under 17 will be admitted, even if accompanied by an adult. The most strictly rated subject is gay sex. The rating system is not set by law, but a voluntary system of controls sponsored by the Motion Picture Association of America and the National Association of Theatre Owners. A system of rating effectually prevents lawsuits. There is no government movie censorship: in 1968 the Supreme Court ruled that ratings boards could only approve films, not ban them. Most movie theater chains, however, will not show unrated films. State and local governments may prohibit the showing of a film if it is in their judgment so offensive as to affront current community standards of decency and is utterly without redeeming social importance. Such action is in practice rare.

Going to the movies in America has always been a ritual. Americans eat popcorn and candy and drink soda at movie theaters while watching the film. They buy these delights in huge packages and cups at stands in the theater lobby. The cinemas make their real money on these items.

Awards

Excellence in film is recognized during the awards season around the turn of the year. The non-profit Hollywood Foreign Press Association's annual *Golden Globes* are awarded in 25 different categories of entertainment filmmaking and television (including foreign language films). The glittering award ceremonies held in January are one of the three most-watched awards shows on television. *The Oscars,* perhaps the best known of such awards, are the small metal statues of the Academy Awards (the Academy of Motion Picture Arts and Sciences), offered each March for many aspects of film-making, principally Best Actor, Best Actress and Best Picture. The three films which have won the most Oscars (11) were *Ben Hur* (1959), *Titanic* (1998) and *The Lord of the Rings: The Return of the King* (2003). Walt Disney has won the most Oscars overall (32).

Just at the moment of its almost complete triumph, however, the film industry is under heavy criticism from American critics. Some even say moviemaking is in decline. First, they say, movies were better 25 years ago. Secondly, the gap between movies people want to see like *Titanic* and movies critics urge them to see like *L.A. Confidential* or *Boogie Nights* has never been greater. Moreover the Oscars tend to celebrate success already achieved rather than lead the industry in a particular direction. To many American critics, Hollywood blockbusters, like the epic *Godzilla* (1987), are boring and pointless, a disposable fireworks display, a long and noisy entertainment that completely disappears from the mind as soon as the credits roll at the end: in one critic's phrase, "kiss kiss bang bang." Most movies have no character development, but are just scenes that are even free to contradict each other, as long as the climax to the explosions and car crashes is noisy enough and flashy enough. Close-ups predominate, because they play well on television. Violence and pornography are also issues. What with the huge production costs of these movies and the skyrocketing salaries paid actors, studio heads, and deal-making agents, movies released today tend to be either huge successes or huge failures. What counts is the potential profit from overseas sales and from such ancillary markets as pay-per-view cable and DVD release.

POPULAR MUSIC

America has not just one, but many musical traditions, most of which feed on and influence each other. Nearly all of America's great musical traditions began in the southern part of the country. The intense, focused group sound of congregational singing has descended through the centuries and can be heard in the majestic hymns that have been adopted as stirring anthems by American civil rights groups, such as "Amazing Grace" and "We Shall Overcome." The huge 19th-century corpus of Protestant songs became part of common American culture for people of all faiths. These include "My Country 'Tis of Thee" and "America the Beautiful" (1899), which became instantly famous and has often been described as America's true national anthem. Wherever rock 'n' roll is played, a shadow of its gospel roots remains. Rock had several sources, but a principal influence was the ecstatic, prophesying, body-shaking style of congregational singing in the camp meetings of religious revivalists from the late 18th century on. All gospel music, including Negro spirituals, descends from those extravaganzas, which drew thousands of people to open-air worship services in woods and groves. In popular music, the spasmodic undulations and ecstatic cries of camp-meeting worshippers were borrowed by performers like Little Richard, Elvis Presley, and the late James Brown, whose career began in gospel and who became the "godfather of soul" as well as of funk, reggae, and rap. Gospel music, passionate and histrionic, with its electrifying dynamics, has been described as "America's grand opera." The continuing impact of gospel music on young African Americans in church may also account for the current greater vitality of hip hop as opposed to hard rock, which has been in creative crisis for well over a decade.

The first major composer of popular music with a uniquely American style was Stephen Foster (1826-1864). He established a pattern that has shaped American music ever since, combining elements of the European musical tradition with African American rhythms and themes. Foster's best songs, which many Americans still know by heart, include "Oh! Susanna," "Camptown Races," and "Old Folks at Home" (better known by its opening line: "Way down upon the Suwannee River.")

America's leading popular songwriter, Irving Berlin (1888-1989) was an immigrant of Russian-Jewish extraction. He wrote some of the best known American songs: "God Bless America" (1918), "White Christmas,"(sung by Bing Crosby in *Holiday Inn* in 1942), "There's No Business Like Show Business," "Let's Face the Music and Dance," "Alexander's Ragtime Band," and "Puttin' on the Ritz." Two songs he wrote for the comedy romance *Top Hat* (1935), "Top Hat, White Tie and Tails" and "Cheek to Cheek" have become song classics. Cole Porter (1891-1964) took the Broadway show song to new heights with his witty lyrics and rousing melodies, combined in such songs as "Anything Goes," "I Get a Kick Out of You," and "It's De-Lovely." Cole Porter's output includes some of the most romantic songs ever written, such as "Let's Do It (Let's Fall In Love)," "You Do Something To Me," "What Is This Thing Called Love?," "I've Got You Under My Skin," "I Love Paris" and many more. Porter's songs are characterized by wit and sophistication with an underlying strain of melancholy and loneliness. Lerner and Loewe were another successful Broadway partnership. Frederick Loewe (1901-88) came from Austria, and wrote the music for Alan Jay Lerner's (1918-86) words and stories. These included *Brigadoon* (1947), *Paint Your Wagon* (1951), *My Fair Lady* (1956), and *Camelot* (1960). Lerner and Loewe also made the musical film *Gigi* (1958).

MUSICALS

The musical is considered by many to be the unique contribution of America to world theater. From humble beginnings, the musical has become one of the world's major forms of entertainment. Musicals are a blend of several theatrical traditions, European and American. The American musical theater is perhaps the only major American musical form that does not have a strong southern connection, though it is influenced by jazz. The chief characteristics of musicals are energy, naturalness and national pride. Though sometimes sentimental, they frequently capture the popular mood, able to capture in song what people are thinking. Normally running between 2½ and 3 hours, a musical is a continuous story with a spoken dialog, songs and dance, following choruses. The standard plot is a simple one: in a series of episodes, boy meets girl, boy loses girl, boy gets girl back. Many musicals are adapted from other works for convenience and cheapness. Most began as plays. These include *Oklahoma* (1943), *Carousel* (1945), *The King and I* (1951), *My Fair Lady* (1956), *Hello, Dolly!* (1964) and *Mame* (1966). Some, like *South Pacific* (1949) and *Fiddler on the Roof* (1964) are based on books. A few, like *The Sound of Music* (1959) and *The Unsinkable Molly Brown* (1960), are biographical. *Little Abner* (1956), *You're A Good Man Charlie Brown* (1967), and *Annie* (1976) were drawn from the funny pages.

Musicals developed from three main sources: the French and Viennese operettas of the 1800s, particularly Offenbach and Strauss the Younger; the English comic operas of Gilbert & Sullivan (1871-1896); and the American musical extravaganza. The only American operetta well-known today is *The Desert Song* (1926), lyrics by Oscar Hammerstein and music by Sigmund Romberg (1887-1951).

The musical in the form we know it today arrived in 1927 with *Show Boat* by Jerome Kern and Oscar Hammerstein (1895-1960). Unlike the musicals of the earlier '20s, which had settings in ballrooms and penthouses, on college campuses, or at the country club, the setting of *Show Boat* was a river boat that sailed up and down the Mississippi bringing its plays and musical entertainment to the population of rural America.

Show Boat paid tribute to the black influence on mainstream American music with a story centered on interracial marriage and, as its most poignant song, the quasi-spiritual show-stopper slave lament "Ol' Man River." (The lyrics of this song and of "Can't Help Loving Dat Man" have been updated as social usages have changed.) This was the first racially integrated show ever to appear on an American stage, and the first to treat a mixed-race love story. The heart of *Show Boat* is a passionate assertion of racial pride and equality. The format that developed is basically: scene, related song or songs; blackout; new scene, continued action, related song, etc. This became the foundation upon which later musicals were built and earned world fame for African American singer, Paul Robeson, when he appeared in the 1928 London transfer. *Show Boat* established the musical as a disturbingly realistic and distinctively American art form with a contemporary social conscience and an enduring capacity for controversy, not to mention an ever-present element of ethnic tension.

The most famous Gershwin musical, *Porgy and Bess* (1935), written by George (1898-1937) and Ira Gershwin and DuBose Heyward, was performed by an all-black cast. The show includes "Summertime," "I Got Plenty O' Nuttin'," and "It Ain't Necessarily So." The Strawberry Woman and Crab Man calls sung in this musical originated as "field hollers" of slaves on the Southern plantations.

Rodgers and Hammerstein's romantic first musical *Oklahoma* was another milestone. This romantic story of Laurey (a farmer's daughter) and Curley (a cowboy) in Oklahoma Territory, was the first musical not to open with a large chorus number. Instead, when the curtain went up, the stage was bare except for a little old lady (Aunt Eller) sitting in a rocking chair on the porch churning butter. The opening notes of the first number, Curley's "Oh What a Beautiful Morning" are sung off stage. Other smash hit songs were "The Surrey With The Fringe On Top," and "I Cain't Say No." When the show was first performed in Boston with its rewritten headline number, "Oklahoma", the audience gave the cast a standing ovation and demanded three encores. *Oklahoma* was also the first musical to have a death scene on stage, when Jud falls on his own knife in a fight with Curley; and it introduced the concept of a "dream ballet" to an American audience.

There followed several of the greatest musicals of all time: *Carousel* (1945); *South Pacific* (1949, film 1958), a romance about Nellie Forbush, a US navy nurse in World War II, a musical now known all over the world for such songs as "Bali Ha'I," "I'm Gonna Wash That Man Right Outta My Hair," "Some Enchanted Evening," and "There's Nothing Like A Dame"; and *The King and I* (1951) ("I Whistle a Happy Tune.") Rodgers and Hammerstein's last show was the world-famous *The Sound of Music* (1959) starring Mary Martin as Maria von Trapp and featuring "My Favorite Things," "Doh-Re-Mi," "The Sound of Music," and "Climb Ev'ry Mountain." Hammerstein's lyrics are characterized by outer simplicity (some think too simple, and out of date), inner depth of feeling, and sharp attention to character.

The first musical to integrate music and dialogue fully with dance was *West Side Story* (1956) by Leonard Bernstein (1918-1990, music) and Stephen Sondheim (1930-, lyrics), based on Shakespeare's *Romeo and Juliet*. Stephen Sondheim is still the reigning genius of today's American musical theatre.

The ever-popular comedy *Guys and Dolls,* based on stories by Damon Runyon, had appeared in 1950. The story is about a group of New York criminals and the efforts of a woman Salvation Army officer to convert them to Christianity. The show's two hit songs were "Luck, Be a Lady" and "Sit Down, You're Rocking the Boat." Marlon Brando and Frank Sinatra appeared in the 1955 film version. In the same decade, Lerner and Loewe's *My Fair Lady* (1956), based on *Pygmalion* by George Bernard Shaw, opened on Broadway starring British actors Rex Harrison as Professor Higgins and Julie Andrews as Eliza Doolittle. The film version (1964) won three Oscars. The 1950s was the decade of big-budget musicals made direct for film, often using music composed years before. Gene Kelly starred successfully in *An American in Paris* (1951) and *Singin' in the Rain* (1952), which features his famous dance twirling an umbrella in a rainstorm.

These were followed in the 1960s and '70s by such famous shows as *Hello, Dolly!* (1969), *Fiddler On The Roof* (1971) and *Hair* (1979), a tribal love rock musical which was the first in the US to feature nude actors. Some uniquely American material, the "Peanuts" comic strip, was also developed into a musical in the 1960s under the title *You're A Good Man, Charlie Brown* (and had a revival in 1999). By the 1970s, musical theater was making extravagant use of advances in technology and design in such hits as *A Little Night Music, A Chorus Line* (1975, film 1985), *No, No, Nanette,* and *Sweeney Todd* (1979).

In recent times British composer Andrew Lloyd Webber's (1948-) musicals have dominated both London's West End as well as the Broadway stage. Ten Webber musicals, including megahit *Cats* have had Broadway productions since 1971. His first show to reach New York was *Jesus Christ Superstar* (1971). His first Broadway hit (1567 performances) was *Evita,* which opened in 1979. A second smash hit for Webber came with *Phantom of the Opera,* which won the 1988 Tony for the year's Best Musical and currently holds the record for the longest running Broadway show.

In the mid-1990s and the beginning of the 21st century, revivals of older plays and blockbuster musicals aimed at recapturing younger audiences from other media dominated commercial theater. In 1996, Jonathan Larson's *Rent,* a musical inspired by Puccini's 1896 opera, *La Bohème,* examined the experiences of disillusioned young Americans looking for meaning in their lives. The following year Disney's hit animated film, *The Lion King,* was imaginatively recreated for the stage.

Indeed, critics feel there is a crisis in the genre. Two recent hits, *Miss Saigon* and *Rent,* were little more than updates on *Madam Butterfly* and *La Bohème.* The most vital musicals are coming off the London stage in such productions as *Billy Elliott* and *Jerry Springer: The Opera.*

FOLK MUSIC

Folk, which is also known as *Americana,* includes bluegrass, country, gospel, old time jug bands, Appalachian folk, blues and Cajun. Folk is also known as *roots music* because it served as the basis of rock and roll, R&B and jazz.

Folk music has no single origin. It is a mixture of traditions. There are folk songs that date so far back they can be considered oral histories. Folk music is the traditional music of many of the early settlers, particularly in the Appalachian region. Many of the best loved American folk tunes are either of blues/gospel derivation, or else have Scots/Irish roots.

From its beginnings, folk music has been the music of the working class. It is community-focused and has rarely enjoyed commercial success. By definition, it is something anyone can understand

and in which everyone is welcome to participate. Folk songs range in subject matter from war, work, civil rights, and economic hardship to nonsense, satire and love songs. The earliest folk songs, such as "Down by the Riverside" and "We Shall Overcome," rose from the slave fields as spirituals. These are songs about struggle and hardship, but they are also full of hope. The 20th century brought folk music back into popular culture, as workers struggled and struck for child labor laws and the eight-hour workday. In the 1940s, bluegrass began to evolve as a distinct genre.

In the '60s American workers again found themselves in struggle. This time, the main concern was not wages or benefits, but civil rights and the war in Vietnam. Folk music underwent a great revival, greatly influencing blues, rock and country music. Out of this rose Folk Rock's superstars, Bob Dylan, Joni Mitchell, Joan Baez and others. Their work dealt with everything from love and war to work and play.

At the start of the 21st century, American folk music has begun to prosper again. Now, the main concerns are Civil Rights for LGBT (Lesbian, Gay, Bisexual and Transgender) workers. Alt-Country has evolved over the past couple of decades. A new generation of bluegrass bands has changed the name of the genre to *newgrass*. Folk festivals are thriving with younger audiences joining their parents' generation.

Woody Guthrie

Woody Guthrie is the original folk hero. It was Guthrie who, in the Thirties and Forties, transformed the folk ballad into a vehicle for social protest and observation. In so doing, he paved the way for Bob Dylan, Bruce Springsteen and a host of other folk and rock songwriters who have been moved by conscience to share experiences and voice forthright opinions. Guthrie wrote literally hundreds of songs, including such revered classics as "This Land Is Your Land," "So Long, It's Been Good to Know You," "Grand Coulee Dam," "I Ain't Got No Home" and "Dust Bowl Refugees."

Gospel and spirituals

A defining characteristic of such songs is their subjectivity, that is, their use of the first-person pronoun to assert an intimate relationship with Jesus, as in "Abide with Me," "I Need Thee Every Hour," "Jesus Loves Me," "He Leadeth Me," "I Love to Tell the Story," or the rousing "Give Me That Old-Time Religion." Out of this gospel tradition came Negro spirituals.

The Blues

Even more influential than jazz is the highly poetic music called "the blues." The blues began in the fields of the South, and for fifty years was performed primarily by black musicians. As black people moved from southern farms to northern cities, the blues moved too. Black music genres such as "Rhythm and Blues" and "Soul" evolved out of both rural and urban blues. Black Gospel church music was a major influence on both blues and jazz. White musicians would adopt and adapt all these musical genres and create their own varieties.

The extent to which American culture is African-derived is widely underestimated. The blues was developed by the children of former slaves in small cities along the Mississippi and Ohio in the 1890s and made its way to the Delta (New Orleans) in the early 1900s, and later spread to urban centers, especially Memphis, St Louis, Chicago and Detroit. Its musical and cultural foundations come from Africa, Europe and the Middle East. Blues characteristics were handed down from cotton pickers' work songs and rhythmic call-and-response field hollers, which were coded in language the white bosses could not understand. Also in the mix are spirituals and early string band sounds.

So influential have the blues become that the way Americans dance, dress, and speak, the music used to sell cars on TV, even their very concept of coolness, can be traced to this distinctive American music form and its African roots. Without the blues, America would not have jazz, rock, gospel, soul, R&B, or rap music, or even George Gershwin's masterpiece, "Rhapsody in Blue." Country father Jimmie Rodgers' catalog is also half blues. Aaron Copland drew on the blues for his classical compositions. Bob Dylan and other '60s folkies - and their Beat poet forebears - reveled in its talking rhythms. The improvising skills so prized by jazz and hip-hop artists are also distilled from blues. The impulse that created the blues, some believe, is the same impulse that created hip-hop, which is to share in a public forum what is essentially private: to take an experience and put it on the line in a performance medium as a warning and a comfort to the people who follow. Even bluegrass, long considered white music, has characteristics of black music. Take its flatted-note fiddling and harmonies, and the laments of displaced rural people mourning the life they had lost, not to mention its use of banjos, an instrument associated with blacks before it was co-opted by whites imitating blacks in minstrel shows. Regardless of the performer's race, the common thread uniting these sounds is the raw expression of human emotion, and the use of music for communication and solidarity. Studies in feminism, race relations, and the sexual revolution point to the role of blues-based rock as the voice of an independent black culture. Thus to understand much of American culture, it is necessary to understand the blues, and the contexts in which it developed and flourished.

Yet there is no universally accepted definition of what makes a blues song. For some it is the chord progressions, for others the instruments, for others the subject, for still others a certain "feeling" to the music they cannot describe. Although often played on the guitar, blues songs have been played on any instrument, from banjos and violins to amplified harmonicas and electric pianos.

Nowadays any night of the week, in big cities and rural outposts, blues bands continue to play. Yet their audience is not getting any younger. Some say the blues is a dying art. And the blues, once fierce and disquieting music, is often marketed as something comfortable, good for selling jeans and beer.

Jazz

W. C. Handy's "St. Louis Blues" is one of the most frequently recorded songs written in the 20th century. Though the meaning of "jazz" is obscure, originally the term almost certainly had to do with sex. The music, which originated in New Orleans early in the 20th century, brought together elements from ragtime, slave songs, and brass bands. Originally played by black musicians in festivals and at street funerals, one of the distinguishing elements of jazz was its fluidity: in live performances, the musicians would almost never play a song the same way twice but would improvise variations on its notes and words. Jazz became popular among both white and black performers and audiences. Blessed with composers and performers of genius, Duke Ellington (1899-1974), Louis Armstrong (1901-1971), Benny Goodman (1909-1986) and Ella Fitzgerald (1918-1996), jazz was the reigning popular American music from the 1920s (the "Jazz Age") through the 1940s.

In the late 1940s a new, more cerebral form of mostly instrumental jazz, called be-bop, began to attract audiences. Its practitioners included trumpeter Dizzy Gillespie (1917-1993) and saxophonist Charlie Parker (1920-1955). Trumpeter Miles Davis (1926-1991) experimented with a wide range of musical influences, including classical music, which he incorporated into such compositions as "Sketches from Spain." Jazz has gone through many phases, more recently modern jazz and fusion, and is constantly evolving. Jazz influenced American popular song, and in turn, particularly through white composers like George Gershwin, the American musical theater.

Ragtime

Ragtime was a combination of folk tunes, African rhythms, and Creole influences. It was played by small groups of African Americans in the streets of New Orleans and on showboats on the Mississippi. Peculiarly American, it was like no other music heard before. Scott Joplin, "the King of Ragtime" (c.1867-1917), was born in Texas and later settled in St Louis, Missouri and finally New York City. When Joplin moved to New York in 1907, he wrote an instruction manual called *The School of Ragtime*. This was an outline of the complex bass patterns, stop-time breaks, harmonic ideas, and sporadic syncopation he used in his compositions. He went on to make many ragtime piano rolls. Joplin's most famous compositions are the *Maple Leaf Rag* and *The Entertainer*, which became popular again when it was heard in the movie *The Sting* in the 1970s.

Rock and Roll

By the early 1950s, however, jazz had lost some of its appeal for a mass audience. A new form of pop music, rock and roll, evolved from rhythm and blues: songs with strong beats and often risqué lyrics. Though written by and for blacks, rhythm and blues also appealed to white teenagers. To make the new music more acceptable to a mainstream audience, white performers and arrangers such as Jerry Lee Lewis began to "cover" rhythm and blues songs, singing them with the beat toned down and the lyrics cleaned up.

Record producers of the time realized that a magnetic white man who could sing with the energy of a black man would have enormous appeal. Just such a figure appeared in the person of Elvis Presley (1935-1977), who had grown up poor in the South. Besides an emotional singing voice, Presley had sultry good looks and a way of shaking his hips that struck adults as obscene but teenagers as natural to rock and roll.

A few years after its debut, rock and roll was well on its way to becoming the crowning jewel of American form of pop music, especially among the young. It spread quickly to Great Britain, where the Beatles and the Rolling Stones got their starts in the early 1960s. Black artists like Chuck Berry, Little Richard, Bo Diddley and Fats Domino also combined genres to create an infectious beat.

Bob Dylan (1941-) extended the reach of folk music by writing striking new songs that addressed contemporary social problems, especially the denial of civil rights to black Americans. The division between the two camps, rock enthusiasts and folk purists, came to a head when Dylan was booed for "going electric" (accompanying himself on electric guitar) at the 1965 Newport Folk Festival. Far from being deterred, Dylan led virtually the entire folk movement into a blend of rock and folk.

This merger was a watershed, setting a pattern that holds true to this day. Rock remains the prevalent pop music of America, and much of the rest of the world, largely because it can assimilate almost any other kind of music, along with new varieties of outlandish showmanship, into its strong rhythmical framework. Whenever rock shows signs of creative exhaustion, it seems to get a transfusion, often from African Americans, as happened in the 1980s with the rise of rap: rhyming, often rude lyrics set to minimalist tunes.

Today, music like urban rap is performed mostly by blacks, progressive rock mostly by whites, but the vast core of American pop music is performed, and enjoyed, by both blacks and whites. Since it began in the 1950s, rock music has moved from the margins of American popular music to become the center of a multi-billion dollar global industry. Closely connected with youth culture, rock music and musicians have helped to establish new fashions, forms of language, attitudes, and political views. Rock music is no longer limited to an audience of teenagers, however, since many current listeners formed their musical tastes during the golden age of rock and roll.

The image of rock is one of rebellion. But when this eclectic music, a fusion of various styles from outside the white middle class mainstream taste, became a mass-produced commodity, rock was caught in a tension between individuality and commercialism. This still looms large in rock music and is reflected in fan distaste for musicians who compromise, or *sell out,* their musical values in order to secure multi-million dollar recording contracts. Shaped by technology, the growth of the mass media, and the social identities of its artists and audiences, rock music continues to play a central role in the popular culture of the US and, increasingly, the world.

Hip Hop

Few changes in American popular culture have been as significant as the rise of hip hop. The genre has radically reshaped the way Americans listen to and consume music. After opposing the pop mainstream, hip hop became it. Through recycling past styles and telling the myth of the self-made black antihero, hip-hop has become a philosophy, a political statement, a way of approaching and remaking culture. Hip hop is now an international language not just among young people in America, and its impact extends beyond the music industry.

The sound of the post-civil rights, post-soul generation has not had to be made safe for white America but has found a global audience on its own terms. Hip hop's capture of the global imagination has bred an unprecedented cultural confidence in its black originators. Whiteness is no longer a threat or an ideal but kitsch to be appropriated. An expansive multiculturalism is replacing the oppositional mentality that lent such edge to hip hop's rise. Thus hip hop has created new identities for its listeners that cross racial boundaries and is helping redefine the American mainstream, which no longer aspires toward a single iconic image of style or class.

Country and Western

Like folk, country music descends from the songs brought from England, Scotland, and Ireland to the Appalachian region. Modern country music, original songs about contemporary concerns, developed in the 1920s, roughly coinciding with a mass migration of rural people to big cities in search of work. Country music tends to have a melancholy sound, and many classic songs are about loss or separation. Like many other forms of American pop music, country lends itself easily to a rock-and-roll beat, and country rock has been yet another successful American merger. Country music lyrics speak of the hopes and troubles of ordinary people in the South and the heartland of America. Country is second only to rock in popularity, and country singer Garth Brooks (1962-) has sold more albums than any other single artist in American musical history including Elvis Presley and the late Michael Jackson.

Cajun Music

Cajun music, a sub-genre of country, represents a mixture of French Acadian traditional music and African strains, sung in Cajun French. It is native to a portion of the southern state of Louisiana, but it has greatly affected blues, rock and modern day country music. Cajun music is infectious. A form of Cajun music sung primarily by black Cajuns is called "Zydeco."

New Age

New age music is another popular genre. This music is thought to be relaxing or otherwise conducive to advanced states of existence or personal enlightenment, and is often used in meditation. New Age has its roots in 1970s free-form jazz. The opening song "This is the dawning of the age of Aquarius" from the 1967 rock musical *Hair* brought the New Age concept to a wide audience. Most New Age music is instrumental and electronic, or vocal arrangements, and often makes use of synthesizers and unique instrumental sounds. This genre of music expresses appreciation of goodness and beauty, and focuses on a vision of a better future rather than current issues.

Military Music

No ticker tape parade or military ceremonial would be complete without a march composed by John Philip Souza (1854-1932), whose "The Stars and Stripes Forever!," the National March of the US, is one of the world's most famous marches.

Satire

The satirical lyrics of Tom Lehrer (1928-) have won him a sizeable cult following all over the world. Although he enjoyed a long, successful career as a mathematics lecturer, latterly working at the University of California, Santa Cruz, his fans know him as the writer and singer of songs with titles like "Poisoning Pigeons In The Park" and 'The Old Dope Peddler." His songs, mostly recorded in the 1950s and 1960s, reveal a deliciously dark wit, though some find them in doubtful taste. As a lyricist he wrote songs as scathingly satirical as some of those written by Bob Dylan or even Jello Biafra. In "Send The Marines" he ridiculed the American government's military interventions overseas:

> *For might makes right,*
> *And till they've seen the light,*
> *They've got to be protected,*
> *All their rights respected,*
> *Till somebody we like can be elected.*

Lehrer was an accomplished piano player and his songs were often musically elegant. Much of the magic of his music came from the way he married withering words to graceful, urbane melodies. Lehrer's songs could be both macabre and hilarious. Unlike the young Dylan, however, Lehrer was never a rocker or a protest singer. In fact, he ridiculed the protest anthems of the 1960s in his song "The Folk Song Army." Lehrer was always a reluctant celebrity. He disliked touring and virtually retired from performing in 1967.

ARCHITECTURE

The iconic architectural form of small town and rural America is the Protestant church building. White and rectangular with a steeple, the typical American church forms the picturesque apex of countless settlements. The boxy-style interiors have been borrowed by town halls and courthouses across the nation. Catholic immigration in the 19th century brought a radically different aesthetic to church architecture and decor.

Skyscrapers

The Brooklyn, Golden Gate and other bridges are icons of America, but America's unique contribution to architecture has not been the bridge but the skyscraper, whose bold, thrusting lines have made it the symbol of capitalist energy. Made possible by new construction techniques and the invention of the elevator, the first skyscraper went up in Chicago in 1884. More than any other phenomenon, the skyscraper has determined the character of the American city, altering its physical and land use patterns; prompting design, technological, and infrastructure developments; creating internal work environments; and redefining boundaries and expectations of individuals and groups defined by gender, class, and ethnicity.

The first skyscraper was the ten-story *Home Insurance Building* in Chicago, built in 1884–85 by William Le Baron Jenney, creator of the first load bearing structural frame. A pupil, Daniel H. Burnham, was largely responsible for shaping the modern city of Chicago. "Make no little plans," he is reported to have said. "They have no magic to stir men's blood." The *Wainwright Building*, St Louis (1890) by Louis Sullivan (1856-1929), however, was the first steel frame building with soaring vertical bands to emphasize its height, and is therefore considered the first true skyscraper.

The prime reason for the original spread of skyscrapers was shortage of land. The two cities most affected were New York City and Chicago, and this is where most early skyscrapers appeared, because of the high ratio of rentable floor space per area of land. These cities are recognized as having among the most compelling skylines in the world. The *Empire State Building*, the first building to have more than 100 floors (102), was completed in 1932. It was designed in the contemporary Art Deco style. The tower takes its name from the nickname of New York State. Upon its completion it took the top spot as tallest building, and at 1,472 feet (448m) to the very top of the antenna, will be the tallest building in NYC until *1 World Trade Center*, replacing the World Trade Center, is completed. Still today New York has the most completed, individual freestanding buildings over 492 ft. (150 m) in the world. Because skyscrapers were such powerful symbols of pride and achievement, they attracted some of the finest architects and artists to their design and decoration. Many of New York's skyscrapers are icons of 20th century architecture. The skyline of Manhattan is many people's first view of America. It has become an emblem of America worldwide.

European architects who emigrated to the US before World War II launched what became a dominant movement in architecture, the International Style. Perhaps the most influential of these immigrants were Ludwig Mies van der Rohe (1886-1969) and Walter Gropius (1883-1969), both former directors of Germany's famous design school, the Bauhaus. Based on geometric form, buildings in their style have been both praised as monuments to American corporate life and dismissed as "glass boxes." The last master of modernist architecture is I. M. Pei (1917-) a pupil of Gropius. Younger architects have rejected the austere, boxy look in favor of "postmodern" buildings with striking contours and bold decoration that allude to historical styles of architecture.

TELEVISION PROGRAMS (for the television industry, see Chapter 6)

Television shows come in many genres that are continually evolving as audience preferences change.

News and Talk Shows

The best known news show is *The Today Show* which airs weekdays on NBC. After *Meet The Press*, which airs on NBC on Sunday mornings, *The Today Show is* the second-longest running American television series. It has spawned imitators such as ABC's *Good Morning America* and *The Early Show* on CBS.

The longest-running daytime TV talk show is *The Oprah Winfrey Show* (also known as *Oprah*), a nationally syndicated program hosted and produced by African American, Oprah Winfrey, which is the highest-rated talk show in American television history. *Oprah* is highly influential, especially with women, and many of its topics penetrate into American pop-cultural consciousness. While early episodes explored sensational social issues, Oprah eventually transformed her series into a more positive experience marked by book clubs, celebrity interviews, self-improvement segments, and philanthropic forays into world events. One of the show's features in recent years has been the "Wildest Dreams" tour, which fulfills the dreams of people reported to her producers by friends and family, be the dream a new house, an encounter with a favorite performer, or a guest role on a popular TV show. To Oprah's chagrin, one of the most repeated and heavily discussed clips is that of her interview with Tom Cruise, which was broadcast on May 23, 2005. Cruise, in the words of *The New York Times*, "jumped around the set, hopped onto a couch, fell rapturously to one knee and repeatedly professed his love for his new girlfriend." This scene quickly became talked about and was heavily parodied. According to *Time* magazine, by confessing intimate details about her weight problems, tumultuous love life, and sexual abuse, and crying alongside her guests, Winfrey has created a new form of media communication known as "rapport talk."

The format of NBC's *The Tonight Show*, which, after the soap opera *Guiding Light*, is the second-longest running entertainment program in US television history, has become the model for late-night talk and variety shows. It features at least two guests each night, usually including a comedian or musician. Meanwhile *Larry King Live* is CNN's longest-running interview program Premiering in 1985 with its now-famous mix of interviews and topical discussions, the show features guests from the whole gamut of business, entertainment and politics. Telecast each weeknight at 9 p.m. ET, the program also features phone calls, e-mails and web cam questions from viewers around the globe. *Saturday Night Live* (SNL) has been a weekly late night 91-minute sketch on NBC on Saturday nights since 1975. A comedy-variety show based in New York, it is one of the longest-running network entertainment programs in American television history.

The five major Sunday political talk shows are NBC's *Meet the Press*, CBS's *Face the Nation*, *Fox News Sunday*, ABC's *This Week*, and CNN's *Late Edition*. Candidates for public office are regular guests, as the shows help them "manage" their message. How much those appearances influence the electorate is debatable, however. The Sunday talk shows influence America's "chattering class"-- journalists and political activists, decision-makers and financial donors -- but only have a big effect if a candidate makes a serious mistake.

Drama

American television presents sophisticated drama such as *The Wire*, *Lost* and *The Sopranos*. *The*

Sopranos is broadcast on the HBO network. It revolves around New Jersey mafia boss Tony Soprano and the difficulties he faces as he tries to balance the often conflicting requirements of his home life and the criminal organization he heads. The series is widely regarded as one of the greatest shows in television history and is often credited with bringing a greater level of artistry to the medium and paving the way for many other successful drama series. When it debuted in 1999, *The New York Times* declared that it "just may be the greatest work of American popular culture of the last quarter century."

Numb3rs, a popular CBS police drama, co-stars Rob Morrow and David Krumholtz, who play FBI Special Agent Don Eppes and his brilliant brother, Charlie, a young math professor who consults for the FBI and NSA. While its storyline involving real math-based crime-busting techniques is unique, *Numb3rs* is typical of several shows in a way not often remarked upon — its rather conservative, humorous endings. For example, after a brilliant piece of math helps apprehend a criminal, the professor sits down at home with his father who, knowing his son has a problem with spelling, insists he plays him at *Scrabble*. Such touches of humor lighten the tension after the violence of the drama and emphasize that the show truly is a comedy. The show helps rebut the stereotype that American popular TV is all sex and violence.

Soap operas

A type of drama particularly associated with American TV is the soap opera, or "soap" for short. The name "soap opera" comes from the radio drama serials originally sponsored and produced by soap manufacturers. They were broadcast in weekday daytime slots when mostly housewives would be listening or watching. What differentiates a soap from other TV drama is stories that span several episodes, with each episode ending on a cliffhanger with a promise that the storyline will be continued in another. An episode generally switches between several different concurrent story threads that may at times interconnect or may run entirely independently. American soap operas have spread throughout the world.

Soap operas are the televised equivalent of paperback novels. The most popular storylines are based on romance, secret relationships, and extramarital affairs, intermixed with family, emotional and moral conflicts, legal dramas, and topical issues. Soaps are usually set in familiar domestic interiors within fictional, medium-sized Midwestern towns, with only occasional excursions to new locations. Soaps mostly either follow the day-to-day lives of a group of characters who live or work in a particular place, or focus on a large extended family. The storylines are marked by chance meetings, missed meetings, coincidences and conversions, rescues and revelations. Previously-unknown children, siblings, and twins (including the evil variety) of established characters often emerge to upset and rejuvenate the relationships between the characters. Unexpected calamities disrupt weddings, childbirths, and other major life events with unusual frequency. These storylines may be made convoluted and confusing to keep audiences hooked as the story unfolds. Crimes such as kidnapping, rape, and even murder may go unpunished if the perpetrator is to be retained in the story. A character's death is not guaranteed to be permanent. In many soaps, the characters are glamorous, seductive and rich. Action scenes, such as car accidents, fights and stunts, are less common, because they are difficult to depict without post production editing, which is not feasible owing to the high output required each week and low budgets.

Aired nearly every weekday since they started, some soap operas have become the longest stories ever told. The longest is *Guiding Light,* which began on radio in 1937 and was later moved to television. Long-running soaps include *As the World Turns*, *General Hospital*, *Days of our Lives*, and *One Life to Live*. Helen Wagner, who has played Hughes family matriarch Nancy Hughes on *As the World Turns* since its debut on April 2, 1956, is in the *Guinness Book of World Records* as the actor with the longest uninterrupted performance in a single role.

Editing techniques have set soap operas apart from other shows since the 1980s. In order to hold the interest of as many sectors of the audience as possible, and to build suspense, a common technique has been to have the action cut between various conversations, returning to each at the precise moment it was left. When a scene is about to end, a character in the concluding scene will often be shown in extreme closeup and deliver a jarring announcement. No other character will respond and there will be no dialogue for several seconds while the music builds before cutting to a commercial or a new scene. This kind of segue is referred to in the industry as a "tag." The soap opera's distinctive open plot structure and complex continuity also increasingly began to be incorporated into prime time programs. The first significant drama series like this were *Hill Street Blues*, *Cagney & Lacey* and *The West Wing*, which used an ensemble cast, multi-episode storylines and extensive character development exploring the personal lives and interpersonal relationships of the regular characters over the series. Probably the most controversial soap opera ever is *Dexter*. Based on the novel *Darkly Dreaming Dexter* by Jeff Lindsay, the show is set in Miami and centers on Dexter Morgan (Michael C. Hall), a serial killer governed by a strict moral code who works for the Miami Metro Police Department as a blood spatter analyst.

Reality TV

Although Reality television has existed in one form or another since the early years of television, the term is most commonly used to describe programs produced since 2000. Reality television presents supposedly unscripted dramatic or humorous situations, documents actual events, and features ordinary people instead of professional actors. Some place cast members, who in most cases previously did not know each other, in artificial living environments.

The Reality television genre embraces a family of shows of similar type. In documentary-style shows, the viewer and the camera are passive observers following people going about their daily personal and professional activities. MTV's *Laguna Beach:The Real Orange County* is the epitome of this style of show, with unscripted situations, real-life locations, and no tasks given to the cast (at least, no known ones). Often "plots" are constructed via editing or planned situations, with the results resembling soap operas, hence the term *docusoap*.

Elimination/Game Shows

Competition provides the interest in two further types of reality TV. These are called "reality-competition," or "reality game shows." In the first, participants compete for a prize. Living together in a confined environment may add to the tension. Participants are removed until only one person or team remains, which is then declared the winner. Usually this is done by eliminating participants one at a time, in balloon debate style, through either disapproval voting or by voting for the most popular choice to win; voting is done by either the viewing audience or by the show's own participants. A well-known example of a reality-competition show is the globally syndicated *Big Brother*, in which cast members live together in the same house, with participants removed at regular intervals by the participants themselves.

Many people classify modern game shows like *Strike It Rich* as a form of reality television because the format includes competition between contestants and/or elimination. The shows are also more expensively produced, the background music is more dramatic, and contestants are either put into physical danger or offered large cash prizes. In addition, there is more interaction between contestants and hosts.

Game Shows

Winning large amounts of money on a show like *Who Wants to Be a Millionaire?* seems to its millions of viewers to be a quick and easy way to achieve the American Dream, equated with financial independence and freedom from work, although the odds against succeeding are in fact long. *The Price Is Right* is the longest continuously running game show in North American television history and also the longest-running five-days-a-week game show in the world. The current version, which has aired for over 35 seasons, is both a spin-off of a previously successful version and the seed for many international versions. *The Price Is Right* is well-known for its signature line of "Come on down!" by which the announcer invites new contestants to take part.

The show centers on contestants guessing the retail prices of featured prizes and other promotional products. Contestants are winnowed down to two in two *Showcase Showdown* rounds, where they vie for a showcase of prizes worth tens of thousands of dollars. Contestants' Row (known to fans as "One-Bid") is the head-on competitive area of the show where the four contestants bid on an offered prize. The one who comes closest to guessing the actual retail price without going over it wins the prize and advances in the competition to play a pricing game. After that, the *Showcase Showdown* determines who will play for the large prize package at the end of the show called the *Showcase*. The Showdown appears twice in the program, once after the third pricing game and again after the sixth. Three contestants spin a large wheel, consisting of twenty sections, each with a different amount of money marked on it ranging from 5¢ to $1.00. The player's goal is to come as close to $1.00 as possible without going over it in one spin or a combination of two spins. At the climax of the show, the final round, the two winners of their *Showcase Showdowns* compete for a single Showcase, a large set of prizes. Each contestant bids on one of the prize packages. The contestant whose bid is closer to, but does not exceed, the price of his or her own showcase wins that showcase. If a contestant succeeds at underbidding i.e., bidding $250 or less away from the price; *and* having the closer bid, that contestant is awarded both showcases. In the event that neither contestant bids less than the price of the showcase, it is called a Double Overbid, and neither one is awarded the grand prize. Criticism of the show as a mindless celebration of greed never seems to be uttered.

Popular variants on the competition-based format include:

Dating-based competition shows, which follow a contestant choosing one out of a group of suitors. These shows have since waned in popularity. Only *The Bachelor* is still on the air.

One of the oldest forms of competition show is job search. In this category, the competitors seek to win a contract for a job requiring a skill they have been pre-screened for. They perform a variety of tasks using that skill and are then judged by one or more experts, who decide whether to keep them on or remove them. Examples include *America's Next Top Model*, *American Idol* (for pop music singers), *Hell's Kitchen* (for chefs), *Project Runway* (for clothing design), and the *MuchMusic VJ Search* (for a new MuchMusic VJ). The *Miss America* Pageant, first aired in 1954, is a competition where the winner gains a scholarship to an institution of her choice.

Some programs create a sporting competition among athletes attempting to establish their name. In *The Amazing Race*, teams of two race around the world in competition with other teams. Self-improvement is a major theme of reality TV. After presenting the subjects in an existing environment that is in need of improvement, the show introduces the subjects to a group of experts, who tell them how to improve things and offer aid and encouragement along the way. Finally, the subjects return to their environment and they, along with their friends and family and the experts, appraise the changes that have occurred. Self-improvement or makeover shows include *Supernanny* (child-rearing), *Made* (attaining difficult goals), *What Not to Wear* (fashion and grooming), and *Trinny & Susannah Undress* (fashion makeover and marriage). Similarly, *Pimp My Ride* shows vehicles being rebuilt. Shows which may be considered an offshoot of the makeover genre make over part or all of a person's living space. *Trading Spaces* was the first such show. Later shows in this category include *Extreme Makeover: Home Edition*, *Debbie Travis' Facelift* and *Designed to Sell*. As with game shows, a gray area exists between such reality TV shows and more conventional formats.

Humor

On TV, humor is represented by the *sitcom*, situational comedy, where the humor comes from the situations the characters get into. A noticeable feature of TV sitcoms is canned laughter, a soundtrack of laughter that is played just after a joke, when a live audience would laugh. In *Friends*, which began in 1994, gentle fun was poked at the funny side of ordinary life. Six friends were shown facing the problems of love, life and friendship. Satire is provided on talk shows such as *The Late Show with David Letterman*. The humor is very direct, but by contrast with some European humor, generally lacks irony.

Hidden cameras

Allen Funt's *Candid Camera* was the first of a long-established type of reality show that used concealed cameras. Debuting in 1948, the show broadcasts unsuspecting ordinary people reacting to pranks. The show was based on concealed cameras filming ordinary people being confronted with unusual situations, sometimes involving trick props, such as a desk with drawers that pop open when one is closed, or a car with a hidden extra gas tank. When the joke was revealed, victims would be told the show's famous catch phrase, "Smile, you're on Candid Camera." On Trash TV, topics are frequently outrageous and are chosen in the interest of creating on-screen drama, tension or outrageous behavior.

Analysis and criticism

Part of reality television's appeal is its ability to place ordinary people in extraordinary situations. For example, on the ABC show *The Bachelor*, an eligible male simultaneously dates a dozen women to scenic locales for extraordinary dates. Reality television also has the potential to turn its participants into national celebrities, as in talent and performance programs such as *American Idol*, though frequently *Survivor* and *Big Brother* participants also reach some degree of celebrity.

Critics say the term "reality television" is something of a misnomer. Such shows frequently portray a modified and highly influenced form of reality, with participants put in exotic locations or abnormal situations, sometimes coached to act in certain ways by off-screen handlers, and with events on screen sometimes manipulated through editing and other post-production techniques. In competition-based programs such as *Big Brother* and *Survivor*, and other special living environment shows like *The Real World*, the producers design the format of the show and control the day-to-day activities and the environment, creating a completely fabricated world in which the competition plays out. Producers select the participants and use carefully designed scenarios, challenges, events, and settings to encourage particular behaviors and conflicts. Some participants in reality shows have also stated afterwards that they altered their behavior to appear more crazy or emotional in order to get more camera time. Some shows have faced speculation that the participants themselves are involved in fakery, acting out storylines that have been planned in advance by producers. Nevertheless, no direct evidence has yet been presented that any such program has been scripted or rigged.

Star Trek

Star Trek was a science fiction series created by Gene Roddenberry which aired from 1966 through 1969. The original *Star Trek* has become such an ingrained part of American speech, values, and sensibilities that someone learning about American culture would do well to become familiar with the look, the feel and the vocabulary of the show. "Beam me up, Scotty" (a reference to the ship's teleportation device), Spock's signature commentary on the "illogic" of human culture, the Vulcan "mind-meld," the Vulcan salute "live long and prosper," and "warp speed" have become part of the American psyche.

The original *Star Trek*, and the motion pictures and television sequels it spawned, command a huge following, including annual conventions of "Trekkies," sales of memorabilia, and every possible variety of book, magazine, audio and video. The show has achieved iconic status as an American - and indeed worldwide - television phenomenon. Ironically *Star Trek* only became really popular when it went into syndication, perhaps the most famous example of this occurrence. It says something about the American mass media that the first pilot of *Star Trek* was turned down because it was "too cerebral."

Cartoons

The Simpsons is an animated half-hour comedy that has redefined the term "cartoon." The show, which started in 1989, is by far the longest-running prime-time animated TV show. Well-known for its excellent writing and bewildering array of around 80 characters, *The Simpsons* has collected 15 Emmy awards and a star on the Hollywood Walk of Fame.

The Simpsons has become one of the most talked-about shows on television. Its popularity is emphasized by the amount of Simpson-related merchandise available, especially anything showing Bart, the grade school under-achiever. He was the star of the first few seasons, and Bart T-shirts became a "must-have" item among youngsters. *The Simpsons* has been successful because of quality writing and a talented cast, but above all because it is an animated program. The characters never age. Animation also allows the writers to introduce a much larger range of characters, which has always been one of *The Simpsons'* strengths.

The Simpsons proved that an animated show could succeed on American television. It is hard to imagine that other successful animated shows such as *Beavis and Butt-Head* (1993-) and *South Park* (1997-) could have found such a large audience without *The Simpsons* laying the groundwork. And there are countless other animated shows that owe *The Simpsons* a debt of gratitude, such as *Family Guy* (1999-).

Children's TV

The most famous children's television program is perhaps *Sesame Street*, an educational series for preschoolers, which is a pioneer of the contemporary educational television standard, combining both education and entertainment. Well-known for its Muppet characters, the series has aired more than 4,000 episodes since it premiered in 1969. *Sesame Street* is one of the most highly-regarded television educational shows for children in the world. No other series has matched its level of international recognition and success. The original series has been televised in 120 countries, including China, and more than 30 international versions have been produced, not including dubbed versions. A study found that 81% of American children under the age of six own a *Sesame Street* toy or game, and 87% own a book based on the series.

The show uses a combination of puppets, animation, and live actors to teach young children letter and word recognition, mathematics (numbers, addition and subtraction), as well as geometric forms, and classification. Since the show's debut, other instructional goals have been basic life skills, such as how to cross the street safely, proper hygiene, healthy eating habits, and social skills. *Sesame Street's* revolutionary format calls for the humans to be intermixed with segments of animation, live-action shorts and Muppets. These segments are created to be like commercials, quick, catchy and memorable, and make the learning experience fun. This format became a model for what is known as *edutainment*.

The show displays a subtle sense of humor that has appealed to older viewers since it first premiered; this was devised as a means to encourage parents and older siblings to watch the series with younger children, thus becoming involved in the learning process, rather than having *Sesame Street* act as a babysitter. Several of the character names used on the program are puns or cultural references aimed at a slightly older audience, including Flo Bear (Flaubert), Sherlock Hemlock (a Sherlock Holmes parody), H. Ross Parrot (based on Reform Party founder H. Ross Perot) and Polly Darton (Dolly Parton). The brownstone architecture of *Sesame Street,* a fictional neighborhood in New York City, as well as the concept of neighbors from different backgrounds living in the same area and sharing their life experiences, was loosely based on Brooklyn Heights, Brooklyn, where several of the founding producers were living at the time.

Multicultural and inclusive casting is a feature of *Sesame Street,* which includes roles for disabled people, young people, senior citizens, Hispanic actors, black actors, and others. While some of the puppets look like people, others are animal or "monster" puppets of different sizes and colors. This encourages children to believe that people come in all different shapes, sizes, and colors, and that no particular physical "type" is any better than another. In line with its multicultural perspective, the show pioneered the idea of occasionally inserting very basic Spanish words and phrases to help young children become acquainted with the concept of a foreign language. The more formalized "Spanish Word of the Day" has been introduced in every episode.

Each of the puppet characters has been designed to represent a specific stage or element of early childhood, and the scripts are written so that the character reflects the development level of children of that age. Human relations, emotions and behaviors are shown through the mostly animal characters. For example, birds, elephants, and bears. Big Bird is often visited by his friend Aloysius Snuffleupagus, who is a very large, brown woolly elephant-like creature.

The show has spawned countless books, movies, videos, toys, apparel, health, body, home and seasonal products, and even two theme parks. There have been two *Sesame Street* feature films. Meanwhile Big Bird has promoted safe seating practices and the wearing of seatbelts for the Ford Motor Company. Major funding for *Sesame Street* is provided by The Corporation for Public Broadcasting and by individual contributors.

Criticisms of American TV programs

Three main criticisms of American television have been made by US and other critics: television is a waste of time; television distorts reality, misrepresenting minorities and glorifying violence; television replaces intelligent discussion with sound bites and images. Television has been attacked because it is an undemanding form of relaxation, "mind-numbing and wasteful," according to one critic. The growing obesity of the nation is blamed on it, as are increased violence and higher levels of teen sex. Finally, we are assured, the "idiot box" is dumbing Americans down. One man even threatened to sue his cable company because he smoked and drank and his wife was overweight, alleging that TV was responsible.

There are plenty of reasons to doubt the validity of those criticisms. Children are watching slightly less television per day than they were a decade ago, although they do continue to grow fatter. Violent crime rates have been falling for over a decade; and rates of teen sexual activity and pregnancy have fallen dramatically since the mid-1990s. Average IQs have been soaring along with TV viewing for decades. And real gross domestic product has more than quintupled since 1950.

Many anti-TV attitudes are based on differences of opinion over what qualifies as a judicious use of one's free time. Critics are constantly hectoring viewers to get out and do something useful, helpful or improving. The assumption behind these injunctions is that any activity will be less wasteful and more edifying than, for example, watching a good episode of *Oprah*. Yet it is not as though two or three generations ago people were sitting around discussing Kierkegaard and Kant with their children over the family dinner table every evening. In fact, most of them were fully engaged in the basic tasks of earning a living or managing a household. In their scarce leisure time, they might go to a baseball game or read a dime novel. In a similar fashion today people might switch on the TV to watch a ball game or an episode of *The Simpsons*. All of which is not to say that watching TV does not have some bad effects, but it is hardly the instrument of mental, cultural, and moral degradation it is so often portrayed as. Indeed TV, far from acting as a narcotic, can actually be said to stimulate the imagination. It offers a magic kaleidoscope onto a wider and more alluring world and enlarges the sense of what is possible.

The effect of TV on children, especially younger ones, is a concern for many parents. It has been calculated, for example, that the average American child sees 40,000 TV advertisements a year. Research published by the American Psychological Association in 2004 shows that while older children and adults understand the inherent bias of advertising, children under the age of eight are unable to comprehend televised advertising messages critically and are prone to accept advertiser messages as truthful, accurate and unbiased. This can lead to unhealthy eating habits as evidenced by today's youth obesity epidemic. For these reasons, a task force of the APA has recommended that advertising targeting children under the age of eight be restricted. Other research, however, shows that the impact of advertising is modest when compared to other factors such as parental influence, trends in family eating habits, school policy, public understanding of nutrition, food labeling, and exercise.

Neil Postman, however, in *Amusing Ourselves To Death* (1986) criticizes television as a medium, which he asserts presents content in the form of entertainment because of the kind of medium it is. Indeed, Portman believes television is dangerous when it attempts to be serious. He argues that television has such "resonance" (power to influence) that our ability to take the world seriously has diminished because of it. Postman believes a new "worldview" (a new ethos or approach to life) has been brought about by the assimilation of television into popular culture.

Postman is concerned that television devalues culture by turning it into entertainment and suggests that we are "amusing ourselves to death." Among the numerous fields he gives as examples are politics, religion, news, athletics, education, and commerce. He laments "the dissolution of public discourse in America and its conversion into the art of show business." For Postman, television provides the explanation for a world obsessed with image to the detriment of content. He argues that television conveys its dialogue in images, not words, and adopts Marshall McLuhan's famous aphorism "the medium is the message." Postman tries to demonstrate how the content of the printing press in America was once "coherent, serious and rational" and how, under the governance of television that tries to be "serious" it has become "shriveled and absurd."

Hence television for Postman is completely devoted to emotional gratification and entertainment. It depends on changing images, and the viewing eye never rests. The problem is not that it is entertaining "but that entertainment is the format through which all experiences are mediated." Postman is particularly critical of TV coverage of the news, and newsreaders who close the program with the words "join us tomorrow," which often fails to reflect the gravity of the content of the news. We should be traumatized by what we have seen, urges Postman. We should not want to "join the program tomorrow." That message is that we should not take the news, which is merely fun, too seriously. The segmented nature of television exacerbates the problem. An earthquake, for example, may be reported on the news, but the next moment we are transported to a fresh and new program. Music also sets the scene for entertainment, as does the brevity with which an average story is covered and the fact that commercial breaks interrupt the coverage. Pictures add to the effect by "short-circuiting introspection." A further contributing factor is that newsreaders often fail to adopt a suitable gravity of tone. Instead they maintain an "ingratiating enthusiasm."

Postman's critique of television is compelling. He does not prove, however, either that society has plummeted to the levels of intellectual deprivation that he describes, or that television has enough "resonance" to alter the truth of our reality; that we now find truth in television, the new form of expression, in the same way that previous generations found truth in the virtues of oratory. While the medium is certainly important to the meaning within the message, there is no proven correlation between a medium whose form allegedly promotes only images and a society that allegedly prioritizes entertainment above, among other things, serious discourse, politics and education.

If Postman is right to lament a lost attitude towards learning, and the presence of "sacred" values, there are also other, less visible factors at work. For example, as society moves in a more liberal direction and away from prescriptive moral codes backed by threats of punishment, it may be that individuals from all classes find "good literature" and "high culture" less compelling. Furthermore, with the triumph of capitalism in Western societies, there may be little room for really radical politics of any hue, and political parties are becoming more similar, replacing diversity with games of one-upmanship and allowing image to take precedence over content. Skeptics doubt, moreover, that Postman's view of public participation in culture before the Age of Television is historically correct.

SPORT

Sport is an important part of American life, but the unique sports Americans prefer and the way professional sport is organized make American sports culture different from that of many other countries. The most popular professional sports are football, basketball, baseball, and ice hockey, whose major leagues enjoy massive media exposure and are considered the preeminent competitions in their sports in the world. The preeminence of the major leagues is partially attributable to their financial muscle and huge domestic market, as well as the fact that relatively few other countries play some of their dominant sports to any significant extent.

Large centers of population made mass audience sport possible. But it was the acceptance of play as a healthy, respectable activity that heralded community-wide involvement in sports. Jack W. Berryman, University of Maryland, has commented, however, that the degree to which children's sports became organized mirrored the American characteristic of being overly regimented, businesslike and competitive. Sports coverage on TV may spur parents to encourage their children to participate. Indeed, most US children spend their summer in private or public camp and play sport there. Some camps are educational, while others are purely recreational. Socialization is seen as an important part of the experience, as is developing a competitive spirit.

While fitness is becoming more popular, Americans remain very interested in all athletic and recreational endeavours. Team sports like lacrosse, rugby, field hockey, and cheerleading are on the rise, while racquet sports such as badminton, racquetball, squash, table tennis, and tennis are gaining participation. The main outdoor sports are freshwater fishing, bicycling (road/paved surface), camping, and day hiking. Canoeing and snorkelling rank one-two among water sports. Since 2000, the top three individual sports have been bowling, roller skating, and martial arts. In winter sports, Alpine skiing remains first in popularity, though snowboarding comes a strong second.

Professional sport

American sports leagues have a particular organization quite unlike that of many countries. The major leagues operate as associations of franchises. They play to a schedule that climaxes with a championship playoff tournament or game after the regular season between the 8 to 16 teams with the best records. Teams are not promoted and relegated as in Europe. American sports, except for soccer, have no equivalent to the cup competitions that run concurrently with leagues in European sports. The same 30 to 32 teams play in the league each year unless they move to another city or the league chooses to expand with new franchises. Competition between national teams is far less important – or in the case of American football effectively non-existent – than in the sporting culture of the rest of the world. International competition is not as important in American sports as it is in the sporting culture of most other countries, although Olympic ice-hockey and basketball tournaments do generate attention. Major league players take part in the World Baseball Classic, an international tournament now played every four years. No government agency is charged with overseeing sports.

American sport is linked to secondary and tertiary education to an extent unknown elsewhere. Millions of students participate in high school and college athletics programs, and many colleges offer athletics scholarships. High school and college sports fill the developmental role that in many other countries would be played by youth teams associated with clubs. The major professional sports leagues operate drafts once a year, when the teams select eligible prospects. Baseball and ice hockey operate minor leagues for players who have finished education but are not good enough for the major leagues. Especially in basketball and football, high school and, even more, college sports are followed with a fervor equaling if not exceeding that felt for professional sports. College football games can draw six-digit crowds and, for upper-tier schools, sports are a significant source of revenue.

Baseball

So many people play baseball as children (or play its close relative, softball, with its larger, softer ball, which is popular with women) that it has become known as "the national pastime." Unlike football and basketball, baseball is a democratic game that can be played well by people of average height and weight. Many American families enjoy going to a Sunday afternoon *double header*, two games between the same two teams in one day. The razzamatazz (colorful, upbeat display) by team supporters led by their baton-twirling cheerleaders has become iconic of American popular culture. The atmosphere of a baseball game is brilliantly evoked in the Prologue to Don DeLillo's novel *Underworld*.

Baseball is the oldest of the major American team sports. It originated before the Civil War (1861-1865) as rounders, a humble game played on sandlots. During the war, Union soldiers from New York City played the game wherever the fighting took them and as they traveled spread the rules used by the first real team, Alexander Cartwright's New York Knickerbocker Baseball Club. Professional baseball dates from 1869.

Baseball's easy scoring system makes it a good game for competitions, and record-keeping soon gave baseball a tradition of its own. Most Americans undoubtedly know that Roger Maris's 61 home runs in one season in 1961 broke Babe Ruth's record of 60 in 1927. (Actually, Maris hit his 61st in the 162nd game, while Ruth's season lasted only 154 games, so many people say Ruth's record still stands.) Afterwards in 1998 Mark McGwire hit 70 homers for the St Louis Cardinals to beat both of them. Likewise the fans know that Cy Young of the Boston Red Sox, whom many consider to be the greatest pitcher ever, won an all-time record 511 Major League games. Cy Young also pitched the first ever perfect game in baseball history, playing against the Philadelphia Athletics. Not a single Philadelphia batter reached first base on either a pitch or a walk. The Cy Young award is now given to each season's best pitcher. The pictures of famous players appear on the backs of baseball cards, which are keenly sought by collectors and can fetch high prices.

The most famous baseball player ever was George Herman Ruth ("Babe Ruth") (1895-1948) from Baltimore, the "Sultan of Swat," who led the New York Yankees to several World Series titles and became a national hero on the strength of his home runs. A huge hitter, he shattered every batting record. His lifetime achievement of 714 home runs was not beaten until 1974. As well as 60 homers in one season, he four times hit more than 50. Actually, he began his career as a pitcher when he set a World Series record of 27 scoreless innings for the Boston Red Sox. In 1920 the Red Sox sold him to the New York Yankees for $125,000, and in 1923 the Yankee Stadium was built with money from the audiences he attracted. He led the Yankees to four World Series. His salary of $80,000 in 1930 was greater than the President's.

Baseball was organized as a professional sport soon after the Civil War. The first professional baseball league was formed in 1871, and by the beginning of the 20th century, most large cities in the eastern US had a professional team. The teams are divided into two Major Leagues, the

National (the older, founded 1876) and the American, each with 14 teams, which are subdivided regionally. During the regular season, April to October, a team plays almost every day, but only against other teams within its division. The most victorious team wins the pennant. The four leading teams in each league play to decide which two will go forward to the World Series at the end of the regular season, where the winner of at least four games (out of a possible seven) is the champion for that year. The first World Series was played in 1903 when Cy Young pitched the Boston Red Sox to a 5-3 victory over Pittsburgh. Racial segregation ended in baseball in 1947 when Jackie Robinson (1919-1972), a gifted and courageous athlete, signed for the Brooklyn Dodgers. Prior to Robinson, black players had been restricted to the Negro League. The New York Yankees have won the most World Series. Other well known teams include the Boston Red Sox, the Cleveland Indians, the Detroit Tigers, the Chicago Cubs, the St Louis Cardinals and the Los Angeles Dodgers.

Starting in the 1950s, baseball expanded its geographical range. Western cities got teams, either by luring them to move from eastern cities or by forming so-called expansion teams with players made available by established teams. Until the 1970s, because of strict contracts, the owners of baseball teams also virtually owned the players; since then, the rules have changed so that players are free, within certain limits, to sell their services to any team. The results have been bidding wars and stars who are paid millions of dollars a year. Disputes between the players' union and the owners have at times halted baseball for months at a time. If baseball is both a sport and a business, late in the 20th century many disgruntled fans viewed the business side as the dominant one.

Baseball has also entered the culture through its unique idioms: a *grand slam* (a home run with three runners on bases); *to throw somebody a curve (ball)* means to trick them, because a curve ball deceives the batter; *not to get to first base* means to get nothing done; and *to take a rain check* is to delay an event, because a free ticket to a later game is given if a game is stopped by rain. Other everyday American expressions taken from baseball include: to make a grandstand play (ostentatious attempt to win approval); to throw a curve (do or say something unexpected); to field something; to be off base (unprepared); to be batting 1,000 (getting everything in a series right); the ground rules; to touch all the bases; to bat for someone; to have strikes against oneself (to be overcome by someone or something); left field (unrelated to the subject); to drive someone up the wall; to be a clutch player (one who plays better when the game is on the line); to be an oddball/screwball/foul ball; ballpark.

Because of its 162-game schedule, baseball attracts more ticket sales and sells more merchandise than any other sport. Baseball had no close rivals in popularity until the 1960s. The shine has gone off baseball's reputation recently, however, because of players taking steroids, and the game is losing gate receipts compared with football, NASCAR (75 million followers) and basketball. Baseball is now second to football in popularity.

Basketball

The most popular American indoor sport is basketball. Professional basketball ranks third behind football and baseball. Spectators at an NBA (National Basketball Association) game can number 20,000 people. Basketball originated in 1891 when Dr James Naismith (1861-1939) was assigned to teach a disorderly physical education class in Springfield, Massachusetts. Naismith was told to invent a new game to keep the young men occupied. Since it was winter and very cold outside, a game that could be played indoors was desirable. Recalling rugby players tossing a ball into a box in a gymnasium, he had the idea of nailing up raised boxes into which players would attempt to throw a ball. When boxes could not be found, he used peach baskets. Naismith drew up the 13 rules for the new game in about an hour. Most of them still apply in some form today.

Basketball caught on because Naismith's students traveled widely, Naismith disseminated the rules freely, and there was a need for a simple game that could be played indoors during winter. Naismith's students included the first great college basketball coach, Forrest "Phog" Allen (1885-1974), who played for Naismith at the University of Kansas and went on to win 771 games as a coach at Kansas himself. Among Allen's star players was Wilt "the Stilt" Chamberlain, who became one of professional basketball's first superstars. One night in 1962, he scored a record 100 points in a game. Julius Erving is another great player in the Basketball Hall of Fame.

The first professional basketball league was formed in 1898 and the NBA in 1949. Players earned $2.50 for home games, $1.25 for games on the road. Not quite 100 years later, Juwan Howard, a star player for the Washington Bullets (now called the Washington Wizards), had competing offers of more than $100 million over seven seasons from the Bullets and the Miami Heat. Basketball's greatest player was Michael Jordan, who earned $30 million a year plus $50 million from sponsorships and advertisements for a career total of $300 million, the most money in sporting history. Known as "His Airness" because of his astonishing ability to change direction in mid-air, Jordan had the highest-ever scoring average, won six NBA Championships with the Chicago Bulls and two Olympic golds. The NBA has 29 teams which play between November and June. At the end of the season, the best eight teams in the Eastern Conference and the best eight in the Western Conference play in the NBA Championship. The Boston Celtics have won this most often, a total of 16 times. The best team recently has been the Chicago Bulls, with five championships since 1991. Women players take part in the American Basketball League and the Women's NBA. The team best known outside the US is the Harlem Globetrotters, an African American team that plays exhibition games all round the world.

Many teams in the NBA now have foreign players, such as the Chinese, Yao Ming, who return home to represent their native countries during the Olympic Games. The so-called Dream Team, made up of the top American professional basketball players, has represented the US in recent Olympic Games. The first Dream Team, in the Barcelona Olympics in 1992, contained Michael Jordan and "Magic" Johnson and won the gold medal. The college basketball championship tournament played in March, known as March Madness, draws enormous attention. Netball, a derivative of basketball invented in the US and usually played by women, is popular in Australia, New Zealand, Sri Lanka, the United Kingdom, and the West Indies.

American Football

Known as *gridiron* or *American football* outside the US and Canada, football now attracts more television viewers than baseball. The play is dangerous, so helmets and thick pads must be worn. Each game has cheerleaders and musicians who march on the field between the halves. Whole families go to watch and violence among spectators is rare. Many games are shown live on television.

The main professional football league is the National Football League, which now has 32 franchises divided into two conferences. After a 16-game season, each conference sends six teams to the NFL Playoffs, which culminates in the league's championship game, the Super Bowl. Super Bowl Sunday is the biggest annual sporting event held in the US. The Dallas Cowboys and San

Francisco 49ers have won the most Super Bowls, five times each. Other well known teams include the Green Bay Packers, the Miami Dolphins, the Pittsburgh Steelers and the Chicago Bears.

Golf

The modern game has been dominated by such players as Arnold Palmer, Jack Nicklaus, Curtis Strange, and Tiger Woods among others. When Woods won his first major in 1997 he was the youngest man by two years to win the Masters and the first black man to win any major. With his score 70-66-65-69-270 (the lowest score in tournament history), he won by 12 shots, an incredible 18 under par.

The PGA Tour, which offers the biggest prizes in the world, together with three of the four major championships in men's golf, and also the richest women's professional tour, the LPGA Tour, are based in the US. America has consistently been the most successful nation in men's professional golf since World War I. The US was also the dominant nation in women's professional golf until around the turn of the 21st century, when Asian and other international golfers began to dominate the LPGA Tour.

Most Americans recognize a fourth major sport—*ice hockey*. Exported to the US from Canada, the sport is commonly referred to simply as "hockey" in the US. The game is most popular in regions with a cold winter, namely New England and the Midwest. In recent years hockey has also become increasingly popular in the Sun Belt due in large part to the expansion of the National Hockey League to cities like Tampa, Dallas, and Phoenix, Arizona.

Tennis is played nationally at high school and college levels, and the country hosts one of the four annual Grand Slam tournaments, the US Open, at the USTA National Tennis Center, Queens, New York City. Many of the of the all-time greats of the sport are American, such as Bill Tilden, Jimmy Connors, John McEnroe, Pete Sampras, Andre Agassi, Billie Jean King, Chris Evert, and Venus and Serena Williams, but the early 21st century has seen a sharp falling off in the number of top ranked American players. *Soccer* participation is highest among under-13s and the women's team ranks high in international events. US *boxers* such as Muhammad Ali and Sugar Ray Robinson rank among the all time greats of the sport. *Mixed martial* arts has recently enjoyed mainstream success. *Track and field* gets little mainstream attention from Americans apart from competition in the Olympic Games, although it is always a mainstay of high school and college athletic departments.

Sports media

Television networks pay millions of dollars for the rights to broadcast sporting events. Because of the advertising slots, broadcasting contracts are very lucrative and account for the biggest chunk of professional teams' revenues. Broadcasters also covet contracts to televise the major sports leagues (especially the NFL) because they are a means to promote programming to the audience, especially young and middle-aged men. Cable and satellite TV have greatly expanded the sports offerings available. Despite the size of the market, however, the country does not have a national daily sports newspaper. This is because the 48 states spread across four time zones, and games on the West Coast may not end until early morning in the East. This makes it difficult to distribute a national newspaper with the scores of late games in time for morning delivery. There are many American sports magazines, however, the best-known being *Sports Illustrated*.

NATIONAL CELEBRATIONS

National holidays

Americans share three national holidays with many countries: Christmas Day, New Year's Day and Easter Sunday. Eight other holidays are uniquely American (although some of them have counterparts in other nations). For most Americans, two holidays stand out above the others as occasions to cherish national origins: Thanksgiving and the Fourth of July.

Thanksgiving Day is the fourth Thursday in November, and many Americans take a day of vacation on the following Friday to make a four-day weekend, during which they may travel long distances to visit family and friends. The holiday dates back to 1621, the year after the Puritans arrived in Massachusetts, determined to practice their dissenting religion without interference. After a rough winter, in which about half of them died, they turned for help to neighboring Indians, who taught them how to plant corn and other crops. The next fall's bountiful harvest inspired the Pilgrims to give thanks by holding a feast. The Thanksgiving feast became a national tradition, not only because so many other Americans have found prosperity but also because the Pilgrims' sacrifices for their freedom still capture the imagination. To this day, Thanksgiving dinner almost always includes some of the foods served at the first feast: roast turkey, cranberry sauce, sweet potatoes (yams), and pumpkin pie. The turkey is filled with stuffing or dressing, sometimes according to a special family recipe. Before the meal begins, families or friends usually pause to give thanks for their blessings, including the joy of being united for the occasion. On Thanksgiving there are special TV programs and sports events. In New York there is Macy's Thanksgiving Day Parade, when a long line of people wearing fancy costumes march through the streets with large balloons in the shapes of imaginary characters. Thanksgiving is considered the beginning of the Christmas period, and the next day many people go out to shop for Christmas presents. *The Fourth of July*, or *Independence Day*, honors the nation's birthday, the signing of the Declaration of Independence on July 4, 1776. It is a day of picnics and patriotic parades, a night of concerts and fireworks. The flying of the American flag (which also occurs on Memorial Day and other holidays) is widespread.

There are six other uniquely American holidays. *Martin Luther King Day*: The Rev. Dr. Martin Luther King, Jr., an African American clergyperson, is considered a great American because of his tireless efforts to win civil rights for all people through nonviolent means. Since his assassination in 1968, memorial services have marked his birthday on January 15. In 1986, that day was replaced by the third Monday of January, which was declared a national holiday. *Presidents' Day*: Until the mid-1970s, the February 22 birthday of George Washington, hero of the Revolutionary War and first President of the US, was a national holiday. In addition, the February 12 birthday of Abraham Lincoln, the President during the Civil War, was a holiday in most states. The two days have been joined, and the holiday has been expanded to embrace all past Presidents. It is celebrated on the third Monday in February. *Memorial Day*: Celebrated on the fourth Monday of May, this holiday honors the dead. Although it originated in the aftermath of the Civil War, it has become a day on which the dead of all wars, and the dead generally, are remembered in special programs held in cemeteries, churches, and other public meeting places. *Labor Day*: The first Monday of September, this holiday honors the nation's working people, typically with parades. For most Americans it marks the end of the summer vacation season, and for many students the opening of the school year. *Columbus Day*: On October 12, 1492, Italian navigator Christopher Columbus landed in the New World. Although most other nations of the Americas observe this holiday on October 12, in the US it takes place on the second Monday in October. *Veterans Day*: Originally called Armistice Day, this holiday was established to honor Americans who had served in World War I. It falls on November 11, the day when that war ended in 1918, but it now honors veterans of all wars in which the US has fought. Veterans' organizations hold parades, and the President customarily places a wreath on the Tomb of the Unknowns at Arlington National Cemetery, across the Potomac River from Washington, D.C.

In addition to the federal holidays, *Loyalty Day* is observed on May 1. Although a legal holiday, it is not a federal holiday. It is set aside for the reaffirmation of loyalty to the US and for the recognition of the heritage of American freedom. The holiday was first observed in 1921 as "Americanization Day" and was intended to counterbalance the celebration of May Day on May 1, an internationally celebrated holiday which was perceived as Communist. Loyalty Day is celebrated with parades and ceremonies in some communities, although many people remain unaware of it. The flag is displayed on all government buildings. May Day commemorates the fight for the eight-hour workday and in particular the Haymarket affair, which occurred in 1886 during a three-day general strike in Chicago. Following an incident in which police opened fire and killed four strikers, a rally was called for the following day at Haymarket Square. The event remained peaceful, yet towards the end, as police moved in to disperse the crowd, an unknown assailant threw a bomb into the police ranks. The bomb and the resulting police response left at least a dozen people dead, including eight policemen. The ensuing trial led to the public hanging of four anarchists, a source of outrage around the globe. The Haymarket Martyrs' Monument in nearby Forest Park was listed on the National Register of Historic Places and as a National Historic Landmark in 1997.

Other celebrations

While not holidays, two other days of the year inspire colorful celebrations in the US. On February 14, Valentine's Day (named after an early Christian martyr) Americans give presents, usually candy or flowers, to the ones they love. On October 31, Halloween (the evening before All Saints or All Hallows Day), American children dress up in funny or scary costumes such as witches, make lanterns out of pumpkins, and go "trick or treating": knocking on doors in their neighborhood. The neighbors are expected to respond by giving them small gifts of candy or money. Adults may also dress in costume for Halloween parties.

Various ethnic groups in America celebrate days with special meaning to them even though these are not national holidays. Jews, for example, observe their high holy days in September, and most employers show consideration by allowing them to take these days off. Irish Americans celebrate the old country's patron saint, St. Patrick, on March 17. This is a high-spirited day on which many Americans wear green clothing in honor of the "Emerald Isle." The celebration of Mardi Gras - the day before the Christian season of Lent begins in late winter - is a big occasion in New Orleans, Louisiana, where huge parades and wild revels take place. Its French name "Mardi Gras" means "Fat Tuesday," and refers to the last day of hearty eating before the penitential season of Lent. The tradition goes back to the city's settlement by French immigrants. There are many other such ethnic celebrations, and New York City is particularly rich in them.

Vacations

Americans get the least annual paid vacation of any developed country. In sharp contrast with

Europeans, for example, Americans mostly get only 10 days (two weeks) each year. They typically have to work five years for a firm to get a third week. The average is 16 days. In addition, they get 10 "federal" one-day holidays. Most of these were moved to Mondays by President Nixon to give people and businesses a three-day weekend in most months. The most common times of year to vacation are the summer or during the Christmas-New Year period.

Vacations in another part of the US are most popular, because there are so many and varied places to visit, and they are cheaper than going abroad. Vacationers, especially families, almost always travel by car, either their own or a rental one, since this is the cheapest and most convenient. It is easy to travel at a steady speed of 50-55 miles (80-88 km) per hour on an interstate highway, stopping for meals or overnight at one of the many roadside motels. Foreign travel is now routine for more Americans, although air travel fell substantially immediately after 9/11. About 20% of Americans hold passports. Canada, Mexico and Britain are the most popular foreign destinations.

National parks (see also Chapter 1)

The early National Parks were created out of the sites of former battlefields or from areas of remote wilderness. The National Parks Service was created in 1916. National Parks now include much of America's natural scenery, Wilderness Areas and Historic Monuments. For most Americans, the combination of car ownership and wilderness which is easily accessible has proved irresistible.

Amusement parks and theme parks

Amusement parks consist of rides and other entertainments for fairly large groups of people. Because amusement parks cater to adults, teenagers, and small children, these parks are more elaborate than city parks or playgrounds. The growth of amusement parks reflects the growth of a mass population in certain cities, and the arrival of immigrants from countries where such parks were popular. Alternatively, a *theme park* will have various "lands" (sections) devoted to telling a particular story. Central Florida, most notably Orlando, boasts more theme parks than any other destination in the world while the northeastern region, most notably Pennsylvania, hosts a slew of traditional amusement parks. Of theme parks, the most famous is Walt Disney World Resort at Orlando, Florida, still the largest theme park and resort complex in the world, which opened in 1971. It has a sister branch at Anaheim, near Los Angeles, California. The theme park operators keep visitors happy with a fantastic range of rides and shows and plentiful places to eat and shop. Disneyland pulled 12.7 million visitors in 2002, and the top 50 theme parks 170 million. Other theme parks include Knott's Berry Farm and the *Six Flags* parks.

Perhaps the most interesting evolution of an attraction into a fully-fledged theme park is that of *Universal Studios Hollywood*. Originally just a backlot tram ride tour of the actual studios, the ride, which started in 1964, slowly evolved into a larger attraction, adding a western stunt show in 1967, "The Parting of the Red Sea" in 1973, a look at props from the movie *Jaws* in 1975, and the "Conan the Barbarian" show in 1984. By 1985, the modern era of the *Universal Studios Hollywood* theme park began with the "King Kong" ride and, in 1990, *Universal Studios Florida* in Orlando opened. *Universal Studios* is now the second-largest theme park company in the world, rivaled in size only by Disney.

So enormous is the range of choice that planning a vacation can be an absorbing winter pastime for the whole family, poring through guidebooks, studying maps and leafing through the sheaves of free leaflets and brochures available from local tourist bureaus, hotel chains and the National Parks Service. Increasingly, whole holiday packages including flight, accommodation and entrance tickets are bought by credit card over the internet.

FOOD

While everyone knows about the American love of steak "n" fries, turkey dinners, and fast food such as fried chicken and hamburgers, America also offers a variety of foods characteristic of its many different traditions and regions. Turkey, served with cranberry sauce made from a small, red, sour berry also native to America, is the classic American dish. (The turkey is an American bird.) Corn is another American classic food and is served in a number of ways. Corn itself can be eaten hot with butter as *corn on the cob*. As well as being baked into corn bread, it can be dried and cooked with oil to make popcorn, which can either be eaten hot, covered with melted butter and salt, or cold straight from the packet. In the South, corn can be roughly ground and boiled in water or milk to make grits, which is often eaten for breakfast. American sandwiches, eaten with mustard and relishes and accompanied by salad, can be magnificent creations composed of several layers and served on a huge variety of breads.

Since the 1980s there has been more interest in food. *Foodies* have promoted a greater variety of dishes and ingredients. Olive oil is now commonly used in cooking, while new sauces have been developed for pasta. Many styles of real coffee have become popular. Even so, Americans rarely cook from raw ingredients. They prefer to heat up pre-prepared meals or bake cakes from cake mixes bought in boxes from stores. They also commonly order in i.e., have a meal delivered to their home by a restaurant.

Southern food

Southern food is characterized by locally grown vegetables, pork, and varying uses of corn. Commonly, vegetables are cooked with meat flavoring, often pork. Cornbread is one Southern favorite which accompanies any main course. Other favorites are various greens, fried chicken, brunswick stew (chicken with cayenne pepper, tomatoes and onions), and calabash-style (for instance, fish and cornmeal pancakes). Another favorite in the South is barbecue. Unlike Southwestern style, barbecue in the South stresses the use of pork, and relies on a flavored sauce composed mainly of vinegar which is thinner and more acidic.

Southwestern cuisine

Southwestern cuisine, influenced by Mexican food, often relies on indigenous ingredients. Common flavors include chilies (green, cayenne, and bell peppers). Of all the regions in the US, the southwest boasts the spiciest food. Tortillas (thin round Mexican bread made from maize flour and eggs) are a staple in many Southwestern foods. All can be made at various levels of heat by altering the amount and types of chilies used. Some Southwest favorites are enchiladas (a thin pancake, filled with meat and covered with a very spicy sauce and topping), tacos (hard, folded tortilla), burritos (a folded tortilla with meat, beans and cheese). A particular favorite is barbecue and chili, a hearty combination of beans and meat in a spicy sauce. Unlike its cousin in the south, southwestern barbecue features beef cooked in a thicker, sweeter, smokier sauce.

The Northeast

Northeastern cuisine retains elements from colonial days. One such is maple syrup, a sweetener introduced to the colonials by the native Indians. Today it is one of the few foods produced exclusively in New England. Another New England staple is apples. Literally dozens of varieties grow in the Northeast and one will find them in both sweet and savory dishes. Chowders, thick soups which were often economical dishes which could feed several people with minimal effort and ingredients, are one of the dishes unique to the Northeast. The most famous chowder, perhaps, is clam chowder, but there are many other varieties. Berries (blueberries, strawberries, and cranberries) grow abundantly in the Northeast and they are often found in *cobblers*, a pastry and fruit dessert, which is said to resemble the cobblestone streets of colonial New England.

The Northwest

Northwest cuisine is harder to characterize because of its relative youth in culinary terms. Its influences are its location and the foods which are found naturally in the area. One new trend in Northwest food is smoking with Alder wood, which gives the food a unique flavor. The Northwest is undoubtedly famous for its seafood: specifically Dungeness crab (a small Pacific coast crab) and salmon. Both can be used in a variety of ways. Salmon can smoked, baked, broiled, or poached with success. The crabs can be used in salads, boiled or steamed. The Northwest, specifically Washington state, is also famous for cherries and apples. Cherries can not only be used in sweet dishes, but also in savory dishes as a sauce that accompanies meat. The cool climate is perfect for growing these fruits. Both fruits are quite versatile and prove to be profitable crops for Northwest farmers.

The Midwest

Midwestern food is perhaps the most eclectic cuisine of all the regional cuisines in the US, perhaps because the Midwest has been influenced by a more diverse group of people than any other region in America. It can aptly be described as a culinary melting pot, influenced by Eastern Europeans, Western Europeans, and Native Americans. Because the Midwest is home to many farms, "family style" dishes are not uncommon. Dishes that please varying tastes and require everyday ingredients are commonly found on Midwest tables. The foods served in Midwest homes often depend on what is grown on the family farm. Vegetables, fresh or pickled, accompany beef, the meat of choice. Other side dishes showcase some of the Midwest's more famous products including potatoes, cheese, and corn.

Eating out in fancy restaurants is not a great part of the American way of life, although the country's cities offer an abundance of fine dining. But Americans often go to burger bars and pizzerias, and to ethnic restaurants such as Italian, Mexican and Chinese. (Ethnic food is not always the same in the US as in the country it comes from.) Restaurant food is varied and inexpensive and provides a quick lunch "on the go" or a relaxing end to a busy day.

Drink

The most famous American contribution to alcohol culture is the cocktail party. The derivation of *cocktail* is not certainly known, but the term now applies to almost any mixed drink containing alcohol. Bourbon whiskey, known worldwide through such famous brands as *Jack Daniels* Tennessee whiskey, is a distinctive product of the US based on corn. Mint julep, made with bourbon, is found in the South, and bourbon and water is sometimes nostalgically called "bourbon and branch": branch was originally clear water from a side stream. A champagne toast is a tradition at every wedding. Americans expect bars to serve ice, generally prefer to put ice in spirits and fruit juices, and have taken to drinking wine chilled. Although Prohibition, when alcohol was banned, ended in 1933, some Americans have reservations about drinking alcohol, for religious, social or health reasons, and either abstain or drink only moderately. The amount of alcohol served at a business function, if any, is rather less than would be usual in some countries, and drinking parties where business people and their clients go in order to get drunk together are unknown. It is a breach of etiquette in America to pressure a person to drink any or more alcohol, if (s)he declines.

Dieting

Americans' obsession with thinness and good health continues to grow. Over half (52%) of consumers Gallup polled in 1998 said they had dieted or were currently dieting. Among dieters, the primary reason to go on a diet was to lose weight (46%), followed by the desire to obtain general good health (16%) and to improve self-esteem (11%). Women tend to diet more often than men; and adults 35 years of age or older are more likely to report being on a diet than adults 18 to 34. While 52 percent of those polled were looking for ways to lose weight, consumers were split on the primary cause of obesity. About as many believed overeating was the cause (35%) as cited lack of exercise (33%). Only 1 percent said it was both. In addition, only 14 percent believed poor nutrition was the cause of obesity. Eighty-six percent of dieters correctly agree that a diet based on grains, fruits and vegetables, is the basis of a healthful eating plan. When dieting, dieters report that they cut back on certain foods, primarily sweets, fats and grains. Unfortunately consumers apparently do not recognize that grain foods are low in fat and calories and provide energy.

With the hope of quick, easy weight loss, Americans spend some $30 billion a year on weight loss, some on diet plans and gimmicks that do not work, according to the American Dietetic Association. Americans are also keen to try the latest foods that are recommended for weight loss, such as olive oil, oats and garlic, and may also take vitamins and mineral supplements. Meanwhile many Americans eat junk food, fast food, snacks such as potato chips, cookies, fizzy drinks and ice cream, and many are overweight from childhood. The contradiction between what people know is healthy to eat and what they actually eat may reflect Americans' pressured lifestyles and their tendency to undisciplined gratification.

Shopping

From the neighborhood store to Wal-Mart, farmers' markets and eBay, shopping is for Americans often as much an experience as a chore. The US has more shopping malls (45,000) than high schools, and the number is increasing each year. Historian James Farrell claims that shopping defines American culture because a mall is the perfect environment for social interaction, aesthetic appreciation and the equality of consumerism. Yet malls are often ugly outside, poorly mapped and short of carts, a scene of self-criticism as well as sales, whose promise of happiness at a low price is largely illusory.

HUMOR

To have a sense of humor and the ability to laugh at oneself are considered essential by most Americans, and America has produced several characteristic genres of humor, many of them derived from ethnic communities, such as Jewish humor. Much of American humor is based on stereotypes, especially those involving groups of people who are believed to be stupid, such as the Poles, or blondes. With the coming of political correctness in the '80s these types of humor have become less common, at least in public, in case they give offense, but it is acceptable for comedians to make fun of their own minority group's customs and attitudes. Jokes are often told at the start of speeches, or on social occasions to break the ice. Lawyer jokes and light bulb jokes, where someone asks how many people of a certain group it takes to change a light bulb, are popular. Light bulb jokes make fun of the worst characteristics of any group of people by suggesting the mistakes they would make in trying to change a light bulb.

Q: How many Marxists does it take to screw in a light bulb?
A: None: The light bulb contains the seeds of its own revolution.

Comic books, small magazines containing a narrative in words and pictures that may or may not be humorous, originated in the US, which still produces the most. *Superman* was also made into a successful movie starring Christopher Reeve. Superheroes like *Daredevil*, *The Hulk* and *The Incredibles* became more popular with the success of feature films such as *X-Men* (2000) and *Spider-Man* (2002). These pull in hefty revenues, aided by advanced computer-generated imagery that makes the heroes look as good as they do on the comic page.

Comic strips and cartoons

Comic strips and cartoons, in newspapers and films, on TV and the internet are perennially popular. Among the best-loved are *Tom and Jerry*, *Peanuts*, and *The Simpsons*. *Tom and Jerry* follows a set format: cat chases mouse, mouse outsmarts cat, cat is punished. The *Peanuts* strip was even listed in the *Guinness Book of World Records* as appearing in more newspapers than any other. Over 40 cartoon films of the Peanuts gang, made-for-television or straight-to-video, were made from the 1960s onwards. The most famous were those where the story was set on major holidays as in *A Charlie Brown Christmas* and *It's the Great Pumpkin, Charlie Brown*. A series of cartoons inspired a hugely popular 1960s TV series, *The Addams Family*.

CHAPTER **11**

CULTURAL DEBATES, SOCIAL PROBLEMS AND SOLUTIONS

Cultural Values

We are free to imagine our country any way we like, but we are not free to deny that it is our country.
Todd Gitlin

America is too varied a place, with a history made up of too many strands, for anyone realistically to set out a one-size-fits-all account of core American values. The values which have most often been held to characterize American culture are those propagated and promoted by those who have possessed the lion's share of economic power, not necessarily the majority of the population. Moreover, accounts of values serve not necessarily as realistic depictions of what happened in the past, or what people believe today, but as "myths" that show to those who hold them and those who hear them how the tellers of the myth see themselves. Even so, myths are important because they say much about what people believe, hence what motivates them, what they will fight for and ultimately die for.

The mainstream American identity is expressed by five key values associated with Protestant Christianity and with the individualism of the English philosopher, John Locke. These are: individual freedom, self-reliance, equality of opportunity, hard work, and material success. The celebrated sociologist, Max Weber, argued that the beliefs of the early Protestant sects played a key role in the establishment of the "spirit" or culture of capitalism, and thereby contributed to the development of the American economic system. Many of the early Protestants subscribed to Calvin's doctrine of predestination, which maintained that the believer's eternal salvation or damnation was determined at birth and that no amount of good works could alter God's decision. This placed a tremendous psychological burden on believers, who had no way of knowing whether they numbered among the Elect, those who achieved eternal salvation in the life hereafter. The practical solution offered by Protestantism lay in the notion of *vocation*, by which the believer was instructed to work long and hard in a vocation to attest his or her confidence that election was assured. Later, the doctrine was relaxed so that systematic labor in a vocation and the material prosperity that accompanied it came to be seen as a sign of election. These beliefs, and the related restrictions on consumption and indulgence, promoted goal-oriented economic activity and facilitated capital formation. Until the middle of the 20th century, Weber's thesis was truest in New England and the northeast; half-true in Appalachia and the middle South, where there were plenty of hard-line Protestants but very little capitalism or progress; partly true but increasingly diluted in much of the rest of the country; and not at all true in the lowland South, where few people ever had anything to do with Calvinism or capitalism, least of all in Louisiana, with its chief city, New Orleans, where the dominant culture was a lax, latitudinarian Catholicism.

The 17th-century English philosophers Thomas Hobbes and John Locke put forward the concept of *possessive individualism*. This meant that the essence of an individual consisted of ownership over his or her own person: people were free insofar as they existed independently of others' wills. Those who were economically dependent on others were therefore not free. An unceasing struggle for hegemony raged between individuals, and the market was the battlefield. Social relations were seen as market relations among proprietors of various selves. The struggle of owners for dominance was said to be the natural condition of man. To safeguard that natural striving, and especially to ensure the security of its outcome, government was instituted. Protection of individually accumulated capital was the fundamental function of government, a function said to be required not by common decision but by the very nature of man.

Under possessive individualism, possession and possessing make the person and make the person free: "I own, therefore I am." Such a person cannot imagine existence apart from possession or the striving after it. Because ownership is the core of the self, the person is not him- or herself but what he or she owns. She is, in a sense, alienated from, without ever having been joined with, herself. As Tönnies wrote: "So far as possible he conducts himself toward others as a merchant and toward himself as a hedonist, but dislikes to go about unmasked."

These values have been given political form through popular sovereignty and find practical expression in the Constitution. The success of the American political experiment is that it has created a set of positive values that have served as the basis for national identity while also being accessible to people who are not white and Christian or in some way related through blood and soil to the Anglo-Saxon Protestant Founders of the country.

In a well-known book, *Albion's Seed,* David Hackett Fischer argues that although less than 20% of the present US population has British antecedents, the British origins of America are still the dominant factor determining its culture. This formative British culture, however, was not monolithic. America still reflects the regional, religious, and class divisions of 17th- and 18th-century Britain. According to Fischer, the foundation of American culture was formed from four mass emigrations from four different regions of Britain by four different socio-religious groups. New England's formative period occurred between 1629 and 1640 when Puritans, mostly from East Anglia, settled there. The next mass migration was of southern English cavaliers and their servants to the Chesapeake Bay region between 1640 and 1675. Then, between 1675 and 1725, thousands of Quakers led by William Penn settled the Delaware Valley. Finally, English, Scots, and Irish from the borderlands settled in Appalachia between 1717 and 1775. Each of these migrations produced a distinct regional culture which can still be seen in America today. Although Fischer is right about the regional and class differences of the colonists, he focuses on the economically dominant section of the colonists in each area. (The large numbers of German Anabaptists in Pennsylvania do not fit into his picture, nor do the thousands of indentured servants and slaves.)

In fact the settlers of America were 60% northern European. Some argue, therefore, that the main reason America has remained so British culturally is because the millions of German, Irish, Scandinavian, Dutch, and other European immigrants and their descendants were close enough racially to assimilate culturally. Millions of Americans who are not ethnically Anglo-Saxon are culturally Anglo-Saxon. Thus many of the country's original values and institutions remain. The open question for the future is how far these will change along with the shifting racial balance of the country, as Hispanics, Asians and Blacks come to form the majority. Much of America's popular culture, the products of the entertainment industry and the mass media, derive from heritages other than the British. In a more recent book, *Liberty and Freedom*, Fischer admits that "what made America free, and keeps it growing more so, was not any single vision of liberty and freedom but the interplay of many visions."

In today's multicultural America, where the mainstream population makes up only about 50% of the whole, traditional values are set alongside other emphases and priorities. In particular, the roles of the English language and the Christian religion are less powerful, although still dominant. Yet personal achievement and wealth still determine one's position in the American class system, where most people aspire to be, and are, middle class.

Until some time after World War II, American values were taken to be the values of the middle class "silent majority" of "Middle America" and were largely unquestioned. These values were especially concerned with personal attitudes and morality, particularly in sex and family relationships, and with traditional institutions, above all religion and democratic government. Mainstream Americans believed that family relationships should be close: couples should get married, not have sex before they did and not divorce if they could help it, and children should grow up with both parents.

Yet major changes in society have meant that these traditional values no longer reflect the way many Americans live. Only 50%-60% of Americans vote in elections, only around 40% regularly attend a place of worship, and over 40% of marriages end in divorce. Meanwhile there is no longer a consensus about sexual behavior and almost one-third of children are living in single parent families. Since the 1960s there have been three watersheds in the evolution of American values, especially people's views on personal issues. Except in the South, majority opinion in the '60s came to accept having sex before marriage and even if marriage was not on the agenda. The "sexual revolution" was in place even in Middle America by the mid-1970s. The notion that it was basically a phenomenon of the Pacific and Northeast coastal areas – California and New York City were usually singled out in political rhetoric – only began to gain currency in the Reagan reaction of the 1980s (the second watershed in the evolution of the values debate). It is notable that the Reagan Administration did not push socially conservative policies. In response, around 1990, substantial numbers of right-wing Protestants, and a few right-wing Catholics, mounted an angry revolt and seized control of the Republican party. The "Moral Majority" campaign of Jerry Falwell was part of that revolt. A narrative of how it happened can be found in *What's the Matter with Kansas?*, by Thomas Frank (2004). This revolt was the third watershed in the debate. In it, conservatives deliberately polarized American society in the hope of achieving an absolute victory for conservative morality. Their attempt failed. One reason was the extremism of the movement, which alarmed and alienated even many Republicans.

As a society, therefore, America is facing major decisions about its future and can be said to be at a crossroads. The American identity, and the history through which it is taught, are coming under penetrating scrutiny and challenge. There is now a trend to highlight the drama inherent in history by presenting different viewpoints and stressing that history is an ongoing process, not merely a collection of often misleading factoids. American history writing is increasingly laying stress on illuminating the interplay of race, gender, and social class rather than the study of heroes and acts of government, a tendency that is disturbing to conservative Americans.

The effects of immigration and multiculturalism are of concern to many Americans, because they seem to have the potential to weaken social bonds, traditional institutions and even national unity. The dilemmas these issues present are argued about from many conflicting points of view. The events of September 11, 2001 brought a renewal of American unity. But already there are signs that this revival is ending because of the Bush Administration's controversial foreign and domestic policies, even though Americans are now facing unprecedented challenges to their security.

Traditionally-minded Americans, such as Harvard professor Samuel P. Huntington (1927-2008), author of *Who Are We? The Challenges to America's National Identity* (2004) argue that America, at heart, has been, and in many ways should remain, a Christian, Anglocentric country. America, he asserts, was founded by British settlers who brought with them a distinct culture including the English language, Protestant values, individualism, religious commitment, hard work and respect for law. Huntington sought to prove that this American creed was the Founders' original intent. The waves of immigrants that later came to the US gradually accepted these values and assimilated into America's Anglo-Protestant culture. More recently, however, national identity has been eroded by the problems of assimilating massive numbers of primarily Hispanic immigrants. Huntington argues that growing class divisions will lead to internal fissures. He also points out that how Americans define themselves determines the US role in the world – national, imperial, cosmopolitan.

Huntington's book begins by putting America's national identity crisis in the context of the collision of ethnicities brought on by higher levels of economic interaction, revolutions in communication and transportation, and increased waves of immigration. *Who Are We?* asks whether recent Mexican immigrants, who are entering the US in record numbers, can adopt America's core identity, characterized by the values planted by America's original English Protestant settlers. The question only takes up one chapter of the book, but is the one that has stirred by far the greatest controversy. To emphasize the importance of core values, Huntington asks a simple question: "Would America be the country it has been if it were settled by French, Spanish, or Portuguese Catholics? No, it would be French Canada, Mexico, or Brazil," he asserts.

Asking "who are we?" is bound to be controversial, if only because so many "I's" make up the collective "we," and each has a stake in defining the group to which he or she belongs. Huntington's definition of America's national identity has been sharply questioned. Some, quoting Max Weber, assert that ethnic identity is "a *subjective* belief in common descent or common origins." These critics maintain that the notion of national identity is normative, not descriptive. It is always a matter of "imagined selves," of what we want to be. In addition, it is pointed out that identities are socially constructed, often in the midst of conflict, to establish lines between insiders and strangers. Identities are dynamic, not static, and subject to contestation between majorities and minorities. Notions of Americanism (as opposed to allegiances to individual states) actually became popular only after the Civil War, while conflict over values abounded even in the early colonial period. Roger Williams, for example, broke with the New England Puritans and went south to found the Rhode Island colony, asserting that atheists, Jews, Muslims, and other non-Christians should not be considered outsiders. Huntington's assertions about the current wave of Latin American (and particularly Mexican) immigration have sparked numerous impassioned responses. From the anthropological point of view, it has been suggested that the phrase *core identity* be replaced by that of the *crossroads*. The notion of a core has the virtues of clarity and simplicity, but the historical and ethnographic record suggests that culture is a crossroads or even a borderland. Even so, Americans see their country as uniquely constituted by the Constitution, which guarantees that, as citizens, they have certain rights.

Disputes over 'rights'

The concept of rights and the role of government are contested between conservatives and liberals, Republicans and Democrats. Under the conservative negative concept of rights, the government must refrain from infringing them. To the contrary, under a liberal positive rights concept, the government must do more to provide individual entitlements, particularly better economic conditions. Civil and political rights (CP rights) are seen as negative because they simply limit government action. As a result, CP rights are thought of by conservatives as "free." By contrast, economic, social and cultural (ESC) rights are seen by conservatives as costly, entailing massive state-provided welfare, while liberals maintain they are nonetheless essential. The implementation of rights is also seen as problematic by some. CP rights are widely seen as capable of, and requiring, immediate application, while ESC rights may be progressively realized, although for many the progress tends to take too long. Similarly, the constitutional provisions related to CP rights are thought to be precise enough for ready application, while ESC provisions have been seen as vague and unenforceable. Thus ESC rights are not seen as rights by conservatives but as "goals" or "aspirations." But liberals argue that the meaningful exercise of political freedoms is impossible if minimum economic needs are not met; and the right to participate in government is limited, if not nonexistent, for a starving, homeless person. This latter view is also beginning to be espoused, as polls by John Zogby have revealed, by political Independents, who are members neither of the Republican nor the Democrat parties, and who were previously perceived as conservative on social issues. Before the Obama administration, the US saw ESC rights as mere aspirations to be met someday in the distant future when they are feasible i.e., affordable without raising taxes or cutting benefits to more politically powerful constituencies. It is predicted that the Obama Administration will take a more liberal attitude to progressing ESC rights.

Influential ideas

Alongside the philosophy, religion and cultural practices which stem from the Judeo-Christian tradition largely brought from the British Isles, a body of quite different ideas and attitudes which have become widely influential has grown up. These were most powerfully articulated by the German philosopher Friedrich Nietzsche (1844-1900). Nietzsche's influence so pervades modern American culture that many who have never read him are influenced by his thought indirectly. The following beliefs are all traceable at least in part to Nietzsche, although many of them are much simpler than similar ideas held by him.

COMMON BELIEFS IN MODERN AMERICAN CULTURE

- The goal of life should be to find yourself. True maturity means discovering or creating an identity for yourself.
- The highest virtue is to be true to yourself. (Consider these song titles from a generation ago: "I Gotta Be Me," "I Did It My Way.")
- When you fall ill, your body is trying to tell you something; listen to the wisdom of your body.

- People who hate their bodies or are in tension with them need to learn how to accept and integrate their physical selves with their minds instead of seeing them as in tension with each other. The mind and body make up a single whole.
- Athletes, musicians, etc., especially need to become so attuned to their bodies that their skills proceed spontaneously from the knowledge stored in their muscles and are not frustrated by an excess of conscious rational thought. (The influence of Zen Buddhism on this sort of thinking is very strong.)
- Sexuality is not the opposite of virtue, but a natural gift that needs to be developed and integrated into a healthy, rounded life.
- Many people suffer from impaired self-esteem; they need to work on being proud of themselves.
- Knowledge and strength are greater virtues than humility and submission.
- Overcoming feelings of guilt is an important step to mental health.
- You cannot love someone else if you do not love yourself.
- Life is short; experience it as intensely as you can or it is wasted.
- People's values are shaped by the cultures they live in; as society changes we need changed values.
- Challenge yourself; do not live passively.

It is notable that none of these ideas flows from the traditional Judeo-Christian culture which dominated Europe for a thousand years and has only recently started to lose its dominance of American culture. Many of them have their roots in Romanticism, with Nietzsche merely articulating impulses that others shared. Thus before considering the non-Christian cultures brought to America by recent immigrants, it is advisable to study the changes brought about in the previously dominant culture by Romanticism and philosophers such as Nietzsche.

Americans' views on the country's place in history

How Americans define their identity determines what role they wish their country to play in the world. But America has not really had a unified vision of itself since the Civil War because the slaveholding South refused to accept defeat, keeping black Americans in a condition as close to slavery as possible for another century and continuing even now to try to hinder blacks from voting and to keep them at every kind of disadvantage. Other rifts have opened up too, especially between the "robber barons" of the so-called Gilded Age of the late 19th and early 20th centuries and the rest of the country, a rift that has opened up again in recent decades. A 2006 analysis of Internal Revenue Service income data by economists Emmanuel Saez at the University of California, Berkeley and Thomas Piketty at the Paris School of Economics showed that the share of income held by the top 1% was as large in 2005 as in 1928. Americans are now acutely aware of those divisions because since about 1980 the Republican Party has included an open alliance between those who accept economic inequality and those who believe in racial inequality. This has all but drowned out the voices of traditional conservatives. But a majority of Americans explicitly rejected that stance in the 2008 election, so that it can be said there are many Americans who do have a unified vision of the country after all. These include many independent voters and the moderate Republicans who voted for Obama.

Today, the unabashed boosterism of America the beautifully harmonious by Commager and the likeminded historians of traditional textbooks is regularly rejected by a new generation of historians who see America's national destiny not so much in consensus as in diversity. Instead of a melting pot, they say, the country functions best as a loose-knit confederacy of independent subcultures with little in common and nothing to be gained from working together. But is the idea of a permanently divided society viable? Will this more radical path lead not to an ethnocentric Eden of equal but totally unlike parts, but instead to the tribalistic bickerings of a New World Balkans? Diversity-within-unity remains both an ideal and an issue.

Public opinion on key issues

Despite the high visibility of cultural issues, there is evidence to suggest that they do not actually amount to "culture wars." In 2006 the Pew Research Center released the findings of a survey of public attitudes on hot-button issues. Its conclusion, broadly, was that describing debates in America over such issues as abortion, gay marriage and stem cell research as "culture wars" may be overblown. There has, according to these results, been no polarization of the public into liberal and conservative camps. Instead, the survey showed that, although the "culture war" issues are divisive, and the country is split fairly evenly on nearly all of them (stem cell research, which had broad support, was the exception), there are not two stark ideological camps. The study looked at five prominent social issues—abortion rights, stem cell research, gay marriage, adoption of children by gay couples, and availability of the "morning-after" pill. Only 12% of poll respondents took the conservative position on all five issues, while 22% took a liberal approach to all five. The reasons (not explored in the Pew research) for the fierce rejection of these options by some religious people may be a reaction to women's equality and a fear of being outnumbered if other groups reproduce faster.

The public's point of view varies from issue to issue, the survey found. They are conservative in opposing gay marriage and gay adoption, liberal in favoring embryonic stem cell research and a little of both on abortion. Along with favoring no clear ideological approach to most social issues, the public expresses a desire for a middle ground on the most divisive social concern of the day: abortion. Indeed, public opinion has moved little on these issues in recent years and continues to be mixed and often inconsistent, reflecting a blend of pragmatism and principle. For instance, a clear majority (56%) continues to oppose allowing gays and lesbians to marry while 35% express support. But nearly as large a majority (54%) supports allowing homosexual couples to enter into legal agreements that would give them many of the same rights as married couples. The survey also found that 55% would prefer abortion laws to be decided at the national level rather than each state deciding for itself. This preference extends to other social issues. Despite growing antipathy toward Congress and low levels of trust in the federal government generally, majorities or pluralities favor a national rather than state-by-state approach to policymaking on stem cell research, gay marriage and whether creationism should be taught in the schools along with evolution.

Abortion continues to split the country nearly down the middle and on occasion hits the headlines when anti-abortion fanatics target abortion clinics and threaten violence against their staff. But there is consensus in one key area: two out of three Americans (66%) support finding "a middle ground" when it comes to abortion. Only three in ten (29%), by contrast, believe "there's no room for compromise when it comes to abortion laws." This desire to find common ground extends broadly across the political and ideological spectrum. Majorities of Republicans (62%), Democrats (70%) and political independents (66%) favor a compromise. So do majorities of liberals, moderates and conservatives. More than six in ten white evangelicals also support compromise, as do 62% of white, non-Hispanic Catholics. Only one group surveyed expressed unwillingness to find a middle way: two-thirds (66%) of those who support an outright ban on abortion say there should be no compromise. In contrast, two-thirds of those who want abortion to be generally available are ready to seek an accommodation.

Public opinion about abortion law is largely unchanged from previous polling. While about one in three (31%) prefer that abortion be generally available to those who want it and one in ten (11%) take the opposite position that abortion should not be permitted at all, most Americans fall in between, preferring what might be described as a "legal but rare" stance. One in five (20%) say that abortion should be available but under stricter limits than it is now, while about one in three (35%) say that abortion should be illegal except in cases of rape, incest or to save the woman's life.

Just as opinions about abortion in general are largely stable, so too are differences of opinion on the issue across demographic, political and religious groups. As polls have often shown, there is no gender gap in opinion about the availability of abortion. College graduates and people in their 50s and early 60s, roughly the first half of the Baby Boom generation, are more supportive of making abortion generally available than are other demographic groups. As in the past, among conservative Republicans, about two-thirds say that abortion should only be available in cases of rape or incest, 50% would permit it when the mother's life is threatened, and 18% would not permit it at all. Many liberal Democrats, by contrast, say abortion either should be generally available (60%) or available but with stricter limits (14%). White evangelicals and black Protestants stand out for their high levels of opposition to abortion. Among seculars and those who rarely attend church, on the other hand, majorities say that abortion should be generally available. A large majority of the public (73%) continues to view abortion as morally wrong in at least some circumstances, while only 24% say that abortion is not a moral issue. But slightly fewer now say that abortion is morally wrong in nearly all circumstances (24% compared with 29% in 2005).

Abortion remains a political hotspot partly because the issue was decided by the Supreme Court, in *Roe v. Wade* 1973, rather than by Congress. Opposition to abortion unites Catholics and evangelical Protestants. "More than any other single cause," says Stephen Bates, "it has been responsible for the mobilization of religious activism in US politics" *op. cit.*, p. 288. The vehement unsettled argument over abortion expresses the moral protest of a significant, though possibly declining, number of Americans about the trend of society away from a broad, fairly restrictive Protestant consensus towards a pluralistic, multicultural, multifaith society. What the court decided, and what Chief Justice Roberts said in his confirmation testimony in 2005, is that a woman's decision to have an abortion is a private one, and hence constitutionally protected. Roberts also made it clear that after more than thirty years he considered the constitutional issue settled, although he himself as a Catholic was in conscience opposed to abortion. Religious activists, however, claim that the freedom to have an abortion is likely to encourage women to choose that option and that the availability of abortion promotes promiscuity and weakens the family. Ironically, there are those who champion limited government in respect of their own lives at the same time as wanting it to regulate the most intimate details of other people's.

An unrefined supply-and-demand argument is used to generate simplistic emotive responses to a many-sided social and moral issue. Liberals retort that the desire to return to social controls over procreation is based on an idealized vision of the family that was never the norm, an attempt to reintroduce male dominance, and in any case is inappropriate to modern life. Older people, who may remember when hundreds of women a year died after illegal abortions, and backstreet abortions were the prime killer of pregnant women, are the group most in favor of abortion rights.

Although abortion is generally available in most states, access to pregnancy advice is not. Six out of seven counties nationwide have no government-funded pregnancy advice center. Meanwhile there are 4,000 crisis pregnancy centers run by pro-life groups that try to persuade women who visit them not to have an abortion. In 2003, President Bush signed an act outlawing partial birth abortions, and in 2004 the Unborn Victims Act, under which a criminal who murders a pregnant woman is also liable for the death of her unborn baby. In fact only 1.4% of abortions are carried out after 21 weeks (21,000) and the number carried out after 26 weeks is about 30 a year. The operations are either performed to save the life of the mother, or because the fetus would not survive.

Abortion statistics may be incomplete because of the unknown number of illegal abortions. A total of over 49 million legal and illegal abortions has been claimed by the Alan Guttmacher Institute for the years since *Roe v. Wade*. Best estimates suggest that about 1.2 million abortions currently take place each year, and one-third of women under 45 have had an abortion. Half of all pregnancies are unplanned and of those half are terminated, although the number has declined over the last decade, probably because of emergency contraception, not because of preaching, protest or propaganda.

A majority of Americans continue to back stem cell research, but public awareness of the issue has not increased recently. Stem cells taken from frozen, five-day-old embryos are so-called because they can be used to develop virtually any other kind of cell in the human body. Scientists want to use them to cultivate specialized cells that could be used to prevent or treat hitherto incurable diseases such as cancers, diabetes and Parkinson's. Stem cells are much more useful than cells taken from fetuses or adults because adult stem cells have developed specialized functions. Since individual embryonic stem cells were first isolated in 1998, their use has been fiercely debated because the Religious Right claim that the cells have the ability to develop into human beings but will not have that opportunity, since they are destroyed in experimentation. In fact they are obtained from fertility clinics which would have discarded them anyway. Federal funding for embryonic stem cell research was controversially banned by President Bush in 2001 but restored by President Obama in 2009.

A clear majority of Americans (56%) say it is more important to continue stem cell research that might produce new medical cures than to avoid destroying the human embryos used in the research. To the contrary, nearly a third (32%) say it is more important to avoid destroying the potential life of human embryos. The proportion favoring stem cell research has increased 13 percentage points, with most of those gains occurring before 2004. For the first time in Pew polling, more white evangelicals favor stem cell research (44%) than oppose it (40%).

By a 56%-35% margin, the majority of Americans continue to oppose allowing gays and lesbians to marry. These figures are largely unchanged over the past several years. Opposition to gay marriage is most pronounced among older Americans, while younger people express relatively high levels of support for legalizing same-sex marriage. Among those 65 and older, three in four (73%) oppose legalizing gay marriage, while more than half (53%) of adults under the age 30 do so. Republicans are relatively united in opposition to gay marriage, with 83% of conservative Republicans and 66% of moderate and liberal Republicans holding this view. The issue splits Democrats, however, with two-thirds of liberal Democrats (66%) in favor of gay marriage and

59% of conservative and moderate Democrats opposed. Independents are evenly divided (46% in favor, 45% opposed). Opinions on this issue are also closely related to religion. White evangelical Protestants (78%) and black Protestants (74%) overwhelmingly oppose gay marriage, as do a majority of white Catholics (58%) and a plurality of white mainline Protestants (47%). Only among seculars does a majority (63%) express support for gay marriage. But while a majority opposes gay marriage, opponents are divided on whether it would be a good idea to amend the Constitution to ban it. The result is that just three in ten Americans (30%) currently oppose gay marriage and think a constitutional amendment would be a good idea. Even among groups most strongly opposed to gay marriage (white evangelicals, Republicans, conservatives and senior citizens) less than a majority favor an amendment.

While only one in three Americans (35%) favor gay marriage, majorities do express support for civil unions. The poll found that 54% of Americans favor allowing gay and lesbian couples to enter into legal agreements giving them many of the same rights as married couples. This figure is nine percentage points higher than it was in October 2003. Evidence of the continuing red state (Republican)/blue state (Democrat) divide can be seen on this question. In the East and West, large majorities (62% and 66% respectively) favor civil unions. In the Midwest and South, by contrast, roughly half (48% and 50% respectively) oppose even this type of legal recognition of same-sex couples. As with gay marriage, white evangelicals (66%), black Protestants (62%) and frequent church attenders (60%) stand out for their opposition to civil unions. But sizeable majorities of white mainline Protestants (66%), Catholics (63%) and seculars (78%) support civil unions.

Despite majority support for civil unions, one such right that the public is not ready to extend to gay people is that of adopting children. By a 52%-42% margin, a majority of the public opposes allowing gays and lesbians to adopt. Here again, the poll finds evidence of a continuing geographic divide: majorities of Midwesterners (57%) and Southerners (60%) oppose gay adoption, while majorities of those in the East (52%) and the West (51%) favor allowing gays to adopt children.

Opinions about the nature of homosexuality have changed slightly since 2003. Somewhat more Americans believe that homosexuality is innate (from 30% in 2003 to 36%) and that homosexuality cannot be changed (from 42% to 49%.). But the majority of the public still rejects the idea that homosexuality is something that people are born with, and see it instead as either a product of the way people are brought up (13%) or as "just the way that some people prefer to live" (38%).

Although the number of Americans who see homosexuality as something people are born with has increased only modestly since 2003, this view is now much more widely held among certain groups than it was previously. There has been a double-digit increase in the view that homosexuality is innate: among college graduates (from 39% to 51%), liberals (46% to 57%), mainline Protestants (37% to 52%) and among those who seldom or never attend church (36% to 52%). In contrast to these groups, majorities of white evangelicals (51%) and black Protestants (52%) continue to view homosexuality as a choice. White evangelicals, in particular, have changed very little in their views on this question over recent years.

Although most Americans reject the notion that homosexuality is innate, a plurality (49%) views sexual orientation as a characteristic that cannot be changed, a seven percentage-point increase since 2003. Views of whether homosexuality can be changed have both a political and a religious component. A small majority of conservatives (52%) say homosexuality can be changed, while the overwhelming majority of liberals (71%) disagree. Similarly, substantial majorities of white evangelicals (56%) and black Protestants (60%) say that homosexuality can be changed, while majorities of white mainline Protestants (67%), Catholics (56%) and seculars (59%) say homosexuality cannot be changed. Views of the nature of homosexuality are closely related to views of gay marriage and civil unions, with those who view homosexuality as innate and unchangeable expressing more support for these policies compared with those who see homosexuality as changeable. Among those who view homosexuality as innate, for instance, a large majority (58%) supports allowing gays and lesbians to marry legally. But among those who see homosexuality as a product of one's upbringing or as a lifestyle choice, overwhelming majorities (82% and 71% respectively) oppose gay marriage. Gay marriage is currently performed in Massachusetts, Connecticut, Iowa, Vermont, New Hampshire, New York and Washington, D.C. It is recognized in Rhode Island and Maryland.

POVERTY AND INEQUALITY

Americans are proud of their economic system, believing it provides opportunities for all citizens to have good lives. With only 4 percent of the world's population, the US's per capita consumption is 14 times greater than the low-income countries which have 40 percent of the world's population. As John Snow, former Treasury Secretary, remarked (Newsweek, September 8, 2008, p. 48) more people in the US and abroad have risen out of poverty over the last 35 years than ever before in history. The picture is clouded, however, by the persistence of poverty. The US is an unequal society, and has one of the highest poverty rates in the industrialized world. The typical low-wage worker in the US earns 44 percent less than counterparts in Europe. And the percentage of American children who are poor is twice as high as in other advanced economies. Just 60 percent of US workers receive health care coverage from their employers (although 2010 legislation aims at 100% coverage of people in work), while over half have no pension plan. A youth between the ages of 18 and 24 from the richest 20 percent of US families is more than 10 times as likely to obtain a college degree than a student from the poorest 20 percent. The private wealth of the top 1 percent of the US population amounts to more than that of the bottom 92 percent of Americans. Government anti-poverty efforts have made some progress but have not eradicated the problem. Indeed there was no serious effort to eradicate poverty by the Bush administration. Similarly, periods of strong economic growth, which bring more jobs and higher wages, have helped reduce poverty but have not eliminated it entirely.

Despite the generally prosperous American economy during the 1980s and 1990s, concerns about inequality continued. Increasing global competition threatened workers in many traditional manufacturing industries, and their wages stagnated. At the same time, the federal government edged away from tax policies that sought to favor lower-income families at the expense of wealthier ones, and it also cut spending on a number of domestic social programs intended to help the disadvantaged. Meanwhile, nearly 75 percent of all the gains from the stock market boom went to the top10 percent of the population. The gap between rich and poor can be measured in a number of ways. According to the most widely used measure, the Gini index, household income inequality remained large in the 2000s. By 2007 the US Gini index had reached 46.3. The gap between rich and poor more than doubled from 1979 to 2000, government data shows, a gulf so large that the richest 1 percent of Americans in 2000 had more money to spend after taxes than the bottom 40 percent. In 2006, income inequality in the US was comparable to that of Russia and Turkey. However, American income inequality, though still large, is rather less when the number of earners per household is considered.

By contrast with the late 1990s, when labor markets were uniquely tight, wages have remained stagnant since 2000, especially among middle- and lower-income earners; and productivity growth has not translated into higher incomes. Despite the expansion after the recession of 2000-2001, the real income of the average family fell by 3%, about $1,600, between 2000 and 2004. This decline during the initial years of expansions appears to be more the norm than the exception in recent recoveries. In both the 1980s and 1990s recoveries, it took seven years for median family income to regain their peak, far longer than in earlier cycles. Indeed, over the past generation, it is the richest families who have experienced the fastest income growth. Between 1979 and 2000, for example, the real income of households in the lowest fifth grew 6.1%; the middle fifth was up 12.3%; the top fifth grew 70%; and the average income of those in the top 1% grew by 184%. In the last recession, some 2.3 million workers lost their jobs, and 2 million their health coverage. The number of full-time workers forced into part-time jobs rose to 4.3 million.

Greater inequality has also been generated by an expansion of capital income and an increased concentration of that income among the very highest income families. Whereas the top 1% received 37.8% of all capital income in 1979, their share rose to 49.1% by 2000 and rose further to 59.4% in 2004. This shift toward greater concentration of capital income reflects an increase in the share of income flowing to corporate profits, and profit rates that in 2005 were the highest in 36 years (excepting 1997). One way that middle-income families have kept their incomes rising over the past few decades has been for women in general and wives in particular to enter the paid labor market. While this has been positive for women's economic independence, it has also put a strain on the balance between work and family.

Another important dimension of income and living standards is income-class mobility, that is, the progress families typically make in income growth over their lifetimes. This raises the question of to what extent children's economic fates are determined by the income position of their parents. Economists find significant income correlations between parents and their children, implying that income-class mobility in America is at least partially restricted by a parent's position in the income scale. In the US it would take a poor family of four with two children approximately nine to 10 generations – over 200 years – to achieve the income of the typical middle-income four-person family. The limited extent of income mobility across generations casts significant doubt on how real the American Dream can be for many Americans.

Traditionally, Americans have sought to realize the American dream of success, fame and wealth through thrift and hard work. As Matthew Warshauer points out, however, the industrialization of the 19th and 20th centuries began to erode the dream, replacing it with a philosophy of "get rich quick." A variety of seductive but elusive strategies have evolved, and today the three leading ways to instant wealth are large-prize television game shows, big-jackpot state lotteries and compensation lawsuits.

American folklore often emphasizes rags-to-riches. The stories of Horatio Alger (1834-99) suggest that anyone with daring and intelligence can lift themselves up by their bootstraps and traverse the income scale in a single generation. For generations, working class parents have told their children that when they grow up they can be anything they want to be. Of course these parents desperately want to believe this but the research shows otherwise. The reality is that very few people who began life at or near the bottom of the social ladder become wealthy. There is much less mobility than in other countries with comparably advanced economies such as Germany, a country with extensive social protections such as universal health coverage. The evidence reveals, moreover, that income mobility in the US has been either flat or diminished over the very period when inequality has been on the rise. Unequal education opportunities and historical discrimination play a role. Children from wealthy families have much greater access to top-tier universities than children from low-income families, even once innate skills are taken into account. Children from upper middle class and affluent families have enormous advantages that those from the lower end of the economic spectrum can rarely overcome. But the American Dream helps to make Americans the most productive people on earth. Why the American people cling to this myth, and what would happen if they ceased to do so are matters for speculation.

Notable in addition to the stunning disparity between productivity growth and pay growth is the tremendous widening of the gap over the last three decades between those at the top of the wage scale, particularly corporate chief executive officers (CEOs), and other wage earners. Between 1995 and 2005, productivity grew a remarkable 33.4%, and over half that growth occurred after 2001. Yet wages for the typical worker and for those with either a high school or a college degree were about the same in 2005 as in 2001. Historically high productivity growth and historically low unemployment have benefited incomes very little. Between 1995 and 2005, health and pension benefits grew at less than half the rate of productivity, and wages for typical workers grew one-third as much. Women are much more likely to earn low wages than men. In 2005, 29.4% of women earned poverty-level wages or less, compared with the 19.9% of men who did so. Women are also much less likely to earn very high wages. In 2005 only 10.1% of women earned at least three times the poverty-level wage compared with 17.6% of men. The proportion of minority workers earning low wages is substantial—33.3% of black workers and 39.3% of Hispanic workers in 2005. Minority women are even more likely to be low earners—37.1% of black women and 45.7% of Hispanic women.

There are three key elements in wage inequality. One is the gap at the "bottom," meaning the difference between median-wage and low-wage workers. Another measure of wage inequality takes into account the "top half" gap, that is, between high-wage (90th or 95th percentile wage earners) and middle-wage earners. The third element is the gap at the very top, the growth of wages for those in the upper 1%, including CEOs. These three elements have had differing histories. The gap at the bottom grew in the 1980s but has been stable or declining ever since, whereas the "top half" wage gap has persistently grown since the late 1970s. The very highest earners have done considerably better than other workers for at least 30 years, and have done extraordinarily well over the last 10 years.

Explaining these shifts in wage inequality requires attention to several factors that affect low-, middle-, and high-wage workers differently. The high levels of unemployment in recent years have disadvantaged wage earners and provided the context in which other forces – specifically, a weakening of labor market institutions and an increase in globalization – have driven up wage inequality. Significant shifts in the labor market, such as the severe drop in the real minimum wage and de-unionization, can explain one-third of the growth in wage inequality. Similarly, the increasing globalization of the economy – immigration, trade, and capital mobility – and the shift toward lower-paying service industries (such as the retail trade) and away from manufacturing can explain, in combination, another third of the total growth in wage inequality.

The erosion of the extent and quality of employer-provided benefits, most notably pensions and health insurance, is another important factor in the deterioration in job quality for many workers.

Employer-provided healthcare coverage eroded from 1979 until 1993-94, when it stabilized, and then began falling again after 2000 through 2007. Coverage dropped from 69.0% in 1979 to 45% in 2007. Employer-provided pension coverage tended to rise in the 1990s but receded by 2.8 percentage points from 2000 to 2004 to 45.5%, 5.1 percentage points below the level in 1979. Pension plan quality also receded, as the share of workers in defined-benefit plans fell from 39% in 1980 to just 8% in 2006. Correspondingly, the share of workers with a defined-contribution plan (and no other plan) rose from 8% to 31%.

The erosion of unionization (from 43.1% of blue collar men in 1978 to just 19.2% in 2005) can account for 65% of the 11.1 percentage-point growth of the blue-collar/white-collar wage gap among men over the 1978-2005 period. Unionized workers earn higher wages than comparable non-union workers and also are 18.3% more likely to have health insurance, 22.5% more likely to have pension coverage, and 3.2% more likely to have paid leave. Young workers' prospects have also declined since 2000. Wages have actually fallen for all entry-level workers since 2000, whether high school or college educated, male or female.

The real value of the minimum wage has been steadily falling also, thereby causing the earnings of low-wage workers to fall significantly behind those of other workers and contributing to the rise in wage inequality. Minimum wage workers make important contributions to their family's economic well-being. They contribute 58% of their family's weekly earnings; in 43% of the affected families the minimum wage earner generated all of the family's earnings. There are 7.3 million children living in these families. While minorities are disproportionately represented among minimum wage workers, 60% are white. These workers also tend to be women (59% of the total) and concentrated in the retail and hospitality industries (46% of all minimum wage earners are employed in those industries, compared to just 21% of all workers.)

Conversely, the 1980s, 1990s, and 2000s have been prosperous times for top executives, especially relative to other wage earners. Between 1992-2005 the average CEO saw pay rise by 186.2%, while the average worker saw wages rise by just 7.2%. In 1965, CEOs in major companies earned 24 times more than an average worker; this ratio grew to 300 at the end of the recovery in 2000. The fall in the stock market reduced the value of CEO stock-related pay (e.g., options), but by 2005 CEO pay had recovered to the point where it was 262 times that of the average worker. The lion's share of the gains for the top 1% in the pay scale accrued to the upper 10% of that elite group (i.e., those in the 99.9th percentile). A similar pattern was seen in the recession which began in 2008. An Associated Press analysis shows the median pay package for CEOs of companies in the Standard & Poor's 500 index fell 7 percent to $7.6 million in 2008, but some boards granted CEOs stock options at low 2009 prices which will likely yield huge gains when the stock market recovers.

Strong job creation that fully utilizes the available workers and skills in the workforce is critical to a strong, lasting, and equitable recovery. A robust job market is what is needed to ensure that the proceeds of economic growth are broadly shared. Historically, it took just less than two years—21 months—to regain the prior employment peak. In the last cycle, it took almost four years (46 months). It is too early to tell how long recovery will take from the 2008 crisis. Persistent long-term unemployment was another problem over the last cycle. Shares of those unemployed 27 weeks or longer, as a proportion of total unemployment, were unusually high at 18.4%. By comparison, the historical share of long-termers was 10.8%. It is still the case that those with less education disproportionately bear the brunt of economic downturns, but it is also the case that higher levels of education no longer provide the same protection against cyclical forces as in prior downturns.

Other trends of note regarding jobs:

- The most jobs being lost in the current recession are in construction, durable goods manufacturing and professional and business services.
- Blue-collar workers made up 43.4% of long-term unemployed in 2005.
- "Perma-temping," that is, the percentage of temporary agency workers who have been on the same work assignment for a year or more, increased from 24.4% in 1995 to 33.7% in 2005.
- Employment rates for men and women at least 55 years old have trended upward since the early 1990s, and the trend even continued over the 2001 recession—the only age cohort so affected.

Wealth

Wealth and its accumulation are very important to a family's financial stability. Wealth, for example, enables a family to invest in a home, education, and retirement. In the short term, wealth reserves can help a family through difficult times, such as job loss. Wealth accumulation and debt often go hand-in-hand—for example, wealth, as well as debt, is generated by home ownership.

Wealth in the US is even more unequally distributed than wages or incomes. Moreover, wealth has become more concentrated at the top of the distribution over time. In 2004, those in the top 1% of the scale held over one-third of all the wealth in the US. The top-fifth controlled 84.7%, while the bottom 80% could claim only 15.3%. Over the 1962-2004 period, the wealth share held by the bottom 80% shrank by 3.8 percentage points, and that 3.8% shifted to the top 5% of households. Wealth inequality has also increased as measured by the ratio of the wealthiest 1% to median wealth. In the early 1960s, the wealthiest Americans held 125 times that of the median wealth holder; in 2004 the wealthiest held 190 times more. As the wealthiest continue to thrive, many households are left behind with little or nothing in the way of assets and often have significant debt. Approximately one in six households had zero or negative net wealth.

The notion that the majority of American households are greatly invested in the stock market is erroneous. Less than half of all households hold stock in any form, including mutual funds and 401(k)–style pension plans. From 2001 to 2004, the share of households holding stock declined – for the first time since 1989 – from 51.9% to 48.6%. Moreover, of those households that held stock, just 34.9% had stock holdings of $5,000 or more. Furthermore, the ownership of stocks was particularly unequal. In 2004, the top 1% of stockowners held 36.9% of all stocks by value, while the bottom 80% of stockholders owned less than 10%. Additionally, stocks are a bigger part of the asset portfolio for wealthier households. For those in the top 1% of the wealth distribution, stock assets made up over 21% of their total assets, while stocks consisted of just 4.8% of all assets for households in the middle fifth of the wealth distribution. While stock market performance is very important, on a daily basis it does not significantly affect average households directly.

Another key factor in family finance is that household debt has consistently trended upward. According to the Federal Reserve Board, the debt service ratio, the proportion of debt payments to household disposable income, was 13.90% in the third quarter of 2008. Predictably, debt-service burdens continue to plague lower-income families disproportionately. By 2004, approximately one in four low-income households had debt-service obligations that exceeded 40% of their income, as did 13.7% of middle-income households. Over 1.1 million filings for personal bankruptcy were made in 2008. Forty percent of personal bankruptcies are due to medical bills. Time will tell how families will cope in the latest recession with large debt burdens often caused by the loss of employment, unmanageable medical bills, or divorce.

Wealth also differs considerably by race. The median wealth of white households is 10 times that of black households. Home ownership rates also vary considerably by race. Less than half of black and Hispanic households own their homes, while 72.7% of white households do. While approximately one in six households had zero or negative net wealth, broken down by race the numbers diverge considerably—13.0% of white households compared to 29.4% of black households.

Income concentration and CEO Pay

Income concentration has been rising in America since 1980. The Gini coefficient rose steadily from 40.3 in 1980 to 46.3 in 2007. Yet the broad data mask wide differences between skilled workers and managers (20% of the nonfarm workforce) and unskilled workers (the remainder). In spring 2007, the supervisory workforce had average hourly salaries of $59 per hour, compared with $17 per hour for nonsupervisory employees. Average hourly earnings for production workers have been going up by 3.4% annually, while those for supervisors have been increasing by 5.6%. Hence, the percentage of total wages of employed Americans earned by supervisory workers rose from 41% in 1997 to 46% in 2007.

Globalization, although a significant benefit to the American standard of living (a 10% addition to GDP since World War II, according to some estimates) is the major cause of income concentration. There is a parallel in the development of America as a national market in the late 19th century. Income concentration in the earlier 20th century was even greater than it is today. Much of the differences in wealth then arose from interest, dividends, and capital gains, rather than salary differentials as it does today. A secondary factor in current income concentration is the low educational achievement of some students, especially minority students.

The shift of manufacturing jobs to their equivalents in computers, telecommunications and information technology has kept America economically competitive but at a heavy cost in layoffs to the workers in older industries. Tariff barriers seem a seductive solution to some and would, for a time at least, preserve jobs. President Bush imposed temporary tariffs in 2002-3 on some steel production, not as part of a fortress economy, but to allow redundant steel workers time to find new jobs. Permanent tariffs barriers, however, would lead to higher prices and less choice of goods, and would risk retaliation from other countries against American exports, and legal challenges within the WTO. Tariff barriers would lead the economy to stagnate, causing more pain to more people, in the opinion of many experts. The challenge for America is to create more well-paying jobs and to mitigate the pain of the losers from economic turbulence, without administering cures that are worse than the disease.

Many Americans have been angered by the dramatic rise in the ratio of CEO compensation packages relative to gains in the salaries of average employees. CEO pay has recently been rising at 10% annually, compared with just over 3% for production and nonsupervisory workers. Outsize CEO compensation is considered by many to be inappropriate and unseemly, especially at a time when so many workers are losing their jobs. There is a widespread feeling that boards of directors should act to cub such excesses or, otherwise, that the government should limit increases in CEO pay. For many, the term "business ethics" has become an oxymoron and some analysts believe that a sour mood of disaffection among middle- and lower-income Americans would be politically dangerous.

Part of the problem, though by no means all of it, is that public perceptions of how companies operate in the globalized world have not caught up with the reality. It is mistakenly assumed that the shareholders are still as involved in corporate management as they used to be a generation ago. Formerly, the shareholders, especially the major ones, would control the strategy of the company and appoint the board, who in turn would hire the CEO and other officers to carry out that strategy. The system seemed in a way democratic. Steadily, however, shareholding became a matter only of investment, not of ownership. Dissatisfied shareholders usually sell their stock rather than intervene in the management of the company. Corporate governance became control by the CEO, and instead of boards hiring the CEO, CEOs began to recommend slates of directors, often CEOs of other corporations, to the shareholders, who usually accepted them. These boards became less challenging of the CEOs' proposals and CEOs became authoritarian. The fact that CEOs appoint the boards, who then determine their compensation, is a major reason for the enormous salaries of CEOs, which many Americans find offensive. Yet CEOs continue to attract huge salaries, because, as Nobel Prize-winning economist Paul Krugman puts it, the "outrage factor" is no longer operative in a society dominated by the cutthroat competition of the affluent.

Government agencies, interest groups and academics have over the years pressed the institutional investors, who are mostly pension funds, to take a more active part in corporate governance but, with few exceptions, the institutions have replied that their duty to their pensioners is simply to invest profitably. The fact that undue compensation should be treated as an unnecessary business expense has not weighed with many institutions, possibly because the sums, although large for individuals, are small for a company. Only the growing but small sector of private equity funds are tending to act as corporate managers.

Defenders of high CEO compensation argue that, in global markets, the results of CEO decisions mean hundreds of millions of dollars profit or loss, and that generous compensation packages are justified to attract the global high flyers who will most often call the right decisions. Yet CEO pay in Europe and Japan has not increased at anything like the rate it has in the US. In fact the rise in CEO compensation tracks pretty closely the rise in the value of companies. The average market capitalization of an S&P 500 company in 2006 was $26 billion, a 13-fold rise since 1980. The average market value of the ten largest S&P 500 companies that year was $260 billion. When actual company performance does not measure up to expectations, compensation may become an issue, whether the result was the fault of the CEO or due to other factors such as a general movement in stock prices. Even so, it has been argued that the stock and options which form major parts of many CEOs' compensation, particularly in the IT sector, should be tied to their company's performance relative to selected competitors over time. That aside, no credible solutions have been found to the problem of perceived inappropriate levels of CEO pay.

According to a report in *The New York Times*, September 8, 2009, data from the Congressional Budget Office and from the National Bureau of Economic Research show that, from 1979 to 2000, the gap between rich and poor almost doubled. The total federal tax burden for the top 1 percent also dropped 3.8 percentage points, but for the middle fifth the decline was only 1.9 percentage points. Tax rates for the poorest fifth declined 1.6 percentage points. Federal tax burdens for most Americans have declined over the previous two decades. Then Congress enacted tax cuts in 2001 and 2003 that were heavily weighted to the top 1 percent, which supporters said would encourage them to invest more to the benefit of all Americans and critics decried as a sop to the already wealthy. The top 1 percent pay a quarter of all federal taxes, while the bottom 40 percent pay 6 percent. Meanwhile the top tax rate is 35% on incomes over $357,700, although President Obama announced a plan in early 2009 to reduce the threshold for this rate to $200,000 for singles and $250,000 for families.

Other key facts about wealth

- Wealth inequality is greater than income inequality: The top 1%, next 9%, and bottom 90% shares of income were 21.8% (2005), 25.6% and 57.5% respectively in 2004. Shares of wealth were 34.3%, 36.9%, and 28.7%, respectively in 2004.
- Average wealth held by the top 1% was close to $15 million, while it was $81,000 for households in the middle-fifth of the wealth distribution.
- Approximately 30% of households have a net worth of less than $10,000.
- About half of those in the bottom quarter of the income distribution own their homes, while 88.9% in the top quarter of the income distribution own homes.

The poverty line

One of the most significant challenges in discussing poverty in America is defining what precisely poverty means. The federal government defines a minimum amount of income necessary for basic maintenance of a family of four. This amount represents three times the cost of an adequate diet and may fluctuate depending on the cost of living and the location of the family. Many analysts, however, consider this definition inadequate and base their analyses of poverty on two times the federal poverty line. The official 2007 threshold for a family of four was $21,027. The official thresholds have fallen well behind income growth among middle and higher income families, creating a situation in which the poor are by definition more economically isolated. For example, the poverty line for a family of four was 48% of median family income in 1960. In 2007 it was 28.5% of the real median household income of $50,233. Trends in poverty are revealing of changes in the living standards of the most economically vulnerable families. After falling steeply throughout the latter 1990s, poverty rates increased not only in the 2001 recession, but in most years through 2007, from 11.3% in 2000 to 12.5%, when 37.3 million persons, including some 13 million children, were in poverty. About 91 million persons were below twice poverty in 2004.

DEPARTMENT OF HEALTH AND HUMAN SERVICES POVERTY GUIDELINES 2007

Persons in Family or Household	48 Contiguous States and D.C.	Alaska	Hawaii
1	$10,210	$12,770	$11,750
2	13,690	17,120	15,750
3	17,170	21,470	19,750
4	20,650	25,820	23,750
5	24,130	30,170	27,750
6	27,610	34,520	31,750

7	31,090	38,870	35,750
8	34,570	43,220	39,750
For each additional person, add	3,480	4,350	4,000

The poverty rate in 2009 (poverty threshold for a family of four, $21,954) was the highest since 1994, but was 8.1 percentage points lower than the poverty rate in 1959, the first year for which poverty estimates are available, the Census Bureau has said. The poverty rate has indeed steadily declined over the last half-century. Since 1978, the percentage of people living below the poverty level has fluctuated in a fairly narrow range around 12 percent, some 36 million people. In its Annual Report for 2009, the Census Bureau said 43.6 million people, or one in seven Americans, lived in poverty, up from 39.8 million in 2008. The poverty rate rose to 14.3 percent from 13.2 percent the year before, the highest level since 1994. But typically one-quarter of these people are African Americans and one-quarter Latinos. This means that these groups are disproportionately represented, as are children, whose poverty rate fluctuates around 17 percent, over 12 million.

What is more, the overall figures mask much more severe pockets of poverty. Families headed by single mothers are particularly susceptible to poverty. Partly as a result of this phenomenon, 29 million children were living in poverty in 2006. The poverty rate was especially high among African American children and Hispanic children, where 60% live in families below twice the federal poverty threshold.

Given their lower incomes, poverty rates for minorities are consistently higher than those of whites. Poverty among blacks and Hispanics, however, was much more responsive than among whites to the faster and more broadly distributed income growth during the 1990s, and by 2000 the poverty rate for blacks was the lowest on record, although, even then, more than a fifth of blacks were poor (22.5%). But by 2007, the rate had increased again to 24.5%. Tight job markets were critical in reducing poverty in the latter 1990s, when overall poverty fell by 2.5 percentage points, with much larger declines for minorities: 6.8 points for blacks and 8.8 points for Hispanics.

Yet, even under the best economic conditions, many poor families need extra help to escape poverty. In the later 1990s, for example, welfare reform and strong labor demand drew many single mothers into the job market. For many of these women, full employment helped generate significant percentage wage gains. But even hourly wage gains of about a third, from around $6 to around $8 dollars an hour, do not provide enough income for these families to meet their basic needs. Fortunately for them, significant work supports – public benefits tied to work – were added or expanded over the 1990s. In 2009 the highest level of Earned Income Tax Credit for a family with at least two children was $5,028. The federal minimum wage was increased to $7.25 from July 24, 2009. More resources were devoted to health and childcare subsidies.

Some analysts have suggested that the official poverty figures overstate the real extent of poverty because they measure only cash income and exclude certain government assistance programs such as Food Stamps, health care, and public housing. Others point out, however, that these programs rarely cover all of a family's food or health care needs and that there is a shortage of public housing. Some argue that even families whose incomes are above the official poverty level sometimes go hungry, skimping on food to pay for such things as housing, medical care, and clothing. Still others point out that people at the poverty level sometimes receive cash income from casual work and in the "underground" sector of the economy, which is never recorded in official statistics (InfoUSA).

Marginalized groups affected by deprivations such as hunger and homelessness cannot effectively exercise the political freedoms necessary to spur the government to action. This alienation partly explains the apathy of the US government in response to poverty. It also explains the high morbidity of African Americans. By income level, even poor African Americans are richer than poor people in much of the rest of the world. But quality of life is influenced by non-economic factors such as social and institutional priorities (e.g., health care and insurance). As a result, African Americans are poorer in terms of the ability to live a long life than many men and women in the developing world. In contrast, families with incomes over $100,000 spend just 3 percent of their incomes on health care, while those earning $45,000 spend 6 percent, but families making under $10,000 spend 17 percent.

The market-driven US economic model is often deemed by Americans to be superior to European economic models. It is asserted, for instance, that the US is the richest country in the world, and it is true that, in per capita (income per head) terms, the US is quite wealthy. Comparing the US economy to similar economies facing the same global conditions with respect to trade, investment, technology, and the environment provides an independent yardstick for gauging economic outcomes derived from different economic models. It is important to note also that what is commonly referred to as the "European model" is actually many different economic models. Not only is each country unique, but unique events – like the reunification of Germany – need to be taken into account. Many EU countries are less market driven and more "interventionist" than the US.

A main determinant of an economy's standard of living is its productivity, which can be compared by the amount of gross domestic product (GDP) per hour worked. In these terms in 2004 several European countries caught up to or surpassed the US. Five countries are above or equal to US levels (US=100)—Norway (125), Belgium (113), France (107), Ireland (104), and the Netherlands (100). The growth rate of productivity is also important, and the US is currently extremely productive. In the cycle 2000-05, US productivity grew at 2.5% per year.

The US is indeed one of the richest countries in the world, with per capita income in 2005 of $39,728, but that was second to Norway's $42,832. Many other economies have per capita incomes above $30,000, approaching the US level—such as Ireland, Switzerland, Austria, Canada, Australia, Denmark, Sweden, Netherlands, Finland, Belgium and the United Kingdom. Many Europeans and Canadians view their social protections as factors that raise their living standards and as such are unmeasured and not captured in income measures. A main reason why per capita incomes in Europe are below US levels is that Europeans value leisure over the consumption of more goods.

While the US is one of the wealthiest countries, it also has the highest degree of inequality of the OECD countries, whether measured in terms of Gini coefficients or the ratio of high earners (90th percentile) to low earners (10th percentile). Low-income earners in the US not only earn relatively lower incomes than their OECD counterparts, but they are also worse off because of limited social policy and safety nets. Access to health care is a good example. The US spends more on health care (whether measured as a percentage of GDP or per capita spending) than any of these other countries. The US spent 17% of its GDP on health care in 2008 – 30% more than the next highest spender (Switzerland at 11.6%) – yet has fewer physicians, nurses and hospital beds than the median. Even with such high spending, 46 million people in the US (18% of the population under 65) do not have health insurance, and access to health care is much more limited than in the countries of its economic peers. In Canada, Japan, and Europe there is essentially universal health care coverage. Moreover the income advantages and high health spending in the US do not produce better outcomes relative to other developed countries in life expectancy, infant mortality, and poverty. The US has the lowest life expectancy, the highest infant mortality rates, and the highest overall and child poverty rates of all the OECD countries.

Other key comparisons with foreign countries
- The US unemployment rate ranks about the middle of OECD countries.
- While productivity is an important factor in relatively higher US incomes, even more significant is that Americans simply work more hours.
- European vacation time is mandated, usually four to five weeks, while there is no mandated vacation time in the US.
- Relative US manufacturing labor costs are below that of seven European countries.

America's working families continue to work hard to make ends meet, improve their living standards, and create better opportunities for their children. New economy or old, this remains the case today much as it was a century ago. Yet there are clearly aspects of today's economy that make it historically unique. Some of these damage the bargaining power of American workers: increased global trade, less union membership, and more low-skilled and high-skilled immigration. There are fewer favorable social norms that guide employer behavior or support policies that provide adequate safety nets, pensions, and health care arrangements. In other words, the biggest challenge in the new economy is not growth itself, but how it is distributed. If Americans do not address this issue, say many analysts, the US risks sacrificing bedrock principles that have historically defined the American economic experience and underpinned the American Dream.

RACIAL DISCRIMINATION (see also Chapter 2)

World War 1 reduced barriers separating Jewish, German, Irish, and Italian ethnic groups in the US. Yet blacks were excluded from this quiet revolution. A century later, a disproportionate number of black Americans are poor, and many argue this is because of a legacy of racial discrimination and because of current discriminatory practices. Since the Civil War, much of the concern over civil rights in the US has focused on efforts to extend them fully to African Americans. The first legislative attempts to assure African Americans an equal political and legal status were the Civil Rights Acts of 1866, 1870, 1871, and 1875. Those acts bestowed upon African Americans such freedoms as the right to sue and be sued, to give evidence, and to hold real and personal property. The 1866 Act was of dubious constitutionality and was reenacted in 1870 only after the passage of the Fourteenth Amendment. The fourth Civil Rights Act attempted to guarantee to the African Americans those social rights that were still withheld. It penalized innkeepers, proprietors of public establishments, and owners of public conveyances for discriminating against African Americans in accommodations, but was invalidated by the Supreme Court in 1883 on the ground that these were not properly civil rights and hence not a field for federal legislation. Blacks also continued to be excluded from some churches.

After the Civil Rights Act of 1875 there was no more federal legislation in this field for nearly a century, until the Civil Rights Acts of 1957 and 1960, although several states passed their own civil rights laws. The Civil Rights Act of 1957 was historically significant because it ended three-quarters of a century of congressional inaction by creating the Civil Rights Division of the Department of Justice, and the Civil Rights Commission, whose actions helped to eradicate much of the institutional discrimination which used to be endemic in the Southern states.

The 20th-century struggle to expand civil rights for African Americans involved the National Association for the Advancement of Colored People (NAACP), the Congress of Racial Equality (CORE), the Urban League, the Southern Christian Leadership Conference, and others. In the late 1950s and early 1960s, African Americans, led by Dr. Martin Luther King, Jr., used boycotts, marches and other forms of nonviolent protest to demand equal treatment under the law and an end to racial prejudice. A high point of the civil rights movement came on August 28, 1963, when more than 200,000 people of all races gathered in front of the Lincoln Memorial in Washington and heard the stirring "I have a dream" speech by King. The civil rights movement, and the executive leadership provided by President Lyndon B. Johnson, encouraged the passage of the most comprehensive civil rights legislation to date, the Civil Rights Act of 1964: it prohibited discrimination for reason of color, race, religion, or national origin in places of public accommodation covered by interstate commerce i.e., restaurants, hotels, motels, and theaters. Besides dealing with the desegregation of public schools, the Act, in Title VII, forbade discrimination in employment. The Equal Employment Opportunity Commission was appointed to enforce the Act, which was strengthened by the Civil Rights Act 1991.

In response to widespread evidence of disfranchisement of black citizens in several southern states, in 1965 Congress passed the Voting Rights Act, which placed federal observers at polls to ensure equal voting rights. The Act protected citizens' right to vote primarily by forbidding the states concerned from using tests of any kind (like literacy tests) to determine eligibility to vote. Until 2007, the Act also required these states to obtain federal approval before enacting any election laws, and assigned federal officials to monitor the registration process in certain localities. Congress has amended the Act several times since 1965 to include other ethnic groups. Even so, the highly controversial result of the voting in Florida at the Presidential election of 2000 strongly suggests that more needs to be done to protect the rights of black citizens to vote. The Civil Rights Act of 1968 dealt with discrimination in housing and real estate. In addition to congressional action on civil rights, there were actions by other branches of the government. The most notable of these were the Supreme Court decisions in 1954 and 1955 declaring racial segregation in public schools unconstitutional and the court's rulings in 1955 banning segregation in publicly financed parks, playgrounds, and golf courses.

Throughout the history of civil rights, there have been Americans opposed to equality for minorities, and some who organized to prevent it. The most notorious of these movements is the Ku Klux Klan (KKK). The KKK was first formed in Tennessee in 1865 to try to deter the blacks from claiming equality after the emancipation of the slaves the previous year. The KKK sometimes burned the Christian symbol of the cross in front of the homes of African Americans and those who supported them. The Klan was virulently opposed to blacks having sex with whites, sharing public places with them, being educated alongside whites and even worshipping together with them. The Klan is a secret organization and members wear long white robes and tall pointed hats to conceal their identity. Klan members have been convicted of many crimes, including murder.

Klan activity has been directed not only against African Americans but also against Jews, Catholics and immigrants. In the 1920s, the Klan had 5 million members and during the 1960s experienced another revival when it opposed the Civil Rights movement, but today it has much less influence.

African Americans constitute 12.7 percent of the population, and in recent decades have made great strides, with the middle class growing significantly. Despite the Civil Rights Movement's successful elimination of state-sponsored racial segregation, however, Georgetown University law professor Sheryll Cashin argues that more needs to be done to overcome private and corporate segregation. Fifty years after the Supreme Court's decision in *Brown v. Board of Education*, modern segregation – based on both voluntary separation and continued racial discrimination – thwarts black citizens' dreams of living in safe, affordable communities with high-quality educational opportunities for their children.

In *The Failures of Integration: How Race and Class are Undermining the American Dream* (Public Affairs Books, 2004), Cashin argues that public and private institutional policies continue to divide neighborhoods along racial and class lines. In addition, Cashin says, both white and black America have grown to accept de facto segregation: whites because segregation from minorities is often seen as necessary to ensuring better opportunities, and blacks simply from ambivalence to integration. This separation provides unequal opportunities to achieve a quality of life most Americans strive for—the ability to live in communities offering attractive neighborhoods, reasonable tax rates, low crime, good schools, and job opportunities. Segregation sets up "winner" and "loser" communities with racial minorities and the poor substantially locked out of the "winner" column (and middle-class whites finding it increasingly harder to stay in).

Cashin warns that continued segregation – whether by choice or longstanding policies – threatens to polarize the nation even further, at a time when coming together as one community would advance everyone's pursuit of the American Dream. Integration, not segregation, continues to be the answer, she says. "In a rapidly diversifying America, the only way to stem our drift toward a 'winner-take-all' society is to jettison the common assumption that separation is okay....Our public policy choices must be premised on an integrationist vision if we are to achieve the dream America says it embraces: full and equal opportunity for all." A further discussion of inequality and race can be found in *The Conscience of a Liberal*, Paul Krugman, W. W. Norton & Co., 2007.

Attitudes to racial disadvantage

The conviction that the US is a melting pot has been an article of faith for generations of Americans. But the gradual process of assimilation that has brought both indigenous peoples and generations of immigrants into the American mainstream has been called in question in recent years. Now it is often said that America is a mosaic, or a salad bowl, and not a melting pot. America is indeed steadily becoming a nation in which no dominant cultural paradigm prevails, one still in the process of developing its own uniquely American culture.

Since the problem of race relations in America predates the Declaration of Independence by some 150 years, its depth and difficulty are unsurprising. It has been said that in large measure Americans live in racial enclaves separated by invisible gates. There are actually two race problems in America: the problem of the severely isolated poorest of the black poor, and the problem of relations between the rest of black America and the country as a whole.

A hotly contested issue – not least among black people themselves – is to what extent the plight of the black underclass comes from "within" the black community (due to failures of "black culture") rather than from "without" (due to white racism). The eminent sociologist, William Julius Wilson, has attempted to reframe the debate on the relationship between race and poverty. He observes that discussions have hardened into two mutually exclusive perspectives. One view regards black poverty as a consequence of social forces such as segregation and the flight of middle-class black residents from urban centers. Alternatively, black poverty has been portrayed as a product of individual and cultural inadequacy. Wilson argues for a symbiosis of these views and wishes to stop seeing the poor as victims. Although he thinks that structural factors (institutional arrangements that largely perpetuate disadvantages) are more influential, he argues that the social position of African Americans is not only the result of such factors, nor only of cultural factors (black family and work arrangements, language, religion, etc.) He points out, for example, that concerns about black violence in the 1970s gave rise to greatly increased incarceration rates for black men. Then, employers' unwillingness to hire black ex-felons, coupled with the rise of service jobs that favored women, led to the decline of opportunities for black men to assume the traditional male provider role that had sustained long-term family commitments. Hence on the one hand, it is true that history has given poor blacks a very raw deal. On the other hand, it is also true that the worst roadblocks to advancement among the underclass derive from their own patterns of behavior regarding family life, work, drug abuse and criminality, and there must be change in these behaviors if progress is to be made. But it is equally obvious that a commitment of resources and support will also be required from the broader society to help these people help themselves. Wilson makes the case that the focus should be on promoting work opportunities and alleviating poverty concentration rather than simply fighting racism or promoting punitive policies.

Wilson explains the behavior of young urban black males – their disdain for low-wage jobs, their use of violence, and their refusal to take responsibility for children – without pointing simplistically to discrimination or a deficit in values. Instead, he argues that many years of exposure to similar situations can create responses that look as if they express individual will or active preference when they are, in fact, adaptations or resigned responses to racial exclusion. A young man who works in the drug economy does not necessarily place little if any value on legitimate work. Employment opportunities are limited in his racially segregated neighborhood. Few of his neighbors and friends have social connections to employers, and most of the good jobs are far away. To complicate matters, many of his friends and neighbors are probably connected to the drug trade. Survival and peer pressure dictate that the man will seek out the dangerous, illegal jobs that are nearby, even while he might prefer a stable, mainstream job. His behavior is delinquent, but more than likely a comprehensible response to lack of opportunity. Wilson applies the same logic to teenage pregnancy. The political left and right both argue that the prospect of welfare payments can motivate young women to have children: conservatives point to delinquent values, while liberals deem this a response to lack of income. Wilson's "socialization" lens makes it appear that learned behaviors take priority over economic need: young women achieve both personal identity and social validation in their community by entering into motherhood. They join others whose lives are similarly defined by early parenting. The receipt of welfare helps them contribute to the household while placing them on a surer moral footing than those who fail to bring income into the home. The actions of both the young man and the teenage mother are "cultural," Wilson suggests, because they follow from the individual's perceptions of how society works. These perceptions are learned, and create powerful expectations that can lead individuals to act in ways that, to the outside world, represent a deficit of values. Three generations of black ghetto dwellers have been relying on welfare and sporadic work and doing so in isolation from the mainstream. Distinctive behaviors, values, and outlooks have arisen as a consequence. Wilson admits it is difficult to engineer cultural change. Evidence of this lies in the many "mobility" programs that move inner-city families to lower-poverty suburbs. Young women continue to have children out of wedlock and, inexplicably, the young men who move out *return* to their communities to commit crime. Those who think they are at a disadvantage (however justified or unjustified that belief may be) internalize their status, so that their low expectations become as durable an obstacle as the discrimination they might be facing. The belief that help is futile can be a powerful deterrent to social change.

Wilson emphasizes the advantages of "race neutral" programs, knowing that Americans and their elected leaders are more likely to support "jobs-first" initiatives that are not identified with poor blacks. He repeatedly points to the benefits that jobs programs and vocational training have on expectations and culture. Increasing employment will tend to reduce the number of people who might promote or condone deviant behavior. Change might not occur overnight, and it may not be wholesale, but it will take place, he asserts.

A key debate is the reasons for the educational under-performance of blacks. Even poor Asians do better on math tests than upper-middle class blacks. Studies show that Asian Americans score higher because they study a lot harder. And one reason for this may be that their two-parent families are in a better position to discipline their children and supervise their study habits than the all-too-typical single-parent households of the black community. The illegitimacy rate in the Asian American community is 2-3 percent, while in the African American community it is 70 percent. The success of these groups (including Asians and also black immigrants, such as West Indians and Nigerians) is claimed to expose the myth that racism will always stifle the aspirations of black people.

Some indeed now argue that racism is no longer the main obstacle to black progress, and that cultural pathologies such as racial paranoia, excessive dependency on government, and high crime and illegitimacy rates are preventing blacks from achieving their full potential. Many people allege that this problem was caused by slavery, because interracial marriage was nowhere legal in the slave states. But in fact the illegitimacy rate for blacks between 1900 and 1960 remained roughly constant at around 20 percent, less than one-third the current rate. The steep increase in black illegitimacy has occurred during the past generation. Similarly, black crime rates were much lower during the first half of the 20th century – even during the Great Depression, even in the Deep South – than during the last three decades. The counter-argument is that these cultural pathologies are themselves the product of oppression, the direct result of slavery, segregation, and racism, so that all Americans, especially the white middle class, owe a continuing obligation to the black underclass that goes beyond an assurance of equal rights under the law. However one analyses the causes, it remains true that black Americans are mired in the worst urban poverty in the industrial West. America's pretensions to being a beacon of hope and freedom to all the world thus seem fraudulent when set alongside the lives of hopelessness and despair lived by so many of those Americans who descend from slaves.

Solutions to racial exclusion

The culture of the ghettos is partly a product of African American history and of government policies denying blacks full citizenship rights. Opinions differ about how much responsibility black people themselves bear for their plight. Americans are also divided as to what extent the problems of the ghettos are the country's responsibility. Reducing crime, improving schools, and getting people into jobs would all clearly help.

How can stereotypes, resentments, and clashes in values be overcome? Progress depends on thoughtful people searching for good ways to do so and rigorously identifying and spotlighting promising practices. At least there are countless people hungry for ideas. Experts say that it is actual experience that changes our sense of connection, or community, by shaping values and perceptions in new ways. Discussion can lay the groundwork by promoting some level of understanding, but the challenge is to go further and seek joint endeavors, such as a multiracial school-reform movement or political coalition. These initiatives are being taken as a result of the *One America* program originally mounted by President Clinton, now a private foundation. Whatever the approach, which varies by community and institution, the goal is to change the sense of who is "us" and who is "them." Progress on race requires that Americans also make painful investments in a better understanding of what divides them in terms of national identity, cultural autonomy, and contested evidence about what works and what does not.

Affirmative action

In recent years, support for affirmative action to help blacks has declined, although surveys still show a small majority in favor. Most whites do not think that either working-class or middle-class blacks really have a legitimate call on public policy any more. For their part, blacks think whites do not care deeply about any problem in African American life. Whites mostly think that blacks automatically defend racial preferences without having demonstrated that they are justified or necessary. The black middle class, whose emergence everyone applauds, has been greatly helped by government in general and affirmative action in particular. Affirmative action is substantially responsible for the integration of the leadership ranks in American society, in fields ranging from police work to high-end medicine.

Affirmative action is a general term which covers a number of strategies whose purpose is to promote and ultimately achieve equality of opportunity. The term "affirmative action" was coined by the Kennedy Administration (1961-1963), which directed US government contractors to take positive steps to have a racially representative workforce. Later, a Republican administration required school districts receiving federal funds to take "affirmative steps" to rectify "language deficiencies" in order to open up their instructional programs to all children.

The prohibition against the use of race as a criterion to exclude blacks did not lead in the years that followed to their inclusion in greater numbers in jobs, professions or housing. In the field of employment, where the numbers of blacks hired had not increased significantly after the Civil Rights Act, numerical goals first appeared as part of the Nixon Administration's (1969-1974) "Philadelphia Plan." In 1972, the Plan was amended to enable the federal government and the courts to require specific measures as a way of compensating for past discriminatory practices. Race now became the basis for determining the extent to which inclusion had been accomplished. The enforcement of affirmative action continued through the Carter Administration (1977-1981), but with the arrival of Ronald Reagan in the White House in 1981, a clear message went out that the initiative had run its course. Enforcement of civil rights laws and regulations was downplayed throughout the 1980s, and critics of affirmative action began to question the wisdom of a policy which they considered to be a form of "reverse discrimination." The term "reverse discrimination" suggests that minorities have enjoyed such advantages over whites that now they are better off than whites or, at least, have achieved parity proportionate to their numbers. The facts do not support this suggestion, however. Affirmative steps to include minorities in the workforce appear to have produced minimal or quite modest gains.

In the current debate, the principle of equal opportunity does not seem to be in question. Even the most ardent opponents of affirmative action support the notion that no one should be discriminated against because of race. But affirmative action is being blamed for other, unacknowledged problems: increased competition for a shrinking pool of largely low-skill jobs; and the need for the public education system to be brought into the 21st century in terms of facilities, curriculum and teacher preparation. The future of affirmative action has long been debated in legal and political arenas. In 1995 the US Supreme Court ruled in *Adarand v. Pe* that any governmental action based on race awarding US government contracts must be subjected to strict scrutiny. This was followed by the approval (in California) of Proposition 209, which ended preferential treatment of women and minorities by government agencies, including colleges and universities. The next year, the US Court of Appeals for the Fifth Circuit, which covers Texas, Louisiana and Mississippi, ruled in *Texas v. Hopwood* that the University of Texas Law School could not apply significantly different criteria when judging minority and non-minority applicants. In 1998 the University of California voted to end the use of affirmative action in the admissions process. The immediate result of these actions was a precipitous drop in the number of minority applicants and enrollees in both the University of California System and at the University of Texas Law School. Meanwhile colleges and universities continued to rely on the Court's decision in *University of California v. Bakke* 1978. There, by a 5-4 vote, the Court said that admissions may not be race-driven, but that schools can consider a student's race as a "plus factor" in addition to other factors which must be equal for all applicants. The Supreme Court has repeatedly frowned on race-based decision-making by the government, and bodies that receive federal funds, but has always stopped just short of outlawing the practice entirely. Finally, in 2003, the issue seemed to be resolved by the Court's decision in *Grutter v. Bollinger,* which arose from the use of affirmation action by the University of Michigan Law School. Justice Sandra Day O'Connor wrote the majority opinion. The Equal Protection Clause of the Constitution (part of the 14th Amendment), she wrote, did not prohibit the Law School's narrowly tailored use of race in admissions decisions to further a compelling interest in obtaining the educational benefits that flow from a diverse student body. At issue was the point value given to minority applicants. The university's policy, which automatically distributed 20 points, or one-fifth of the points needed to guarantee admission, to every single "underrepresented minority" applicant solely because of race, was not narrowly tailored to achieve the interest in educational diversity that the university claimed justified their program, and although the system itself was not unconstitutional, it had to be amended. Experts say that by upholding the Law School's admissions policy, the court has approved a model for how to enroll a student body that is both academically excellent and racially integrated. The question is no longer whether affirmative action is legal; it is how to hasten the day when affirmative action is no longer needed.

But even if narrowly tailored affirmative action is legal, it is losing popular favor, and its proponents are arguing that America must implement some other positive strategies to increase the participation of all groups in national life. It is in the self-interest of all Americans, they say, to ensure that inequality is reduced, and economic and social benefits are distributed more fairly among the groups that make up society. Not to do so will lead to increased conflict between the well-to-do and the have-nots, with the attendant social and economic costs to the nation. The US cannot afford a large population of unprepared, underprepared and excluded workers and expect its economy to prosper in direct competition with other countries.

Developmental action

Even after a quarter-century, the plight of the inner city underclass, the most intractable aspect of racial inequality, has not been mitigated by affirmative action. There are thus compelling reasons to question the wisdom of relying on racial preferences as heavily as Americans now do to bring about civic inclusion for African Americans. Some middle-class American blacks are now turning to a new policy, developmental action, to raise the status of blacks. They point out that the widespread use of preferences can logically be expected to erode the perception of black competence both among beneficiaries and neutral observers. Affirmative action can also undercut the incentives for blacks to develop their competitive abilities. Thirdly, preferences are humiliating. Preferential treatment can lead to the patronization of black workers and students, that is, the setting of a lower standard of expected accomplishment for blacks than whites because of the belief that blacks are not as capable of meeting a higher, common standard. Behavior of this kind can be a self-fulfilling prophecy. In other words, observed performance among blacks may be lower precisely because blacks are being patronized to meet affirmative action guidelines. Such behavior could undermine the ability of black workers to identify and correct their deficiencies, encouraging them to think they can get ahead without reaching the same level of proficiency as their white co-workers. A similar situation can arise among applicants for admission to graduate schools.

One way to resolve or avoid this dilemma is for employers or schools to meet their desired level of black participation through a concerted effort to enhance performance while maintaining common standards of evaluation. This is called *developmental affirmative action*. For example, black students are far scarcer than white and Asian students in advanced studies in math and science. They could be encouraged through summer workshops, support for curriculum development at historically black colleges, or the financing of research assistant grants. Similarly, management assistance could be provided to new black-owned businesses, which would then be expected to bid competitively for government contracts. Black students could be admitted to the state university conditional on a rise in their academic scores to competitive levels after a year or two of study at a local community college. The key is that the racially targeted assistance be short-lived, and preparatory to the entry of its recipients into an arena of competition where they would be assessed by the same standards as everyone else.

Young black students and entrepreneurs are in fact among the richest young people of African descent anywhere on the globe. There is no achievement to which they cannot legitimately aspire. Whatever degree of success they attain in life, the fact that some of their ancestors were slaves and others faced outrageous bigotry will have little to do with it. The generation coming of age during the 1960s, now ensconced in the burgeoning black middle class, enjoy their status primarily because their parents and grandparents faithfully discharged their responsibilities. The benefits of affirmative action, whatever they may have been, pale in comparison to this inheritance.

In favor of developmental action, it is argued that previous generations of blacks, from slavery onward, managed to educate their children, acquire land, found communal institutions, and mount a successful struggle for equal rights. It is time now that their children begin to do the same. With their far greater freedoms, some middle class blacks argue, they should now not look to whites, of whatever political persuasion, to ensure that their dreams are realized. The children of today's black middle class will live their lives in an era of equal opportunity. While racial discrimination has not disappeared, the historic barriers to black participation in the political, social and economic life of the nation have been lowered dramatically over the past four decades, especially for the wealthiest 20 percent of the black population.

None of this is to deny that Americans must work together as a nation to address the country's problems, including its race problem. But arguably the best way to do so is to appeal to the goodwill of whites and other citizens, since they are unlikely to respond favorably to moral intimidation. Human nature dictates that those who are not black are more likely to want to help if they see that blacks acknowledge the nature of the problem, and are taking concrete actions to do something about it. Meanwhile, as a practical matter, African American preachers, teachers, and parents are often in the best position to reform the mores of the black community.

ACCESS TO HEALTHCARE

The number of people with health insurance fell for the first time in 2009 since the Census Bureau began collecting the data in 1987. Some 194.5 million people had private health coverage in 2009, compared to 201 million in 2008. (The newly enacted healthcare overhaul will require most people to obtain health insurance by 2014, and the government will offer subsidies to help them afford it.) The number of people without health insurance jumped to 50.7 million in 2009 from 46.3 million a year earlier, leaving 16.7 percent of the population without health coverage, the Census Bureau said in its 2009 annual report on income, poverty and health coverage. The number has increased 22 percent since 2000, from 38.4 million. The number of uninsured Americans exceeds the cumulative population of 24 states and the District of Columbia.

According to the Commonwealth Fund, the difficulty of obtaining and keeping health insurance coverage has resulted in major increases in the numbers of uninsured younger adults ages 25–34 and uninsured older adults ages 45–64. Census data reveals that those hardest hit in 2006 were families with incomes between $25,000 and $75,000, but even when family income exceeded $75,000, the numbers of uninsured Americans grew by 1.3 million, suggesting that family premiums are becoming increasingly unaffordable, especially when employers do not provide coverage. The number of uninsured full-time workers increased from 20.8 million in 2005 to 22 million in 2006, while the number of uninsured part-time workers, 5.6 million, remained the same. The number of Americans insured by Medicaid and Medicare also remained the same, at 38.3 million and 40.3 million respectively.

People living in the nation's largest cities had a higher rate of uninsurance than people living in the suburbs. The Midwest had the lowest uninsured rate in 2006, with 11.4 percent of Midwesterners lacking coverage, as compared with 12.3 percent of people in the Northeast, 17.9 percent of people in the West and 19 percent of people in the South. Based on a three-year average from 2004 to 2006, Texas was home to the highest percentage of uninsured people, 24.1 percent. Conversely, the nation's lowest uninsurance rates were in Minnesota, Hawaii, Iowa, Wisconsin and Maine.

Also of note, more children were without health insurance. The percentage of uninsured children younger than 18 rose from 10.9 percent in 2005 to 11.7 percent in 2006. The number of uninsured children younger than 18 rose from 8 million to 8.7 million. Children ages 12–17 were more likely to be uninsured than younger children. More than 6.6 million children were covered by the federally-funded State Children's Health Insurance Program, known as SCHIP, at some point during 2006. Since Congress first authorized SCHIP in 1997, the number of uninsured children in America has fallen by 24 percent. The number would have been much worse if Medicaid and SCHIP had not covered an additional 5 million children over the six-year period from 2000 to 2006, because that was when employers were dropping dependent coverage. Among children, the likelihood of health care coverage in 2006 varied by poverty status, age and race. While 7.3 percent of white children were uninsured, 22.1 percent of Hispanic children lacked coverage, as did 14.1 percent of black children and 11.4 percent of Asian children.

Enrollment in Medicaid grew by 2.1% in 2008, according to the Kaiser Family Foundation, while enrollment in SCHIP increased by 4% in 2007-2008 to 7.4 million, according to the Department of Health and Human Services (not including children counted as Medicaid beneficiaries). Medicaid covers pregnant women, children and teens, and aged, blind and disabled people. Each state decides who is eligible. Medicaid's ability to respond during economic downturns to cover substantial numbers of newly eligible people who would otherwise be uninsured depends directly on its status as an entitlement program, under which funding levels increase when need grows. During 2009 the Congress engaged in intense negotiations over President Obama's plan to extend health insurance coverage to the uninsured, a plan which caused considerable public controversy, not least because it was claimed that the plan would increase healthcare spending from 18 percent to 20 percent of GDP (see Chapter 4).

FAMILY BREAKDOWN

Divorce, abuse, and domestic violence directly affect many families in America and have an especially bad influence on the social behavior of young people. Statistics have shown that 40 to 50 percent of children will reach the age of 18 without both biological parents. Divorce impacts young people tremendously. The actual effect depends mostly on their age as well as other factors such as the level of parental conflict they have witnessed, the degree of subsequent contact with the parent they do not continue to live with, and how any step-family works. Children of divorcees are less likely to graduate high school, are more likely to have lower earnings and become dependant on welfare, and they may marry at an early age. Daughters that grow up out of these divorce families are more likely to have a child out of wedlock and be divorced as well. There is more chance that they will be delinquent, have problems in peer relationships and lack school performance. The boys, on the other hand, become more aggressive and start behaving badly. Many times these adolescents have to deal with economic hardships because the parent who has custody of them is not financially stable, which often leads them to move into crime-ridden neighborhoods where the teens are pressured into crime by their peers. Another problem that influences the social behavior of young people is domestic violence, which many times leads to child abuse. This can psychologically harm the child. Indeed experts have estimated that abused children are 30% more likely to be abusive parents themselves. Many of these young people tend to grow up believing that violence is acceptable. Sexual abuse is another form of suffering that can ruin the child's interaction with other people.

Causes

There is evidence that worsening job opportunities for men somewhat increases divorce and single parenthood. But economic reasons seem to be outweighed by social and cultural factors. Contraceptive technology, access to abortion, and attitudes to premarital sex and the family all changed during the 1960s and early 1970s and into the 1990s. Yet on a broad view of the trends and findings, it is fairly plausible to suggest that the main reason for the increase in single parenthood is that the relationship between economic opportunity and marriage has changed over the years.

A study by David T. Ellwood and Christopher Jencks of the John F. Kennedy School of Government at Harvard in 2002 suggested that three factors have likely altered the preferred timing of marriage and parenthood. First, the pill and legalized abortion gave couples, and particularly women, far more control over the timing of births, and thus allowed other factors (including economic incentives) to play more of a role. Previous forms of contraception were often less reliable, required interruption of sexual activity, or gave males control. The pill and abortion weakened the link between marriage and childbearing. Second, changing sexual mores made it far more acceptable for unmarried couples to engage in sexual activity and live together. The non-economic incentives to marry therefore fell. All else equal, this change could make economic considerations more important and allow them to influence the timing of marriage and childbearing. Finally, gender roles and expectations changed dramatically, particularly with respect to maternal employment. As late as March 1968, less than a quarter of married mothers whose youngest child was under five were working. This varied little by education. Even among those with elementary school children, only about 40% worked, and even fewer worked full-time. By 2007, of the 120 million women age 16 years and over, 71 million, 59.3%, were working or looking for work. Despite welfare reform, moreover, maternal employment rose sharply with education. Because potential mothers expect to work far more over their lifetime, they know that their decisions about the timing of fertility have greater financial implications. Thus women are finding it advantageous to delay childbearing. If women are delaying childbearing, many will delay marriage as well.

Why should these changes lead college-educated women to delay childbearing more than women with less schooling? First, college-educated women have more attractive labor market options, so they may choose to postpone motherhood simply because it would interfere with another satisfying activity. Second, the career costs associated with early childbearing may be greater for more skilled women. College-educated women may need to invest more heavily in the early parts of their careers in order to maximize their lifetime earnings (by becoming a partner in a law firm, for example). There is strong evidence that early childbearing reduces the earnings of educated women more than the earnings of less educated women. Finally, college-educated women may be more likely to expect to use paid childcare and may therefore want to wait until they can afford such help. Less educated women who want to have children at a relatively early age are faced with the problem that their male counterparts have fared increasingly badly in the labor market. As a result, the women see few economically attractive mates. This might lead them to delay marriage but not childbearing. More educated women, who are in no rush to have children, would also be in no rush to get married. Hence they would delay both marriage and childbearing, even though their prospective husbands are doing relatively well economically.

The changing economic benefits of marriage can also help to explain the recent sudden change in many marriage trends during the late 1990s. For the first time in almost 30 years, both delayed marriage and childbearing became more common. Wages of less skilled men and women rose sharply. Jobs became plentiful. The Earned Income Tax Credit and other supports made work even more lucrative for parents. Welfare reform pushed many more women into paid employment. And perhaps welfare reform also signaled a modest shift in attitudes toward single-parenthood as well.

The state of marriage in America

The median age for marriage for males is 27, for females 25. In a given year, nearly half of all marriages are remarriages for one or both partners. The marriage rate (the annual number of marriages per 1,000 unmarried adult women) continues to decline. By 2003 it had dropped 50% (to 45.6) in fifty years. The marriage rate for African Americans is considerably lower than for any other group, according to the Census. There has been a modest decline in the divorce rate since it reached an all-time high in 1980; there are now 18 divorces (rather than 22) per 1,000 married women. The projected rate of divorce still stands at around 50%—this represents the percentage of marriages (first and remarriage) entered into during a particular year that are projected to end in divorce or separation before one spouse dies. Approximately 60%-67% of second marriages end in divorce, and about 74% of third marriages end in divorce. About one-third of adults who have ever been married and are still living have experienced a divorce. This percentage rises to 46% for the baby boom generation. Catholics are substantially less likely than Protestants to get divorced (25% versus 39%). Twenty percent of first marriages end within the first five years. One's chances of divorce are diminished by such factors as: older age, higher income, more education, having a religious affiliation, absence of divorce in family of origin, and having a child after marriage. Cohabitation (sexual partners sharing a household) has increased 1100% in forty years. Over 50% of first marriages are preceded by cohabitation. Almost 40% of cohabiting households have children in them.

American households 2006

- Average household size was 2.57 people, down from 3.14 in 1970.
- Slightly more than one in four households (26 percent) consisted of a person living alone, up from 17 percent in 1970.
- About 5.7 million children, or 8 percent of the total, lived in a household that included a grandparent. The majority of these children (3.7 million) lived in the grandparent's home, and of these, about 60 percent had a parent present.
- Among the 13 million children 15 to 17, about 2.3 million were working, and of these, 2.2 million worked part time.
- 33 percent of males and 26 percent of females 15 and older had never married, up from 28 and 22 percent in 1970.
- The majority of men and women had been married by the time they were 30 to 34 (71 percent), and among men and women 65 and older, 96 percent had been married.

CHILDREN IN SINGLE-PARENT FAMILIES BY RACE 2005

Non-Hispanic White	23%
Black or African American	65%
American Indian	49%

Asian and Pacific Islander	17%
Hispanic or Latino	36%
Total	32%

Single parent families

Single parent households have showed little variation since 1994, the Census Bureau reported in 2007. The percentage of households headed by single parents remained around 9 percent, up from 5 percent in 1970, according to the latest data on America's families and households published in *Families and Living Arrangements: 2006*. There were 12.9 million one-parent families, 10.4 million single-mother families and 2.5 million single-father families. Just over two-thirds (67 percent) of the nation's 73.7 million children younger than 18 lived with two married parents. Also, there were an estimated 5.8 million stay-at-home parents: 5.6 million mothers and 159,000 fathers. To help with the problem of single-parent families, the Harvard study recommended increasing opportunities for less skilled men; if wages rose for unskilled men and women, as they did in the late 1990s, one might expect more marriage and less single-parenthood, which is what was observed in the late 1990s. Finally, support for existing two parent families would seem to reduce their vulnerability to divorce.

BANKRUPTCIES

There are an average of 1.4 million bankruptcy filings every year. And according to a disturbing study from Harvard, more people are ending up in bankruptcy than suffering a heart attack, being diagnosed with cancer, or graduating from college. Bankruptcy has become deeply entrenched in American life. And, in an era when traditionalists decry the demise of the institution of marriage, Americans file more petitions for bankruptcy than for divorce.

The dance of financial ruin starts slowly but picks up speed quickly, exhausting the dancers before it ends. Few families have substantial savings, and usually run out of cash within a month or so after a job loss. Soon the charges start mounting up for the basics of life—food, gasoline, and whatever else can go on "the [credit] card." When there still is not enough to go around, the game of impossible choices begins. Pay the mortgage or keep the heat on? Cancel the car insurance or the health insurance? Meanwhile, interest and late payment fees have piled on, making everything more expensive.

Over the past generation, the number of American families who have found themselves in serious financial trouble has grown shockingly large. In 1981, about 69,000 women filed for bankruptcy. By 1999, the figure had jumped to nearly 500,000 and remains around there. Divorced and single women are not the only ones in trouble; several hundred thousand married women filed for bankruptcy along with their husbands. The families in the worst financial trouble are not the very young, tempted by the freedom of their first credit cards. They are not the elderly, trapped by failing bodies and declining savings accounts. And they are not simply people who lack the self-control to keep their spending in check. Rather, the people who consistently rank in the worst financial trouble are united by one characteristic. They are parents with children at home. Having a child is now the single best predictor that a woman will end up in financial collapse. Married couples with children are more than twice as likely to file for bankruptcy as their childless counterparts; a divorced woman raising a youngster is nearly three times more likely to file for bankruptcy than her single friend who never had children.

Middle Class financial distress

Over the past generation, the signs of middle class financial distress have continued to grow, in good times and in bad, in recession and in boom. If those trends persist, more than 5 million families with children will file for bankruptcy by the end of the decade. That would mean that across the country nearly one of every seven families with children would have declared itself flat broke, losers in the great American economic game.

The lines at the bankruptcy courts are not the only signs of financial distress. A family with children is now 75 percent more likely to be late on credit card payments than a family with no children. The number of car repossessions doubled in the five years 1997-2002. Home foreclosures have more than tripled in less than 25 years, and soared during the latest recession: families with children are now more likely than anyone else to lose the roof over their heads. Economists estimate that for every family that officially declares bankruptcy, there are seven more whose debt loads suggest they should.

Who are the families in so much trouble? Most are ordinary, middle class people united by their determination to provide a decent life for their children. Many had been felled by a layoff or a business failure. In addition, Senator Tom Daschle claimed at a news conference (December 11, 2008) that half of bankruptcies and foreclosures were caused by medical bills. Few people in foreclosure are chronically poor. For most, poverty is only temporary, a setback in an otherwise solidly middle class life. When membership in the middle class is defined by enduring criteria that do not disappear when a pink slip arrives – criteria such as going to college, owning a home, or having held a good job – more than 90 percent of those in bankruptcy would qualify as middle class. By every measure except their balance sheets, these families are as solidly middle class as any in the country. And they are united by another common thread: most of these families sent two parents into the workforce.

Logically, sending a second parent into the workforce should make a family more financially secure, not less. But when mothers joined the workforce, the family gave up something of considerable (although unrecognized) economic value: an extra skilled and dedicated adult, available to help save the family during times of emergency. When Junior got sick, the stay-at-home mother was there to care for him full-time, without the need to hire a nurse. If Dad was laid off, Mom could enter the workforce, bringing in a new income until Dad found another job. And if the couple divorced, the mother who had not been working outside the home could get a job and add new income to support her children. The stay-at-home mother gave her family a safety net, an all-purpose insurance policy against disaster.

If the two-income families had saved the second paycheck, they would have built a different kind of safety net—money in the bank. But families did not save that money. Even as millions of mothers entered the workforce, savings declined, not because families were frittering away their paycheck. Instead, families were swept up in a bidding war, competing furiously with one another for their most important possession: a house in a decent school district. As confidence in the school system crumbled, the bidding war for family housing intensified, and parents soon found themselves bidding up the price for other opportunities for their children, such as a slot in a decent preschool or admission to a good college. Mom's extra income fitted in perfectly, coming at just the right time to give each family extra ammunition to compete in the bidding wars—and to drive the prices even higher for the things they all wanted.

The average two-income family earns far more today than did the single-breadwinner family of a generation ago. And yet, once they have paid the mortgage, the car payments, the taxes, the health insurance, and the day-care bills, today's dual-income families have less discretionary income – and less money to save – than that single-income family. Mom's paycheck has been pumped directly into the basic costs of keeping the children in the middle class.

At the same time that millions of mothers went to work, the family needed the stay-at-home mom (or a costly replacement) more than ever. The number of frail elderly, most of whom must depend on family for daily care, spiraled upward. Hospitals began discharging patients "quicker and sicker," expecting the family to pick up the task of nursing them back to health. With Mom in the workforce, parents were faced with a painful choice between paying for expensive care and taking time off work. At the same time, the divorce rate continued its upward climb. This situation was compounded by a leaner-and-meaner business climate that closed plants and laid off workers with alarming frequency. In this tougher world, millions of two-income families learned the price of living without a safety net.

One-income families

The two-income trap affects the one-income family too. When millions of mothers entered the workforce, they ratcheted up the price of a middle-class life for everyone, including families that wanted to keep Mom at home. A generation ago, a single breadwinner who worked diligently and spent carefully could assure his family a comfortable position in the middle class. But bidding wars, fuelled by families with two incomes, changed the game for single-income families as well, pushing them down the economic ladder.

Under conditions of competitive consumption, single-parent families are in even worse shape than their married counterparts. And if current trends persist, more than one of every six single mothers will go bankrupt by the end of the decade [2010]. The usual explanations for why these women are in trouble – "deadbeat dads" who do not pay child support, discrimination in the workplace, and so forth – cannot account for this growing distress. Today's middle class single mothers have better legal protection, higher salaries, more child support, and more opportunities in the workplace than their divorced counterparts of a generation ago, yet they face a much greater likelihood of financial collapse.

Changes in the family balance sheet before a couple divorces explain much about the vulnerability of today's single mothers. Married parents are in trouble because they have spent more than they earn, and have not been able to save, in order to buy a middle class life for their children. As a result, today's newly divorced mother is already teetering over a financial abyss the day she signs her divorce papers. She cannot compete with double-income families to provide her children with what have come to be seen as the basic requirements of a middle class upbringing.

Causes of financial distress

Women now need paychecks to pay the mortgage and the health insurance bills. Their incomes are committed, and calling for them to abandon those financial commitments would mean forcing them to give up their families' spot in the middle class. Ironically, middle class mothers went into the workforce in a calculated effort to give their families an economic edge. Instead, millions of them are now in the workplace just so their families can break even. At a time when women are getting college diplomas and entering the workforce in record numbers, their families are in more financial trouble than ever. Partly these women were the victims of bad timing. Despite general economic prosperity, the risks facing their families jumped considerably. Partly they were the victims of optimistic myopia: they saw the rewards a working mother could bring, without seeing the risks associated with that newfound income. And partly they were the victims of one another. As millions of mothers poured into the workplace, it became increasingly difficult to put together a middle class life on a single income. The combination has taken these women out of the home and away from their children, and simultaneously made family life less, not more, financially secure. Today's middle class mother is trapped: she cannot afford to work, and she cannot afford to quit. The resulting extraordinary changes in family life have gone almost completely unaccounted for in American economic policy. Instead of helping families, government power helped big business extort more hours for less pay and less security.

According to survey data reported by Public Agenda in 2000, 80 percent of mothers would prefer to stay at home with their children if they could. The profound lack of employer and government support for working mothers in the US is a factor in this attitude; how much so is a central point of contention between conservatives and feminists. Clearly, however, many working mothers take jobs out of necessity, not choice, and to ignore this coercive reality, as both conservatives and feminists generally do, is at odds with the culture's high regard for "family values." The problem is ultimately a question of wage distribution within the private economy—something no American government has challenged or even seriously contemplated since the early days of the New Deal.

The effect on women

It is mothers who have been the special targets of change over the past generation. It is mothers who left the home en masse, transforming generations of family economics. It is mothers who must do it all, tending to home and children while managing full-time jobs outside the home. And it is nearly always mothers who preserve the remnants of the family in the aftermath of divorce. Even for a married couple, financial failure is disproportionately a woman's problem. In this age of nominal equality between husbands and wives, in the most intimate aspect of their lives – family finance – couples reveal a surprising traditionalism. Research shows that, on average, a husband is three times more likely than a wife to take primary responsibility for managing the family's money. But as a couple sinks into financial turmoil, this responsibility tends to shift to wives.

This shift is a signal of serious discord within a marriage. In financially troubled families, women who managed the money alone were twice as likely to describe themselves as very dissatisfied with the arrangement than the men who took on that task. Men, for their part, often feel that their failure to provide for their families calls into question not just their abilities in the labor force but also their identities as husbands, as fathers, and as men. Hence financial problems and marital problems are statistically linked. Study after study shows that money is a source of contention in most marriages, but it is particularly problematic for couples that are financially unstable. It is all too easy to turn frustration and anger on one another. For some, words give way to physical blows in an ever-escalating battle to assess blame.

Financial distress is a problem for both men and women. But these phenomena are not gender-neutral. Mothers are 35 percent more likely than childless homeowners to lose their homes, three times more likely than men without children to go bankrupt, and seven times more likely to head up the family after a divorce. Having children has become the dividing line between the solvent and the insolvent. Today's parents are working harder than ever and falling desperately behind even with two incomes. Yet this state of affairs is not an unavoidable feature of the modern economy or the inevitable by-product of women's entry into the workforce. It is mostly a question of proper family money management.

Source: The section above is a shortened version of an excerpt from Elizabeth Warren and Amelia Warren Tyagi, *The Two-Income Trap: Why Middle-Class Mothers And Fathers Are Going Broke*, Basic Books, a member of Perseus Books Group, 2003. The excerpt appeared on the msnbc. com *Today, Tech & Money* page at http://www.msnbc.msn.com/id/3079221/ and is reprinted by permission.

Young people struggle to deal with debt

People in their 20s are carrying an unprecedented burden of debt: college loans, credit card debt, personal loans, on average $16,120. Nearly two-thirds carry some debt, and those with debt have taken on more in recent years, according to an analysis by Experian, the credit-reporting agency, for *USA TODAY* in 2007. Their late payments are rising, and they are more likely to be late with their payments than other Americans. Nearly half of twenty-somethings have actually stopped paying a debt, had cars repossessed or sought bankruptcy protection.

Debt is causing these young people anxiety. A poll of twenty-somethings by *USA TODAY* and the National Endowment for Financial Education (NEFE) found that 60% feel they are facing tougher financial pressures than young people did in previous generations, and 30% say they worry frequently about their debt. Debt is creating a sense that no matter what they do, they are not going to be able to get ahead. Debt has forced some to change their career plans; and 22% say they have taken a job they otherwise would not have in order to pay off student loan debt. Twenty-nine percent say they have put off or chosen not to pursue more education because of debt. And 26% have put off buying a home for the same reason. A smaller percentage say they have put off marrying (11%) or having children (14%). The Boomerang Generation –young adults who return to live with their parents – is real too. In the poll, 19% said they had moved back with parents to cut costs. The 2000 Census found that more than 25% of 18-to-34-year-olds had moved back in with family. Experience Inc., which provides career services to link college graduates with jobs, found that 58% of twenty-somethings it surveyed had moved back home after college. Of those, 32% stayed for more than a year. Many young people cannot save early for their retirement, and most do not. Fifty-five percent are not saving in either an individual retirement account or a 401(k) account, and 40% do not have a savings account they contribute to regularly.

The root cause of the problem is that the average price of college has grown much faster than the rate of inflation. Average annual tuition at public four-year colleges and universities was $5,836 in 2006-07, up 268% from 1976-77, according to the U.S. Education Department and NCES. Private college tuition was up 248% to $22,218 a year. At the same time, although total federal student aid has grown sharply, so has the proportion of people in college. In 2004, 67% of high school graduates enrolled in college; in 1972, only 49% did. As a result, student grants cover only 39% of the costs of a four-year college compared with nearly 80% in the mid-1970s. Students have generally made up the gap between what colleges charge and what they can afford by borrowing. The percentage of students who borrowed for college jumped to 65% in 2000-01 from 34% in 1977, says NCES. Half of all students also use credit cards to help pay for books and other items, the American Council on Education has found. Moreover, after graduation, jobs pay slightly less than they used to. Thirty years ago, a male college graduate could make the equivalent of $51,223 a year in 2004 inflation-adjusted dollars. In 2004, he earned *less*: $50,700. Wages for women, though, have risen. But it takes a greater portion of the average income to buy a median-price home today. In 1970, it was 17%; in 2005, 22.4%. The median price of a home was $23,000 in 1970. Adjusted for inflation, that is $115,770—barely more than half the median price of $219,000 in 2005. The U.S. Student Association (USSA) wants the government to boost student Pell grants, cut interest rates on government-backed loans, and offer more forgiving repayment options, including graduated payments so that those who earn less early in their careers are not unduly burdened. And they want payment plans that consider the effect of children on a family's monthly student loan payment. At present, student loan debt is like a fixed-rate mortgage.

THE WOMEN'S RIGHTS MOVEMENT

1998 marked the 150th anniversary of a movement started by Elizabeth Cady Stanton to achieve full civil rights for women in the US. The Women's Rights movement originated at the Seneca Falls Conference in 1848. Over the past seven generations, dramatic social and legal changes have been accomplished that are now so accepted that they go unnoticed by the people whose lives they have utterly changed. Many people who have lived through the recent decades of this process have come to accept without question what has transpired. And younger people, for the most part, can hardly believe life was ever otherwise. The staggering changes for women that have come about in family life, religion, government, employment and education happened because women themselves made these changes happen through meetings, petition drives, lobbying, public speaking, and nonviolent resistance.

The First Wave
One of the most interesting of the early feminist statements is a speech by Elizabeth Cady Stanton, appearing before the Judiciary Committee in 1892 on behalf of the women's suffrage Amendment (to be the19th.) Rather than present her well-known case yet again after 20 years of such appearances, she instead drew out the basic attitude toward life implicit in feminism. Her speech, entitled "The Solitude of Self," claims that human beings live in radical isolation from one another. Women require full opportunities for individual development to enable them to face (or even better to outface) the horrors of existence. For that reason it is wrong to deprive anyone, woman or man, of any natural right:

"We ask no sympathy from others in the anxiety and agony of a broken friendship or shattered love. When death sunders our nearest ties, alone we sit in the shadows of our affliction. Alike mid the greatest triumphs and darkest tragedies of life we walk alone. On the divine heights of human attainments, eulogized and worshiped as a hero or saint, we stand alone. In ignorance, poverty, and vice, as a pauper or criminal, alone we starve or steal …. Whatever the theories may be of woman's dependence on man, in the supreme moments of her life he cannot bear her burdens. Alone she goes to the gates of death to give life to every man that is born into the world. No one can share her fears, no one can mitigate her pangs; and if her sorrow is greater than she can bear, alone she passes beyond the gates into the vast unknown....Seeing then that life must ever be a march and a battle, that each soldier must be equipped for his own protection, it is the height of cruelty to rob the individual of a single natural right." First wave feminists like Susan B. Anthony and Elizabeth Cady Stanton were also prominent in the temperance movement, which called for a ban on the public sale of alcohol, a long campaign that finally succeeded with the ratification in 1920 of the 18th amendment to the Constitution, which began thirteen years of Prohibition.

The Second Wave

It is often forgotten that the Women's Rights Movement did not begin in the 1960s. What occurred then was actually a second wave of activism powered by several seemingly independent events of that turbulent decade, each of which brought a different segment of the population into the movement. First, encouraged by Esther Peterson, Director of the Women's Bureau of the Department of Labor, President Kennedy in 1961 convened a Commission on the Status of Women, naming Eleanor Roosevelt as its chair. The report issued by that commission in 1963 documented discrimination against women in virtually every area of American life. State and local governments quickly established their own commissions for women, to research conditions and recommend changes that could be initiated. Then in 1963, Betty Friedan published a landmark book, *The Feminine Mystique*. This evolved out of a survey she had conducted for her 20-year college reunion. In it she documented the emotional and intellectual oppression that educated middle-class women were experiencing because of limited life options. The book became an immediate bestseller, and inspired thousands of women to look for fulfillment beyond the role of homemaker. Next, as part of the 1964 Civil Rights Act, Title VII prohibited discrimination in employment on the basis of sex as well as race, religion, and national origin, and the Equal Employment Opportunity Commission was established to investigate discrimination complaints. But although it received 50,000 sex discrimination complaints in its first five years, it did not pursue them with sufficient vigor, and feminists agreed to form a civil rights organization for women similar to the NAACP. In 1966, the National Organization for Women was organized, soon to be followed by an array of other mass-membership organizations addressing the needs of specific groups of women, including blacks, Latinas, Asian Americans, lesbians, welfare recipients, business owners, aspiring politicians, and tradeswomen and professional women of every sort. The federal Equal Pay Act was passed in 1963, and by the early 1970s over 40 states had passed equal pay laws.

New Issues Come to the Fore

These various parts of the re-emerging Women's Rights Movement addressed a wide range of issues. Small groups of women in hundreds of communities worked on grassroots projects like establishing women's newspapers, bookstores and cafes. They created battered women's shelters and rape crisis hotlines to care for victims of sexual abuse and domestic violence. They came together to form child care centers so that women could work outside their homes. Women health care professionals opened women's clinics to provide birth control and family planning counseling, and to offer abortion services, for low-income women.

With the inclusion of Title IX in the Education Codes of 1972, equal access to higher education and to professional schools became the law. The long-term effect of that one single reform has been phenomenal. The number of women doctors, lawyers, engineers, architects and other professionals has doubled and doubled again as quotas which limited women's enrollment in graduate schools were outlawed. Athletics has probably been the most hotly contested area of Title IX, as it has also been one of the hottest areas of improvement. In 1972, only one in twenty-seven high school girls played sports; today one in three do. The whole world has seen how much American women athletes can achieve during the last few Olympic Games, measured in their huge numbers of medals.

The changes brought about by the Women's Rights Movement are reflected in attitudes held in society at large. In 1972, 26% of men and women said they would not vote for a woman for President. By 1996 only just over 5% of women and 8% of men took that view. But perhaps the most dramatic impact of the Women's Rights Movement of the past few decades has been women's financial liberation. Married women can now get credit cards in their own name, and obtain a bank loan without a male co-signer.

The Supreme Court has made it possible for a woman to hold any job for which she is qualified. Women have been appointed to the Supreme Court itself: Ruth Bader Ginsburg, Sandra Day O'Connor and in 2009 Sonia Sotomayor. Now women work in literally thousands of trades, professions and businesses which would have been almost unthinkable just a generation ago. More than three million women now work in occupations considered "nontraditional" until very recently. Women have now also entered the clergy, the military (excluding ground infantry and submarines), and the newsroom. Many of these changes came about because of legislation and court cases promoted by women's organizations. But many of the advances women achieved in the 1960s and 1970s were personal: getting husbands to help with the housework or regularly take responsibility for family meals; getting a long-deserved promotion at work; gaining the financial and emotional strength to leave an abusive partner.

The Equal Rights Amendment is Reintroduced

The Equal Rights Amendment, which had languished in Congress since 1923, was reintroduced in 1972 and ratified by 35 of the necessary 38 states. The ERA was introduced again in 2007, because as it failed to achieve ratification by the necessary three-quarters of the states last time, it has to be passed by the Congress again. The ERA states: "Equality of rights under the law shall not be denied or abridged by the United States or by any state on account of sex." Women's rights activists have chosen a Constitutional Amendment to obtain their objectives because women have not received sufficient protection from the equal rights clause of the 14th Amendment. The reason for this is that the Supreme Court has based its judgments upon cases under that Amendment on a formal model of equality, where women and men are equally situated, and has not extended its protection to cases which affect women more heavily or uniquely. Meanwhile ERAs passed by states, although interpreted inconsistently by judges, have been an extremely important way of advancing women's rights.

The first campaign for the ratification of the ERA mobilized millions of women in communities across the nation to take part in grassroots activity on behalf of the Women's Rights Movement. The National Council of Women's Organizations (NCWO) has nearly 200 member organizations, which have a collective total of more than twelve million members. Women's organizations organized their members to help raise money and generate public support. House meetings, walk-a-thons, door-to-door canvassing and marches were staged in key states that brought out hundreds of thousands of supporters. Massive lobbying, petitioning, countdown rallies, White House picketing and even hunger strikes and civil disobedience took place. The ranks of NOW and other women's rights organizations swelled to historic sizes. When the extended deadline for ratification expired in 1982, the ERA had come just three states short of the 38 needed to write it into the Constitution. Seventy-five percent of the women legislators in those three pivotal states supported the ERA, but only 46% of the men voted to ratify. The decisive issue was abortion. Opponents argued that if the ERA passed, it would mean that abortion would become a constitutional right. The reasoning goes that since only women become pregnant, discrimination against pregnancy by not funding abortions is sex-oriented discrimination. Supreme Court Justice Ruth Bader Ginsburg is on record as asserting that abortion funding would be a constitutional right if the ERA passed. By 2003, 18 states were paying for Medicaid abortions, 15 of which did so under court order because they had an ERA in their state constitutions. The 15 not-yet-ratified states are Alabama, Arizona, Arkansas, Florida, Georgia, Illinois, Louisiana, Mississippi, Missouri, Nevada, North Carolina, Oklahoma, South Carolina, Utah, and Virginia.

The ERA was promptly reintroduced into Congress, and has been in every subsequent session, on the basis that the ERA would have to be passed again by two-thirds majorities in Congress and three-quarters of the states. Each time the process has stalled. Now, in the belief that only three more states need ratify and the other states need not be asked to vote again, despite the passage of time, women's organizations are pursuing a "three-state strategy." The new strategy was chosen because the Madison Amendment, concerning congressional pay raises, became the 27th Amendment to the Constitution on May 7, 1992, after a ratification period of 203 years. This established the precedent that there should be no constitutional objection to an ERA ratification period longer than the current few decades. Also, Congress, when it first passed the ERA in 1972, chose to impose a time limit, but not in the text of the Amendment itself, and later, a different session of Congress extended that time limit, thus establishing a further precedent. A strong argument can therefore be made that any session of Congress could, by a simple majority in both Houses, extend (or eliminate) the currently expired ratification time limit on the ERA, so that just three more state ratifications would add the ERA to the Constitution. It is argued further that the 35 existing state ratifications should stand, because under Article V of the Constitution and confirmed by precedent, states that have once ratified an Amendment do not have the power to rescind that ratification. These arguments have yet to be adjudicated by the Supreme Court, to which they would assuredly go if the "three state strategy" were successful.

The Women's Rights Agenda today

Significant progress has been made on the topics discussed at the original Seneca Falls Convention in 1848. Therefore much of the discussion has moved beyond the issue of equal rights and into territory that is controversial, even among feminists. There are four main currents within modern feminist thought: Liberal (concerned with attaining economic and political equality within the context of capitalism); Radical (focused on men and patriarchy as the main causes of the oppression of women); Socialist (critical of capitalism and Marxism, postulating various forms of interaction between capitalism and patriarchy); Marxist Feminism (a theoretical position held by relatively few feminists in the US which seeks to develop the potential of Marxist theory to understand the capitalist sources of the oppression of women).

The feminist agenda:

- Although the Supreme Court ruling in *Roe v. Wade* in 1973 affirmed a woman's right to terminate her pregnancy in the first two trimesters, the right is still controversial.

- Women's enrollment in military academies and service in active combat is being debated.
- The presence of women in leadership roles in religious worship is controversial for some, natural for others.
- Affirmative action. Is help in making up for past discrimination appropriate? Do qualified women now have a level playing field?
- Woman's dual role as workers and mothers. Should businesses accommodate women's family responsibilities, or should women compete equally for advancement with men, most of whom still assume fewer family obligations?
- The US government should undertake a gender impact assessment of the effect of economic liberalization on women, taking into account women's varying ethnic and economic backgrounds; provide greater funding for trade-related adjustment assistance programs, and collect and disseminate gender disaggregated i.e., analyzed labor and economic data.
- Pornography. Is it degrading, even dangerous, to women, or is it simply a free speech issue?
- Sexual harassment. Just where does flirting leave off and harassment begin?
- Surrogate motherhood. Is it simply the right of a free woman to hire out her womb for this service?
- Should Social Security benefits be allocated equally for homemakers and their working spouses, to keep surviving wives from poverty as widows?

When US representatives in Beijing joined in the unanimous adoption of the Beijing Platform for Action in 1995, they committed the US government to actions which included: revising laws and administrative practices to ensure women's equal rights and access to economic resources; developing gender-based methodologies to conduct research to address the feminization of poverty; promoting women's economic rights and independence, including access to employment, appropriate working conditions and control over economic resources; facilitating women's equal access to resources, employment, markets and trade; eliminating occupational segregation and all forms of employment discrimination; promoting harmonization of work and family responsibilities for women and men (i.e., labor protections, job benefits, parental leave, education reform and technological innovation). Since then, however, women's rights advocates have found progress disappointing. Little action has been taken since 2001, changes in employment patterns have had an adverse effect on women, unions have become weaker, and cuts to some government programs have also had a particularly heavy effect. According to the AFL-CIO, one quarter to one third of working women lack basic benefits: affordable health care, prescription drug coverage, pension, retirement benefits, and equal pay. Many women work irregular hours and most (3 in 5) contribute half or more of their families' incomes, increasing their daily pressure. Today, young women proudly calling themselves "the third wave" are confronting these and other thorny issues.

While many women prefer not to label themselves "feminist" because the term may provoke hostility, few would give up the personal freedoms and expanded opportunities women have won over the last 150 years. Whatever choices Americans make for their own lives, most of them envision a world for their daughters, nieces and granddaughters where all girls and women will have the opportunity to develop their unique skills and talents and pursue their dreams.

Today women hold some 15% of the seats in Congress. They also hold 24.3% of the state legislative seats. Yet, despite such small numbers, women have successfully changed thousands of local, state, and federal laws that had limited women's legal status and social roles. Substantial barriers to the full equality of America's women still remain, however, and the women's rights movement lost some of its impetus toward the end of the 20th century. Political scientist Steven P. Schacht argues that this was because feminism has lacked mass support, probably due to negative labeling by conservative critics. To some extent feminism became polarized by class, with the wealthy and upwardly mobile leaders pushing some agendas that were of no interest to working-class women, and to some extent a generation gap developed between the leaders of the baby boomer generation and women of "generation X" who had different priorities. The remaining injustices are, however, being tackled daily in the courts and conference rooms, the homes and organizations, in the workplaces and on the playing fields.

ALCOHOL ABUSE AND ILLEGAL DRUGS

Underage drinking

Too many young people in America begin drinking alcohol when they are as young as 12. In 1998, about 10.4 million drinkers in the US were less than 21 years old. A study shows a four-in-one (25%) chance that children who begin drinking at 13 will become problem drinkers—and most likely impaired drivers—as opposed to young people who do not drink until the age of 21. By the time teenagers get to college, their rate of consumption has increased dramatically: 4.4 million of them are binge drinkers and another 1.8 million are heavy drinkers (consuming five or more drinks on one occasion at least five times in the past month).

Some of the social pattern of abuse is predictable. Youth in depressed rural areas (such as Appalachia) and in small towns where there is little for young people to do start drinking very early, and so do youth in poor urban neighborhoods. But it also seems to be true that the children of rich families are far more prone to alcohol and drug abuse than middle class youngsters. In part this is because the parents are not enough involved with their teenagers, but there also seems to be a culture of permissiveness that goes with wealth, a sense that if you are rich the ordinary rules of behavior do not apply.

In some cases, such as school vacation trips, parents are not aware that underage and excessive drinking is taking place. These trips may become drinking junkets or "'booze cruises." Other parents sometimes acknowledge the drinking and help their teens plan parties, hoping to ensure their safety by controlling their drinking environment. Parents may feel it is hard to communicate with their children about alcohol, but talking to them and setting clear boundaries are the most effective things they can do. Survey after survey shows that young people rank parents among the top reasons for not using alcohol.

Young people alone are not at the root of the underage drinking issue. Adults often facilitate youth drinking by providing the drinks. Indeed, 75 percent of teens say that alcohol is easy to acquire. Approximately two-thirds of teenagers who drink report that they buy their own alcohol. Whether they buy it from stores or at bars that sell without checking IDs, from home delivery services or from friends and siblings, alcohol is everywhere and easily within youths' reach. A study of underage drinking showed that 48 percent of all salespeople never asked to see the buyers' identification. Of those sellers who asked, 50 percent of them sold the alcohol even after the buyers said they had no ID. And it seems that underage drinkers make alcohol a priority in their budgets.

Each year, college students spend approximately $5.5 billion on alcohol—more than they spend on soft drinks, milk, tea, coffee and books combined. Laws holding parents liable for underage drinking incidents are becoming more common.

Adult alcohol abuse

Alcohol consumption among Americans is declining, according to research published by Yuqing Zhang and colleagues of Boston University School of Medicine in the *American Journal of Medicine* (August, 2008). Yet there does not appear to be any significant decline in alcohol-related health disorders. According to the 1999 Household Survey on Drug Abuse, alcohol is the most widely abused drug among working adults, especially among full-time workers aged 18 to 25—more than 1 in 3 (38%) are binge drinkers. Rates of binge drinking among those soon to enter the workforce (ages 15-17) show a steady climb from 12% to 22%. Rates of binge drinking and heavy drinking (bingeing at least 5 times a month) are consistently higher among men than women. For example, 43% of men aged 18 to 25 are binge drinkers, compared to 21% of women. Many more employees drink to a lesser degree. A common misconception is that alcoholics are responsible for most alcohol-related workplace problems. But casual drinkers, in aggregate, account for far more incidents of absenteeism, tardiness, and poor quality of work than the alcohol dependent. Alcohol is also a factor in nearly 40% of road traffic fatalities.

DRUGS

Illegal drugs exact an enormous toll on American society. Drugs take 52,000 lives annually and drain the economy of $181 billion dollars a year, according to the National Institute on Drug Abuse and the American College of Emergency Physicians. Sixteen million Americans currently use drugs, and seven million meet the criteria for needing treatment for drug abuse. Of those, 62 percent are dependent on marijuana. Recreational drugs, including cocaine and heroin, are responsible for an estimated 10,000 deaths per year. Despite tougher anti-drug laws than some countries, a WHO survey in 2008 showed the US had the highest level of illegal drug use, particularly cocaine and marijuana, in the world. People with higher incomes were more likely to use both legal and illegal drugs.

America's "war on drugs" – interdiction, stiff mandatory sentences, and more vigorous enforcement of drug laws – has so far failed. The reason, say some commentators, is that the desire to solve problems by taking drugs is a product of American culture. When a child is taught that the appropriate response to pain or discomfort is taking a pill, it increases the chances that such a child, when faced with the challenges of adolescence, will seek comfort by taking drugs. Some believe the portrayal of the illegal drug trade in movies, TV series and novels attracts some young people to try drugs, although others dispute this.

Drugs are dangerous, pushed or prescribed, experts point out. An article in the *Journal of the American Medical Association* (JAMA) reports that an estimated 106,000 hospitalized patients die each year from drugs which, by medical standards, are properly prescribed and administered. More than two million suffer serious side effects. Reactions to prescription drugs kill more than twice as many Americans as HIV/AIDS or suicide. Fewer die from accidents or diabetes than adverse drug reactions. (The study did not include outpatients, cases of malpractice, or instances where the drugs were not taken as directed.) According to another AMA publication, *American Medical News,* drug related problems kill as many as 198,815 people, put 8.8 million in hospitals, and account for up to 28% of hospital admissions. If these figures are accurate, only cancer and heart disease kill more patients than drugs.

Despite harsh mandatory minimum laws that send many low-level drug offenders to prison, drug use as evidenced by survey information and emergency room admissions remains a significant problem. One proposed solution to the illegal drug problem was encouraging potential users to ignore peer pressure and "just say no." This strategy is not being recommended for prescription drugs, however, and doctors are beginning to debate such double standards. Some are calling for the "real drug problem" to be addressed—the cultural notion that the first solution to seek for relief of life's problems is a drug.

The Bureau of Justice Statistics has published the results of surveys of drug use by youth, the general population and in the workplace.

The University of Michigan Monitoring the Future Study found in 2007 that 31.7% of high school seniors had used marijuana in the previous 12 months, and 42.3% had used it at some time. Reported use of marijuana by high school seniors during the past month peaked in 1978 at 37% and declined to its lowest level in 1992 at 12%.

Such self-reports may underrepresent drug use because dropouts and truants are not included, and these groups may use drugs more than those who stay in school. But it is also possible that some respondents exaggerate their use to impress their peers. Past year marijuana use by college students has ranged from a low of 31.2% in 1995 to a high of 35.9% in 1998. The use of cocaine within the past month of the survey by high school seniors peaked in 1985 at 6.7%, up from 1.9% in 1975. Cocaine use declined to a low of 1.3% in 1992 and 1993. In 2006, 2.5% of high school seniors reported past-month cocaine use. Rates of past year cocaine use by college students have varied over the past 11 years from a low of 2.9% in 1996 to a high of 5.1% in 2006, with 8.5% reporting they had used it at some time. Overall there has been a gradual decline in the use of illegal drugs by teens in recent years.

In the general population, according to data from the *2006 National Household Survey on Drug Use and Health* (NSDUH), 112 million Americans age 12 or older (45% of the population) reported illicit drug use at least once in their lifetime, 15% within the past year, and 8% within the past month. Marijuana had been used by 28% of people age 18-25 in the previous year. In the workplace, a study focusing on findings from 2002 through 2004 from the NSDUH reported that 9.4 million (8.2%) of full time workers were illicit drug users; 57.5% of illicit drug users aged 18 to 64 were employed full-time; and nearly one out of five (19%) workers aged 18 to 25 used illicit drugs during the past month.

A total of 32 million (29.6%) of full-time workers reported random drug testing in their workplace. For each age group, past month illicit drug users were about 12% less likely than nonusers to report working for employers who conducted pre-hire drug tests. Illicit drug use among full-time employees was most prevalent in food preparation and serving-related occupations (17.4%), followed by construction and extraction occupations. After increasing more than 1,200% from 1987 (22%) to 1996 (81%), the percentage of employers conducting drug testing has dropped in recent years to a current level of 66%, according to the American Management Association. The AMA's 10,000 members cover approximately 25% of the nation's workforce.

The statistics should be considered with care. Headline figures may not discriminate between casual experimentation and full-blown addiction.

Legalizing marijuana

About one-third of Americans, according to Gallup, say marijuana should be legalized. They claim that the laws against the use of marijuana place undue burdens on law enforcement resources, punish ill Americans whose doctors have prescribed the substance, and unfairly affect African Americans. In 2008, Rep. Barney Frank introduced a proposal H.R. 5843 to end federal penalties for Americans carrying fewer than 100 grams, almost a quarter-pound, of the substance and for the "nonprofit transfer" of up to an ounce of marijuana. Rob Kampia, director of the Marijuana Policy Project, says marijuana arrests outnumber arrests for all violent crimes combined, taking up inordinate amounts of police time. Some reformers want resources diverted to stop the trafficking of narcotics into the US. Bill Piper of the Drug Policy Alliance Network points out that those found guilty of marijuana use can lose their jobs, financial aid for college, their food stamp and welfare benefits, or their low-cost housing. About a dozen states, like California, have approved some degree of medical marijuana use. But the Office of National Drug Control Policy has long opposed marijuana legalization, for medical purposes or otherwise, saying the drug has a high potential for abuse and no accepted medical use. The Drug Enforcement Administration says people charged with simple possession are rarely incarcerated. Legalization of marijuana, it claims, will create dependency and treatment issues, and open the door to use of other drugs, impaired health, delinquent behavior, and drugged drivers.

Those most at risk

Among employed adults, the highest rates of current drug use are reported by white, non-Hispanic males, 18-25 years old, with less than a high school education. Among juvenile drug addicts, substance abuse usually is just one among several problem behaviors such as gang membership, gun possession, violence, and general delinquency. Many of these reflect an effort to identify with a peer group.

Yet there is some good news. The nation is moving steadily in the right direction in the fight against illegal drugs. After a decade-long surge in illicit drug use in the 1990s, the National Drug Control Strategy achieved a 23 percent reduction in youth illegal drug use from 2002 to 2007 as measured by the Monitoring the Future (MTF) study. Marijuana use has fallen by 25 percent, and youth use of drugs such as MDMA/Ecstasy, LSD, and methamphetamine dropped precipitously over the same period, cutting the use of these drugs by more than 50 percent. Approximately 900,000 fewer young Americans are using illicit drugs today than in 2001. The percentage of adolescents aged 12 to 17 who used inhalants in the previous year was lower in 2007 (3.9 percent) than in 2003, 2004, and 2005 (4.5, 4.6, and 4.5 percent respectively). Inhalants are often the first drug for new users. Lesser declines in drug use are shown by the National Survey on Drug Use and Health, where adolescent past month use of cigarettes, alcohol, and illicit drugs declined between 2002 and 2007. Use of illicit drugs fell from 11.6% to 9.5%, primarily due to a decline in marijuana use: 8.2% used marijuana in 2002 compared with 6.7% in 2007. Illicit drug dependence or abuse declined from 5.6% to 4.3%. Among young adults ages 18 to 25, the level of nonmedical use of prescription pain relievers rose 12 percent to 4.6 percent in 2007. Moreover, workforce drug testing data from Quest Diagnostics indicate that drug test positives show the lowest levels of drug use in the US workforce since 1988. Positive drug tests for cocaine declined by 38 percent from 2006 to 2008. The percentage testing positive for methamphetamine had been rising quickly, but dropped by 50 percent from 2005 to 2007.

A new, coordinated approach

One in five state prisoners has committed an offence to obtain money to buy drugs. Young people who use drugs are several times more likely to commit various crimes, such as assault and property destruction, as those who do not use drugs. For more than 8 million children, one or both parents are dependent on alcohol and illicit drugs, and many have a mental illness or are involved in criminal activity as well. Indeed, it is becoming unusual for an offender not to have a substance abuse and/or mental health problem. Public health and public safety agencies are co-operating to address the related problems of substance abuse and crime in a comprehensive way, pooling information and funding, and adopting a common approach which places more emphasis on treatment.

The treatment aims to help offenders come to terms with their pasts and generate the capacity to lead productive lives. More than 96 percent of prisoners eventually return to society, at a rate of about 500,000 each year from state prisons. They can return drug-free and able to contribute to society, or they can return likely to abuse substances and commit crimes. Thus, the argument for treatment rests largely on a need to protect the public. Ultimately, though, modern policy is based on science. In the last few years, research has established that treatment works, and what kind of treatment works for whom. There is no longer any doubt that addiction is a brain disease in which repeated drug use impairs the capacity of the brain to function even after drug use ceases, and that treatment yields enormous benefits for the addict, his or her family, and society.

A federal study found that 18 months after release, an inmate who receives treatment is 73 percent less likely to be rearrested and 44 percent less likely to return to drug use than one who receives no treatment. Repeatedly, studies have found substantial declines—of 40, 60, even 80 percent—in drug selling, prostitution, homelessness and welfare receipt, and substantial increases in employment, among those receiving treatment. Treatment also produces financial savings. While a year of outpatient treatment costs less than $5,000 per participant, and comprehensive residential treatment programs range between $5,000 and $15,000, a 6-year prison term can cost as much as $150,000.

Offenders with substance abuse problems, however, often have a variety of other problems that make it difficult for them to sustain compliance with treatment programs or otherwise maintain productive behavior: mental illness, the effects of physical or emotional abuse, poverty, homelessness, educational and work skill deficits, difficulties in parenting or, for juveniles, abusive parents. Juveniles are often following the path of their parents into substance abuse. Treatment of the whole family may be indicated, and intensive aftercare is always necessary.

The National Drug Control Strategy

The National Drug Control Strategy is based on partnership with parents, educators, and community leaders to prevent drug use through education and social disapproval. The Strategy commits unprecedented resources to the treatment of drug abuse. The Strategy builds on the existing approach, which focuses on preventing drug use before it starts, healing America's drug users, and disrupting the market for illegal drugs. Solid progress has already been made toward reducing drug use by 25 percent. Yet in 2006, 23.6 million persons aged 12 or older needed treatment for an illicit drug or alcohol abuse problem (9.6 percent of the persons aged 12 or older). Of these, only 2.5 million (10.8 percent of those who needed treatment) received it. Thus, 21.2 million persons (8.6 percent of the population aged 12 or older) needed treatment but did not receive it. Other programs address the needs of the six million Americans who need treatment for drug addiction but cannot afford it. The overwhelming majority of these users fail to recognize their need for treatment. Such people are issued vouchers for appropriate services to be provided by an organization approved by their state. The costs are borne 55% by the state and 45% by the patient.

While focusing heavily on reducing demand for illegal drugs, the Strategy recognizes the importance of eroding the economic base of the drug trade. Steps are being taken to make the drug trade more dangerous and less profitable for drug dealers, and ultimately to break the international and domestic market for illegal drugs. The Strategy is designed to make drugs scarce, expensive, and of unreliable quality. Success in preventing the importation of illegal drugs (mostly from Mexico) has so far been limited.

Complementing the Strategy is the award-winning National Youth Anti-Drug Media Campaign. This is the largest integrated (multimedia) social marketing program ever undertaken by the federal government. Besides the television, radio, and print advertisements, the Campaign has created websites and publications detailing information about drugs and how communities can fight back. The Campaign's messages have become ubiquitous in the lives of America's youth and their parents. From network television advertisements to school-based educational materials, from playground basketball backboards to internet websites, and from parenting skills brochures to ads in movie theatres, the Campaign's messages reach Americans wherever they live, work, learn, and play. Over 35 million people have visited the Media Campaign websites and more than four tons of material a month is shipped to parents, educators, and youth inquiring about facts regarding drugs. Studies have shown that the Campaign has had a significant affect on youth attitudes and behavior.

The gun culture

Armed in America

These figures are offered for reflection and research and not as headlines for debating a complex problem. It is important to distinguish between figures for all firearms and figures for handguns, which are the guns most commonly used in crime.

The US is one of the most violent countries in the developed world. America has some of the world's weakest gun control laws and at the same time has a constitutional protection for gun owners. In 1995 the Bureau of Alcohol, Tobacco and Firearms estimated that there were 223 million guns in private ownership. In other wealthy countries fewer people are likely to own a gun than in America; gun control laws are a public health question.

- In 2006 there were over 10,177 homicides by guns and the majority of homicides involve guns (FBI).

In a single year, 3,000 children and teens are killed by gunfire, and at least 4 to 5 times as many children and teens suffer from non-fatal firearm injuries (Children's Defense Fund and National Center for Health Statistics). The rate of firearm deaths among children under age 15 is almost 12 times higher in the US than in 25 other industrialized countries combined (Centers for Disease Control and Prevention).

- On average, approximately 57% of annual firearm deaths are suicides, 40% are homicides, and 3% are unintentional shootings.
- There were 52,447 deliberate non-fatal firearms injuries and 23,237 accidental non-fatal injuries in 2000 (Centers for Disease Control and Prevention).
- In 2004, firearm homicide was the leading cause of death for black males ages 15-34 (CDC).
- Concealable weapons kill more Americans every year than all household and recreational products combined.
- Suicide is the leading cause of death by firearms. There were 16,907 such deaths in 2004 and the total number of deaths by firearms that year was 32,436.
- Stolen guns are used in about 30 percent of crimes (Bureau of Justice Statistics).
- A person living in a home with a gun is three times more likely to die by homicide and five times more likely to die by suicide than someone in a gunless household.
- Americans use guns defensively more than 2 million times each year, five times more frequently than the 430,000 times guns were used to commit crimes in 1997.
- Ninety-eight percent of the time, simply brandishing a gun is sufficient to stop a violent attack.
- Some 35% of US homes and about 25% of adults have guns, most commonly for recreation and self-protection (National Institute of Justice).

As studies have shown, 2 to 2.5 million Americans use guns to protect themselves and their families, and some 400,000 of them state that they would almost certainly have lost their lives if they had not defended themselves. Nevertheless, a recent study found that 69 percent of all Americans, and 57 percent of the nation's gun owners, want stricter gun control laws. The NRA, the National Rifle Association, the largest gun rights organization, is opposed to such controls, and refers to the Second Amendment's "right to bear arms," but the NRA does support certain gun control measures to suppress crime. Some organizations such as Gun Owners of America, however, campaign against all gun control on law abiding citizens, arguing that one control will lead to another and eventually to the end of the right to keep and bear arms. Organizations that campaign for more gun control include the Coalition to Stop Gun Violence and the Brady Campaign to Prevent Gun Violence. Ranked by filings, gun rights lobbyists outnumber gun control advocates by 3:1, according to the Center for Public Integrity. The disparity in dollars spent on campaigns is even greater.

Male juveniles, regardless of race, are more likely to die from gunshot wounds than from all natural causes combined. This record rate of violence has various causes such as family or neighborhood concerns, poverty, joblessness, drug abuse, and the ready availability of guns. Many ascribe the high abuse of firearms to the glorification of violence in the media. It is notable that in 2005, 75% of the 10,100 homicides committed using firearms were committed using handguns, compared to 4% with rifles, 5% with shotguns, and the rest with a type of firearm not specified

The gun culture is perhaps the most hotly debated of America's enduring political issues. The arguments center on disagreements that range from the practical – does gun ownership cause or prevent crime? – to the constitutional – how should the Second Amendment be interpreted?

– to the ethical – what should the balance be between an individual's right of self-defense through gun ownership and the people's interest in maintaining public safety? Political arguments about gun rights fall into two basic categories: first, does the government have the authority to regulate guns? and second, if it does, is gun regulation effective public policy? The first category, collectively known as rights-based arguments, focus on the Second Amendment, state constitutions/states' rights, the right of self-defense, and security against tyranny and invasion. Public policy arguments, the second category, revolve around the importance of a militia, the reduction of gun violence and firearm deaths, and also can include arguments based on security against foreign invasions.

The debate has been deadlocked for decades between upholders of an individual's right to firearms under the Constitution and the duty of government to prevent crime and maintain order. Repeated polling has found that a majority of Americans believe they have a right to own a gun, while at the same time a majority also believes there is a need for stricter firearms law enforcement. Only a minority support new gun laws rather than stricter enforcement. Generally, Democrats support gun control proposals and Republicans do not, although the votes on the Brady bill in 1993 show that this is not a strictly partisan issue. The partisan divide on this issue is somewhat reflected by public opinion. Democrats overwhelmingly support gun control and Republicans are divided on the issue. Gun control was not a major issue in the 2008 election campaign, as hardly any Americans consider it to be one. Apart from the activists on both sides, it sometimes seems to be of more interest to foreigners. Yet gun control remains what politicians consider a "wedge issue," as many opponents are passionate about their right to unfettered gun ownership and may make voting decisions on this issue alone.

There are 60 million gun owners. No country has anywhere near the rate of gun ownership as the US and there is a correspondingly high gun homicide rate. But countries such as Canada have a significant level of gun ownership but a low rate of gun homicide. The number of guns in the US is 25 times higher than in Canada, which has 10% of the population of the US. In any case, the majority of guns owned by Canadians are not handguns, which are strictly regulated – and most gun homicides are caused by handguns. Although cultural and economic factors may contribute to the homicide rate, the association between the number of weapons and the number of homicides caused by these weapons seems inescapable. The typical gun owner is male, middle class, college educated and lives in a small town or rural area. Gun ownership varies greatly by region.

The gun culture in America stems from the Revolutionary War, the frontier experience, and the widespread practice of hunting and sport shooting. Guns also figure frequently in movies and the media. Some Americans, especially in the West and South, regard the right to own a gun and to use it in self-defense as central to American identity. In the days when America was an agrarian country, the value of shooting skills for survival against Native Americans, wild animals and (rarely) foreign armies meant that achieving proficiency with a gun marked a "rite of passage" for entering manhood. There is still a widespread false perception that guns won the West, ignoring the roles of homesteaders, ranchers, miners, tradespeople and businesspeople. Meanwhile in urban areas, gun ownership is nowadays associated by some with the "redneck" stereotype of rural, white, working class men.

Guns in popular culture

The gun has long been a symbol of power and masculinity in America. The figure of the gun-toting frontiersman in popular literature was created by James Fenimore Cooper in his adventure tales *The Last of the Mohicans* (1826) and *The Deerslayer* (1840). By the late 1800s, cowboy and Wild West imagery had become part of the collective imagination. A female cowboy, Calamity Jane (1852-1903) featured in Edward Wheeler's *Deadwood Dick* dime novels from 1877. The first American female superstar, Annie Oakley (1860-1926) was a sharpshooter from Ohio who toured the country from 1885 as a performer in *Buffalo Bill's Wild West Show*. (The musical *Annie Get Your Gun* (1946) was a fictional account of her life.) The archetypal cowboy hero was established largely by Theodore Roosevelt's *The Winning of the West* (1889-95), a history of the early frontier, and by Owen Wister in stories and novels, most notably *The Virginian* (1902). The image of the swaggering, gunslingng cowboy was also popularized by early cinema, notably through such classics as *The Great Train Robbery* (1903) and *A California Hold Up* (1906), the most commercially successful film of the pre-nickelodeon era. Since the 1930s, gangster films have flaunted the image of the tough, wily, gun-wielding urban lawbreaker. To some extent this image was replaced in and after World War II by the patriotic combat film that emphasized group efforts and individual sacrifice for a larger cause. These movies often featured groups of men from diverse backgrounds who were thrown together, tested on the battlefield and molded into a dedicated fighting unit. The use of guns continued to feature in late 20th century action films such as *Bonnie and Clyde* (1967), *The Godfather* (1972), *Dirty Harry* (1979) and *Robocop* (1987). In the 1970s, films like *Taxi Driver* (1976) and *Apocalypse Now* (1979) portrayed men apparently sent mad by the Vietnam war, while other movies such as *Coming Home* and *The Deer Hunter* (both 1978) told of fictitious veterans supposedly in need of rehabilitation after their Vietnam experiences. The negative role of the gun in fictionalized modern urban violence has been explored in such films as *Boyz n the Hood* (1991) and *Menace to Society* (1993).

School violence

Gun control has become more of an issue because of school violence. Since January 1, 1989, 14 deaths have occurred at primary schools, 106 at secondary and 130 at colleges or universities, in five, 59 and 24 separate incidents respectively. The worst incident at a secondary school took place at Columbine High School, Colorado, on April 20, 1999, where 15 were killed, and the worst at a college at Virginia Tech on April 16, 2007, where there were 33 victims. This was the deadliest peacetime shooting incident anywhere by a single gunman in US history. Almost all the victims died from shooting. The massacre prompted rapid changes in Virginia law that had allowed the student responsible, who had been adjudged mentally unsound, to purchase handguns without detection by the National Instant Criminal Background Check System (NICS). It also led to passage of the first major federal gun control measure in more than 13 years, a law that strengthened the NICS in 2008. An extreme, albeit unique reaction, was that of the small, rural Harrold Independent School District in Texas, covering 110 students near Fort Worth, which in 2008 voted unanimously to allow teachers to bring guns to class. Those who do will have to be certified to carry a concealed handgun, receive crisis training and obtain permission from school officials. There have also been calls for students to have permission to carry concealed handguns to class. Congress once barred guns from schools nationwide, but the law was struck down by the Supreme Court.

Gun control

The right to bear arms, seen mainly as a community right, was an issue in the Revolutionary War.

Ironically, the interpretation of the Second Amendment as an individual right arose in response to early gun control laws. This standpoint was first contested in a Kentucky court case, *Bliss v. Commonwealth* (1822, KY) in which the state court held that "the right of citizens to bear arms in defense of themselves and the State must be preserved entire." The right to bear arms was absolute and unqualified. A generation later, in an Arkansas case, *State v. Buzzard* (1842, Ark) the Arkansas high court adopted a community-based interpretation, holding that the plain words of the US and Arkansas Constitutions enacted a political and not an individual right and that the State had the right to regulate and control it. There was thus no absolute right to keep and bear arms, individually or collectively, and this has since been the orthodox view. Until the 14th Amendment, the right to keep and bear arms did not apply to African Americans who had been slaves. Modern weapons technology has posed challenges of a different kind. Under the National Firearms Act of 1934, citizens may only keep and bear fully automatic weapons under stringent regulations and only in states which permit citizens to have such weapons. The Gun Control Act of 1968 generally prohibits interstate firearms transfers except among licensed manufacturers, dealers and importers. Armor-piercing projectiles are banned. Today the US has the least restrictive gun control laws in the developed world, except for Switzerland, in part due to the strength of the gun lobby, particularly the NRA. The NRA does, however, support gun laws intended to prevent criminals from obtaining firearms, while generally opposing new restrictions that affect law abiding citizens.

The Right to Bear Arms
Amendment II to the US Constitution

A well regulated Militia, being necessary to the security of a free State, the right of the people to keep and bear Arms, shall not be infringed. (1791)

Since the late 19th century, the Supreme Court has consistently ruled that the Second Amendment restricts only the Congress, and not the states, in the regulation of guns. Until recently, there had been only one modern Supreme Court case that dealt directly with the Second Amendment, *United States v. Miller* 307 U.S. 174 (1939). Miller had been jailed by a state court for a breach of the 1934 National Firearms Act by taking an unregistered sawed-off shotgun without a stamp-affixed written order for it across the state line from Oklahoma to Arkansas. The Supreme Court upheld the law, though, strictly speaking, *Miller* did not uphold gun control but states' rights.

Gun control laws

Gun control legislation exists at all levels of government. According to the NRA, there are 20,000 gun laws nationwide, while there are 300 federal and state laws regarding the manufacture, design, sale, purchase, or possession of guns, according to the *American Journal of Preventive Medicine*. In fact the vast majority of laws are local codes, which vary widely.

Federal Gun Control

The first major gun control legislation was the National Firearms Act of 1934 which mandated that short-barrel shotguns and fully automatic firearms like machine guns be taxed and registered. This was followed in 1938 by the Federal Firearms Act, which required gun sellers to be licensed and which prohibited persons convicted of violent felonies from purchasing guns.

The Gun Control Act of 1968 prohibited the ownership of machine guns by civilians and also required that guns carry serial numbers. This was the law that introduced a tracking system to identify the purchaser of a gun by make, model, and serial number. The 1968 Act further restricted access to guns by regulating imported guns, extending gun dealer licensing requirements, prohibiting mail order sales, and expanding the list of persons not eligible to purchase guns to include persons convicted of any non-business related felony, minors, persons found to be mentally incompetent, and users of illegal drugs.

The transfer of newly manufactured machine guns to private citizens was banned with the passage of the Firearm Owners Protection Act 1986, which also established mandatory penalties for the use of a gun in the commission of a federal crime, and prohibited "cop killer" bullets capable of penetrating bulletproof clothing. In 1990, the Crime Control Act banned the manufacturing and importation of semi-automatic assault weapons.

In 1994, Congress passed the best known national gun control law, the Brady Handgun Control Act, named for the press aide who was seriously injured in the assassination attempt on President Reagan in 1981. This law originally imposed a five-day waiting period for purchasers of handguns, and required local law enforcement authorities to conduct background checks of all purchasers. The Supreme Court struck down the waiting period as unconstitutional because it infringed on states' rights. The law was revised so that the background check is instantly accomplished by gun dealers through a national computer system and there is no longer a waiting period. (There are no background checks when purchasing guns in a private transaction.) The Domestic Violence Offender Gun Ban of 1996 prohibited ownership and use of guns by individuals convicted of misdemeanor domestic violence. In response to a number of school shootings, requirements for background checks for firearm purchases were strengthened by the School Safety And Law Enforcement Improvement Act 2007, commonly known as the NICS Improvement Amendments Act. The Obama administration will likely seek to restore the ban on assault weapons which lasted from 1994-2004 and make it indefinite, and expand the list of banned weapons.

Gun control in Washington D.C.

In the iconic case of firearms law in the nation's capital, a city that has one of the highest murder rates in the country, the Supreme Court recently made a landmark decision.

In 2007 the Supreme Court said in *District of Columbia v. Heller*, 07-290, that an individual's right to bear arms was protected under the Second Amendment, ruling that Americans have an individual right to possess firearms "for traditionally lawful purposes, such as self-defense within the home." The court made it clear, however, that, like other rights, the right to bear arms is not unlimited, leaving open the prospect of reasonable governmental regulation.

The circumstances of the case are well known. The government of Washington, D.C. had asked the court to uphold Washington's 31-year ban on handgun ownership in the face of a federal appeals court ruling that struck down the ban as incompatible with the Second Amendment. City officials said the law was designed to reduce gun violence, noting that four out of every five homicides was committed with a gun. According to the District's medical examiner, there were 177 homicides in 2006. Of those, 135 were firearm-related. The city also said the ban was constitutional because it limited the choice of firearms but did not prohibit residents from owning any guns at all. Rifles and shotguns were legal, if kept under lock or disassembled. Businesses might have guns for protection. Chicago had a similar handgun ban, but few other gun-control laws were as strict as the District's. Opponents of the ban pointed to the level of violence to make their case that Washington D.C. residents should be allowed to have guns to protect themselves in their homes.

As widely reported, the main issue before the justices was whether the Second Amendment protects an individual's right to own guns or instead sets forth the collective right of states to maintain militias. The former interpretation would permit fewer restrictions on gun ownership. Gun control advocates argued that the Second Amendment was intended to ensure that states could maintain militias, a response to 18th-century fears of an all-powerful national government. Gun control opponents hoped the Court would make it clear that the Constitution does not prevent communities from having the gun laws they believe are needed to protect public safety. They argued that laws like Washington's have not worked because guns still are readily available, through legal and illegal means. Although the city's homicide rate has declined dramatically since peaking in the early 1990s, the murder rate in Washington still ranks among the nation's highest.

At present 44 state constitutions contain some form of gun rights, which are not affected by the court's consideration of Washington's restrictions. The Court declined to rule on the incorporation of the Second Amendment into state law: "While the status of the Second Amendment within the 20th-century incorporation debate is a matter of importance for the many challenges to state gun control laws, it is an issue that we need not decide."

The D.C. government has since complied with most of the decision. A bipartisan bill H.R. 6691 was introduced into the House of Representatives in 2008 to require the D.C. government to comply with the entire decision in Heller and eliminate most gun restrictions in the District.

State and local gun control

Child access prevention laws
It is illegal in many states to leave a loaded weapon within easy access of a minor.

Concealed weapon laws
The number of states allowing the concealed carry of weapons has increased to 48 since 1986. Many require an individual to obtain a license. Licensing requirements vary widely. In over half the states, all non-felons are able to obtain licenses. Vermont and Alaska have no licensing or permit requirement for non-felons aged 16 or 21 respectively. Two states prohibit concealed weapons. Mutual recognition of licenses is negotiated between the states.

Regulation of private sales to minors
Under federal law, minors under 18 are prohibited from owning guns and minors under 21 are prohibited from purchasing guns from dealers. Unless regulated by state law, however, minors 18 and over are able to buy weapons through private sales. Currently 21 states either prohibit or substantially regulate the purchase of guns by minors.

Regulating all secondary market sales
Over 20 states regulate all secondary sales through registration or licensing requirements. In the states that have no such regulation, the secondary market allows minors and criminals to obtain weapons easily at gun shows (the "gun show" loophole).

Ban on "assault" weapons
In 1989, California was the first state to ban certain types of automatic weapons. Bans have since been enacted in New York, Massachusetts, New Jersey, Hawaii, Connecticut and Maryland. The expiration of the Assault Weapons Ban has been shown to have had little effect on crime rates throughout the US, at least in those areas that do not have their own laws on assault weapons.

"One handgun a month" laws

Many purchasers (felons and minors) have circumvented federal law by purchasing firearms from individuals who have legally made bulk purchases of handguns. Four states (South Carolina, Virginia, Maryland, and California) have laws that limit legal purchases of handguns to one a month per individual buyer.

Ban on "Saturday Night Specials" and other "junk guns"

These are small, easily concealed guns which, although unreliable, appeal to some criminals because of their portability. A minority of states have laws which regulate the purchase and use of these weapons. Additionally, local laws in a number of cities outlaw the possession of these weapons.

Preemption

The majority of states have laws which prohibit local authorities from passing gun control ordinances. Officials in cities which are able to pass such ordinances, such as New York, credit a dramatic reduction in violent crime to their existence.

Waiting periods

About half the states still use state data in addition to federal data to conduct background checks prior to issuing a handgun permit. Eleven states impose waiting periods as well.

Effect of laws

The general opinion of criminologists about gun control is summarized by Don Kates: "Unfortunately, an almost perfect inverse correlation exists between those who are affected by gun laws, particularly bans, and those whom enforcement should affect. Those easiest to disarm are the responsible and law abiding citizens whose guns represent no meaningful social problem. Irresponsible and criminal owners, whose gun possession creates or exacerbates so many social ills, are the ones most difficult to disarm." *Tennessee Law Review*, "Guns and Public Health: Epidemic of Violence or Pandemic of Propaganda?" 1994.

Since the Brady bill was enacted, the number of deaths due to guns has significantly decreased. This is partly due to the overall decrease in the crime rate, but it is also clear that the domestic production and importation of handguns has decreased. Handgun ownership has remained fairly constant in the past three decades. The surge in gun ownership in the late 80's and early 90's probably was more related to public concerns about crime rather than a reaction to gun control legislation. Although fewer than 3% of gun applications have been denied since the enactment of the Brady bill, most of the denials have kept guns from felons.

Key Gun Control Issues

The biggest component of the gun control debate is whether existing gun laws are sufficient, or whether more gun laws are needed. Liberals and populists generally favor more gun laws, in the form of more registration or more licensing, to close loopholes in the law and restrict access. Moderate liberals and populists generally favor more restrictions on ownership while acknowledging "sportsmen's rights" or "the right of self-protection." Moderate compromises are to extend waiting periods before allowing ownership, and to perform "background checks" of varying degrees of severity. Conservatives and libertarians generally oppose gun laws, while acknowledging that restrictions are inevitable. They are content to enforce existing gun laws, which implies not passing any new ones. They refer to Second Amendment rights and favor laws to allow "concealed carry." A call for "instant background checks" appears to tighten gun control but actually means allowing purchasing guns on the spot. Centrists and moderates from both the right and left generally support restrictions on juvenile access to guns, especially in light of the school shootings.

"Smart guns"

Trigger Locks require entering a combination to use the gun (or some other locking method). They are intended to reduce inadvertent use by children or other unauthorized users. While low-tech gun safety locks have been sold for years, efforts are underway to create a "smart gun," which would make handguns accessible only to the gun's owners. Prototypes have been developed for such guns with features that include wristbands that must be worn by the gun owner to transmit a radio signal that allows the gun to fire, and personalized identification codes that the owner must enter before the gun will function. Gun manufacturers have begun to develop such safety technology, both to prevent future lawsuits and in hope of revitalizing a saturated handgun market. Maryland mandates that all handguns sold in that state have built-in locks, the first state to pass such a law. While researchers agree that smart guns are scientifically possible, most manufacturers claim that current models are highly flawed, and it will be years before marketable and convenient smart guns can be developed.

Proponents argue that guns should be subject to the same consumer safety standards that apply to aspirin bottles, automobiles or any other product. New personalized gun technology will protect against accidental firearms-related injuries, and go a long way toward eliminating the high rate of shooting deaths among children in the US. By making the gun useless to anyone but its owner, new locking technology would also prevent criminals from using stolen guns.

Opponents of smart gun technology say it would sharply increase the price of handguns and would make guns inaccessible for many law abiding citizens who need gun protection. Also, these new devices may not be as smart as they are made out to be. New high-tech safety features could malfunction and prevent the gun from firing when its owner is using it for self-defense. Some gun manufacturers have claimed that criminals could use jamming devices to disable police versions of the weapons.

Another new technology that could affect gun control is *microstamping,* a ballistics identification device. This uses a laser to leave an imprint on the firing pin and the barrel of a weapon, and any gun that discharges a cartridge would leave an imprint on it. The identification number of a cartridge at a crime scene would in effect identify the gun dealer who last sold that weapon, and from there the person who last bought the weapon.

Public attitudes

Regional differences in gun politics tend to be greater than partisan ones. Gun control is most favored along the eastern seaboard in such states as New York, New Jersey, Maryland and the District of Columbia. States with major metropolitan areas, notably California and Illinois, also favor controls to reduce crime. Meanwhile, gun rights are favored in northwestern states, such as Montana, Idaho and Washington; the Deep South, including Alabama, Georgia and Florida; and southwestern states such as Texas, New Mexico and Utah, both in the interests of suppressing crime and because hunting and sport shooting is more popular there. In the stereotypical gun rights state of Texas, opinions are divided, since the state contains three of the nation's largest cities. In other areas, including the midwest and plains states, opinions are mixed. Alaska and Vermont do not require any license to carry concealed weapons in public places, but do have laws prohibiting concealed weapons in certain places such as bars or taverns. The spread of concealed carry laws since 1986 in those states that tend to be in support of gun rights has led to the widespread, legally permitted, carrying of concealed handguns by civilians in many parts of the US. While gun control is not strictly a partisan issue, there is more support for increased gun control in the Democratic Party, while the Republican Party favors gun rights. The Libertarian Party, whose campaign platforms favor classical liberal government and individual rights, is outspokenly pro-gun.

A survey released by the Pew Center on April 23, 2007, just after the shootings at Virginia Tech (April 16) showed that the most recent mass shooting had had little impact on public opinion about gun control. Six in ten Americans say it is more important to control gun ownership, while 32% say it is more important to protect the right of Americans to own guns. Opinion has changed little since 2004, when 58% said it was more important to control gun ownership than to protect the rights of gun owners. At the same time, a 55% majority opposes a ban on the sale of handguns, while just 37% favor such a ban. There was greater support for gun control in the late 1990s and in 2000. Support for controlling gun ownership peaked in March 2000, less than a year after the shootings at Columbine High School. At that time, 66% said it was more important to control gun ownership, while just 29% thought it was more important to protect the rights of gun owners. The public was evenly split over a handgun ban (47% favor/47% opposed). The survey found deep public differences about whether mass shootings like those at Virginia Tech reflect broader problems in society or are just the isolated acts of individuals. Roughly half (47%) say such shootings are isolated acts, while about as many (46%) say they reflect broader social problems. Opinions on this issue are divided politically; a solid majority of conservative Republicans (57%) say shootings like the one at Blacksburg are just the isolated acts of troubled individuals. Most liberal Democrats (59%) assign the blame to broader problems in American society. Those who say the shootings reflect fundamental social problems offer a variety of explanations. Overall, 37% volunteer problems related to morality or social values, while 23% cite shortcomings in the mental health, legal, or school systems. Just 14% mention gun laws or issues related to gun control. There is a sizable gender gap in opinions about whether the Virginia Tech shootings and others like them are isolated acts of troubled individuals, or represent broader social problems. By 55%-39%, men generally believe that such shootings are just isolated acts. By a nearly identical margin (54%-37%), women say shootings like the one at Blacksburg reflect broader problems in American society. Notably, residents of the West are more likely than those in other regions to say that large-scale shootings are the acts of troubled people. People in the Northeast, by contrast, mostly point to broader social problems. People who said that the shootings at Virginia Tech and similar tragedies reflect broader problems in society differ in their views about those problems. Nearly half of Republicans who say the shootings reflect broader social problems cite issues with morality or social values; that compares with just 26% of Democrats. Democrats who say the shootings reflect broader social problems are much more likely than Republicans to mention gun laws or the ease with which people can buy guns (22% v. 8%). Another issue not specifically addressed in the survey is the failure of educational institutions to control bullying, which has been alleged to be a factor in school shootings. Bullying may be unduly tolerated by the oppressive conformism of small town America, which is suspicious of anyone who appears to be "different."

Gun Control Trends

There is somewhat less support for gun owners' rights than in 2004, though the overall balance of opinion has not changed substantially. Yet there is somewhat greater opposition to a law banning the sale of handguns than there was in 2000 or the late 1990s. Currently, 55% say they oppose such a ban, compared with 47% in 2000. There are deep differences in opinion. For instance, men oppose a ban on handgun sales by more than two to one (64%-30%). Women are evenly divided over such a ban, with 47% opposed and 44% in favor. By a wide margin (75%-21%), Republicans oppose a law banning handgun sales. Half of Democrats support a law prohibiting them, while 43% are opposed. Most independents (54%) oppose a ban on handgun sales, while 38% support a ban.

It is very much in doubt if new calls for gun controls will be successful. This is partly because of US history and the power of the gun lobby, whose campaign donations in 2000, the election year after the Columbine massacre, rose to $4 million. While gun control groups put pressure on candidates in the 2008 election, Republicans looking at the 40 million NRA membership, as well as Democrats seeking broad support from moderate and even conservative voters, may be still inclined to resist more control. The new generation of Democrats, who entered Congress in 2007, come mostly from states in which the "right to bear arms" is regarded as a civil right. Many of these young Democrats are, like their Republican colleagues, against further gun control. Psephologists (election analysts) say that his position on gun control was a factor in the defeat of Al Gore in 2000. That is why in 2004 the Democratic candidate John Kerry made it clear that he was a gun owner.

Lax laws alone are not to blame for gun violence in America. The deeper problem is America's "culture of violence," as President Obama called it during the 2008 campaign. The causes for this are as diverse as they are disputed. Unemployment, poverty, movies, video games, rap music, have been blamed as well as the winner-takes-all society with its harsh consequences for losers, outsiders, and those who are different or do not fit in. There is no end in sight for this debate and, above all, there is little likelihood of a solution.

But gun control activists still believe that it is too easy for criminals to obtain guns and that an alarming proportion of the population remains armed. Their concern has been fueled by an unprecedented rash of school shootings. Many experts are blaming this phenomenon on violent video games and poor parenting, but in each case the youths involved had easy access to the weapons they used. Gun control advocates support measures which would require trigger locks on all guns and which would apply the provisions of the Brady bill to gun shows. They also advocate a federal law authorizing only one handgun purchase per month and raising the age for gun ownership from 18 to 21.

On the other hand, opposition to gun control led by the National Rifle Association (NRA) remains fierce. Opponents of gun control argue that gun owners often use their weapons to deter crime and that handguns are most commonly used for this purpose. Some studies have shown that such defensive use of weapons occurs at a much greater rate than the extent to which weapons are used in criminal activity although the validity of these studies is in dispute. Gun control opponents are usually law-abiding citizens who put greater trust in individualism than in the government to protect their safety. Some of them are concerned that each step toward greater gun control will lead to the eventual confiscation of all firearms. During the 2008 election, gun rights groups spent nearly $4 million to support candidates. This was almost four times the amount contributed by gun control supporters.

CRIME

The US has a reputation for a high rate of crime, especially violent crime. But though the crime rate rose sharply in the late 1960s and early 1970s, bringing it to a constant all-time high during much of the 1970s and 1980s, it has dramatically declined since 1991 from 5,897 crimes per 100,000 population to 3,730 in 2007, a 36% fall. The overall crime rate was about the same in 2007 as in 1969. This is the more remarkable since the population increased by 17% in the period. There is no obvious explanation. Donohue and Levitt suggest the legalization of abortion in 1973 accounts for one-half of the fall in crime during the 1990s. (They point out that equivalent reductions in crime could in principle be obtained through alternatives for abortion, such as more effective birth control, or providing better environments for those children at greatest risk for future crime.) The authors also note that when imprisonment rose 50% from 1991 to 1997, crime fell by 10%. Crime rates are highly localized within regions, states and cities.

Violent crime
According to the FBI's annual survey *Crime in the United States,* for every 100,000 people there were 547 violent crimes in 1980, rising to 713.6 in 1994, but falling to 466.9 in 2007. Violent crime overall is at its lowest rate since 1976, having decreased steadily since 1991. The murder rate, at 5.6 per 100,000, has held almost steady since 1999 after falling 57% from a peak of 9.8 in 1991, and now stands at its lowest level since 1965. A report by the Department of Justice in 2006 noted that most murders were intraracial, with 86% of white murders committed by whites, and 94% of black murders committed by blacks. The other categories of violent crime - robbery, rape, and aggravated assault – are also at their lowest levels for a generation. Robberies cost victims $588 million, an average of $1,321 for each offense. Part of the 1990s crime wave was carjacking. Criminals with guns held up cars that had stopped at traffic lights and made the driver leave or drive to a place where no-one was around. They then stole the car and any money and valuables but usually left the driver unharmed. About half the attempts failed. There have been no national statistics on carjacking since 1996.

The fall in violent crime may be the result of concerted action by law enforcement at all levels to break up gangs and to take drug dealers and gun criminals off the streets. Other factors include the number of young males, the rate of incarceration, and the chances that in a recession more adults are home to supervise young people. Even so, the U.S. Conference of Mayors says there is a murder committed every 31 minutes, a rape every 5 minutes. While many cities are raising concerns about gang violence and an increase in juvenile crime, the general downward trend appears to be continuing. Crime in certain cities may reflect the economic crisis. African Americans are more likely to be victims of violent crime than whites.

According to the FBI, property crime also fell in 2007 for the fifth year in a row, to 3,263 per 100,000 population, the lowest since 1968. These crimes, which include burglary, larceny and motor vehicle theft, cost an estimated $17.6 billion. Even so, across America, a burglary takes place every 14.5 seconds, and a larceny or theft every 4.8 seconds. Crime is worse in cities, especially in the inner cities. Property crime was also more prevalent in the South.

Poorer people, men, those younger than 25 and non-European Americans were more likely to be victims. Income, sex and age had the most effect on vulnerability, while the effect of race depended on the crime. In 2005, African Americans were 35% more likely to experience a violent crime. The likelihood of being murdered was dramatically higher for them (49% of victims). Sexual assault, rape and simple assault rates, however, were roughly the same for all races. All households had about the same chance of becoming victims of theft. But people living in households with an annual income of less than $7,500 were far more likely to be assaulted, robbed and have their homes burgled.

It should be noted that the FBI figures represent crimes reported *voluntarily* by more than 17,700 city, county, college and university, state, tribal, and federal agencies, representing nearly 95 percent of the population. Thus crime may be underreported. On the other hand, critics have claimed that law enforcement agencies and others exaggerate crime by selective reporting of the data. Numbers may rise, for example, because the population does, while the crime *rate* may fall. Moreover, critics point out, some cities have poorly managed police departments and have seen big drops in arrest rates. It is thus not surprising that violent crime and murder rates have gone up there.

The US crime rate is similar to that of other developed countries. Yet the homicide rate is substantially higher. The rate per 100,000 population is three times that of Canada (1.9) and five times that of Germany (1.0). Most industrialized countries have homicide rates below 2.5. There is an even more marked disparity between the rates of murder committed with firearms. UN data show that the proportion of Americans killed by firearms per year is several times greater than that of residents in the 10 developed countries with the next highest rates of firearm homicides. Comparing homicide rates by themselves, however, may not be representative of the overall crime rate of a country. Rates may also reflect the presence of law enforcement and readiness to report a crime. Reported property crime is lower in the US than in Canada or Germany. International comparisons of crime statistics should in any case be treated with caution, as the definitions of crimes vary between countries.

Incarceration

The US has the highest incarceration rate in the world. According to the Department of Justice, in 2006 over 7.2 million people were in prison, on probation, or on parole. The International Centre for Prison Studies at King's College, London (ICPS), estimates that 2.3 million of these are in jail. Additionally, a report from the Office of Juvenile Justice and Delinquency Prevention, January 2009, said there were 94,000 juveniles held in facilities as of October 27, 2004. China, with a population over four times that of the US, is far second with 1.6 million, although that figure is disputed and may be much higher. With a rate of 750 for every 100,000 population, incarceration in America exceeds that in Russia (627) and greatly outnumbers that in England and Wales (148), Germany (88) and Japan (63). The world average is 125. As of 2004, the three states with the lowest ratio of imprisoned to 100,000 civilian population were Maine (148), Minnesota (171) and Rhode Island (175). The three states with the highest ratios are Louisiana (816), Texas (694), and Mississippi (669). Non-whites comprise 70% of prisoners. In 2002, 93.2% of prisoners were male. About 10% of black males in the US between the ages of 25 and 29 were in prison, compared to 2.4% of Hispanic males and 1.3% of white males. A 2005 report estimated that 27% of federal prison inmates are noncitizens. But federal prisoners are only 6% of the incarcerated population;

noncitizen populations in state and local prisons are more difficult to establish. ICPS estimates 5.9% as of June 2007. Incarceration is one of the main forms of punishment for felonies (where the sentence is more than one year.) Alternative penalties for less serious crimes (misdemeanors) include community corrections (halfway house), house arrest, probation, and restitution. But it is not the number of people sent to prison every year but the length of the sentences – much longer than anywhere else in the world – that is mainly responsible for American rates of incarceration.

Even though crime rates declined by about 25 percent from 1988-2008, the US prison population has multiplied fourfold since 1980. A major reason is said by analysts to be the result of mandatory sentences passed during the "war on drugs." Currently, the US houses over 500,000 prisoners for drug crimes. In contrast, Japan and Sweden have zero tolerance for illicit drugs at the same time as they have few people in prison for drug crime and low drug use. Another significant cause of high incarceration is that the US jails people, some for a long time, for nonviolent and victimless crimes. The US is one of the only advanced nations that imprison people for minor property crimes such as writing bad checks. Nearly one million of those imprisoned are serving time for non-violent crimes. Half of all state prison inmates are non-violent offenders and 20% are drug offenders.

Jails and prisons are mostly run by the states. The federal government also operates detention centers in big cities or near federal courthouses to hold criminal defendants appearing in federal court. In most states, cities operate small jails used only for very short-term incarceration – up to five days – until the prisoner comes before a judge for the first time, or receives a summons to do so before being released or transferred to a larger jail. Many of the smaller county and city jails do not classify prisoners by offense. While some of these facilities operate with close security to prevent prisoner-on-prisoner violence, others may put prisoners into the same cells without regard to their criminal histories. Other local jails, for example, Cook County Jail in Chicago, one of the largest in the US, are large and have many different security levels, including medical units and units for women. In California, prisoners are segregated by race, ethnicity, and sexual orientation while held in county jails and state reception centers, where newly committed prisoners are assessed before being transferred to where they will serve their sentences.

Sentencing

The primary goals of sentencing are punishment, deterrence, incapacitation, and rehabilitation. In some states, juries recommend the sentence, but in most states, and in federal court, sentencing is performed only by a judge. Criminal defendants are sentenced at a sentencing hearing, where the prosecutor and the defender present arguments regarding the penalty. In the hearing, the judge may consider all relevant evidence, testimony, and a presentence report from a probation or court services officer. The rules of evidence do not apply, and hearsay and other fallible evidence may be introduced. Death penalty sentences are usually delivered by a jury, not a judge, and only after a hearing. For violations and other minor charges, sentencing is either predetermined or pronounced immediately after conviction. Where the sentence is indeterminate, it will be for a range of years (e.g., 5-15 years). The legislature generally sets a relatively short minimum (e.g., 1/3 of the sentence) after which a parole board sets the actual date of release. Some states establish criteria the parole board must follow; in others, the decision is discretionary. An impressive portrayal of the workings of the jury room is presented in the critically acclaimed film *12 Angry Men* (1957) starring Henry Fonda.

In the 1950s, Congress passed laws requiring judges to impose specified minimum sentences to prison for drug offenses. Judges were precluded from reducing sentences in light of mitigating factors. In the 1960s, these laws came under attack for failing to deter drug crimes. Moreover, prosecutors were reluctant to prosecute some cases because the mandatory minimums were considered unjustly severe. By the late 1970s, all indeterminate sentencing had fallen into disfavor. Many perceived that crime rates were soaring, and a powerful lobby emerged demanding sentencing reform. These critics argued for longer prison sentences, and also pushed for uniformity in sentencing, noting that discretionary sentencing produced widely varied sentences for the same crime.

Several states enacted sentencing guidelines in the 1970s and early 1980s. These increased punishments for criminal offenses and limited judicial discretion in sentencing by specifying the punishment required. Under many sentencing statutes, parole for prison inmates was either abolished or restricted to certain offenses. Criminals given life sentences in some states may thus stay in prison for life, without the possibility of parole. Subsequently Congress passed the Sentencing Reform Act of 1984 (SRA). The SRA abolished parole for federal prisoners and reduced the amount of time off granted for good behavior. The SRA also established the U.S. Sentencing Commission to create a new sentencing system. Between 1984 and 1987, the USSC crafted the Federal Sentencing Guidelines. These shifted the focus in sentencing from the offender to the offense. The guidelines categorize offenses and identify the sentence required upon conviction. Judges are allowed to increase or decrease sentences or depart from the guidelines, but only if they have a very good explanation and clearly state the reasons on the record. Upward departures, or increases in sentences, are permitted. The judge may consider all "relevant conduct," including the circumstances surrounding the conviction, offenses that were committed at the same time as the charged offense but were not charged, prior convictions, and acts for which the defendant was previously tried but acquitted. In limited circumstances, judges may decrease a sentence, for example, if the defendant accepts responsibility for the crime or committed the crime to avoid a more serious offense. Prosecutors often challenge decreased sentences on appeal, and they usually win because the guidelines call for adherence in all but exceptional cases.

Prosecutors exercise wide discretion in sentencing in federal court. They may increase or decrease a sentence by changing the number of counts either in the initial charge or by a plea agreement. A notable feature of the American justice system is that the vast majority of criminal convictions arise from plea bargains, in which an agreement is made between prosecutors and defense counsel for the defendant to plead guilty to a lesser charge for a shorter sentence than they would receive if found guilty at trial. For example, a prosecutor may not use evidence of certain conduct at trial. But upon conviction or a guilty plea, the prosecutor can introduce that evidence in the sentencing hearing. If the prosecutor is able to prove by a preponderance of the evidence that the defendant committed the acts, the court is obliged to increase the defendant's sentence. Furthermore, state police officers and prosecutors can decide which cases to refer to federal prosecutors. They can thus pressure defendants to enter a guilty plea in state court to avoid federal sentencing. The decision on whether to ask the court for a lesser sentence in exchange for substantial assistance to law enforcement is also left to the prosecutor. At first, many federal judges refused to recognize the Federal Sentencing Guidelines. But after the U.S. Supreme Court held that the guidelines did not violate the separation of powers doctrine and were not an excessive delegation of legislative power, federal courts abandoned the indeterminate approach to sentencing and have used the sentencing guidelines to determine criminal sentences.

Congress has also increased the use of minimum sentences. The Comprehensive Crime Control Act of 1984 requires minimum sentences for drug and firearm offenses. In 1986, as public fears of drug abuse increased, Congress enacted the Anti-Drug Abuse Act. This created mandatory minimum sentences for drug trafficking and distribution, using the quantity of the drug involved to determine the minimum terms of imprisonment. In 1994, Congress moved to limit the applicability of mandatory minimums in the case of low-level, nonviolent drug offenders. Also in 1994, Congress exercised its power over sentencing by passing the Violent Crime Control and Law Enforcement Act. Under this Act, violent offenders convicted of their third felony must be sentenced to life imprisonment. Mandatory minimums are not the same as the Federal Sentencing Guidelines. Mandatory minimum sentences remove all discretion from the sentencing judge, whereas the guidelines allow for some leeway. Critics point to the procedural advantages enjoyed by prosecutors, and allege that defendants do not receive the Constitutional protection of due process, but they admit that there is a lack of political will for change.

The most common punishments identified in state statutes are community service, probation, fines, restitution, and imprisonment. In the 1990s, some southeastern states authorized sentences of hard labor on chain gangs. Many states have also reinstated the death penalty. In both federal and state courts, the sentencing hearing is preceded by a presentence investigation and report. These are conducted by a court services or probation officer, who then submits the report to all parties to the prosecution. At the hearing, the prosecutor and defendant are entitled to argue against the recommendations. In many states, courts still possess the authority to craft sentences within the minimums and maximums set by sentencing statutes.

Opponents of determinate sentencing claim that it will result in increased crowding of prisons and greater costs. As a result of three strikes laws, for example, the number of life sentences increased by 83% between 1992 and 2003. Proponents note that enhanced sentencing will result in long-term cost savings because repeat offenders will no longer be on the street. Supporters of indeterminate sentencing say that it provides prisoners with an incentive to take advantage of rehabilitation programs and allows prison authorities to release someone once rehabilitation occurs. Some judges have exercised their sentencing discretion by meting out innovative punishments intended to address the specific criminal conviction or the conviction history of the specific criminal. Juvenile court judges possess wide discretion in sentencing.

Nearly half the states have adopted various strategies to reduce corrections costs by lowering the number of people imprisoned. The largest reported declines in prison populations have occurred in states such as Texas and California, which changed parole policies to allow the release of thousands of inmates. In comparison, local jail populations have grown, outstripping the annual average increase of 4.3 percent since 1995. Jails are locally controlled and less subject to state-wide policy changes.

Prison conditions

Prisons have various levels of security. Supermax prison facilities provide the highest. These units hold many of the most dangerous inmates, who have committed murders or assaults, or are known to be or accused of being prison gang members. Inmates are held with 23-hour confinement and abridged amenities. Most states have either a supermax section of a prison or an entire supermax prison. The U.S. Federal Bureau of Prisons operates a number of supermax facilities across the country. One Federal supermax is deserving of special note: ADX Florence, located in Florence,

Colorado, also known as the "Alcatraz of the Rockies," is widely considered to be the most secure prison in the US. As well as a standard supermax section, ADX Florence has a special section where international and domestic spies, traitors and terrorists are held in harsh conditions. Each maximum security prisoner has his or her own cell which has sliding doors controlled from a secure remote control station. While out of their cells, prisoners remain in the cell block or an exterior cage. Movement out of the cell block or "pod" is tightly restricted using restraints and escorts by correctional officers. Maximum security may feature permanent 24-hour solitary confinement with no human contact or opportunity to earn better conditions through good behavior.

Prisoners in a close security prison are usually housed one or two to a self-contained cell each with its own toilet and sink. The doors are operated from a remote control station. Inmates may leave their cells for work assignments or correctional programs and otherwise may be allowed in a common area in the cellblock or an exercise yard. The fences are generally double fences with watchtowers, housing armed guards, plus often a third, lethal-current electric fence in the middle. Prisoners that fall into the medium security group may sleep in dormitories on bunk beds with lockers to store their possessions. They may have communal showers, toilets and sinks. Dormitories are locked at night with one or more correctional officers supervising. There is less supervision over the internal movements of prisoners. The perimeter is generally double fenced and regularly patrolled.

The lowest level of prison security is minimum security. White collar criminals, who pose little physical risk to the public, are mostly housed there under the supervision of correctional officers, who regularly patrol the dormitories. As in medium security facilities, they have communal showers, toilets, and sinks. A minimum-security facility generally has a single fence that is watched, but not patrolled, by armed guards. At facilities in very remote and rural areas, there may be no fence at all. Prisoners may often work on community projects, such as wilderness or roadside litter cleanup. Many minimum security facilities are small camps located in or near military bases, larger prisons (outside the security perimeter) or other government institutions and provide a convenient supply of convict labor. Many states allow persons in minimum-security facilities access to the internet.

Criticism of prisons

Overcrowding, gang violence, rape, and health issues such as tuberculosis, Hepatitis C, lower rates of fertility, and HIV/AIDS among inmates, and lack of medical care, are among concerns that have been raised about American prisons. Critics also allege that segregation of gang members from other inmates has the effect of turning prisons into schools of crime. Some advocate more focus on rehabilitation to cut the numbers of repeat offenders. The US spends an estimated $60 billion per year on corrections. In 2005, the average annual cost per prisoner was $23,876. Yet a 2002 study showed that among 275,000 prisoners released in 1994, 67.5% were rearrested within 3 years, and 51.8% were back in prison. Those serving the longest time, 61 months or more, had a significantly lower re-arrest rate (54.2%) than every other category of prisoner. This is most likely explained by the older average age of those released after the longest sentences. Criminal justice policy has also been criticized for the disproportionate representation of African Americans and other minorities among prisoners. Another issue is the increasing cost of housing and healthcare for prisoners aged over 55. In recent years, there has been much debate over the privatization of prisons. The argument for privatization stresses cost reduction, whereas the arguments against it focus on standards of care. The three leading corporations in the private prison business are the

Corrections Corporation of America, the GEO Group, and Cornell Companies. The National Criminal Justice Commission Act of 2009, S.714, was introduced into the Senate by Senator Jim Webb (D-Virginia) to set up a commission to review all areas of federal and state criminal justice costs, practices, and policies. At the time of writing, the Bill had passed out of the Judiciary Committee and been placed on the Senate Legislative Calendar; and a similar bill had already been passed by the House.

The 'three strikes' law

Habitual or prior and persistent offender laws, popularly known as *three strikes* laws, have been enacted by 26 states and the federal government. These laws mandate the state courts to hand down long jail terms to persons who have been convicted of a serious criminal offense on three or more separate occasions. *Three strikes* comes from baseball, and basically means three balls being swung at by the batter and missed and the last one caught, which results in the batter being declared "out." They are based on the principle that offenders who have committed serious or violent felonies and who continue to do so must be incapacitated. The scope of such laws is determined by the definition of *felony*. California classifies any of 500 felonies as a "third strike" carrying a sentence of 25-years-to-life. Proponents say the resulting increase in prison populations is evidence that justice is being done and future crime prevented. Opponents of three strikes laws, particularly that in California, enacted in 1995, say the laws are disproportionate in some cases and not responsible for the fall in crime. A report on California's three strikes law published by the Sentencing Project in 2002 concluded that the law had not contributed to the reduction of crime to any significant extent. The study also showed that the law had increased the number and severity of sentences for nonviolent offenders and the law was rapidly expanding an aging and costly prison population. The study projected that by 2026, 30,000 offenders would be imprisoned for a third strike, costing $750 million per year. Fully 83 percent of inmates would be at least 40 years of age. According to the Sentencing Project, California's considerable drop in crime between 1993 and 1999 (41 percent) was based on a number of factors: an improved economy, declines in gang and drug activity, community policing, and the aging of prime crime populations, not the three strikes laws. Numerous additional studies have reached the same conclusion. In fact, other jurisdictions have had similar crime rate declines without instituting "three-strikes": New York (40.9%), Massachusetts (33.3%), and Washington, D.C. (31.4%).

Youth incarceration

The US incarcerates more of its youth than any other country. Throughout 2007, more than 126,000 were serving time. Approximately 500,000 per year are brought to detention centers, up to 70% for non-violent offenses. The system was created under the 1974 Juvenile Justice and Delinquency Prevention Act. The Act required states holding youth within adult prisons to remove most of them. The Act also provided grants to states for programs for children in the juvenile justice system. The programs include assistance for learning disabled children, juvenile boot camps and community juvenile crime prevention. Recently, however, 47 states have made it easier to be tried as an adult, a policy criticized by many, but favored by the public despite documented decreases in youth crime, especially violent crime, including a 68% decline in homicide in the 1990s. Probably due to media coverage, though, most Americans believe youth crime is in fact increasing.

Critics of juvenile justice, like the National Council on Crime and Delinquency, hold the system is unjust, ineffective, and counter-productive. They claim the system is stacked against minority youth at every point. Juvenile detention facilities are often overcrowded and understaffed. Young people are subject to fights, stabbings and rapes from their peers and violence from staff. Congregating delinquent youth also delays their maturation and makes their behavior worse, according to social scientists. Additionally, incarceration can aggravate mental illness, according to administrators who testified to the House of Representatives in 2004. Incarcerated youth have higher school dropout rates on release and consequently are more likely to be under-achievers in the labor market. Previous incarceration is the leading indicator for a repeat offence among youth. It is a greater predictor even than weapon possession, gang membership, and bad relationships with parents. According to studies, incarceration is actually leading to more criminality among youth and more serious crimes. Alternative policies have been shown to be more effective in reducing youth offending in practical and economic terms.

There is a widespread movement to reduce and eventually put an end to youth incarceration. Meanwhile the worst prisons and detention centers are being shut down, youth in the system are being treated better, and young people are receiving better representation. Legislation is being promoted to curb youth incarceration, abolish arrest warrants for young people, limit zero tolerance policies, and promote alternatives to incarceration. Targets have included the Cheltenham Juvenile Detention Center in Maryland and the Tallulah Correction Center for Youth in Louisiana (which was actually sued by the U.S. Department of Justice for violating the civil rights of youth held in its confines.)

In 2003, Louisiana became nationally recognized for its leadership in reforming a broken juvenile justice system. Under the Juvenile Justice Reform Act, Tallulah was shut down, conditions were improved in other abusive youth prisons, and a commitment was made to increased use of alternatives to incarceration, and to revamping secure care prisons into small, therapeutic facilities throughout the state that kept children closer to their families. Before the passage of the Act, over 2,000 children were held in prison in Louisiana. Now the system holds just over 500. In 1998, the rate of children returning to prison after release was 56%. Now it is 11%.

The leading initiative promoting treatment as an alternative to incarceration is the JDAI—The Juvenile Detention Alternatives Initiative. This is a private-public partnership being implemented nationwide, with pilot programs in California, Oregon, New Mexico and Illinois. Their goal is to make sure that locked detention is used only when absolutely necessary. Alternatives to confinement are sensitive to family and culture, and treatment is often built around the strengths of the youth and their families. Alternative treatment methods include diversion, mentorship, Aggression Replacement Training, Functional Family Therapy, and multi-systemic therapy. The JDAI has produced some large reductions in arrest rates, incarceration and crime.

The Death Penalty

Capital punishment is legal in 35 states. It is applied rarely, in practice only for aggravated murder, and even more rarely for felony murder or contract killing. Since 1976 there have been 1,160 executions. There were 52 executions in 2009, and the number may increase when lethal injection cases are decided. There are 3,316 inmates on death row, including 667 in California, 397 in Florida, 373 in Texas and 228 in Pennsylvania.

Policy on capital punishment is going in opposite directions in different states. Most states are moving towards abolishing the death penalty, or limiting its use, and some have already done so; others meanwhile are seeking to make more use of capital punishment. In 2007, New Jersey became the first state to repeal the death penalty since 1976, and New Mexico followed in 2009 (although not retroactively), replacing the death penalty with life without parole. Capital punishment has been illegal in Michigan since 1846. Michigan was the first English-speaking government in the world to abolish the death penalty, when it did so for all crimes except treason. Massachusetts in 1984 and New York in 2004 closed down their death rows. They had last performed executions in 1947 and 1963 respectively. New Hampshire and Kansas have populated death rows but have not executed since 1976, although both have constitutional death penalty statutes. But in states with a large death row population and regular executions, like California and Texas, the death penalty is unlikely to end any time soon. Capital punishment was suspended in all states from 1972 through 1976, primarily as a result of the Supreme Court's decision in *Furman v. Georgia*, where the court found the imposition of the death penalty unconstitutional, on the ground of cruel and unusual punishment, in violation of the Eighth Amendment. Furman and others had been convicted under Georgia's death penalty statute in a "unitary trial," in which the jury was asked to return a verdict of guilt or innocence and, simultaneously, determine whether the defendant would be punished by death or life imprisonment. Justice Marshall and Justice Brennan have always held that the death penalty is against the Eighth Amendment. After the judgment, 37 states enacted new death penalty statutes. In 1976 the Court clarified Furman in *Woodson v. North Carolina*, and *Roberts v. Louisiana*, which explicitly forbade punishing a specific form of murder (such as that of a police officer) with a mandatory death penalty. That same year the Court decided *Gregg v. Georgia* and upheld a procedure in which the trial of capital crimes was split into guilt-innocence and sentencing phases. A decision in 1977, *Coker v. Georgia* banned the death penalty for rape and, by implication, for any offense other than murder. In 2008 in *Kennedy v. Louisiana*, the Supreme Court ruled against Louisiana's child rape death penalty, saying "there is a distinction between intentional first-degree murder on the one hand and non-homicide crimes against individual persons."

At sentencing hearings, the jury must be instructed to weigh mitigating factors such as the defendant's mental health. Between 1984 and 2002, however, forty-four mentally retarded inmates were executed. In the latter year, however, it was held by the Supreme Court in *Atkins v. Virginia* (2002) that executions of mentally retarded criminals are "cruel and unusual." In 2007, Texas executed James Lee Clark despite an IQ of 65 after a controversial expert witness stated he believed Clark was faking his retardation. After the Supreme Court's 2005 decision in *Roper v. Simmons*, the minimum age at time of crime to be subject to the death penalty was raised to 18. State laws have not been updated to conform with this decision. Under the US system, unconstitutional laws do not need to be repealed, but are instead held to be unenforceable. No one has been under age 19 at time of execution since at least 1964.

Crimes subject to capital punishment
the highest grade of murder, mostly with aggravating circumstances

Federal
- treason
- the use of a weapon of mass destruction resulting in death
- espionage
- terrorism
- certain violations of the Geneva Conventions that result in death

State
- aggravated rape in Louisiana, Florida, and Oklahoma
- extortionate kidnapping in Oklahoma
- aggravated kidnapping in Georgia, Idaho, Kentucky and South Carolina
- aircraft hijacking in Alabama
- drug trafficking resulting in a person's death in Connecticut
- train wrecking which leads to a person's death, and perjury which leads to a person's death in California

In the Armed Services, the death penalty is on the books but has not been applied for many years. Under the Uniform Code of Military Justice, capital punishment is available for a number of offenses committed during wartime including: desertion, mutiny, spying, and misconduct before the enemy. In practice, no one has been executed for a crime other than murder or conspiracy to murder since James Coburn was executed for robbery in Alabama in 1964. As of November 2008, there was only one person on death row facing capital punishment who has not been convicted of murder. Demarcus Ali Sears remains under a death sentence in Georgia for kidnapping with bodily injury.

Sentencing and appeals
TV and the movies may give the impression that direct appeal to the governor or President for clemency is the typical route to avoid a death sentence in America. But the actual route is a complex legal appeals process in the courts. The death penalty is subject to a complex system of review. The stages of review are typically: sentencing; direct review; state collateral review; and federal habeas corpus. Recently, a new type of collateral review, making a fifth level in all—the Section 1983 challenge—has become increasingly important. (Clemency or pardon, through which a state governor or the President can reduce or abrogate a death sentence, is an executive rather than legal process.) In direct review, an appeal court examines the record of evidence presented in the trial and the law the court applied. If the appeal court finds that the trial court made significant legal errors, then the judgment will be reversed, or the sentence nullified and a new sentencing hearing ordered. In the rare case where the appellate court finds that no reasonable juror could find the defendant eligible for the death penalty, it will order the defendant acquitted of the crime for which the death penalty was given, and order a sentence passed for the next most severe punishment for which the offense is eligible. A majority of death sentences, however, about 60%, survive direct review and are usually considered final. Where the prisoner receives the death sentence in a state-level trial, as is usually the case, state collateral review takes place. (If the case

is a federal one, it proceeds immediately from direct review to federal habeas corpus.) The purpose of collateral proceedings is to permit the prisoner to challenge the sentence on grounds that could not reasonably have been raised at trial or on direct review. Most often these are claims, such as ineffective assistance of counsel, which require the court to consider new evidence outside the original trial record, something courts may not do in an ordinary appeal. State collateral review is rarely successful. Only around 6% of all death sentences are overturned. After a death sentence is affirmed in state collateral review, the prisoner may file for federal habeas corpus, which is a type of collateral review. The scope of federal habeas corpus is governed by the Antiterrorism and Effective Death Penalty Act. The purpose is to ensure that the state courts have done at least a reasonable job in protecting the prisoner's constitutional rights. Prisoners may also use federal habeas corpus to bring new evidence that they are innocent, though to be a valid defense at this late stage, the evidence must be truly compelling. Federal habeas corpus is narrow in theory, but important in practice, as 21% of death penalty cases are reversed through this review. Some studies have put the success rate as high as 40% or more. Under the Antiterrorism and Effective Death Penalty Act, a state prisoner is ordinarily allowed only one suit for habeas corpus in federal court. If the federal courts refuse to issue a writ of habeas corpus, an execution date may be set. In recent times, however, prisoners have postponed execution through a final round of federal litigation using the Civil Rights Act 1871 (a Section 1983 suit) which allows people to bring lawsuits to protect their civil rights, in this case challenging a state's method of execution as cruel and unusual punishment. In fact, a fifth level of appeal exists, a petition for *certiorari* to the U.S. Supreme Court to review the case after direct review and state collateral review. A shortage of lawyers has meant that long backlogs of appeals have built up.

Although hundreds of death sentences were passed, only 11 executions took place between 1977 and 1984, owing to the use by defense lawyers of delaying tactics, such as filing repeated writs for habeas corpus. The procedures were expedited in federal cases by the Antiterrorism and Effective Death Penalty Act. From 1976 to 2008, 1,125 people have been executed, almost all by the states and most after 1990. Texas has accounted for over a third of modern executions (431 as of 2009). The federal government has executed only three people in the last 27 years. California has the greatest number of prisoners on death row, but has held relatively few executions.

A wide variety of methods are used in executions. The principal method (35 states) is lethal injection. Other methods include electrocution, gas chambers, hanging, and the firing squad. Since 1976, there have been 954 executions by lethal injection, 155 by electrocution, 11 by gas chamber, 3 by hanging, and 2 by firing squad. The method of execution of federal prisoners is that of the state in which the conviction took place. If the state has no death penalty, the judge must choose a state which has one. The remaining two states that allow hanging are New Hampshire, which allows it by decision of the Corrections officials, and in Washington state, at the choice of the defendant. Regardless of the method, an hour or two before the execution, the condemned person is offered religious services and a last meal. Executions are carried out in private with only invited persons able to view the proceedings.

Application of sentences

Despite the continual publicity about the issue, the death penalty is not widely or routinely used, and is applied more in some states than in others, and more in some counties than others. On a national basis, the death penalty has been applied on average in one in 700 cases of murder, or

1 for about every 325 murder convictions. The death penalty is sought and applied more often in some jurisdictions, not only between states but within states. A 2004 Cornell study showed that while 2.5% of murderers convicted nationwide were sentenced to death, in Nevada 6% were given the death penalty. Texas gave 2% of murderers the death sentence but executed 40% of those sentenced, about four times the national average. California executed only 1% of those sentenced. Only 1.4% of those executed since 1976 have been women. African Americans have made up 34% of those actually executed. Whether blacks are in fact more likely to be convicted of and executed for murder is a matter of fierce debate. Studies indicate that the single greatest predictor of whether a death sentence is given is not the race of the defendant but the race of the victim. Although blacks and whites are the victims of murder in almost equal numbers, 80% of the people executed since 1977 have been convicted of murders involving white victims. Between 1976 and 2003, fewer than 2% of death row prisoners were exonerated, while others had their sentences reduced for other reasons. This amounted to 112 prisoners released. There are always witnesses to executions, sometimes numerous witnesses, but it is the law, not the number of witnesses present, which determines whether the execution is "public." The execution of Timothy McVeigh, the Oklahoma bomber, on June 11, 2001, was witnessed by some 300 people (some by closed circuit television).

Controversy over the death penalty

Capital punishment is a controversial issue among Americans. A wide range of arguments is deployed on both sides of the debate, and many prominent individuals and organizations take part. The arguments include moral, practical, religious, and emotional arguments.

- *Pro:* Advocates of the death penalty argue that it:
  deters crime; helps prosecutors in plea bargaining (practice of promising leniency in exchange for pleading guilty to a lesser charge or becoming a prosecution witness); prevents repeat offenses; provides closure to surviving victims and loved ones; is less expensive to try because some defendants plead guilty to avoid it; is just.
- *Con:* does not deter; cheapens human life; puts the government on the same moral level as the criminal; is unfairly applied across racial and class lines; is more expensive because of appeals; excludes new evidence.

Campaigning for and against the death penalty, and on behalf of death row inmates, is active. Opinion polls consistently show that a majority of Americans support the death penalty. Among the groups that oppose capital punishment, Amnesty International and some religions oppose it on moral grounds, while the Innocence Project works to free wrongly convicted prisoners, including death row inmates, based on newly available DNA tests. Other groups, such as the Southern Baptists, law enforcement organizations, and some victims' rights groups support capital punishment.

Anti-death penalty

- Death Penalty Information Center (opposition not stated)
- The Innocence Project—to exonerate wrongfully convicted people through DNA testing
- Truth in Justice—to educate the public about vulnerabilities in the justice system
- Campaign to end the Death Penalty—grassroots campaign

Pro-death penalty

- The Ultimate Punishment—a professor defends the death penalty

- The Death Penalty : a Defense—book by David Anderson
- Death Penalty Information—News, arguments and links
- Criminal Justice Legal Foundation—articles on the death penalty cases and deterrence

Extremist movements

Political extremism in the US takes three main forms—the Militia Movement, the Sovereign Citizen movement, and the Tax Protest movement—all of them negligible.

The Militia Movement

The militia movement is a relatively new right-wing extremist movement consisting of armed paramilitary groups, both formal and informal, with an anti-government, conspiracy-oriented ideology. Militia groups began to form not long after the deadly standoff between agents of the Bureau of Alcohol, Tobacco and Firearms and the FBI, and the Branch Davidians at Waco, Texas in 1993. By the spring of 1995, they had spread to almost every state. Although the militia movement has declined from its peak in early 1996, it remains active, especially in the Midwest, and continues to cause a number of problems for law enforcement and the communities in which militia groups are active.

A series of events in the early 1990s angered people on the extreme right sufficiently to start the movement. The events that angered them ranged from the election of Bill Clinton to the Rodney King riots in Los Angeles (when African Americans protested the beating of Rodney King by police) to the passage of the North American Free Trade Agreement. More than any other issue, though, the deadly standoffs at Ruby Ridge, Idaho, in 1992 and Waco ignited widespread passion. To most Americans, these events were tragedies, but to the extreme right, they were examples of a government willing to stop at nothing to stamp out people who refused to conform. In using the term "militia," these groups imply that they are not only legal but are a constitutional arm of the government. They claim that militia groups are equivalent to the statutory militia, not, however, controlled by the government, and designed to oppose the government should it become tyrannical.

The fact that both the Ruby Ridge and Waco incidents involved illegal firearms added considerable fuel to the fire that formed the militia movement. Many militia members and leaders were radical gun rights advocates, people who believed that in fact there could be no such things as illegal firearms, and whose anti-government ire was fueled largely by fear and suspicion that guns would soon be confiscated. Militias emerged on the basis that members of the "militia" were exempt from federal gun laws. Many people initially joined the fledgling movement largely as a way to protect more aggressively their right to bear arms; even today, gun-related issues dominate many of the newsletters published by militia groups.

A third defining feature of the militia movement is a fascination with conspiracies. Conspiracy theories were easily accepted by people who believed that the federal government deliberately murdered people at Ruby Ridge and Waco and that gun confiscation could begin any day. The conspiracy theories described a shadowy movement intent on creating a one-world socialist government no matter what the cost. This "New World Order," using the United Nations as its primary tool, had already taken over most of the planet. The US was still a bastion of freedom, but its own government was collaborating with New World Order forces to strip Americans slowly of their freedoms in preparation for the final takeover.

The combination of anger at the government, fear of gun confiscation and susceptibility to conspiracy theories formed the core of the militia movement's ideology. Although there were white supremacists in the movement, and although groups and individuals within the movement often made common cause with or at least tolerated hate groups, the orientation of the militia movement remained primarily anti-government and conspiratorial. The movement appealed to many radical libertarians just as it appealed to traditional proponents of extreme right-wing causes.

Their extreme anti-government ideology, along with their elaborate conspiracy theories and fascination with weaponry and paramilitary organization, led many members of militia groups to behave in ways that justified the concerns expressed about them by public officials, law enforcement and the general public. The militias have embroiled themselves since 1994 in a variety of bombing plots, conspiracies and serious violations for which a number of members have been jailed. Multiple members of at least eight groups have been arrested and convicted, usually on weapons, explosives, or conspiracy charges. No confrontation with the authorities, however, has so far been violent.

The militia movement has declined overall in the past several years, though in many areas it remains at least as strong it was. In Michigan, Ohio, Indiana, Illinois and Kentucky, active militias regularly meet and train. New militia groups continue to form, as in Georgia and West Virginia. Perhaps the most active militia group in the country is the Kentucky State Militia (KSM). Yet the movement is not a serious threat to law and order, let alone to any level of government.

Sovereign Citizens

The "sovereign citizen" movement is a loosely organized collection of groups and individuals who have adopted a right-wing anarchist ideology originating in the theories of a group called the *Posse Comitatus* in the 1970s. Its adherents believe that virtually all existing government in the US is illegitimate and they seek to "restore" an idealized, minimalist government that never actually existed. To this end, sovereign citizens wage "war" against the government and other forms of authority using "paper terrorism" harassment and intimidation tactics, and occasionally resorting to violence.

Tax protest

The tax protest movement is a relatively long-lived anti-government movement arising from opposition to federal income taxes. Tax protesters generally believe that either the income tax laws are in some way invalid or that they do not apply to most citizens; therefore, they believe they have a legal and moral right not to pay taxes. Many tax protesters suspect that the government covers up the "truth" about the income tax in order to continue oppressing the people and taking their money. Tax protesters engage in a wide variety of tax evasion strategies that range from simple refusal to pay taxes to complicated schemes using onshore and offshore trusts in order to hide income from the government. Tax protesters are also violent on occasion, attacking IRS agents or property or others charged with enforcing the law.

Law enforcement

Movies like *Bullitt* (1968), *Beverly Hills Cop* (1984) and *LA Confidential* (1997), and TV shows like *Dragnet* and *NYPD Blues*, have spread images of the fast driving, quick shooting American cop around the world. Police work in America can be fast-paced and dangerous in cities, but in rural areas a sheriff might make only a handful of arrests each year.

Law enforcement in the US acts independently of all other branches of government, but the police themselves are subject to the law. In addition to law enforcement, the police provide first response to emergencies and other threats to public safety. For many years, police forces were plagued with corruption. They became more professional in the 1920s. Officers were promoted strictly on merit and received higher salaries. They concentrated on dealing with felonies and other serious crimes. Since then they have successively adopted three main types of policing strategy: reactive policing responding to calls for service; community policing; and problem-oriented policing. Police forces are supervised by non-partisan police boards.

The police long had, and to some extent still have, lack of respect from minority communities. Following urban unrest in the 1960s, police placed more emphasis on community relations, and increased diversity in hiring. In the 1990s, finding that reactive policing, based on cars, two-way radio and the telephone, was ineffective, many law enforcement agencies began to adopt community policing, and others problem-orientated strategies. Forces also began to make use of computerized systems for tracking and mapping crime patterns and trends, and databases on criminals and stolen property.

Federal police

The federal government empowers a wide range of law enforcement agencies to maintain law and public order in matters affecting the country as a whole. These agencies are a mixture of direct law enforcement agencies, for example, the FBI; regulatory authorities with law enforcement powers, for example, the Environmental Protection Agency; and other agencies with police units, for example, the Department of Veterans Affairs Police.

Although federal law enforcement officers are naturally mostly concerned with enforcing federal law, they are also often involved at state, county, and local level. The investigatory powers of federal officers have become very broad, especially since the passage of the USA Patriot Act. The Department of Justice is the largest and most prominent federal law enforcement agency. It includes the FBI, the Drug Enforcement Administration, and the Bureau of Alcohol, Tobacco, Firearms, and Explosives (renamed in 2002 but still known as ATF). At a crime or disaster scene affecting large numbers of people, multiple jurisdictions, or broad geographic areas, many police agencies may be involved by mutual aid agreements. Command in such situations remains a complex and flexible issue.

The Federal Bureau of Investigation

Perhaps the most famous law enforcement agency in the world, the Federal Bureau of Investigation (FBI) originated in a corps of special agents formed in 1908 to investigate federal crimes. Their first major task was to track down white slavers who were believed to be abducting women and girls across state lines and forcing them into a life of prostitution. The FBI became famous fighting gangsters during Prohibition. From 1932, the FBI's best known Director, J. Edgar Hoover, began to publicize the Bureau to build up support for it among the public and enlist public cooperation in catching wanted criminals. The Bureau was given its present name in 1935.

Two events in late 1992 and early 1993 set the stage for public and congressional inquiries into the FBI's ability to respond to crises and had a major impact on its policies and operations. In August 1992, the FBI responded to the shooting death of a Deputy U.S. Marshal, who was killed at Ruby Ridge, Idaho, while participating in a surveillance of federal fugitive Randall Weaver. In the course of the standoff, Weaver's wife was accidentally shot and killed by an FBI sniper. Eight months later, at a remote compound outside Waco, Texas, FBI Agents sought to end a 51-day standoff with members of a heavily armed religious sect who had killed four officers of the Bureau of Alcohol, Tobacco and Firearms. Instead, as Agents watched in horror, the compound burned to the ground from fires lit by members of the sect. Eighty persons, including children, died in the blaze. In response to the public outcry, the Bureau formed the Critical Incident Response Group (CIRG) to deal more efficiently with such situations.

During the years 1993 through 1996, the Bureau successfully investigated incidents as diverse as the World Trade Center bombing in New York City (1993); the bombing of the Murrah Federal Building in Oklahoma City (1995); and the UNABOMBER, Theodore Kaczynski (1996). The FBI also addresses crime in cyberspace, and physical and cyber attacks against infrastructure. It monitors the dissemination of computer viruses, worms, and other malicious programs, and warns government and business computer users of these dangers. In addition, the Bureau has identified and stopped large numbers of pedophiles who have used the internet to purvey child pornography and to lure children into situations where they could be harmed. In 2009 President Obama announced the appointment of a civilian Cyber Command in the White House and a military Cyber Command in the Pentagon to counteract efforts to damage the information infrastructure vital to America's economic and military security.

The FBI has responsibility for protecting the American people against future terrorist attacks, countering foreign intelligence operations against the US, and addressing cyberattacks and other high-technology crimes. In addition, the Bureau remains dedicated to protecting civil rights, and combating public corruption, organized crime, white-collar crime, and major acts of violent crime.

State police

The federal government is prohibited under the Constitution from exercising general police powers. Each state retains its police, military and domestic law-making powers. The Constitution gives the federal government the power to deal with affairs between the states, however. For policing, this means that if a domestic crime such as murder is committed and the fugitive does not flee the state, the federal government has no jurisdiction. If a fugitive crosses a state line, however, federal law enforcement agencies may become involved. Almost all states operate statewide agencies that provide law enforcement, including investigations and patrols. They may be called state police, state patrol or highway patrol, and are normally part of the state Department of Public Safety. In addition, the Attorney General's office of each state has its own bureau of investigation. Various departments of state governments may also have an enforcement division such as capitol police, Department of Correction, water police, or environmental (fish and game/wildlife) police.

Sheriffs' Departments and County (Parish, Borough) police

Sheriffs' departments

Many Westerns feature sheriffs of frontier towns who are either corrupt weaklings, or glorious heroes who eventually rid their towns of their mean elements, as in *Destry Rides Again* (1932, 1939) and *Dodge City* (1939). Real-life sheriffs include Pat Garrett, who shot dead Billy the Kid (1881), and Grover Cleveland, formerly sheriff of Erie County, New York, the only sheriff to be elected President (1884). A sheriff is usually the highest law enforcement officer of a county and commander of the militia. By an almost uniquely American tradition, sheriffs are usually elected. Sheriff's departments range from one- or two-member forces to the 16,400-member (plus 400 reserve deputies) of the Los Angeles County Sheriff's Department. In many rural areas, particularly in the South, the sheriff has traditionally been viewed as one of a county's most influential political office holders, while in the northeastern states, the role of sheriff has been considerably reduced. Officers of the sheriff's department are known as *deputies* or similar. Sheriffs' departments normally provide a full service, including accident and criminal investigations and traffic patrol, irrespective of municipal boundaries. They sometimes do limited or restricted duties. On restricted duties they may provide basic court services such as keeping the county jail, transporting prisoners, providing courthouse security, and service of papers for the county and state courts. Sheriffs also often conduct civil process duties such as auction sales of real property (mostly dwellings) in foreclosure, and conduct seizures of chattels (possessions) to satisfy a court judgment. In other jurisdictions, these duties are performed by officers such as a marshal or constable.

County police

In some counties, the sheriff's department assumes only minor duties such as the service of papers. In others, such duties may be done by a constable. County police are mostly found in metropolitan counties and have countywide jurisdiction. Hawaii has only county police. But in most counties, there are no county police and the local sheriff is the sole law enforcement officer. County police may provide full service, limited service (for unincorporated areas of the county) or restricted service (security for county facilities and parks, or road patrols). Some northeastern states maintain county detectives in their county attorneys' offices.

U.S. Marshals

The U.S. Marshals Service is a federal agency within the Department of Justice. Marshals played an important part in maintaining law and order and suppressing crime in the expanding western territories. Famous marshals of that era included Wild Frederick Douglass (1819-95), Bill Hickok (1837-76), and Wyatt Earp (1848-1929). Since the 1920s, marshals have become mainly court bailiffs. They still carry out a wide range of duties, however, particularly in tracing and apprehending fugitive felons. Fictionally, "Rooster Cogburn" was played by John Wayne in three films including *True Grit* (1969), and Colton "Cole" White is played on the Playstation, Xbox and Xbox360 game *Gun*.

Municipal

The largest and best-known municipal police department is that of New York City with its 40,000 officers. In small country towns, by contrast, there may be just a single officer (sometimes still called the *town marshal*). Metropolitan departments have usually have been formed by a merger between local agencies to provide greater efficiency by centralizing command and resources and to resolve jurisdictional problems. This may happen in communities experiencing rapid population growth and urban sprawl, or in neighboring communities too small to afford individual police departments. In addition there are Special District police such as transit police, campus police, airport police, park police, or police departments responsible for protecting government property. Some agencies, such as the Port Authority of New York and New Jersey Police Department, have multi-state powers.

Police duties

Police have three main duties. They have a broad mandate to keep the peace and prevent behaviors which might disturb others. This typically includes minor incidents ranging from a barking dog to a fist-fight. Police are usually called on to deal with these situations with discretion, rather than as violations of law. Where the law has been violated and a suspect must be identified and apprehended, as in murder, robbery or burglary, police act to enforce the law. How often they need to do so varies greatly with the type of area they are policing. Police also provide a range of services such as first aid, tourist information, or acting as educators on topics such as drugs. Because police are traditionally available all the time, citizens often call upon them for roadside assistance, finding lost pets or property, or checking locks on vacationers' homes.

Styles of policing

The pattern of policing reflects many factors including the Constitution, the size of the country, the diversity of the community, historical factors, demography and political decisions over budgets. There are three styles of American policing – *watchman*, *legalistic*, and *service*. These are chosen according to a district's social and economic characteristics, government organization, and the policy of police administrators. The *watchman* style emphasizes maintaining order. This is usually found in communities with a declining industrial base, and a blue-collar population of mixed ethnicity. This style is less pro-active, and certain offenses may be disregarded on social or cultural grounds, as long as public order is maintained. The broad discretion exercised in this style of policing can result in discrimination whereby some groups get better treatment than others. The *legalistic* style emphasizes law enforcement and professionalism. This style is usually adopted in reform-minded cities with mixed socioeconomic composition. Officers are expected to write a large number of citations and make many arrests, acting as if there were a single community standard for conduct, rather than different standards for different groups. The fact that certain groups are more likely to have contact with police means that this style of policing may seem harsh to them. The *service* style emphasizes the service functions of police work, and is usually found in homogeneous suburban, middle-class communities where residents demand individual treatment. Police in these communities may view their work as protecting their citizens against "outsiders," making frequent but often informal interventions. The uniformity of the community means crimes are usually more obvious, and therefore less frequent, leaving police free to deal with service functions and traffic control. At any given time, police officers may be acting in a watchman, service, or legalistic style according to what they are doing, their temperament, or mood. Certain tactics, such as hot pursuit car chases, may be restricted or forbidden. Police usually carry a handgun, often semi-automatic, on duty. Many are required to be armed on-duty and off-duty. They also often carry batons known as *nightsticks*, or collapsible batons. Somewhat controversially, they may also use Tasers, stun guns that give electric shocks. Most large police departments have SWAT (Special Weapons and Tactics) units to deal with barricaded suspects, hostage-taking and other high-risk incidents. Most officers are dispatched from a centralized communications center by radio. Police cars are also routinely equipped with portable computers linked by radio to databases. Intelligence-Led Policing (ILP) is a management and resource allocation approach to law enforcement using data collection and intelligence analysis to set specific priorities for all manner of crimes, including those associated with terrorism. ILP is a collaborative approach based on improved intelligence operations and community-oriented policing and problem solving, which the field of law enforcement has considered beneficial for many years. Today it is being adopted by a variety of law enforcement entities.

Scandals

Police forces with staffing problems have at times recruited unqualified or unsuitable individuals such as the so-called "gypsy cops," who may have histories of poor performance or misconduct in other departments. Several serious cases of police misconduct have raised questions over the screening of potential recruits. In the late 1990s, robbery and drugs offenses by LAPD officers gave rise to the Rampart Division scandal. The films *Colors* (1988), *Training Day* (2001) and *Dirty* (2006) were based on these events. The 1999 Tulia, Texas mass drug arrests (also made into films) led to several innocent people being jailed for some years because of false allegations by an undercover "gypsy cop." The 2004 torture of Lester Eugene Siler led to the imprisonment of five Tennessee officers for 51 to 72 months.

Values in a post-religious society

The British philosopher, Isaiah Berlin, famously made the distinction between "negative" and "positive" freedom, the first being "freedom from" tyranny and interference and the second being "freedom to" do what one will, the freedom of self-realization. Most conflicts in American culture now are over positive freedoms. Americans have hitherto been able to avoid the question of what positive freedoms they want to encourage because they have not been challenged to answer it. But now they are being challenged to do so by the presence of large minorities, whose numbers are boosted by immigration, legal and illegal, and who may have a strong sense of their own values.

The issue of immigration and identity converges with the larger problem of the valuelessness – relativism, secularism, permissiveness, materialism – of postmodernity, what Europe's most famous secular liberal philosopher, Jürgen Habermas, has called "unbridled subjectivity," and American thinker Leo Strauss "the crisis of modernity." The rise of relativism has made it harder to assert positive values and therefore the shared beliefs Americans demand of immigrants and of themselves. Postmodern elites have evolved beyond identities defined by religion and nation to what they regard as a superior place. But aside from their celebration of endless diversity and tolerance, they find it difficult to agree on the substance of the good life to which they aspire, and on positive virtues that set boundaries to behavior, be it misogynist rap lyrics, Madonna's crucifix act or cloning. There has been debate among Americans for a long time over values. Cultural conservatives and the religious right have long criticized Hollywood especially for undermining the values of family and faith. There is still, however, a basic framework of liberal tolerance within which America's cultural debates take place. White supremacists and Muslim extremists have remained within their cultural ghettoes.

As Francis Fukuyama has observed, the problem of how America's post-religious society can come up with values was the critical issue for two celebrated thinkers from the University of Chicago, Allan Bloom, author of *The Closing of the American Mind,* and Leo Strauss. The question is whether there is a way of establishing values through reason and philosophical discourse without reverting to religion. Strauss's central argument was that classical political philosophy, the Greek emphasis on "natural right," or nature deciphered by reason as a source of values, had been prematurely rejected by modern philosophy. The deep philosophical problem is whether it is feasible for philosophy to overcome the objections of Heidegger and Nietszche and say that reason does permit the establishment of positive values, in other words that the truth of certain ideas can be demonstrated. The practical political problem is whether a set of values can be generated that will serve integrative purposes. These values must at one and the same time be positive and meaningful yet not provide the basis for excluding certain groups. In the end, the debate is about positive virtues, what kind of people are found admirable in the nation's common story, the story that builds the community, and what kinds of behavior are assigned dignity in American culture. This kind of definition of the good life may possibly be achieved without resolving the deeper philosophical issue, but Strauss worried about the stability of such a practical solution in the absence of a philosophical resolution about how to arrive at truths. Tentative and unstable though such a solution may be, a solution of sorts is necessary because Americans live in a large national community that is progressively globalizing amid ever-increasing flows of people and information. In this situation, America requires civility, deliberation and democratic discourse. However much the "factions" that Madison so much dreaded may wish it, the country cannot federalize into a multiplicity of self-regarding communities. The American republic, to remain true to the flag to which it pledges allegiance, must remain one nation whatever its citizens' various beliefs about God.

CHAPTER 12

THE US AND THE WORLD

Peace, commerce, and honest friendship with all nations, entangling alliances with none.
Thomas Jefferson, First Inaugural Address, March 4, 1801

American attitudes to the world

Americans have a deep sense that their country is not just a geographical entity but a moral and spiritual symbol, a nation set apart and specially chosen by God. Thus the American understanding of liberty and democracy, justice and freedom of religion is to many Americans self-evident, universal and unchallengeable because these concepts were handed down by God first to Americans. Hence Americans believe they have a mission to be a beacon to mankind. Before the Puritan exiles even stepped ashore at Boston in 1630, John Winthrop, their leader, told them '...we shall be as a city upon a hill.'

In modern times this point of view was perhaps best expressed by the mid-20th century historian, Henry Steele Commager (1902-1998). Born in Pittsburgh and raised in the Midwest, Commager studied history at the University of Chicago. His late-1920s collaboration with historian Samuel E. Morison, *The Growth of the American Republic,* quickly became the most popular college textbook of its time. To these historians, the world's future was as one great democracy modeled after the American experience. America's role was to lead the world by example into the next millennium, holding fast to its first, commonly-held principles of justice, equality and mutual respect. But to those who do not share this vision, the American way of talking about their country's place in history and its role in the world can seem sanctimonious and hubristic. Actually nearly half the American electorate, far more than a decade ago, can be said to doubt the conservative view of American exceptionalism, and that half disproportionately includes the well-educated, those who have lived abroad, recent immigrants, and young voters – just about everyone who wants to see change in America.

Ever since President Woodrow Wilson (1913-21), liberals and conservatives, Democrats and Republicans have zealously embraced the earnest but breathtakingly extravagant foreign policy style of his "New Diplomacy," which was based on moral exceptionalism and the ensuing obligation to export democracy to the world. This view has been reflected in the tenor of much of the last hundred years of American diplomacy, including President Kennedy's (1961-63) stirring but rather hazardous notion that "to assure the survival and the success of liberty" throughout the globe, the

US would "pay any price, bear any burden" and the Clinton administration's hubristic proposition that America was "the indispensable nation."

By contrast, Americans sometimes adopt a solipsistic, isolationist outlook, based as they are in a large country geographically far removed from most of the rest of the world. Since America is better, many think, why not go it alone? Americans sometimes find it difficult to understand an outside world they see as strange and menacing, especially one not motivated by Christianity. But in a globalized world it has become no longer feasible to hunker down in "fortress America" since it can no longer exist as an oasis of prosperity regardless of the outside world (Bates, *op. cit.*, pp. 1-2, 275-277.)

Americans have often believed that their distinctive moral consciousness might prove the salvation of mankind. Today, however, they may find that same characteristic at least as likely to legitimate invidious discrimination as to inspire utopian strivings. They are torn between Victorian censoriousness and Social Gospel communalism. The first arises from Puritan fears of witchcraft and debauchery and inspired the fervor of 19th-century abolitionists and 20th-century prohibitionists. The Social Gospel also springs from the Puritans, their pledges of mutual love, stirring the visionary hopes behind the New Deal, the civil rights movement and the Obama vision of revival.

In the 1950s and early '60s, when the US had emerged as the world's leading power, the American attitude to the rest of the world was articulated in the "modernization theory," probably the most ambitious American attempt to create a complete empirical theory of social change. Walt Rostow's *The Stages of Economic Growth: a non-Communist manifesto* (1960) was a key text. Modernization theory had its origins in the works of late 19th-century European social theorists like Emile Durkheim, Karl Marx, Ferdinand Tönnies and Max Weber. These authors sought to describe the changes in social norms and relationships that took place as human societies made the transition from agricultural to industrial production. The Department of Comparative Politics at Harvard, led by Weber's protégé Talcott Parsons, hoped to create an integrated, interdisciplinary social science that would combine economics, sociology, political science and anthropology. Modernization theorists made being modern the goal of development and, in their view, the various benefits of modernity tended to go together. Economic development, urbanization, the breakdown of primary kinship groups and higher education, together with shifts towards values like "achievement" and rationality, secularization and democracy, were seen as an interdependent whole. Economic development would fuel better education, which would lead to value change, which would promote modern politics, and so on in a virtuous circle.

Samuel P. Huntington's *Political Order in Changing Societies* (1968) was an alternative general theory of political development. Huntington argued, as Aristotle had many centuries before, that political decay was at least as likely as political development, and that the actual experience of newly independent countries was one of increasing social and political disorder. He also suggested that the good things of modernity often operated at cross-purposes. In particular, if social mobility outpaced the development of political institutions, there would be frustration as new social actors found themselves unable to participate in the political system. This was the leading cause of insurgencies, military coups, and weak or disorganized governments in the developing world. Without political order, neither economic nor social development could proceed successfully. The different constituents of modernization needed to be sequenced. Premature increases in political participation, such as early elections, could destabilize fragile political systems. This analysis laid the foundation for a development strategy that came to be called the "authoritarian transition," whereby a modernizing dictatorship provided political order, a rule of law, and the conditions for successful economic and social development. Once these institutions were in place, further aspects of modernity like democracy and civic participation could be introduced. Other critics of modernization theory alleged that it was an ethnocentric Western model of social development rather than a universal one. Huntington's book drew considerable opposition in the US but it was exactly this kind of leader – Park Chung-Hee in Korea, Lee Kwan Yew in Singapore, and Suharto in Indonesia – who brought about the so-called "Asian Miracle."

In a second major volume, *The Third Wave*, Huntington noted that almost all of what he called "third wave" transitions to modernity and democracy in the late 20th century had occurred in culturally Christian countries. The Catholic world, in particular, was catching up to the Protestant first movers, just as Catholic societies had come late to the capitalist revolution. The Third Wave was not, however, a manifestation of a cross-cultural modernization process that would eventually encompass all societies, but one rooted in a particular set of values inherited from Western Christianity. Huntington was convinced of the durability of cultural values and the primacy of religion as a shaper of both national political development and international relations. By contrast, globalization was a superficial force that created the thinnest cosmopolitan veneer and would not in the end guarantee peace or prosperity. The US did not represent the vanguard of a universalizing democratic movement; rather, it was successful due to its origins as an "Anglo-Protestant" society.

From the viewpoint of Francis Fukuyama, culture is more useful in explaining the provenance than the durability of democracy. For him the appeal of living in modern, free societies with accountable governments is universal. Fukuyama believes that modernization and Westernization are closely related. Cultural conflict is not a feature of contemporary China or India, and most Muslims and Russians, for example, are peaceable. For Fukuyama, nation-states and not civilizations remain the primary actors in world politics, and they are motivated by a host of interests and incentives that often override inherited cultural outlooks.

Attitudes to geopolitics have recently shown sharply contrasting opinions. After the end of the Cold War, there was widespread optimism that a peaceful new international order would emerge. Many Americans at that time thought the world had arrived at "the end of history," that the future would take one inevitable shape, liberal democracy, and that, through globalization, nations would just peacefully engage in commerce, with nationalism and geopolitical confrontation things of the past. Most pundits believed that China and Russia were well on their way to becoming liberal democracies. The theory was that once their respective middle classes reached a certain level of wealth they would be demanding the legal and political rights that are required of constitutional liberalism.

In *The Return of History and the End of Dreams*, Robert Kagan challenged this optimism, reminding his readers of the competitive nature of human beings striving for honor and influence, and of the "stubborn traditions" once again resurgent in many nation states. He drew particular attention to autocracy in Russia and China, and to Islamist radicalism. For Kagan, power politics still obtained and war was not impossible. Kagan argued that the Chinese and Russian ruling classes were not so much concerned with human rights as with satisfying public needs. In both countries a relatively small ruling class controlled all the levers of power. Even though they had problems with corruption, they had served their populations rather well.

Kagan predicted that the future would see the return of nationalism, with growing tensions and confrontation between the forces of democracy and autocracy. What determined its stance in world politics was a nation's type of government, not its culture, religion or geographic location. While not dismissing terrorism, he pointed out that modernity had never lost against traditionalism. Kagan foresaw closer ties between the USA, India and Japan, rather than a larger role for NATO. He proposed an international organization consisting of democratic states coordinating their policies. Regarding the EU, he paid little attention to the prospects of at least an inner core pursuing a single foreign policy. For thinkers like Kagan, the US would follow its traditional isolationism at its peril.

Fareed Zakaria, by contrast, argued in *The Post-American World* that the autocracies were simply pragmatists who would eventually become stakeholders in the global economy. Kagan did not agree. He asserted that autocrats believed in autocracy and would continue to reject the demands of meddlesome Western governments and NGOs. They were providing economic success for their people and as a result gaining international respect.

Zakaria argues that the "rise of the rest" – the growth of countries like China, India, Brazil, Russia, and many others – will reshape the world. Their economic growth is producing political confidence, national pride, and competition for resources. But Zakaria's central thesis is that the world is changing, and the change is largely for the better and caused by the benign development of other power centers, not the decline of the US. The biggest challenge for America, he argues, is not terrorism or nuclear proliferation or a rising China, but rather Americans' own ability to adapt successfully to the new environment. He favors confidence and openness rather than insecurity and barriers

As Zakaria sees it, the global dominance the US has enjoyed is rapidly coming to an end, not because of its own missteps, though there are many, but because of extraordinary economic growth in other countries. Zakaria believes that the "flattening" of the world – a metaphor for the rise of middle-class citizens in the Second World who are beginning to consume like Americans – promises global stability and global growth. Except for a few pockets of poverty, he thinks globalization has been largely successful. He predicts that despite its record of recent blunders at home and abroad, America will stay strong, buoyed by a stellar educational system and the influx of young immigrants, who give the US a more youthful demographic than Europe and much of Asia, whose workers support an increasing population of unproductive elderly. In the post-American world, the rise of the world population by another billion by 2020 and the accompanying growth in consumption, together with global warming, will create an energy technology industry at least as big as the IT industry that will provide an enormous opportunity for the US if it can dominate the new industry. America will, however, need to adopt new ways of doing business with the world, one that is based on "consultation, cooperation, and even compromise" as opposed to go-it-alone unilateralism. Already, in a speech to students of Moscow's New Economic School on July 8, 2009, President Obama said that "in 2009, a great power does not show strength by dominating or demonizing other countries. The days when empires could treat sovereign states as pieces on a chess board are over." American success in the 21st century will also depend on how the newly ascendant powers will be integrated into existing institutions such as the G8, the IMF, the World Bank and the WTO.

Meanwhile, two books have made a scathing critique of US foreign policy. *Incoherent Empire* by Michael Mann portrays the US as a military giant but political dwarf, incapable of ruling foreign lands or controlling its client states. Unable to steer the world economy, the US is a backseat driver, prodding poorer foreign states toward often-inappropriate free market politics. In Mann's opinion, the US seduces with promises of freedom, democracy, and material plenty while bringing only militarism and stagnation. Mann's thesis is that military unilateralism is not the policy of realism it is made out to be. To Mann, US foreign policy is based on simplistic views and a lack of understanding of the cultures and aspirations of the rest of the world. It also assumes that the US has the right to judge, and to impose its ways upon other nations. The American people, though honest, hardworking and patriotic are almost always misinformed and cannot see that some of those displayed by the US media as fanatic terrorists view themselves as patriotic nationalist fighters. Hence the US has not been winning any friends worldwide. Indeed, burdened as they are with a particularly parochial viewpoint, Americans do not even know how isolated they are, and many do seem not to care. Additionally, Chalmers Johnson's *The Sorrows of Empire* makes a powerful case that the roots of American militarism lie far back in the past and, by implication, that the new unilateralism is simply a product of neoconservatism. Johnson prophesies that unless the US makes some necessary course corrections, it will be in a state of perpetual war, inspiring more terrorism than it can defeat. Americans themselves will lose some of their democratic and constitutional rights, as truthfulness in public discourse is replaced by propaganda and disinformation. Ultimately, excessive military commitments will bankrupt the nation.

Since the early 1990s, the US has described itself as the sole superpower. But in reaction to the ongoing campaigns in Iraq and Afghanistan, there has been a swing back in American opinion to the view that statecraft's modest but arduous task is to enable one's country to survive and prosper in the world as it exists, rather than to transform international relations and promote liberty and democracy.

US diplomatic strategies

The goal of US diplomatic strategy is to defend the safety of America, promote the interests of America and maintain the leading position of America in the world. According to the National Security Council, US diplomatic strategy pursues eight main goals through trade, aid, foreign relations, intelligence and the military to:

1. champion aspirations for human dignity.
2. strengthen alliances to defeat global terrorism and work to prevent attacks against the US and its friends.
3. work with others to defuse regional conflicts.
4. prevent enemies from threatening the US, its allies, and its friends with weapons of mass destruction.
5. ignite a new era of global economic growth through free markets and free trade.
6. expand the circle of development by opening societies and building the infrastructure of democracy.
7. develop agendas for cooperative action with the other main centers of global power.
8. transform America's national security institutions to meet the challenges and opportunities of the twenty-first century.

Diplomacy has a key role in supporting the military and intelligence functions. American diplomats, for example, are addressing issues of domestic governance around the world, including public health, education and law enforcement. The US is also helping to build police forces, court systems and legal codes, local and provincial government institutions and electoral systems.

For the US, trade and investment liberalization is a key component of the national security strategy. Section four of the U.S. National Security Strategy states: "A strong world economy enhances our national security by advancing prosperity and freedom in the rest of the world. We will promote economic growth and economic freedom beyond America's shores." Later in the section, it is explained that this will be realized through global, regional and bilateral free trade initiatives. The connection between US promotion of free trade and national security interests became even more explicit when US Trade Representative Robert Zoellick stated that countries seeking a free trade agreement with the US had to cooperate with the US on its foreign policy and national security goals. As Henry Kissinger has observed, America in recent years has seen itself as the source and guarantor of democracy, setting itself up as the judge of the fairness of foreign elections and applying economic sanctions if they are not met. Thus America has succeeded in imposing neoliberal economic reforms on a number of oil-rich countries to open them up to its multinational energy companies.

Critics allege that this increasing linkage in US foreign policy between national security interests, the neoliberal economic model of trade liberalization, privatization and deregulation is encouraging increased militarism in the US and abroad. For example, US forces are being used to protect corporate interests, as in the case of the Occidental oil pipeline in Colombia, under the guise of the "war on terror." This blurring of security and economic policy is believed by some to threaten to destabilize parts of the world and limit the scope for realizing a sustainable model of development that supports environmental conservation, economic well-being and equity for all.

International trade

Imports and exports

The rising trade deficit was one of the few negatives as the American economy boomed over the 1990s. The deficits on goods trade and current account have roughly doubled over recent years and are now at record-breaking levels, although trade flows are being altered by the recession. The merchandise trade balance (imports plus exports) is the most widely known and frequently used indicator of US international economic activity. Year 2008 trade performance produced an $821 billion merchandise trade deficit, the second-largest negative trade balance in history. The broadest measure of US international economic transactions, however, is the balance on current account. In addition to merchandise trade, it includes trade in services and unilateral transfers. The deficit fell sharply in 2008 for the second consecutive year, to 3.7 percent of GDP, the lowest since the figure was 3.4 percent in the fourth quarter of 2001, due partly to a larger surplus in services trade. Economists expect the improvement in the current account to continue, mostly due to rapid falls in imports as the recession cuts into consumers' buying power. The US finances the deficit by borrowing from foreigners, so a smaller deficit reduces the need for such borrowing. Trade balances by themselves, however, may or may not indicate underlying problems with the competitiveness of particular industries or of a nation. The reason is that overall trade flows are determined, broadly speaking, primarily by macroeconomic factors such as rates of growth, savings and investments, government budget deficits and surpluses, international capital flows, and exchange rates.

US trade deficits reflect a shortage of savings in the domestic economy and a reliance on capital imports to finance that shortfall. The world's richest country has become by far the world's biggest borrower, with a net debt to the rest of the world (assets minus liabilities) of more than $2 trillion. These borrowings are a concern for Congress for several reasons besides the diplomatic. Financial, budgetary and other policies may affect the size of the trade deficit, while trade and capital flows affect the exchange value of the dollar. A large overall trade deficit may also indicate that certain industries are having difficulty competing with imports at home and in markets abroad. This may generate trade friction and pressures for the government to do more to open foreign markets, shield US producers from foreign competition, or assist US industries to become more competitive. On the large trade deficit with China, it should be kept in mind that 60% of the content of Chinese exports to the US originated in the US and were assembled in China.

Self-interest ought to dictate that the US be a net lender to the rest of the world rather than a borrower. Its ageing population ought to be saving for retirement in real assets abroad. Yet recent years have seen a consumption frenzy fuelled by imports. The federal government and state governments are running big deficits. California's deficit alone is bigger than the budgets of many countries. Meanwhile American consumers save less of their income than consumers in any other rich economy. China's citizens save more than 40 percent of their income; the United States is unlikely according to experts ever to reach half that rate. The numbers strongly suggest that some day this borrowing will have at least to slow down, as it has perforce during the recession, and that could mean a steep fall in the value of the dollar. But a sharp further rise in the euro-dollar or yen-dollar exchange rates – making European and Japanese exports much more expensive – could halt European growth and Japanese recovery in its tracks. Leading economists are warning that the only long-term answer is for US governments and citizens to stop spending more than they can afford and start saving.

TOP TEN COUNTRIES WITH WHICH THE U.S. TRADES MAY 2009

The values given are for imports and exports added together. These countries represent 66.99% of U.S. imports, and 64.69% of U.S. exports in goods.

Country Name	Total in billions of U.S. $
Canada	32.79
China	27.98
Mexico	22.74
Japan	10.41
Germany	8.60
United Kingdom	6.78
Korea, South	5.67
France	4.51
Netherlands	4.10
Taiwan	3.63

Trade negotiations

FACTFILE 17 US TRADE AGREEMENTS

As well as WTO and NAFTA, the following trade agreements are in effect in the US:

Free Trade Agreements
- Australia
- Bahrain
- Canada
- Chile
- Costa Rica
- Dominican Republic
- El Salvador
- Guatemala
- Honduras
- Israel
- Jordan
- Mexico
- Morocco
- Nicaragua
- Oman
- Peru
- Singapore

The US has signed free trade agreements with Colombia, Korea, and Panama, but Congress must enact legislation to approve and implement each individual agreement in order for them to go into effect.

Trade and Investment Framework Agreements (TIFAs) provide strategic frameworks and principles for dialogue on trade and investment issues between the US and the other parties to the TIFA. Topics for consultation and possible further cooperation include market access issues, labor, the environment, protection and enforcement of intellectual property rights, and, in appropriate cases, capacity building.

Although the names of Framework Agreements may vary e.g., the Trade, Investment, and Development Agreement (TIDCA) with the South African Customs Union, or the United States-Icelandic Forum, these agreements all serve as a forum for the US and other governments to meet and discuss issues of mutual interest with the objective of improving cooperation and enhancing opportunities for trade and investment. The US has 56 TIFAs with countries at different levels of development and trade and investment interests.

The U.S. is currently negotiating or considering ratification of the following:
- Andean Free Trade Agreement
- Asia-Pacific Economic Cooperation
- Central America-Dominican Republic Free Trade Agreement
- Enterprise for ASEAN Initiative - provides the impetus for the negotiation of bilateral FTAs

with individual countries of the Association of Southeast Asian Nations (ASEAN): Brunei, Cambodia, Indonesia, Laos, Malaysia, Myanmar, Philippines, Singapore, Thailand and Vietnam.

- Free Trade Area of the Americas
- Middle East Free Trade Area Initiative
- Southern African Customs Union Free Trade Agreement

The 1994 North American Free Trade Agreement (U.S.-Canada-Mexico) continues to serve as the template for U.S. trade agreements.

The *US bilateral investment treaty* (BIT) program helps to protect private investment, to develop market-oriented policies in partner countries, and to promote US exports. The BIT program's basic aims are: to protect investment abroad in countries where investor rights are not already protected through existing agreements (such as modern treaties of friendship, commerce, and navigation, or free trade agreements); encourage the adoption of market-oriented domestic policies that treat private investment in an open, transparent, and non-discriminatory way; and to support the development of international law standards consistent with these objectives.

The US is involved in an unprecedented number of trade negotiations. Most of the current ones began after trade promotion authority (fast track authority) legislation was enacted in 2002. Under that legislation, if the President meets notification requirements and other conditions, Congress will consider a bill to implement a trade agreement under an expedited procedure (no amendment, deadlines for votes). President Obama wishes to amend the legislation to cover labor and environmental standards.

The WTO

The broadest initiative is the multilateral trade negotiations in the World Trade Organization (WTO). In November 2001, trade ministers from the 142 member countries of the WTO agreed to launch a new round of trade talks (the "Doha Round") covering market access, WTO institutional rules, and developing-country issues. The talks have so far failed to reach agreement, mostly because of agriculture, which, although it accounts for only 8% of world trade, is a sensitive issue in the US and many other countries.

Background

For over 50 years, US trade officials have negotiated multilateral trade agreements to achieve lower trade barriers and rules to cover international trade. In the past two decades, US officials also negotiated seven free-trade agreements (FTAs) with neighboring countries or strategic partners. Four of these have so far come into effect: the US-Israel FTA (effective 1985), the Canada-US FTA (effective 1989), the North American FTA (effective 1994), the US-Jordan FTA (effective 2001). The Bush Administration made bilateral and regional free trade agreements more important elements of its trade policy. The multilateral arena is no longer the only means, or perhaps even the principal means, by which the US is pursuing the benefits of trade.

US Negotiating Strategy

US negotiating strategy is based on a concept known as "competitive liberalization." This is designed to push forward trade liberalization on multiple fronts – bilateral, regional and multilateral – to further trade negotiations by liberalizing trade with countries willing to join free trade agreements, and to put pressure on other countries to negotiate in the WTO. Some fear that the accent on regional and bilateral negotiations will undermine the World Trade Organization (WTO) and increase the risk of "trade diversion." Trade diversion occurs when the lower tariffs under a trade agreement cause trade to be diverted away from a more efficient producer outside the trading bloc to a producer inside the bloc.

Traditionally, regional and bilateral trade agreements have been negotiated for a mixture of economic, political, and development reasons. The US-Canada Free-Trade Agreement (FTA) was primarily economic in nature, recognizing the largest bilateral trade relationship in the world between two countries at a similar stage of development. The partnership with Mexico to create NAFTA brought in a country at a different stage of development and gave attention to trade as a lever to encourage economic advancement. It also had a geopolitical rationale of encouraging stability in the US neighbor to the south. The FTA with Israel is seen as an affirmation of US commitment to the State of Israel, while the FTA with Jordan can be seen as a reward for Jordan's cooperation in the Middle East peace process. Cooperation with the US in its foreign and security policies is becoming a more important consideration, as is the ability to counteract free trade agreements among other countries or trading blocs that disadvantage American firms.

NAFTA

The North American Free Trade Agreement (NAFTA) among the US, Canada, and Mexico went into effect on January 1, 1994 under President Clinton. Based on a longstanding bipartisan consensus, it was the first FTA the US had entered into with a lower-wage and lower-income developing country. Its economic impact on US communities and workers, however, remains controversial. Perceptions of NAFTA's benefits and costs mirror and affect debate on extending NAFTA to other countries or negotiating similar FTAs such as the Free Trade Area of the Americas. In addition, ongoing implementation issues affecting specific industries such as agriculture and trucking remain controversial and dispute-prone. Most studies indicate that NAFTA has had a relatively small effect on the US economy, in part because Mexico's is only 6% the size of the US economy. Most economists, however, believe that NAFTA has had a modest positive impact on productivity and a discernible impact on stimulating two-way trade. Nevertheless, certain communities and industries have been adversely affected as a result of US-Mexican economic integration. Although the numbers are small relative to the size of the US workforce, the economic hardship and job losses are significant to those affected. The effectiveness of NAFTA's side agreements on labor and the environment are a source of considerable debate. Running for President, Mr Obama said he would add binding obligations to NAFTA, WTO and other free trade agreements to protect the right to collective bargaining and other core labor standards recognized by the International Labor Organization. He would also add binding environmental standards so that companies from one country could not gain an economic advantage by damaging the environment. Thirdly, he would amend NAFTA to make clear that fair laws and regulations written to protect citizens in any of the three countries could not be overridden simply at the request of foreign investors.

Trade with Latin America

Trade is one of the driving issues in US relations with Latin America, which is the nation's fastest growing regional trade partner, with the exception of Africa. According to the Congressional Research Service, between 1996 and 2006, US merchandise trade with Latin America grew by

118% compared to 96% for Asia (driven largely by China), 95% for the EU, 239% for Africa and 104% for the world. The region's increasing importance as a US trade partner is also an important trend in globalization. In the US, merchandise trade has become an increasingly important part of the economy, growing from 7.9% of GDP in 1970 to 21.4% in 2006.

US export growth to some of the larger Latin American markets – Venezuela, Chile, Brazil, Colombia, Argentina and Costa Rica – has been positive but imports have grown more than twice as fast as exports. The dollar value of US imports rose because of price increases in commodities, particularly petroleum and metals, but this likely also contributed to the region's increased demand for US exports. Most of the growth in imports was due to Mexico, the largest US regional trade partner in dollar terms and second largest export market, accounting for 11.5% of US trade in 2006 and 60% of the region's trade with the US. In Costa Rica there is strong production-sharing trade in certain industries. By contrast, the rest of Latin America makes up only 7.7% of US trade. Brazil, for example, has the second largest economy in Latin America and is the second largest Latin American trading partner of the US, but accounts for only 8.2% of US trade with Latin America, or one-seventh that of Mexico.

Since the 1980s, many Latin American countries have adopted trade liberalization, and tariffs have declined, although spottily, from 45% in 1985 to 9.3% by 2002. Trade reform has not been embraced with equal vigor, however, by all countries and US exports are not treated equally under all liberalization schemes. Also, trade reform has been delayed or even reversed in some countries when faced with economic instability or changing political philosophy. Total merchandise trade accounted for relatively small percentages of GDP in Brazil and Argentina, two countries generally associated with lagging or incomplete trade reforms.

Free Trade Area of the Americas (FTAA)

The vision of free trade in the Americas was put forward initially by President George H. W. Bush in June 1990. He envisaged the creation of a "free trade system that links all of the Americas: North, Central, and South." Given that the timing, terms, and actual dimensions of the proposal were uncertain, the main significance was an offer of a special relationship with the countries of the Western Hemisphere.

Upon assuming office, President Clinton backed the hemispheric free trade concept as supportive of US economic and political interests. Once NAFTA was approved in late 1993, the Administration restated its intention of negotiating an FTA with Chile first, but named no other specific countries. At the Summit of the Americas in Miami in December, 1994, however, President Clinton hailed the proposal by the 34 countries to build a Free Trade Area of the Americas (FTAA) spreading from Alaska to Argentina by the end of 2005 as producing more jobs in the US and improving the quality of life for residents of the western hemisphere. After Miami, the vision of hemispheric free trade was embraced by President Bush and promoted both by formal negotiations, and by the expansion of sub-regional groups and the proliferation of bilateral FTAs.

If created, the FTAA would be a $13 trillion market of 34 countries (Cuba would not be included) and nearly 800 million people. The population alone would make it the largest free trade area in the world with nearly twice the 450 million population of the 27-nation European Union. Trade with the US comprises about 50 percent of the region's global trade volume. In the years following the 1994 summit, western hemisphere trade ministers have met several times to advance the negotiating process. At the sixth meeting in Buenos Aires in April 2001, the ministers made public a draft FTAA agreement that included preliminary chapters on all nine negotiating groups: market access, agriculture, intellectual property rights, services, investment, government procurement, competition policy, dispute settlement, and subsidies.

A key political and social issue raised by the FTAA negotiations on services is governments' role and responsibilities in providing essential services to their populations. These include health, education, water, electricity and social safety nets. These services have been widely understood as governments' responsibility within social contracts. Some services are also human rights which, under the Universal Declaration of Human Rights, governments are required to ensure for all persons living within their jurisdiction.

Since 2001, progress has stalled owing to political and economic objections by a number of countries, particularly Brazil and Venezuela. Many Brazilian companies are concerned that they would be overwhelmed by US competition in an FTAA. In addition, US actions protecting steel and textiles and subsidizing farm production have been highlighted by those in Latin America who support a return to protectionist and more interventionist economic policies. As the region has been hard hit over recent years by economic recessions, rising political instability (particularly in Argentina, Venezuela and Bolivia), declining capital inflows, and an increase in unemployment, pressures have intensified for more nationalistic policies.

The US views hemispheric integration as bolstering US economic and political interests in a variety of ways. Movement towards freer markets is seen as supportive of US prosperity, while the strengthening of democratic regimes is viewed as supportive of US values and security. Closer economic ties are also seen as improving cooperation on a range of bilateral issues, including environmental concerns and anti-drug efforts. In the most general terms, a reciprocal reduction of trade barriers by two or more countries usually contributes to improved efficiency and higher living standards for both. As average tariffs in Latin America are roughly three times higher than US tariffs, supporters argue that the lowering of tariffs and other trade barriers should facilitate significant increases in US trade.

The progress of economic and political reforms throughout the hemisphere as a result of economic integration is also of concern to US policymakers. The reforms have already made Latin America to some extent a more attractive setting for US investment. US opponents of an FTAA, however, are concerned that hemispheric free trade would lead to the export of jobs and capital from the US, as businesses took advantage of much lower wages and weaker safety and environmental standards. Many opponents of the FTAA have argued that free trade with poorer countries will put pressure on the US to lessen its own workforce protections and environmental requirements. Other critics are concerned that an FTAA will inevitably involve the US in the instabilities, class tensions, and economic turmoil of many southern hemisphere societies. According to this view, the costs of an FTAA would include a deterioration in the US trade balance, an increase in immigration pressures, and the need to extend a large amount of credit. From a very different perspective, some opponents also argue that hemispheric free trade could undermine the achievement of a stronger and more open multilateral world trading system. In this view, regional free trade agreements do not serve the interests of the US because it has major commercial interests in all regions of the world. Furthermore, it is argued that a multilateral agreement offers far greater economic benefits than regional agreements.

Few Latin American countries today still show an interest in FTAA. The model of development the US is pursuing is not generally acceptable to Latin American governments and their peoples. Critics say that it is unsustainable; it rewards the wealthy but is niggardly toward those in poverty; it is highly competitive; and it does not put human and social development at the center of policy making. At the heart of the current US approach is a faith in market-based solutions and a consequent bias toward the privatization of services. President Chavez of Venezuela has described FTAA as a "tool of imperialism." and is promoting a Bolivarian Alternative for the Americas known as ALBA, which advocates a socially-oriented trade block in direct opposition to FTAA.

The US and Latin America have pursued trade liberalization through multilateral, regional, and bilateral negotiations, with mixed results. In part this reflects their divergent priorities. For many Latin American countries, reducing barriers to agricultural trade is top of the list for a successful agreement. In contrast, the US has made clear its unwillingness to address most agricultural and antidumping issues in a regional agreement like the FTAA to preserve its bargaining leverage in the WTO against other subsidizers like the EU and Japan. Latin American countries meanwhile have a concern for easing subsidized agricultural sectors slowly toward liberalization. In addition to market access, the US focuses its trade negotiating goals on areas where it is most competitive, such as services (financial, tourism, technology, professional, among others); intellectual property rights (IPR); government procurement; and investment. Hence, there is a near reversal of priorities that has slowed the progress of negotiations. The result in the Western Hemisphere has been the proliferation of bilateral and plurilateral agreements. FTAs are permanent, unlike the unilateral benefits extended under the Andean Trade Preference Act (ATPA), the Caribbean Basin Trade Partnership Act (CBTPA), and the Generalized System of Preferences (GSP), which must be periodically reauthorized by Congress. Brazil, the major regional economy not in an agreement with the US, has in fact moved in a different direction by adding associate members to Mercosur, supporting Venezuela's accession to Mercosur as a full member, and leading in the formation of the South American Community of Nations. (Argentina, Brazil, Paraguay and Uruguay are full members of Mercosur, the Common Market of the South; Bolivia, Chile, Colombia, Ecuador and Peru are associate members.) Although these are neither deep nor comprehensive trade arrangements, they do signal a political will to consolidate regional bargaining interests in juxtaposition to the US-backed FTAA.

Recent nationalizations of key industries and other efforts to increase the role of the state in managing the economies of Venezuela, Bolivia, and Ecuador also do not bode well for broadening support for market-based trade. Meanwhile, multiple FTAs, by definition, promote a cumbersome trading system with each FTA having its own rules of origin (to deter transshipment of goods) and related customs administration and enforcement requirements that can complicate investment and trading decisions.

Resolving this situation will not be easy. For example, without progress on agriculture at the WTO, a comprehensive FTAA is unlikely. Moreover, Brazil and the US will need to make compromises. A less than comprehensive FTAA, meanwhile, may not be considered worth the political capital needed to get it approved, and offers a far less attractive alternative to a multilateral agreement. Thus, an FTAA will likely not emerge soon, despite the benefits of integrating a complex web of subregional FTAs. Notwithstanding these difficulties, the effort has not been abandoned because trade issues are unavoidably part of larger concerns with economic reform, development, and globalization at the forefront of US and Latin American foreign economic policy.

The Andean Trade Promotion and Drug Eradication Act (ATPDEA) authorizes the US President to grant certain unilateral preferential tariffs to the Andean countries of Bolivia, Colombia, Ecuador and Peru. Often considered as the trade component of the "war on drugs," this legislation attempts to encourage the economic development of Andean countries and economic alternatives to drug production and trafficking. It has had some success in encouraging a move away from narcotics trade to legitimate business in the region and in increasing US exports. Since previous legislation was signed in 1991, the four Andean countries have increased their exports to the US by 80%. Products benefiting from tariff preferences include cut flowers from Colombia, Ecuador and Bolivia; precious metals and jewelry from Colombia, Bolivia and Peru; and fish and fish products from Ecuador. By some estimates, 140,000 new jobs have been created in these four countries (CRS, *Trade and the Americas*).

Free Trade Agreements

Middle East - North African Free Trade Agreement. President Bush announced an initiative to create a US–Middle East FTA by 2013. Countries would begin the process by negotiating accession to the WTO and subsequently concluding Bilateral Investment Treaties and Trade and Investment Framework Agreements with the US. As domestic reforms progressed, countries would then negotiate FTAs with the US, possibly linking to existing or planned FTAs, such as those with Jordan, Morocco or Bahrain. The rationale was to provide an incentive for the transformation of the economies of the Middle East and their integration into the world economy, thus raising the standard of living in the region. One study reports that, since 1980, the share of world exports from Middle Eastern countries has dropped from 13.5% to 4%, and that per capita income in the Arab world has fallen by 25% (*Middle East Free Trade Area: Progress Report*, Congressional Research Service, Library of Congress, 2006).

An FTA with Taiwan has been proposed. Taiwan is the 8th largest trading partner of the US, exporting $24.9 billion in 2008; the US is Taiwan's largest trading partner, importing $36.3bn in 2008. From Taiwan, the US imports computers, circuitry, vehicle parts, television transmission and telecommunications equipment. US exports to Taiwan include integrated electronic circuits, electrical machinery, aircraft parts, corn and soybeans. While the Bush administration indicated support for the concept of a US-Taiwan FTA, several outstanding trade disputes remain, including Taiwan's enforcement of intellectual property rights; the imposition of excessive standards; testing, certification and labeling requirements; and Taiwanese rice import quotas. Taiwan signed a TIFA with the US in 1994 and acceded to the WTO on January 1, 2002.

Intellectual Property Rights (IPR)

Ideas and knowledge are an increasingly important part of trade. Most of the value of new medicines and other high technology products lies in the amount of invention, innovation, research, design and testing involved. Films, music recordings, books, computer software and online services are bought and sold because of the information and creativity they contain, not usually because of the plastic, metal or paper used to make them. Many products that used to be traded as low-technology goods or commodities, for example brand named clothing or new varieties of plants, now contain a higher proportion of invention and design in their value. Creators can be given the right to prevent others from using their inventions, designs or other creations. They can also be given the right to negotiate payment in return for others using their creations. These are "intellectual property rights." They usually give the creator an exclusive right over the use of his/her creation for a certain period of time. They take a number of forms. For example books, paintings and films come under copyright; inventions can be patented; brand names and product logos can be registered as trademarks. Governments have given creators these rights as an incentive to produce ideas that will benefit society as a whole, especially when the period of protection expires and the creations and inventions enter the public domain. Intellectual property protection is also designed to contribute to technical innovation and the transfer of technology.

The extent of protection and enforcement of these rights has varied widely around the world; and as intellectual property has become more important in trade, these differences have created a new source of tension in international economic relations. With the growth of globalization, new internationally agreed trade rules for intellectual property rights were seen as a way to introduce more order and predictability, and for disputes to be settled more systematically. The WTO Agreement on Trade-Related Aspects of Intellectual Property Rights (TRIPS) is an attempt to narrow the gaps in the way IPR are protected around the world, and to bring them under common international rules. It establishes minimum levels of protection that each government has to give to the intellectual property of fellow WTO members. A country's own nationals and foreigners must be treated equally. Similarly, fellow members of the WTO must be given *most favored nation* treatment i.e., nationals of all trading partners in the WTO must receive equal treatment. Governments are allowed to reduce any short-term costs through various exceptions, for example to tackle public health problems. When there are trade disputes over IPR, the WTO's dispute settlement system is available.

There had been some degree of protection for intellectual property before TRIPS through various agreements of the WIPO (World Intellectual Property Organization). These included the Paris Convention for the Protection of Industrial Property (patents, industrial design, etc.) and the Berne Convention for the Protection of Literary and Artistic Works (copyright). China has joined virtually all major international IPR Conventions. Some types of intellectual property, however, are not covered by these conventions; and in some cases, the standards of protection prescribed were thought inadequate. The TRIPS agreement added a significant number of new or higher standards. China enacted new copyright and trademark laws on October 27, 2001 to bring it into conformity with TRIPS and an amended Patent Law came into effect in July 2001. China had already issued new regulations for protecting plant varieties and layout designs of integrated circuits, effective October 1, 1997. Trade secrets are protected under Article 10 of the Chinese Unfair Competition Law.

Intellectual property rights are customarily divided into two main areas:

(i) Copyright and rights related to copyright
The rights of authors of literary and artistic works (such as books and other writings, musical compositions, paintings, sculpture, computer programs and films) are protected by copyright for a minimum period of 70 years after the death of the author. Also protected through copyright and related rights (sometimes referred to as "neighboring" rights) are the rights of performers (e.g., actors, singers and musicians), producers of phonograms (sound recordings) and broadcasting organizations. The main social purpose of protection of copyright and related rights is to encourage and reward creative work.

(ii) Industrial property
Industrial property can usefully be divided into two main areas. One area can be characterized as the protection of distinctive signs, in particular trademarks (which distinguish the goods or services

of one undertaking from those of other undertakings) and geographical indications (which identify a good as originating in a place where a given characteristic of the good is essentially attributable to its geographical origin.

The protection of such distinctive signs aims to stimulate and ensure fair competition and to protect consumers by enabling them to make informed choices between various goods and services. The protection may last indefinitely, provided the sign in question continues to be distinctive. Other types of industrial property are protected primarily to stimulate innovation, design and the creation of technology. Into this category fall inventions (protected by patents), industrial designs, integrated circuit layouts and trade secrets. The social purpose is to provide protection for the results of investment in the development of new technology, thus giving the incentive and means to finance research and development activities. A functioning intellectual property regime should also facilitate the transfer of technology in the form of foreign direct investment, joint ventures and licensing.

The protection is usually given for a finite term (typically 20 years in the case of patents). The WTO agreement recognizes that the terms of a licensing contract could restrict competition or impede technology transfer. Under certain conditions, therefore, governments have the right to take action to prevent abuses. The agreement also says that governments must be prepared to consult each other on controlling anti-competitive licensing. Special flexibilities exist to protect the development of medicines. The "one-size-fits-all" standard will, however, sometimes produce too much IPR protection too early and is likely to be a source of further disputes.

The US and the world environment

Although the US has been severely criticized for not ratifying the Kyoto Protocol (1997) – neither has the EU – it is working to strengthen international action under the auspices of the United Nations Framework Convention on Climate Change (1992), the parent document of the Protocol. The perspective of the US on climate change is informed by its economic prosperity, the diversity of its climate and natural resources, and the demographic trends of its over 300 million residents. Because of its diverse climatic zones, climate change will not affect the country uniformly.

The US is taking action to reduce projected growth in its greenhouse gas emissions cost-effectively and to enhance its ability to cope with climate change. The US is committed to reduce its greenhouse gas intensity (the ratio of emissions to economic output) by 18 percent by 2012, a 4.5 percent reduction from forecast emissions. Previously, emissions were projected to increase by 43 percent between 2000 and 2020. Meanwhile, the US is leading global investment and research to enhance understanding of the science of climate change. America is also helping to develop technologies to address climate change such as clean energy and "sequestration" technologies. Clean energy substitutes cleaner for carbon-based fuels, while sequestration technologies promote economic and environmentally sound methods for the capture and storage of greenhouse gases. In addition, the US is working with other countries to increase climate observation systems and to finance more demonstration projects of advanced energy technologies in developing countries, providing over $1 billion in climate change-related assistance to developing countries.

The US continues to make progress in limiting its own emissions of greenhouse gases by becoming more energy efficient. While robust economic growth led to higher greenhouse gas emissions during the 1990s, investments in technology led to increases in energy efficiency which partly offset the increases. In the last decade, emissions per unit of economic output have declined by 17%. Energy use per unit of output compares relatively well with the rest of the world. In addition, much of the economic growth in the US has occurred in less energy-intensive sectors e.g., computer technologies. Consequently, the correlation between economic growth and greenhouse gas emissions has changed. While the US is the world's largest consumer of energy, it is also the world's largest producer of energy, with vast reserves of coal, natural gas and crude oil.

The US funds approximately half of the world's climate change research. Furthermore, the US is a world leader in addressing and adapting to a variety of national and global problems that could be worsened by climate change. Examples include reducing the spread of malaria, increasing agricultural and forest productivity, overcoming hunger and malnourishment, reducing the damage from extreme weather, and improving methods to forecast the timings and locations of such weather. Other programs are directed to preventing habitat loss and other threats to biological diversity. On coming to office, President Obama declared that combating climate change would have a much higher priority. For example, he allowed states like California to set their own, tougher standards of vehicle emissions. Most Americans welcomed this change of policy, although many remain reluctant to modify their lifestyles, particularly in the absence of adequate mass transit.

Even so, the US insists that efforts to combat climate change must be economically sustainable, although what is sustainable may be said to vary with economic and political circumstances. The US economy remains a critically important engine of global prosperity; and global economic development is key to protecting the environment. The *New Energy Policy* involves expanded nuclear power generation; improved energy efficiency; development of hydrogen fuels and renewable technologies; expanded use of cleaner fuels; and more use of renewable energy forms. President Obama has given particular priority to alternative energy and tighter emission standards. He is also continuing the cap-and-trade system for limiting emissions which was developed by President Bush.

Under a cap-and-trade system, the government sets a cap on the total amount of carbon that can be emitted nationally; companies then buy or sell permits to emit CO2. The cap is reduced over time to reduce total emissions.Cap-and-trade harnesses the power of markets and technology to reduce greenhouse gas emissions. Critics, however, say that the cost of permits will increase energy prices and cut consumer spending and industrial production, leading to cuts in GDP and perhaps to more production being outsourced overseas. The system is indeed creating new partnerships with the developing world. New energy policy includes an enhanced emission reduction registry; creation of transferable credits for emission reduction; tax incentives for investment in low-emission energy equipment; support for research for energy efficiency and sequestration technology; emission reduction agreements with specific industrial sectors, with particular attention to reducing transportation emissions; international outreach, in tandem with funding, to promote climate research globally; carbon sequestration on farms and forests; and, importantly, review of progress in 2012 to determine if additional steps are needed in light of further scientific research. These strategies are expected to achieve emission reductions comparable to the average reductions prescribed by the Kyoto agreement, but without the threats to economic growth that American policymakers believe rigid national emission limits would bring. In 2009, the Obama Administration's stimulus package included measures to promote clean energy, and the House of Representatives passed legislation to cut carbon dioxide emissions from 2005 levels by 17 percent by 2020 and by 83% by 2050. At the G8 meeting in July, 2009, it was agreed that by 2050 global greenhouse gases would be cut by 50%.

The US is also active in technology transfer. Hard technology transfer, such as equipment to control emissions and increase energy efficiency, can be particularly effective in reducing emissions, while the transfer of soft technologies, such as capacity building and strengthening institutions through the sharing of technical expertise, can help countries reduce their vulnerability to the impacts of climate change. But whether hard or soft, US technology transfer programs are approached in collaboration with the development objectives and established legal framework of the partner country. Moreover, the US undertakes and supports a broad range of activities aimed at enhancing public understanding and awareness of climate change. The US is committed to providing citizens with access to the information necessary to evaluate the consequences of policy options.

Foreign aid

According to the testimony of Secretary of State Hillary Rodham Clinton before the Senate Appropriations Committee on April 30, 2009, the State Department and USAID work with the military in two crucial ways. They complement and build upon the military's efforts in conflict areas, and use diplomatic and development tools to build stable and peaceful societies, work that is far less costly in lives and dollars than military action later. In Iraq, as the US prepares to withdraw its troops, it is reinforcing security gains while supporting the Iraqi government and people as they strengthen public institutions, promote economic growth and job creation, and assist Iraqis who fled their communities because of violence and want to return home. In Afghanistan, the US is helping the Afghans move toward sustained economic and political progress. In Pakistan, the US is supporting the government's efforts to stabilize the economy, strengthen law enforcement, alleviate poverty, and help displaced citizens find safe shelter. The US is also giving humanitarian, economic, and security assistance to the Palestinian Authority and the Palestinian people. Finally, the US is assisting developing countries hardest hit by the global financial crisis, not simply as a moral imperative but also as an investment in US security and prosperity. The State Department and USAID also give emergency food aid. Other supplemental budget requests made in 2009 covered international peacekeeping in Africa, humanitarian needs in Burma, the dismantlement of North Korea's nuclear program (assuming optimistically that they come back to the Six-Party Talks), assistance for Georgia, support for the Lebanese government, and funding for critical air mobility support in Mexico as part of the Merida Initiative, which links the US, Mexico and Central American countries in efforts against drug trafficking, transnational crime, and money laundering. Official development assistance accounts for less than half the US international affairs budget, consisting primarily of allocations to USAID, the Peace Corps, multilateral institutions, and certain programs sponsored by the State Department and Department of Defense.

Despite reservations about government aid, Americans have a long tradition of domestic and international generosity. Money finds its way from the US to developing countries through churches, private charities, foundations, and remittances by US workers to their homelands. Over the past 25 years US private giving has grown significantly. Churches and other religious congregations initially played the largest role in international giving through relief and humanitarian assistance as well as overseas missions. Then colleges, universities, and foundations began responding to international development needs with scholarships and support for foreign universities and research centers. The number and budgets of private voluntary organizations have grown too. With globalization and changing immigration patterns, US corporations have increased their philanthropy to developing countries. And US immigrants, many from developing countries, have been sending more and more money back to their homelands.

America and China

Since US-Chinese relations were normalized three decades ago, Americans have both idealized and demonized the drive of China's leadership to preserve social and political stability by raising the Chinese people's material living standards, the level of China's technology, and the strength of its security forces. Overly optimistic forecasts of profits from private US investments in China remain unfulfilled, and a peaceful settlement between Taiwan and China does not appear imminent. As a result, Americans' views of China have become increasingly sober and stable since the thawing of the Cold War.

Geopolitics became more fluid in the 1990s. America's concerns about China's possible use of force against Taiwan have grown, and the US has also focused more sharply on China's acquisition, application, and export of strategic technologies. At the same time, popular opposition to freer trade with China during time of economic change and recession in the US has also grown, especially among lower-income Americans. Public opinion surveys even suggest that four out of five Americans believe the US should introduce environmental and labor standards into the WTO. Booming US demand for imports from China have boosted trade deficits, reinforcing American frustrations with China's barriers to US exports and investments. In fact, these feelings are exaggerated, since it has been estimated that 60% of US imports from China contain parts and materials made in the US.

Most Americans favored China's joining the WTO, assuming that it would live by the rules. This is both because prospective exporters and investors saw great opportunities in China's growing market, and because Americans also expected China's participation in the WTO to accelerate the reform of its economic and legal institutions, and ultimately also develop direct, cross-straits trade links between Taiwan and China. The US remains keenly interested in China's institutional as well as economic reform, its progressive integration into the global community, and the peaceful course of its cross-straits relations.

Although strategic bonds between the US and China weakened after the end of the Cold War, since there was no longer any need to contain Soviet expansion, they have been strengthened recently by mutual interests in the defeat of terrorism, and combating climate change and avian flu. America's strategic interests in China have been constant, namely peace, security, prosperity, and a healthy environment. Chinese interests in the US have also been constant and largely compatible, notwithstanding sharp differences over Taiwan, strategic technology transfers, trade, intellectual property and human rights. In particular, US-Chinese relations have been consistently driven by strong common interests in preventing mutually damaging wars in Asia that could involve nuclear weapons; in ensuring that Taiwan's relations with the mainland remain peaceful; in sustaining the growth of the US, China, and other Asian-Pacific economies; and, in preserving natural environments that sustain healthy and productive lives.

Americans have a great stake in China's successful reform and opening policy. China's growing economy is a valuable market to many workers, farmers, and businesses across America, not just to large multinational firms like Boeing, Microsoft, and Motorola, and it will become much more valuable as China's markets open further. That is why the US has an interest in China's participation in the WTO, its opening to the global economy, and its compliance with international rules and norms. The American and Chinese economies are in fact complementary: the lack of savings in the US is complemented by a lack of demand in China. The two countries are solid business partners.

China also affects America's security. Through its participation in the six-nation talks, China is helping to stabilize the currently peaceful but sometimes tense and dangerous situation in the Korean peninsula, where US troops are on the front line; and in nuclear-armed South Asia, where renewed warfare could lead to terrible consequences. The development of China also affects America's environment. Indeed, how China meets its rising energy needs and protects its dwindling habitats will affect the global atmosphere and currently endangered species. In future, US firms hope to market environmental technologies to China.

Yet issues remain between the two countries. The US has serious concerns about the recent big increases in China's military spending. China insists on its right to modernize its armed forces and to buy or sell strategic technologies without disclosing how it does so. The Chinese also point out that China has more bordering countries than any other state. But Americans do not want China to acquire, deploy, or export strategic technologies that could be used against the US or its allies in Northeast Asia, the Persian Gulf, or elsewhere. Already China is limiting American freedom of action in Asia and the Pacific Rim. The US would feel more comfortable if there were greater transparency about military goals and strategies, systems, doctrine and training on the Chinese side. At least a hotline has been opened. Nor do US companies wish to transfer certain technologies to China without adequate protection of their intellectual property. The two countries also continue to have different approaches to human rights. Thirdly, Americans feel that China should strengthen its property laws to meet international market standards, and avoid disputes over the intellectual, financial, and tangible property rights of Americans in China. Great common interests and the risks of serious disagreements will keep raising difficult new challenges. They will require new initiatives for mutually beneficial cooperation and continuous efforts to avoid potentially critical misunderstandings over unforeseeable events in Taiwan, Korea, Japan, the Persian Gulf, the former Yugoslavia, or elsewhere.

To pursue this course amid unexpected difficulties, both countries will need to pay close attention to many issues, conduct frank dialogues, and participate in constructive statesmanship. Ups and downs in US-Chinese relations will likely recur, but they need not be as volatile as they have been in recent years. This puts a large premium on ensuring that there are clear communications between China and America to help keep the relationship on an even keel. There is room for strategic partnership over climate change and the control of bird-borne diseases. Already the US and China are business partners with increasing engagement between companies, NGOs and universities, which is having a favorable effect throughout the US on how China is perceived.

Since 1991 four bilateral agreements between China and the US have addressed Chinese protection of intellectual property rights (IPRs) and US complaints have generally focused on China's enforcement of IPRs rather than seeking changes in their content. US Trade Representatives have complained to the Chinese government that Chinese firms have violated US copyrights on a variety of goods, including computer software, CDs, laser discs, and audiocassettes. Chinese media laws restricted the lawful distribution of imported CDs and cassette tapes, yet a large majority of the 75 million CDs produced in China contained copyrighted songs used without permission of their owners. Outdoor markets near major universities, such as in the *Zhongguancun* district near Beijing University, openly sold pirated software programs. The Computer Software Association reported that China purchased just $1 of software per desktop computer, the lowest rate in the world.

The Chinese government responded to US complaints by shutting down several CD factories producing pirated discs. The US said this was not enough, and both sides threatened to impose tariffs on selected goods from the other country. Perhaps more important, the US threatened to withhold support for China to join the WTO. After that, China carried out thousands of raids on retail outlets selling pirated products, upgraded enforcement efforts, and closed seven pirate CD factories. Increased judicial protection of IPRs was highlighted by the court judgment won by the Walt Disney Corporation against several Chinese companies for producing works showing Disney characters without a license. Even so, because of the scale of the problem and further complaints from US firms, similar disputes have continued. Chinese customs officials, however, have participated in several US-organized IPR training sessions. In light of these efforts, the US authorities have been willing to enter into more cooperative arrangements to tackle continuing problems such as the importation into China of counterfeit VCDs/DVDs. A case settled by the Beijing No.1 Intermediate People's Court was that between the Educational Testing Service of Princeton (New Jersey) and the New Oriental School over use by the School of copyright materials such as TOEFL and GRE papers.

THE US MILITARY

The US possesses unprecedented and unequalled strength and influence in the world. As Americans see it, the US is now threatened less by conquering states than by failing ones, less by fleets and armies than by catastrophic technologies in the hands of the embittered few. The American vision is of decades of peace, prosperity, and liberty. The distinction between domestic and foreign affairs is meanwhile diminishing: in a globalized world, events beyond America's borders have a greater impact inside them. The US national security strategy is based on a distinctly American internationalism that reflects the union of their values and national interests. They say their goals are peaceful relations with other states, and respect for human dignity. Yet to many Americans, the country's interventions in countries such as Iraq and Afghanistan have been blatant misuses of American power by a government no longer in tune with its people's best interests.

Even before the terrorist attacks on the World Trade Center and the Pentagon on September 11, 2001, the accession of Republican President George W. Bush had brought about major changes in both the reality and the rhetoric of US international relations. In his inaugural address, Mr. Bush said: "We will build our defenses beyond challenge, lest weakness invite challenge. We will confront weapons of mass destruction, so that a new century is spared new horrors. The enemies of liberty and our country should make no mistake: America remains engaged in the world by history and by choice, shaping a balance of power that favors freedom." Following the 9/11 attacks, in an address to both Houses of Congress on September 20, 2001, Bush made this policy more explicit: "We will direct every resource at our command - every means of diplomacy, every tool of intelligence, every instrument of law enforcement, every financial influence and every necessary weapon of war - to the destruction and to the defeat of the global terror network.... From this day forward, any nation that continues to harbor or support terrorism will be regarded by the United States as a hostile regime."

Changes in US military doctrine were announced by the then Secretary of Defense, Donald Rumsfeld, in a speech delivered at the American Military University on January 31, 2002. Rumsfeld reaffirmed America's role as the only remaining global power. He also stated that its position required that the American military be able to fight four major conflicts simultaneously, while preserving its ability to face challenges posed by terrorist organizations and the countries that sponsor or shelter them. This was a significant departure from the defense policy pursued by preceding administrations, which established that the US needed to be able to fight only two major wars at once. Rumsfeld also outlined how the traditional range of the US army might need to be extended beyond the US territories and its military bases to include near-earth space and cyberspace.

To achieve these objectives would require what is known as "Strategic Dominance." According to this concept, the US must always be able to assess its adversaries' military capabilities and reduce their ability to react through the planned destruction of the enemy's industrial, military, and political infrastructures. In the first phase of conflict, the strategy does not require the US to occupy the contested territory or the enemy's country, or to engage in any ground operations whatsoever. The US has already experimented with and refined this doctrine – as well as the new high-tech weapons that make it possible – in Iraq, Bosnia, Kosovo and Afghanistan. As demonstrated in the Iraq campaign in 2003, the US military is now able to secure victory in a conventional conflict swiftly, with a negligible number of losses, both in terms of soldiers and equipment, although the same cannot be said of the asymmetrical conflict that followed. The innovations being made within the armed forces rest on experimentation with new approaches to warfare, strengthening joint operations, exploiting US intelligence advantages, and taking full advantage of science and technology. The management of the Department of Defense (DOD) is also being transformed.

In his speech, Rumsfeld explained that the application of the new doctrine would be tailored to specific conditions on the ground. The first step was suppression of enemy air defenses, primarily through the use of aircraft and cruise missiles. These are able to place 50% of their ordnance within 10m of their aim points. The second step was attacks on enemy command, control, communications and intelligence (C^3I) facilities. Then came precision targeting of enemy combat forces throughout the entire theatre of operations. Finally, the ground forces moved in for the mopping up phase. There was some overlap between these phases, with C^3I being hit simultaneously with air defenses, and some ground forces (primarily special operations types) might be on the ground providing targeting from the beginning.

In the case of Afghanistan, for example, after an initial phase in which the priority was forming a local government that could take over the country from the Taliban, the US attacked mainly military installations using high-precision weapons, surgical air strikes, and unmanned long-range weapons like Cruise and Tomahawk missiles. In the second phase, when the Northern Alliance was moving to occupy the territory abandoned by the Taliban, the US switched to carpet bombings, allowing the Alliance and the US special forces who supported them to advance without having to face real battles.

The Rumsfeld reforms

The object of the reforms was to confront the increased threat from lightly armed, highly agile adversaries in what Rumsfeld called "an era of the unexpected and unpredictable." He sought to prepare for multiple futures, stop training for Cold War threats and start concentrating on a variety of new threats, including wars in space. He focused on alertness to the futures ahead, agility in response to threats and opportunities, adaptability, and alignment around a clear mission. The *agility* to go anywhere on a moment's notice means increased mobility. That means faster ships, new fighting vehicles, and a much more responsive civil service. *Adaptability* involves a range of new operating protocols, increased investment in research and development, and more flexible personnel and administrative systems. Whereas the Air Force and Navy used to plan the number of sorties per target, they now plan targets per sortie. Whereas the Navy used to deploy ships on a rigid, six-month schedule, it now maintains a surge capability to move five or six carrier strike groups into combat in 30 days, with another two available for action 60 days later. *Alignment* around a clear mission includes joint operations across the services and among allies.

Rumsfeld also advocated a military able to fight two more traditional regional wars, in addition to Iraq. With $20 billion annual increases planned through 2009, Rumsfeld's budget ended the "procurement holiday" that followed the Cold War, which in turn ended the "personnel holiday" that had shaved nearly 2 million full-time-equivalent jobs from the uniformed military, civil service, and contractor workforces between 1990 and 1999. Rumsfeld moved to invest in new technologies such as unmanned aerial vehicles, space-based weaponry and information warfare. More than 80 new weapons systems are under development. Despite the problems encountered in Iraq, boots on the ground were considered less important than precision weapons in the air. He also introduced pay-for-performance for the more than 600,000 civilian DOD employees and increased outsourcing.

Rumsfeld slated for closure the famous Walter Reed Medical Center, Ellsberg Air Force base in South Dakota, and the Portsmouth Naval Shipyard in Maine, and undertook a massive restructuring of forces abroad. Under the proposal, 22 major bases were closed, others realigned around new missions, and some 800 smaller installations cut. All totaled, more than 200,000 military and civilian employees moved to new locations, while 18,000 lost their jobs altogether. Abroad, Rumsfeld started to reposition forces to new "lilypad" bases that could serve as staging points for quick engagements in the Middle East and Central Asia. Rumsfeld did, however, take criticism for sending an underequipped, under-trained fighting force to police post-war Iraq, and angered Congress with his base closing plans. Moreover the military needs to improve its success in meeting its recruiting targets. It has proved difficult to fight even two wars at once (Iraq and Afghanistan). Also the extreme reliance on technology assumed by Rumsfeld has proved insufficient; troops and civilian staff are needed on the ground to suppress insurgencies and win hearts and minds.

Electronics

US ground warfare capability has been transformed by new electronics. Circuitry has shrunk to the point that a satellite ground station can be carried by hand, rather than on the back of a truck. The satellites are both smaller and in lower orbits, thus less expensive to build and launch. Navigation simply requires hitting a button on a hand-held GPS receiver, which returns a position that can be accurate to within one meter. Communications and targeting systems that once required several people to transport, operate and defend, and which were too bulky and expensive to use on the front lines, can now be carried and operated by one person. People on the ground can find targets and communicate their location in real time. In Afghanistan, operations that once would have required hundreds of ground troops were done with five-man special operations teams. Because of the declining cost of satellite communications it is now possible to send real time imagery and communications intelligence directly to commanders in the field fast enough for it to be useful. Imaging satellites that are militarily useful are now inexpensive enough to be built and launched by private industry.

In addition to a tremendous intelligence (C³I) capability, the US possesses an unmatched force projection capability. No other country, or reasonable combination of countries, has long-range heavy bombers (B-2s and B-52s) carrying precision munitions (JDAMs). None have stealth technologies (F-117, B-2, and the *Zumwalt*-class destroyer (DDG-1000), due to enter service in 2013). None come close to equivalent naval air power (12 carrier battle groups). The 1990's saw the achievement of precision high altitude and long range bombing. Precision is now measured in meters. The million dollar cruise missile has been replaced with the $18,000 GPS-guided Joint Direct Attack Munition (JDAM) or "smart bomb." The cost of imprecision, high in lives and higher in dollars, has declined as the precision has increased. The normalization of Iraq, however, has proved complex, and costly in both casualties and capital, with the outcome yet to be seen.

GPS

The Global Positioning System (GPS) is at present the only fully functional Global Navigation Satellite System (GNSS) in the world. Developed by the DOD, and fully functional from 1995, it currently uses 31 satellites to transmit microwave signals which enable GPS receivers to determine their location, speed, direction and time. The GPS satellites also carry a set of nuclear detonation detectors which form a major portion of the US Nuclear Detonation Detection System. The official name of GPS is NAVSTAR GPS. (NAVSTAR is not an acronym.) The GPS satellites are managed by the U.S. Air Force (USAF) 50th Space Wing at Schriever Air Force Base, Colorado Springs, Colorado.

In 1983, after Korean Air Lines Flight 007 strayed into the USSR's prohibited airspace and was shot down, President Reagan made GPS available for civilian use. GPS has since become a widely used aid to navigation, and a useful tool for map-making, land surveying, commerce, scientific uses, and hobbies such as geocaching (land treasure hunting). Its precise timing is used in many applications including the scientific study of earthquakes. GPS is also a key synchronization resource for cell phone networks. GPS is embedded in cars, watches and cell phones. When approaching a monument, for example, a tour vehicle's GPS system can display information about it. GPS has also moved into cell phones. The Federal Communications Commission mandates handset positioning for emergency calls. GPS is vital to the functioning of the world's financial markets. GPS also plays a role in aviation safety.

To help prevent civilian GPS guidance from being used in an enemy's military or improvised weaponry, the US government controls the export of civilian receivers. A US-based manufacturer cannot generally export a GPS receiver unless the receiver contains limits restricting it from functioning when it is simultaneously (1) at an altitude above 18 km (60,000 ft) and (2) traveling at over 515 m/s (1,000 knots). These parameters are well above the operating characteristics of the typical cruise missile, but would be characteristic of the reentry vehicle from a ballistic missile.

Robots and Unmanned Aerial Vehicles (UAVs)

By the end of 2008, there were about 12,000 robots of some two dozen varieties operating on the ground in Iraq. Robots often have faster reaction times and better aim than human beings. They can be ideal for dull, dirty, or dangerous roles, and can perform boring tasks with unstinting accuracy for long periods. They battle in zones filled with biological or chemical weapons, in rough seas, or in flights with very high gravitational pressures. Robots can scout ahead for improvised explosive devices (IEDs) and ambushes. Soldiers use them to drive up to IEDs and, using the gripper, disassemble the bomb. In addition, *PackBots* serve as mine detectors and chemical and biological weapons sensors. A *PackBot* is about the size of a lawn mower. Remote controlled, they can drive themselves and even climb stairs, over rocks and down tunnels, and swim under six feet. The Special Weapons Observation Reconnaissance Detection System, *SWORDS*, with its five cameras, is the first armed robot designed to roam the battlefield. It has proved especially useful for urban warfare, going first into buildings and alleyways where insurgents might hide. *SWORDS* can even drive underwater at depths of one hundred feet.

In the air, the *Predator* is a twenty-seven-foot-long plane that can spend some 24 hours in the air, flying at heights of up to 26,000 feet. The *Predator* strikes at everything from suspected insurgent safe houses to cars being prepped for suicide attacks. The little drone has quickly become perhaps the busiest US asset in the air. There are many other drones such as the *Global Hawk,* which can look at an entire region. *Predators* and *Global Hawks* are mostly directed from the US, but many UAVs are controlled by troops on the ground, although they mainly operate autonomously rather than being remotely piloted. Other UAVs include the *Shadow* and the eight-inch long *Raven*, which is like a javelin with three cameras in its nose. The small UAVs fly just above the rooftops, sending back video images. There were 5,331 US drones in 2008, almost double the number of manned fighter planes.

The *Spartan Scout*, an unmanned sea vehicle (USV) can inspect small civilian boats without risking sailors' lives. The boat mounts a loudspeaker and microphone, so that a linguist on the "mothership" can interrogate any suspicious boats. The other type of navybots are UUVs (unmanned underwater vehicles) designed mainly to search for mines. Some are mini-submarines or converted torpedoes the *REMUS* (Remote Environmental Monitoring Unit), which was used to clear Iraqi waterways of mines and explosives.

In favor of robotic warfare, it is argued that the operator can thus lessen the likelihood of civilians being killed. Moreover, a robot can enter a room and only shoot at someone who shoots first, without endangering a soldier's life. To the contrary, it is arguable that disconnecting a person via distance makes killing easier, and abuses and atrocities more likely. Also, while the use of robots may have reduced casualties, it has not enabled the US to defeat insurgencies.

America's military

The armed forces have traditionally enjoyed high public support, although their popularity fell during and immediately after the Vietnam War. Since the terrorist attacks of 9/11, the military budget has greatly expanded, and although Congress has proposed conditions on appropriations (funds), politicians of both parties have been careful not to appear to be denying essential supplies for forces in the field. America's military budget is reckoned to be almost as much as the rest of the world's defense spending put together.

Strategy

The US military has been forced to evolve to meet non-traditional threats (terrorism) since 9/11 and to handle the continuing resistance to the US presence in Afghanistan and Iraq.

Military (Army) strategy

Most of America's military history is that of the army and its leaders. Americans' pride in their military leaders is shown by the fact that Washington, Andrew Jackson, Grant and Eisenhower all became Presidents, and Colin Powell has often been touted as a future President. The army is organized into field armies, army corps, divisions, brigades, battalions, companies, platoons and (smallest of all) squads. Special forces have included the Green Berets. The most famous officers' training college is the US Military Academy at West Point, New York. Trainee officers are called *cadets*.

The current training of US military forces is a rising concern of military planners, as they seek to prepare troops for the demands that new electronic, network, and unmanned technologies will heap on them in the future. On the modern battlefield, everybody must think, even at the most junior levels. Future warriors may find themselves on a battlefield with no sense of the presence of their comrades except as icons on a computer screen. Electronic warfare has created a class of problems that are not only complicated, detailed and have no intuitive connection with our bodily senses, but technology itself changes so rapidly that soldiers need to learn whole new generations of software commands on an almost yearly basis. Claims are made that technology will make the tasks of troops easier, but according to the Defense Science Board, the opposite is likely to be true.

Key facts about the US military

The military branches consist of the Department of the Army, Department of the Navy (including the Marine Corps), and Department of the Air Force. The Coast Guard is normally subordinate to the Department of Transportation, but in wartime reports to the Department of Homeland Security. The US military receives $711 billion per year in funding, constituting approximately 50 percent of world military expenditures. The military is all-volunteer. The draft (compulsory military service) was ended in 1973 after protests against using it for the Vietnam War had split the country. Women comprise 13% of the armed forces, and 80% of jobs are open to them. Blacks serve on equal terms with others. The first black Chairman of the Joint Chiefs was Colin Powell, appointed 1989. Homosexuals may serve. President Clinton said they should not reveal their sexuality and the authorities should not ask ("Don't ask, don't tell".) President Obama abolished the ban in 2010. There are 25,000 military veterans, whose welfare is looked after by the Veterans' Administration (VA). At the end of the Cold War in 1989, the US closed its peacetime bases in other countries, although, controversially, it has maintained one at Guantanamo Bay in Cuba, which President Obama has vowed to close. The commander-in-chief is the President. Then comes the Secretary of Defense, then a civilian secretary for each service, and then the Joint Chiefs of Staff, who are the military chiefs of the four services, the Army, Navy, Air Force and Marine Corps.

US MILITARY PERSONNEL, MAY 2009

Component	Military	Enlisted	Officer	Female	Civilian
Army	548,000	456,651	88,093	73,902	243,172
Marine Corps	201,031	180,443	20,588	12,290	
Navy	332,000	276,276	51,093	50,008	182,845
Air Force	323,000	261,193	64,370	64,137	154,032
Coast Guard	41,000	32,647	8,051	4,965	7,396
Total Active	**1,445,000**	**1,174,563**	**224,144**	**200,337**	**580,049**
Army National Guard	353,000				
Army Reserve	205,000				

Marine Forces Reserve	40,000				
Navy Reserve	67,000				
Air National Guard	107,000				
Air Force Reserve	67,000				
Coast Guard Reserve	11,000				
Forced Total Reserve	**850,000**				
Other DOD Personnel					97,976

Of the men and women on active service, 41% are non-white. Current plans are to increase the Army to 547,400 and the Marine Corps to 202,000 by 2012.

Naval strategy

The service has 350 ships and 5,000 aircraft. The US nuclear aircraft carriers such as the *USS* (United States Service) *Nimitz*, *Enterprise,* and *Constellation*, are the largest ships in the world. Nuclear submarines are equipped with Trident missiles. Ships and sailors are divided between different fleets. Special forces include the Seals and the Seabees. Officers are trained at the US Naval Academy at Annapolis, Maryland. Trainee officers are called *midshipmen*.

The battlefield is no longer the size of a country or the deep oceans of the world. Today's battlefield is the littorals, the land-sea interface where over 70% of the earth's population resides and which teem with merchant ships. To win on this 21st century battlefield, a state must be able to dominate the littorals, ready to strike on a moment's notice, anywhere, anytime. This shift in paradigm has caused many to rethink US capabilities and their employment. This is why the Navy has been set on the course of *Sea Power 21*, which reflects the US assessment of the kind of Navy they will need to face the challenges of the 21st century. The program is about projecting decisive joint and combined capabilities from the sea, operating in an information rich environment. This calls for the projection of precise, persistent, responsive combat power through enhanced warfighting effectiveness, better education and training, sustained readiness and greater efficiency. Higher pay and better career opportunities have helped raise recruitment and retention to record levels. An important concept is *alignment*. When an organization is aligned, everyone from junior to senior shares an understanding of the goals and purposes of that organization, allowing them to contribute to their fullest.

Winning the global war on terrorism is the current number one priority. Operations will often be joint with other US services and with the services of partner countries. Major objectives are to strengthen deterrence with advanced defensive technologies, and to increase operational independence through sea basing i.e., naval bases at sea known as *global fleet stations*. Striking power will be distributed to the furthest corners of the earth and the Fleet will be ready to "surge" additional warfighting power on short notice. The Global Concept of Operations, in concert with the US Marine Corps, requires a fleet of approximately 375 ships and procurement of 11 ships per year. Some will be armed with 100-mile guns. Personnel development is a priority second only to warfighting effectiveness. Every leader is expected to be deeply involved in developing their shipmates.

A significant new development in US strategy is the projection of power through a worldwide coalition of military and law enforcement organizations. This coalition will share information to track shipping around the world to end the illegal exploitation of sea lines of communication and thus, naval planners believe, stop terrorism at its root. In this coalition, intelligence will be just as important, and in some cases, more important, than force structure.

Air Force strategy

The U.S. Air Force is organized into numbered air forces which are each divided into wings, squadrons and flights. The USAF has a reputation among the services for providing the best food, accommodation, clubs and other comforts. Officers are educated at the Air Force Academy, Colorado Springs, CO. Trainee officers are called *cadets*. Cadets graduate with a bachelor of science after their four years' training.

The vision statement of the USAF is "global vigilance, reach and power." Operationally, the USAF relies on agility, rapid response, and the integration of all relevant units, those of the US and of its partner countries. In the USAF, as in all the US Services, a major re-think is underway of how forces are organized, trained, and equipped. The focus is on four areas: Europe, North East Asia, Southwest Asia and Asian coastal areas. The US now thinks in terms of capabilities to deliver air and space power. Skeptics have long criticized the National Missile Defense initiative as the opening salvo in a long-range plan to extend US military power into space. Statements from the US Space Command defining US strategy until the year 2020 leave little doubt that policy planners are looking at space as the next battlefield. To achieve this, it is developing three competences: developing airmen; technology-to-warfighting; and integrating operations. According to USAF, air and space are the largest growth areas for security and will play an increasing role in its warfighting. The US is no longer promising that it will not use nuclear weapons to retaliate against a non-nuclear attack. In 2009, however, the US and Russia agreed to sign a treaty each reducing their nuclear weapons stocks to 1,500. Previously, President Obama had made a statement in Prague outlining the way ahead for further progress in global nuclear non-proliferation. His administration has highlighted the issues of strategic arms reductions among existing nuclear powers, enforcement of the Non-Proliferation Treaty among non-nuclear powers, and better control of materials which could be used to make nuclear weapons. Noting that Brazil, South Africa and Libya had decided not to go down the nuclear road, Obama hopes a new global framework would make non-nuclear options the norm.

Military Facilities

The US military manages approximately 24 million acres of federal land, of which the Army manages about half. Much of the land is located in wetlands along coastlines, some of the most ecologically significant areas in the world. The US has 820 installations in 39 countries, controlling an empire greater than any in history, although Americans do not see their power as imperial.

Army and Air Force installations

The term "military installation" means a base, camp, post, station, port or ship that comes under the Department of Defense. An installation is a grouping of facilities, located in the same vicinity, which support the same defense operations. Some are *major installations*. These are self-supporting centers of operations for actions of importance to combat, combat support, or training. A main operating base has all the necessary land and facilities. On average an installation has 5000 or more service members. A *minor installation* will have between 1000 and 5000 service members and may include a military hospital. There are in addition *support sites* such as missile tracking sites and radio relay sites.

Naval installations

Naval installations primarily comprise harbors. Harbors afford safe moorings and protection for vessels during storms. They may also provide accommodations for activities such as resupply, refueling, repairs, or the transfer of cargo and personnel. When all or part of a harbor is used to transfer commercial cargo or passengers, it is referred to as a "port." Military harbors generally include the landside areas that provide functional support to waterborne naval activity. In these cases, they are variously termed: *naval base, naval station, naval depot,* or *naval shipyard*, depending upon the support activity involved. Ocean water terminals include general cargo terminals, container terminals, and roll-on/roll-off (RO/RO) terminals. At the latter, all cargo remains on wheels. A RO/RO terminal can typically unload and reload a ship in 18 to 36 hours. The mooring facilities are designed to withstand local storm fronts and sometimes hurricane force wind and tidal conditions. The port manager controls logistics and establishes the workload for all Army elements within the port complex that unload vessels and transport materials inland. An efficient container terminal equipped with gantry cranes can usually discharge and reload a container ship in 24 to 48 hours. The Navy is now streamlining its base operating support services. While previously each base managed its own logistics, now under the new policy of regionalization, base operating support is organized regionally.

The US Marine Corps

The US Marine Corps is a separate service, although it is managed by the Department of the Navy. Its chief is the Commandant of the Marine Corps. The service takes part in land, sea and air operations and is proud that it is known as the most physically tough. The service is famous for its capture during World War II of Wake Island, Guam and Guadalcanal from the Japanese. Marine Corps officers are educated at the US Naval Academy.

The Marine Corps has often been used for large amphibious landings and has come to be regarded as America's shock troops. Originally conceived to provide shipboard security and amphibious warfare, the Marine Corps nowadays fulfills a unique role within the military. The Marine Corps serves as an all-purpose, fast-response task force in any part of the world where emergency intervention is required. The Marines' mission is to hold an area until heavy reinforcements such as the U.S. Army arrive. Marines are trained to be versatile, adapted to a wide variety of operations. They have a unique mission statement and, alone among the branches of the U.S. armed forces, "shall, at any time, be liable to do duty in the forts and garrisons of the United States, on the seacoast, or any other duty on shore, *as the President, at his discretion, shall direct.*" (author's italics) The Marine Corps possesses ground and air combat forces, but relies upon the US Navy to provide sea combat elements to fulfill its mission. The ground combat elements are largely contained in three Marine divisions, or "MarDivs." The 1st Marine Division is based at Camp Pendleton, California, the 2nd at Camp LeJeune, North Carolina, while the third is based on Okinawa, Japan. Reconnaissance (recon) battalions are composed of Marines. Their mission is to scout the enemy or even penetrate the enemy line. The air combat elements are similarly grouped in the first, second and third Marine wings.

Marine tactics and doctrine lay special emphasis on aggression and taking the offensive. The Marines have been central in developing groundbreaking tactics for maneuver warfare, particularly in the use of helicopters and modern amphibious assault. The training and operational culture of the Marines emphasizes the infantry combat abilities of every Marine. All Marines receive training first and foremost as riflemen, summed up in their saying "Every Marine is a rifleman." As a force, the Marines consistently use all essential elements of combat (air, ground, sea) together. The Marine Corps' ability to maintain permanent integrated multi-element task forces under a single command provides a special ability to respond flexibly and urgently.

Sustaining a skilled, motivated, and ready force is the foundation for the future of the Navy-Marine Corps team. A variety of means are utilized to retain the best and brightest sailors and marines. For example, the Navy's Homebasing Initiative, introduced in 1996, gives naval families more stability by allowing personnel to serve in a single Fleet Concentration Area (FCA). Shore duty is based on at-sea requirements plus sea/shore rotation goals (3 years ashore/ 4 years at sea with 70% of rotation postings within the same FCA).

America as a superpower

America is the richest country and the most sophisticated high-tech military power in the world, and is spending more on defense in real terms than at any time since the end of the Second World War. Yet it is being exhausted by insurgents armed with AK-47 assault rifles, rocket-propelled grenades, and improvised explosive devices (IEDs) i.e., roadside bombs. With the phased withdrawal from Iraq, and inconclusive fighting in Afghanistan, America faces humiliation at the hands of jihadist militants as momentous as the eviction of Soviet forces from Afghanistan in 1989, a defeat that helped to dissolve the Soviet empire.

True, America has recovered from previous disasters, not least the Vietnam war. But its military troubles come at a time when the global strategic balance appears to be tilting away from the US. Iran is filling the vacuum created in Iraq, and is accelerating its nuclear program. China's military punch is growing along with its booming economy. Russia is more belligerent. The transatlantic relationship is loveless. Across the world, anti-Americanism has increased to the point where the US is often regarded as a threat to world peace rather than its guarantor.

Strategists wonder whether the Iraq war has damaged America so badly as to set it on a path to "imperial decline." Is the post-Soviet "unipolar" world, established after America's first war against Saddam Hussein in 1991, coming prematurely to an end as a result of the second war to topple him? For Richard Haass, president of the Council on Foreign Relations, "the American era in the Middle East is over," and because of the importance of the Middle East, American global power has also been weakened, for years if not for decades.

Zbigniew Brzezinski, national security adviser to President Carter, blames all three post-Cold War Presidents for wasting America's moment of supremacy. In his recent book, *Second Chance*, he praises President Bush senior for his handling of the collapse of Soviet communism with "delicacy

THE US AND THE WORLD

and skill" but gives him only a B grade for failing to exploit the victory in Kuwait in 1991 to resolve the Arab-Israeli conflict. He gives President Clinton a mediocre C for his vacillation. President George Bush junior gets an unforgiving F for his "catastrophic leadership." The most powerful image of America, says Mr. Brzezinski, is no longer the Statue of Liberty but the prison camp at Guantanamo Bay. Unless Mr. Bush's successor takes urgent steps to restore America's political and moral standing, he says, "the crisis of American superpower will become terminal," and the epoch of American dominance will be shortened.

As noted, former defense secretary Rumsfeld planned to slim down the army and invest the money in high-tech weapons, reconnaissance systems, and data links. Speed, stealth, and accuracy would substitute for mass. After 9/11, a new political doctrine also crystallized: leadership would substitute for consensus. America would free itself of the encumbrance of formal alliances and multilateral diplomacy. Rumsfeld lived by the dictum that "the mission determines the coalition," not the other way around. The swift removal of the Taliban from control in most of Afghanistan in 2001 by a "coalition of the willing," relying on special forces backed by air power, seemed to validate such concepts. But in Iraq the light, mobile force that smashed its way to the center of Baghdad was plainly inadequate for the task of garrisoning the country, securing the borders and arms dumps, confronting the insurgency, and preventing the slide to sectarian war. America's decision to go to war without formal United Nations support left it with few friends when things went wrong.

Many will argue over the parallels between the failures in Iraq and Vietnam, but there is at least one connection. For decades after the fall of Saigon, traumatized American commanders gave up the study of messy "small wars" to concentrate on fighting the decisive "big war" against the massed armies of the Soviet bloc. Commanders assumed, wrongly, that forces trained to fight high-intensity battles could also handle low-intensity conflicts.

One cavalry officer, Lt-Colonel Paul Yingling, has denounced the failure of America's generals— in Iraq as in Vietnam—to prepare the army for counter-insurgency. Calling, in the *Armed Forces Journal*, for Congress to hold the top brass to account, he wrote: "As matters stand now, a private who loses a rifle suffers far greater consequences than a general who loses the war." In fact, some changes have been made to adapt to the new face of warfare. Army and marine training centers have been reconfigured. Brigades now exercise in mock Iraqi villages, with thousands of actors playing civilians, Iraqi forces and insurgents. Gone are old-style clashes of massed steel on steel, and some commanders now worry that they are losing the skills to fight big conventional wars.

The joint army and marines counter-insurgency manual says the central aim is not to destroy the enemy but to protect civilians. Fighting insurgents involves "armed social work," with key decisions often taken not by the general at headquarters, but by the corporal on the street. In other words, the main task for the 82nd Airborne Division and other army units for the foreseeable future will be nation-building in Iraq and Afghanistan, although, such are the lost opportunities, even that may prove impossible. Above all, says the manual, counter-insurgency requires large quantities of two resources that America is short of: boots on the ground and time.

The Pentagon says America has the best-led, best-trained and best-equipped army ever fielded. "We are not a broken army, but we are working very hard," insists one senior officer. "If you ask a marathon runner how he feels after 19 miles,[30.4 km] he will say he is tired. That does not mean he is not in shape." The trouble, though, is that America's forces were designed for sprints, not marathons. This strategy matches the short attention-span of the American public for foreign affairs. Americans expect their wars to be over quickly with minimum inconvenience to them.

The US has some 1.5 million men and women under arms, including nearly 750,000 in the army and marine corps. But only a fraction can be deployed on long tours of duty because some units are unsuitable for counter-insurgency, while deployed troops need to be rotated periodically to give them time to recover. The army calculates it needs at least two brigades at home to sustain one in a war zone. That means the current total of about 50 army combat brigades and marine equivalents in the full-time forces should support about 17 in the field. But with the surge of five extra brigades to Iraq, America in 2007 had 25 such brigades deployed around the world. The pressure is alleviated with part-time units from the National Guard and reserves (about two combat brigades), but their use is increasingly unpopular at home.

In the ongoing "war on terror," deployments in war zones are ever longer, while "dwell time" at home to recover is shorter. These days American units get nothing like the recommended 2:1 ratio of dwell time to deployment. Some army brigades currently get barely a year to rest and re-train after serving 15 months, a ratio of 0.8:1. By this measure, American ground forces get a fifth as much rest as their British counterparts; and British commanders say that anything less than two years at home for each six-month deployment (a 4:1 ratio) could "break the army."

With some units now on their fourth deployment, an army medical survey in Iraq in 2007 found higher levels of mental health problems, including a 24% level of post traumatic stress disorder among those on multiple combat tours. Less than half agreed that "all non-combatants should be treated with respect" and more than a third thought torture should sometimes be allowed.

Some units no longer have time to rehearse major assault operations, and their training for counter-insurgency is hampered by equipment shortages. For example, about half the Marines' pre-positioned kit, stored on ships around the world and in vast Norwegian caves, has been drawn down to give front-line fighters what they need. The army and marines say morale remains strong but, equally, they say the current tempo cannot go on indefinitely. At some point either the resources must increase, or demands on the forces must be reduced.

Even before the 2007 surge was announced, Colin Powell, the former Secretary of State and an ex-Chairman of the Joint Chiefs of Staff, said that the active army was "about broken." The outgoing military chief, General Peter Pace, also warned Congress in 2007 that America's ability to deal with another crisis in the world was being eroded. He said there was a "significant" risk that America would not be ready to respond properly to a series of possible military conflicts from Korea to Taiwan, Cuba or Iran. America could still beat any likely enemy, said the general, but its response would be slower and bloodier.

All this does not take into account America's need to keep forces ready to deal with unexpected developments elsewhere. A study by the Congressional Budget Office (CBO) in 2007 calculated that if the surge in Iraq lasted until April 2008 (the option floated by commanders in Iraq), only between three and 11 brigades would be available to deal with another crisis in the following 18 months, depending on how much time units need to recover. But American plans for a major war to, say, defend South Korea have in the past envisaged dispatching 20 or 21 brigades, noted the CBO. With time, America could build up its forces for another campaign by sending or training lower-readiness units, mobilizing reservists or, in extreme emergency, by reinstating the draft.

Clearly America needs a bigger army. The new defense secretary, Robert Gates, has announced plans to expand ground forces by an extra 62,000 troops—nearly a tenth of the total—to bring the army up to 547,000 and the marines to 202,000 by 2012. This will not immediately ease the strain, as it will take years to prepare new units. And even this rise may not be enough. According to the CBO, the increase would still not sustain the current surge in Iraq without breaching the rotation guidelines.

Some want an even bigger expansion, perhaps as many as 200,000 more troops. But can America find more soldiers? The army is already short of captains and majors, who take years to train. And despite more generous bonuses, the quality of new recruits is starting to drop, with more in the lowest aptitude ranking, more high-school dropouts, and more receiving waivers from disqualification (for example, for using drugs or having a criminal record). The age limit for recruitment has risen from 35 to 42, while fitness levels are lower. Some complain that training standards have also suffered, as the army adopts gentler means to get more recruits through boot camp.

But even though recruitment is difficult, particularly at a time of high employment, the army is growing steadily, from 482,000 in 2001 to about 548,000. The army says it sees no need for some of the more radical proposals, such as a return of the draft or recruiting foreigners with the promise of American citizenship. In the 1980s the army alone had 780,000 soldiers, all of them volunteers. The army says the profile of its recruits remains above the average for the American population. The number of soldiers re-enlisting—often during service in war zones—remains high. Indeed, the striking thing about the army and marines is not their morale problems, but their resilience.

Even if the troops can be found, equipping them remains a problem. The army says it entered the war on terror with $56 billion-worth of equipment shortages, and kit is being worn out or destroyed much faster than expected. Everything from night-vision goggles to new body armor and armored Humvees has to be shuffled around so that deployed units are fully kitted out, leaving those at home with even bigger gaps. The shortages are especially acute in the National Guard, which has only about half the equipment it needs, and part of that is in Iraq. State governors complain that their ability to deal with emergencies, such as tornadoes and hurricanes, is being compromised.

As matters stand, America can probably consider only limited and short-lived interventions, for instance to bring disaster relief. Given time, it could build up its forces for a major crisis. What seem out of the question for the foreseeable future are the medium-scale "wars of choice."

For some time to come, the burden of projecting American power will fall even more heavily on the air force and navy. This may be enough to deter hostile governments, but insurgents and militias might be less worried. Air power alone cannot win a war.

Military spending

America, the only superpower, still spends roughly as much on defense as the rest of the world put together, and remains the only country able to project military power globally. Its military spending, over $700 billion, represents 4% of GDP, which is low by historical standards. Military commanders often say that "the nation is not at war; the military is at war," that is, the American public is not yet making real sacrifices. Taxes remain low, while the casualties are moderate enough not to be greatly felt, particularly by the urban elite.

The defense budget request submitted by President Obama to Congress for fiscal year 2010 would, if implemented, dramatically reshape America's military. The budget shifts about 10 percent of funds to irregular warfare. It also cuts programs, including delaying the interceptor and radar sites in Poland and the Czech Republic planned by President Bush. Mr. Obama plans to deploy smaller SM-3 interceptors by 2011, first aboard ships and later in Europe. Production of F-22A

Raptor fighters will be capped. The F22 was intended to provide air dominance, while the F-35 Joint Strike Fighter (JSF) was optimized for ground attacks. It is a fine judgment whether the planned F-22 numbers are sufficient to ensure that America's Air Force can maintain an effective conventional deterrent in the decades ahead. Indeed, the Chinese and Russians are continuing to acquire large numbers of new generation fighter aircraft. Without adequate numbers of F-22s, the US will lose the ability to achieve air dominance in places like the Middle East and the straits of Taiwan. The budget also proposes ending C-17 Cargo Aircraft production at 205 frames. The C-17, which can carry 169,000 pounds of equipment, including the Abrams tank and Apache helicopter, is also ideal for operating from austere airfields, including dirt runways. Given the danger of rockets, improvised explosive devices, and guerrilla attacks on truck convoys, the C-17 has become the preferred means for moving men and materiel in theaters like Afghanistan. The Obama Administration has also reduced the Army's Future Combat Systems program. It is not clear from this decision how the Army is going to update its medium-weight forces, the aging Humvees, and the heavy Abrams and the Bradley. Finally, the Navy's next-generation cruiser, known as the CG(X), is being delayed in order to revisit both the requirements and the acquisition strategy. China and Russia have acquired large numbers of carrier-killer and other missiles against which the US Navy, in the opinion of some analysts, currently has no effective defense.

America has ample reserves to defend its global role and potential rivals also have weaknesses. European countries are rich, but for the most part they are unwilling to spend money on military power; Russia's production of oil and gas, although significant, tends to make its currency, the ruble, appreciate, damaging other sectors of its economy, and its population is in a demographic down-spiral. Russia is, however, modernizing its military and flexing its muscles in its "near abroad," prompting Poland to sign an agreement for the US to station a missile defense system on its soil. In July 2009, the US apparently moved closer to cooperation with Russia over the threats from North Korea and Iran, which implies that the missile defense system may not be deployed. America faces stronger regional antagonists, but none is yet competing for global supremacy, whether alone or in concert. If anything, many states want America's help to "balance" a rising China and a growling Russia.

HOMELAND SECURITY

The US is at war with terrorist enemies who are intent on attacking the Homeland and destroying the American way of life. Currently, the most dangerous manifestation of the threat from violent Islamic terrorist groups remains al-Qaida, which has a persistent desire for weapons of mass destruction—chemical, biological, radiological, or nuclear. Al-Qaida's plotting focuses on prominent political, economic, and infrastructure targets in order to produce mass casualties, visually dramatic destruction, significant economic damage, fear, and loss of confidence in government among the population. In addition, there are a host of other terrorist groups and individuals including Lebanese Hizballah. Moreover there are potential threats from groups often referred to as "single-issue" groups, who include white supremacists, animal rights extremists, and eco-terrorists. The lives and livelihoods of the American people also remain at risk from natural catastrophes, including naturally occurring infectious diseases and hazards such as hurricanes and earthquakes, and from man-made accidents. Americans in 39 States face significant risk from earthquakes. Additionally, although each incident is often less significant than major hurricanes and earthquakes, floods have been the most frequently occurring natural disaster and the leading cause of property damage and death from natural disasters in the Homeland over the past century. An example of a man-made accident occurred in August 2003. An estimated 50 million people across eight States and the Canadian province of Ontario were left without electrical power when a utility in Ohio experienced problems that began a chain of events leading to power outages lasting, in some places, several days. This incident, known as the "Northeast Blackout of 2003," cost roughly $6 billion and caused at least 265 power plants to shut down. America's vast land and long maritime borders make it difficult to deny terrorists and their weapons complete access to the Homeland. Nor is the US immune to the emergence of home-grown radicalization and violent Islamic extremism. Naturally occurring infectious diseases also pose a significant ongoing hazard. Increasing human contact with domesticated and wild animals (from which many human diseases emerge), the growing speed and volume of global travel and commerce, and a decline in the development of new infectious disease therapeutics complicate this challenge.

Working with partners and allies, the US has broken up terrorist cells, disrupted attacks, and saved American lives; enemies have not succeeded in launching another attack on US soil since 9/11. The US has also applied the lessons of Hurricane Katrina to make sure that America is safer, stronger, and better prepared. Homeland security is a responsibility of local, Tribal, State, and federal governments, faith-based and community organizations, and businesses. Dozens of federal departments and agencies, as well as state and local governments, are involved. At federal level, Homeland Security includes border security; intelligence missions; and detecting, tracking, and rendering safe weapons of mass destruction (WMD). The State, local and Tribal first response to incidents is through law enforcement, fire, public health, and emergency medical services. The private and non-profit sectors are also full partners, as the country's principal providers of goods and services, and the owners or operators of approximately 85 percent of the nation's critical infrastructure. These efforts are now coordinated through a Cabinet level agency reporting directly to the President, the Department of Homeland Security (DHS). Its establishment has involved the most extensive reorganization of the federal government in the past fifty years. And since many of the threats the US faces – pandemic diseases, the proliferation of weapons of mass destruction, terrorism, and natural disasters – also demand multinational effort and cooperation, the US has strengthened homeland security through foreign partnerships. The US has greatly increased worldwide counterterrorism efforts since 9/11, constraining the ability of al-Qaida to attack the Homeland, and making the Homeland a harder target to strike. These measures have helped disrupt multiple potentially deadly plots.

The strategic objectives of homeland security are to: prevent and disrupt terrorist attacks; protect the American people, critical US infrastructure, and key resources; respond to and recover from incidents that do occur; and continue to strengthen the foundation to ensure long-term success. The last goal entails creating and transforming homeland security principles, systems, structures, and institutions. This includes applying a comprehensive approach to risk management, building a culture of preparedness, developing a comprehensive Homeland Security Management System coordinating the responses of America's 87,000 federal, state and local governments to deal with security, improving incident management, better utilizing science and technology, and leveraging all instruments of national power and influence.

Border Security and Interior Enforcement

America historically has relied heavily on two vast oceans and two friendly neighbors for border security, and on the private sector for most forms of domestic transportation security. The increasing mobility and destructive potential of modern terrorism has required the US to rethink and renovate fundamentally its systems for border and transportation security. Indeed, they must work hand in hand because domestic transportation systems are inextricably intertwined with the global transport system. Better border security includes improving the ability to detain and remove criminal and fugitive aliens and visa violators. The US will continue to hire, train, and deploy additional Border Patrol agents, Customs and Border Protection officers, and Immigration and Customs Enforcement officers, as well as to build on the substantial improvements to the infrastructure and technology deployed at the borders. At the same time, the US is enhancing interior enforcement efforts, including worksite enforcement programs. In addition, the US is continuing to step up efforts to verify the status of non-immigrants studying in the US through the Student and Exchange Visitor Information System (SEVIS) and to follow up where there may be violations.

America's rivals

The dilemma for the Pentagon is how to improve its ability to fight today's insurgencies while preparing for tomorrow's conventional threats. Russia, enriched by high oil prices, is becoming more authoritarian at home and aggressive abroad. It still has a large arsenal of nuclear weapons. But its conventional forces are badly out of date, although they were quickly successful against Georgia, a weak opponent, in 2008. Large-scale exercises are a rarity for its conscript army, which in any case is heavily committed in Chechnya. The fleet does not put to sea in big numbers. Indeed, Russia's real means of projecting power is not its armed forces, but its sale of cheap advanced weaponry to other countries, although the conflict with Georgia showed that they have not given up military adventures close to home.

India, though growing fast, seems more interested in a strategic partnership with America than rivalry. China is the country that most worries the Pentagon. America says it encourages the peaceful rise of China as a "responsible stakeholder" in the world. But China's rulers are investing heavily in a blue-water navy, which may one day include aircraft carriers, apparently to establish a defensive perimeter deep in the Pacific along a chain of islands that runs from Japan to Guam and Papua. China is also modernizing its nuclear arsenal.

For the moment, China seems interested mainly in regional dominance, particularly keeping America at bay in any future conflict over Taiwan. Its leaders are emphasizing "asymmetrical" means designed to blunt America's technological superiority: hoping to deny America the use of the seas with long-range anti-ship missiles and submarines, paralyze its highly computerized forces through cyber-warfare and neutralize spy and communications satellites. In 2007, China tested an anti-satellite missile. Its defense budget is thought to be expanding by around 12% a year, though its real size is the subject of conjecture. According to the Stockholm International Peace Research Institute, China in 2006 overtook Japan to become the world's fourth-largest defense spender, after America, Britain and France.

This military expansion is made possible by startling economic growth. China's GDP now surpasses that of Britain or France. According to Goldman Sachs, China will overtake America around 2027 and become by far the world's biggest economy by 2050. Even now, it is helping to prop up the dollar by buying large chunks of American debt. It holds $1 trillion in foreign reserves. China is pushing America aside as the world's biggest exporter, and last year it produced more cars than the US. China is also taking advantage of America's unpopularity to project its own "soft" power, although the current popularity abroad of President Obama is counteracting this. Europe, too, poses challenges to America: London is vying to replace New York as again the world's most important financial center, and the euro has displaced the dollar as the main currency of the international bond market. Meanwhile, North Korea is demonstrating progress in its nuclear weapons program; Iran is apparently still seeking to develop its own nuclear weapons; and insurgents and terrorists are fighting for control of Pakistan and its substantial nuclear arsenal.

Soft power: the force of good example

Important as "hard" military and economic power may be, these factors are not all that has made America a superpower. The "soft power" (a term first coined by Joseph Nye) of its open culture and liberal democracy, the success of American business methods, the American way of life portrayed in television, movies and music, and the international ties with America resulting from immigration from many countries, have provided an attractive model and encouraged others to see the world America's way (Henry Kissinger, *Does America Need a Foreign Policy?* p.18). In the realm of values and ideas, admiration leads to imitation. It has allowed America to multiply its influence through an unrivalled network of alliances. The abuses of prisoners at Abu Ghraib and Guantanamo, however, have clouded perceptions of America as a humane and law-abiding power and lessened US moral authority. Polls taken abroad by the Pew Charitable Trust, and Gallup International, widely reported, show that the attractiveness of the US has been negatively impacted in many countries by its use of hard power. In fact it has been claimed that US military intervention has destabilized embattled nations, spurred civil unrest, and further incited terrorism.

"Smart power"

President Obama, in adopting what analysts call "smart diplomacy," has announced that the mix of hard and soft power in American foreign policy will be rebalanced. Critics like former Vice-President Dick Cheney retort that returning to more use of soft power in current circumstances is hypocrisy, and might even be taken to signal a weakening of America's political will to pursue its strategic aim. Even so, as long ago as September, 2007, Defense Secretary Gates pointed to the mismatch between the $1 trillion spent annually on the military and the $36 million on soft power, and advocated for a "dramatic increase in spending on civilian instruments of national security—— diplomacy, strategic communications, foreign assistance, civic action, and economic reconstruction and development."

Successive Presidents have believed that they can project American soft power through use of their constitutional right to appoint ambassadors, naming up to 30% of them from among their friends and fundraisers. Such people usually have outstanding track records in business and take an active, entrepreneurial approach to diplomacy. Career diplomats, however, such as the American Academy of Diplomacy, point out that non-career ambassadors generally lack the requisite knowledge and skills and do not know local languages. Probably both types of ambassador will continue to be appointed, not least because business leaders often have the skills to sell capitalism, democracy and American culture.

At one point it looked as if muscular unilateral military action, however controversial, had made the world safer, encouraged democracy in the Middle East, and enhanced American power. The

Taliban were gone; al-Qaeda was on the run; America had new military bases in Central Asia; Saddam Hussein was captured, and Iraqis voted freely. Moreover, Libya gave up its weapons of mass destruction; Palestinians elected the moderate Mahmoud Abbas after the death of Yasser Arafat; Israel left Gaza; and Syria withdrew from Lebanon. Peaceful revolutions in Ukraine and Georgia brought new pro-Western leaders.

But many of these gains have been reversed. Russia denounces America's "diktat and imperialism," talks of a new arms race, threatens oil and gas supplies to neighbors regarded as unfriendly, and says it wants to overturn the Western-inspired world economic order. America is being rolled back from parts of Central Asia, while Ukraine and the Caucasus are in turmoil. In the Middle East, a defiant Iran has been stoking the insurgency in Iraq. Its Lebanese proxy, Hizbullah, survived Israel's military onslaught in 2006 with greater prestige. Above all, al-Qaeda has reconstituted itself, and exploits Muslim resentment over the "war on terror" to recruit new followers to its global *jihad*. Piracy in the Indian Ocean has added a new threat. Meanwhile, Iran draws ever closer to having a nuclear capability; the threat of that by itself bids to change the balance of power in the region.

The "forward strategy of freedom" intended to democratize the Middle East has stalled, not least because elections have, at least temporarily, worsened sectarian tensions in Iraq and brought Hamas to power in the Palestinian territories. America will stay strong but whether it can use its power is a different question. The dilemma for America is whether the withdrawal from Iraq will restore America's strength or signal greater weakness.

The most urgent US diplomatic mission thus is to repair its international image and moral position. President Obama immediately announced after his inauguration that he would close Guantanamo Bay prison and also gradually withdraw US soldiers from Iraq. Meanwhile, the Obama administration has introduced the notions of smart power and 3D—Diplomacy, Development and Defense. In contrast to the previous President's strategy of unilateralism, Obama's diplomatic strategy is to form wide partner relationships to face global challenges together. The concept of partnership is divided into three layers: the first is to consolidate relationships with traditional allies, that is European countries, Japan and South Korea; the second is to strengthen relationships with countries with regional influence, like India, Indonesia, Brazil and Egypt; the third is to build frank and constructive relationships with countries with international influence, like China and Russia. In addition, there is a fourth layer called "effective use of international organizations." Obama regards the improvement of US relations with Muslim communities as a priority. His elaborate speech at Cairo University addressed some issues of deep concern in the Muslim world and represented a soft diplomacy style totally different from his predecessor: Obama humbly recognized mistakes made by America and expressed his intention to make "a sustained effort to listen to each other, to learn from each other, to respect one another, and to seek common ground." Obama's humble diplomacy style has softened the aggressive image of the US and has to some extent repaired the US's relationship with other countries. However, people are more concerned as to how the US will act on its diplomatic transformation and whether or not the US will build equal partner relationships with other countries based on mutual interests and respect.

Instead of threatening to topple rogue regimes, the US administration has re-opened a diplomatic dialogue of sorts with North Korea, Syria and, most recently, Iran. There is now unanimity among US policymakers that peace in the Middle East is in their and Israel's interest. It is President Obama's belief that the best way to achieve that is to create the necessary conditions on the ground and set the stage for a Palestinian state as well. Obama's speech in Cairo, together with firm pressure on Israel to stop building settlements in the West Bank, made a great impression in the Middle East. America has rediscovered multilateralism, not least to keep a united front in imposing limited sanctions on Iran.

Meanwhile, exercising hard power, President Obama has ordered 4,000 more troops into Afghanistan, vowing to "disrupt, dismantle and defeat" the terrorist al-Qaida network there and in neighboring Pakistan. He has also announced plans to send hundreds of additional civilians to Afghanistan and additional help to train the Afghan army and police. In a region that Obama has called "increasingly perilous" more than seven years after the Taliban was removed from power, the fresh infusion of forces is designed to bolster the Afghan army and turn up the heat on terrorists that Obama says are plotting new attacks against Americans from safe havens in Pakistan. The plan takes aim at terrorist havens in Pakistan, and challenges the government there and in Afghanistan to show results. Obama says Pakistan and Afghanistan will be held to account, using benchmarks for progress, although the consequences if not met remain unclear. If the campaign fails, and the Afghanistan government falls to the Taliban or allows al-Qaida to go unchallenged, that country will again be a base for terrorists. The strategy fits with Obama's premise that the US failed mightily in the years following 9/11 by focusing on Iraq instead of Afghanistan.

Transnational issues
A prolonged drought in the Mexico border region has strained water-sharing arrangements between the two countries. This adds to longstanding differences over the rights of Mexican migrant workers in the US. There are also disagreements with other Central and South American countries, principally Mexico and Colombia, over the traffic in illegal drugs and the associated money laundering.

The US continues to keep to the three agreements with China about the status of Taiwan. The influence of Taiwan in the US, despite active lobbying, continues to grow less and less. The US hopes that China will show more transparency about the goals and strategies of its military build-up and about its military systems, doctrine and training. A hotline between the two militaries is now in place.

Meanwhile the US awaits ratification by the Russian Duma (Parliament) of the 1990 agreement over the Maritime Boundary in the Bering Sea. Presidents Obama and Medvedev have appointed a joint commission to study the area. There are also outstanding issues with Canada over the precise maritime boundary in the waters off the US/Canadian northwest coastline at Dixon Entrance, Beaufort Sea, and the Strait of Juan de Fuca near Vancouver Island. It is also one of those facts, strange but true, that the US leases from Cuba a naval base at Guantanamo Bay, which can only be terminated by mutual agreement or US abandonment of the area. The US has made no territorial claim in Antarctica (but has reserved the right to do so) and does not recognize the claims of any other state.

The US signed both the International Convention on Civil and Political Rights (ICCPR) and the International Convention on Economic, Social and Cultural Rights (ICESCR) in 1977. It ratified the ICCPR (with significant reservations) in 1992. However, there is no likelihood of, or even much effort toward, Senate ratification of the ICESCR. Nonetheless, the US has been an insistent voice in denouncing other countries for choosing one class of rights (ESC rights) over another (CP rights). The US has used violations of CP rights committed by some countries to justify the US rejection of ESC rights. According to the US, authoritarian governments invented ESC rights to excuse their indefinite delay in protecting political freedoms. The US contends that CP rights are universal and that the need for economic advancement cannot justify their repression. Thus the US supports universalism, so long as universal human rights do not include ESC rights. This stance betrays an ignorance of history, particularly President F. D. Roosevelt's calls for an Economic Bill of Rights including the freedom from want.

Afterword

It is easy to be carried away with excitement, fear, indignation or sorrow, according to one's point of view, by news of international disputes, military action, and weapons development. But these events only go to show how important it is for the nations of the world to learn to live together in peace. As Winston Churchill put it, "Jaw, jaw is better than war, war." In other words, the sort of continuous international dialogue in which President Obama is engaged is better than continual fighting. And as Kofi Annan, former Secretary-General of the United Nations, said when he received the Centennial Nobel Peace Prize in 1999: "Peace must be sought, above all, because it is the condition for every member of the human family to live a life of dignity and security." Let us hope that in the 21st century the nations of the world co-operate to follow the paths of justice and of peace, and that people everywhere learn to honor one another and seek the common good. Even while we do so, however, we should ponder America's dilemma as an open, democratic society challenged by terrorists who do not wish or intend to negotiate, but plan to maim, murder, and destroy in order to replace American values and the American way of life with their own.

Yet the US remains the largest, richest and most powerful of developed nations, with a unique culture of freedom, equality and openness safeguarded by its Constitution that will ensure its strength and stability against all competitors, and a unique dream that in America all earthly things are possible that will continue to inspire its own people and many others around the world. Successive waves of immigrants inspired by the American Dream continue to arrive to make America their home and realize that Dream for themselves and for their families, even though the US, like the rest of the world, is currently facing severe problems due to the financial crisis and recession. But what perhaps above all makes America special is its unique power to regenerate its society and so prove to itself the truth of Abraham Lincoln's words that America, under God, is the last, best hope of earth. Throughout US history, adaptability has been perhaps the best and most quintessential of American attributes. Americans have made mistakes and misjudgments both recently and in the past. But American culture keeps focused on what it needs to do to be true to itself and how to set about doing what needs to be done. The American spirit springs up resurgent with new hope as each generation gazes once again across the American panorama and moves out toward the frontier that lies ahead.

QUESTIONS FOR REFLECTION AND DISCUSSION

Chapter 1. The American Panorama: The Regions, The Cities, and the Environment

Before you read: 1. How has geography affected US history and culture? 2. Which are the economically and culturally most important regions in America? 3. What are the characteristics of America's leading cities? 4. What issues motivate the modern environmental movement in the US?

After you read: 1. What effect do you think the geography of the US has on American attitudes? 2. How significant do you think regional differences are in American culture? 3. How successful do you think American cities have been in revitalizing themselves? 4. What do you consider should be the priorities of the American environmental movement?

Chapter 2. The Peoples of America

Before you read: 1. How did immigrants from many different countries create American culture? Is there in fact a single American culture nowadays? 2. Which groups had the greatest influence in shaping the dominant American culture? 3. How is the American population changing? 4. What do you know about the history of Native Americans, African Americans, Hispanic Americans and Asian Americans?

After you read: 1. To what extent is America a multicultural society? What are the advantages and disadvantages of such a society? 2. How important do you think English is in creating American national unity? 3. To what extent are the stereotypes of older Americans true? 4. What are the likely effects of the aging of the American population?

Chapter 3. Government

Before you read: 1. What part does the Constitution play in making America a unique culture? 2. What are the basic ideas of American political philosophy? 3. Does having three branches of government ensure a balance of power or can it make government ineffective? 4. What part has the Constitution played in making the US a stable and unified country?

After you read: How successfully do you think the US political process has adapted to a large, diverse population spread over a continent? 2. Do you think the Supreme Court should confine itself narrowly to interpreting the text of the Constitution, or should it be active in laying down judicial principles? 3. Why do you think relatively few Americans vote? 4. Is it because Tocqueville made a better analysis of American culture and society that Marxism has never taken root in the US?

Chapter 4. Capital and Labor: The Economic System and Social Security Net

Before you read: 1. Why is the American economy best described as a "capitalist economy?" 2. Why does the American economy produce more goods and services per person than any other? 3. How great a threat to the American Dream are changes to the economy? 4. What is the role of welfare in the American economy?

After you read: 1. How efficient do you think stock markets are as a means of sharing commercial risks? 2. What do you think accounts for Americans' mixed feelings about government regulation of the economy? 3. How significant do you believe the public sector will be in the US economy in the future? 4. How fair is the balance between capital and labor in the US economy?

Chapter 5. Study, Science, Space and Medicine

Before you read: 1. What are the chief characteristics of education in the US? 2. Why do American teenagers score less well on math and science tests than their peers in other countries? 3. What do Americans think about the space program? 4. How important are American discoveries in medicine?

After you read: 1. Is American higher education too narrow in its focus? 2. Is the space program more likely to foster international co-operation or competition? 3. To what extent does it still make sense to speak of "American science" as distinct from international scientific research? 4. Should the US usually fund its own scientific research or cooperate with partners?

Chapter 6. The Media and Transportation

Before you read: 1. How important is freedom of information in the US? 2. What do you know about the economic problems of American newspapers? 3. What role do the media play in American popular culture? 4. What are the costs and benefits of Americans' love affair with the car?

After you read: 1. How "free" do you think information is in America? 2. How significant is blogging as a medium of communication? 3. Do you think the internet and other media i.e., multimedia, will replace television in America? 4. What is your reaction to the fact that there are now more vehicles in the US than people to drive them?

Chapter 7. The American Character

Before you read: 1. What impressions do you have of the American character? 2. What values do you believe Americans hold most strongly? 3. What do you think are the main differences between American families and families in other cultures? 4. What do you think Americans believe about marriage and child-raising?

After you read: 1. Which personal characteristics of Americans do you find most attractive and why?

2. Why are Americans so conservative in their values? 3. What are the benefits and disadvantages of American individualism? 4. Why is abortion so controversial?

Chapter 8. American Religion

Before you read: 1. What is the relationship between church and state in the US? 2. What are the most common forms of American religion? 3. What do you know about forms of religion created in America? 4. Why are there so many religions in America?

After you read: How religious is America? 2. How Christian is America? 3. Why is the Religious Right a significant political force? 4. What is the future of traditional American Christianity?

Chapter 9. The Arts and Literature

Before you read: 1. What are the chief American co contributions to the arts? 2. What are the distinctive features of American popular culture? 3. What are the distinctive themes of American literature? 4. How strong are the arts in American culture?

After you read: 1. How healthy are the arts in America? 2. To what extent have the arts in America rejected their European heritage? 3. Have the arts in America become simply another form of entertainment? 4. What do the arts in America tell us about Americans' idea of the good life?

Chapter 10. Music and movies, skylines and screens, food and fun

Before you read: 1. What are the distinctive features of American popular culture? 2. How far does Hollywood present a true picture of America? 3. What does American popular culture owe to African Americans? 4. Why has American popular culture spread around the globe?

After you read: 1. How far do you agree with Neil Postman's claim that television has dumbed down American culture? 2. How significant is the musical as an art form? 3. What is the role of festivals in America? 4. Would America be a healthier society if people enjoyed more leisure and did less work?

Chapter 11. Cultural Debates, Social Problems and Solutions

Before you read: 1. Why is there so much economic inequality in the US? 2. Why have efforts to overcome the race problem not succeeded? 3. What are the aims and achievements of the Women's Rights Movement? 4. What are the main causes of crime in the US, and how effective are efforts to overcome them?

After you read: 1."America's pretensions to being a beacon of hope and freedom to all the world … seem fraudulent when set alongside the lives of hopelessness and despair lived by so many of those Americans who descend from slaves." Do you agree? Why or why not? 2. Do you believe affirmative action programs should be continued? Why or why not? 3. How far do you think globalization is a cause of unemployment in America? 4. What can be done to tackle family breakdown in America?

Chapter 12. The U.S. and the World

Before you read: 1. What do you know about the US as a trading economy? 2. How do you think Americans view the world environment? 3. What do you know about relations between the US and China? 4. What do you know about the US as a military power?

After you read: 1. What will be the effects of US international trade agreements? 2. What do you think is the future for relations between the US and China? 3. What do you think should be the balance between "hard" and "soft" power in American diplomacy? 4. How long do you think America will be able to continue to act unilaterally?

BIBLIOGRAPHY

Chapter 1: The American Panorama

Bishop, Bill, *The Big Sort: Why the Clustering of Like-Minded America Is Tearing Us Apart*, Houghton Mifflin Harcourt, 2008

Blatt, Harvey, *America's Environmental Report Card: Are We Making the Grade?* The MIT Press, 2004

Brooks, David, *Bobos in Paradise: The New Upper Class and How They Got There*, Simon & Schuster, 2001

Campbell, Neil, *The Cultures of the American New West*, Routledge, 2000

Carson, Rachel, and Linda Lear, (Introduction) and Edward O. Wilson (Afterword), *Silent Spring*, Mariner Books, 2002

Caughey, John, *Los Angeles: Biography of a City*, University of California Press, 1977

Clark, Terry Nichols (ed.), *Urban Innovation: Creative Strategies for Turbulent Times* (Innovation Series), Sage Publications, Inc., 1994

Florida, Richard, *Who's Your City?: How the Creative Economy Is Making Where to Live the Most Important Decision of Your Life*, Basic Books, 2009

Gordon, Colin, *Mapping Decline: St. Louis and the Fate of the American City* (Politics and Culture in Modern America), University of Pennsylvania Press, 2008

Jacobs, Jane, *Cities and the Wealth of Nations*, Random House USA, Inc., 1988

Kempton, Willett M., James S. Boster and Jennifer A. Hartley, *Environmental Values in American Culture*, The MIT Press, 1996

Kotkin, Joel, *The Next Hundred Million*, Penguin Press, 2010

_____ "The Luxury City vs. the Middle Class", American online magazine, Wednesday, May 13, 2009

Pinsky, Robert, *Thousands of Broadways: Dreams and Nightmares of the American Small Town*, University of Chicago Press, 2009

Primm, James, *Lion of the Valley: St Louis, Missouri, 1764-1980*, University of Missouri Press, 1998

Reitano, Joanne, *The Restless City: A Short History of New York from Colonial Times to the Present*, Routledge, 2007

Scardino, Barrie, William F. Stern and Bruce C. Webb (eds.), *Ephemeral City: Cite Looks at Houston*, University of Texas Press, 2003

Smith, Carl, *The Plan of Chicago: Daniel Burnham and the Remaking of the American City* (Chicago Visions and Revisions), University of Chicago Press, 2007

Watters, Ethan, *Urban Tribes: A Generation Redefines Friendship, Family, and Commitment*, Bloomsbury USA, 2003

Weiss, Michael J., *The Clustered World: How we live, what we buy and what it all means about who we are*, Little, Brown and Company, 2000

Where Did They Go? The Decline of Middle-Income Neighborhoods in Metropolitan America, Brookings Institution, 2008

Cultural maps, http://xroads.virginia.edu/~MAP/map_hp.html

National Resources Defense Council, http://www.nrdc.org

New Geography, http://www.newgeography.com

Service Learning Northwest. Environment Tools for Students, High Impact Project. (2004, December 13). [Online]. Available: http://www.tcoek12.org/tcoeforms/curriculum/HighImpact_Enviro.pdf

Chapter 2: The Peoples of America

Beasley, Vanessa B. (ed.), *Who Belongs in America?: Presidents, Rhetoric, And Immigration*, Texas A&M University Press, 2006

Beeghley, L., *The Structure of Social Stratification in the United States*, Pearson, Allyn & Bacon, 2004

Birmingham, Stephen, *Our Crowd - The Great Jewish Families of New York and The Rest of Us: The Rise of America's Eastern European Jews*, Syracuse University Press, 1996

Bommes, Michael and Andrew Geddes, *Immigration and Welfare: Challenging the Borders of the Welfare State* (Routledge/Eui Studies in the Political Economy of Welfare, 1), Routledge, 2001

Borjas, George. J., *Heaven's Door: Immigration Policy and the American Economy*, Princeton University Press, 1999

Breidlid, Anders, *American Culture*, Routledge, 2007

Briggs, Vernon M., Jr., *Immigration and the American Labor Force*, Johns Hopkins University Press, 1984

Camarota, Steven, *100 Million More: Projecting the Impact of Immigration on the U.S. Population, 2007 to 2060*, Center for Immigration Studies, 2007

Daniels, Roger, *Coming to America: A History of Immigration and Ethnicity in American Life* (2nd edn.), Harper Perennial, 2005

_____*Guarding the Golden Door: American Immigration Policy and Immigrants since 1882*, Hill and Wang, 2005

Diner, Hasia, *The Jews of the United States, 1654 to 2000* (Jewish Communities in the Modern World), University of California Press, 2006

Ehrenreich, B., *The Inner Life of the Middle Class*, Harper-Collins, 1989

Eltis, David, *Coerced and Free Migration: Global Perspectives* (The Making of Modern Freedom), Stanford University Press, 2002

Erickson, Charlotte J., *Leaving England: Essays on British Emigration in the Nineteenth Century*, Cornell University Press, 1994

Ferenczi, Imre, *International Migrations*, Arno Press, 1970

Foner, Nancy, *In A New Land: A Comparative View Of Immigration*, NYU Press, 2005

Gilbert, D., *The American Class Structure: In An Age of Growing Inequality*, Wadsworth Thompson, 2002

Glassner, Barry, Hilary Taub Lachoff and Tom Teicholz, *The Jewish Role in American Life: an annual review*, Casden Institute for the Study of the Jewish Role in American Life, University of Southern California, 2001

Greene, Victor R., *A Singing Ambivalence: American Immigrants Between Old World and New, 1830-1930*, Kent State University Press, 2004

Hämäläinen, Pekka, *The Comanche Empire* (The Lamar Series in Western History), Yale University Press, 2009

Hansen, Marcus L., *The Atlantic Migration, 1607-1860*, Harvard University Press, 1940

Hickey, W. & J., *Society in Focus*, Pearson, Allyn & Bacon, 2005

Ignatiev, Noel, *Race Traitor*, Routledge, 1996

Jacobson, Matthew Frye, *Roots Too: White Ethnic Revival in Post-Civil Rights America*, Harvard University Press, 2008

Jones, Maldwyn Allen, *American Immigration*, University of Chicago Press, 2nd edn., 1960

Kennedy, John Fitzgerald, *A Nation of Immigrants*, Harper Perennial, 2008

Kingston, Maxine Hong, *The Woman Warrior: Memoirs of a Girlhood Among Ghosts*, Vintage,1989

Lareau, Annette and Dalton Conley (eds.), *Social Class: How Does It Work?* Russell Sage Foundation Publications, 2008

Le May, Michael C., *From Open Door to Dutch Door: An Analysis of U.S. Immigration Policy Since 1820*, Praeger, 1987

The Measure of America: American Human Development Report 2008-2009, Columbia University Press, 2008

Mendes-Flohr, Paul and Yehuda Reinhart (eds.), *The Jew in the Modern World*, Oxford University Press, 1995

Miller, Kerby A., *Emigrants and Exiles: Ireland and the Irish Exodus to North America*, (Oxford Paperbacks), Oxford University Press USA, 1988

Miyares, Ines M. and Christopher A. Airess, *Contemporary Ethnic Geographies in America*, Rowman & Littlefield Publishers, Inc., 2006

Musicant, I., *Divided Waters: The Naval History of the Civil War*

Nugent, Walter, *Crossings: The Great Transatlantic Migrations, 1870-1914*, Indiana University Press, 1992

Passel, Jeffery S. and D'Vera Cohn, *U.S. Population Projections: 2005-2050*, Pew Research Center, 2008

Portes, Alejandro and Ruben G. Rumbaut, *Immigrant America: A Portrait*, University of California Press, 2006

Ray, Paul H. and Sherry Ruth Anderson, *The Cultural Creatives: How 50 Million People Are Changing the World*, Three Rivers Press, 2001

Roediger, David, *How Race Survived U.S. History: From Settlement and Slavery to the Obama Phenomenon*, Verso, 2008

Roszak, Theodore, "Senior Citizens: Social and Political Impact," *Civilization*, October/November 1998

Schofield, Brian, *Selling Your Father's Bones: America's 140-Year War against the Nez Perce Tribe*, Simon & Schuster, 2009

Smith, James P. and Barry Edmonston, *The New Americans: Economic, Demographic, and Fiscal Effects of Immigration*, National Academies Press, 1997

Taylor, Philip, *The Distant Magnet*, Harper & Row, 1971

Walker, Mack, *Germany and the Emigration, 1816-1885*, Harvard University Press, 1964

Wimsatt, William Upski, *Bomb the Suburbs: Graffiti, Race, Freight-Hopping and the Search for Hip-Hop's Moral Center*, Soft Skull Press, 2008

Zia, Helen, *Asian American Dreams: The Emergence of an American People*, Farrar, Strauss and Giroux, 2001

African Americans

Dray, Philip, *At the Hands of Persons Unknown: The Lynching of Black America*, Modern Library Paperbacks, 2003

Franklin, John Hope and Alfred A. Moss, Jr., *From Slavery to Freedom with Study Guide*, Knopf, 2000

Gomez, Michael A., *Exchanging Our Country Marks: The Transformation of African Identities in the Colonial and Antebellum South*, University of North Carolina Press, 1998

Hewitt, Lawrence L. (ed.), Arthur W. Bergeron (ed.) and Arthur W. Bergeron, Jr. (ed.), *Louisianians in the Civil War* (Shades of Blue and Gray Series), University of Missouri Press, 2002

Hollandsworth, James G., *The Louisiana Native Guards: The Black Military Experience During the Civil War*, Louisiana State University Press, 1998

Jordan, Ervin L., Jr., *Black Confederates and Afro-Yankees in Civil War Virginia* (A Nation Divided: New Studies in Civil War History), University of Virginia Press, 1995

Kolchin, Peter, *American Slavery: 1619-1877*, Penguin, 1995

Lemann, Nicholas, *Redemption: The Last Battle of the Civil War*, Farrar, Strauss & Giroux, 2007

Levine, Bruce, *Confederate Emancipation: Southern Plans to Free and Arm Slaves during the Civil War*, Oxford University Press USA, 2005

Litwack, Leon F., *Trouble in Mind: Black Southerners in the Age of Jim Crow*, Knopf, 1998

McPherson, J., *The Negro's Civil War: How American Blacks Felt and Acted during the War for the Union* (Vintage Civil War Library), Vintage Books, 2003

Ramold, Steven J., *Slaves, Sailors, Citizens: African Americans in the Union Navy*, Northern Illinois University Press, 2002

Verney, Kevern, *African Americans and US Popular Culture*, Routledge, 2003

Willis, John C., *Forgotten Time: The Yazoo-Mississippi Delta after the Civil War*, University of Virginia, 2000

Hispanic and Latino Americans

Acosta-Belén, Edna, et al, *"Adíos, Borinquen Querida": The Puerto Rican Diaspora, Its History, and Contributions*, Center for Latino, Latin American and Caribbean Studies, State University of New York at Albany, 2000

_____ and Carlos E. Santiago (eds.), *Puerto Ricans in the United States: A Contemporary Portrait*, Lynne Rienner Publishers, 2006

Pérez y González, María, *Puerto Ricans in the United States*, Greenwood Press, 2000

Asian Americans

Chan, Sucheng, *Asian Americans: an interpretive history* (Immigrant Heritage of America Series), Twayne Publishers, 1991

_____Remapping Asian American History, Rowman Altamira, 2003

Chin, Gabriel J. (ed.), *U.S. Commission on Civil Rights: Reports on Asian Pacific Americans*, 2005

Lowe, Lisa, *Immigrant Acts: On Asian American Cultural Politics*, Duke University Press, 1996

Min, Pyong Gap, *Asian Americans: Contemporary Trends and Issues*, Pine Forge Press, 2006

Takaki, Ronald, *Strangers from a Different Shore: A History of Asian Americans*, Little, Brown, 1998

Wu, Frank H., *Yellow: Race in American Beyond Black and White*, Basic Books, 2003

Zia, Helen, *Asian American Dreams: The Emergence of an American People*, Farrar, Strauss and Giroux, 2001

Zhou, Min and Carl L. Bankston III, *Growing Up American: How Vietnamese Children Adapt to Life in the United States*, Russell Sage Foundation, 1999

An extensive bibliography on the American Dream by Robert Delaney can be found at http://www.liu.edu/cwis/cwp/library/amdream.htm

Chapter 3: Government

Abelson, Donald E., *Do Think Tanks Matter?: Assessing the Impact of Public Policy Institutes*, McGill-Queens University Press, 2009

Bailyn, Bernard, *The Ideological Origins of the American Revolution*, Belknap Press of the Harvard University Press, 1992

Barber, James David, *Presidential Character: Predicting Performance in the White House*, Longman Classics in Political Science (4th edn.), Prentice Hall, 2008

Bennett, James C., *The Anglosphere Challenge: Why the English-Speaking Nations Will Lead the Way in the Twenty-First Century*, Rowman & Littlefield Publishers, Inc., 2007

Black, Eric, *Our Constitution: The Myth That Binds Us*, Westview Press, 1988

Bovard, James, *Lost Rights: The Destruction of American Liberty*, Palgrave Macmillan, 1995

Brinkley, Alan, Nelson W. Polsby and Kathleen M. Sullivan, *New Federalist Papers: Essays in Defense of the Constitution* (Twentieth Century Fund Book), W.W. Norton & Co., 1997

Caplan, Bryan, *The Myth of the Rational Voter: Why Democracies Choose Bad Policies*, Princeton University Press, 2008

Cohen, Nick, *What's Left: How Liberals Lost Their Way*, HarperCollins UK, 2007

Dionne, E. J. , Jr., *Why Americans Hate Politics*, Simon & Schuster, 2004

_____*They Only Look Dead: Why Progressives Will Dominate the Next Political Era*, Simon & Schuster, 1997

_____ *Souled Out: Reclaiming Faith and Politics After the Religious Right,* Princeton University Press, 2008

Franz, Michael M., Paul B. Freedman, Kenneth M. Goldstein and Travis N. Ridout, *Campaign Advertising and American Democracy*, Temple University Press, 2007

Gitlin, Todd, *The Intellectuals and the Flag*, Columbia University Press, 2007

_____*The Twilight of Common Dreams: Why America Is Wracked by Culture Wars*, Holt Paperbacks, 1996

Guinier, Lani, *The Tyranny of the Majority: Fundamental Fairness in Representative Democracy,* Free Press, 1970

Goodwin, Doris Kearns, *Lyndon Johnson and the American Dream,* St. Martin's Griffin,1991

Hacker, Jacob S., *The Great Risk Shift*: *The New Economic Insecurity and the Decline of the American Dream,* Oxford University Press USA, 2008

Holmes, David L., *The Faiths of the Founding Fathers*, Oxford University Press USA, 2006

Jumonville, Neil, Kevin Mattson, E. J. Dionne, Jr., *Liberalism for a New Century,* University of California Press, 2007

Katz, Richard S., *Political Institutions in the United States* (Comparative Political Institutions), Oxford University Press USA, 2007

Kernell, Samuel, Gary C. Jacobson and Thad Kousser, *The Logic of American Politics,* CQ Press, 2008

Kopel, David and Paul H. Blackman, *No More Wacos: What's Wrong with Federal Law Enforcement and How to Fix It.* Prometheus Books, 1997

Lane, Eric and Michael Oreskes, *The Genius of America: How the Constitution Saved Our Country--and Why it Can Again*, Bloomsbury USA, 2008

Lilla, Mark, *The Stillborn God: Religion, Politics and the Modern West*, Vintage, 2008

McGann, James, *Think Tanks and Policy Advice in the U.S.: Academics, Advisors and Advocates* (Routledge Research in American Politics), Routledge, 2007

McGuire, Robert A., *To Form A More Perfect Union: A New Economic Interpretation of the United States Constitution*, Oxford University Press USA, 2003

McHugh, Michael, *The Second Gilded Age: The Great Reaction in the United States 1973-2001,* University Press of America, 2006

Nugent, Margaret Lotus and John R. Johannes, *Money, Elections, and Democracy: Reforming Congressional Campaign Finance*, Westview Press, 1990

Purdy, Jedediah, *A Tolerable Anarchy: Rebels, Reactionaries, and the Making of American Freedom*, Knopf, 2009

Schlesinger, Arthur M., Jr., *The Imperial Presidency,* Mariner Books, 2004

Starr, Paul, *Freedom's Power: The True Force of Liberalism,* Basic Books, 2008

Smith, James A., *The Idea Brokers: Think Tanks and The Rise of the New Policy Elite*, Free Press, 1993

Sunstein, Cass R., *Going to Extremes: How Like Minds Unite and Divide,* Princeton University Press, 2009

Surowiecki, James, *The Wisdom of Crowds,* Anchor, 2005

Tocqueville, Alexis de, *Democracy in America*, ed. Phillips Bradley, Knopf, 1980

Wicker, Tom, *One of Us: Richard Nixon and the American Dream*, Random House, 1991

Wolfe, Alan, *The Future of Liberalism*, Knopf, 2009

Accuracy in Media, www.aim.org

ACLU - The American Civil Liberties Union, the leading civil liberties organization, www.aclu.org

American Enterprise Institute - conservative think tank, www.aei.org

American Federation of State, County and Municipal Employees (AFSCME) – includes arguments against privatization of government services, www.afscme.org

American Memory - a variety of links on selected presidential writings and articles, http://memory.loc.gov/ammem/index.html

American National Election Studies - high quality data on voting, public opinion, and political participation, www.electionstudies.org

The Anti-Federalist Papers - online version from the West El Paso Information Network (WEPIN), http://wepin.com/articles/afp/index.htm

Brookings Institution - the nation's oldest think tank - information and recommendations on emerging policy challenges, including federal-state issues, www.brookings.edu/

Cato Institute - a libertarian perspective on issues such as federalism, www.cato.org

Center for Democracy and Technology - discusses how new computer and communications technologies are affecting the constitutional rights and liberties of Americans, www.cdt.org

Center for the Study of the American Electorate, www1.american.edu/ia/cdem/csae/

Center for Voting and Democracy - critical views of the Electoral College, www.fairvote.org/

CNN All Politics - news, news analysis, polling data, and news articles dating back to 1996, www.cnn.com/ALLPOLITICS

The Constitution - hypertext links to amendments and other changes, www.law.cornell.edu/constitution/

Constitutions of the United States - the constitutions of almost all of the states are now online, www.findlaw.com/11stategov/index.html

Cornell University Law School Legal Information Institute - index of Supreme Court cases, http://supct.law.cornell.edu/supct

CQ (Congressional Quarterly) - campaign finance, http://moneyline.cq.com/pml/home.do

The Democratic Party, www.democrats.org

Democracy Institute, www.democracyinstitute.org

Federal Agencies - information on the federal agencies, www.firstgov.gov

Federal Election Commission - the law on campaign financing, www.fec.gov

The Federal Register - the official publication for executive branch documents, www.gpoaccess.gov/fr/index.html

Federal World - links to numerous federal agencies and government information, www.fedworld.gov

FindLaw - Supreme Court decisions since 1907, www.findlaw.com

Free Expression Network Clearinghouse - legislation updates, legal briefings, and news on cases of censorship in local communities, www.FREEExpression.org

Foundation for the Defense of Democracies – researches terrorism, www.defenddemocracy.org/

The Gallup Organization - results of recent polls and an archive of past polls and information on how polls are conducted, www.gallup.com/Home.aspx

GovTrack.us - enables progress of legislation and details of votes to be tracked, www.govtrack.us

Governing Magazine - news about state and local governments, www.governing.com

The Greens/Green Party USA, www.greenparty.org/index.php

House of Representatives - email addresses and home pages for members of the House of Representatives, www.house.gov

Inaugural Addresses - the inaugural addresses of American Presidents from George Washington to George W. Bush, www.bartleby.com/124

InfoUSA: Outline of U.S. Government, http://usinfo.org/enus/government/overview/ch1.html

Institution of Global Communications - lobbying and public-interest activities on conflict, race and women's issues, www.igc.apc.org

The Internet Public Library Association provides links to hundreds of professional and trade associations, www.ipl.org/ref/AON

The Libertarian Party, www.lp.org

The Liberty Counsel – a nonprofit religious civil liberties education and legal defense organization established to preserve religious freedom (pro-life, pro-family), www.lc.org

Librarians' Internet Index – a search facility, www.lii.org

Miller Center of Public Affairs - documents and academic resources concerning the Presidency, www.americanpresident.org

Moving Ideas:The Electronic Policy Network - "timely information and leading ideas about federal policy and politics." It also has links to dozens of sites, www.care2.com/causes/politics/

The National Archive - the site offers access to the various presidential libraries, www.archives.gov/presidential_libraries/index.html

National Conference of State Legislatures - information on some of the challenges state governments are currently facing, www.ncsl.org

National Constitution Center - basic facts about the Constitution, an online version of the *Federalist Papers,* other information, and a Constitution quiz, www.constitutioncenter.org

National Governors Association - extensive information on developments among the states, state policy positions on various issues, and other state information, www.nga.org

National Issues Forums - nonpartisan articles on current issues, www.nifi.org

National Right to Life Committee - a special interest group opposed to legalized abortion, www.nrlc.org

Newspapers, www.newspapers.com

NRA - The National Rifle Association, www.nra.org/home.aspx

OMB - The Office of Management and Budget offers information ranging from new developments in administrative policy to the costs of the bureaucracy to paperwork- reduction efforts, www.whitehouse.gov/omb/

PBS by the People - contains a section "PBS by the People" which provides tips on how to analyze a poll, www.pbs.org/elections/savvyanalyze.html

The Pew Forum on Religion and Public Life Issues – highly respected nonpartisan views on religion and politics, http://pewforum.org/religion-politics

The Pew Research Center for the People & the Press offers survey data on a number of topics relating to American politics and government, http://people-press.org

Political Science Resources – links, www.lib.umich.edu/govdocs/psusp.html

The Polling Report - polling results on a number of issues, www.pollingreport.com

Project for the New American Century - neoconservative organization supporting greater American militarization, challenging hostile governments, advancing democratic and economic freedom, www.newamericancentury.org

Project Vote Smart - information on campaign financing and voting, www.votesmart.org

Public Agenda - links to poll data and other sources on public opinion, www.publicagenda.org

RealClear Politics - independent source of political news and resource, www.realclearpolitics.com

The Reason Foundation's proposals for privatizing government services, www.privatization.org

Reform Party, www.rpusa.org

Republican National Committee, www.gop.com/

Roll Call - the newspaper of Capitol Hill since 1955, www.rollcall.com

Roper Center for Public Opinion Research, www.ropercenter.uconn.edu

The Rothenberg Political Report – a nonpartisan analysis of American Politics and Elections, http://rothenbergpoliticalreport.blogspot.com

Smithsonian Museums: *Vote: the Machinery of Democracy,* http://americanhistory.si.edu/vote/

Socialist Party USA, http://sp-usa.org

Source Watch - information about attack ads, etc., www.sourcewatch.org/index. php?title=Empower_America

State and Local Government, a directory of official state, county and city government websites, www.statelocalgov.net/statefaq.cfm

State News, state policy and politics, updated daily, www.stateline.org/live/

Statehouse News Bureau - information on state governments and issues concerning federalism, www.statenews.org

Supreme Court Opinions, http://supremecourtus.gov

The UCLA Online Institute for Cyberspace Law and Policy, www.gseis.ucla.edu/iclp/hp.html

The White House, www.whitehouse.gov/

This Nation.com - nonpartisan coverage of current political questions. James Madison's notes are a major source for the debates of the Constitutional Convention, www.thisnation.com/library/madison/index.html

THOMAS - named for Thomas Jefferson, maintained by the Library of Congress, provides a record of all bills introduced into Congress, information about each member of Congress and how he or she voted on specific bills, and other data, http://thomas.loc.gov/

US Code - Cornell University Law School Legal Information Institute, www.law.cornell.edu/uscode/

The United States Government Manual - information on the functions, organization, and administrators of every federal department, www.gpoaccess.gov/gmanual/index.html

United States Senate - email addresses and home pages for members of the Senate, www.senate.gov

US Courts The Federal Judiciary, www.uscourts.gov

US GPO - the Government Printing Office offers information on Congress in session, bills pending and passed, and a history of the bills, www.gpo.gov

US Presidency and Supreme Court Data - assesses the political beliefs of Supreme Court Justices, www.sunysb.edu/polsci/jsegal/data/pressc_main.htm

US Supreme Court media, www.oyez.org

USA.gov - extensive information on the federal government and the services it provides for citizens, www.firstgov.gov

WashLaw - texts of state cases, federal cases and state and federal laws, www.washlaw.edu

Yale University Library - sources relating to American politics and government, www.library.yale.edu/socsci

Chapter 4: Capital and Labor: The Economic System and Social Safety Net

Akerlof, George A. and Robert J. Schiller, *Animal Spirits: How Human Psychology Drives the Economy, and Why It Matters for Global Capitalism*, Princeton University Press, 2009

Bain, Jeffrey K., *Social Security Solvency*, Nova Science Publishers, Inc., 2009

Banker, David E. and James M. MacDonald, (eds.), *Structural and Financial Characteristics of U.S. Farms: 2004 Family Farm Report*, Agriculture Information Bulletin No.797, USDA, March 2005

Chossudovsky, Michel, *The Globalization of Poverty and the New World Order*, Global Research, Centre for Research on Globalization, 2005

Conley, Dalton, *Elsewhere, U.S.A.: How We Got from the Company Man, Family Dinners, and the Affluent Society to the Home Office, BlackBerry Moms, and Economic Anxiety*, Pantheon, 2009

Conley discusses the subject at http://fora.tv/2009/01/27/Dalton_Conley_Elsewhere_USA

Dobelstein, Andrew, *Understanding the Social Security Act: The Foundation of Social Welfare for America in the Twenty-First Century*, Oxford University Press USA, 2009

Dyer, Joel, *Harvest of Rage: Why Oklahoma City Is Only the Beginning*, Basic Books, 1998

Economic Policy Institute/Cornell University Press, *The State of Working America* (annual)

Farber, David, *Sloan Rules: Alfred P. Sloan and the Triumph of General Motors*, University of Chicago Press, 2005

Ferguson, Neil, *The Ascent of Money: A Financial History of the World*, The Penguin Press, 2008
_____ *The Cash Nexus: Money and Power in the Modern World*, Basic Books, 2002

Freeman, Richard B., *Working Under Different Rules* (Sla Occasional Papers Series), Russell Sage Foundation, 1994

Friedman, Thomas L., *The World Is Flat 3.0: A Brief History of the Twenty-first Century*, Picador, 2007

Geisst, Charles R., *Visionary Capitalism: Financial Markets and the American Dream in the Twentieth Century*, Praeger, 1990

Gilbert, Neil, *Transformation of the Welfare State: The Silent Surrender of Public Responsibility*, Oxford University Press USA, 2004

Goldberg, Steven H., *Billions of Drops in Millions of Buckets: Why Philanthropy Doesn't Advance Social Progress*, Wiley, 2009

Gordon, John Steele, *Empire of Wealth: The Epic History of American Economic Power*, Harper Perennial, 2005

Greenspan, Alan, *The Age of Turbulence: Adventures in a New World*, Allen Lane, 2007

Hacker, Jacob S., *The Divided Welfare State: The Battle over Public and Private Social Benefits in the United States*, Yale, 2002

Hamilton, Kirk (ed.), *Where Is the Wealth of Nations? Measuring Capital for the 21st Century*, World Bank Publications, 2005

Hirsch, Fred and M. J. Rosaant, *The Social Limits to Growth*. iUniverse.com, 1999

Huffington, Arianna, *Pigs at the Trough: How Corporate Greed and Political Corruption Are Undermining America*, Three Rivers Press, 2004

Lal, Deepak, *Reviving the Invisible Hand: The Case for Classical Liberalism in the Twenty-first Century*, Princeton University Press, 2008

McConnell, Campbell R. and Stanley Brue, *Economics: Principles, Problems and Policies*, McGraw Hill/Irwin, 2008

Newman, Katherine S., *Declining Fortunes: The Withering of the American Dream*, Basic Books, 1993

Nickels, William, James McHugh and Susan McHugh, *Understanding Business*, Mc-Graw-Hill, 2008

Pew Oceans Commission, *America's Living Oceans: Charting a Course for Sea Change*, 2003

Posner, Richard A., *A Failure of Capitalism: The Crisis of '08 and the Descent into Depression*, Harvard University Press, 2009

Putnam, Robert D., *Bowling Alone: The Collapse and Revival of American Community*, Simon & Schuster, 2001

Reich, Robert, *Super Capitalism: The Transformation of Business, Democracy, and Everyday Life*, Vintage, 2008

Rivlin, Alice M., *Reviving the American Dream: The Economy, the States & the Federal Government*, Brookings Institute, 1992

Schlosser, Eric, *Fast Food Nation: The Dark Side of the All-American Meal*, Houghton Mifflin, 2001

Schumpeter, Joseph A., *The Theory of Economic Development: An Inquiry into Profits, Capital, Credit, Interest, and the Business Cycle (Social Science Classics Series)*, Transaction Publishers, 1982

Smick, David, *The World is Curved: Hidden Dangers to the Global Economy*, Marshall Cavendish, 2009

Solow, Robert H., *Growth Theory: An Exposition*, Oxford University Press USA, 2000

Sorkin, Andrew Ross, *Too Big to Fail: The Inside Story of How Wall Street and Washington Fought to Save the Financial System*, Viking Adult, 2009

Steingart, Gabor, *The War for Wealth: The True Story of Globalization, or Why the Flat World is Broken*, McGraw-Hill, 2008

Trump, Donald, *The Art of the Deal*, Mass Market Paperback, 2004

Weber, Max, *The Protestant Ethic and the Spirit of Capitalism*, Roxbury Publishing Company, 2001

Whyte, William H. and Joseph Nocera, *The Organization Man*, University of Pennsylvania Press, 2002

Human Rights Watch. Unfair Advantage: Workers' Freedom of Association in the United States Under International Human Rights Standards. [Online]. Available: http://www.hrw.org/en/node/79051/section/3 [2009, June 15]

Chapter 5: Study, Science, Space and Medicine

College Guide, College Board (annual)

Fiske Guide to Colleges, Sourcebooks (annual)

Sacks, Peter, *Tearing Down the Gates: Confronting the Class Divide in American Education*, University of California Press, 2007

Schleppler, Judith A. et. al., *Portraits of Great American Scientists*, Prometheus Books, 2001

U.S. News Ultimate College Guide, Sourcebooks (annual)

Chronicle of Higher Education (forum for debate over hiring and promotion of faculty), www.chronicle.com

Education USA your guide to U.S. higher education, http://www.educationusa.state.gov/

Scholarship Scams, FinAid.org

For information on visa procedures and traveling to the United States, see www.travel.state.gov

Chapter 6: The Media and Transportation

Boehlert, Eric, *Bloggers on the Bus: How the Internet Changed Politics and the Press*, Free Press, 2009

Brennan, Elizabeth A. and Elizabeth C. Clarage, *Who's Who of Pulitzer Prize Winners*, The Oryx Press, 1999

Buell, Hal, *Moments: The Pulitzer Prize-Winning Photographs: A Visual Chronicle of Our Time*, Revised and Updated, Tess Press, 2006

Jacobs, James B., *Drunk Driving: An American Dilemma* (Studies in Crime and Justice), University of Chicago Press, 1992

McChesney, Robert W., *The Problem of the Media: U.S. Communication Politics in the 21st Century*, Monthly Review Press, 2004

Mindich, David T.Z., *Tuned Out: Why Americans Under 40 Don't Follow the News*, Oxford University Press USA, 2005

Nordahl, Darrin, *My Kind of Transit: Rethinking Public Transportation in America*, Center for American Places, 2009

Tichi, Cecelia, *Exposés and Excess: Muckraking in America, 1900/2000*, University of Pennsylvania Press, 2005

Clay Shirky, "Newspapers and Thinking the Unthinkable," March 13, 2009: *shirky.com/weblog/2009/03/newspapers-and-thinking-the-unthinkable*

Chapter 7: The American Character

Berman, Dr. Jenn (Author), Donna Corwin (Foreword), *The A to Z Guide to Raising Happy, Confident Kids*, New World Library, 2007

Carter, Robert A., *Buffalo Bill Cody: The Man Behind the Legend*, Wiley, 2002

Cherlin, Andrew J., *The Marriage-Go-Round: The State of Marriage and the Family in America Today*, Knopf, 2009

Churchyard, Charles, *National Lies: The Truth About American Values*, Axroide Publishing, 2009

Claire, Elizabeth, *American Manners and Customs: A Guide for Newcomers*, Eardley Publications, 2004

Connell, Evan S., *Son of the Morning Star: Custer and The Little Bighorn*, North Point, 1997

Grossman, James R., *The Frontier in American Culture: Essays by Richard White and Patricia Nelson Limerick,* University of California Press, 1994

O'Connor, Karen, *No Neutral Ground?: Abortion Politics In An Age Of Absolutes* (Dilemmas in American Politics), Westview Press, 1996

Rosa, Joseph G., *Wild Bill Hickok: The Man and His Myth*, University Press of Kansas, 2007

Turner, Frederick Jackson (author) and John Mack Faragher, (ed.), *Re-reading Frederick Jackson Turner: "The Significance of the Frontier in American History" and Other Essays*, Yale University Press, 1999

Tefertiller, Casey, *Wyatt Earp: The Life Behind the Legend*, Wiley, 1999

Williams, Mary E. (ed.), *Opposing Viewpoints Series - American Values*, Greenhaven Press, 2004

The Association for Wedding Professionals International, www.afwpi.com/wedstats

TheKnot,www.theknot.com/au_industrystats.shtml

Chapter 8: American Religion

Bates, Richard Stephen, *God's Own Country: Religion and Politics in the USA*, Hodder, 2008

Blaker, Kimberly, Edward M. Buckner, Bobbie Kirkhart and John Suarez, *The Fundamentals of Extremism: The Christian Right in America,* New Boston Books, 2003

Bloom, Harold, *The American Religion,* Chu Hartley Publishers LLC, 2006

Bull, Malcolm and Keith Lockhart, *Seeking a Sanctuary: Seventh-day Adventism and the American Dream*, Indiana University Press, 2006

Brodie, Fawn M., *No Man Knows My History: The Life of Joseph Smith*, Vintage, 1995

Givens, Terryl, *By the Hand of Mormon: The American Scripture that Launched a New World Religion,* Oxford University Press USA, 2003

Gottschalk, Stephen, *Rolling Away the Stone: Mary Baker Eddy's Challenge to Materialism* (Religion in North America), Indiana University Press, 2005

Holifield, E. Brooks, *Theology in America: Christian Thought from the Age of the Puritans to the Civil War,* Yale University Press, 2005

Hudnut-Beumler, James, *Looking for God in the Suburbs: The Religion of the American Dream and its Critics*, 1945-1965, Rutgers University Press, 1994

Loveland, Anne C. and Otis B. Wheeler, *From Meeting House to Megachurch: A Material and Cultural History*, University of Missouri Press, 2003

Lee, Shayne and Philip Sinitiere, *Holy Mavericks: Evangelical Innovators and the Spiritual Marketplace* [Joel Osteen, Paula White, T. D. Jakes, Rick Warren, and Brian McLaren], NYU Press, 2009

Marsden, George M., *Religion and American Culture*, Wadsworth Publishing, 2000

Miller, Donald E., *Reinventing American Protestantism: Christianity in the New Millennium*, University of California Press, 1999

Morone, James A., *Hellfire Nation: The Politics of Sin in American History,* Yale University Press, 2004

Ruthven, Malise, *Fundamentalism: A Very Short Introduction* (Very Short Introductions), Oxford University Press, 2007

Wigger, John H. and Nathan O. Hatch, *Methodism and the Shaping of American Culture,* Abingdon Press, 2001

Wolfe, Alan, *The Transformation of American Religion: How We Actually Live Our Faith*, University of Chicago Press, 2005

Hartford Institute for Religion Rsearch, http://hirr.hartsem.edu/research/fastfacts/fast_facts.html

Chapter 9: The Arts and Literature

Drama

Bigsby, C. W. E., *A Critical Introduction to Twentieth-Century American Drama*, Cambridge University Press, 1982-1985

Bordman, Gerald, *Oxford Companion to American Theatre.* Oxford University Press USA, 2004

Marsh-Lockett, Carol (ed.), *Black Women Playwrights: Visions on the American Stage*, Garland, 1998

Meserve, Walter J., *An Outline History of American Drama, Littlefield*, Adams, 1965

Miller, Jordan (ed.), *American Drama between the Wars: a Critical History* (Critical History of American Drama Series), Twayne Publishers, 1997

Wainscott, Ronald, *The Emergence of the Modern American Theater: 1914-1929*, Yale University Press, 1997

Wilmeth, Don B. and Tice L.Miller, *The Cambridge Guide to American Theatre*, Cambridge University Press, 1996

Classical Music and Opera

Butterworth Neil, *Dictionary of American Classical Composers*, Routledge, 2004

Leonard Bernstein http://www.leonardbernstein.com/

OPERA America http://www.operaamerica.org/

Schirmers (composers) http://www.schirmer.com/

Painting

Baigell, Matthew, *A Concise History of American Painting and Sculpture*, Westview Press, 2006

Corn, Wanda M., *The Great American Thing: Modern Art and National Identity, 1915-1935,* University of California Press, 1999

Craven, Wayne, *American Art: History and Culture*, McGraw-Hill Humanities/Social Sciences/ Languages, 2002

Doss, Erika Lee, *Twentieth-Century American Art* (Oxford History of Art), Oxford University Press USA, 2002

Gerdts, William H., *American Impressionism*, 2nd ed., Abbeville Press, 2001

Groseclose, Barbara S., *Nineteenth-Century American Art* (Oxford History of Art), Oxford University Press USA, 2002

Haskell, Barbara, *The American Century: Art and Culture, 1900-2000*, 2 vols., W.W. Norton & Co., 2000

Hughes, Robert, *American Visions: The Epic History of Art in America*, Harville Press, 1997

Lewis, Samella S., Mary Jane Hewitt and Floyd Coleman, *African American Art and Artists*, University of California Press, 2003

Pohl, Frances K., *Framing America: A Social History of American Art*, Thames & Hudson, 2007

Wilton, Andrew and Tim Barringer, *American Sublime: Landscape Painting in the United States 1820-1880,* Princeton University Press, 2003

The Armory Show http://xroads.virginia.edu/~MUSEUM/Armory/entrance.html

Emporis Buildings http://corporate.emporis.com/

New York Skyscrapers 100 years of high rises http://www.in-arch.net/NYC/nyc.html

The Skyscraper Page http://skyscraperpage.com/

Whitney Museum of American Art http://whitney.org/http

Photography

Gaimond, James, *American Photography and the American Dream* (Cultural Studies of the United States), University of North Carolina Press, 1991

Orvell, Miles, *American Photography* (Oxford History of Art), Oxford University Press USA, 2003

Respini, Eva, *Into the Sunset: Photography's Image of the American West,* The Museum of Modern Art, New York, 2009

American Photography: A Century of Images http://www.pbs.org/ktca/americanphotography/

National Endowment for the Arts, *How the United States Funds the Arts* http://arts.endow.gov/pub/pubAbout.php

American Literature

General

Bloom, Harold and Blake Hobby (eds.) (Bloom's Literary Themes), *The American Dream,* Bloom's Literary Criticism, 2009

Gray, Richard, *History of American Literature*, Blackwell, 2004

Kazin, Alfred, *On Native Grounds: An Interpretation of Modern American Prose Literature,* Harcourt, 1995

Long, Elizabeth, *The American Dream and the Popular Novel*, Routledge and Kegan Paul, 1985

Showalter, Elaine, *A Jury of Her Peers: American Women Writers From Anne Bradstreet to Annie Proulx,* Knopf, 2009

Hypertexts, American Studies, University of Virginia http://xroads.virginia.edu/~hyper/hypertex.html

Parini, Jay, *The Oxford Encyclopedia of American Literature*, Oxford, 2004 www.oxford-americanliterature.com

Simonds, William Edward, *A Student's History of American Literature,* (N.B. published 1902) http://www.bibliomania.com/2/3/270/frameset.html

The Yellow Pages – Literature http://xroads.virginia.edu/~YP/yplitgen.html

Voice of the Shuttle (general website for the humanities) http://vos.ucsb.edu/index.asp

Puritans and the Colonial period

Hayes, Kevin J.(ed.), *The Oxford Handbook of Early American Literature*, Oxford University Press, 2008

Miller, Perry, *Errand Into the Wilderness*, Belknap Press of Harvard University Press, 1956

Shucard, Alan, *American Poetry: The Puritans through Walt Whitman*, University of Massachusetts Press, 1990

Romantics and Transcendentalists

Buell, Lawrence, *The American Transcendentalists: Essential Writings* (Modern Library Classics), Modern Library, 2006

Gura, Philip F., *American Transcendentalism: A History*, Hill and Wang, 2008

Phillips, Jerry, Andrew Ladd and Michael Anesko Ph.D., *Romanticism and Transcendentalism:(1800-1860)* (Background to American Literature), Facts on File, 2005

Realism

Berthoff Warner, *The Ferment of Realism; American Literature, 1884-1919*, Cambridge University Press, 1981

Pizer, Donald, *The Cambridge Companion to American Realism and Naturalism: From Howells to London* (Cambridge Companions to Literature), Cambridge University Press, 2008

Early 20th century, Modernism, Lost Generation

Curnutt, Kirk, *A Historical Guide to F. Scott Fitzgerald* (Historical Guides to American Authors), Oxford University Press USA, 2004

Lamb, Robert Paul and G. R. Thompson (eds.), *A Companion to American Fiction 1865 - 1914* (Blackwell Companions to Literature and Culture), Wiley-Blackwell, 2005

Meltzer, Milton, *Willa Cather: A Biography* (Literary Greats), Twenty-First Century Books, 2007

Tate, Mary Jo (Author) and Matthew Joseph Bruccoli (Foreword), *Critical Companion to F. Scott Fitzgerald: A Literary Reference to His Life And Work*, Facts on File, 2007

F. Scott Fitzgerald Centenary *http://www.sc.edu/fitzgerald/index.html*

Baldwin, James, *Notes of a Native Son*, Beacon Press, 1990 [Harlem Renaissance]

The Postwar Novel

Arnold, Edwin T. and Dianne C. Luce (eds.), *Perspectives on Cormac McCarthy*, Cormac McCarthy Society, 1999

Weisenburger, Steven C., *A Gravity's Rainbow Companion: Sources and Contexts for Pynchon's Novel*, University of Georgia Press, 2006

Poetry

Davidson, Michael, *The San Francisco Renaissance: Poetics and Community at Mid-Century* (Cambridge Studies in American Literature and Culture), Cambridge University Press, 1991

Gooch, Brad, *Flannery: a Life of Flannery O'Connor*, Little, Brown and Company, 2009

Gordon, Lyndall, *Eliot's New Life*,

Ackroyd, Peter, *T. S. Eliot*, Penguin,1998

Matthiessen, F. O., *The Achievement of T. S. Eliot*, Oxford University Press, 1947

Gardner, Helen, *The Art of T. S. Eliot*, Faber & Faber, 1980

Kane, Daniel, *All Poets Welcome: The Lower East Side Poetry Scene in the 1960s*, University of California Press, 2003

Lehman, David, *The Last Avant-Garde: The Making of the New York School of Poets*, Anchor, 1998

Philosophy

Borradori, Giovanna, *The American Philosopher,* University of Chicago Press, 1994

Flower, Elizabeth and Murray G. Murphy, *A History of Philosophy in America*, two vols., G. P. Putnam's Sons, 1977

Harris, Leonard, *Philosophy Born of Struggle: Anthology of African American Philosophy from 1917*, Kendell/Hunt, 1983

Harris, Leonard, Scott L. Pratt and Anne S. Waters (eds.), *American Philosophies,*Blackwell, 2002

Hollinger, David A. and Charles Capper, *The American Intellectual Tradition*, two vols., Oxford University Press USA, 1993

Kuklick, Bruce, *A History of Philosophy in America, 1720-2000*, Clarendon Press, 2001

MacKinnon, Barbara (ed.), *American Philosophy: A Historical Anthology*, SUNY Press, 1985

Pratt, Scott L., *Native Pragmatism*, Indiana University Press, 2002

Stanlick, Nancy A. and Bruce S. Silver (eds.), *Philosophy in America: Primary Readings*, Pearson Prentice Hall, 2004

Stuhr, John J. (ed.), *Classical American Philosophy*, Oxford University Press USA, 1987

____ *Pragmatism and Classical American Philosophy, second edition.*Oxford University Press USA, 2000

Boersma, David, "American Philosophy," *The Internet Encyclopedia of Philosophy*, http://www.iep.utm.edu/

Jonathan Edwards

The Works of Jonathan Edwards, Yale University Press (26 vols.)

Crisp, Oliver (ed. with Paul Hem), *Jonathan Edwards: Philosophical Theologian*, Ashgate, 2003

Gura, Philip F., *Jonathan Edwards: America's Evangelical*, Hill and Wang, 2006

Hatch, Nathan O. and Harry S. Stout (eds.), *Jonathan Edwards and the American Experience*, Oxford University Press USA, 1988

Jenson, Robert W., *America's Theologian: A Recommendation of Jonathan Edwards*, Oxford University Press USA, 1992

Kimnach, Wilson H. and Douglas A. Sweeney (eds.), *The Sermons of Jonathan Edwards: A Reader*, Yale University Press, 2000

McDermott, Gerald R., *Understanding Jonathan Edwards: An Introduction to America's Theologian*, Oxford University Press USA, 2008

Reinhold Niebuhr

Niebuhr, Reinhold, *Leaves from the Notebook of a Tamed Cynic*, Westminster/John Knox Press, 1990.

_____*Moral Man and Immoral Society: A Study in Ethics and Politics*, Kessinger Publishing LLC, 2006

_____*An Interpretation of Christian Ethics*, Seabury Press, 1979

_____*Beyond Tragedy: Essays on the Christian Interpretation of History*, Scribner Book Company, 1979

_____*Christianity and Power Politics*, Gazelle Book Services Ltd, 1969

_____*The Children of Light and the Children of Darkness: A Vindication of Democracy and a Critique of Its Traditional Defense*, Prentice Hall College Div., 1974

_____*Faith and History: A Comparison of Christian and Modern Views of History*, Nord Press, 2008

_____*The Irony of American History*, University of Chicago Press, 2008

_____*Pious and Secular America*, Wipf & Stock Publishers, 2001

Brown, Charles C., *Niebuhr and His Age: Reinhold Niebuhr's Prophetic Role in the Twentieth Century*, Trinity Press International, 1992

Ford, David F., (ed.), *The Modern Theologians: An introduction to Christian theology in the twentieth century*, Vol. II, Basil Blackwell Ltd., 1989

Fox, Richard Wightman, *Reinhold Niebuhr: A Biography*, Pantheon Books, 1985

"Reinhold Niebuhr," by Yun Jung Moon, *The Boston Collaborative Encyclopedia of Modern Western Theology*, http://people.bu.edu/wwildman/bce/mwt_themes_770_niebuhrreinhold.htm

C. Wright Mills

Mills, C. Wright, *White Collar: The American Middle Classes*, Oxford University Press USA, 1951

_____*The Power Elite*, Oxford University Press USA, 2000

_____*The Sociological Imagination*, Oxford University Press USA, 2000

_____*The Marxists*, Penguin Books Ltd., 1969

_____Mills, Kathryn with Pamela Mills (eds.), *C. Wright Mills: Letters and Autobiographical Writings*, University of California Press, 2001

Chapter 10: Movies and Music, Skylines and Screens, Food and Fun

Movies

Cousins, Mark, *The Story of Film*, Thunder's Mouth Press, 2006

Gabler, Neal, *An Empire of Their Own: How the Jews Invented Hollywood*, Crown Publishers, 1988

_____*Walt Disney: The Triumph of the American Imagination*, Knopf, 2007

Jones, K. Maurice, *Spike Lee and the African-American Filmmakers: A Choice of Colors*, Millbrook, 1996

Mast, Gerald and Bruce F. Kawin, *A Short History of the Movies*, Longman, 2002

Nowell-Smith, Geoffrey (ed.), *The Oxford History of World Cinema*. rev. edn., Oxford University Press USA, 1999

Osborne, Robert and Bruce Davis (eds.), *70 Years of the Oscar: The Official History of the Academy Awards*, Abbeville, 1999

Sklar, Robert, *Film: An International History of the Medium*, Prentice Hall, 2002

_____*Movie-Made America*, Random House, 1994

Thomson, David, *The New Biographical Dictionary of Film*, Knopf, 2002

_____*The Whole Equation: A History of Hollywood*, Knopf, 2004

Music

Cooper, B. Lee and Wayne S. Haney, *Rock Music in American Popular Culture*, Harrington Park Press, 1995

Hoffmann, Frank, B., Lee Cooper and Wayne S. Haney, *Rock Music in American Popular Culture*, Routledge, 1995. Vol II, 1997, Vol. III, 1999

Erenberg, Lewis A., *Swingin' the Dream: Big Band Jazz and the Rebirth of American Culture*, University of Chicago, 1998

Greil, Marcus, *Mystery Train: Images of America In Rock 'N Roll* 4th edn., Penguin, 1997

McKeen, William, *Rock and Roll is Here to Stay: An Anthology*, Norton, 2000

Pratt, Ray, *Rhythm and Resistance: The Political Uses of Popular Music*, Smithsonian Books, 1994

Rose, Tricia, *Black Noise: Rap Music and Black Culture in Contemporary America*, University Press of New England for Wesleyan University Press, 1994

Ross, Andrew, Tricia Rose and Andrew Rose (eds.), *Microphone Fiends: Youth Music and Youth Culture.* Routledge, 2003

Zukin, Sharon, *Dangerous Crossroads: Popular Music, Postmodernism and the Poetics of Place*, Verso, 1994

Architecture

Harris, Cyril M., *American Architecture: An Illustrated Encyclopedia*, Norton, 2002

Kidder Smith, G. E., *Source Book of American Architecture*, Princeton Architectural Press, 2009

Leblanc, Sydney, *The Architecture Traveler: A Guide to 250 Key 20th-Century American Buildings*, Norton, 2000

McCullough, David, *The Great Bridge: The Epic Story of the Building of the Brooklyn Bridge*, Simon & Schuster, 2001

Moudry, Roberta (ed.), *The American Skyscraper: Cultural Histories*, Cambridge University Press, 2005

Roth, Leland M., *A Concise History of American Architecture*, Harper & Row, 1980

Upton, Dell, *Architecture in the United States*, Oxford University Press USA, 1998

Wiseman, Carter, *Twentieth-Century American Architecture: The Buildings and Their Makers*, Norton, 2000

A Digital Archive of American Architecture, Boston College, http://www.bc.edu/bc_org/avp/cas/fnart/fa267/20_sky.html

Television Programs

Barnouw, Erik, *Tube of Plenty: The Evolution of American Television*, Oxford University Press USA, 1982

Engelman, Ralph, *Public Radio and Television in America: A Political History*, Sage, 1996

Fiske, John and John Hartley, *Reading Television*, Routledge, 2004

Gamson, Joshua, *Claims to Fame: Celebrity in Contemporary America*, University of California Press, 1994

Gunter, Barrie and Jill L. McAleer, *Children and Television*, Routledge, 1997

Jones, Gerard, *Honey, I'm Home! Sitcoms: Selling the American Dream*, Grove Weidenfeld, 1992

Lears, Jackson, *Something for Nothing: Luck in America*, Viking, 2003

Lipsitz, George, *Time Passages: Collective Memory and American Popular Culture*, University of Minnesota Press, 1990

Marc, David, *Comic Visions: Television Comedy and American Culture*, Unwin Hyman, 1997

Newcomb, Horace (ed.), *Museum of Broadcast Communications Encyclopedia of Television*, Fitzroy Dearborn, 1997

Postman, Neil, *Amusing Ourselves to Death: Public Discourse in the Age of Show Business*, 1986

Scanlan, Tom, *Family, Drama, and American Dreams*, Greenwood, 1978

Schickel, Richard, *Intimate Strangers: The Culture of Celebrity*, Doubleday, 1985

Verney, Kevern, *African Americans and US Popular Culture*, Routledge, 2003

Wakin, Edward, *How TV Changed America's Mind*, Lothrop, Lee & Shepard, 1996

Fun

Coogan, Peter, *Superhero: The Secret Origin of a Genre*, MonkeyBrain, 2006

Farrell, James, *One Nation Under Goods: The Seductions of American Shopping*, Smithsonian, 2003

Hajdu, David, *The Ten-Cent Plague: The Great Comic-Book Scare and How It Changed America*, Picador, 2009

Hoffmann, Frank, et. al., *Baseball and American Culture*, Routledge, 2003

Kirsch, George B., *Golf in America*, University of Illinois Press, 2009

Mandelbaum, Michael, *The Meaning of Sports: Why Americans Watch Baseball, Football, and Basketball and What They See When They Do*, Public Affairs, 2005

Nilsen, Alleen Pace and Don L.F. Nilsen, *Encyclopedia of 20th-Century American Humor*, Oryx Press, 2000

Zukin, Sharon, *Point of Purchase: How Shopping Changed American Culture*, Routledge, 2003

The Yellow Pages – Popular Culture http://xroads.virginia.edu/~YP/yppop.html

Chapter 11: Cultural Debates, Social Problems and Solutions

American Management Association, *Survey on Workplace Testing*, New York, 2000

Bellah, Robert N., Richard Madsen, William M. Sullivan and Ann Swidler, *Habits of the Heart: Individualism and Commitment in American Life*, University of California Press, 2007

Branham, Lynn S., *The Law of Sentencing, Corrections, and Prisoners' Rights in a Nutshell*, 6th ed., West Group, 2002

Cashin, Sheryll, *The Failures of Integration: How Race and Class are Undermining the American Dream*, Public Affairs Books, 2004

Cole, George F. and Christopher E. Smith, *The American System of Criminal Justice*, 10th edition, Wadsworth/Thomson Learning, 2004

Conley, Dalton, *Being Black, Living in the Red: Race, Wealth, and Social Policy in America*, University of California Press, 1999

_____ *Wealth and Poverty in America: A Reader*, Wiley-Blackwell, 2002

Donohue, John and Steven Levitt, "The Impact of Legalized Abortion on Crime," Berkeley Program in Law & Economics, Working Paper Series 2000 (2): 69

Dow, David R. and Mark Dow (eds.), *Machinery of Death: The Reality of America's Death Penalty Regime*, Routledge, 2002

Draut, Tamara, *Strapped: Why America's 20- and 30- Somethings Can't Get Ahead*, Anchor, 2007

Ellwood, David T. and Christopher Jencks, *The Spread of Single-Parent Families in the United States since 1960,* John F. Kennedy School of Government, Harvard University, October 2002

Fischer, David Hackett, *Albion's Seed: Four British Folkways in America*, Oxford University Press USA, 1989

Frank, Thomas, *What's the Matter with Kansas?* Henry Holt, 2004

Friedan, Betty, *The Feminine Mystique,* (Penguin Women's Studies), 1992

Hartley, John and Roberta E. Roberta (eds.), *American Cultural Studies: A Reader*, Oxford University Press USA, 2000

Hofstadter, Richard, "America as a Gun Culture," *American Heritage Magazine*, October 1970, Vol. 21, Issue 6, pp. 4 – 11, 81-85

Huntington, Samuel P., *Who Are We? The Challenges to America's National Identity: America's Great Debate,* Free Press, 2005

Krugman, Paul, *The Conscience of a Liberal,* W. W. Norton & Co., 2007

Lawrence, Mishel, Jared Bernstein, and Heidi Shierholz, (2009), The State of Working America 2008/2009. [Online]. Economic Policy Institute. Available:http://www.epinet.org/content.cfm/webfeatures_econindicators_income20050831. [2009, July 14]

Megivern, James J., *The Death Penalty: An Historical and Theological Survey*, Paulist Press, 1997 (2006, January 27).

Mind the Gap: Income Inequality, state by state. [Online]. CNN Money.com. Available: http://money.cnn.com/2006/01/25/news/economy/income_gap/index.htm [2009, July 14]

(1996, April 5).

The Causes of Income Inequality. [Online]. National Center for Policy Analysis. Available: http://www.ncpa.org/~ncpa/pd/economy/ecob2.html [2009, July 14]

National Institutes of Health, National Institute on Alcohol Abuse and Alcoholism & the Robert Woods Johnson Foundation, *Worksite Alcohol Study,* Rockville, MD, 1998

Peterson, Wallace S., *Silent Depression:* Twenty-Five Years of Wage Squeeze and Middle Class Decline, W. W. Norton & Co.,1995

Regoli, Robert M. Ph.D. and John D. Hewitt, Ph.D., *Exploring Criminal Justice: The Essentials,* Jones & Bartlett Publishers, 2009

Schacht, Steven P. and Doris W. Ewing, *Feminism with men: bridging the gender gap*, Rowman & Littlefield, 2004

Sentencing - Sentencing Guidelines: Fair Or Unfair, Further Readings. [Online]. Available: http://law.jrank.org/pages/10153/Sentencing.html" [2009, July 14]

Spohn, Cassia C., *How Do Judges Decide?: The Search for Fairness and Justice in Punishment,* Sage, 2002

Executions in the U.S.1608-2002: The Espy File. [Online].Death Penalty Information Center. Available:http://www.deathpenaltyinfo.org/executions-us-1608-2002-espy-file {2002, June 20}.

The Yellow Pages – American Identities. [Online}. Available: http://xroads.virginia.edu/~YP/ethnic.html [2009, July 14]

U.S. Department of Health and Human Services, SAMHSA, *Results from the 1999 National Household Survey on Drug Abuse,* Office of Applied Studies, Rockville, MD, September, 2000.

United States Gun Control. [Online]. US Legal Law Digest, Law Summaries. Available: http://lawdigest.uslegal.com/criminal-laws/gun-control/7096/ [2009, July 14]

Warren, Elizabeth and Amelia Warren Tyagi, *The Two-Income Trap: Why Middle-Class Mothers And Fathers Are Going Broke*, Basic Books, 2003

Warshauer, M., Who Wants to Be a Millionaire? Changing Conceptions of the American Dream. [Online]. Available: http://www.americansc.org.uk/online/American_Dream.htm [2009, June 17]

White, John Kenneth, *The Values Divide: American Politics and Culture in Transition*, CQ Press, 2002

Wilson, William Julius, *More than Just Race: Being Black and Poor in the Inner City* (Issues of Our Time), W. W. Norton & Co., 2009

Chapter 12: The U.S. and the World

Brzezinski, Zbigniew, *Second Chance: Three Presidents and the Crisis of American Superpower*, Basic Books, 2007

Bush, George W., *Decision Points*, Crown Publishers, 2010

Eland, Ivan, *The Empire Has No Clothes: US Foreign Policy Exposed*, The Independent Institute, 2006

Fukuyama, Francis, *State Building: Governance and the World Order in the 21st Century*, Cornell University Press, 2004

Harvey, Robert (ed.), *The World Crisis: The Way Forward after Iraq*, Constable, 2008

Hertsgaard, Mark, *The Eagle's Shadow: Why America Fascinates and Infuriates the World*, Picador, 2003

Hirsch, Michael, *At War with Ourselves: Why America is Squandering its Chance to Build a Better World*, Oxford University Press USA, 2003

Huntington, Samuel P., *Political Order in Changing Societies* (The Henry L. Stimson Lectures Series), Yale University Press, 2006

Kagan, Robert, *The Return of History and the End of Dreams*, Knopf, 2008

Killcullen, David, *The Accidental Guerrilla*, Oxford University Press USA, 2009

Kissinger, Henry, *Does America Need a Foreign Policy?* Simon & Schuster, 2001

La Croix, Sumner J. and Denise Eby Konan, "Intellectual Property Rights in China: the changing political economy of Chinese-American interests," University of Hawaii, Department of Economics, Working Paper No. 02-1, January 2002

Layne, Christopher, *The Peace of Illusions: American Grand Strategy from 1940 to the Present*, Cornell University Press, 2006

Leach, Garry, *Crude Interventions: The US, Oil and the New World*, (Dis)order, Zed Books, 2006

Madsen, Richard, *China and the American Dream: A Moral Inquiry*, University of California Press, 1995

Mann, Michael, *Incoherent Empire*, Verso, 2005

Nye, Joseph, *Soft Power: The Means to Success in World Politics*, PublicAffairs, 2006

Rumsfeld, Donald, *Known and Unknown*, Sentinel Books, 2011

Singer, P. W., *Wired for War: The Robotics Revolution and Conflict in the 21st- Century,* Penguin Press, 2009

Wolfe, Alan, *Return to Greatness: How America Lost Its Sense of Purpose and What It Needs to Do to Recover It*, Princeton University Press, 2005

Zakaria, Fareed, *The Post-American World*, W.W. Norton & Co., 2009

SOURCES

Chapter 1: The American Panorama: The Regions, the Cities, and the Environment

CIA, *The World Factbook*

Environmental Protection Agency. 2008 Electronic Report on the Environment (eRoe). [Online]. Available: http://www.epa.gov/roe/ [September 1, 2009]

Kotkin, Joel. (2009, May 13).The Luxury City vs. the Middle Class. [Online]. Available: http://www.american.com/author_search?Creator=Joel%20Kotkin. Reproduced by permission of AEI online magazine.

U.S. Census Bureau, Census 2006 estimates, 2000 Census, 1990 Census, http:www.census.gov/

USIA. (1997, September). Portrait of the USA. [Online]. Available: http://usa.usembassy.de/etexts/factover/ch2.htm

The White House, http://www.whitehouse.gov/issues/energy_and_environment/

Chapter 2: The Peoples of America

American Jewish Committee, http://www.ajc.org/

Anti-Defamation League, http://www.adl.org/

Aptheker, H., "Negro Casualties in the Civil War," *The Journal of Negro History*, Vol. 32, No. 1. (January, 1947), p. 12

Asian-Nation: The Landscape of Asian America, http://www.asian-nation.org/

Centers for Disease Control and Prevention, *Journal of Population Growth,* National Vital Statistics Reports, Vol. 57, No. 7

CIA, *The World Factbook*

Cohn, Raymond. Immigration to the United States. EH.Net Encyclopedia, edited by Robert Whaples. August 14, 2001. [Online]. Available: http://eh.net/encyclopedia/article/cohn.immigration.us

Congressional Record. Military Report on Colfax Riot, 1875. [Online]. Available: http://files.usgwarchives.net/la/state/history/military/uncat/colfaxr.txt [September 5, 2009]

Congressional Research Service, *The Changing Demographic Profile of the United States,* June 7, 2006 http://aging.senate.gov/crs/aging1.pdf

Cottrol, Robert J. and Diamond, Raymond T. The Second Amendment: Toward an Afro-Americanist Reconsideration. [Online]. Available: http://www.guncite.com/journals/cd-recon.html. [September 5, 2009]

Council of Economic Advisers for the President's Initiative on Race, *Changing America: Indicators of Social and Economic Well-Being by Race and Hispanic Origin,* Chapter 2, September 1998

Department of Homeland Security, Office of Immigration Statistics, *Yearbook of Immigration Statistics*

Dray, Philip, *At the Hands of Persons Unknown: The Lynching of Black America,* Modern Library, 2003

Gomez, Michael A., *Exchanging Our Country Marks: The Transformation of African Identities in the Colonial and Antebellum South,* The University of North Carolina Press, 1998, pp. 27, 29

Hewitt, Lawrence L. (ed.), Arthur W. Bergeron (ed.), Arthur W. Bergeron, Jr. (ed.), *Louisianians in the Civil War,* University of Missouri Press, 2002, p. 10

Hollandsworth, James G., *The Louisiana Native Guards: The Black Military Experience During the Civil War,* Louisiana State University Press, 1998

Jordan, Ervin L., Jr., *Black Confederates and Afro-Yankees in Civil War Virginia* (A Nation Divided: New Studies in Civil War History), University of Virginia Press,1995

Kolchin, Peter, *American Slavery: 1619-1877,* Hill and Wang, 2003, pp. 78-83

Lemann, Nicholas, *Redemption: The Last Battle of the Civil War,* Farrar, Straus and Giroux, 2007, p. 17

Lester, Connie L. Tennessee Encyclopedia of History and Culture. Disfranchising Laws. [Online]. Available: http://tennesseeencyclopedia.net/imagegallery.php?EntryID=D033 [September 4, 2009]

Levine, Bruce, *Confederate Emancipation: Southern Plans to Free and Arm Slaves during the Civil War,* Oxford University Press USA, 2007, pp. 4,19,62-63,125

Library of Congress, The Chinese in California 1850-1925, http://lcweb2.loc.gov/ammem/award99/cubhtml/cichome.html

Litwack, Leon F., *Trouble in Mind: Black Southerners in the Age of Jim Crow,* Vintage, 1999

Longacre, Edward G., "Black Troops in the Army of the James 1863-65," *Military Affairs,* Vol. 45, No. 1 (February 1981), p.3

McPherson, J., *The Negro's Civil War: How American Blacks Felt and Acted During the War for the Union,* Vintage, 2003, pp.165-16

Musicant, I., *Divided Waters: The Naval History of the Civil War,* Book Sales, 2000, p. 74

National Center for Health Statistics (NCHS), a component of the National Institutes of Health (NIH), *65+ in the United States: 2005*

NumbersUSA, based on U.S. Census data, http://www.numbersusa.com/ PBS. Brotherly Love. Growth and Entrenchment of Slavery. [Online]. Available: http://www.pbs.org/wgbh/aia/part3/3narr6.html [September 4, 2009]

PBS. The Terrible Transformation. New World Exploration and English Ambition. [Online]. Available: http://www.pbs.org/wgbh/aia/part1/1narr2.html. [September 4, 2009]

PBS. The Terrible Transformation. From Indentured Servitude to Racial Slavery. [Online]. Available: http://www.pbs.org/wgbh/aia/part1/1narr3.html. [September 4, 2009]

Perry, James A. The Black Collegian Online. African Roots of African-American Culture. [Online]. Available: http://www.black-collegian.com/issues/1998-12/africanroots12.shtml [September 9, 2009]

Pew Hispanic Center, a Pew Research Center Project, http://www.pewhispanic.org/

The Philippine History Site, http://opmanong.ssc.hawaii.edu/filipino/riots.html

Pildes, Richard H. Constitutional Commentary, Vol.17, 2000, pp. 12,13, 27. Democracy, Anti-Democracy, and the Canon. [Online]. Available: http://papers.ssrn.com/sol3/papers.cfm?abstract_id=224731 [September 5, 2009]

Ramold, Steven J., *Slaves, Sailors, Citizens: African Americans in the Union Navy*, Northern Illinois University Press, 2002, pp. 3-4, 55,76-77, 82-84, 92-99

State Department, Bureau of International Information Programs (IIP) at http://www.america.gov/

U.S. Census Bureau, http:www.census.gov/

_____ 1920-2000 figures, *Time Almanac* 2005, p. 377

_____ 1980 Census of population, vol. 1, chap. D, pt. 1; *Language spoken at home and ability to speak English for United States, regions, and states: 1990*; Census 2000, Summary File 3, Table DP-2

USIA: *Portrait of the USA*, September 1997; *U.S. Society & Values*, Electronic Journal of the U.S. Information Agency, Vol. 4, No. 2, June 1999

Willis, John C., *Forgotten Time: The Yazoo-Mississippi Delta after the Civil War* (The American South Series), University of Virginia Press, 2000

Chapter 3: Government

Bates, Richard Stephen, *God's Own Country: Religion and Politics in the USA*, Hodder, 2008, p. 97

History Learning Site, http://www.historylearningsite.co.uk/

National Public Radio, http://www.npr.org/

Sabato, Larry J. "PACs and Parties" in *Money, Elections, and Democracy: Reforming Congressional Campaign Finance*, Nugent, Margaret Lotus and Johannes, John R. (eds.), Westview Press, 1990, pp. 187–204

U.S. Congress, *How our Laws are made*

Chapter 4: Capital and Labor: The Economic System and Social Security

Bureau of Labor Statistics, http://www.bls.gov/

CIA, *The World Factbook*

Congressional Budget Office, http://www.cbo.gov/

Constitutional Rights Foundation, http://www.crf-usa.org/bill-of-rights-in-action/bria-14-3-a.html

Council on Foundations, http://www.cof.org/

The Dahlem Report ("The Financial Crisis and the Systemic Failure of Academic Economics.") [Online]. Available: http://www.debtdeflation.com/blogs/wpcontent/uploads/papers/Dahlem_Report_EconCrisis021809.pdf [June 18, 2009]

Department of the Treasury, Office of Public Affairs, http://ustreas.gov/offices/public- affairs/

Economic Policy Institute, http://www.epi.org/

Families and Work Institute. National Study of the Changing Workforce 2008. [Online]. Available: http://www.familiesandwork.org/site/research/reports/Times_Are_Changing.pdf [September 23, 2009]

Futures Industry Association, http://www.futuresindustry.org/

Government Accountability Office, http://www.gao.gov/

Greenspan, Alan, *The Age of Turbulence: Adventures in a New World*, Allen Lane, 2007, pp. 8-10, 18, 48, 141, 169-70, 181, 233, 348-62, 369, 374-75, 461, 474n, 481, 489

Leslie Hossfeld, Mac Legerton and Gerald Keuster. The Economic and Social Impact of Job Loss in Robeson County, North Carolina 1993-2003. Sociation Today, Vol. 2, Fall, 2004 [Online]. Available: http://www.ncsociology.org/hossfeld.htm [September 23, 2009]

InfoUSA 2008-2009, http://usinfo.org/zhtw/

Kaiser Commission on Medicaid and the Uninsured, http://www.kff.org/uninsured/index.cfm

Kaiser Family Foundation, http://www.kff.org/

McKinsey Quarterly, http://www.mckinseyquarterly.com/home.aspx

National Association of Housing and Redevelopment Officials, http://www.nahro.org/programs/phousing/index.cfm

National Bureau of Economic Research, http://www.nber.org/

The National Debt, http://www.ustreas.gov/education/faq/markets/national-debt.shtml

(National Industrial) Conference Board, http://www.conference-board.org/

Ray, Darryl. (2003, September). University of Tennessee Agricultural Policy Analysis Center. Re-thinking US Agricultural Policy: Changing Course to Secure Farmer Livelihoods Worldwide. [Online]. Available: Robert Gordon University, http://www2.rgu.ac.uk/publicpolicy/introduction/socpolf.htm

Securities and Exchange Commission, http://www.sec.gov/

Social Security Administration, http://www.ssa.gov/

The Concord Coalition, http://www.concordcoalition.org/

The Economic Report of the President, http://www.gpoaccess.gov/eop

The Social Security Network: a Century Foundation project, http://www.socsec.org/

Urban Institute, National Center for Charitable Statistics, http://nccs.urban.org/

U.S. Department of Agriculture, http://www.usda.gov/wps/portal/usdahome

U.S. Department of Commerce, http://www.doc.gov/

U.S. Department of Labor, http://www.dol.gov/

U.S. Department of Labor, Bureau of Labor Statistics, http://www.bls.gov/

U.S. Department of Transportation, http://www.dot.gov/new/index.htm

CHAPTER 5: Study, Science, Space and Medicine

Gladwell, Malcolm, *Outliers*, Little, Brown, 2008

National Aeronautics and Space Administration (NASA), http://www.nasa.gov/home/index.html

National Center for Education Statistics, http://nces.ed.gov

National Education Association, http://www.nea.org/

National Institute for Literacy, http://www.nifl.gov/

National Institutes for Health, http://www.nih.gov/

TIMSS & PIRLS International Study Center, *Comparative studies in educational achievement,* http://timss.bc.edu/

U.S. Census Bureau, American Community Survey, 2006, Census 2000, http://www.census.gov

U.S. Information Agency, http://dosfan.lib.uic.edu/usia/

CHAPTER 6: The Media and Transportation

Air Transport Association, http://www.airlines.org/

American Bus Association, http://www.buses.org/

American Public Transportation Association, http://www.apta.com/Pages/default.aspx

Americans for Transportation Mobility, http://www.fasterbettersafer.org/

Bureau of Labor Statistics, http://www.bls.gov/

Bureau of Transportation Statistics, http://www.bts.gov/

Burrelles*Luce*/Audit Bureau of Circulations figures for six-month period ending 3/31/08, http://www.burrellesluce.com/

CIA, World Factbook

The Claremont Institute, an interactive community that aims to bring internet users together with public policy organizations under "the broad umbrella of 'conservative' thoughts, ideas, and actions," http://www.claremont.org/

Columbia Journalism Review - lists who owns which media. http://www.cjr.org/

Electronic Privacy Information Center - information on privacy issues relating to the internet. http://epic.org/

Federal Aviation Administration, http://www.faa.gov/

Greenspan, Alan, *The Age of Turbulence: Adventures in a New World,* Allen Lane, 2007, pp. 460, 462

Take Back the Media - combats corporate bias in the media, http://www.takebackthemedia.com/

Technorati, http://technorati.com/ TotalNEWS - a directory of more than a thousand news sources, including ABC, CBS, Fox News, MSNBC, and USA Today, http://totalnews.com/

UCLA Center for Communication Policy, *The UCLA Internet Report: Surveying the Digital Future Year Three,* 2003, http://www.digitalcenter.org/pdf/InternetReportYearThree.pdf

U.S. Army Corps of Engineers, http://www.usace.army.mil/Pages/default.aspx

U.S. Department of Transportation, http://www.dot.gov/new/index.htm

U.S. Information Agency, http://dosfan.lib.uic.edu/usia/

Vanderbilt University Television News Archive – the Television News Archive holds abstracts of news stories covered by ABC, CBS, and NBC television since 1968. http://tvnews.vanderbilt.edu/

CHAPTER 7: The American Character

Bates, Richard Stephen, *God's Own Country: Religion and Politics in the USA*, Hodder, 2008, p. 58
Gouge, Catherine. (Spring 2007)."The American Frontier: History, Rhetoric, Concept," *Americana: The Journal of American Popular Culture (1900-present*.[Online]. Volume 6, Issue 1. Available: http://www.americanpopularculture.com/journal/articles/spring_2007/gouge.htm [2007, August 9]
Greenspan, Alan, *The Age of Turbulence: Adventures in a New World*, Allen Lane, 2007, p. 505
International Student Resources, *Life in America*, http://www.leaderu.com/isr/lifeinamerica/lifeinamerica.html
National Center for Policy Analysis, http://www.ncpa.org/
National Public Radio, http://www.npr.org

CHAPTER 8: American Religion

Bates, Richard Stephen, *God's Own Country: Religion and Politics in the USA*, Hodder, 2008, pp. 37, 57, 111-112, 138-141, 147, 253, 266, 326, 348
USIA, *Portrait of America*, Chapter 8, http://usa.usembassy.de/etexts/factover/ch8.htm
The Yearbook of Canadian and American Churches 2003, 2007

CHAPTER 9: The Arts and Literature

American Film Institute http://www.afi.com/
American Photography. A Century of Images, http://www.pbs.org/ktca/americanphotography/
The Armory Show http://xroads.virginia.edu/~MUSEUM/Armory/entrance.html
Arnold, Edwin T. and Dianne C. Luce (eds.), *Perspectives on Cormac McCarthy*, Cormac McCarthy Society, 1999
Berthoff, Warner, *The Ferment of Realism: American Literature, 1884-1919*, Cambridge University Press, 1981
Bigsby, C. W. E., *A Critical Introduction to Twentieth-Century American Drama*, Cambridge University Press, 1982-1985
Boller, Paul F., *American Transcendentalism, 1830-1860: An Intellectual Inquiry*, Putnam,1974
Bordman, Gerald, *Oxford Companion to American Theatre*, Oxford University Press USA, 1992
Bruccoli, Matthew J. (ed.), *F. Scott Fitzgerald: A Life in Letters: A New Collection*, Cambridge University Press, 1995
Butterworth, Neil, *Dictionary of American Classical Composers*, Routledge, 2004
Carter, Everett, *Howells and the Age of Realism*, Lippincott, 1954
Craven, Wayne, *American Art: History and Culture*, Abrams, 1994, 2003
Davidson, Michael, *The San Francisco Renaissance: Poetics and Community at Mid-Century*, (Cambridge Studies in American Literature and Culture), Cambridge University Press, 1991
Doss, Erika Lee, *Twentieth-Century American Art*, Oxford University Press USA, 2002
Emporis Buildings http://www.emporis.com

F. Scott Fitzgerald Centenary http://www.sc.edu/fitzgerald/

Gerdts, William H., *American Impressionism*, 2nd ed., Abbeville, 2001

Gitlin, Todd. C. Wright Mills, Free Radical. Peace and Conflict Studies, Institute of Sociology, University of Münster. [Online]. Available: http://www.uni-muenster.de/PeaCon/dgs-mills/mills-texte/GitlinMills.htm [September 14, 2009]

Gray, Richard, *History of American Literature*, Blackwell, 2004

Groseclose, Barbara S., *Nineteenth-Century American Art* (Oxford History of Art), Oxford University Press USA, 2002

Harris, Cyril M., *American Architecture: An Illustrated Encyclopedia*, Norton, 2002

Haskell, Barbara and Lisa Phillips, *The American Century: Art and Culture, 1900-2000*, 2 vols., Norton, 2000

Hayes, Kevin J. (ed.), *The Oxford Handbook of Early American Literature*, Oxford University Press USA, 2008

Hughes, Robert, *American Visions: The Epic History of Art in America*, Knopf, 1997

Hypertexts (University of Virginia) http://xroads.virginia.edu/~hyper/hypertex.html

Kane, Daniel, *All Poets Welcome: The Lower East Side Poetry Scene in the 1960s*, University of California Press, 2003

Kingman, Russ, *A Pictorial Life of Jack London*, Crown Publishers, Inc.,1979

Koster, Donald, *Transcendentalism in America*, Twayne Publishers, 1975

Lauter, Paul (ed.), *The Heath Anthology of American Literature*, Vol. 2, 4th edn., Wadsworth Publishing, 2002

Leblanc, Sydney, *The Architecture Traveler: A Guide to 250 Key 20th-Century American Buildings*, Norton, 2000

Lehman, David, *The Last-Avant Garde: The Making of the New York School of Poets*, Anchor, 1999

Lewis, Samella S. and Floyd Coleman, *African American Art and Artists*, University of California Press, 2003

Lucie-Smith, Edward, *American Realism*, Thames & Hudson, 2002

Marchand, Roland. *Advertising the American Dream*, University of California Press, 1985

------- *Creating the Corporate Soul: The Rise of Public Relations and Corporate Imagery in American Big Business*, University of California Press, 1998

Maynard, W. Barksdale, *Walden Pond: A History*, Oxford University Press USA, 2006

Meserve, Walter J., *An Outline History of American Drama*, Littlefield, Adams, 1965

Miller, Jordan (ed.), *American Drama between the Wars: a Critical History* (Critical History of American Drama Series), Twayne Publishers, 1997

Miller, Perry, *Errand Into the Wilderness*, Belknap Press of Harvard University Press, 1956

Moon, Yun Jung. Reinhold Niebuhr. *The Boston Collaborative Encyclopedia of Modern Western Theology*. [Online]. Available: http. //people.bu.edu/wwildman/bce/ [July 8, 2008]

Murphy, Brenda (ed.), *The Cambridge Companion to American Women Playwrights*, Cambridge University Press, 1999

National Endowment for the Arts, *How the United States Funds the Arts* http://arts.endow.gov/pub/how.pdf

New York Skyscrapers 100 years of high rises http://www.in-arch.net/NYC/nyc.html

The Official Leonard Bernstein Website http://www.leonardbernstein.com/

OPERA America http://www.operaamerica.org/

Orvell, Miles, *American Photography* (American History of Art), Oxford University Press USA, 2003

Panini, Jay, *The Oxford Encyclopedia of American Literature*, Oxford, 2004 www.oxford-americanliterature.com/

Pizer, Donald, *Realism and Naturalism in Nineteenth-Century American Literature*, Southern Illinois University Press, 1966

Pohl, Francis K., *Framing America: A Social History of American Art*, Thames & Hudson, 2002

Roth, Leland M., *A Concise History of American Architecture*, Harper & Row, 1980

Schirmers http://www.schirmer.com/

Schudson, Michael, *Advertising, the Uneasy Persuasion*, Basic Books, 1984

Shucard, Alan, *American Poetry: The Puritans through Walt Whitman*, University of Massachusetts Press, 1988

Simonds, *History of American Literature* http://www.bibliomania.com/2/3/270/frameset.html

Skyscraper Page, http://skyscraperpage.com/ © Emporis Corporation 6/2009

Smith, G. E. Kidder, *Source Book of American Architecture: 500 Notable Buildings from the 10th Century to the Present*, Princeton Architectural Press, 1996

Stasz, Clarice, *American Dreamers: Charmian and Jack London*, iUniverse, Lincoln, Nebraska, 2000

The Emergence of Advertising in America: 1850 - 1920 (EAA) http://scriptorium.lib.duke.edu/eaa/

Twitchell, James, *Adcult USA: The Triumph of Advertising in America*. Columbia University Press, 1995

Upton, Dell, *Architecture in the United States*, Oxford University Press USA, 1998

U.S. State Department, Bureau of International Information Programs.(2006). Outline of American Literature (revised edition). [Online]. Available: http://www.america.gov/media/pdf/books/outline_us_lit.pdf [September 13, 2009]

USIA, *Portrait of America*, Chapter 10, http://usinfo.org/potraitamerica/ch10.htm

USIA. U.S. Society & Values. (June 1998). Electronic Journals of the U.S. Information Agency, Vol. 3, Number 1. [Online]. Available: http://usa.usembassy.de/etexts/art/ijse0698.pdf [September 13, 2009]

Voice of the Shuttle http://vos.ucsb.edu/index.asp

Wainscott, Ronald, *The Emergence of the Modern American Theater: 1914-1929*, Yale University Press, 1997

Wilmeth, Don B. and Tice L. Miller, *The Cambridge Guide to American Theatre*, Cambridge University Press, 1996

Wilton, Andrew and Tim Barringer, *American Sublime: Landscape Painting in the United States, 1820-1880*, Princeton University Press, 2002, 2003

Wiseman, Carter, *Twentieth-Century American Architecture: The Buildings and Their Maker.*, Norton, 2000

The Yellow Pages – Literature http://xroads.virginia.edu/~YP/yplitgen.html

CHAPTER 10: Movies and Music, Skylines and Screens, Food and Fun

42explore Thematic Pathfinders for all ages, http://42explore.com/folkmusic.htm

Academy of Country Music (Western states), http://www.acmcountry.com/content/index.php

All Music Guide, http://www.allmusic.com/

American Gospel Music Directory, http://www.americangospel.com/

Barnouw, Erik, *Tube of Plenty: The Evolution of American Television,* Oxford University Press, 1982, 1990

Berlin, Edward A., *King of Ragtime: Scott Joplin and His Era,* Oxford, 1994

Blues Foundation, http://www.blues.org/

Clarke, Donald, *The Penguin Encyclopedia of Popular Music,* 2nd ed., Penguin, 1999

Country Music Association (Nashville and Southern states), http://www.cmaworld.com/

The Country Music Foundation, *The Encyclopedia of Country Music: The Ultimate Guide to the Music,* Oxford, 1998

Engelman, Ralph, *Public Radio and Television in America: A Political History,* Sage, 1996

Fiske, John and John Hartley, *Reading Television,* Routledge, 2003

Garofalo, Reebee, *Rockin' Out: Popular Music in the USA,* 4th edn., Pearson Education, 2007

Gunter, Barrie and Jill L. McAleer, *Children and Television: One eyed Monster?,* Routledge, 1990

Woody Guthrie, http://www.woodyguthrie.org/

Jazz Corner, http://www.jazzcorner.com/

Jazz Review, http://www.jazzreview.com/

Kastin, David, *American Popular Music: Rock, Jazz, Rap, and Roots,* Pearson, 2001

Larkin, Colin, ed., *The Guinness Encyclopedia of Popular Music.* Stockton, 2002

Lissauer, Robert, *Lissauer's Encyclopedia of Popular Music in America, 1888 to the Present,* Facts On File, 1996

Malone, Bill C., *Country Music USA,* University of Texas Press, 2002

Marcus, Greil, *Mystery Train: Images of America In Rock 'N Roll,* 4th ed., Penguin, 1997

McKeen, William, *Rock and Roll is Here to Stay: An Anthology,* Norton, 2000

McNeil, W. K., *Encyclopedia of American Gospel Music,* Routledge, 2005

National Curve Bank, http://curvebank.calstatela.edu/newmath/newmath.htm

Newcomb, Horace, ed., *Museum of Broadcast Communications Encyclopedia of Television.* Fitzroy Dearborn, 1997

Nilsen, Alleen Pace and Don L.F. Nilsen, *Encyclopedia of 20th-Century American Humor,* Oryx Press, 2000

NPR 'America's Folk Music Anthology', http://www.npr.org/programs/morning/features/2002/jul/anthology/

PBS The Blues Teachers Guide, http://www.pbs.org/theblues/classroom.html

PBS *Broadway: The American Musical,* http://www.pbs.org/wnet/broadway/

Rees, Dafydd and Luke Crampton, 'Q Magazine', *Encyclopedia of Rock Stars,* 1999

Roughstock's History of Country Music, http://www.roughstock.com/history/

Rourke, Constance, *American Humor: A Study of the National Character,* ACLS History E-Book Project, 2008

Seeger, Ruth Crawford, *The Music of American Folk Song and Selected Other Writings on American Folk Music* (Eastman Studies in Music), University of Rochester Press, 2003

Smithsonian Center for Folklife and Cultural Heritage, http://www.folklife.si.edu/index.html

Szatmary, David P., *Rockin' in Time: A Social History of Rock and Roll,* 4th ed., Prentice, 1999

Top 10 Best Labor Songs, http://folkmusic.about.com/od/toptens/tp/BestLaborSongs.htm

Townsend, Peter, *Jazz in American Culture,* University of Mississippi Press, 2000

Wakin, Edward, *How TV Changed America's Mind,* Lothrop, Lee & Shepard, 1996

Werkhoven, Henk N., *The International Guide to New Age Music: A Comprehensive Guide to the Vast and Varied Artists and Recording of New Age Music,* Billboard Books, U. S., 1997

Americana: The Institute for the Study of American Popular Culture, http://www.americanpopularculture.com

Digital Archive of American Architecture, Boston College, http://www.bc.edu/bc_org/avp/cas/fnart/fa267/20_sky.html

Kingwood College Library AMERICAN POPULAR MUSIC1900 to 1950, http://kclibrary.nhmccd.edu/music-2.html

A guide to American popular music, 1900-1950, Popular Culture: Resources for Critical Analysis, http://www.wsu.edu/~amerstu/pop/tvrguide.html

The Skyscraper Page, http://skyscraperpage.com/

CHAPTER 11: Cultural Debates, Social Problems and Solutions

AARP, http://www.aarp.org/

ADA (Americans with Disabilities Act), http://www.ada.gov/

American Association of Pro-Life Obstetricians and Gynecologists (AAPLOG), http://www.aaplog.org/

Anti-Defamation League, http://www.adl.org/

Brady Campaign to Prevent Gun Violence, http://www.bradycampaign.org/

Branham, Lynn S., *The Law and Policy of Sentencing and Corrections* (Nutshell Series).West, 2005

Bureau of Justice Statistics, *The Source Book of Criminal Justice Statistics,* http://www.albany.edu/sourcebook/

Census Bureau. (2008, August 2008). Income, Poverty and Health Insurance Coverage in the United States. [Online]. Available: http://www.census.gov/prod/2008pubs/p60-235.pdf [September 9, 2009

Centers for Disease Control and Prevention, http://www.cdc.gov/

Community Food Security Coalition, http://www.foodsecurity.org/

Death Penalty Information Center, http://www.deathpenaltyinfo.org/

Department of Health and Human Services: Centers for Disease Control and Prevention, http://www.cdc.gov/

EEOC (The Equal Employment Opportunity Commission), http://www.eeoc.gov/

Ellwood, David T. and Jencks, Christopher, "The Spread of Single-Parent Families in the United States since 1960," in Moynihan, Daniel Patrick, Lee Rainwater and Timothy Smeeding (eds.), *The Future of the Family,* Russell Sage, 2004, pp .25-65

Ellwood, David T. and Jenks, Christopher. John F. Kennedy School of Government, Harvard University. The Spread of Single-Parent Families in the United States since 1960. [Online]. Available: http://www.hks.harvard.edu/inequality/Seminar/Papers/ElwdJnck.pdf [September 9, 2009

Ethnic Majority, http://www.ethnicmajority.com/

Family Research Council, *The Family Portrait*, 2002, http://www.frc.org/get.cfm?i=BK04C01

Federal Bureau of Investigation, http://www.fbi.gov/

Federal Register, Vol. 72, No. 15, January 24, 2007, pp. 3147–3148

For Your Marriage, http://www.foryourmarriage.org /

Gay and Lesbian Alliance Against Defamation, http://www.glad.org/

Gitlin, Todd, "C. Wright Mills, Free Radical," University of Münster, Peace & Conflict Studies, http://www.uni-muenster.de/PeaCon/dgs-mills/mills-texte/GitlinMills.htm

Greenspan, Alan, *The Age of Turbulence: Adventures in a New World*, Allen Lane, 2007, pp. 392-408, 423-436

Gun Control, http://www.guncite.com/

Handgun Control Inc.,

Inequality.org, http://www.demos.org/inequality/

InfoUSA, Bureau of International Information Programs (IIP), U.S. Department of State.[Online]. Available: http://usinfo.org/enus/government/forpolicy/chap2.html [September 8, 2009]

Loury, Glenn C. The Divided Society and the Democratic Idea. University Lecture, Boston University, October 7, 1996. [Online]. Available: http://www.bu.edu/irsd/articles/divided.htm

The Martin Luther King, Jr. Research and Education Institute, http://mlk-kpp01.stanford.edu/

Ministry to Interchurch Marriages: A National Study, 1999, http://www.interchurchfamilies.org/resource/ministry.shtm NAACP, http://naacp/

The National Marriage Project: *The State of Our Unions 2003, 2004, 2006,* http://marriage.rutgers.edu/; Testimony of Barbara Dafoe Whitehead before the US Senate, 2004, http://marriage.rutgers.edu/Publications/Pub%20Whitehead%20Testimony%20Apr%2004.htm

NOW (National Organization for Women), http://www.now.org/

Pew Research Center for the People & the Press, http://people-press.org/reports/ August 3, 2006, reproduced by permission Pro-Death Penalty.com, http://www.prodeathpenalty.com/

Proctor, Bernadette D. and Joseph Dalaker, U.S. Census Bureau, Current Population Reports, *Poverty in the United States: 2002*, U.S. Government Printing Office, Washington, DC, 2003, pp. 60-222

Public Agenda, http://www.publicagenda.org/

Spohn, Cassia C., *How Do Judges Decide?: The Search for Fairness and Justice* in Punishment, Sage Publications, Inc., 2008

This Nation (nonpartisan site dealing with current political questions), http://www.thisnation.com/

U.S. Census Bureau, http:www.census.gov/

USIA. An Outline of the U.S. Economy. [Online]. Available: http://guangzhou.usembassy-china.org.cn/uploads/images/qfgZh_IgIYLkXBEPBkXZxQ/Outline of_the_U.S._Economy.doc [September 8, 2009]

Violence Policy Center, http://www.vpc.org/

Waite, Linda and Gallagher, Maggie, The Case for Marriage: Why Married People Are Happier, Healthier, and Better Off Financially, Broadway, 2001 *Washington Times,* http://www.washingtontimes.com/

Women's Policy Inc., http://www.womenspolicy.org/site/PageServer

Women's Web World, Virtual Quincy Directory, http://www.virtualquincy.com/quincy/women/women.html

CHAPTER 12: The U.S. and the World

Armed Forces Journal, http://www.armedforcesjournal.com/

Bates, Richard Stephen, *God's Own Country: Religion and Politics in the USA,* Hodder, 2008, pp. 1-2, 275-277

Center for Strategic and Budgetary Assessments, http://www.csbaonline.org/2006-1/index.shtml

Clark, Admiral Vern. (2003, October 27). Edited remarks of the Chief of Naval Operations at the International Sea Power Symposium, Naval War College, Newport, R.I. [Online]. Available: http://www.navy.mil/navydata/cno/speeches/clark031027.txt [July 10, 2009]

Congressional Budget Office, http://www.cbo.gov/

Congressional Research Service, *Trade and the Americas,* Issue Brief for Congress, Library of Congress, 2002, http://fpc.state.gov/documents/organization/10865.pdf

_____*Trade Negotiations During the 109th Congress,* Library of Congress, 2006, http://italy.usembassy.gov/pdf/other/RL33463.pdf

_____ *U.S.-Latin America Trade: Recent Trends and Policy Issues,* 2009, http://www.fas.org/sgp/crs/row/98-840.pdf

Council on Foreign Relations, http://www.cfr.org/

Despres, John. Rand Organization. American Interests and Concerns with China. (2001) [Online]. Available http://www.rand.org/pubs/monograph_reports/MR1300/MR1300/ [September 7, 2009]. © Reprinted with permission of RAND Corporation, Santa Monica, California.

Globemaster US military aviation database, http://www.globemaster.de/

Goldman Sachs, http://www2.goldmansachs.com/

International Institute for Strategic Studies (IISS), http://www.iiss.org/

International Monetary Fund, http://www.imf.org/external/index.htm

The Modern Tribune, http://www.themoderntribune.com/

NAFTA Claims, http://www.naftaclaims.com/

OECD, http://www.oecd.org/home/0,2987,en_2649_201185_1_1_1_1_1,00.html

Office of the United States Trade Representative OMB, http://www.whitehouse.gov/omb/

Peterson Institute for International Economics, http://www.iie.com/

Singer, P. W. (Winter 2009). Military Robots and the Laws of War. *The New Atlantis, A Journal of Technology and Society.* [Online]. Available: http://www.thenewatlantis.com/publications/military-robots-and-the-laws-of-war (September 8, 2009)

Stockholm International Peace Research Institute (SIPRI), http://www.sipri.org/

UN World Population Prospects, http://esa.un.org/unpp/

Understanding the WTO: The Agreements. Intellectual property: protection and enforcement. [Online]. Available: http://www.wto.org/english/theWTO_e/whatis_e/tif_e/agrm7_e.htm [September 7, 2009]

The United States Navy official website, http://www.navy.mil/swf/index.asp

U.S. Air War College, http://www.au.af.mil/au/awc/awchome.htm

U.S. Census Bureau, http:www.census.gov/

U.S. Department of Commerce, http://www.commerce.gov/

U.S. Department of Defense DefenseLINK site, http://www.defenselink.mil/

U.S. Department of Homeland Security, http://www.dhs.gov/index.shtm

U.S. Department of Labor, Bureau of Labor Statistics, http://www.bls.gov/

U.S. Department of State, http://www.state.gov/

_____ Bureau of Educational and Cultural Affairs, EducationUSA, http://educationusa.state.gov/, http://exchanges.state.gov

_____ Bureau of International Information Programs, http://www.state.gov/r/iip/

_____ International Information Programs. U.S. Climate Report Says Protecting Economy has High Priority. (03 June, 2002) [Online]. Available: http://www.gcrio.org/OnLnDoc/pdf/climate_economy020603.pdf) [September 7, 2009]

_____Bureau of Population, Refugees and Migration, http://www.state.gov/g/prm/

U.S. Department of Transportation, http://www.dot.gov/new/index.htm

USAID. The full measure of U.S. development assistance. [Online]. Available: http://www.usaid.gov/fani/overview/overview_devassistance.htm [September 7, 2009]

Washington University School of Law, http://www.law.washington.edu/

The White House, http://www.whitehouse.gov/

The World Bank, http://www.worldbank.org/ World Trade Organization, http://www.wto.org/

The following sources were also used and were accessed on May 4, 2009:

Drug Enforcement Administration, http://www.usdoj.gov/dea/index.htm

Office of Juvenile Justice and Delinquency Prevention, http://ojjdp.ncjrs.org/

Office of National Drug Control Policy, http://www.whitehousedrugpolicy.gov/

The Supreme Court, http://www.supremecourtus.gov/

U.S. Census Bureau USA Statistics in Brief, http://www.census.gov/compendia/statab/brief.html

U.S. Central Intelligence Agency, https://www.cia.gov/library/publications/the-world-factbook/

U.S. Citizenship and Immigration Services, http://www.uscis.gov/portal/site/uscis

U.S. Department of Homeland Security Office of Immigration Statistics, http://www.dhs.gov/ximgtn/statistics/

U.S. Department of Justice, http://www.usdoj.gov/

U.S. Department of Justice Bureau of Justice Statistics, http://www.ojp.usdoj.gov/bjs/

U.S. Energy Information Administration, http://www.eia.doe.gov

U.S. Patent and Trademark Office, http://www.uspto.gov/index.html

USA.gov, http://www.usa.gov

INDEX

Book titles may be found under author's name.

Lightning Source UK Ltd.
Milton Keynes UK
UKHW050623310822
408116UK00004B/497